STREET ATLAS
Greater
Manchester

First published in 1997

Philip's, a division of
Octopus Publishing Group Ltd
2–4 Heron Quays, London E14 4JP

Second edition 2001
Second impression 2001

ISBN 0-540-07969-3

© Philip's 2001

oîs Ordnance Survey®

This product includes mapping data licensed
from Ordnance Survey® with the permission
of the Controller of Her Majesty's Stationery
Office. © Crown copyright 2001. All rights
reserved. Licence number 100011710

Printed and bound in Spain
by Cayfosa-Quebecor

Contents

II   **Railways and Metrolink**

III   **Key to map symbols**

IV   **Key to map pages**

VI   **Route planning**

VIII   **Administrative and Postcode boundaries**

1   **Street maps** at 2½ inches to 1 mile

138   **Street maps** of selected areas at 5 inches to 1 mile

172   **Index** of towns and villages

173   **Index** of streets, hospitals, industrial estates, railway
stations, schools, shopping centres and universities

Digital Data

The exceptionally high-quality mapping found in this atlas is available as digital
data in TIFF format, which is easily convertible to other bit mapped (raster) image
formats.

The index is also available in digital form as a standard database table. It contains
all the details found in the printed index together with the National Grid reference
for the map square in which each entry is named and feature codes for places of
interest in eight categories such as education and health.

For further information and to discuss your requirements, please contact
Philip's on 020 7531 8440 or george.philip@philips-maps.co.uk

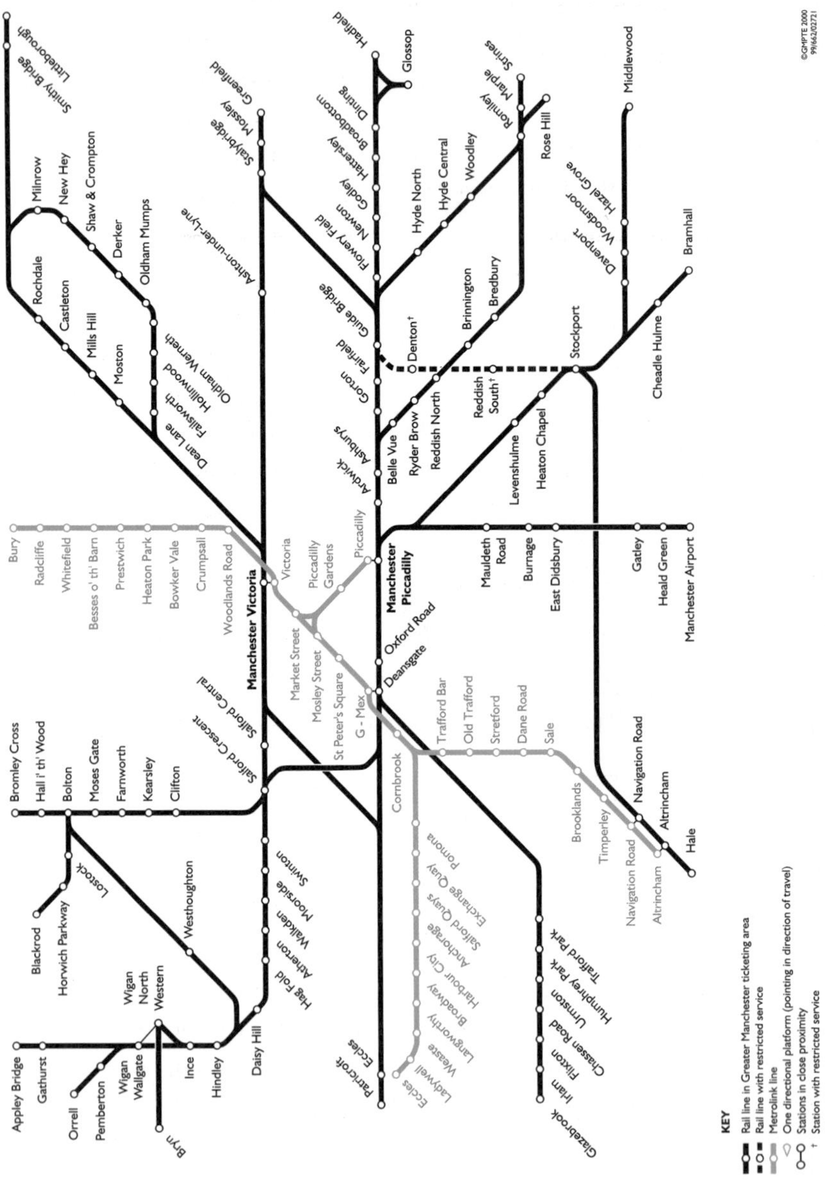

	Motorway with junction number
	Primary route - dual carriageway and single
	A road - dual carriageway and single
	B road - dual carriageway and single
	Minor road - dual carriageway and single
	Other minor road - dual carriageway and single
	Road under construction
	Pedestrianised area
DY7	**Postcode boundaries**
	County and unitary authority boundaries
	Railway
	Tramway, miniature railway
	Rural track, private road or narrow road in urban area
	Gate or obstruction to traffic (restrictions may not apply at all times or to all vehicles)
	Path, bridleway, byway open to all traffic, road used as a public path
	The representation in this atlas of a road, track or path is no evidence of the existence of a right of way
84	**Adjoining page indicators** (The colour of the arrow indicates the scale of the page - see scales below)
157	
148	**The map area within the pink band is shown at a larger scale on the page indicated by the red block and arrow**

Walsall	**Railway station**
(M)	**Metrolink**
	Private railway station
	Bus, coach station
	Ambulance station
	Coastguard station
	Fire station
	Police station
+	**Accident and Emergency entrance to hospital**
H	**Hospital**
+	**Places of worship**
i	**Information Centre** (open all year)
P	**Parking**
P&R	**Park and Ride**
PO	**Post Office**
X	**Camping site**
	Caravan site
	Golf course
	Picnic site
Prim Sch	**Important buildings, schools, colleges, universities and hospitals**
River Medway	**Water name**
	Stream
	River or canal - minor and major
	Water
	Tidal water
	Woods
	Houses
Balls Park	**Non-Roman antiquity**
VILLA	**Roman antiquity**

Abbr	Full	Abbr	Full
Allot Gdns	**Allotments**	Meml	**Memorial**
Acad	**Academy**	Mon	**Monument**
Cemy	**Cemetery**	Mus	**Museum**
C Ctr	**Civic Centre**	Obsy	**Observatory**
CH	**Club House**	Pal	**Royal Palace**
Coll	**College**	PH	**Public House**
Crem	**Crematorium**	Recn Gd	**Recreation Ground**
Ent	**Enterprise**	Resr	**Reservoir**
Ex H	**Exhibition Hall**	Ret Pk	**Retail Park**
Ind Est	**Industrial Estate**	Sch	**School**
Inst	**Institute**	Sh Ctr	**Shopping Centre**
Ct	**Law Court**	TH	**Town Hall/House**
L Ctr	**Leisure Centre**	Trad Est	**Trading Estate**
LC	**Level Crossing**	Univ	**University**
Liby	**Library**	Wks	**Works**
Mkt	**Market**	YH	**Youth Hostel**

■ The dark grey border on the inside edge of some pages indicates that the mapping does not continue onto the adjacent page

■ The small numbers around the edges of the maps identify the 1 kilometre National Grid lines

The scale of the maps is 3.92 cm to 1 km
2½ inches to 1 mile 1: 25344

0	¼	½	¾	1 mile
0	250m	500m	750m	1 kilometre

The scale of the maps on pages numbered in red is 7.84 cm to 1 km 5 inches to 1 mile 1: 12672

0	220 yards	440 yards	660 yards	½ mile
0	125m	250m	375m	½ kilometre

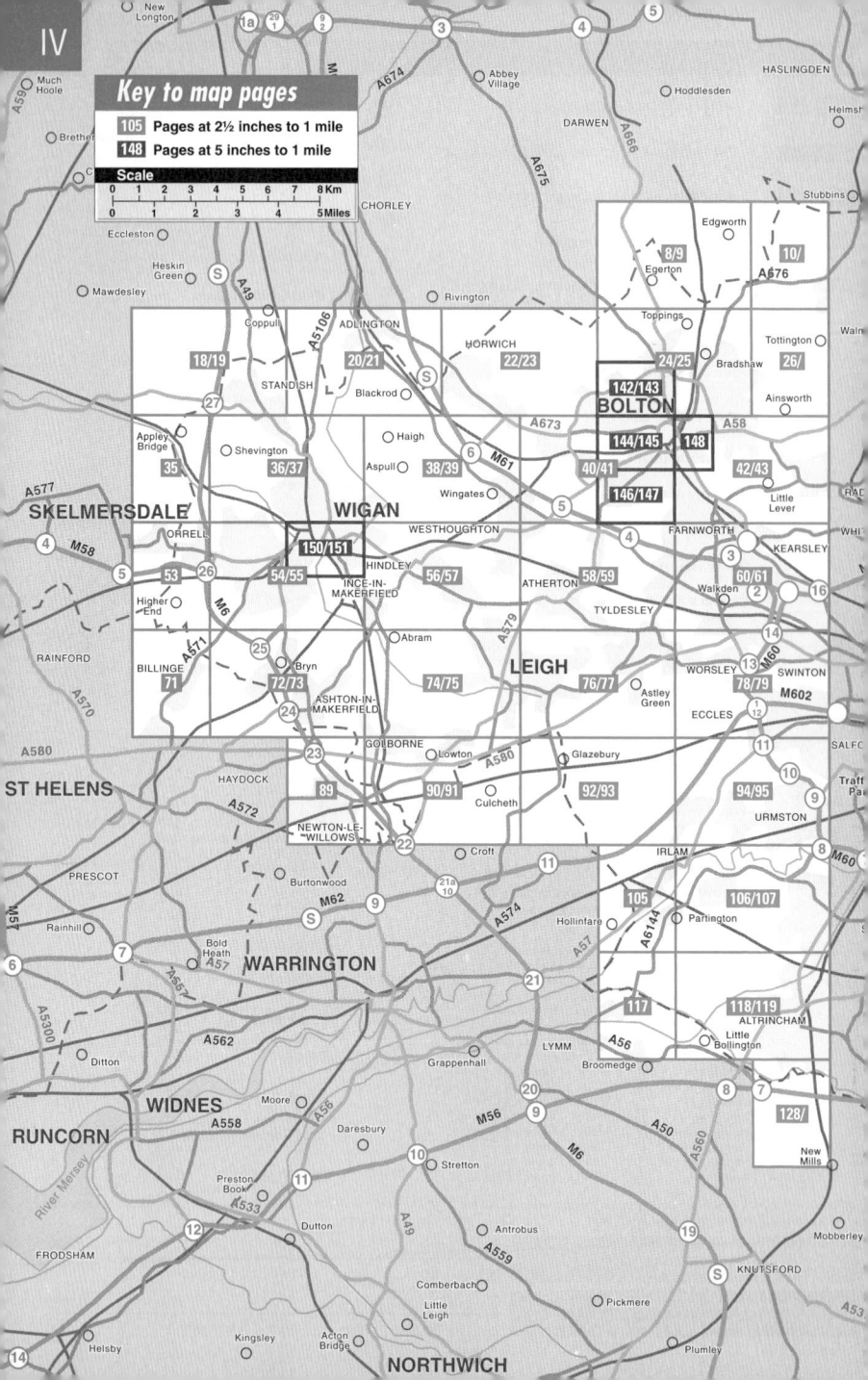

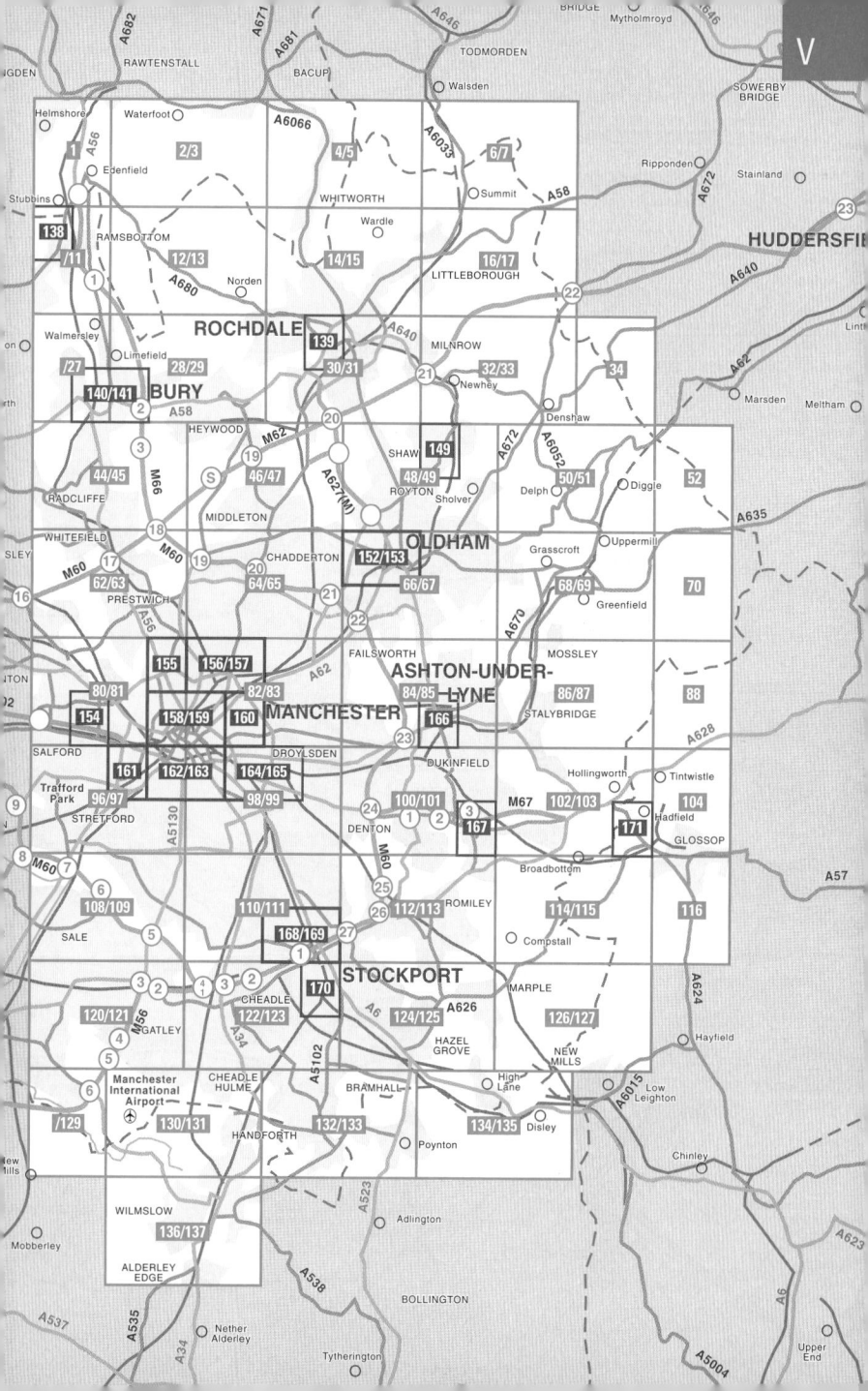

Route planning

Scale

| 0 | 1 | 2 | 3 | 4 | 5 | 6 | 7 | 8 km |
| 0 | | 1 | 2 | 3 | | 4 | | 5 miles |

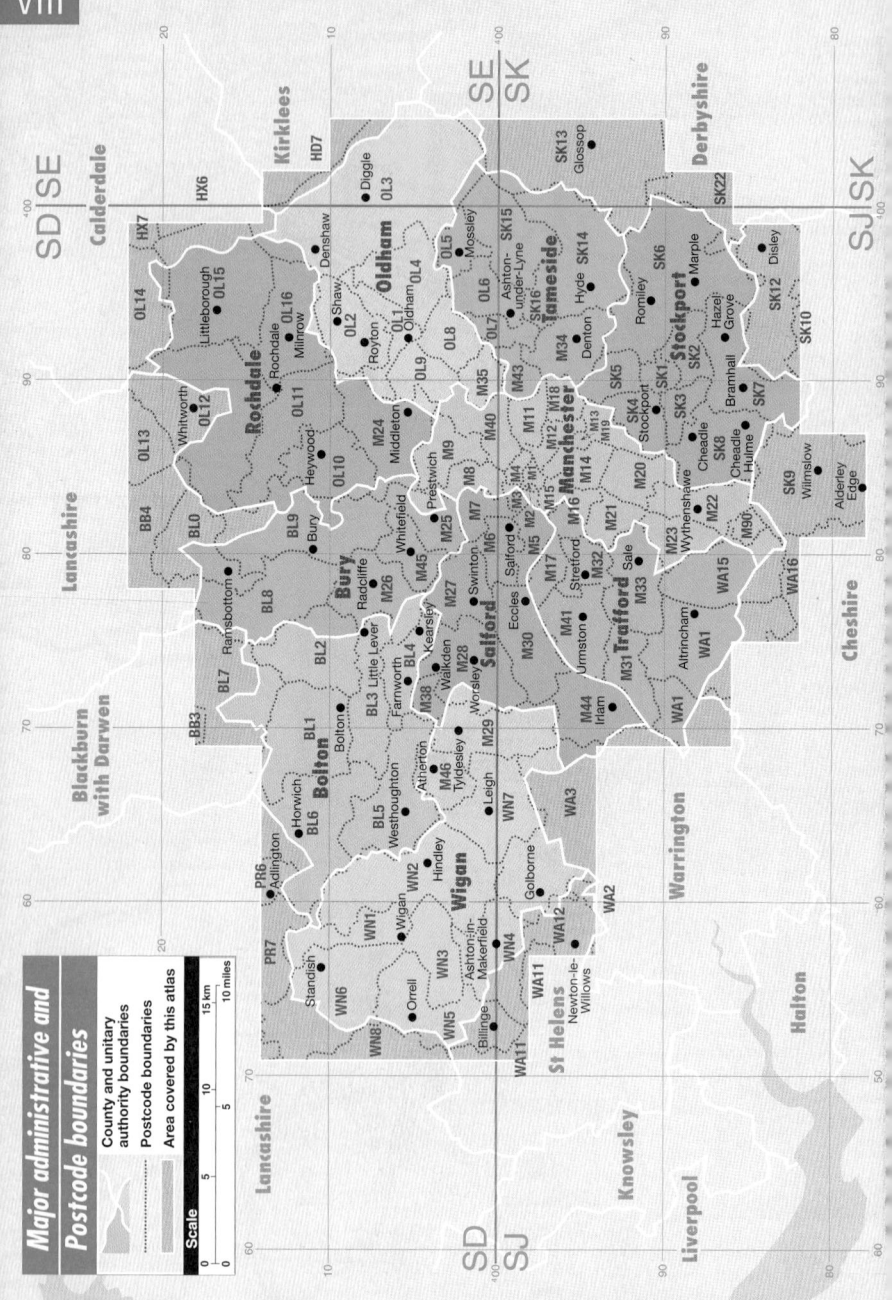

Major administrative and Postcode boundaries

County and unitary authority boundaries
Postcode boundaries
Area covered by this atlas

Scale

0   5   10   15 km
0   5   10 miles

Map Grid References

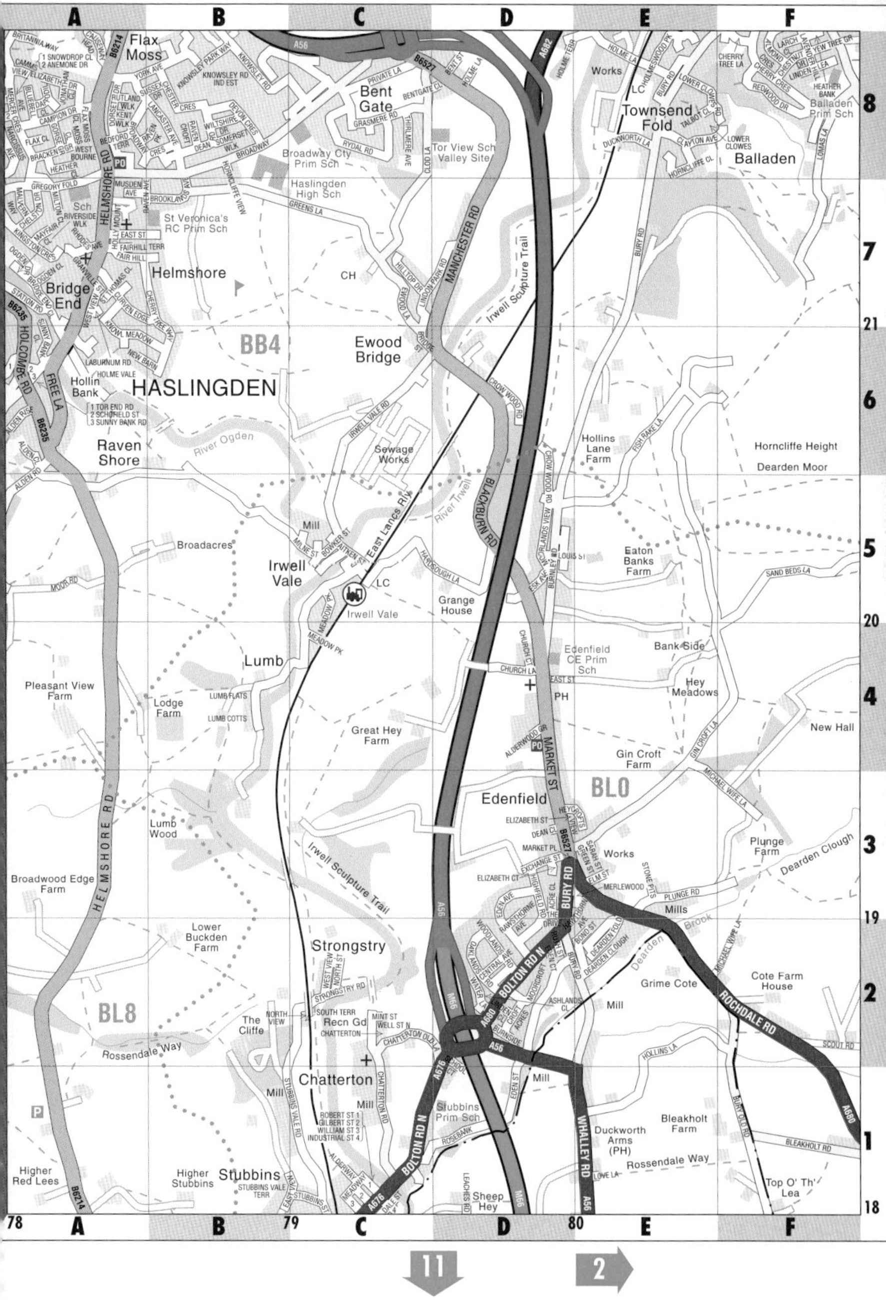

	A	B	C	D	E	F

8
Britannia Way, Flax Moss, Bent Gate, Knowsley Rd Ind Est, A56, Works, Townsend Fold, Balladen Prim Sch, Cherry Tree La, Heather Bank

7
Helmshore, Helmshore Rd, Broadway City Prim Sch, Tor View Sch Valley Site, Haslingden High Sch, St Veronica's RC Prim Sch, Manchester Rd, CH, Irwell Sculpture Trail

21

6
Bridge End, Hollin Bank, HASLINGDEN, BB4, Ewood Bridge, Raven Shore, 1 Tor End Rd, 2 Schofield St, 3 Sunny Bank Rd, River Ogden, Sewage Works, Hollins Lane Farm, Horncliffe Height, Dearden Moor, Blackburn Rd

5
Broadacres, Mill, Irwell Vale, River East Lancs Rly, River Twell, LC, Eaton Banks Farm, Sand Beds La

20
Pleasant View Farm, Lodge Farm, Lumb, Lumb Flats, Lumb Cotts, Meadow Pk, Irwell Vale, LC, Grange House, Church Rd, Edenfield CE Prim Sch, Bank Side, Hey Meadows

4
Great Hey Farm, Market St, PH, PO, Gin Croft Farm, New Hall

3
Broadwood Edge Farm, Lumb Wood, Irwell Sculpture Trail, Edenfield, BL0, Elizabeth St, Dean St, Market St, Elizabeth Cl, Works, Stone Fold, Merlewood, Plunge Farm, Dearden Clough, Plunge Rd

19
Lower Buckden Farm, Strongstry, Strongstry Rd, Bolton Rd N, Mills, Mill, Cote Farm House, Rochdale Rd

2
BL8, The Cliffe, North View, South Terr, Rec Gd, Chatterton, Mint St, Well St, Chatterton Dean, A56, Grime Cote, Rossendale Way, Scout Rd

1
Higher Red Lees, Rossendale Way, Higher Stubbins, Stubbins, Stubbins Vale Terr, 1 Robert St, 2 Gilbert St, 3 William St, 4 Industrial Est, Mill, Chatterton, Bolton Rd S, Stubbins Prim Sch, Sheep Hey, Whalley Rd, Duckworth Arms (PH), Love La, Bleakholt Farm, Bleakholt Rd, Top O' Th' Lea, A680

18

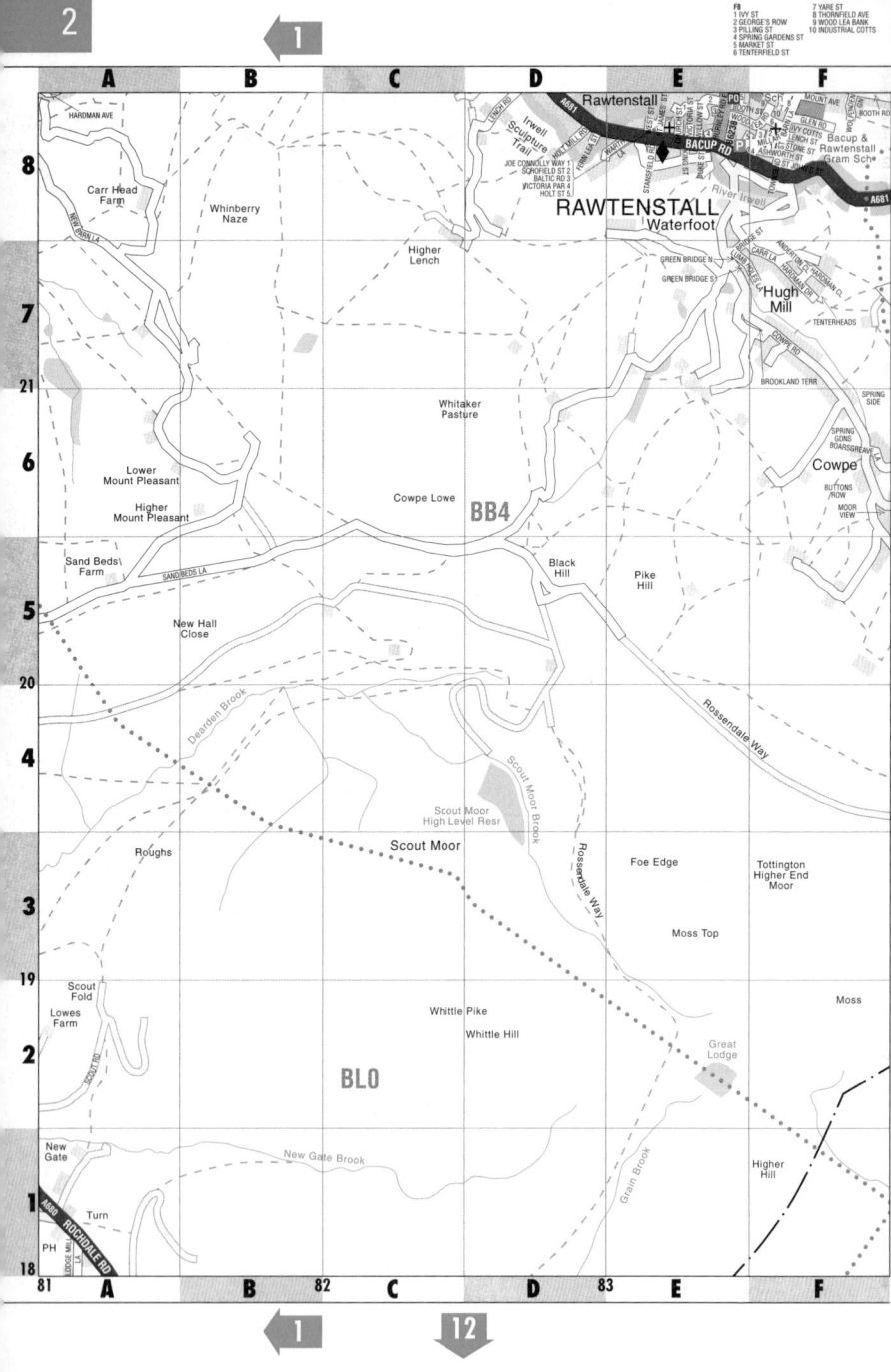

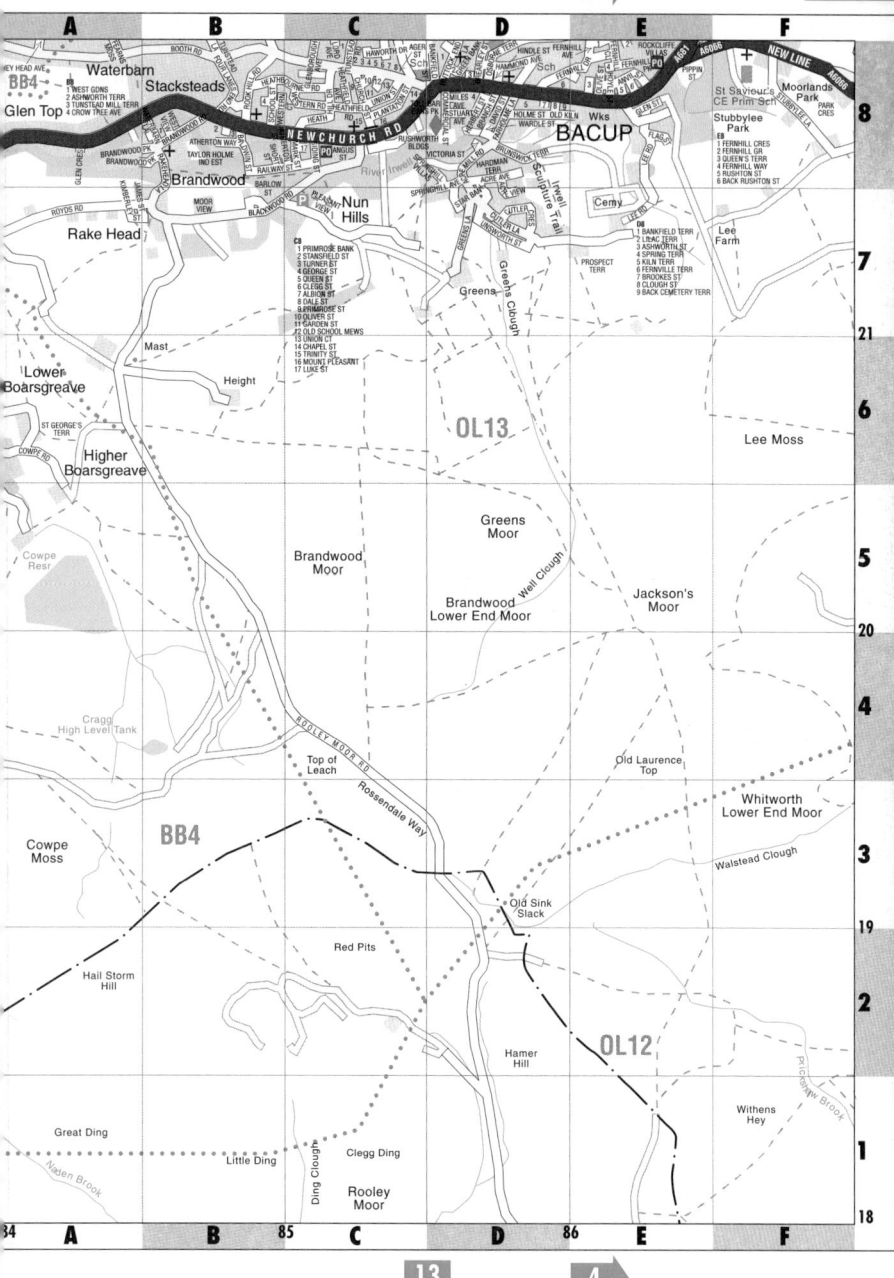

3

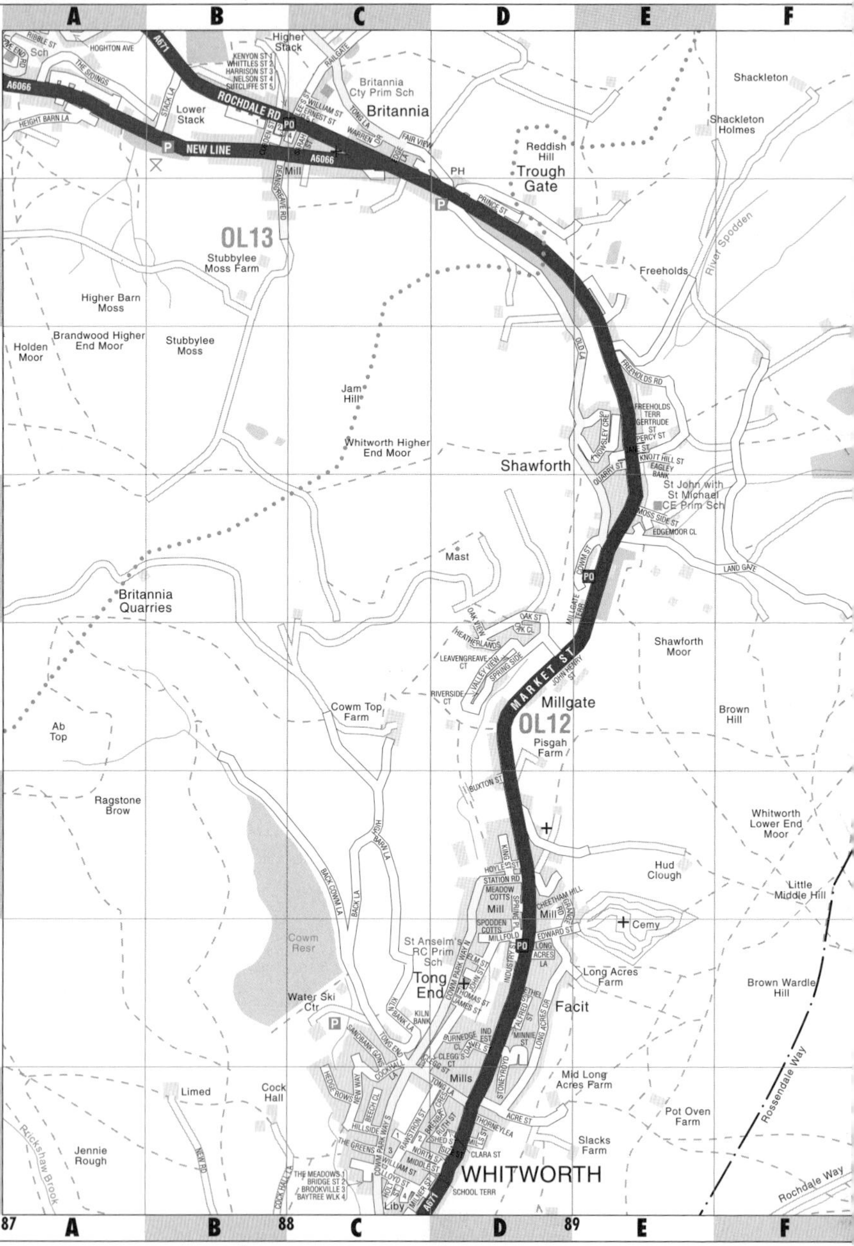

A
B
C
D
E
F
8
7
21
6
5
20
4
3
19
2
1
18
87
88
89
A6066
A671
ROCHDALE RD
NEW LINE
Lower Stack
Higher Stack
Britannia
Britannia Cty Prim Sch
Reddish Hill
Trough Gate
Shackleton
Shackleton Holmes
PH
Mill
OL13
Stubbylee Moss Farm
Higher Barn Moss
Holden Moor
Brandwood Higher End Moor
Stubbylee Moss
Jam Hill
Whitworth Higher End Moor
Freeholds
River Spodden
Shawforth
St John with St Michael CE Prim Sch
Mast
Britannia Quarries
Shawforth Moor
MARKET ST
Millgate
OL12
Pisgah Farm
Brown Hill
Cowm Top Farm
Ab Top
Ragstone Brow
Whitworth Lower End Moor
Hud Clough
Little Middle Hill
Cemy
Cowm Resr
St Anselm's RC Prim Sch
Tong End
Water Ski Ctr
Long Acres Farm
Facit
Brown Wardle Hill
Mills
Mid Long Acres Farm
Limed
Cock Hall
Pot Oven Farm
Rossendale Way
Jennie Rough
Slacks Farm
WHITWORTH
Rochdale Way
Rickshaw Brook
Liby
SCHOOL TERR

3

14

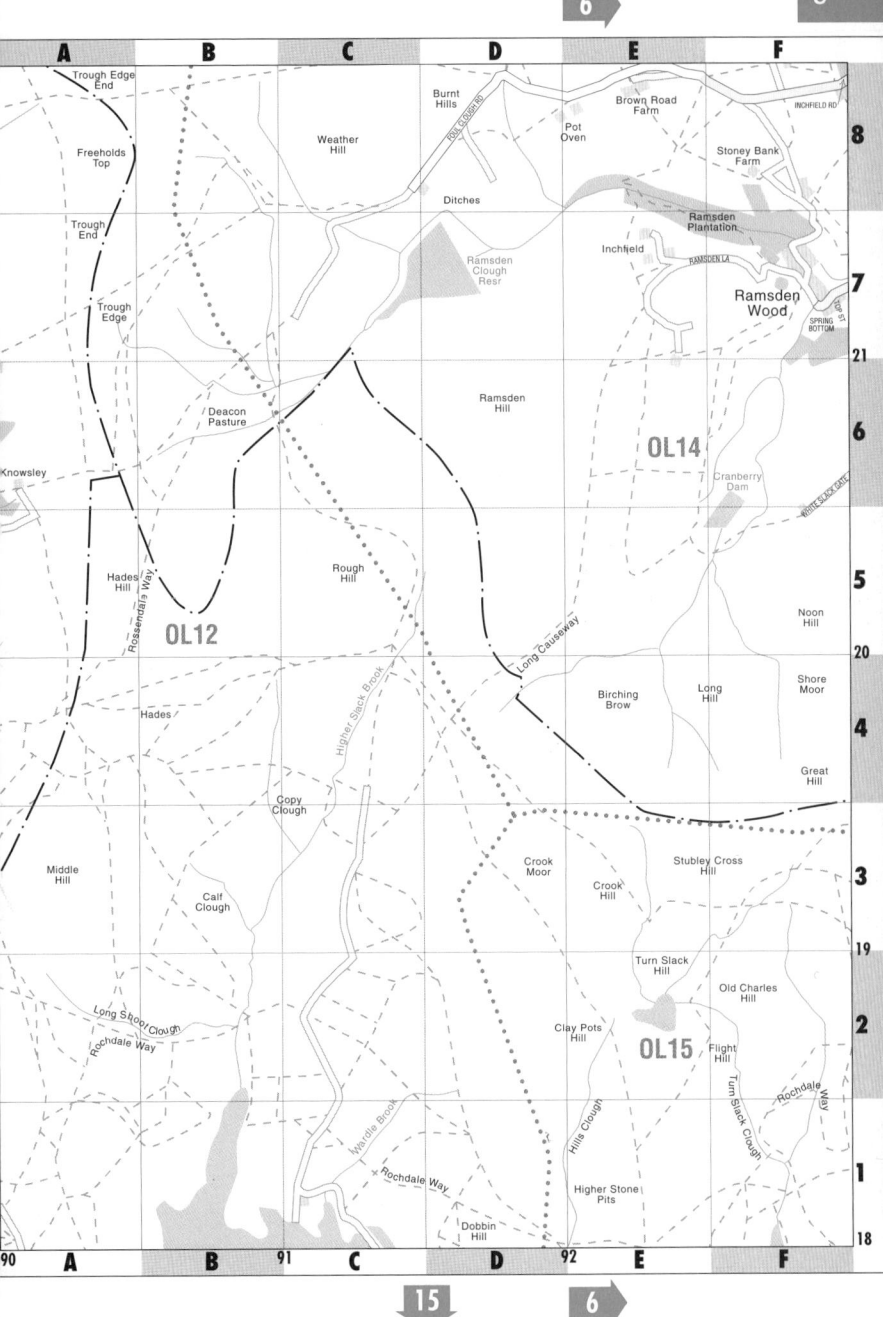

A   B   C   D   E   F

Trough Edge End
Burnt Hills
FOUL CLOUGH RD
Brown Road Farm
INCHFIELD RD

8

Weather Hill
Pot Oven
Stoney Bank Farm

Freeholds Top
Ditches
Ramsden Plantation

Trough End
Ramsden Clough Resr
Inchfield
RAMSDEN LA

7

Trough Edge
Ramsden Wood
SPRING BOTTOM

21

Deacon Pasture
Ramsden Hill

Knowsley
OL14

6

Cranberry Dam

Hades Hill
Rossendale Way
WHITE SLACK GATE

OL12
Rough Hill

5

Noon Hill

Long Causeway
20

Hades
Higher Slack Brook
Birching Brow
Long Hill
Shore Moor

4

Copy Clough
Great Hill

Middle Hill
Crook Moor
Crook Hill
Stubley Cross Hill

3

Calf Clough
Turn Slack Hill

19

Long Shoot Clough
Clay Pots Hill
OL15
Old Charles Hill

Rochdale Way
Flight Hill

2

Wardle Brook
Hills Clough
Turn Slack Clough
Rochdale Way

Rochdale Way
Higher Stone Pits

1

Dobbin Hill

18

90   A   B   91   C   D   92   E   F

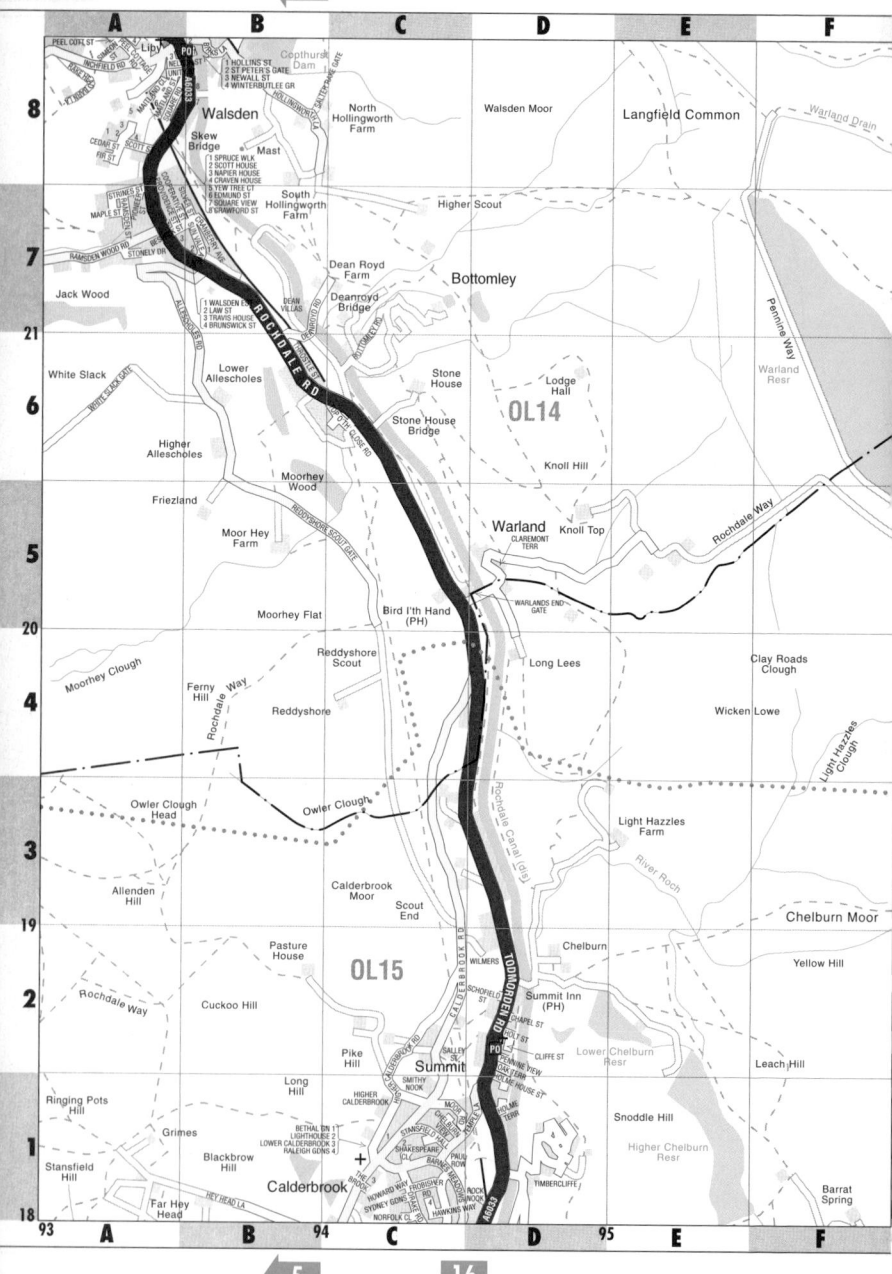

A **B** **C** **D** **E** **F**

8

Liby
Peel Cote St
Inchfield Rd
1 Hollins St
2 St Peter's Gate
3 Newall St
4 Winterbutlee Gr
Cophurst Dam
Walsden
North Hollingworth Farm
Walsden Moor
Langfield Common
Warland Drain

Skew Bridge
Mast
1 Spruce Wlk
2 Scott House
3 Napier House
4 Craven House
5 Yew Tree Ct
6 Edmund St
7 Square View
8 Crawford St
South Hollingworth Farm
Higher Scout

7

Strong St
Maple St
Ramsden Wood Rd
Stoney Dr
Dean Royd Farm
Bottomley
Pennine Way

21

Jack Wood
1 Walsden Est
2 Law St
3 Travis House
4 Brunswick St
Dean Villas
Deanroyd Bridge
Stone House
Lodge Hall
Warland Resr

White Slack
Lower Allescholes
Stone House Bridge
OL14
Knoll Hill

6

Higher Allescholes
Moorhey Wood
Warland
Knoll Top
Claremont Terr
Rochdale Way

Friezland
Moor Hey Farm
Bird I'th Hand (PH)
Warlands End Gate

5

Moorhey Flat
Reddyshore Scout
Long Lees
Clay Roads Clough

20

Moorhey Clough
Ferny Hill
Rochdale Way
Reddyshore
Wicken Lowe
Light Hazzles Clough

4

Owler Clough Head
Owler Clough
Light Hazzles Farm

3

Allenden Hill
Calderbrook Moor
Scout End
River Roch
Chelburn Moor

19

Rochdale Way
Pasture House
OL15
Chelburn
Yellow Hill

2

Cuckoo Hill
Wilmers
Summit Inn (PH)
Lower Chelburn Resr
Leach Hill

Pike Hill
Sally St
Cliffe St
House St

Long Hill
Summit
Smithy Nook
Snoddle Hill
Higher Chelburn Resr

1

Ringing Pots Hill
Higher Calderbrook
Bethal Dn 1
Lighthouse 2
Lower Calderbrook 3
Raleigh Gdns 4
Shakespeare St
Paul Row
Timbercliffe
Barrat Spring

Stansfield Hill
Grimes
Blackbrow Hill
Calderbrook
Far Hey Head
Hey Head La
Howard Way
Sydney Gdns
Norfolk Cl
Hawkins Way

18

93 **A** **B** 94 **C** **D** 95 **E** **F**

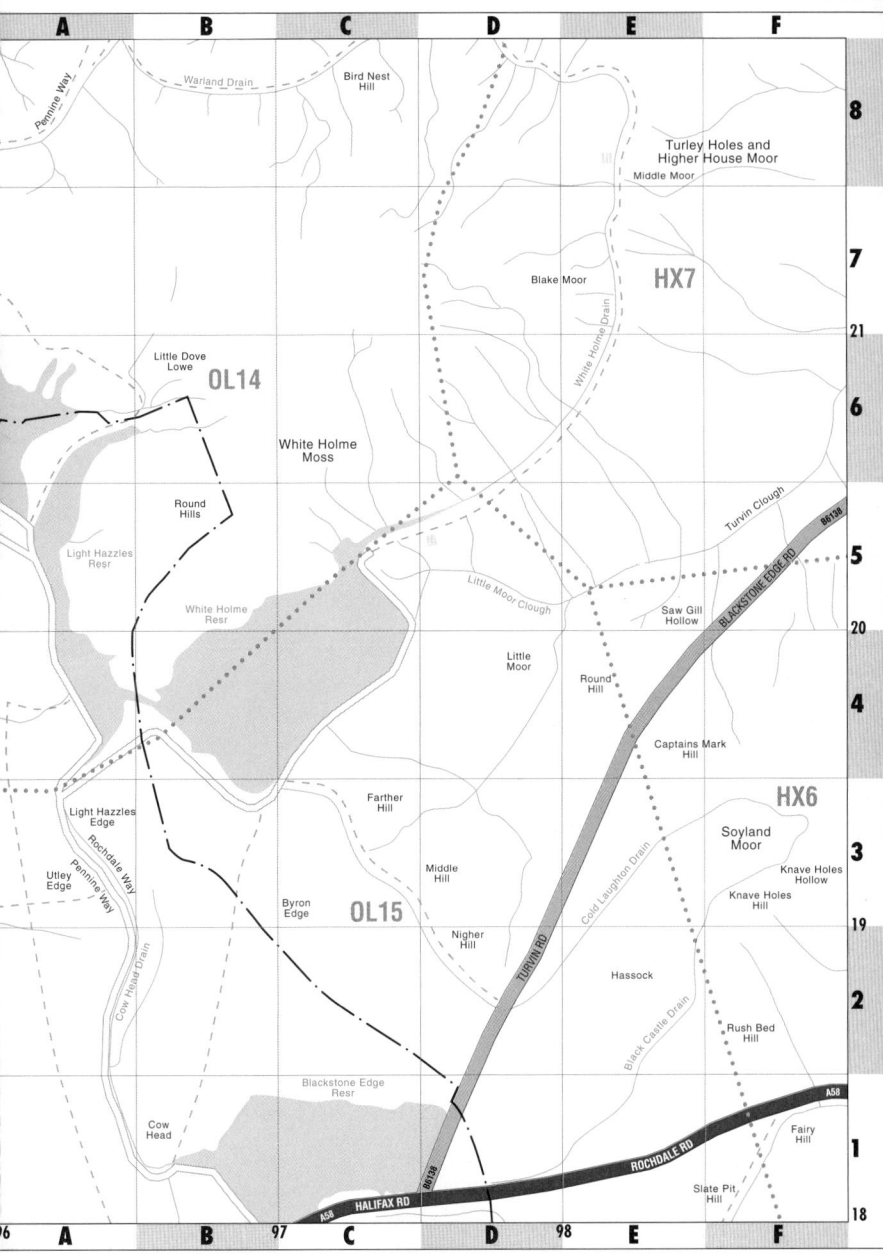

Warland Drain

Bird Nest Hill

Pennine Way

Turley Holes and Higher House Moor

Middle Moor

8

Blake Moor

HX7

White Holme Drain

7

21

Little Dove Lowe

OL14

White Holme Moss

6

Round Hills

Turvin Clough

B6138

Light Hazzles Resr

Little Moor Clough

5

White Holme Resr

Saw Gill Hollow

BLACKSTONE EDGE RD

20

Little Moor

Round Hill

4

Captains Mark Hill

Farther Hill

HX6

Light Hazzles Edge

Soyland Moor

3

Rochdale Way

Middle Hill

Cold Laughton Drain

Knave Holes Hollow

Utley Edge

Pennine Way

Knave Holes Hill

19

Byron Edge

OL15

Nigher Hill

TURVIN RD

Cow Head Drain

Hassock

2

Black Castle Drain

Rush Bed Hill

Blackstone Edge Resr

A58

Cow Head

ROCHDALE RD

Fairy Hill

1

Slate Pit Hill

B6138

18

A58 HALIFAX RD

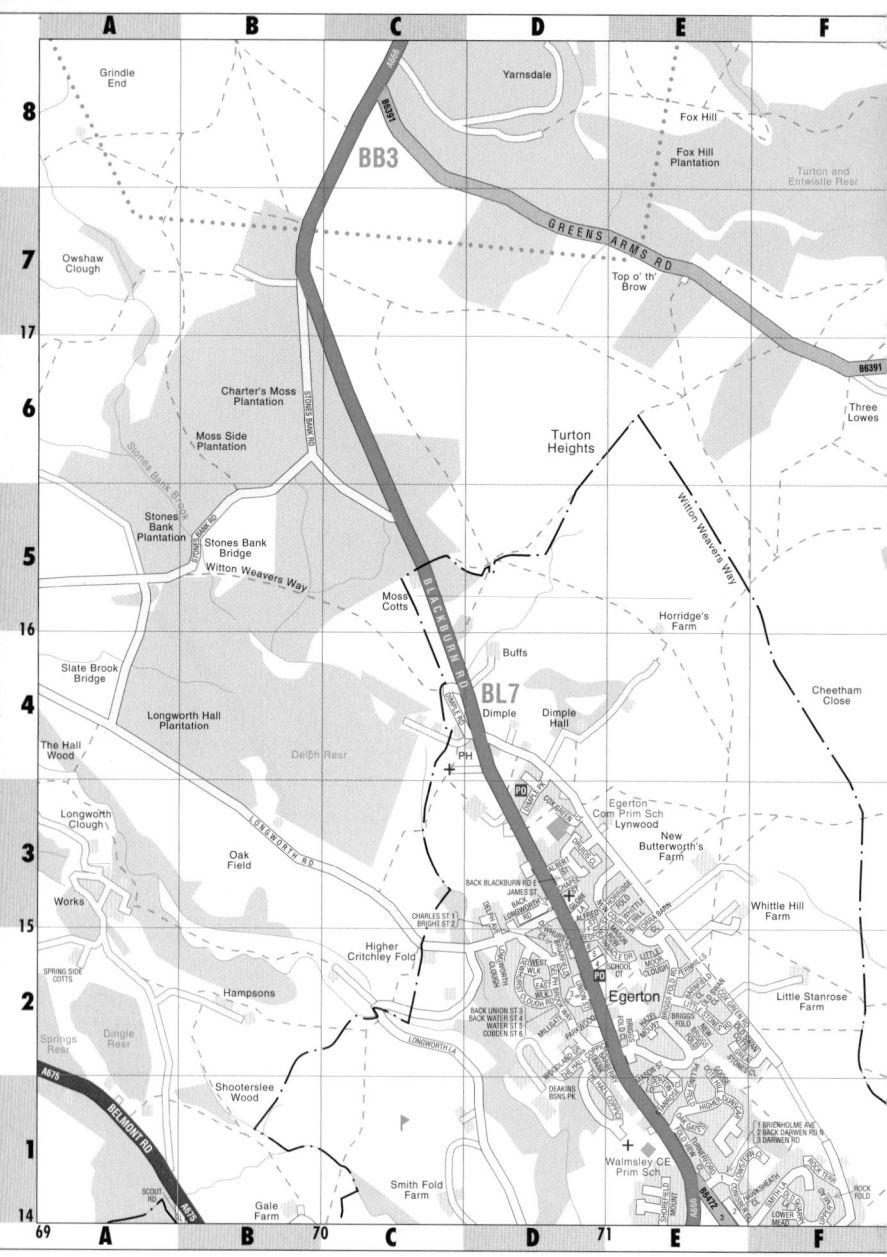

New House Farm
Strawbury Duck (PH)
Entwistle
EDGE LA
GREENROFD RD
RAILWAY TERR
ENTWISTLE HALL LA

Entwistle

Hill Top
Dingle Farm
SCHOOL VIEW
SCHOOL LA

Pleasant View
Wheatsheaf Farm

Hazel Clough Farm

Hob Lane Farm
Isherwood Fold

Horrocks Fold Farm

Greenthorne

Nabbs Farm
Armsgrove Farm
DEER HOUSES

Edgworth
Thomason Fold
MAY ST PH

Mill

GREENS ARMS RD

Billy Brook

Wayoh Resr

BL7

Temple Farm

Spring Bank Farm

Higher Barn Farm

Clough House Farm

Fir Trees
Chetham Arms Hotel (PH)

Chapeltown

Edgworth Prim Sch
MOUNT PLEASANT

Pallet Farm

Victoria Mill
LC

HIGH ST
KAY ST
CHAPEL FIELDS
CHARLOTTE ST
STATION RD

Wellington St

Turton Bottoms

Witton Weavers Way

BACK HIGH ST

Quarlton Fold Farm

Turton Tower

Tower Farm

Lithermans Bridge

Jumbles

Birches

Walves Resr

CHAPELTOWN RD

Horrobin Lodge
THE COPSE
HORROBIN LA

LEES COTTS

Jumbles Country Park

Bull's Head Inn (PH)
RAMSBOTTOM RD A676
TURTINGTON
B6213

Turra Barn

HORROBIN FOLD

Jumbles Resr

Turton Heights (PH)

Hazelhurst Brook

King William Inn (PH)

WALSH FOLD

BL2

Lamb Inn (PH)

BRADSHAW RD

BL8

Toye Farm

The Last Drop Village
Top of Turton
CH

Holts Fold
Bromley Cross
BOLT RD

A676

9

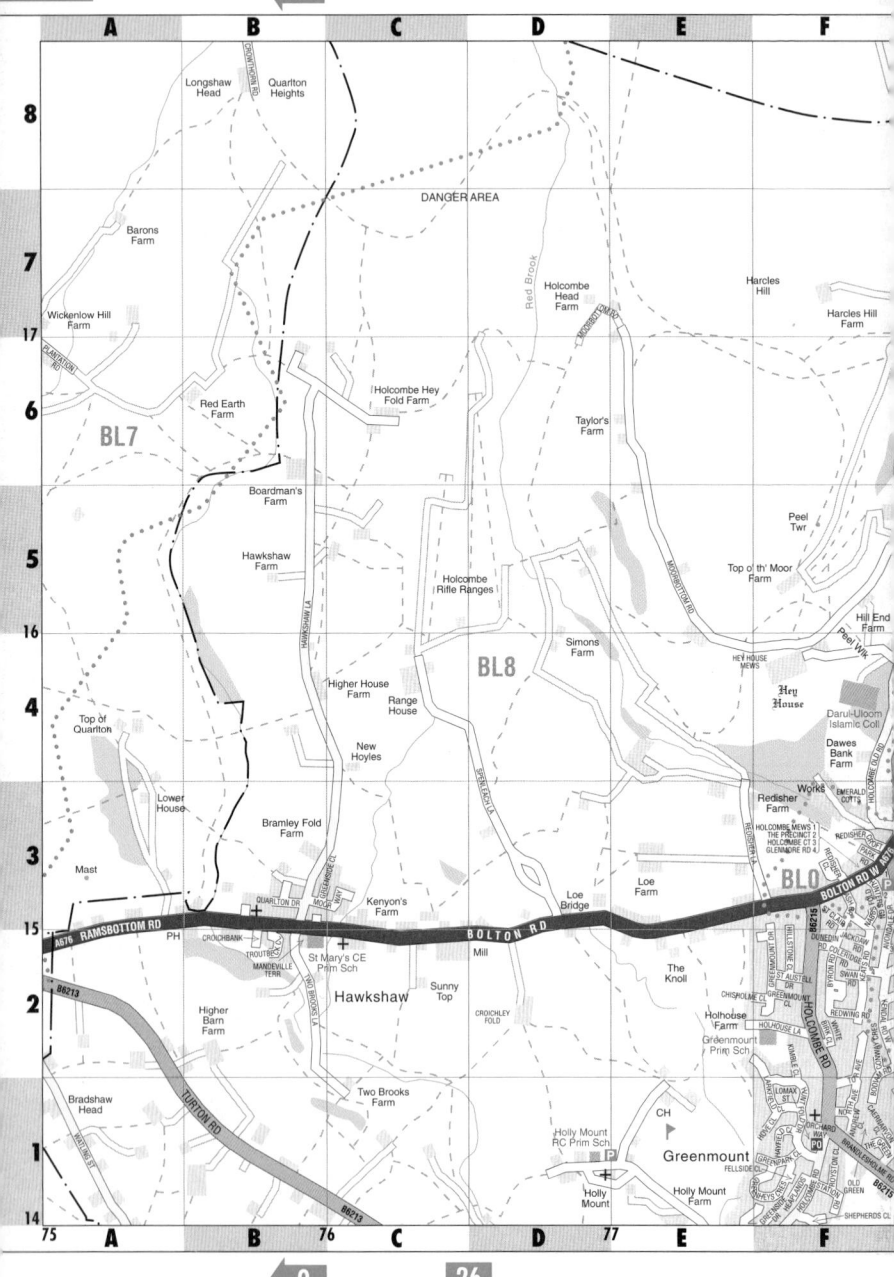

8

DANGER AREA

Longshaw Head

Quarlton Heights

Red Brook

Holcombe Head Farm

Harcles Hill

7

Barons Farm

Harcles Hill Farm

17

Wickenlow Hill Farm

Holcombe Hey Fold Farm

Taylor's Farm

6

BL7

Red Earth Farm

Peel Twr

Boardman's Farm

5

Hawkshaw Farm

Holcombe Rifle Ranges

Top of th' Moor Farm

Simons Farm

Hill End Farm

Peel Wk

16

BL8

HEY HOUSE MEWS

Hey House

4

Higher House Farm

Darul-Uloom Islamic Coll

Top of Quarlton

Range House

Dawes Bank Farm

New Hoyles

Works

Redisher Farm

Emerald Cotts

Redisher Cl

3

Lower House

Bramley Fold Farm

BLO

Mast

Kenyon's Farm

Loe Bridge

Loe Farm

HOLCOMBE MEWS 1
THE PRECINCT 2
HOLCOMBE CT 3
GLENMORE RD 4

BOLTON RD W

QUARLTON DR

15

A676 **RAMSBOTTOM RD**

PH

CROICHBANK

TROUTBECK

Mill

BOLTON RD

The Knoll

HILLSTONE CL

AUSTELL

CATERHAM CL

DENEDIN

HOLCOMBE RD

2

B6213

MANDEVILLE TERR

St Mary's CE Prim Sch

Sunny Top

Hawkshaw

CROICHLEY FOLD

Holhouse Farm

Greenmount Prim Sch

CHISHOLME CL

GREENMOUNT CL

WHITE...

REDWING RD

SWAN...

Higher Barn Farm

Two Brooks Farm

CH

Holly Mount RC Prim Sch

Greenmount

FELLSIDE CL

ORCHARD

1

Bradshaw Head

TURTON RD

Holly Mount

Holly Mount Farm

OLD GREEN

14

B6213

SHEPHERDS CL

For full street detail of the highlighted area see page 138.

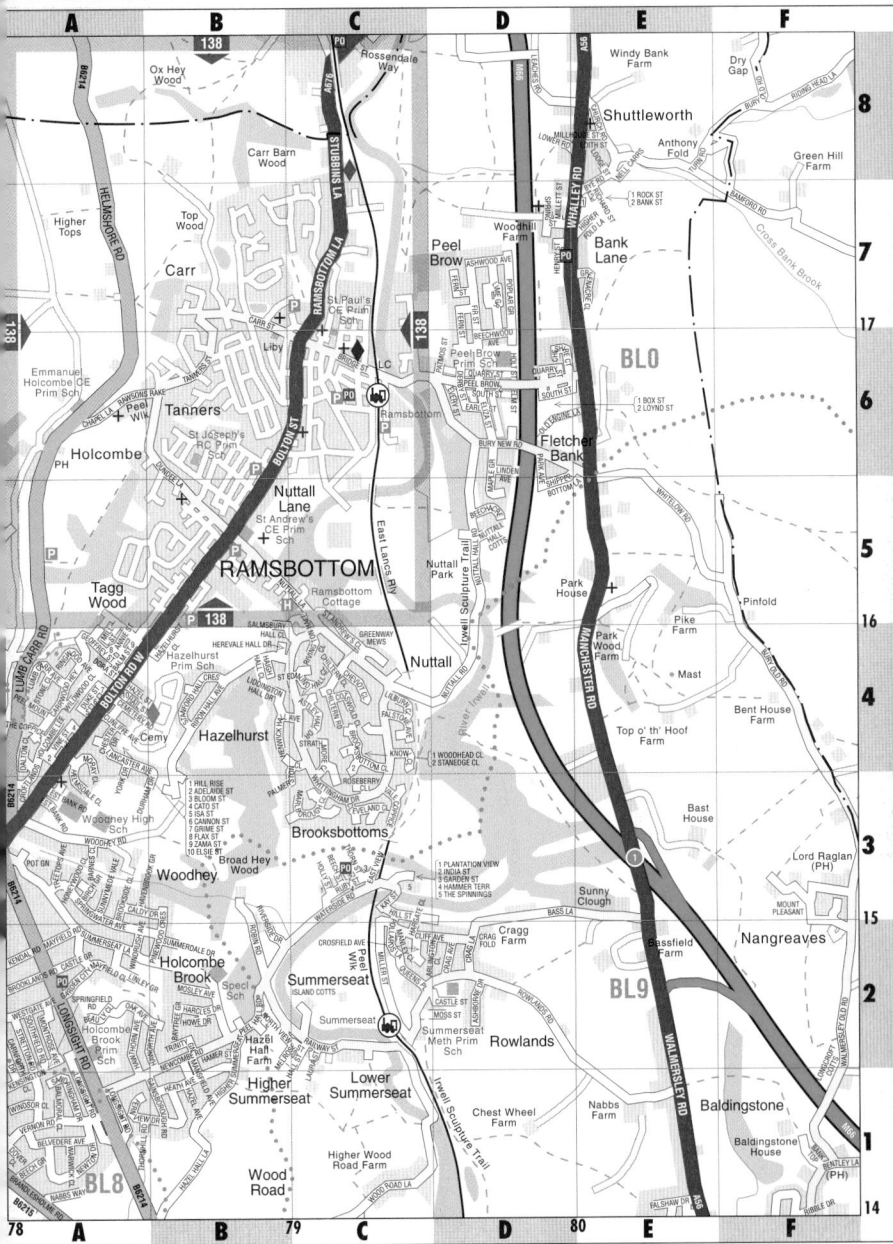

A B C D E F

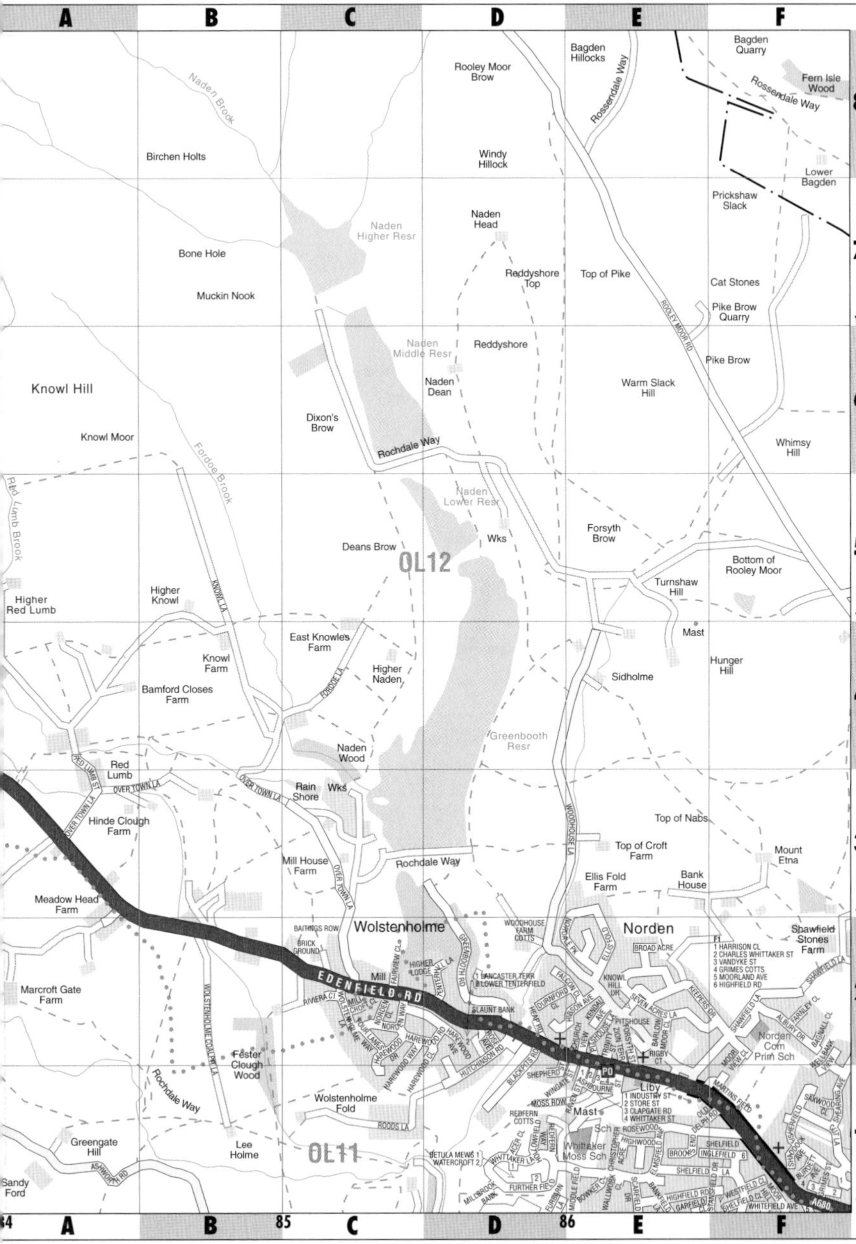

Naden Brook

Rooley Moor Brow

Bagden Hillocks

Bagden Quarry

Fern Isle Wood

Rossendale Way

8

Birchen Holts

Windy Hillock

Lower Bagden

Prickshaw Slack

7

Naden Higher Resr

Naden Head

Reddyshore Top

Top of Pike

Cat Stones

Bone Hole

Muckin Nook

Pike Brow Quarry

17

Naden Middle Resr

Reddyshore

Pike Brow

Knowl Hill

Naden Dean

Warm Slack Hill

6

Knowl Moor

Dixon's Brow

Rochdale Way

Whimsy Hill

Foldie Brook

Naden Lower Resr

Higher Red Lumb

Deans Brow

Wks

OL12

Forsyth Brow

Bottom of Rooley Moor

5

Reb Lumb Brook

Higher Knowl

Knowl La

Turnshaw Hill

16

East Knowles Farm

Higher Naden

Mast

Hunger Hill

Knowl Farm

Sidholme

4

Bamford Closes Farm

Naden Wood

Greenbooth Resr

Red Lumb

Over Town La

Rain Shore

Wks

Top of Nabs

Top of Croft Farm

Mount Etna

3

Hinde Clough Farm

Mill House Farm

Rochdale Way

Ellis Fold Farm

Bank House

Meadow Head Farm

Woodhouse La

Baithings Row

Wolstenholme

Woodhouse Farm Cotts

Norden

Shawfield Stones Farm

15

Brick Ground

Mill

Broad Acre

1 HARRISON CL
2 CHARLES WHITTAKER ST
3 VANDYKE ST
4 GRIMES COTTS
5 MOORLAND AVE
6 HIGHFIELD RD

Marcroft Gate Farm

EDENFIELD RD

Knowl Hill

2

Wolstenholme Chapel La

Fester Clough Wood

Beaunt Bank

Lancaster Terr
Lower Tenterfield

Rigby

Norden Com Prim Sch

Rochdale Way

Wolstenholme Fold

OL11

Lee Holme

Roods La

Shepherd

PO

Liby

Moss Row

Mast

1 INDUSTRY ST
2 STORE ST
3 CLAPGATE RD
4 WHITTAKER ST

Greengate Hill

Betuka Mews 1
Watercroft 2

Whittaker Moss Sch

Rosewood

Shelfield

1

Sandy Ford

Millbridge Bank

Further Field

Highfield Rd

A680

14

A B C D E F

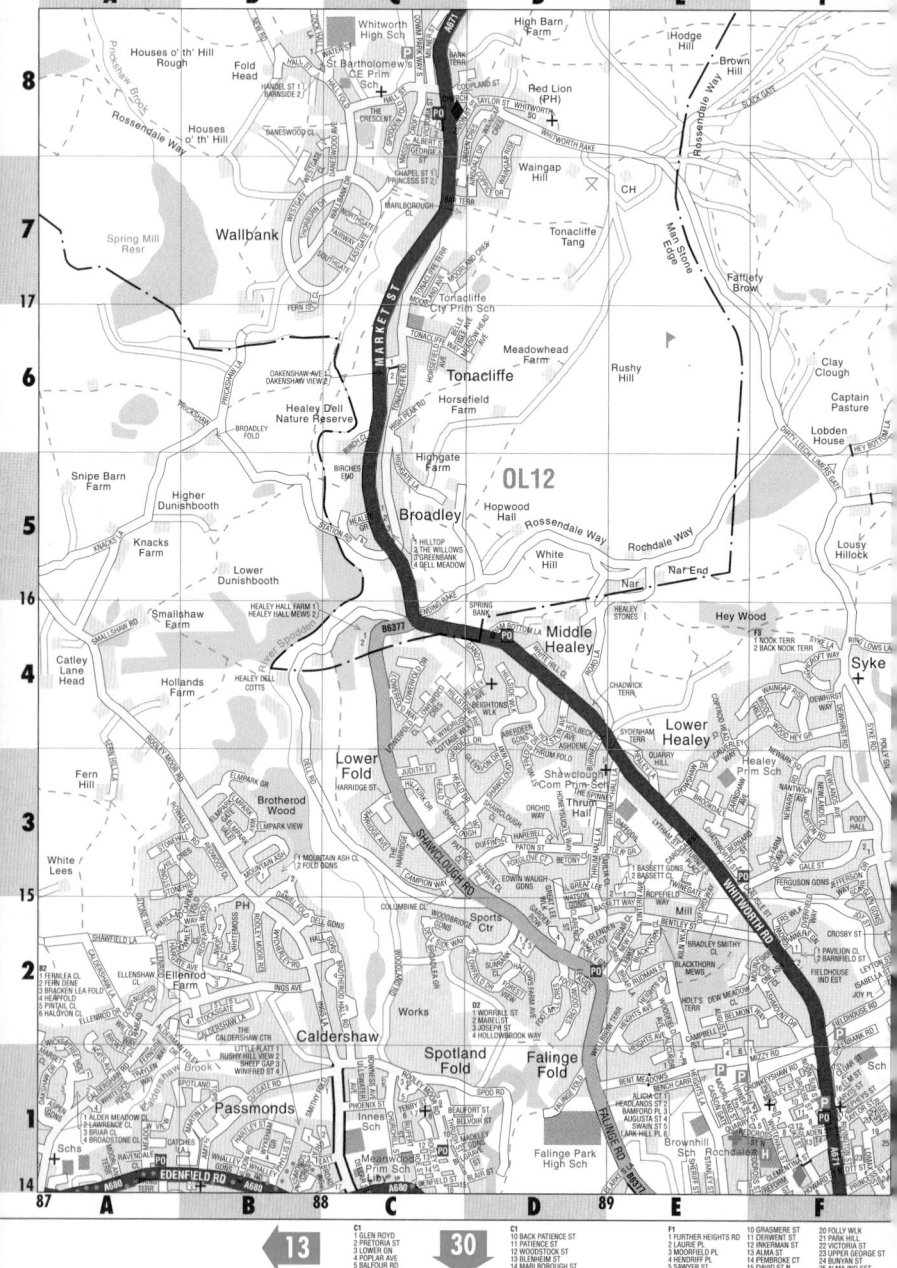

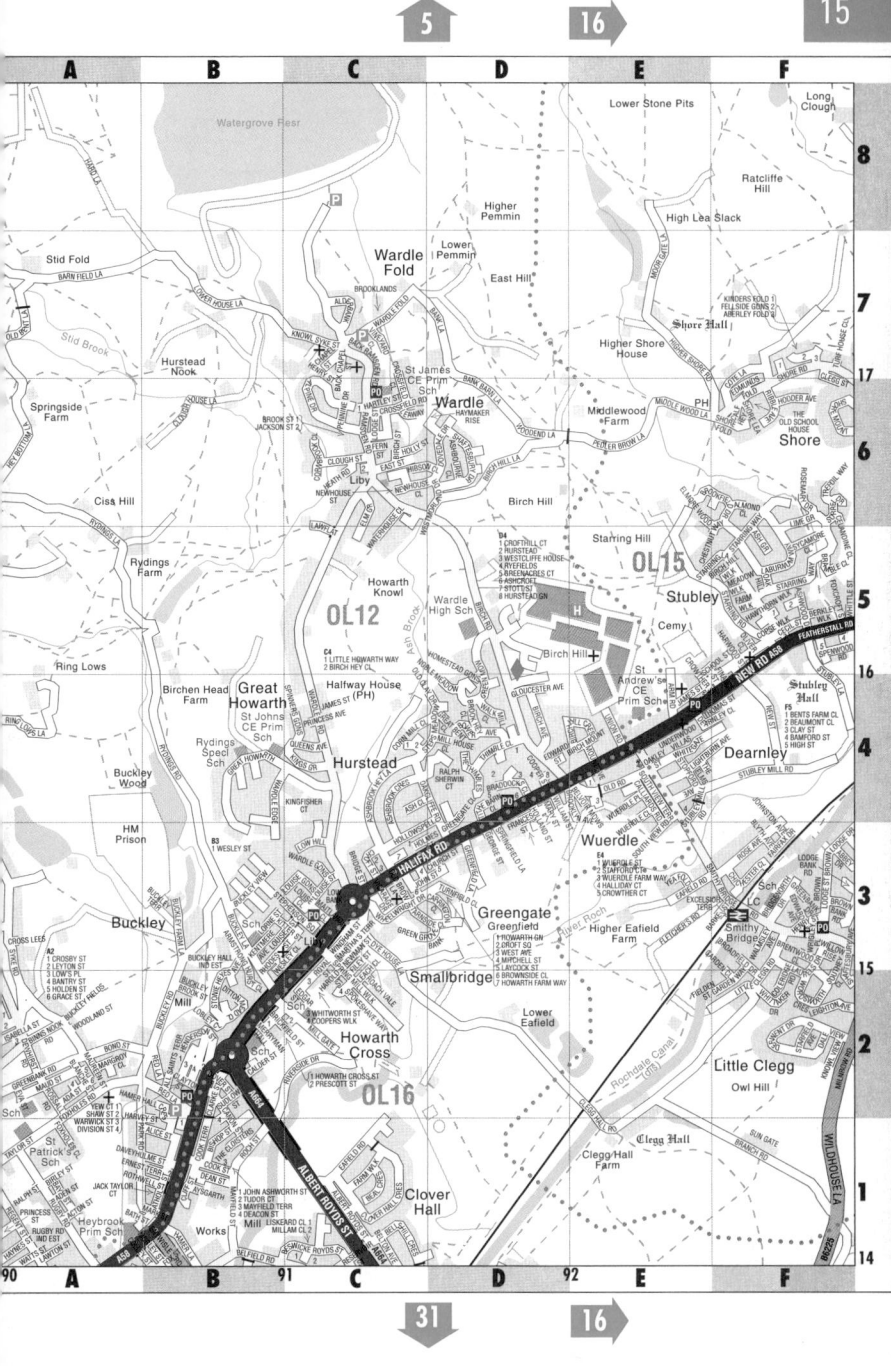

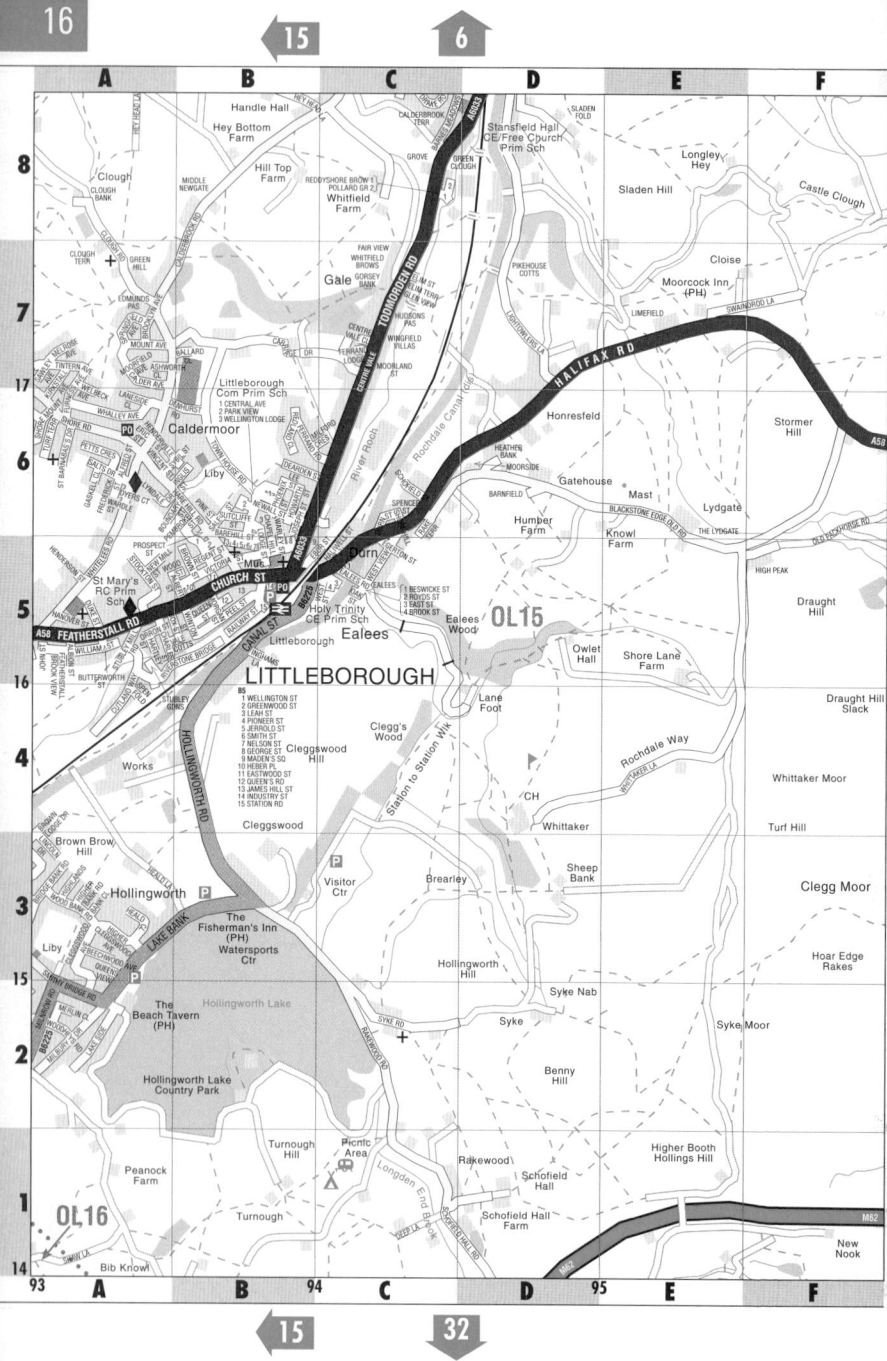

15
6

A **B** **C** **D** **E** **F**

Handle Hall

Hey Bottom
Farm

Hill Top
Farm

MIDDLE
NEWGATE

Clough
CLOUGH
BANK

Whitfield
Farm

REDDYSHORE BROW 1
POLLARD GR 2

Stansfield Hall
CE Free Church
Prim Sch

CALDERBROOK
TERR

GROVE

GREEN
CLOUGH

SLADEN
FOLD

Longley
Hey

Castle
Clough

Sladen Hill

8

FAIR VIEW
WHITFIELD
BROWS
GORSEY
BANK

Gale

Cloise

Moorcock Inn
(PH)

SWAINROAD LA

CLOUGH
TERR

GREEN
HILL

EDMUNDS
PAS

CENTRAL
VALE

HUDSONS
PAS

WINGFIELD
VILLAS

PIKEHOUSE
COTTS

LIMEFIELD

7

MOUNT AVE

BALLARD

WOODLAND
ST

HALIFAX RD

17

Littleborough
Com Prim Sch
1 CENTRAL AVE
2 PARK VIEW
3 WELLINGTON LODGE

Honresfeld

Stormer
Hill

Caldermoor

Liby

HEATHER
BANK

MOORSIDE

Gatehouse

Mast

Lydgate

A58

BARNFIELD

BLACKSTONE EDGE OLD RD

THE LYDGATE

6

Humber
Farm

Knowl
Farm

HIGH PEAK

Draught
Hill

PROSPECT
ST

Durn

1 BESWICKE ST
2 INDYCS ST
3 EAST ST
4 BROOK ST

St Mary's
RC Prim
Sch

Holly Trinity
CE Prim Sch

Ealees

OL15

Ealees
Wood

Owlet
Hall

Shore Lane
Farm

5

A58 FEATHERSTALL RD

CHURCH ST

Littleborough

16

WILLIAM ST

BUTTERWORTH

LITTLEBOROUGH

B5
1 WELLINGTON ST
2 GREENWOOD ST
3 LEAH ST
4 PIONEER ST
5 JERROLD ST
6 SMITH ST
7 NELSON ST
8 GEORGE ST
9 MADEN'S SQ
10 HEBER PL
11 EASTWOOD ST
12 QUEEN'S RD
13 JAMES HILL ST
14 INDUSTRY ST
15 STATION RD

Clegg's
Wood

Cleggswood
Hill

Lane
Foot

Rochdale Way

Draught Hill
Slack

Whittaker Moor

Works

Cleggswood

CH

Whittaker

Turf Hill

4

Brown Brow
Hill

Hollingworth

HEALD

LANE BANK

Visitor
Ctr

Brearley

Sheep
Bank

Clegg Moor

3

Liby

The
Fisherman's Inn
(PH)
Watersports
Ctr

Hollingworth
Hill

Syke Nab

Hoar Edge
Rakes

15

The
Beach Tavern
(PH)

Hollingworth Lake

SYKE RD

Syke

Syke Moor

2

Hollingworth Lake
Country Park

Benny
Hill

Peanock
Farm

Turnough
Hill

Picnic
Area

Rakewood

Schofield
Hall

Higher Booth
Hollings Hill

1

OL16

Turnough

Schofield Hall
Farm

M62

New
Nook

14

SWAN LA

Bib Knowl

M62

93 **A** **B** 94 **C** **D** 95 **E** **F**

15
32

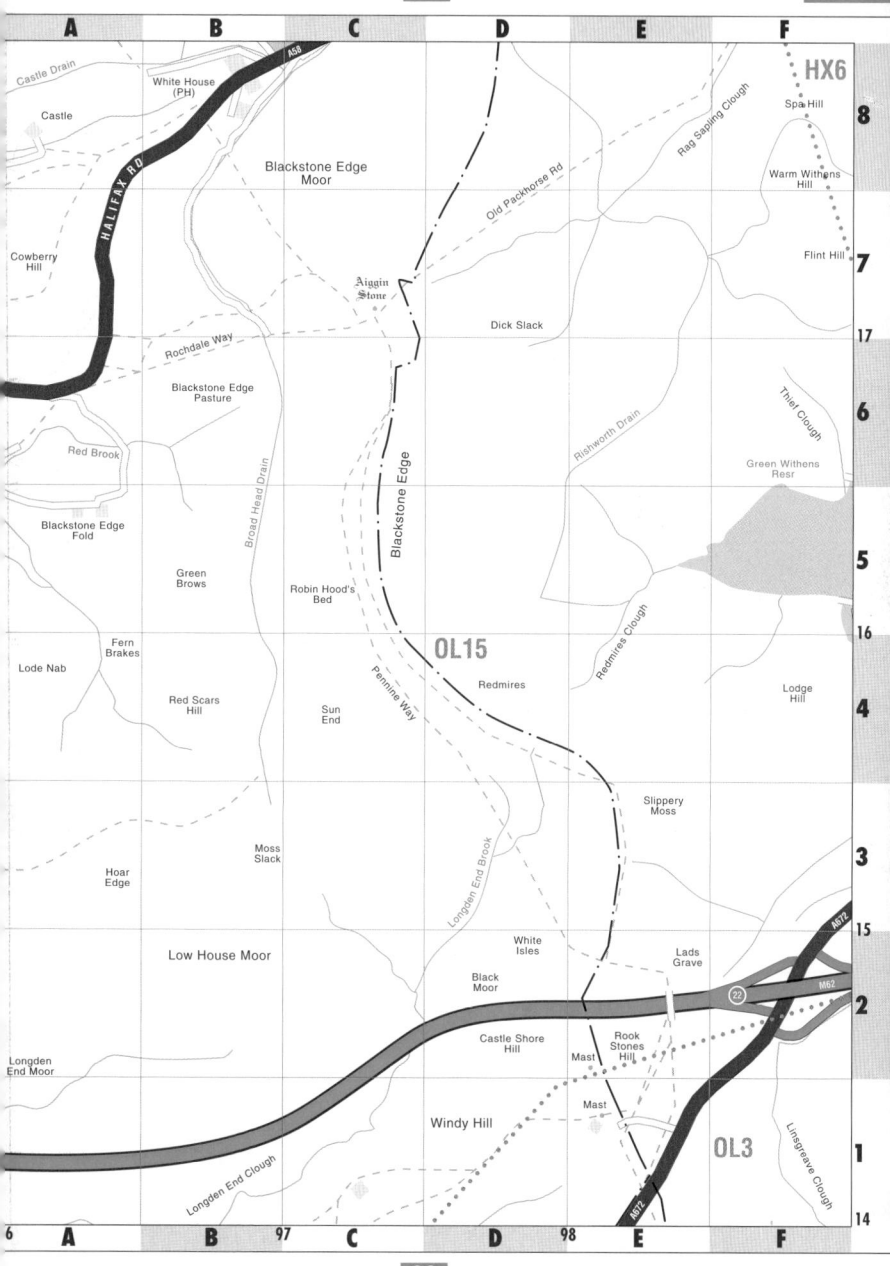

Castle Drain

White House (PH)

Castle

A58

HALIFAX RD

Blackstone Edge Moor

Spa Hill

8

Warm Withens Hill

Rag Sapling Clough

Old Packhorse Rd

Cowberry Hill

Flint Hill

7

Aiggin Stone

Dick Slack

17

Rochdale Way

Blackstone Edge Pasture

Thief Clough

6

Rishworth Drain

Red Brook

Broad Head Drain

Green Withens Resr

Blackstone Edge Fold

Blackstone Edge

Green Brows

5

Robin Hood's Bed

Redmires Clough

16

Fern Brakes

OL15

Lode Nab

Pennine Way

Redmires

Lodge Hill

4

Red Scars Hill

Sun End

Slippery Moss

3

Moss Slack

Hoar Edge

Longden End Brook

M62

15

White Isles

Lads Grave

Low House Moor

Black Moor

22

M62

2

Longden End Moor

Castle Shore Hill

Mast

Rook Stones Hill

Windy Hill

Mast

OL3

Linsgreave Clough

1

Longden End Clough

M62

14

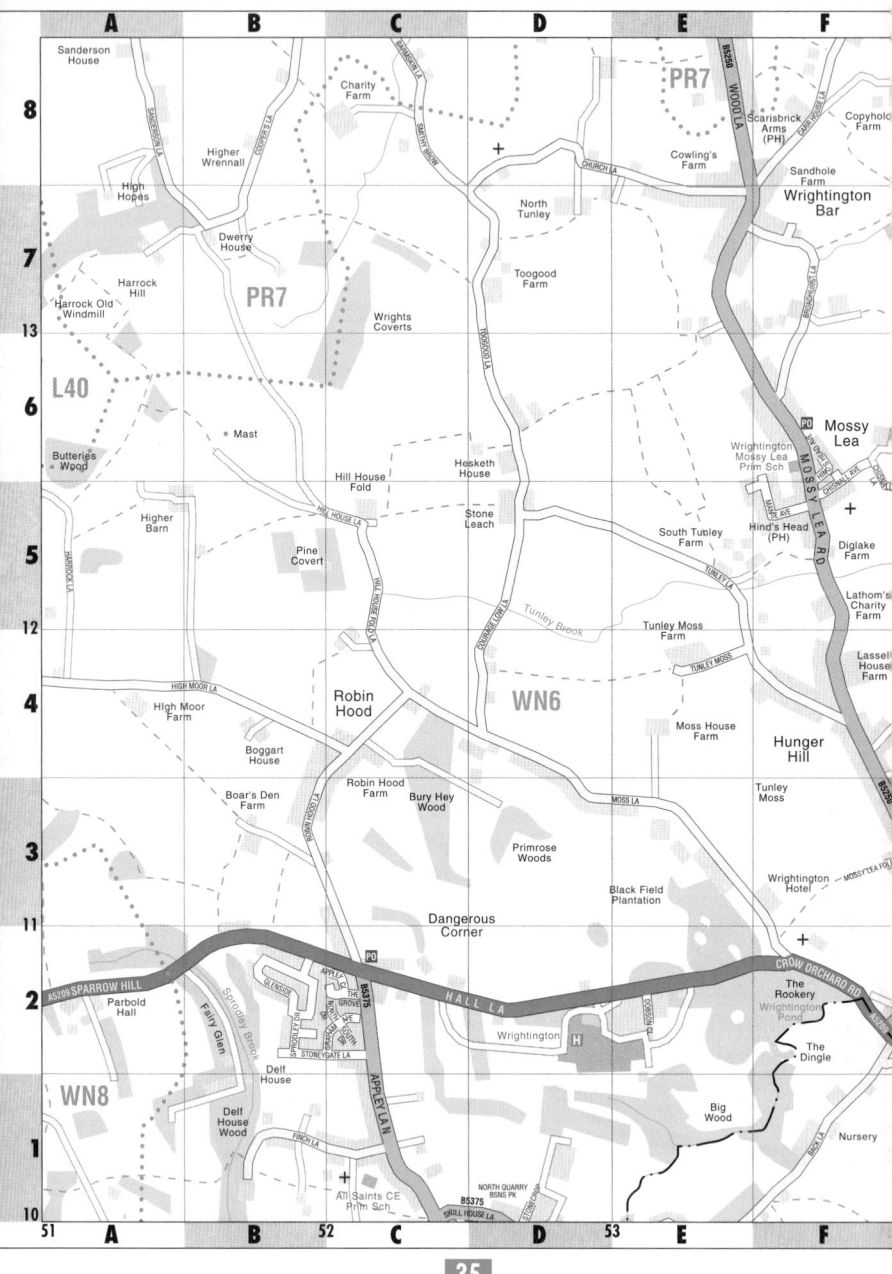

8

Coppull

Elmhurst
Farm

Blainscough
Hall

Wet Oaks
Wood

Vause
Farm

Coppull Moor
Farm

PR7

7

Alison Arms
(PH)

Bridge
Farm

13

Patrick
Farm

St John's
CE Prim Sch

CHISNALL LA

Chisnall
Wood

Coppull Moor

COPPULL MOOR LA

Coppull
Hill

6

Moorhouse
Farm

The
Grange

CHISNALL LA

Stars Brook

Bogburn Hall
Farm

5

Langtree
Old Hall
Farm

New
Seven Stars
(PH)

12

PRESTON RD

WN1

Cross
Farm

4

Lone
Farm

WN6

Chadwick
Farm

Gorse Hall

St Joseph's
Wrightington
RC Prim Sch

Potters
Farm

Thompson
House

Pepper Lane
Farm

QUAKERS
TERR

Langtree Hall

MOSSY
LEA
FOLD

PEPPER LA

Saddle Hill
Farm

LANGTREE LA

3

MOSSY LEA RD

Harris
Rd

Standish
Com High Sch

11

Shevington
Moor

STANDISH

St Marie's
RC Prim Sch

2

Hotel

Chamberlain's
Farm

CROW ORCHARD RD

ALMOND BROOK RD

Black Horse
Farm

St
Stephen's
Rd

SCHOOL LA

RECTORY LA

B5239

Lark
Hill

1

CRIPPLE
GATE

ASHURST RD 1
GREENSWARD CL 2

HIGH LA

B5239

A49

Schs

10

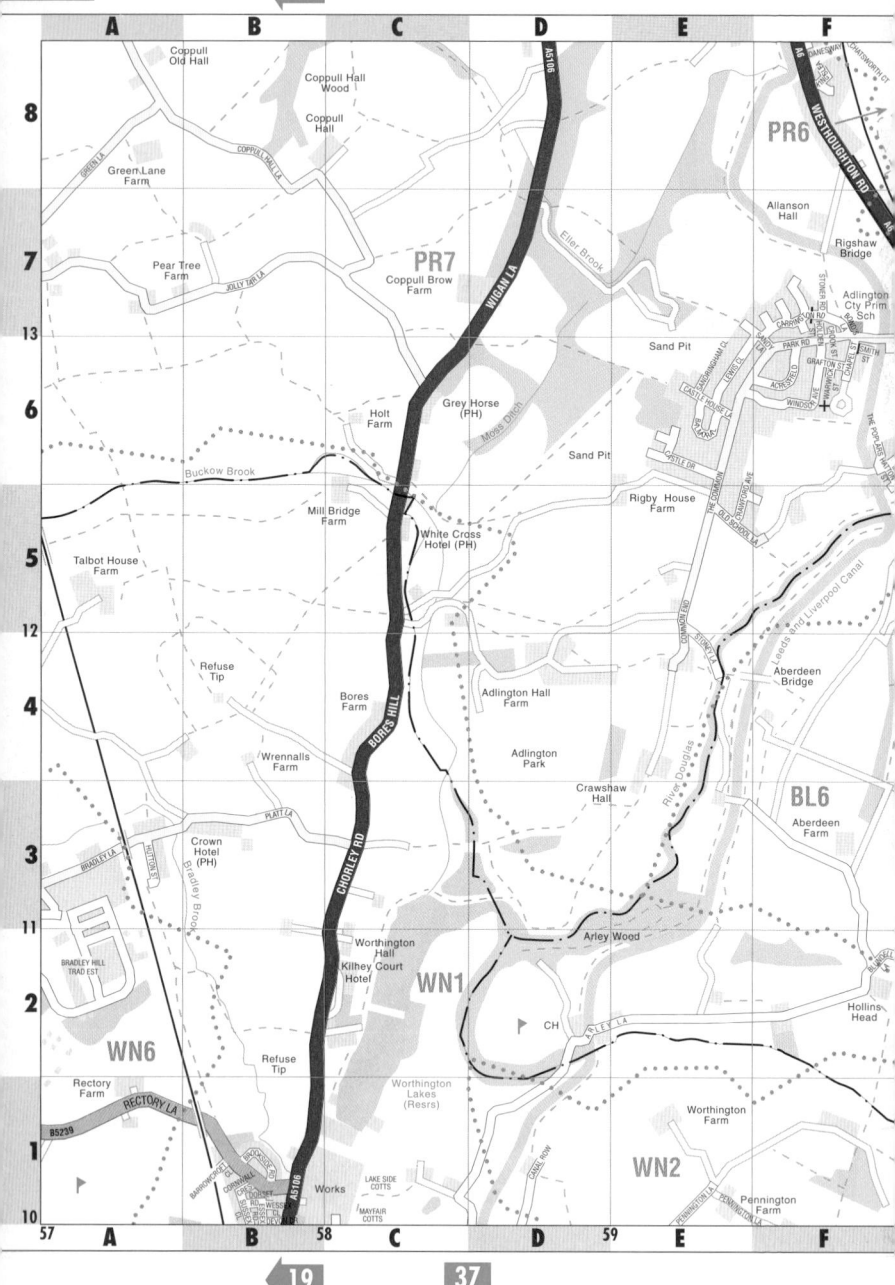

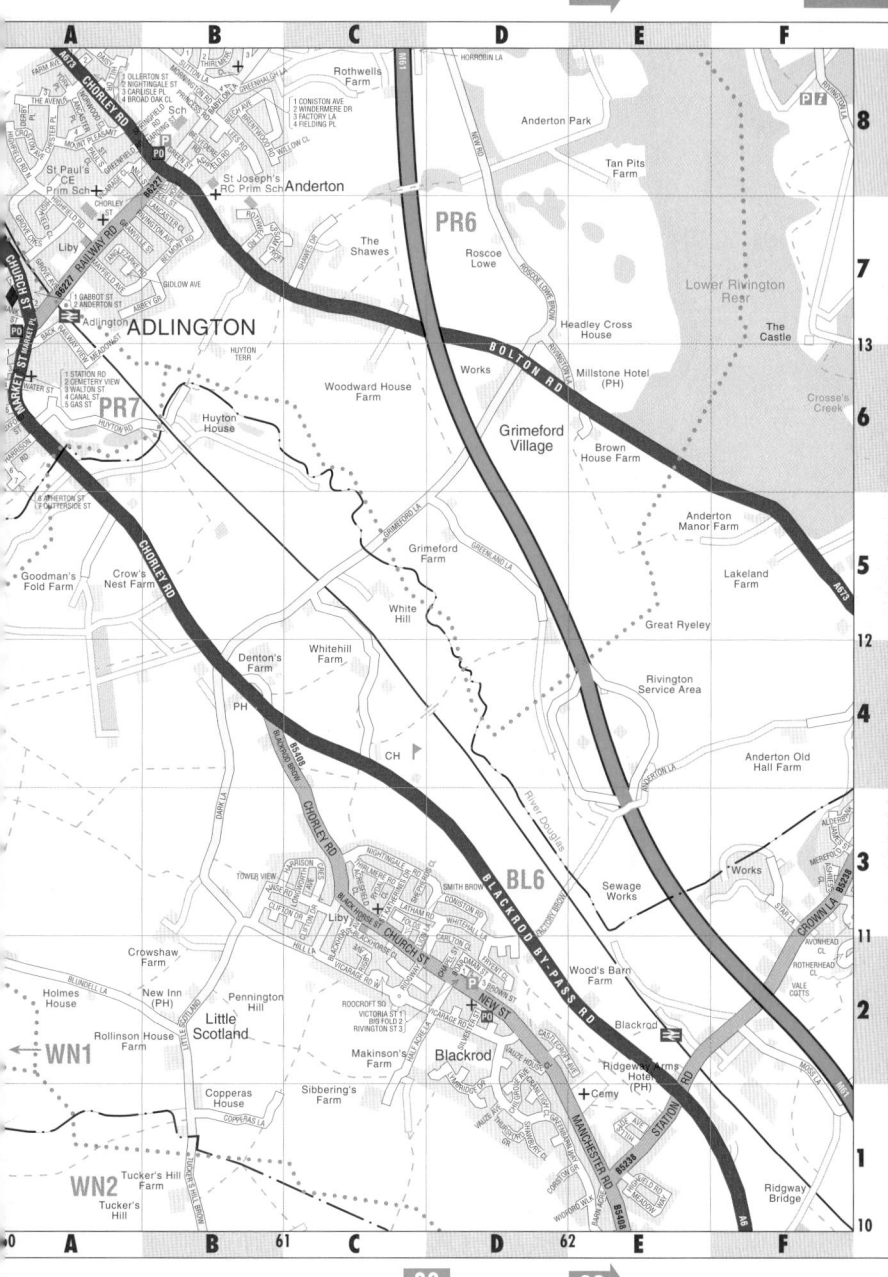

21

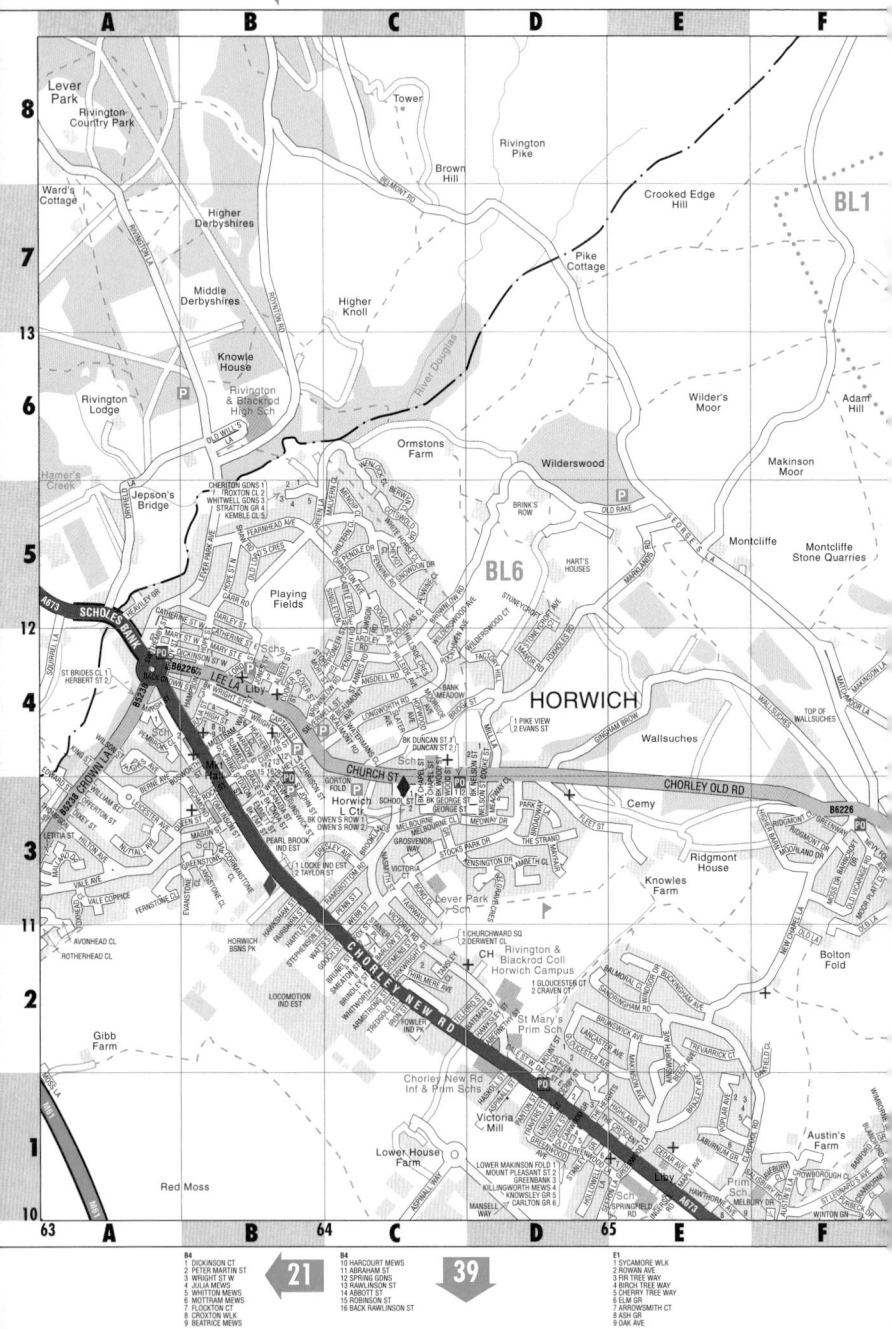

21 39

B4
1 DICKINSON CT
2 PETER MARTIN ST
3 WRIGHT ST W
4 JULIA MEWS
5 WHITTON MEWS
6 MOTTRAM MEWS
7 FLOCKTON CT
8 CROXTON WLK
9 BEATRICE MEWS

B4
10 HARCOURT MEWS
11 ABRAHAM ST
12 SPRING GDNS
13 RAWLINSON ST
14 ABBOTT ST
15 ROBINSON ST
16 BACK RAWLINSON ST

E1
1 SYCAMORE WLK
2 ROWAN AVE
3 FIR TREE WAY
4 BIRCH TREE WAY
5 CHERRY TREE WAY
6 ELM GR
7 ARROWSMITH CT
8 ASH GR
9 OAK AVE

A B C D E F

BL6

Smithills Moor

BL7

Whimberry Hill

8

Holden's Farm

Gilligant's Farm

COAL PIT RD

Green Nook

Lomax Wifes Farm

Haslam's Farm

7

13

Brown Lowe

Sheep Cote Green Farm

Chadwick's Close Farm

Smithills Dean

BL1

New Collier's Row

6

Hampsons Farm

Burnt Edge

COLLIER'S ROW

Cunliffe's Farm

White Brow

Slack Hall

BURNT EDGE LA

Walker Fold

Walker Fold Farm

COLLIERS ROW RD

Higher Tongs

LONGSHAW FORD RD

Pendlebury's Farm

5

Mast

EDGE LA

Lower Tongs

12

Hole Hill Farm

Little Dakins Farm

Dakin's Brook

BARROW BRIDGE RD

P

Horwich Moor

MATCHMOOR LA

Fleet's Moor

Old Harts Farm

WALKER FOLD RD

4

Barrow Bridge

Harpers

BL6

Harwood's Farm

3

Ivy Model Farm

SHEPHERDS DR

Blundell Arms (PH)

Yate Fold

Bob's Smithy Inn (PH)

CHORLEY OLD RD

CH

MONTSERRAT BROW

Fly Bus

BOWLAND RD

MONTSERRAT RD

Johnson Fold Com Prim Sch

Johnson Fold

11

Bottom o' th' Moor

Green Hill

Grundy Fold

B6226

CRAVEN

GARDEN

Delph Hill

DELPH

PO

2

Colemans

Coal Brow

Rants Farm

Delph Hill

BOLT

DELPH HILL

Doffcocker

1

High Rid Resr

Hawthorn Plantation

OLD KILN LA

MOSS BANK WAY

Doffcocker Lodge

Doffcocker

Wilson Fold Farm

BLANDFORD RISE

Fall Birch

H

High Rid Farm

HIGH RID LA

OLD HALL LA

Old Hall

NEW HALL MEWS

B6402

THE SICKLE

OLD KILN LA

Sch

10

96 A B 67 C D 68 E F

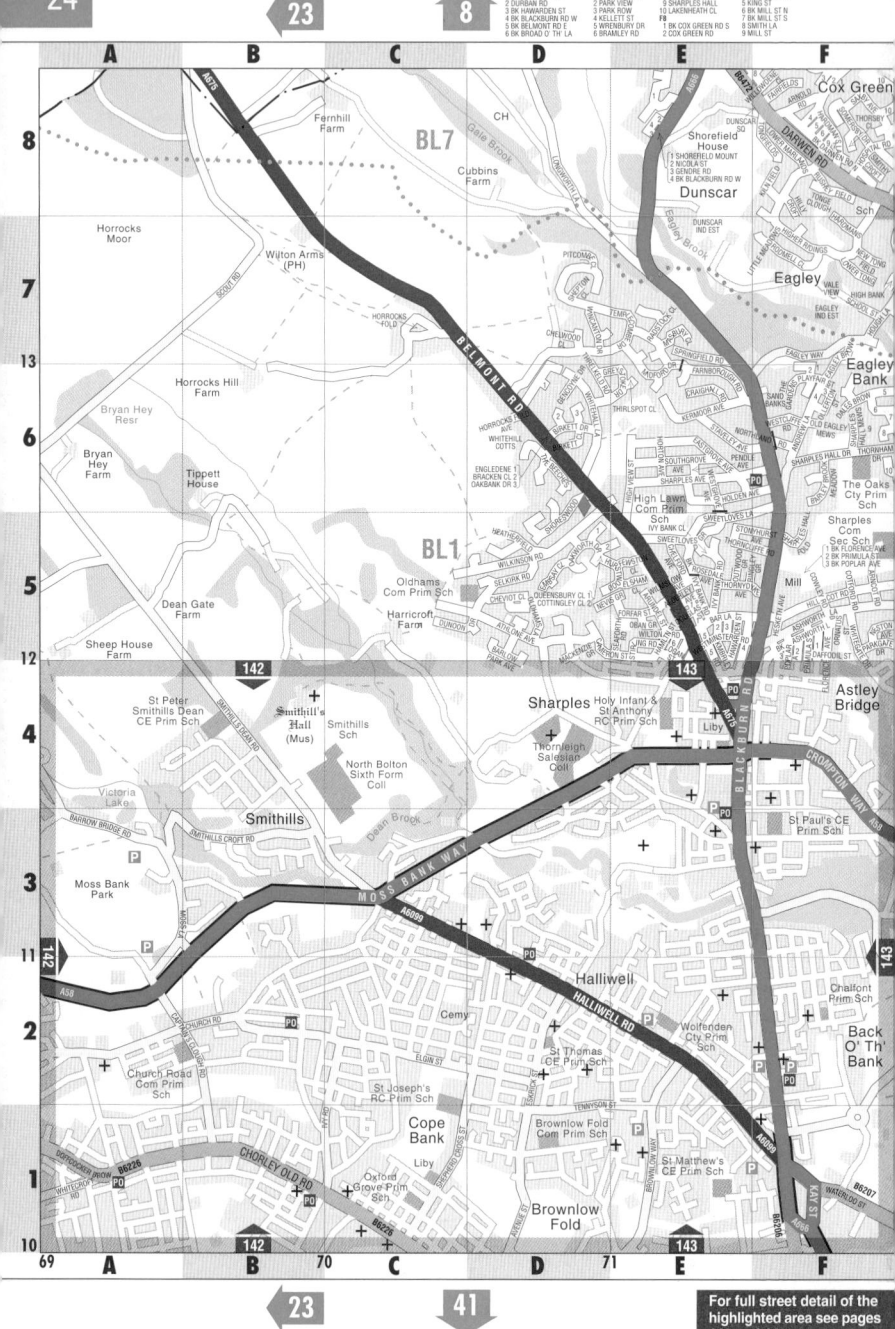

23

8

23   41

For full street detail of the highlighted area see pages 142 and 143.

BK DARWEN RD 1
BLAIR ST 2
WESLEY ST 3
Inst of Islamic H Ed 4

BL7

Toppings
Eagley Inf Sch
Eagley Jun Sch

Bromley Cross
Toppings Gn

Turton High Sch
BLAKE ST

Bromley Cross

Birtenshaw Farm

Birtenshaw Hall Sch

Sharples Sch
Sharples Com Prim Sch

Bank Top

Great Oak Farm

Playing Field

BL1

Hall i' th' Wood

Hall i' th' Wood (Mus)

Hall i' th' Wood

Works

BEWICK ST 1
PADGLEY ST 2
ROWTON ST 3
BK DELPH ST 4
COLMORE GR 5
ASHWELL ST 6
LEVER ST 7
ELSDON GR 8

Castle Hill

Castle Hill Com Prim Sch

Denvale Mills

BRITANNIA WAY

GLAISDALE ST 1
CASTLE HILL ST 2
FURNESS SQ 3
SADDLE ST 4
HAVERHILL GR 5
WEALDSTONE GR 6
DALYMOUNT CL 7
CONNAUGHT SQ 8

Works

Tonge Moor

SLATER LA 1
RYEFIELD ST 2
BK RYEFIELD ST 3
BRASSINGTON PL 4

WATERLOO ST

Moss Hill Farm

Water Field

Brown Barn Farm

Harry Fold

Harry Fold

SLACK LA

Cromptons

Meadow Barn

Lower Knotts

Top o' th' Knotts

Side of the Moor

St Maxentius Sch

Bradshaw Chapel

Bradshaw

KERSHAW ST

COTTAGE CROFT

MOOR GATE

Harwood Lee

SCARTHWOOD CL 1
BK TOTTINGTON RD E 2
HELMARTON CL 3
RECREATION ST 4
ROBERT ST 5

Hill Farm

LEE GATE

Liby

PO

St Brendan's RC Prim Sch

Brook Fold

BOLTON RD

BK BRADSHAW BROW W 1
BK TURTON RD W 2
JETHRO ST 3
GALINDO ST 4
ORMROD ST 5

Bradshaw Brow

Canon Slade Sch

Longsight Com Prim Sch

Harwood

GREENWOODS LA

Hardy Mill Com Prim Sch

Longworths

BL2

HILLSDALE GR 1
SPRINGWATER CL 2
CARLETON CL 3
HIGH MOUNT 4

NEWBRIDGE GDNS 1
OLD NURSERY FOLD 2
HAWTHORN BANK 3
FOUR LANE ENDS 4

HARWOOD VALE

Brook Bank

Jolly Brows

BOLTON

Firwood Fold

Spinney Nook

Firwood Specl Sch

HARTWELL

Christ's Church CE Prim Sch

Earls Farm

Withins Sch

Withins Sports Ctr

Top o' th' Brow

Top o' th' Brow Com Prim Sch

BRIDSON LA

Thicketford Brow

LE GENDRE ST 1
CANUTE ST 2
CASTLEWOOD SQ 3
BK BANBURY ST 4
PARKSIDE ST 5
HUNTROYDE AVE 6
ST AUGUSTINE'S CT 7
HARWOOD GR 8
ALEXANDER RD 9
BK ALEXANDER RD 10
BK BRISTOL AVE 11
BK ABINGDON RD 12
BK CROMER AVE 13
KIRKHAM ST 14

Red Lane Com Prim Sch

DALE GDNS

A B C D E F

8

BL0

Tower Farm

Stephen's St

Walmersley
STRATFORD AVE 1
LEAMINGTON ST 2

Carr Bank

Bevis Green

Springside Farm

Banks Farm

Bank Top Farm

Springside Prim Sch

7

13

Moss Farm

Brandlesholme Hall Farm

Kirklees

Old Hall Prim Sch

BL9

Limefield

Touch Road Farm

Recn Gd

Playing Field

Our Lady of Lourdes RC Prim Sch

BK WALMERSLEY RD W 1
PURDON ST 2
GREYMINT RD 3

6

Burrs Country Park

Brown Cow Inn (PH)

Burrs

Higher Woodhill

Seedfield

F5
1 LITTLEWOOD AVE
2 BK LINTON AVE
3 BK MOSTYN AVE
4 BK WALMERSLEY RD E
5 BK MALVERN AVE
6 BK RAYMOND AVE
7 BK MONMOUTH AVE
8 BK ARGYLE ST

5

BURY RD

BL8

Woolfold

Mill

Bolholt

The Elton High Sch

Owler Barrow

The Nurseries

Woodhill

1 BK TODDINGTON RD N
2 DAVID ST
3 STEWART ST

1 WENTWORTH ST
2 WOODLANDS GR

Woodbank Prim Sch

Irwell Sculpture Trail

140

12

River Irwell

Fernhill

4

TOTTINGTON RD

NEWBOLD ST

CROSTONS RD

Woodhill Fold

Woodfields

BURY

3

Chantlers Prim Sch

Elton

1 BK AINSWORTH RD S
2 DALTON ST 3
3 BK AINSWORTH RD N 3
ELLIS ST 4

B6196

Bury Ground

140

ASB

BOLTON RD

PEEL WAY

ASB

THE ROCK

140

Mus

P

Mkt
Hall

Rochdale Rd

11

2

AINSWORTH RD

BOLTON RD

Tentersfield

JUBILEE WAY

Cts
Bury

TENTERDEN ST

Mus, Art Gall & Lib

Sch of Arts

MANCHESTER RD

Bury Gram Sch

St Gabriel's RC High Sch

ANGOULEME WAY

Holy Trinity Sch

St Marie's Sch

Bury Coll

St Stephen's CE Prim Sch

Mus

DAISYFIELD CT

Buckley Wells

Florence Nightingale

Bury Coll

B6219

WELLINGTON RD

1

140

10

WOLSELEY ST
WARREN ST
ELTON ST
WHARNSIDE ST
WELLINGTON SQ
WELLINGTON CT

3 HILL'S CT
4 MILL LA
5 BK TOTTINGTON RD
6 BK GOODLAD ST
7 SMETHURST ST
8 BK BYROM ST
9 BYROM ST
10 BK BYROM ST S
11 BONHOLT IND EST

C2
1 BK AINSWORTH RD S
2 BK STEPHEN ST
3 BK BELBECK ST
4 BK KNIGHT CT
5 BK PEERS ST
6 DAISY ST
7 STEPHEN CL
8 BELBECK ST S
9 ALDER CL

C3
1 BK TOTTINGTON RD S
2 BK HAYWARD ST
3 BK WALSHAW RD N
4 BK MAYOR ST
5 BK COTTAM ST
6 BK WHITTLE ST
7 HILLYARD ST
8 NEW GEORGE ST
9 BK NEW GEORGE ST

10 BK ASHWORTH ST
11 BOOTHFIELD

WALMSLEY ST
K OLIVE BANK

For full street detail of the highlighted area see page 140.

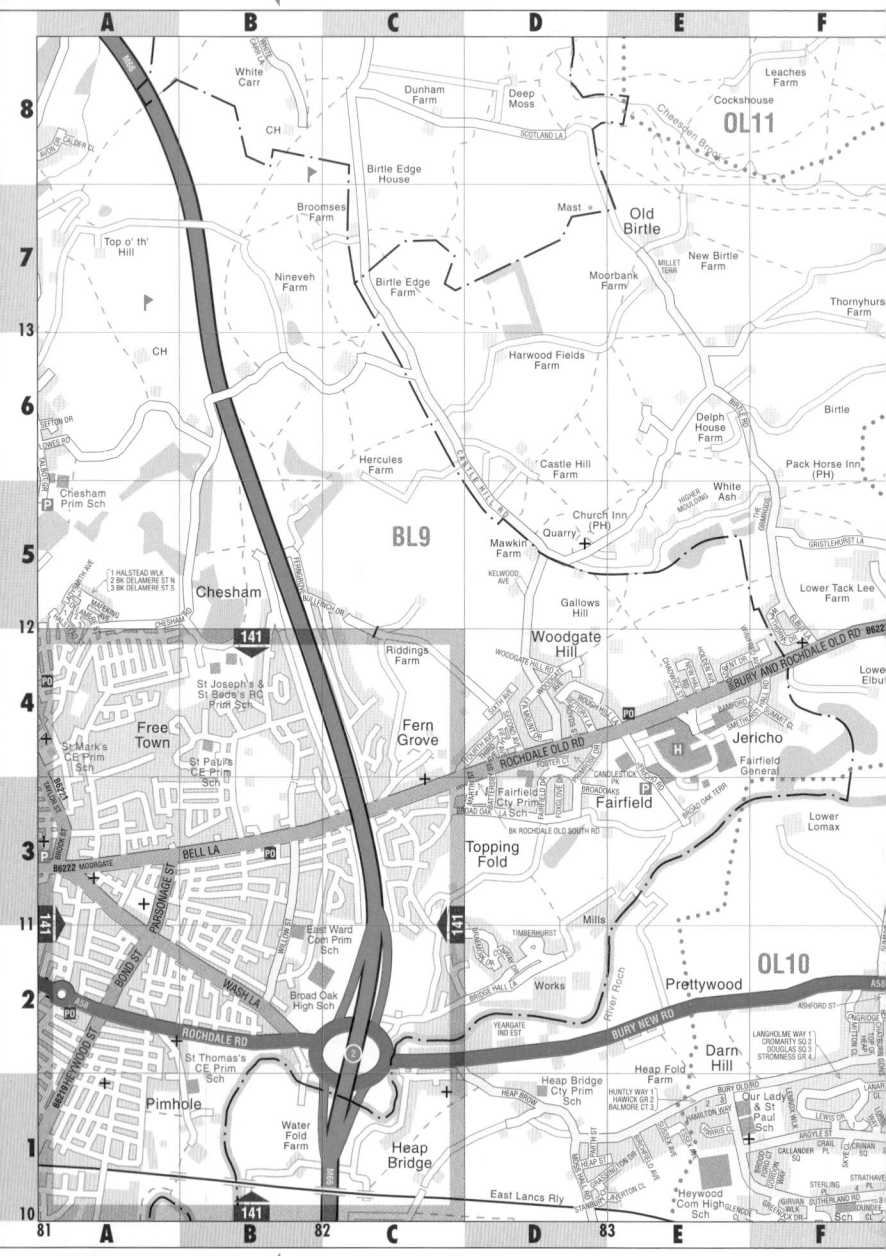

27
12

OL11

Cockshouse
Leaches Farm

White Carr

Dunham Farm

Deep Moss

CH

Birtle Edge House

SCOTLAND LA

Cheesden Brook

Broomses Farm

Mast

Old Birtle

New Birtle Farm

Top o' th' Hill

Nineveh Farm

Birtle Edge Farm

Moorbank Farm

MILLET TERR

Thornyhurst Farm

CH

Harwood Fields Farm

Delph House Farm

Birtle

Hercules Farm

CASTLE HILL RD

Castle Hill Farm

White Ash

Pack Horse Inn (PH)

BL9

Mawkin Farm

Quarry

Church Inn (PH)

HIGHER MOULDING

GRISTLEHURST LA

Chesham Prim Sch

Chesham

KELWOOD AVE

Gallows Hill

Lower Tack Lee Farm

1 HALSTEAD WLK
2 BK DELAMERE ST N
3 BK DELAMERE ST S

Riddings Farm

Woodgate Hill

Lowe Elbu

BURY AND ROCHDALE OLD RD

B9622

Free Town

Fern Grove

St Joseph's & St Bede's RC Prim Sch

St Mark's CE Prim Sch

St Paul's CE Prim Sch

ROCHDALE OLD RD

Jericho

Fairfield General

Lower Lomax

Fairfield Cty Prim Sch

Fairfield

BELL LA

Topping Fold

BK ROCHDALE OLD SOUTH RD

BROAD OAK TERR

MOORGATE

B6222

East Ward Com Prim Sch

Mills

OL10

TIMBERHURST

Prettywood

A58

East Ward Com Prim Sch

Broad Oak High Sch

WASH LA

Works

Darn Hill

ASHFORD ST

LANGHOLME WAY 1
CROMARTY SQ 2
DOUGLAS SQ 3
STROMNESS GR 4

ROCHDALE RD

BURY NEW RD

YEARGATE IND EST

St Thomas's CE Prim Sch

Pimhole

Water Fold Farm

Heap Bridge

Heap Fold Farm

Heap Bridge Cty Prim Sch

HUNTLY WAY 1
HAWICK GR 2
BALMORE CT 3

Our Lady & St Paul Sch

LEWIS DR

ARGYLE CL

CALLANDER SQ

CRAIL PL

CLORINAN

East Lancs Rly

Heywood Com High Sch

STERLING

GIRVAN WLK

SUTHERLAND RD

STRATHAVE

For full street detail of the highlighted area see page 141.

27

45

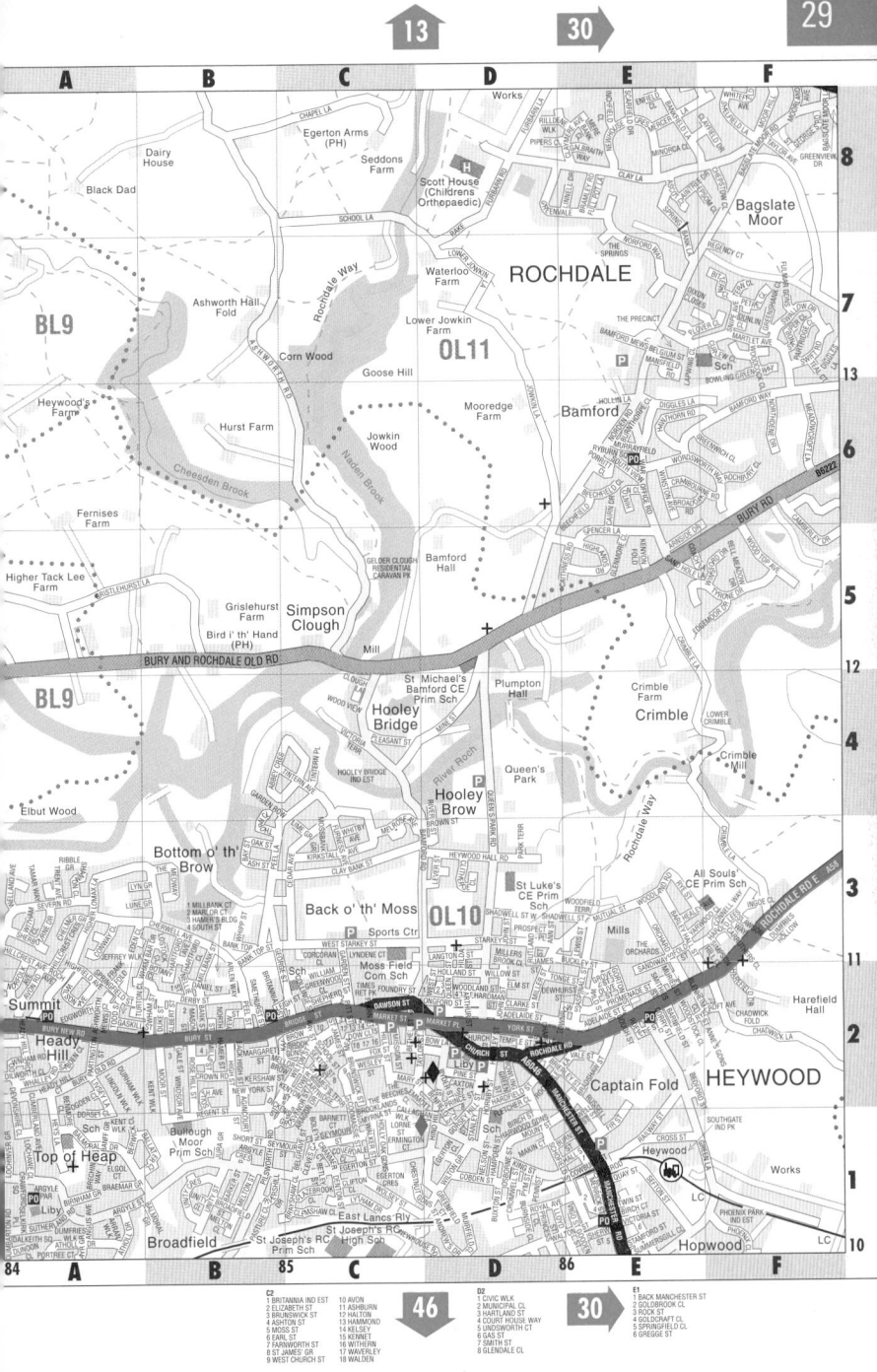

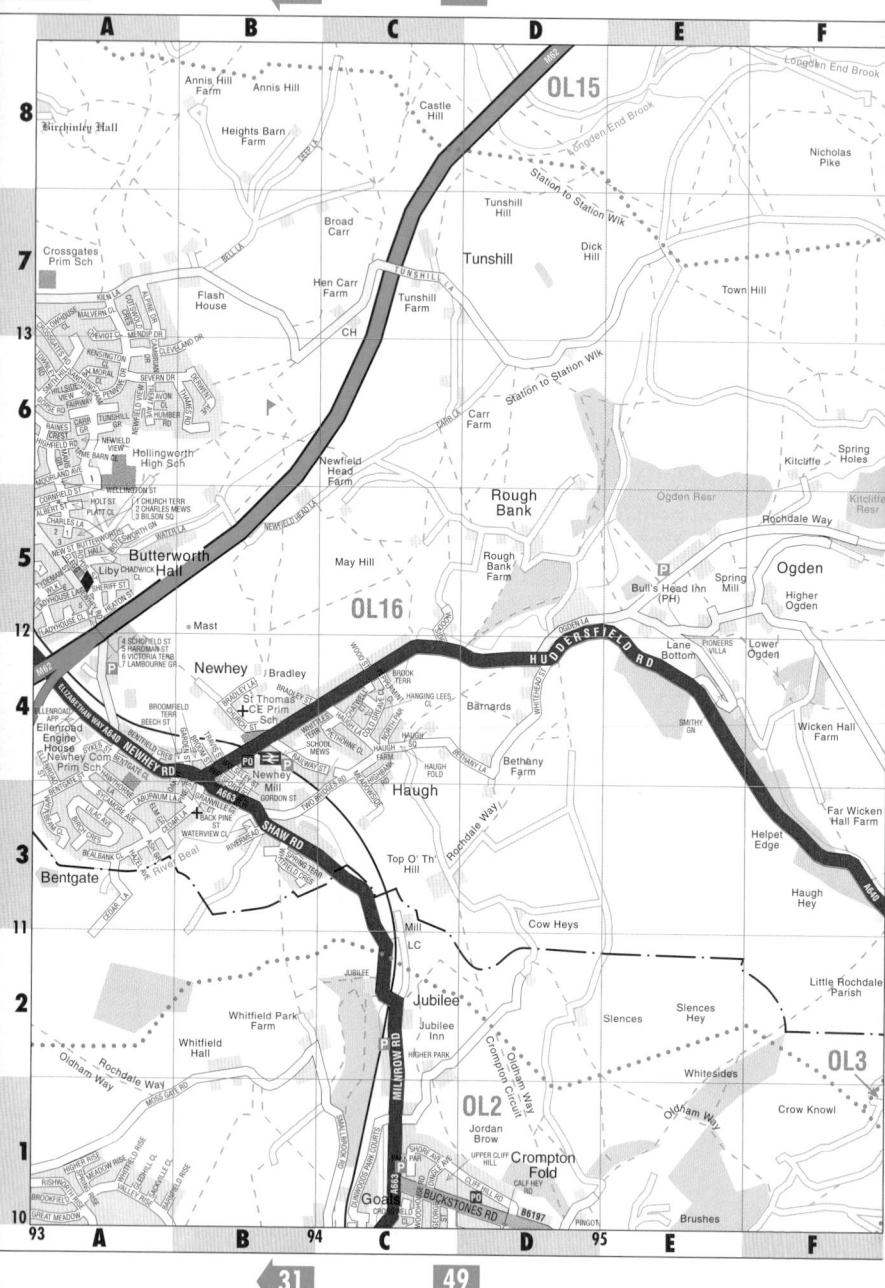

A   B   C   D   E   F

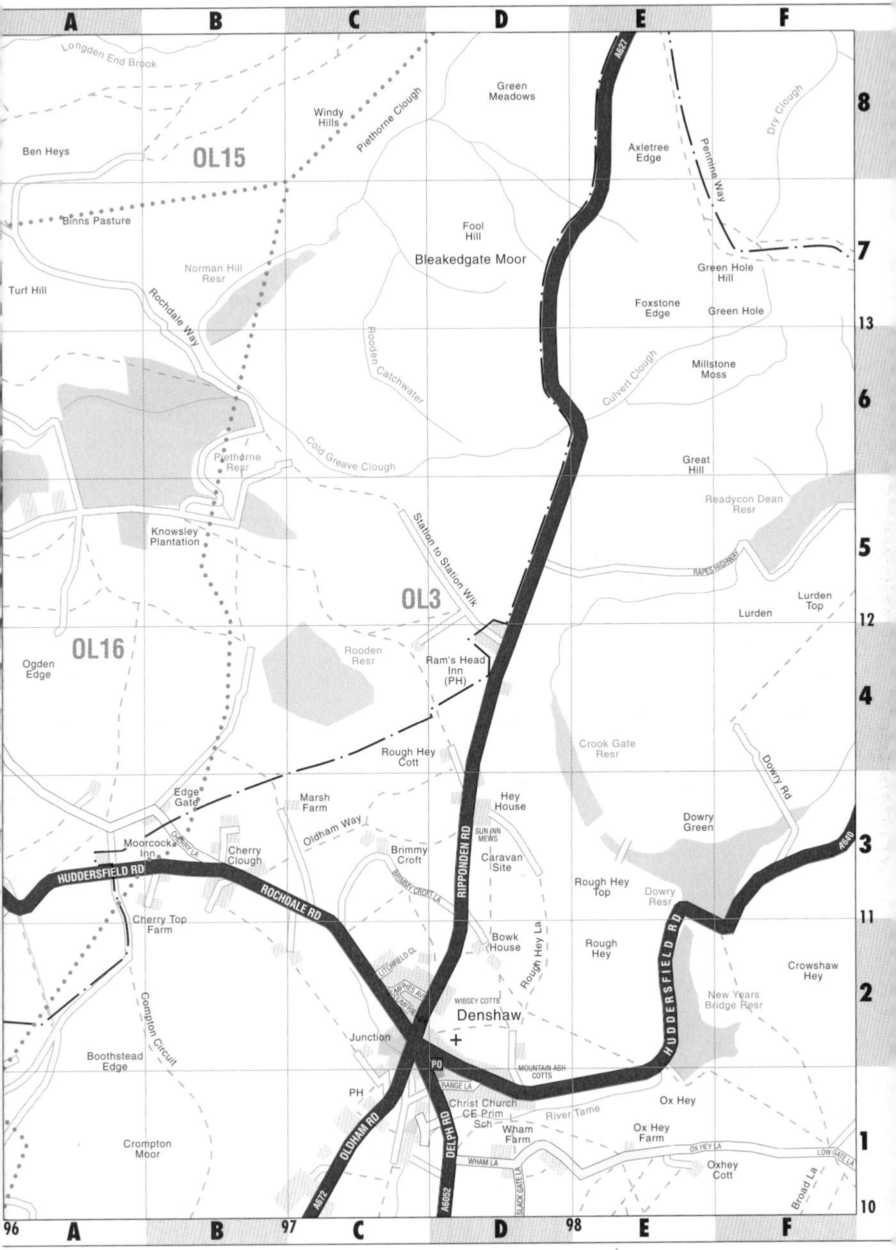

8

Longden End Brook

Ben Heys   OL15

Windy Hills   Piethorne Clough   Green Meadows

Binns Pasture

Norman Hill Resr   Fool Hill   Axletree Edge   Pennine Way   Dry Clough   7

Turf Hill   Bleakedgate Moor   Green Hole Hill   13

Rochdale Way   Rooden Catchwater   Foxstone Edge   Green Hole

Millstone Moss   6

Piethorne Resr   Cold Greave Clough   Culvert Clough

Knowsley Plantation   Great Hill   5

Readycon Dean Resr

Ogden Edge   OL16   Station to Station Wlk   OL3   Lurden Top   12

Rooden Resr   Ram's Head Inn (PH)   Lurden   4

Rough Hey Cott   Crook Gate Resr   Dowry Rd

Edge Gate   Marsh Farm   Oldham Way   Hey House   Dowry Green   A640   3

Moorcocks Inn   Cherry Clough   Brimmy Croft   SUN INN MEWS   Rough Hey Top   Dowry Resr

HUDDERSFIELD RD   ROCHDALE RD   BRIMMY CROFT LA   Caravan Site   Rough Hey   HUDDERSFIELD RD   11

Cherry Top Farm   Bowk House   Rough Hey La   Crowshaw Hey   2

Campton Circuit   WIBSEY COTTS   Denshaw   New Years Bridge Resr

Boothstead Edge   Junction   PO   MOUNTAIN ASH COTTS   Ox Hey   1

PH   ORANGE LA   Christ Church CE Prim Sch   River Tame   Ox Hey Farm

OLDHAM RD   DELPH RD   Wham Farm   OX HEY LA   LOW GATE LA

Crompton Moor   WHAM LA   SLACK GATE LA   Oxhey Cott   Broad La

96   A   B   97   C   D   98   E   F   10

A627   A672   A670   A662   A6052

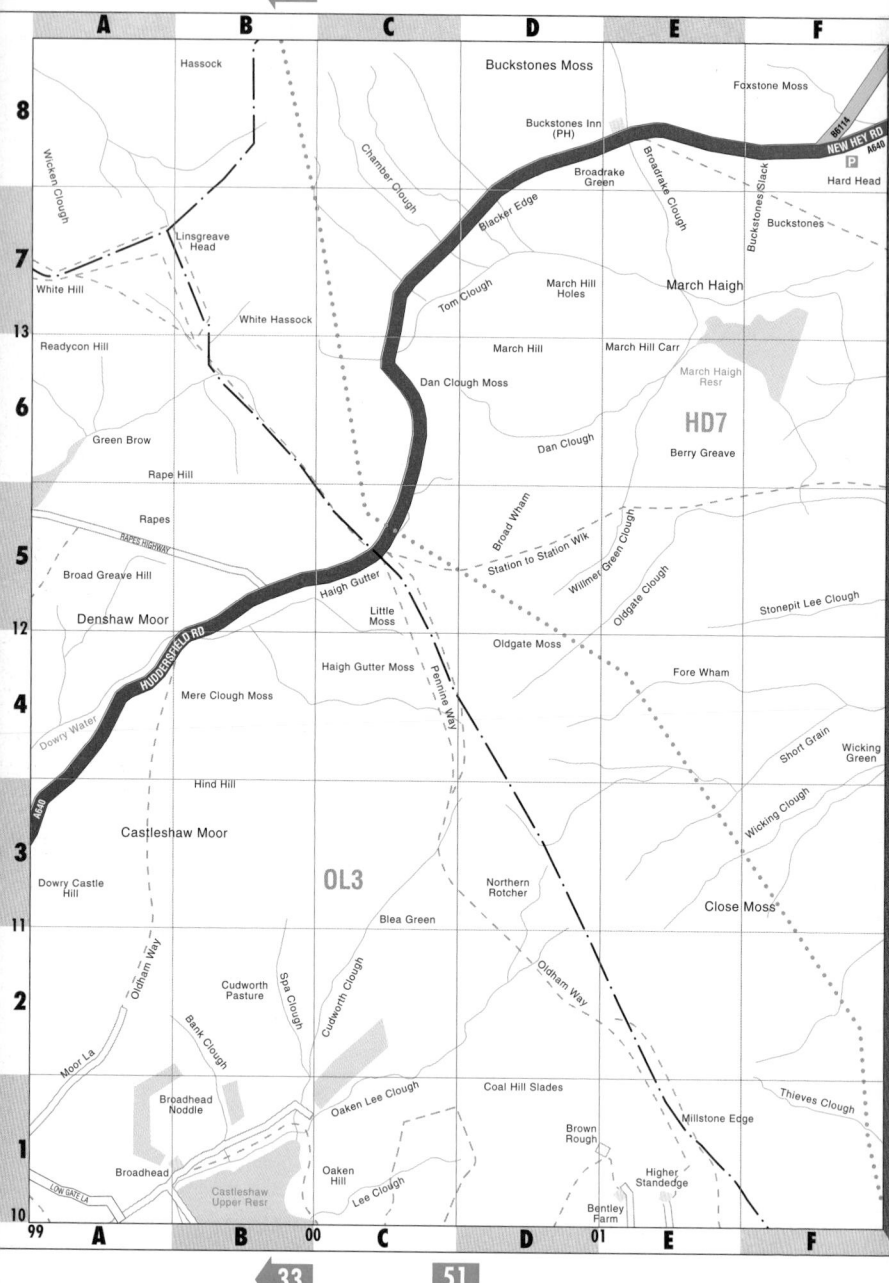

A   B   C   D   E   F

Hassock

Buckstones Moss

Foxstone Moss

8

Wicken Clough

Buckstones Inn
(PH)

Broadrake
Green

Broadrake Clough

NEW HEY RD

B6114

A640

Hard Head

Linsgreave
Head

Blacker Edge

Buckstones

Buckstones Slack

7

White Hill

Chamber Clough

Tom Clough

March Hill
Holes

March Haigh

13

White Hassock

Readycon Hill

March Hill

March Hill Carr

March Haigh
Resr

6

Green Brow

Dan Clough Moss

HD7

Berry Greave

Rape Hill

Dan Clough

Rapes

Broad Wham

5

RAPES HIGHWAY

Broad Greave Hill

Haigh Gutter

Station to Station Wlk

Willmer Green Clough

Oldgate Clough

Stonepit Lee Clough

Denshaw Moor

HUDDERSFIELD RD

Little
Moss

12

Haigh Gutter Moss

Pennine Way

Oldgate Moss

Fore Wham

4

Mere Clough Moss

Dowry Water

Short Grain

Wicking
Green

Hind Hill

Wicking Clough

A640

3

Castleshaw Moor

OL3

Northern
Rotcher

Close Moss

Dowry Castle
Hill

11

Blea Green

2

Oldham Way

Cudworth
Pasture

Spa Clough

Cudworth Clough

Oldham Way

Bank Clough

Coal Hill Slades

Thieves Clough

Broadhead
Noddle

Oaken Lee Clough

Brown
Rough

Millstone Edge

1

Broadhead

LOW GATE LA

Oaken
Hill

Lee Clough

Higher
Standedge

10

Moor La

Castleshaw
Upper Resr

Bentley
Farm

A   B 00 C   D 01 E   F

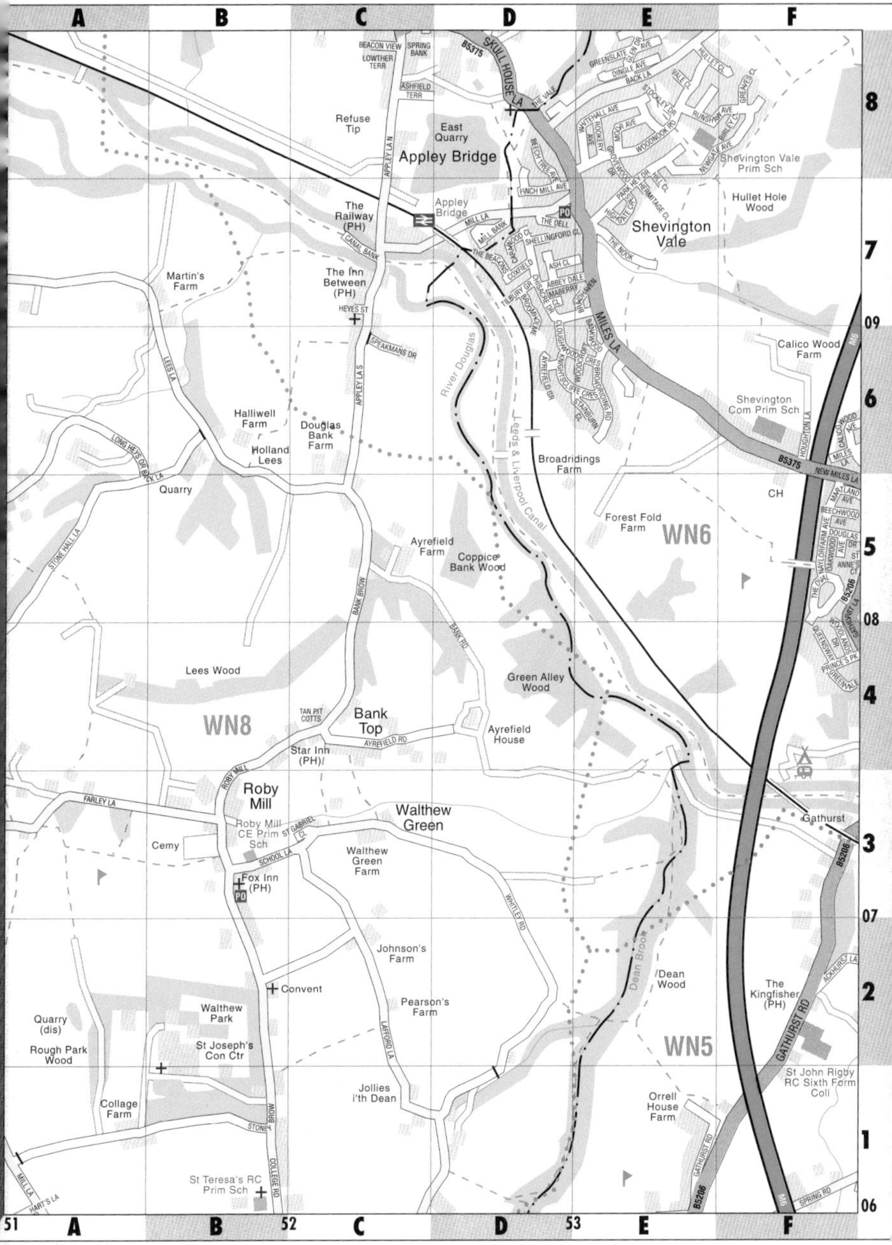

WN6

WN5

Shevington

Crooke

Standish Lower Ground

Beech Hill

Marsh Green

White Hill Farm

Merrybone Farm

Paradise Farm House

Shevington High Sch

Stockley Hill Wood

Ppg Sta

Woodfold Prim Sch

Resr

Victoria Cres

Resrs

Strickland House Farm

Convent

Wakefields

Standish Hall Farm

Millbrook Prim Sch

St Bernadett's RC Prim Sch

Elnup Wood Nature Reserve

Standish Park

Upper Wood Farm

Lower Wood Farm

Birley Wood

Ridges Wood

Brockhurst

Giant's Hall Farm

Greaves Wood

Works

Otters Croft Wood

St Anne's CE Prim Sch

Leeds & Liverpool Canal

River Douglas

Gathurst

Gathurst Station Inn (PH)

Ackhurst Hall

Ackhurst Brook

Martland Mill

John Fisher RC High Sch

Sacred Heart RC Prim Sch

St Andrew's Sch

Works

Works

Dumbarton Gn

Lancaster Wlk

Libv Sch

TA Ctr

Newsham Wlk 1
Hillreed 2
Brookvale 3

Pagefield Ind Est

GATHURST LA

BROAD TH LA

CHURCH LA

WIGAN RD

WIGAN LOWER RD

WOODHOUSE DR

SHEVINGTON LA

B5206

B5375

54   55   56

WN6 · **WN2** · **WN1**

Boar's Head · Thorn Hill · Hampson Green · Red Rock · Winstanleys · Astleys · School Coverts · Home Farm · Zoo · Haigh Hall · Haigh Upper Plantations · Haigh Country Park · Rothwells Farm · Brock Wood · Longhurst · Haigh Upper Plantations · Woodfield Prim Sch · Leyland Mill Brow · Haigh Lower Plantations · Whitley · Marylebone · Bottling Wood · St John the Baptist CE Sch · Springfield · Gidlow · Swinley · Whelley · Wigan & Leigh Coll (Pagefield Bldg) · Bull Hey · Water Heyes · Longshoot

Brimelow Farm · Mere Oaks Sch · Boar's Head

A1
1 HEARDMAN AVE
2 WHITESIDE AVE
3 WATERLOO ST
4 BROOKHOLE
5 HEDGEMEAD
6 FOSTER ST
7 MEADOW CT
8 BERESFORD ST
9 GORMAN ST
10 KINGFISHER CT
11 NIGHTINGALE CT
12 FALCONWOOD CL
13 LOWER ST STEPHEN ST
14 TERNAN LO
15 PAGEFIELD CL

B3
1 RIPON AVE
2 PATELEY SQ
3 YEWDALE CRES

4 MONTON MEWS

C1
1 SANDYCROFT AVE
2 CHARLES ST
3 SCARISBRICK ST
4 CLIFTON ST
5 LITTLE LONDON
6 DICCONSON CRES
7 BRICK KILN LA
8 BK MESNES ST

9 MESNES TERR
10 POWELL ST

C2
1 INGLEWHITE CRES
2 INGLEWHITE PL
3 WARNFORD ST
4 EVEREST PL
5 ASHLAND AVE
6 MONUMENT MANSIONS
7 HOLME CT

8 ST MICHAEL'S CT

E1
1 SALMON ST
2 CUMBERLAND ST
3 WESTMORLAND ST
4 PERCH ST
5 WINDERMERE ST
6 WRIGHT ST
7 SEDWYN ST

F2
1 VIGO ST
2 LONGSHED ST
3 CHELTENHAM ST
4 MILFORD RD
5 BORDEN CL

37 21

BL6

BL5

WN2

WN1

BL5

Nightingale's Farm

Willoughby Farm

Harts

MEADOW PIT LA

B5239

RILEY LA

HAIGH RD

St David's CE Prim Sch

Haighlands

COPPERAS LA

Windmill

CROSS ST 1
THOMAS ST 2

Haigh

VICTORIA CL

SCHOOL LA

PROSPECT COTTS

Curfew House

Haig Country Park

Hilton Farm

TARNBROOK DR

MANOR DR

Our Lady's RC Sch

SHOEMAKER SONS

Liby

P PO

BALCARRES RD

FRENCHWOOD CT

Aspull Church Sch

WIGAN RD

High St

W WOODFIELD ST

New Springs

B5238

St Leeds & Liverpool Canal

Top Lock

COALFIELD Sch

Sch

1 SILVINGTON WAY
2 MARCHBANK
3 DRYTON WLK

KIRKLESS VILLAS

Commercial Inn (PH)

Kirkless Hall Inn (PH)

Works

CAMBERWELL CRES

FINDHLEY CRES

Kirkless Hall

BRANTHWAITE

Toddington Farm

Freezeland Farm

Gorses Farm

Stanley Nook Farm

Aspull

1 EDINBURGH WLK
2 BRAEMAR WLK
3 CARLISLE WAY
4 INVERNESS CL

Walkers Higher Farm

Walkers Lower Farm

Shaw's Fold Farm

Rugby Football Gd

Bradshaw Hall

Marsh Farm

HALL LA

Bank House Farm

Hindley Hall Golf Course

GREENBARN WAY

Blackrod Cty Prim Sch

MANCHESTER RD

B5408

BL6

Yate's Farm

Scot Lane End Sch

Scot Lane End

Works

Borsdane Brook

SCOT LA

Shepherds Farm

BOLTON RD

Ainscow's Farm

Dodd's Farm

DODD'S FARM LA

PENNINGTON GREEN LA

BADSHAW LA

FIRS COTTAGES

The Firs Farm

Pennington Green

School Farm

Borsdane Wood

Borsdane

CHORLEY RD

A6

BLACKROD BY-PASS RD

Park Hall Farm

Hotel

Landlord's Farm

B5239

PO

FLESTON DR

BROOMHOLM LA

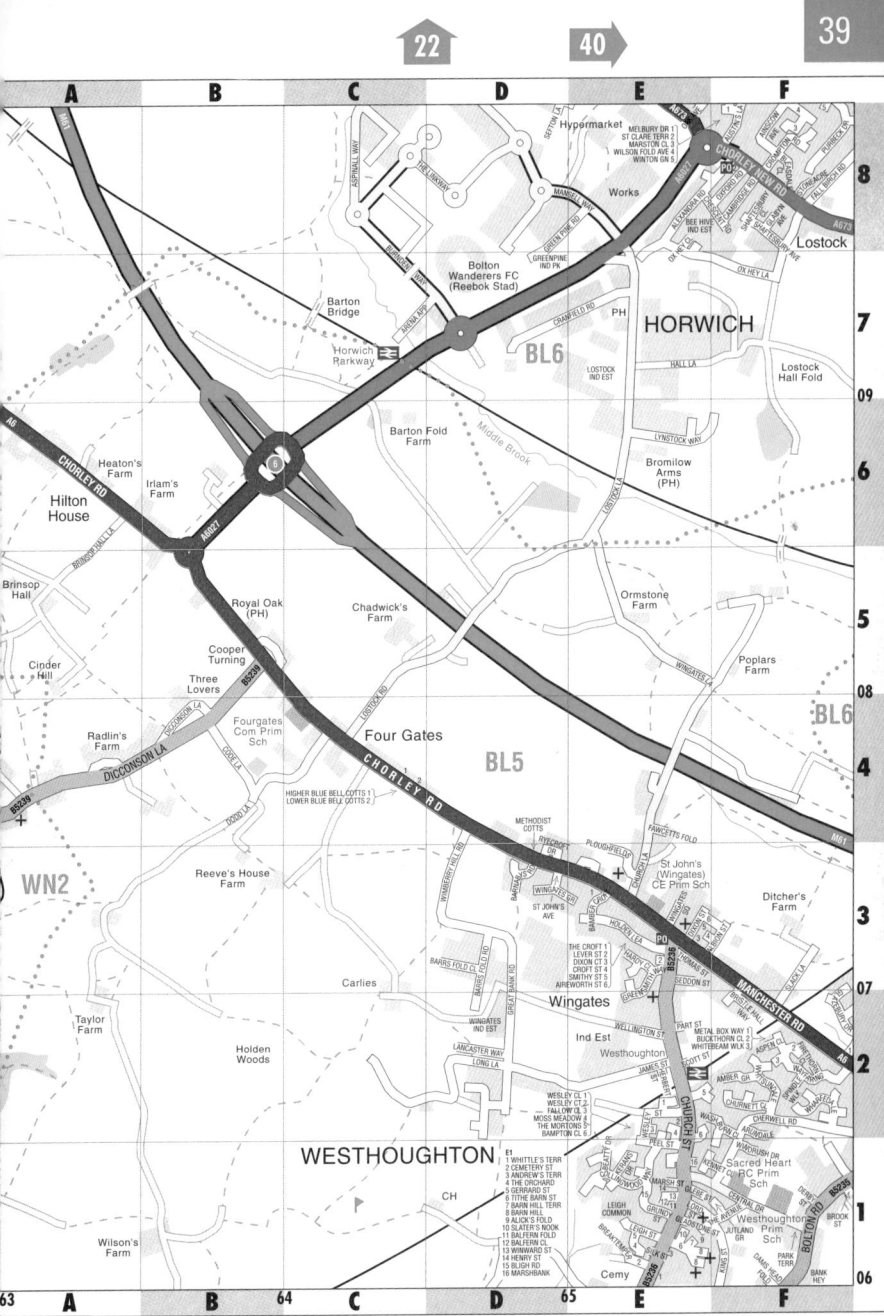

A   B   C   D   E   F

8
7
09
6
5
08
4
3
07
2
1
06

Hypermarket
MELBURY DR 1
ST CLARE TERR 2
MARSTOR CL 3
WILSON FOLD AVE 4
WINTON GN 5

Works

CHORLEY NEW RD
PO
Lostock

HORWICH

BL6

Bolton
Wanderers FC
(Reebok Stad)

Barton
Bridge

Horwich
Parkway

PH

LOSTOCK
IND EST

HALL LA

Lostock
Hall Fold

LYNSTOCK WAY

09

Heaton's
Farm

CHORLEY RD

Irlam's
Farm

Hilton
House

Barton Fold
Farm

Middle Brook

Bromilow
Arms
(PH)

A6

Brinsop
Hall

Royal Oak
(PH)

Chadwick's
Farm

Ormstone
Farm

Cinder
Hill

Cooper
Turning

Poplars
Farm

Three
Lovers

WINGATES LA

BL6

Radlin's
Farm

Fourgates
Com Prim
Sch

Four Gates

BL5

HIGHER BLUE BELL COTTS 1
LOWER BLUE BELL COTTS 2

CHORLEY RD

B61

WN2

Reeve's House
Farm

METHODIST
COTTS

FAWCETTS FOLD

PLOUGH FIELD

St John's
(Wingates)
CE Prim Sch

Ditcher's
Farm

3

Taylor
Farm

Carlies

THE CROFT 1
LEVER ST 2
DIXON CT 3
CROFT ST 4
SMITHY ST 5
AIREWORTH ST 6

Wingates

SEDDON ST

PO

07

MANCHESTER RD
A6

Holden
Woods

WINGATES
IND EST

LANCASTER WAY

LONG LA

Ind Est
Westhoughton

METAL BOX WAY 1
BUCKTHORN CL 2
WHITEBEAM WLK 3

2

WESTHOUGHTON

E1
1 WHITTLE'S TERR
2 CEMETERY ST
3 ANDREW'S TERR
4 THE ORCHARD
5 GERRARD ST
6 TITHE BARN ST
7 BARN HILL TERR
8 BARN HILL
9 ALICK'S FOLD
10 SLATER'S NOOK
11 BALFERN FOLD
12 BALFERN CL
13 WINWARD ST
14 HENRY ST
15 BLIGH RD
16 MARSHBANK

WESLEY CL 1
WESLEY CT 2
FALLOW CL 3
MOSS MEADOW 4
THE MORTONS 5
BAMPTON CL 6

Sacred Heart
RC Prim
Sch

CHURCH ST

Westhoughton
Prim Sch

BOLTON RD

CH

LEIGH
COMMON

Westhoughton

Park
Terr

BANK
HEY

Wilson's
Farm

Cemy

1

63   A   B   64   C   D   65   E   F

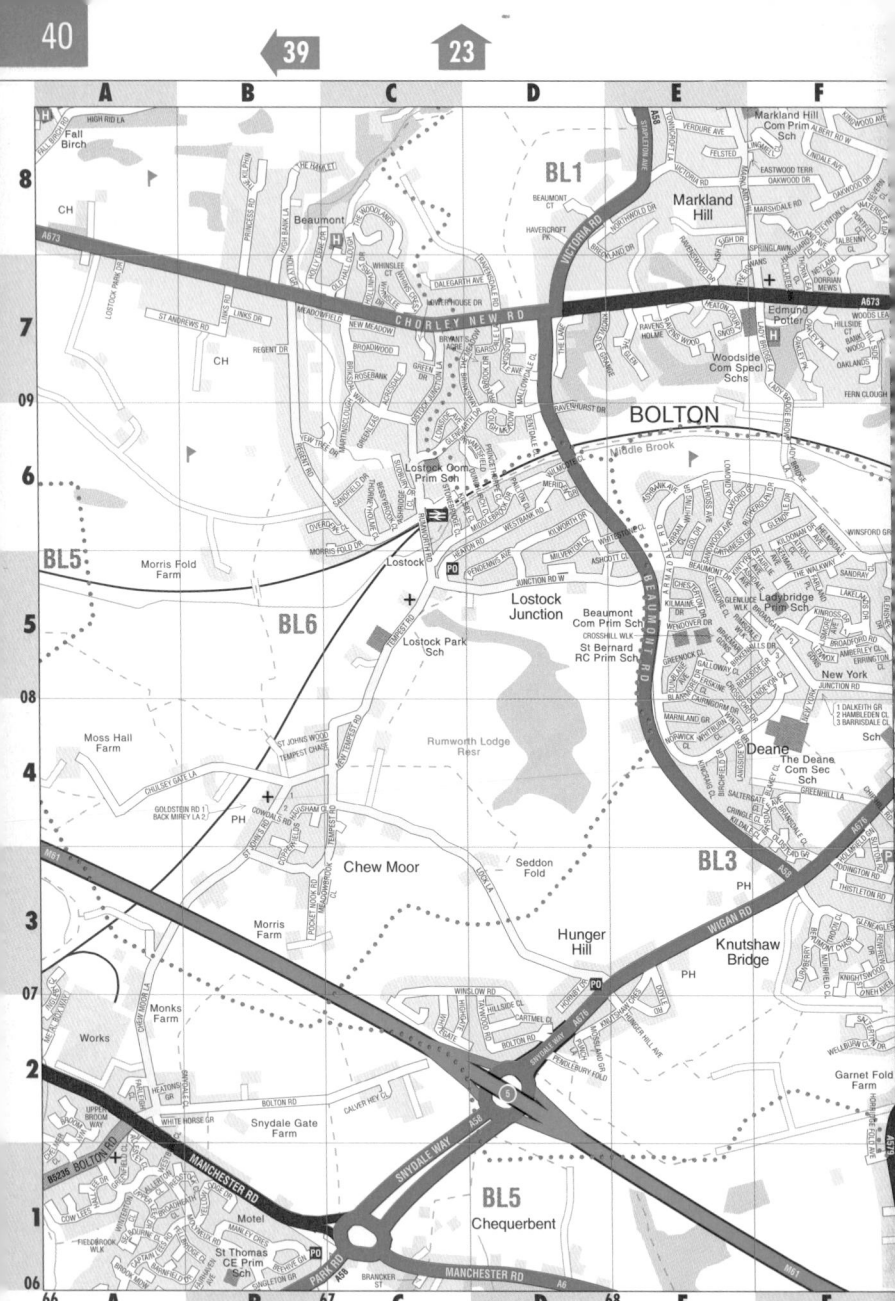

For full street detail of the highlighted area see pages 144, 145, 146 and 147.

24
42
59
42

BOLTON

Victory

Heaton

Gilnow Park

Queen's Park

Gilnow

Pocket

Willows

Dene

Fernhill Gate

Daubhill

Lever Edge

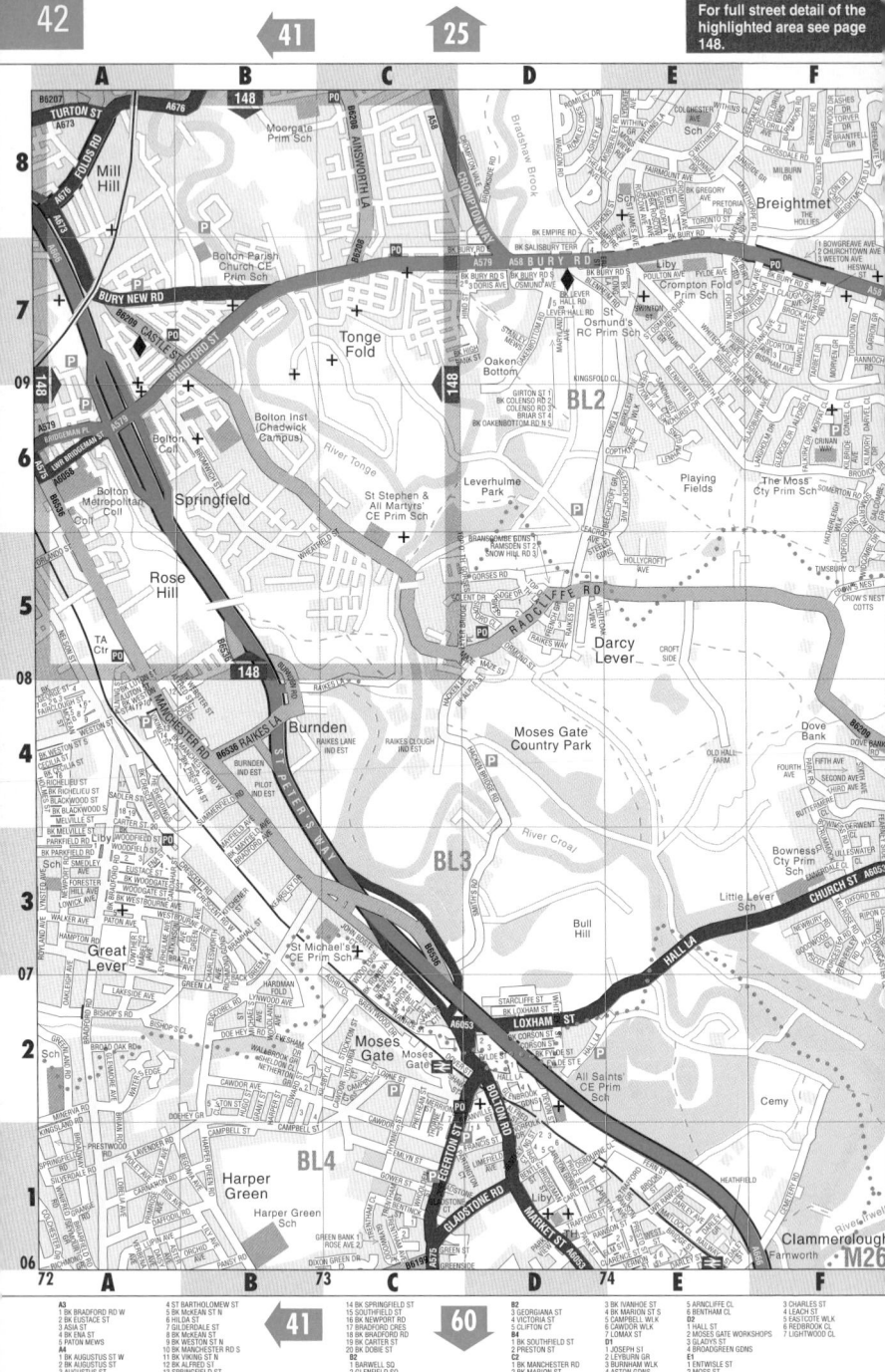

42

41 25

For full street detail of the
highlighted area see page
148.

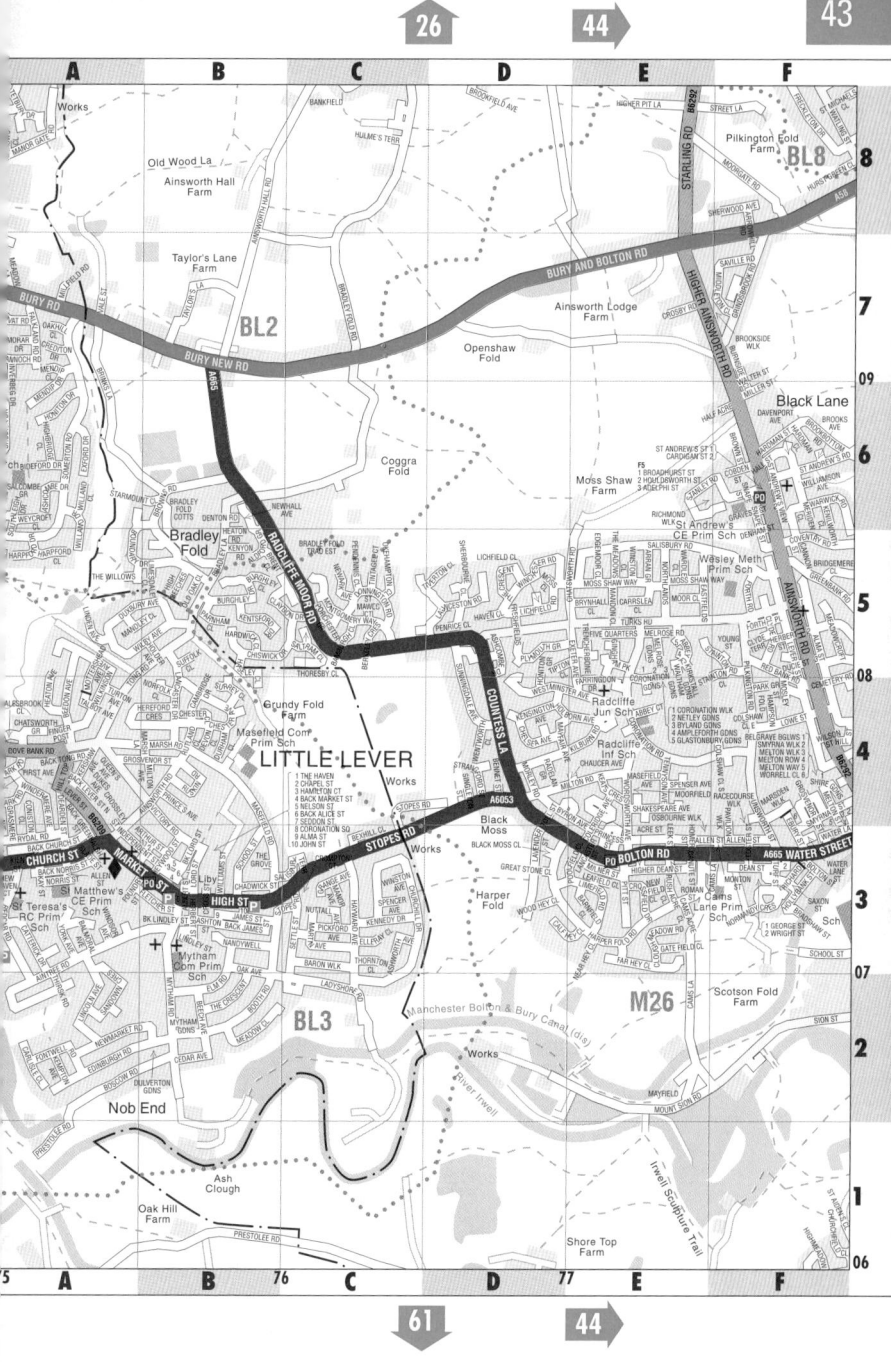

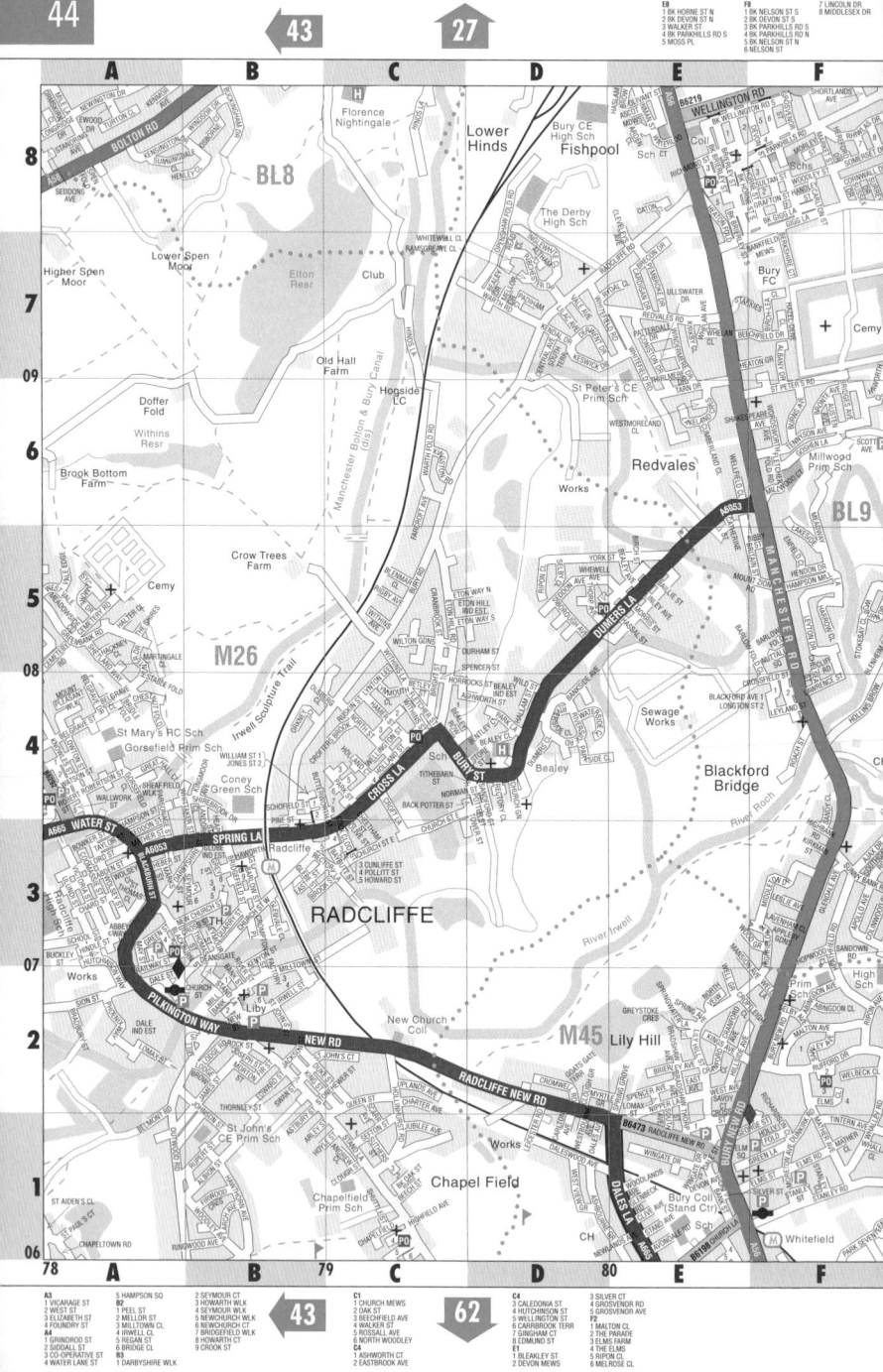

A   B   C   D   E   F

East Lancs Rly

GREENOCK DR

Water Farm

HEYWOOD DISTRIBUTION PK

8

Resr

Gigg

River Roch

Jackson Fold

THREE LANE ENDS

PILSWORTH RD

7

Superstore

Lomax's

PILSWORTH RD

Hill Top

Three Arrows Inn (PH)

09

Goshen Sports Ctr

Captains Farm

Brightley Brook

6

PH

THE CROFT

BORDEN WAY BEECHWOOD

Higher Barn

Hollins Brook

PILSWORTH COTTS

OL10

Hollins Vale

GAWTHORPE CL WILTON CL HEATON CL

Meadow Croft Fold

Broom Hill Farm

5

Hollins Grundy Prim Sch

HAWESWATER CRES

Castle House

08

Hollins

BL9

HOLLINS LA

Whittle Brook

Thurston Fold

4

CH

Sunny Bank

Cemy

BLEASDALE CL WENSLEYDALE CL

ST GEORGE'S CT

QUEEN ANN CL

Brick House

Sunny Bank Prim Sch

M24

Unsworth Moss

M62

3

Liby

Castlebrook High Sch

POLE LANE CT

Back o' th' Moss

Moss Side

07

Bury & Whitefield Prim Sch

Unsworth

CH

Unsworth Prim Sch

Bury Music Ctr

HILLS LA

The Hills

2

All Saints CE Prim Sch

Mersey Drive Com Sch

PILKINGTON WLK

DOUGLAS WLK

LOSTOCK WLK

ALT WLK

Egypt Farm

M25

Brookvale Farm

1

Ribble Drive Com Prim Sch

CALDER WAY ROOM WLK DOUGLAS MERSEY SQ

M45

Nursery

CHAPEL WLK

POLE LA

M66

18

Same Yet (PH)

06

ST MICHAELS GDNS Prim Sch

81   A   B   82   C   D   83   E   F

45 29

A B C D E F

8

7

09

6

5

08

4

3

07

2

1

06

84 A B 85 C D 86 E F

45 64

M25

M62

OL10

M24

St Joseph's RC Prim & High Schs

St Andrew's Dr

Siddal Moor Sports Coll

Hares Hill Farm

HARESHILL RD

Higher Fields

Heywood Distribution Pk

PILSWORTH RD

GLOUCESTER DR

ATHOLL DR

CUMBERTON DR

Stock Nook

New Gap Farm

Gardner's Arms (PH)

Lower Whittle

Birch Service Area

Top o' th' Hill

White Hart Hotel (PH)

Birch

BIRCH IND EST

Whittle Fold

WHITTLE LA

Greenhill Farm

Green Lane End

Rochdale Way

HEYWOOD OLD RD

The Jolly Butcher Inn (PH)

Bowlee

Sports Ctr

CALDER WLK

Siddal Farm

Siddal Fold

Oakridge Farm

Rochdale Way

OAKEN BANK RD

Mast

Hatters Farm

The Queen Elizabeth Sch

Dingle Farm

MANCHESTER RD

MIDDLETON RD

Lane End

M62

HOLLIN LA

Top of Hebers

A6046

A6045

Langley Prim Sch

St Mary's RC Prim Sch

Langley

Furrow Com Prim Sch

Liby

Middleton Parish CE Prim Sch

Parkfield Prim Sch

PO

1 CASSIDY GDNS
2 BISHOP MARSHALL WAY

1 LAKELAND CT
2 LONGTHWAITE CL
3 KESWICK CT
4 MILLBECK CT
5 BOWNESS CT

RUSCOMBE FOLD 1
RIMINGTON FOLD 2
BISHOPS MDW 3

BENFOLD WLK 1
CLIFTON WLK 2

E2
1 DUFTON WLK
2 DUDDON WLK
3 SEASCALE WLK
4 MOWBRAY WLK
5 HAWESWATER MEWS
6 WINSTER DR
7 D OLIVERA CT
8 DOVEDALE CT
9 ST BEES WLK

F1
1 THROSTLE HALL CT
2 NINIAN CT
3 EXETER CT
4 KIO ST
5 WATER ST
6 MARKET ST
7 CHAPEL ST
8 WOOD ST
9 CROSS ST

10 CHISHOLM CT
11 WEAVERS CT
12 GREAT ARBOR WAY
13 SCHOLARS WAY

8

7

09

6

08

5

4

3

07

2

06

1

A   B   C   D   E   F

Trub

OL11

OL10 ▶

OL9

Sewage Wks

Newhey Farm

Thornfields

Thornham Fold

Tandle Hill Tavern (PH)

Garden Ctr

Slattocks

St John's CE Prim Sch

Hopwood Arms (PH)

Rochdale Way

HILLBANK ST

Glade Wood

CH

Hopwood Hall

Lords Wood

Stake Hill

Hopwood Hall Coll

BENTLEY AVE

Woodside Farm

Rochdale Way

M24

Higher Stake Hill

Cardinal Langley RC High Sch

STAKEHILL IND EST

Hollins

Alderman Kay Sch

St John Fisher RC Prim Sch

Chadderton Heights Farm

Hollin Prim Sch

Stanycliffe

Heald's Green

Boarshaw Com Prim Sch

OL1

Black Pits

Crem

Acres

Chadderton Fold

Cemy

Higher Boarshaw

St Matthew's CE Sch

Oldham Way

River Irk

Chadderton Hall Park

OL9

Sch

Mills Hill

HAIGH LA

MIDDLETON

HAIGH LA

OLDHAM RD

A669

A627(M)

A62

M62

ROCHDALE RD

MANCHESTER RD

CHADDERTON HALL RD

LONG ST

A576

A1
1 WATER ST
2 SADLER ST
3 ST LEONARD'S SQ
4 BARROWFIELD WLK
5 ASSHETON ST

A2
1 WALTON ST
2 WHITE HART MEADOW
3 CHURCH STREET IND EST
4 BREWSTER ST
5 NORMAN WEALL CT
6 BACK SPRING GDNS
7 LOWER BAMFORD CL
8 PETERLOO TERR
9 ASSHETON ST

10 ST STEPHEN'S GDNS
11 WICKHAM TERR

OL11

OL16

High
Crompton

Plumpton

Thornham St James'
CE Prim Sch

Summit

Gravel
Hole

Puckersley Inn
(PH)

Low
Crompton

M24

Hanging
Chadder

Narrowgate
Farm

Fir Bank
Com Prim Sch

Oozewood
Clough

Tandle Hill
Country Park

Oozewood

OL2

1 CAMERON CT
2 DEVINE CL
3 HIGHBURY WAY

Cemy

High Barn
Com Prim Sch

Luzley
Brook

Hough

Thorp
Com Prim Sch

Thorp

1 BERKLEY ST
2 LANCASTER SQ
3 LANCASTER HOUSE

Milton
Street
Day
Sch

Cinder Hill
Farm

Crofters

RACEFIELD
HAMLET

ROYTON

Haggate

Shaw Rd

Horton Arms
(PH)

OL1

Middleton Rd

Sch

Our Lady's
RC Comp
Sch

Royley

St
Anne's
CE Prim
Sch

Superstore

Holden
Fold

Broadway

Ind Est

Chadderton
Hall Com
Prim Sch

Oldham Rd

North
Chadderton
Sch

Oldham Athletic AFC
(Boundary Pk)

Long
Sight

OL9

Chadderton Way

Superstore

A663

The
Royal
Oldham

West
Hulme

Oldham
Edge

Mast

90

A

B

91

C

D

92

E

F

06

07

08

09

2

3

4

5

6

7

8

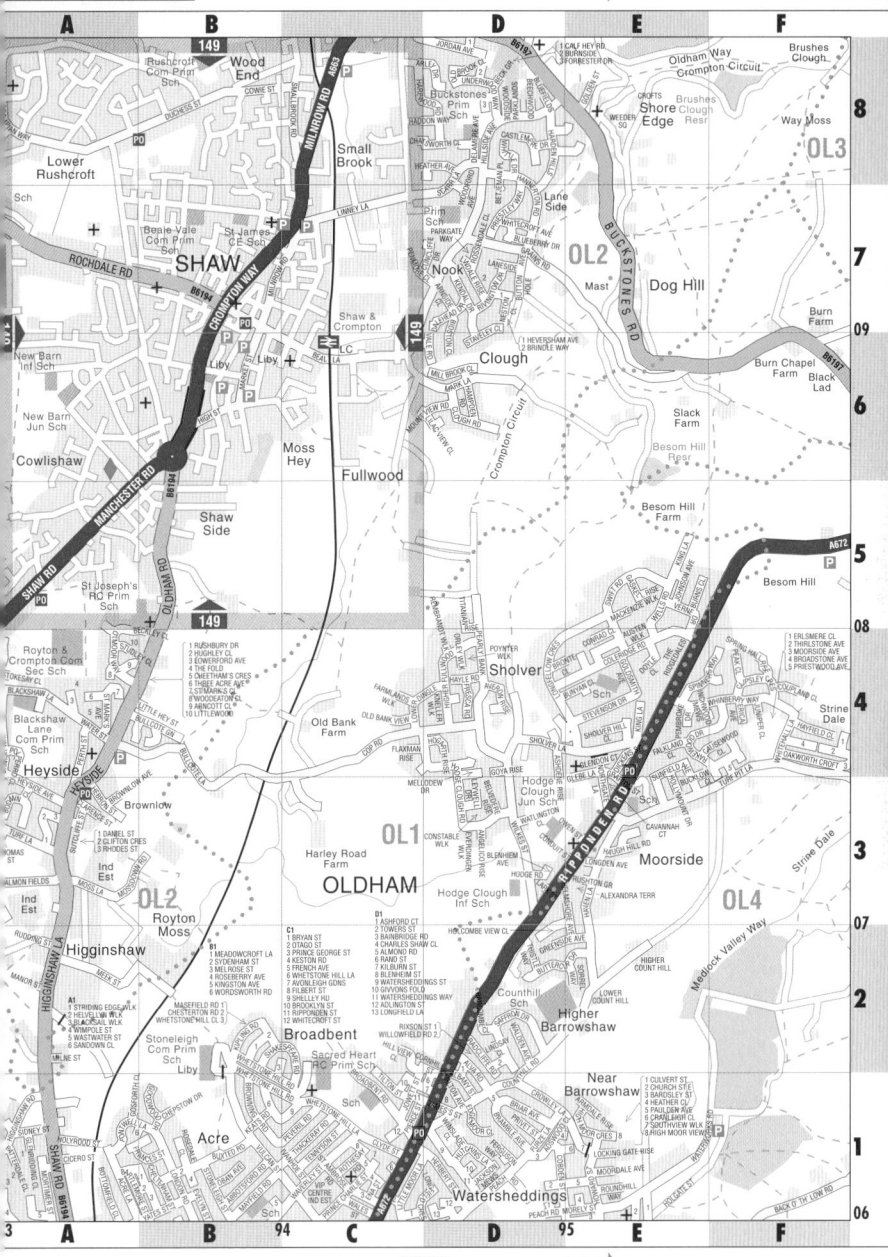

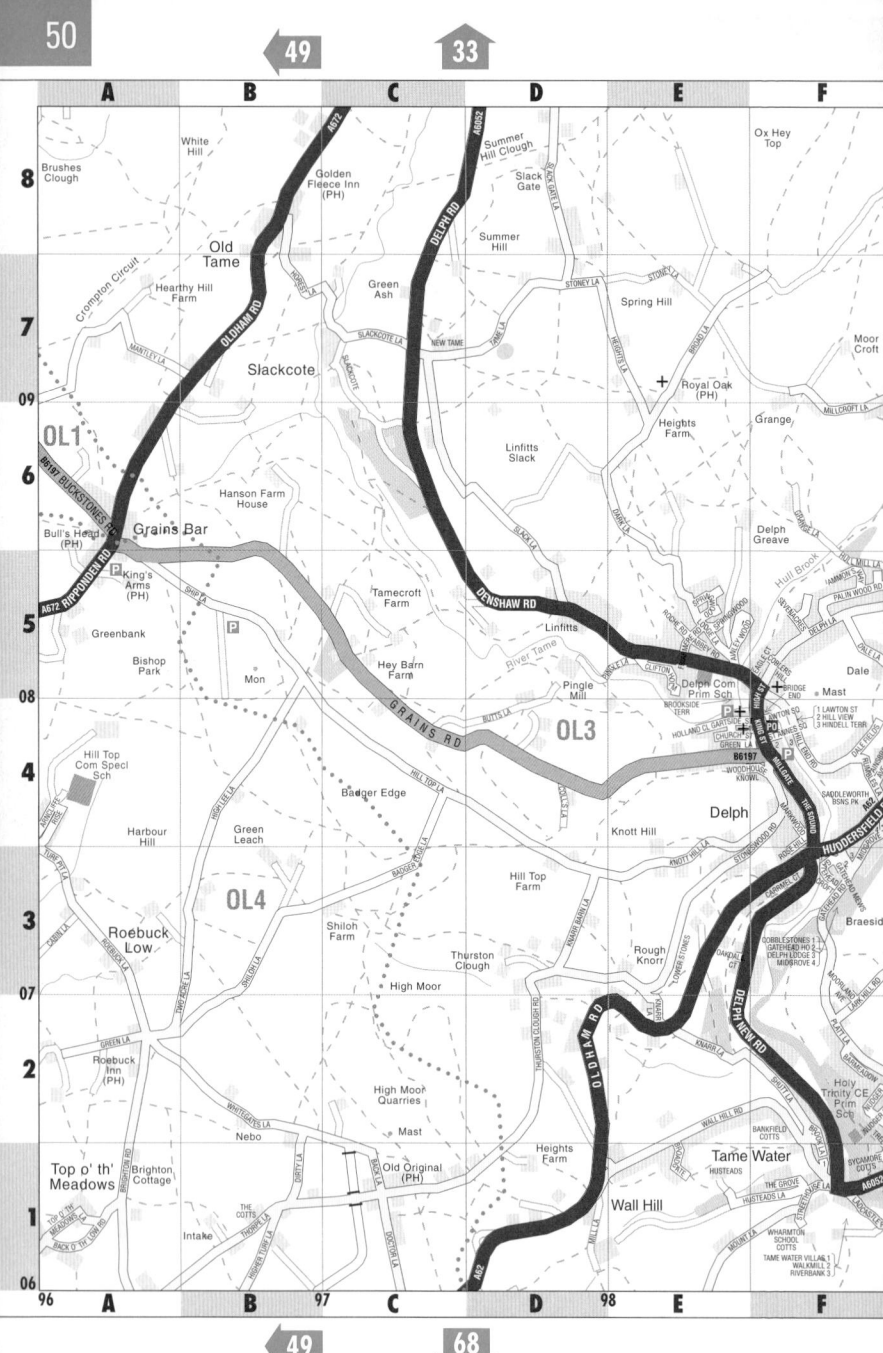

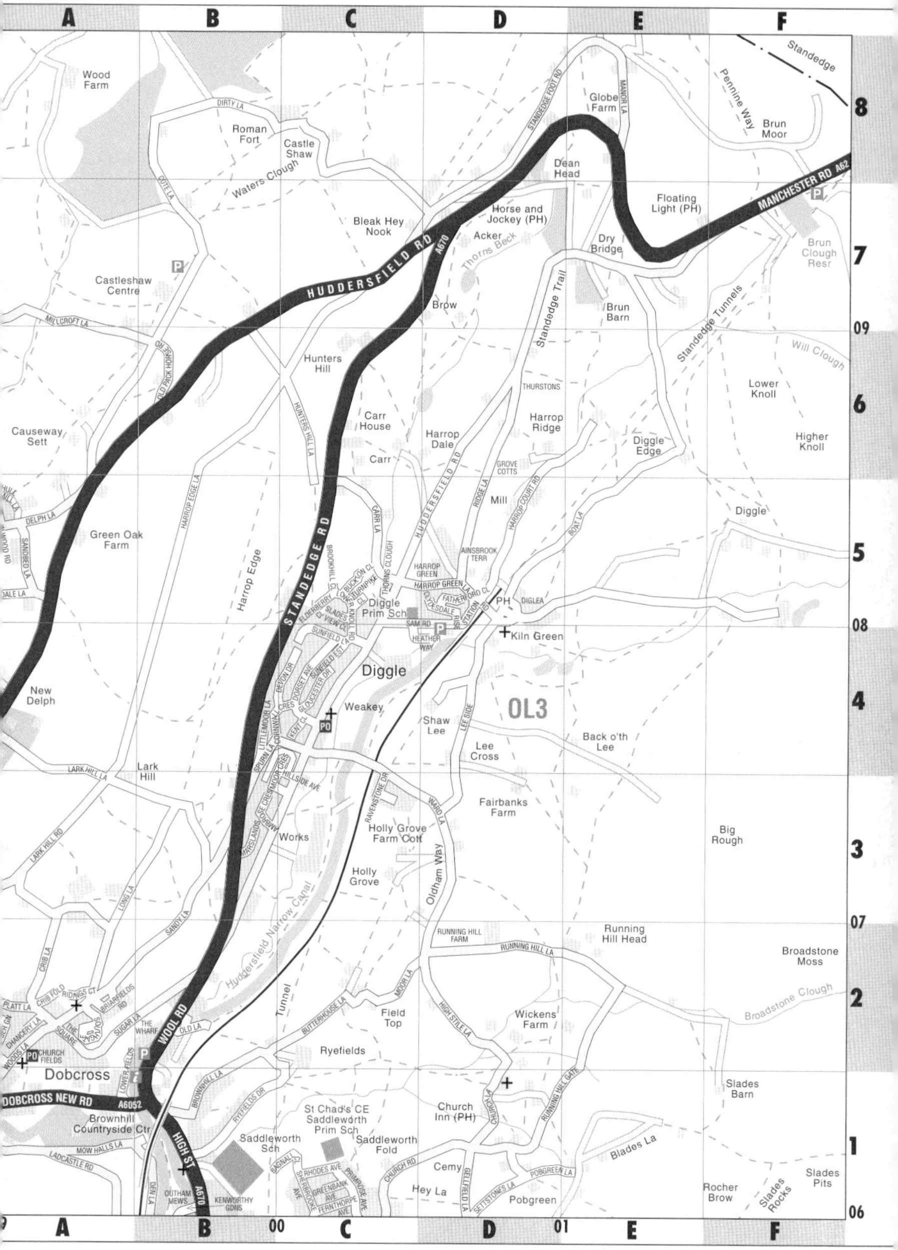

A	B	C	D	E	F

Wood Farm

DIRTY LA

Roman Fort

Castle Shaw Hill

Waters Clough

Bleak Hey Nook

Globe Farm

Dean Head

Standedge

Brun Moor

Pennine Way

8

Horse and Jockey (PH)

Acker

Thorns Beck

Floating Light (PH)

MANCHESTER RD A62

Dry Bridge

Brun Clough Resr

7

Castleshaw Centre

HUDDERSFIELD RD A670

Brow

Brun Barn

Standedge Trail

Standedge Tunnels

Will Clough

09

Causeway Sett

Hunters Hill

Harrop Edge

Carr House

Harrop Dale

THURSTONS

Harrop Ridge

Diggle Edge

Lower Knoll

Higher Knoll

6

Green Oak Farm

Carr

GROVE COTTS

Mill

Diggle

5

DELPH LA

Harrop Edge

STANDEDGE RD

AINSBROOK TERR

HARROP GREEN

Harrop Green

Diggle Prim Sch

PH

DIGLEA

Kiln Green

08

New Delph

Diggle

Weakey

Shaw Lee

Lee Cross

Back o'th Lee

OL3

4

LARK HILL LA

Lark Hill

WOOL RD

Works

Holly Grove Farm Cott

Holly Grove

Oldham Way

Fairbanks Farm

Big Rough

3

Huddersfield Narrow Canal

Tunnel

RUNNING HILL FARM

RUNNING HILL LA

Running Hill Head

Broadstone Moss

Broadstone Clough

07

2

Field Top

Wickens Farm

Slades Barn

Dobcross

DOBCROSS NEW RD A6052

Ryefields

HIGH ST A670

Church Inn (PH)

Blades La

Slades Pits

Slades Rocks

1

Brownhill Countryside Ctr

St Chad's CE Saddleworth Prim Sch

Saddleworth Sch

Saddleworth Fold

Cemy

Hey La

Pobgreen

Rocher Brow

06

A	00	B	C	01	D	E	F

8

Poul Moss

Warcock

Redbrook
Resr

Warcock
Hill

MANCHESTER RD A62

Standedge Tunnel

Standedge Trail

Butterly

Great Butterly
Hill

Butterly Clough

Bobus

Little Butterly
Hill

7

Round
Hill

Swellands
Resr

HD7

09

Rocher Moss

Black Moss
Resr

Blakely Clough

6

Little Black
Moss Resr

Pennine Way

Black Moss

Rocher Brow

5

Rifle Range

Hoar Clough

Broadhead
Brow

08

Diggle
Resr

Ravenstone
Brow

4

Ravenstone
Rocks

Wicken Clough

OL3

Broadhead
Moss

White Moss

3

Wicken Clough
Moss

South Clough

Broadstone
Moss

07

Broadstone
Hill

South Clough
Moss

2

Broad Stones

Diggle
Rake

Featherbed
Moss

Hollin Brown
Knoll

1

Near Wain
Stones

Boggart Stones

Far Wain
Stones

A635

HOLMFIRTH RD

A635

06

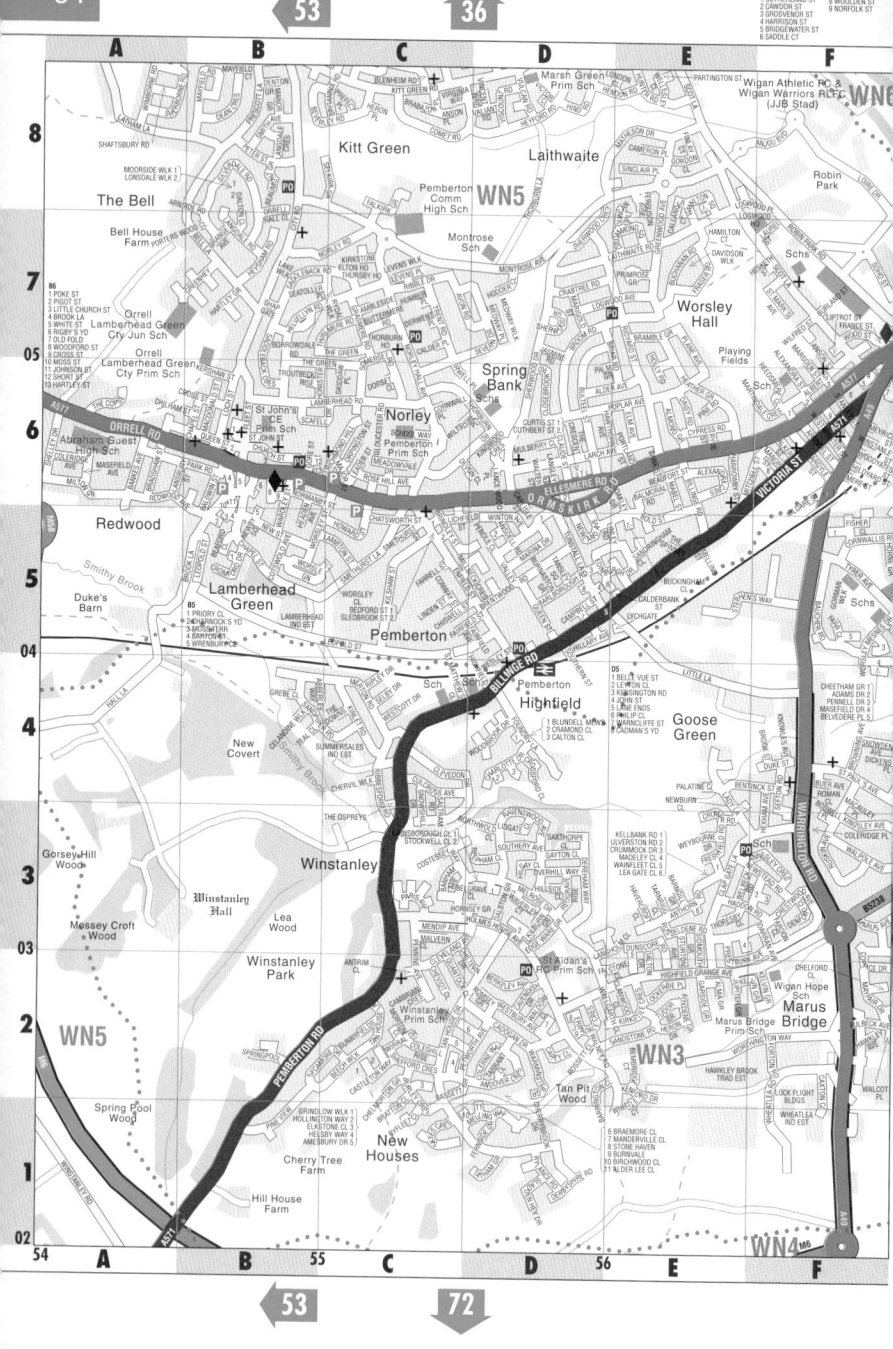

F6
1 SUTHERLAND ST
2 CAWDOR ST
3 GROSVENOR ST
4 HARRISON ST
5 BRIDGEWATER ST
6 SADDLE CT

7 ATHERTON ST
8 WOOLDEN ST
9 NORFOLK ST

8

Kitt Green

Laithwaite

Wigan Athletic FC &
Wigan Warriors RLFC
(JJB Stad)

WN6

The Bell

Robin
Park

WN5

Pemberton
Comm
High Sch

Montrose
Sch

Worsley
Hall

Schs

7

M6
1 POKE ST
2 PIGOT ST
3 LITTLE CHURCH ST
4 BROOK LA
5 WHITE ST
6 RIGBY'S YD
7 OLD FOLD
8 WOODFORD ST
9 CROSS ST
10 MOSS ST
11 JOHNSON ST
12 SHORT ST
13 HARTLEY ST

Orrell
Lamberhead Green
Cty Jun Sch

Orrell
Lamberhead Green
Cty Prim Sch

Spring
Bank

Playing
Fields

05

Norley

St John's
Prim Sch

ORRELL RD

6

Redwood

ORMSKIRK RD S

ELLESMERE RD S

VICTORIA ST

Abraham Guest
High Sch

5

Smithy Brook

Lamberhead
Green

Worsley
Hall

Duke's
Barn

Pemberton

Schs

04

B5
1 PRIORY CL
2 BILLBROOK'S YD
3 MOSSFIRR
4 BARTONFI
5 WRENBURY CT

BILLINGE RD

Pemberton
Highfield

D5
1 BELL VUE ST
2 LEWTON CL
3 KENSINGTON RD
4 JOHN ST
5 LANE ENDS
6 PHILIP CL
7 WARNCLIFFE ST
8 CADMAN'S YD

4

New
Covert

1 BLUNDELL MEWS
2 DRAMOND CL
3 CALTON CL

Goose
Green

03

Gorsey Hill
Wood

Winstanley

Lea
Wood

KELLBANK RD 1
ULVERSTON RD 2
DRUMMOCK DR 3
MADELEY CL 4
WAINFLEET CL 5
LEA GATE CL 6

Messey Croft
Wood

Winstanley
Hall

PO Sch

St Aidan's
RC Prim Sch

3

Winstanley
Park

Wigan Hope
Sch

Marus Bridge
Prim Sch

Marus
Bridge

2

WN5

WN3

Spring Pool
Wood

Tan Pit
Wood

Hawkley Brook
Trad Est

PEMBERTON RD

6 BRAEMORE CL
7 MANDERVILLE CL
8 STONE HAVEN
9 BURNVALE
10 BIRCHWOOD CL
11 ALDER LEE CL

1

Cherry Tree
Farm

New
Houses

GRUNDLOW WLK 1
HOLLINGTON WAY 2
ELKSTONE CL 3
HELSBY WAY 4
AMESBURY DR 5

Hill House
Farm

02

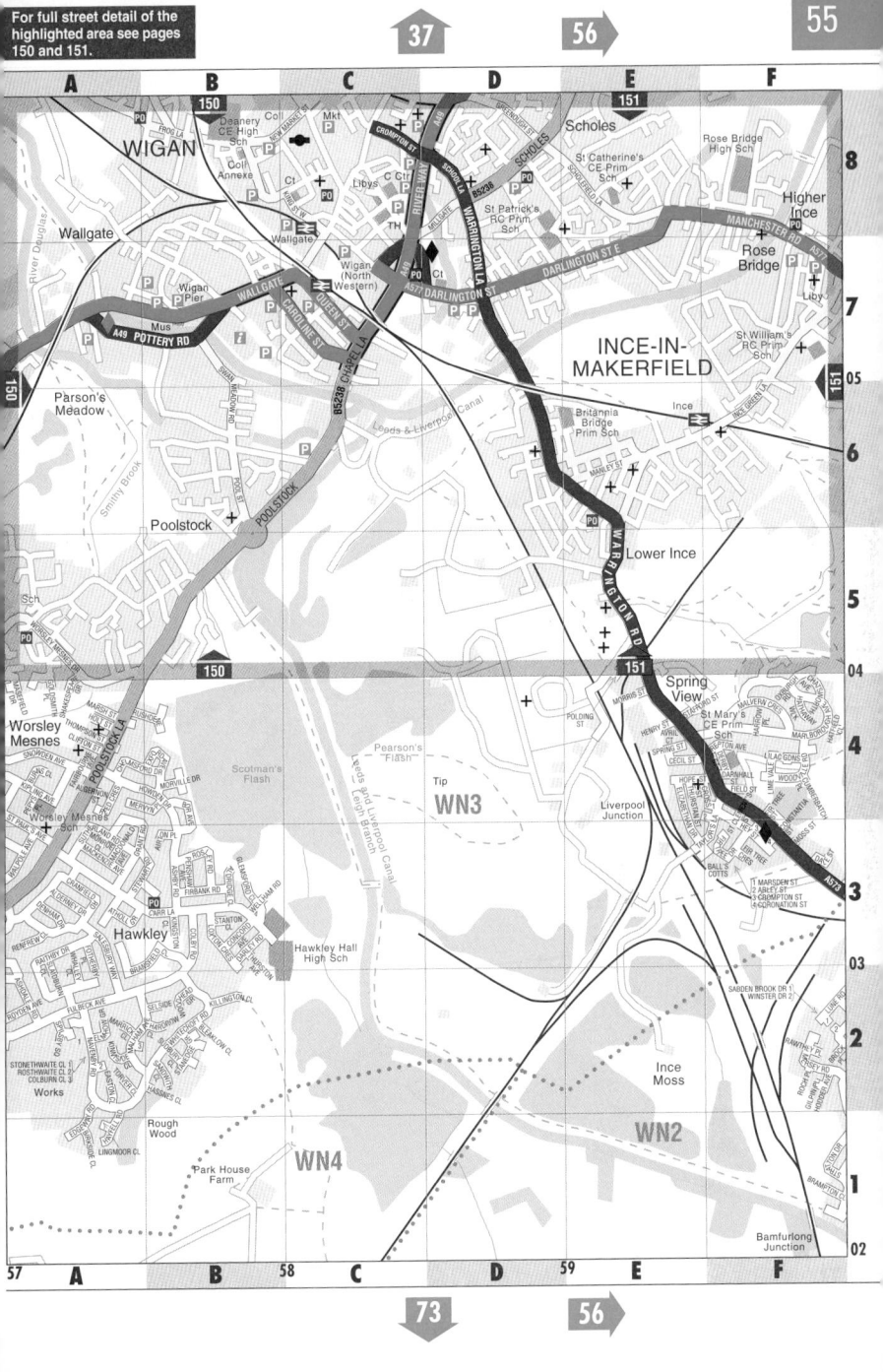

A2
1 ELIZABETHAN WLK
2 GEORGIAN SQ
3 WENNING WLK
4 ALBION ST
5 ASPINALL ST
6 DARWEN DR
B1
1 WILLOW LODGE
2 WILLOW ST

3 DIXON PL
4 DOOTSON ST
5 ST JOHN'S CT
6 BURNS RD
7 KEATS WAY
B2
1 SYRESHAM ST
2 GREEN ST
3 TABERNER ST
4 LOMAX ST

3 SILVER ST
4 GRAMPIAN WAY
7 LUNEDALE
D4
1 WOODGREEN CL
2 UNSWORTH ST
3 ALDRED ST
4 WENLOCK GR
5 ARMITSTEAD ST

D5
1 MORRIS ST
2 EMLYN ST
3 REGENT ST
4 MEADOWS CL
5 WINANSCLIFFE ST
6 CRANBY ST
7 BEAUFORT ST
8 FOLEY ST
9 WENLOCK ST

D5
10 PUMP ST
11 FIRST AVE
12 THE MEWS
13 BYRON AVE
14 ALBERT ST
15 PROSPECT IND CTR
16 HINDLEY BSNS CTR

D6
1 RANDLE ST
2 LANGSET AVE
3 GOLLIER ST
4 GIDLOW ST
5 QUEEN ST
6 PRESBYTERIAN FOLD
7 PENNINGTON ST
8 NELSON ST

E5
1 GRANVILLE ST
2 BAMBER'S BLDGS
3 DURHAM RD
4 CASTLE RISE
5 CORBET ST
6 EGERTON CT
E6
1 HILL TOP FOLD
2 CHADWICK ST

3 WOODFORD CT
4 WOODFORD ST

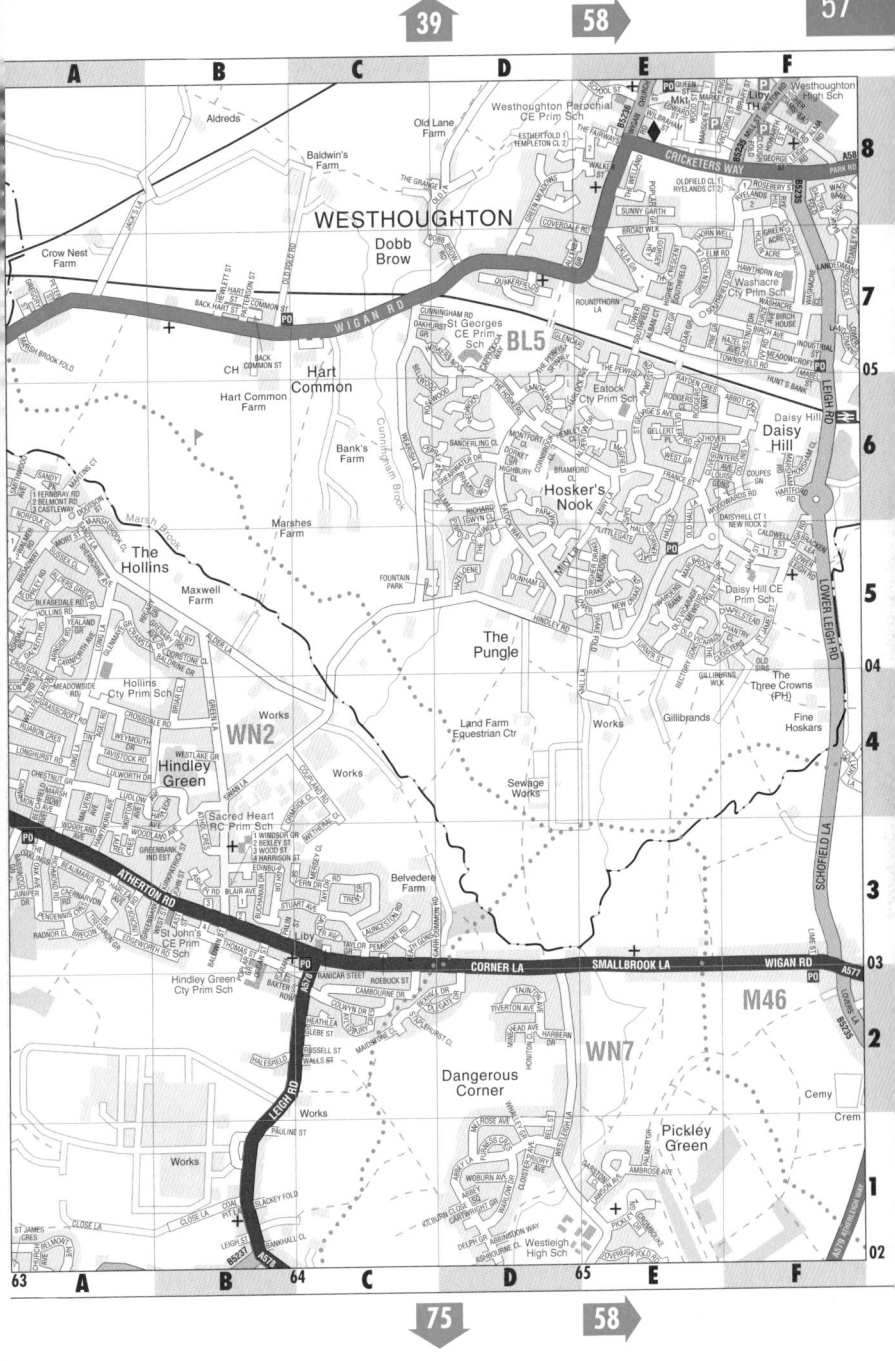

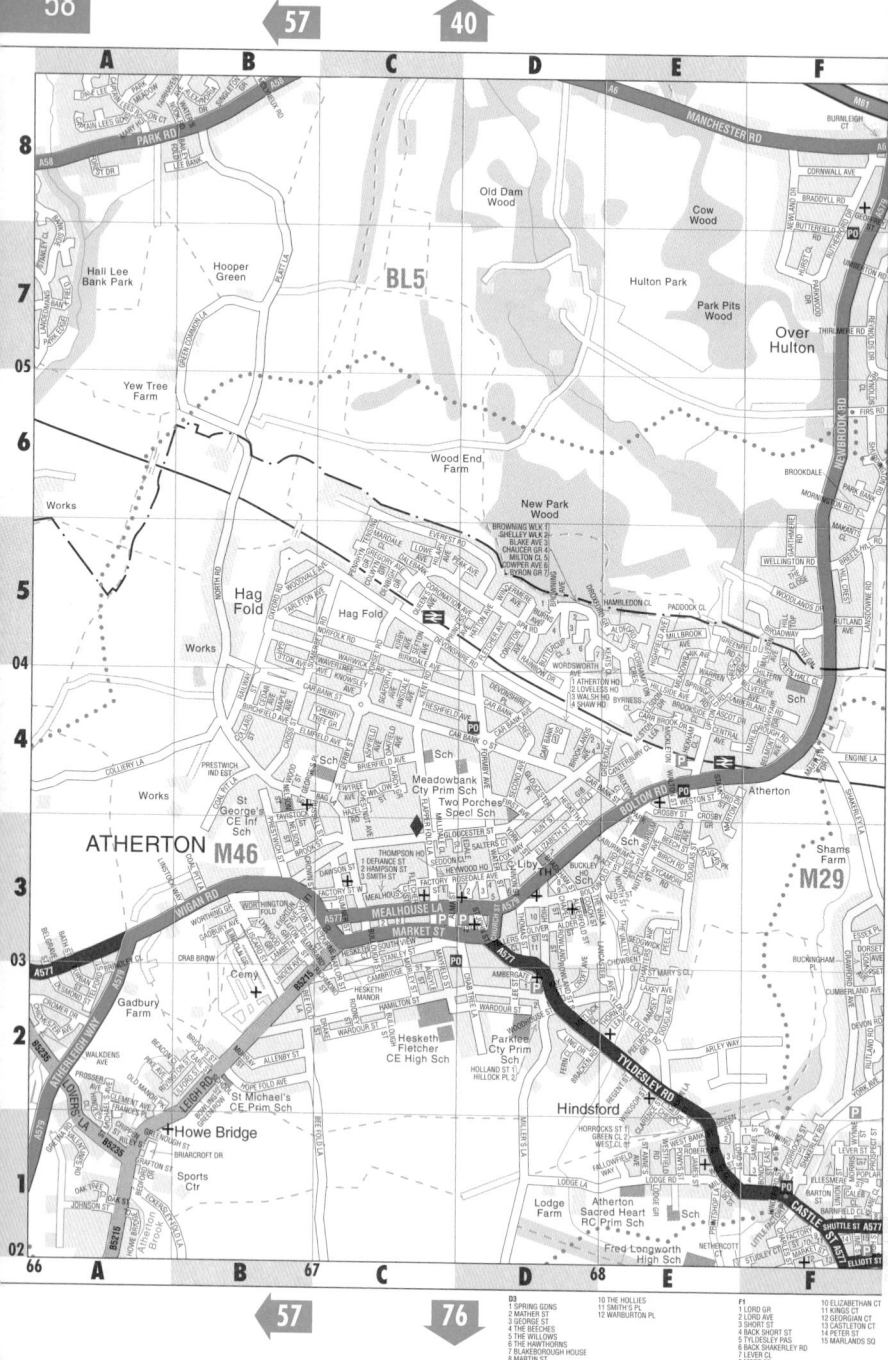

D3
1 SPRING GDNS
2 MATHER ST
3 GEORGE ST
4 THE BEECHES
5 THE WILLOWS
6 THE HAWTHORNS
7 BLAKEBOROUGH HOUSE
8 MARTIN ST
9 BRAMPTON ST

10 THE HOLLIES
11 SMITH'S PL
12 WARBURTON PL

F1
1 LORD GR
2 LORD AVE
3 SHORT ST
4 BACK SHORT ST
5 TYLDESLEY PAS
6 BACK SHAKERLEY RD
7 LEVER CL
8 MORT ST
9 ALFRED ST

10 ELIZABETHAN CT
11 KINGS CT
12 GEORGIAN CT
13 CASTLETON CT
14 PETER ST
15 MARLANDS SQ

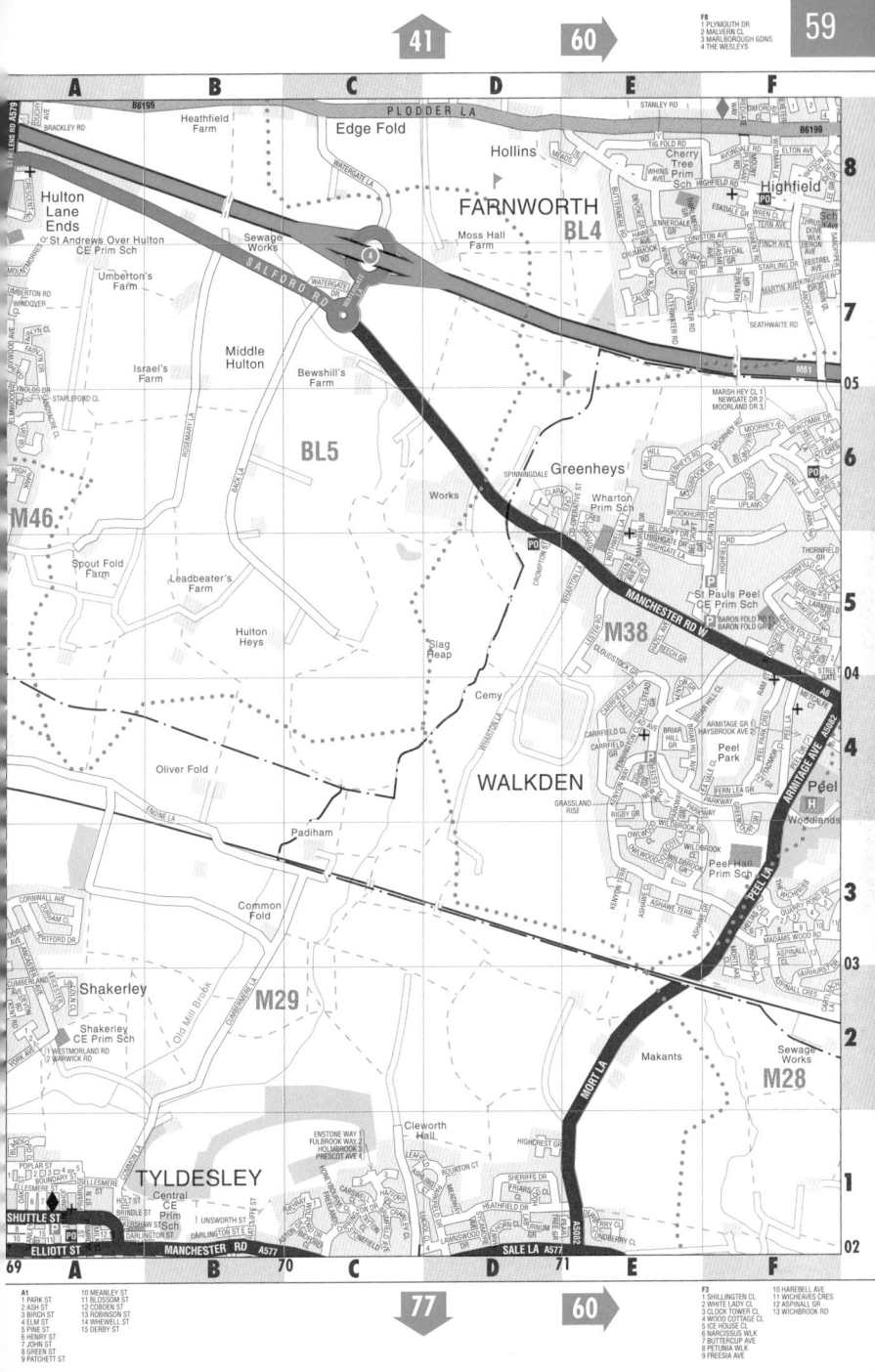

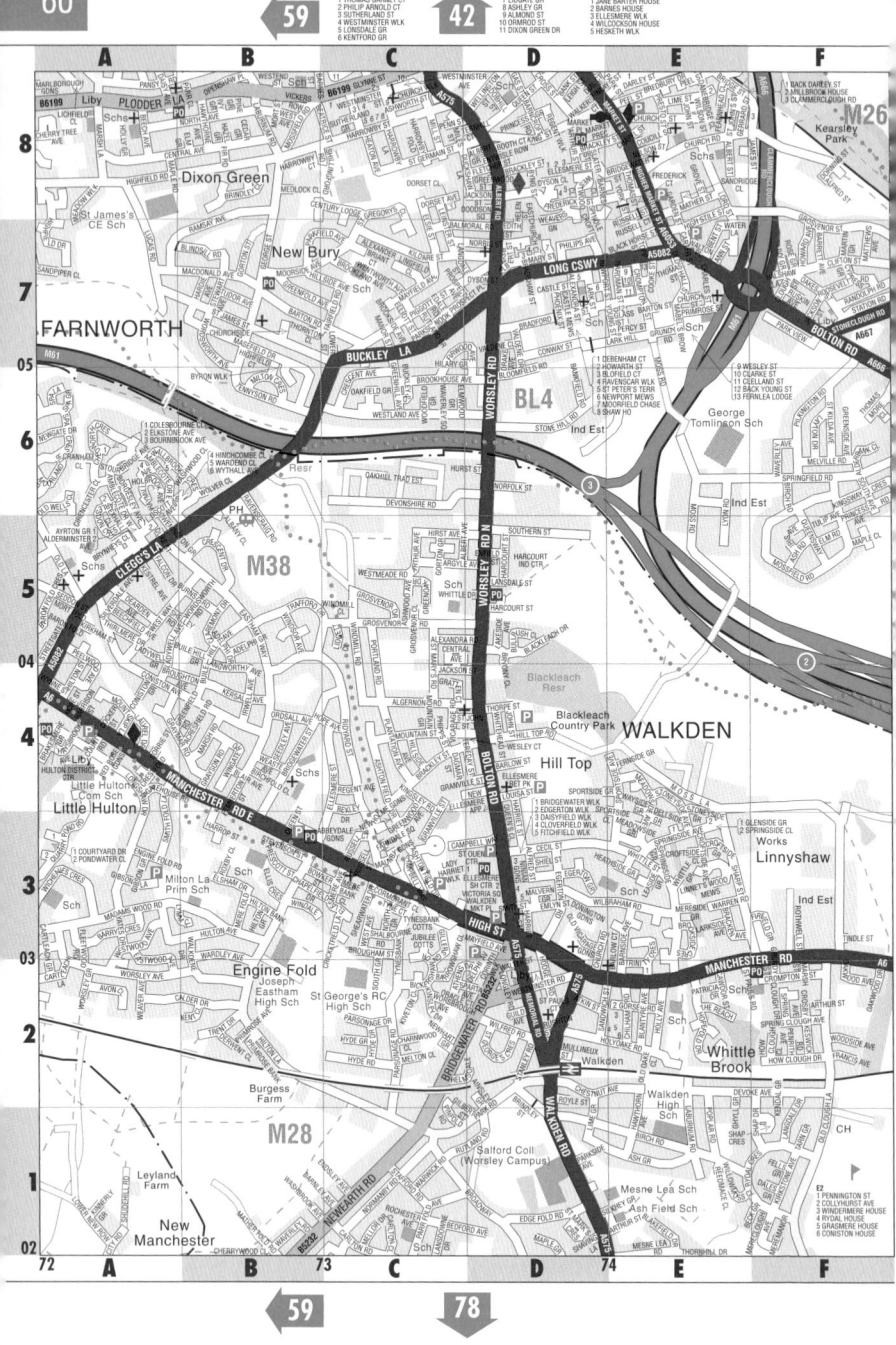

59
42

C8
1 THOMAS GARNET CT
2 PHILIP ARNOLD CT
3 SUTHERLAND ST
4 WESTMINSTER WLK
5 LONSDALE GR
6 KENTFORD GR

C8
7 LIDGATE GR
8 ASHLEY GR
9 ALMOND ST
10 ORMROD ST
11 DIXON GREEN DR

D8
1 JANE BARTER HOUSE
2 BARNES HOUSE
3 ELLESMERE WLK
4 WILCOCKSON HOUSE
5 HESKETH WLK

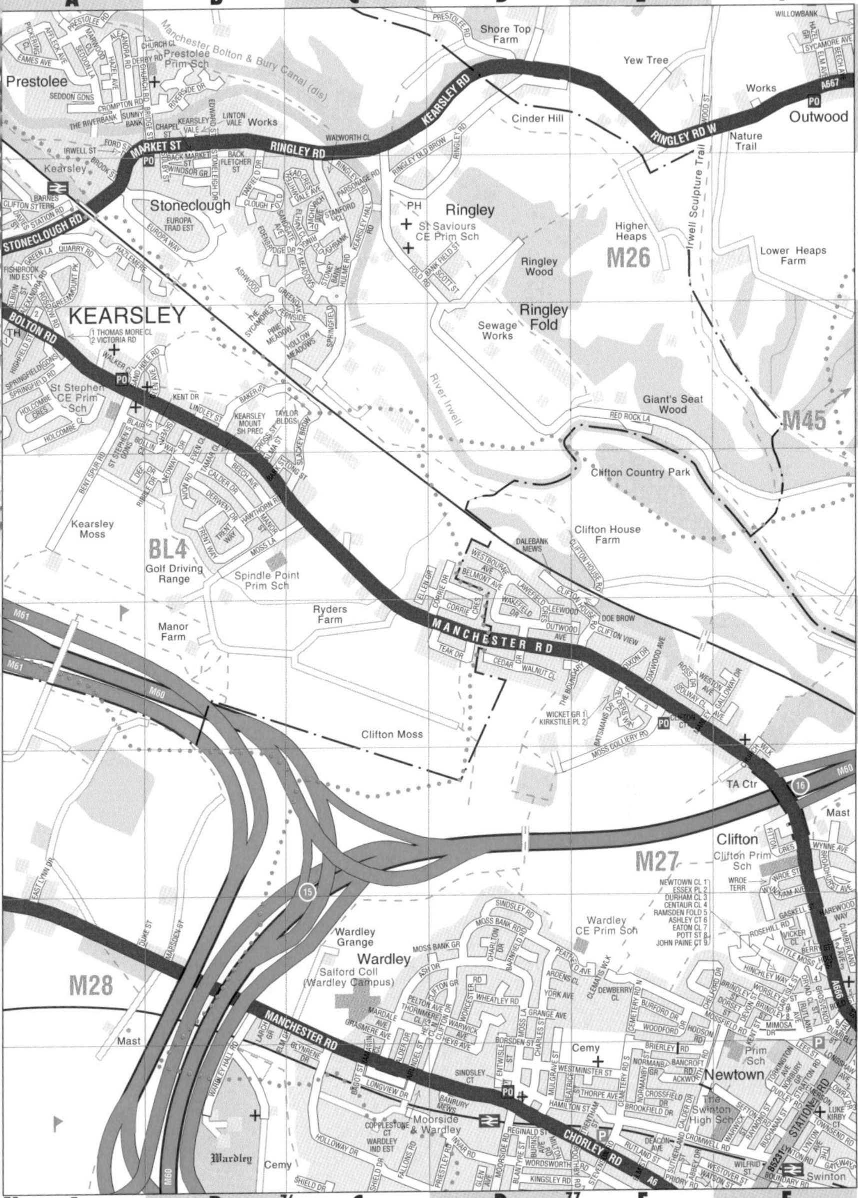

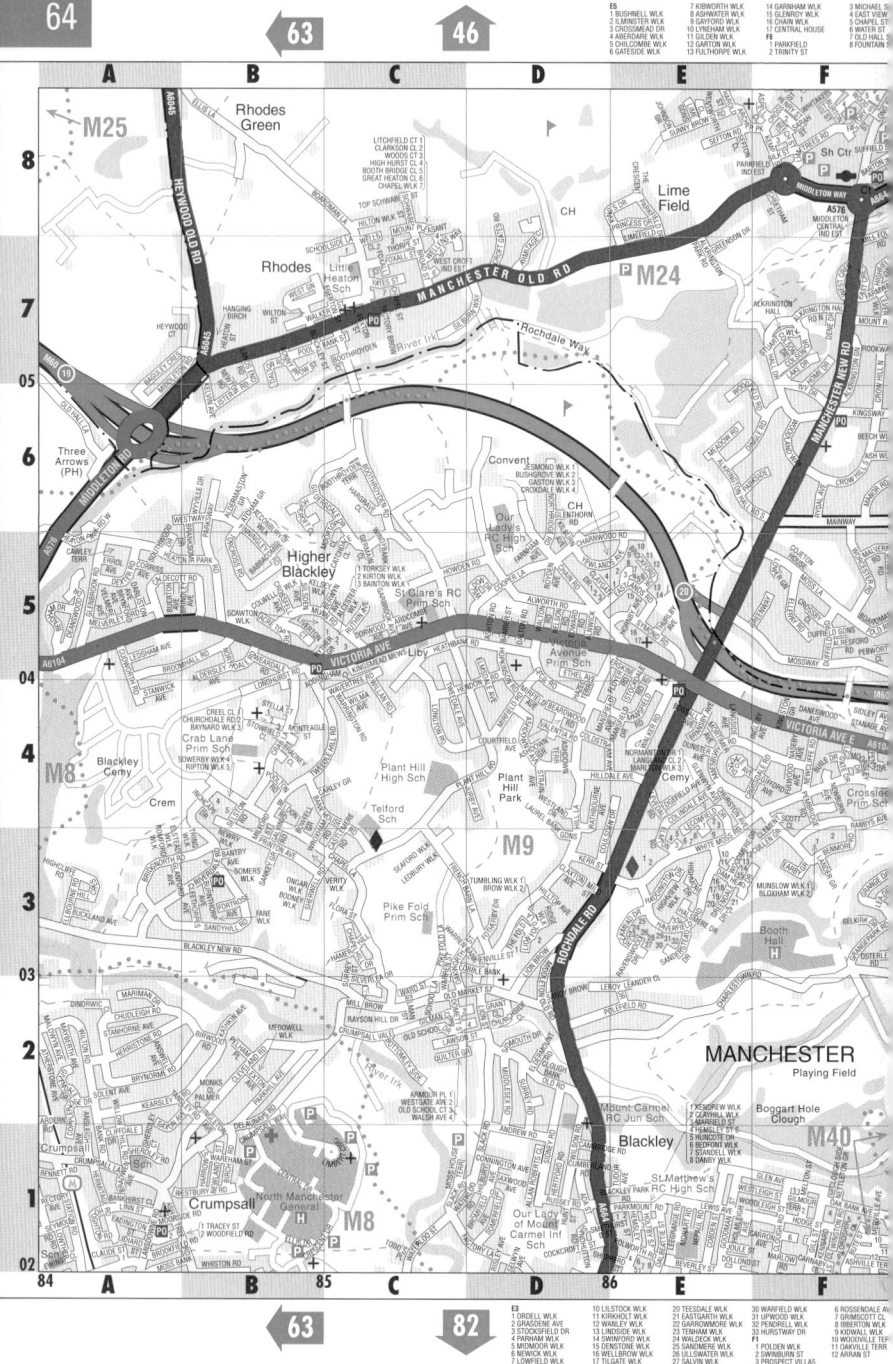

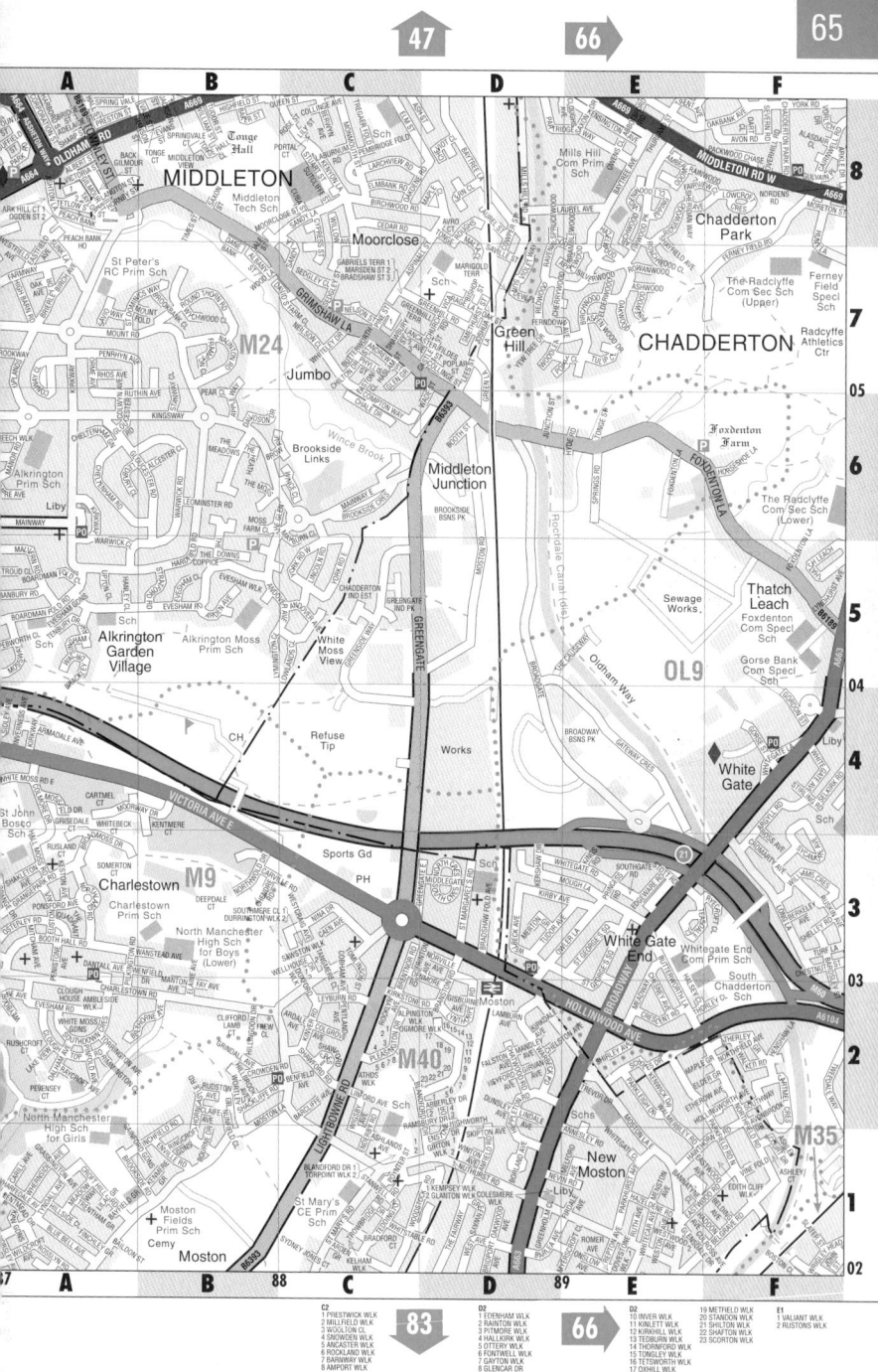

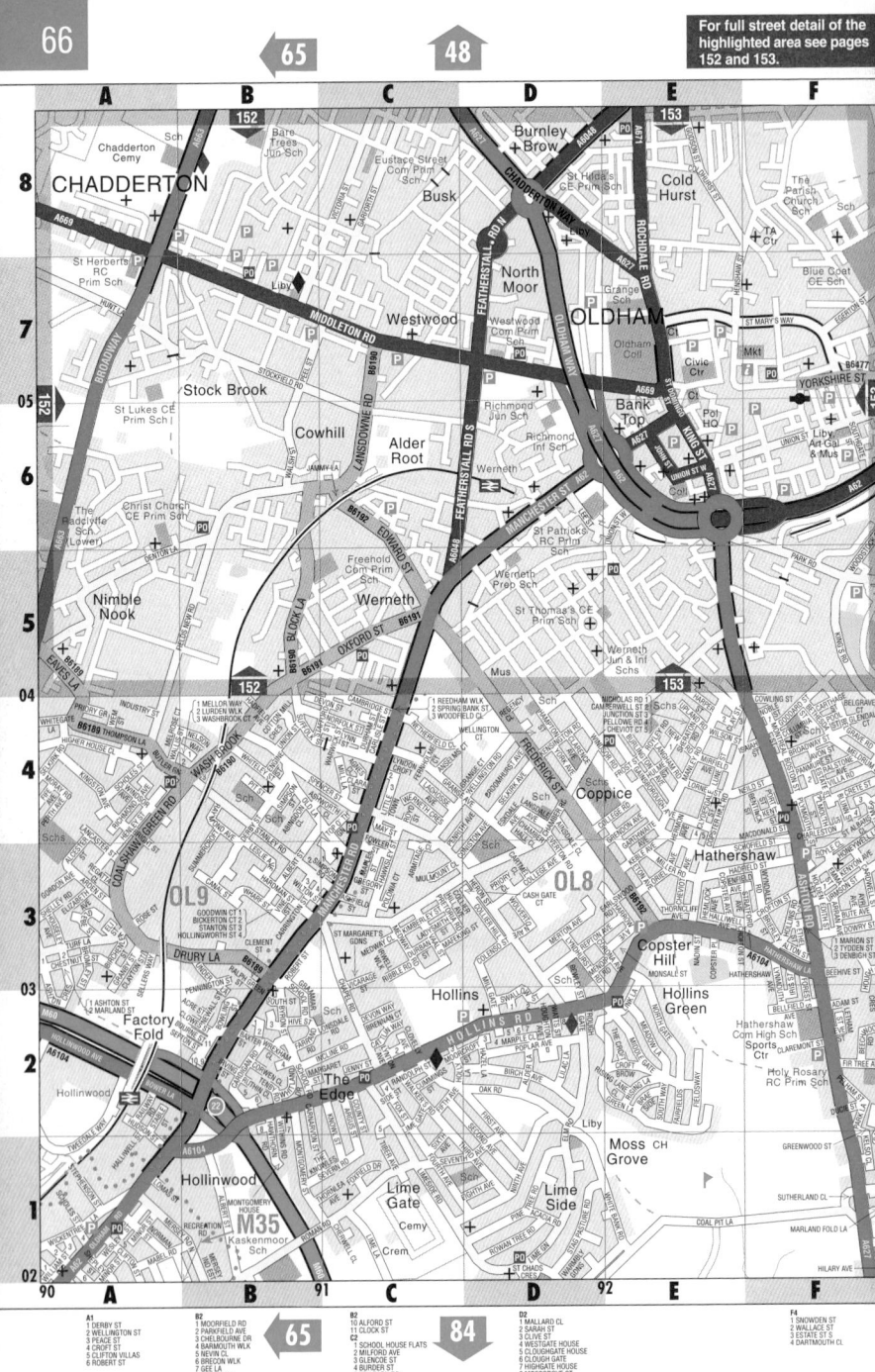

65   48

For full street detail of the
highlighted area see pages
152 and 153.

A   B   C   D   E   F

8

Sch
Chadderton
Cemy

CHADDERTON

St Herberts
RC Prim Sch

Bare
Trees
Jun Sch

Eustace Street
Com Prim
Sch

Busk

152

Burnley
Brow

St Hilda's
CE Prim Sch

CHADDERTON WAY

Cold
Hurst

153

The
Parish
Church
Sch

TA
Ctr

Blue Coat
CE Sch

7

BROADWAY

St Lukes CE
Prim Sch

MIDDLETON RD

Westwood

North
Moor

Westwood
Com Prim
Sch

FEATHERSTALL RD N

OLDHAM RD

ROCHDALE RD

OLDHAM

Oldham
Coll

Grange
Ave

Civic
Ctr

ST MARY'S WAY

Mkt

B6477

YORKSHIRE ST

153

05   152

Stock Brook

Cowhill

Alder
Root

LANSDOWNE RD

Richmond
Jun Sch

FEATHERSTALL RD S

A669

Bank
Top

Pol
HQ

KING ST

Ct

Liby
Art Gal
& Mus

A62

6

The
Radclyfe
Sch
(Lower)

DENTON LA

Christ Church
CE Prim Sch

BLOCK LA

EDWARD ST

Freehold
Com Prim
Sch

OXFORD ST

B6195

B6191

Richmond
Inf Sch

Werneth

St Patricks
RC Prim
Sch

MANCHESTER ST

UNION ST W

UNION ST

A627

PARK RD

5

EAVES LA

B6189

Nimble
Nook

Werneth

B6191

St Thomas's CE
Prim Sch

Werneth
Prep Sch

Werneth
Jun & Inf
Schs

Mus

04

WHITEGATE LA

B6189 THOMPSON LA

PRIORY AVE

INDUSTRY ST

WASH BROOK

1 MELLOR WAY
2 LURDEN WLK
3 WASHBROOK CT

CAMBRIDGE ST

152

WELLINGTON
CT

1 REEDHAM WLK
2 SPRING BANK ST
3 WOODFIELD CT

FREDERICK ST

NICHOLAS RD
CASHMEWELL ST
JUNCTION ST 3
FELLOWE RD 4
CHEVIOT CT 3

Sch

COWLING ST

BELGRAVE

ASHTON RD

GLENDALE

4

COAL SHAW GREEN RD

Sch

Coppice

Hathershaw

3   **OL9**

GOODWIN CT 1
BICKERTON CT 2
STANTON ST 3
HOLLINGWORTH ST 1

DRURY LA

CLEMENT

ST MARGARET'S
GDNS

OL8

CASH GATE
CT

A6104

**Copster
Hill**

MONSALE ST

THORNCLIFF

HATHERSHAW

MARION ST
TYDDEN ST
DENBIGH ST

BEEHIVE ST

03

1 ASHTON ST
2 MARLAND ST

PENNINGTON ST

Factory
Fold

HOLLINWOOD AVE

A6104

Hollinwood

M60

Hollins

VICARAGE

HOLLINS RD

1 MARKET PL
2 POPLAR AVE

A627

**Hollins
Green**

BELLFIELD

Hathershaw
Com High Sch
Sports
Ctr

ADAM ST

FIR TREE AV

Holy Rosary
RC Prim Sch

2

A6104

**The
Edge**

Liby

**Moss
Grove**

CH

GREENWOOD ST

SUTHERLAND CL

1

PEACE

A6104

Hollinwood

MONTGOMERY
HOUSE

M35

RECREATION RD

Kaskenmoor
Sch

**Lime
Gate**

Cemy

**Lime
Side**

OAK AVE

BIRCH AVE

ACACIA AVE

ST CHADS
CRES

Crem

COAL PIT LA

MARLAND FOLD LA

HILARY AVE

02

90   A   **91**   B   C   D   **92**   E   F

65   84

A1
1 DERBY ST
2 WELLINGTON ST
3 PEACE ST
4 CROFT ST
5 CLIFTON VILLAS
6 ROBERT ST

B2
1 MOORFIELD RD
2 PARKFIELD AVE
3 CHELBURNE DR
4 BARMOUTH WLK
5 NEVIN CL
6 BRECON WLK
7 GEE LA
8 CARDIFF CL
9 PUMP ST

B2
10 ALFORD ST
11 CLOCK ST
C2
1 SCHOOL HOUSE FLATS
2 MILFORD AVE
3 GLENCOE ST
4 BURDER ST
5 FOX PARK RD

D2
1 MALLARD CL
2 SARAH ST
3 CLIVE ST
4 WESTGATE HOUSE
5 CLOUGHGATE HOUSE
6 CLOUGH GATE
7 HIGHGATE HOUSE
8 MOSSGROVE ST

F4
1 SNOWDEN ST
2 WALLACE ST
3 ESTATE ST 5
4 DARTMOUTH CL

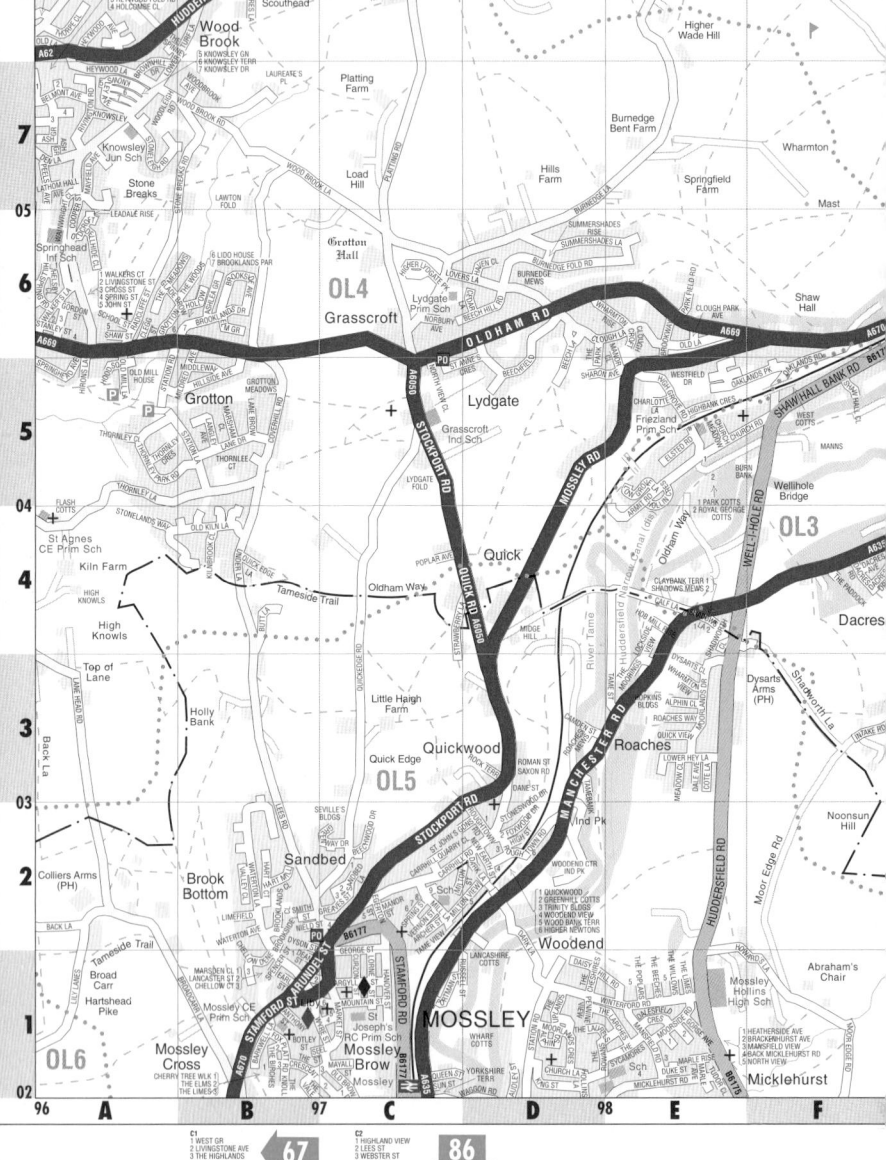

C1
1 WEST GR
2 LIVINGSTONE AVE
3 THE HIGHLANDS
4 CRADDOCK ST
5 CHAPEL CT
6 CHAPEL ST

C2
1 HIGHLAND VIEW
2 LEES ST
3 WEBSTER ST
4 CROSS ST
5 WILD'S SQ
6 SPRING COTTS
7 BACK MILL LA
8 HAWTHORN TERR
9 WOODMEADOW CT

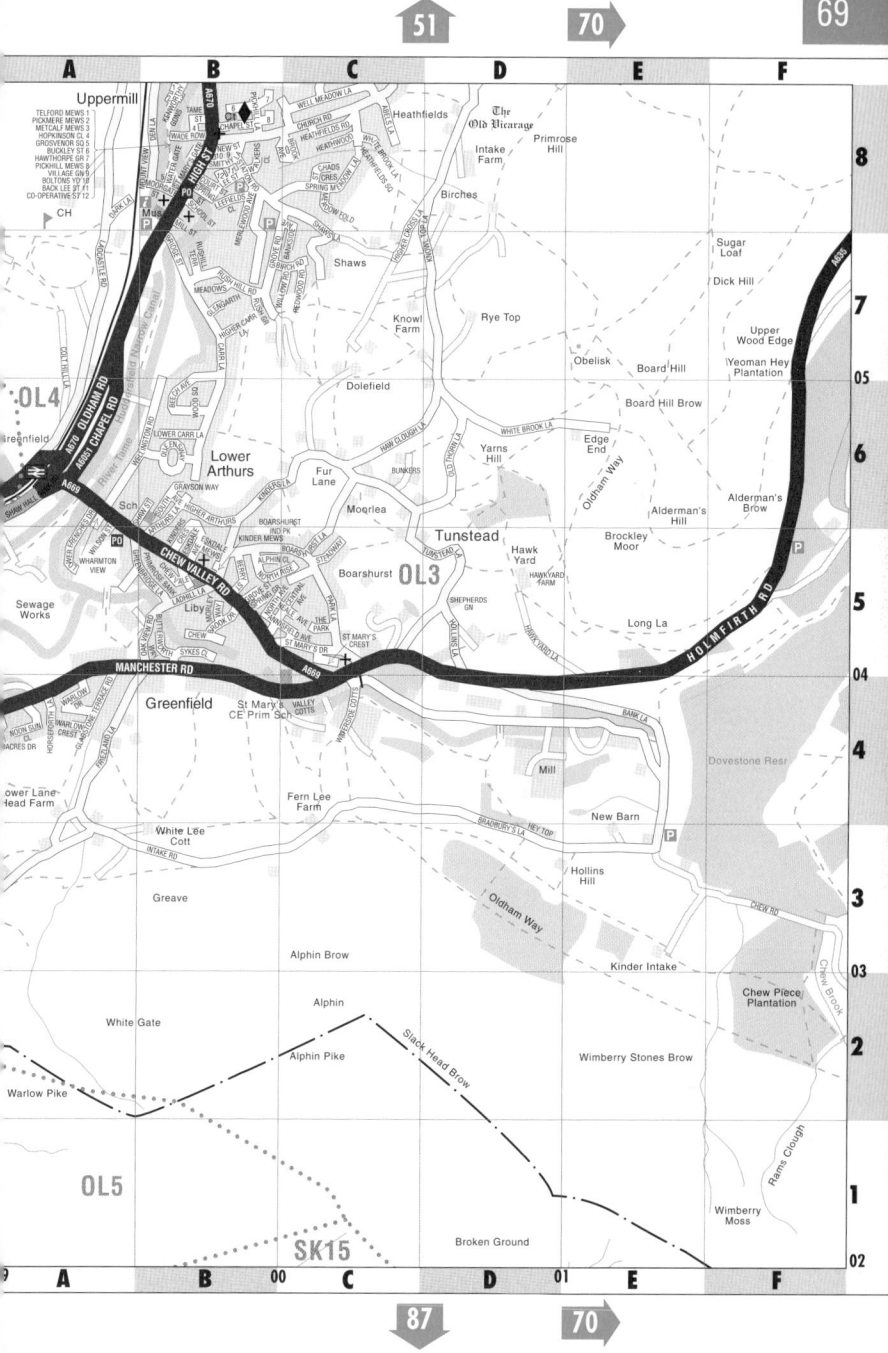

A B C D E F

Uppermill

CH

OL4

Greenfield

Heathfields

The Old Vicarage

Intake Farm

Primrose Hill

Birches

8

Shaws

Knowl Farm

Rye Top

Sugar Loaf

Dick Hill

Upper Wood Edge

7

Obelisk

Board Hill

Yeoman Hey Plantation

05

Dolefield

Board Hill Brow

White Brook La

Yarns Hill

Edge End

6

Lower Arthurs

Fur Lane

Bunkers

Oldham Way

Alderman's Hill

Alderman's Brow

Moorlea

Boarshurst

Tunstead

Hawk Yard

Brockley Moor

Boarshurst

OL3

Shepherds Gn

Hawkyard Farm

Long La

5

Lib'y

The Park

St Mary's Crest

04

MANCHESTER RD

A669

St Mary's Dr

Greenfield

St Mary's CE Prim Sch

Valley Cotts

Bank La

HOLMFIRTH RD

Dovestone Resr

4

Lower Lane Head Farm

Fern Lee Farm

White Lee Cott

Bradbury La

Hey Top

Mill

New Barn

Intake Rd

Greave

Hollins Hill

Chew Rd

3

Oldham Way

03

Alphin Brow

Kinder Intake

Chew Piece Plantation

Chew Brook

Alphin

White Gate

Alphin Pike

Slack Head Brow

Wimberry Stones Brow

Rams Clough

2

Warlow Pike

OL5

SK15

Broken Ground

Wimberry Moss

1

02

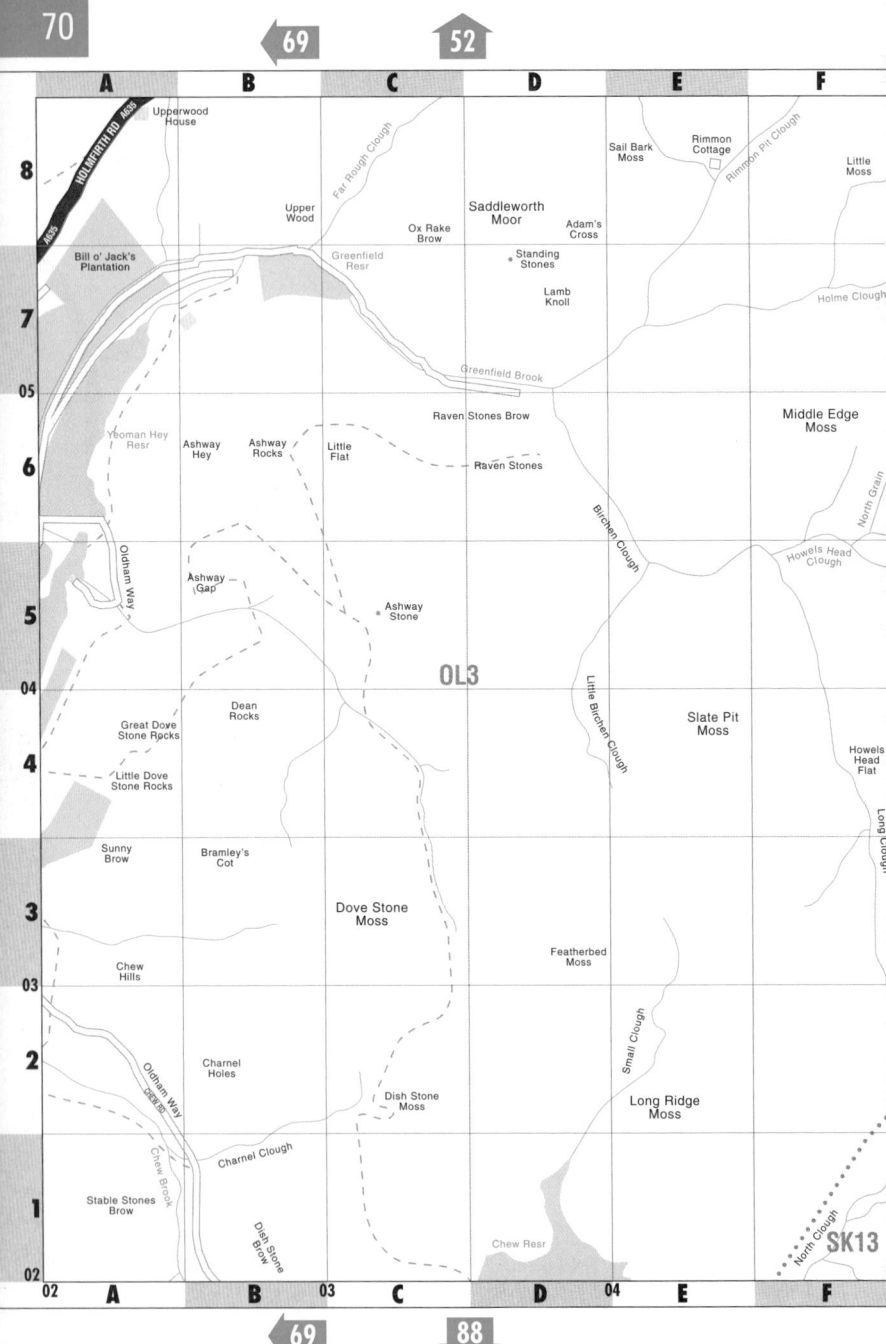

Upperwood House

HOLMFIRTH RD A635

A635

Bill o' Jack's Plantation

Upper Wood

Far Rough Clough

Greenfield Resr

Ox Rake Brow

Saddleworth Moor

Sail Bark Moss

Rimmon Cottage

Rimmon Pit Clough

Little Moss

Adam's Cross

Standing Stones

Lamb Knoll

Holme Clough

Greenfield Brook

Yeoman Hey Resr

Raven Stones Brow

Middle Edge Moss

Ashway Hey

Ashway Rocks

Little Flat

Raven Stones

Oldham Way

Ashway Gap

Ashway Stone

OL3

Birchen Clough

North Grain

Howels Head Clough

Great Dove Stone Rocks

Dean Rocks

Slate Pit Moss

Howels Head Flat

Little Dove Stone Rocks

Little Birchen Clough

Sunny Brow

Bramley's Cot

Long Clough

Chew Hills

Dove Stone Moss

Featherbed Moss

Oldham Way

Charnel Holes

Small Clough

Chew Brook

Dish Stone Moss

Long Ridge Moss

Charnel Clough

Stable Stones Brow

Dish Stone Brow

Chew Resr

North Clough

SK13

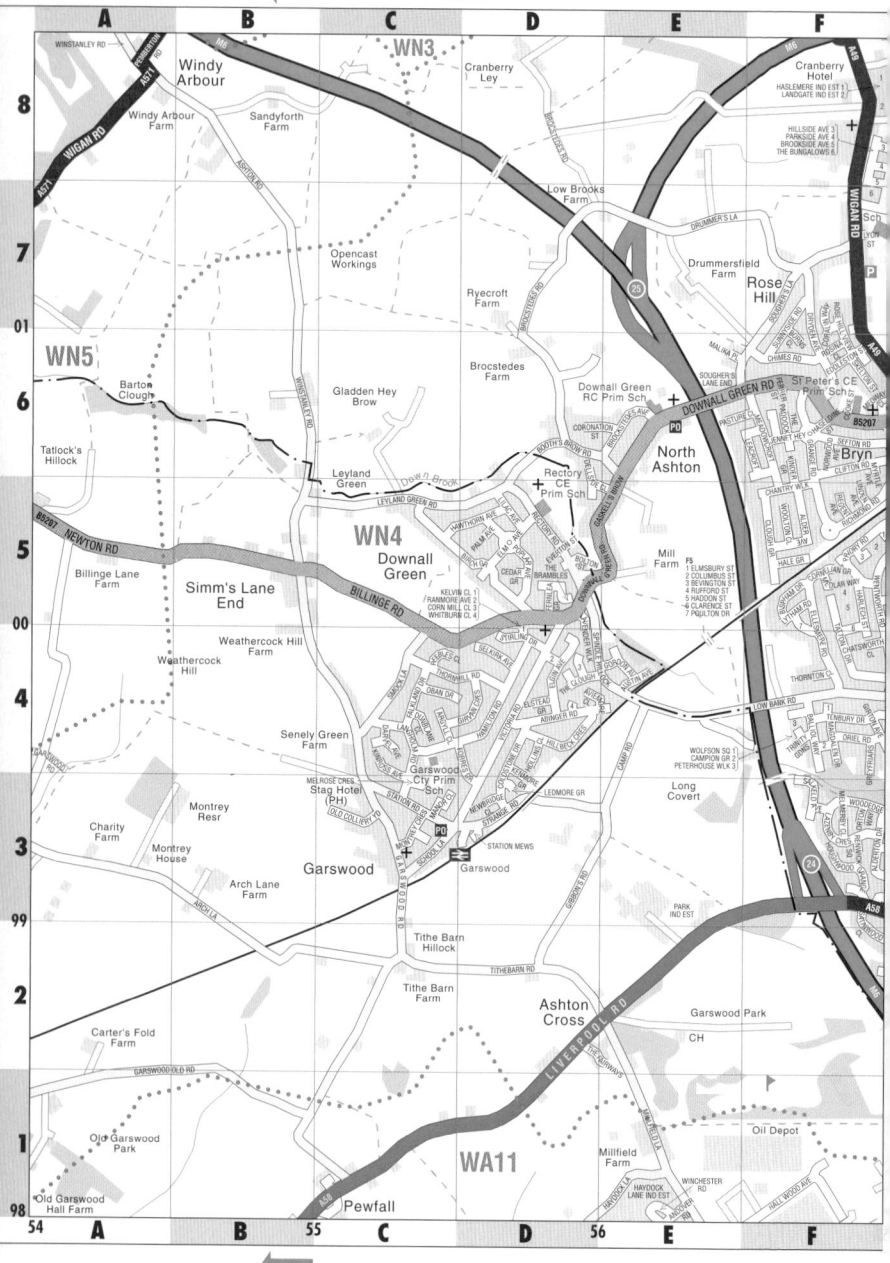

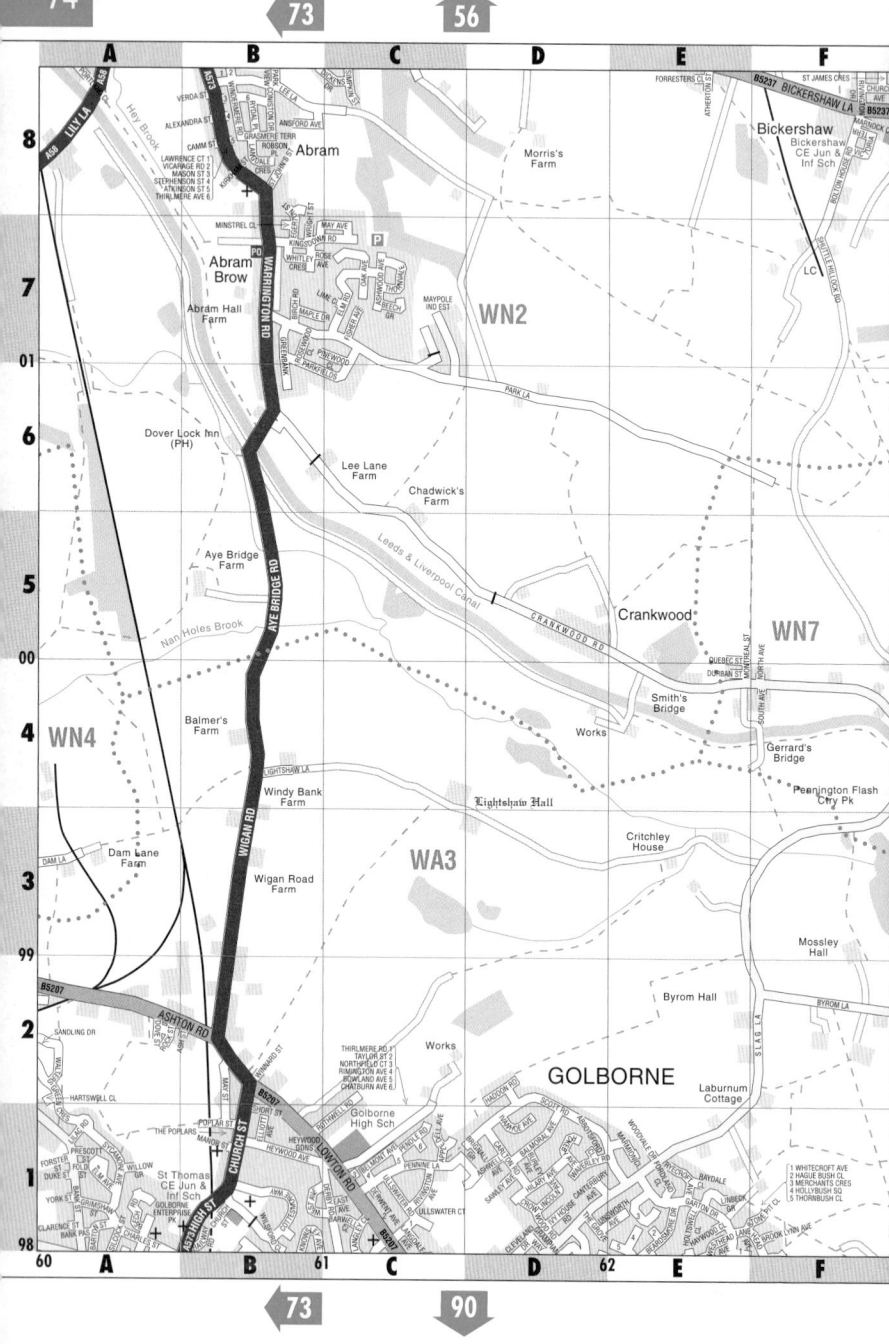

57

75

D5
1 COWBURN ST
2 OWEN ST
3 HARRY'S CT
4 PRIMROSE ST
5 CO-OPERATIVE ST
6 PINGOT CT

7 MERE ST
E8
1 BROOKS HOUSES
2 NORTHWELL ST
3 WESTWELL GR
4 COAL PIT LA

F5
1 ENDSLEIGH GDNS
2 ST MARY'S WAY
3 HILDEN ST
4 DOWNING ST
5 PORTLAND ST
6 BRADSHAWGATE SH ARC

7 ALBION ST

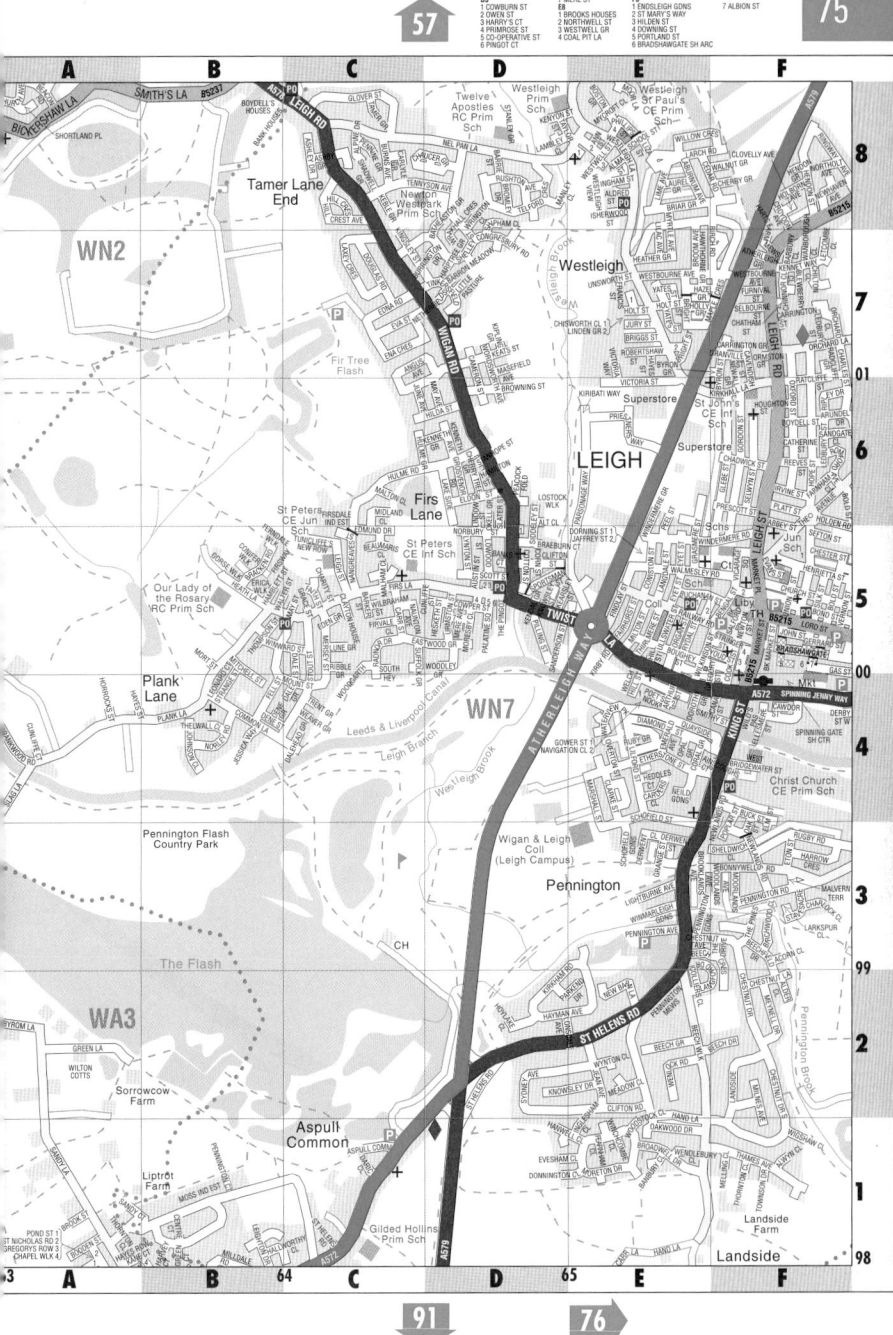

75 58

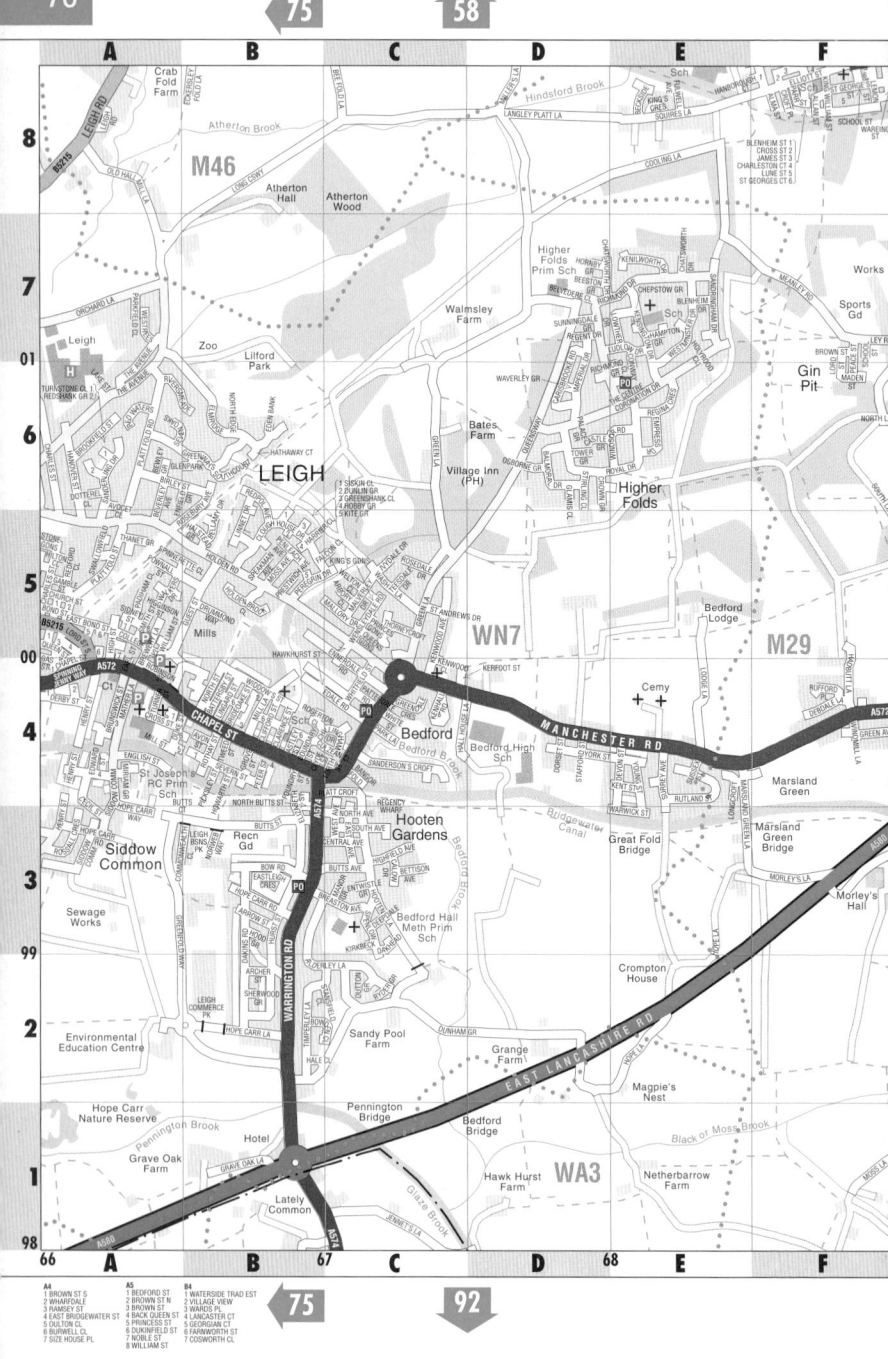

8

Crab Fold Farm

Hindsford Brook

Langley Platt La

Sch

KING'S GRN

SQUIRES LA

HANBURY CT

ST GEORGE

SCHOOL ST
WAREING

Atherton Brook

M46

Long Shoot

Cooling La

BLENHEIM ST 1
CROSS ST 2
JAMES ST 3
CHARLESTON CT 4
LUNE ST 5
ST GEORGES CT 6

Old Hall Mill La

Atherton Hall

Atherton Wood

7

Higher Folds Prim Sch

Walmsley Farm

Works

Sports Gd

01

Leigh

Zoo

Lilford Park

Gin Pit

H

TURLESTONE CL 1
REDSHANK GR 2

Bates Farm

WAVERLEY GR

NORTH LA

6

Hathaway Ct

LEIGH

Village Inn (PH)

1 SISKIN CL
2 DUNLIN GR
3 GREENSHANK CL
4 HOBBY GR
5 KITE GR

Higher Folds

5

ST ANDREWS DR

WN7

Bedford Lodge

Mills

Hawkhurst St

KERFOOT ST

M29

RUFFORD

DESDALE

00

A572

P

P

PO

Cemy

A572

4

CHAPEL ST

Bedford

MANCHESTER RD

Bedford High Sch

York St

Marsland Green

St Joseph's RC Prim Sch

Bedford Brook

Sanderson's Croft

Bedford B

Kent St

Rutland St

Marsland Green Bridge

3

Siddow Common

Recn Gd

Hooten Gardens

Warwick St

Bridgewater Canal

Great Fold Bridge

Morley's La

Morley's Hall

Sewage Works

PO

Bedford Hall Meth Prim Sch

99

WARRINGTON RD

Archer

Crompton House

2

Environmental Education Centre

Leigh Commerce Pk

Hope Carr La

Sandy Pool Farm

Grange Farm

EAST LANCASHIRE RD

Magpie's Nest

Netherbarrow Farm

Hope Carr Nature Reserve

Pennington Brook

Hotel

Pennington Bridge

Bedford Bridge

Black or Moss Brook

1

Grave Oak Farm

GRAVE OAK LA

Lately Common

Glaze Brook

Hawk Hurst Farm

WA3

Netherbarrow Farm

Jenkel's La

98

A588

A574

66 A 67 B C 68 D E F

75 92

A4
1 BROWN ST S
2 WHARFDALE
3 RAMSEY ST
4 EAST BRIDGEWATER ST
5 OULTON CL
6 BURWELL CL
7 SIZE HOUSE PL

A5
1 BEDFORD ST
2 BROWN ST N
3 BROWN ST
4 BACK QUEEN ST
5 PRINCESS ST
6 DUKINFIELD ST
7 NOBLE ST
8 WILLIAM ST

B4
1 WATERSIDE TRAD EST
2 VILLAGE VIEW
3 WARDS PL
4 LANCASTER CT
5 GEORGIAN CT
6 FARNWORTH ST
7 COSWORTH CL

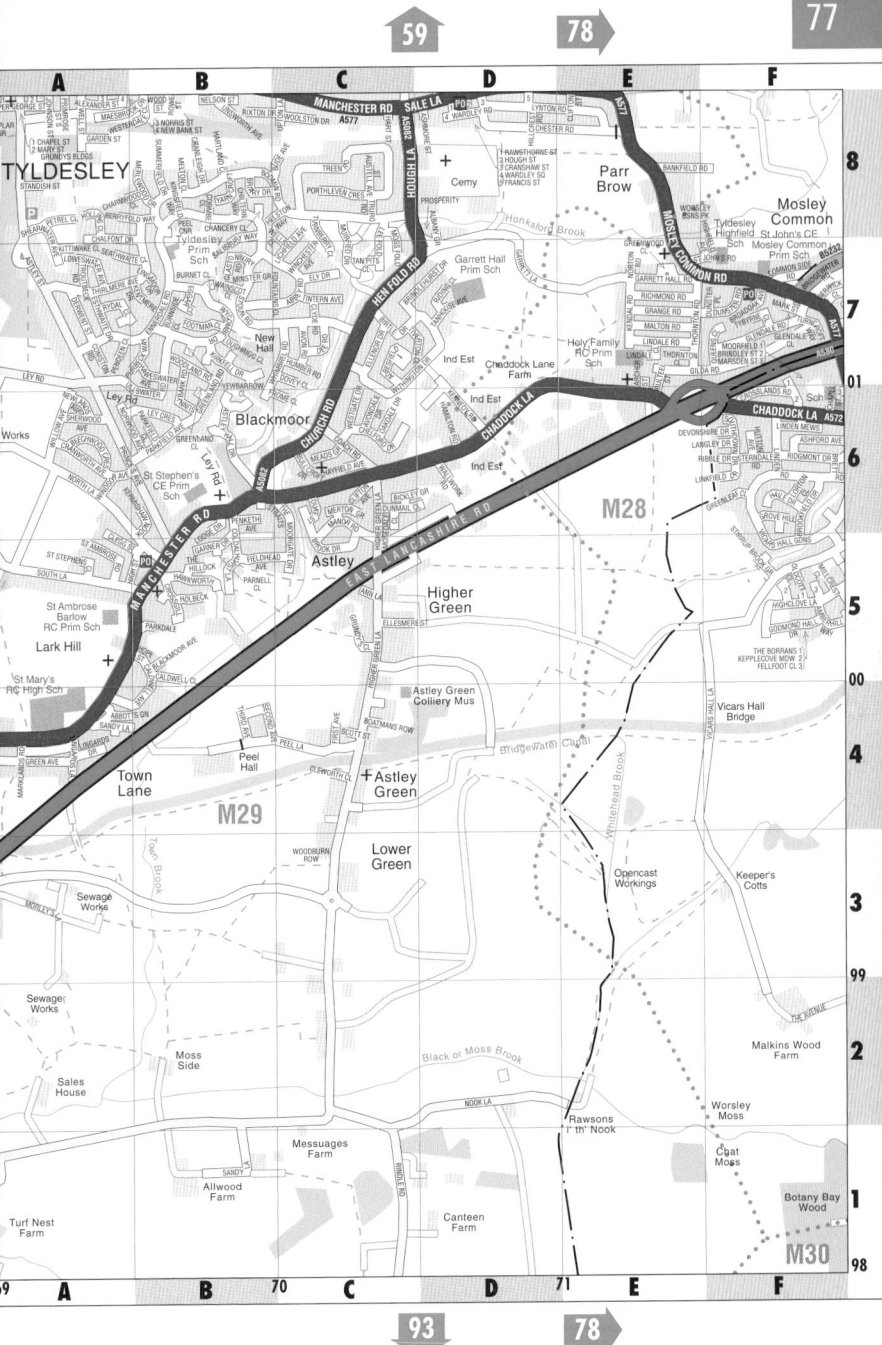

E7
1 BEDFORD AVE
2 PADDISON ST
3 STOCKTON ST
4 THORNFIELD DR
5 ALBERMARLE RD
6 COLLIER ST
7 LINCOLN RD

F7
1 GORSEFIELD DR
2 WAGGONERS CT
3 ROSETTE WLK
4 MAIDEN MEWS
5 LIGHTBOURNE AVE

B1
1 SARAH ST
2 WINIFRED ST
3 BEECH HOUSE
4 ATHERTON WAY
5 HAMPSON CL
6 GREEN ST

C1
1 WILLOW TREE CT
2 CORNWALL ST
3 CHAPEL ST
4 THOMAS JOHNSON CL
5 ELIZA ANN ST
6 SPOONER RD
7 GREENWATCH CL
8 OLD STATION ST

D1
1 ST JOHN ST
2 BRADBURN CL
3 MOORFIELD CL
4 BRADBURN AVE
5 BRADBURN GR
6 DORRING ST
7 WILHAM AVE
8 WADE HOUSE
9 WALKER HOUSE

E1
10 O'KANE HOUSE
11 UVEDALE HOUSE
12 PITCAIRN HOUSE
13 DE TRAFFORD HOUSE
14 ELLESMERE ST

E2
1 ABERDEEN
2 MONTROSE
3 DUNDEE
4 PERTH
5 EDINBURGH
6 STERLING
7 BUCKLE HO
8 GARDNER HO

F2
1 CHAPEL ST
2 FAIRHILL PL
3 KEMBALL
4 NORTHWAY
5 THE MALL
6 SHUTTLE ST
7 SOUTHWAY
8 BOOTHWAY
9 BACK CHAPEL ST
10 COLLEGE CROFT
11 ST MARY'S RD
12 EWOOD
13 CRAUNTON

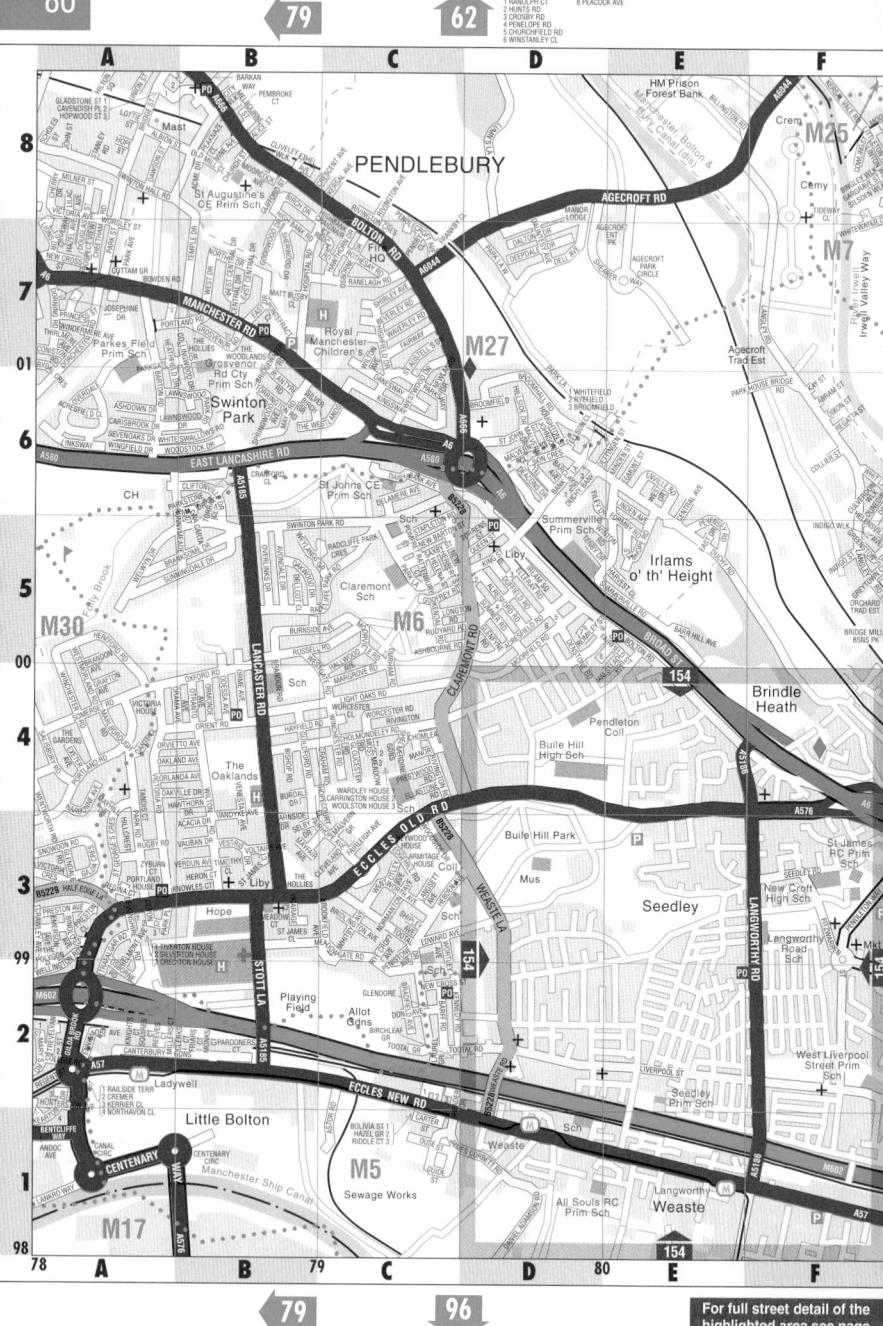

D5
1 RANULPH CT
2 HUNTS RD
3 CROSBY RD
4 PENELOPE RD
5 CHURCHFIELD RD
6 WINSTANLEY CL.

7 NORBURY AVE
8 PEACOCK AVE

PENDLEBURY

HM Prison
Forest Bank

Swinton
Park

Irlams
o' th' Height

Brindle
Heath

M30

M6

Seedley

The
Oaklands

Buile Hill Park

Buile Hill
High Sch

Hope

Little Bolton

M5
Sewage Works

Weaste

Langworthy
Weaste

For full street detail of the
highlighted area see page
154.

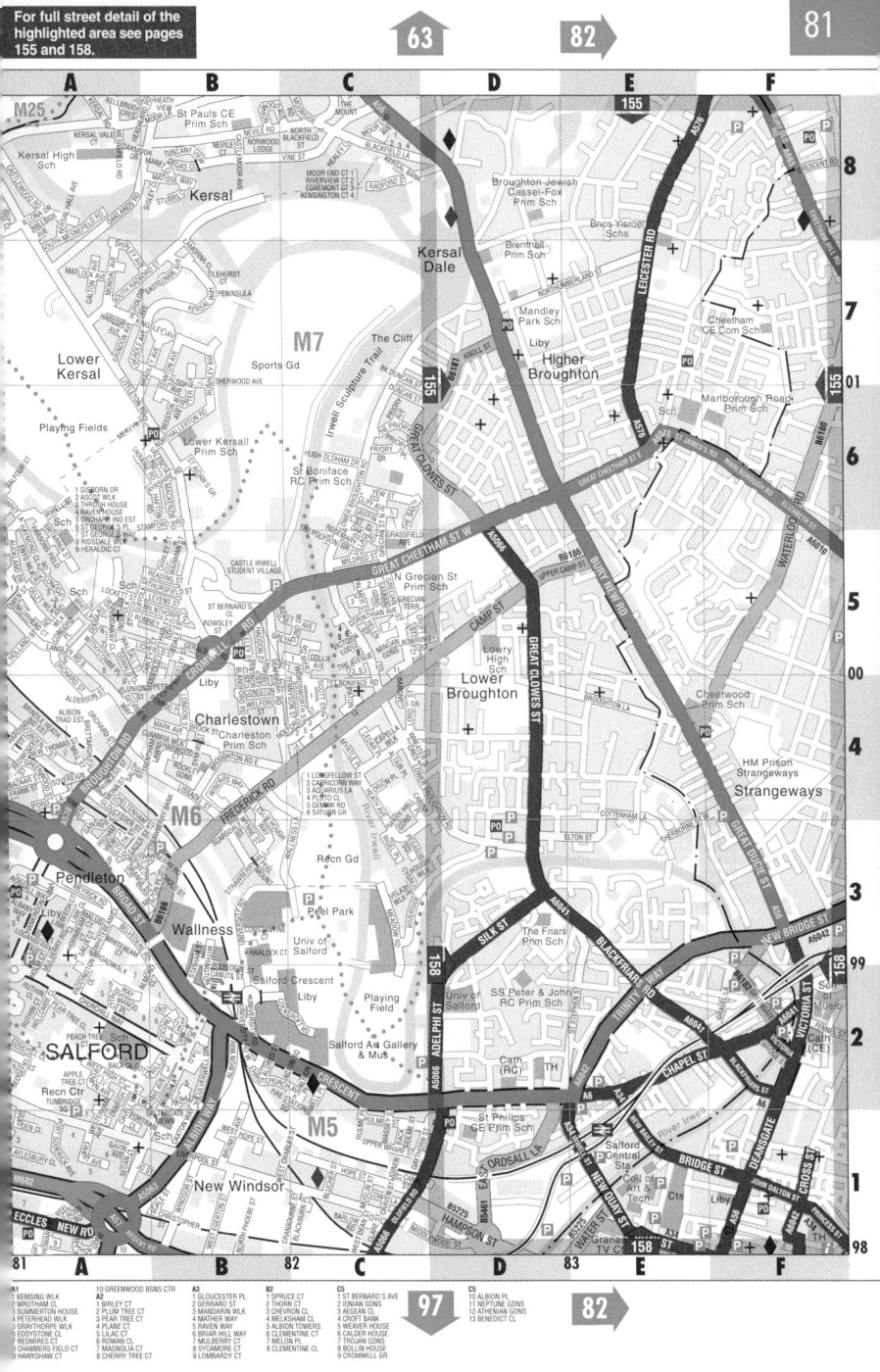

For full street detail of the highlighted area see pages 155 and 158.

63 82 81

For full street detail of the highlighted area see pages 156, 157, 159 and 160.

Harpurhey

Cheetham Hill

Collyhurst

Miles Platting

MANCHESTER

Ancoats

Bradford

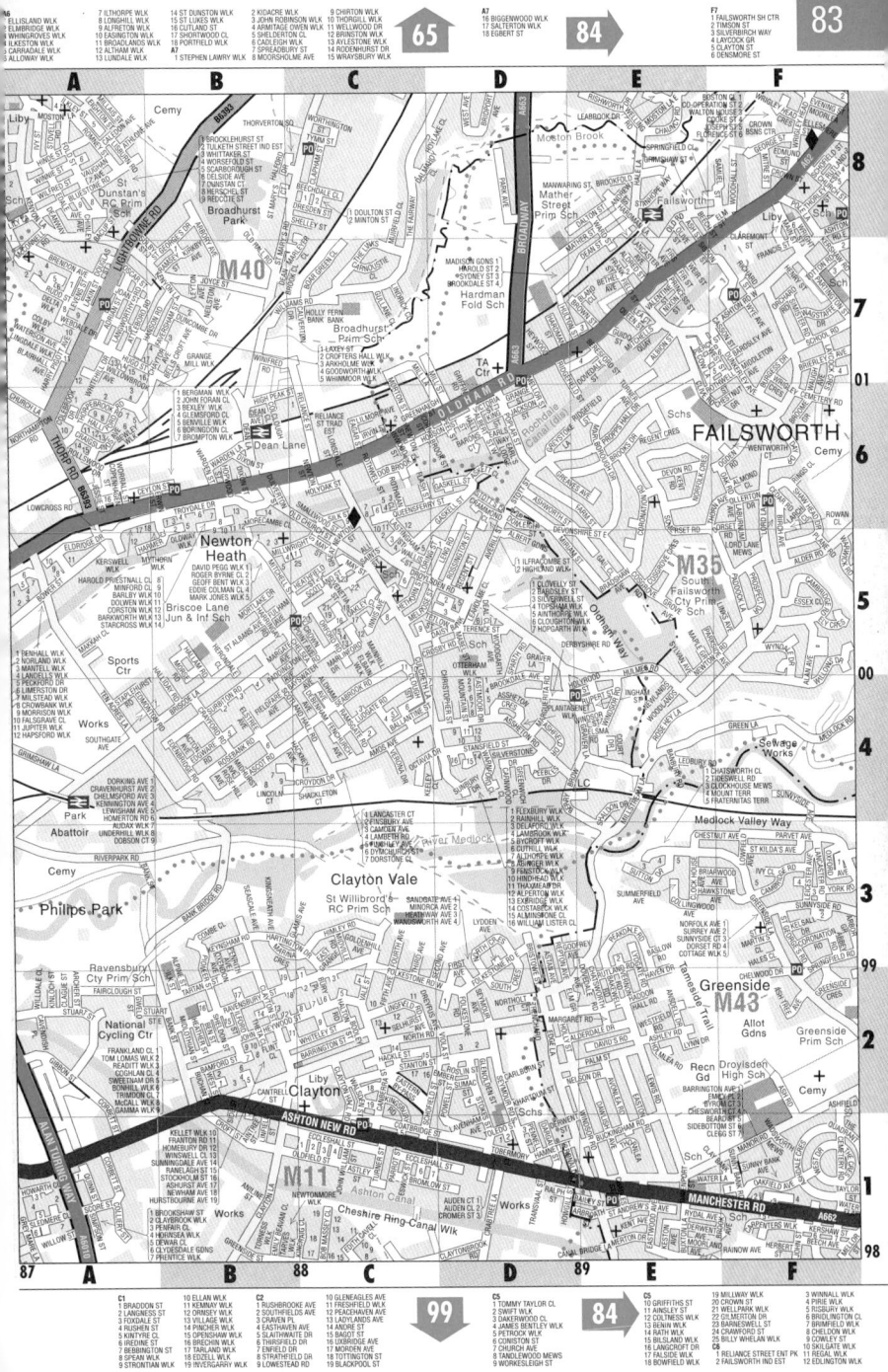

A6
1 ELLISLAND WLK
2 ELMBRIDGE WLK
3 WHINGROVES WLK
4 ILKESTON WLK
5 CARRADALE WLK
6 ALLOWAY WLK
7 ILTHORPE WLK
8 LONGHILL WLK
9 ALFRETON WLK
10 EASINGTON WLK
11 BROADLANDS WLK
12 ALTHAM WLK
13 LUNDALE WLK
14 ST DUNSTAN WLK
15 ST LUKES WLK
16 CUTLAND ST
17 SHORTWOOD CL
18 PORTFIELD WLK
A7
1 STEPHEN LAWRY WLK

A7
9 CHIRTON WLK
10 THORGILL WLK
11 WELLWOOD DR
12 BRINSTON WLK
13 AYLESTONE WLK
14 RODENHURST ST
15 WRAYSBURY WLK

1 KIDACRE WLK
2 JOHN ROBINSON ST
3 ARMITAGE OWEN WLK
4 SHELDSTON CL
5 CADLEIGH WLK
6 SPREADBURY ST
7 MOORSHOLME AVE

65

A7
16 BIGGENWOOD WLK
17 SALTERTON WLK
18 EGBERT ST

84

F7
1 FAILSWORTH SH CTR
2 TIMSON ST
3 SILVERBIRCH WAY
4 LAYCOCK AVE
5 CLAYTON ST
6 DENSMORE ST

Place names
Newton Heath, Failsworth, Clayton Vale, Clayton, Philips Park, Greenside, Droylsden

M40, M35, M43, M11

Bottom index

C1
1 BRADDON ST
2 LANGNESS ST
3 FOXDALE ST
4 RUSHEN ST
5 KINTYRE CL
6 IREDINE ST
7 BEBINGTON ST
8 SPEAN WLK
9 STRIONTIAN WLK
10 ELLAM WLK
11 KEMNAY WLK
12 ORMSEY WLK
13 VILLAGE WLK
14 PINCHER WLK
15 OPENSHAW WLK
16 BREDON WLK
17 TARLAND WLK
18 EDZELL WLK
19 INVERGARRY WLK

C2
1 RUSHBROOKE AVE
2 SOUTHFIELDS AVE
3 CRAVEN PL
4 EASTHAVEN AVE
5 SLAITHWAITE DR
6 THIRLEMERE DR
7 ENFIELD DR
8 STRATHFIELD DR
9 LOWESTEAD RD
10 GLENEAGLES AVE
11 FRESHFIELD AVE
12 PEASGHAVEN AVE
13 LADYLANDS AVE
14 ANDREW ST
15 BAGOT ST
16 UXBRIDGE AVE
17 MORDEN AVE
18 TOTTINGTON ST
19 BLACKPOOL ST

C5
1 TOMMY TAYLOR CL
2 SWIFT WLK
3 DAKERWOOD CL
4 JAMES BENTLEY WLK
5 PETROCK WLK
6 CONISTON ST
7 CHURCH AVE
8 TANDLEWOOD MEWS
9 WORKESLEIGH ST

C5
10 GRIFFITHS ST
11 AINSLEY ST
12 COLTNESS WLK
13 BEKIN WLK
14 RATH WLK
15 BILSLAND WLK
16 LANGCROFT DR
17 FALSIDE WLK
18 BOWFIELD WLK
19 MILLWAY WLK
20 CROWN ST
21 WELLPARK WLK
22 GLENESTON DR
23 BARNESWELL ST
24 CRAWFORD ST
25 BILLY WHELAN WLK

D8
1 RELIANCE STREET ENT PK
2 FAILSWORTH IND EST
3 WINNALL WLK
4 PIRIE WLK
5 RUSBURY WLK
6 BRIDLINGTON CR
7 BRIMFIELD WLK
8 CHELDON WLK
9 COWLEY ST
10 SKILGATE WLK
11 REGAL WLK
12 EDLINGTON WLK

99
84

Grid references: 87, 88, 89, 98, 99, 00, 01
A, B, C, D, E, F

83 66

A B C D E F

8

Stansfield Road
Jun & Inf Schs
Kaskenmoor Sch
Landsberg Terr
Street End

Holy Family RC Prim Sch

Limehurst Prim Sch
Wood Park

HILARY AVE

VICTORIA ST

OL8

Knott Lanes
KNOTT LANES Works

Bardsley House

7

St John's CE Jun Sch

Falsworth

CHARLES HALL MORRIS HOUSE

Crime Lake

Crime View Inn

Crime Farm

Valley Bridge

Holt Lane End

M35

Woodhouse Green

Daisy Nook Country Park

Tameside Trail

TREE HOUSE LA
OAKEN CLOUGH TERR
OAKEN CLOUGH

6

New Bank Farm
Woodhouses Prim Sch

Daisy Nook

Medlock Vale (National Trust)

Woodhouses

Bottom Field Farm

River Medlock

Visitor Ctr

Medlock Hall

Oldham Way

5

Bottom of Woodhouses

CH

Branch (dis)

Ashton & Stockport Junction Canal (dis) Hollinwood

Oldham Way

Taunton

KESWICK AVE

00

Nook View Farm

Littlemoss

Willow Bank Farm

Buckley Hill Farm

Hope Fold

Playing Fields

Crowhill

4

Medlock Valley Way

Medlock Vale

Tameside Trail

Littlemoss High Sch for Boys

ANDREW ST

WOODLEIGH DR

Baum Farm

Athletics Gd

OL7

3

Lumb Clough

DROYLSDEN

M43

Medlock Sports Ctr

LITTLEMOSS BSNS PK

1 THROSTLES CL
2 CONDOR CL
3 WOODCOCK CL
4 STONECHAT CL
5 BROOKSIDE AVE

Moss Side Farm

Masts

99

SHAKESPEARE CRES Sch

Masts

KAYLEY IND EST

2

CASTLE CL

Lees Park

Moorside Prim Sch

PAULIN DR

1 MOSS BANK CT
2 MYRTLE GR
3 ROBERT OWEN ST
4 RICHMOND ST
5 JASMINE AVE

Masts

Ashton Moss

1 HINDLEY CL
2 FAIRTHORNE GRANGE
3 BACK CAMBRIDGE ST
4 CECIL ST
5 GORTON ST
6 HAMILTON ST
7 TRAFALGAR SQ

West End Prim Sch

1

Hypermarket

1 HILSON CT
2 BROWNING AVE
3 MILTON AVE
4 MASEFIELD CRES

EDMUND ST FAIRFIELD HOUSE

Aldwyn Cty Prim Sch

M34

Factory

98

MANCHESTER RD A662

ASHTON RD **DROYLSDEN RD** A662

Lidy

FRANKLIN RD

MANCHESTER RD A6140

SNIPE RET PK

90 A 91 B C 92 D E F

B1
1 MOORCROFT ST
2 BUDWORTH GDNS
3 TABLEY GDNS
4 PICKMERE CL
5 BESWICK ST
6 MERLEWOOD AVE

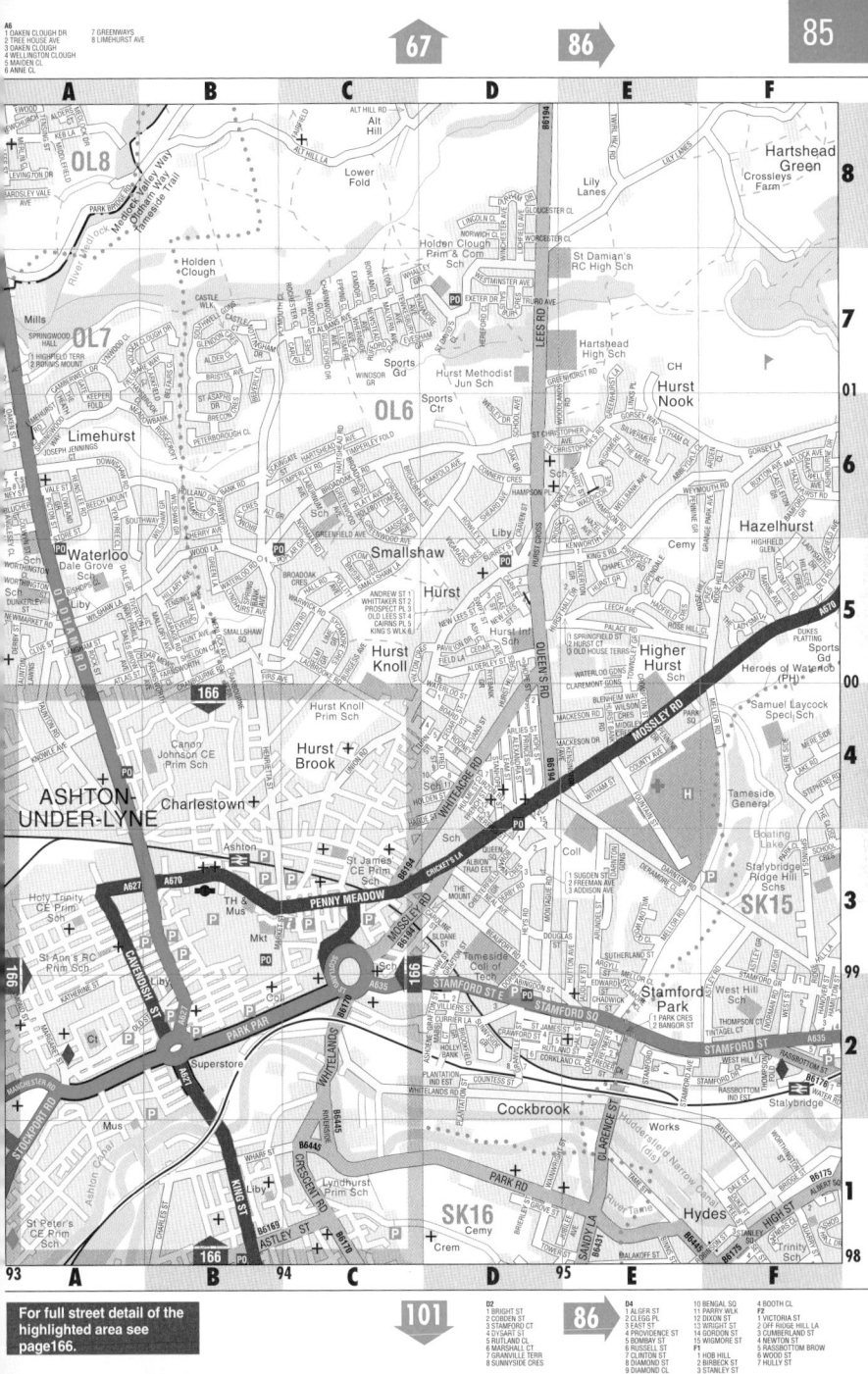

A6
1 OAKEN CLOUGH DR   7 GREENWAYS
2 TREE HOUSE AVE   8 LIMEHURST AVE
3 OAKEN CLOUGH
4 WELLINGTON CLOUGH
5 MAIDEN CL
6 ANNE CL

A   B   C   D   E   F

OL8

Hartshead Green
Crossleys Farm

Alt Hill

Lower Fold

Holden Clough

Lily Lanes

St Damian's RC High Sch

Mills Springwood Hall

OL7

Limehurst

Holden Clough Prim & Com Sch

Hartshead High Sch

Sports Gd

Hurst Methodist Jun Sch

Sports Ctr

Hurst Nook

CH

Hurst Knoll

OL6

Waterloo

Dale Grove Sch

Liby

Smallshaw

Hazelhurst

Hurst

Hurst Knoll

166

Higher Hurst Sch

Dukes Plating Sports Gd

Heroes of Waterloo (PH)

Samuel Laycock Speci Sch

Hurst Knoll Prim Sch

Canon Johnson CE Prim Sch

Hurst Brook

Charlestown

Ashton

Tameside General

H

ASHTON-UNDER-LYNE

Holy Trinity CE Prim Sch

St James CE Prim Sch

Coll

SK15

Stalybridge Ridge Hill Schs

St Ann's RC Prim Sch

Liby

PENNY MEADOW

TH & Mus

Mkt

The Mount

166

166

Tameside Coll of Tech

Stamford Park

West Hill Sch

Superstore

166

Mus

PARK PAR

STAMFORD ST

Stamford Sq

1 PARK CRES
2 BANGOR RD

STAMFORD ST

Cockbrook

Plantation Ind Est

St Peter's CE Prim Sch

King St

166

Lyndhurst Prim Sch

SK16

Cemy

Crem

Works

Hydes

Trinity Sch

PARK RD

93   A   B   94   C   D   95   E   F   98

For full street detail of the highlighted area see page166.

101   86

D2
1 BRIGHT ST
2 COBDEN ST
3 STAMFORD CT
4 DYSART ST
5 RUTLAND CL
6 MARSHALL CT
7 GRANVILLE TERR
8 SUNNYSIDE CRES

D4
1 ALGER ST
2 CLEGG PL
3 EAST ST
4 PROVIDENCE ST
5 BOMBAY ST
6 RUSSELL ST
7 CLINTON ST
8 DIAMOND ST
9 DIAMOND CL

10 BENGAL SQ
11 PARRY WLK
12 DIXON ST
13 WRIGHT ST
14 GORDON ST
15 WIGMORE ST

F1
1 HOB HILL
2 BIRBECK ST
3 STANLEY ST

4 BOOTH CL
F2
1 VICTORIA ST
2 OFF RIDGE HILL LA
3 CUMBERLAND ST
4 NEWTON ST
5 RASSBOTTOM BROW
6 WOOD ST
7 HULLY ST

85 68

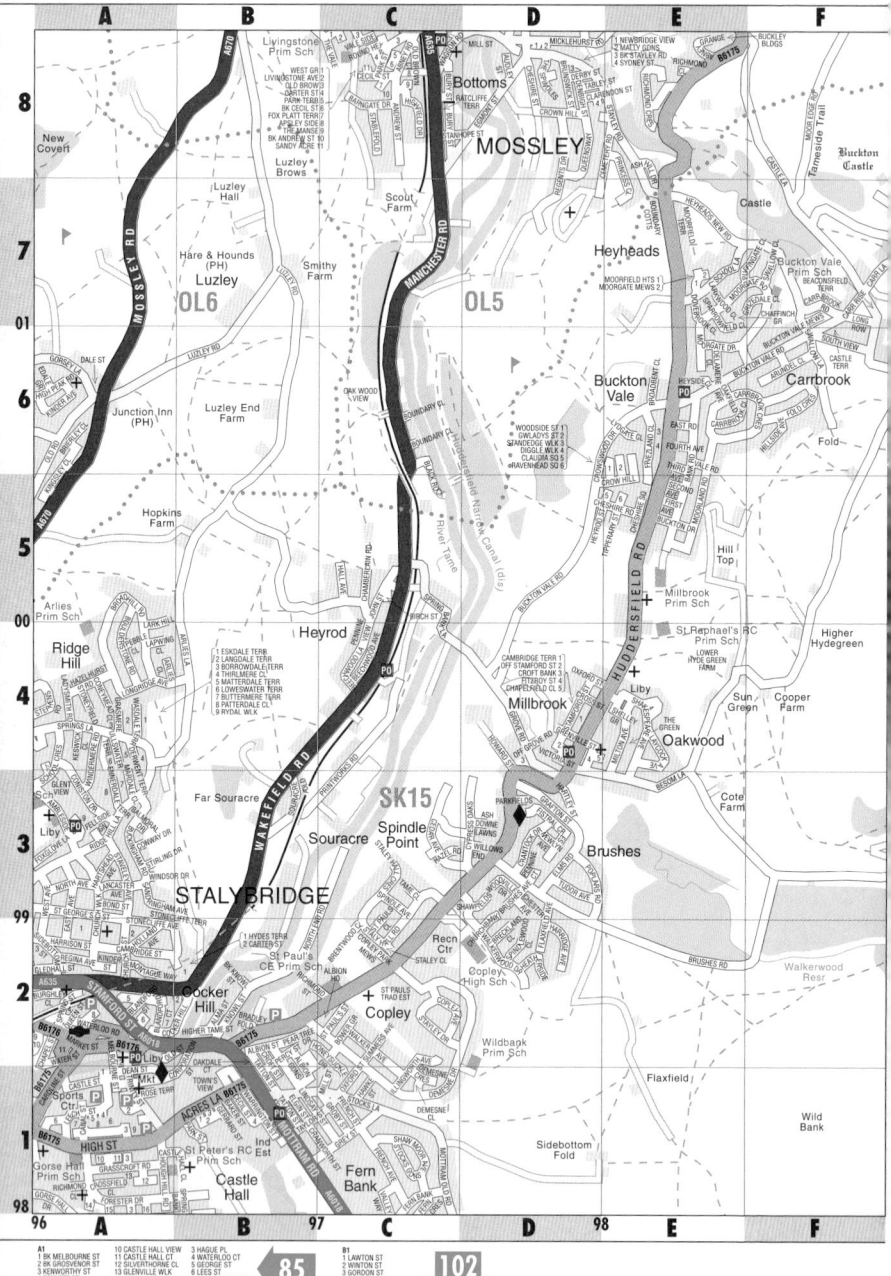

85 102

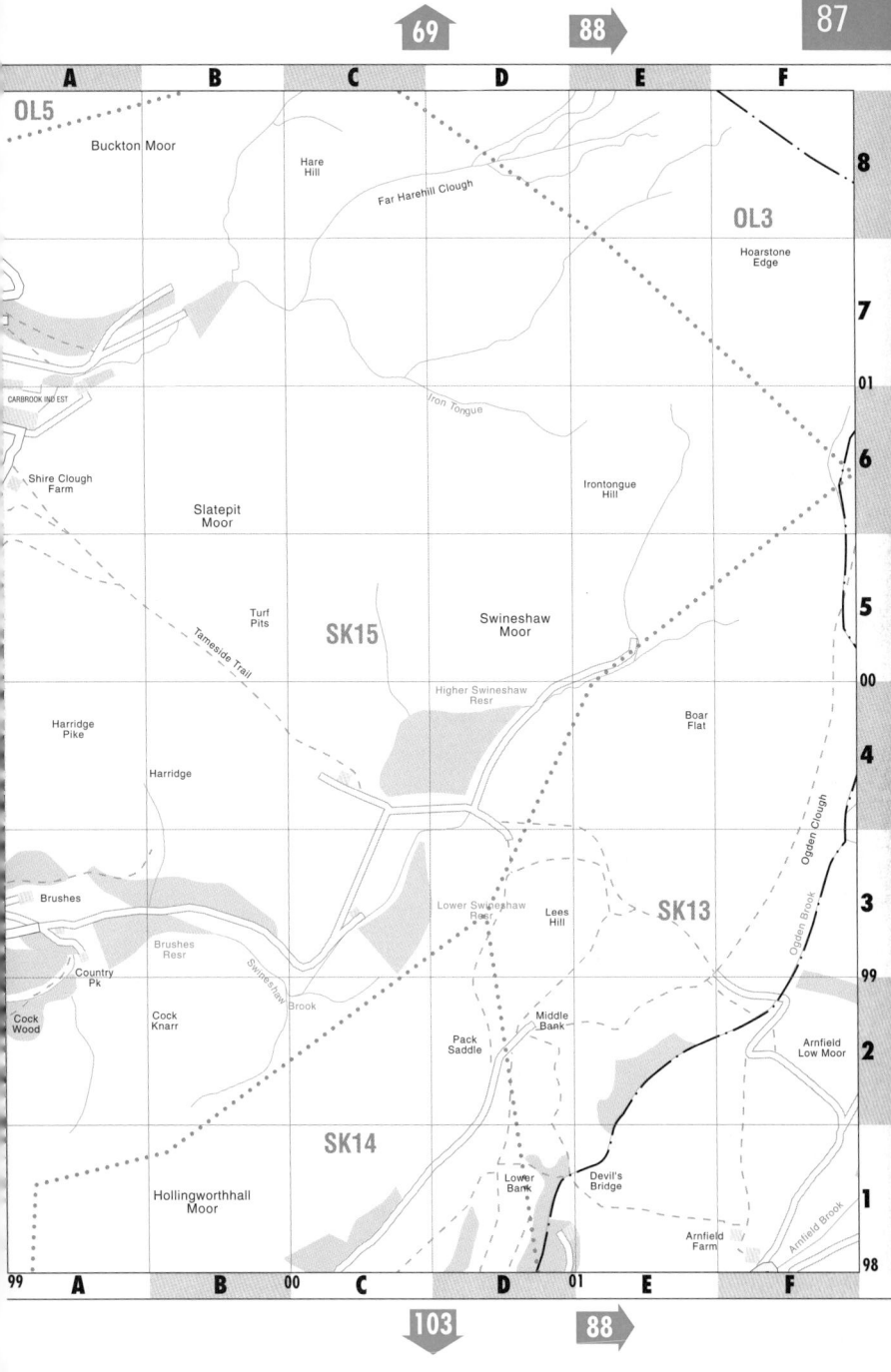

A   B   C   D   E   F

OL5

Buckton Moor

Hare Hill

Far Harehill Clough

OL3

Hoarstone Edge

8

7

01

CARBROOK IND EST

Shire Clough Farm

Iron Tongue

Irontongue Hill

6

Slatepit Moor

Turf Pits

SK15

Swineshaw Moor

5

Tameside Trail

00

Higher Swineshaw Resr

Harridge Pike

Boar Flat

4

Harridge

Brushes

Lower Swineshaw Resr

Lees Hill

SK13

Ogden Clough

Ogden Brook

3

Brushes Resr

Swineshaw Brook

99

Country Pk

Cock Wood

Cock Knarr

Middle Bank

Pack Saddle

Arnfield Low Moor

2

SK14

Hollingworthhall Moor

Lower Bank

Devil's Bridge

Arnfield Brook

1

Arnfield Farm

98

99 A   B 00 C   D 01 E   F

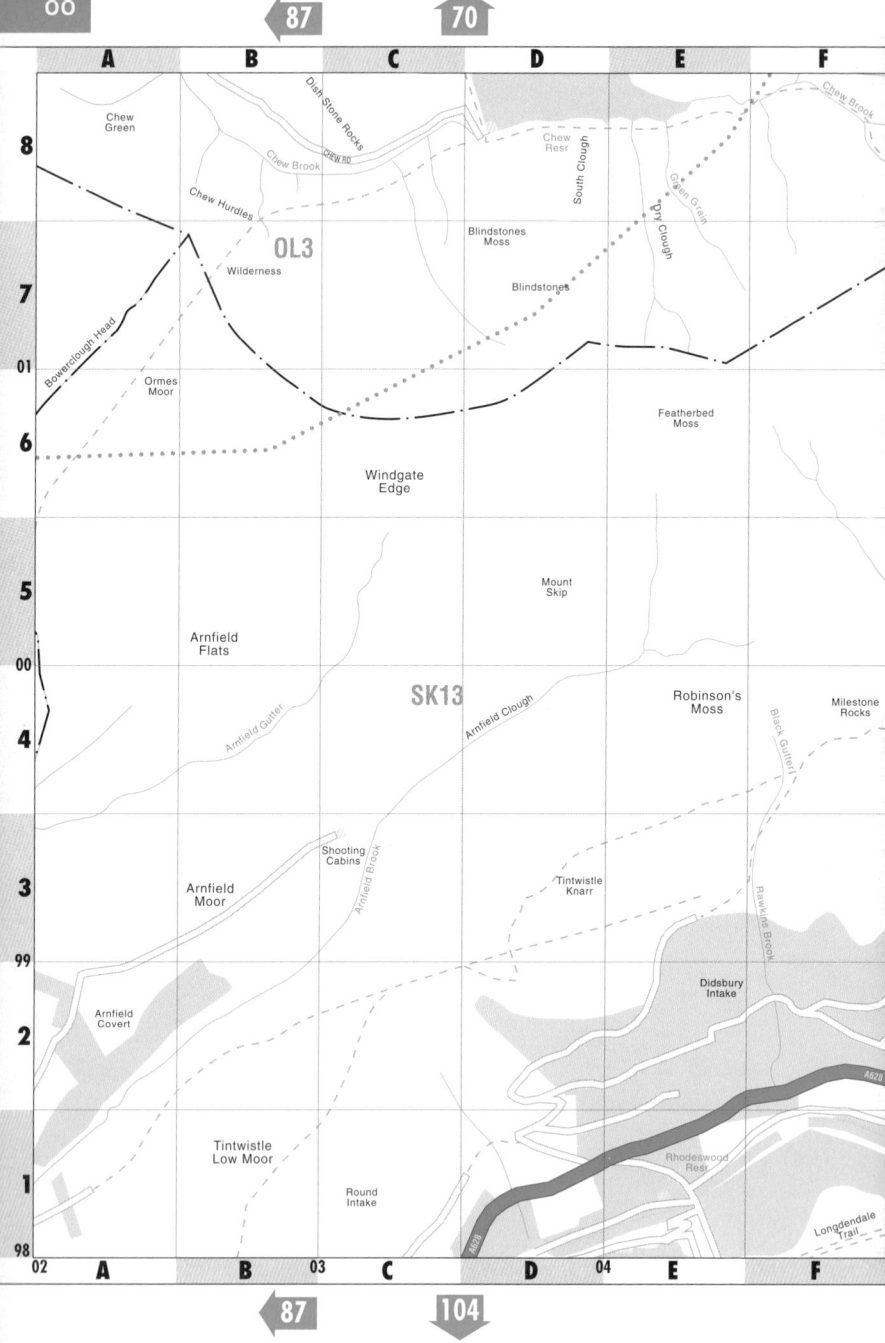

A B C D E F

Chew
Green

Dish Stone Rocks

CHEW RD.

Chew Brook

Chew Brook

Chew Hurdles

Chew
Resr

South Clough

Green Grain

Dry Clough

OL3

Wilderness

Blindstones
Moss

Blindstones

Bowerclough Head

8

7

01

6

Ormes
Moor

Windgate
Edge

Featherbed
Moss

5

Mount
Skip

Arnfield
Flats

Arnfield Gutter

SK13

Arnfield Clough

Robinson's
Moss

Milestone
Rocks

00

4

Black Gutter

Shooting
Cabins

Arnfield
Moor

Arnfield Brook

Tintwistle
Knarr

Rawkins Brook

Didsbury
Intake

3

99

Arnfield
Covert

2

A628

Tintwistle
Low Moor

Round
Intake

Rhodeswood
Resr

1

A628

Longdendale
Trail

98

A 02 B 03 C D 04 E F

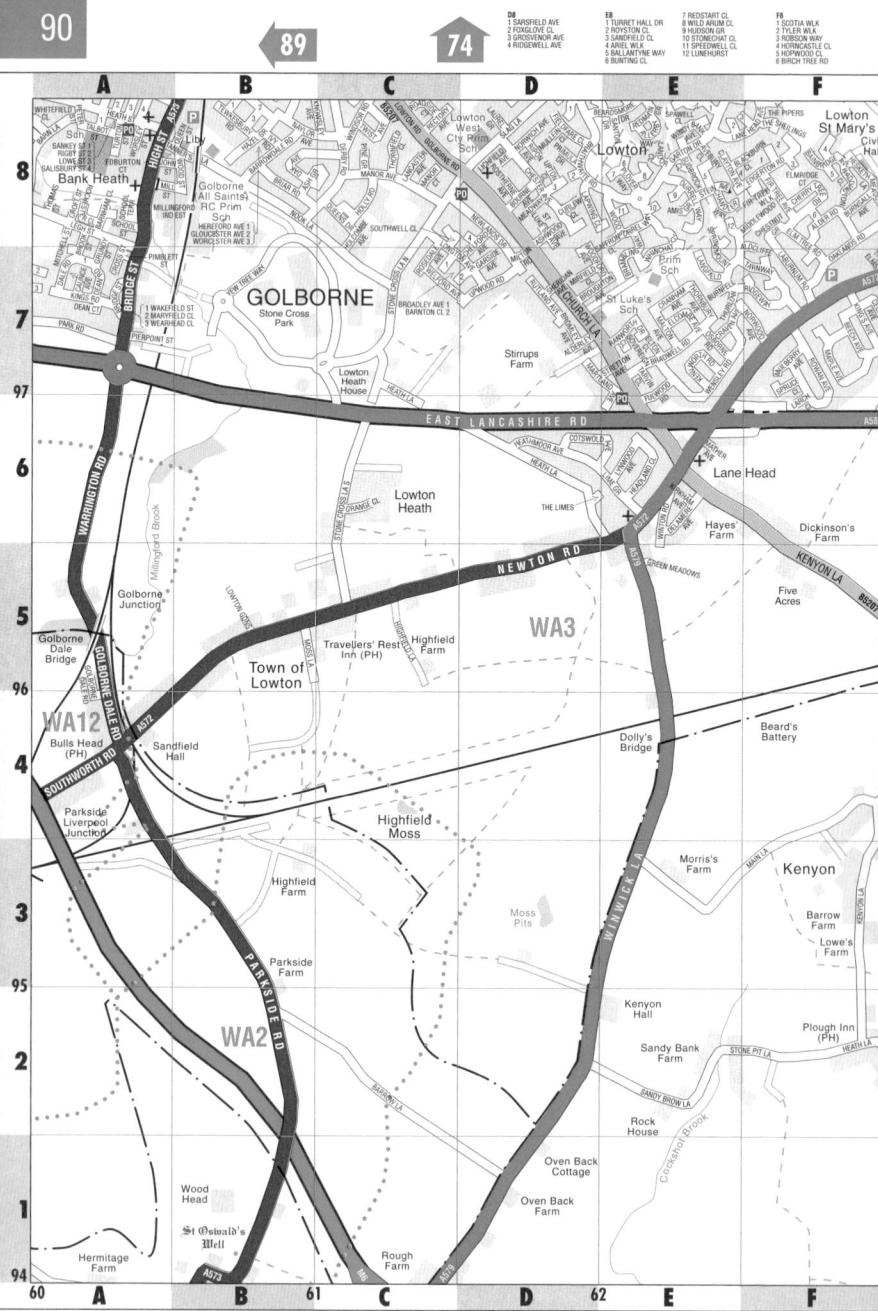

91 76

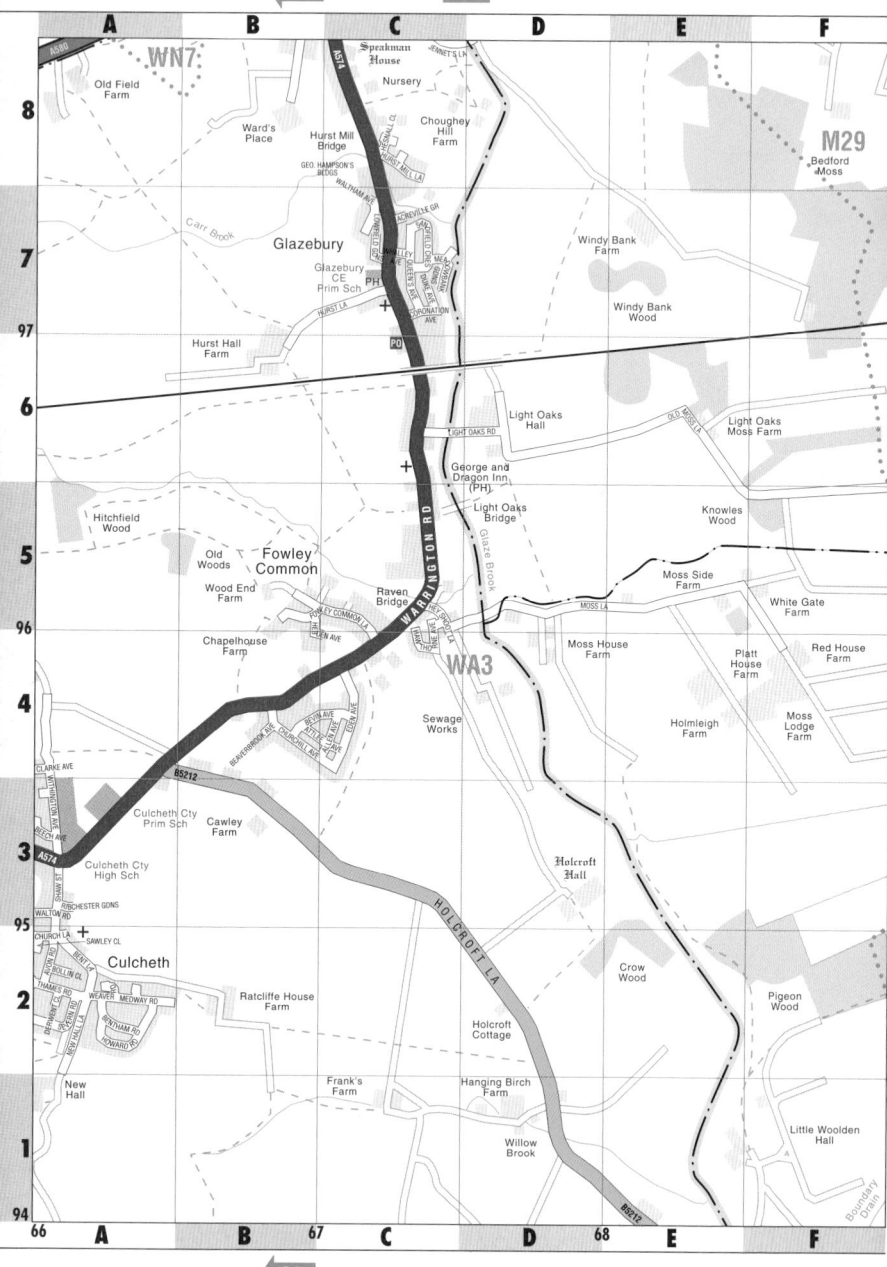

A   B   C   D   E   F

8

Moss
Bank

Shooter's
Grove

RIDGE RD

Astley Moss

M30

M29   7

97

LC

Four Winds
Farm

Birch
Farm   6

Chat Moss

Olive Mount
Farm

Railway View
Farm   5

96

Moss
Farm

Mosslands
Farm

TWELVE YARDS RD

Woodbarn
Farm

CLIFTON

RASPBERRY LA

New
Farm   4

Birch View
Farm

Oakfield

WA3

Irlam
Moss

ASTLEY RD

M44

Ebenezer
Farm

Larkhill
House   3

Hope Cottage
Farm

Hepzibah
Farm

ROCHDALE DR

CRANBOURNE DR

BALSHAW CT.

Little Woolden
Moss

95

PARRS CT.

BROOKLANDS CL.

Woodstock
Farm

BALSHAW

Boundary Drain

Springfield   2

SPRINGFIELD LA

STUART AVE.

Ringing Pits
Farm

Plant Cottage
Farm

CALDER AVE.

ELSINORE
AVE.

Birch
Court

Little
Haven

MOSS RD

VICTORIA DR

LEADER WILLIAMS RD

GREENORE DR

Birch Tree
Farm

Worsley View
Farm   1

Mast

HOWARD DR.

Great Molden
Moss

WA3

Prospect
Grange

ROSCOE RD

WALKER RD

69   A   B   70   C   D   71   E   F   94

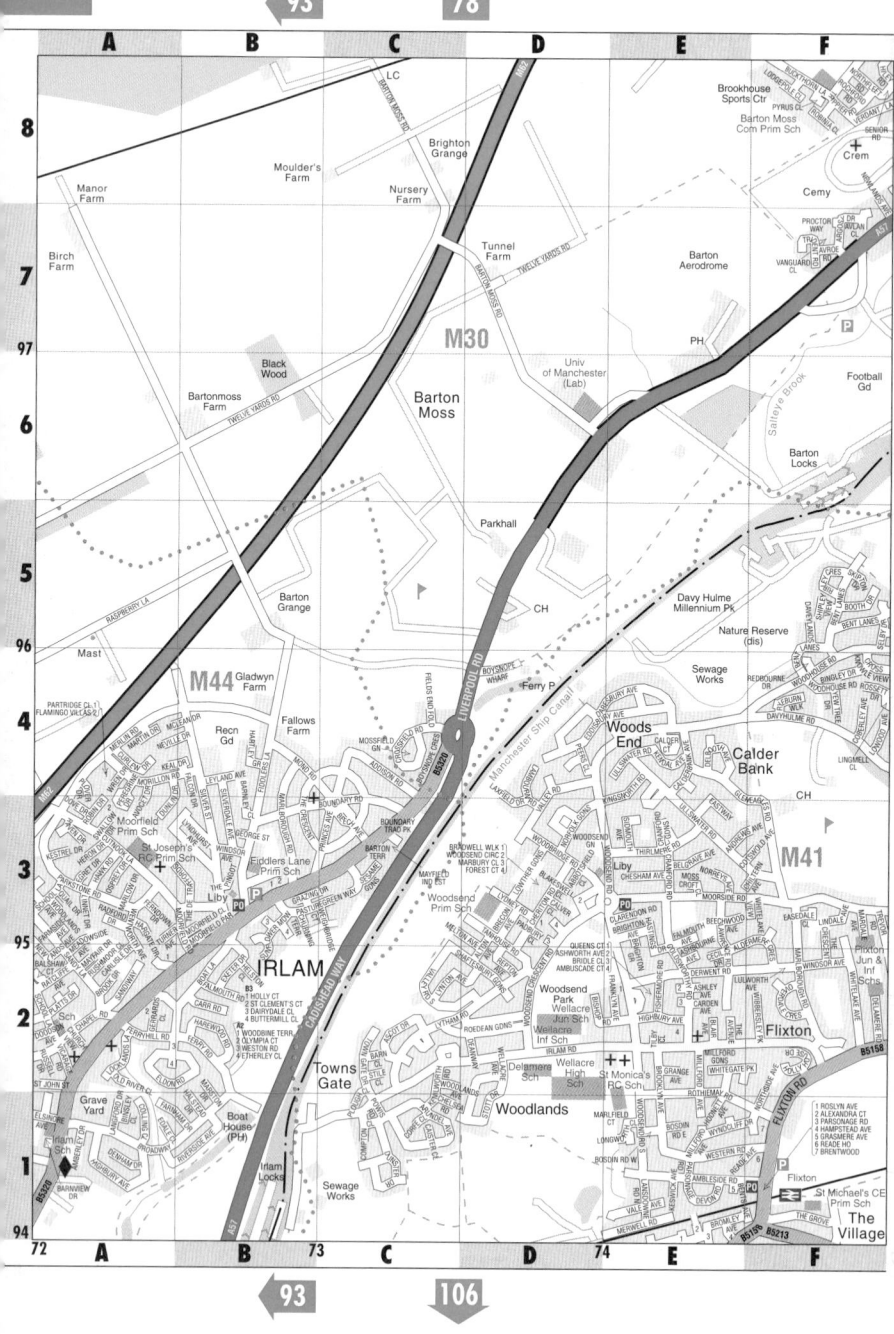

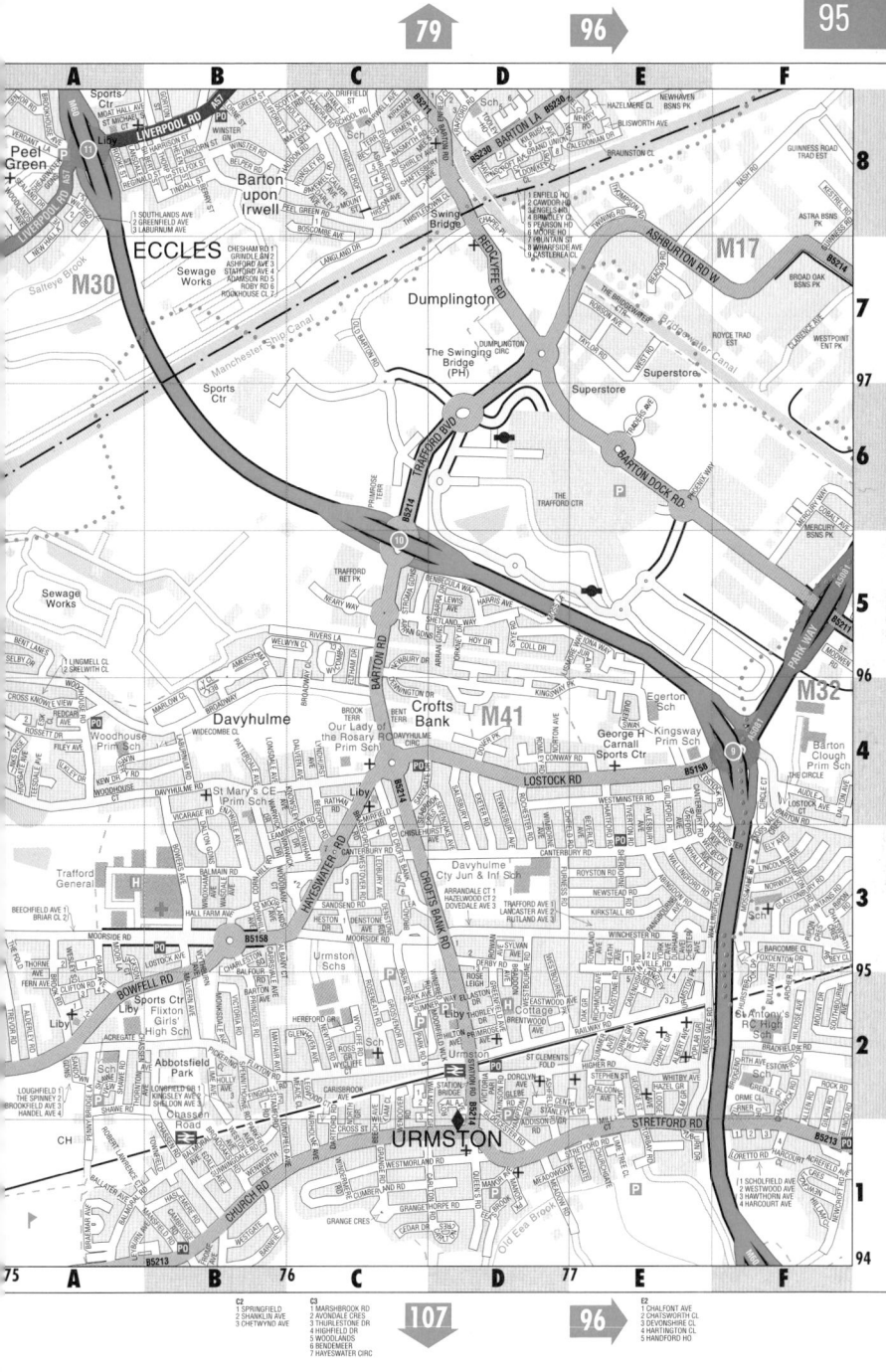

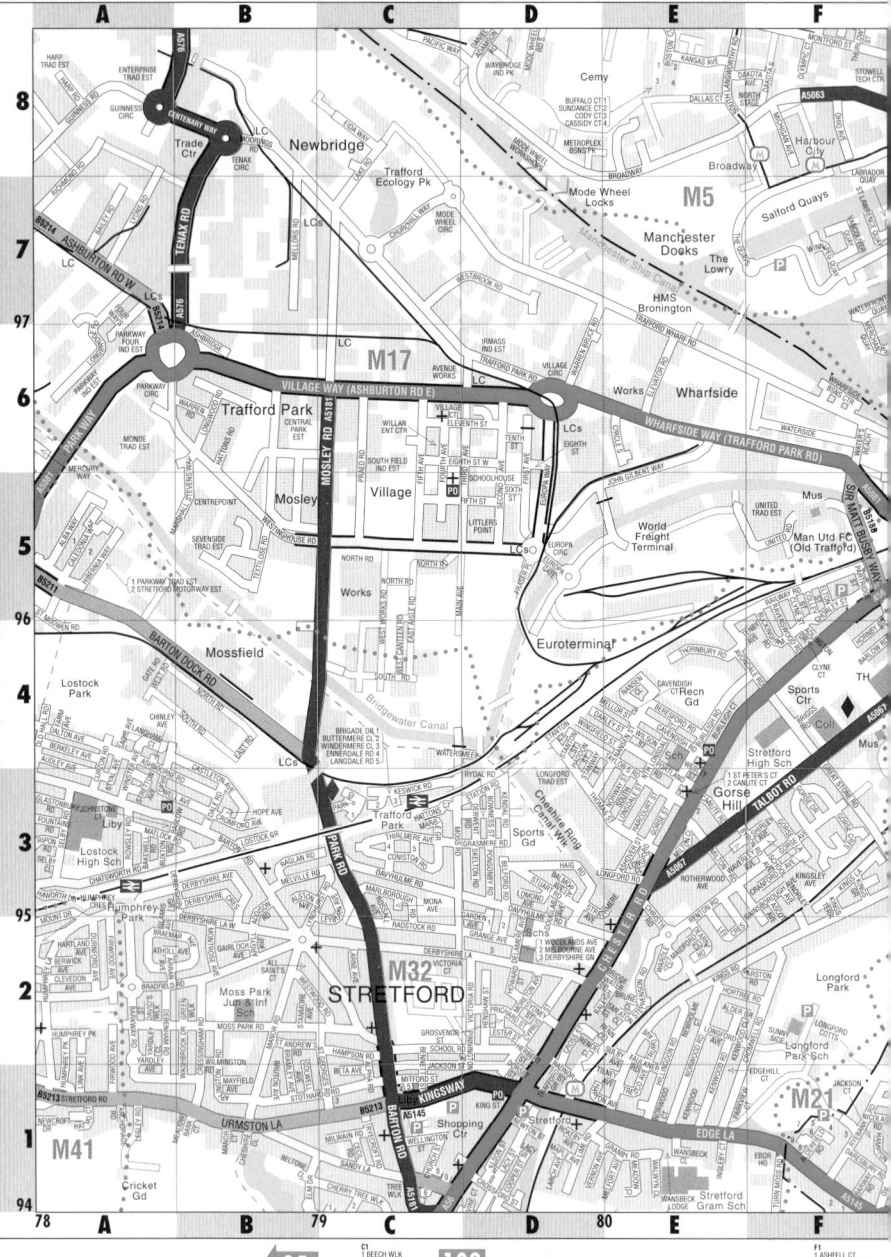

C1
1 BEECH WLK
2 WALNUT WLK
3 ST GEORGE'S CT
4 PINFOLD CT
5 THOMAS GIBBON CL
6 COB HALL RD
7 STRETFORD HO
8 SOUTHWELL CT
9 ST MATHEWS CT

F1
1 ASHFELL CT
2 SUMMERFIELD CT
3 RYEBANK MEWS
4 LONGFORD HO
5 ALDERFIELD HO
6 CRESCENT CT
7 PARK VIEW
8 ALDER EDGE
9 BEECH CT

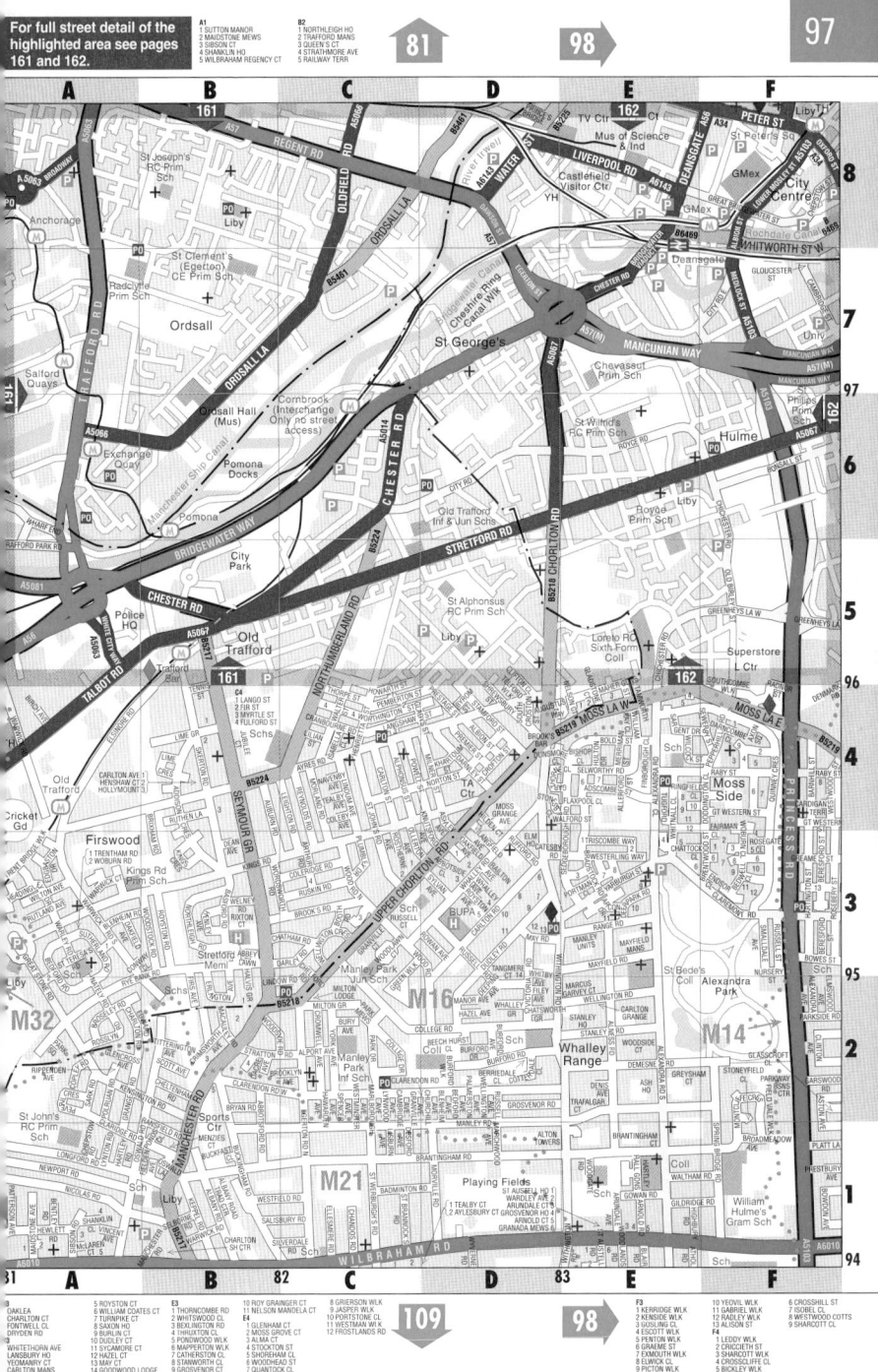

For full street detail of the highlighted area see pages 161 and 162.

A1
1 SUTTON MANOR
2 MAIDSTONE MEWS
3 SIBSON CT
4 SHANKLIN HO
5 WILBRAHAM REGENCY CT

B2
1 NORTHLEIGH HO
2 TRAFFORD MANS
3 QUEEN'S CT
4 STRATHMORE AVE
5 RAILWAY TERR

81
98
97

OAKLEA
CHARLTON CT
FOXTWELL CL
DRYDEN RD

WHITETHORN AVE
LANSBURY HO
YEOMANRY CT
CARLTON MANS

5 ROYSTON CT
6 WILLIAM COATES CT
7 TURNPIKE CT
8 SAXON HO
9 BURLIN CT
10 DUDLEY CT
11 SYCAMORE CT
12 HAZEL CT
13 MAY CT
14 GOODWOOD LODGE

E3
1 THORNCOMBE RD
2 WHITSWOOD CL
3 BEXLINGTON RD
4 THRUXTON CL
5 PONDWOOD WLK
6 MAPPERTON WLK
7 CATHERSTON CL
8 STANWORTH CT
9 GROSVENOR CT

10 ROY GRAINGER CT
11 NELSON MANDELA CT

E4
1 GLENHAM CT
2 MOSS GROVE CT
3 ALMA CT
4 STOCKTON ST
5 SHOREHAM CL
6 WARDLEY WLK
7 QUANTOCK CL

8 GRIERSON WLK
9 JASPER WLK
10 PORTSTONE CL
11 WESTMAN WLK
12 FROSTLANDS RD

F3
1 KERRIDGE WLK
2 KENSIDE WLK
3 GOSLING CL
4 ESCOTT WLK
5 PENTON WLK
6 GRAEME ST
7 EXMOUTH WLK
8 ELWICK CL
9 PICTON WLK

10 YEOVIL WLK
11 GABRIEL WLK
12 RADLEY WLK
13 ALISON ST

F4
1 LEDDY WLK
2 CRUCHETH ST
3 SHARCOTT WLK
4 CROSSCLIFFE CL
5 BICKLEY WLK

6 CROSSHILL ST
7 ISOBEL CL
8 WESTWOOD COTTS
9 SHARCOTT CL

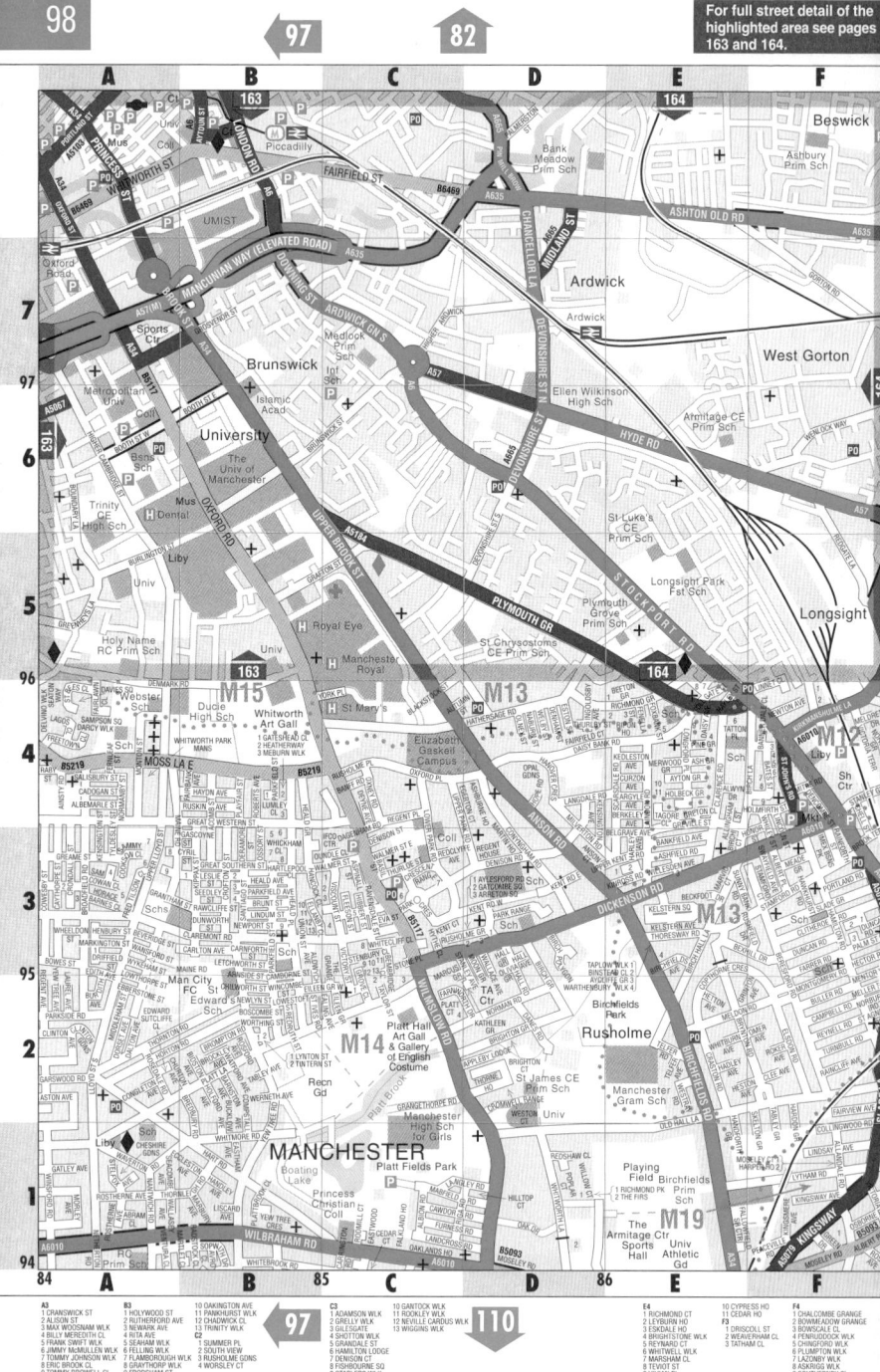

98

97

82

For full street detail of the highlighted area see pages 163 and 164.

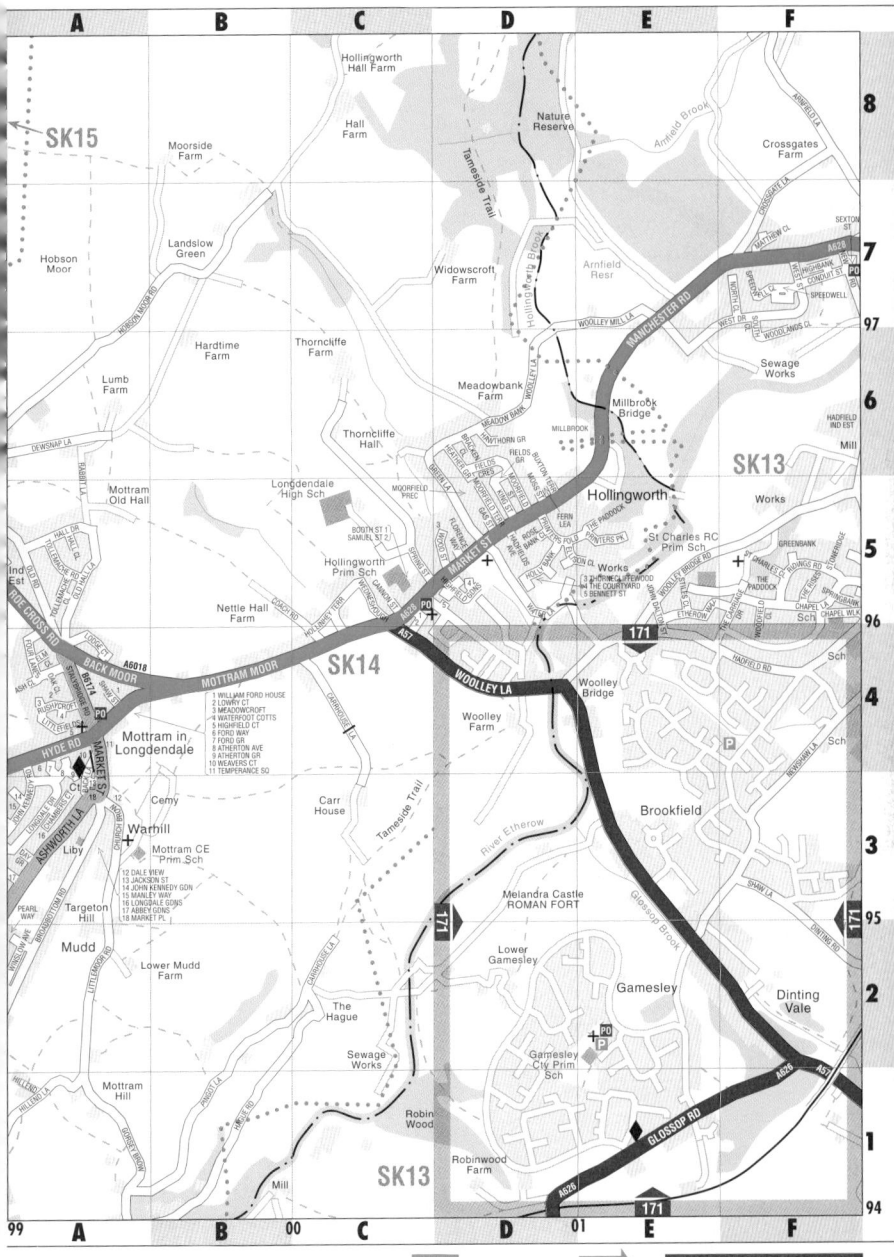

A B C D E F

8

SK15

Hobson Moor

Moorside Farm

Landslow Green

Hollingworth Hall Farm

Hall Farm

Nature Reserve

Tameside Trail

Amfield Brook

Crossgates Farm

7

SEXTON ST

A628

PO

MATTHEW CL

SPEEDBANK

CONDUIT ST

SPEEDWELL

WEST DR

WOODLANDS CL

MANCHESTER RD

97

Lumb Farm

Hardtime Farm

Thorncliffe Farm

Widowscroft Farm

Meadowbank Farm

WOOLLEY MILL LA

Arnfield Resr

Sewage Works

6

Thorncliffe Hall

Longdendale High Sch

MOORFIELD PREC

Millbrook Bridge

Millbrook

HADFIELD IND EST

Mill

Hollingworth

Works

SK13

Works

5

Mottram Old Hall

MARKET ST

BOOTH ST 1
SAMUEL ST 2

Hollingworth Prim Sch

FERN LEA

THE PADDOCK

PRINTERS PK

St Charles RC Prim Sch

GREENBANK

THE PADDOCK

Sch

CHAPEL WLK

96

Nettle Hall Farm

3 THORNELEY WOOD
4 THE COURTYARD
6 BENNETT ST

171

Ind Est

A6018

BACK MOOR

MOTTRAM MOOR

SK14

A57

WOOLLEY LA

Woolley Bridge

ETHEROW

171

HADFIELD RD

Sch

4

HYDE RD

PO

Mottram in Longdendale

1 WILLIAM FORD HOUSE
2 LOWRY CT
3 MEADOWCROFT
4 WATERFOOT COTTS
5 HIGHFIELD CT
6 FORD WAY
7 FORD GR
8 ATHERTON AVE
9 ATHERTON GR
10 WEAVERS CT
11 TEMPERANCE SQ

Woolley Farm

Brookfield

P

171

Cemy

Warhill

Liby

Carr House

Tameside Trail

River Etherow

Glossop Brook

95

MARKET ST

ASHWORTH LA

Mottram CE Prim Sch

12 DALE VIEW
13 JACKSON ST
14 JOHN KENNEDY GDN
15 MANLEY WAY
16 LONGDALE GDNS
17 ABBEY GDNS
18 MARKET PL

Melandra Castle ROMAN FORT

Lower Gamesley

Gamesley

Dinting Vale

PEARL WAY

Targeton Hill

Mudd

Lower Mudd Farm

The Hague

PO
P

Gamesley Cty Prim Sch

A626

A57

Mottram Hill

Sewage Works

Robin Wood

GLOSSOP RD

DINTING RD

2

Robinwood Farm

SK13

Mill

A628

171

1

99 A B 00 C D 01 E F 94

For full street detail of the highlighted area see page 171.

SK13

Townhead Farm
Valehouse Wood
Valehouse Resr
Deepclough
Higher Deepclough

WOODHEAD RD
A628

LOWER SQ
Cockerhill
OLD RD
MANCHESTER RD
CHURCH ST A628
Tintwistle
CE Prim Sch
Tintwistle

Valehouse Farm

Trans Pennine Trail

Nell's Pike

Devil's Elbow
Ogden Clough

River Etherow

Tintwistle Bridge

Bottoms Resr

Peak Naze

Resr

Resrs

WOODHEAD RD

A6 1 NEW BANK ST
2 OLD HALL SQ
3 THE CROSS
4 EVESHAM AVE
5 PINGOTT LA
6 BLENHEIM CL.

Padfield Cty Prim Sch
Padfield
Little Padfield Farm

Hadfield

TEMPLE AVE
LEES ROW

Blackshaw

PLATT ST
HOLLINS IND PK
Hadfield
RAILWAY

Upper Swineshaw Resr

PARK RD

Cemy

Swineshaw Resr

Banks Wood
Glossop Dale Com Coll
Mouselow
Mast
Castlehill Wood
Bettenhill
DEMETER RD

Cat Wood
Broom Hill

Laneside Farm
Shire Hill
H

Mouselow Quarry
Hilltop
Wimberryhill
Wood's H
Moorside

Shaw
PARTINGTON FIELDS

All Saints' RC Prim Sch

Shire Hill

Howard Park

Higher Dinting
Dinting Junc
Dinting

Glossop Dale Com Coll

Duke of Norfolk's CE Prim Sch
Old Glossop

Manor Park

Dinting Lane Trad Est
Dinting Vale
Works

St Luke's CE Prim Sch
Liby
Duke of Norfolk's CE Prim Sch

PO
Shelf Brook

Dinting CE Prim Sch

GLOSSOP
Glossop Brook

SHEFFIELD RD
A57
MILLERSDALE CT 1
ISLWOOD DR 2
PARTINGTON CT 3
DOVEDALE CT 4
HATHERSAGE RD 5

SHEFFIELD RD
A57

HIGH ST W
Mill
Heritage Ctr
HIGH ST E
L Ctr
REGENT ST

C1
1 ST MARY'S RD
2 BROOK ST
3 HALL'S CT
4 HAYDEN CT
5 CROSS ST
6 CENTRAL STORE
7 MARKET ST

8 7 97 6 5 96 4 3 95 2 1 94
02 A B 03 C D 04 E F
A B C D E F

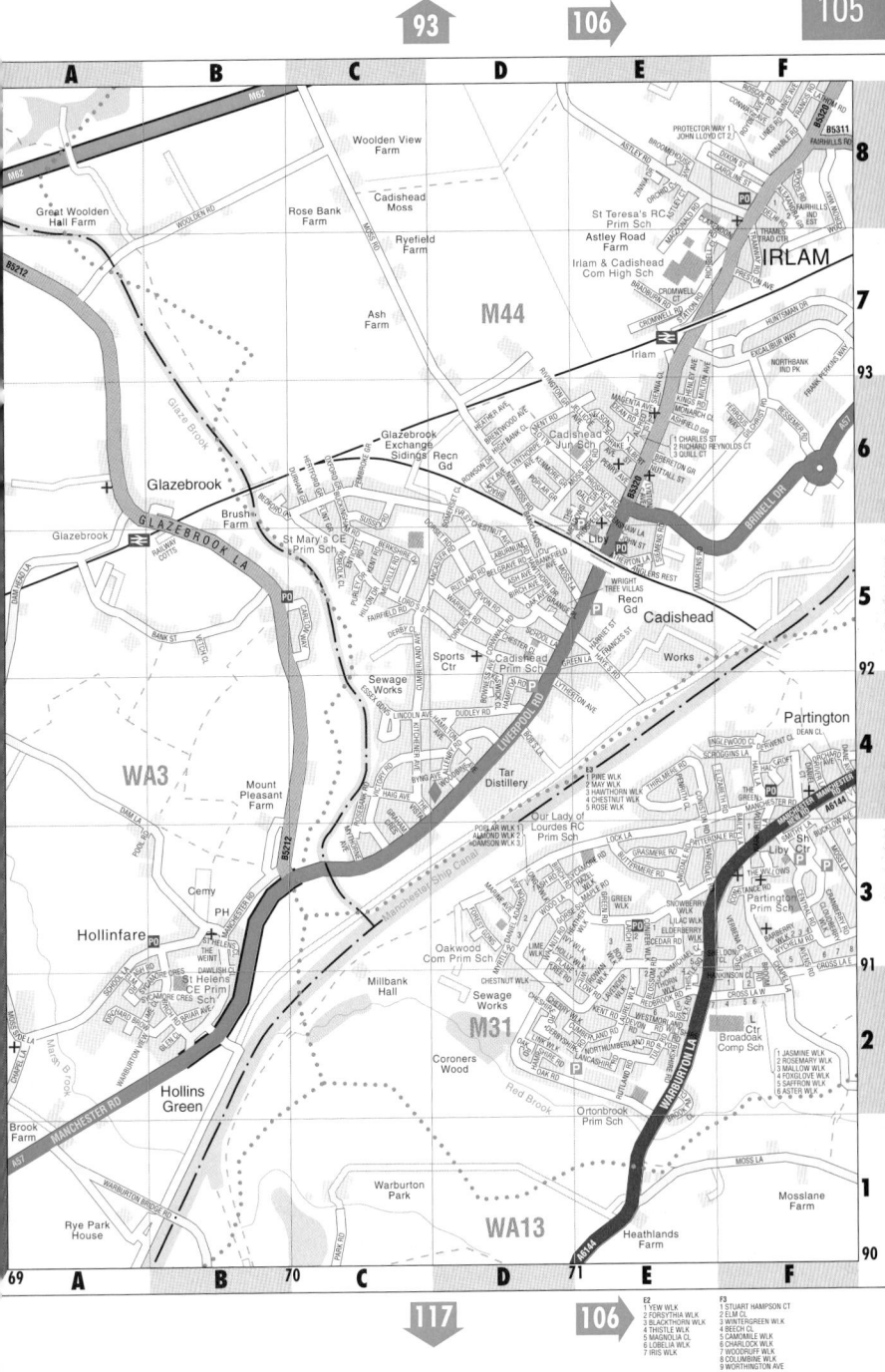

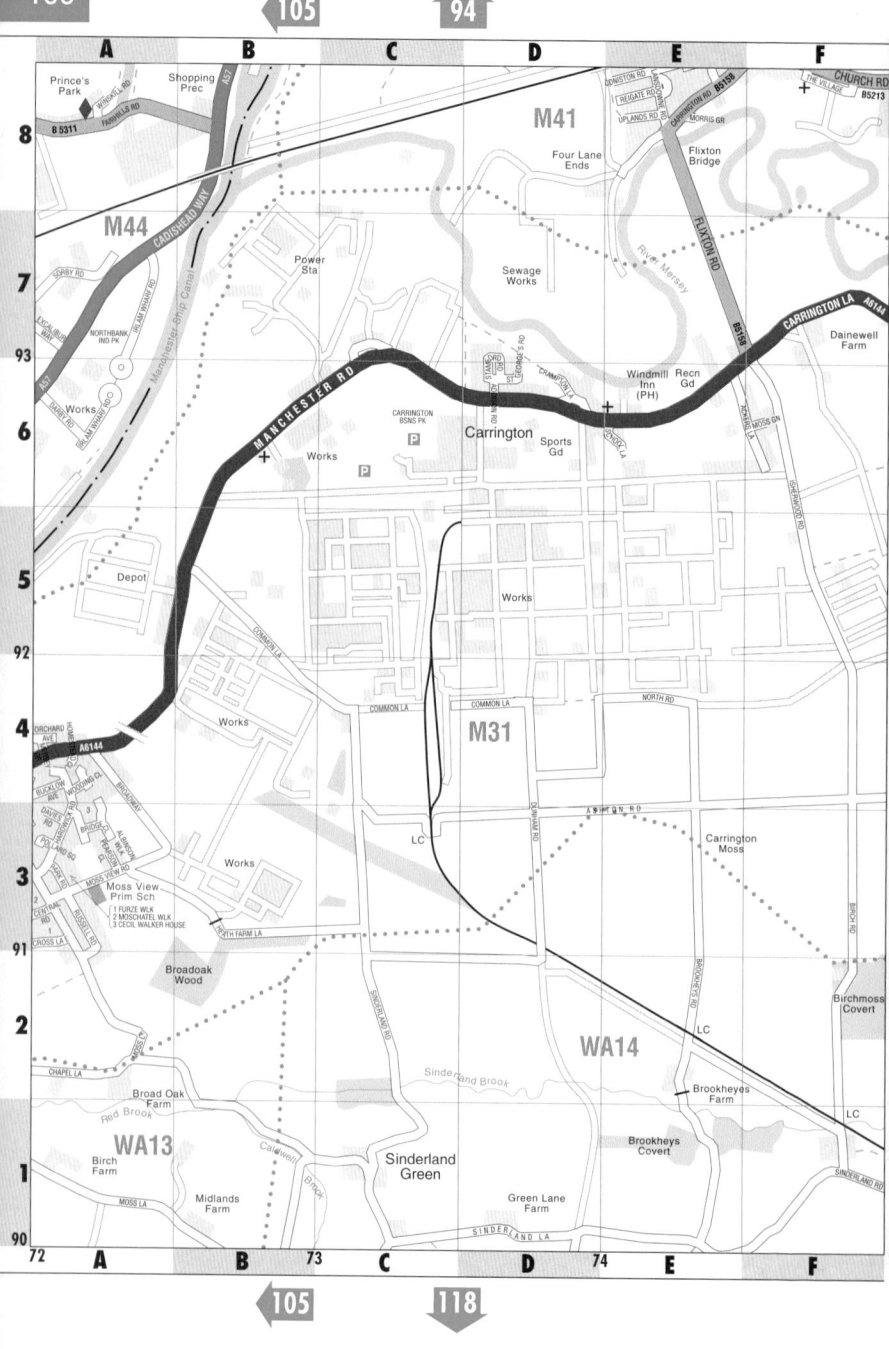

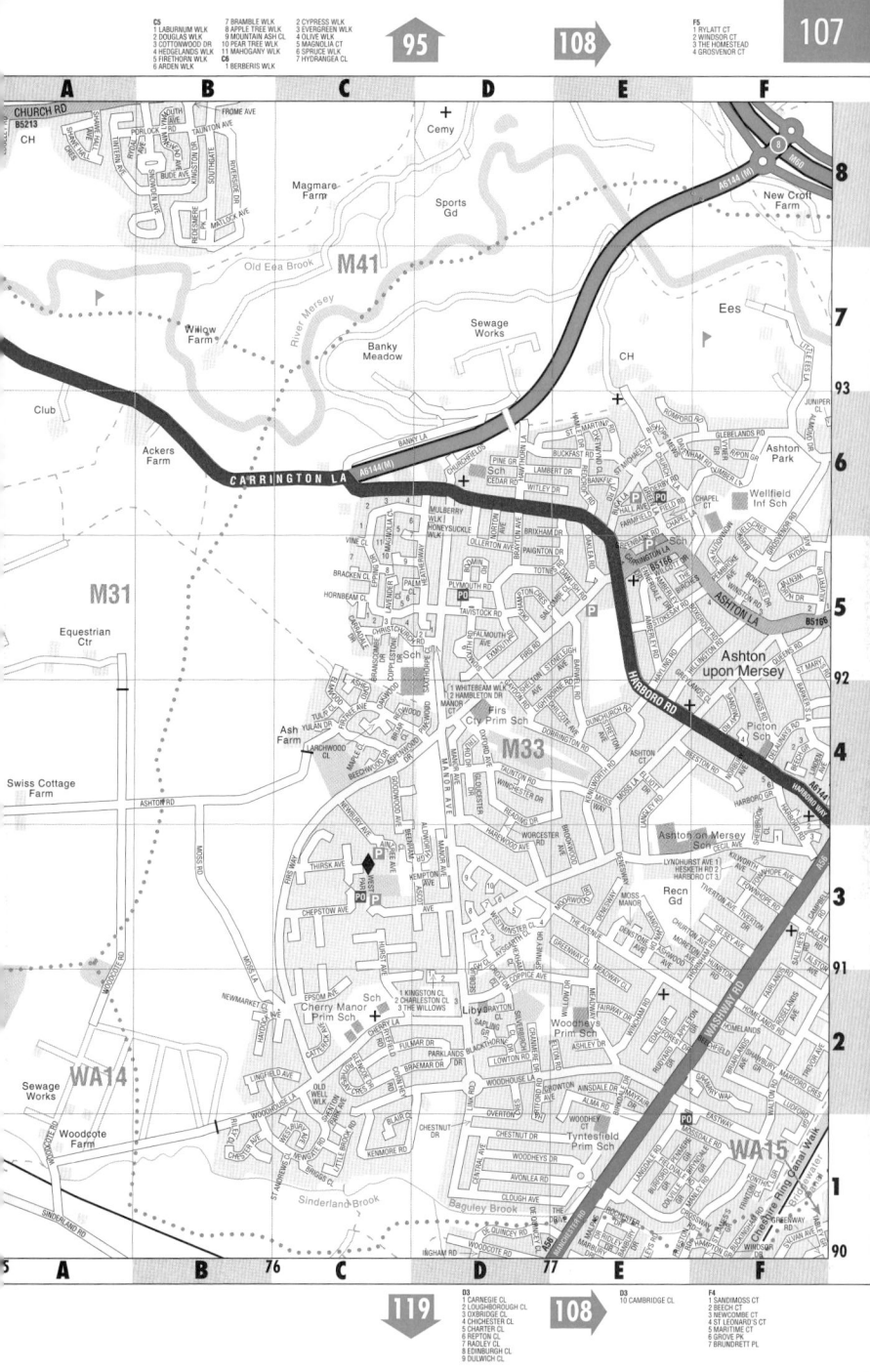

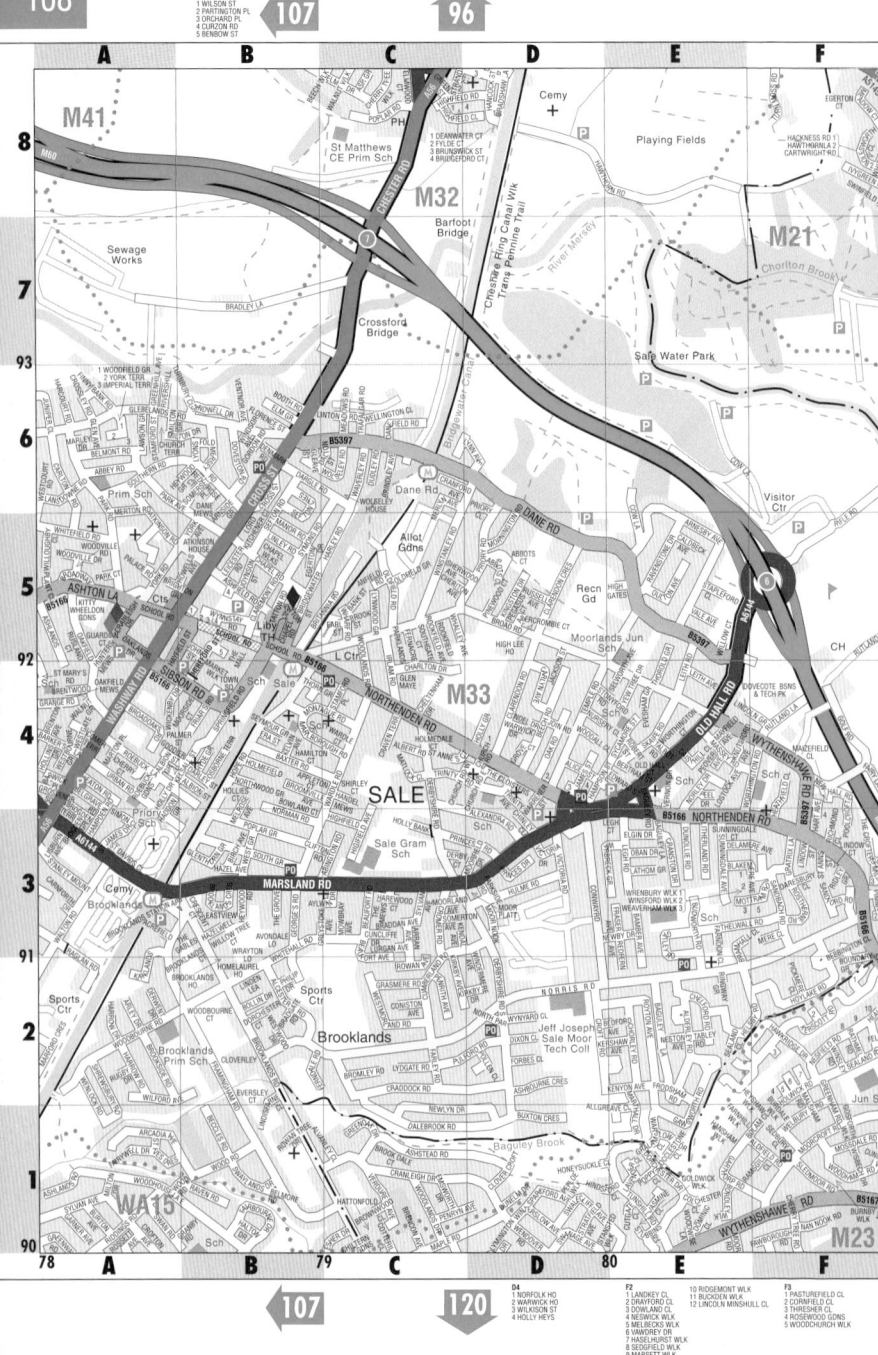

B5
1 WILSON ST
2 PARTINGTON PL
3 ORCHARD PL
4 CURZON RD
5 BENBOW ST

107

96

D4
1 NORFOLK HO
2 WARWICK HO
3 WILKISON ST
4 HOLLY HEYS

F2
1 LANSKEY CL
2 DRAYFORD CL
3 DOWLAND CL
4 NESWICK WLK
5 MELBECKS WLK
6 VAWDREY DR
7 HASELHURST WLK
8 SEDGFIELD WLK
9 MARSETT WLK

10 RIDGEMONT WLK
11 BUCKDEN WLK
12 LINCOLN MINSHULL CL

F3
1 PASTUREFIELD CL
2 CORNFIELD CL
3 THRESHER CL
4 ROSEWOOD GDNS
5 WOODCHURCH WLK

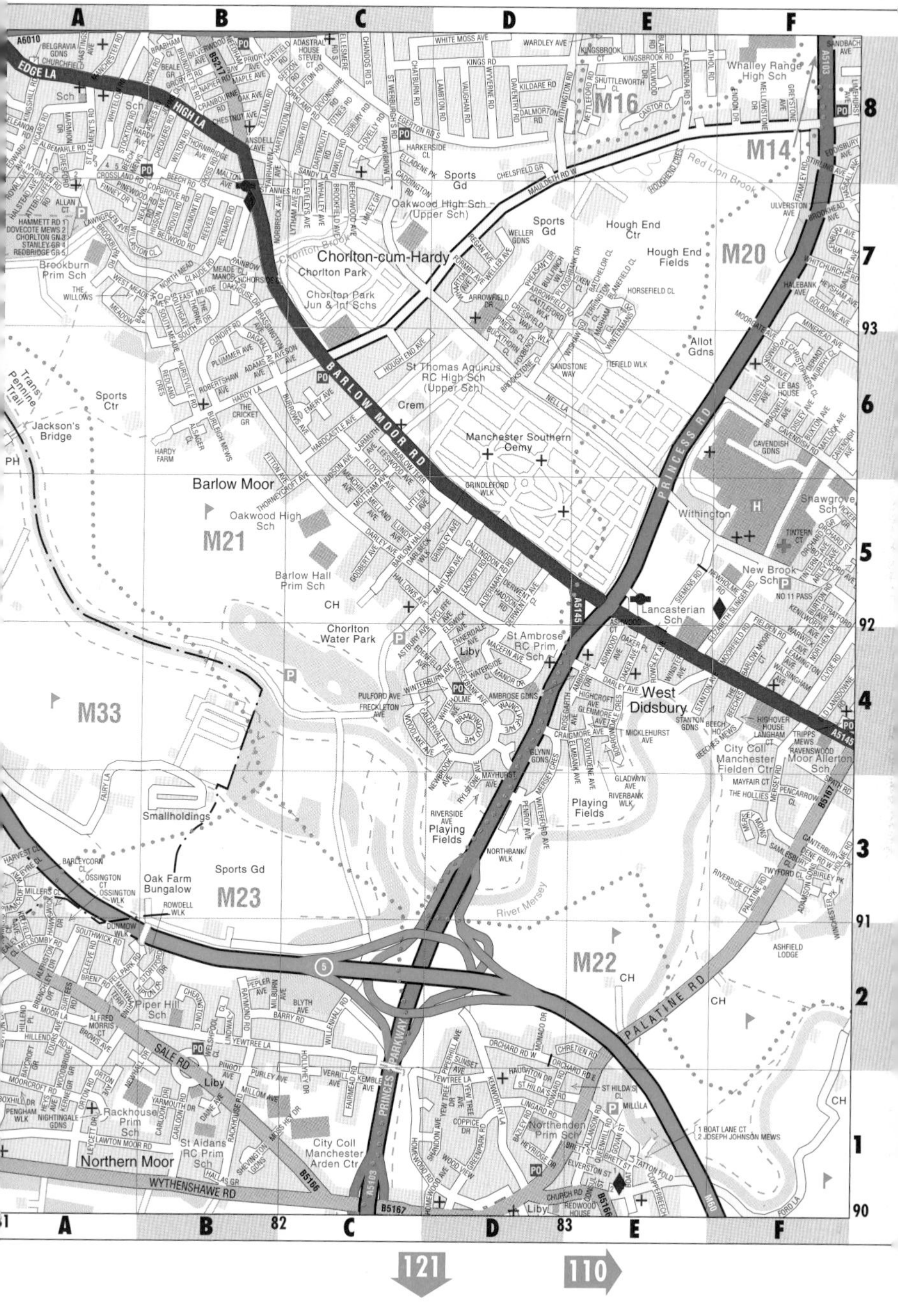

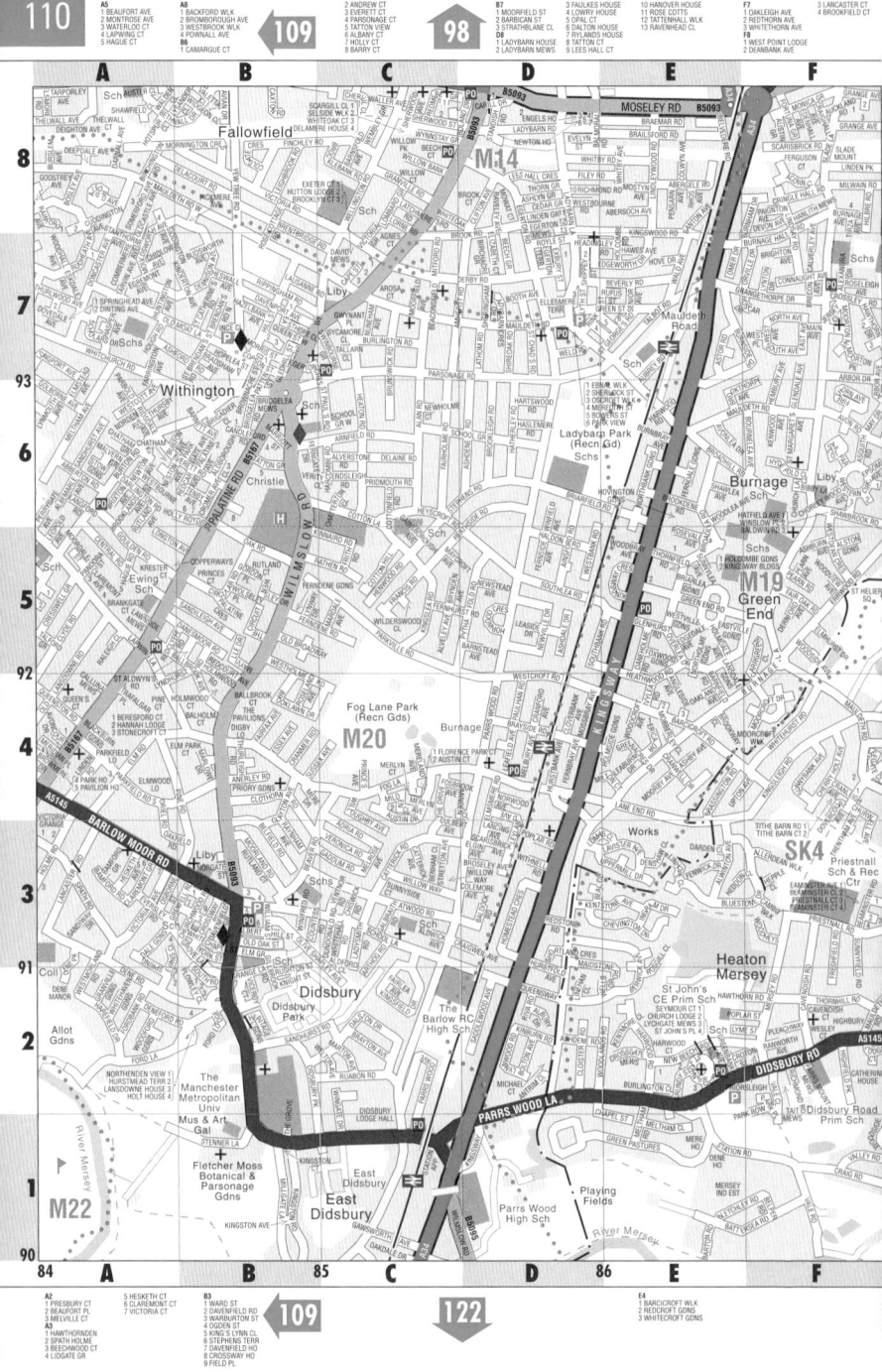

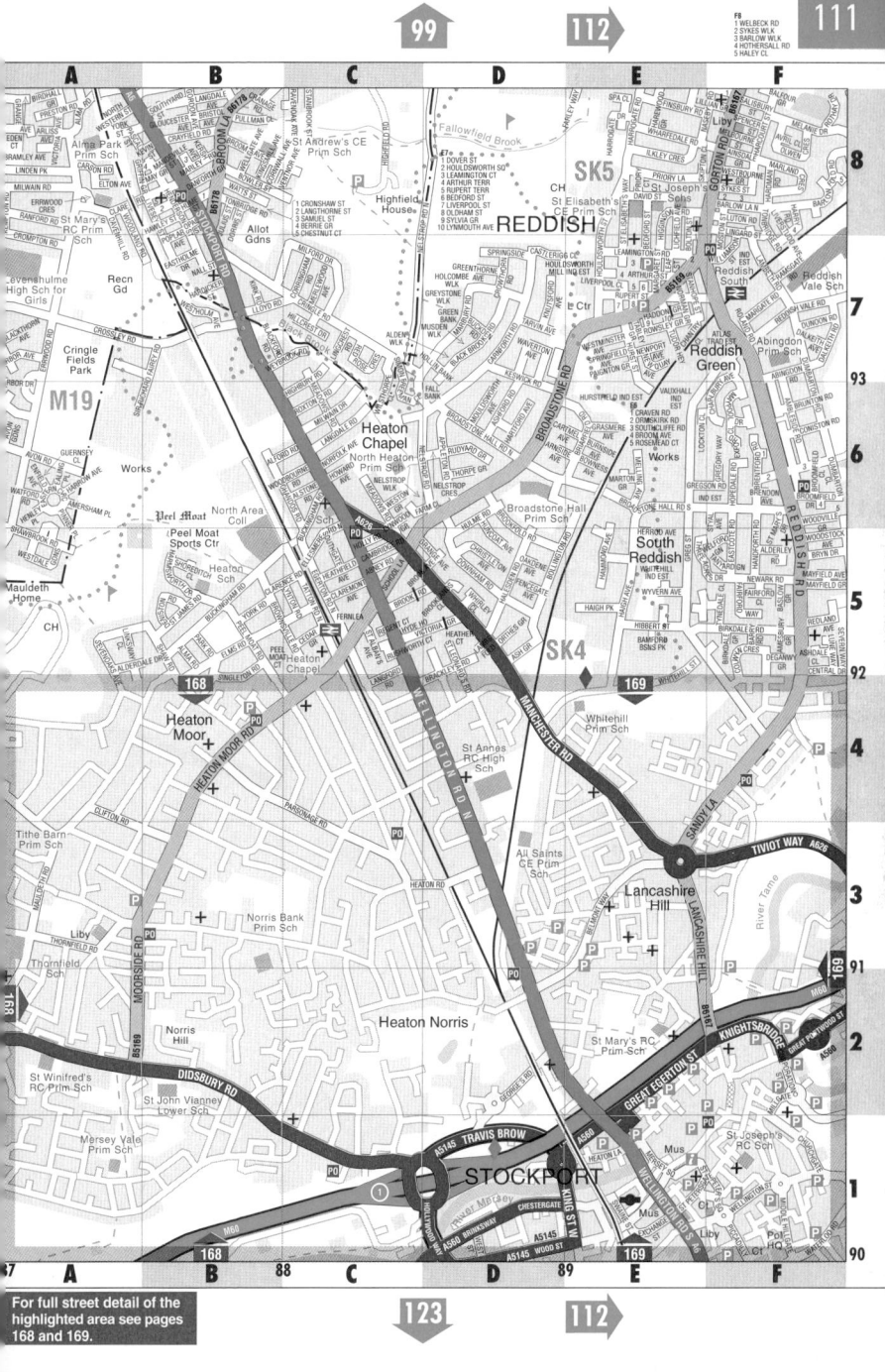

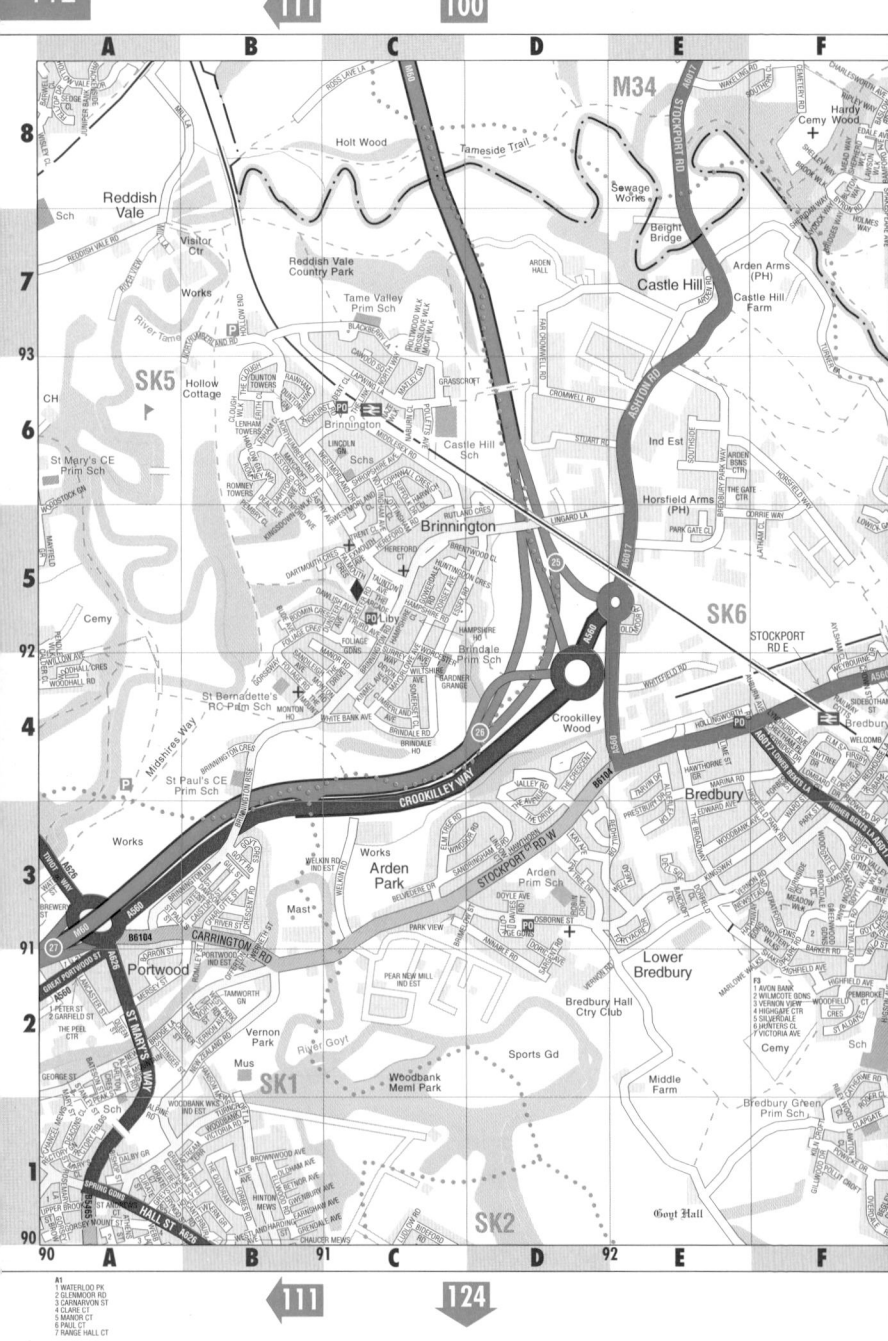

A1
1 WATERLOO PK
2 GLENMOOR RD
3 CARNARVON ST
4 CLARE CT
5 MANOR CT
6 PAUL CT
7 RANGE HALL CT

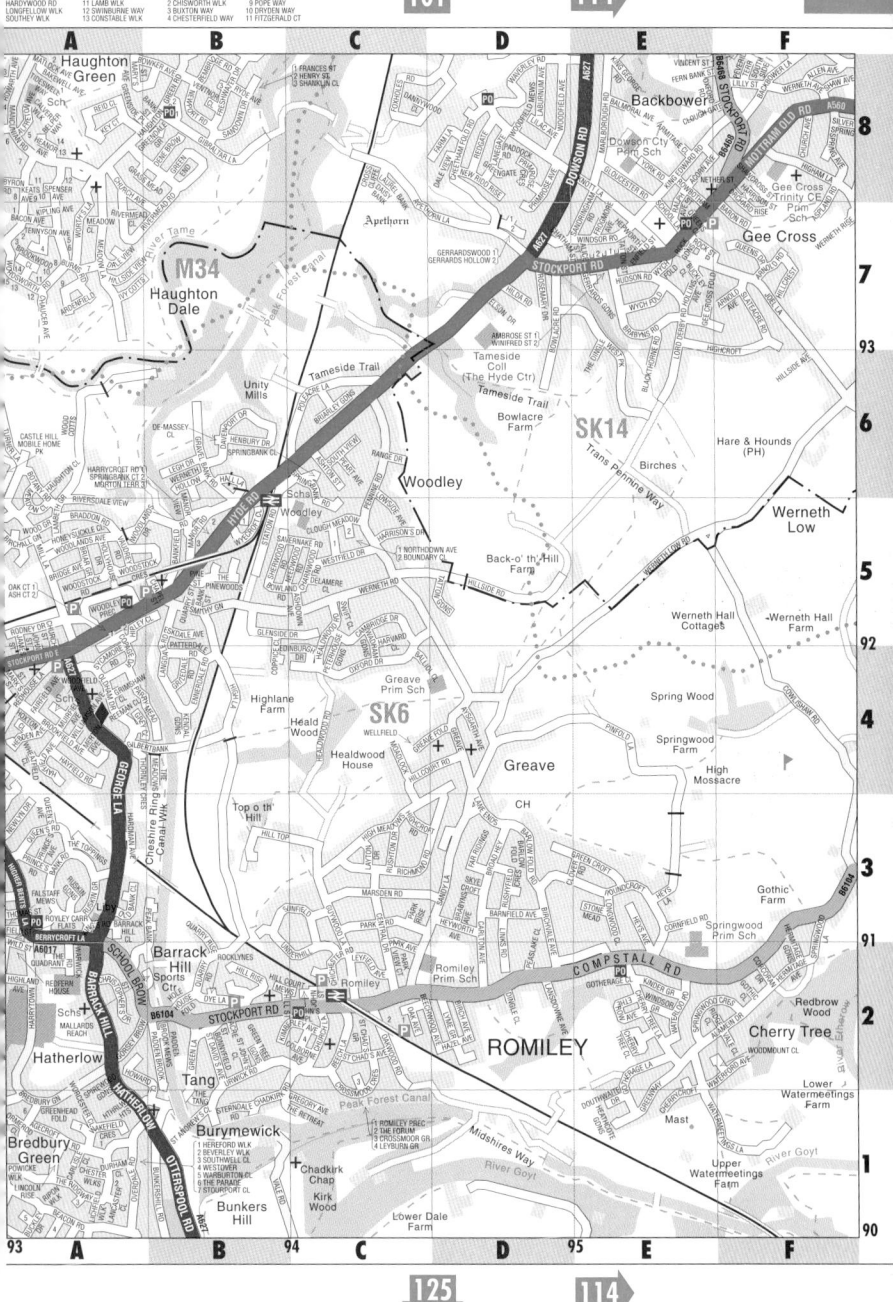

7 SYLVESTER WAY
8 ROSSETTI WAY
9 HOAD WLK
10 HARDYWORTH RD
11 LONGFELLOW WLK
13 SOUTHEY WLK

7 MAYFIELD AVE
8 GOLDSMITH WAY
9 ARNOLD WAY
10 MOORE WLK
11 LAMB WLK
12 SWINBURNE WAY
13 CONSTABLE WLK

14 BRACKENHILL TERR
15 MARLOWE WLK
A8
1 HAYFIELD WLK
2 CHISWORTH WLK
3 BUXTON WAY
4 CHESTERFIELD WAY

5 ILKESTON WLK
6 HATHERSAGE WAY
7 MACAULAY WAY
8 CAMPION WAY
9 POPE WAY
10 DRYDEN WAY
11 FITZGERALD CT

12 SOUTHEY CT
13 CASTLETON CT
14 CASTLETON WAY

Haughton
Green

M34

Haughton
Dale

Apethorn

Backbower

Gee Cross

SK14

Unity
Mills

Tameside Trail

Tameside Coll
(The Hyde Ctr)

Tameside Trail

Bowlacre
Farm

Woodley

Hare & Hounds
(PH)

Birches

Trans Pennine Way

Werneth
Low

Woodley

Back-o' th' Hill
Farm

Werneth Hall
Cottages

Werneth Hall
Farm

Highlane
Farm

Greave
Prim Sch

Spring Wood

Heald
Wood

SK6

WELLFIELD

Springwood
Farm

Healdwood
House

Greave

High
Mossacre

CH

Top o th'
Hill

Gothic
Farm

Springwood
Prim Sch

Barrack
Hill
Sports
Ctr

ROMILEY

COMPSTALL RD

Romiley
Prim Sch

Redbrow
Wood

Cherry Tree

Lower
Watermeetings
Farm

STOCKPORT RD

Romiley

Hatherlow

Tang

THE
TANG

Mast

Burymewick

Midshires Way

Upper
Watermeetings
Farm

Bredbury
Green

Chadkirk
Chap

Kirk
Wood

River Goyt

River Goyt

Bunkers
Hill

Lower Dale
Farm

Peak Forest Canal

8
7
93
6
5
92
4
91
3
2
90
1

A B C D E F

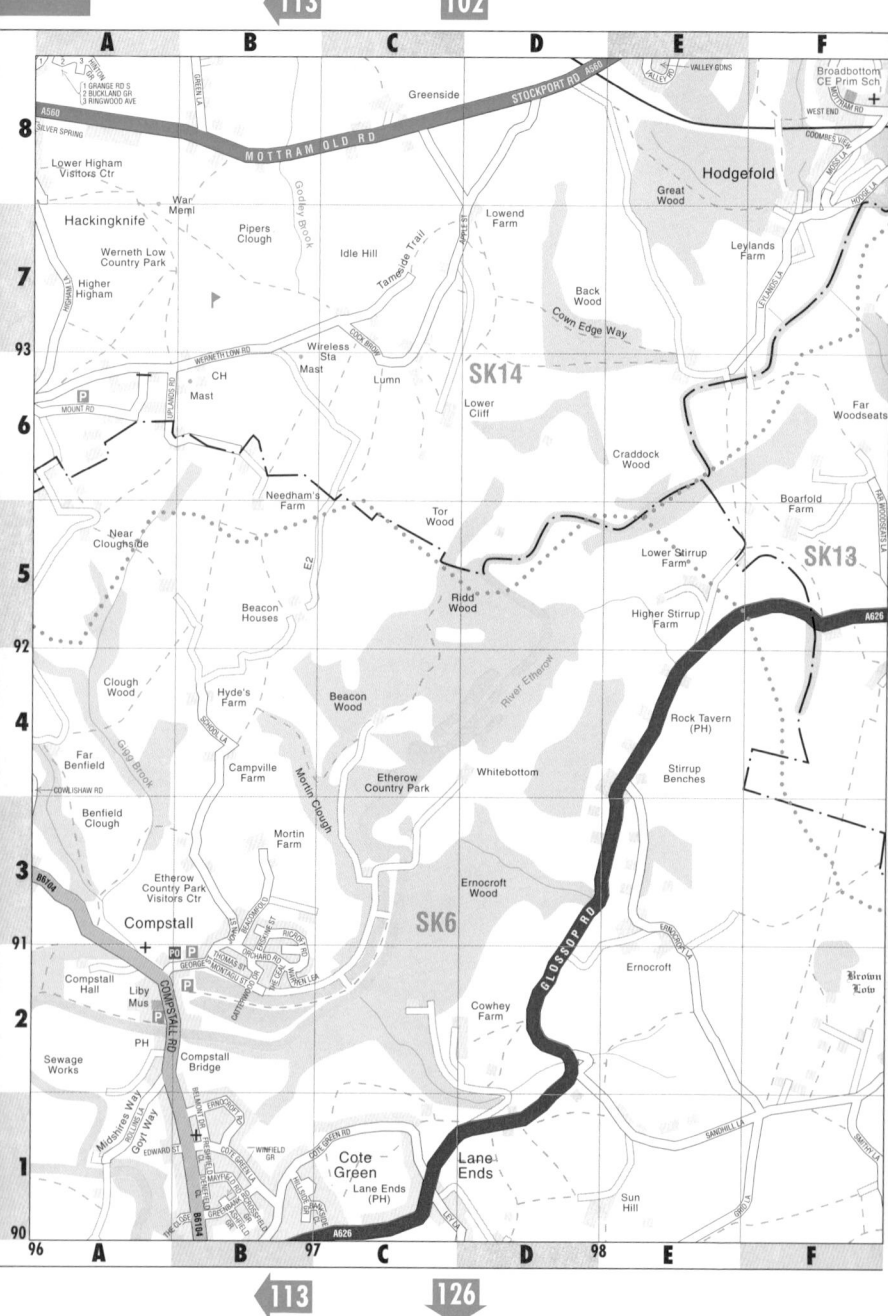

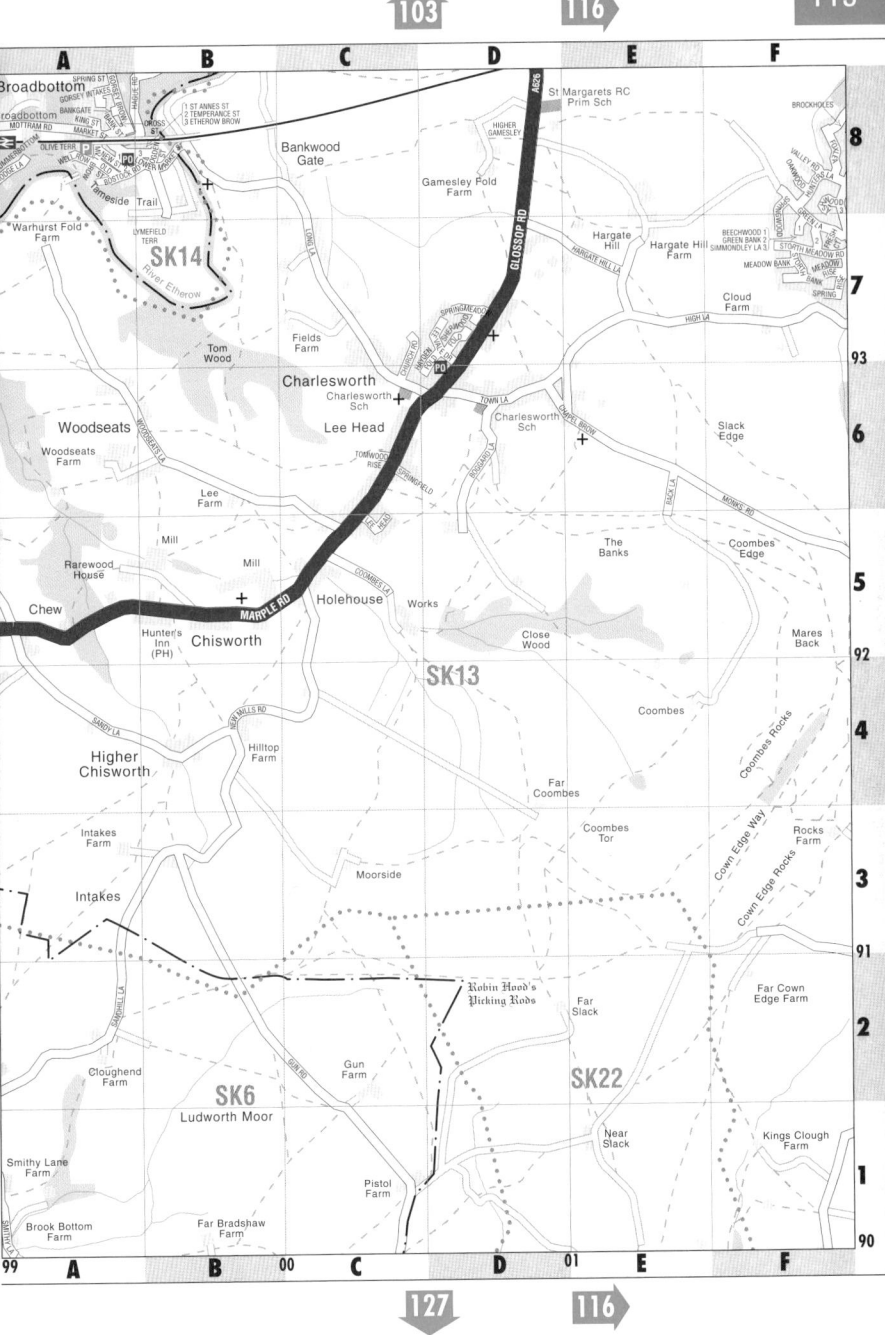

A   B   C   D   E   F

8

Broadbottom
UPPING ST
GORSEY ST
BANKGATE
KING ST
MARKET ST
1 ST ANNES ST
2 TEMPERANCE ST
3 ETHEROW BROW
CROSS ST

St Margarets RC
Prim Sch

A626

BROCKHOLES

Broadbottom
MOTRAM RD

OLIVE TERR

JOSSE LA

P
PO

LYMEFIELD
TERR

Tameside Trail

Bankwood
Gate

HIGHER
GAMESLEY

VALLEY RD LA

OHAYS RD LA

STOTTH MEADOW RD
BEECHWOOD 1
GREEN BANK 2
SIMMONDLEY LA 3

MEADOW BANK

Warhurst Fold
Farm

SK14

River Etherow

Tom
Wood

Fields
Farm

Gamesley Pold
Farm

Hargate
Hill

Hargate Hill
Farm

Cloud
Farm

MEADOW
BANK

SPRING

7

93

Charlesworth

Charlesworth
Sch

SPRINGMEADOW

GLOSSOP RD

LONG LA

HARGATE HILL LA

HIGH LA

Woodseats

Charlesworth
Sch

TOWN LA

CHAPEL BROW

Slack
Edge

6

Woodseats
Farm

Lee Head

Lee
Farm

TOM WOOD
RISE

GLOSSOP RD

SPRING LA

BLACK LA

MOSS RD

+

Charlesworth

Mill

Mill

COOMBES LA

The
Banks

Coombes
Edge

5

Rarewood
House

MARPLE RD

Holehouse

LEE LA

Works

Close
Wood

Coombes

Mares
Back

Coombes Rocks

Chew

Hunter's
Inn
(PH)

Chisworth

SK13

92

SANDY LA

Higher
Chisworth

BACK MILLS RD

Hilltop
Farm

Far
Coombes

Coombes

Coombes Rocks

Coombes Edge Way

Rocks
Farm

4

Intakes
Farm

Moorside

Coombes
Tor

Cown Edge Way

Cown Edge Rocks

3

Intakes

LA THOMAS

DUN RD

Robin Hood's
Picking Rods

Far
Slack

Far Cown
Edge Farm

91

Cloughend
Farm

SK6

Ludworth Moor

Gun
Farm

SK22

Kings Clough
Farm

2

Smithy Lane
Farm

Near
Slack

SMITHY LA

Brook Bottom
Farm

Far Bradshaw
Farm

Pistol
Farm

1

90

99   A   B   00   C   D   01   E   F

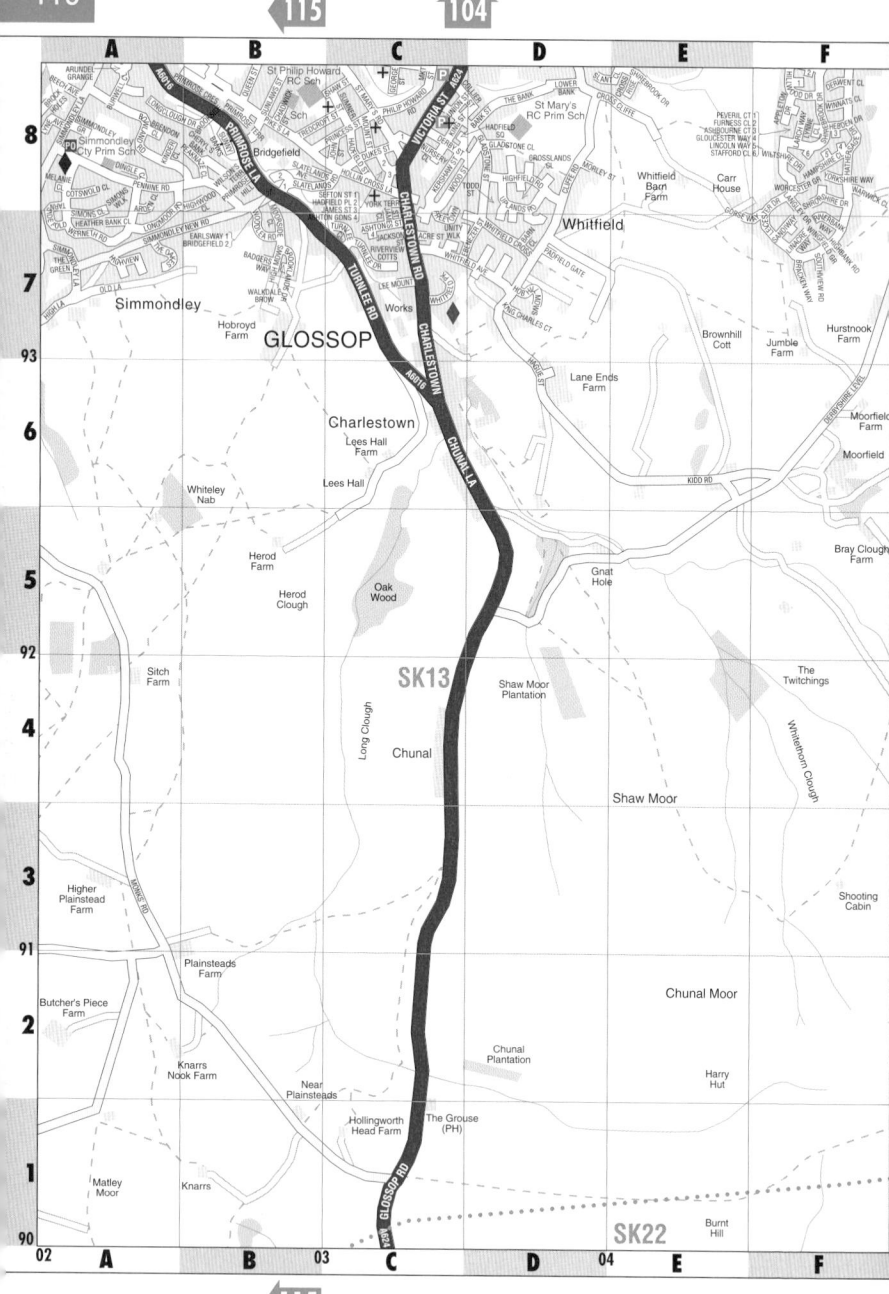

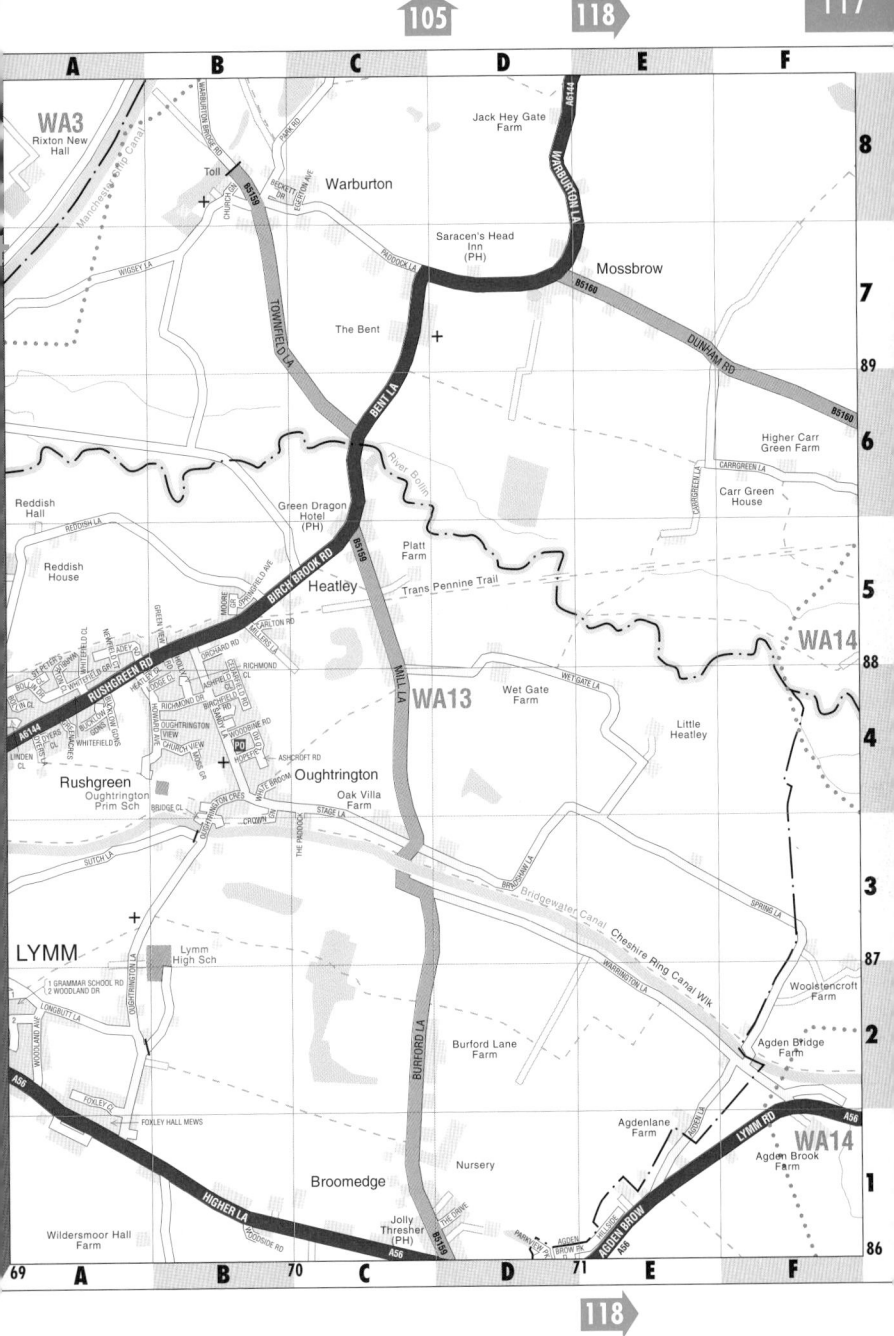

WA3
Rixton New Hall

Jack Hey Gate Farm

Warburton

Toll

Saracen's Head Inn (PH)

Mossbrow

The Bent

Higher Carr Green Farm

Reddish Hall

Green Dragon Hotel (PH)

Carr Green House

Reddish House

Platt Farm

Heatley

Trans Pennine Trail

WA14

Rushgreen

Wet Gate Farm

WA13

Little Heatley

Oughtrington Prim Sch

Oughtrington

Oak Villa Farm

Rushgreen

Bridgewater Canal Cheshire Ring Canal Wlk

Woolstencroft Farm

LYMM

Lymm High Sch

Agden Bridge Farm

1 GRAMMAR SCHOOL RD
2 WOODLAND DR

Burford Lane Farm

Agdenlane Farm

Agden Brook Farm

WA14

Broomedge

Nursery

LYMM RD

Jolly Thresher (PH)

AGDEN BROW

Wildersmoor Hall Farm

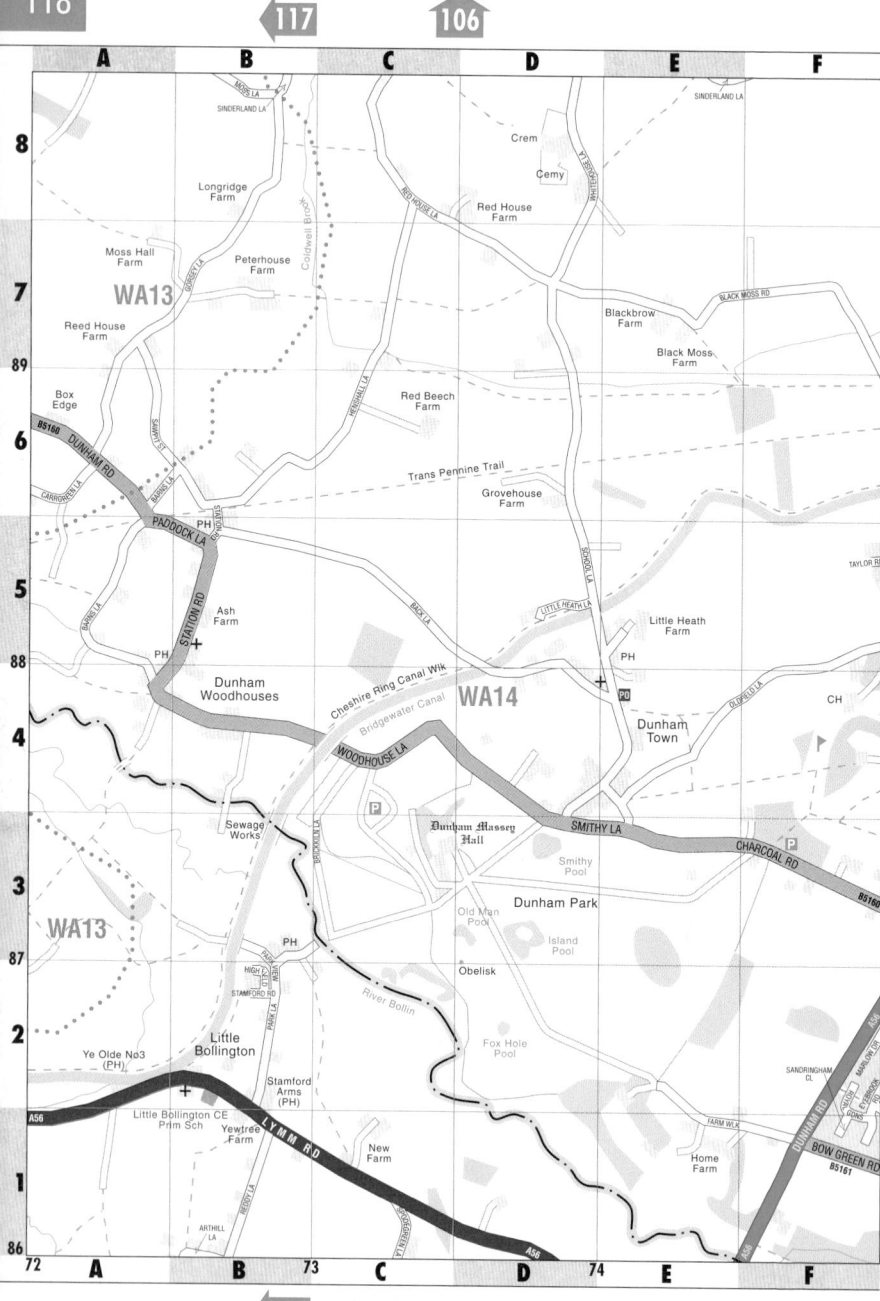

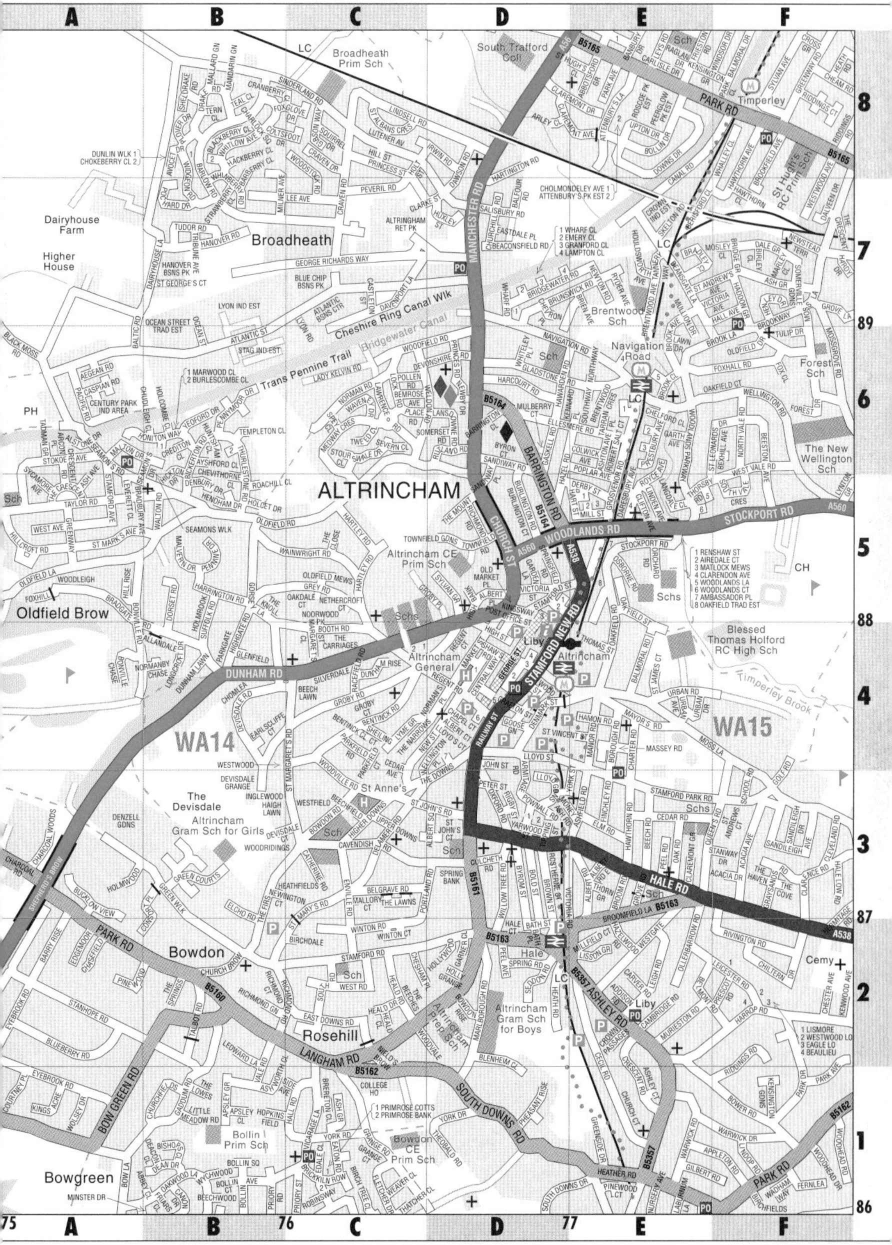

107

D5
1 POLICE ST
2 STAMFORD WAY
3 STAMFORD SQ

120

E9
1 LYNGARTH HO
2 ASTBURY CL
3 THELWALL CL
4 THE WOODS
5 SELWORTH CL

128

C4
1 STAMFORD GRANGE
2 EASINGWOLD

120

D3
1 ROSTHERNE ST
2 WILLIAM WLK

D4
1 GREENWOOD ST
2 THE CAUSEWAY
3 CROSS ST
4 BREWERY ST
5 GRAFTON MALL
6 LLOYD SQ
7 OSBOURNE PL

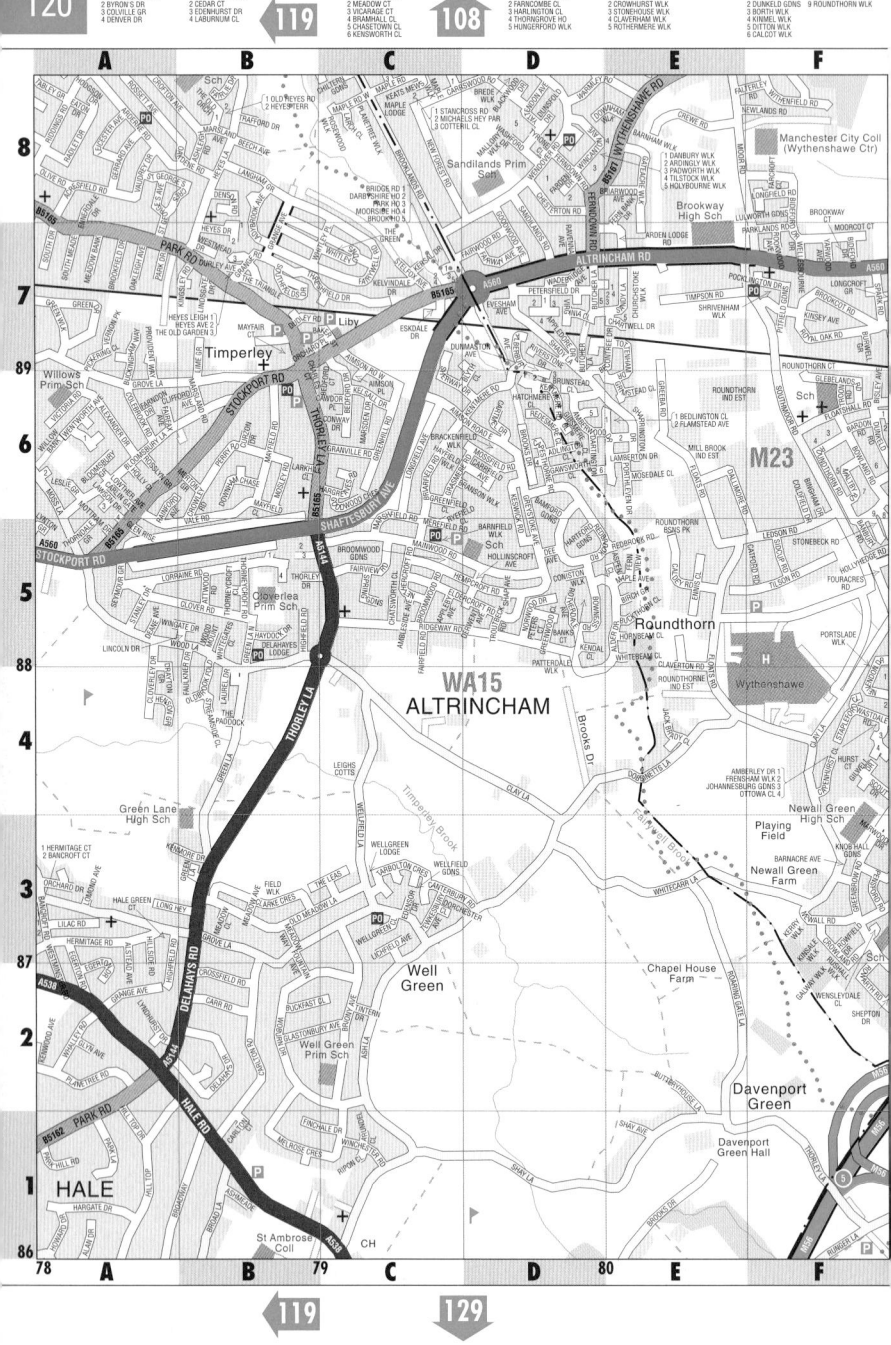

A6
1 CRANBOURNE CL
2 BYRON S DR
3 COLVILLE GR
4 DENVER DR

B5
1 CHERRY TREE CL
2 CEDAR CT
3 EDENHURST DR
4 LABURNUM CL

D6
1 SHAFTSBURY CT
2 MEADOW CT
3 VICARAGE CT
4 BRAMHALL CL
5 CHASETOWN CL
6 KENSWORTH CL

D7
1 THORNGROVE AVE
2 FARINCOMBE CL
3 HARLINGTON CL
4 THORNGROVE RD
5 HUNGERFORD WLK

E7
1 BUSHFIELD CL
2 CROWHURST WLK
3 STONEHOUSE WLK
4 CLAVERHAM WLK
5 ROTHERMERE WLK

F6
1 ECKERSLEY CL
2 DUNKELD GDNS
3 BORTH WLK
4 KINNIEL WLK
5 DITTON WLK
6 CALCOT WLK

7 LARGS WLK
8 HOCKLEY RD
9 ROUNDTHORN WLK

119
108
119
129

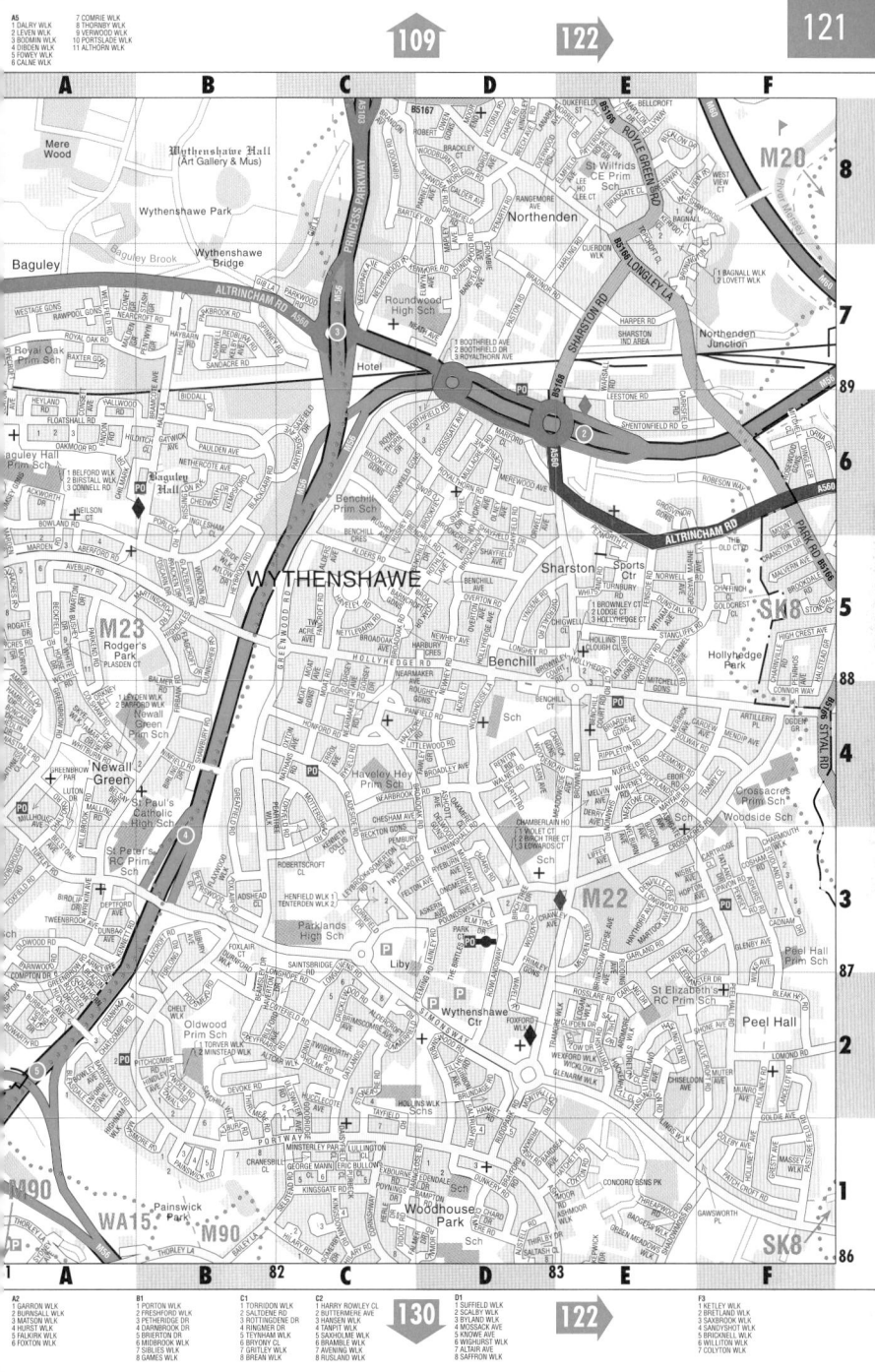

A5
1 DALRY WLK
2 LEVEN WLK
3 BODMIN WLK
4 DIBDEN WLK
5 FOWEY WLK
6 CALNE WLK
7 COMRIE WLK
8 THORNEY WLK
9 VERWOOD WLK
10 PORTSLADE WLK
11 ALTHORN WLK

109
122
130
122

A2
2 GARRON WLK
3 BURNSALL WLK
3 MATSON WLK
4 HURST WLK
5 FALKIRK WLK
6 FOXTON WLK

B1
1 PORTON WLK
2 FRESHFORD WLK
3 PETHERIDGE DR
4 OARNBROOK DR
5 BRIERTON DR
6 MISBROOK WLK
7 SIBLES WLK
8 GAMES WLK

C1
1 TORRIDON WLK
2 SALTDENE RD
3 ROTTINGDENE DR
4 RINGMER DR
5 TEYNHAM WLK
6 BRYONY CL
7 GRITLEY WLK
8 BREAN WLK

C2
1 HARRY ROWLEY CL
2 BUTTERMERE AVE
3 HANSEN WLK
4 TANPIT WLK
5 SAXHOLME WLK
6 BRAMBLE WLK
7 AVENING WLK
8 RUSLAND WLK

D1
1 SUFFIELD WLK
2 SCALBY WLK
3 BYLAND WLK
4 MOSSACK AVE
5 KNOWE AVE
6 WIGHURST WLK
7 ALTAIR AVE
8 SAFFRON WLK

F3
1 KETLEY WLK
2 BRETLAND WLK
3 SAXBROOK WLK
4 SANDYSHOT WLK
5 BRICKNELL WLK
6 WILLITON WLK
7 COLYTON WLK

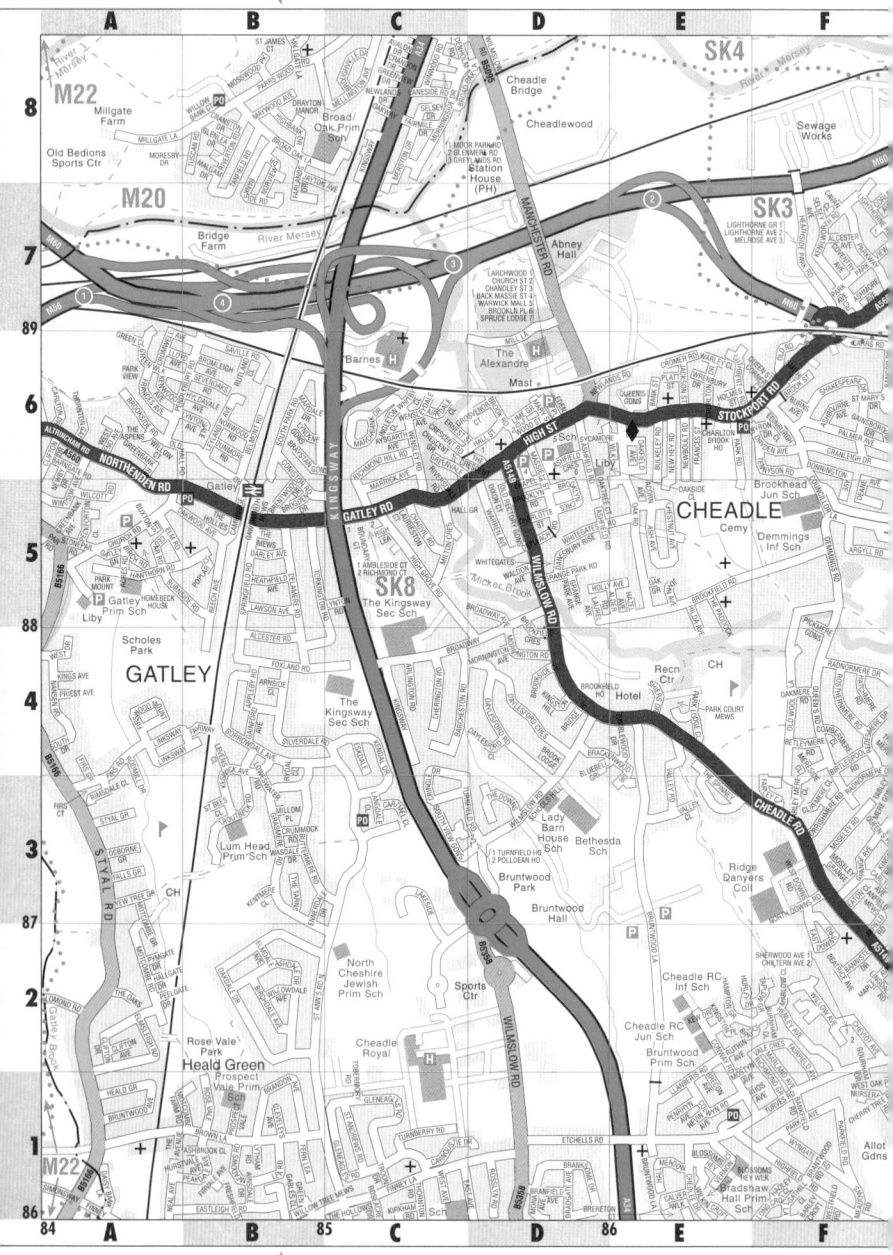

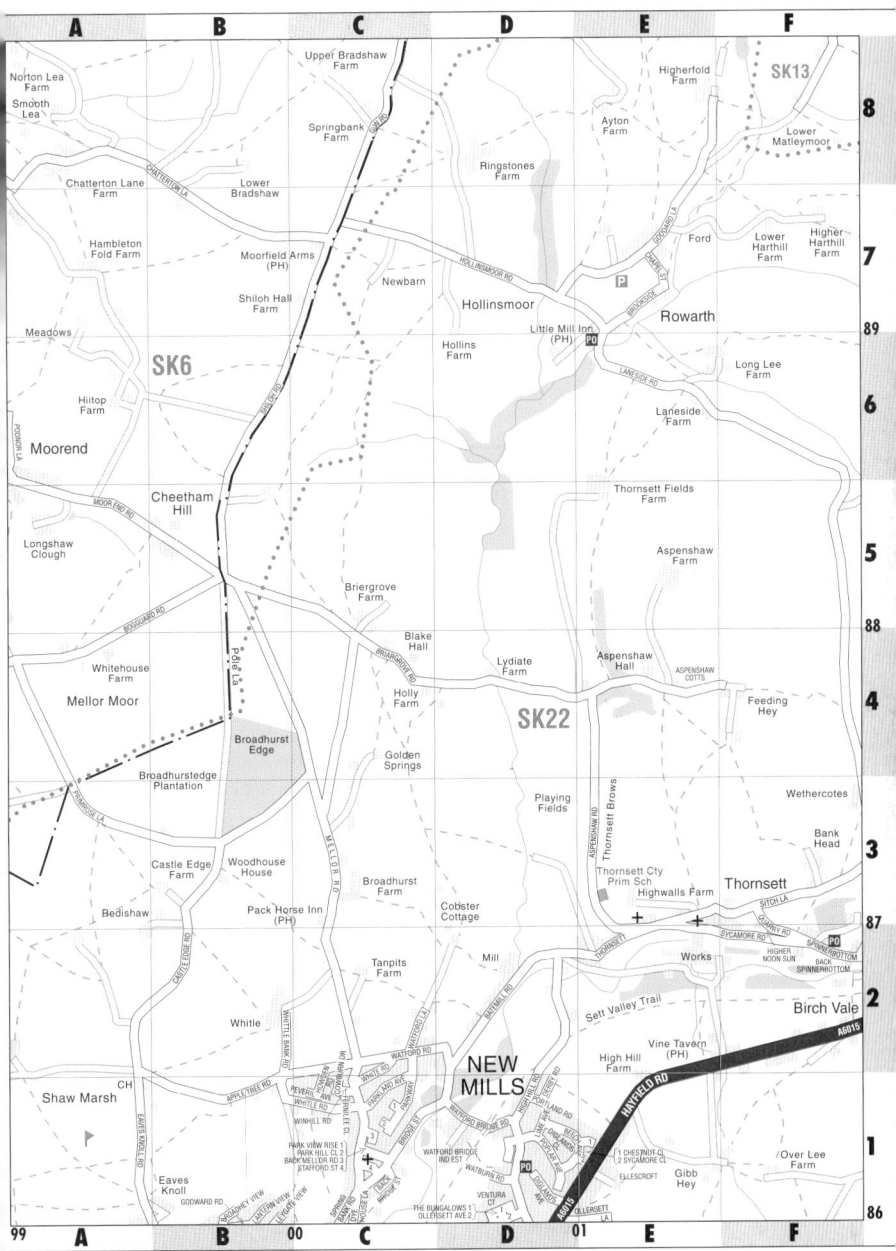

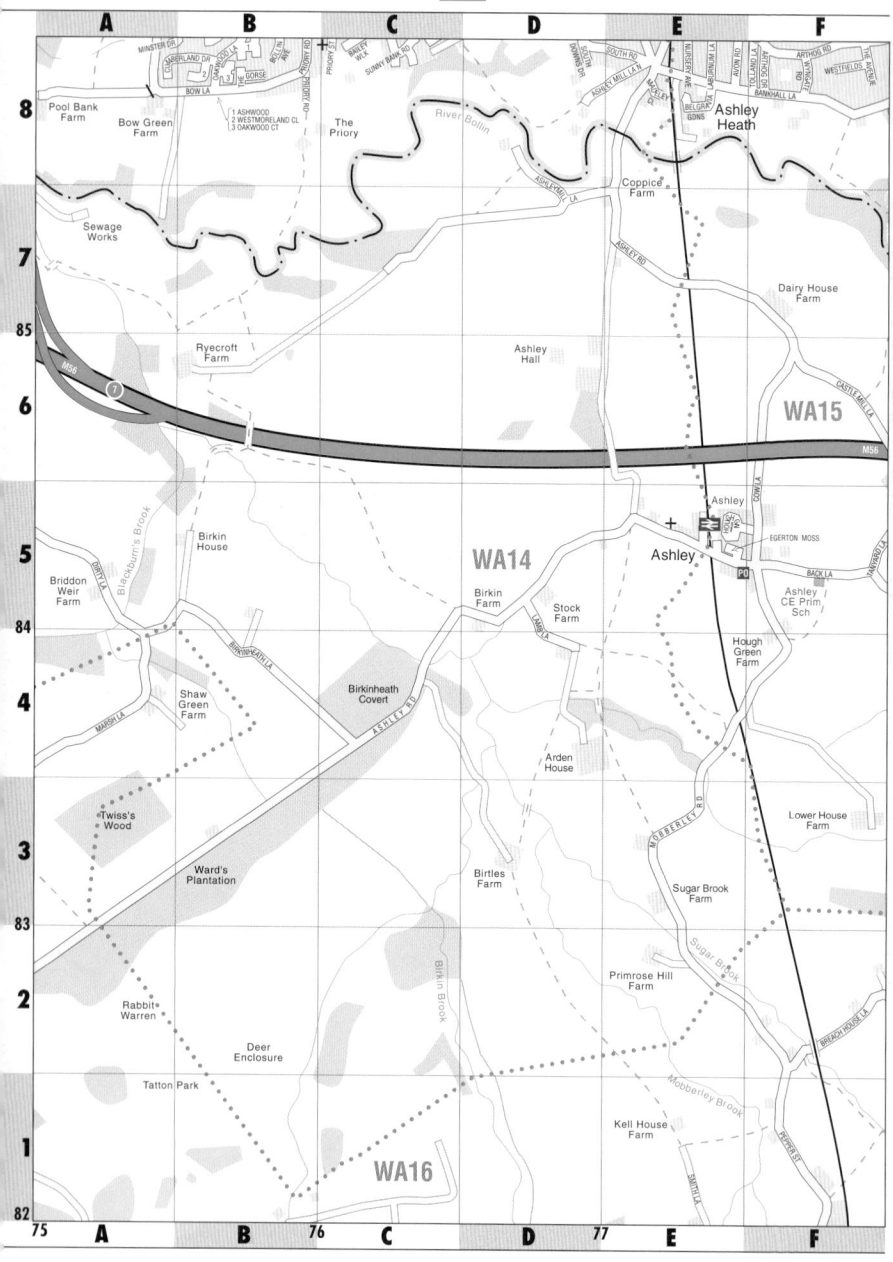

128

119

	A	**B**	**C**	**D**	**E**	**F**

8

Pool Bank Farm

Bow Green Farm

MINSTER DR

SUNDERLAND DR

GOLF LA

OLD HALL DR

BOW LA

PRIORY RD

1 ASHWOOD
2 WESTMORELAND CL
3 OAKWOOD CT

BAILEY
WLK

SUNNY BANK RD

The Priory

River Bollin

SOUTH RD

DOWNS DR

ASHLEY MILL LA S

NURSERY RD

PINGLEY

BELGRAVE GDNS

ARTHOG RD
WESTFIELDS AVE
BANKHALL LA
RING RD

Ashley Heath

7

Sewage Works

M56

Ryecroft Farm

ASHLEYHALL LA

Coppice Farm

ASHLEY RD

Dairy House Farm

85

6

M56

7

Ashley Hall

CASTLE MILL LA

M56

WA15

5

Briddon Weir Farm

TINTY LA

Blackburn's Brook

Birkin House

Ashley

Egerton Moss

Ashley

PO

BACK LA

Ashley CE Prim Sch

WA14

Birkin Farm

Stock Farm

LONG LA

K MOOR

YARDEN LA

84

4

MARSH LA

BIRKINHEATH LA

Shaw Green Farm

Birkinheath Covert

ASHLEY RD

Arden House

Hough Green Farm

MOBBERLEY RD

3

Twiss's Wood

Ward's Plantation

Birtles Farm

Sugar Brook Farm

Lower House Farm

83

2

Rabbit Warren

Deer Enclosure

Birkin Brook

Primrose Hill Farm

Sugar Brook

Mobberley Brook

BREACH HOUSE LA

1

Tatton Park

Kell House Farm

SMITH LA

PEDLEY LA

WA16

82

75	**A**	**B**	**76**	**C**	**D**	**77**	**E**	**F**

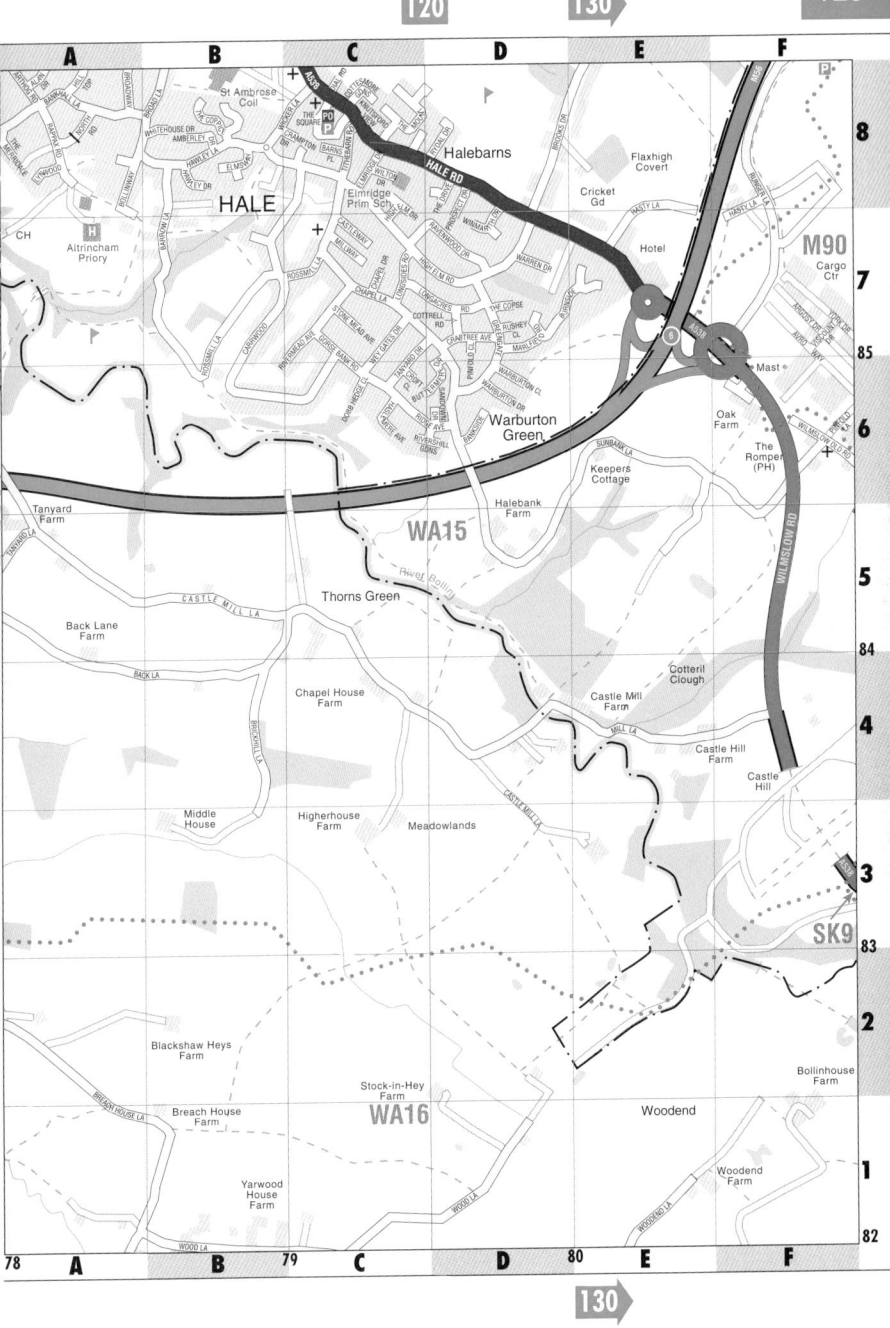

8

Halebarns

Flaxhigh
Covert

HALE

Cricket
Gd

St Ambrose
Coll

THE
SQUARE

HALE RD

Elmridge
Prim Sch

Hotel

M90
Cargo
Ctr

7

CH

Altrincham
Priory

85

Mast

6

Oak
Farm

WILMSLOW RD

The
Romper
(PH)

Warburton
Green

Tanyard
Farm

Keepers
Cottage

WA15

Halebank
Farm

River Bollin

5

Back Lane
Farm

CASTLE MILL LA

Thorns Green

Castle Mill
Farm

84

BACK LA

Cotteril
Clough

Chapel House
Farm

Castle Mill
Farm

Castle Hill
Farm

BRICKKILN LA

4

CASTLE MILL LA

Castle
Hill

Middle
House

Higherhouse
Farm

Meadowlands

SK9

3

83

Blackshaw Heys
Farm

Bollinhouse
Farm

2

Stock-in-Hey
Farm

BREACH HOUSE LA

Breach House
Farm

WA16

Woodend

Woodend
Farm

1

Yarwood
House
Farm

WOOD LA

WOODEND LA

82

78

A

B

79

C

D

80

E

F

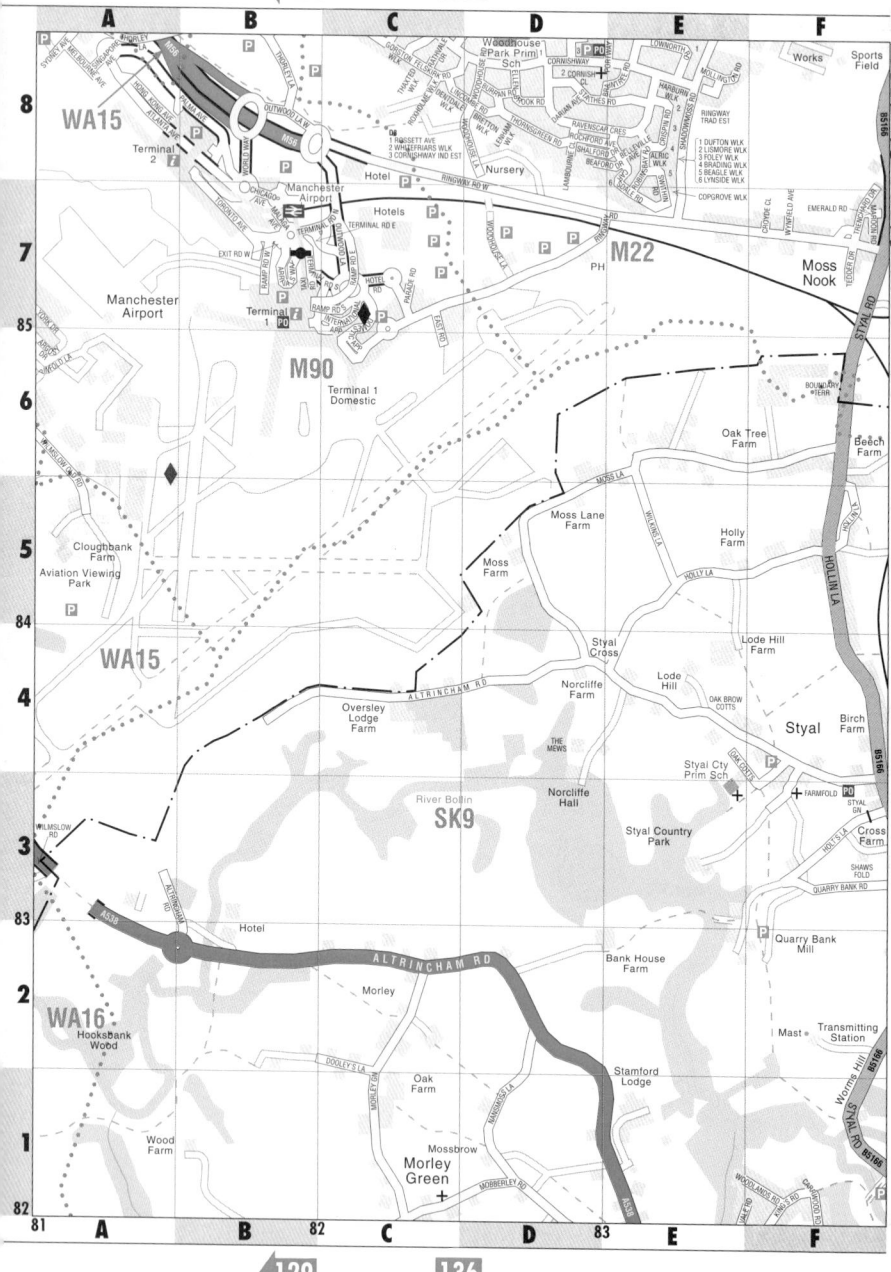

WA15

Terminal 2

Manchester Airport

M90

Terminal 1 Domestic

WA15

Cloughbank Farm

Aviation Viewing Park

Manchester Airport

Terminal 1

Woodhouse Park Prim Sch

CORNISHWAY

Nursery

Hotel

Hotels

1 ROSSETT AVE
2 WHITEFRIARS WLK
3 CORNISHWAY IND EST

RINGWAY RD W

PH

M22

RINGWAY TRAD EST

1 DUFTON WLK
2 LISMORE WLK
3 FOLEY WLK
4 BRADING WLK
5 BEAGLE WLK
6 LYNSIDE WLK

COPGROVE WLK

Works

Sports Field

Moss Nook

EMERALD RD

B5166

Oak Tree Farm

Beech Farm

Moss Lane Farm

Holly Farm

Moss Farm

Moss Farm

MOSS LA

HOLLY LA

HOLLIN LA

Lode Hill Farm

Styal Cross

Norcliffe Farm

Lode Hill

OAK BROW COTTS

Styal

Birch Farm

B5166

Oversley Lodge Farm

ALTRINCHAM RD

THE MEWS

Styal Ctry Prim Sch

FARMFOLD

Cross Fold

STYAL GN

River Bollin

SK9

Norcliffe Hall

Styal Country Park

SHAWS FOLD

QUARRY BANK RD

WILMSLOW RD

Hotel

A538

ALTRINCHAM RD

Bank House Farm

Quarry Bank Mill

WA16

Hooksbank Wood

Morley

DOOLEY'S LA

Oak Farm

MOBBERLEY LA

Stamford Lodge

Mast

Transmitting Station

Worms Hill

STYAL RD B5166

Wood Farm

Mossbrow

Morley Green

MOBBERLEY RD

WOODLANDS RD

CARRWOOD RD

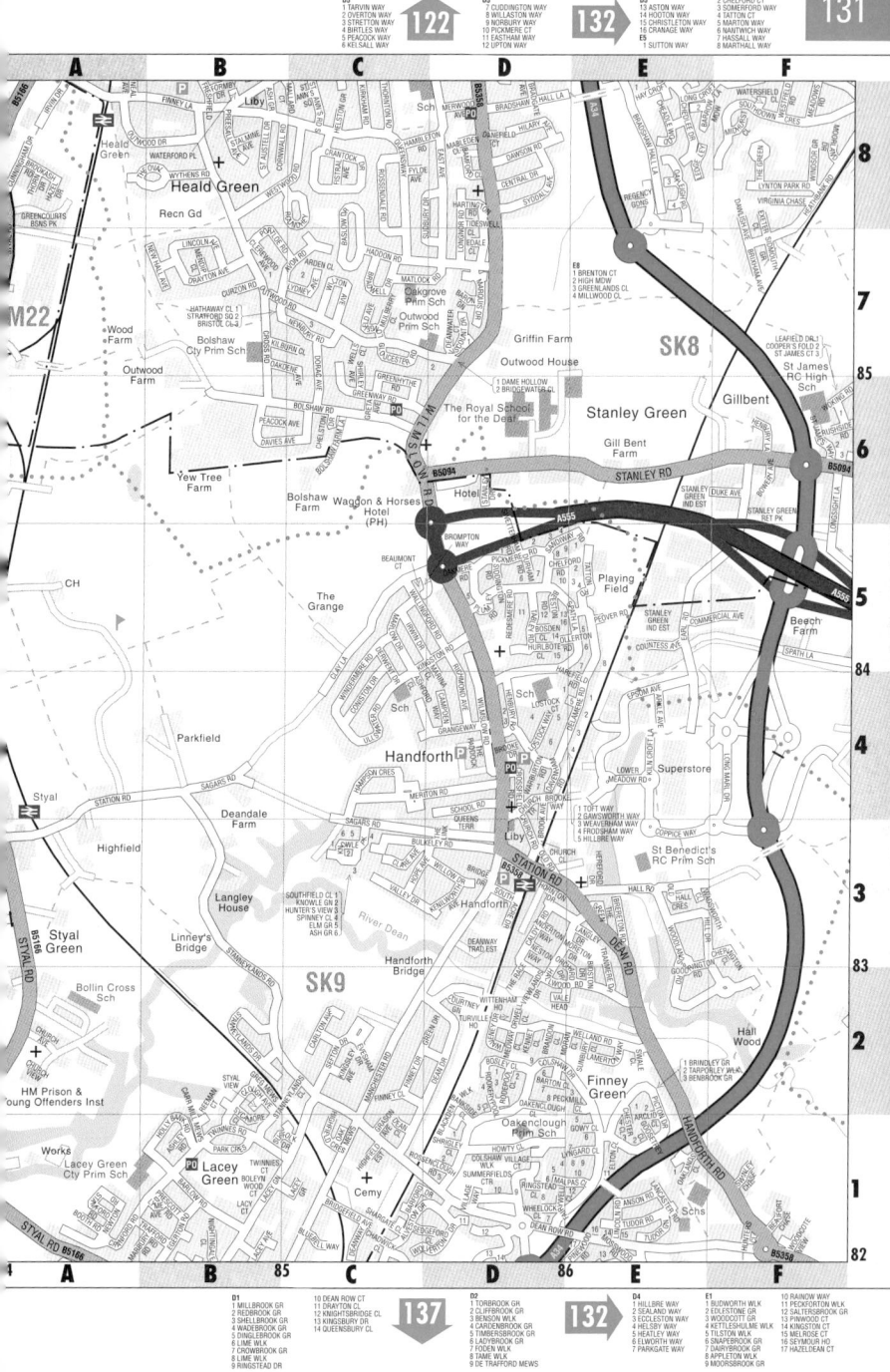

122

D5
1 TARVIN WAY
2 OVERTON WAY
3 STRETTON WAY
4 BIRTLES WAY
5 PEACOCK WAY
6 KELSALL WAY

132

D5
7 CUDDINGTON WAY
8 WILLASTON WAY
9 NORBURY WAY
10 PICKMERE CT
11 EASTHAM WAY
12 UPTON WAY

D5
13 ASTON WAY
14 HOOTON WAY
15 CHRISTLETON WAY
16 CRANAGE WAY
E5
17 SUTTON WAY

2 CHELFORD CT
3 SOMERFORD WAY
4 TATTON CT
5 MARTON WAY
6 NANTWICH WAY
7 HASSALL WAY
8 MARTHALL WAY

137

D1
1 MILLBROOK GR
2 REDBROOK GR
3 SHELLBROOK GR
4 WADEBROOK GR
5 DINGLEBROOK GR
6 LIME WLK
7 CROWBROOK GR
8 LIME WLK
9 RINGSTEAD DR

10 DEAN ROW CT
11 DRAYTON CL
12 KNIGHTSBRIDGE CL
13 KINGSBURY DR
14 QUEENSBURY CL

132

D2
1 TORBROOK GR
2 CLIFBROOK GR
3 BENSON WLK
4 CARDENBROOK GR
5 TIMBERBROOK GR
6 LADYBROOK GR
7 PEOVER WLK
8 TAME WLK
9 DE TRAFFORD MEWS

D4
1 HILLBRE WAY
2 SEALAND WAY
3 ECCLESTON WAY
4 HELSBY WAY
5 HEATLEY WAY
6 ELWORTH WAY
7 PARKGATE WAY

E1
1 BUDWORTH WLK
2 EDLESTONE GR
3 WOODCOTT GR
4 KETTLESHULME WLK
5 TILSTON WLK
6 SNAPEBROOK GR
7 DAIRYBROOK GR
8 MOORSBROOK GR

11 RAINOW WAY
12 SALTERSBROOK GR
13 PINWOOD CT
14 KINGSTON CT
15 MELROSE CT
16 SEYMOUR HO
17 HAZELDEAN CT

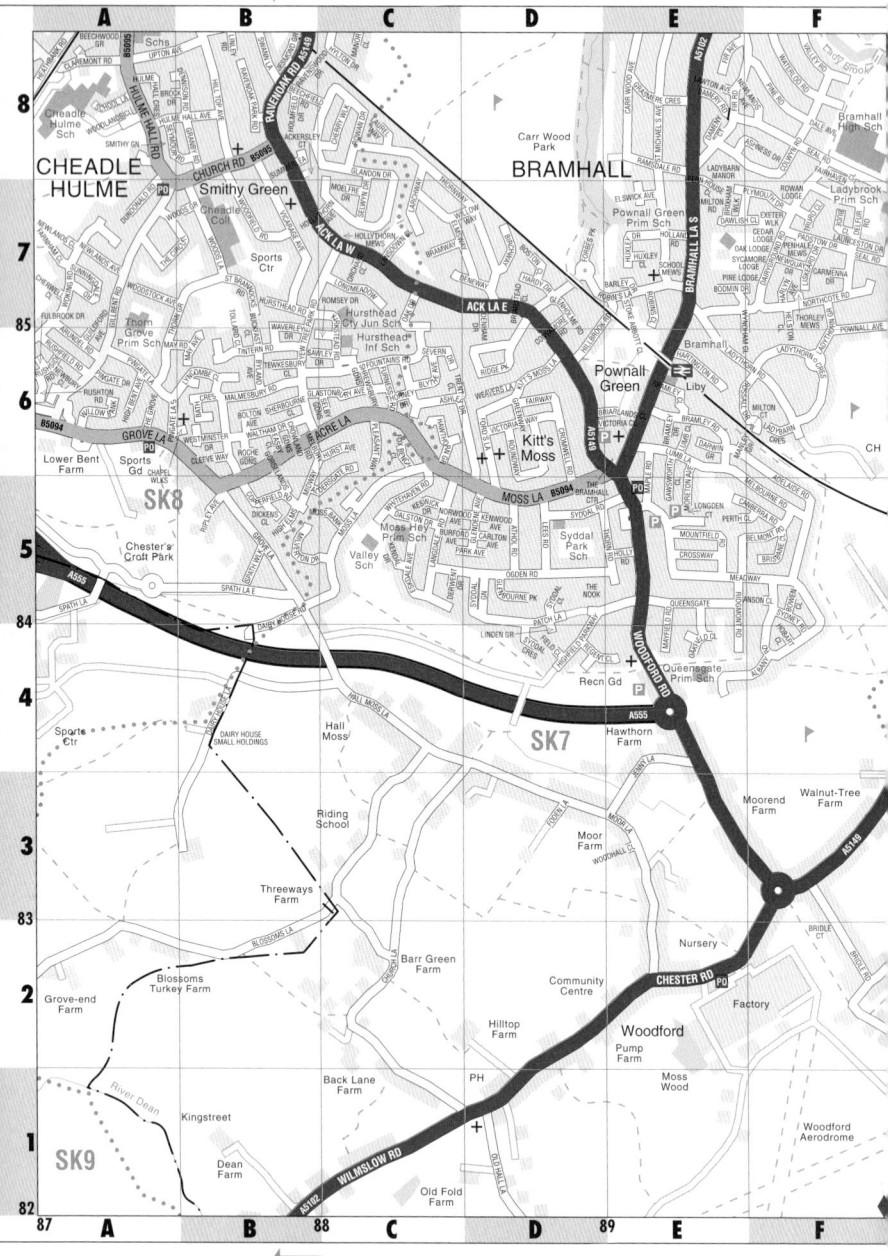

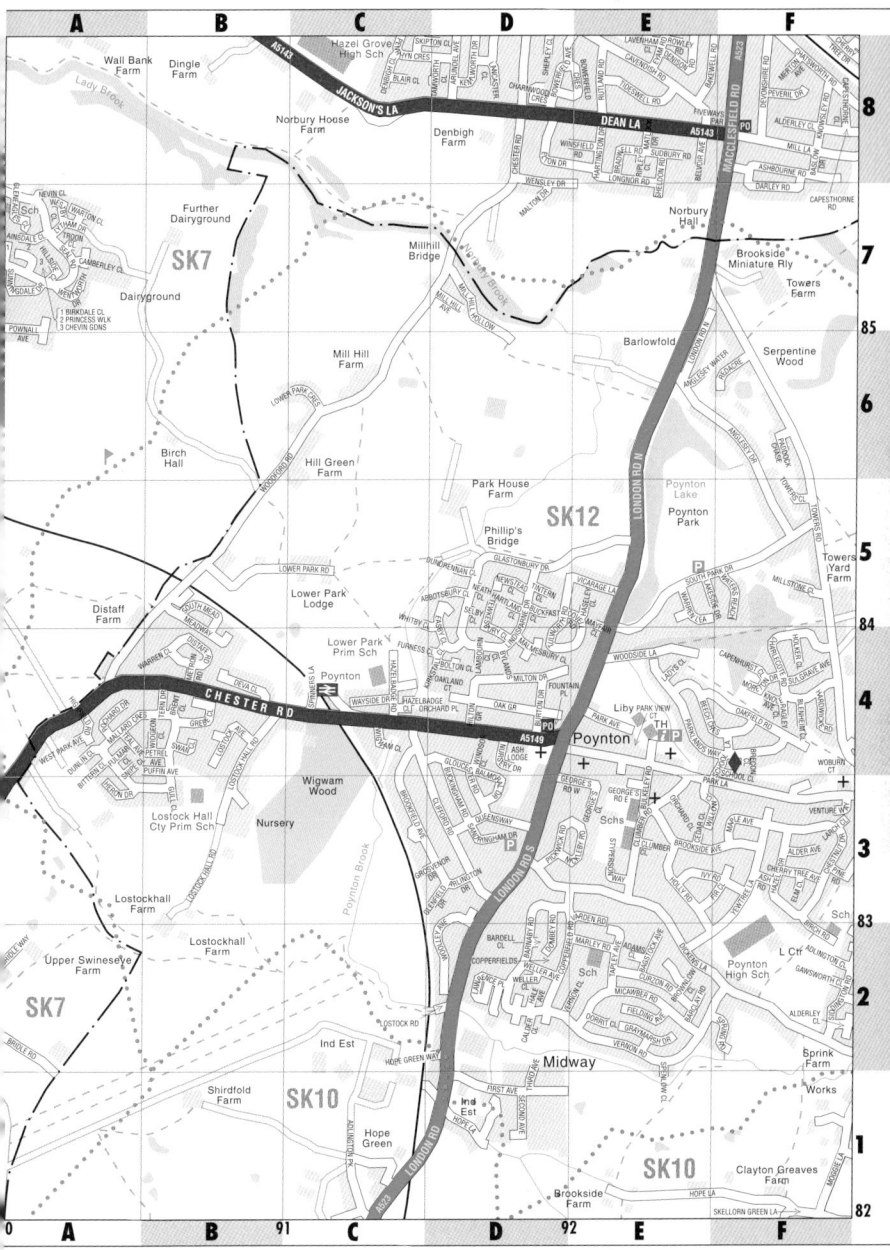

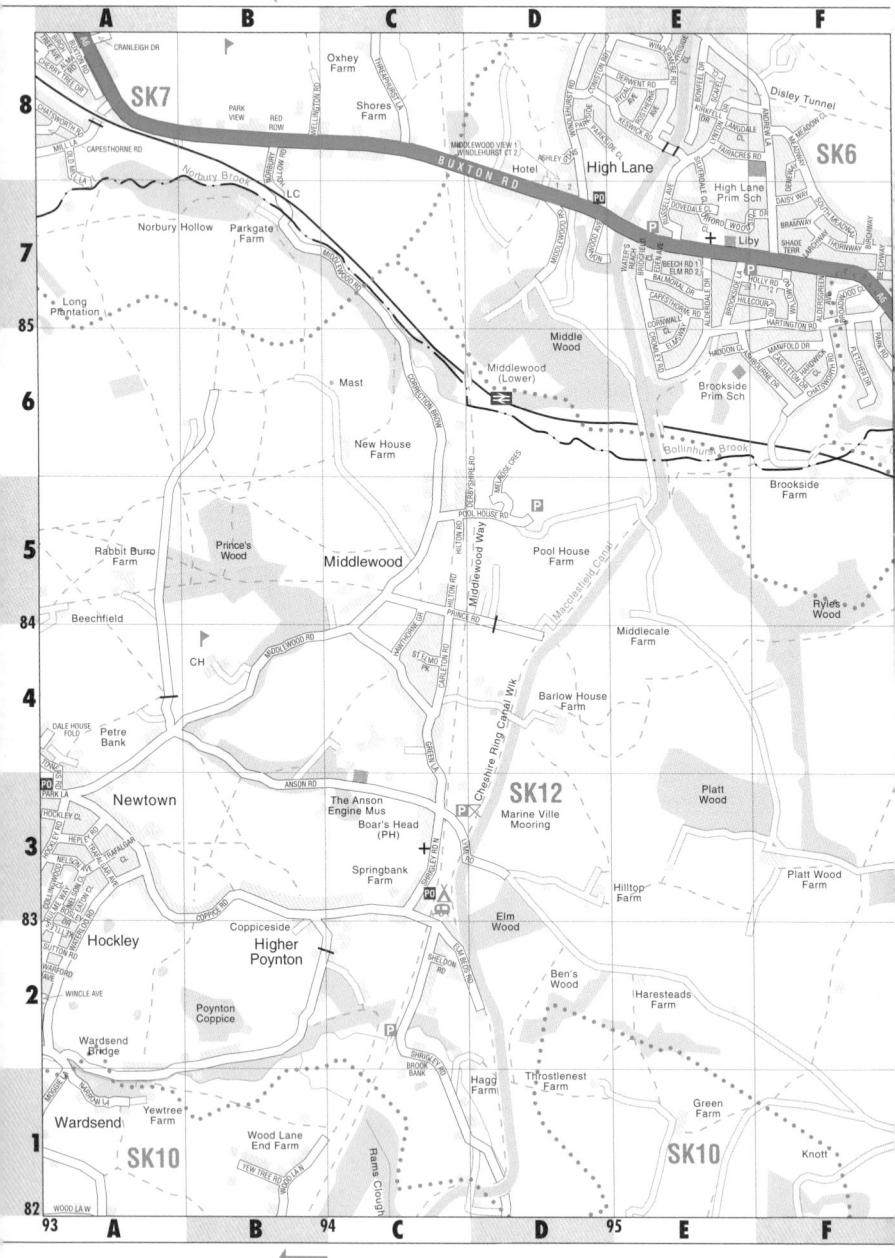

SK7

SK6

SK12

SK10

SK10

High Lane

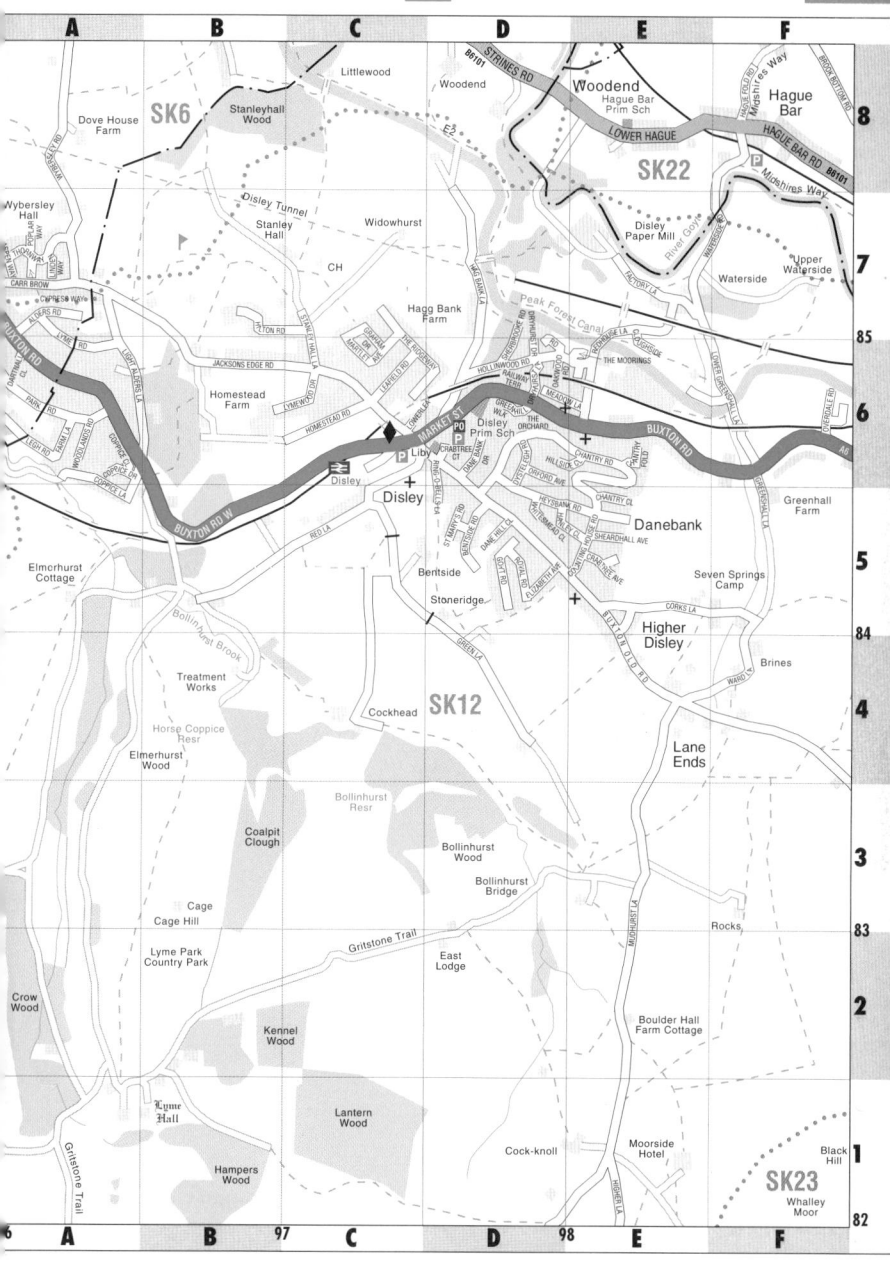

A B C D E F

8

Littlewood

Woodend

STRINES RD
B6101

Woodend
Hague Bar
Prim Sch

Hague
Bar

SK6

Dove House
Farm

Stanleyhall
Wood

LOWER HAGUE

SK22

Midshires Way

HAGUE BAR RD B6101

Wybersley
Hall

Disley Tunnel

E3

Widowhurst

Stanley
Hall

Disley
Paper Mill

River Goyt

Upper
Waterside

7

CARR BROW

CHINLEY WAVE

CYPRESS WAVE

CH

Midshires Way

Waterside

85

Hagg Bank
Farm

Peak Forest Canal

THE MOORINGS

BUXTON RD

JACKSONS EDGE RD

Homestead
Farm

RAILWAY RD

Disley
Prim Sch

THE ORCHARD

Greenhall
Farm

6

HOMESTEAD RD

MARKET ST

Liby

P

Disley

Danebank

Greenhall
Farm

Elmerhurst
Cottage

BUXTON RD W

RED LA

Bertside

Stoneridge

Seven Springs
Camp

5

Bollinhurst Brook

Treatment
Works

Cockhead

GREEN LA

SK12

Higher
Disley

Brines

84

Horse Coppice
Resr

4

Elmerhurst
Wood

Lane
Ends

Bollinhurst
Resr

Coalpit
Clough

Bollinhurst
Wood

Bollinhurst
Bridge

3

Rocks

83

Cage
Cage Hill

Gritstone Trail

East
Lodge

Boulder Hall
Farm Cottage

Crow
Wood

Lyme Park
Country Park

2

Kennel
Wood

Lyme
Hall

Lantern
Wood

Cock-knoll

Moorside
Hotel

Black
Hill

1

Gritstone Trail

Hampers
Wood

SK23

Whalley
Moor

82

6 A B 97 C D 98 E F

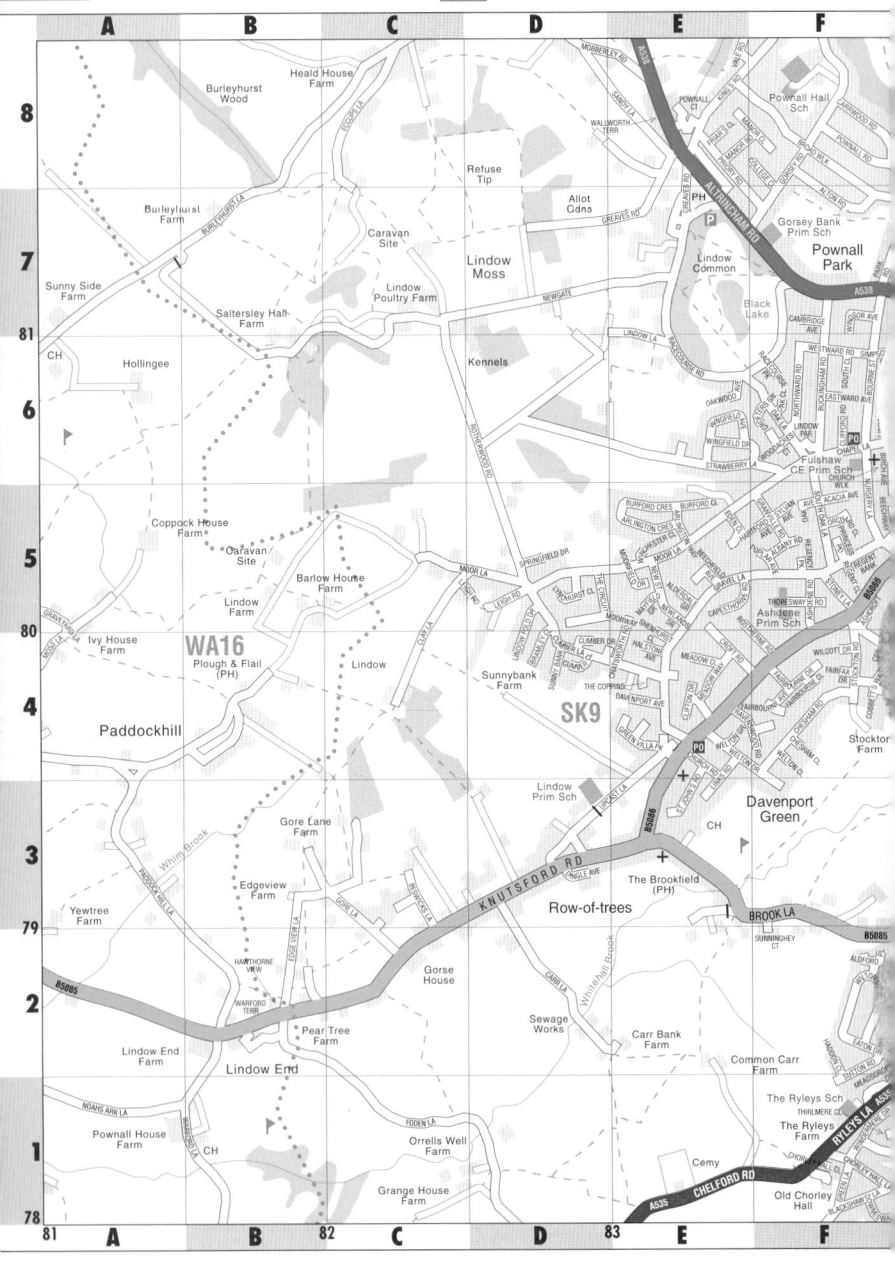

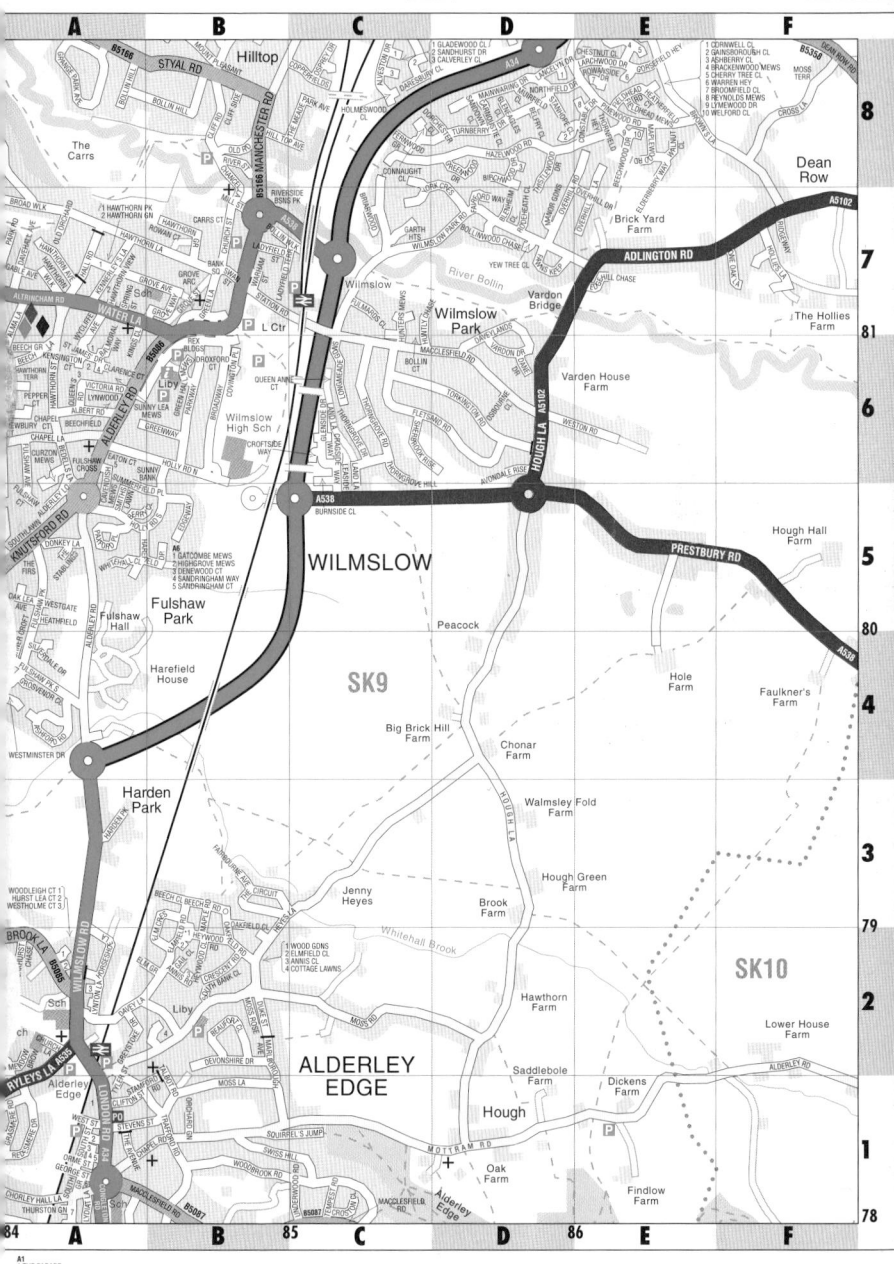

A1
1 THE PARADE
2 BROWN ST
3 GREEN ST
4 MASSEY ST
5 CHAPEL ST
6 HUBERT WORTHINGTON HO
7 CARLISLE ST

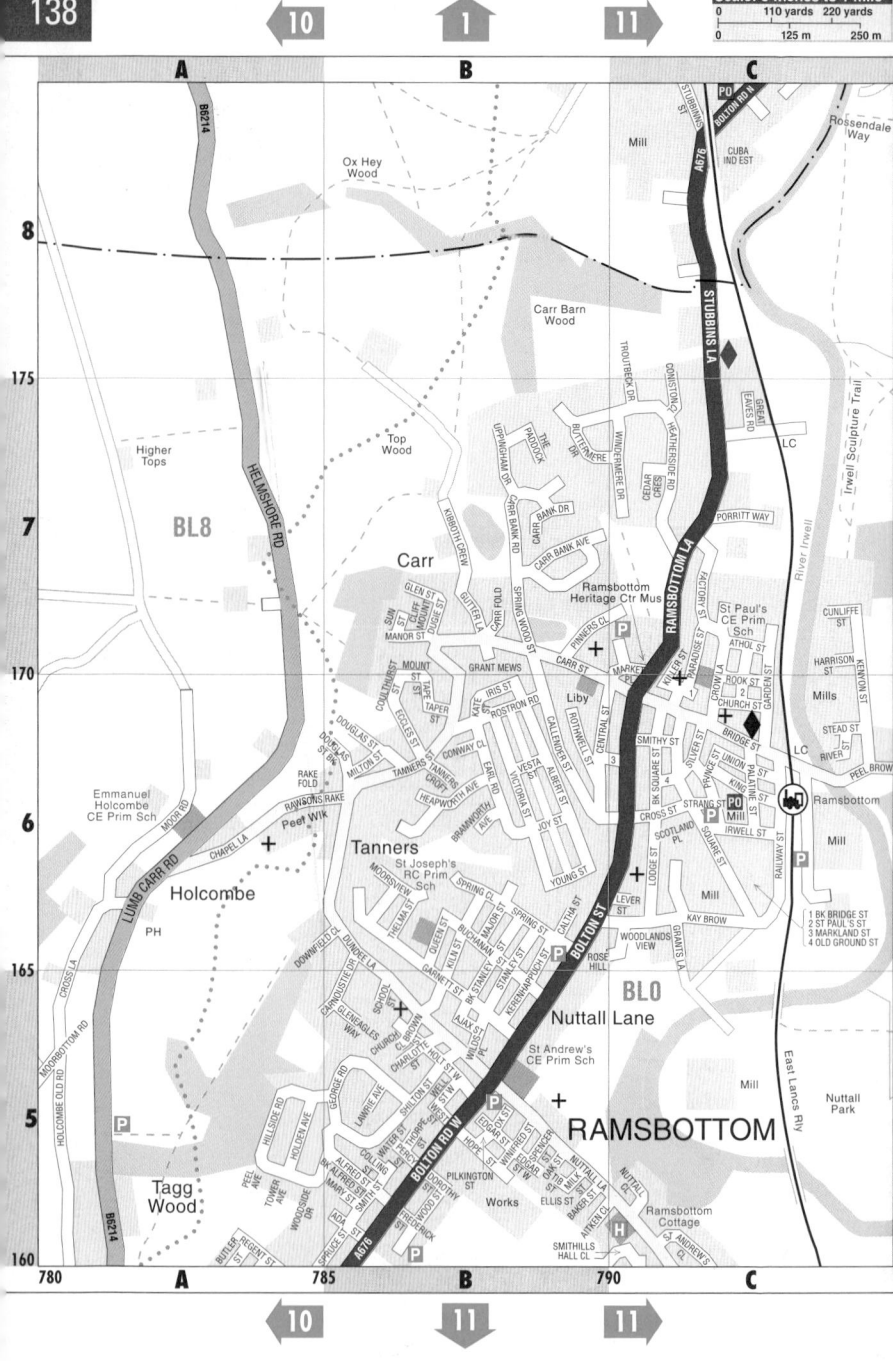

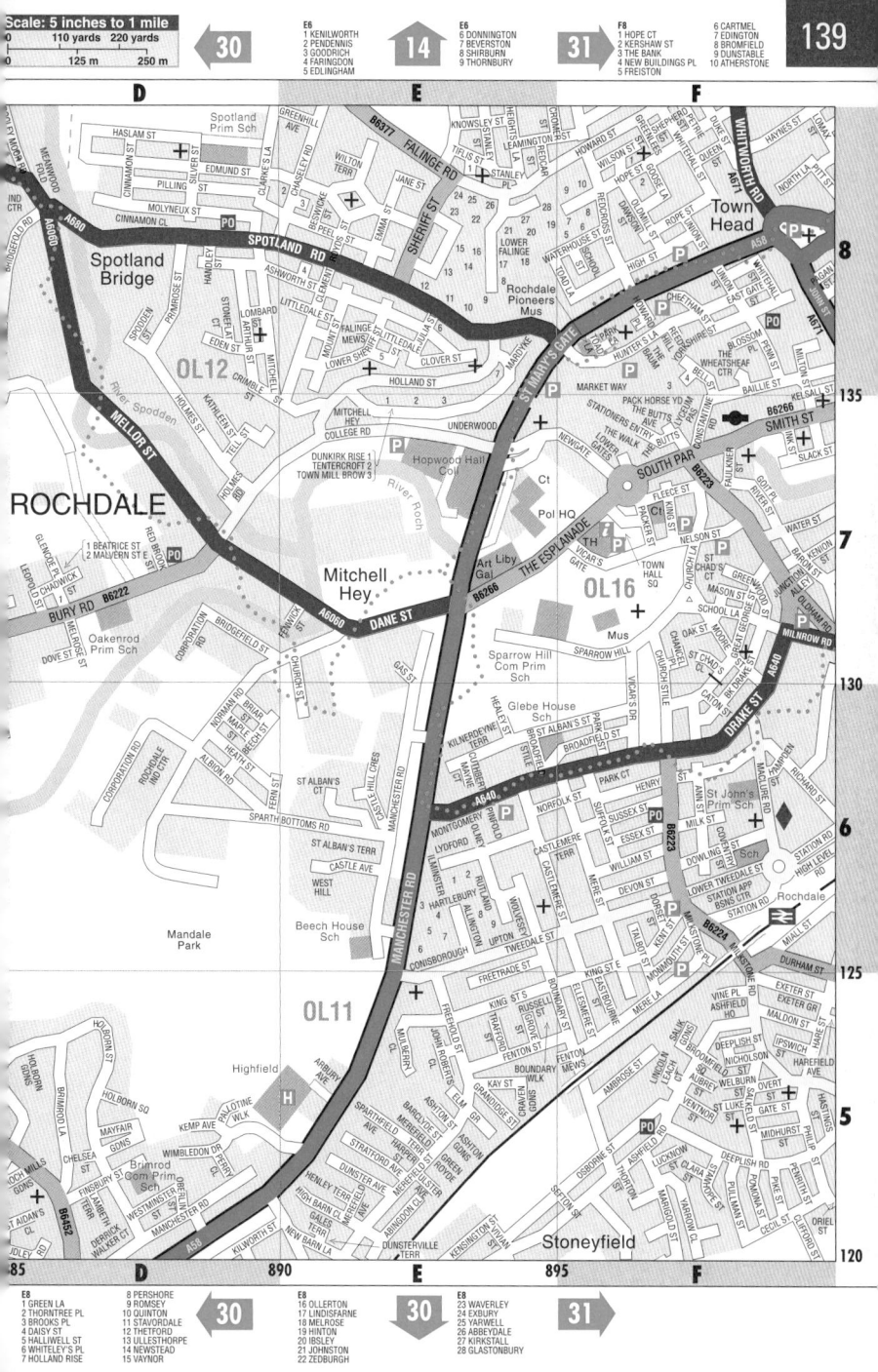

Scale: 5 inches to 1 mile
0   110 yards   220 yards
0   125 m   250 m

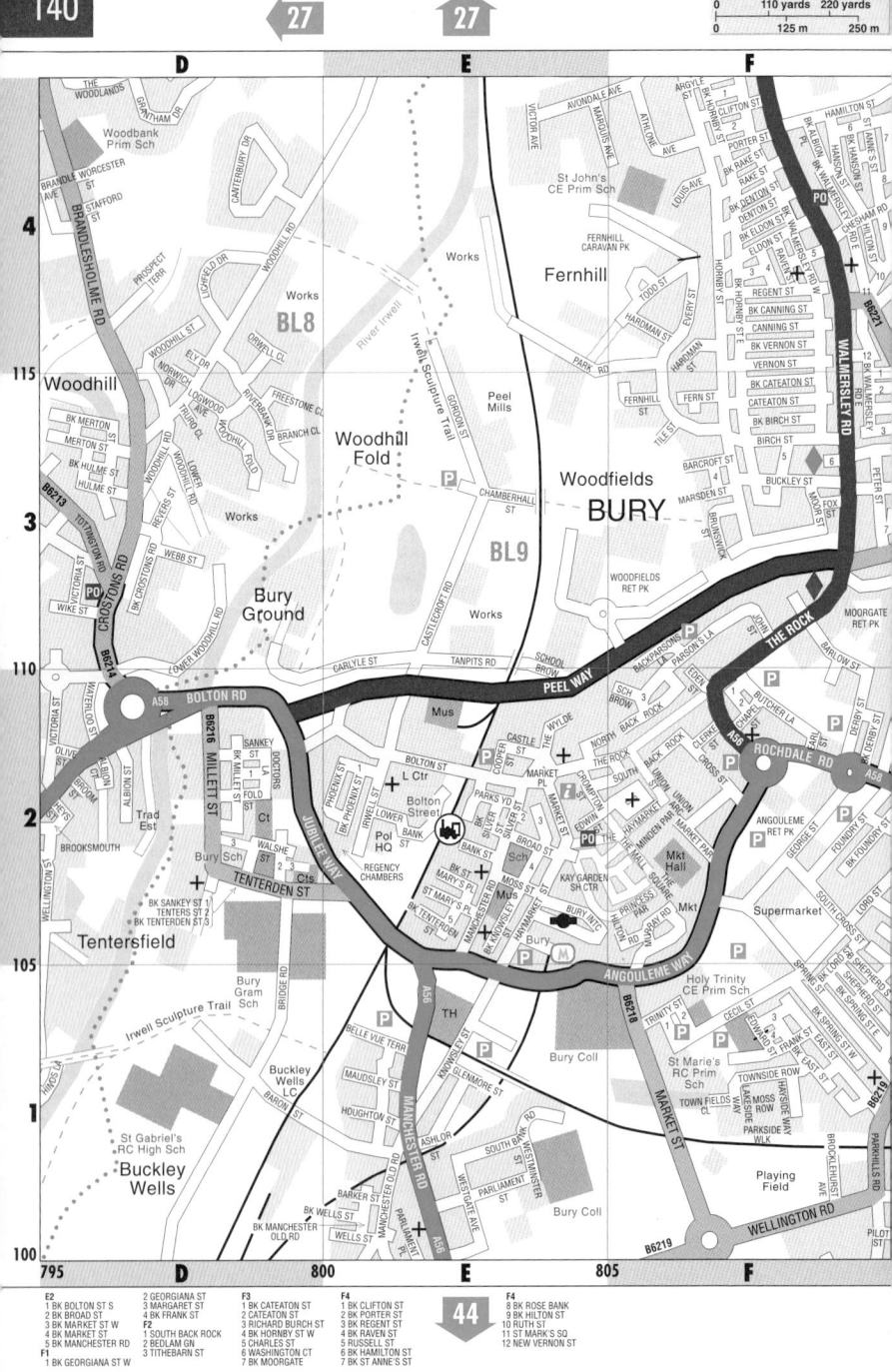

E2
1 BK BOLTON ST S
2 BK BROAD ST
3 BK MARKET ST W
4 BK MARKET ST
5 BK MANCHESTER RD

F1
1 BK GEORGIANA ST W

2 GEORGIANA ST
3 MARGARET ST
4 BK FRANK ST

F2
1 SOUTH BACK ROCK
2 BEDLAM GN
3 TITHEBARN ST

F3
1 BK CATEATON ST
2 CATEATON ST
3 RICHARD BURCH ST
4 BK HORNBY ST W
5 CHARLES ST
6 WASHINGTON CT
7 BK MOORGATE

F4
1 BK CLIFTON ST
2 BK PORTER ST
3 BK REGENT ST
4 BK RAVEN ST
5 RUSSELL ST
6 BK HAMILTON ST
7 BK ST ANNE'S ST

F4
8 BK ROSE BANK
9 BK HILTON ST
10 RUTH ST
11 ST MARK'S SQ
12 NEW VERNON ST

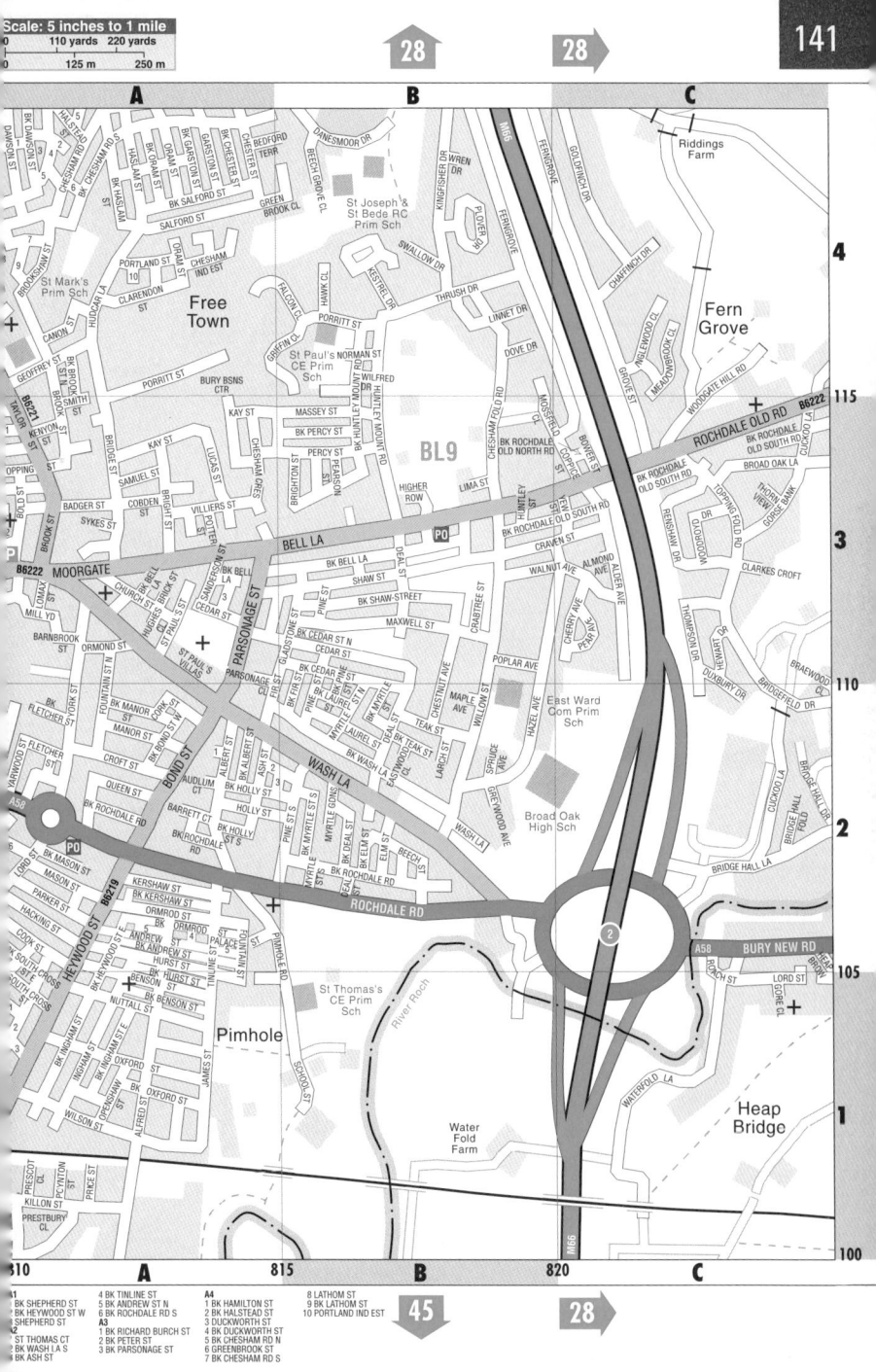

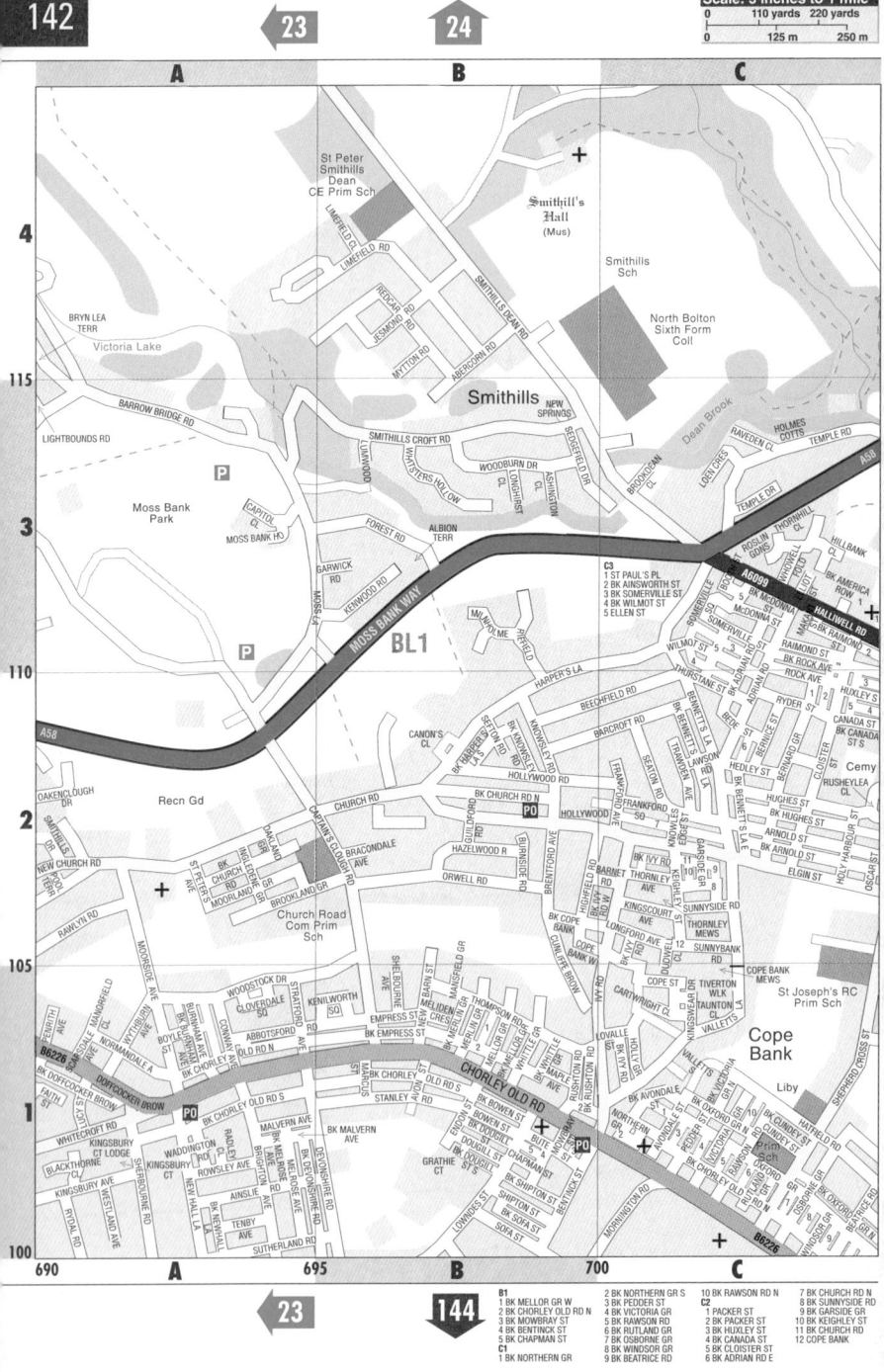

Scale: 5 inches to 1 mile

B1
1 BK MELLOR GR W
2 BK CHORLEY OLD RD N
3 BK MOWBRAY ST
4 BK BENTINCK ST
5 BK CHAPMAN ST

C1
1 BK NORTHERN GR

2 BK NORTHERN GR S
3 BK PEDDER ST
4 BK VICTORIA ST
5 BK RAWSON RD
6 BK RUTLAND ST
7 BK OSBORNE GR
8 BK WINDSOR GR
9 BK BEATRICE RD

10 BK RAWSON RD N

C2
1 PACKER ST
2 BK PACKER ST
3 BK HUXLEY ST
4 BK CANADA ST
5 BK CLOISTER ST
6 BK ADRIAN RD E

7 BK CHURCH RD N
8 BK SUNNYSIDE RD
9 BK GARSIDE GR
10 BK KEIGHLEY ST
11 BK CHURCH RD
12 COPE BANK

D2
1 WORDSWORTH TRAD EST
2 BK ESKRICK ST E
3 BK CHAUCER ST
4 BK LYTTON ST
5 MILES ST

6 BK GLEN BOTT ST
7 BK ESKRICK ST E
8 BK FRANCES ST
9 BK GROVE ST
10 BK ST THOMAS ST E
11 BK DARWIN ST

D2
12 ST JOSEPH ST
13 BK BOUNDARY ST
14 HALLIWELL ST
15 BK HAYON ST
16 BK UTTLEY ST

17 BK HALLIWELL RD S
18 BK ST AUGUSTINE ST
19 BK ESKRICK ST
20 BK CARL ST
21 BK WAPPING ST
22 BK WORDSWORTH ST

23 BK VICKERMAN ST
24 RUSHEY FOLD CT
25 BK AINSWORTH ST

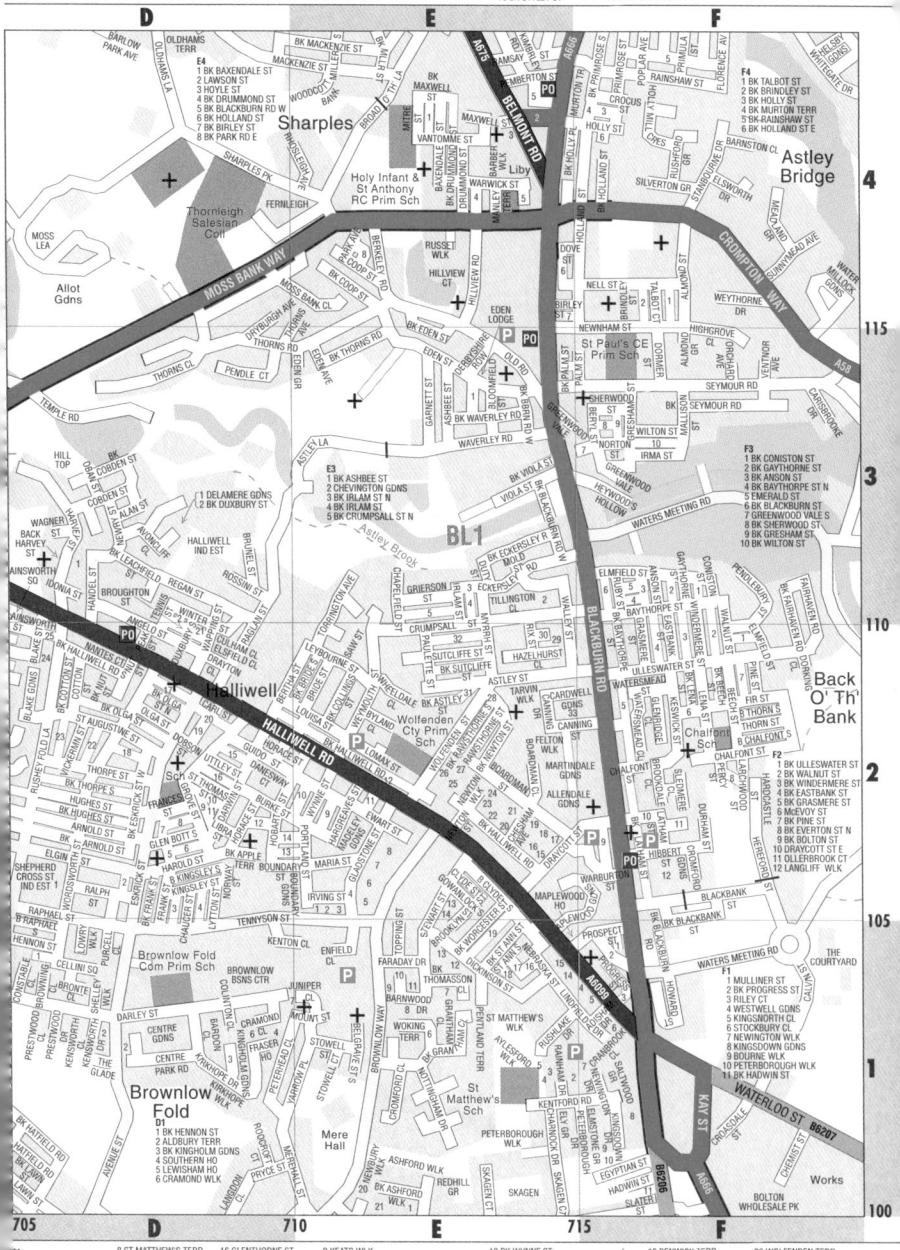

E1
1 MIDHURST CL
2 RAINHAM GR
3 WOODCHURCH CL
4 WESTMARSH CL
5 MOUNTFIELD WLK
6 BK WOKING GDNS
7 THOMASSON CL

8 ST MATTHEW'S TERR
9 FOSTER TERR
10 BARNWOOD CL
11 BARNWOOD CL
12 DICKINSON TERR
13 DICKINSON CL
14 HIGHBROOK GR
15 FERNHURST GR

16 GLENTHORNE ST
17 BK NEVADA ST
18 NEVADA ST
19 WORCESTER ST
20 SHAFTSBURY CL
21 FARNHAM CL
E2
1 IRVING HOUSE

2 KEATS WLK
3 TENNYSON WLK
4 BELGRAVE ST
5 BELGRAVE GDNS
6 GLADSTONE CL
7 LONGTOWN GDNS
8 WHITCHURCH GDNS
9 BK HARGREAVES ST

10 BK WYNNE ST
11 BK EWART ST
12 MARSH ST
13 BK STEWART ST
14 BOSTON ST
15 WITNEY CL
16 WATFORD CL
17 WESTWICK TERR

18 BENWICK TERR
19 YORK TERR
20 CHESTER WLK
21 HUNTINGDON WLK
22 LANCASTER WLK
23 NEWTON TERR
24 LANCASTER TERR
25 KEMPSTON GDNS

26 WOLFENDEN TERR
27 TANWORTH WLK
28 CHARLOTTE ST
29 HOLYHURST WLK
30 PENWOOD CL
31 BK WOLFENDEN ST
32 BK CRUMPSALL ST
33 BK CARDWELL ST

145

25

Scale: 5 inches to 1 mile

| 0 | 110 yards | 220 yards |
| 0 | 125 m | 250 m |

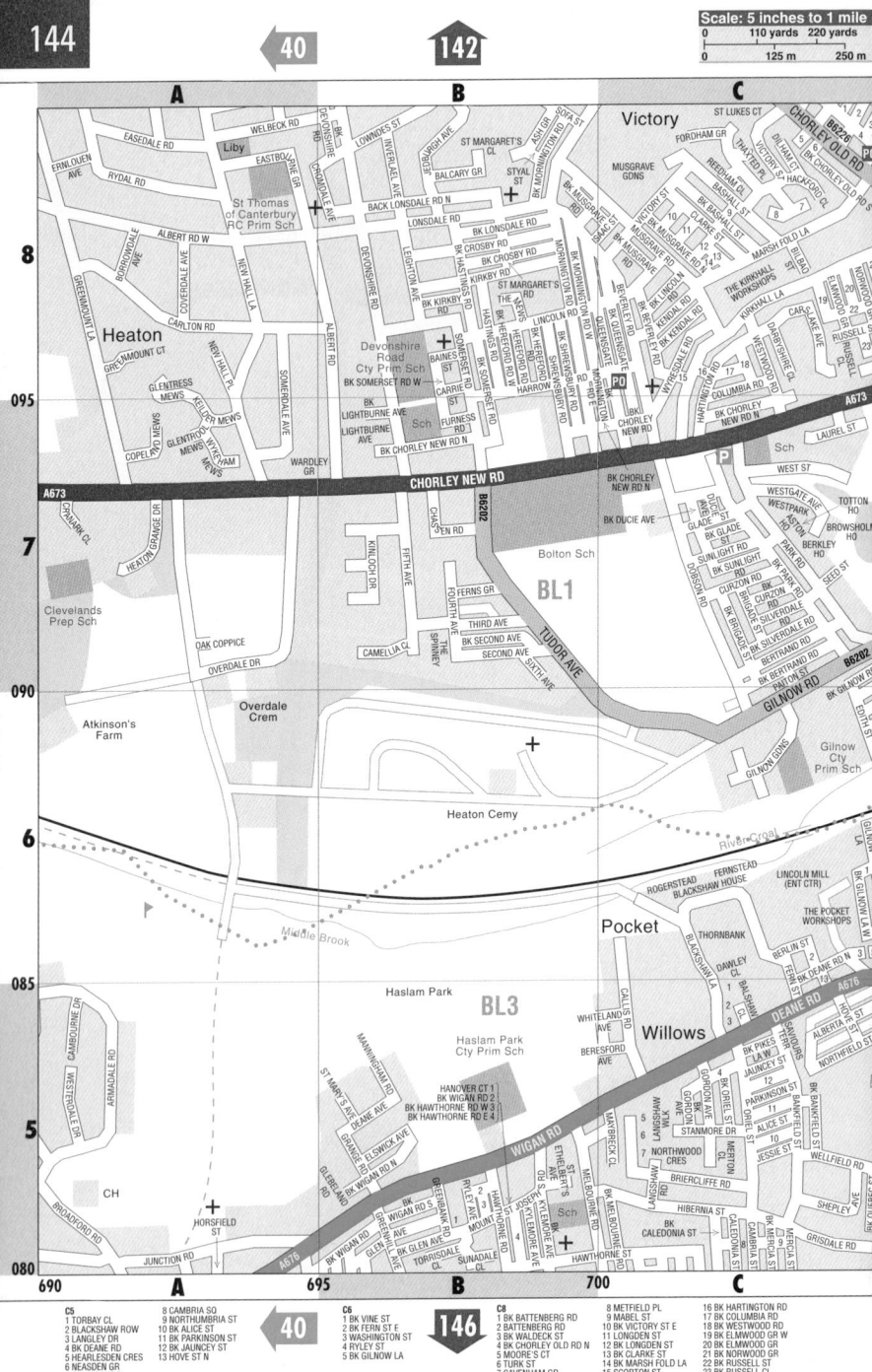

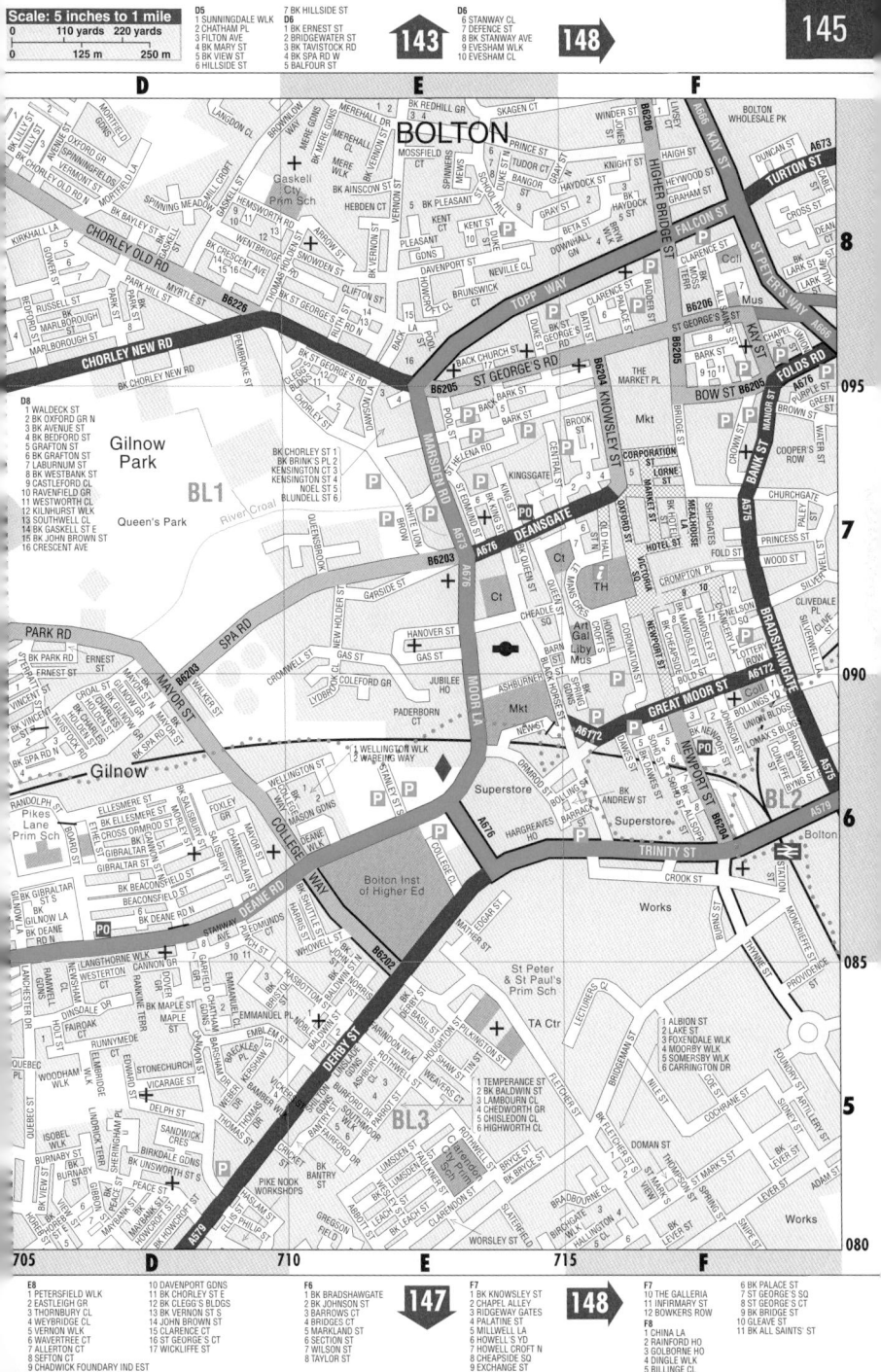

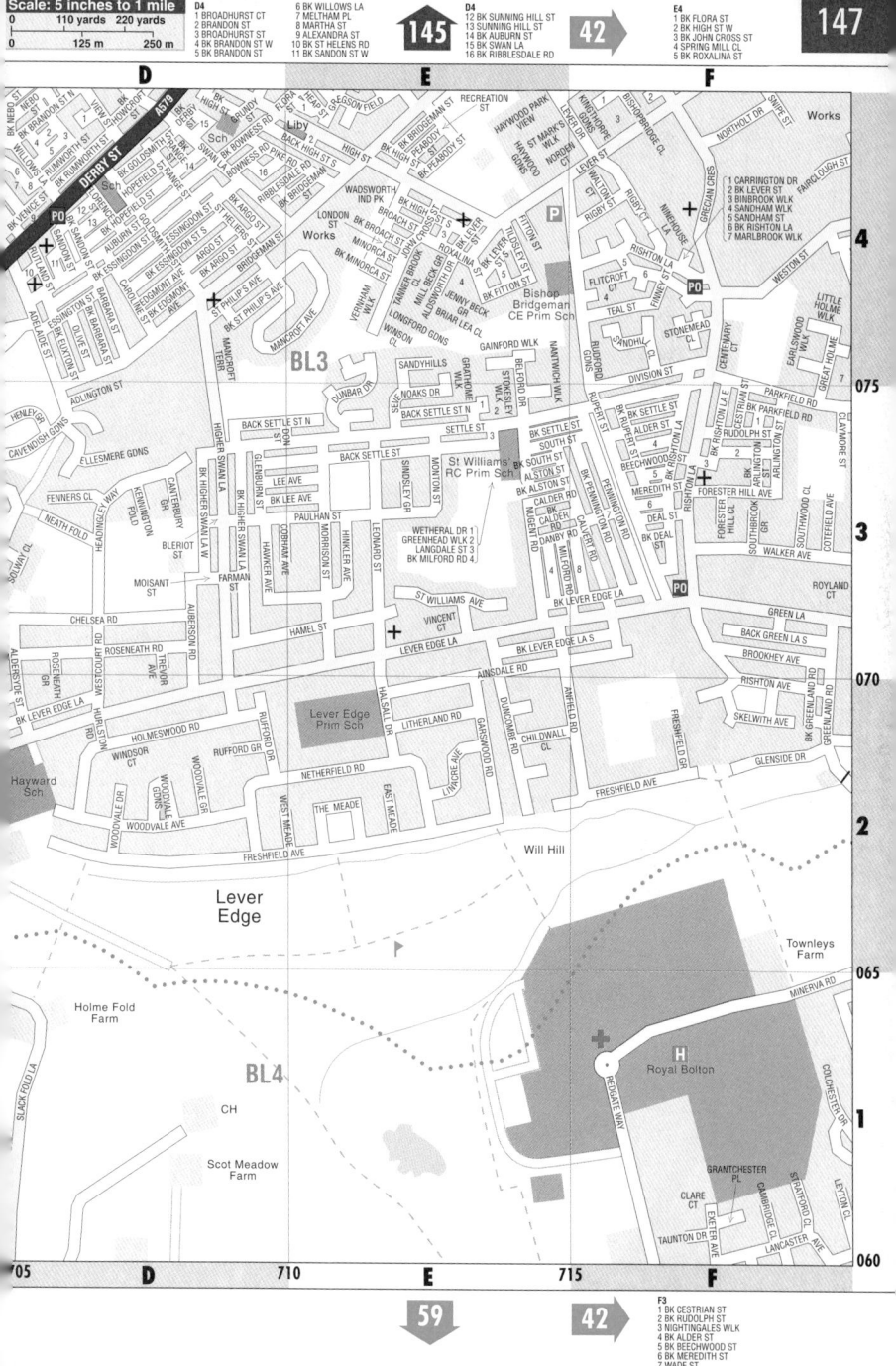

145
25
42

Scale: 5 inches to 1 mile
0   110 yards   220 yards
0   125 m   250 m

A   B   C

145
42
42

A6
1 COCKERELL SPRINGS
2 BK LOWER BRIDGEMAN ST
3 TURNSTONE RD
4 BK BRADFORD ST S
A7
1 THORNTON ST
2 BK BURY OLD RD

3 GLOSTER ST
4 BK CASTLE ST
A8
1 TURTON HOUSE
2 CHARLES ST
3 KESTREL ST
B7
1 BK RADCLIFFE RD E

B7
2 FAWCETT ST
3 BK BURY RD S
4 WESLEY MEWS
C7
1 BK DUNSTAN ST
2 SACKVILLE ST
3 CHURCHILL ST

C7
4 COLENSO CT
5 BK HENGIST ST
6 BK EDDITCH GR N
7 TOMLIN SQ
8 BK CLARENDON RD
9 BK SOUTH VIEW ST

C8
1 ROSSALL ST
2 PRESALL ST
3 BARNARD ST

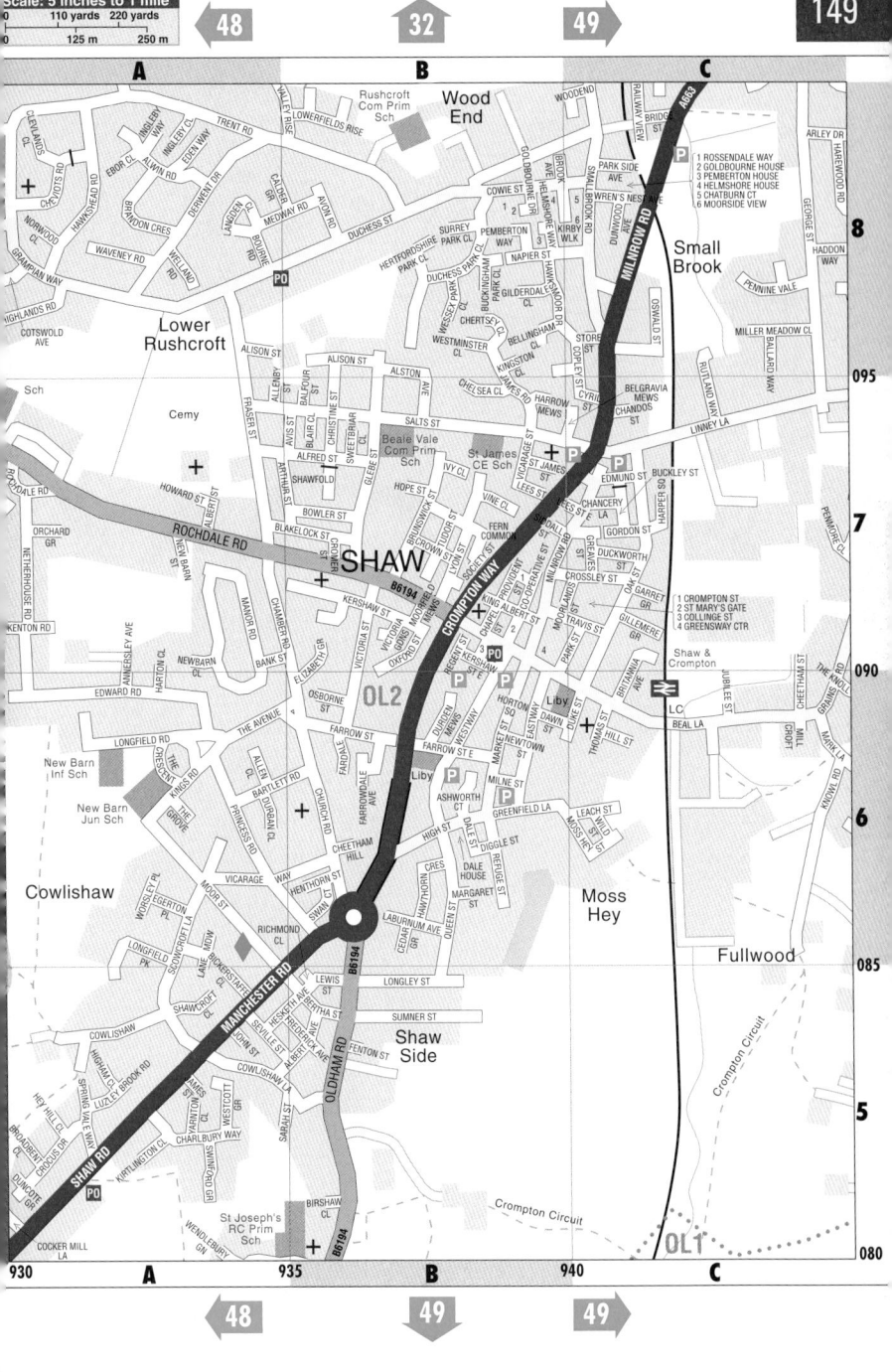

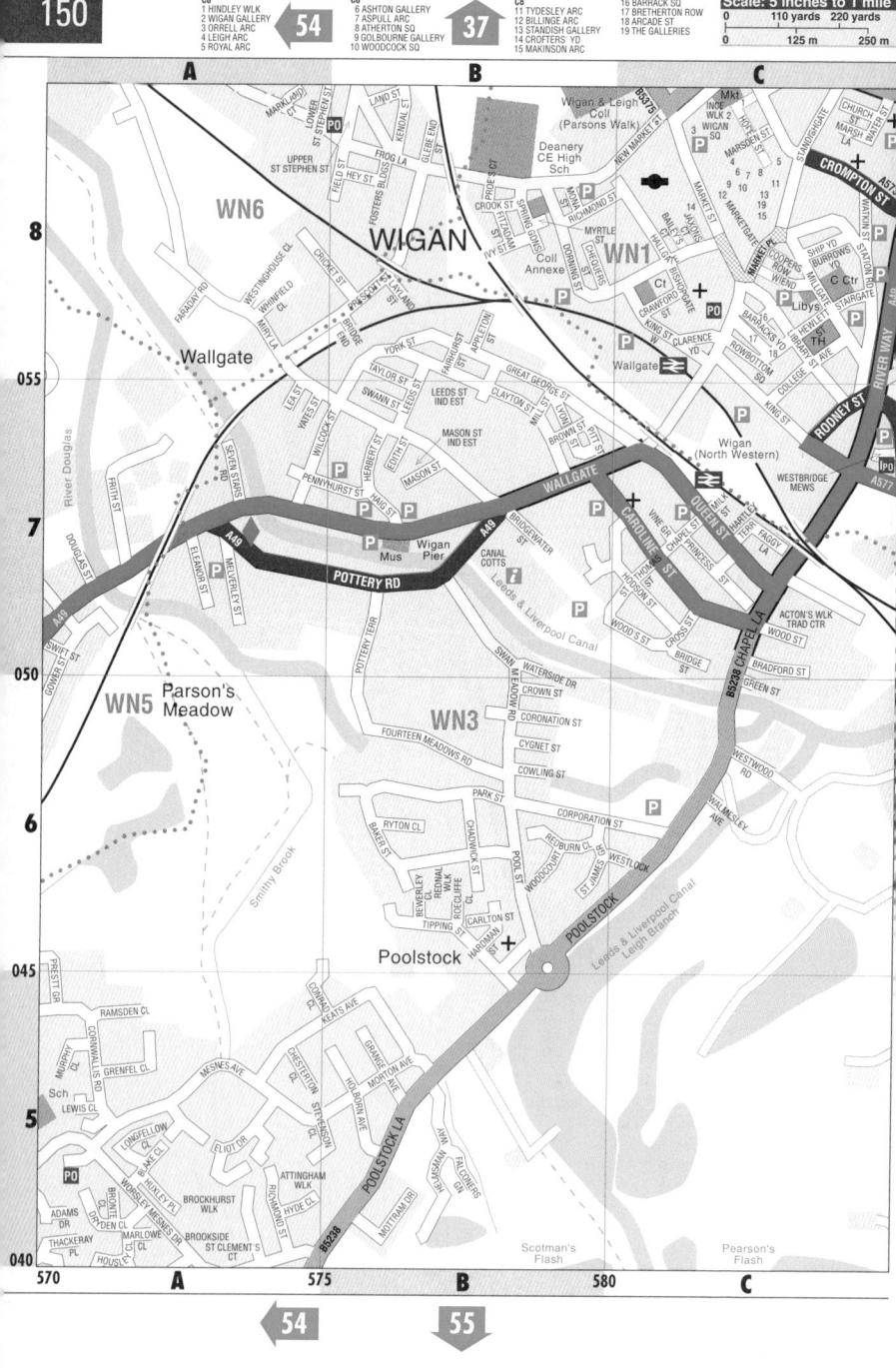

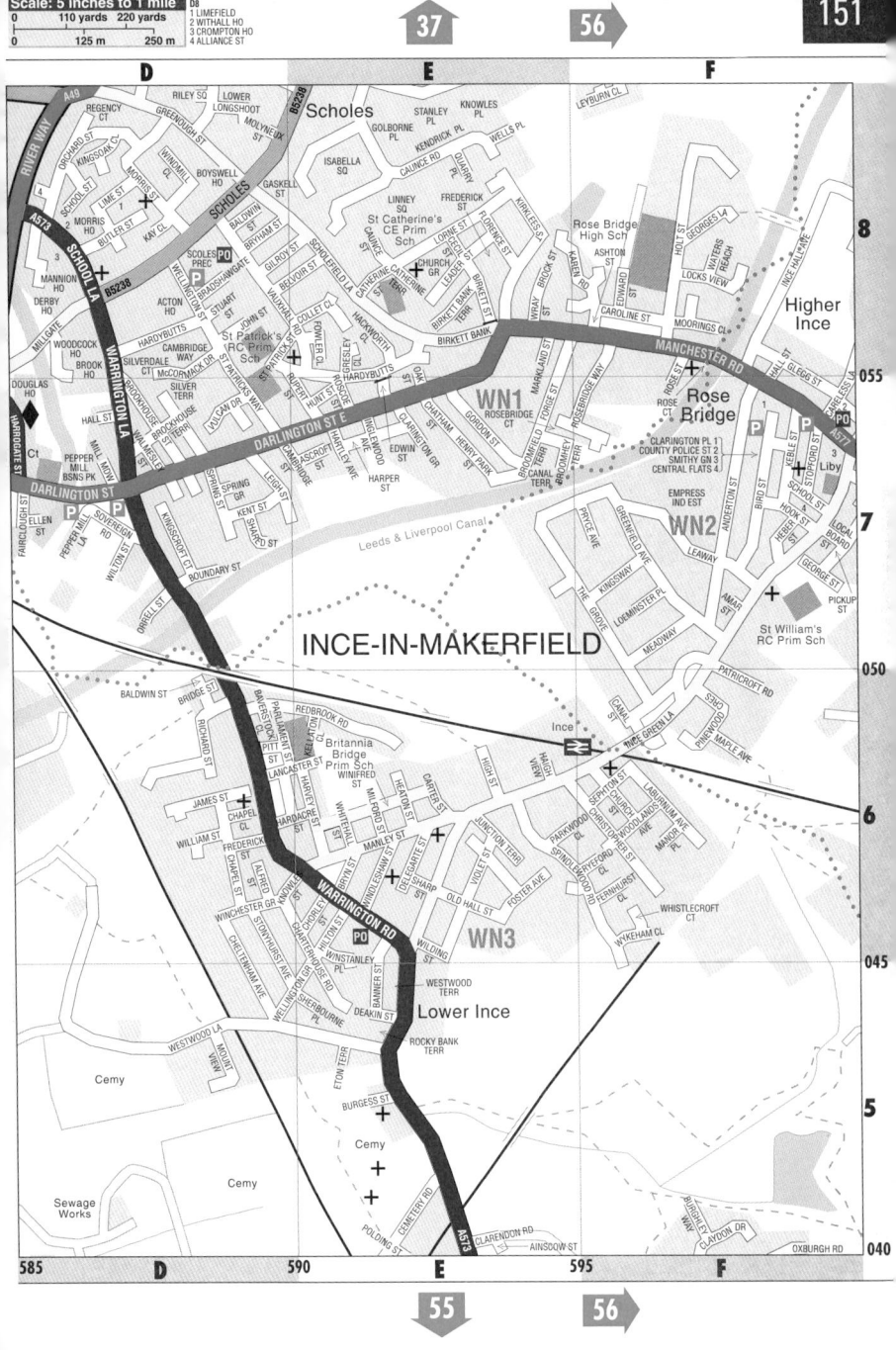

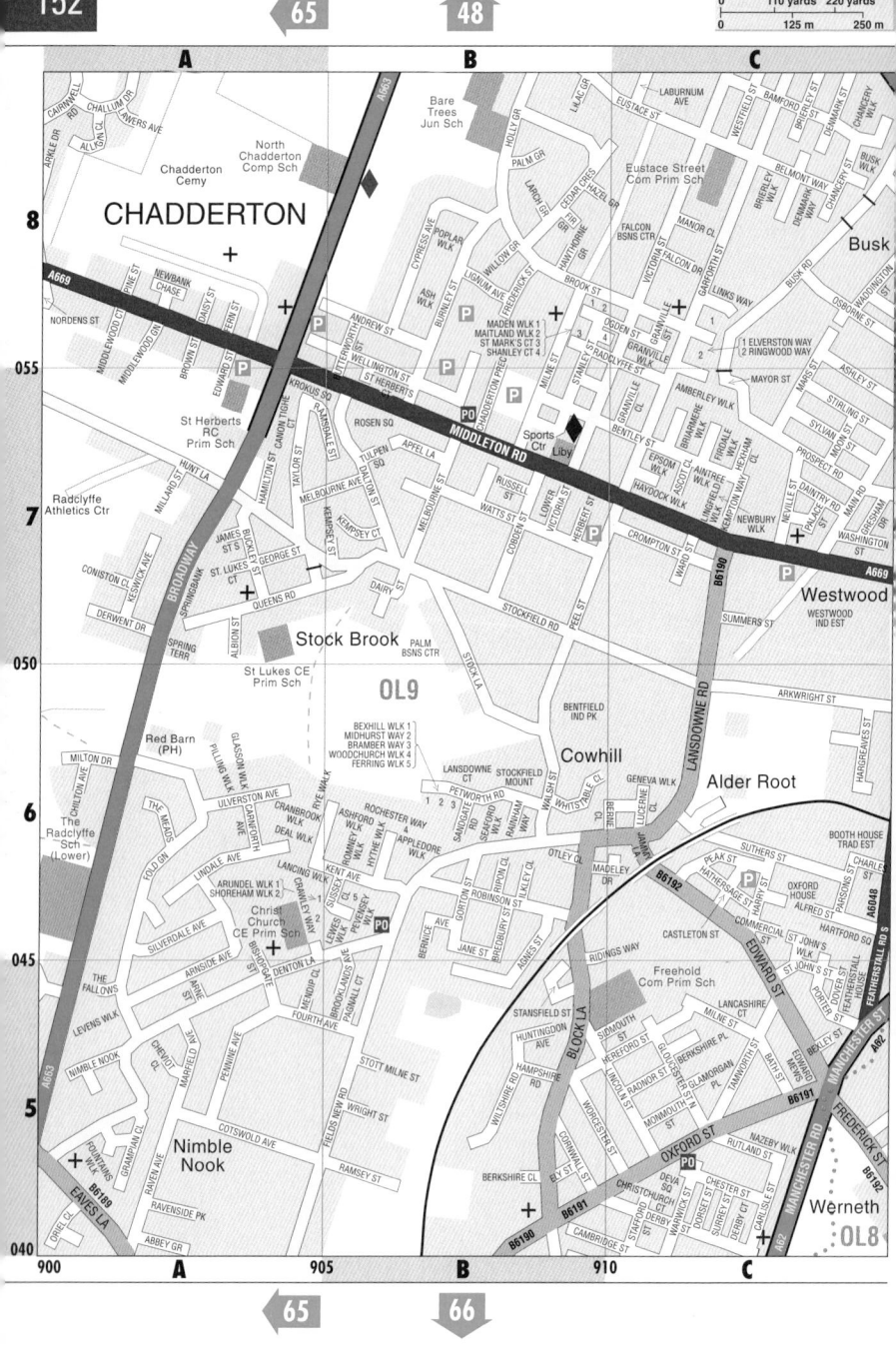

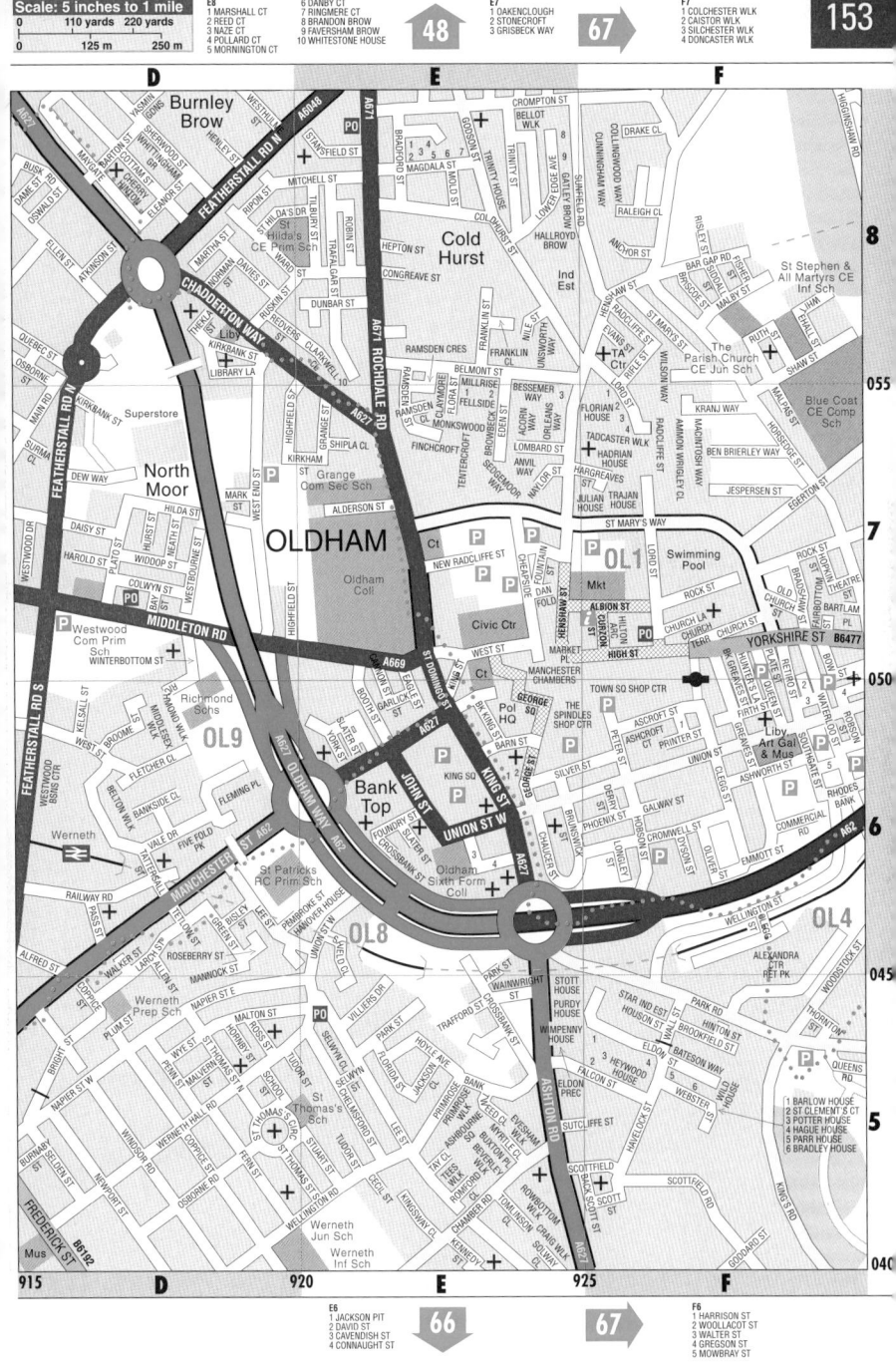

Scale: 5 inches to 1 mile

0   110 yards   220 yards
0   125 m   250 m

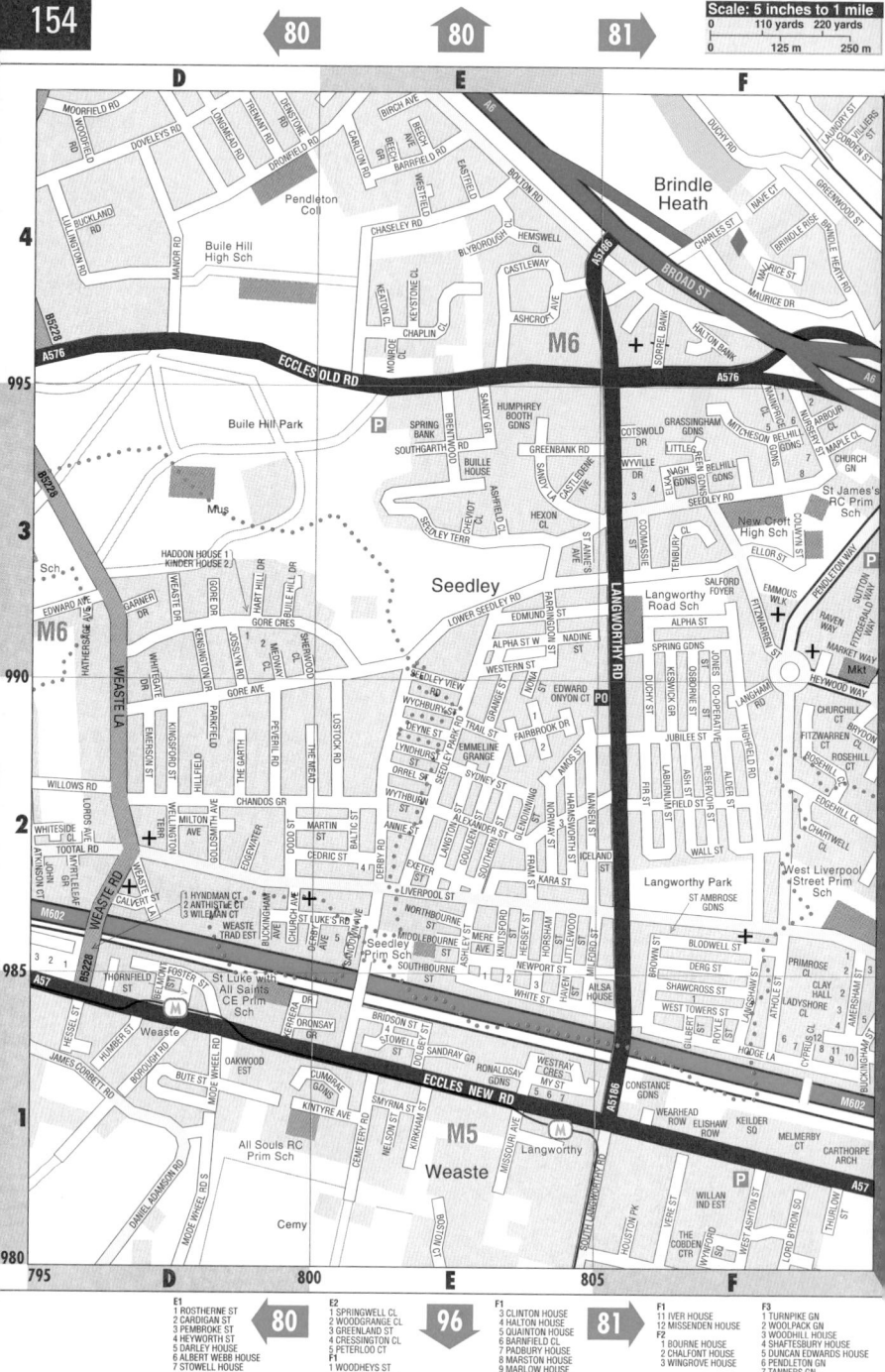

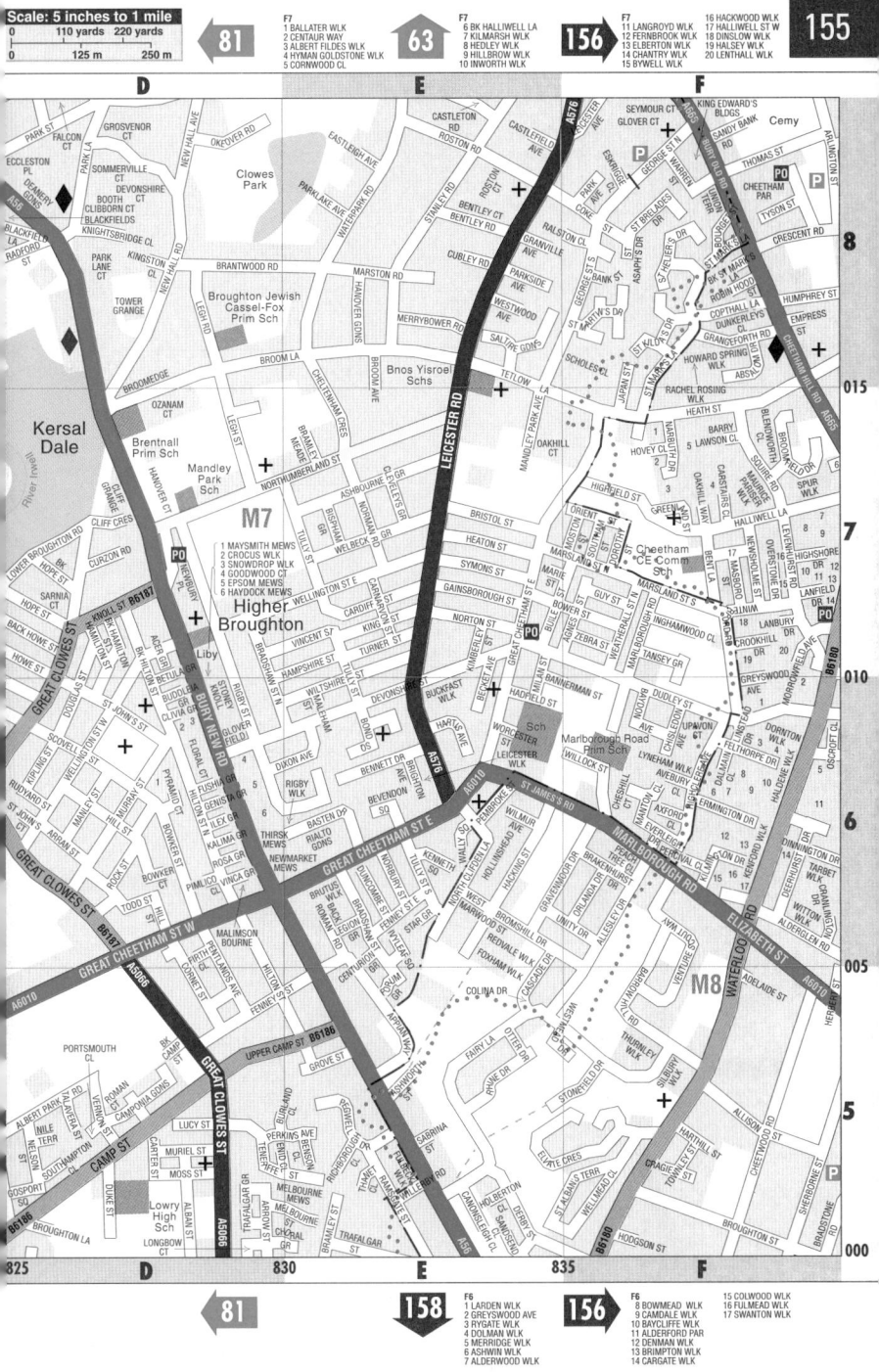

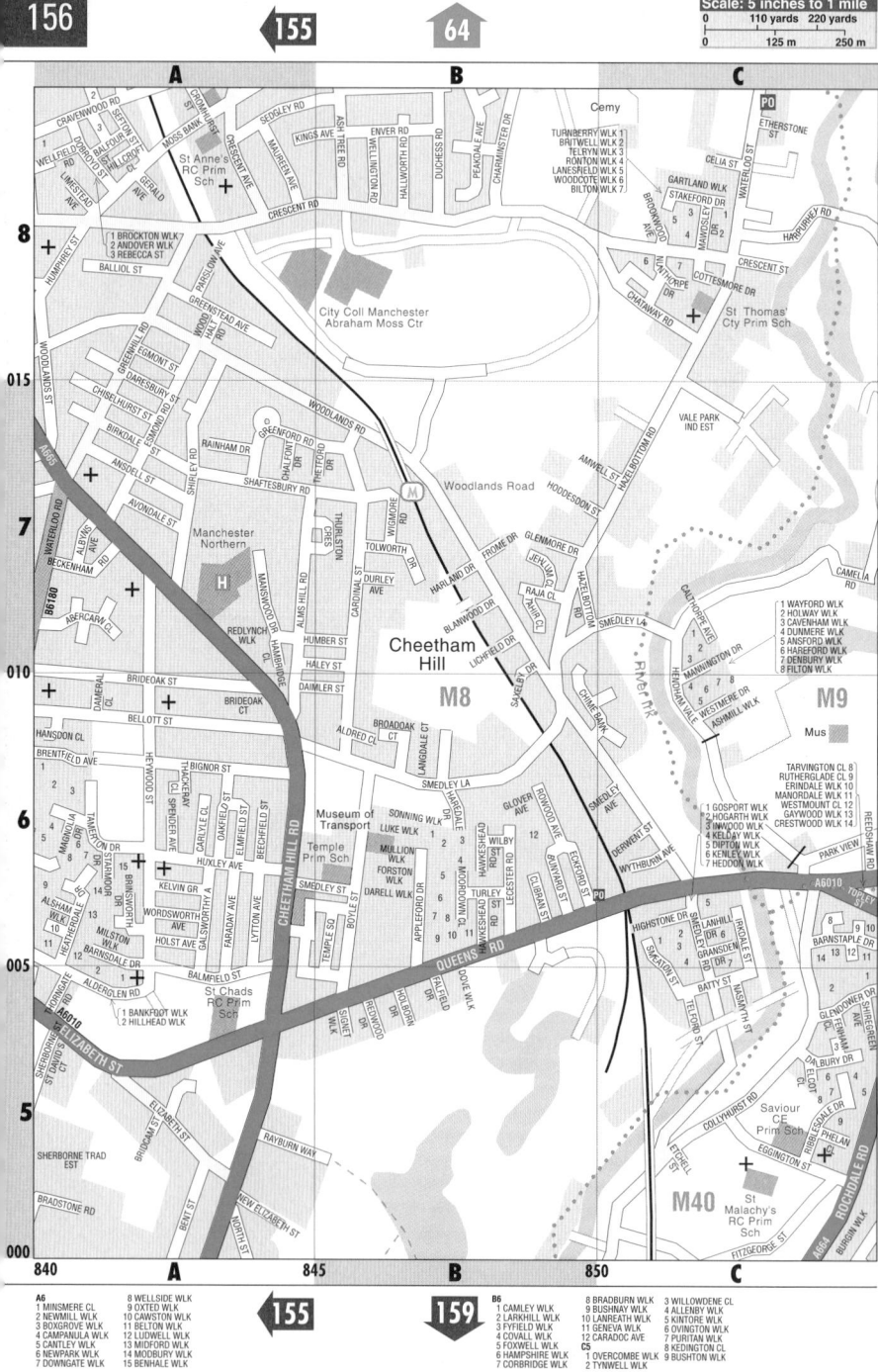

Cemy

St Anne's RC Prim Sch

TURNBERRY WLK 1
BRITWELL WLK 2
TELRYN WLK 3
RONTON WLK 4
LANESFIELD WLK 5
WOODCOTE WLK 6
BILTON WLK 7

PO

ETHERSTONE ST

GARTLAND WLK
STAKEFORD DR

City Coll Manchester Abraham Moss Ctr

St Thomas' Cty Prim Sch

VALE PARK IND EST

Woodlands Road

Manchester Northern

Cheetham Hill

M8

M9

Mus

1 WAYFORD WLK
2 HOLWAY WLK
3 CAVENHAM WLK
4 DUNMERE WLK
5 ANSFORD WLK
6 HAREFORD WLK
7 DENBURY WLK
8 FILTON WLK

TARVINGTON CL 8
RUTHERGLADE CL 9
ERINDALE WLK 10
MANORDALE WLK 11
WESTMOUNT CL 12
GAYWOOD WLK 13
CRESTWOOD WLK 14

1 GOSPORT WLK
2 HOGARTH WLK
3 INWOOD WLK
4 KELDAY WLK
5 DIPTON WLK
6 KENLEY WLK
7 HEDDON WLK

Museum of Transport

Temple Prim Sch

MULLION WLK
FORSTON WLK
DARELL WLK

St Chads RC Prim Sch

1 BANKFOOT WLK
2 HILLHEAD WLK

SHERBORNE TRAD EST

BRADSTONE RD

Saviour CE Prim Sch

St Malachy's RC Prim Sch

M40

D7
1 BROMWICH DR
2 CLATFORD WLK
3 OAKRIDGE WLK
4 BINDON WLK
5 WATFIELD WLK
6 HOLMFOOT WLK

7 LINSLADE WLK
8 SELWOOD WLK
9 PORTWOOD WLK
10 TREMAIN WLK
11 CALDERBROOK WLK
D8
1 MILLPOOL WLK

2 PATHFIELD WLK
3 MURROW WLK
4 DERVILLE WLK
5 SHAPWICK CL
6 HARROWDENE WLK
7 BRENLEY WLK
8 ROXWELL WLK

9 PORTAL WLK
10 HAYGROVE WLK
11 MAYBROOK WLK
E7
1 WILLOW BANK
2 ORPINGTON RD
3 OSBORNE RD

64

E8
4 ASHGILL WLK
5 GLENPARK WLK
6 DRYGATE WLK
7 BELSYDE WLK
8 NORBET WLK
9 PURTON WLK

83

E7
10 BANKHALL WLK
11 LOWREY WLK
12 DURHAM ST
13 EVANTON WLK
14 MERTON WLK
15 TRONGATE WLK

16 VIEWFIELD WLK
17 FIRDON WLK

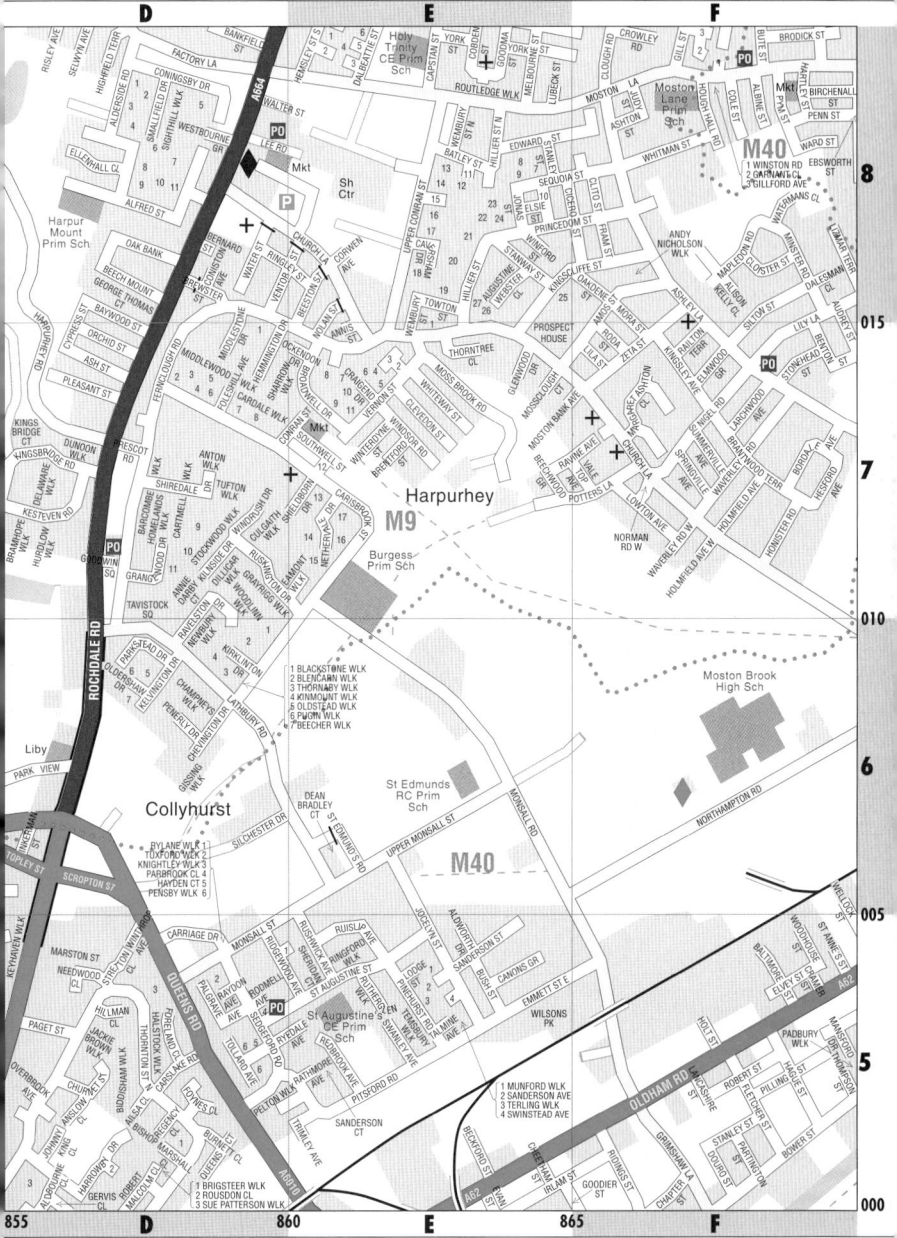

Scale: 5 inches to 1 mile
0   110 yards   220 yards
0   125 m   250 m

E7
1 HERSHAM WLK
2 RADFORD DR
3 MONKWOOD DR
4 LONGDELL WLK
5 ROCKFIELD DR
6 DENESIDE WLK
7 BROWNSON WLK

8 PRIMLEY WLK
9 DARLTON WLK
10 SIMISTER ST
11 THORNSETT CL
12 KINGCOMBE WLK
13 TIPTREE WLK
14 HANSLOPE WLK
15 SWAINSTHORPE DR

160

E8
16 BOOKHAM WLK
17 FARNDALE WLK
18 APPRENTICE CT
19 WADCROFT WLK
20 BRAXTON WLK
21 LODDEN WLK
22 BURNTWOOD WLK

83

E8
23 SALTBURN WLK
24 NAUNTON WLK
25 CROCKER WLK
26 HIGHDOWN WLK
27 ROUNDHAM WLK

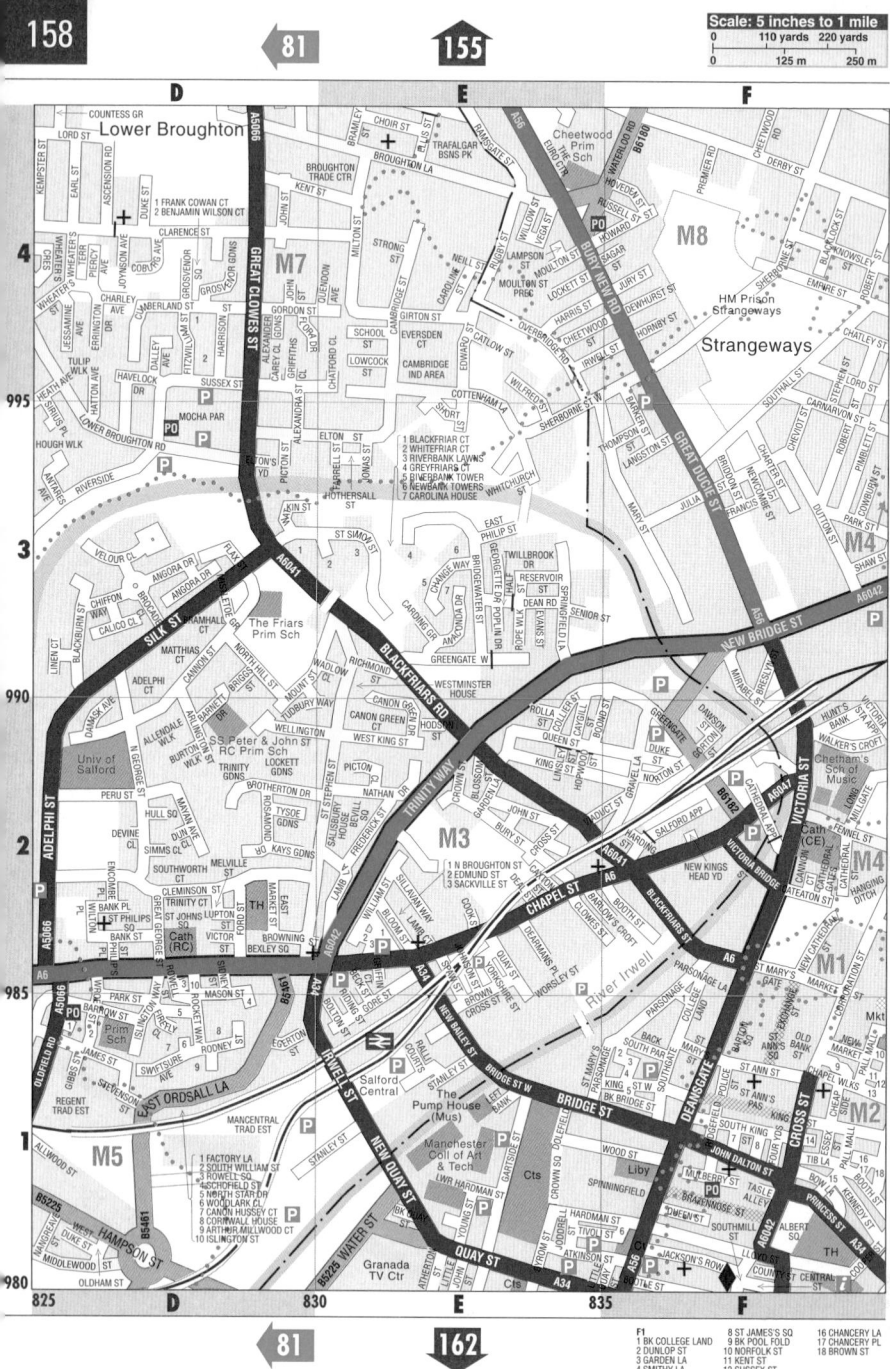

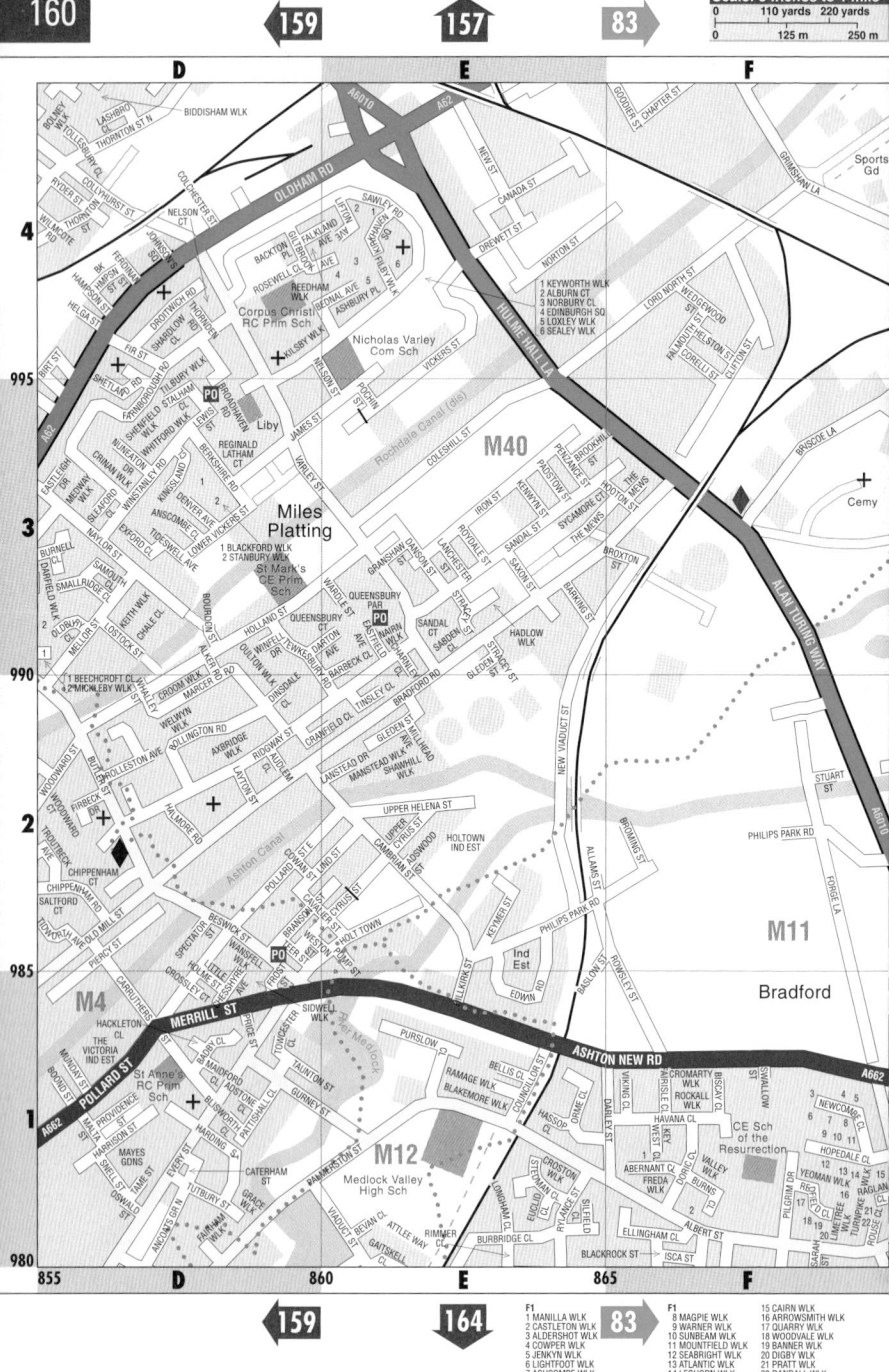

Scale: 5 inches to 1 mile
| 0 | 110 yards | 220 yards |
| 0 | 125 m | 250 m |

D E F

M5
ORDSALL LA
River Irwell
WATER ST
PRINCE'S BRIDGE B5225
Mus of Science & Ind
TV Ctr
GREAT JOHN ST
C1
ARTILLERY ST
A34 A56
PETER ST
TH
St Peter's
Sq
Liby
M2

8
REGENT RD
A6143
A57
DAWSON ST
OLD MEDLOCK ST
LIVERPOOL RD
Castlefield Visitor Ctr.
Mus
DEANSGATE
GMex
City Centre
The Bridgewater Hall
OXFORD RD A34
A5103

M3
Deansgate
B6469
GMex
Great Bridge
Rochdale Canal
M1
WHITWORTH ST W
B6469

975
DERWENT IND AREA
D7
1 MEDLOCK HO
2 IRWELL HO
3 EGERTON HO
4 BLANTYRE HO
Bridgewater Canal
CASTLE ST
SLATE WHARF
HEWITT ST
LITTLE PETER ST

Cheshire Ring Canal Wlk
CATFIELD WLK
BRAMFELL WLK
KIMBERLEY WLK
WESTCOTT CT
THOMAS CT
ST GEORGES CT
Deansgate
F7
1 GLOUCESTER ST
2 EBENEZER ST
3 NEWCASTLE ST
4 VALERIE WLK
5 CONMERE SQ
MEDLOCK ST
A5103
Univ

7
St George's
CLEWORTH WLK
CHESTER RD
A5067
HULME
River Medlock
MANCUNIAN WAY
MANCUNIAN WAY
A57(M)

Chevassut Prim Sch
BENTLEY HO
M15
St Wilfrid's RC Prim Sch

970
VIRGIL ST
PRINCESS CT
CORNBROOK
STRETFORD RD
Hulme
A5067

6
CHORLTON RD
B5218
MOSSHALL CL
Royce Prim Sch
LINGMOOR WLK 1
WASNIDGE WLK 2
OCEAN WLK 3
RAKEHEAD WLK 4
PEATFIELD WLK 5
GREENTHORN WLK 6
BROWNBANK WLK 7
HEBDEN WLK 8
CROWBOROUGH WLK 9
CARVER WLK 10
CAREY WLK 11
PRINCESS RD

965
DENBIGH WLK 1
ALLIOTT WLK 2
WHITEACRE WLK 3
ALAMBROOKE WLK 4
ACADEMY WLK 5
Loreto Coll

M16
1 HAMILTON GR
2 CLIFTON GR
St Alphonsus RC Prim Sch
CORNBROOK WAY
GRAFTON ST

5
Liby
GLOBE CT
PICKFORD
EAGLE
FALCON
OSPREY
RAVEN
Superstore
L Ctr

825 D 830 E 835 F
960

D6
1 MALVERN ROW
2 THAMES CT
3 AVON CT
4 WELLAND CT
5 TAMAR CT
6 BOLLIN CT
7 TRAFFORD CT
8 RYLANDS CT
9 MILLINGTON WLK
10 TOWNFIELD WLK
11 BOWGREEN WLK
12 MERESIDE WLK
13 WARDSEND WLK
14 HEYROSE WLK
15 NORCOT WLK

D6
16 PLATTWOOD WLK
17 OLDGATE WLK
18 TOWNCLIFFE WLK
19 DILLMASS WLK
20 STOCKLEY WLK
21 WINCHAM CL
22 ROYCE CT

D6
23 SPRINGSIDE WLK
24 DUDLOW WLK
25 HILLFOOT WLK
26 ROSSHILL WLK

F6
1 KNOWLES PL
2 HORNCHURCH CT

3 MORAN WLK
4 PINDER WLK
5 RAGLAN WLK
6 HOWBROOK WLK
7 SALUTATION ST

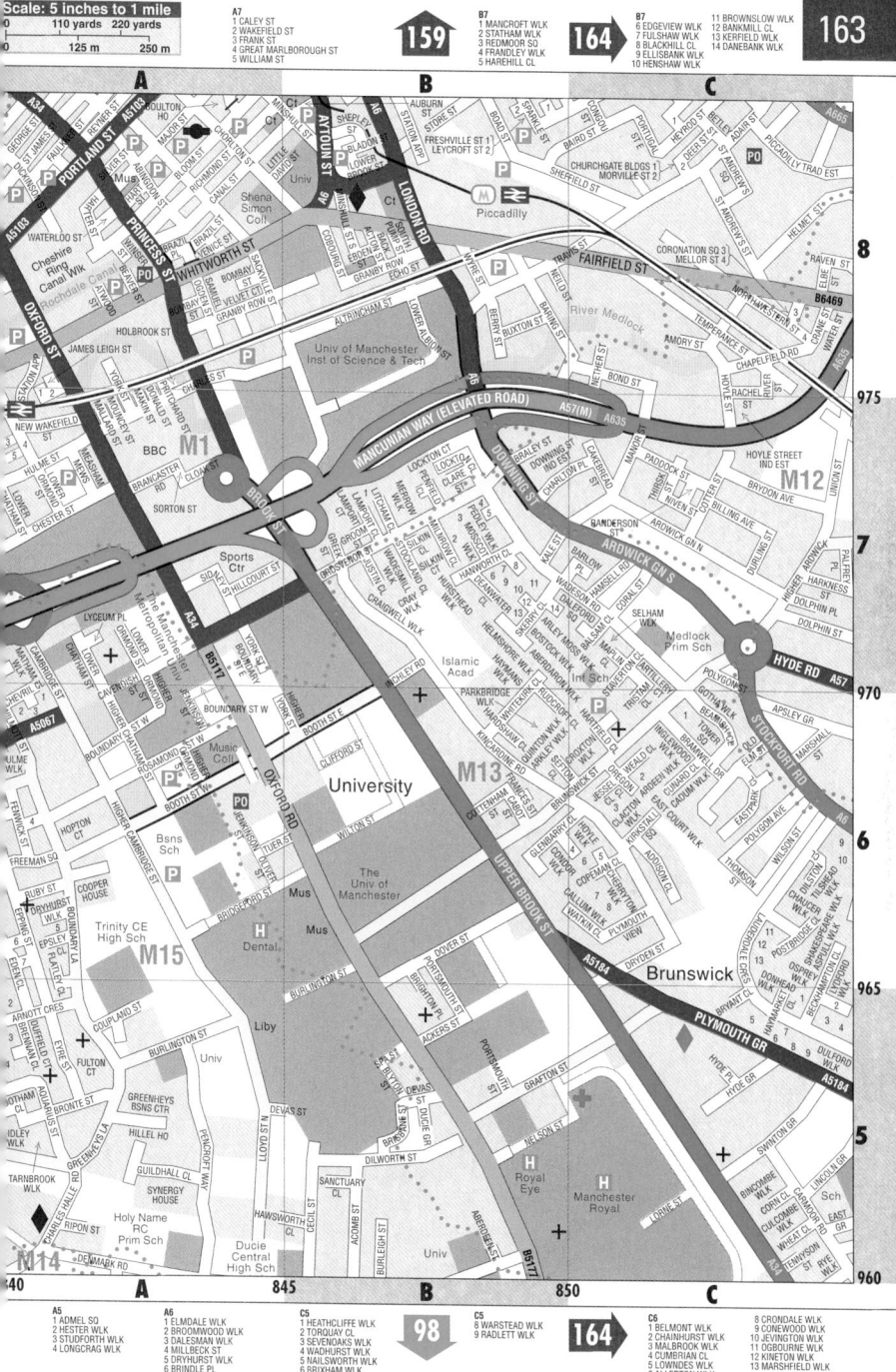

159

164

98

164

A7
1 CALEY ST
2 WAKEFIELD ST
3 FRANK ST
4 GREAT MARLBOROUGH ST
5 WILLIAM ST

B7
1 MANCROFT WLK
2 STATHAM CL
3 REDMOOR SQ
4 FRANDLEY WLK
5 HAREHILL CL

B7
6 EDGEVIEW WLK
7 FULSHAW WLK
8 BLACKHILL CL
9 ELLISBANK WLK
10 HENSHAW WLK

11 BROWNSLOW WLK
12 BANKMILL CL
13 KERFIELD WLK
14 DANEBANK WLK

A5
1 ADMEL SQ
2 HESTER WLK
3 STUDFORTH WLK
4 LONGCRAG WLK

A6
1 ELMDALE WLK
2 BROOMWOOD WLK
3 DALESMAN WLK
4 MILLBECK ST
5 DRYHURST WLK
6 BRINDLE PL
7 RAIL PL

C5
1 HEATHCLIFFE WLK
2 TORQUAY CT
3 SEVENOAKS WLK
4 WADHURST WLK
5 NAILSWORTH WLK
6 BRIXHAM WLK
7 BEAMINSTER WLK

C5
8 WARSTEAD WLK
9 RADLETT WLK

C6
1 BELMONT WLK
2 CHAINHURST WLK
3 MALBROOK WLK
4 CUMBRIAN CL
5 LOWNDES WLK
6 ALLERTON WLK
7 HUTTON WLK

8 CRONDALE WLK
9 CONEWOOD WLK
10 JEVINGTON WLK
11 OGBOURNE WLK
12 KINETON WLK
13 MARSHFIELD WLK

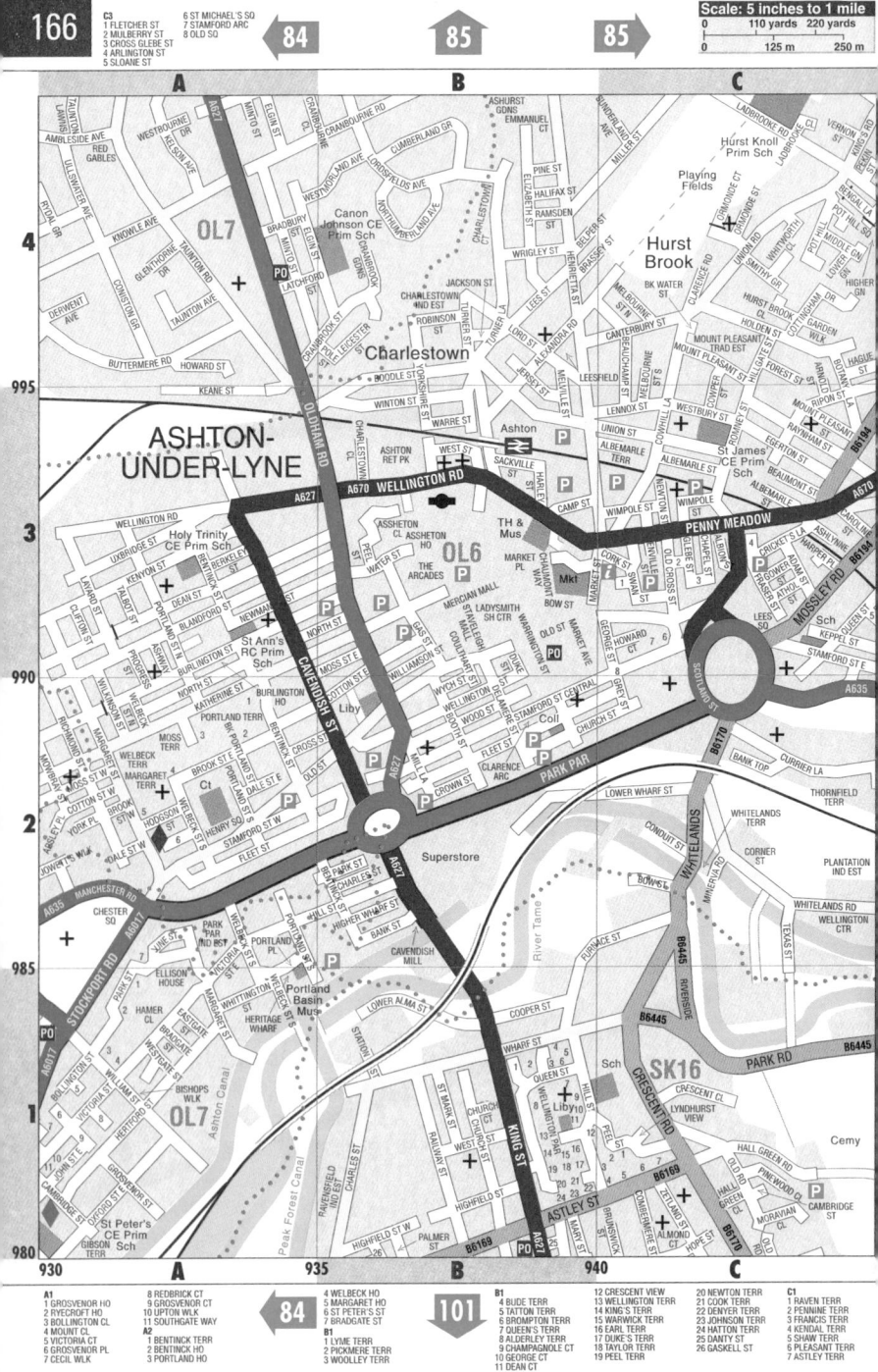

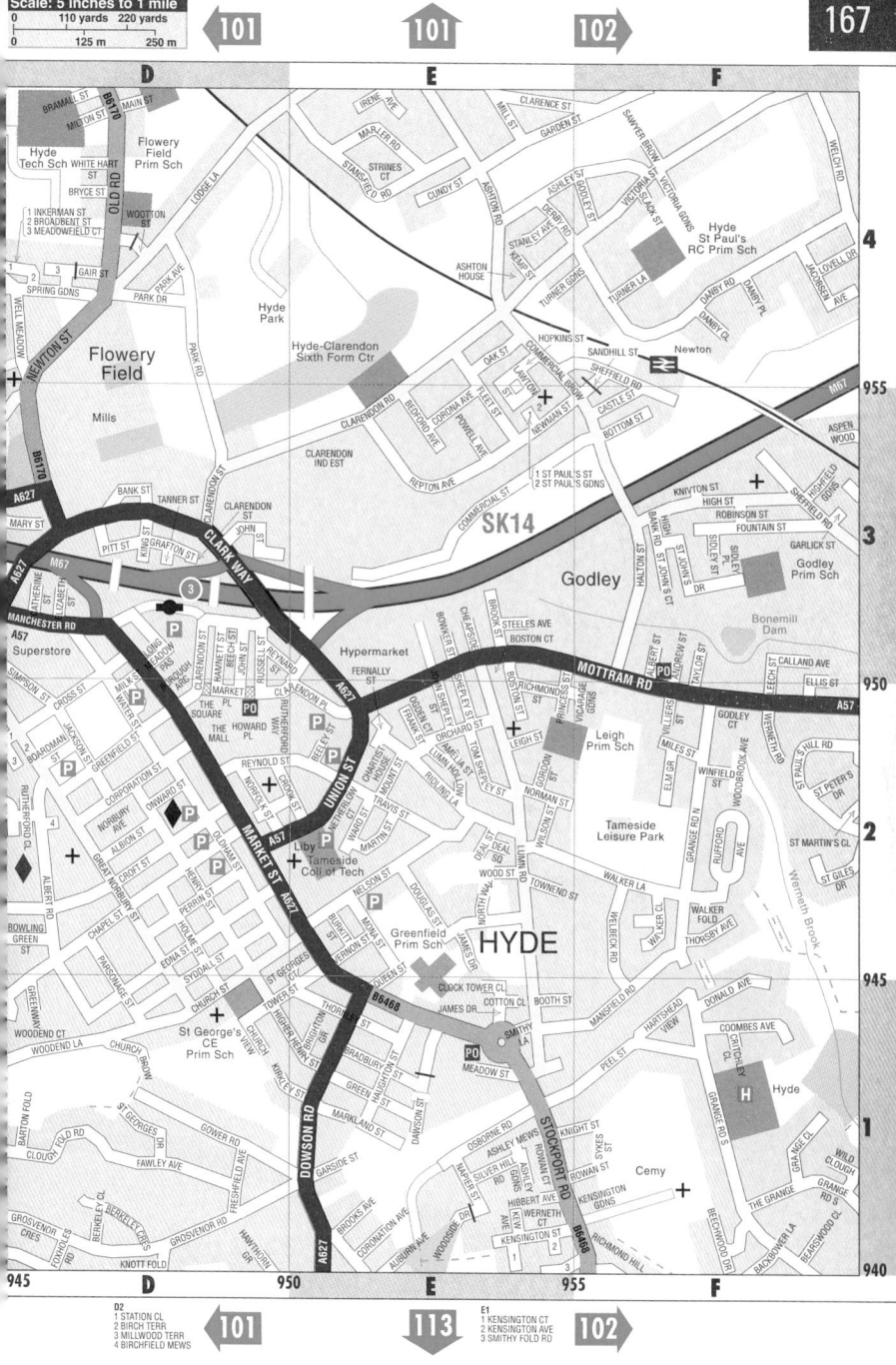

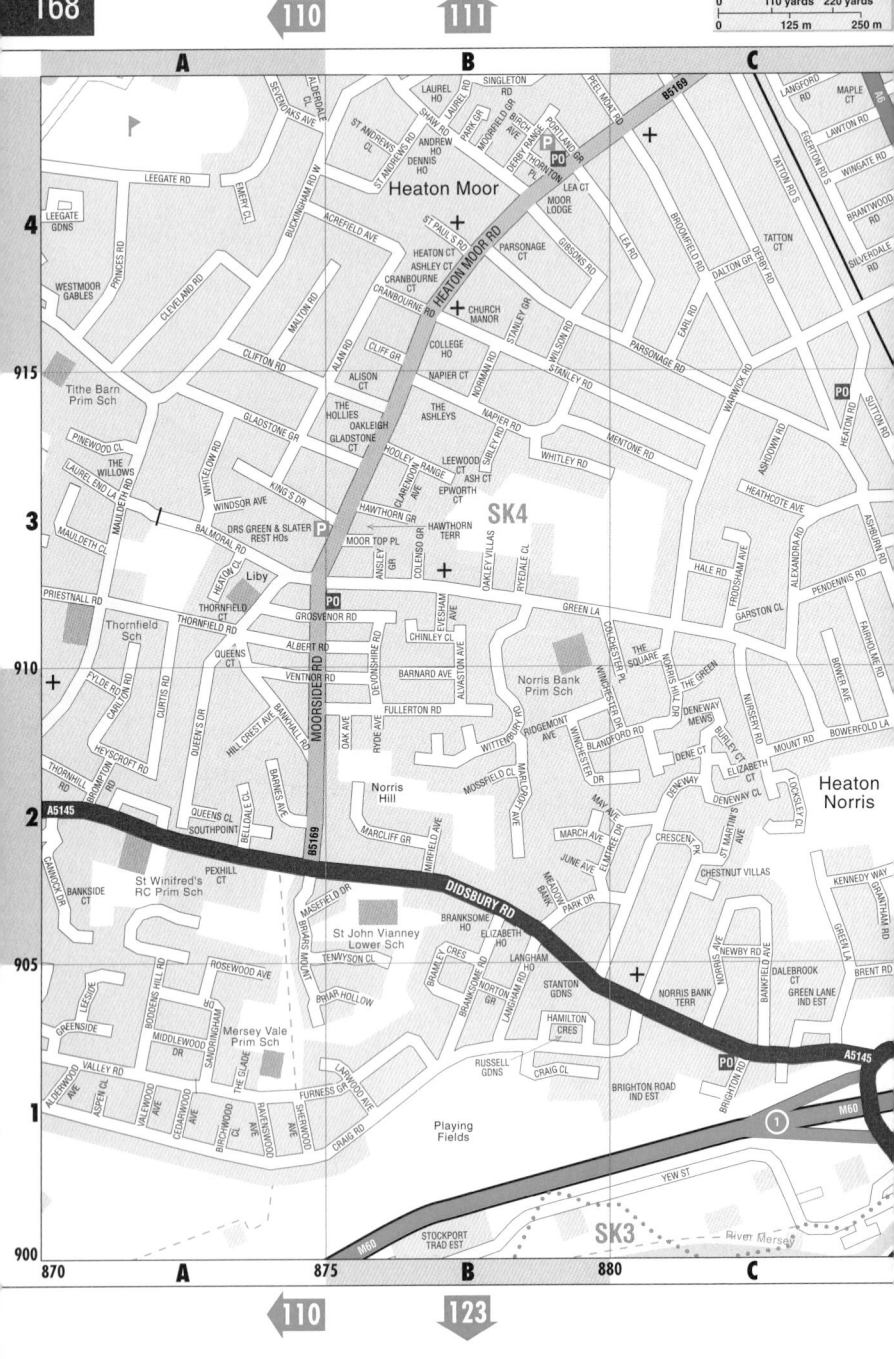

Scale: 5 inches to 1 mile

0   110 yards   220 yards
0   125 m   250 m

123
E8
1 CHATHAM HO
2 BOWDON HO
3 PEMBROKE HO
4 PALATINE HO

169
E8
5 LANCASTER HO
6 DURHAM HO
7 FRANCES ST

124
F8
1 LOONIES CT
2 JOULES CT
3 OLD GARDENS ST
4 HOLLINGWORTH CL

5 MOTTRAM ST
6 RATCLIFFE ST
7 GROSVENOR ST

Scale: 5 inches to 1 mile

0   110 yards   220 yards

0   125 m   250 m

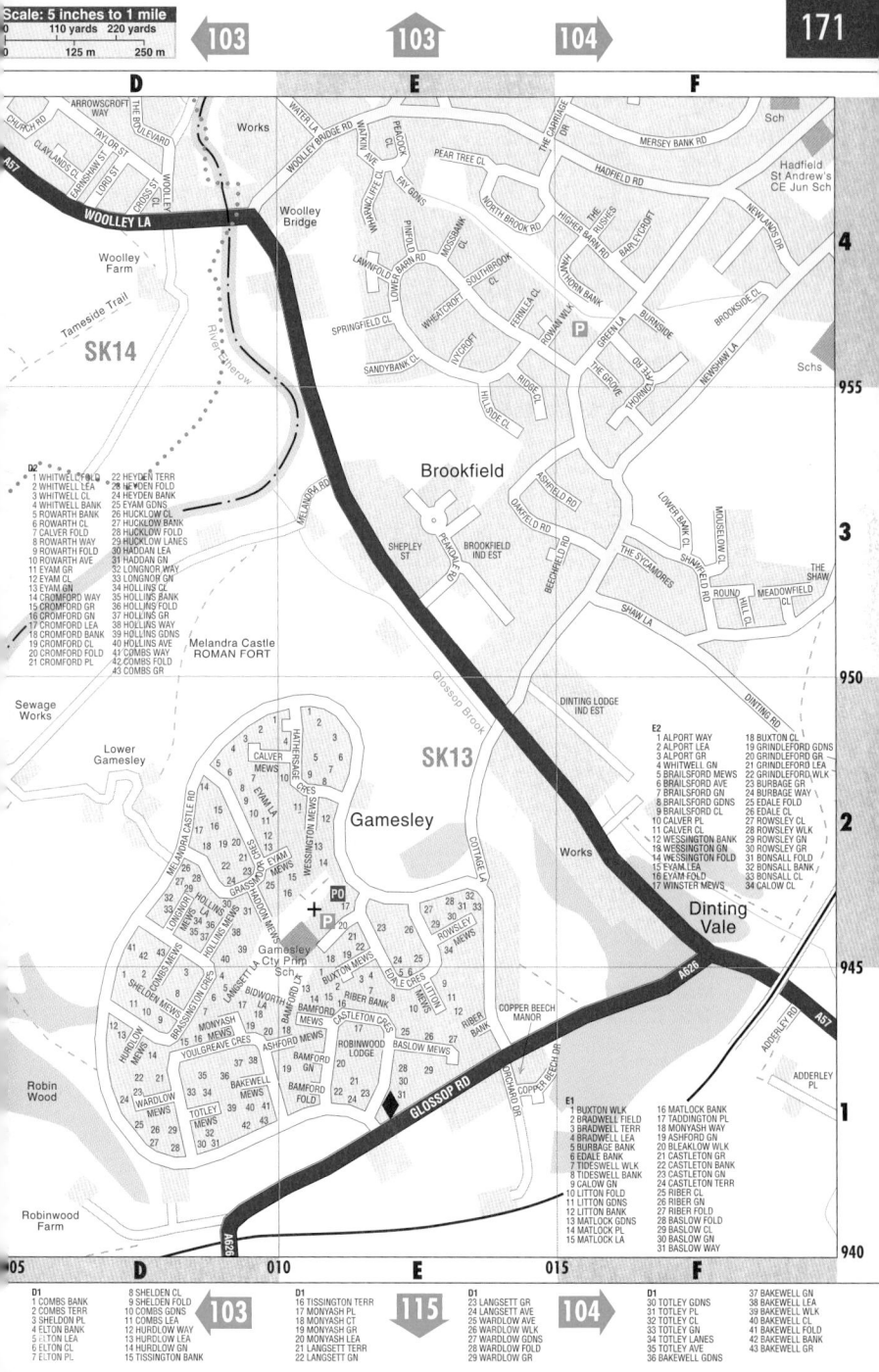

Index

Street names are listed alphabetically and show the locality, the Postcode District, the page number and a reference to the square in which the name falls on the map page

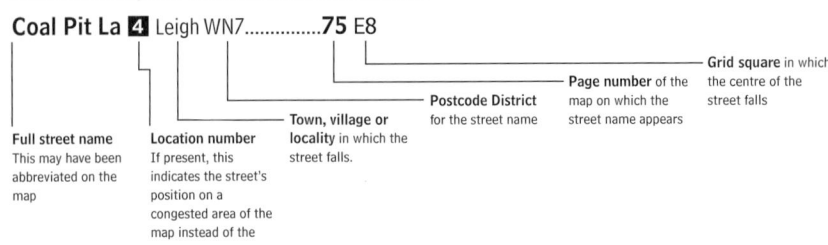

Coal Pit La 4 Leigh WN7..............75 E8

Grid square in which the centre of the street falls

Page number of the map on which the street name appears

Postcode District for the street name

Town, village or locality in which the street falls.

Full street name
This may have been abbreviated on the map

Location number
If present, this indicates the street's position on a congested area of the map instead of the name

Abbreviations used in the index

App	Approach	Cl	Close	Espl	Esplanade	N	North	S	South
Arc	Arcade	Comm	Common	Est	Estate	Orch	Orchard	Sq	Square
Ave	Avenue	Cnr	Corner	Gdns	Gardens	Par	Parade	Strs	Stairs
Bvd	Boulevard	Cotts	Cottages	Gn	Green	Pk	Park	Stps	Steps
Bldgs	Buildings	Ct	Court	Gr	Grove	Pas	Passage	St	Street, Saint
Bsns Pk	Business Park	Ctyd	Courtyard	Hts	Heights	Pl	Place	Terr	Terrace
Bsns Ctr	Business Centre	Cres	Crescent	Ind Est	Industrial	Prec	Precinct	Trad	Trading Est
Bglws	Bungalows	Dr	Drive		Estate	Prom	Promenade	Wlk	Walk
Cswy	Causeway	Dro	Drove	Intc	Interchange	Ret Pk	Retail Park	W	West
Ctr	Centre	E	East	Junc	Junction	Rd	Road	Yd	Yard
Cir	Circus	Emb	Embankment	La	Lane	Rdbt	Roundabout		

Town and village index

Abram Brow 74 B7	Culcheth 91 E3	Heywood 29 E2	Oldham 66 E7	Tintwistle 104 A7
Adlington 21 A7	Delph 50 E4	High Lane 134 D8	Orrell 53 E7	Tyldesley 59 B1
Ainsworth 26 B1	Denshaw 33 D2	Hindley 56 D6	Partington 105 F4	Uppermill 69 A8
Alderley Edge 136 C2	Denton 100 D3	Hollinfare 105 A3	Pendlebury 80 C8	Urmston 95 C1
Altrincham 118 C5	Diggle 51 C4	Hollingworth 103 E5	Pennington Green 38 E1	Walkden 60 D4
Appley Bridge 35 D8	Disley 135 C5	Horwich 22 D4	Platt Bridge 56 A2	Walsden 6 B8
Ashley 128 E5	Downall Green 72 C5	Hyde 101 E2	Poynton 133 E4	Westhoughton 57 C8
Ashton-in-Makerfield ..73 C5	Droylsden 84 B3	Ince-in-Makerfield 55 E7	Prestwich 63 A4	Whitefield 62 E7
Ashton-under-Lyne ...85 A4	Dukinfield 101 D7	Irlam 105 F7	Radcliffe 44 C3	Whitworth 4 D1
Aspull 38 C6	Eccles 79 E1	Kearsley 61 A7	Ramsbottom 11 B5	Wigan 55 B8
Atherton 58 E2	Edenfield 1 D3	Leigh 75 E6	Rawtenstall 2 E8	Wilmslow 137 C5
Bacup 3 E8	Edgworth 9 D6	Little Bollington ...118 B2	Reddish 111 D8	Windy Arbour 72 B8
Bickershaw 74 F8	Failsworth 83 F6	Little Lever 43 B4	Rochdale 30 D7	Woodford 132 E2
Billinge 71 E4	Fairsworth 60 A7	Littleborough 16 B5	Romiley 113 D2	Worsley 78 E6
Blackrod 21 D2	Flixton 94 E2	Longshaw 25 E1	Rowarth 127 E7	Wrightington Bar 18 F7
Bolton 41 E8	Fowley Common 92 B5	Lymm 117 A3	Royton 48 E4	Wythenshawe 121 C5
Boothstown 78 A5	Gamesley 171 E2	Manchester 82 C2	Sale 108 C4	
Bramhall 132 D8	Garswood 72 C3	Marple 125 D5	Salford 81 A2	
Bredbury 112 E4	Gatley 122 A4	Middleton 65 B8	Shaw 49 B7	
Brinnington 112 C5	Glazebury 92 B7	Milnrow 31 E4	Shevington 36 B5	
Broomedge 117 C1	Glossop 104 B1	Moorend 127 A6	Shevington Moor 19 A2	
Bury 27 E3	Golborne 90 B8	Mossley 68 C1	Stalybridge 86 B3	
Carrington 106 D6	Hadfield 104 B5	Mottram-in-	Standish 19 F2	
Chadderton 65 F8	Handforth 131 C4	Longdendale 103 A4	Stockport 111 D1	
Charlesworth 115 C6	Haslingden 1 A6	New Mills 127 D2	Stretford 96 C2	
Cheadle 122 E5	Hattersley 102 E2	Newhey 32 B4	Styal 130 F4	
Coppull 19 E8	Hazel Grove 124 E2	Newton-le-Willows 89 B2	Swinton 79 F8	

1

1st St WN2 . . . . .73 E7

3

3rd St WN2 . . . . .73 E7

4

4th St WN2 . . . . .73 F7

'a'

'a' Ct WN4 . . . . .73 B2

A

Abberley Dr M40 . . . . .65 D2
Abberley Way WN3 . . . . . .54 B4
Abberton Rd M20 . . . . . . .110 A6
Abbey Cl Altrincham WA14 . 119 B1
Denton M34 . . . . .102 F3
Orrell WN8 . . . . .53 C7
Radcliffe M26 . . . . .43 E5
Urmston M32 . . . . .95 F3
Abbey Cres OL10 . . . . .29 B4
Abbey Ct Manchester M18 . . .99 E6
Radcliffe M26 . . . . .43 E4
Wigan WN5 . . . . .36 E2
Abbey Dale WN6 . . . . .35 D7
Abbey Dr Bury BL8 . . . . . . .27 A1
Littleborough OL15 . . . . . . .15 F3
Orrell WN5 . . . . .53 E6
Swinton M27 . . . . .61 E1
Abbey Gdns SK14 . . . . . . .103 A3
Abbey Gr Adlington PR6 . . . .21 B7
Eccles M30 . . . . .79 E2
Mottram-in-L SK14 . . . . . . .102 F3
Oldham OL9 . . . . .152 A5
Stockport SK1 . . . . .124 B8
Abbey Hey Inf & Jun Schs
M18 . . . . .99 E5
Abbey Hey La M11,M18 . . . .99 F6
Abbey Hills Rd OL4,OL8 . . . .67 C4
Abbey La WN7 . . . . .57 D1
Abbey Lawn M16 . . . . .97 B3
Abbey Rd Cheadle SK8 . . . . .122 A3
Delph OL3 . . . . .50 E5
Droylsden M43 . . . . .83 F3
Failsworth M35 . . . . .84 B8
Golborne WA3 . . . . .91 C8
Middleton M24 . . . . .46 F4
Sale M33 . . . . .108 A6
Tyldesley M29 . . . . .77 C7
Abbey Sq WN7 . . . . .57 D1
Abbey St WN7 . . . . .75 F6
Abbey Way M26 . . . . .44 A3
Abbeycourt M30 . . . . .79 E2
Abbeydale BL2 OL12 . . . . . .139 E8
Abbeydale Cl OL6 . . . . .85 E6
Abbeydale Gdns M28 . . . . . .60 C3
Abbeyfield Sq M11 . . . . . . .165 B8
Abbeyfields WN6 . . . . .36 E2
Abbeyville Wlk M15 . . . . . .162 E5
Abbeyway N WA11 . . . . .89 A7
Abbeyway S WA11 . . . . .89 A7
Abbeywood Ave M18 . . . . . .99 E4
Abbingdon Way WN7 . . . . . .57 D1
Abbot Croft BL5 . . . . .57 F6
Abbot's Fold Rd M28 . . . . . .78 B7
Abbots Cl M33 . . . . .108 D5
Abbots Ct M33 . . . . .108 D5
Abbotsbury Cl
Manchester M12 . . . . .165 A6
Poynton SK12 . . . . .133 D5
Abbotsfield Cl M41 . . . . .94 D3
Abbotsford Cl WA3 . . . . . . .74 D1
Abbotsford Dr M24 . . . . . . .46 D4
Abbotsford Gr WA14 . . . . . .119 E8
Abbotsford Prep Sch M41 . .95 A2
Abbotsford Rd Bolton BL1 . .142 A1
Chadderton OL9 . . . . .65 E8
Manchester M21 . . . . .97 B1
Oldham OL1 . . . . .49 B1
Abbotside Cl M16 . . . . .97 D3
Abbotsleigh Dr Sk7 . . . . . .123 F2
Abbott Prim Sch M40 . . . . .159 C3
Abbott St Bolton BL3 . . . . .145 E5
Hindley WN2 . . . . .56 C6
14 Horwich BL6 . . . . .22 B4
Rochdale OL11 . . . . .30 B3
Abbotts Gn M29 . . . . .77 A4
Abbotts Way WN5 . . . . .71 D3
Abden St M26 . . . . .44 A3
Abels La OL3 . . . . .69 C8
Aber Ave SK2 . . . . .124 C4
Aber Rd SK8 . . . . .123 A6
Abercarn Cl M8 . . . . .156 A7
Abercorn Rd BL1 . . . . .143 D1
Abercorn St **7** OL4 . . . . . . .67 D6
Abercrombie Ct M33 . . . . .108 D5
Abercorn Wlk **4** M9 . . . . . .64 E5
Aberdaron Wlk M13 . . . . . .163 B7
Aberdeen **1** M30 . . . . .79 E2
Aberdeen Cres SK3 . . . . . .170 D8
Aberdeen Gdns OL12 . . . . . .14 D4
Aberdeen Gr SK3 . . . . .170 D8
Aberdeen St M13,M15 . . . . .163 B5
Aberford Rd M23 . . . . .121 A5
Abergele Rd M14 . . . . .110 E8
Abergele St SK2 . . . . .124 A5
Aberley Fold OL15 . . . . .15 F7

Abernant Cl M11 . . . . .160 F1
Abernethy St BL6 . . . . .22 D2
Abersoch Ave M14 . . . . . . .110 E8
Abingdon Ave M45 . . . . . . .44 F2
Abingdon Cl Oldham OL9 . . . .66 B4
Rochdale OL11 . . . . .139 E5
Whitefield M45 . . . . .44 F2
Abingdon Prim Sch SK5 . . .111 F7
Abingdon Rd Bolton BL2 . . . .25 E6
Reddish SK5 . . . . .111 F7
Stockport SK7 . . . . .123 E3
Urmston M41 . . . . .95 E3
Abington St
Ashton-u-L OL6 . . . . .85 D2
Manchester M1 . . . . .163 A8
Abinger Rd WN4 . . . . .72 D4
Abinger Wlk M40 . . . . .83 D4
Abington Dr WN2 . . . . .56 A1
Abington Rd M33 . . . . .108 C3
Abney Grange OL5 . . . . .86 E8
Abney Rd Mossley OL5 . . . . .86 C8
Reddish SK4 . . . . .111 C5
Aboukir St OL16 . . . . .31 B8
Abraham Guest High Sch
WN5 . . . . .54 A1
Abraham St **11** BL6 . . . . . . .22 B4
Abram Bryn Gates
Prim Sch WN2 . . . . .73 F7
Abram CE Prim Sch WN2 . . .56 B1
Abram Cl M14 . . . . .98 A1
Abram St M6 . . . . .80 F6
Abraham Wlk BM8 . . . . . . .155 F8
Acacia Ave
Altrincham WA15 . . . . .119 F3
Cheadle SK8 . . . . .123 A1
Denton M34 . . . . .101 A3
Swinton M27 . . . . .79 E6
Wigan WN5 . . . . .136 F5
Acacia Cres WN6 . . . . .36 F3
Acacia Dr
Altrincham WA15 . . . . .119 F3
Salford M6 . . . . .80 B3
Acacia Gr SK5 . . . . .169 F4
Acacia Rd OL8 . . . . .66 D1
Acacias Prim Sch M19 . . . . .110 F7
Academy Wlk M15 . . . . . . .162 E5
Acer Cl Hyde SK14 . . . . . . .102 A2
Rochdale OL11 . . . . .13 C2
Acer Gr M7 . . . . .155 D7
Acheson St **3** M18 . . . . . . .99 F5
Ack La E SK7 . . . . .132 D7
Ack La W SK7,SK8 . . . . . . .132 C7
Ackers La M31 . . . . .106 F6
Ackers St M13 . . . . .163 B5
Ackersley Cl SK8 . . . . .132 B8
Ackhurst La WN5 . . . . .36 A2
Ackroyd Ave M18 . . . . .99 F6
Ackroyd St M11 . . . . .99 E7
Ackworth Dr M23 . . . . .121 A6
Ackworth Rd M27 . . . . .61 E1
Acme St M27 . . . . .80 B8
Acomb St Manchester M14 . . .98 B4
Manchester M15 . . . . .163 A6
Acorn Bsns Ctr SK4 . . . . . .169 D1
Acorn Cl Leigh WN7 . . . . . . .75 F3
Manchester M19 . . . . .110 F8
Whitefield M45 . . . . .62 F6
Acorn Ctr OL1 . . . . .67 B8
Acorn St
Newton-le-W WA12 . . . . . . .89 D3
Oldham OL4 . . . . .67 E6
Acorn Way OL1 . . . . .153 E7
Acre Ave OL13 . . . . .3 D8
Acre Barn OL2 . . . . .48 E8
Acre Cl BL0 . . . . .1 D3
Acre Field BL2 . . . . .25 F6
Acre La Bramhall SK7,SK8 . .132 C6
Oldham OL1 . . . . .49 A1
Acre Mill Rd OL13 . . . . .3 D8
Acre St Denton M34 . . . . . .100 E3
Glossop SK13 . . . . .116 C7
Oldham OL9 . . . . .66 B2
Radcliffe M26 . . . . .43 E3
Romiley SK6 . . . . .113 B2
Whitworth OL12 . . . . .4 D1
Acre Top Rd M9 . . . . .64 B5
Acre View OL13 . . . . .3 D7
Acrefield OL3 . . . . .108 A3
Acrefield Ave
Manchester SK4 . . . . .168 B4
Urmston M41 . . . . .95 F1
Acregate M41 . . . . .95 A2
Acres Ct M22 . . . . .121 D4
Acres La SK15 . . . . .86 B1
Acres Rd Gatley SK8 . . . . . .122 A5
Manchester M21 . . . . .109 B8
Acres St BL8 . . . . .26 F1
Acresbrook SK15 . . . . .102 C7
Acresbrook Wlk BL8 . . . . . .26 F5
Acresdale BL6 . . . . .40 C7
Acresfield Adlington PR7 . . . .20 F6
Tyldesley M29 . . . . .77 C7
Acresfield Ave M34 . . . . .84 C1
Acresfield Cl Blackrod BL6 . . .21 C3
Pendlebury M27 . . . . .80 A6
Acresfield Rd
Dukinfield SK14 . . . . .101 F5
Middleton M24 . . . . .47 C3
Sale WA15 . . . . .120 A8
Salford M6 . . . . .80 D5
Walkden M38 . . . . .60 B4
Acreswood Cl PR7 . . . . .19 E8
Acreville Gr WA3 . . . . .92 E7
Acton Ave M40 . . . . .83 B4
Acton Ho WN1 . . . . .151 D8
Acton Sq M5 . . . . .81 B2

Acton St Oldham OL1 . . . . . .67 B8
Rochdale OL12 . . . . .15 A1
Wigan WN1 . . . . .37 C1
Acton Terr WN1 . . . . .37 C1
Acton's Walk Trad Ctr
WN1 . . . . .150 C7
Ada St Manchester M9 . . . . . .64 D1
Ramsbottom BL0 . . . . .138 B5
Rochdale OL12 . . . . .15 A2
Adair St Manchester M1 . . . .159 C1
Manchester M1 . . . . .163 C8
Rochdale OL11 . . . . .30 B2
Adam Cl SK8 . . . . .123 B4
Adam St Ashton-u-L OL6 . . .166 C3
Bolton BL3 . . . . .148 A5
Oldham OL8 . . . . .66 F2
Adams Ave M21 . . . . .109 B6
Adams Cl
Newton-le-W WA12 . . . . . . .89 D2
Poynton SK12 . . . . .133 E2
Adams Dr WN3 . . . . .150 A5
Adamson Gdns M20 . . . . . .109 F3
Adamson Rd M30 . . . . .95 C8
Adamson St
Ashton-in-M WN4 . . . . .73 A3
Dukinfield SK16 . . . . .101 C6
Adamson Wlk **11** M14 . . . . .98 C3
Adastral Ho M11 . . . . .109 C8
Adcroft St SK1 . . . . .170 F7
Adderley Pl SK13 . . . . .171 F1
Adderley Rd SK13 . . . . .171 F1
Addingham Cl M9 . . . . .64 B5
Addington Rd BL3 . . . . .40 F3
Addington St M4 . . . . .159 B2
Addison Ave OL6 . . . . .85 D3
Addison Cl M13 . . . . .163 C6
Addison Cres M16 . . . . .97 B4
Addison Dr M24 . . . . .47 C3
Addison Rd
Altrincham WA15 . . . . .119 E2
Carrington M31 . . . . .106 D6
Irlam M44 . . . . .94 C4
Stretford M32 . . . . .96 B3
Urmston M41 . . . . .95 D1
Adelaide Rd Bramhall SK7 . .132 F5
Stockport SK3 . . . . .170 D8
Adelaide St Bolton BL3 . . . .147 D6
Eccles M30 . . . . .79 D1
Heywood OL10 . . . . .29 D2
Manchester M8 . . . . .155 F5
Middleton M24 . . . . .65 A8
Ramsbottom BL0 . . . . .11 A4
Swinton M27 . . . . .79 D7
Adelaide St E OL10 . . . . . . .29 E2
Adelphi Ct M3 . . . . .158 D3
Adelphi Dr M38 . . . . .60 B5
Adelphi Gr M38 . . . . .60 B5
Adelphi St Manchester M3 . .158 D2
8 Radcliffe M26 . . . . .43 F5
Standish WN6 . . . . .19 E2
Aden Cl M12 . . . . .164 D8
Aden St Oldham OL4 . . . . . .67 D5
Adey Rd WA13 . . . . .117 A5
Adisham Dr BL1 . . . . .143 F1
Adlington Cl
Altrincham M23,WA15 . . . .120 D6
Bury BL8 . . . . .27 A1
Poynton SK12 . . . . .133 F2
Adlington Cty Prim Sch
PR7 . . . . .20 F7
Adlington Dr M32 . . . . .96 F4
Adlington Pk SK10 . . . . . . .133 C1
Adlington Rd SK9 . . . . .137 E7
Adlington St Bolton BL3 . . . .147 D3
Manchester M12 . . . . .164 D8
12 Oldham OL4 . . . . .49 D1
Adlington Sta PR6 . . . . .21 A8
Adlington Way M **16** M34 . .101 A1
Adlington Wlk SK1 . . . . . . .169 E1
Adlow Ind Pk M12 . . . . . . .164 D8
Adria Rd M20 . . . . .110 C3
Adrian Rd BL1 . . . . .142 C2
Adrian St M40 . . . . .83 A7
Adrian Terr OL16 . . . . .31 C7
Adscombe St M16 . . . . .97 E4
Adshall Rd SK8 . . . . .123 A5
Adshead Cl M22 . . . . .121 B3
Adstock Wlk **7** M40 . . . . . .159 C3
Adstone Cl M4 . . . . .160 E4
Adswood Cl OL4 . . . . .67 D8
Adswood Gr SK3 . . . . .170 D6
Adswood La E SK2 . . . . . . .170 F6
Adswood La W SK2,SK3 . . .170 F6
Adswood Old Hall Rd
SK8 . . . . .123 D4
Adswood Prim Sch SK3 . . .170 E5
Adswood Rd SK3,SK8 . . . . .170 D5
Adswood St M40 . . . . .160 E2
Adswood Terr SK3 . . . . . . .170 E6
Adwell Cl WA3 . . . . .91 A8
Aegean Cl **3** M7 . . . . .81 C5
Aegean Rd WA14 . . . . .119 A6
Affetside Dr BL8 . . . . .26 E2
Affleck Ave M20 . . . . .61 A8
Afghan St OL1 . . . . .67 B8
Agden Brow WA13 . . . . . . .117 E1
Agden Brow Pk WA13 . . . . .117 D1
Agden La WA13 . . . . .117 E1
Age Croft OL8 . . . . .67 C3
Agecroft Ent Pk M27 . . . . . .80 E7
Agecroft Park Circle M27 . . .80 E7
Agecroft Rd
Manchester M25,M27 . . . . . .80 E8
Romiley SK6 . . . . .113 A1
Agecroft Rd E M25 . . . . .63 A2
Agecroft Rd W M25 . . . . . . .63 A2

Agecroft Trad Est M6 . . . . . .80 F7
Ager St OL13 . . . . .3 C8
Agincourt St OL10 . . . . .29 B2
Agnes Ct OL4 . . . . .66 C4
Agnes St M13 . . . . .110 C7
Agnes St Manchester M19 . . .99 A2
Manchester M7 . . . . .155 F7
Oldham OL9 . . . . .152 B6
Agnew Pl M6 . . . . .81 A4
Agnew Rd M18 . . . . .165 C5
Aigburth Gr SK5 . . . . .99 F2
Ailsa Cl M40 . . . . .157 D5
Ailsa Ho M6 . . . . .154 F1
Aimson Pl WA15 . . . . .120 C6
Aimson Road E WA15 . . . . .120 C6
Aimson Road W WA15 . . . .120 C7
Aines St M12 . . . . .165 A7
Ainley Rd M22 . . . . .121 D3
Ainley Wood Delph OL3 . . . .50 E5
Dukinfield SK16 . . . . .101 D7
Ainsbrook Ave OL3 . . . . .50 F4
Ainsbrook Terr OL3 . . . . . . .51 D5
Ainscough Ct WN7 . . . . .75 F4
Ainscow Ave BL6 . . . . .39 F8
Ainscow St WN3 . . . . .151 E5
Ainsdale Ave Atherton M46 . .58 C4
Bury BL8 . . . . .27 B2
Edgworth BL7 . . . . .9 E6
Manchester M7 . . . . .63 D1
Ainsdale Cl Bramhall SK7 . .133 A7
Oldham OL8 . . . . .66 D8
Ainsdale Cres OL2 . . . . .48 E2
Ainsdale Dr Gatley SK8 . . . .122 B1
Sale M33 . . . . .107 E2
Whitworth OL12 . . . . .14 D7
Ainsdale Gr SK5 . . . . .111 F8
Ainsdale Rd BL2 . . . . .147 E3
Ainsdale St M12 . . . . .164 F6
Ainse Rd BL6 . . . . .21 B3
Ainsford Rd M20 . . . . .110 D5
Ainsley Gr M28 . . . . .60 D2
Ainsley St **1** M40 . . . . .83 C5
Ainslie Rd BL1 . . . . .142 A1
Ainsty Rd M14 . . . . .98 A4
Ainsworth Ave BL6 . . . . .22 B3
Ainsworth Cl M34 . . . . .100 B3
Ainsworth Ct OL11 . . . . .29 E8
Ainsworth Hall Rd BL2 . . . . .43 B8
Ainsworth La BL2 . . . . .148 C8
Ainsworth Rd Bury BL8 . . . .27 B2
Little Lever BL3 . . . . .43 A8
Radcliffe M26 . . . . .43 F5
Ainsworth Sq BL1 . . . . .143 D3
Ainsworth St Bolton BL1 . . .142 C2
Rochdale OL16 . . . . .31 A6
Ainthorpe Wlk M40 . . . . . . .83 D5
Aintree Ave M33 . . . . .107 C3
Aintree Cl SK7 . . . . .124 F2
Aintree Dr OL11 . . . . .29 E8
Aintree Gr SK3 . . . . .170 E5
Aintree Rd BL3 . . . . .43 A3
Aintree St M11 . . . . .165 B8
Aintree Wlk OL9 . . . . .152 C7
Air Hill Terr **8** OL12 . . . . . .14 C1
Airedale Cl SK8 . . . . .122 C6
Airedale Ct WA14 . . . . .119 E5
Aireworth St BL5 . . . . .39 F3
Airton Cl M40 . . . . .159 C3
Airton Pl WN3 . . . . .153 B8
Aitken Cl BL0 . . . . .138 B5
Aitken St Haslingden BL0 . . . .1 C5
Reddish M19 . . . . .99 C1
Ajax Dr BL9 . . . . .45 A4
Ajax St Ramsbottom BL0 . . .138 B5
Rochdale OL11 . . . . .30 B3
Aked Cl M12 . . . . .164 D6
Akesmoor Dr SK2 . . . . .124 C6
Alamein Dr SK6 . . . . .113 F2
Alan Ave M35 . . . . .83 F5
Alan Dr Altrincham WA15 . . .120 A1
Marple SK6 . . . . .125 F6
Alan Rd Manchester M20 . . .110 C4
Stockport SK4 . . . . .168 B4
Alan St BL1 . . . . .143 D3
Alan Turing Way
Droylsden M11 . . . . .83 A1
Manchester M10,M40 . . . . .160 F3
Alanbrooke Wlk M15 . . . . .162 E5
Alandale Ave M34 . . . . .100 C7
Alandale Rd SK3 . . . . .123 C7
Alasdair Cl OL9 . . . . .65 F8
Alba Cl M30 . . . . .79 D1
Alba Way M32 . . . . .96 A5
Alban Ct BL5 . . . . .57 E7
Alban St M7 . . . . .155 D5
Albany Ave M11 . . . . .99 F7
Albany Cl M38 . . . . .60 B5
Albany Ct
Manchester M20 . . . . .110 B6
Urmston M41 . . . . .95 B3
Albany Dr BL9 . . . . .44 F7
Albany Gr M29 . . . . .77 D8
Albany Rd Bramhall SK7 . . .132 F4
Eccles M30 . . . . .79 B3
Manchester M21 . . . . .97 B1
Wilmslow SK9 . . . . .136 F5
Albany Road Trad Est M21 . .97 B1
Albany St Middleton M24 . . .65 B7
Oldham OL4 . . . . .49 D1
10 Rochdale OL11 . . . . . . .31 A5
Albany Way
Hattersley SK14 . . . . .102 E2
Salford M6 . . . . .81 A3
Albemarle Ave M20 . . . . . . .110 A6
Albemarle Rd M21 . . . . . . .109 A8
Albemarle St
Ashton-u-L OL6 . . . . .166 C3

Albemarle St continued

Manchester M14 . . . . .98 A4
Albemarle Terr OL6 . . . . . .166 C3
Alberbury Ave M23 . . . . . . .120 D7
Albermarle Rd **5** M27 . . . . .79 E7
Albert Ave Dukinfield SK16 . .101 C6
Manchester M25 . . . . .63 D1
Reddish M18 . . . . .99 F4
Shaw OL2 . . . . .149 B5
Urmston M41 . . . . .95 E2
Walkden M28 . . . . .60 C5
Albert Cl Cheadle SK8 . . . . .123 A2
Whitefield M45 . . . . .63 A8
Albert Ct WA14 . . . . .119 D4
Albert Fildes Wlk **3** M8 . . .155 F7
Albert Gr Farnworth BL4 . . . .60 D8
Manchester M12 . . . . .164 F5
Albert Hill St M20 . . . . .110 B3
Albert Park Rd M7 . . . . .81 D7
Albert Pl Altrincham WA14 . .119 D5
Manchester M13 . . . . .98 F3
Whitefield M45 . . . . .45 B1
Albert Rd
Altrincham WA15 . . . . .119 E3
Cheadle SK8 . . . . .123 A2
Eccles M30 . . . . .79 F2
Farnworth BL4 . . . . .60 D8
Hyde SK14 . . . . .167 D2
Manchester M19 . . . . .99 A1
Manchester SK4 . . . . .168 A3
Sale M33 . . . . .108 C4
Whitefield M45 . . . . .63 A8
Wilmslow SK9 . . . . .137 A6
Albert Rd E WA15 . . . . .119 E3
Albert Rd W Bolton BL1 . . . .144 A8
Bolton BL1 . . . . .40 F8
Albert Royds St OL12,OL16 . .15 B2
Albert Sq
Altrincham WA15 . . . . .119 D3
Manchester M2 . . . . .158 F1
Stalybridge SK15 . . . . .85 F1
Albert St Ashton-in-M WN4 . .73 B3
Bolton BL3 . . . . .D3
Bury BL9 . . . . .141 A2
Denton M34 . . . . .100 F3
Droylsden M43 . . . . .84 B1
Eccles M30 . . . . .79 F2
Farnworth BL4 . . . . .60 D7
Farnworth BL4 . . . . .60 E8
Hadfield SK13 . . . . .104 A5
Hazel Grove SK7 . . . . .124 D3
Heywood OL10 . . . . .29 B2
14 Hindley WN2 . . . . .56 D5
Horwich BL6 . . . . .22 B4
Hyde SK14 . . . . .167 F3
Irlam M44 . . . . .105 E6
Little Lever BL3 . . . . .43 B3
Littleborough OL15 . . . . . . .16 B5
Manchester M11 . . . . .160 F1
Middleton M24 . . . . .65 A8
Milnrow OL16 . . . . .32 A5
Oldham OL4 . . . . .67 E5
Oldham OL8 . . . . .66 B3
Prestwich M25 . . . . .63 C4
Ramsbottom BL0 . . . . .138 B6
Royton OL2 . . . . .48 D4
Shaw OL2 . . . . .149 A7
Stockport SK3 . . . . .169 D1
Whitworth OL12 . . . . .14 C8
Wigan WN5 . . . . .54 F6
Albert St W M35 . . . . .83 F6
Albert Webb Ho **6** M5 . . . .154 E1
Alberta St Bolton BL3 . . . . .144 C5
Stockport SK1 . . . . .170 F8
Alberton Cl WN2 . . . . .38 C6
Albine St M40 . . . . .157 F8
Albinson Wlk M31 . . . . .106 A3
Albion Cl SK4 . . . . .169 E3
Albion Ct BL8 . . . . .140 D2
Albion Dr Apsull WN2 . . . . . .38 B2
Droylsden M43 . . . . .84 A2
Albion Fold M43 . . . . .84 A2
Albion Gardens Cl OL2 . . . . .48 F4
Albion Gr BL3 . . . . .145 E5
Bury BL8 . . . . .140 D2
Farnworth M35 . . . . .83 E7
Hyde SK14 . . . . .167 D2
Kearsley BL4 . . . . .60 E8
7 Leigh WN7 . . . . .75 F5
Littleborough OL15 . . . . . . .16 A5
Manchester M19 . . . . .162 F8
Manchester M16 . . . . .97 D4
Oldham OL1 . . . . .153 F7
Oldham OL3 . . . . .152 A7
Pendlebury M27 . . . . .80 A8
4 Platt Bridge WN2 . . . . .56 A2
Radcliffe M26 . . . . .44 B1
Rochdale OL11 . . . . .30 B3
Sale M33 . . . . .108 B4
Stalybridge SK15 . . . . .86 B2
Westhoughton BL5 . . . . .39 F3
Wigan WN1 . . . . .151 D8
Albion Terr BL1 . . . . .142 B3

Albion Towers **5** M5 . . . . .81 B2
Albion Trad Est
 Ashton-u-L OL6 . . . . .85 D3
 Salford M6 . . . . .81 A4
Albion Way M5,M6 . . . . .81 B1
Alburn Ct M40 . . . . .64 E4
Albury Dr Manchester M19 .110 D2
 Rochdale OL12 . . . . .13 F2
Albury Way WN2 . . . . .37 F2
Albyns Ave M8 . . . . .156 A7
Alcester Ave SK3 . . . . .122 F7
Alcester Cl Bury BL8 . . . . .27 B3
 Middleton M24 . . . . .65 B6
Alcester Rd Gatley SK8 . . . . .122 B4
 Sale M33 . . . . .108 B2
Alcester St OL9 . . . . .66 A3
Alcester Wlk M9 . . . . .64 C5
Alconbury Ct M43 . . . . .100 B8
Alconbury Wlk M9 . . . . .64 B6
Aldborough Cl M20 . . . . .110 B6
Aldbourne Cl M40 . . . . .157 D5
Aldbury Terr **2** BL1 . . . . . . .143 D1
Aldcliffe WN3 . . . . .90 F8
Aldcroft St **3** M18 . . . . .99 F6
Alden Cl Haslingden BB4 . . . . .1 A6
 Whitefield M45 . . . . .63 A8
Alden Rd BB4 . . . . .1 A5
Alden Rise BB4 . . . . .1 A6
Alden Wlk SK4 . . . . .111 D7
Alder Ave Ashton-in-M WN4 .72 F5
 Billinge WN5 . . . . .71 D5
 Bury BL9 . . . . .141 C3
 Poynton SK12 . . . . .133 F3
 Wigan WN5 . . . . .54 D6
Alder Cl Ashton-u-L OL6 . . . .85 B7
 2 Bury BL8 . . . . .27 C2
 Dukinfield SK16 . . . . .102 A7
 Wigan WN7 . . . . .75 F2
Alder Ct M8 . . . . .63 F1
Alder Dr Altrincham WA15 .120 D5
 Swinton M27 . . . . .61 C1
Alder Edge **8** M21 . . . . .96 F1
Alder Forest Ave M30 . . . . . .79 A4
Alder Gr Bolton BL7 . . . . .25 C6
 Denton M34 . . . . .101 A3
 Stockport SK3 . . . . .123 C8
 Stretford M32 . . . . .96 F2
Alder La Hindley WN2 . . . . . .57 B5
 Oldham OL8 . . . . .66 F2
Alder Lee Cl WN3 . . . . .54 D1
Alder Meadow Cl OL12 . . . . .14 A1
Alder Moor Cl M11 . . . . .99 D8
Alder Park Prim Sch M30 . . .79 A4
Alder Rd Cheadle SK8 . . . . . .122 E5
 Failsworth M35 . . . . .83 F5
 Golborne WA3 . . . . .90 F8
 Middleton M24 . . . . .47 C2
 Rochdale OL11 . . . . .30 D2
Alder St Atherton M46 . . . . . .58 D3
 Bolton BL3 . . . . .147 F3
 Eccles M30 . . . . .79 A4
 Newton-le-W WA12 . . . . .89 C3
 Salford M6 . . . . .154 F2
Alderbank Horwich BL6 . . . . .21 F3
 Littleborough OL12 . . . . .15 C7
Alderbank Cl BL4 . . . . .60 F6
Aldercroft Ave Bolton BL2 . .25 D1
 Wythenshawe M22 . . . . .121 C2
Alderdale Dr
 Droylsden M43 . . . . .83 E2
 High Lane SK6 . . . . .134 E7
 Manchester SK4 . . . . .111 A5
Alderdale Gr SK9 . . . . .136 E5
Alderdale Rd SK8 . . . . .123 C4
Alderfield Ho **5** M21 . . . . . .96 F1
Alderfield Rd M21 . . . . .96 F1
Alderfold St M46 . . . . .58 D3
Alderford Par **11** M8 . . . . .155 F6
Aldergate Gr OL6 . . . . .85 F5
Alderglen Rd M8 . . . . .156 A5
Alderley Ave Bolton BL1 . . . .24 E5
 Golborne WA3 . . . . .90 D7
Alderley Cl Billinge WN5 . . . .71 E5
 Hazel Grove SK7 . . . . .133 F8
 Poynton SK12 . . . . .133 F2
Alderley Dr SK6 . . . . .112 E3
Alderley Edge SK9 . . . . .137 D1
Alderley Edge
 Com Prim Sch SK9 . . . . .137 F2
Alderley Edge Jun Sch
 for Girls SK9 . . . . .137 A1
Alderley Edge Sch
 for Girls SK9 . . . . .137 A2
Alderley La WN7 . . . . .76 B2
Alderley Lo SK9 . . . . .137 A1
Alderley Rd
 Alderley Edge SK10,SK9 . . .137 F2
 Hindley WN2 . . . . .57 A3
 Reddish SK5 . . . . .111 F5
 Sale M33 . . . . .108 E2
 Urmston M41 . . . . .95 A2
 Wilmslow SK9 . . . . .137 A6
Alderley St OL6 . . . . .85 F5
Alderley Terr **6** SK16 . . . .166 B1
Alderman Foley Dr OL12 . . . .14 A2
Alderman Kay Sch M24 . . . . .47 A3
Alderman Sq M12 . . . . .164 E8
Aldermary Rd M21 . . . . .109 B6
Aldermaston Gr M9 . . . . .64 B6
Aldermere Cres M41 . . . . . . .94 F3
Alderminster Ave M38 . . . . . .60 A5
Alderney Dr WN2 . . . . .55 A3
Alders Ave M22 . . . . .121 C5
Alders Ct OL8 . . . . .85 A8

Alders Green Rd WN2 . . . . . .57 A5
Alders Rd High Lane SK12 . .135 A7
 Wythenshawe M22 . . . . .121 C5
Alders The WN6 . . . . .36 D4
Aldersgate Rd
 Bramhall SK7,SK8 . . . . .132 C5
 Stockport SK3 . . . . .124 B6
Aldersgreen Ave SK6 . . . . . .134 F7
Aldershot Wlk **3** M11 . . . . .160 F1
Alderside Rd M9 . . . . .157 D8
Alderside Ave M9 . . . . .64 B5
Alderson St Oldham OL9 . . .153 E7
 Salford M6 . . . . .81 A4
Aldersyde St BL3 . . . . .147 D3
Alderton Dr BL5 . . . . .57 E6
Alderue Ave M22 . . . . .121 D6
Alderway BL0 . . . . .1 C1
Alderwood Ave SK4 . . . . . . .168 A1
Alderwood Fold OL4 . . . . . . .67 F5
Alderwood Gr BL0 . . . . .1 D4
Alderwood Wlk **7** M8 . . . .155 F6
Aldfield Rd M23 . . . . .108 F1
Aldford Cl M20 . . . . .110 C3
Aldford Dr M46 . . . . .58 E5
Aldford Gr BL3 . . . . .43 B5
Aldford Pl SK9 . . . . .136 F2
Aldford Way WN6 . . . . .36 F1
Aldham Ave M40 . . . . .83 C4
Aldred Cl M8 . . . . .156 B6
Aldred St Bolton BL3 . . . . . .146 B3
 Eccles M30 . . . . .79 C1
 Failsworth M35 . . . . .83 E7
 3 Hindley WN2 . . . . .56 D8
 Leigh WN7 . . . . .75 E8
 Salford M5 . . . . .81 B2
Aldridge Cl WN3 . . . . .55 B3
Aldridge Wlk M11 . . . . .164 F8
Aldsworth Dr BL3 . . . . .147 E4
Aldwick Ave M20 . . . . .110 C3
Aldwinians Cl M34 . . . . .100 E5
Aldworth Dr M40 . . . . .157 E5
Aldworth Gr M33 . . . . .107 D3
Aldwych OL11 . . . . .30 F3
Aldwych Ave M14 . . . . .98 B3
Aldwyn Cl M34 . . . . .100 E5
Aldwyn Cres SK7 . . . . .124 C2
Aldwyn Cty Prim Sch M34 . .84 C1
Aldwyn Park Rd M34 . . . . . .100 C8
Alexander Ave M35 . . . . .84 A8
Alexander Briant Ct BL4 . . . .60 C7
Alexander Ct M5 . . . . .161 A8
Alexander Dr
 Altrincham WA15 . . . . .120 A6
 Milnrow OL16 . . . . .31 F6
 Whitefield M45 . . . . .45 A2
Alexander Gdns M7 . . . . . . .158 D4
Alexander Rd **8** BL2 . . . . . .25 C1
Alexander St Rochdale OL11 .30 B2
 Salford M6 . . . . .154 E2
 Tyldesley M29 . . . . .77 A8
Alexandra Ave Hyde SK14 . .101 C2
 Manchester M14 . . . . .97 F3
 Whitefield M45 . . . . .63 A8
Alexandra Cl SK3 . . . . .123 C6
Alexandra Cres
 1 Oldham OL1 . . . . .67 B8
 Wigan WN5 . . . . .54 D6
Alexandra Ct M41 . . . . .94 E1
Alexandra Ctr Ret Pk
 OL4 .153 F6
Alexandra Dr M19 . . . . .110 F7
Alexandra Gr M44 . . . . .105 F8
Alexandra Ho **6** OL1 . . . . .67 B8
Alexandra Hospl The
 SK8 .122 D6
Alexandra Mews OL4 . . . . . .67 C6
Alexandra Park Inf Sch
 SK3 .123 C7
Alexandra Park Prim Sch
 OL4 . . . . .67 A5
Alexandra Rd
 Ashton-in-M WN4 . . . . .73 B4
 Ashton-u-L OL6 . . . . .85 D4
 Dukinfield M34 . . . . .101 A4
 Eccles M30 . . . . .95 C8
 Horwich BL6 . . . . .39 E8
 Kearsley BL4 . . . . .61 A7
 Kearsley M26 . . . . .61 A4
 Manchester M16 . . . . .97 E4
 Manchester SK4 . . . . .168 C3
 Oldham OL8 . . . . .67 A4
 Sale M33 . . . . .108 D3
 Walkden M28 . . . . .60 C5
Alexandra Rd S M16 . . . . . . .97 E2
Alexandra St Abram WN2 . . .74 B8
 Ashton-u-L OL6 . . . . .85 D4
 8 Bolton BL3 . . . . .147 D4
 Farnworth BL4 . . . . .60 D7
 Heywood OL10 . . . . .29 D2
 Hyde SK14 . . . . .101 C1
 Manchester M7 . . . . .158 D3
 Oldham OL8 . . . . .67 A4
 Wigan WN5 . . . . .54 F6
Alexandra Terr
 14 Manchester M19 . . . . . .99 A1
 Oldham OL4 . . . . .49 E3
Alexandria Dr BL5 . . . . .58 A7
Alf Kaufman Specl Sch
 OL11 .13 E1
Alford Ave M20 . . . . .110 A8
Alford Cl BL2 . . . . .42 F6
Alford Rd SK4 . . . . .111 C6
Alford St **10** OL9 . . . . .66 B2
Alfred Ave M28 . . . . .79 A7
Alfred James Cl **17** M40 . .109 F2
Alfred Morris Ct M23 . . . . . .109 A2
Alfred St Ashton-u-L OL6 . . .85 D4

Alfred St continued
 Bolton BL3 . . . . .42 B4
 Bolton BL7 . . . . .8 D3
 Bury BL9 . . . . .141 A1
 Dukinfield SK14 . . . . .101 C3
 Eccles M30 . . . . .79 D3
 Farnworth BL4 . . . . .42 D2
 Ince-in-M WN3 . . . . .151 D6
 Irlam M44 . . . . .105 E6
 Kearsley BL4 . . . . .60 F8
 Littleborough OL15 . . . . .16 A6
 Manchester M9 . . . . .157 D8
 Newton-le-W WA12 . . . . .89 E3
 Oldham OL9 . . . . .152 C6
 Platt Bridge WN2 . . . . .56 A3
 Ramsbottom BL0 . . . . .138 B5
 Shaw OL2 . . . . .149 B7
 9 Tyldesley M29 . . . . .58 F1
 Walkden M28 . . . . .60 D3
 Whitworth OL12 . . . . .4 D2
 Wigan WN1 . . . . .37 D2
Alfreton Ave M34 . . . . .113 A8
Alfreton Rd SK2 . . . . .124 E5
Alfreton Wlk **9** M40 . . . . . .83 A6
Alfriston Dr M23 . . . . .109 A2
Alger St **3** BL4 . . . . .60 D8
Algernon Rd M28 . . . . .60 C4
Algernon St Eccles M30 . . . .79 D3
 Hindley WN2 . . . . .56 D5
 Swinton M27 . . . . .79 D8
 Wigan WN3 . . . . .55 A4
Algreave Rd SK3 . . . . .123 A8
Alice Ingham RC Prim Sch
 OL16 .15 C2
Alice St Bolton BL3 . . . . .144 C5
 Hyde SK14 . . . . .113 E7
 Pendlebury M27 . . . . .80 B8
 Rochdale OL12 . . . . .14 B1
 Sale M33 . . . . .108 D4
Alicia Ct OL12 . . . . .14 E1
Alicia Dr OL12 . . . . .14 E1
Alick's Fold **4** BL5 . . . . .39 E1
Alison Cl SK4 . . . . .168 B3
Alison Kelly Cl M9 . . . . .157 F8
Alison St
 13 Manchester M14 . . . . . .97 F3
 2 Manchester M40 . . . . . . .98 A3
 Shaw OL2 . . . . .149 B8
Alker Rd M40 . . . . .160 D3
Alker St WN5 . . . . .54 F6
Alkrington Cl BL9 . . . . .45 A2
Alkrington Gn M24 . . . . .64 F7
Alkrington Hall Rd N M24 . .64 F7
Alkrington Hall Rd S M24 . .64 E7
Alkrington Moss Prim Sch
 M24 . . . . .65 B5
Alkrington Park Rd M24 . . . .65 A6
Alkrington Prim Sch M24 . . .65 A6
All Saint's CE Prim Sch
 M40 .83 C5
All Saint's Cl M32 . . . . .48 D5
All Saint's St M32 . . . . .96 B2
All Saints
 Catholic High Sch SK16 .101 D7
All Saints CE Prim Sch
 Appley Bridge WN6 . . . . .18 C1
 Marple SK6 . . . . .126 A5
 Rochdale OL12 . . . . .15 A2
 Stockport SK4 . . . . .169 E3
 Whitefield BL9 . . . . .45 A2
All Saints Jun Sch SK18 . . .165 B6
All Saints RC Prim Sch
 M33 .107 B6
All Saints Terr OL12 . . . . . . .15 B7
All Saints' CE Prim Sch
 BL4 . . . . .42 D2
All Saints' RC Prim Sch
 SK13 . . . . .104 D2
All Saints' Rd SK4 . . . . .169 E4
All Saints' St Bolton BL1 . . .145 E8
 Failsworth M40 . . . . .83 C5
All Souls RC Prim Sch
 M5 . . . . .154 D1
All Souls' CE Prim Sch
 OL10 .29 F3
Allams St M11 . . . . .160 E2
Allan Ct M21 . . . . .109 A7
Allan Roberts Cl M9 . . . . . . .64 D1
Allan St M9 . . . . .76 F8
Allanadale Ct **10** M7 . . . . .63 E1
Allandale M14 . . . . .119 B4
Allandale Dr OL2 . . . . .48 A5
Allandale Rd M19 . . . . .98 F1
Allanson Rd M22 . . . . .109 E1
Alldis Cl M12 . . . . .164 E5
Alldis St SK2 . . . . .124 B5
Allen Ave
 Fowley Common WA3 . . . . . . .92 C4
 Hyde SK14 . . . . .113 F8
Allen Cl OL2 . . . . .149 A6
Allen Rd M41 . . . . .95 F2
Allen St Bury BL8 . . . . .27 C3
 Little Lever BL3 . . . . .43 A8
 Oldham OL8 . . . . .153 D6
 Radcliffe M26 . . . . .43 E4
 Rochdale OL16 . . . . .31 A5
Allenby Gr BL5 . . . . .57 D7
Allenby Rd Irlam M44 . . . . . .105 D4
 Swinton M27 . . . . .79 C6
Allenby St Atherton M46 . . . .58 B2
 Shaw OL2 . . . . .149 A7
Allenby Wlk **4** M40 . . . . . .156 C5
Allendale Dr BL9 . . . . .45 A3
Allendale Gdns BL1 . . . . . . .143 E2
Allendale Wlk M3 . . . . .154 F3
Allerby Way WA3 . . . . .90 E8

Allerdean Wlk SK4 . . . . .110 F3
Allerford St M16 . . . . .97 E4
Allerton Cl BL5 . . . . .40 A1
Allerton Ct **7** BL1 . . . . .145 E8
Allerton Wlk **8** M13 . . . . . .163 C6
Alleschoes Rd OL14 . . . . .6 B7
Allesley Cl BL5 . . . . .40 A1
Allesley Dr M7 . . . . .155 F6
Allgreave Cl M33 . . . . .108 E1
Allaine St **4** WN1 . . . . .151 D8
Alligin Cl OL9 . . . . .152 A8
Allingham St M13 . . . . .98 E4
Allington OL11 . . . . .139 E6
Allington Dr M30 . . . . .79 E4
Allison St M8 . . . . .155 F5
Allison Wlk M15 . . . . .162 E5
Allison Gr M30 . . . . .79 E4
Allott St OL10 . . . . .29 D1
Allonby Wlk M24 . . . . .46 C2
Allotment Rd M44 . . . . .105 D6
Alloway Wlk **6** M40 . . . . . . .83 A6
Allscott Way WN4 . . . . .73 C4
Allsopp St BL3 . . . . .145 F6
Allwood St M5 . . . . .158 D1
Alma Cl WN8 . . . . .53 C7
Alma Ct **3** Manchester M15 .97 E4
 Orrell WN8 . . . . .53 C7
Alma Gr WN3 . . . . .54 E2
Alma Hill WN8 . . . . .53 C7
Alma Hill Est WN8 . . . . .53 C7
Alma Ind Est **29** OL12 . . . .14 F1
Alma La SK9 . . . . .137 A7
Alma Par WN8 . . . . .53 C7
Alma Park Prim Sch M19 . .111 A8
Alma Rd Hazel Grove SK7 . .134 A8
 Manchester M19 . . . . .111 A8
 Orrell WN8 . . . . .53 C7
 Sale M33 . . . . .107 E2
 Westhoughton BL5 . . . . .57 F8
Alma St Atherton M46 . . . . . .58 C3
 Bolton BL3 . . . . .146 C4
 Eccles M30 . . . . .79 F1
 Kearsley BL4 . . . . .61 B5
 Leigh WN7 . . . . .75 E8
 Little Lever BL3 . . . . .43 B3
 Newton-le-W WA12 . . . . .89 B3
 Radcliffe M26 . . . . .44 C3
 16 Rochdale OL12 . . . . . . .14 F1
 Stalybridge SK15 . . . . .86 B2
 Tyldesley M29 . . . . .76 F8
Alminstone Cl M40 . . . . .83 D4
Almond Ave Bury BL9 . . . . . .45 A3
Almond Brook Rd WN6 . . . . .19 C1
Almond Cl Failsworth M35 . .83 F6
 Littleborough OL15 . . . . .15 F6
 Salford M6 . . . . .81 B2
 Stockport SK3 . . . . .123 C8
Almond Cres Rawtenstall BB4 .1 B8
 Standish WN6 . . . . .36 F7
Almond Ct SK16 . . . . .166 C1
Almond Dr M33 . . . . .107 F6
Almond Gr Bolton BL1 . . . . .143 F3
 Wigan WN5 . . . . .54 D6
Almond Rd **8** OL4 . . . . .49 D1
Almond St Bolton BL1 . . . . .143 F4
 9 Farnworth BL4 . . . . .60 C8
 Manchester M40 . . . . .159 B4
 Tottington BL8 . . . . .26 E7
Almond Tree Rd SK8 . . . . . .123 A1
Almond Way **11** SK14 . . . .102 A2
Almond Wlk M31 . . . . .105 E2
Alms Hill Rd M8 . . . . .156 A7
Alness Rd M16 . . . . .97 E2
Alnwick Cl WN2 . . . . .38 D5
Alnwick Dr BL9 . . . . .45 A5
Alnwick Rd M9 . . . . .64 D5
Alperton Wlk M40 . . . . .83 D4
Alpha Court Ind Est M34 . .100 C3
Alpha Ct M34 . . . . .100 C3
Alpha PI M15 . . . . .162 E7
Alpha Rd M32 . . . . .96 E1
Alpha St Manchester M11 . . .99 E7
 Salford M6 . . . . .154 E3
Alpha St W M11 . . . . .99 D7
Alphagate Dr M34 . . . . .100 C3
Alphin Cl Oldham OL3 . . . . . .69 B5
 Uppermill OL5 . . . . .68 E3
Alphin Sq OL5 . . . . .68 D1
Alphonsus St M16 . . . . .97 C4
Alpine Dr Leigh WN7 . . . . . . .75 C8
 Littleborough OL12 . . . . .15 C6
 Milnrow OL16 . . . . .32 A7
 Royton OL2 . . . . .48 E3
Alpine Rd Stockport SK1 . . .112 A1
 Stockport SK1 . . . . .112 A2
Alpine St Droylsden M11 . . . .83 B2
 Newton-le-W WA12 . . . . .89 A3
Alpington Wlk M40 . . . . .65 C2
Alport Ave M16 . . . . .97 C2
Alport Gr BL5 . . . . .39 D4
Alport Lea **2** SK13 . . . . . . .171 E2
Alport Way **1** SK13 . . . . . .171 E2
Alresford Rd Middleton M9 . .64 F5
 Salford M6 . . . . .80 D5
Alric Wlk M22 . . . . .130 E8
Alsager Cl M21 . . . . .109 B6
Alsham Wlk M8 . . . . .156 A6
Alsop Ave M7 . . . . .81 B7
Alstead Ave WA15 . . . . .120 A3
Alston Ave Sale M33 . . . . . .107 F3
 Shaw OL2 . . . . .149 B8
 Stretford M32 . . . . .96 B3
Alston Cl SK7 . . . . .124 A1
Alston Gdns M19 . . . . .110 F5
Alston Lea M46 . . . . .58 D5
Alston Rd Manchester M18 . .99 E5
 Wigan WN2 . . . . .37 F2
Alston St Bolton BL8 . . . . . .147 E3
 Bury BL8 . . . . .27 C4

Alston Wlk M24 . . . . .46 C2
Alstone Dr WA14 . . . . .119 A6
Alstone Rd SK4 . . . . .111 C6
Alt Cl WN7 . . . . .75 D6
Alt Fold Dr OL8 . . . . .67 C3
Alt Gr OL6 . . . . .85 B6
Alt Hill La OL6,OL7 . . . . .85 C8
Alt Hill Rd OL6 . . . . .67 C1
Alt La OL8 . . . . .67 C3
Alt Prim Sch OL8 . . . . .67 C2
Alt Wlk M45 . . . . .45 C2
Altair Ave **7** M22 . . . . .121 D1
Altair Pl M7 . . . . .81 C4
Altcar Gr SK5 . . . . .99 E2
Altcar Wlk M22 . . . . .121 C2
Altham Cl BL9 . . . . .44 D7
Altham Wlk **8** M40 . . . . . . .83 A6
Althorn Wlk **11** M23 . . . . .121 A5
Althorpe Wlk M40 . . . . .83 D4
Alton Ave M41 . . . . .94 D2
Alton Cl Ashton-in-M WN4 . . .73 C4
 Ashton-u-L OL6 . . . . .85 D7
 Whitefield BL9 . . . . .45 A5
Alton Rd SK9 . . . . .136 F7
Alton Sq M11 . . . . .99 E7
Alton St OL8 . . . . .66 F3
Alton Towers M16 . . . . .97 D1
Altrincham CE Prim Sch
 WA14 . . . . .119 D5
Altrincham General Hospl
 WA14 . . . . .119 D4
Altrincham Gram Sch
 for Boys WA14 . . . . .119 D2
Altrincham Gram Sch
 for Girls
 Altrincham WA14 . . . . .119 B3
 Altrincham WA14 . . . . .119 B3
Altrincham Prep Sch
 WA14 . . . . .119 D2
Altrincham Priory Hospl
 WA15 . . . . .129 A7
Altrincham Rd
 Manchester M23 . . . . .120 E7
 Wilmslow SK9 . . . . .130 C2
 Wythenshawe M23 . . . . .121 E5
 Wythenshawe M23 . . . . .121 B7
 Wythenshawe M22 . . . . .130 C4
 Altrincham St M1 . . . . .163 B8
 Altrincham Sta WA15 . . . . .119 E4
 Altringham Ret Pk WA14 . .119 C7
Alum Cres M13 . . . . .45 A3
Alva Rd OL4 . . . . .49 D2
Alvan Sq **1** M11 . . . . .99 D7
Alvanley Cl Sale M33 . . . . . .108 C1
 Shevington WN5 . . . . .36 C1
Alvanley Cres **1** SK3 . . . .123 C6
Alvaston Ave SK4 . . . . .168 B2
Alvaston Rd M18 . . . . .99 F4
Alveley Ave M20 . . . . .110 C5
Alverstone Rd M20 . . . . .110 C6
Alveston Dr SK9 . . . . .137 C8
Alvington Gr SK7 . . . . .124 A1
Alwin Rd OL2 . . . . .48 A4
Alwinton Ave SK4 . . . . .110 E3
Alworth Rd M9 . . . . .64 D5
Alwyn Cl WN3 . . . . .75 F1
Alwyn Dr M13 . . . . .98 E4
Alwyn St WN1 . . . . .37 D1
Alwyn Terr WN1 . . . . .37 D1
Amar St WN2 . . . . .151 F7
Ambassador PI WA15 . . . . .119 E5
Amber Gdns
 Dukinfield SK16 . . . . .101 B8
 Wigan WN6 . . . . .56 E4
Amber Gr BL5 . . . . .39 F2
Amber St M4 . . . . .159 A2
Ambergate M40 . . . . .58 D2
Ambergate St M11 . . . . .160 F2
Amberhill Way
 Boothstown M28 . . . . .77 F5
 Boothstown M28 . . . . .78 A5
Amberley Cl Bolton BL3 . . . .144 C5
 Wigan WN2 . . . . .37 F2
Amberley Dr
 Altrincham WA15 . . . . .129 B8
 Irlam M44 . . . . .94 A1
 Sale M33 . . . . .107 E5
 Wythenshawe M23 . . . . .121 A4
Amberley Rd M33 . . . . .107 E5
Amberley Wlk OL9 . . . . .152 C7
Amberwood Cl WN2 . . . . . . .56 B7
Amberwood Dr
 Manchester M23 . . . . .120 D6
Amblecote Dr E M40 . . . . . . .60 A6
Amblecote Dr W M38 . . . . . .60 A6
Ambleside Ince-in-M WN3 . .56 B7
 Stalybridge SK15 . . . . .86 A3
 Wigan WN5 . . . . .54 C7
Ambleside Ave
 Altrincham WA15 . . . . .120 C5
 Ashton-u-L OL7 . . . . .84 F4
Ambleside Cl Bolton BL2 . . . .25 B4
 Middleton M24 . . . . .46 E1
Ambleside Ct SK8 . . . . .122 C5
Ambleside PI WA11 . . . . .71 B1
Ambleside Rd
 Reddish SK5 . . . . .111 F6
 Urmston M41 . . . . .94 E1
Ambleside Wlk M9 . . . . .65 A2
Amblethorn Dr **2** BL1 . . . . .23 E2
Ambrey Cl **4** SK9 . . . . .57 E1
Ambrose Cres OL3 . . . . .51 B3
Ambrose Ct Hyde SK14 . . . .113 E7
 Manchester M21 . . . . .165 A7
Ambrose Dr M20 . . . . .109 C5
Ambrose Gdns M20 . . . . . . .109 E4
Ambrose St Hyde SK14 . . . .113 E7
 Rochdale OL16 . . . . .31 B5
 Wigan WN1 . . . . .37 C2
Ambuscade Ct M41 . . . . .94 E2
Ambush St M11 . . . . .99 F7

Amelia St Denton M34 100 F4
Hyde SK14 167 E2
Amersham Cl M41 95 B5
Amersham Pl M19 111 A6
Amersham St M5 154 F1
Amesbury Dr WN3 54 C2
Amesbury Gr SK5 111 F5
Amesbury Rd M9 64 E4
Amethyst Cl WN2 38 A2
Amherst Rd M14,M20 110 D7
Amis Gr WA3 90 E8
Amlwch Ave SK2 124 D6
Ammon Wrigley Cl OL1 153 F7
Ammon's Way OL3 50 F5
Amory St M12 163 C8
Amos Ave M40 83 C4
Amos St Manchester M9 157 F8
Salford M6 154 E2
Ampleforth Gdns M26 43 E5
Ampney Cl M30 79 B1
Amport Wlk 8 M40 65 C2
Amwell St M8 156 C7
Amy St Middleton M24 47 B1
Rochdale OL12 14 B1
Anaconda Dr M3 158 E3
Ancaster Wlk 5 M40 65 C2
Anchor Cl M19 99 C1
Anchor Ct M8 63 F1
Anchor La BL4,M38 59 F7
Anchor St OL1 153 F8
Anchorage Quay M5 161 A8
Anchorage Rd M32 96 A1
Anchorage Sta M5 161 A8
Anchorage Wlk M18 165 C6
Anchorside Cl M21 109 B7
Ancoats Gr
Manchester M4 160 D1
Manchester M4 164 D8
Ancoats Gr N M4 160 D1
Ancoats Hospl M4 159 C1
Ancoats St 5 OL4 67 E6
Ancroft Gdns BL3 146 C2
Ancroft St M15 162 E6
Anderton Cl Bury BL8 26 F1
Rawtenstall BB4 2 F7
Anderton Gr OL6 85 E5
Anderton La BL6 21 E4
Anderton Prim Sch PR6 21 B8
Anderton St Adlington PR7 21 A7
Ince-in-M WN2 151 F7
Anderton Way Aspull WN2 38 B2
Handforth SK9 131 D3
Andoc Ave M30 80 A1
Andover Ave M24 65 C5
Andover Cres WN3 54 D2
Andover Rd WA11 72 E1
Andover St M30 79 C1
Andover Wlk M8 156 A8
Andre St 14 M11 83 C2
Andrew Ave WN5 71 F5
Andrew Cl Radcliffe M26 44 C1
Ramsbottom BL8 10 F1
Andrew Ct 2 M20 110 B6
Andrew Gr SK16 101 D8
Andrew Ho SK4 168 B4
Andrew La Bolton BL1 24 F6
High Lane SK6 134 F8
Andrew Rd M9 64 D1
Andrew St Ashton-u-L OL6 85 D5
Bury BL9 141 A2
Chadderton OL9 152 B8
Droylsden M43 84 C4
Failsworth M35 83 E8
Hyde SK14 167 F3
Middleton M24 65 C7
Mossley OL5 86 C8
Stockport SK4 169 D2
Andrew's Terr 3 BL5 39 E1
Andrews Ave M41 94 E3
Andy Nicholson Wlk M9 157 F8
Anemone Dr BB4 1 A8
Anerley Rd M20 110 B4
Anfield Cl BL9 45 B3
Anfield Mews SK8 122 F3
Anfield Rd Bolton BL3 147 F2
Cheadle SK8 122 F3
Failsworth M40 65 D1
Sale M33 108 C5
Angel Cl SK16 101 B8
Angel St Dukinfield M34 101 A4
Hazel Grove SK7 124 D3
Manchester M4 159 A3
Angel Trad Est 4 M4 159 A3
Angela Ave OL1,OL2 48 E2
Angela St M15 162 D7
Angelico Rise OL1 49 D3
Angelo St BL1 143 D2
Angle St BL2 25 B1
Angler Gr M34 100 F3
Anglers Rest M44 105 E5
Anglesea Ave SK2 170 F6
Anglesey Cl OL7 85 A6
Anglesey Dr SK12 133 F6
Anglesey Gr SK8 123 A6
Anglesey Rd OL7 84 F6
Anglesey Water SK12 133 E6
Angleside Ave M19 110 E4
Anglezarke Rd PR6 21 A7
Anglia Gr BL3 146 C4
Angora Dr M3 158 D3
Angouleme Ret Pk BL9 140 F2
Angouleme Way BL9 140 F1
Angus Ave Heywood OL10 29 A1
Leigh WN7 75 C7
Angus St OL13 3 C8
Aniline St M11 83 B1
Anita St M4 159 B2
Anjou Bvd WN5 54 F8
Ann La M29 77 C5
Ann Sq OL4 67 D8
Ann St Denton M34 100 E3
Dukinfield OL7 100 F8
Dukinfield SK14 101 C3
Farnworth BL4 60 E7
Heywood OL10 29 D3
Leigh WN7 75 E8
Reddish SK5 169 E4
Rochdale OL11 139 F6
Annable Rd Bredbury SK6 112 D3
Droylsden M43 84 B1
Irlam M44 105 F8
Manchester M18 99 E6
Annald Sq M43 100 A8
Annan Gr WN4 73 E5
Annan St M34 100 F4
Annandale Gdns WN8 53 A7
Anne Cl 6 OL7 85 A6
Anne Line Cl 3 OL11 31 A5
Anne Nuttall St M15 162 D7
Anne St SK16 101 D8
Annecy Cl BL8 27 B4
Annersley Ave OL2 149 A6
Annesley Cres WN3 54 F3
Annesley Gdns 1 M18 99 D6
Annesley Rd M40 65 E1
Annette Ave WA12 89 A5
Annie Darby Ct M9 157 D7
Annie St Ramsbottom BL0 11 A4
Salford M5,M6 154 E2
Annis Cl SK9 137 B2
Annis Rd
Alderley Edge SK9 137 B2
Bolton BL3 146 B4
Annis St M9 157 E7
Annisdale Cl M30 79 B2
Annisfield Ave OL3 69 C5
Anscombe Cl M40 160 D3
Ansdell Ave M21 109 C8
Ansdell Dr M43 83 E2
Ansdell Rd Horwich BL6 22 C4
Reddish SK5 100 A1
Rochdale OL16 31 B4
Wigan WN5 54 D5
Ansdell St M8 156 A7
Ansell Cl M18 99 D6
Anselms Ct OL8 66 C4
Ansford Ave WN2 74 B8
Ansford Wlk M9 156 C6
Ansleigh Ave M8 64 A1
Ansley Gr SK4 168 B3
Anslow Cl M40 157 D5
Anson Ave M27 79 E6
Anson Cl SK7 132 F5
Anson Ct M14 98 D3
Anson Engine Mus The
SK12 134 C3
Anson Pl WN5 54 C8
Anson Rd Handforth SK9 131 E1
Manchester M14 98 D3
Poynton SK12 134 B3
Reddish M34,SK5 100 A2
Swinton M27 79 E6
Anson St Bolton BL1 143 F3
Eccles M30 79 B4
Wigan WN5 54 F7
Answell Ave M8 64 A2
Antares Ave M7 158 D3
Anthistle Ct M5 154 D2
Anthony Cl M12 164 E7
Anthony St OL5 68 B1
Anthorn Rd WN3 54 E3
Antilles Cl M12 99 A4
Antler Ct WN4 73 B6
Anton Wlk M9 157 D7
Antrim Cl Manchester M19 110 D2
Wigan WN3 54 C2
Anvil Cl WN5 53 D5
Anvil St OL13 3 E8
Anvil Way OL1 153 E7
Apethorn La SK14 113 D7
Apfel La OL9 152 B7
Apollo Ave BL9 44 F3
Apollo Wlk M12 165 A6
Apperley Grange M30 79 E4
Appian Way M7 155 E5
Apple Cl OL8 67 C3
Apple Dell Ave WA3 74 C1
Apple St SK14 114 D7
Apple Tree Ct M5 81 A2
Apple Tree Rd SK22 127 B1
Apple Tree Wlk 8 M33 107 C5
Apple Way M24 65 B6
Appleby Ave
Altrincham WA15 120 C5
Dukinfield SK14 101 C5
Manchester M12 99 A3
Appleby Cl Bury BL8 26 F2
Stockport SK3 170 D5
Appleby Gdns
1 Bolton BL2 25 B1
Whitefield M45 44 F3
Appleby Lo M14 98 D2
Appleby Rd SK8 122 B4
Appleby Wlk 4 OL2 48 E4
Applecross Wlk M11 165 C8
Appledore Dr
Altrincham M23 120 D7
Bolton BL2 25 F3
Appledore Wlk OL9 152 B6
Appleford Dr M8 156 B6
Applethwaite WN2 56 B8
Appleton Ct M33 108 B4
Appleton Dr SK13 116 F8
Appleton Gr M33 107 E2
Appleton Rd
Altrincham WA15 119 F1
Appleton Rd *continued*
Reddish SK4 111 D6
Appleton St WN3 150 B8
Appleton Wlk 8 SK9 131 E1
Applewood OL9 65 E7
Appley Bridge Sta WN6 35 C7
Appley Cl WN6 18 C2
Appley La N WN6 18 C1
Appley La S WN6,WN8 35 C6
Apprentice Ct 18 M9 157 E8
April Cl OL8 67 C4
Apsley Cl WA14 119 B1
Apsley Gr
Altrincham WA14 119 B1
Manchester M12 163 C6
Apsley Pl OL6 166 A2
Apsley Rd M34 100 F4
Apsley Side OL5 86 C8
Apsley St SK1 169 F1
Aquarius La M6 81 C4
Aquarius St M15 163 A5
Aqueduct Rd BL3 148 C5
Aquinas Coll SK2 124 A6
Aragon Dr OL10 29 C2
Aragon Way SK6 125 E6
Arbor Ave M19 110 F6
Arbor Dr M19 110 F7
Arbor Gr Droylsden M43 83 F3
Walkden M38 59 E4
Arbory Ave M40 83 B7
Arbory Cl WN7 76 C5
Arbour Cl Bury BL9 27 E6
Salford M6 154 F3
Arbour La WN6 19 B1
Arbour Rd OL4 67 E4
Arbroath St M43 83 E1
Arbury Ave Cheadle SK3 123 A7
Rochdale OL11 139 E5
Arcade St 18 WN1 150 C8
Arcade The
Brinnington SK5 112 C5
2 Stalybridge SK15 101 F8
Arcades The OL6 166 B3
Arcadia Ave M33 108 A1
Arch La WN4 72 B3
Arch St Bolton BL1 148 A8
Bolton BL1 25 A1
Archer Ave BL2 148 C8
Archer Gr BL2 148 C8
Archer Pk M24 64 E8
Archer Pl M32 95 F3
Archer St Boothstown M28 77 E7
Droylsden M11 83 A2
Leigh WN7 76 B2
Mossley OL5 68 C2
Stockport SK2 124 C5
Archie St M5 161 A7
Arclid Cl SK9 131 E1
Arcon Cl OL16 31 E6
Arcon Dr M16 97 E3
Arcon Pl WA14 119 A6
Ardale Ave M40 65 C2
Ardcombe Ave M9 64 C5
Ardeen Wlk M13 163 C6
Arden Ave M24 65 B5
Arden Bsns Ctr SK6 112 E6
Arden Cl Ashton-u-L OL6 85 E6
Bury BL9 44 E8
Gatley SK8 131 C7
Glossop SK13 116 A8
Arden Ct SK7 123 D1
Arden Gr M40 65 C1
Arden Hall SK6 112 D7
Arden Ho OL2 48 E4
Arden Lodge Rd M23 120 E7
Arden Prim Sch SK6 112 D3
Arden Rd SK6 112 E7
Arden St OL9 66 A3
Arden Wlk 6 Sale M33 107 C5
Stockport SK1 169 E1
Ardenfield M34 113 A7
Ardenfield Dr M22 121 E3
Ardens Cl M27 61 D2
Ardent Way M25 63 B1
Ardern Gr SK1 170 F8
Ardern Rd M8 63 F2
Arderne Rd WA15 120 A8
Ardingly Wlk M23 120 D8
Ardley Rd BL6 22 C4
Ardmore Wlk M22 121 E2
Ardwick Gn N M12 163 C7
Ardwick Gn S M12,M13 163 C7
Ardwick Sta M12 164 D7
Arena App BL6 39 C7
Argo St BL3 147 D4
Argosy Dr Eccles M30 94 F7
Wythenshawe M90 129 F7
Argus St OL8 66 C2
Argyle Ave Manchester M14 98 E4
Walkden M28 60 C5
Whitefield M45 63 A8
Argyle Cres OL10 29 B1
Argyle Par OL10 29 A1
Argyle St Atherton M46 58 C2
Bury BL9 140 F4
Droylsden M43 84 A1
Hazel Grove SK7 124 E2
Heywood OL10 29 A1
Hindley WN2 56 E5
Manchester M18 99 D5
Oldham OL1 67 B8
14 Rochdale OL11,OL16 31 A4
Swinton M27 79 E7
Wigan WN5 54 F6
Argyll Ave M32 96 B2
Argyll Cl Failsworth M35 84 B7
Garswood WN4 72 C4
Argyll Park Rd M35 84 B7
Argyll Rd Cheadle SK8 122 F5
Oldham OL9 65 F4
Argyll St Ashton-u-L OL6 85 E3
Mossley OL5 68 C1
Ariel Wlk 4 WA3 90 E8
Ark St 3 M19 99 A2
Arkendale Cl M35 84 C7
Arkholme M28 78 A8
Arkholme Wlk M40 83 B7
Arkle Ave SK8,SK9 131 E4
Arkle Dr OL9 65 F8
Arkley Wlk M13 163 B6
Arkwright Dr SK6 126 A6
Arkwright Rd SK6 126 A6
Arkwright St Horwich BL6 22 C2
Oldham OL9 152 C6
Arkwright Way OL11 31 A2
Arlen Ct BL2 148 B5
Arlen Rd BL2 148 B5
Arlen Way OL10 29 B2
Arley Ave Bury BL9 27 F6
Manchester M20 109 F5
Arley Cl Altrincham WA14 119 D8
Aspull WN2 38 B2
Dukinfield SK16 101 D6
Arley Dr Sale M33 108 A2
Shaw OL2 49 D8
Arley Gr SK3 123 D4
Arley La WN1,WN2 20 D2
Arley Mere Cl SK8 122 F3
Arley Moss Wlk M13 163 B7
Arley St Ince-in-M WN3 55 F4
Radcliffe M26 44 B1
Arley Way Atherton M46 58 E2
22 Denton M34 101 A1
Arlies Cl SK15 86 A4
Arlies La SK15 86 B4
Arlies Prim Sch SK15 86 A4
Arlies St OL6 85 D4
Arlington Ave Denton M34 101 A2
Manchester M25 63 B2
Swinton M27 79 D6
Arlington Cl BL9 11 C2
Arlington Cres SK9 136 E5
Arlington Dr
Golborne WA3,WN7 91 C8
Poynton SK12 133 D3
Stockport SK2 124 A3
Arlington Rd Cheadle SK8 122 C4
Stretford M32 96 B1
Arlington St 4
Ashton-u-L OL6 166 C3
Bolton BL3 147 F3
Manchester M3 158 D2
Manchester M8 155 F8
Arlington Way SK9 136 E5
Arliss Ave M19 111 A8
Arm Rd OL15 15 E4
Armadale Ave M9 65 A4
Armadale Cl SK3 170 F5
Armadale Rd Bolton BL3 40 E5
Dukinfield SK16 101 D7
Armdale Rise OL4 49 E1
Armit Rd OL3 68 E5
Armitage Ave M38 59 F4
Armitage CE Prim
Sch M12 164 E6
Armitage Cl Hyde SK14 113 E8
Middleton M24 64 D7
Oldham OL8 66 C3
Armitage Ct M12 164 F6
Armitage Gr M38 59 F4
Armitage Ho M6 80 C3
Armitage Owen
Wlk 4 M40 83 A7
Armitage Rd WA14 119 D3
Armitage St M30 79 D1
Armitstead St 5 WN2 56 D4
Armour Pl M9 64 C2
Armoury Bank WN4 73 B3
Armoury St SK3 170 E8
Armstrong Hurst Cl OL12 15 B2
Armstrong St Aspull WN2 38 A3
Horwich BL6 22 C2
Arncliffe Cl 5 BL4 42 D1
Arncliffe Dr M23 121 A3
Arncliffe Rise OL4 50 A4
Arncot Rd BL1 24 F5
Arncott Cl OL2 49 A4
Arne Cl SK2 125 A5
Arne St OL9 152 A5
Arnesby Ave M33 108 E5
Arnesby Gr BL2 148 B8
Arnfield Dr 1 M28 78 B6
Arnfield La SK13 103 F8
Arnfield Rd
Manchester M20 110 C6
Stockport SK3 170 D5
Arnold Ave Heywood OL10 46 E7
Hyde SK14 113 F7
Arnold Cl SK16 102 A7
Arnold Ct M16 97 E1
Arnold Dr Droylsden M43 84 A1
Middleton M24 47 C3
Arnold Rd Bolton BL7 24 F8
Hyde SK14 113 F7
Manchester M16 97 E1
Arnold St Ashton-u-L OL6 166 C3
Bolton BL1 142 C2
Oldham OL1 67 A8
Stockport SK3 170 E7
Arnold Wlk 9 M34 113 A7
Arnott Cres M15 162 F5
Arnside Ave
Hazel Grove SK7 124 C2
Ince-in-M WN2 56 A7
Oldham OL9 152 A5
Reddish SK4 111 E6
Arnside Cl Gatley SK8 122 B4
High Lane SK6 134 E8
Shaw OL2 49 D7
Arnside Dr Dukinfield SK14 101 C4
Rochdale OL11 29 E5
Salford M6 80 B3
Arnside Gr Bolton BL2 42 E8
Sale M33 108 B6
Arnside Rd Hindley WN2 57 A5
Wigan WN5 54 B8
Arnside St M14 98 B2
Arosa Ct M20 110 C7
Arran Ave Oldham OL8 66 F3
Sale M33 108 C3
Stretford M32 96 A2
Arran Cl BL3 40 E6
Arran Gdns M41 95 C5
Arran Gr M26 43 E5
Arran Rd SK16 101 C7
Arran St 12 Manchester M40 64 F1
Manchester M7 155 D6
Arran Wlk OL10 29 A1
Arrandale Ct M41 95 D3
Arras Gr M34 99 F3
Arreton Sq M14 98 D3
Arrivals Way M90 130 B7
Arrow St Bolton BL1 145 E8
Leigh WN7 76 B3
Manchester M7 155 D5
Arrow Trad Est M34 100 D5
Arrowfield Dr M21 109 D7
Arrowfield Rd M21 109 D7
Arrowhill Rd BL8 43 F8
Arrowscroft Way SK14 171 D4
Arrowsmith Ct 7 BL6 22 E1
Arrowsmith Wlk 16 M11 160 F1
Arthill La WA14 118 B1
Arthington St OL16 31 B8
Arthog Dr WA15 128 F8
Arthog Rd
Altrincham WA15 128 F8
Manchester M20 110 C3
Arthur Ave M28 60 C5
Arthur La BL2 26 B2
Arthur Millwood Ct M3 158 D1
Arthur Rd M16 97 C3
Arthur St Bury BL8 27 C2
Eccles M30 79 C1
Farnworth BL4 60 D8
Heywood OL10 29 D2
Hindley WN2 56 E5
Hyde SK14 101 C1
Leigh WN7 75 E4
Little Lever BL3 43 B3
Prestwich M25 62 F4
Reddish SK5 111 E7
Rochdale OL12 139 D8
Shaw OL2 149 B7
Swinton M27 79 D7
Walkden M28 60 E1
Walkden M28 60 F2
Arthur Terr 4 SK5 111 E7
Arthurs La OL3 69 B6
Artillery Ct M13 163 C7
Artillery Pl M22 121 F4
Artillery St Bolton BL3 145 F5
Manchester M3 162 E8
Arundale BL5 39 F2
Arundale Ave M16 97 E1
Arundale Cl SK14 102 F3
Arundale Ct M16 97 E1
Arundale Gr SK14 102 F3
Arundale Prim Sch SK14 102 F3
Arundel Ave
Hazel Grove SK7 133 D8
Prestwich M45 63 B7
Rochdale OL11 30 E4
Urmston M41 94 C1
Arundel Cl
Altrincham WA15 120 C1
Bury BL8 27 C6
Mossley SK15 86 F6
Arundel Dr WN7 75 F6
Arundel Gr SK2 124 B4
Arundel Grange SK13 104 A1
Arundel Rd SK8 132 A6
Arundel St Ashton-u-L OL6 85 E3
Bolton BL1 24 E5
Glossop SK13 104 C1
Hindley WN2 56 E5
Manchester M15 162 D7
Mossley OL5 68 B1
Oldham OL4 67 C7
Rochdale OL11 30 E4
Swinton M27 61 C1
Wigan WN5 54 F6
Arundel Wlk OL9 152 A6
Asby Cl M24 46 D2
Ascension CE Prim
Sch M7 158 D4
Ascension Rd M7 158 D4
Ascot Ave Sale M33 107 D3
Stretford M32 96 F3
Ascot Cl Oldham OL9 152 C7
Rochdale OL11 29 E8
Ascot Dr Atherton M46 58 E4
Hazel Grove SK7 125 A2
Urmston M41 94 C2
Ascot Mdws BL9 44 E8
Ascot Par M19 110 F6
Ascot Rd Failsworth M40 83 B4
Little Lever BL3 42 F3
Ascot Wlk M6 81 A5
Ascroft Ave WN6 36 F3
Ascroft St Oldham OL1 153 F6

Ascroft St continued
Wigan WN1 . . . . .151 E7
Asgard Dr M5 . . . . .161 C8
Asgard Gr M5 . . . . .161 C8
Ash Ave Altrincham WA14 . .119 A5
Cheadle SK8 . . . . .122 E5
Irlam M44 . . . . .105 D5
Newton-le-W WA12 . . . . . . .89 C2
Ash Cl Appley Bridge WN6 . .35 D7
Ashton-u-L OL6 . . . . .85 D5
Littleborough OL12 . . . . . . .15 C4
Mottram-in-L SK14 . . . . . . .103 A4
Ash Ct Manchester SK4 . . . .168 B3
Romiley SK6 . . . . .113 A5
Ash Dr M27 . . . . .61 C2
Ash Field Sch M28 . . . . . . .60 E1
Ash Gr Altrincham WA14 . . .119 C1
Altrincham WA15 . . . . .119 F7
Bolton BL1 . . . . .144 B8
Bolton BL2 . . . . .25 F3
Bury BL8 . . . . .27 A5
Droylsden M43 . . . . .100 A8
Gatley SK8 . . . . .131 B8
Golborne WA3 . . . . .90 B8
Handforth SK9 . . . . .11 C3
Horwich BL6 . . . . .22 E1
Littleborough OL15 . . . . . . .15 F5
Manchester M14 . . . . .98 E4
Marple SK6 . . . . .125 E5
Newhey OL16 . . . . .32 A3
Oldham OL4 . . . . .68 A7
Orrell WN5 . . . . .53 F6
Prestwich M25 . . . . .63 A6
Ramsbottom BL0 . . . . .10 F3
Reddish M34 . . . . .111 D5
Royton OL2 . . . . .48 D6
Stalybridge SK15 . . . . .85 F3
Standish WN6 . . . . .36 F8
Stretford M32 . . . . .108 C8
Swinton M27 . . . . .79 D5
Walkden M28 . . . . .60 E1
Westhoughton BL5 . . . . . . .57 F2
Ash Grove Cres WN5 . . . . .71 E6
Ash Hill Dr OL5 . . . . .86 E8
Ash Ho M16 . . . . .97 E2
Ash La Altrincham WA15 . .120 C2
Aspull WN2 . . . . .38 A2
Ash Leigh Dr BL1 . . . . .40 E8
Ash Lo SK12 . . . . .133 D4
Ash Rd Coppull PR7 . . . . . .19 E8
Droylsden M43 . . . . .83 F2
Hollinfare WA3 . . . . .105 A2
Kearsley BL4 . . . . .60 F5
Partington M31 . . . . .105 D3
Poynton SK12 . . . . .133 F3
Reddish M34 . . . . .99 F3
Ash Sq OL4 . . . . .67 D8
Ash St Bolton BL2 . . . . . . .148 A6
Bury BL9 . . . . .141 A2
Denton M34 . . . . .100 D7
Failsworth M35 . . . . .83 E8
Golborne WA3 . . . . .74 B2
Hazel Grove SK7 . . . . .124 D3
Heywood OL10 . . . . .29 B3
Manchester M9 . . . . .157 D7
Middleton M24 . . . . .65 C8
Oldham OL4 . . . . .67 B6
Rochdale OL11 . . . . .30 C2
Salford M6 . . . . .154 F2
Stockport SK3 . . . . .123 B8
2 Tyldesley M29 . . . . .59 A1
Ash Tree Ave M43 . . . . . . .83 F2
Ash Tree Dr Sm16 . . . . . . .101 F7
Ash Tree Rd Hyde SK14 . . .102 B5
Manchester M8 . . . . .64 A1
Ash Wlk Chadderton OL9 . .152 B8
Middleton M24 . . . . .64 F6
Ashawe Cl M38 . . . . .59 E3
Ashawe Gr M38 . . . . .59 E3
Ashawe Terr M38 . . . . .59 E3
Ashbank Ave BL3 . . . . .40 E6
Ashbee St BL1 . . . . .143 E3
Ashberry Cl SK9 . . . . .137 D8
Ashborne Dr BL9 . . . . .11 D2
Ashbourne Ave Aspull WN2 .38 A2
Bolton BL2 . . . . .148 B6
Cheadle SK8 . . . . .122 F6
Denton M34 . . . . .100 F1
Urmston M41 . . . . .94 E2
Ashbourne Cl Leigh WN7 . .57 D1
Littleborough OL12 . . . . . . .15 D6
Ashbourne Cres M33 . . . .108 D2
Handforth SK13 . . . . .116 F8
Ashbourne Dr
Ashton-u-L OL6 . . . . .85 F6
High Lane SK6 . . . . .134 F6
Ashbourne Gdns WN2 . . . .56 F5
Ashbourne Gr
Manchester M7 . . . . .155 E7
Whitefield M45 . . . . .44 D1
Worsley M28 . . . . .78 E8
Ashbourne Rd
Denton M34 . . . . .100 E2
Eccles M30 . . . . .79 E1
Hazel Grove SK7 . . . . .133 F8
Pendlebury M6 . . . . .80 C5
Stretford M32 . . . . .96 A3
Ashbourne Sq OL8 . . . . . .153 E5
Ashbourne St OL10 . . . . . .13 E1
Ashbridge M17 . . . . .96 B6
Ashbridge Rd M35 . . . . . . .84 B6
Ashbrook Ave M34 . . . . . .100 D4
Ashbrook Cl Gatley SK8 . . .122 B1
Reddish M34 . . . . .100 B3

Ashbrook Cl continued
Whitefield M45 . . . . .63 B8
Ashbrook Cres OL12 . . . . .15 C4
Ashbrook Farm Cl SK5 . . .99 F2
Ashbrook Hey La OL12 . . .15 C4
Ashbrook La SK5 . . . . .99 F2
Ashbrook St M11 . . . . . . .100 A7
Ashburn OL10 . . . . .29 C2
Ashburn Ave M19 . . . . . . .110 F5
Ashburn Gr SK4 . . . . .169 D3
Ashburn Rd SK4 . . . . .169 D3
Ashburne Ho M14 . . . . .98 D4
Ashburner St BL1 . . . . . . .145 E6
Ashburton Cl SK14 . . . . . .102 E2
Ashburton Rd SK3 . . . . . .170 E6
Ashburton Rd W M17,M41 . .95 E7
Ashbury Cl BL3 . . . . .145 E5
Ashbury Pl M40 . . . . .160 E4
Ashbury Prim Sch M11 . . .164 F8
Ashbury's Sta M12 . . . . . .165 A7
Ashby Ave M19 . . . . .110 E4
Ashby Cl BL3 . . . . .42 C2
Ashby Gr Leigh WN7 . . . . .75 C8
Whitefield M45 . . . . .63 B7
Ashby Rd WN3 . . . . .55 B3
Ashcombe Dr Bolton BL2 . .43 A6
Radcliffe M26 . . . . .43 D1
Ashcombe Wlk **7** M11 . . .160 F1
Ashcroft Ave M22 . . . . . . .121 D4
Ashcott Cl BL6 . . . . .40 E5
Ashcroft
6 Littleborough OL12 . . . . .15 D4
Wilmslow SK9 . . . . .136 F5
Ashcroft Ave M6 . . . . .154 E4
Ashcroft Cl OL1 . . . . .153 F6
Ashcroft Rd WA13 . . . . . .117 B4
Ashcroft St WN2 . . . . .56 E4
Ashdale Ave BL3 . . . . .40 E5
Ashdale Cl SK5 . . . . .111 F5
Ashdale Cres M43 . . . . . . .83 F1
Ashdale Dr Gatley SK8 . . .122 B2
Manchester M20 . . . . .110 D5
Ashdale Rd Hindley WN2 . .57 A5
Ashdene SK5 . . . . .111 F5
Ashdene Ashton-u-L OL6 . . .85 D2
Rochdale OL12 . . . . .14 D4
Ashdene Cl
Oldham OL1,OL9 . . . . .48 C1
Oldham OL4 . . . . .67 F7
Ashdene Cres BL2 . . . . . . .25 D4
Ashdene Prim Sch SK9 . . .136 F5
Ashdene Rd
Manchester M20 . . . . .110 D6
Manchester M24 . . . . .110 D2
Wilmslow SK9 . . . . .136 F5
Ashdene Rise OL1 . . . . . . .49 D4
Ashdown Ave
Manchester M9 . . . . .64 D4
Romiley SK6 . . . . .113 C5
Ashdown Dr Bolton BL2 . . .25 C3
Boothstown M28 . . . . .78 A7
Pendlebury M27 . . . . .80 A6
Ashdown Gr M9 . . . . .64 D4
Ashdown Rd SK4 . . . . .168 A3
Ashdown Way OL2 . . . . . . .48 E8
Ashdowne Lawns SK15 . . .86 D3
Asher St BL3 . . . . .146 C2
Ashes Cl SK15 . . . . .102 C8
Ashes Dr BL2 . . . . .42 F8
Ashes La Glossop SK13 . .104 B2
Milnrow OL16 . . . . .31 F7
Oldham OL4 . . . . .67 F6
Stalybridge SK15 . . . . .102 C8
Ashfell Ct **1** M21 . . . . .96 F1
Ashfield M34 . . . . .100 A1
Ashfield Ave Atherton M46 . .58 C4
Hindley WN2 . . . . .56 F4
Rochdale OL11 . . . . .139 F5
Ashfield Cl Lymm WA13 . . .117 B4
Ashfield Cres Billinge WN5 . .71 E4
Cheadle SK8 . . . . .122 D6
Ashfield Dr Aspull WN2 . . .38 C5
Failsworth M40 . . . . .83 C4
Ashfield Gr Bolton BL1 . . . .25 A6
Irlam M44 . . . . .105 E6
Reddish M18,M34 . . . . .99 F4
Romiley SK6 . . . . .114 B1
Stockport SK3 . . . . .123 C8
Ashfield Ho OL11 . . . . .139 F5
Ashfield House Gdns WN6 . .36 F8
Ashfield Lo OL16 . . . . .31 F4
Ashfield Lo M20 . . . . .109 F2
Ashfield Park Dr WN6 . . . .36 E1
Ashfield Rd Adlington PR6 . .21 B8
Altrincham WA15 . . . . .119 E5
Cheadle SK8 . . . . .122 D5
Hadfield SK13 . . . . .171 E3
Manchester M13 . . . . .98 E3
Rochdale OL11 . . . . .139 F5
Sale M33 . . . . .108 B5
Stockport SK4 . . . . .123 F4
Urmston M41 . . . . .95 D2
Ashfield Sq M43 . . . . .83 F2
Ashfield St
Manchester M11 . . . . .160 F2
Oldham OL8 . . . . .66 C3
Ashfield Terr WN6 . . . . . . .18 B3
Ashfield Valley Prim Sch
OL11 . . . . .30 E4
Ashford W33 . . . . .107 C4
Ashford Ave
Boothstown M28 . . . . .77 F6
Eccles M30 . . . . .95 C8
Reddish SK5 . . . . .99 F2

Ashford Ave continued
Swinton M27 . . . . .79 C7
Ashford Cl Bolton BL2 . . . . .25 E4
Bury BL8 . . . . .27 B1
Handforth SK9 . . . . .131 C4
Ashford Ct **8** SK13 . . . . . .171 E1
Ashford Mews SK13 . . . . .171 E1
Ashford Rd
Manchester M20 . . . . .110 B7
Reddish SK4 . . . . .111 D6
Wilmslow SK9 . . . . .137 A4
Ashford Rise WN1 . . . . . . .37 B4
Ashford St OL10 . . . . .28 F2
Ashford Wlk Bolton BL1 . . .143 E1
Oldham OL9 . . . . .152 B6
Ashgate Ave M22 . . . . . . .121 E4
Ashgill Wlk **4** M9 . . . . . .157 E7
Ashgrove OL16 . . . . .31 B1
Ashia Cl OL16 . . . . .31 B6
Ashill Wlk M3 . . . . .162 E8
Ashington Cl BL1 . . . . . . .142 B3
Ashington Dr BL8 . . . . .26 F2
Ashington Way WN5 . . . . . .36 B1
Ashkirk St **4** M18 . . . . . . .99 D5
Ashland Ave
Ashton-in-M WN4 . . . . .73 A4
5 Wigan WN1 . . . . .37 C2
Wigan WN3 . . . . .108 A5
Ashlands Ave
Boothstown M28 . . . . .78 A7
Failsworth M40 . . . . .65 C1
Swinton M27 . . . . .79 D6
Ashlands Dr M34 . . . . .100 E6
Ashlands Rd WA15 . . . . . . .108 A1
Ashlar Dr M12 . . . . .164 E8
Ashlea Gr OL4 . . . . .68 B6
Ashleigh Ave SK13 . . . . . .104 B2
Ashleigh Cl OL2 . . . . .48 E2
Ashleigh Rd WA15 . . . . . . .120 B8
Ashley Ave Bolton BL2 . . . .42 D8
Manchester M16 . . . . .97 D4
Swinton M27 . . . . .79 A6
Urmston M41 . . . . .94 E2
Ashley CE Prim Sch
WA15 . . . . .128 F5
Ashley Cl OL11 . . . . .30 C4
Ashley Court Dr M40,OL9 . .65 F1
Ashley Cres M27 . . . . .79 A6
Ashley Ct Altrincham WA15 .119 E1
Failsworth M40 . . . . .65 C1
Manchester SK4 . . . . .168 B4
Swinton M27 . . . . .61 F2
Ashley Dr Bramhall SK7 . . .132 C6
Leigh WN7 . . . . .75 C8
Sale M33 . . . . .107 E2
Swinton M27 . . . . .79 D6
Ashley Gdns
High Lane SK6 . . . . .134 D8
Hyde SK14 . . . . .167 E1
Ashley Gr **8** BL4 . . . . .60 C8
Ashley La M9 . . . . .157 F8
Ashley Mews Hyde SK14 . .167 E1
Whitefield M45 . . . . .63 B7
Ashley Mill La N WA14 . . .128 E8
Ashley Rd
Altrincham WA15 . . . . .119 E2
Ashley WA14,WA15,WA16 . .128 E4
Dukinfield SK16 . . . . .83 E2
Handforth SK9 . . . . .131 B1
Hindley WN2 . . . . .57 B3
Stockport SK2 . . . . .124 C8
Ashley St Hyde SK14 . . . . .167 E3
Manchester M4 . . . . .159 B3
Oldham OL9 . . . . .152 C7
Salford M6 . . . . .154 E2
Ashley Sta WA15 . . . . .128 E5
Ashleymill La WA14 . . . . . .128 D7
Ashleys The SK4 . . . . .168 B3
Ashling St M32 . . . . .108 B3
Ashlor St **5** BL9 . . . . .140 E1
Ashlyn Gr M14 . . . . .110 D8
Ashlynne OL6 . . . . .166 C3
Ashmeade WA15 . . . . .120 B1
Ashmill Wlk M9 . . . . .156 C6
Ashmond Rd **12** OL4 . . . . .67 F6
Ashmoor Rd M22 . . . . . . .121 E1
Ashmoor Wlk M22 . . . . . . .121 E1
Ashmore Ave SK3 . . . . . . .122 F7
Ashmore St M29 . . . . .77 D8
Ashmount Dr OL12 . . . . . . .14 F2
Ashness Cl BL6 . . . . .21 D5
Ashness Dr Bolton BL2 . . . .25 E1
Bramhall SK7 . . . . .132 E8
Middleton M24 . . . . .46 B3
Ashness Gr BL2 . . . . .25 E1
Ashness Pl BL2 . . . . .25 E1
Ashover Ave M12 . . . . .164 F6
Ashover Cl **8** BL1 . . . . .24 F6
Ashover St M32 . . . . .96 E3
Ashridge Cl BL6 . . . . .40 C6
Ashridge Dr
Dukinfield SK16 . . . . .101 B7
Eccles M30 . . . . .95 D8
Ashridge Way WN5 . . . . . .36 B1
Ashstead Rd M33 . . . . . . .108 C1
Ashton Ave WA14 . . . . . . .119 E6
Ashton Cres OL9 . . . . .66 A2
Ashton Ct Denton M34 . . .100 E6
Sale M33 . . . . .107 E4
Ashton Field Dr M28 . . . . . .60 D3
Ashton Gallery **6** WN1 . . .150 C8
Ashton Gdns
Glossop SK13 . . . . .116 C7
Rochdale OL11 . . . . .139 E5

Ashton Grange Ind Est
WN4 . . . . .73 B6
Ashton Heath WN4 . . . . . . .73 D2
Ashton Hill La M43 . . . . . .100 A8
Ashton Ho
Manchester M15 . . . . .162 E8
Hyde SK14 . . . . .167 E3
Ashton La Middleton M24 . .65 A8
Sale M33 . . . . .107 F5
Ashton New Rd
Droylsden M11,M43 . . . . . . .83 C1
Manchester M11,M40 . . . . .160 F1
Ashton Nichol Mere
Cty Prim Sch WN4 . . . . . . .73 B5
Ashton Old Rd
Manchester M11 . . . . .99 D7
Manchester M11,M12 . . . . .164 E8
Ashton on Mersey Sch
M33 . . . . .107 F3
Ashton Pl SK7 . . . . .124 F1
Ashton Rd Bredbury SK6 . .112 E6
Carrington M31,M33 . . . . .106 C3
Denton M34 . . . . .100 E6
Droylsden M43 . . . . .84 B1
Dukinfield SK14 . . . . .101 E5
Failsworth M35 . . . . .84 C7
Golborne WA3 . . . . .74 A2
Manchester M9 . . . . .64 D5
Newton-le-W WA12 . . . . . . .89 C5
Oldham OL6,OL7 . . . . .67 B3
Windy Arbour WN4 & WN5 . .72 B8
Ashton Rd E M35 . . . . .84 A7
Ashton Rd W M35 . . . . . . .83 F7
Ashton Ret Pk OL6 . . . . . .166 B3
Ashton St Bolton BL3 . . . .146 B4
Dukinfield SK16 . . . . .101 A7
Glossop SK13 . . . . .116 C7
4 Heywood OL10 . . . . .29 C2
Little Lever BL3 . . . . .43 B3
Manchester M9 . . . . .157 F8
Oldham OL9 . . . . .66 A3
Rochdale OL11 . . . . .139 E5
Romiley SK6 . . . . .113 C6
Wigan WN1 . . . . .151 F8
Ashton Sta OL6 . . . . .166 B3
Ashton-under-Lyne
Sixth Form Coll OL6 . . . . .85 E3
Ashurst Ave M11 . . . . .83 B2
Ashurst Cl Bolton BL2 . . . . .25 F3
Hyde SK14 . . . . .167 E3
Ashurst Dr SK3,SK8 . . . . . .123 B5
Ashurst Gdns OL6 . . . . . . .166 B4
Ashurst Rd
Shevington Moor WN6 . . . . .19 B2
Wythenshawe M22 . . . . . . .121 F3
Ashville Terr M40 . . . . .64 F1
Ashwater Wlk **8** M40 . . . . .64 A5
Ashway OL6 . . . . .166 A3
Ashway Clough N SK2 . . . .124 D5
Ashway Clough S SK2 . . . .124 D5
Ashwell Ave WA3 . . . . .74 D1
Ashwell Rd M23 . . . . .121 B7
Ashwell St BL2 . . . . .25 B3
Ashwin Wlk **6** M8 . . . . . . .155 F6
Ashwood Altrincham WA14 .128 B8
Chadderton OL9 . . . . .65 E7
Glossop SK13 . . . . .115 F8
Kearsley M26 . . . . .61 B7
Ashwood Ave
Abram Brow WN2 . . . . .74 C7
Ashton-in-M WN4 . . . . .73 A2
Golborne WA3 . . . . .90 D8
Manchester M20 . . . . .109 E4
Ramsbottom BL0 . . . . .11 D7
Reddish M34 . . . . .100 B3
Sale M33 . . . . .107 E3
Walkden M28 . . . . .60 C5
Ashwood Cres SK3 . . . . . .170 D6
Ashwood Ct M20 . . . . .109 E4
Ashwood Dr Bury BL8 . . . . .27 B6
Littleborough OL15 . . . . . . .15 E5
Royton OL2 . . . . .48 D4
Ashwood Rd SK12 . . . . . . .135 D6
Ashworth Ave Denton M34 .100 F7
Little Lever BL3 . . . . .43 C3
Urmston M41 . . . . .94 E2
Ashworth Cl
Altrincham WA14 . . . . .119 B1
Littleborough OL15 . . . . . . .16 A4
Oldham OL9 . . . . .66 C4
Royton OL2 . . . . .48 F4
Ashworth Ct
5 Radcliffe M26 . . . . .44 C4
Shaw OL2 . . . . .149 B6
Ashworth La Bolton BL1 . . .24 E5
Mottram-in-L SK14 . . . . . .102 F2
Ashworth Mews OL10 . . . . .29 A2
Ashworth Rd
Rochdale OL10,OL11 . . . . . .29 B7
Rochdale OL16 . . . . .12 E2
Ashworth St Aspull WN2 . . .38 E4
3 Bacup OL13 . . . . .3 D8
Bury BL8 . . . . .27 C3
Denton M34 . . . . .100 E4
Failsworth M35 . . . . .83 D6
Farnworth BL4 . . . . .60 C8
Heywood OL10 . . . . .46 D8
Manchester M7,M8 . . . . . .155 E5
Oldham OL1 . . . . .153 F6
Radcliffe M26 . . . . .44 C4
Rawtenstall BB4 . . . . .2 F8
Rochdale OL12 . . . . .139 E8
Ashworth Terr
3 Bacup OL13 . . . . .3 B8
Bolton BL2 . . . . .25 E4
Ashworth View M5 . . . . . .161 C1
Ashworth Way **6** SK14 . . .102 F2
Asia St **3** BL3 . . . . .42 A3

Askern Ave M22 . . . . .121 D3
Askett Cl M40 . . . . .83 D6
Askrigg Wlk **8** M13 . . . . . . .98 F4
Askwith Dr WN2 . . . . .56 F4
Askwith Rd M24 . . . . .56 F3
Aspell Cl M24 . . . . .64 F8
Aspen Cl Altrincham WA15 .120 E5
Stockport SK4 . . . . .168 A1
Westhoughton BL5 . . . . . . .57 F7
Aspen Gdns OL12 . . . . .14 A1
Aspen Gn M34 . . . . .101 A2
Aspen Way SK6 . . . . .135 A7
Aspen Wood SK14 . . . . . . .167 F3
Aspen Wood Dr OL9 . . . . . .65 E7
Aspens The SK8 . . . . .122 A6
Aspenshaw Cotts SK22 . . .127 E4
Aspenshaw Rd SK22 . . . . .127 E3
Aspenwood WN4 . . . . .73 A2
Aspenwood Cl SK6 . . . . . .125 E7
Aspenwood Dr M33 . . . . . .107 C4
Aspin La M4 . . . . .159 A3
Aspinal Prim Sch M18 . . . .99 E2
Aspinall Cl M28 . . . . .59 F3
Aspinall Cres M28 . . . . . . .59 F2
Aspinall Gr **12** M28 . . . . . .59 F3
Aspinall Rd WN6 . . . . .19 B1
Aspinall St Heywood OL10 . .29 E2
Horwich BL6 . . . . .22 D1
Manchester M14 . . . . .98 C3
Middleton M24 . . . . .65 C7
6 Platt Bridge WN2 . . . . . . .56 A2
Aspinall Way BL6 . . . . .22 C1
Aspland Rd SK14 . . . . .113 F8
Aspull Arc **8** WN1 . . . . . . .150 C8
Aspull Church Sch WN2 . . .38 C4
Aspull Comm WN7 . . . . . . .75 C1
Aspull New Springs Inf Sch
WN2 . . . . .38 A2
Aspull St OL4 . . . . .67 C5
Aspull Wlk M13 . . . . .163 C6
Asquith Ave M34 . . . . .101 C6
Asquith Rd M19 . . . . .110 F6
Asquith St SK5 . . . . .99 F1
Assheton Ave M34 . . . . . . .84 C1
Assheton Cl OL6 . . . . .166 B3
Assheton Cres M40 . . . . . . .83 D4
Assheton Ho OL6 . . . . .166 B3
Assheton Rd
Failsworth M40 . . . . .83 D4
Shaw OL2 . . . . .48 F7
Assheton St
8 Middleton M24 . . . . .47 A1
9 Middleton M24 . . . . .47 A2
Assheton Way M24 . . . . . . .65 A8
Assisi Gdns M12 . . . . .165 B6
Assumption Rd M24 . . . . . .46 D3
Astan Ave M43 . . . . .83 C2
Astbury Ave Droylsden M34 .84 D1
Manchester M21 . . . . .109 C4
Astbury Cl
4 Altrincham WA15 . . . . . .119 E6
Golborne WA3 . . . . .91 B8
Oldham OL4 . . . . .67 F6
Astbury Cres SK3 . . . . . . .170 D6
Astbury St M46 . . . . .58 D4
Astbury Wlk SK8 . . . . .123 A5
Aster Ave BL4 . . . . .42 A1
Aster Ho OL1 . . . . .48 E1
Aster St OL1 . . . . .48 E1
Aster Wlk M31 . . . . .105 F2
Astley Cl OL7 . . . . .84 F5
Astley Ct M44 . . . . .105 E8
Astley Gdns SK16 . . . . . . .101 B8
Astley Gr SK15 . . . . .86 A3
Astley Green Colliery Mus
M29 . . . . .77 C4
Astley Hall Dr
Ramsbottom BL0 . . . . .11 C4
Tyldesley M29 . . . . .77 B6
Astley High Sch SK6 . . . . .101 E6
Astley La BL1 . . . . .143 E2
Astley Rd Bolton BL2 . . . . . .25 E5
Irlam M44 . . . . .93 C3
Stalybridge SK15 . . . . .85 F2
Astley St Bolton BL1 . . . . .143 E2
Droylsden M11 . . . . .83 C1
Dukinfield SK16 . . . . .101 A8
Leigh WN7 . . . . .76 B4
Stalybridge SK15 . . . . .102 A8
Stockport SK4 . . . . .169 E1
Tyldesley M29 . . . . .77 A7
Astley Terr **3** SK16 . . . . . .166 C1
Aston Ave M14 . . . . .98 A2
Aston Cl SK3 . . . . .123 C6
Aston Gdns **4** BL4 . . . . . . .42 D1
Aston Gr M29 . . . . .59 C1
Aston Ho BL1 . . . . .144 C2
Aston Way **28** SK9 . . . . . . .131 D5
Astor Rd Manchester M19 . .110 E7
Salford M5 . . . . .80 C1
Astra Bsns Pk M17 . . . . . . .95 F8
Astra Ind Ctr OL11 . . . . . . .30 C3
Atcham Gr M9 . . . . .64 B6
Athenian Gdns **12** M5,M7 . .81 C1
Athens Dr M28 . . . . .60 C2
Athens St SK1 . . . . .124 A8
Athens Way OL4 . . . . .67 E6
Atherfield BL2 . . . . .42 F8
Atherfield Cl **8** M18 . . . . . . .99 F6
Atherleigh Gr WN7 . . . . . . .75 F7
Atherleigh Way M29 . . . . . .58 F1
Atherley Gr OL9 . . . . .65 F7
Atherstone **3** OL12 . . . . . .139 F8
Atherstone Ave M8 . . . . . . .64 A2
Atherstone Cl BL8 . . . . .27 C4
Atherton Ave M44 . . . . . . .103 A4
Atherton Cl M35 . . . . .84 B5
Atherton Gr SK14 . . . . . . .103 A4

Atherton Green Hall Sch
M46 .58 F4
Atherton Ho M46 . . . . .58 D4
Atherton La M44 . . . . .105 E5
Atherton Rd WN7 . . . . .56 D5
Atherton Sacred Heart
RC Prim Sch M46 . . . . .58 E1
Atherton Sq Adlington PR7 . . .21 A6
Bacup OL13 . . . . .3 C8
Bickershaw WN2 . . . . .74 E8
Eccles M30 . . . . .79 B1
Manchester M3 . . . . .158 E1
Oldham OL4 . . . . .67 C5
Oldham OL4 . . . . .67 E5
5 Oldham OL4 . . . . .67 F6
Stockport SK3 . . . . .170 D8
7 Wigan WN5 . . . . .54 F6
Atherton St George's
Prim Sch M46 . . . . .58 C4
Atherton Sta M46 . . . . .58 E4
Atherton Way Bacup OL13 . . . .3 B8
4 Eccles M30 . . . . .79 B1
Athlone Ave Bolton BL1 . . . . .24 D5
Bury BL9 . . . . .140 F4
Cheadle SK8 . . . . .123 C5
Manchester M40 . . . . .83 A8
Athol Cres WN2 . . . . .57 B3
Athol Rd Bramhall SK7 . . . . .132 D5
Manchester M16 . . . . .109 E8
Athol St Ashton-u-L OL6 . . . .166 C3
Eccles M30 . . . . .79 C1
Ramsbottom BL0 . . . . .138 C7
Reddish M18 . . . . .99 E3
Rochdale OL12 . . . . .15 B1
Stockport SK4 . . . . .169 D3
Athole St M5,M6 . . . . .154 F1
Atholl Ave M32 . . . . .96 A2
Atholl Cl BL3 . . . . .40 F6
Atholl Dr OL10 . . . . .46 A8
Atholl Gr WN3 . . . . .55 A3
Athos Wlk M40 . . . . .65 C2
Atkin St M28 . . . . .60 D2
Atkinson Ave BL3 . . . . .42 B3
Atkinson Ho M33 . . . . .108 B5
Atkinson Rd Sale M33 . . . . .108 A5
Urmston M41 . . . . .95 D2
Atkinson St Abram WN2 . . . .74 B8
Manchester M3 . . . . .158 E1
Oldham OL9 . . . . .153 D8
2 Rochdale OL11 . . . . .30 C2
Stockport SK1 . . . . .124 A7
Atlanta Ave M90 . . . . .130 A8
Atlantic Bsns Ctr WA14 . . .119 C7
Atlantic St WA14 . . . . .119 B6
Atlantic Wlk **11** M11 . . . . . .160 F1
Atlas St Ashton-u-L OL7 . . . . .85 A5
Dukinfield SK16 . . . . .101 D8
Atlas Trad Est SK5 . . . . .111 F7
Atlow Dr M23 . . . . .121 B5
Attenbury's La WA14 . . . . . .119 E8
Attenbury's Pk Est WA14 . .119 E8
Attercliffe Rd M21 . . . . .109 A7
Attewell St M11 . . . . .165 A8
Attingham Wlk
Denton M34 . . . . .100 E1
Salford M6 . . . . .80 A4
Attleboro Rd M40 . . . . .83 A7
Attlee Ave WA3 . . . . .92 C4
Attlee Way M12 . . . . .160 E1
Attwood Rd WA15 . . . . .120 B5
Attwood St M12 . . . . .99 A3
Atwood Rd M20 . . . . .110 C3
Atwood St M1 . . . . .163 A8
Auberson Rd BL3 . . . . .147 D3
Aubrey Rd M14 . . . . .110 E2
Aubrey St Rochdale OL11 . .139 F5
Salford M5 . . . . .161 A7
Auburn Ave Bredbury SK6 . .112 F4
Hyde SK14 . . . . .167 E1
Auburn Dr M41 . . . . .95 E1
Auburn Rd Denton M34 . . . .100 E2
Manchester M16 . . . . .97 B4
Auburn St Bolton BL3 . . . . .147 D4
Manchester M1 . . . . .159 B1
Manchester M1 . . . . .163 B8
Auckland Dr M6 . . . . .81 A5
Auckland Rd M19 . . . . .110 F8
Audax Wlk M40 . . . . .83 B4
Auden Cl M11 . . . . .83 D1
Auden Ct M11 . . . . .83 D1
Audenshaw Hall Gr M34 . .100 B7
Audenshaw Prim Sch
M34 .100 D7
Audenshaw Rd
Ashton-u-L M34 . . . . .100 D7
Ashton-u-L M34 . . . . .100 E8
Audenshaw St Stephen's
CE Prim Sch
M34 .100 E8
Audlem Cl M40 . . . . .160 D2
Audlem Wlk SK8 . . . . .123 A5
Audley Ave M32 . . . . .95 F4
Audley Rd M19 . . . . .99 B2
Audley St Ashton-u-L OL6 . . .85 E2
Mossley OL5 . . . . .68 D1
Audlum Ct B19 . . . . .141 A2
Audrey Ave M18 . . . . .99 E5
Audrey St M9 . . . . .157 F7
Aughton Cl WN5 . . . . .71 E4
Aughton St WN2 . . . . .56 D4
Augusta Cl OL12 . . . . .14 E2
Augusta St OL12 . . . . .14 E1
Augustine Webster Cl
M9 . . . . .157 E8
Augustus St **3** BL3 . . . . .42 A4
Manchester M3,M8 . . . . .159 A4

Augustus Way M15 . . . . .97 E4
Austell Rd M22 . . . . .121 D1
Austen Ave BL9 . . . . .44 F6
Austen Rd M30 . . . . .79 D1
Austen Wlk OL10 . . . . .49 E4
Auster Cl M14 . . . . .110 A8
Austin Ave WN4 . . . . .72 E4
Austin Ct M20 . . . . .110 C4
Austin Dr M20 . . . . .110 C4
Austin Gr M10 . . . . .110 F8
Austin St WN7 . . . . .75 D5
Austin's La BL6 . . . . .22 F1
Autumn St M13 . . . . .98 C4
Avallon Cl BL8 . . . . .26 F7
Avalon Dr M20 . . . . .122 C8
Avalon Pk OL4 . . . . .67 D6
Avebury Cl Golborne WA3 . . .90 E8
Horwich BL6 . . . . .22 F1
Manchester M7 . . . . .155 F6
Avebury Rd M23 . . . . .121 A5
Avenham Cl M15 . . . . .162 E5
Avening Wlk **7** M22 . . . . . .121 C2
Avens Rd M31 . . . . .105 F3
Avenue St Bolton BL1 . . . . .143 D1
Stockport SK1 . . . . .169 F2
Avenue The Adlington PR6 . .21 A8
Alderley Edge SK9 . . . . .137 A1
Altrincham WA15 . . . . .128 F8
Bolton BL2 . . . . .148 B7
Boothstown M28 . . . . .78 B3
Bredbury SK6 . . . . .112 D4
Bury BL9 . . . . .27 F5
Eccles M30 . . . . .79 D1
Gatley SK8 . . . . .122 A1
Hadfield SK13 . . . . .104 A4
Leigh WN7 . . . . .76 A6
Manchester M7 . . . . .81 C5
Newton-le-W WA12 . . . . .89 D4
Orrell WN5 . . . . .53 D3
Sale M33 . . . . .107 E3
Shaw OL2 . . . . .149 A6
Urmston M41 . . . . .94 E2
Westhoughton BL5 . . . . .39 F1
Wigan WN1 . . . . .37 D2
Wigan WN6 . . . . .36 E4
Worsley M28 . . . . .78 D4
Avenue Works M17 . . . . . . .96 C6
Averham Wlk M17 . . . . .73 B2
Averhill M40 . . . . .78 B8
Averill St M40 . . . . .83 D5
Averon Rise OL1 . . . . .49 D4
Aveson Ave M21 . . . . .109 B6
Avian Dr M14 . . . . .110 B8
Aviary Rd M28 . . . . .78 F6
Aviary The M28 . . . . .79 A6
Aviemore Cl WN4 . . . . .72 D4
Avis St OL2 . . . . .149 B7
Avlan Cl M30 . . . . .94 F7
Avocet Cl Leigh WN7 . . . . . . .76 A6
Newton-le-W WA12 . . . . .89 C4
Avocet Dr
Altrincham WA14 . . . . .119 B8
Irlam M44 . . . . .94 A4
Avon **6** OL10 . . . . .29 C2
Avon Bank **1** SK6 . . . . .112 F3
Avon Cl Marple SK6 . . . . .125 E5
Milnrow OL16 . . . . .32 A6
Walkden M28 . . . . .60 A2
Avon Ct **3** M15 . . . . .162 D6
Avon Dr B19 . . . . .28 A8
Avon Gdns M19 . . . . .111 A6
Avon Rd Altrincham WA15 . .128 E8
Ashton-in-W WN4 . . . . .73 E5
Billinge WN5 . . . . .71 D3
Chadderton OL9 . . . . .65 F8
Culcheth WA3 . . . . .92 A2
Gatley SK8 . . . . .122 B1
Heywood OL10 . . . . .29 A2
Kearsley BL4 . . . . .61 B5
Manchester M19 . . . . .111 A6
Shaw OL2 . . . . .149 B8
Tyldesley M29 . . . . .77 C1
Wigan WN5 . . . . .54 C7
Avon St Bolton BL1 . . . . .142 B1
Leigh WN7 . . . . .76 B4
Oldham OL8 . . . . .66 F2
Stockport SK3 . . . . .170 E7
Avonbrook Dr OL9 . . . . .65 F2
Avoncliff Cl BL1 . . . . .143 D3
Avoncourt Dr M20 . . . . .110 A4
Avondale
Ramsbottom BL0 . . . . .10 F3
Salford M6 . . . . .80 B5
Tyldesley M29 . . . . .77 C6
Avondale Lo M33 . . . . .108 B3
Avondale Ave Farnworth BL4 .59 F8
Hazel Grove SK7 . . . . .124 F2
Stockport SK3 . . . . .123 A6
Stretford M32 . . . . .96 F4
Whitefield M45 . . . . .44 E1
Wigan WN1 . . . . .37 C1
Avondale Rise SK9 . . . . .137 D6
Avondale Sch SK3 . . . . .123 B7
Avondale St Bolton BL1 . . . .142 C1
Manchester M8 . . . . .156 A7
Standish WN6 . . . . .19 E2
Avonhead Cl BL6 . . . . .21 F3
Avonlea Dr M19 . . . . .110 E6
Avonlea Rd Droylsden M43 . .83 E2
Sale M33 . . . . .107 D1
Avonleigh Gdns **7** OL1 . . . .49 C1
Avril Cl SK5 . . . . .111 F8
Avril Ct WN3 . . . . .55 E4

Avro Cl M14 . . . . .98 B1
Avro Ct M24 . . . . .65 D8
Avro Way M90 . . . . .129 F7
Awburn Rd SK14 . . . . .102 E1
Axbridge Wlk M40 . . . . .160 D2
Axford Cl M7 . . . . .155 F6
Axon Sq M16 . . . . .97 F4
Aycliffe Ave M23 . . . . .109 D5
Aycliffe Gr M13 . . . . .98 E3
Aye Bridge Rd WA3 . . . . .74 B5
Aylesbury Ave
Denton M34 . . . . .100 F1
Urmston M41 . . . . .95 E3
Aylesbury Cl **2** M5 . . . . . . .81 A1
Aylesbury Cres WN2 . . . . . . .57 C2
Aylesbury Gr M21 . . . . .97 C1
Aylesby Ave M18 . . . . .99 B4
Aylesford Rd M14 . . . . .98 D3
Aylesford Wlk BL1 . . . . .143 E1
Aylestone M M40 . . . . .83 A7
Aylsham Cl SK6 . . . . .112 F4
Aylsham Mews M27 . . . . .79 D5
Aylwin Dr M33 . . . . .108 C3
Ayr Ave OL8 . . . . .66 F3
Ayr Cl SK7 . . . . .125 A2
Ayr Gr OL10 . . . . .29 A1
Ayr St BL2 . . . . .25 C4
Ayrefield Gr WN6 . . . . .35 D6
Ayrefield Rd WN8 . . . . .35 C4
Ayres Rd M17 . . . . .97 C4
Ayrshire Rd M7 . . . . .81 B6
Ayrton Gr M38 . . . . .60 A5
Aysgarth Cl OL16 . . . . .15 B1
Aysgarth Ave Cheadle SK8 .122 C6
Droylsden M18 . . . . .99 E5
Romiley SK6 . . . . .113 D4
Aysgarth Cl M33 . . . . .107 D3
Ayshford Cl WA14 . . . . .119 B6
Ayton Gr M14 . . . . .98 E4
Aytoun St M1 . . . . .159 B1
Azalea Ave M18 . . . . .99 D6

B
Babbacombe Gr M9 . . . . .64 B5
Babbacombe Rd SK2 . . . . . .124 C6
Babylon La PR6 . . . . .21 B8
Back Abingdon Rd M12 . . . . .25 B1
Back Acton St M1 . . . . .163 B8
Back Adrian Rd BL1 . . . . . . .142 C3
Back Adrian Rd E **6** BL1 . .142 C2
Back Ainscow St BL1 . . . . . .145 E8
Back Ainsworth La BL2 . . . . .25 C1
Back Ainsworth La E BL2 . . .25 C1
Back Ainsworth St BL1
Bury BL8 . . . . .27 B2
BL8 . . . . .27 C2
Back Ainsworth St N
BL8 . . . . .27 C2
Back Ainsworth Rd
BL8 . . . . .142 C3
22 Bolton BL1 . . . . .143 D2
Back Albert St BL9 . . . . .141 A1
Back Albion Pl BL9 . . . . .140 F4
Back Alder St **4** BL3 . . . . . .147 F3
Back Alexander Rd **10** BL2 . .25 C1
Back Alexandra St BL3 . . . .146 C4
Back Alfred St **12** BL3 . . . . .42 A4
Back Alice St
10 Bolton BL3 . . . . .144 C5
Little Lever BL3 . . . . .43 B3
Back Alicia St BL3 . . . . .42 D5
Back All Saints' St **11**
BL3 . . . . .145 F8
Back Alston St BL3 . . . . .147 E3
Back America Row BL1 . . . .142 C3
Back Andrew St
Bolton BL3 . . . . .145 F6
Bury BL9 . . . . .141 A2
Back Andrew St N 5
BL9 . . . . .141 A2
Back Anglia Gr BL3 . . . . .146 C4
Back Annis Rd **3** BL3 . . . . .146 B4
Back Anson St **1** BL1 . . . . .143 F3
Back Apple Terr BL1 . . . . . . .143 D2
Back Argo St BL3 . . . . .147 D4
Back Argyle St **3** BL9 . . . . . .27 F5
Back Arlington St BL3 . . . . .147 F3
Back Arnold St **1** BL1 . . . . .142 C2
Back Arnold Terr BL1 . . . . . . .23 F1
Back Ash St Bolton BL2 . . . .148 A6
3 Bury BL9 . . . . .141 A2
Back Ashbee St **1** BL1 . . . .143 E3
Back Ashford Wlk BL1 . . . . .143 E1
Back Ashley St BL1 . . . . .143 D3
Back Ashton St BL3 . . . . .146 B4
Back Ashworth La **10** BL1 . .24 F5
Back Ashworth St **10** BL8 . .27 C3
Back Astley St BL1 . . . . .143 E2
Back Auburn St **14** BL3 . . . .147 D4
Back Augustus St **3** BL3 . . .42 A4
Back Augustus St W **1**
BL3 . . . . .42 A4
Back Avenue St **3** BL1 . . . .145 D8
Back Avondale St BL1 . . . . .142 C1
Back Baldwin St BL3 . . . . . .145 E5
Back Baldwin St N BL3 . . . .145 E5
Back Balloon St M4 . . . . . . .159 A2
Back Banbury St **2** BL3 . . . .25 C1
Back Bank St **1** M8 . . . . . .158 F1
Back Bankfield St BL3 . . . . .144 C5
Back Bantry St BL3 . . . . .145 E5
Back Barbara St BL3 . . . . . .147 D4
Back Bark St BL1 . . . . .145 E7
Back Bashall St BL1 . . . . . . .144 C8

Back Battenberg Rd **1**
BL1 . . . . .144 C8
Back Baxendale St **1**
BL1 . . . . .143 E4
Back Bayley St BL1 . . . . .145 D8
Back Baythorpe St BL1 . . . .143 E4
Back Baythorpe St N **4**
BL1 . . . . .143 F3
Back Beaconsfield St
BL3 . . . . .145 D6
Back Beaconsfield Terr
BL2 . . . . .25 B1
Back Beatrice Rd **9** BL1 . . .142 C1
Back Bedford St **1** BL1 . . .145 D8
Back Beech St BL1 . . . . .143 F2
Back Beechwood St 5
BL3 . . . . .147 F3
Back Belbeck St **3** BL8 . . . .27 C2
Back Bell La Bury BL9 . . . . .141 A3
Bury BL9 . . . . .141 B3
Back Belmont Rd **1** BL1 . . .24 E5
Back Belmont Rd E **5** BL1 . .24 E5
Back Bennett's La **1** 142 C1
Back Bennett's La E BL1 . . .142 C2
Back Benson St BL1 . . . . . . .141 A1
Back Bentinck St **4** BL1 . . .142 B1
Back Bentley St BL2 . . . . . . .148 C5
Back Beverley Rd BL1 . . . . .144 C8
Back Birch St BL9 . . . . .140 F3
Back Birley St **7** BL1 . . . . . .143 E4
Back Blackbank St BL1 . . . .143 F2
Back Blackburn Rd BL1 . . . .143 F1
Back Blackburn Rd E BL7 . . .8 D3
Back Blackburn Rd W
Bolton BL1 . . . . .143 E4
Bolton BL1 . . . . .143 E4
4 Bolton BL1 . . . . .24 E8
Bolton BL7 . . . . .24 E8
Back Blackburn St 6
BL1 . . . . .143 F3
Back Blackwood St BL3 . . . .42 A4
Back Bolton Rd N BL8 . . . . . .27 C1
Back Bolton Rd S Bury BL8 . .27 C1
Bury BL8 . . . . .27 C2
Back Bolton St **5** BL1 . . . . .143 F2
Back Bolton St S **1** BL1 . . .140 E2
Back Bond St W **1** 141 A2
Back Boundary St 10 BL1 .143 D2
Back Bowen St BL1 . . . . .142 B1
Back Bowness Rd BL3 . . . . .147 D4
Back Bradford Rd
Bolton BL3 . . . . .42 A3
18 Bolton BL1 . . . . .42 A4
Back Bradford Rd W 1
BL3 . . . . .42 A3
Back Bradford St E BL2 . . . .148 B7
Back Bradford St E BL2 . . . .148 B7
Back Bradford St **4**
BL2 . . . . .148 A6
Back Bradford St W
Bolton BL2 . . . . .148 A7
Bolton BL2 . . . . .148 B7
Back Bradshaw Brow E
BL2 . . . . .25 C4
Back Bradshaw Brow W
BL2 . . . . .25 D5
Back Bradshaw St **7** OL16 .31 A8
Back Bradshawgate
Bolton BL1 . . . . .143 E2
New Mills SK22 . . . . .127 C1
Newton-le-W WA12 . . . . .89 B3
Ramsbottom BL0 . . . . .138 C6
Back Bridgeman St BL3 . . . .147 E4
Back Brierley St BL9 . . . . .44 E8
Back Brierley St S BL9 . . . . . .44 E8
Back Brindley St **3** BL3 . . . .147 F4
Back Brink's Pl BL1 . . . . .145 F7
Back Bristol Ave **11** BL2 . . .25 C1
Back Bristol St BL3 . . . . .145 D5
Back Broach St BL3 . . . . .147 E4
Back Broad o' th' La **2**
BL1 . . . . .24 E5
Back Broad St **2** BL9 . . . . .140 E2
Back Bromwich St BL2 . . . .148 B6
Back Brook St N BL9 . . . . . .141 A4
Back Brookfield St BL2 . . . .148 B7
Back Broom St BL2 . . . . .148 A7
Back Brow WN8 . . . . .53 C7
Back Bryce St BL3 . . . . .145 E5
Back Burnaby St BL3 . . . . . .147 D4
Back Burnham Ave BL1 . . . .142 A1
Back Bury New Rd E BL2 . .148 A7
Back Bury New Rd E BL2 . .148 B7
Back Bury Old Rd **2** BL2 . .148 A7
Back Bushell St BL3 . . . . . . .147 D4
Back Byrom St S **10** BL8 . . .27 B4
Back Byrom St **1** BL8 . . . . . .27 B4
Back Calder Rd BL3 . . . . . . .147 E3
Back Caledonia St BL3 . . . .144 C5
Back Calvert Rd **8** BL3 . . . .147 F3

Back Cambridge St OL7 . . . .84 F1
Back Camp St M7 . . . . .155 D5
Back Canada St
4 Bolton BL1 . . . . .142 C2
Horwich BL6 . . . . .22 B3
Back Canada St S BL1 . . . . .142 C2
Back Canning St BL1 . . . . . .140 F4
Back Carl St **25** BL1 . . . . . .143 D2
Back Carter St **19** BL3 . . . . .42 A4
Back Castle St
4 Bolton BL2 . . . . .148 A7
Bolton BL2 . . . . .148 B6
Back Cateaton St **1** BL1 . .158 F3
Back Cecil St BL2 . . . . .148 B7
Back Cecilia St BL3 . . . . .42 A4
Back Chapman St **5** BL1 . .142 C2
Back Charles Holden St
BL1 . . . . .145 D6
Back Chaucer St **3** BL1 . . .143 D2
Back Cheapside BL1 . . . . . . .145 F7
Back Chesham Rd N 5
BL9 . . . . .141 A4
Back Chesham Rd S **7**
BL9 . . . . .141 A4
Back Chester St BL9 . . . . . .141 A4
Back China La M1 . . . . .159 B1
Back Chorley New Rd
Bolton BL1 . . . . .144 B7
Bolton BL1 . . . . .145 B8
Back Chorley New Rd N
Bolton BL1 . . . . .144 C7
BL1 . . . . .144 C7
Back Chorley Old Rd
Bolton BL1 . . . . .142 A1
BL1 . . . . .23 F1
Back Chorley Old Rd N
2 Bolton BL1 . . . . .142 A1
3 Bolton BL1 . . . . .142 A1
Bolton BL1 . . . . .144 C8
4 Bolton BL1 . . . . .144 C8
Back Chorley Old Rd S
Bolton BL1 . . . . .142 A1
Bolton BL1 . . . . .23 F1
Back Chorley St BL1 . . . . . . .145 E7
Back Chorley St **11** BL1 . . .145 E8
Back Church La M46 . . . . . .146 C4
Back Church Rd
Bolton BL1 . . . . .142 A2
4 Bolton BL1 . . . . .142 A2
7 Bolton BL1 . . . . .142 B2
Back Church St
Bolton BL1 . . . . .145 E8
Little Lever BL3 . . . . .43 A3
Back Clarendon Rd 8
BL2 . . . . .148 C7
Back Clarke St **13** BL1 . . . .144 C8
Back Clay St E BL7 . . . . .25 A7
Back Clay St W BL7 . . . . .25 A7
Back Clegg St **8** BL1 . . . . . .143 E2
Back Clegg's Bldgs 12
BL1 . . . . .145 E8
Back Clifton St **8** BL9 . . . . .140 F4
Back Cloister St **8** BL1 . . . .142 C2
Back Clyde St BL1 . . . . .143 E2
Back Cobden St M11 . . . . . .143 D3
Back Colenso Rd BL2 . . . . . .42 D7
Back College Land 1
BL1 . . . . .158 F1
Back College Way BL1 . . . . .145 E6
Back Collings St BL1 . . . . . .143 E2
Back Columbia Rd 17
BL1 . . . . .144 C8
Back Common St BL5 . . . . . .57 B7
Back Coniston St **1** BL1 . . .143 F3
Back Coop St BL1 . . . . .143 E4
Back Cope Bank BL1 . . . . . .142 B2
Back Cornall St BL8 . . . . .27 C3
Back Corson St BL4 . . . . .42 D2
Back Cottam St BL8 . . . . .27 C3
Back Cotton St BL1 . . . . .143 D2
Back Cox Green Rd N **3**
BL7 . . . . .24 F8
Back Cox Green Rd S
BL7 . . . . .24 F8
Back Crawford Ave BL2 . . . .148 B6
Back Crawford St BL2 . . . . .148 B6
Back Crescent Ave BL1 . . . .145 D8
Back Crescent Rd BL3 . . . . . .42 C4
Back Crescent Rd W BL3 . . .42 C4
Back Croft La BL3 . . . . .148 B5
Back Cromer Ave BL2 . . . . . .25 C1
Back Crosby Rd BL1 . . . . . . .144 B8
Back Cross La WA12 . . . . .89 B4
Back Crostons Rd **2** BL8 . .140 C3
Back Crostons Rd BL8 . . . . .140 D3
Back Crowther St **11** BL3 . .147 E3
Back Crumpsall St **12**
BL1 . . . . .143 E2

Back Crumpsall St N **5**
BL1 . . . . .143 E3
Back Cundey St BL1 . . . . . .142 C1
Back Curzon Rd BL1 . . . . . .144 C7
Back Cyril St BL3 . . . . .148 A5
Back Daisy St BL3 . . . . .146 C4
Back Dale St OL16 . . . . .31 F5
Back Darley St BL4 . . . . .60 E8
Back Darwen Rd N
Bolton BL7 . . . . .24 F8
Bolton BL7 . . . . .25 A7
Bolton BL7 . . . . .25 B7
Bolton BL7 . . . . .8 E1
Back Darwen Rd S BL7 . . . .25 A7
Back Darwin St **11** BL1 . . .143 D2
Back Dawes St BL3 . . . . . . .145 F6
Back Deal St Bolton BL3 . .147 F3
Bury BL9 . . . . .141 B2
Back Deane Church La
BL3 . . . . .146 B4
Back Deane Church La W
BL3 . . . . .146 B4
Back Deane Rd **4** BL3 . . .144 C5
Back Deane Rd N
Bolton BL3 . . . . .144 C6
Bolton BL3 . . . . .145 D6
Back Delamere St N BL9 . . .28 A5
Back Delamere St S BL9 . . . .28 A5
Back Denton St BL9 . . . . . .140 F4
Back Derby St Bolton BL3 . .145 E5
Bolton BL3 . . . . .147 D4
Bury BL9 . . . . .140 F2
Back Design St BL3 . . . . . . .146 B4
Back Devon St N **2** BL9 . . .44 E8
Back Devon St S **2** BL9 . . .44 F8
Back Devonshire Rd BL1 . .142 A1
Back Dijon St BL3 . . . . .146 C4
Back Dijon St N BL3 . . . . . .146 C4
Back Dobie St **20** BL3 . . . . .42 A4
Back Doffcocker Brow
BL1 . . . . .142 A1
Back Dorset St BL2 . . . . . . .148 A7
Back Dougill St BL1 . . . . . .142 B1
Back Dougill St S BL1 . . . . .142 B1
Back Drake St OL16 . . . . . . .139 F7
Back Drummond St **4**
BL1 . . . . .143 E4
Back Ducie Ave BL1 . . . . . .144 C7
Back Duckworth St
BL9 . . . . .141 A4
Back Duncan St
Horwich BL6 . . . . .22 C3
Manchester M7 . . . . .81 C7
Back Dunstan St **1** BL2 . .148 C7
Back Durham St OL11 . . . . .31 A5
Back Duxbury St BL1 . . . . . .143 D3
Back Earnshaw St BL3 . . . .146 B3
Back East St BL9 . . . . .140 F1
Back Eastbank St **4** BL1 . .143 F2
Back Eckersley Rd BL1 . . . .143 E3
Back Edditch Gr BL2 . . . . . .148 C7
Back Edditch Gr N **6**
BL2 . . . . .148 C7
Back Eden St BL1 . . . . .143 E3
Back Edgmont Ave BL3 . . .147 D4
Back Eldon St BL9 . . . . .140 F4
Back Elgin St BL1 . . . . .143 D2
Back Ellesmere Rd BL3 . . .144 B3
Back Ellesmere St BL3 . . . .145 D6
Back Elm St BL9 . . . . .141 B2
Back Elmwood Gr **24** BL1 .144 C8
Back Elmwood Gr W **19**
BL1 . . . . .144 C8
Back Elsworth St M3,M4 . .159 A4
Back Emmett St BL6 . . . . . . .22 B3
Back Empire Rd BL2 . . . . . . .42 D7
Back Empress St BL1 . . . . . .142 B1
Back Ena St **2** BL3 . . . . .42 A3
Back Ernest St **1** BL1 . . . .145 D6
Back Eskrick St **2** BL1 . . .143 D2
Back Eskrick St E **7** BL1 . .143 D2
Back Eskrick St S **10** BL1 .143 D2
Back Eskrick St W BL1 . . . .143 D2
Back Essington St BL3 . . . . .42 B4
Back Essington St S BL3 . .147 D4
Back Eustace St **2** BL3 . . . .42 A3
Back Euxton St BL3 . . . . . . .147 D4
Back Everton St N **8** BL1 .143 F2
Back Ewart St **11** BL1 . . . .143 E2
Back Fair St BL3 . . . . .146 C2
Back Fairhaven Rd BL1 . . . .143 F3
Back Fenton St BL8 . . . . .27 C1
Back Fern St **2** BL3 . . . . . .144 C5
Back Fir St BL9 . . . . .141 B2
Back Fitton St BL3 . . . . .147 E4
Back Fletcher St
Bury BL9 . . . . .141 A2
Kearsley M26 . . . . .61 B8
Back Fletcher St S **3** BL3 .145 F5
Back Flora St **1** BL3 . . . . .147 E4
Back Florence Ave BL1 . . . . .24 F5
Back Fortune St BL3 . . . . . . .24 B5
Back Foundry St BL9 . . . . . .140 F2
Back Frances St **6** BL1 . . .143 D2
Back Frank St Bolton BL1 . .143 D2
4 Bury BL9 . . . . .140 F1
Back Fylde St BL4 . . . . .42 D2
Back Gainsborough Ave
BL3 . . . . .146 C3
Back Garside Gr **9** BL1 . . .143 E2
Back Garston St BL3 . . . . . .141 A4
Back Gaskell St BL1 . . . . . .145 D8
Back Gaskell St E **14** BL1 .145 D8
Back Gaythorne St **2**
BL1 . . . . .143 F3

Back George Barton St
BL2 . . . . .25 B1
Back George St Bolton BL3 .42 A4
Horwich BL6 . . . . .22 C3
Manchester M1 . . . . .159 A1
Back Georgiana St W **1**
BL9 . . . . .140 F1
Back Georgina St BL3 . . . . .146 B3
Back Gibraltar St BL3 . . . . .145 D6
Back Gibraltar St S BL3 . . .145 D6
Back Gigg La BL9 . . . . .44 F8
Back Gilmour St M24 . . . . . .65 A8
Back Gilnow Gr **1** BL1 . . .145 D6
Back Gilnow La
Bolton BL3 . . . . .144 C6
Bolton BL3 . . . . .145 D6
Back Gilnow La W BL3 . . . .144 C7
Back Gilnow Rd BL1 . . . . . .144 C7
Back Glade St BL1 . . . . .144 C7
Back Gladstone St **4**
OL4 .67 B6
Back Glen Ave BL3 . . . . . . .144 B5
Back Glen Bott St **3** BL1 .143 D2
Back Glenboro Ave BL3 . . . .27 C2
Back Gloster St BL2 . . . . . . .148 A7
Back Goldsmith St BL3 . . . .147 D4
Back Goodlad St **6** BL8 . . .27 B7
Back Gordon Ave BL3 . . . . .144 C5
Back Gorses Mount BL2 . . .148 C5
Back Grafton St **6** BL1 . . .145 D8
Back Grantham Cl BL1 . . . .143 E1
Back Grasmere St **5** BL1 .143 F2
Back Greaves St OL1 . . . . . .153 F6
Back Green La BL3 . . . . .42 B3
Back Green La S BL3 . . . . . .147 F3
Back Green St M24 . . . . .47 B1
Back Greenhalgh St BL3 . . .43 A3
Back Greenland Rd BL3 . . .147 F2
Back Gregory Ave BL2 . . . . .42 E8
Back Grendon St BL3 . . . . .146 C3
Back Gresham St **9** BL1 . .143 F3
Back Grove St **9** BL1 . . . . .143 D2
Back Hadwin St **11** BL1 . .143 F1
Back Halliwell La M8 . . . . .155 F7
Back Halliwell Rd BL1 . . . .143 E2
Back Halliwell Rd S BL1 . . .143 D2
Back Halstead St
Bolton BL3 . . . . .148 A7
Bury BL9 . . . . .141 A4
Back Hamilton St
Bolton BL3 . . . . .148 A7
Manchester M7 . . . . .155 D7
Back Hampson St M40 . . . .160 D4
Back Hanson St BL1 . . . . . . .143 D1
Back Hargreaves St **9**
BL3 . . . . .143 E2
Back Harper's La **1** BL1 . .142 B2
Back Hart St BL5 . . . . .57 B7
Back Hartington Rd **18**
BL1 . . . . .144 C8
Back Harvey St
Bolton BL1 . . . . .143 D3
Bury BL8 . . . . .27 C3
Back Haslam St BL3 . . . . . .144 B3
Back Haslam Terr BL2 . . . .148 C7
Back Hastings Rd BL1 . . . .142 A1
Back Hatfield Rd BL1 . . . . .143 D1
Back Hawthorne Rd **5**
BL3 . . . . .144 B6
Back Hawthorne Rd E
BL3 . . . . .144 B5
Back Hawthorne Rd W
BL3 . . . . .144 B5
Back Hawthorne St **4**
BL3 . . . . .146 B4
Back Haydn St **18** BL1 . . .143 D2
Back Haydock St BL1 . . . . .145 F8
Back Hayward St **2** BL3 . . .27 C3
Back Hengist St **5** BL2 . . .148 C7
Back Hennon St **1** BL1 . . .143 D1
Back Henrietta St BL3 . . . .146 C3
Back Henry Lee St BL3 . . .146 C3
Back Hereford Rd BL1 . . . .144 B8
Back Hereford Rd W BL1 . .144 B8
Back Heywood St E BL1 . . .141 A2
Back Heywood St W **2**
BL9 . . . . .141 A1
Back High Bank St BL2 . . . .148 C7
Back High St Bolton BL3 . .147 E4
Edgworth BL7 . . . . .9 C4
Heywood OL10 . . . . .29 B2
Back High St S **1** BL3 . . . .147 E4
Back High St W **2** BL3 . . .147 E4
Back Higher Darcy St
BL3 . . . . .148 C5
Back Higher Shady La W
BL7 . . . . .25 B7
Back Higher Swan La
BL3 . . . . .147 D3
Back Higher Swan La W
BL3 . . . . .147 D3
Back Hilden St BL2 . . . . . . .148 A6
Back Hilden St W BL2 . . . . .148 A6
Back Hillside St **2** BL3 . . .145 D5
Back Hilton St Bolton BL2 . .148 C7
7 Bury BL9 . . . . .140 F4
Manchester M7 . . . . .155 D7
Back Hind St **2** BL3 . . . . .148 C7
Back Holland St
6 Bolton BL1 . . . . .143 E4
Bolton BL1 . . . . .143 F4
Back Holland St S BL1 . . . .143 F4
Back Holly Pl BL1 . . . . .143 E4
Back Holly St
3 Bolton BL1 . . . . .143 F4
Bury BL9 . . . . .141 A1
Back Holly St S BL9 . . . . . .141 A2

Back Hope St
Manchester M7 . . . . .155 D7
7 Oldham OL1 . . . . .67 B7
Back Hopefield St BL3 . . . .147 D4
Back Horbury St BL3 . . . . . .27 C2
Back Horeb St **2** BL3 . . . . .145 D5
Back Hornby St BL9 . . . . . .140 F4
Back Hornby St E BL9 . . . .140 F3
Back Hornby St W **4** BL9 .140 F3
Back Horne St N **1** BL9 . . .44 E8
Back Horne St S **1** BL9 . . .44 E8
Back Horsa St BL2 . . . . .25 B1
Back Horsa St N **17** BL2 . . .25 B1
Back Hotel St BL1 . . . . .145 F7
Back Hough La E BL7 . . . . . .25 A7
Back Howarden St **3** BL1 . .24 C5
Back Howcroft St BL3 . . . . .147 D4
Back Howe St M7 . . . . .155 D7
Back Hughes St BL1 . . . . . .142 C2
Back Hulbert St BL8 . . . . . . .27 C2
Back Hulme St Bury BL8 . .140 D3
Manchester M5 . . . . .81 C1
Back Hulton St
BL3 . . . . .146 A3
Bolton BL3 . . . . .146 A4
Back Hulton La S BL3 . . . .146 A4
Back Hulton La W BL3 . . . .146 A4
Back Huntley Mount Rd
BL9 . . . . .141 B3
Bury BL9 . . . . .141 A1
Back Hurst St Bolton BL3 . .146 C3
Back Huxley St **3** BL1 . . . .142 C2
Back Ingham St BL9 . . . . . .141 A1
Back Ingham St E BL9 . . . .141 A1
Back Irlam St **4** BL1 . . . . .143 E3
Back Irlam St N **1** BL1 . . .143 E3
Back Ivanhoe St **2** BL3 . . .43 A3
Back Ivy Bank Rd BL1 . . . . .24 E5
Back Ivy Rd Bolton BL1 . . .142 C1
Back Jack Ivy Rd W BL1 . .142 B2
Back James St BL3 . . . . .43 B3
Back Jauncey St **12** BL3 . .144 C5
Back John Brown St **15**
BL1 . . . . .145 D8
Back John Cross St **3**
BL3 . . . . .147 E4
Back John St **3** BL1 . . . . . .145 E6
Back Johnson St **2** BL1 . .145 F6
Back Jubilee St BL3 . . . . . . .145 D5
Back Junction St N BL1 . . .159 A1
Back Keighley St **10** BL1 .142 C2
Back Kendal Rd BL1 . . . . . .144 C8
Back Kershaw St BL9 . . . . .141 A2
Back King St Bolton BL1 . .145 E7
Back King St N **4** BL7 . . . .24 F8
Back King St S BL2 . . . . .25 D5
Back Kingholm Gdns **3**
BL1 . . . . .143 D1
Back Kingsley St BL1 . . . . .143 D2
Back Kirkby Rd BL1 . . . . . .144 B8
Back Knight St **4** BL8 . . . . .27 C2
Back Knowsley Rd BL1 . . . .142 C1
Back Knowsley St
BL1 . . . . .145 F7
Bury BL9 . . . . .140 E2
Back Kylemore Ave BL3 . . .144 B5
Back La Altrincham WA15 . .129 B4
Appley Bridge WN6 . . . . .35 E8
Ashton-u-L OL7 . . . . .84 E5
Atherton BL5 . . . . .90 E8
Bolton BL1 . . . . .145 E8
Charlesworth SK13 . . . . . . .115 C6
Mossley OL5,OL6 . . . . .68 A2
Mottram-in-L SK14 . . . . . . .103 A4
Oldham OL4 . . . . .50 C1
Partington WA14 . . . . .118 C5
Whitworth OL12 . . . . .4 C3
Back Lark St BL1 . . . . .145 E8
Back Latham St BL1 . . . . . .143 F2
Back Lathom St **19** BL9 . .141 A4
Back Lawn St BL9 . . . . .141 B2
Back Lawn St BL1 . . . . .143 D1
Back Leach St BL3 . . . . .145 E5
Back Leachfield St BL1 . . . .143 D3
Back Lee Ave BL3 . . . . .147 D3
Back Lee St Bolton BL1 . . .148 A8
11 Oldham OL3 . . . . .69 B8
Back Legh St WA12 . . . . .89 A3
Back Lena St BL1 . . . . .143 F2
Back Lenora St **1** BL3 . . .146 B4
Back Lever Edge La
BL3 . . . . .146 C2
Bolton BL3 . . . . .147 F3
Back Lever Edge La S
BL3 . . . . .147 D3
Back Lever Hall Rd BL2 . . . .42 D7
Back Lever St Bolton BL3 . .145 F5
Bolton BL3 . . . . .147 E4
Back Lever St N BL3 . . . . . . .43 A4
Back Lever St S BL3 . . . . . .147 E4
Back Lightburne Ave BL1 . .142 A1
Back Lilly St BL1 . . . . .145 D8
Back Lincoln Rd BL1 . . . . . .144 C8
Back Lindley St BL3 . . . . . . .43 B3
Back Linton Ave **2** BL9 . . .27 F5
Back Long La BL2 . . . . .42 E7
Back Longden St **2** BL1 . .144 C8
Back Longfellow Ave
BL3 . . . . .146 B3
Back Longfield Rd BL3 . . . .146 B3
Back Longsight S BL2 . . . . . .25 E5
Back Longsight BL2 . . . . .25 E5
Back Longworth Rd BL7 . . . .25 D7
Back Lonsdale Rd BL1 . . . .144 B8
Back Lonsdale Rd N BL1 . .144 B8
Back Lonsdale St BL8 . . . . . .27 C2

Back Lord St Bury BL9 . . . .140 F2
Little Lever BL3 . . . . .43 B3
Back Lower Bridgeman St
2 BL2 . . . . .148 A6
Back Loxham St BL4 . . . . . . .42 D2
Back Lumsden St BL3 . . . . .145 E5
Back Luton St BL3 . . . . .145 D6
Back Lytton St **4** BL1 . . . .143 D2
Back Mackenzie St BL1 . . .143 E4
Back Malvern Ave
Bolton BL1 . . . . .142 A1
5 Bury BL9 . . . . .27 F5
Back Manchester Old Rd
BL9 . . . . .140 E1
Back Manchester Rd
BL2 . . . . .148 A6
5 Bury BL9 . . . . .140 E2
1 Farnworth BL3 . . . . . . .42 C2
Back Manchester Rd E
BL3 . . . . .148 A5
Back Manchester Rd S
BL3 .42 A4
Back Manchester Rd W
BL3 .42 B4
Back Manchester St **1**
OL10 . . . . .29 E1
Back Maple St BL3 . . . . . . .145 D5
Back Marion St **2** BL3 . . . .42 C2
Back Marion St S **4** BL3 . .42 C2
Back Market St
4 Bury BL9 . . . . .140 E2
Hindley WN2 . . . . .56 D5
Kearsley M26 . . . . .61 B8
Leigh WN7 . . . . .75 F5
Little Lever BL3 . . . . .43 B3
Newton-le-W WA12 . . . . .89 A3
Back Market St W **3** BL9 .140 E2
Back Markland Hill La
BL1 .23 F1
Back Markland Hill La W
BL1 .23 F1
Back Marlborough St
BL1 . . . . .145 D8
Back Marsh Fold La **14**
BL1 . . . . .144 C8
Back Mary St **4** BL3 . . . . .145 D5
Back Mason St BL9 . . . . . . .141 A2
Back Massie St SK8 . . . . . . .122 D6
Back Mawdsley St BL1 . . . .145 F7
Back Maxwell St BL1 . . . . . .143 E4
Back Maybank St BL3 . . . . .145 D5
Back Mayfield Ave BL3 . . . .42 B3
Back Mayor St Bolton BL1 .145 D6
6 Bury BL8 . . . . .27 C3
Back Mayor St N BL1 . . . . .145 D6
Back Maze St BL3 . . . . .148 C5
Back McDonna St BL1 . . . .142 C3
Back McKean St **8** BL3 . . . .42 A4
Back McKean St N BL3 . . . . .42 A4
Back Melbourne Rd BL3 . . .144 C5
Back Mellor Gr BL1 . . . . . . .142 B3
Back Mellor Gr W **1** BL1 .142 B1
Back Melrose Ave BL1 . . . .142 A1
Back Melville St BL3 . . . . . . .42 A3
Back Mercia St BL3 . . . . . . .144 B5
Back Mere Gdns BL1 . . . . . .145 E8
Back Meredith St **6** BL3 . .147 F3
Back Merlin Gr BL1 . . . . . . .142 B1
Back Merton St BL3 . . . . . .140 D3
Back Mesnes St
Wigan WN3 . . . . .150 C8
8 Wigan WN1 . . . . .37 C1
Back Methwold St BL3 . . . .146 C4
Back Micklehurst Rd OL5 . .68 E1
Back Milford Rd BL3 . . . . . .147 E3
Back Mill La OL5 . . . . .68 C2
Back Mill St N **6** BL7 . . . . .24 F8
Back Mill St S **6** BL7 . . . . .24 F8
Back Miller St BL3 . . . . .143 E4
Back Millet St BL9 . . . . .140 D2
Back Milner Ave BL9 . . . . . . .27 F5
Back Minorca St BL3 . . . . . .147 E4
Back Mirey La BL6 . . . . .40 B4
Back Monmouth Ave
BL9 .27 F5
Back Moor SK14 . . . . .103 A4
Back Moorfield Gr BL2 . . . . .25 B1
Back Moorgate S BL1 . . . . .140 D3
Back Mornington Rd
BL1 . . . . .144 C7
Back Mornington Rd E
BL1 . . . . .144 C7
Back Mornington Rd W
BL1 . . . . .144 B8
Back Morris Green La
Bolton BL3 . . . . .146 C2
Bolton BL3 . . . . .146 C3
Back Morris Green La E
BL3 . . . . .146 C3
Back Mortfield La **1**
BL1 . . . . .144 C8
Back Moss Terr BL1 . . . . . .145 D8
Back Mostyn Ave **3** BL9 . . .27 F5
Back Mowbray St **3** BL1 . .142 B1
Back Murton Terr **4** BL1 . .143 F4
Back Musgrave Rd
BL1 . . . . .144 B8
Back Musgrave Rd N
BL1 . . . . .144 C8
Back Myrtle St BL9 . . . . . . .141 B2
Back Myrtle St S BL9 . . . . .141 B2
Back Nebo St BL3 . . . . .147 D4
Back Nelson St BL6 . . . . . . .22 C2
Back Nelson St N **5** BL9 . . .44 F8
Back Nelson St S **1** BL9 . . .44 F8
Back Nevada St **17** BL1 . . .143 E1

Back New George St **9**
BL8 .27 C3
2 BL2 . . . . .27 C3
Back Newbold St BL8 . . . . . .27 C2
Back Newhall La BL1 . . . . .142 A1
Back Newport Rd **11** BL3 . .42 A4
Back Newport St BL1 . . . . .145 F6
Back Newton St BL1 . . . . . .143 E2
Back Nixon Rd BL3 . . . . . . .146 C3
Back Norbury Rd BL4 OL12 .144 F3
Back Normanby St BL3 . . .146 C2
Back Norris St BL3 . . . . .43 A3
Back Northern Gr **1** BL1 . .142 C1
Back Northern Gr S **2**
BL1 . . . . .142 C1
Back Nunnery Rd BL3 . . . .146 B4
Back Nut St BL1 . . . . .143 D2
Back o' th' Low Rd OL4 . . . .49 F1
Back Oak St M26 . . . . .44 C1
Back Oakenbottom Rd N
BL2 .42 D7
Back Olaf St **14** BL2 . . . . . .25 B1
Back Oldham Rd OL16 . . . . .31 A6
Back Olga St **5** BL1 . . . . . .143 D2
Back Olga St N BL1 . . . . . . .143 D2
Back Olive Bank **2** BL8 . . .27 B4
Back Oram St **9** BL9 . . . . .141 A4
Back Osborne Gr **7** BL1 . .143 E1
Back Oriel St BL3 . . . . .144 C5
Back Ormrod St BL3 . . . . . .141 A2
Back Owen's Row BL6 . . . . .22 C3
Back Oxford Gr N
BL1 . . . . .142 C1
2 Bolton BL1 . . . . .145 D8
Back Oxford St BL9 . . . . . . .141 A1
Back Packer St **8** BL1 . . . .143 D2
Back Palace St BL1 . . . . . . .145 F8
Back Palm St BL1 . . . . .143 E3
Back Park Rd Bolton BL1 . .144 C7
Back Park Rd E **8** BL1 . . . .143 E4
Back Park St BL1 . . . . .145 D8
Back Park View BL9 . . . . . . .24 F6
Back Park View Rd **1** BL3 .146 C4
Back Parkdale Rd BL2 . . . . .25 C1
Back Parkfield Rd
BL3 . . . . .147 F3
Bolton BL3 . . . . .42 A3
Back Parkhills Rd N **4**
BL9 .44 F8
Back Parkhills Rd S
4 BL9 . . . . .44 F8
5 Bury BL9 . . . . .44 F8
Back Parkinson St **11**
BL1 . . . . .144 C5
Back Parsonage St **9**
BL1 . . . . .141 A3
Back Partington St BL3 . . .146 C2
Back Patience St **10** OL12 .14 C1
Back Patterson St BL3 . . . .146 A4
Back Peabody St BL3 . . . . .147 E4
Back Peace St BL3 . . . . .145 D5
Back Pedder St **2** BL1 . . . .142 B3
Back Peers St **8** BL8 . . . . . .27 C2
Back Penarth Rd **6** BL3 . . .146 B4
Back Pennington Rd BL3 . .147 F3
Back Percy St BL1 . . . . .141 B3
Back Peter St E **2** BL9 . . . .141 B3
Back Peveril St BL3 . . . . . . .146 B3
Back Phoenix St BL1 . . . . . .140 E2
Back Piccadilly M1 . . . . .159 B1
Back Pikes La W BL3 . . . . . .144 C5
Back Pine St
7 Bolton BL1 . . . . .143 F2
Bury BL9 . . . . .141 B2
Newhey OL16 . . . . .32 B4
Back Pleasant St BL1 . . . . .145 E8
Back Pool Fold **9** M2 . . . .158 F1
Back Poplar Ave BL3 . . . . . .147 F3
Back Porter St **33** BL9 . . . .140 F4
Back Portugal St **2** BL2 . .148 B7
Back Potter St M26 . . . . . . .44 D4
Back Preston St BL3 . . . . . . .42 B4
Back Primrose St BL1 . . . . .143 E4
Back Primula St BL1 . . . . . . .24 F5
Back Proctor St BL3 . . . . . . .27 C1
Back Progress St **2** BL3 . .143 F1
Back Quay St M3 . . . . .158 E1
Back Quebec St BL3 . . . . . .144 C5
Back Queen St Bolton BL1 .145 E7
4 Leigh WN7 . . . . .76 A5
Back Queensgate BL1 . . . . .144 C7
Back Radcliffe Rd **1**
BL2 . . . . .148 B7
Back Railway View PR7 . . . .21 A7
Back Raimond St BL1 . . . . .142 C3
Back Rainshaw St **5** BL1 .143 F4
Back Rake St BL9 . . . . .140 F4
Back Ramsden Rd OL12 . . .15 C7
Back Range St BL3 . . . . .147 E4
Back Raphael St BL1 . . . . . .143 D1
Back Rathbone St WA12 . . .89 A3
Back Raven St **4** BL9 . . . . .140 F4
Back Rawlinson St **1** BL6 .22 B4
Back Rawson Rd N BL1 . . .142 C1
Back Rawson Rd N
BL1 . . . . .142 C1
Back Rawsthorne St BL1 . .143 E2
Back Raymond Ave **6** BL9 .27 F5
Back Redfearn Rd BM4 . . .159 C3
Back Redhill Gr **1** BL1 . . . .145 E8
Back Reginald St BL3 . . . . .140 F4
Back Ribblesdale Rd **18**
BL3 . . . . .147 D4
Back Richard Burch St
BL9 . . . . .141 A3
Back Richelieu St BL3 . . . . .42 A4
Back Rigby La N BL2 . . . . . .25 C6
Back Rigby La S BL2 . . . . . .25 C6

Back Rishton La
Bolton BL3 147 F3
Bolton BL3 147 F4
Back Rishton La E BL3 147 F3
Back Rochdale
Old North Rd BL9 141 C3
Back Rochdale Old Rd S
BL9 141 B3
Back Rochdale
Old South Rd BL9 28 D3
Back Rochdale Rd
Bury BL9 141 A2
Bury BL9 141 B2
Back Rochdale Rd S 6
BL9 141 A2
Back Rock Ave BL1 142 C3
Back Roland Rd 3 BL3 146 C4
Back Roman Rd M7 155 E6
Back Romer St BL2 148 C7
Back Rosamond St BL3 146 C4
Back Roscow Ave BL2 42 E8
Back Rose Bank 8 BL9 140 F4
Back Roseberry St 7
BL3 146 C4
Back Rowena St BL3 42 C2
Back Rowland St BL3 146 B3
Back Roxalina St 5 BL3 147 E4
Back Royal Ave BL9 27 F5
Back Rudolph St 2 BL3 147 F3
Back Rumworth St BL3 147 D4
Back Rupert St BL3 147 F3
Back Rushton Rd BL1 142 B1
Back Rushton St 6 OL13 3 E8
Back Russell Cl 2 BL1 144 C8
Back Russell St 22 BL1 144 C8
Back Rutland Gr 6 BL1 142 C1
Back Ryefield St BL1 25 A1
Back Salford WN7 75 F5
Back Salford St BL9 141 A4
Back Salisbury St BL3 145 D6
Back Salisbury Terr BL2 42 D7
Back Sandon St BL3 147 D4
Back Sandon St W 11
BL3 147 D4
Back Sandy Bank Rd BL7 9 D5
Back Sankey St BL9 140 D2
Back Sapling Rd BL3 146 C2
Back Sapling Rd S BL3 146 C2
Back Scholes St BL8 27 C3
Back School La WN8 53 C7
Back Scott St OL8 153 F5
Back Scowcroft St 22 BL2 25 B1
Back Second Ave BL1 144 B7
Back Settle St Bolton BL3 147 E3
Bolton BL3 147 F3
Back Settle St N
Bolton BL3 147 D3
Bolton BL3 147 E3
Back Seymour Rd BL1 143 F3
Back Shakerley Rd 6 M29 58 F1
Back Sharman St BL3 148 B5
Back Shaw-Street BL9 141 B3
Back Shepherd St 1 BL9 141 A1
Back Sherwood St 8
BL1 143 F3
Back Shipton St BL1 142 B1
Back Short St 4 M46 58 F1
Back Shrewsbury Rd BL1 144 B8
Back Shuttle St BL3 145 E6
Back Silver St BL9 140 E2
Back Silverdale Rd BL1 144 C7
Back Skipton St BL2 148 C8
Back Smethurst La BL3 146 B2
Back Smethurst La W
BL3 146 B2
Back Sofa St BL1 142 B1
Back Soho St BL3 145 F6
Back Somerset Rd BL1 144 B8
Back Somerset Rd W
BL1 144 B8
Back Somerville St 3
BL1 142 C3
Back South Cross St E
BL9 141 A2
Back South Par M3 158 F1
Back South St BL3 147 E3
Back South View St 9
BL2 148 C7
Back Southfield St 1 BL3 42 B4
Back Spa Rd BL1 145 D6
Back Spa Rd N BL1 145 D6
Back Spa Rd W 4 BL1 145 D6
Back Spear St 6 M1,M4 159 B2
Back Spinnerbottom
SK22 127 F2
Back Spring Gdns
Bolton BL1 145 F6
6 Middleton M24 47 A2
Back Spring St E BL9 140 F1
Back Spring St W BL9 140 F1
Back Springfield St 14
BL3 42 A4
Back Square St BL0 138 C6
Back St Ann St BL1 143 E1
Back St Anne's St 7 BL9 140 F4
Back St Augustine St
BL1 143 D2
Back St George's Rd
Bolton BL1 145 E8
Manchester M4 159 B3
Back St George's Rd N
BL1 145 E8
Back St Helens Rd
Bolton BL3 146 B3
10 Bolton BL3 147 D4
Back St Helens Rd S
Bolton BL3 146 A2
Bolton BL3 146 B2
Back St Helens Rd S *continued*
Bolton BL3 146 B3
Bolton BL3 146 C3
Back St James's St 8 OL1 67 B7
Back St Mark's La M8 155 F8
Back St Mary's Pl BL9 140 E2
Back St Philip's Ave BL3 147 D4
Back St Thomas St E 10
BL1 143 D2
Back Stainsbury St BL3 146 C4
Back Stanley St BL0 138 B5
Back Stanway Ave 8
BL3 145 D6
Back Stephen St 2 BL8 27 C2
Back Stewart St 13 BL1 143 E2
Back Stone St 15 BL2 25 B1
Back Sunlight Rd BL1 144 C7
Back Sunning Hill St 12
BL3 147 D4
Back Sunnyside Rd 8
BL1 142 C2
Back Sutcliffe St BL1 143 E2
Back Swan La 15 BL3 147 D4
Back Talbot St 1 BL1 143 F4
Back Tavistock Rd 3
BL1 145 D6
Back Teak St BL9 141 B2
Back Tenterden St
Bury BL9 140 D2
Bury BL9 140 E2
Back Thicketford Rd BL2 25 C1
Back Thicketford Rd W
BL2 25 B1
Back Thomas St 8 M4 159 A2
Back Thomasson Cl BL1 143 E1
Back Thorn St BL1 143 F2
Back Thorns Rd BL1 143 E3
Back Thorpe St BL1 143 D2
Back Thurnham St 3
BL3 146 C3
Back Tinline St 4 BL9 141 A2
Back Tonge Moor Rd BL2 25 B3
Back Tonge Moor Rd E
Bolton BL2 25 B1
Bolton BL2 25 B2
Bolton BL2 25 C3
Back Tonge Old Rd BL2 148 C7
Back Tottington Rd 5
BL8 27 B4
Back Tottington Rd E BL2 25 E5
Back Tottington Rd N BL8 27 C4
Back Tottington Rd S 1
BL8 27 C3
Back Tudor St 8 BL3 146 C4
Back Turner St M4 159 A2
Back Turton Rd E BL2 25 C5
Back Turton Rd W BL2 25 C5
Back Uganda St BL3 146 C2
Back Ulleswater St 1
BL1 143 F2
Back Union Rd BL2 25 B1
Back Union St BL7 8 D2
Back Unsworth St S BL3 145 D5
Back Uttley St 16 BL1 143 D2
Back Venice St BL3 147 D4
Back Vernon St
Bolton BL1 145 E8
Bury BL9 140 F4
Back Vernon St S 13 BL1 145 E8
Back Vickerman St 23
BL1 143 D2
Back Victoria Gr 4 BL1 142 C1
Back Victoria Gr N BL1 142 C1
Back Victory St E 10 BL1 144 C8
Back View St 5 BL3 145 D5
Back Viking St N 11 BL3 42 A4
Back Vincent St BL1 145 D6
Back Vine St 1 BL3 144 C6
Back Viola St BL1 143 E3
Back Waldeck St 3 BL1 144 C8
Back Walmersley Rd E
Bury BL9 140 F3
Bury BL9 140 F4
4 Bury BL9 27 F5
Bury BL9 27 F6
Back Walmersley Rd W
Bury BL9 140 F4
Bury BL9 27 F6
Back Walnut St 2 BL1 143 F2
Back Walshaw Rd N 3
BL8 27 C3
Back Walshaw Rd S BL8 27 C3
Back Wapping St 21 BL1 143 D2
Back Wardle St BL2 148 C5
Back Wash La BL9 141 B2
Back Wash La S 2 BL9 141 A2
Back Water St Bolton BL7 8 D2
Stockport SK1 169 F2
Back Waverley Rd BL1 143 E3
Back Webster St BL3 148 B5
Back Wellington Rd S BL9 44 F8
Back Wells St BL9 140 E1
Back Westbank St 8
BL1 145 D8
Back Westbourne Ave
BL3 42 A3
Back Weston St N 9 BL3 42 A4
Back Weston St S BL3 42 A4
Back Westwood Rd 18
BL1 144 C8
Back Wheatfield St BL2 148 C5
Back Whittle Gr BL1 142 B1
Back Whittle St 6 BL8 27 C3
Back Wigan Rd
Bolton BL3 144 B5
Bolton BL3 146 A4
Back Wigan Rd N
Bolton BL3 144 B5
Back Wigan Rd N *continued*
Bolton BL3 146 A4
Back Wigan Rd S BL3 144 B5
Back Willis St 6 BL3 146 C4
Back Willows La 6 BL3 147 D4
Back Willows La N
Bolton BL3 146 B4
Bolton BL3 146 C4
Back Willows La S
Bolton BL3 146 B4
Bolton BL3 146 C4
Back Wilmot St 4 BL1 142 C3
Back Wilton St 10 BL1 143 F3
Back Windermere St 3
BL1 143 F2
Back Windsor Gr 8 BL1 142 C1
Back Woking Gdns 6
BL1 143 E1
Back Wolfenden St 31
BL1 143 E2
Back Wood St Bury BL8 27 C3
Horwich BL6 22 C3
Back Woodbine Rd BL3 146 C3
Back Woodbine Rd N
BL3 146 C3
Back Woodfield St BL3 42 A3
Back Woodgate St BL3 42 A3
Back Worcester St BL1 143 E1
Back Wordsworth St 22
BL1 143 D2
Back Worsel St N BL3 146 C4
Back Wright St BL6 22 B4
Back Wynne St 10 BL1 143 E2
Back Yates St BL2 25 B1
Back Young St BL4 60 E7
Backbower La SK14 113 F8
Backford Wlk 1 M20 110 A8
Backparsons La BL9 140 F3
Backton Pl M40 160 D4
Baclaw Cl WN1 37 F1
Bacon Ave M34 113 A7
Bacup & Rawtenstall
Gram Sch BB4 2 F8
Bacup Rd BB4,OL13 2 E8
Bacup St M40 83 A8
Badby Cl M4 160 D1
Baddeley Cl SK3 170 D5
Badder St BL1 145 F8
Baden St M11 164 E8
Bader Dr OL10 46 D7
Badger Cl OL16 31 C3
Badger Edge La OL3,OL4 50 C3
Badger La Rochdale OL16 31 B2
Rochdale OL16 31 C3
Badger St BL9 141 A3
Badgers Way SK13 116 B7
Badgers Wlk M22 121 E1
Badminton Rd M21 97 C1
Bag La M46 58 C4
Bagnall Cl Rochdale OL12 13 F2
Uppermill OL3 51 C1
Bagnall Ct M22 121 E8
Bagnall Wlk M22 121 E8
Bagot St 15 Droylsden M11 83 C2
Swinton M27 61 C1
Bagshaw La WN2 38 E2
Bagshaw St SK14 101 E5
Bagslate Moor La OL11 29 F8
Bagslate Moor Rd OL11 29 F8
Bagstock Ave SK12 133 E2
Baguley Cres
Middleton M25 64 A7
Stockport SK3 170 D6
Baguley Dr BL9 45 A2
Baguley Hall Prim Sch
M23 121 A6
Baguley La Sale M33 108 E2
Sale M33 108 E3
Baguley Rd M33 108 E4
Baguley St M43 84 B1
Baildon Rd OL12 14 B1
Baildon St M40 65 A1
Bailey Fold BL5 58 B8
Bailey La Bolton BL2 25 E1
Partington M31 105 F3
Wythenshawe M22,M90 121 B1
Bailey Rd M17 96 A7
Bailey St Droylsden M43 83 E1
8 Oldham OL1 67 A7
Prestwich M25 63 C4
Bailey Wlk WA14 128 C8
Bailey's Ct WN1 150 C8
Baillie St Radcliffe BL9 44 E5
Rochdale OL16 139 F8
Baillie St E 18 OL16 31 A8
Bails The M7 81 C6
Bain St M27 79 F7
Bainbridge Ave WA3 90 F8
Bainbridge Cl M12 164 D6
Bainbridge Rd 3 OL4 49 D1
Bainburgh Clough OL8 67 C4
Baines Ave M44 93 F1
Baines St BL1 144 B8
Bainton Wlk M9 64 C5
Baird St M1 163 C8
Baitings Row OL12 13 C2
Baker St Heywood OL10 46 E8
Kearsley BL4 61 B6
Middleton M24 65 B8
Ramsbottom BL0 138 B5
Sale WA15 120 C7
Stalybridge SK15 86 B1
Stockport SK4 169 E3
Wigan WN3 150 B6
Bakewell Ave
Ashton-u-L OL6 85 F6
Denton M34 113 A8
Bakewell Bank 42 SK13 171 D1
Bakewell Cl 40 SK13 171 D1
Bakewell Dr WN6 37 A4
Bakewell Fold 41 SK13 171 D1
Bakewell Gdns 36 SK13 171 D1
Bakewell Gn 37 SK13 171 D1
Bakewell Gr 43 SK13 171 D1
Bakewell Lea 38 SK13 171 D1
Bakewell Mews SK13 171 D1
Bakewell Rd Droylsden M43 83 E2
Eccles M30 95 C8
Hazel Grove SK7 133 E8
Stretford M32 96 A3
Bakewell St
Manchester M18 99 C4
Stockport SK3 170 D7
Bakewell Wlk 39 SK13 171 D1
Bala Cl M5 81 A2
Balcarres Ave WN1 37 E2
Balcarres Rd WN2 38 C5
Balcary Gr BL1 144 B8
Balcombe Cl BL8 27 C7
Balderstone Com High Sch
OL11 31 A3
Balderstone Rd OL11 31 A3
Baldock Rd M20 110 D3
Baldrine Dr WN2 57 B5
Baldwin Rd M19 110 F6
Baldwin St Bacup OL13 3 B8
Bolton BL3 145 E5
Hindley WN2 57 B3
Ince-in-M WN3 151 D6
Wigan WN1 151 D8
Wigan WN5 54 B6
Bale St M1,M2 162 F8
Balfern Cl 12 BL5 39 E1
Balfern Fold 11 BL5 39 E1
Balfour Gr SK5 111 F8
Balfour Rd
Altrincham WA14 119 D7
5 Rochdale OL12 14 C1
Urmston M41 95 B3
Balfour St 5 Bolton BL3 145 D6
Manchester M8 156 A8
Oldham OL4 67 C7
Salford M6 81 A6
Shaw OL2 149 B7
Balham Wlk M12 164 F6
Balholm Ct M20 110 B4
Ball St Rochdale OL16 31 A8
Shevington WN6 36 E2
Ball Wlk SK14 102 F1
Ball's Cotts WN3 55 F3
Balladen Prim Sch BB4 1 F8
Ballantine St M40 83 C4
Ballantyne Way 5 WA3 90 E8
Ballard Cl OL15 16 B7
Ballard Way OL2 149 C8
Ballater Ave M41 95 A1
Ballater Cl OL10 29 B1
Ballater Wlk 1 M8 155 F7
Ballbrook Ave M20 110 B5
Ballbrook Ct M20 110 B4
Balleratt St M19 99 A1
Balliol Cl SK6 113 C4
Balliol St Manchester M8 156 A8
Swinton M27 79 E8
Balliol Way WN4 72 F4
Balloon St M4 159 A2
Balm St BL0 11 A4
Balmain Ave M18 99 C3
Balmain Rd M41 95 B3
Balmer Rd M23 121 B4
Balmfield St M8 156 A5
Balmforth St M15 162 D7
Balmoral PR7 20 E6
Balmoral Ave Cheadle SK8 123 A2
Denton M34 100 D7
Golborne WA3 74 D1
Hyde SK14 113 E8
Little Lever BL3 43 A3
Rochdale OL11 30 B8
Royton OL2 48 F4
Stretford M32 96 D3
Urmston M41 95 B1
Whitefield M45 63 A7
Balmoral Cl Horwich BL6 22 E2
Milnrow OL16 32 A6
Ramsbottom BL8 11 A1
Whitefield BL9 45 A5
Balmoral Dr Heywood OL10 29 A1
Heywood OL10 29 B1
High Lane SK6 134 E7
Hindley WN2 56 C4
Leigh WN7 76 D6
Poynton SK12 133 D3
Reddish M34 100 A3
Sale WA14 119 F8
Stalybridge SK15 86 A3
Balmoral Gr SK7 124 F3
Balmoral Grange M25 63 E3
Balmoral Ho M30 79 C2
Balmoral Rd
Altrincham WA15 119 E4
Ashton-in-M WN4 73 A4
Farnworth BL4 60 D7
Manchester M14 110 D8
Manchester SK4 168 A3
Swinton M27 62 A2
Urmston M41 95 A1
Wigan WN5 54 E6
Balmoral St M18 99 C4
Balmoral Way SK9 137 A6
Balmore Cl BL3 146 A3
Balmore Ct OL10 28 E1
Balniel Wlk WN1 37 E2
Balsam Cl M13 163 C7
Balshaw Ave M44 93 F2
Balshaw Cl BL3 144 C5
Balshaw Ct M44 94 A2
Baltic Rd Altrincham WA14 119 A6
Rawtenstall BB4 2 E8
Baltic St M5 154 E2
Baltimore St M10,M40 157 F5
Bamber Ave M33 108 E3
Bamber Croft BL5 39 E3
Bamber St M9 64 D5
Bamber Wlk BL3 145 D5
Bamber's Bldgs 2 WN2 56 E5
Bamburgh Cl M26 43 C5
Bamburgh Dr OL7 84 E5
Bamburgh Pl 3 WN4 73 A5
Bamford Ave Denton M34 112 F8
Middleton M24 47 A2
Bamford Bsns Pk SK4 111 E5
Bamford Cl Bury BL9 28 E4
Gatley SK8 131 D8
Bamford Ct OL11 30 C6
Bamford Dr WN2 37 F2
Bamford Fold SK13 171 E1
Bamford Gdns WA15 120 D6
Bamford Gn SK13 171 E1
Bamford Gr Ashton-u-L OL6 85 F6
Manchester M20 110 A3
Bamford La SK13 171 E1
Bamford Mews
Gamesley SK13 171 E1
Rochdale OL11 29 E7
Bamford Pl OL12 14 E1
Bamford Prim Sch OL11 29 F7
Bamford Rd Heywood OL10 29 D3
Manchester M20 110 A3
Ramsbottom BL0 12 B6
Bamford St Droylsden M11 83 B2
4 Littleborough OL15 15 F5
Oldham OL9 152 C8
Royton OL2 48 E3
Stockport SK1 170 F8
Bamford Way OL11 29 F6
Bampton Ave WA11 71 B1
Bampton Cl Stockport SK2 124 B7
Westhoughton BL5 39 E2
Bampton Rd M22 121 D1
Bampton Wlk M24 46 E2
Banastre Dr WA12 89 F3
Banbury Cl WN7 75 E1
Banbury Dr WA14 119 E8
Banbury Mews M27 61 D1
Banbury Rd
Failsworth M35,M40 83 E4
Longshaw WN5 53 D2
Middleton M24 65 A5
Wythenshawe M23 120 F5
Banbury St 5 Bolton BL2 25 C1
Stockport SK1 169 F1
Bancroft Ave SK8 123 A1
Bancroft Cl SK6 112 E3
Bancroft Ct WA15 120 A3
Bancroft Fold SK14 102 B5
Bancroft Rd
Altrincham WA15 120 A3
Swinton M27 61 E1
Banff Gr OL10 29 A1
Banff Rd M14 98 C4
Bangor Fold WN7 76 C4
Bangor Rd SK8 122 F6
Bangor St Ashton-u-L OL6 85 E2
Bolton BL1 145 E8
Reddish SK5 169 F4
Rochdale OL16 31 B6
Banham Ave WN3 54 C3
Bank Ave WN5 53 D5
Bank Barn La OL12 15 D6
Bank Bridge Rd M11,M40 83 B3
Bank Brow WN8 35 C5
Bank Cl OL15 16 A3
Bank Field BL5 58 A7
Bank Field St M26 61 D7
Bank Gr M38 59 F6
Bank Hall BL8 27 A2
Bank Hey BL5 39 F1
Bank Hill St OL4 67 C7
Bank Ho WN2 75 B8
Bank House Rd M9 64 C4
Bank La Littleborough OL12 15 D7
Oldham OL3 69 E4
Pendlebury M6,M27 80 D6
Tintwistle SK13 104 A7
Walkden M38 59 F6
Bank Mdw BL6 22 C4
Bank Meadow Prim Sch
M12 164 D8
Bank Pas WA3 74 A1
Bank Pl Bury BL8 27 C3
Manchester M3 158 D2
Bank Rd Appley Bridge WN8 35 D4
Manchester M8 64 A1
Mossley SK15 86 E6
Romiley SK6 113 A3
Bank Side BL5 58 A7
Bank Sq SK9 137 B7
Bank St Adlington PR7 21 A7
Ashton-u-L OL6 166 B2
Bolton BL1 145 F7
Bury BL8 26 F4
Bury BL9 140 E2
Cheadle SK8 122 E6
Denton M34 100 F6
Denton M34 113 B8
Droylsden M11 83 B2
Droylsden M43 99 F8
Edgworth BL7 9 C4
Failsworth M40 83 A3
Farnworth BL4 60 D8

Bank St continued
Glossop SK13 ......116 D8
Golborne WA3 ......74 A1
Heywood OL10 ......29 B2
Hollinfare WA3 ......105 B5
Hyde SK14 ......167 D3
Manchester M3 ......158 D2
Manchester M7 ......155 F8
⑧ Oldham OL4 ......67 D6
Platt Bridge WN2 ......56 A3
Radcliffe M26 ......44 B2
Ramsbottom BL0 ......11 E7
Rochdale OL11 ......31 A4
Romiley SK6 ......113 B5
Sale M33 ......108 C5
Shaw OL2 ......149 A7
Whitefield M45 ......44 E1
Wigan WN5 ......54 E6
Bank Terr OL12 ......14 C8
Bank The Glossop SK13 ......116 D8
Bank Top Ashton-u-L OL6 ......166 C2
Bury BL9 ......11 F1
Heywood OL10 ......29 B3
Bank Top Gr BL1 ......25 A5
Bank Top Pk OL4 ......67 D6
Bank Top St OL10 ......29 E5
Bank Wood BL1 ......40 F7
Bankbottom SK13 ......104 A5
Bankbrook WN6 ......36 D4
Banker St BL3 ......148 C5
Bankes Ave WN5 ......54 A6
Bankfield Ainsworth BL2 ......43 C8
Dukinfield SK14 ......101 D5
Bankfield Ave
Droylsden M43 ......84 A2
Irlam M44 ......105 D5
Manchester M13 ......98 E3
Stockport SK4 ......168 C1
Bankfield Cl BL2 ......26 C1
Bankfield Cotts OL3 ......50 F2
Bankfield Dr
Boothstown M28 ......78 B7
Oldham OL8 ......67 B2
Bankfield La OL11 ......29 E8
Bankfield Mews BL9 ......44 F7
Bankfield Rd Cheadle SK8 ......122 F1
Farnworth BL4 ......60 D6
Romiley SK6 ......113 B5
Sale M33 ......107 E6
Tyldesley M29 ......77 B8
Bankfield St Bacup OL13 ......3 B8
Bolton BL3 ......144 C5
Bolton BL3 ......146 C4
Manchester M9 ......157 D8
Reddish SK4 ......169 E3
Bankfield Terr ① OL13 ......3 D8
Bankfield Trad Est SK6 ......169 E4
Bankfoot Wlk M8 ......156 A5
Bankgate SK14 ......115 A8
Bankhall Cl WN2 ......56 A2
Bankhall Cl WA14,WA15 ......128 F8
Bankhall Rd SK4 ......168 A2
Bankhall Wlk ⑩ M9 ......157 E7
Bankhirst Cl M8 ......64 A1
Bankhouse Rd BL8 ......27 C4
Banklands SK14 ......101 D5
Bankley St M19 ......99 A1
Bankmill Cl ⑱ M13 ......163 B7
Banks Croft OL10 ......46 D7
Banks Ct Altrincham WA15 ......120 D5
Leigh WN7 ......75 D5
Banks La SK1 ......124 B8
Banks Lane Inf Sch SK1 ......124 B8
Banks Lane Jun Sch SK1 ......124 B8
Bankside Altrincham WA15 ......129 D6
Hattersley SK14 ......102 D1
Bankside Ave
Ashton-in-M WN4 ......73 A8
Oldham OL3 ......69 C7
Radcliffe M26 ......44 D4
Bankside Cl
Handforth SK9 ......131 D1
Oldham OL9 ......153 D6
Romiley SK6 ......114 C1
Bankside Ct
Manchester M12 ......99 A4
Stockport SK4 ......168 A2
Bankside Rd M20 ......122 B7
Bankside Tutorial Unit
M43 ......84 A2
Bankside Wlk ⑤ SK14 ......102 D2
Bankswood SK13 ......104 A4
Bankswood WN6 ......35 E6
Banky La M33 ......107 D6
Bann St M3 ......170 E8
Bannatyne Cl M40 ......65 E1
Banner Dale Cl M13 ......98 F4
Banner St Hindley WN2 ......56 E5
Ince-in-M WN3 ......151 E5
Banner Wlk ⑩ M11 ......160 F1
Bannerman Ave M25 ......63 C3
Bannerman Rd M43 ......84 B1
Bannerman Sq M40 ......97 F4
Bannerman St M7 ......155 E6
Bannister Dr SK8 ......122 F2
Bannister St Bolton BL2 ......42 E8
Stockport SK1 ......170 F7
Banstead Ave M22 ......121 D7
Bantry Ave M9 ......64 B3
Bantry St Bolton BL3 ......145 E5
④ Rochdale OL12 ......15 A2
Baptist St M4 ......159 B3
Bar Gap Rd OL1 ......153 F8
Bar La 24 E5

Bar St WN2 ......56 A1
Bar Terr OL12 ......14 C7
Barathea Cl OL11 ......30 B3
Barbara Rd BL3 ......146 A2
Barbara St BL3 ......147 D4
Barbeck Cl M40 ......160 E3
Barber St ⑤ Droylsden M11 ......99 E7
Hadfield SK13 ......104 A5
Barber Wlk BL1 ......143 E4
Barberry Bank BL7 ......8 E2
Barberry Cl WA14 ......119 B7
Barberry Wlk M31 ......105 F3
Barbican St ⑥ M20 ......110 B7
Barbon Wlk ⑧ M40 ......159 C2
Barbrook Cl WN6 ......19 B2
Barbury Cl WN7 ......75 F7
Barchester Ave BL2 ......25 E1
Barcheston Rd SK8 ......122 C4
Barcicroft Rd M19,SK4 ......110 E4
Barcicroft Wlk ① M19 ......110 E4
Barclay Rd SK12 ......133 E2
Barclays Ave M46 ......80 D6
Barcliffe Ave M40 ......65 C2
Barcombe Cl Oldham OL4 ......49 D2
Urmston M32 ......95 F3
Barcombe Wlk M9 ......157 D7
Barcroft Rd BL1 ......142 C2
Barcroft St BL9 ......44 D5
Bardale Gr WN4 ......73 A3
Bardell Cl SK12 ......133 D2
Bardney Ave WA3 ......73 F2
Bardon Cl BL1 ......143 D1
Bardon Rd M23 ......120 F6
Bardsea Ave M22 ......121 D1
Bardsley Ave M35 ......83 F7
Bardsley Cl Bolton BL2 ......25 D5
① Hattersley SK14 ......102 E2
Orrell WN8 ......53 A7
Bardsley Gate Ave SK13 ......102 E6
Bardsley St Failsworth M40 ......83 D5
Middleton M24 ......47 A1
Oldham OL4 ......49 E1
Oldham OL4 ......67 E5
Oldham OL9 ......65 F3
Stockport SK4 ......169 D3
Bardsley Vale Ave OL8 ......85 A8
Bare St 148 A8
Bare Trees Jun Sch OL9 ......152 B8
Barehill St SK15 ......16 B6
Barff Rd M5 ......80 C2
Barfold Cl SK2 ......125 A5
Barford Cl WN8 ......53 A7
Barford Dr Golborne WA3 ......91 A8
Hansforth SK9 ......131 C1
Barford Gr BL6 ......21 D1
Barford Wlk M23 ......121 B4
Baric Cl M30 ......79 F1
Baring St M1,M12 ......163 B8
Barke St Bolton BL1 ......145 E7
Bolton BL1 ......145 F8
Kearsley BL4 ......61 B5
Barkan Way M27 ......80 B8
Barke St OL15 ......15 F3
Barker Rd SK4 ......168 C3
Barker St Bury BL9 ......140 E1
Heywood OL10 ......29 B1
Leigh WN7 ......75 C5
Manchester M3 ......158 F3
Barker's La M33 ......107 F4
Barking St M40 ......160 D2
Barkway Rd M22 ......96 A2
Barkwell La OL5 ......68 B1
Barkworth Wlk M40 ......83 B6
Barlborough Rd WN5 ......54 D5
Barle Ave M46 ......65 D1
Barlea Ave M40 ......65 D1
Barley Brook Mdw BL1 ......24 F6
Barley Brook St WN6 ......37 B1
Barley Croft SK8 ......122 F1
Barley Croft Rd SK14 ......101 E6
Barley Dr SK7 ......132 E2
Barley Hall St OL10 ......29 E2
Barleycorn Cl M33 ......109 A3
Barleycroft SK14 ......171 F4
Barleyfield Wlk M24 ......46 F1
Barleywood Wlk SK15 ......102 E7
Barlow Cres SK6 ......125 F4
Barlow Ct Edgworth BL7 ......9 F5
Walkden M28 ......60 E3
Barlow Fold Bury BL9 ......44 F5
Romiley SK6 ......113 D3
Barlow Fold Cl BL9 ......44 F5
Barlow Fold Rd
Reddish SK5 ......111 F8
Romiley SK6 ......113 D3
Barlow Hall Prim Sch
M21 ......109 C5
Barlow Hall Rd M21 ......109 C5
Barlow Ho ⑧ OL8 ......153 F5
Barlow La M30 ......79 C2
Barlow La N SK5 ......111 F8
Barlow Moor Cl OL11 ......13 E2
Barlow Moor Ct M20 ......109 F4
Barlow Moor Rd M21 ......109 C6
Barlow Park Ave BL1 ......24 D5
Barlow Pl M13 ......163 C2
Barlow RC High Sch The
M20 ......110 C2
Barlow Rd
Altrincham WA14 ......119 B7
Dukinfield SK16 ......101 D6
Handforth SK9 ......131 B1
Manchester M5 ......81 C1
Reddish M19 ......99 C1
Stretford M16,M32 ......96 F4
Barlow St Bacup OL13 ......3 B7
Bury BL9 ......140 F3

Barlow St continued
Eccles M30 ......79 D1
Heywood OL10 ......46 B8
Horwich BL6 ......22 C2
Oldham OL4 ......67 A6
Radcliffe M26 ......44 B3
Rochdale OL16 ......31 A7
Walkden M28 ......60 D4
Barlow Terr M21 ......109 C6
Barlow Wlk ③ SK5 ......111 F8
Barlow Wood Dr SK6 ......126 B3
Barlow's Croft M3 ......158 E2
Barlow's La S SK7 ......124 C3
Barmhouse Cl M34 ......50 F2
Barmhouse Cl SK14 ......102 A3
Barmhouse La SK14 ......102 A3
Barmhouse Mews SK14 ......102 A3
Barmouth St M11 ......164 F8
Barmouth Wlk ④ M11 ......164 F8
Barmskin La WN6 ......18 C8
Barn Acre BL6 ......21 E1
Barn Cl Glossop SK13 ......116 D7
Urmston M41 ......94 C2
Barn Field La OL12 ......15 A7
Barn Fold OL4 ......67 E5
Barn Gr M34 ......100 E7
Barn Hill ⑥ BL5 ......39 E1
Barn Hill Terr ⑦ BL5 ......39 E1
Barn La WA3 ......89 F8
Barn Mdw BL7 ......9 D5
Barn St Bolton BL1 ......145 E7
Oldham OL1 ......153 E6
Whitefield M45 ......62 F7
Barn Way WA12 ......89 B3
Barn Wlk ⑧ M11 ......99 E7
Barnaby Rd SK12 ......133 D2
Barnabys Rd BL5 ......39 D3
Barnacre Ave Bolton BL2 ......42 F7
Wythenshawe M23 ......120 F3
Barnard Ave
Manchester SK4 ......168 B2
Prestwich M45 ......63 B7
Barnard Cl OL7 ......84 F4
Barnard Rd M18 ......99 B3
Barnard St ⑧ BL3 ......148 C8
Barnbrook St BL9 ......141 A3
Barnby St M12 ......99 A3
Barnclose Rd M22 ......121 D1
Barncroft Dr BL6 ......22 F3
Barncroft Gdns M22 ......121 C5
Barncroft Rd BL4 ......60 D8
Barnes Ave SK4 ......168 A2
Barnes Ho ⑧ M4 ......60 D8
Barnes Hospl SK8 ......122 C6
Barnes Mdws OL15 ......6 C1
Barnes St ⑧ BL4 ......60 B8
Barnes Terr ⑧ M40 ......83 A7
Barnet Rd BL1 ......142 C2
Barnett Ave M20 ......110 B6
Barnett Ct OL10 ......29 C1
Barnett Dr M3 ......158 D2
Barnfield
Littleborough OL15 ......16 D6
Urmston M41 ......95 B1
Barnfield Cl Bolton BL7 ......8 E2
Radcliffe M26 ......43 E3
⑧ Salford M5 ......154 F1
Tyldesley M29 ......58 F1
Barnfield Cres M33 ......107 F6
Barnfield Dr
Boothstown M28 ......78 B6
Westhoughton BL5 ......40 A1
Barnfield Rd Hyde SK14 ......102 B5
Manchester M19 ......110 E4
Swinton M27 ......61 D2
Barnfield Rd E SK3 ......123 F4
Barnfield Rd W SK3 ......123 D4
Barnfield Rise OL2 ......32 A1
Barnfield St Denton M34 ......100 D4
Heywood OL10 ......29 E2
Rochdale OL12 ......14 F2
Barngate Dr OL5 ......86 D8
Barngate Gr BL5 ......122 A6
Barngill Gr WN3 ......54 E3
Barnham Cl WA3 ......90 A8
Barnham Wlk M23 ......120 E8
Barnhill Ave M25 ......63 B2
Barnhill Dr M25 ......63 B3
Barnhill Rd M25 ......63 B3
Barnhill St M14 ......97 F4
Barnley Cl M44 ......94 B3
Barns La Partington M44 ......118 A5
Partington WA14 ......118 A4
Barns Pl WA15 ......129 C8
Barnsdale Cl BL2 ......26 C1
Barnsdale Dr M8 ......156 A6
Barnsfold Ave M14 ......110 C8
Barnsfold Rd SK6 ......125 D7
Barnside 14 B8
Barnside Ave M28 ......60 E3
Barnside Cl BL9 ......27 F6
Barnside Way M35 ......84 C6
Barnsley St SK14 ......124 B8
Wigan WN6 ......37 B2
Barnstaple Dr M40 ......156 C6
Barnstead Ave M20 ......110 D5
Barnston Ave M14 ......98 B2
Barnston Cl BL1 ......143 E2
Barnton Cl WA3 ......90 D7
Barnview Dr M44 ......94 A1
Barnway Wlk ⑦ M40 ......83 A7
Barnwell Ave WA3 ......91 D4
Barnwood Dr BL1 ......143 D1

Barnwood Cl ⑪ BL1 ......143 E1
Barnwood Dr BL1 ......143 E1
Barnwood Rd M23 ......120 E6
Barnwood Terr ⑧ BL1 ......143 E1
Baron Fold M38 ......60 A4
Baron Fold Cres M38 ......59 F5
Baron Fold Gr M38 ......59 F5
Baron Fold Rd M38 ......59 F5
Baron Gn SK8 ......131 D7
Baron Rd SK14 ......113 F7
Baron St Bury BL9 ......140 D1
Rochdale OL16 ......139 F7
Baron Wlk BL3 ......43 C3
Baroness Gr M7 ......81 C4
Barons Cl M35 ......83 D6
Barr All Ave M6 ......80 E5
Barra Dr M41 ......95 D5
Barrack Hill SK6 ......113 A2
Barrack Hill Cl SK6 ......113 A2
Barrack Hill Prim Sch
SK6 ......113 A2
Barrack Sq ⑯ WN1 ......150 C8
Barrack St Bolton BL3 ......145 F6
Manchester M15 ......162 D7
Barracks Rd WN2 ......56 D1
Barracks Yd WN1 ......150 C8
Barrass St ⑪ M11 ......99 D7
Barratt Gdns M24 ......46 D4
Barrett Ave BL4 ......60 F7
Barrett Ct BL4 ......141 A2
Barrett St OL4 ......67 B5
Barfield Rd M6 ......154 E4
Barrhill Cl M15 ......162 E6
Barrie St WN7 ......75 D8
Barrie Way BL1 ......25 B4
Barrington Ave
Cheadle SK8 ......123 A1
Droylsden M43 ......83 F1
Barrington Cl
Altrincham WA14 ......119 D6
Wigan WN1 ......54 D2
Barrington Rd WA14 ......119 D5
Barrington St M11 ......83 C2
Barrington Wlk ⑦ BL2 ......25 B1
Barrisdale Cl BL3 ......40 F5
Barron Mdw WN7 ......76 A5
Barrow Bridge Rd
Bolton BL1 ......142 A3
Bolton BL1 ......23 F4
Barrow Hill Rd M8 ......155 F5
Barrow La
Altrincham WA15 ......129 B7
Golborne WA2 ......90 C2
Barrow Mdw SK8 ......131 D8
Barrow St Ashton-in-M WN4 ......73 D5
Manchester M3,M5 ......158 D1
Barrowcroft Cl WN1 ......20 B1
Barrowdale Rd M23 ......90 B8
Barrowdene Ho BL1 ......25 E2
Barrowfield Rd M22 ......121 A2
Barsmark St M27 ......61 C4
Barowfields M24 ......47 A2
Barrows Ct ⑧ BL1 ......145 F6
Barrowshaw Cl M28 ......60 C2
Barrs Fold Cl BL5 ......39 D3
Barrs Fold Rd BL5 ......39 D3
Barrule Ave SK7 ......124 E1
Barry Cres M28 ......60 A3
Barry Ct ⑧ M20 ......110 B6
Barry Lawson Cl ⑧ M8 ......155 F7
Barry Rd Reddish SK5 ......111 F5
Wythenshawe M23 ......109 C2
Barry Rise WA14 ......119 A2
Barry St OL1 ......67 B8
Barsham Dr BL3 ......145 D5
Bartlemore St OL1 ......153 F7
Bartlett Rd OL2 ......149 A6
Bartlett St M11 ......165 B8
Bartley Rd M22 ......121 C8
Barton Ave Urmston M41 ......95 B2
Wigan WN1 ......37 B2
Barton Bsns Pk M30 ......79 C1
Barton Cl SK9 ......131 D2
Barton Clough WN5 ......71 E5
Barton Clough Prim Sch
M32 ......95 F8
Barton Ct SK14 ......101 C1
Barton Dock Rd Eccles M41 ......95 E6
Stretford M32 ......96 B4
Barton Fold SK14 ......167 D1
Barton Hall Ave M30 ......79 A1
Barton La Eccles M30 ......79 C1
Eccles M30 ......79 B1
Barton Moss Com Prim Sch
M30 ......94 F8
Barton Moss Rd M30 ......94 D7
Barton Rd
Dukinfield SK14,SK16 ......101 C6
Eccles M30 ......79 C1
Farnworth BL4 ......60 C8
Manchester SK4 ......110 E1
Middleton M24 ......64 B8
Pendlebury M27 ......80 A6
Stretford M32 ......96 B3
Stretford M32 ......96 B3
Urmston M41 ......95 C5
Swinton M28 ......78 F5
Barton Sq ⑧ M2 ......158 F1
Barton St Farnworth BL4 ......60 E7
Golborne WA3 ......74 A1
Manchester M3 ......162 E8
Oldham OL1 ......153 D8
Platt Bridge WN2 ......56 B2
Tyldesley M29 ......58 F1
④ Swinton M27 ......54 B5
Barton Terr M44 ......94 C3
Barway Rd M21 ......96 F1

Barwell Cl Golborne WA3 ......74 C1
Reddish SK5 ......112 A8
Barwell Rd M23 ......107 E5
Barwell Sq ⑨ BL4 ......42 B2
Barwick Pl M43 ......108 A4
Basechurch Wlk M40 ......164 F6
Basford Rd M16 ......97 B3
Bashall St BL1 ......144 C8
Basil Ct OL16 ......31 B6
Basil St Bolton BL3 ......145 E5
Manchester M14 ......98 C3
Rochdale OL16 ......31 B6
Stockport SK4 ......169 E3
Basildon Cl M13 ......164 D5
Baslam Wlk ⑧ M4 ......159 C2
Basle Cl SK7 ......123 E4
Baslow Ave Hindley WN2 ......56 F3
Manchester M19 ......99 C2
Baslow Cl SK13 ......171 E1
Baslow Dr Gatley SK8 ......131 C8
Hazel Grove SK7 ......133 F8
Baslow Fold ⑳ SK13 ......171 E1
Baslow Gr SK5 ......111 F5
Baslow Mews SK13 ......171 E1
Baslow Rd Denton M34 ......112 F8
Droylsden M43 ......83 E3
Stretford M32 ......96 A3
Baslow St M11 ......160 F2
Baslow Way ⑧ SK13 ......171 E1
Bass La BL9 ......11 D3
Bass St Bolton BL2 ......148 C7
Dukinfield SK16 ......101 B8
Basset Ave M6,M7 ......81 C5
Bassett Gr WN5 ......54 C2
Bassett Way OL12 ......14 C2
Basswood Gr WN2 ......57 A3
Basten Dr M7 ......155 E6
Batchelor Cl M21 ......109 E7
Bateman St BL6 ......22 D2
Batemill Rd SK22 ......127 D2
Bates Cl OL11 ......30 D1
Bates St Dukinfield SK16 ......101 C8
Manchester M13 ......98 F4
Bateson Dr OL4 ......67 F6
Bateson St SK1 ......112 A2
Bateson Way OL8 ......153 F5
Bath Cl SK7 ......125 A2
Bath Cres Bramhall SK8 ......132 B6
Manchester M16 ......161 C5
Bath La SK7 ......125 A1
Bath St Altrincham WA14 ......119 D2
Atherton M46 ......58 A3
Bolton BL1 ......145 F8
Oldham OL9 ......152 C5
Wigan WN7 ......37 F2
Batheaston Gr WN7 ......75 D8
Batley St M9 ......157 E8
Batridge Rd BL7 ......9 A7
Batsmans Dr M27 ......61 C4
Battenberg Rd BL1 ......144 C8
Battersbay Gr SK7 ......124 C2
Battersby St Bury BL9 ......28 D3
Droylsden M11 ......99 F7
Ince-in-M WN2 ......56 A2
Leigh WN7 ......76 B4
Rochdale OL11 ......30 D3
Battersea Rd SK4 ......110 F1
Batty St M8 ......156 C5
Baucher Rd WN3 ......54 F1
Baum The OL16 ......139 F8
Baverstock Cl WN3 ......151 D6
Baxendale St BL1 ......143 E4
Baxter Gdns M23 ......121 A7
Baxter Rd M33 ......108 B4
Baxter St Oldham OL8 ......66 D2
Standish WN6 ......19 E1
Baxters Row WN2 ......57 C2
Bay St Heywood OL10 ......29 B3
Oldham OL9 ......153 D7
Rochdale OL12 ......15 A1
Bay Tree Ave M28 ......79 A5
Baybutt St M26 ......44 C3
Baycliffe Cl WN2 ......56 F3
Baycliffe Wlk ⑩ M8 ......155 F6
Baycroft Gr M23 ......109 A1
Baydon Ave M7 ......155 F6
Bayfield Gr M40 ......65 A1
Bayley St SK14 ......101 E5
Baynard Wlk M9 ......64 B8
Baysdale Cl 48 C5
Baysdale Ave BL3 ......40 F4
Bayston Wlk M12 ......164 F6
Bayswater Ave M40 ......83 C4
Bayswater St BL3 ......146 C2
Baythorpe St BL1 ......143 F3
Baytree Ave
Chadderton OL9 ......65 E8
Dukinfield M34 ......101 A4
Baytree Gr BL6 ......21 B2
Baytree La M24 ......65 D8
Baytree Rd M6 ......36 F2
Baytree Wlk OL12 ......4 C1
Baywood St M9 ......157 D8
Bazaar St M6 ......81 A4
Bazley Rd M22 ......109 D1
Bazley St M3 ......23 F4
Beacomfold SK6 ......114 B3
Beacon Ave M34 ......58 B2
Beacon Dr M23 ......121 A2
Beacon Gr OL9 ......47 C4
Beacon Hts WN8 ......43 D7
Beacon Rd Billinge WN5 ......71 E6
Eccles M17 ......95 E7

Beacon Rd continued
Leigh WN2 ....**75** A8
Romiley SK6 ....**113** A1
Shevington Moor WN6 ....**19** B2
Beacon View
Appley Bridge WN6 ....**35** C3
Marple SK6 ....**125** F8
Beacon View Dr WN8 ....**53** B7
Beacons The WN6 ....**35** D7
Beaconsfield M14 ....**110** C7
Beaconsfield Rd WA14 ....**119** D7
Beaconsfield St BL3 ....**145** D6
Beaconsfield Terr SK15 ...**86** F7
Beadham Dr M9 ....**64** A5
Beaford Cl WN5 ....**54** B5
Beaford Dr M22 ....**130** E8
Beagle Wlk M22 ....**130** E8
Beal Cl SK4 ....**110** D3
Beal Cres OL16 ....**15** C1
Beal Dr WN2 ....**56** A2
Beal La SK5 ....**149** C6
Beal Vale Com Prim Sch
OL2 ....**149** B7
Beal Wlk M45 ....**63** C8
Bealbank Cl OL16 ....**32** A3
Bealcroft Cl OL16 ....**31** E7
Bealcroft Wlk OL16 ....**31** E7
Beale Gr M21 ....**109** B8
Bealey Ave BL9 ....**44** E5
Bealey Cl Manchester M18 **165** B5
   Radcliffe M26 ....**44** D4
Bealey Dr BL9 ....**44** D7
Bealey Hospl M26 ....**44** D4
Bealey Ind Est M26 ....**44** D4
Bealey Row M26 ....**44** C4
Beaminster Ave SK4 ....**110** F3
Beaminster Cl SK4 ....**110** F3
Beaminster Ct SK4 ....**110** F3
Beaminster Rd SK4 ....**110** F3
Beaminster Wlk 7 M13 .....**163** C5
Beamish Cl M12,M13 ....**163** C6
Beamsley Dr M22 ....**121** B2
Bean Leach Ave SK2 ....**124** F6
Bean Leach Dr SK2 ....**124** F6
Bean Leach Rd SK2,SK7 .....**124** F5
Beanfields M28 ....**78** F5
Beard Rd M18 ....**99** C4
Beard St Droylsden M43 ......**83** F1
   Royton OL2 ....**48** E3
Beardsmore Dr WA3 ....**74** E1
Beardwood Rd M9 ....**64** D4
Bearswood Cl WA14 ....**167** F1
Beathwaite Dr SK7 ....**123** C1
Beatrice Ave Cheadle SK8 ..**122** F2
   Reddish M18 ....**99** F4
Beatrice Mews 9 BL6 ....**22** B4
Beatrice Rd Bolton BL1 .....**142** C1
   Swinton M28 ....**79** B7
Beatrice St Denton M34 .....**100** E3
   Farnworth BL4 ....**60** C8
   Rochdale OL11 ....**139** D7
   Swinton M27 ....**61** D1
Beatrice Wignall St M43 ...**100** A8
Beatson Wlk 2 M4 ....**159** C1
Beattock St M15 ....**162** D7
Beatty Dr BL5 ....**39** E1
Beauchamp St OL6 ....**166** C4
Beaufont Dr OL4 ....**67** C5
Beaufort Ave
   1 Manchester M20 ....**110** A5
   Sale M33 ....**108** C2
   Swinton M27 ....**79** D7
Beaufort Chase SK9 ....**131** F1
Beaufort Cl
   Alderley Edge SK9 ....**137** B2
   Hattersley SK14 ....**102** D2
Beaufort Pl 2 M20 ....**110** A2
Beaufort Rd Ashton-u-L OL6 ..**85** D3
   Hattersley SK14 ....**102** E2
   Sale M33 ....**108** C3
   Stockport SK2 ....**124** D5
Beaufort St Eccles M30 ......**79** B3
   1 Hindley WN2 ....**56** D5
   Manchester M3 ....**162** E8
   Prestwich M25 ....**63** C4
   Rochdale OL12 ....**14** C1
   Wigan WN5 ....**54** E6
Beaufort Way 3 SK14 ....**102** E1
Beaulieu WA15 ....**119** F2
Beauly Cl BL0 ....**11** A2
Beaumaris Cl Leigh WN7 ....**75** C5
   Manchester M12 ....**164** F6
Beaumaris Cres SK7 ....**124** C1
Beaumaris Rd WN2 ....**57** A3
Beaumonds Way OL11 ....**30** A6
Beaumont Ave BL6 ....**22** C4
Beaumont Cl Bredbury SK6 ..**40** F3
Beaumont Cl 2 OL15 ....**15** F5
Beaumont Com Prim Sch
   BL3 ....**40** E5
Beaumont Ct Bolton BL1 .....**40** D8
   Handforth SK9 ....**131** C5
Beaumont Dr BL3 ....**40** E5
Beaumont Gr WN5 ....**54** C4
Beaumont Hospl BL6 ....**40** C8
Beaumont Rd
   Bolton BL1,BL3,BL6 ....**40** E5
   Horwich BL6 ....**22** C4
   Manchester M21 ....**109** B7
Beaumont St OL6 ....**166** C3
Beauvale Ave SK2 ....**124** C7
Beaver Cir WN4 ....**73** C6
Beaver Dr BL9 ....**45** B4
Beaver Ho SK1 ....**124** B8
Beaver Rd M20 ....**110** B3
Beaver Road Prim Sch
   M20 ....**110** B3
Beaver St M1 ....**163** A8

Beaver Wlk SK14 ....**102** D1
Beaverbrook Ave WA3 ....**92** B4
Bebbington Cl M33 ....**108** F3
Bebbington St 1 M11 ......**83** C1
Beccles Rd M33 ....**108** B1
Beck Gr Shaw OL2 ....**49** D8
   Walkden M28 ....**60** F1
Beck Ho SK14 ....**102** D1
Beck St Droylsden M11 ....**99** E7
   Manchester M3 ....**158** E1
Beckenham Cl BL8 ....**27** B1
Beckenham Rd M8 ....**156** A7
Becket Ave M7 ....**155** E6
Becket Mews OL4 ....**67** B6
Becket Meadow St OL4 ......**67** B6
Beckett Dr WA13 ....**117** B8
Beckett St
   Manchester M18 ....**165** C5
   Oldham OL4 ....**67** B6
Beckfield Rd M23 ....**121** A5
Beckfoot Dr M13 ....**98** E3
Beckford St M40 ....**157** E5
Beckhampton Cl M13 ....**163** C6
Beckley Ave M25 ....**63** A2
Beckside Reddish SK5 ....**100** A1
   Tyldesley M29 ....**76** E8
Beckton Gdns M22 ....**121** C3
Beckwith WN2 ....**56** A6
Becontree Ave M34 ....**101** A4
Becontree Dr M23 ....**120** E7
Bede St BL1 ....**142** C2
Bedells La SK9 ....**137** A6
Bedfont Wlk M9 ....**64** E1
Bedford Ave Hyde SK14 .....**167** E3
   Manchester M16 ....**97** D2
   Sale M33 ....**108** D2
   Shaw OL2 ....**48** F7
   1 Swinton M27 ....**79** E7
   Walkden M28 ....**60** C1
Bedford Cl WA15 ....**120** C6
Bedford Dr
   Altrincham WA15 ....**120** C6
   Atherton M46 ....**58** A1
Bedford Gdns WN2 ....**56** F6
Bedford Gn M44 ....**105** B6
Bedford Hall
   Meth Prim Sch WN7 ....**76** C3
Bedford High Sch WN7 ......**76** D4
Bedford Pl WN4 ....**73** A6
Bedford Rd Eccles M30 ......**79** E3
   Manchester M16 ....**97** A3
   Urmston M41 ....**95** C4
Bedford St Bolton BL1 ......**145** D8
   Bolton BL7 ....**9** D2
   Heywood OL10 ....**29** E2
   1 Leigh WN7 ....**76** A5
   Prestwich M25 ....**63** C5
   6 Reddish SK5 ....**111** E7
   Reddish SK5 ....**111** E8
   Wigan WN1 ....**37** E1
   Wigan WN5 ....**54** C5
Bedford Terr Bury BL9 .....**141** A4
   Haslingden BL4 ....**1** A8
Bedlam Gn 2 BL9 ....**140** F2
Bedlington Cl M23 ....**120** E6
Bednal Ave M40 ....**160** E4
Bedwell Cl M16 ....**97** F3
Bedworth Cl BL2 ....**148** B5
Bee Fold La M46 ....**58** C1
Bee Hive Ind Est BL6 ....**39** E8
Beech Ave Adlington PR6 ....**21** B8
   Atherton M46 ....**58** E3
   Boothstown M28 ....**78** A6
   Chadderton OL1,OL9 ....**48** A2
   Culcheth WA3 ....**92** A3
   Denton M34 ....**100** D4
   Droylsden M43 ....**83** F1
   Farnworth BL4 ....**60** A8
   Gatley SK8 ....**122** B5
   Glossop SK13 ....**116** A8
   Golborne WA3 ....**90** F7
   Hazel Grove SK7 ....**124** E2
   Horwich BL6 ....**22** E1
   Irlam M44 ....**94** C3
   Kearsley BL4 ....**61** B5
   Little Lever BL3 ....**43** B4
   Marple SK6 ....**125** D6
   New Mills SK22 ....**127** D1
   Oldham OL3 ....**69** B6
   Oldham OL4 ....**67** D8
   Radcliffe M26 ....**61** B8
   Sale M33 ....**120** B8
   Salford M6 ....**154** E4
   Stockport SK2,SK3 ....**170** F6
   Urmston M41 ....**95** C2
   Whitefield M45 ....**62** F6
   Wythenshawe M22 ....**121** D8
Beech Cl
   Alderley Edge SK9 ....**137** B3
   Bolton BL2 ....**25** C6
   Newton-le-W WA12 ....**89** C2
   4 Partington M31 ....**105** F3
   Prestwich M25 ....**63** C3
   Whitworth OL12 ....**4** C1
Beech Cres Leigh WN7 ....**75** F3
   Poynton SK12 ....**133** E4
   Standish WN6 ....**36** E8
Beech Ct Manchester M14 ..**110** C8
   1 Manchester M21 ....**96** F1
   Manchester M8 ....**63** F1
   2 Sale M33 ....**107** F4
Beech Dr WN7 ....**75** E2
Beech Gr Abram WN2 ....**74** C7
   Ashton-u-L OL7 ....**84** F1
   Leigh WN7 ....**75** E2
   Manchester M14 ....**110** D7

Beech Gr continued
   Ramsbottom BL8 ....**11** A1
   Sale M33 ....**107** F4
   Salford M6 ....**154** E4
   Stalybridge SK15 ....**101** F8
   Walkden M38 ....**59** E5
   Wigan WN6 ....**36** E3
   Wilmslow SK9 ....**137** A6
Beech Grove Cl BL9 ....**141** B4
Beech Hall St WN6 ....**37** A2
Beech Hill Ave WN6 ....**36** F3
Beech Hill La WN6 ....**36** E3
Beech Hill Prim Sch WN6 ...**37** A3
Beech Hill Rd OL4 ....**68** D6
Beech Ho M20 ....**109** F4
Beech Holme Gr SK2 ....**124** C8
Beech House Sch
   OL11 ....**139** C6
Beech Hurst Cl M16 ....**97** D2
Beech La Romiley SK6 ......**113** C2
   Uppermill OL4 ....**68** D5
   Wilmslow SK9 ....**137** A6
Beech Lawn WA14 ....**119** C4
Beech Mews
   Manchester M21 ....**109** A8
   Stockport SK2 ....**124** A5
Beech Mount
   Ashton-u-L OL7 ....**85** A6
   Manchester M9 ....**157** D8
Beech Range 13 M19 ....**99** A1
Beech Rd
   Alderley Edge SK9 ....**137** B3
   Altrincham WA15 ....**119** C3
   Cheadle SK8 ....**123** B1
   Golborne WA3 ....**74** A1
   High Lane SK6 ....**134** F7
   Manchester M21 ....**109** B7
   Sale M33 ....**108** D4
   Stockport SK2,SK3 ....**124** A5
Beech St Ashton-in-M WN4 ..**73** A6
   Atherton M46 ....**58** E3
   Bolton BL1 ....**143** F2
   Bury BL9 ....**141** B2
   Eccles M30 ....**79** D5
   Edgworth BL7 ....**9** D5
   Failsworth M35 ....**83** E8
   Hyde SK14 ....**167** D3
   Middleton M24 ....**64** F8
   Newhey OL16 ....**32** B4
   8 Oldham OL1 ....**67** A7
   Radcliffe M26 ....**44** C1
   Ramsbottom BL9 ....**11** C3
   Rochdale OL11 ....**139** D6
   Swinton M27 ....**79** F7
Beech Street
   Com Prim Sch M30 ....**79** B1
Beech Tree Ave M6 ....**35** D8
Beech Tree Ho WN7 ....**73** F7
Beech View SK14 ....**102** A2
Beech Wlk Leigh WN7 ....**75** F1
   Middleton M24 ....**65** A6
   Standish WN6 ....**36** D8
   1 Stretford M32 ....**96** C1
   Wigan WN3 ....**54** C2
Beechacre BL0 ....**11** C8
Beechbank M9 ....**63** C3
Beechcroft M25 ....**42** E6
Beechcroft Cl M40 ....**160** D3
Beechcroft Gr BL2 ....**42** E6
Beechdale Cl M40 ....**83** C8
Beecher Wlk M9 ....**157** D6
Beeches Mews M20 ....**109** F4
Beeches The
   Altrincham WA14 ....**119** C2
   4 Atherton M46 ....**58** D3
   Bolton BL1 ....**24** D6
   Cheadle SK8 ....**123** B1
   Eccles M30 ....**79** F3
   Heywood OL10 ....**29** C2
   Manchester M20 ....**109** F4
   Mossley OL5 ....**68** E1
Beechey Sq OL1 ....**67** A7
Beechfield
   Altrincham WA14 ....**119** C3
   Rochdale OL11 ....**29** E6
   Sale M33 ....**107** F2
   Uppermill OL4 ....**68** D5
   Wilmslow SK9 ....**137** A6
Beechfield Ave
   Hindley WN2 ....**57** A4
   1 Radcliffe M26 ....**44** C1
   Urmston M41 ....**95** A3
   Walkden M38 ....**60** A5
   Wilmslow SK9 ....**136** E5
Beechfield Cl
   1 Oldham OL4 ....**67** F6
   Rochdale OL11 ....**29** E6
Beechfield Dr Bury BL9 ......**44** F7
Beechfield Rd Bolton BL1 ...**142** A3
   Cheadle SK8 ....**132** B8
   Hadfield SK13 ....**171** F3
   Milnrow OL16 ....**31** F4
   Stockport SK3 ....**170** F5
   Swinton M27 ....**79** D5
Beechfield St M8 ....**156** B6
Beechhill Dr M23 ....**91** E3
Beechpark Ave M22 ....**121** C7
Beechurst Rd SK8 ....**123** B5
Beechway High Lane SK6 ....**134** F7
   Wilmslow SK9 ....**136** F5
Beechwood
   Altrincham WA14 ....**119** B1
   Glossop SK13 ....**116** A8
   Shaw OL2 ....**49** D8
   Whitefield BL9 ....**45** A6

Beechwood Ave
   Ashton-in-M WN4 ....**73** A2
   Littleborough OL15 ....**16** A3
   Manchester M21 ....**109** C7
   Newton-le-W WA12 ....**89** D4
   Ramsbottom BL0 ....**11** D6
   Reddish SK5 ....**169** F4
   Romiley SK6 ....**113** D2
   Stalybridge SK15 ....**35** F5
   Stalybridge SK15 ....**86** C4
   Urmston M41 ....**94** E3
Beechwood Cres
   Orrell WN5 ....**53** E6
   Tyldesley M29 ....**77** A6
Beechwood Ct Bury BL8 ......**27** A5
   Coppull PR7 ....**19** F8
   3 Manchester M20 ....**110** A4
Beechwood Dr Hyde SK14 ..**167** F1
   Marple SK6 ....**125** E6
   Mossley OL5 ....**68** C2
   Royton OL2 ....**48** C6
   Sale M33 ....**107** C4
   Swinton M28 ....**79** B6
   Wilmslow SK9 ....**137** E8
Beechwood Gr
   Cheadle SK8 ....**132** A8
   Manchester M9 ....**157** E7
Beechwood La
   Culcheth WA3 ....**91** D4
   Stalybridge SK15 ....**86** C4
Beechwood Rd
   Manchester M25 ....**63** D3
   Oldham OL6 ....**66** F2
Beechwood Sch BL3 ....**147** F3
Beede St M11 ....**165** B8
Beedon Ave BL3 ....**43** A4
Beehive Gn BL5 ....**40** B1
Beehive St OL8 ....**66** F3
Beeley St Hyde SK14 ....**167** E2
   Salford M6 ....**81** B5
Beenham Cl M33 ....**107** C3
Beeston Ave
   Altrincham WA15 ....**119** F6
   Manchester M7 ....**81** B6
Beeston Cl BL8 ....**25** B3
Beeston Gr Leigh WN7 ....**76** D7
   Prestwich M45 ....**63** B7
   Stockport SK5 ....**170** E5
Beeston Rd Handforth SK9 .**131** D5
   Sale M33 ....**107** F4
Beeston St M9 ....**157** E8
Beeth St M11 ....**99** D7
Beeton Gr M13 ....**98** E4
Beever Prim Sch OL1 ....**67** A8
Beever St Manchester M16 ..**97** D4
   Oldham OL1 ....**67** A7
Begley Cl SK6 ....**112** F1
Begonia Ave BL4 ....**42** B1
Begonia Wlk M12 ....**164** F6
Beightons Wlk OL12 ....**14** D4
Beis Yaakov High Sch M7 ...**81** C8
Belbeck St BL8 ....**27** C2
Belcroft Dr M38 ....**59** E6
Belding Ave M40 ....**65** F1
Beldon Rd M9 ....**64** B4
Belfairs Cl OL7 ....**85** B7
Belfield Cl OL16 ....**31** C8
Belfield Com Sch OL16 ......**31** C8
Belfield La OL16 ....**31** D8
Belfield Mill La OL16 ....**31** D8
Belfield Old Rd OL16 ....**31** C8
Belfield Rd
   Manchester M20 ....**110** B3
   Manchester M25 ....**63** E2
   Reddish SK5 ....**99** F3
   Rochdale OL16 ....**31** C8
Belfield Trad Est OL16 ....**31** D8
Belford Ave M34 ....**100** A3
Belford Dr BL3 ....**147** E3
Belford Rd M32 ....**96** D3
Belford Wlk M23 ....**121** A6
Belfort Dr M5 ....**161** B8
Belfry Cl SK9 ....**137** D8
Belfry Cres WN6 ....**19** F2
Belgate Cl M12 ....**99** A4
Belgium St OL11 ....**29** E7
Belgrave Ave
   Failsworth M35 ....**84** B8
   Manchester M14 ....**98** E3
   Marple SK6 ....**125** F6
   Oldham OL8 ....**67** A4
   Urmston M41 ....**94** E3
Belgrave Bglws M26 ....**43** F4
Belgrave Cl Golborne WN7 ..**91** C8
   Radcliffe M26 ....**44** A4
   Wigan WN3 ....**54** D2
Belgrave Cres Eccles M30 ..**79** F2
   Horwich BL6 ....**22** C2
   Stockport SK2 ....**124** B4
Belgrave Ct Denton M34 ...**100** D4
   Oldham OL8 ....**66** F1
Belgrave Dr M26 ....**43** E3
Belgrave Gdns 5 BL1 ....**143** E2
Belgrave Rd
   Altrincham WA14 ....**119** B3
   Failsworth M40 ....**65** F1
   Irlam M44 ....**105** D5
   Oldham OL8 ....**66** F4
   Sale M33 ....**108** D4
Belgrave St Atherton M46 ...**58** E2
   Bolton BL1 ....**143** E2
   Denton M34 ....**100** D4
   Heywood OL10 ....**29** C1
   Oldham OL4 ....**67** A6
   Rochdale OL12 ....**14** D1
Belgrave St S BL1 ....**143** E1

Beechwood Ave continued
Belgravia Gdns
   Altrincham WA15 ....**128** E8
   Manchester M21 ....**109** A8
Belgravia Mews OL2 ....**149** C7
Belhaven Rd M8 ....**63** F2
Belhill Gdns M6 ....**154** F3
Bell Clough Rd M43 ....**84** B3
Bell Cres M11 ....**164** F8
Bell La Bury BL9 ....**141** B3
   Milnrow OL16 ....**32** B7
Bell Mdw Dr OL11 ....**29** F5
Bell St Bolton BL2 ....**148** A6
   Droylsden M43 ....**84** B2
   Wigan WN3 ....**56** E6
   Leigh WN7 ....**53** B7
   Oldham OL1 ....**67** A7
   Rochdale OL16 ....**139** F8
Bell Terr M30 ....**95** C8
Bella St BL3 ....**146** C4
Bellairs St BL3 ....**146** B3
Bellamy Ct M18 ....**99** E5
Bellamy Dr WN7 ....**76** B5
Bellcroft M22 ....**121** E8
Belldale Cl SK4 ....**168** A2
Belldean WN2 ....**56** B8
Belle Green CE Prim Sch
   WN2 ....**56** B8
Belle Green La WN2 ....**56** A8
Belle Isle Ave OL12 ....**14** C6
Belle Vue Ave M12 ....**164** F5
Belle Vue St
   Manchester M12 ....**165** A6
   Manchester M12 ....**99** C4
Belle Vue Sta M18 ....**165** C5
Belle Vue Terr BL9 ....**140** E1
Belleville Ave M22 ....**62** E8
Bellew St M11 ....**164** E8
Bellfield Ave Cheadle SK8 ..**123** B1
   Oldham OL8 ....**66** F2
Bellingham Ave WN1 ....**37** C2
Bellingham Cl Bury BL8 ......**26** F2
   Shaw OL2 ....**149** B8
Bellingham Dr WN1 ....**37** D2
Bellingham Mount WN1 .....**37** D2
Bellis Cl M12 ....**160** A1
Bellot Wlk OL1 ....**153** E8
Bellott St M8 ....**156** A6
Bellpit Cl M28 ....**78** C7
Bells Croft Ave M40 ....**83** B7
Bellshill Cres OL16 ....**15** C1
Bellwood BL5 ....**57** C6
Belmont Ave Atherton M46 ..**58** F4
   Denton M34 ....**100** D4
   Golborne WA3 ....**74** C1
   Kearsley M27 ....**61** C5
   Wigan WN5 ....**57** A1
   Oldham OL4 ....**67** F7
   Orrell WN5 ....**53** D3
   Salford M6 ....**80** A2
Belmont Ch Ctr SK4 ....**169** E3
Belmont Cres M30 ....**79** D3
   Manchester M16 ....**162** D4
   Oldham OL1 ....**153** E8
   Oldham OL4 ....**67** E5
   Salford M5 ....**154** D1
   Stockport SK4 ....**169** E3
Belmont Way Oldham OL9 ..**152** C4
   Rochdale OL12 ....**14** E2
   Stockport SK4 ....**169** E3
Belmont Wlk 1 M13 ....**163** C6
Belmore Ave M8 ....**156** A3
Belmore Rd M33 ....**108** B1
Belper Rd Eccles M30 ....**95** B8
   Manchester SK4 ....**110** F1
Belper St M18 ....**166** B4
Belper Way M34 ....**113** A8
Belper Wlk M18 ....**165** C6
Belroy Ct M25 ....**63** B3
Belsay Cl OL7 ....**84** F5
Belsay Dr M23 ....**121** A4
Belstone Ave M23 ....**121** A3
Belstone Cl SK7 ....**123** F2
Belstyde W 7 SK14 ....**167** E2
Belthorne Ave M9 ....**65** B2
Belton Ave OL16 ....**15** C1
Belton Wlk 11
   Manchester M8 ....**156** A6
   Oldham OL9 ....**153** D6
Beltone Cl M32 ....**96** B1
Belvedere Ave
   Atherton M46 ....**58** F4
   Ramsbottom BL8 ....**11** A1
   Reddish SK5 ....**99** F2
Belvedere Ct WN7 ....**75** C6
Belvedere Ct M25 ....**63** A3
Belvedere Dr
   Bredbury SK6 ....**112** C3
   Dukinfield SK15,SK16 ......**101** E8

Belvedere Pl **5** WN3 . . . . .54 F5
Belvedere Rd Adlington PR6 .21 B8
  Ashton-in-M WN4 . . . . .73 C4
  Manchester M14 . . . . .110 E8
  Newton-le-W WA12 . . . . .89 B5
  Salford M6 . . . . .81 A3
Belvedere Rise OL1 . . . . .49 D3
Belvedere St M6 . . . . .81 B2
Belvoir Ave
  Hazel Grove SK7 . . . . .133 E8
  Manchester M19 . . . . .99 A2
Belvoir Mdws OL16 . . . . .15 E4
Belvoir St Bolton BL2 . . . . .148 C7
  Rochdale OL12 . . . . .14 C1
  Wigan WN1 . . . . .151 E8
Belvor Ave M34 . . . . .100 E7
Belwood Rd M21 . . . . .109 B7
Bembridge Cl M14 . . . . .98 C3
Bembridge Ct WN3 . . . . .54 E2
Bembridge Dr BL3 . . . . .42 D5
Bembridge Rd M34 . . . . .113 B8
Bempton Cl SK2 . . . . .125 A5
Bemrose Ave WA14 . . . . .119 C6
Bemsley Pl M5 . . . . .161 A8
Ben Brierley Way OL2 . . . . . . .153 F7
Ben St M11 . . . . .83 B2
Benbecula Way M41 . . . . .95 D5
Benbow Ave M12 . . . . .164 F5
Benbow St **3** M33 . . . . .108 B5
Benbrook Gr SK9 . . . . .131 E2
Bench Carr OL12 . . . . .14 E1
Benchill Ave M22 . . . . .121 D5
Benchill Court Rd M22 . . . . . . .121 E4
Benchill Cres M22 . . . . .121 C5
Benchill Dr M22 . . . . .121 E4
Benchill Dr M22 . . . . .121 C6
Benchill Prim Sch M22 . . . . . . .121 C6
Benchill Rd M22 . . . . .121 D5
Bendall St M11 . . . . .99 E8
Bendemeer **8** M41 . . . . .95 C3
Bendix St M4 . . . . .159 B2
Benedict Cl **5** M7 . . . . .81 C5
Benedict Dr SK16 . . . . .101 D6
Benfield Ave M40 . . . . .65 C2
Benfleet Cl OL10 . . . . .29 D1
Benfleet Cl M12 . . . . .165 A6
Benfold Wlk M24 . . . . .46 D3
Bengairn Cl WN1 . . . . .37 F1
Bengal La OL6 . . . . .166 C4
Bengal Sq **10** OL6 . . . . .85 D4
Bengal St Leigh WN7 . . . . .75 F5
  Manchester M4 . . . . .159 C2
  Stockport SK3 . . . . .170 E8
Benhale Wlk **15** M8 . . . . .156 A6
Benin Wlk **26** M40 . . . . .83 C5
Benjamin Fold WN4 . . . . .73 B5
Benjamin Wilson Ct M7 . .158 D4
Benmore Cl OL10 . . . . .29 A1
Benmore Rd M9 . . . . .64 F3
Bennet Mews **3** SK14 . . . . . . .101 D5
Bennet St M26 . . . . .43 D4
Bennett Cl **4** SK3 . . . . .170 D8
  Orrell WN5 . . . . .53 D4
Bennett Rd M8 . . . . .63 F1
Bennett St Ashton-u-L OL7 . . . .84 F1
  Dukinfield SK14 . . . . .101 D5
  Hollingworth SK14 . . . . .103 D5
  Manchester M12 . . . . .164 E6
  4 Stalybridge SK15 . . . . .86 A1
  6 Stockport SK3 . . . . .123 C8
  Stretford M32 . . . . .96 C1
Bennett's La BL1 . . . . .142 C2
Benny La M43 . . . . .84 D3
Benson Cl M7 . . . . .155 E5
Benson St Bury BL9 . . . . .141 A1
  Edgworth BL7 . . . . .9 E5
Benson Wlk **3** SK9 . . . . .131 D2
Bent Fold Dr BL9 . . . . .45 A1
Bent Hill St Bolton BL3 . . . . . . .146 A4
  Bolton BL3 . . . . .40 F4
Bent La Culcheth WA3 . . . . .92 A2
  Lymm WA13 . . . . .117 C6
  Manchester M8 . . . . .155 F7
  Prestwich M25 . . . . .63 C4
Bent Lanes M41 . . . . .94 F5
Bent Spur Rd BL4 . . . . .61 A5
Bent St Farnworth BL4 . . . . .60 E7
  Haslingden BB4 . . . . .1 D8
  Manchester M3,M8 . . . . .159 A4
Bent Terr M41 . . . . .95 C4
Bentcliffe Way M30 . . . . .80 A1
Bentfield Cres OL16 . . . . .32 A4
Bentfield Ind Pk OL9 . . . . .152 B6
Bentgate Cl Haslingden BB4 . .1 D8
  Newhey OL16 . . . . .32 A4
Bentgate St OL16 . . . . .32 A4
Benthall Wlk M34 . . . . .100 E1
Bentham Cl Bury BL8 . . . . .26 E3
  6 Farnworth BL4 . . . . .42 D1
Bentham Pl WN6 . . . . .19 F2
Bentham Rd Culcheth WA3 . . . .92 A2
  Standish WN6 . . . . .19 F2
Bentinck Cl WA14 . . . . .119 C4
Bentinck Ho **2** OL6 . . . . .166 A2
Bentinck Rd WA14 . . . . .119 C4
Bentinck St

Bentinck Terr **1** OL6 . . . . . . .166 A2
Bentley Ave M24 . . . . .47 D5
Bentley Cl M26 . . . . .44 D4
Bentley Ct Farnworth BL4 . . . . .42 D1
  Manchester M7 . . . . .155 E8
Bentley Fold BL8 . . . . .26 F4
Bentley Hall Rd BL2,BL8 . .26 D4
Bentley Ho M15 . . . . .162 E6
Bentley La BL9 . . . . .11 E2
Bentley Rd Denton M34 . . . . . .100 F3
  Manchester M21 . . . . .97 A1
  Manchester M7 . . . . .155 E8
Bentley St Bolton BL2 . . . . . . .148 C5
  Farnworth BL4 . . . . .42 D1
  8 Oldham OL1 . . . . .67 B8
  Oldham OL9 . . . . .152 C7
  Rochdale OL12 . . . . .14 E2
Bentleys The SK5 . . . . .169 F3
Bentmeadows OL12 . . . . .14 E1
Benton Dr SK6 . . . . .126 C8
Benton St M9 . . . . .157 F7
Bents Ave Bredbury SK6 . . . . .112 F3
  Urmston M41 . . . . .94 F1
Bents Farm Cl **1** OL12 . . . . .15 F5
Bentside Rd SK12 . . . . .135 D5
Benville Wlk M40 . . . . .83 B6
Benwick Terr **10** BL1 . . . . . . .143 E2
Benyon St OL4 . . . . .67 E6
Berberis Wlk **3** M33 . . . . . . .107 C6
Beresford Ave BL3 . . . . .144 C5
Beresford Cres
  Oldham OL4 . . . . .67 D8
  Reddish SK5 . . . . .99 E3
Beresford Ct M20 . . . . .110 A4
Beresford Rd
  Manchester M13 . . . . .98 F3
  Stretford M32 . . . . .96 E4
Beresford St
  Failsworth M35 . . . . .83 E7
  Manchester M14 . . . . .97 F3
  Newhey OL16 . . . . .32 B4
  Oldham OL4 . . . . .67 B8
  8 Wigan WN6 . . . . .37 A1
Bergman Wlk M40 . . . . .83 B6
Berigan Cl M12 . . . . .164 E5
Berisford Cl WA15 . . . . .119 E7
Berkeley Ave
  Manchester M14 . . . . .98 E4
  Oldham OL9 . . . . .65 F3
  Stretford M32 . . . . .96 A4
  Wigan WN3 . . . . .54 D2
Berkeley Cl Golborne WN7 . . . .91 C8
  Hyde SK14 . . . . .113 E6
  Stockport SK2 . . . . .124 C8
Berkeley Cres Hyde SK14 . .167 D1
  Little Lever M26 . . . . .43 C5
Berkeley Ct **1** M7 . . . . .63 E1
Berkeley Dr Oldham OL2 . . . . . .48 D2
  Rochdale OL16 . . . . .31 B4
Berkeley Rd Bolton BL1 . . . . . .143 E4
  Hazel Grove SK7 . . . . .124 F3
Berkeley St OL6 . . . . .166 A3
Berkley Ave M19 . . . . .99 A1
Berkley Ho BL1 . . . . .144 C7
Berkley St OL2 . . . . .48 D5
Berkley Wlk OL15 . . . . .15 F5
Berkshire Cl OL9 . . . . .152 B5
Berkshire Ct BL9 . . . . .44 F7
Berkshire Dr M44 . . . . .105 C5
Berkshire Pl OL9 . . . . .152 C5
Berkshire Rd M40 . . . . .160 D3
Berlin Rd SK3 . . . . .170 D6
Berlin St BL3 . . . . .144 A4
Bermondsay St M5 . . . . .161 B8
Bernard Gr BL1 . . . . .142 C2
Bernard St Glossop SK13 . . . .104 C1
  Manchester M9 . . . . .157 D8
  Rochdale OL12 . . . . .14 D3
Berne Ave BL6 . . . . .22 A3
Berne Cl Oldham OL9 . . . . .152 C6
  Stockport SK7 . . . . .123 E4
Bernice Ave OL9 . . . . .152 B6
Bernice St BL1 . . . . .142 C2
Berrie Gr M19 . . . . .111 B8
Berriedale Cl M16 . . . . .97 D2
Berrington Gr WN4 . . . . .73 A3
Berry Brow M40 . . . . .83 D4
Berry Cl SK9 . . . . .137 A5
Berry St Eccles M30 . . . . .95 B8
  Manchester M1 . . . . .163 B8
  Oldham OL3 . . . . .69 B5
  Stalybridge SK15 . . . . .102 C8
  Swinton M27 . . . . .61 F2
Berrycroft La SK6 . . . . .113 A3
Berryfold Way M29 . . . . .77 B8
Bert St BL3 . . . . .146 B3
Bertha Rd OL16 . . . . .31 C7
Bertha St Bolton BL1 . . . . .143 D2
  Manchester M11 . . . . .83 D1
  Shaw OL2 . . . . .49 B5
Bertie St OL11 . . . . .30 D4
Bertram St
  Manchester M12 . . . . .165 A6
  Newton-le-W WA12 . . . . .89 A3
  Sale M33 . . . . .108 E4
Bertrand Rd BL1 . . . . .144 C7
Berwick Ave
  Manchester SK4 . . . . .110 E2
  Stretford M41 . . . . .96 A3
  Whitefield M45 . . . . .63 A7
Berwick Cl Boothstown M28 . .77 F7
  Heywood OL10 . . . . .29 A1
Berwick Pl WN1 . . . . .37 E1
Berwick St OL16 . . . . .31 B6
Berwyn Ave Cheadle SK8 . . . .123 B5
  Manchester M9 . . . . .64 C5
  Middleton M24 . . . . .65 C8
Berwyn Cl BL6 . . . . .22 C5

Beryl Ave BL8 . . . . .26 F7
Beryl St BL1 . . . . .143 F3
Besom La SK15 . . . . .86 E3
Bessemer Rd M44 . . . . .105 F6
Bessemer St M11,M18 . . . . . . .165 C7
Bessemer Way OL1 . . . . .153 E7
Besses o' th' Barn Sta
  M45 . . . . .63 A7
Bessie's Well Pl WN6 . . . . .36 F8
Bessybrook Cl BL6 . . . . .40 C6
Beswick Dr M35 . . . . .84 A6
Beswick Row M4 . . . . .159 A3
Beswick St
  5 Droylsden M43 . . . . .84 B1
  Manchester M4 . . . . .160 D2
  Oldham OL4 . . . . .48 E2
  Walsden OL14 . . . . .6 A7
Beswicke Royds St OL16 . . . . .15 C1
Beswicke St
  Littleborough OL15 . . . . .16 C5
  Rochdale OL12 . . . . .139 E8
Beswicks La SK9 . . . . .136 C3
Beta Ave M32 . . . . .96 C1
Beta St BL1 . . . . .145 F8
Bethal Gn OL6 . . . . .6 C1
Bethany La OL16 . . . . .32 D4
Bethel Ave M35 . . . . .83 E7
Bethel St OL10 . . . . .29 C2
Bethersden Rd WN1 . . . . .37 B4
Bethesda Sch SK8 . . . . .122 D3
Bethesda St OL8 . . . . .66 A1
Bethnall Dr M14 . . . . .110 B8
Betjeman Pl OL2 . . . . .49 D8
Betley Rd SK5 . . . . .99 F1
Betley St Heywood OL10 . . . . . .29 C1
  Manchester M1 . . . . .163 C8
  Radcliffe M26 . . . . .44 C4
Betleymere Rd SK8 . . . . .122 F4
Betnor Ave SK1 . . . . .112 B1
Betony Cl OL12 . . . . .14 D3
Bettison Ave WN7 . . . . .76 A4
Bettwood Dr M8 . . . . .63 F2
Betty Nuppy's La OL16 . . . . . .31 C5
Betula Gr M7 . . . . .155 D7
Betula Mews OL11 . . . . .13 D1
Beulah Ave WN5 . . . . .71 D4
Beulah St M18 . . . . .165 C7
Bevan Cl M12 . . . . .160 E1
Bevendon Sq M7 . . . . .155 E6
Beveridge St M14 . . . . .98 A3
Beverley Ave Denton M34 . .101 A2
  Leigh WN7 . . . . .76 A6
  Longshaw WN5 . . . . .71 B5
  Urmston M41 . . . . .95 E3
Beverley Cl M45 . . . . .45 B1
Beverley Pl OL16 . . . . .31 A8
Beverley Rd Bolton BL1 . . . . . .144 C8
  Little Lever BL3 . . . . .42 F3
  Pendlebury M27 . . . . .80 C7
  Stockport SK2 . . . . .124 C8
  Wigan WN5 . . . . .54 B8
Beverley St M9 . . . . .157 D8
Beverley Wlk Oldham OL8 .153 E5
  Romiley SK6 . . . . .113 A1
Beverly Cl OL6 . . . . .85 B7
Beverly Rd M14 . . . . .110 E7
Beverston **7** OL11 . . . . .139 E6
Bevill Sq M3 . . . . .158 E2
Bevin Ave WA3 . . . . .92 B4
Bevington St **3** WN4 . . . . . . .72 F5
Bevis Gn BL9 . . . . .27 F8
Bewerley Cl WN3 . . . . .150 B6
Bewick St BL2 . . . . .25 B3
Bewley Gr WN7 . . . . .76 A6
Bewley St OL8 . . . . .66 D2
Bexhill Ave WA15 . . . . .119 F6
Bexhill Cl BL3 . . . . .43 C3
Bexhill Dr Hindley WN7 . . . . . . .57 C2
  Manchester M13 . . . . .98 F3
Bexhill Rd SK3 . . . . .123 E4
Bexhill Wlk OL9 . . . . .152 B6
Bexley Cl Glossop SK13 . . . . .104 C3
  Urmston M41 . . . . .94 E3
Bexley Dr Bury BL8 . . . . .27 B1
  Walkden M38 . . . . .60 C4
Bexley Sq M3 . . . . .158 D2
Bexley St Hindley WN2 . . . . . . .57 B3
  Oldham OL9 . . . . .152 C5
Bexley Wlk M40 . . . . .83 B6
Bexington Rd M16 . . . . .97 E3
Beyer Cl M18 . . . . .165 C5
Bibby La M19 . . . . .110 F6
Bibby St Bury BL9 . . . . .44 F5
  Dukinfield SK14 . . . . .101 D5
Bibury Ave M22 . . . . .121 B3
Bickerdike Ave M12 . . . . .99 B3
Bickerdike Ct **1** M12 . . . . . . .99 B3
Bickersdale
  CE Jun & Inf Sch WN2 . . . . . .74 F8
Bickershaw Dr M28 . . . . .60 C2
Bickershaw La
  Bickershaw WN2 . . . . .74 F8
  Leigh WN7 . . . . .56 D1
Bickerstaffe Cl OL2 . . . . .149 A5
Bickerton Ct OL9 . . . . .153 A7
Bickerton Dr SK7 . . . . .124 A1
Bickerton Rd WA14 . . . . .119 B6
Bickley Gr M29 . . . . .77 C6
Bickley Wlk **3** M16 . . . . .97 F4
Biddall Dr M23 . . . . .121 B6
Biddisham Wlk M40 . . . . .157 D5
Biddulph Ave SK2 . . . . .124 C5
Bideford Rd
  Altrincham M23 . . . . .120 F7
  Bolton BL2 . . . . .43 A6
  Wythenshawe M23 . . . . .120 F8
Bideford Rd Rochdale OL11 . .30 B3

Bideford Rd continued
  Stockport SK2,SK1 . . . . .124 C8
Bidford Cl M29 . . . . .59 C1
Bidston Ave M14 . . . . .98 B2
Bidston Cl Bury BL8 . . . . .27 A2
  Shaw OL2 . . . . .49 D8
Bidston Dr SK9 . . . . .131 E2
Bidworth La SK13 . . . . .171 D1
Big Fold BL6 . . . . .21 D2
Biggerwood Wlk **18** M40 . .83 A7
Bignor St M8 . . . . .156 A6
Bilbao St M4 . . . . .160 D1
Bilberry St Rochdale OL16 . . .31 A6
  Rochdale OL16 . . . . .31 B6
Bilbrook St M4 . . . . .159 B3
Bill La M45 . . . . .62 F8
Bill Williams Cl M11 . . . . .165 C8
Billberry Cl M45 . . . . .63 B8
Billing Ave M12 . . . . .163 C7
Billing Arc **8** WN1 . . . . .150 C8
Billinge Chapel End
  Cty Prim Sch WN5 . . . . .71 E4
Billinge Cl **5** BL1 . . . . .145 F8
Billinge Hospl WN5 . . . . .53 D2
Billinge Rd Garswood WN4 .72 C5
  Wigan WN3,WN5 . . . . .54 D4
  Wigan WN5 . . . . .54 E6
Billinge St Aidan's
  CE Prim Sch WN5 . . . . .71 E5
Billington Ave WA12 . . . . .89 C5
Billington Rd M27 . . . . .62 A1
Billy La M27 . . . . .62 A2
Billy Meredith Cl **4** M14 . . .98 A3
Billy Whelan Wlk **25** M40 . .83 C5
Bilsland Wlk **18** M40 . . . . . . .83 C5
Bilson Dr SK3 . . . . .123 B7
Bilton Sq OL16 . . . . .32 A5
Bilton Wlk M8 . . . . .156 C8
Binbrook Wlk BL3 . . . . .147 F4
Bincombe Wlk M13 . . . . .163 C5
Bindloss Ave M30 . . . . .80 E3
Bindon Wlk **4** M9 . . . . .157 D7
Bingham Dr M23 . . . . .120 F6
Bingham St M27 . . . . .79 F8
Bingley Cl M11 . . . . .164 F8
Bingley Dr M41 . . . . .94 F4
Bingley Rd OL16 . . . . .31 C7
Bingley Sq OL16 . . . . .31 C7
Bingley Terr OL16 . . . . .31 C7
Bingley Wlk M7 . . . . .80 F8
Binns Nook Rd OL12 . . . . .15 A2
Binns Pl M4 . . . . .159 B1
Binns St SK15 . . . . .85 E1
Binsley Cl M44 . . . . .94 A1
Binstead Cl M14 . . . . .98 E3
Birbeck St **2** SK15 . . . . .85 F1
Birch Ave Bury BL8 . . . . .27 A5
  Chadderton OL1,OL9 . . . . .48 A2
  Failsworth M35 . . . . .83 F5
  Irlam M44 . . . . .105 D5
  Littleborough OL12 . . . . .15 D8
  Manchester M16 . . . . .97 A4
  Manchester SK4 . . . . .168 B4
  Middleton M24 . . . . .65 A7
  Oldham OL8 . . . . .66 D2
  Romiley SK6 . . . . .113 D2
  Sale M33 . . . . .108 B6
  Salford M6 . . . . .154 F4
  Standish WN6 . . . . .36 F8
  Westhoughton BL5 . . . . .57 F7
  Whitefield M45 . . . . .62 F7
  Wilmslow SK9 . . . . .136 F6
Birch Brook Rd WA13 . . . . . . .117 C5
Birch Cl OL12 . . . . .14 C6
Birch Cres OL16 . . . . .32 A3
Birch Ct Dukinfield SK16 . . . .101 D8
  Heywood OL10 . . . . .29 B3
  Manchester M13 . . . . .98 E3
  Marple SK6 . . . . .125 E5
Birch Dr Hazel Grove SK7 . . .124 C2
  Oldham OL4 . . . . .67 F5
  Pendlebury M27 . . . . .80 B8
Birch Gr Denton M34 . . . . .100 E3
  Manchester M13 . . . . .98 E3
  Manchester M8 . . . . .64 A3
  Middleton M24 . . . . .47 C2
  Oldham OL3 . . . . .69 C7
  Partington M31 . . . . .105 D3
  Poynton SK12 . . . . .133 F2
  Swinton M27 . . . . .79 D5

Birch Rd continued
  Walkden M43 . . . . .60 E1
Birch St Ashton-u-L OL7 . . . . .100 F8
  Ashton-u-L OL7 . . . . .84 E1
  Bolton BL2 . . . . .148 B6
  Bury BL9 . . . . .140 F3
  Droylsden M43 . . . . .100 B8
  Heywood OL10 . . . . .29 D1
  Manchester M12 . . . . .165 A6
  Radcliffe BL9 . . . . .44 E5
  Stalybridge SK15 . . . . .86 C5
  3 Tyldesley M29 . . . . .59 A1
  Wigan WN6 . . . . .37 A1
Birch Terr **2** SK14 . . . . .167 D2
Birch Tree Ave SK7 . . . . .134 A8
Birch Tree Cl WA14 . . . . .119 C1
Birch Tree Ct M22 . . . . .121 D3
Birch Tree Dr M22 . . . . .121 D3
Birch Tree Rd **6** WA3 . . . . . . .90 F8
Birch-Lea Cl BL9 . . . . .44 F7
Birchacre Gr M14 . . . . .110 D7
Birchall Ave WA3 . . . . .91 E4
Birchall Cl SK16 . . . . .101 D6
Birchall Gn SK6 . . . . .113 A5
Birchdale WA14 . . . . .119 C2
Birchdale Ave SK8 . . . . .122 B2
Birchen Bower Wlk BL8 . . . . . .26 F5
Birchenall St M40 . . . . .157 F8
Birchenlea St OL9 . . . . .66 A3
Birches End OL12 . . . . .14 C5
Birches Rd BL7 . . . . .9 D4
Birches The Mossley OL5 . . . . .68 B1
  Sale M33 . . . . .107 E5
Birchfield Bolton BL2 . . . . .25 E6
  Dukinfield OL7 . . . . .100 F8
Birchfield Ave
  Atherton M46 . . . . .58 B4
  Heywood BL9 . . . . .28 E1
Birchfield Dr
  Boothstown M28 . . . . .78 A7
  Rochdale OL11 . . . . .30 C4
Birchfield Gr BL3 . . . . .40 E4
Birchfield Mews **4** SK14 . .167 D2
Birchfield Rd Cheadle SK3 .123 A2
  Lymm WA13 . . . . .117 B4
Birchfields WA15 . . . . .119 F1
Birchfields Ave M13 . . . . .98 E3
Birchfields Prim Sch
  M14,M19 .98 E2
Birchfields Rd M13,M14 . . . . . .98 E2
Birchfold Cl M38 . . . . .60 B4
Birchgate Wlk BL3 . . . . .145 F5
Birchin La M4 . . . . .159 A1
Birchin Pl M4 . . . . .159 A1
Birchington Rd M14,M20 . . . .110 A8
Birchinlee Ave OL2 . . . . .48 C3
Birchleaf Gr M5 . . . . .80 C2
Birchley Ave WN5 . . . . .71 C3
Birchley Rd WA11,WN5 . . . . . . .71 C4
Birchley St Mary's
  RC Prim Sch WN5 . . . . .71 D4
Birchley View WA11 . . . . .71 B2
Birchside Ave SK13 . . . . .104 B2
Birchvale Ave SK6 . . . . .113 D3
Birchway Bramhall SK7 . . . . . .132 D7
  High Lane SK6 . . . . .134 F7
Birchwood OL9 . . . . .65 E7
Birchwood Cl Leigh WN7 . . . . .75 F3
  Stockport SK4 . . . . .168 A1
  Wigan WN3 . . . . .54 D2
Birchwood Dr SK9 . . . . .137 D8
Birchwood Rd M24 . . . . .65 C8
Birchwood Way SK16 . . . . .101 D6
Bird Hall Ave SK8 . . . . .123 B6
Bird Hall La SK3,SK8 . . . . .123 B6
Bird Hall Rd SK8 . . . . .123 C5
Bird St WN2 . . . . .151 F7
Birdhall Gr M19 . . . . .111 A8
Birdlip Dr M23 . . . . .121 A3
Birkby Dr M24 . . . . .46 E2
Birkdale Ave Atherton M46 . .58 C5
  Oldham OL2 . . . . .48 E2
  Whitefield M45 . . . . .62 D6
Birkdale Cl Bramhall SK7 . . . .133 A7
  Dukinfield SK16 . . . . .101 F5
  Heywood OL10 . . . . .46 D8
Birkdale Dr Bury BL8 . . . . .27 B2
  Sale M33 . . . . .107 E2
Birkdale Gdns BL3 . . . . .145 D5
Birkdale Gr Eccles M30 . . . . . . .79 C3
  Reddish SK5 . . . . .111 F5
Birkdale Rd Reddish SK5 . . . . .111 F5
  Rochdale OL16 . . . . .31 C4
Birkdale St M8 . . . . .156 A7
Birkenhills Dr BL3 . . . . .40 E5
Birkett Bank WN1 . . . . .151 E8
Birkett Bank Terr WN1 . . . . . .151 E8
Birkett Cl BL1 . . . . .24 D6
Birkett Dr BL1 . . . . .24 D6
Birkett St WN1 . . . . .151 E8
Birkinbrook Cl M45 . . . . .45 A1
Birkinheath La WA14 . . . . .128 B4
Birkleigh Wlk BL2 . . . . .42 E4
Birks Ave OL4 . . . . .67 F8
Birks Dr BL8 . . . . .27 B6
Birks La OL14 . . . . .6 B8
Birkside Cl WN3 . . . . .55 A1
Birkworth Ct SK2 . . . . .124 D6
Birley Cl Altrincham WA15 . .119 F7
Birnham Gr BL3 . . . . .42 C5
Birley Ct **1** M5 . . . . .81 A2
Birley Pk M20 . . . . .109 F3
Birley St Bolton BL1 . . . . .143 E4
  Bury BL9 .27 F5
  Leigh WN7 . . . . .76 A6

Birley St continued
Newton-le-W WA12 ....89 D4
Rochdale OL12 ....15 A1
Birling Dr M23 ....121 B4
Birnham Gr OL10 ....29 A1
Birshaw Cl OL2 ....149 B5
Birstall Wlk M23 ....121 A6
Birt St M40 ....160 D4
Birtenshaw Cres BL7 .....25 B7
Birtenshaw Hall Sch BL7 .25 B6
Birtle Dr M29 ....7 C7
Birtle Rd BL9 ....28 E6
Birtle View Sch OL10 ....29 C2
Birtles Ave SK5 ....99 F3
Birtles Cl Cheadle SK8 .123 A5
 Dukinfield SK16 ....101 D6
Birtles The M22 ....121 D3
Birtles Way **4** SK9 ..131 D5
Birtlespool Rd SK8 ....122 F4
Birtley Wlk **14** M40 .159 C3
Birwood Rd M8 ....64 B2
Biscay Cl M11 ....160 F1
Bishop Bilborrow
 Meml RC Prim Sch M14 ..97 F3
Bishop Bridgeman
 CE Prim Sch BL3 ......147 E4
Bishop Cl M10 ....97 E4
Bishop Marshall Cl M40 .157 D5
Bishop Marshall Way M24 .46 D4
Bishop Rd Salford M6 ...80 B4
 Urmston M41 ....94 D2
Bishop St Middleton M24 .65 D7
 Rochdale OL16 ....15 B1
 Stockport SK1 ....112 A1
Bishop's Cl Bolton BL3 .42 A2
 Cheadle SK8 ....123 A5
Bishop's Rd BL3 ....42 A2
Bishopbridge Cl BL3 ...147 F4
Bishopdale Cl OL2 ......48 D5
Bishopgate WN1 ....150 C8
Bishopgate St OL9 .....152 A5
Bishops Cl
 Altrincham WA14 ......119 B1
 Ashton-u-L OL7 ....85 A5
Bishops Gate M2 ....162 F8
Bishops Mdw M24 ....46 D3
Bishops Mews M33 ......107 E6
Bishops Rd M25 ....63 C1
Bishops Wlk OL7 ....166 A1
Bishopsgate Wlk OL16 ...31 C4
Bishopton Cl M19 ....99 C1
Bisley Ave M23 ....120 F6
Bisley St OL8 ....153 D6
Bismarck St OL4 ....67 A5
Bispham Ave Bolton BL2 .42 F7
 Reddish SK5 ....99 F3
Bispham Cl BL8 ....26 F1
Bispham Dr WN4 ....72 F5
Bispham Gr M7 ....155 E7
Bispham Hall Bsns Pk
 WN5 ....53 C2
Bispham St BL2 ....148 C8
Bittern Cl Poynton SK12 .133 A4
 Rochdale OL11 ....29 F7
Bittern Dr M43 ....84 C3
Bk Adcroft St SK1 .....170 F7
Bk Alfred St BL0 ......138 B5
Bk Andrew St OL5 ....86 C8
Bk Cardwell St **8** BL1 .143 E2
Bk Cecil St OL5 ....86 C8
Bk Chapel St Bury BL8 ..26 F7
 12 Manchester M19 ..99 A1
Bk Drummond St BL3 ....143 E4
Bk Grosvenor St **9** SK15 .86 A1
Bk Halliwell Rd S **17** BL1 143 D2
Bk Knowl St SK15 ....86 B2
Bk Melbourne St **1** SK15 .86 A1
Bk Nut St BL1 ....143 D2
Bk Portland St OL9 ....166 A2
Bk Stayley Rd OL5 ......86 D8
Bk Water St OL6 ....166 C4
Black Brook Rd SK4 ....111 D7
Black Horse St
 Blackrod BL6 ....21 C3
 Bolton BL1 ....145 E6
 Farnworth BL4 ....60 E7
Black La BL0 ....12 B7
Black Moss Cl M26 ......43 D3
Black Moss Rd WA14 ....118 F7
Blackbank St BL1 ......143 F2
Blackberry Cl M44 .....119 B8
Blackberry Dr WN2 ......56 C4
Blackburn St OL5 ......112 C7
Blackburn Cl WA3 ....90 E8
Blackburn Gdns M20 ....110 A4
Blackburn Pl M5 ....81 C1
Blackburn Rd Bolton BL1 .143 F2
 Bolton BL7 ....8 C4
 Edenfield BL0,BB4 .....1 D5

Blackburn St
 Manchester M3 ....161 C5
 Manchester M26 ....158 D3
 Prestwich M25 ....63 C4
 Radcliffe M26 ....44 A3
 Radcliffe M26 ....44 B2
Blackcap Cl M28 ....78 B7
Blackcarr Rd M23 .....121 B6
Blackchapel Dr OL16 ...31 B3
Blackcroft Cl M27 .....79 E8
Blackfield La M7 ....81 C8
Blackfields M7 ....155 D8
Blackford Ave BL9 .....44 F4
Blackford Rd M19 .....111 B7
Blackford Wlk M40 ....160 D2
Blackfriar Ct M3 .....158 D3
Blackfriars Rd M3 ....158 E2
Blackfriars St M3 ....158 F2
Blackhill Cl **8** M13 .163 B7

Blackhorse Ave BL6 .....21 C2
Blackhorse Cl BL6 ......21 C3
Blackleach Ctry Pk M28 .60 D4
Blackleach Dr M28 ......60 D5
Blackledge Cl WN5 ......53 E5
Blackledge St BL3 ....146 C4
Blackley Cl BL9 ....45 A2
Blackley New Rd M9,M25 .64 B3
Blackley Park Rd M9 ....64 D1
Blackley St
 Manchester M16 ......161 C5
 Middleton M24 ....64 B7
Blackleyhurst Ave WN5 ..71 E5
Blacklock St M3,M8 ...158 F4
Blackmoor Ave M29 .....77 B5
Blackpits Rd OL11 .....13 D1
Blackpool St **11** M11 .83 C2
Blackrock OL5 ....86 C6
Blackrock St M11 .....164 F8
Blackrod Brow BL6 .....21 B4
Blackrod By-Pass Rd BL6 .21 D2
Blackrod Cty Prim Sch
 BL6 ....38 E8
Blackrod Dr BL8 ....26 F1
Blackrod Sta BL6 ......21 E2
Blacksail Wlk **8** OL1 .49 A1
Blackshaw Ho BL3 .....144 C6
Blackshaw La
 Alderley Edge SK9 ...136 F1
 Bolton BL3 ....144 C6
 Royton OL2 ....49 A4
Blackshaw Lane
 Com Prim Sch OL2 ....49 A4
 6 Hadfield SK13 ..104 A5
Blackshaw Prim Sch BL2 .43 A6
Blackshaw Row **2** BL3 144 C5
Blackshaw St SK3 .....170 E8
Blacksmith La OL11 ....30 B4
Blackstock St M13 .....98 C4
Blackstone Ave OL16 ...31 C8
Blackstone Edge Old Rd
 OL15 ....16 E6
Blackstone Edge Rd
 HX6,HX7 ....7 F5
Blackstone Rd SK2 ....124 D5
Blackstone Wlk M9 ....157 D6
Blackthorn Ave
 Manchester M19 ......111 A7
 Wigan WN6 ....36 F3
Blackthorn Cl OL12 ....14 E2
Blackthorn Mews OL12 ..14 E2
Blackthorn Rd OL8 .....84 C8
Blackthorne Cl BL1 ...105 E2
Blackthorne Dr M33 ...107 D2
Blackthorne Rd M33 ...107 D2
Blackwell Wlk **3** M4 .159 C2
Blackwin St M12 ......165 A6
Blackwood Dr M23 ....120 D8
Blackwood Rd OL13 .....3 B7
Blackwood St BL3 ......42 A4
Bladen Cl SK8 ....123 A4
Bladon St M1 ....163 C8
Blainscough Rd PR7 ....19 E8
Blair Ave Hindley WN2 ..57 B3
 Urmston M41 ....94 E2
 Walkden M38 ....60 B4
Blair Cl Hazel Grove SK7 .133 C8
 Sale M33 ....107 C1
 Shaw OL2 ....149 B7
Blair La BL2 ....25 D1
Blair Rd M16 ....97 E1
Blair St Bolton BL7 ...25 A8
 Kearsley BL4 ....61 B6
 Manchester M16 ......162 D5
 Rochdale OL12 ....14 D1
Blairhall Ave M40 .....83 A7
Blairmore Dr BL3 ......40 E5
Blake Ave WN4 ....58 D5
Blake Cl WN3 ....150 A5
Blake Dr SK2 ....124 E7
Blake Gdns BL1 ....143 D2
Blake St Bolton BL1 ..143 D2
 BL7 ....25 A8
 Rochdale OL16 ....31 A8
Blakeborough Ho **7** M6 .58 D3
Blakedown Wlk M12 ....164 E5
Blakefield Dr M28 .....60 E1
Blakelock St OL2 .....149 B7
Blakemere Ave M33 ....108 E3
Blakemore Wlk M12 ....160 E1
Blakeswell Cl M41 .....94 D3
Blakey Cl BL3 ....42 A4
Blakey St M12 ....99 A4
Blanchard St M15 .....162 E5
Blanche St BL0 ....12 A2
Blandan Wlk **10** OL1 .49 A4
Bland Cl M35 ....83 E7
Bland Rd M25 ....80 A2
Blandford Ave M28 .....79 A2
Blandford Cl Bury BL8 .27 C5
 Tyldesley M29 ....59 A1
Blandford Ct SK15 .....86 A2
Blandford Dr M40 ......65 D2
Blandford Ho **7** SK15 .86 A2
Blandford Rd Eccles M30 .79 B2
 Salford M6 ....81 B4
 Stockport SK4 ....168 C2
Blandford Rise BL6 ....22 F1
Blandford St
 Ashton-u-L OL6 ......166 A3
 Stalybridge SK15 ....86 A2
Blanefield Cl M21 ....109 E7
Blantyre Ave M28 .....60 C3
Blantyre Ho **4** M15 .162 D7
Blantyre Rd M27 ....80 B6
Blantyre St Eccles M30 .79 A3
 Hindley WN2 ....56 E6

Blantyre St continued
 Manchester M15 ......162 D7
 Swinton M27 ....61 D1
Blanwood Dr M8 ....156 B7
Blaquebus Bank SK2 ...124 D5
Blaven St SK3 ....170 F5
Blaydon Cl WN2 ....38 D5
Blazemoss Bank SK2 ...124 D5
Bleach St WN2 ....56 C4
Bleackley St M24 .....64 B7
Bleak Hey Rd M22 ....121 E2
Bleak St BL2 ....25 B2
Bleakholt Rd BL0 .....1 F1
Bleaklow Cl OL6 ......85 E3
Bleakley St **1** M45 .44 E1
Bleaklow Cl WN3 ......55 B2
Bleasby St OL4 ....67 B7
Bleasdale Cl Horwich BL6 .39 F8
 Whitefield BL9 ......45 A3
Bleasdale Rd Bolton BL1 .23 F2
 Newton-le-W WA12 ....89 C4
 Wythenshawe M22 ....121 A2
Bleasefield Chase M28 .78 A5
Bleatarn Rd SK1 .....124 B7
Bledlow Cl M30 ....79 E3
Blencarn Wlk M9 .....157 D6
Blendworth Cl M8 ....155 F7
Blenheim Ave M16 .....97 D2
Blenheim Cl
 Altrincham WA14 ....119 D2
 6 Hadfield SK13 .104 A5
 Heywood OL10 ....29 E2
 Poynton SK12 ....133 F4
 Whitefield BL9 ......45 A5
 Wilmslow SK9 ....137 D7
Blenheim Rd
 Ashton-in-M WN4 ....73 C2
 Cheadle SK8 ....123 B2
Blenheim St
 8 Oldham OL4 ....49 D1
 10 Rochdale OL12 .14 C1
Blenheim Way OL6 .....85 E4
Bleriot St BL3 ......147 D3
Blessed Thomas Holford
 RC High Sch
 WA14 ....119 C4
Bletchley Cl M13 ....164 D5
Bletchley Rd SK4 ....110 D3
Blethyn St BL3 ......146 B2
Bligh Rd **3** BL5 ...39 E1
Blinco Rd M41 ....95 F2
Blind La M12 ....164 D7
Blindsill Rd BL4 ....60 B7
Blisford Ct WN2 .....56 D4
Blisworth Ave M30 ...95 E8
Blisworth Cl M4 .....160 D1
Blithfield Wlk M11 ..160 D1
Block La OL9 ....152 B5
Blocksage St M34 ....101 D7
Blodwell St M5,M6 ...154 F2
Blofield Ct BL4 .....60 D7
Blomley St OL11 .....30 C2
Bloom St Manchester M1 .163 A8
 Manchester M3 ......158 E2
 Salford M6 ....154 D3
 Stockport SK3 ......170 D8
Bloomfield Dr
 Boothstown M28 .....78 A7
 Whitefield BL9 .....44 B3
Bloomfield Rd BL4 ...60 D8
Bloomfield St BL1 ...143 E3
Bloomsbury Gr WA15 .120 A6
Bloomsbury La WA15 .120 A6
Blossom Gr
 Manchester M31 ....105 E2
Blossom Pl OL16 ....139 F8
Blossom Rd M31 ....105 E2
Blossom St
 Manchester M4 .....159 A2
 11 Tyldesley M29 .59 A1
Blossoms Hey SK8 ...122 E1
Blossoms Hey Wlk SK8 .122 E1
Blossoms La SK7 ....132 B2
Blossoms St SK2 ....170 F7
Bloxham Wlk M9 .....64 F3
Blucher St Ashton-u-L OL7 .85 A6
 Manchester M12 ....164 E6
 Salford M5 ....81 C5
Blue Bell Ave
 Manchester M40 ....65 A1
 Manchester M40 ....83 A8
Blue Chip Bsns Pk WA14 .119 C7
Blue Coat CE Comp Sch
 OL1 ....153 F7
Blue Ribbon Wlk M27 .80 A8
Bluebell Ave BB4 ...1 A8
Bluebell Cl OL11 ...30 E3
Bluebell Dr OL16 ...31 B3
Bluebell Gr SK8 ....122 D4
Bluebell Way SK9 ...131 C1
Blueberry Dr OL2 ...49 D7
Blueberry Rd WA14 ..119 A7
Bluefields OL2 .....48 D8
Bluestone Dr SK4 ...110 D3
Bluestone Rd
 Manchester M40 ....65 A1
 Reddish M34 ....100 A3
Blundell La BL6 ....21 A3

Blundell Mews WN3 ....54 D4
Blundell St BL1 .....145 E7
Blundering La SK15 ..102 D6
Blunn St OL8 ....64 F4
Blyborough Cl M6 ...154 E4
Blyth Ave Littleborough OL15 .15 F3
 Wythenshawe M23 ...109 C2
Blyth Cl WA15 ......120 D6
Blythe Ave SK7 .....132 C6
Blyton St M15 ......163 B5
Blyton Way M34 .....118 F8
Bnos Yisroel Schs M7 .155 E8
Boad St M1 ....163 B8
Boar Green Cl M40 ..65 D3
Board St Ashton-u-L OL6 .85 D4
 Bolton BL3 ....147 E4
Boardale Dr M24 ....46 E1
Boardman Cl BL1 ....143 E2
Boardman Fold Cl M24 .65 A5
Boardman Fold Rd M24 .65 A5
Boardman La M24 ....64 C8
Boardman Rd M8 ....63 F2
Boardman St Blackrod BL6 .21 D2
 Eccles M30 ....79 F1
 Hyde SK14 ....167 D2
Boars Head Ave WN6 .37 A7
Boarsgreave La BB4 .2 F6
Boarshaw Clough M24 .47 B2
Boarshaw Clough Way
 M24 ....47 B2
Boarshaw Cres M24 ..47 B3
Boarshaw Ind Est M24 .47 C3
Boarshaw La M24 ....47 D3
Boarshaw Rd M24 ....47 B2
Boarshurst Ind Pk OL3 .69 B6
Boarshurst La OL3 ..69 C5
Boat La Diggle OL3 .51 E5
 Irlam M44 ....94 B2
 Wythenshawe M22 ..109 C1
Boatman Rd M29 .....77 C4
Boatmans Row M29 ..77 C4
Bob Massey Cl M11 ..83 C1
Bob's La M44 ....105 D4
Bobbin Wlk
 4 Manchester M4 .159 C1
 7 Oldham OL1 ....67 A6
Boddens Hill Rd SK4 .168 A1
Boddington Rd M30 ..79 A1
Bodiam Rd BL8 ......10 F3
Bodley St M11 ......83 C2
Bodmin Cl OL2 ......49 A4
Bodmin Cres SK5 ...112 B5
Bodmin Dr Bramhall SK7 .132 E7
Bodmin Rd Sale M33 .107 D5
 Tyldesley M29 .....59 A1
Bodmin Wlk **8** M23 .121 A5
Bodney Wlk M9 .....64 B3
Boggart Hole Clough
 Country Park M9 ...64 E4
Boggard La PR7 ....19 D6
Boland Dr M14 .....110 D6
Bolam Cl M23 ......108 F1
Bold St Altrincham WA14 .119 D3
 Bury BL9 ....141 A3
 Leigh WN7 ....75 F5
 11 Manchester M15 .162 E5
 Manchester M16 ...162 D5
 Swinton M27 ......61 F2
 Wigan WN5 ....54 D7
Bolderod Pl SK2 ...124 E4
Bolderwood Dr WN2 .56 D4
Boldsworth Cl M21 .109 C8
Boleyn Ct OL10 ....29 C1
Boleyn Wood Ct SK9 .131 B1
Bolholt Terr BL8 ..27 B4
Bolivia St M5 .....80 C2
Bollin Ave WA14 ..119 B3
Bollin Cl Culcheth WA3 .92 A2
 Kearsley BL4 .....61 B6
 Lymm WA13 ....117 A4
Bollin Ct Altrincham WA14 .119 B3
 11 Manchester M15 .162 D6
Bollin Dr Altrincham WA14 .119 A4
 Lymm WA13 ....117 A4
 Sale M33 ....108 A2
Bollin Hill SK9 ...137 B8
Bollin Ho **8** M7 .81 C5
Bollin Prim Sch WA14 .119 C7
Bollinway WA15 ...128 A8
Bollinwood Chase SK9 .137 D7
Bollington Rd
 Manchester M40 ...160 D2
 Stockport SK4 ....111 E5
Bolney St M11...
Bolney Wlk M40 ...160 D2
Bolshaw Prim Sch SK8 .131 C5
Bolshaw Farm La SK8 .131 C5

Bolshaw Rd SK8 ....131 C6
Bolton Ave Bramhall SK8 .132 B6
Bolton Cl Golborne WA3 .91 B8
 Poynton SK12 .....133 D1
 Prestwich M25 ....62 F2
Bolton Coll BL2 ...148 A6
Bolton District
 General Hospl BL4 .147 F1
Bolton Gates Ret Pk BL1 .148 A8
Bolton House Rd WN2 .74 F8
Bolton Inst
 (Chadwick Campus) BL2 .148 B6
Bolton Inst of H Ed BL3 .145 E6
Bolton Metropolitan Coll
 Bolton BL1 ....145 F8
 Bolton BL3 ....148 A6
Bolton Muslim Girls Sch
 BL3 ....147 D8
Bolton Old Rd M46 .58 E3
Bolton Parish Church
 CE Prim Sch BL2 ..148 B7
Bolton Rd
 Adlington BL6,PR6 .21 D6
 Ashton-in-M WN2,WN4 .73 D5
 Aspull WN2 ....38 A4
 Atherton M46 .....58 E4
 Bolton BL2 ....25 C5
 Bolton BL3 ....40 D2
 Bolton BL7 ....9 D5
 Bury BL8 ....140 C2
 Bury BL8 ....27 C1
 Farnworth BL4 ....42 D2
 Kearsley BL4 .....60 F7
 Pendlebury M27 ...80 C7
 Radcliffe M26 ....43 E3
 Salford M6 ....80 E5
 Swinton M27 ......62 A1
 Walkden M28 ......60 D4
 Westhoughton BL5 .39 F1
Bolton Rd W
 Ramsbottom BL0 ...10 F3
 Ramsbottom BL1 ...11 A4
Bolton Royal Infmy BL1 .145 D7
Bolton Sch BL1 ...144 B7
Bolton St Bury WN4 .37 E1
 Bury BL9 ....140 E2
 Downall Green WN4 .72 D5
 Manchester M3 ....158 E1
 Oldham OL4 ....67 B6
 Radcliffe M26 ....43 F3
 Reddish SK5 ......111 E7
Bolton Street Sta BL9 .140 E2
Bolton Wanderers FC
 (Reebok Stad) BL6 .39 D7
Bolton Wholesale Pk
 BL3 ....143 F1
Boltons Yd **10** OL13 .69 B8
Bombay Rd
 Shevington WN5 ...36 C1
 Stockport SK3 ....123 C7
Bombay St
 Ashton-u-L OL6 ...85 D3
 Manchester M1 ....163 A8
Bonar Cl **6** SK3 .123 C8
Bonar Rd SK3 .....123 C8
Boncarn Dr M23 ...121 A4
Bonchurch Wlk M18 .165 B6
Bond Cl BL6 ......22 C3
Bond Sq M7 ....155 E6
Bond St Bury BL9 .141 A3
 Denton M34 ......100 F3
 Edenfield BL0 ....1 E2
 Leigh WN7 ....75 F5
 Manchester M12 ...163 C8
 Rochdale SK15 ....86 A3
 Stalybridge SK15 .86 A3
 8 Westhoughton BL5 .39 D7
Bondmark Rd M18 ..165 C6
Bongs Rd SK2,SK6 .125 A6
Bonhill Wlk M11 ..83 B2
Bonholt Ind Est **11** BL8 .27 B4
Bonington Rise SK6 .126 B8
Bonis Cres SK2 ...124 C4
Bonny Brow St M24 .64 B7
Bonnywell Rd WN7 .75 D4
Bonsall Bank **8** SK13 .171 E2
Bonsall Cl **8** SK13 .171 E2
Bonsall Fold **8** SK13 .171 E2
Bonsall St M15 ...162 F6
Bonscale Cres M24 .46 E3
Bonville Chase WA14 .119 A4
Bonville Rd WA14 .119 A4
Boodle St OL6 ....166 B4
Bookham Wlk **16** M9 .157 E8
Boond St Manchester M3 .158 E2
 Manchester M4 ...160 D1
Boonfields BL7 ...25 A8
Booth Ave M14 ...110 D7
Booth Bridge Cl M24 .64 C7
Booth Cl Bury BL8 .27 B4
 8 Stalybridge SK15 .85 F1
Booth Clibborn Ct M7 .155 D8
Booth Ct BL4 .....60 D8
Booth Dr M41 ....94 F5
Booth Hall Dr BL8 .26 F5

Booth Hall Hospl M9 .... 64 F3
Booth Hall Rd M9 .... 65 A3
Booth Hill La OL1 .... 48 E1
Booth House Trad Est
OL9 .... 152 C6
Booth Rd Altrincham WA14 .. 119 C4
Bacup OL13 .... 3 B8
Droylsden M34 .... 100 A7
Handforth SK9 .... 131 A1
Little Lever BL3 .... 43 B2
Manchester M16 .... 97 C3
Sale M33 .... 108 B6
Booth St Ashton-u-L OL6 .... 166 B2
Bolton BL1 .... 142 C3
Bury BL8 .... 26 F5
Denton M34 .... 100 F5
Hollingworth SK14 .... 103 C5
Hyde SK14 .... 167 E1
Manchester M2 .... 158 F1
Manchester M3 .... 158 F2
Middleton M24 .... 65 D6
2 Oldham OL4 .... 67 E6
Oldham OL9 .... 153 E6
Rawtenstall BB4 .... 2 E8
Stalybridge SK15 .... 101 F8
Stockport SK3 .... 170 E7
Booth St E M13 .... 163 B6
Booth St W M13,M15 ...... 163 A6
Booth Way BL8 .... 26 F5
Booth's Brow Rd WN4 ..... 72 D6
Booth's Hall M28 .... 78 B6
Booth's Hall Gr 2 M28 ..... 78 B6
Booth's Hall Rd M28 .... 78 B6
Booth's Hall Way M28 ...... 78 B6
Boothby Rd M27 .... 61 E1
Boothby St SK2 .... 124 C4
Boothcote M34 .... 100 D6
Boothfield 11 Bury BL8 ...... 27 C3
Eccles M30 .... 79 A3
Boothfield Ave M22 .... 121 D6
Boothfield Dr M22 .... 121 D6
Boothfield Rd M22 .... 121 D6
Boothroyden Cl M24 .... 64 C7
Boothroyden Rd M24,M9 .. 64 C6
Boothroyden Terr M9 ...... 64 C6
Boothsbank Ave M28 .... 78 B6
Boothshall Paddock M28 ... 78 B5
Boothshall Way M28 .... 78 A5
Boothstown Dr M28 .... 78 A5
Boothstown Meth Sch
M28 .... 77 F6
Boothway 8 M30 .... 79 F2
Bootle St M2 .... 162 F8
Bor Ave WN3 .... 55 B4
Bordale Ave M9 .... 157 F7
Bordan St M11 .... 164 F8
Borden Cl 5 WN2 .... 37 F2
Borden Way BL9 .... 45 A6
Border Brook La M28 ...... 78 A6
Bordesley Ave M38 .... 60 A6
Bordley Wlk M23 .... 108 E1
Bordon Rd SK3 .... 123 B7
Bores Hill WN1 .... 20 C4
Boringdon Cl M40 .... 83 B6
Borland Ave M40 .... 65 D1
Borough Arc SK14 .... 167 D2
Borough Ave Radcliffe BL9 .. 44 D5
Swinton M27 .... 62 A1
Borough Rd
Altrincham WA15 .... 119 E4
Salford M5 .... 154 D1
Borough St 5 SK15 .... 86 A1
Borrans The M28 .... 77 F5
Borron Rd WA12 .... 89 B5
Borron St SK1 .... 112 A2
Borrowdale Ave
Bolton BL1 .... 144 A8
Gatley SK8 .... 122 B4
Borrowdale Cl OL2 .... 48 D6
Borrowdale Cres
Ashton-u-L OL7 .... 84 F4
Manchester M20 .... 109 E4
Borrowdale Dr
Rochdale OL11 .... 30 C4
Whitefield BL9 .... 45 A3
Borrowdale Rd
Middleton M24 .... 46 E2
Stockport SK2 .... 124 B6
Wigan WN5 .... 54 B7
Borrowdale Terr SK15 ...... 86 A4
Borsdane Ave WN2 .... 56 F5
Borsdane Brook Sch WN2 .. 56 C5
Borsden St M27 .... 61 D2
Borth Ave SK2 .... 124 C7
Borth Wlk 3 M23 .... 120 F6
Borwell St M18 .... 99 D5
Boscobel Rd BL3 .... 42 B2
Boscombe Ave M30 .... 95 C8
Boscombe Dr SK7 .... 124 C1
Boscombe Pl WN2 .... 56 E4
Boscombe St
Manchester M14 .... 98 B2
Reddish SK5 .... 99 F2
Boscow Rd BL3 .... 43 A2
Bosden Ave SK7 .... 124 F3
Bosden Cl Handforth SK9 .. 131 D5
Stockport SK1 .... 170 F8
Bosden Fold SK1 .... 170 F8
Bosden Hall Rd SK7 ...... 124 E3
Bosdenfold Rd SK7 .... 124 E3
Bosdin Rd E M41 .... 94 E1
Bosdin Rd W M41 .... 94 E1
Bosley Ave M20 .... 110 A8
Bosley Cl SK9 .... 131 D2
Bosley Dr SK12 .... 134 A3
Bosley Rd SK3 .... 123 A8
Bossall Ave M9 .... 64 E4
Bossington Cl SK2 .... 124 C8
Bostock Rd SK14 .... 115 A8
Bostock Wlk M13 .... 163 B7
Boston Cl Bramhall SK7 ... 132 D7
Culcheth WA3 .... 91 F4
Failsworth M35 .... 83 F8
Boston Ct Hyde SK14 ...... 167 E3
Salford M5 .... 96 E8
Boston Gr WN7 .... 75 E8
Boston St 14 Bolton BL1 .... 143 E2
Hyde SK14 .... 167 E2
Manchester M15 .... 162 F5
Oldham OL8 .... 66 F4
Boston Wlk 8 M34 .... 101 A1
Boswell Ave M34 .... 84 D1
Boswell Pl WN3 .... 54 F3
Boswell Way M24 .... 47 E4
Bosworth Cl M45 .... 63 C8
Bosworth Sq OL11 .... 30 D4
Bosworth St Horwich BL6 .. 22 B4
Manchester M11 .... 165 A8
Rochdale OL11 .... 30 D4
Botanical Ave M16 .... 161 A5
Botany Cl Aspull WN2 ...... 38 B2
Heywood OL10 .... 29 B2
Botany La OL6 .... 166 C3
Botany Rd Eccles M30 ...... 79 A4
Romiley SK6 .... 113 A6
Botesworth Gn OL16 .... 32 A5
Botha Cl 4 M11 .... 99 D7
Botham Cl M15 .... 162 F5
Bothwell Rd M40 .... 159 C3
Botley St OL5 .... 68 B1
Bottesford Ave M20 ...... 109 F5
Bottom o' th' Knotts Brow
BL7 .... 9 E3
Bottom o' th' Moor
Horwich BL6 .... 23 A3
Oldham OL1,OL4 .... 67 B7
Bottom O'Th Moor BL2 ..... 25 D2
Bottom St SK14 .... 167 F3
Bottomfield Cl OL1 .... 49 A1
Bottomley Rd OL14 .... 6 C6
Bottomley Side M9 .... 64 C2
Bougainvillea Gdns M12 ... 99 A4
Boughey St WN7 .... 75 E5
Boulden Dr BL8 .... 27 C5
Boulder Dr M23 .... 121 A2
Boulderstone Rd SK15 ..... 86 A4
Boulevard The
Hazel Grove SK7 .... 124 E2
Hollingworth SK14 .... 171 D4
Bouley Wlk M12 .... 165 A6
Boulton Ho M1 .... 163 A8
Boundary Cl Mossley OL5 .. 86 C6
Romiley SK6 .... 113 C5
Boundary Cotts SK15 ..... 86 E7
Boundary Ct SK8 .... 122 C5
Boundary Dr BL2,BL3 ...... 43 A5
Boundary Gdns
Bolton BL1 .... 143 E2
Oldham OL1 .... 48 E1
Boundary Gr M33 .... 108 F2
Boundary La
Manchester M15 .... 163 A6
Shevington Moor WN6 ..... 19 A3
Boundary Park Rd OL1 .... 48 C1
Boundary Rd Cheadle SK8 .. 123 A6
Irlam M44 .... 94 C3
Swinton M27 .... 61 F1
Boundary St Bolton BL1 ... 143 D2
Leigh WN7 .... 76 B4
Littleborough OL15 .... 16 B6
Manchester M12 .... 165 A6
Rochdale OL11 .... 139 F5
Tyldesley M29 .... 59 A1
Wigan WN1 .... 151 D7
Boundary St E M1,M13 ..... 163 A7
Boundary St W M15 .... 163 A6
Boundary Terr SK9 .... 130 F6
Boundary The M27 .... 61 E4
Boundary Trad Pk M44 ..... 94 C3
Boundary Wlk OL11 .... 139 E5
Boundry Gn M34 .... 100 E4
Bourdon St M40 .... 160 D3
Bourget St M7 .... 155 F8
Bournbrook Ave M38 .... 60 A6
Bourne Ave Golborne WA3 .. 90 D8
Swinton M27 .... 79 F7
Bourne Dr M40 .... 65 B1
Bourne Ho 1 M6 .... 154 F2
Bourne Rd OL2 .... 149 A8
Bourne St Oldham OL9 ...... 66 B2
Stockport SK4 .... 169 E4
Wilmslow SK9 .... 136 F6
Bourne Wlk 9 BL1 .... 143 F1
Bournelea Ave M19 .... 110 F6
Bourneville Dr BL8 .... 27 A2
Bournville Ave SK4 .... 169 E4
Bournville Gr M19 .... 99 C1
Bourton Cl BL8 .... 27 B3
Bourton Ct M29 .... 59 D1
Bourton Dr M18 .... 99 B4
Bow Green Rd WA14 ...... 119 A1
Bow La Altrincham WA14 ... 128 B8
Heywood OL10 .... 29 D2
Manchester M2 .... 158 F1
Bow Rd WN7 .... 76 B3
Bow St Ashton-u-L OL6 ..... 166 B3
Bolton BL1 .... 145 F7
Dukinfield OL6,SK16 .... 166 C2
7 Manchester M2 .... 158 F1
Oldham OL1 .... 153 F7
Rochdale OL11 .... 30 D3
Stockport SK3 .... 123 C8
Bowden Cl Culcheth WA3 .... 91 F4
Bowden Cl *continued*
Leigh WN7 .... 76 C2
Middleton OL11 .... 47 D8
Mottram-in-L SK14 .... 102 E1
Bowden La SK6 .... 125 E7
Bowden Rd Glossop SK13 .. 104 C3
Pendlebury M27 .... 80 A7
Bowden St Denton M34 .... 100 E3
Hazel Grove SK7 .... 124 E3
Bowdon Ave M14 .... 97 F1
Bowdon CE Aided
Prim Sch WA14 .... 119 C1
Bowdon Ho 2 SK3 .... 170 E8
Bowdon Prep Sch WA14 .. 119 C2
Bowdon Rd WA14 .... 119 C3
Bowdon Rise WA14 .... 119 D2
Bowdon St SK3 .... 170 E8
Bowen Cl SK7 .... 132 F5
Bowen St BL1 .... 142 B1
Bower Ave
Hazel Grove SK7 .... 124 D1
Littleborough OL12 .... 15 D4
Stockport SK4 .... 168 C2
Bower Ct SK14 .... 102 A5
Bower Gdns SK15 .... 102 D8
Bower Gr SK15 .... 86 C2
Bower La OL9 .... 66 A2
Bower Rd WA15 .... 119 F1
Bower St Bury BL9 .... 141 C3
Failsworth M40 .... 83 A5
Manchester M7 .... 155 F7
Oldham OL1 .... 67 B8
Reddish SK5 .... 99 F2
Bower Terr M43 .... 84 C3
Bowerfield Ave SK7 ...... 133 D8
Bowerfield Cres SK7 ..... 133 E8
Bowerfold La SK4 .... 169 D2
Bowers Ave M41 .... 95 B3
Bowers St M14 .... 110 E7
Bowery Ave SK8 .... 131 F6
Bowes Cl BL8 .... 27 B5
Bowes St M14 .... 97 F3
Bowfell Dr SK6 .... 134 E8
Bowfell Gr M9 .... 64 B4
Bowfell Rd M41 .... 95 B2
Bowfield Wlk 13 M40 ...... 83 C5
Bowgreave Ave BL2 .... 42 F7
Bowgreen Wlk 11 M15 .... 162 D6
Bowker Ave M34 .... 113 B8
Bowker Bank Ave M8 ...... 63 F2
Bowker Cl OL11 .... 13 E1
Bowker Ct M7 .... 155 D6
Bowker St Haslingden BL0 .... 1 C5
Hyde SK14 .... 167 E3
Manchester M7 .... 155 D6
Radcliffe M26 .... 44 A3
Walkden M28 .... 60 B3
Bowker Vale Gdns M9 ...... 63 F3
Bowker Vale Prim Sch M8 .. 63 F4
Bowker Vale Sta M8 .... 63 F3
Bowkers Row 12 BL1 ..... 145 F7
Bowlacre Rd SK14 .... 113 D7
Bowland Ave
Ashton-in-M WN4 .... 73 B4
Golborne WA3 .... 74 C1
Reddish M18 .... 100 A4
Bowland Cl Ashton-u-L OL6 .. 85 C7
Bury BL8 .... 26 F3
Shaw OL2 .... 48 E7
Stockport SK2 .... 124 E5
Bowland Ct M33 .... 108 B4
Bowland Dr BL1 .... 23 E2
Bowland Gr OL16 .... 31 F4
Bowland Rd Glossop SK13 .. 116 A8
Reddish M34 .... 100 B3
Romiley SK6 .... 113 B5
Wythenshawe M23 .... 121 A6
Bowlee Cl BL9 .... 45 A2
Bowler St Manchester M19 .. 111 B8
Shaw OL2 .... 149 B7
Bowlers Wlk OL12 .... 14 F2
Bowley Ave M22 .... 121 A2
Bowling Green Row M46 ... 58 B2
Bowling Green St
Heywood OL10 .... 29 D2
Hyde SK14 .... 167 D2
Bowling Green Way OL11 .. 29 F7
Bowling Rd M18 .... 99 E3
Bowling St OL9 .... 66 B2
Bowlings The WN6 .... 37 A2
Bowman Cres OL6 .... 85 D3
Bowmead Wlk 8 M8 ...... 155 F6
Bowmeadow Grange 2
M12 .... 98 F4
Bowmont Cl SK8 .... 123 A4
Bowness Ave Cheadle SK8 .. 123 B1
Irlam M44 .... 105 D4
Reddish SK4 .... 111 E6
Rochdale OL12 .... 14 C1
Bowness Ct 5 M24 .... 46 D2
Bowness Cty Prim Sch
BL3 .... 42 F3
Bowness Dr M33 .... 107 F5
Bowness Pl WN2 .... 56 B8
Bowness Rd
Altrincham WA15 .... 120 D5
Ashton-u-L OL7 .... 84 F4
Bolton BL3 .... 147 D4
Little Lever BL3 .... 42 F4
Middleton M24 .... 46 D1
Bowness St Droylsden M11 .. 99 F7
Stretford M32 .... 96 D3
Bowness Wlk 7 OL2 .... 48 E4
Bowring St M7 .... 81 C5
Bowscale Cl 3 M13 .... 98 F4
Bowstone Hill Rd BL2,BL8 .. 26 B5
Box St Littleborough OL15 .. 16 A5
Ramsbottom BL0 .... 11 D6
Box Wlk M31 .... 105 E3
Boxgrove Rd M33 .... 107 F5
Boxgrove Wlk 3 M8 ...... 156 A6
Boxhill Dr M23 .... 109 A1
Boxtree Ave M18 .... 99 D4
Boyd Cl WN6 .... 19 F1
Boyd St M12 .... 165 A7
Boyd's Wlk SK16 .... 101 C7
Boydell St WN7 .... 75 F6
Boydell's Ho WN2 .... 75 B8
Boyer St M16 .... 161 B5
Boyle St Bolton BL1 ...... 142 A1
Manchester M8 .... 156 B6
Boysnope Cres M30 .... 94 C4
Boysnope Wharf M30 ...... 94 D4
Boyswell Ho WN1 .... 151 D8
Brabant Rd SK8 .... 123 B2
Brabazon Pl WN5 .... 54 C8
Brabham Cl M21 .... 109 B8
Brabyns Ave SK6 .... 113 D3
Brabyns Brow SK6 .... 126 A7
Brabyns Rd SK14 .... 113 E7
Brabyns Sch SK6 .... 126 B7
Bracadale Dr SK3 .... 170 F5
Bracewell Cl M12 .... 165 B5
Bracken Ave M28 .... 60 E3
Bracken Cl Bolton BL1 ..... 24 D6
Droylsden M43 .... 84 D2
Heywood OL10 .... 46 D8
Hollingworth SK14 .... 103 D6
Marple SK6 .... 126 C7
Oldham OL4 .... 67 F6
Sale M33 .... 107 C5
Bracken Dr M23 .... 121 B5
Bracken Gr BB4 .... 1 A8
Bracken Lea BL5 .... 57 F5
Bracken Lea Fold 3 OL12 .. 14 B2
Bracken Rd Atherton M46 ... 58 D2
Leigh WN7 .... 75 B5
Bracken Way SK13 .... 116 F7
Brackenfield Wlk WA15 .. 120 D6
Brackenhill Terr 14 M34 .. 113 A7
Brackenhurst Ave OL5 ..... 68 E1
Brackenlea Pl SK3 .... 170 D5
Brackenside SK5 .... 112 A8
Brackenwood Cl OL1 ...... 48 C2
Brackenwood Dr SK8 ..... 122 E4
Brackenwood Mews SK9 .. 137 E8
Brackley Ave Irlam M44 ... 105 D6
Manchester M15 .... 162 D7
Brackley Ct M22 .... 121 D8
Brackley Dr M24 .... 65 A5
Brackley Lo M30 .... 79 F3
Brackley Rd Atherton BL5 .. 59 A8
Eccles M30 .... 79 D4
Reddish SK4 .... 111 D5
Brackley Sq 5 OL1 .... 67 A8
Brackley St Farnworth BL4 .. 60 D8
9 Oldham OL1 .... 67 A8
Walkden M28 .... 60 C4
Bracondale Ave BL1 ...... 142 B2
Bradbourne Cl BL3 .... 145 F5
Bradburn Ave 4 M30 ...... 79 D1
Bradburn Cl 2 M30 .... 79 D1
Bradburn Gr 5 M30 .... 79 D1
Bradburn Rd M44 .... 105 E7
Bradburn St M30 .... 79 D1
Bradburn Wlk 8 M8 ...... 156 B6
Bradbury Ave WA14 ...... 119 A5
Bradbury St
Ashton-u-L OL7 .... 166 A4
Hyde SK14 .... 167 E1
Radcliffe M26 .... 44 A2
Bradbury Wlk 10 OL2 ...... 48 E4
Bradbury's La OL3 .... 69 D3
Bradda Mount SK7 .... 124 A2
Braddan Ave M33 .... 108 C3
Bradden Cl M5 .... 81 A1
Braddocks Cl OL12 .... 15 D4
Braddon Ave M41 .... 95 D2
Braddon Rd SK6 .... 113 A5
Braddon St 1 M11 .... 83 C1
Bradfyll Rd BL5 .... 58 F8
Brade Cl M11 .... 165 C8
Bradfield Ave M6 .... 80 C2
Bradfield Cl SK5 .... 99 E2
Bradfield Rd M32,M41 ...... 96 A2
Bradford Ave BL3 .... 42 B3
Bradford Cres 17 BL3 ...... 42 A4
Bradford Ct M40 .... 65 C1
Bradford Park Dr BL2 .... 148 B6
Bradford Rd Bolton BL3,BL4 .. 42 A2
Eccles M30 .... 79 E4
Manchester M4,M40 ...... 160 E2
Bradford St Bolton BL2 .... 148 B7
Farnworth BL4 .... 60 D7
Oldham OL1 .... 153 E8
Wigan WN3 .... 150 C7
Bradgate Ave SK8 .... 122 D1
Bradgate Cl M22 .... 121 E8
Bradgate Rd
Altrincham WA14 .... 119 A5
Sale M33 .... 108 B2
Bradgate St
Ashton-u-L OL7 .... 166 A1
7 Ashton-u-L OL7 .... 166 A2
Bradgreen Rd M30 .... 79 C3
Brading Wlk M22 .... 130 E8
Bradlegh Rd WA12 .... 89 B1
Bradley Ave M7 .... 81 B7
Bradley Cl WA15 .... 119 E7
Bradley Dr BL9 .... 45 B2
Bradley Fold SK15 .... 86 B2
Bradley Fold Cotts BL2 .... 43 B6
Bradley Fold Rd
BL2,BL3,BL8,M26 .... 43 C7
Bradley Fold Trad Est BL2 .. 43 C5
Bradley Green Rd SK14 ... 101 F6
Bradley Green Road
Prim Sch SK14 .... 101 F6
Bradley Hall Trad Est
WN6 .... 19 F2
Bradley Hill Trad Est WN6 .. 20 A2
Bradley Ho OL8 .... 153 F5
Bradley La Little Lever BL3 .. 43 B5
Newhey OL16 .... 32 B4
Newton-le-W WA5,WA12 .... 89 A1
Sale M32, M33 .... 108 B7
Standish WN6 .... 19 F2
Bradley Smithy Cl OL12 .... 14 E2
Bradley St
7 Manchester M1 .... 159 B2
Newhey OL16 .... 32 B4
Bradleys Ct M1 .... 159 B1
Bradney Cl M9 .... 64 B4
Bradnor Rd M22 .... 121 D7
Bradshaw Ave
Failsworth M35 .... 83 E5
Manchester M20 .... 110 B7
Whitefield M45 .... 44 E2
Bradshaw Brow BL2 .... 25 C4
Bradshaw Cl WN6 .... 19 D1
Bradshaw Cres SK6 ...... 126 A7
Bradshaw Fold Ave M40 ... 65 D3
Bradshaw Hall Dr BL2 ..... 25 C6
Bradshaw Hall La
Cheadle SK8 .... 131 E8
Gatley SK8 .... 131 D8
Bradshaw Hall Prim Sch
SK8 .... 122 E1
Bradshaw La Lymm WA13 .. 117 D3
Stretford M32 .... 108 D8
Bradshaw Mdws BL2 .... 25 D6
Bradshaw Rd Bolton BL2 ... 25 D7
Bury BL8 .... 26 D5
Marple SK6 .... 125 F7
Bradshaw St Atherton M46 .. 58 D3
Bolton BL2 .... 145 F6
Farnworth BL4 .... 60 D7
Heywood OL10 .... 29 E2
2 Manchester M4 .... 159 A2
Manchester M7 .... 155 E6
Middleton M24 .... 65 C7
Oldham OL1 .... 153 F7
Radcliffe M26 .... 43 F3
9 Rochdale OL16 .... 31 A8
Wigan WN1 .... 37 E2
Wigan WN5 .... 54 A6
Bradshaw St N M7 .... 155 D7
Bradshawgate
Bolton BL1,BL3 .... 145 F7
Leigh WN7 .... 75 F5
Wigan WN1 .... 151 D8
Bradshawgate Sh Arc 7
WN7 .... 75 F5
Bradstock Rd M16 .... 97 E3
Bradstone Rd M8 .... 156 A5
Bradwell Ave
Manchester M20 .... 109 F6
Stretford M32 .... 96 A3
Bradwell Dr SK8 .... 131 C7
Bradwell Field 2 SK13 ... 171 E1
Bradwell Lea 4 SK13 .... 171 E1
Bradwell Pl 7 BL2 .... 25 B1
Bradwell Rd Golborne WA3 .. 90 E7
Hazel Grove SK7 .... 133 E8
Bradwell Terr 3 SK13 .... 171 E1
Bradwell Wlk M41 .... 94 D3
Bradwen Ave M8 .... 64 A1
Bradwen Cl M34 .... 101 A1
Brady St BL6 .... 22 A4
Brae Side OL8 .... 66 E2
Braeburn Ct WN7 .... 75 D5
Braemar Ave Stretford M32 .. 96 A2
Urmston M41 .... 95 A1
Braemar Dr M33 .... 107 C2
Braemar Gdns BL3 .... 40 E5
Braemar Gr OL10 .... 29 A1
Braemar La M28 .... 78 B6
Braemar Rd
Hazel Grove SK7 .... 124 F3
Manchester M14 .... 110 E8
Braemar Wlk WN2 .... 38 D5
Braemore Cl Shaw OL2 .... 48 E8
Wigan WN3 .... 54 D2
Braemore Dr Bury BL9 ..... 28 D2
Mottram-in-L SK14 .... 102 F1
Braeside Cl SK2 .... 124 F6
Braeside Cres WN5 .... 71 D5
Braeside Gr BL3 .... 40 F5
Braewood Cl BL9 .... 28 D2
Bragenham St M18 .... 165 C5
Braidhaven WN6 .... 35 E7
Brailsford Ave 6 SK13 .... 171 E2
Brailsford Cl 9 SK13 ..... 171 E2
Brailsford Gdns 8 SK13 .. 171 E2
Brailsford Gn 7 SK13 .... 171 E2
Brailsford Mews 5 SK13 .. 171 E2
Brailsford Rd Bolton BL2 .. 25 C3
Manchester M14 .... 110 E8
Braintree Rd M22 .... 130 E8
Braithwaite WN6 .... 36 A6
Braithwaite Rd
Golborne WA3 .... 90 D8
Middleton M24 .... 46 D4
Brakehouse Cl OL16 .... 31 E6
Brakenhurst Dr M7 .... 155 F6
Brakesmere Gr M28 .... 60 A4
Braley St M12 .... 163 B7
Bramall Cl BL9 .... 45 B2
Bramall Hall (Mus) SK7 .. 123 E1
Bramall St SK14 .... 167 D4
Bramber Way OL9 .... 152 B6
Bramble Ave Oldham OL4 .. 49 D1
Salford M5 .... 161 C7
Bramble Cl OL15 .... 15 F5

Bramble Gr WN5 ....54 E7
Bramble Wlk [7] Sale M33 ....107 C5
[6] Wythenshawe M22 ....121 C2
Brambles The WN4 ....72 D5
Bramblewood OL9 ....65 E8
Brambling Cl
  Droylsden M34 ....84 C2
  Hazel Grove SK2 ....125 A5
Brambling Dr BL5 ....57 D6
Brambling Way WA3 ....90 E7
Bramcote Ave Bolton BL2 ....148 B6
  Wythenshawe M23 ....121 B6
Bramdean Ave BL2 ....25 E5
Bramfield Wlk M15 ....162 D7
Bramford Cl BL5 ....57 E6
Bramhall Ave BL2 ....26 A4
Bramhall Cl
  [4] Altrincham WA15 ....120 D6
  Dukinfield SK16 ....101 D6
  Milnrow OL16 ....31 E5
  Sale M33 ....108 E3
Bramhall Ct M3 ....158 D3
Bramhall Ctr The SK7 ....132 E6
Bramhall High Sch M27 ....132 F8
Bramhall La SK2,SK3 ....170 F5
Bramhall La S
  Bramhall SK7 ....132 E7
  Stockport SK3,SK7 ....123 E2
Bramhall Moor Ind Est SK7 ....124 E2
Bramhall Moor La SK7 ....124 C2
Bramhall Mount SK7 ....170 F5
Bramhall Park Rd SK7,SK8 ....123 D1
Bramhall St Bolton BL3 ....42 B3
  Manchester M18 ....99 E5
Bramhall Sta SK7 ....132 E6
Bramham Rd SK6 ....26 C6
Bramhope Wlk M9 ....157 D7
Bramley Ave
  Manchester M19 ....111 A8
  Stretford M32 ....96 B1
Bramley Cl Bramhall SK7 ....132 E6
  Swinton M27 ....79 C6
  Wilmslow SK9 ....136 D4
Bramley Cres SK4 ....168 B1
Bramley Dr Bramhall SK7 ....132 E6
  Bury BL8 ....27 C6
Bramley Meade M7 ....155 E7
Bramley Rd [6] Bolton BL1 ....24 F6
  Bolton BL1 ....25 A6
  Bramhall SK7 ....132 E6
  Rochdale OL11 ....29 E8
Bramley St M7 ....155 E5
Brammay Dr BL8 ....26 E6
Brampton Cl WN2 ....55 F1
Brampton Rd Bolton BL3 ....146 A2
  Stockport SK7 ....123 F2
Brampton St [8] M46 ....58 D3
Bramway Bramhall SK7 ....132 C7
  High Lane SK6 ....134 F7
Bramwell Dr M13 ....163 C6
Bramwell St SK1 ....124 B8
Bramworth Ave BL0 ....138 B6
Brancaster Dr WA3 ....91 A7
Brancaster Rd M1 ....163 A7
Branch Cl BL6 ....140 D3
Branch Rd OL15 ....15 F1
  Ince-in-M WN2 ....56 A7
Brancker St BL5 ....40 C1
Brandish Cl M13 ....164 D5
Brandle Ave BL8 ....27 C4
Brandlehow Dr M24 ....46 C2
Brandlesholme Cty Prim Sch BL8 ....27 C6
Brandlesholme Rd BL8 ....27 C6
Brandon Ave Gatley SK8 ....122 B1
  Reddish M34 ....99 F3
  Salford M30 ....80 A5
  Wythenshawe M22 ....121 C8
Brandon Brow [1] OL1 ....153 E8
Brandon Cl Bury BL8 ....27 D5
  Handforth SK9 ....131 D2
  Orrell WN8 ....P B3
Brandon Cres OL2 ....149 A8
Brandon Rd M6 ....80 B5
Brandon St [3] Bolton BL3 ....147 D4
  Milnrow OL16 ....31 D6
Brandram Rd M25 ....63 C4
Brandreth Pl WN6 ....19 F1
Brandsby Gdns M15 ....161 A8
Brandwood OL1 ....47 E1
Brandwood Ave M21 ....109 D4
Brandwood Cl M28 ....78 A8
Brandwood Cty Prim Sch BL3 ....146 C4
Brandwood Fold BL7 ....9 E5
Brandwood Pk OL13 ....3 B8
Brandwood St OL13 ....3 B8
Brandwood St BL3 ....146 C4
Branfield Ave SK8 ....122 D1
Brankgate Cl M20 ....110 A5
Branksome Ave M25 ....63 B4
Branksome Dr
  Cheadle SK8 ....122 D1
  Manchester M9 ....64 B6
  Salford M6 ....80 B5
Branksome Ho SK4 ....168 B2
Branksome Rd SK4 ....168 B1
Bransby Ave M9 ....64 E4
Branscombe Dr M33 ....107 C5
Branscombe Gdns BL3 ....42 D5
Bransdale Ave OL2 ....48 C4
Bransdale Cl BL3 ....40 F4
Bransdale Dr WN4 ....73 D3
Bransfield Cl WN5 ....55 B3

Bransford Cl WN4 ....73 C2
Bransford Rd
  Droylsden M11 ....99 E8
  Urmston M41 ....95 C3
Branson St M4,M40 ....160 D2
Branson Wlk WA15 ....120 C6
Branston Rd M40 ....65 D2
Brantfell Gr BL2 ....42 F8
Branthwaite WN2 ....38 B1
Brantingham Ct M16 ....97 E1
Brantingham Rd M16,M21 ....97 D1
Brantwood Cl OL2 ....48 C4
Brantwood Dr BL2 ....42 F8
Brantwood Rd
  Cheadle SK8 ....122 F1
  Manchester M7 ....155 D8
  Manchester M7 ....168 C4
Brantwood Terr M9 ....157 F7
Branwood Prep Sch M30 ....79 E3
Brassey St Ashton-u-L OL6 ....166 B4
  Middleton M24 ....47 A1
Brassington Ave
  Manchester M21 ....109 B7
  Salford M5 ....161 B8
Brassington Cres SK13 ....171 D1
Brassington Gdns M5 ....161 B8
Brassington Rd SK4 ....110 E4
Brathay Cl BL2 ....25 F2
Bratton Cl WN3 ....54 C2
Bratton Wlk M13 ....164 D6
Brattray Dr M24 ....46 E3
Braunston Cl M30 ....95 E8
Braxton Wlk [6] M9 ....157 E8
Bray Ave M30 ....79 B3
Bray Cl SK8 ....122 E2
Braybrook Dr M9 ....40 D7
Brayford Dr WN2 ....38 C5
Brayford Rd M22 ....121 D1
Brayshaw Cl OL10 ....29 C1
Brayside Rd M19,M20 ....110 D4
Brayston Gdns SK8 ....122 B6
Brayton Ave
  Manchester M20 ....110 C2
  Sale M33 ....107 D5
Brazennose St WN2 ....158 F1
Brazil Pl M1 ....163 A8
Brazil St M1 ....163 A8
Brazley Ave Bolton BL3 ....42 B3
  Horwich BL6 ....22 E1
Breach House La WA16 ....129 A7
Bread St M18 ....99 E6
Breaktemper BL5 ....39 E1
Brean Wlk [8] M22 ....121 C1
Brearley St OL13 ....3 D8
Breaston Ave WN7 ....76 C3
Brechin Way OL10 ....29 A1
Brechin Wlk [8] M11 ....83 C1
Breck Rd M30 ....79 B2
Breckland Cl SK15 ....86 D2
Breckland Dr BL1 ....40 D8
Breckles Pl BL3 ....145 D5
Brecon Ave Cheadle SK8 ....122 E1
  Denton M34 ....100 F1
  Manchester M19 ....110 F7
  Urmston M41 ....94 D3
Brecon Cl Platt Bridge WN2 ....56 B2
  Poynton SK12 ....133 F4
  Royton OL2 ....48 C6
Brecon Cres OL6 ....85 B6
Brecon Dr Bury BL9 ....44 E7
  Hindley WN2 ....57 A3
Brecon Wlk [8] OL8 ....66 B2
Bredbury Dr BL4 ....60 E8
Bredbury Gn SK6 ....113 A1
Bredbury Green Prim Sch SK6 ....112 F1
Bredbury Hall Ctry Club SK6 ....112 D2
Bredbury Park Way SK6 ....112 E6
Bredbury Rd M14 ....98 B2
Bredbury St
  Dukinfield SK14 ....101 D5
  Oldham OL9 ....152 B6
Bredbury Sta SK6 ....112 F4
Brede Wlk M23 ....120 D8
Breeze Hill WN6 ....37 B7
Breeze Hill Rd
  Atherton M46 ....58 F5
  Oldham OL4 ....67 D5
Breeze Hill Sch OL4 ....67 D5
Breeze Mount M25 ....63 C3
Breightmet Dr BL2 ....42 E7
Breightmet Fold La BL2 ....42 F8
Breightmet St BL2 ....148 A7
Brellafield Dr OL2 ....48 F8
Brenbar Cres OL12 ....4 D1
Brenchley Dr M23 ....109 A2
Brendall Cl M23 ....108 C1
Brendon Ave SK2 ....125 A5 [Brendon Cl]
Brendon Ave
  Manchester M40 ....83 A7
  Reddish M34 ....100 A3
  Reddish SK5 ....111 F6
Brendon Dr M34 ....84 D1
Brendon Hills OL2 ....48 D3
Brenley Wlk [7] M9 ....157 D8
Brennan Cl M15 ....163 A5
Brennan Ct OL8 ....66 C2
Brennock Cl M11 ....164 F8
Brent Cl Little Lever BL3 ....43 B5
  Poynton SK12 ....133 B4
Brent Moor Rd SK7 ....124 A3
Brent Rd Stockport SK4 ....168 C1
  Wythenshawe M23 ....109 A2
Brentbridge Rd M14 ....110 B8
Brentfield Ave M8 ....156 A6
Brentford Ave BL1 ....142 B2

Brentford Rd SK5 ....111 F6
Brentford St M9 ....157 E7
Brentnall Prim Sch M7 ....155 D7
Brentnall St SK1 ....170 F7
Brentnor Rd M40 ....65 C3
Brenton Ave M33 ....108 A4
Brenton Ct [4] SK8 ....131 E8
Brentwood Sale M33 ....108 A4
  Salford M6 ....154 E3
  Urmston M41 ....94 F1
  Wigan WN5 ....54 D5
Brentwood Ave
  Altrincham WA14 ....119 E7
  Irlam M44 ....105 D6
  Swinton M28 ....79 B6
  Urmston M41 ....95 D2
Brentwood Cl
  Brinnington SK5 ....112 D5
  Littleborough OL15 ....15 F3
  Stalybridge SK15 ....86 C2
Brentwood Cres M41 ....119 E6
Brentwood Ct M25 ....62 F3
Brentwood Dr Eccles M30 ....79 D4
  Farnworth BL3,BL4 ....42 C2
  Gatley SK8 ....122 B5
Brentwood Rd
  Adlington PR6 ....21 B8
  Swinton M27 ....79 B6
Brentwood Sch WA14 ....119 E7
Brentwood St M14 ....97 F3
Brereton Cl WA14 ....119 C1
Brereton Ct [8] SK8 ....122 E1
Brereton Dr M28 ....79 F7
Brereton Gr M44 ....105 E6
Brereton Rd Eccles M30 ....78 F1
  Handforth SK9 ....131 E3
Breslyn St M3 ....158 F3
Bretherton Row [7] WN1 ....150 C8
Bretherton St WN6 ....56 C6
Brethren's Ct M43 ....100 A8
Bretland Ave M22 ....121 F3
Bretland Wlk [8] M22 ....121 F3
Brett Rd M28 ....77 F6
Brett St M22 ....109 C1
Brettargh St M6 ....81 A4
Bretton Wlk M22 ....130 D8
Brewer St M1 ....159 B1
Brewer's Gn SK7 ....124 D3
Brewerton Rd OL4 ....67 C6
Brewery La WN7 ....76 A5
Brewery St
  [4] Altrincham WA14 ....119 D4
  [4] Middleton M24 ....47 A2
  Milnrow OL16 ....31 F6
  New Mills SK22 ....127 C1
  Newton-le-W WA12 ....89 B3
  [8] Oldham OL1 ....67 A6
  Oldham OL3 ....69 B7
  Pendlebury M27 ....80 A8
  Ramsbottom BL0 ....138 C6
  [6] Rochdale OL12 ....14 F1
  Rochdale OL11 ....30 C1
  Stockport SK1 ....169 F2
  Wigan WN3 ....150 C7
Brewster St
  Manchester M9 ....157 D8
  [4] Middleton M24 ....47 A2
Brian Ave M43 ....84 C3
Brian Redhead Ct M15 ....162 E7
Brian St OL11 ....30 B2
Briar Ave
  Hazel Grove SK7 ....124 F2
  Hollinfare WA3 ....105 B2
  Oldham OL4 ....67 F5
Briar Cl Ashton-in-M WN4 ....73 A4
  Hindley WN2 ....57 B4
  Sale M33 ....107 C3
  Urmston M41 ....95 A3
Briar Cres M22 ....121 C5
Briar Gr Leigh WN7 ....75 E8
  Oldham OL1 ....48 B1
  Romiley SK6 ....113 A5
Briar Hill Ave M38 ....59 E4
Briar Hill Cl M38 ....59 E4
Briar Hill Gr M38 ....59 E4
Briar Hill Way [8] M6 ....81 A3
Briar Hollow SK4 ....168 B1
Briar Lea Cl BL3 ....147 E4
Briar Rd Golborne WA3 ....90 B8
Briardene WN1 ....37 C1
Briardene Gdns M22 ....121 E4
Briarfield BL7 ....8 D2
Briarfield Rd
  Altrincham WA14 ....120 C6
  Cheadle SK8 ....123 A5
  Farnworth BL4 ....42 A1
  Manchester M19,M20 ....110 B6
  Reddish SK4 ....111 E6
  Worsley M28 ....78 F7
Briarlands Ave M33 ....107 F2
Briarlands Cl SK7 ....132 D6
Briarley Gdns M33 ....110 E5 [Briarlea Gdns]
Briarlea Gdns SK6 ....113 C6
Briarly WN6 ....37 A7
Briarmere Wlk [4] OL9 ....152 C7
Briars Mount SK4 ....168 A2
Briars Pk SK7 ....123 C1
Briarstead Cl SK7 ....131 D1
Briarwood SK9 ....137 C7
Briarwood Ave
  Droylsden M43 ....84 A3
  Sale M23 ....120 E8
Briarwood Chase SK8 ....123 B1
Briarwood Cres SK6 ....126 A3
Briary Dr M29 ....77 B8
Brick Ground OL12 ....13 C2
Brick Kiln La [4] WN1 ....37 C1
Brick St Bury BL9 ....141 A3
  [8] Manchester M4 ....159 A3
Brickbridge Rd SK6 ....126 A5

Brickfield St
  Hadfield SK13 ....104 B5
  Rochdale OL16 ....15 B2
Brickhill La WA15 ....129 B4
Brickiln La WA14 ....118 C3
Brickiln Row WA14 ....119 C1
Brickley St WA14 ....159 A3
Brickworth Ave M22 ....121 F3
Bridcant St M8 ....156 A1
Briddon St M3 ....158 F3
Bride St BL1 ....143 E2
Brideoak St M8 ....156 A6
Brideoake St Leigh WN7 ....76 B4
  Oldham OL4 ....67 E8
Bridestowe Ave SK14 ....102 C3
Bridestowe Wlk SK14 ....102 C3
Bridge Ave M6 ....113 A5
Bridge Bank Rd OL15 ....16 A3
Bridge Cl Lymm WA13 ....117 B4
  Partington M31 ....106 A3
  [4] Radcliffe M26 ....44 B2
Bridge Coll SK2 ....124 D8
Bridge Dr Cheadle SK8 ....122 D4
  Handforth SK9 ....131 D3
Bridge End Delph OL3 ....50 F4
Bridge End Cl BB4 ....1 A7
Bridge Gr WA15 ....119 F7
Bridge Hall Dr BL9 ....141 C2
Bridge Hall Fold BL9 ....141 C2
Bridge Hall La BL9 ....28 D2
Bridge Hall Prim Sch SK3 ....170 D6
Bridge La SK7 ....123 F1
Bridge Mills Bsns Pk M6 ....80 F5
Bridge Rd Bury OL10 ....140 D1
  Sale M23 ....120 C7
Bridge St Aspull WN2 ....38 A3
  Bolton BL1 ....145 F7
  Droylsden M43 ....99 E8
  Dukinfield M34 ....100 F7
  Dukinfield SK16 ....101 A6
  Farnworth BL4 ....42 E1
  Golborne WA3 ....90 A7
  Haslingden BB4 ....1 C6
  Heywood OL10 ....29 D2
  Hindley WN2 ....56 E6
  Ince-in-M WN3 ....151 D6
  Kearsley M26 ....61 B8
  Littleborough OL12 ....15 C3
  Manchester M3 ....158 E1
  Middleton M24 ....65 A8
  Milnrow OL16 ....31 F6
  New Mills SK22 ....127 C1
  Newton-le-W WA12 ....89 B3
  [8] Oldham M35 ....67 A6
  Oldham OL3 ....69 B7
  Radcliffe M26 ....44 A3
  Ramsbottom BL0 ....138 C6
  Rawtenstall BB4 ....2 E7
  Rochdale OL11 ....30 C1
  Sale M33 ....108 A5
  Stalybridge SK15 ....85 D1
  Stockport SK1 ....169 F2
  Whitworth OL12 ....4 C1
  Wigan WN3 ....150 C7

Bra–Bri **185**

Bridge St continued
  Hindley WN2 ....56 E6
  Manchester M3 ....158 E3
  Manchester M3 ....162 E8
  [8] Oldham OL1 ....67 A8
  Sale M33 ....108 B5
  Stretford M32 ....96 E2
  Walkden M38 ....60 B4
  Wigan WN3 ....150 B7
  [6] Wigan WN5 ....54 B2
Bridge St W M3 ....158 E1 [Bridgewater Viaduct]
Bridgewater Viaduct M15,M3 ....162 E7
Bridgewater Way M15,M16 ....161 B5
Bridgewater Wlk M28 ....60 D3
Bridgfield Cl SK6 ....134 E7
Bridgnorth Rd M9 ....64 A3
Bridle Cl Droylsden M43 ....84 F3
  Urmston M41 ....94 E2
Bridle Ct SK7 ....132 F2
Bridle Fold M26 ....44 A3
Bridle Rd Prestwich M25 ....63 E7
  Woodford SK7,SK10 ....132 F2
Bridle Way M33 ....133 A2
Bridlington Ave M6 ....80 C3
Bridlington Cl [4] M40 ....83 D8
Bridson La M40 ....83 B8
Bridson St [4] M5 ....154 E1
Brien Ave WA14 ....119 F7
Briercliffe Cl M18 ....99 D6
Briercliffe Rd BL3 ....144 C5
Brierfield Ave M46 ....58 C4
Brierfield Dr BL7 ....27 E8
Brierholme Ave BL7 ....8 E1
Brierley Ave Failsworth M35 ....84 A7
  Whitefield M45 ....44 E2
Brierley Cl Ashton-u-L OL6 ....86 A6
  Denton M34 ....100 E1
Brierley Dr M24 ....65 A2
Brierley Rd M27 ....61 E1
Brierley St Bury BL9 ....44 E8
  Heywood OL10 ....29 D2
  Oldham OL8 ....66 F3
  Oldham OL9 ....152 C8
  Stalybridge SK15 ....85 D1
Brierley Wlk OL9 ....152 C8
Brierwood Cl OL11 ....48 E1
Brierton Dr [5] M22 ....121 B1
Brigade Dr M32 ....96 C3
Brigade St BL1 ....144 C7
Brigadier Cl M20 ....110 B6
Brigantine Cl M5 ....161 A8
Brigg Cl M33 ....107 C1
Briggs Fold Cl BL7 ....8 E2
Briggs Fold Rd BL7 ....8 E2
Briggs Rd M32 ....96 F4
Briggs St Leigh WN7 ....75 E7
  Manchester M3 ....158 D3
Brigham St M11 ....165 C8
Bright Rd M30 ....79 E2
Bright St [1] Ashton-u-L OL6 ....85 D2
  Bolton BL7 ....9 D3
  Droylsden M43 ....84 B1
  Leigh WN7 ....75 E7
  Oldham OL8 ....153 D5
  Oldham OL9 ....66 A4
  [4] Radcliffe M26 ....44 C4
  [1] Rochdale OL16 ....31 A5
Brightman St M18 ....99 E6
Brighton Ave Bolton BL1 ....142 A1
  Manchester M7 ....110 F7
  Reddish SK5 ....99 F6
  Urmston M41 ....94 E3
Brighton Cl SK8 ....123 C4
Brighton Gr Hyde SK14 ....167 E1
  Manchester M14 ....98 D2
  Sale M33 ....108 B5
  Wigan WN3 ....94 E3
Brighton Pl M13 ....163 A6
Brighton Range M18 ....99 F4
Brighton Rd Oldham OL4 ....50 A1
  Stockport SK4 ....168 C4
Brighton St [4] M4 ....159 B2
Brignall Gr WA3 ....74 D1
Brigsteer Wlk M40 ....157 D8
Brigstock Ave M18 ....165 C5
Briksdal Way BL6 ....40 C7
Brimelow St SK6 ....112 D3
Brimfield Ave M40 ....59 C1
Brimfield Wlk [4] M40 ....83 C6
Brimmy Croft La OL3 ....33 C3
Brimpton Wlk [2] M8 ....155 F6
Brimrod Com Prim Sch OL11 ....139 D5
Brimrod La OL11 ....139 D5
Brimscombe Ave M22 ....121 C2
Brindale Ho SK5 ....112 C4
Brindale Prim Sch SK5 ....112 C4
Brindale Rd SK5 ....112 C4

Brindl Rise M6 154 F4
Brindle Heath Ind Est M6 81 A4
Brindle Heath Rd M6 154 F4
Brindle Pl (6) M15 163 A6
Brindle Rise M6 154 F4
Brindle St Hindley WN2 56 F6
Tyldesley M29 59 A1
Brindle Way OL2 49 D7
Brindlehurst Dr M29 77 D7
Brindley Ave
(7) Boothstown M28 78 A6
Manchester M9 64 B5
Marple SK6 125 F5
Sale M33 108 C6
Brindley Cl Atherton M46 58 A2
Eccles M30 95 D8
Farnworth BL4 60 B8
Brindley Gr SK9 131 E2
Brindley Rd M16 161 B5
Brindley St Bolton BL1 143 F4
Boothstown M28 77 F6
Eccles M30 79 B3
Horwich BL6 22 C2
Swinton M27 61 F2
Walkden M28 60 D2
Wigan WN5 54 C5
Brinell Dr M44 105 F6
Brink's Row BL6 22 D5
Brinkburn Rd SK7 125 A3
Brinklow Cl M11 99 E7
Brinks La BL2 43 A6
Brinkshaw Ave M22 121 E2
Brinksway Bolton BL1 40 D7
Stockport SK3 123 C8
Brinksway Trad Est (1)
SK3 123 C8
Brinksworth Cl BL2 43 A8
Brinnington Cres SK5 112 B4
Brinnington Rd
Brinnington SK5 112 C4
Stockport SK1 112 A3
Brinnington Rise SK1,SK5 112 B4
Brinnington Sta SK5 112 C6
Brinsop Hall La BL5 39 A6
Brinsop Sq M12 165 B6
Brinston Wlk (12) M40 83 A7
Brinsworth Dr M8 156 A6
Briony Ave WA15 120 C2
Briony Cl OL2 48 E2
Brisbane Cl SK7 132 F5
Brisbane St M13,M15 163 B5
Brisco Wlk M24 46 C2
Briscoe La M40 83 B4
Briscoe Lane Jun & Inf Sch
M40 83 B5
Briscoe St OL1 153 F8
Bristle Hall Way BL5 39 F2
Bristol Ave Ashton-u-L OL6 85 B7
(8) Bolton BL2 25 C1
Manchester M19 111 B8
Bristol Cl SK8 131 C7
Bristol Ct (2) M7 63 E1
Bristol St M7 155 E7
Bristowe St M11,M43 83 D3
Britain St BL9 44 F5
Britannia Ave OL2 149 C6
Britannia Bridge Prim Sch
WN3 151 E6
Britannia Cty Prim Sch
OL13 4 C8
Britannia Ind Est (1) OL10 29 C2
Britannia Rd Sale M33 108 C5
Wigan WN5 54 B8
Britannia St Dukinfield OL7 100 F8
Heywood OL10 29 B2
(1) Oldham OL1 67 A7
Salford M6 81 A5
Britannia Way Bolton BL1 25 A2
Haslingden BB4 1 A8
Britnall Ave M12 164 F5
Briton St Oldham OL2 48 E2
(6) Rochdale OL16 31 A8
Britwell Wlk M8 156 C8
Brixham Ave SK8 131 F7
Brixham Dr M33 107 D6
Brixham Rd M16 97 B4
Brixham Wlk
Bramhall SK7 132 E7
(6) Manchester M13 163 C5
Brixton Ave M20 110 A6
Brixworth Wlk (19) M9 64 E3
Broach St BL3 147 E4
Broad Acre OL12 13 E2
Broad Hey SK6 113 D3
Broad Hill Cl SK7 124 A2
Broad Ing OL12 14 C1
Broad La Altrincham WA15 120 B1
Billinge WA11 71 B1
Delph OL3 50 E7
Rochdale OL16 31 B3
Rochdale OL16 31 D2
Broad Lea M41 95 C3
Broad o' th' La Bolton BL1 143 E4
Shevington WN6 36 A6
Broad Oak Bsns Pk M17 95 F7
Broad Oak Cl PR6 21 A8
Broad Oak Cres OL8 67 A2
Broad Oak High Sch BL9 141 B2
Broad Oak La Bury BL9 28 D3
Manchester M20 122 B8
Manchester M20 122 C8
Broad Oak Pk Eccles M30 79 D4
Swinton M28 79 B6
Broad Oak Prim Sch
M20 122 C8
Broad Oak Rd BL3 42 A2
Broad Oak Terr BL9 28 E3
Broad Rd M33 108 D5
Broad Shaw La
Rochdale OL16 31 D2
Rochdale OL16 31 D3
Broad St Bury BL9 140 E2
Middleton M24 64 C7
Salford M6 80 E5
Salford M6 81 A4
Broad Wlk
Westhoughton BL5 57 E7
Wilmslow SK9 136 F8
Broadacre Orrell WN8 53 A6
Shevington Moor WN6 19 B2
Stalybridge SK15 102 E6
Broadacre Rd M18 99 E3
Broadbent Ave
Ashton-u-L OL6 85 C6
Dukinfield SK16 101 D8
Broadbent Cl Mossley SK15 86 E6
Shaw OL2 149 A5
Broadbent Dr BL9 28 E4
Broadbent Fold Prim Sch
SK16 102 A7
Broadbent Gr SK14 102 E1
Broadbent Rd OL1 49 C1
Broadbent St Hyde SK14 167 D4
Swinton M27 79 D7
Broadbottom CE Prim Sch
SK14 114 F8
Broadbottom Rd SK14 103 A3
Broadbottom Sta SK14 115 A8
Broadcarr La OL5 68 B1
Broadfield Cl M34 101 A2
Broadfield Com Prim Sch
OL8 66 F4
Broadfield Dr OL15 15 F3
Broadfield Gr SK5 99 E3
Broadfield Rd
Manchester M14 98 A3
Reddish SK5 99 E3
Broadfield St
Heywood OL10 29 B1
Rochdale OL16 139 F6
Broadfield Stile OL16 139 E6
Broadford Rd BL3 40 F5
Broadgate Bolton BL3 40 F5
Middleton M24,OL9 65 D5
Uppermill OL3 50 E1
Broadgate Mdw M27 79 F6
Broadgreen Gdns (4) BL4 42 D2
Broadhalgh Ave OL11 30 A7
Broadhalgh Rd OL11 30 A6
Broadhaven Rd M40 160 D3
Broadhead Rd BL7 9 E7
Broadhead Wlk M45 45 B1
Broadheath Cl BL5 40 A1
Broadheath Prim Sch
WA14 119 C8
Broadhey View SK22 127 B1
Broadhill Rd
Manchester M19 110 E6
Stalybridge SK15 86 A5
Broadhurst M34 101 A5
Broadhurst Ave
Culcheth WA3 91 F2
Swinton M27 61 F3
Broadhurst Ct (1) BL3 147 D4
Broadhurst Gr OL6 85 C6
Broadhurst La WN6 18 F7
Broadhurst Prim Sch M40 83 C7
Broadhurst St
(3) Bolton BL3 147 D4
(1) Radcliffe M26 43 F5
Stockport SK3 170 F7
Broadlands WN6 36 B6
Broadlands Rd M28 79 C6
Broadlands Wlk (11) M40 83 A6
Broadlea Gr OL12 14 C2
Broadlea Rd M19 110 E5
Broadley Ave
Golborne WA3 90 C7
Wythenshawe M22 121 D4
Broadley Fold OL12 14 B6
Broadmeadow BL7 25 B8
Broadmeadow Ave M16 97 F1
Broadmoss Dr M9 65 A3
Broadmoss Rd M9 65 A3
Broadoak Ave
Boothstown M28 77 F7
Wythenshawe M22 121 C5
Broadoak Comp Sch
M31 105 F2
Broadoak Cres OL6 85 B5
Broadoak Ct M8 156 B6
Broadoak Dr M22 121 D5
Broadoak Prim Sch
Ashton-u-L OL6 85 C6
Swinton M27 79 C6
Broadoak Rd
Ashton-u-L OL6 85 C6
Rochdale OL11 29 E6
Stockport SK7 123 F2
Wythenshawe M22 121 C5
Wythenshawe M22 121 D4
Broadoaks BL9 28 D3
Broadoaks Rd Sale M33 108 A4
Urmston M41 95 B1
Broadriding Rd WN6 35 E6
Broadstone Ave OL4 49 F4
Broadstone Cl
Prestwich M25 63 A3
Rochdale OL12 14 A1
Broadstone Hall Prim Sch
SK4 111 D6
Broadstone Hall Rd N
SK4 111 D6
Broadstone Hall Rd S
SK4,SK5 111 E6
Broadstone Rd Bolton BL2 25 D5
Reddish SK4,SK5 111 D6
Broadwalk M6 81 A3
Broadway
Altrincham WA15 120 B1
Atherton M46 58 F5
Chadderton OL9 152 A7
Cheadle SK8 122 C4
Droylsden M43 100 A8
Dukinfield SK14,SK16 101 B5
Failsworth M35,M40 83 D8
Failsworth M40,OL9 65 E2
Farnworth BL4 42 A1
Haslingden BB4 1 B8
Hindley WN2 57 A5
Horwich BL6 22 D3
Irlam M44 94 A1
Oldham OL9 48 B1
Partington M31 106 A4
Royton OL1,OL2 48 D2
Sale M33 108 A5
Salford M5 96 E8
Stockport SK2 124 C7
Stockport SK7 123 F2
Urmston M41 95 B4
Walkden M28 60 D1
Wilmslow SK9 137 B6
Broadway Ave SK8 122 D5
Broadway Bsns Pk OL9 65 E4
Broadway Cl M41 95 C5
Broadway Cres BB4 1 A8
Broadway Cty Prim Sch
BB4 1 C8
Broadway Ind Est
Dukinfield SK16 101 B6
Salford M5 161 A8
Broadway N M43 100 A8
Broadway St OL8 66 F4
Broadway Sta M5 96 F8
Broadway The SK6 112 E3
Broadwell Dr Leigh WN7 75 E1
Manchester M9 157 E7
Broadwood BL6 40 C7
Broadwood Cl SK6 134 F7
Brocade Cl M3 158 D3
Broche Cl OL11 30 B3
Brock Ave BL2 42 F7
Brock Cl M11 99 D7
Brock Dr SK8 132 B8
Brock Mill La WN1 37 C4
Brock Pl WN2 55 F2
Brock St Manchester M1 159 B1
Wigan WN1 151 E8
Brockenhurst Dr BL2 25 F3
Brockford Dr M9 64 E5
Brockholes SK13 115 F8
Brockhurst Wlk WN3 150 A5
Brocklebank Rd
Manchester M14 110 C8
Rochdale OL16 31 D7
Brocklehurst Ave BL9 140 F1
Brocklehurst St M9,M40 83 A8
Brockley Ave M14 98 B2
Brockstedes Ave WN4 72 E6
Brockton Wlk M8 156 A8
Brockway OL16 31 C3
Brocstedes Rd WN4 72 D7
Brocton Ct M7 63 D1
Brodick Dr BL2 42 F6
Brodick St M40 157 F8
Brodie Cl M30 79 B2
Brogan St (9) M18 99 D5
Brogden Ave WA3 91 E4
Brogden Dr SK8 122 B5
Brogden Gr M33 108 A3
Brogden Terr M33 108 A3
Bromborough Ave (2)
M20 110 A8
Bromfield (8) OL12 139 F8
Bromfield Ave M9 64 D1
Broming St M11 160 F2
Bromleigh Ave SK8 122 B6
Bromley Ave Golborne WA3 90 D7
Royton OL2 48 C6
Urmston M41 94 E1
Bromley Cl WN2 38 A2
Bromley Cres OL6 85 B6
Bromley Cross BL7 9 B1
Bromley Cross Rd BL7 25 B7
Bromley Cross Sta BL7 25 B7
Bromley Dr WN7 75 D8
Bromley Rd M33 108 C2
Bromley St Denton M34 100 F3
Manchester M4,M40 159 B3
Oldham OL9 66 A3
Bromlow St M11 83 C1
Brompton Ave M35 84 B8
Brompton Rd
Manchester M14 98 B2
Manchester SK4 168 A2
Urmston M32 95 F3
Brompton St OL4 67 A5
Brompton Terr (6) SK16 166 B1
Brompton Way SK9 131 E5
Brompton Wlk M40 83 B6
Bromsgrove Ave M30 79 B2
Bromshill Dr M7 155 E6
Bromwich Dr (1) M9 157 D7
Bromwich St BL2 148 B6
Bronington Cl M22 121 E7
Bronte Ave BL9 44 F6
Bronte Cl Bolton BL1 143 D1
Oldham OL1 49 D4
Rochdale OL12 14 A1
Wigan WN3 150 A5
Bronte St M15 163 A5
Bronville Cl OL1 48 C1
Brood Ford Ct OL10 28 F1
Brook Ave
Altrincham WA15 119 E6
Droylsden M43 83 E1
Handforth SK9 131 D4
Manchester M19 99 B2
Oldham OL3 69 C8
Reddish SK4 111 D5
Shaw OL2 149 B8
Swinton M27 79 F7
Brook Bank Bolton BL2 25 D3
Disley SK12 134 C2
Brook Bottom Rd SK22 126 F1
Brook Cl Altrincham WA15 119 E6
Whitefield M45 63 B8
Brook Ct Manchester M14 110 D8
Prestwich M7 63 C1
Brook Dale Ct M33 108 C1
Brook Dr Marple SK6 125 F4
Tyldesley M29 77 C5
Whitefield M45 63 B8
Brook Fm Cl M31 105 E2
Brook Fold La SK14 102 B1
Brook Gdns Bolton BL2 25 E4
Heywood OL10 29 C2
Brook Gr M44 94 A2
Brook Green La M34 99 F3
Brook Hey Cl OL12 15 D4
Brook Ho Sale WA15 120 C7
Wigan WN1 151 D8
Brook House Cl Bolton BL2 25 E3
Bury BL8 26 E8
Brook La Alderley Edge SK9 136 F3
Altrincham WA15 119 F6
Oldham OL4 67 E6
Oldham OL8 67 B4
Rochdale OL16 31 B3
Uppermill OL3 50 F2
Whitefield BL9 45 A4
Wigan WN5 54 B5
Brook Lo SK8 122 D4
Brook Lynn Ave WA3 74 F1
Brook Mdw Glossop SK13 104 E1
Westhoughton BL5 40 A1
Brook Rd Cheadle SK8 122 D6
Manchester M14 110 D7
Reddish SK4 111 C5
Urmston M41 95 A2
Brook St Ashton-in-M WN4 73 C2
Atherton M46 58 B3
Bolton BL1 145 F7
Bury BL9 141 A3
Cheadle SK8 122 F6
Failsworth M35 83 D6
Farnworth BL4 42 E1
(2) Glossop SK13 104 C1
Golborne WA3 75 A1
Golborne WA3 90 A8
Hazel Grove SK7 124 E2
Hyde SK14 167 E3
Ince-in-M WN2 56 A7
Kearsley M26 61 A7
Littleborough OL12 15 C6
Littleborough OL15 16 C5
Manchester M1 163 A7
Oldham OL1 67 A7
Oldham OL9 152 B8
Radcliffe M26 44 B3
Royton OL2 48 D3
Sale M33 108 C5
Salford M6 81 B4
Swinton M27 79 D8
Westhoughton BL5 39 F1
Wigan WN3 54 F4
Brook St E OL6 166 A2
Brook St W OL6 166 A2
Brook Terr Manchester M13 98 F3
Newhey OL16 32 C4
Urmston M41 95 C4
Brook The OL15 6 C1
Brook Wlk M34 112 F8
Brook's Bar M16 97 D4
Brook's Pl (3) OL12 139 E8
Brook's Rd M16 97 C3
Brookash Rd M22 131 A8
Brookbank Cl M24 65 B7
Brookbottom Rd M26 43 F6
Brookburn Prim Sch
M21 109 A7
Brookburn Rd M21 109 A7
Brookcot Rd M23 120 F7
Brookcroft Ave M22 121 D5
Brookcroft Rd M22 121 D5
Brookdale Atherton M46 58 F6
Rochdale OL12 14 E3
Brookdale Ave
Denton M34 100 E7
Denton M34 101 B2
Failsworth M40 83 D4
Marple SK6 126 A4
Brookdale Cl Bolton BL1 143 F2
Bredbury SK6 112 F3
Brookdale Cotts SK2 124 F7
Brookdale Rd
Bramhall SK7 123 F1
Hindley WN2 56 F5
Wythenshawe SK8 121 F5
Brookdale Rise SK7 123 F1
Brookdale St M35 83 E7
Brookdean Cl BL1 142 C3
Brookdene Rd
Manchester M19 110 E6
Whitefield BL9 45 A2
Brooke Dr SK9 131 D4
Brooke Way SK9 131 D4
Brookes St (7) Bacup OL13 3 D8
Middleton M24 47 B2
Brookfield Prestwich M25 63 B4
Shaw OL2 32 A1
Brookfield Ave
Ainsworth BL2 26 C1
Ainsworth BL2 43 D8
Altrincham WA15 119 F8
Manchester M21 109 C7
Poynton SK12 133 C3
Romiley SK6 113 A4
Royton OL2 48 D3
Salford M6 80 C3
Stockport SK1 124 A7
Urmston M41 95 A2
Brookfield Cl SK1 124 A7
Brookfield Cres SK8 122 D4
Brookfield Ct (4) M19 110 F8
Brookfield Dr
Altrincham WA15 120 A7
Boothstown M28 77 F6
Littleborough OL15 15 F6
Swinton M27 61 E1
Brookfield Gdns
Wythenshawe M22 121 C6
Wythenshawe M22 121 D6
Brookfield Gr OL6 85 D2
Brookfield Ho SK8 122 D4
Brookfield Ind Est SK13 171 E3
Brookfield Rd Bury BL9 27 E8
Cheadle SK8 122 E5
Culcheth WA3 91 D3
Eccles M30 79 B4
Manchester M8 64 A1
Orrell WN8 53 B7
Shevington Moor WN6 19 B2
Brookfield St Bolton BL2 148 B7
Leigh WN7 76 A6
Newton-le-W WA12 89 B3
Oldham OL8 153 F5
Brookfold M35 83 E8
Brookfold La BL2 25 F5
Brookfold Rd SK4 111 D6
Brookhead Ave M20 109 F7
Brookhead Dr SK8 123 A6
Brookhead Jun Sch SK8 122 F5
Brookhey Ave BL3 147 F3
Brookheys Rd M31,WA14 106 E2
Brookhill Cl OL3 51 C5
Brookhill St M40 160 E3
Brookhouse Ave
Eccles M30 95 A8
Farnworth BL4 60 C6
Brookhouse Sports Ctr
M30 94 F8
Brookhouse St WN1 151 D7
Brookhouse Terr WN1 151 D7
Brookhurst La M38 59 E6
Brookhurst Rd M18 99 D4
Brookland Ave
Denton M34 100 D2
Farnworth BL4 60 C7
Hindley WN2 56 D5
Brookland Gr BL1 142 A2
Brookland Rd WN1 37 B3
Brookland St OL16 31 B3
Brookland Terr BB4 2 F7
Brooklands Horwich BL6 22 C3
Littleborough OL12 15 C7
Brooklands Ave
Ashton-in-M WN4 73 D2
Atherton M46 58 D4
Haslingden BB4 1 B7
Leigh WN7 75 E3
Manchester M20 110 A6
Oldham OL9 152 B5
Brooklands Cl
Denton M34 100 D4
Irlam M44 93 F2
Mossley OL5 68 B2
Reddish SK4 111 D5
Brooklands Cres M33 108 B3
Brooklands Ct
Manchester M8 63 F2
Rochdale OL11 30 C6
Sale M33 108 B3
Brooklands Dr
Droylsden M43 84 C3
Glossop SK13 116 B7
Oldham OL4 68 B6
Orrell WN5 53 D5
Brooklands Ho M33 108 B2
Brooklands Par OL4 68 B6
Brooklands Prim Sch
M33 108 A2
Brooklands Rd
Hazel Grove SK7 124 E1
Manchester M25,M8 63 E2
Orrell WN8 53 C7
Ramsbottom BL0 11 A2
Reddish SK5 99 E2
Sale M23,M33 108 B2
Swinton M27 79 D6
Brooklands St
Middleton M24 47 A1
Royton OL2 48 D5
Brooklands Sta M33 108 A3
Brooklands Station App
M33 108 A3
Brooklands The OL10 29 C2
Brooklawn Dr
Manchester M20 110 B4
Prestwich M25 63 C6
Brookleigh Rd M20 110 D6
Brooklet Cl OL4 67 F5
Brookln Pl SK8 122 D6
Brooklyn Ave
Littleborough OL15 16 A7
Littleborough OL16 15 E4
Manchester M16 97 C2

Brooklyn Ave continued
Urmston M41 ....94 E1
Brooklyn Cres SK8 ....122 D5
Brooklyn Ct M14 ....110 C7
Brooklyn Rd Cheadle SK8 ...122 D5
Stockport SK2 ....124 C6
16 Oldham OL1 ....49 C1
Brooks Ave
Hazel Grove SK7 ....124 D3
Hyde SK14 ....167 E1
Radcliffe M26 ....43 F6
Brooks Dr
Altrincham M23,WA15 .....120 D6
Altrincham WA15 ....129 D8
Failsworth M35 ....83 E6
Brooks End OL11 ....13 E1
Brooks Ho 1 WN7 ....75 E8
Brooks St SK1 ....170 F7
Brooksbottom Cl BL0 ....11 C4
Brookshaw St Bury BL9 ....141 A4
Droylsden M11 ....83 A1
Brookside Glossop SK13 ...116 B8
Mossley OL5 ....68 B2
Oldham OL4 ....67 D6
Rawtenstall SK22 ....127 E7
Wigan WN3 ....150 A5
Brookside Ave
Ashton-in-M WN4 ....72 F8
Droylsden M43 ....84 C3
Farnworth BL4 ....60 C7
Oldham OL4 ....68 B6
Poynton SK12 ....133 E3
Stockport SK2 ....124 F7
Brookside Bsns Pk M24 ....65 D6
Brookside Cl Atherton M46 ..58 E4
Billinge WN5 ....71 E5
Bolton BL2 ....D5 D5
Cheadle SK8 ....122 D4
Hadfield SK14 ....171 F4
Hyde SK14 ....102 A3
Rochdale OL11 ....11 A3
Brookside Cres Bury BL8 ...25 E8
Middleton M24 ....65 C6
Walkden M28 ....60 E3
Brookside Ct M19 ....99 A2
Brookside Dr Hyde SK14 ..102 A3
Manchester M25,M7 ....63 D1
Brookside La Sa6 ....134 E7
Brookside Miniature Rly
SK12 ....133 F7
Brookside Prim Sch SK6 ...134 E6
Brookside Rd Bolton BL2 ...42 D8
Gatley SK8 ....122 A6
Manchester M40 ....65 A1
Sale M33 ....108 A2
Standish WN1 ....20 B1
Brookside Terr OL3 ....50 E4
Brookside Wlk BL8 ....43 F7
Brooksmouth BL8 ....140 D2
Brookstone Cl M21 ....109 D6
Brookthorn Cl SK2 ....124 F5
Brookthorpe Ave M19 ......110 E6
Brookthorpe Rd BL8 ....27 A3
Brookvale 4 WN6 ....37 A1
Brookview WN2 ....56 D4
Brookville OL12 ....4 C1
Brookwater Cl BL8 ....26 F6
Brookway
Altrincham WA15 ....119 F7
Oldham OL4 ....67 E5
Uppermill OL4 ....68 E6
Brookway Cl M19 ....110 E4
Brookway Cl M23 ....120 F7
Brookway High Sch M23 ...120 E7
Brookwood Ave
Manchester M8 ....156 C8
Sale M33 ....107 E3
Brookwood Cl M34 ....113 A7
Broom Ave Leigh WN7 ......75 E7
Manchester M19 ....111 B8
Manchester M7 ....155 E8
4 Reddish SK5 ....111 F6
Broom La Manchester M19 ..111 B8
Manchester M7 ....155 D8
Broom Rd
Altrincham WA15 ....119 E3
Partington M31 ....105 F2
Broom Way 54 D7
Broom St Bury BL8 ....140 D2
Newhey OL16 ....32 B4
Swinton M27 ....79 F7
Broom Way BL5 ....40 A2
Broome Gr OL9 ....153 D6
Broome St OL9 ....153 D6
Broomedge M7 ....155 D8
Broomehouse Ave M44 ....105 E8
Broomfield M6 ....80 D6
Broomfield Cl
Ainsworth BL2 ....26 C1
Reddish SK5 ....111 F6
Wilmslow SK9 ....137 E8
Broomfield Cres
Middleton M24 ....46 D1
Stockport SK2,SK3 ....124 A4
Broomfield Dr
Manchester M8 ....155 F7
Reddish SK5 ....111 F6
Broomfield La WA15 ....119 E3
Broomfield Pl WN6 ....119 E1
Broomfield Rd
4 Bolton BL3 ....146 C4
Manchester SK4 ....168 C4
Standish WN6 ....19 E2
Broomfield Sq OL11 ......139 F5
Broomfield Terr
Newhey OL16 ....32 B4
Wigan WN1 ....151 E7

Broomfields M34 ....101 A5
Broomflat Cl WN6 ....19 E1
Broomgrove La M34 ....101 A4
Broomhall Rd
Manchester M9 ....64 B5
Pendlebury M27 ....80 D6
Broomhey Ave WN1 ....37 C4
Broomhey Terr WN1 ......151 E7
Broomhill Dr SK7 ....123 D1
Broomholme WN6 ....35 D7
Broomhurst Ave OL8 ....66 D4
Broomstair Rd M34 ....100 F6
Broomville Ave M33 ......108 B4
Broomwood Gdns WA15 ...120 C5
Broomwood Prim
Sch WA15 ....120 D5
Broomwood Rd WA15 .....120 C5
Broomwood Wlk 2 M15 ...163 A6
Broseley Ave
Culcheth WA3 ....91 D4
Manchester M20 ....110 D3
Broseley La WA3 ....91 D5
Broseley Rd M16 ....97 A2
Brosscroft SK13 ....104 A6
Brosscroft Village SK13 ...104 A6
Brotherdale Cl OL2 ....48 D5
Brotherod Hall Rd OL12 ...14 C2
Brotherton Dr M3 ....162 D6
Brotherton Dr M3 ....158 D2
Brough Cl WN2 ....56 E3
Brough St 4 M11 ....99 E7
Brougham St M28 ....60 C3
Broughton Ave
Golborne WA3 ....90 D7
Walkden M38 ....60 B4
Broughton Cl M24 ....46 D2
Broughton
Jewish Cassel-Fox
Prim Sch M7 ....155 D8
Broughton La
Manchester M5,M7 ....155 D5
Manchester M7,M8 ....158 E4
Broughton Rd
Reddish SK5 ....169 F4
Salford M6 ....81 A4
Broughton Rd E M6 ....81 B4
Broughton St Bolton BL1 ..143 D2
Manchester M8 ....159 A4
Broughton Trade Ctr M7 ...158 E4
Broughville Dr M20 ....122 C8
Brow Ave M24 ....65 C6
Brow St OL11 ....31 A4
Brow Wlk M9 ....64 D3
Browbeck OL11 ....153 E7
Browfield M5 ....161 B8
Browfield Ave M5 ....161 B8
Browfield Way OL1 ....48 E1
Browmere Dr M20 ....110 A4
Brown Bank Rd OL16 ......15 F3
Brown Edge Rd OL4 ....67 E4
Brown La SK8 ....122 B1
Brown Lodge Dr OL15 .....15 F3
Brown Lodge St OL15 .....15 F3
Brown St
2 Alderley Edge SK9 .....137 A1
Blackrod BL6 ....21 D2
Bolton BL1 ....145 F7
Chadderton OL9 ....152 A8
Failsworth M35 ....83 E7
Heywood OL10 ....29 D3
Ince-in-M WN2 ....56 A7
3 Leigh WN2 ....56 F4
3 Leigh WN7 ....76 A5
Littleborough OL15 ....16 B5
18 Manchester M2 ....158 F1
Manchester M24 ....159 A1
Middleton M24 ....47 A2
Radcliffe M26 ....43 F6
Ramsbottom BL0 ....138 B5
Salford M6 ....154 F1
Stockport SK1 ....169 E2
Tyldesley M29 ....76 F7
Wigan WN3 ....150 B7
Brown St N 2 WN7 ....76 A5
Brown St S 1 WN7 ....76 A4
Brown's La SK9 ....137 E8
Brownacre St M20 ....110 B6
Brownbank Wlk M15 ......162 F5
Browncross St M3 ....158 E1
Brownhill Countryside Ctr
OL3 ....51 B1
Brownhill Dr OL4 ....68 A7
Brownhill La OL3 ....51 B1
Brownhill Sch OL12 ....14 E1
Brownhill St M11 ....165 A8
Brownhills Cl BL8 ....27 A5
Browning Ave
Atherton M46 ....58 D5
Droylsden M43 ....84 A1
Wigan WN3 ....54 F4
6 Wythenshawe M22 .....121 C1
Bryson Wlk M18 ....165 C5
Buchan St M11 ....83 B2
Buchanan Dr WN2 ....38 B4
Buchanan Rd WN5 ....54 E7
Buchanan St Leigh WN7 ...75 E5
Ramsbottom BL0 ....138 B5
Swinton M27 ....61 F1
Buck La M33 ....92 F7
Buckden Rd SK4 ....111 D7
Buckden Wlk 11 M23 .....108 F2
Buckfast Ave
Ashton-in-M WA11 ....89 A7
Oldham OL4 ....67 C4
Oldham OL8 ....67 D3

Brownlow Ave
Ince-in-M WN2 ....56 B7
Royton OL2 ....49 A3
Brownlow Bsns Ctr BL1 ...143 D1
Brownlow Cl SK12 ....133 E2
Brownlow Fold
Com Prim Sch BL1 ....143 D1
Brownlow La WN5 ....53 C1
Brownlow Rd BL6 ....22 C5
Brownlow Way BL1 ....143 E1
Brownmere WN6 ....36 F2
Browns Rd BL1,BL3 ....43 B6
Brownside Cl OL16 ....15 C3
Brownslow Wlk 11 M13 ...163 B7
Brownson St M7 ....157 E8
Brownsville Rd SK4 ......111 C5
Brownsville Gr SK16 .....101 E7
Brownswood Ave M11 ....112 B1
Brownwood Cl M33 ......108 C1
Brows Ave M23 ....109 A2
Browsholme Ho BL1 ......144 C7
Broxton Ave Bolton BL3 ..146 B3
Orrell WN5 ....53 F7
Broxton St M40 ....160 F3
Broxwood Cl 8 M18 ....99 D5
Bruce St OL11 ....30 C4
Bruce Wlk 2 M11 ....99 D7
Brundage Rd M22 ....121 D2
Brundrett Pl 7 M23 ......107 F4
Brundrett St SK1 ....124 A8
Brundrett's Rd M21 ......109 B8
Brunel Ave M5 ....81 A2
Brunel Cl M32 ....96 E2
Brunel St Bolton BL1 .....143 D3
Horwich BL6 ....22 C2
Brunet Wlk M12 ....164 F6
Brunstead Cl M23 ....120 D6
Brunswick Ave BL6 ....22 E2
Brunswick St BL1 ....145 E8
Brunswick Rd
Altrincham WA14 ....119 D7
Manchester M20 ....110 D3
Brunswick St Hyde SK14 ..140 F3
Dukinfield SK16 ....101 C8
3 Heywood OL10 ....29 C2
Leigh WN7 ....76 A4
Manchester M13 ....163 B6
Mossley OL5 ....68 A8
Oldham OL1 ....153 E6
Rochdale OL16 ....31 A8
Shaw OL2 ....149 B7
Stretford M32 ....108 D8
Walsden OL14 ....6 A7
Brunswick Terr OL13 ......3 D8
Brunt St M13 ....98 B3
Brunton Rd SK5 ....111 F6
Bruntwood Ave SK8 ......122 A1
Bruntwood La
Cheadle SK8 ....122 E1
Cheadle SK8 ....122 E2
Bruntwood Prim Sch
SK8 ....122 E2
Brushes Ave SK15 ....86 D3
Brushes Rd SK15 ....86 D3
Brussels Rd SK3 ....170 D6
Bruton Ave M32 ....96 B1
Brutus Wlk M7 ....155 E6
Bryan Rd M21 ....97 B2
Bryan St 11 OL4 ....67 C8
Bryant Cl M13 ....163 C5
Bryant's Acre BL1 ....40 D7
Bryantsfield BL1 ....40 D6
Bryce St Bolton BL3 ......145 E5
Hyde SK14 ....167 D4
Brydges Rd SK6 ....125 E5
Brydon Ave M12 ....163 C7
Brydon Cl Salford M6 ....154 F2
Bryham St WN1 ....151 D8
Bryn Cross WN4 ....73 A6
Bryn Dr SK5 ....111 E5
Bryn Gates La WN2,WN4 ..73 D8
Bryn Lea Terr BL1 ....142 A4
Bryn Rd WN4 ....73 B5
Bryn St WN4 ....73 C4
Bryn St
Ashton-in-M WN4 ....73 B3
Ince-in-M WN3 ....151 E6
Bryn Sta WN4 ....73 A6
Bryn Wlk BL1 ....145 F8
Bryndale Gr M33 ....107 F1
Brynden Ave M20 ....110 C5
Brynford Ave M9 ....64 A5
Bryngs Dr BL2 ....25 F4
Brynhall Cl M26 ....43 E5
Brynheys Cl M38 ....60 A5
Brynn St M7 ....73 F7
Bryone Dr SK2 ....124 B5
Bryony Cl Orrell WN5 ......53 D5
Walkden M28 ....60 D5
6 Wythenshawe M22 ....121 C1

Buckfast Cl
Altrincham WA15 ....120 B2
Bramhall SK8 ....132 B6
Manchester M21 ....97 B1
Poynton SK12 ....133 D5
Buckfast Rd Middleton M24 ..46 F3
Sale M33 ....107 E6
Buckfast Wlk M7 ....155 E6
Buckfield Ave M5 ....161 B7
Buckhurst Rd
Manchester M19 ....99 A1
Ramsbottom BL0 ....12 C3
Buckingham Ave
Denton M34 ....101 B2
Horwich BL6 ....22 E2
Salford M6 ....154 D2
Whitefield M45 ....63 A2
Buckingham Cl WN5 ......54 E5
Buckingham Dr Bury BL8 ..44 B8
Dukinfield SK16 ....101 F7
Buckingham Park Cl OL2 ..149 B8
Buckingham Pl M29 ....58 F3
Buckingham Rd
Cheadle SK8 ....123 A3
Droylsden M43 ....83 E1
Irlam M44 ....105 C6
Manchester M21 ....97 B1
Manchester M25 ....63 C2
Manchester SK4 ....111 B5
Manchester SK4 ....111 C6
Poynton SK12 ....133 D3
Sale WA14 ....107 F1
Stalybridge SK15 ....86 A4
Stretford M32 ....96 F4
Swinton M27 ....62 A2
Wilmslow SK9 ....136 F6
Buckingham Rd W SK4 ...168 A4
Buckingham St
12 Rochdale OL16 ....31 A8
Salford M5 ....154 F1
Stockport SK2 ....124 A6
Buckingham Way
Altrincham WA15 ....120 A7
Stockport SK2 ....170 F6
Buckland Ave M9 ....64 A3
Buckland Dr WN5 ....36 B1
Buckland Gr SK14 ....114 A8
Buckland Rd M6 ....80 A4
Buckley View M44 ....105 C6
Buckle Ho 7 M30 ....79 C2
Buckley Ave M18 ....99 C4
Buckley Barn Ct OL11 .....30 C1
Buckley Bldgs OL5 ....86 E8
Buckley Brook St OL12 ....15 B2
Buckley Chase OL16 ....15 E6
Buckley Cl SK14 ....113 E7
Buckley Dr SK6 ....113 A1
Buckley Farm La OL12 ....15 B3
Buckley Fields OL12 ....15 A2
Buckley Hall Ind Est OL12 ..15 B3
Buckley Hall La OL16 ......31 E5
Buckley Ho M46 ....58 D3
Buckley La Farnworth BL4 ..60 C7
Prestwich M25 ....62 E3
Rochdale OL12 ....15 B3
Buckley Rd
Manchester M18 ....99 C4
Oldham OL16 ....67 D8
Rochdale OL12 ....15 B2
Buckley Sq BL4 ....60 C6
Buckley St Bury BL9 .....140 F3
Chadderton OL9 ....152 A7
Denton M34 ....100 D7
Droylsden M43 ....84 A1
Heywood OL10 ....29 E2
Manchester M11 ....99 E8
6 Oldham OL4 ....69 B8
Oldham OL4 ....67 E5
Radcliffe M26 ....44 A3
Reddish SK5 ....99 E2
Rochdale OL16 ....31 A8
Shaw OL2 ....149 C7
Stalybridge SK15 ....101 F8
Wigan WN6 ....37 B2
Buckley St W WN6 ....37 A2
Buckley Terr OL12 ....15 B3
Buckley View OL12 ....15 B3
Bucklow Ave
Manchester M14 ....98 B1
Partington M31 ....105 F4
Bucklow Cl
Mottram-in-L SK14 ......102 F1
Oldham OL4 ....49 E4
Bucklow Dr M22 ....121 E8
Bucklow View WA14 ......119 A4
Bucknell Ct M40 ....159 C4
Bucksones Com Prim Sch
OL2 ....49 D8
Bucksones Rd
Shaw OL1,OL2 ....49 E7
Shaw OL2 ....32 D1
Buckthorn Cl
Altrincham WA15 ....120 E5
Oldham OL9 ....109 D6
Westhoughton BL5 ....39 F2
Buckthorn La M30 ....94 F8
Buckton Cl OL3 ....51 C5
Buckton Dr SK15 ....86 E4
Buckton Vale Mews SK15 ..86 F7
Buckton Vale Prim Sch
SK15 ....86 F7
Buckton Vale Rd
Mossley SK15 ....86 D5
Mossley SK15 ....86 F6
Buckwood Cl SK7 ....125 A3
Buddleia Gr M7 ....155 D6
Bude Ave Brinnington SK5 ..112 B5
Tyldesley M29 ....77 C8

Bro–Bur 187

Bude Ave continued
Urmston M41 ....107 B8
Bude Cl SK7 ....132 F7
Bude Terr 4 SK16 ....166 B1
Bude Wlk M23 ....121 B5
Budsworth Ave M20 ......110 B7
Budworth Gdns 2 M43 ....84 B1
Budworth Rd M33 ....108 C3
Budworth Wlk 1 SK9 .....131 E1
Buer Ave WN3 ....54 F4
Buersil Ave OL16 ....31 B4
Buersil St OL16 ....31 B3
Buerton Ave M9 ....64 A5
Buffalo Ct M5 ....78 A1
Bugle La M5 ....99 B1
Bugle St M1 ....162 E8
Buile Dr M9 ....64 F4
Buile Hill Ave M38 ....60 B5
Buile Hill Dr M5 ....154 D3
Buile Hill Gr M38 ....60 B5
Buile Hill High Sch M6 ...154 D4
Buile St M7 ....155 E7
Builne Ho M6 ....154 E3
Bulford Ave M22 ....121 B2
Bulkeley Rd Cheadle SK8 ..122 E6
Handforth SK9 ....131 D3
Poynton SK12 ....133 E3
Bulkeley St SK3 ....170 D8
Bull Hill Cres M26 ....62 B8
Bullcote Gn OL2 ....49 B4
Bullcote La OL1,OL2 ....49 B4
Bullcroft Dr M29 ....77 C6
Buller Mews BL8 ....27 B1
Buller Rd M13 ....98 F2
Buller St 7 Bury BL8 ......27 C1
Droylsden M43 ....100 B8
Farnworth BL3 ....42 C2
Oldham OL4 ....67 D8
Bullfinch Dr BL9 ....28 B5
Bullfinch Wlk M21 ....109 D7
Bullock St SK1 ....170 F7
Bullough Moor Prim Sch
OL10 ....28 C2
Bullough St Atherton M46 ..58 C1
Atherton M46 ....58 C3
Bullows Rd M38 ....59 D8
Bullrush Cl M28 ....60 D5
Bulteel St Bolton BL3 ....146 C2
Boothstown M28 ....77 E7
Eccles M30 ....79 B3
Wigan WN5 ....54 D6
Bulwer St OL16 ....31 A8
Bungalow Rd WA12 ....89 E1
Bungalows The
Ashton-in-M WN4 ....72 F7
New Mills SK22 ....130 C3
Bunkers Hill M45 ....69 C6
Bunkers Hill Rd SK14 ....102 E1
Bunkershill Rd SK6 ......113 B1
Bunsen St M1 ....159 A1
Bunting Dr 6 WA3 ....90 E8
Bunting Mews M28 ....78 B8
Bunyan Cl OL1 ....49 E4
Bunyan St 24 OL12 ....14 F1
Bunyard St M8 ....156 B6
BUPA Hospl Manchester
M16 ....97 D3
Burbage Bank 3 SK13 ...171 E1
Burbage Gr 28 SK13 .....171 E2
Burbage Rd M23 ....121 A2
Burbage Way SK13 ....171 E2
Burbridge Cl M11 ....160 E1
Burchall Field OL16 ....31 B7
Burdale Dr M6 ....80 B4
Burdale Wlk M23 ....108 F1
Burder St 4 OL8 ....66 C2
Burdett Ave OL12 ....13 F1
Burdett Way M12 ....164 E5
Burdith Ave M14 ....98 A2
Burdon Ave M22 ....121 E3
Burford Ave Bramhall SK7 ..132 D5
Manchester M16 ....97 E4
Urmston M41 ....95 E4
Burford Cl SK9 ....136 E5
Burford Cres SK9 ....136 E5
Burford Dr Bolton BL3 ...145 E5
Manchester M16 ....97 E4
Swinton M27 ....61 E2
Burford Gr M33 ....107 E1
Burford La M13 ....117 C2
Burford Rd M16 ....97 D2
Burford Wlk M16 ....97 D2
Burgate Cl WN3 ....54 E2
Burgate WA16 ....159 C2
Burgess Ave OL6 ....85 C5
Burgess Dr M35 ....83 F7
Burgess Prim Sch M40 ...157 E7
Burgess St WN3 ....151 E5
Burghley Ave OL4 ....49 B4
Burghley Cl Bolton BL3 ....43 B5
Stalybridge SK15 ....86 A2
Burghley Dr BL3 ....43 B5
Burgin Wlk M40 ....156 C5
Burgundy Dr BL8 ....26 F7
Burke St BL1 ....143 D2
Burkhardt Dr WA12 ....89 E3
Burkitt St SK14 ....167 E2
Burland Cl M7 ....155 E6
Burland St WN5 ....54 F7
Burleigh Cl SK7 ....124 A1
Burleigh Ct M32 ....96 E4
Burleigh Mews M21 ......109 B6
Burleigh Rd M32 ....96 E4
Burleigh St M15 ....163 B5
Burlescombe Cl WA14 ...119 B6

Burley Ave WA3 . . . . .74 D1
Burley Cres WN3 . . . . .54 C2
Burley Ct SK4 . . . . .168 C2
Burleyhurst La SK9,WA16 . .136 B7
Burlin Ct **8** M16 . . . . .97 D3
Burlington Ave OL8 . . . . .66 E4
Burlington Cl SK4 . . . . .110 E2
Burlington Ct WA14 . . . . .119 D5
Burlington Dr SK3 . . . . .123 F4
Burlington Gdns SK3 . . . . .123 F4
Burlington Ho OL6 . . . . .166 A3
Burlington Mews SK3 . . . . . . .123 F4
Burlington Rd
  Altrincham WA14 . . . . .119 D5
  Eccles M30 . . . . .79 E4
  Manchester M20 . . . . .110 C7
Burlington St
  Ashton-u-L OL6,OL7 . . . . . . .166 A3
  Hindley WN2 . . . . .56 D5
  Hindley WN2 . . . . .56 E5
  Manchester M13,M15 . . . . . .163 B5
  Manchester M15 . . . . .163 A5
  12 Rochdale OL11 . . . . .31 A4
  Burlton Gr WN2 . . . . .38 A2
  Burman St M11,M43 . . . . .99 F7
  Burn Bank OL3 . . . . .68 F5
Burnaby St Bolton BL3 . . . . . .145 D5
  Oldham OL8 . . . . .153 D5
  Rochdale OL11 . . . . .30 C4
Burnage Ave M19 . . . . .110 F8
Burnage Hall Rd M19 . . . . . . .110 F7
Burnage High Sch
  for Boys Manchester M19 . .110 E5
  Manchester M20 . . . . .110 D6
Burnage La M19 . . . . .110 F4
Burnage Range M19 . . . . .99 A1
Burnage Sta M20 . . . . .110 D4
Burnaston Gr WN5 . . . . .54 D5
Burnbray Ave M19 . . . . .110 E6
Burnby WN6 M13 . . . . .108 E1
Burndale Dr BL9 . . . . .45 A3
Burnden Ind Est BL3 . . . . .42 B4
Burnden Rd BL3 . . . . .148 B5
Burnden Way BL6 . . . . .39 C7
Burnedge Cl OL2 . . . . .4 D2
Burnedge Fold Rd OL4 . . . . . . .68 D6
Burnedge La OL4 . . . . .68 D7
Burnedge Mews OL4 . . . . .68 D6
Burnell Cl M40 . . . . .160 D3
Burnell Cl OL10 . . . . .46 D7
Burneside Cres M24 . . . . .46 E3
Burnet Cl Rochdale OL16 . . . . .31 C4
  Tyldesley M29 . . . . .77 B7
Burnett Ave M5 . . . . .161 B8
Burnett Cl M40 . . . . .157 D5
Burnett Gdns M5 . . . . .161 B8
Burnfell WA3 . . . . .90 E7
Burnfield Rd
  Manchester M18 . . . . .99 D3
  Reddish SK5 . . . . .99 F1
Burnham Ave Bolton BL1 . . . .142 A1
  Reddish SK5 . . . . .99 F1
Burnham Cl Cheadle SK8 . . . .122 F2
  Culcheth WA3 . . . . .91 E4
Burnham Dr
  Manchester M19 . . . . .110 F8
  Urmston M41 . . . . .95 C3
Burnham Gr WN2 . . . . .37 F2
Burnham Rd M34 . . . . .100 A3
Burnham Wlk **3** BL4 . . . . .42 D1
Burnhill Ct WN6 . . . . .36 E8
Burnleigh Ct BL5 . . . . .58 F8
Burnley La
  Chadderton OL1,OL9 . . . . .48 A2
  Oldham OL1,OL9 . . . . .48 C1
Burnley Rd Bury BL9 . . . . .28 E1
  Edenfield BL0 . . . . .1 D5
Burnley Rd E BB4 . . . . .2 E8
Burnley St Chadderton OL9 . .152 B8
  Failsworth M35 . . . . .83 A8
Burnmoor Rd BL2 . . . . .42 F8
Burns Ave Atherton M46 . . . . .58 D5
  Bury BL9 . . . . .44 F6
  Cheadle SK8 . . . . .122 F6
  Leigh WN7 . . . . .75 C8
  Swinton M27 . . . . .61 D1
Burns Cl Ashton-in-M WN4 . . . .72 F6
  Longshaw WN5 . . . . .53 D1
  Manchester M11 . . . . .160 F1
  Oldham OL1 . . . . .49 E5
  Wigan WN3 . . . . .55 A4
Burns Cres SK2 . . . . .124 C7
Burns Fold SK16 . . . . .102 A7
Burns Gdns M25 . . . . .62 F3
Burns Gr M43 . . . . .84 A2
Burns Rd **6** Abram WN2 . . . .56 B1
  Denton M34 . . . . .100 E3
  Walkden M38 . . . . .60 A5
Burns St Bolton BL3 . . . . .145 F6
  Heywood OL10 . . . . .29 D2
Burnsall Ave Golborne WA3 . .90 F8
  Whitefield M45 . . . . .62 D6
Burnsall Gr OL2 . . . . .48 D4
Burnsall Wlk **2** M22 . . . . . . .121 A2
Burnside Altrincham WA15 . .129 D7
  Edenfield BL0 . . . . .1 D2
  Hadfield SK14 . . . . .171 F4
  Shaw OL2 . . . . .49 D8
  Stalybridge SK15 . . . . .102 D7
Burnside Ave Reddish SK4 . .111 E6
  Salford M6 . . . . .80 B5
Burnside Cl Bredbury SK6 . . . .112 F3
  Heywood OL10 . . . . .29 D1
  Radcliffe M26 . . . . .43 F7
  Stalybridge SK15 . . . . .102 D7

Burnside Cl continued
  Tyldesley M29 . . . . .77 B7
  Wilmslow SK9 . . . . .137 C6
Burnside Dr M19 . . . . .110 F7
Burnside Rd Bolton BL1 . . . . .142 B2
  Gatley SK8 . . . . .122 B5
  Rochdale OL16 . . . . .31 C6
Burnt Edge La BL6 . . . . .22 B5
Burnthorp Ave M9 . . . . .64 B3
Burnthorpe Cl OL11 . . . . .29 E6
Burntwood Wlk **2** M9 . . . . . .157 E8
Burnvale WN3 . . . . .54 D2
Burran Rd M22 . . . . .130 D8
Burrington Dr WN7 . . . . .75 D7
Burrows Ave OL11 . . . . .109 C6
Burrows Yd WN1 . . . . .150 C8
Burrs Cl BL8 . . . . .27 C6
Burrs Ctry Pk BL8 . . . . .27 D6
Burrs Lea Cl BL8 . . . . .27 E6
Burrswood Ave BL9 . . . . .27 F6
Bursar Cl WA12 . . . . .89 D4
Burslem Ave M14 . . . . .110 A8
Burstead St M18 . . . . .99 E7
Burstock St M4 . . . . .159 B3
Burston St M18 . . . . .165 C6
Burtinshaw St **7** M18 . . . . . . .99 D5
Burton Ave Bury BL8 . . . . .26 F4
  Manchester M20 . . . . .110 B6
  Sale M33 . . . . .108 A1
Burton Cl WA3 . . . . .91 F3
Burton Dr SK12 . . . . .133 D4
Burton Gr M28 . . . . .79 C8
Burton Rd M20 . . . . .110 A6
Burton St Manchester M40 . .159 B4
  Middleton M24 . . . . .64 F8
  Oldham OL4 . . . . .67 E5
  Stockport SK4 . . . . .169 E3
Burton Wlk
  Manchester M3 . . . . .158 D2
  Stockport SK4 . . . . .169 E3
Burtonwood Ct M24 . . . . .46 F1
Burtree St M12 . . . . .165 A6
Burwell Ave PR7 . . . . .19 D8
Burwell Cl Glossop SK13 . . . .116 A8
  6 Leigh WN7 . . . . .76 A4
  Rochdale OL12 . . . . .14 D4
Burwell Gr M23 . . . . .120 F7
Bury & Bolton Rd BL8 . . . . . . .43 E7
Bury & Rochdale Old Rd
  BL9,OL10 . . . . .29 B5
Bury & Whitefield Prim Sch
  BL9 . . . . .45 B3
Bury Art Gall & Mus BL9 . . . .140 D2
Bury Ave M16 . . . . .97 C2
Bury Bsns Ctr BL9 . . . . .141 A4
Bury Catholic Prep Sch
  BL9 . . . . .44 E8
Bury CE High Sch BL9 . . . . . . .44 D8
Bury Coll OL9 . . . . .148 A5
Bury Coll (Stand Ctr) M45 . . .44 E1
Bury FC (Gigg La) BL9 . . . . . . .44 F7
Bury General Hospl BL9 . . . . . .27 F6
Bury Gram Jun Sch BL9 . . . . .140 D2
Bury Gram Sch BL9 . . . . .140 D2
Bury Intc BL9 . . . . .148 A7
Bury New Rd
  Bolton BL1,BL2 . . . . .148 A7
  Bolton BL2,BL8 . . . . .43 B7
  Bury BL9 . . . . .44 B5
  Heywood BL9,OL10 . . . . .28 E2
  Manchester M7,M8,M25 . . . .155 E5
  Prestwich M25 . . . . .63 B3
  Ramsbottom BL0 . . . . .11 D6
  Whitefield M45 . . . . .62 E7
Bury Old Rd Ainsworth BL2 . . .26 B1
  Bolton BL2 . . . . .148 A7
  Bolton BL2,BL8 . . . . .148 B7
  Edenfield BL0 . . . . .1 F1
  Heywood BL9,OL10 . . . . .28 E1
  Prestwich M25,M45,M7,M8 . .63 C4
  Ramsbottom BL9 . . . . .11 F4
Bury Pl M11 . . . . .83 C2
Bury Rd Bolton BL2 . . . . .42 D7
  Bury BL8 . . . . .27 A5
  Edenfield BL0 . . . . .1 D3
  Edgworth BL7 . . . . .9 E3
  Radcliffe BL9,M26 . . . . .44 C5
  Rawtenstall BB4 . . . . .1 A6
  Rochdale OL11 . . . . .30 B6
Bury Sch of Arts & Crafts
  BL9 . . . . .140 E2
Bury St Heywood OL10 . . . . . . .29 B2
  Manchester M3 . . . . .158 E2
  Mossley OL5 . . . . .86 C8
  Radcliffe M26 . . . . .44 D4
  Reddish SK5 . . . . .169 F3
Bury Sta M19 . . . . .140 E2
Bush Moor Wlk M13 . . . . .164 D5
Bush St M40 . . . . .157 E5
Bushell St BL3 . . . . .146 B4
Bushey Dr M23 . . . . .121 A5
Busheyfield Cl SK14 . . . . .101 D5
Bushfield Wlk **1** M23 . . . . . .120 E7
Bushgrove Wlk M9 . . . . .64 D5
Bushnay Wlk **8** M8 . . . . .156 B6
Bushton Wlk **8** M9 . . . . .64 E5
Bushton Wlk **3** M40 . . . . . . .156 C5
Busk Rd OL9 . . . . .152 C8
Busk Wlk OL9 . . . . .152 C8
Butcher La
  Altrincham M23 . . . . .120 D7
  Bury BL9 . . . . .140 F2
  Royton OL2 . . . . .48 C5
Butchers La WN4 . . . . .73 B3
Bute Ave OL8 . . . . .66 F3
Bute St Bolton BL1 . . . . .142 B1
  Glossop SK13 . . . . .104 E3
  Manchester M40 . . . . .157 F8

Bute St continued
  Manchester M40 . . . . .64 F1
  Salford M5 . . . . .154 D1
Butler Ct **11** M40 . . . . .159 C3
Butler Gn OL9 . . . . .66 A4
Butler La M4,M40 . . . . .159 C3
Butler St
  Manchester M4,M40 . . . . . . .160 D2
  Ramsbottom BL0 . . . . .138 A5
  Wigan WN1 . . . . .151 D8
Butley St Bury SK7 . . . . .124 E4
Butman St M4 . . . . .99 F6
Butt Hill Ave M25 . . . . .63 B3
Butt Hill Cl M25 . . . . .63 B3
Butt Hill Ct M25 . . . . .63 B3
Butt Hill Dr M25 . . . . .63 B3
Butt Hill Rd M25 . . . . .63 B3
Butt La OL4 . . . . .68 B4
Butter La **8** M3 . . . . .158 F1
Buttercup Ave **7** M28 . . . . . .59 F3
Buttercup Cl M46 . . . . .58 D5
Buttercup Dr Oldham OL4 . . . .49 D2
  Rochdale OL11 . . . . .30 B3
  Stockport SK3 . . . . .170 D5
Butterfield Cl SK8 . . . . .123 B1
Butterfield Rd BL5 . . . . .58 F8
Butterhouse La OL3 . . . . .51 C2
Butterley Cl SK16 . . . . .101 F7
Buttermere Ave
  Ashton-in-M WN4 . . . . .73 B5
  Heywood OL10 . . . . .46 D8
  Swinton M27 . . . . .79 F6
  8 Wythenshawe M22 . . . . .121 C2
Buttermere Cl Bolton BL3 . . . .42 F4
  Stretford M32 . . . . .96 C3
Buttermere Dr
  Altrincham WA15 . . . . .129 D6
  Middleton M24 . . . . .46 E2
  Ramsbottom BL0 . . . . .138 B7
Buttermere Gr OL2 . . . . .48 D7
Buttermere Rd
  Ashton-u-L OL7 . . . . .166 A4
  Gatley SK8 . . . . .122 B3
  Oldham OL4 . . . . .67 D8
  Partington M31 . . . . .105 E3
  Wigan WN5 . . . . .54 C7
Buttermere Terr SK15 . . . . . .86 A4
Buttermill Cl **4** M44 . . . . .94 B3
Butterstile La M25 . . . . .63 A2
Butterstile Prim Sch M25 . . . .63 A2
Butterwick Cl M12 . . . . .99 B3
Butterworth Hall OL16 . . . . . .32 A5
Butterworth La M40,OL9 . . . . .65 E2
Butterworth St
  Chadderton OL9 . . . . .152 B8
  Littleborough OL15 . . . . .16 A5
  Manchester M11 . . . . .165 A8
  Manchester M24 . . . . .65 C7
  2 Oldham OL4 . . . . .67 C7
  Radcliffe M26 . . . . .44 B4
Butterworth Way OL3 . . . . . . .69 B5
Butteryhouse La WA15 . . . . . .120 E2
Button La M23 . . . . .109 A2
Button La Jun Sch M23 . . . . .108 F2
Buttons Row M28 . . . . .2 F6
Buttress St M18 . . . . .165 C6
Butts Ave WN7 . . . . .75 E4
Butts The OL16 . . . . .139 F7
Butts Ct WN7 . . . . .76 A4
Butts La SK17 . . . . .50 D4
Butts St WN7 . . . . .76 B3
Butts The OL16 . . . . .139 F7
Buxted Rd OL1 . . . . .49 B1
Buxton Ave Ashton-u-L OL6 . .85 F6
  Manchester M20 . . . . .109 F6
Cairn Dr Rochdale OL11 . . . . .29 E6
Buxton Cres Rochdale OL16 .31 B4
  Sale M33 . . . . .108 D1
Buxton La Droylsden M43 . . . .83 E1
  Marple SK6 . . . . .125 E5
Buxton Mews SK13 . . . . .171 E2
Buxton Old Rd SK12 . . . . .135 E4
Buxton Pl OL8 . . . . .153 E5
Buxton Rd Disley SK12 . . . . . .135 E6
  High Lane SK12,SK6,SK7 . . . .134 D8
  Stockport SK2 . . . . .124 B5
  Stretford M32 . . . . .96 A3
  Whaley Br SK12 . . . . .135 B5
Buxton St Bury BL8 . . . . .27 C2
  Gatley SK8 . . . . .122 A5
  Hazel Grove SK7 . . . . .124 D3
  Heywood OL10 . . . . .29 D2
  Manchester M1 . . . . .163 B8
  Whitworth OL12 . . . . .4 D3
Buxton Terr SK14 . . . . .103 D5
Buxton Way **3** M34 . . . . .113 A8
Buxton Wlk **1** SK13 . . . . . . .171 E2
Bycroft Wlk M40 . . . . .83 D4
Bye St M34 . . . . .100 F7
Byfield Rd M22 . . . . .121 C4
Byfleet Cl WN3 . . . . .54 C1
Byland Ave Bramhall SK8 . .132 B6
  Oldham OL4 . . . . .67 D4
Byland Cl BL1 . . . . .143 E2
Byland Gdns M26 . . . . .43 E5
Byland Wlk **9** M22 . . . . .121 D1
Bylands Cl SK12 . . . . .133 D4
Bylands Fold SK16 . . . . .101 D6
Byley Rise WN6 . . . . .36 E8
Byng Ave M44 . . . . .105 D4
Byng St Farnworth BL4 . . . . . . .60 D8
  Heywood OL10 . . . . .46 D8
Byng St E **2** WA15 . . . . .145 F6
Byrchall High Sch WN4 . . . . . .73 B1
Byrcland Cl M12 . . . . .164 E8

Byre Cl M23 . . . . .109 A3
Byrness Cl M46 . . . . .58 E4
Byrom Ave M19 . . . . .99 C1
Byrom St Altrincham WA14 . .119 D3
Byrom St Bury M3 . . . . .83 F1
Byrom La WA3 . . . . .74 F2
Byrom St Alrincham WA14 . .119 D3
  9 Bury BL8 . . . . .27 B4
  Manchester M16 . . . . .97 D4
  Manchester M3 . . . . .162 E8
  Salford M5 . . . . .168 A4
Byron Ave Droylsden M43 . . . .84 A2
  26 Hindley WN2 . . . . .56 D5
  Prestwich M25 . . . . .62 F3
  Radcliffe M26 . . . . .43 E4
  Swinton M27 . . . . .79 F8
Byron Ct M7 Abram WN2 . . . . .56 B1
  3 Orrell WN5 . . . . .53 F7
  Wigan WN5 . . . . .36 E3
Byron Cres PR7 . . . . .19 F8
Byron Ct WA14 . . . . .119 D6
Byron Dr SK8 . . . . .122 F6
Byron Gr Atherton M46 . . . . . .58 D5
  Leigh WN7 . . . . .75 E7
  Reddish SK5 . . . . .99 E1
Byron Rd Denton M34 . . . . . . .112 F8
  Middleton M24 . . . . .46 F2
  Ramsbottom BL8 . . . . .10 F2
  Stretford M32 . . . . .96 F3
Byron St Eccles M30 . . . . .79 D2
  Leigh WN7 . . . . .75 F7
  Oldham OL8 . . . . .66 B2
  Royton OL2 . . . . .48 E4
Byron Street Com Prim Sch
  OL2 . . . . .48 E4
Byron Wlk Farnworth BL4 . . . .60 B6
  6 Royton OL2 . . . . .48 E4
Byron's Dr **2** WA15 . . . . .120 A6
Byrth Rd OL8 . . . . .84 F8
Bywell Wlk **15** M8 . . . . .155 F7

C

Cabin La OL4 . . . . .50 A3
Cable St Bolton BL1 . . . . .145 F8
Cabot Pl SK5 . . . . .169 F4
Cabot St M13 . . . . .163 B6
Caddington Rd M21 . . . . .109 C8
Cadishead Jun Sch M44 . . . .105 D6
Cadishead Prim Sch
  M44 . . . . .105 D5
Cadishead Way M41,M44 . . . .94 C2
Cadleigh Wlk **6** M40 . . . . .83 A7
Cadman Gr WN2 . . . . .56 D4
Cadman's Yd **8** WN5 . . . . .54 D5
Cadmium Wlk M18 . . . . .99 C4
Cadnam Dr M22 . . . . .121 F3
Cadogan Dr WN3 . . . . .54 D2
Cadogan Pl **7** M7 . . . . .63 E1
Cadogan St M14 . . . . .98 A4
Cadum Wlk M13 . . . . .163 C6
Caen Ave M45 . . . . .63 C3
Caernarvon Cl BL8 . . . . .10 F1
Caernarvon Dr SK7 . . . . .124 C1
Caernarvon Rd WN2 . . . . .57 A3
Caernarvon Way **2** M34 . . . .100 F1
Caesar St OL11 . . . . .31 A2
Cairn Dr Rochdale OL11 . . . . .29 E6
Cairn St BL6,M7 . . . . .81 C5
Cairn Wlk **15** M11 . . . . .160 F1
Cairngorm Dr BL3 . . . . .40 E5
Cairns Pl OL6 . . . . .85 D5
Cairnwell Rd OL9 . . . . .65 F8
Caister Ave M45 . . . . .63 A7
Caister Cl M41 . . . . .94 C1
Caistor Cl M16 . . . . .109 E8
Caistor St SK1 . . . . .112 B3
Caistor Wlk **8** OL1 . . . . .153 F7
Caithness Cl M23 . . . . .121 A4
Caithness Dr BL3 . . . . .40 E6
Caithness Rd OL11 . . . . .29 E5
Cakebread St M12 . . . . .163 C7
Calbourne Cres M12 . . . . .99 B3
Calcot Wlk **6** M23 . . . . .120 F6
Calcutta Rd SK3 . . . . .123 C7
Caldbeck Ave Bolton BL1 . . . . .23 F1
  Sale M33 . . . . .108 A5
Caldbeck Cl
  Ashton-in-M WN4 . . . . .73 B4
  Platt Bridge WN2 . . . . .56 B2
Caldbeck Dr Farnworth BL4 . .59 E7
  Middleton M24 . . . . .46 E2
Caldecott Rd M9 . . . . .64 C3
Calder Ave Hindley WN2 . . . . .57 C3
  Irlam M44 . . . . .93 F1
  Littleborough OL15 . . . . .16 A7
Calder Cl Bury BL9 . . . . .28 A8
  Poynton SK12 . . . . .133 D2
  Reddish SK5 . . . . .112 A4
Calder Cres M45 . . . . .45 B2
Calder Ct **1** SK13 . . . . .171 D1
Calder Dr Kearsley BL4 . . . . .61 B5
  Platt Bridge WN2 . . . . .56 A2
  Swinton M27 . . . . .61 E1
  Walkden M28 . . . . .60 C6
Calder Gr OL2 . . . . .48 D7
Calder Ho M7 . . . . .81 C5
Calder Pl WN5 . . . . .54 C7
Calder Rd BL3 . . . . .147 E3

Calder St Manchester M5 . . . .162 D8
  Rochdale OL16 . . . . .15 B2
Calder Way M45 . . . . .45 B2
Calder Wlk Middleton M24 . .46 C2
  Whitefield M45 . . . . .45 B2
Calderbank Ave M41 . . . . .94 E4
Calderbank St WN5 . . . . .54 E5
Calderbrook Dr SK8 . . . . .123 A4
Calderbrook Rd OL15 . . . . .6 C2
Calderbrook Ter OL15 . . . . . . .16 C8
Calderbrook Way M46 . . . . . . .67 B5
Calderbrook Wlk **11** M40 . . .157 D7
Calderdale Ct OL8 . . . . .48 C5
Caldershaw Ctr The OL12 . . . .14 B2
Caldershaw La OL12 . . . . .14 A2
Caldershaw Prim Sch
  OL12 . . . . .14 A1
Caldershaw Rd OL11,OL12 . .14 A1
Caldervale Ave M21 . . . . .109 C4
Calderwood Cl BL8 . . . . .27 A6
Caldon Cl M29 . . . . .58 F1
Caldwell Ave M29 . . . . .77 A8
Caldwell Cl M29 . . . . .77 B5
Caldwell St BL5 . . . . .57 F5
Caldy Dr BL0 . . . . .11 A3
Caldy Rd Handforth SK9 . . . . .131 D3
  Salford M6 . . . . .154 D4
Cale Gn SK2 . . . . .170 F6
Cale Green Prim Sch
  SK3 . . . . .170 F6
Cale La WN2 . . . . .38 B2
Cale St SK2 . . . . .170 F6
Caleb Cl M29 . . . . .58 F1
Caledon Ave M40 . . . . .83 A8
Caledonia St Bolton BL3 . . . .144 C5
  3 Radcliffe M26 . . . . .44 C4
Caledonia Way M32 . . . . .96 A5
Caledonian Dr M30 . . . . .95 E8
Caley St Bolton BL1 . . . . .23 F2
  1 Manchester M1 . . . . .163 A7
Calf Hey OL15 . . . . .15 F6
Calf Hey Cl M26 . . . . .43 D3
Calf Hey N **7** OL11 . . . . .31 A4
Calf Hey Rd OL2 . . . . .49 D8
Calf Hey S **8** OL11 . . . . .31 A4
Calf La OL3,OL5 . . . . .68 E4
Calgarth Dr M24 . . . . .46 D3
Calgary St M18 . . . . .165 C5
Calico Cl M3 . . . . .158 D3
Calico Wood Ave WN6 . . . . . . .35 F6
Callaghan Wlk OL10 . . . . .29 C1
Calland Ave SK14 . . . . .167 F3
Callander Ct WN5 . . . . .54 E8
Callander Sq OL10 . . . . .28 F1
Callander St BL0 . . . . .138 B6
Callards Rd OL16 . . . . .15 E4
Callingdon Rd M21 . . . . .109 D5
Callington Cl **4** SK14 . . . . . .102 E2
Callington Dr SK14 . . . . .102 E2
Callington Rd **8** SK14 . . . . .102 E2
Callis Rd BL3 . . . . .144 C5
Callum Wlk M13 . . . . .163 C6
Caluna Mews M20 . . . . .110 A4
Calne Wlk **6** M23 . . . . .121 A5
Calow Cl **2** SK13 . . . . .171 E2
Calow Dr WN7 . . . . .76 C3
Calow Gn **9** SK13 . . . . .171 E1
Caltha St BL0 . . . . .138 B6
Calthorpe Ave M9 . . . . .156 C7
Calton Ave M7 . . . . .81 A7
Calve Croft Rd M22 . . . . .121 F2
Calveley Wlk M9 . . . . .36 E8
Calver Ave M30 . . . . .95 C8
Calver Cl
  11 Gamesley SK13 . . . . .171 E2
  Urmston M41 . . . . .94 D3
Calver Fold **7** SK13 . . . . .171 D2
Calver Hey Cl BL5 . . . . .40 C2
Calver Mews SK13 . . . . .171 D2
Calver Pl **8** SK13 . . . . .171 D2
Calver Wlk Cheadle SK8 . . . .122 E1
  Denton M34 . . . . .113 A8
  13 Manchester M40 . . . . . .159 C3
Calverhall Way WN4 . . . . .73 A3
Calverleigh Cl BL3 . . . . .146 C4
Calverley Ave M19 . . . . .110 F7
Calverley Cl SK9 . . . . .137 C8
Calverley Way OL12 . . . . .14 E4
Calverly Rd SK8 . . . . .123 A5
Calvert Rd BL3 . . . . .146 C4
Calvert St M5 . . . . .154 D2
Calverton Dr M40 . . . . .83 C7
Calvin St BL1 . . . . .143 F1
Calvine Wlk **4** M40 . . . . .159 C3
Camarque Ct **11** M20 . . . . . .110 B6
Cambeck Cl M45 . . . . .45 B1
Cambeck Wlk M45 . . . . .45 A1
Cambell Rd M30 . . . . .79 B2
Camberley Cl SK7 . . . . .133 A7
Camberley Dr OL11 . . . . .29 F5
Cambert La
  Manchester M18 . . . . .165 C5
  Manchester M18 . . . . .99 D5
Camberwell Cres WN2 . . . . . . .37 F1
Camberwell Dr OL7 . . . . .85 A7
Camberwell St
  Manchester M3,M8 . . . . .159 A4
  Oldham OL8 . . . . .66 E4
Camberwell Way OL2 . . . . .48 D3
Cambo Wlk SK4 . . . . .110 F3
Camborne Rd SK14 . . . . .102 E3
Camborne St M14 . . . . .98 B3
Cambourne Dr Bolton BL3 . .144 A5
  Hindley WN2 . . . . .57 C2

Cambrai Cres M30 ....79 A4
Cambria Sq 8 BL3 ....144 C5
Cambria St Bolton BL3 ..144 C5
　Oldham OL4 ....67 D7
Cambrian Cres WN3 .....54 C2
Cambrian Dr Milnrow OL16 ..32 A6
　Royton OL2 ....48 C3
Cambrian Rd SK3 ......123 C8
Cambrian St M11,M40 ..160 E2
Cambridge Ave
　Manchester M16 ....97 C2
　Rochdale OL11 ....30 A6
　Wilmslow SK9 ....136 F7
Cambridge Cl
　Farnworth BL4 ....147 F1
　16 Sale M33 ....107 D3
Cambridge Dr
　Little Lever BL3 ....43 B4
　Reddish M34 ....100 A3
　Romiley SK6 ....113 C5
Cambridge Gr Eccles M30 ..79 F2
　Whitefield M45 ....63 A7
Cambridge Ind Area M7 ..158 E4
Cambridge Rd
　Altrincham WA15 .....119 E2
　Droylsden M43 ....83 F3
　Failsworth M35 ....83 F5
　Gatley SK8 ....122 B5
　Horwich BL6 ....39 F8
　Manchester M9 ....64 D1
　Orrell WN5 ....53 F8
　Reddish SK4 ....111 C5
　Manchester M41 ....95 B1
Cambridge St
　Ashton-u-L OL7 ....84 F1
　Atherton M46 ....58 C2
　Dukinfield SK16 ......166 C1
　Manchester M1,M15 ..162 F7
　Manchester M7,M8 ...158 E4
　Oldham OL9 ....66 C4
　Stalybridge SK15 ......86 A2
　Stockport SK2 ....124 A6
　Wigan WN1 ....151 D7
Cambridge Terr SK15 ....86 D4
Cambridge Way WN1 ...151 D8
Camdale Wlk 9 M8 ....155 F6
Camden Ave M40 ....83 C4
Camden Cl BL2 ....26 C1
Camden St OL5 ....68 D3
Camelia Rd M9 ....156 C7
Camellia Cl BL1 ....144 B7
Cameron Ct OL2 ....48 D6
Cameron Pl WN5 ....54 E8
Cameron St Bolton BL1 ..143 D4
　Bury BL8 ....27 C2
　Leigh WN7 ....75 D7
　Manchester M1,M15 ..162 F8
Camley Wlk 1 M8 .....156 B6
Camden St OL5 ....74 B8
Camms View BB4 ....1 A8
Camomile Wlk 5 M31 ..105 F3
Camp Rd M7 ....72 E4
Camp St Ashton-u-L OL6 ..166 B3
　Bury BL8 ....27 C3
　Manchester M3 ......162 D8
　Manchester M5,M7 ...155 D5
Campania St OL2 ....48 E2
Campanula Wlk 4 M8 ..156 A6
Campbell Cl BL8 ....26 F4
Campbell Cl BL4 ....42 C2
Campbell Rd Bolton BL3 ..146 A2
　Manchester M13 ....98 F2
　Sale M33 ....107 F3
　Swinton M27 ....79 D7
Campbell St Farnworth BL4 ..42 B1
　Reddish SK5 ....99 F1
　Rochdale OL12 ....14 E2
　Wigan WN5 ....54 D5
Campbell Way M28 ......60 D3
Campbell Wlk 6 BL4 ....42 C2
Campden Way SK9 .....131 D4
Campion Dr BB4 ....1 A8
Campion Way WN4 ......72 F4
Campion Way
　8 Denton M34 ......113 A8
　Rochdale OL12 ....14 C3
Campion Wlk M11 .....164 F8
Camponia Gdns M7 ....155 D5
Camrose Wlk M13 .....164 D5
Cams La M26 ....43 E3
Cams La M26 ....43 E2
Cams Lane Prim Sch M26 ..43 F3
Canaan WA3 ....91 C8
Canada St Bolton BL1 ..142 C2
　Horwich BL6 ....22 B3
　Manchester M40 ......160 E4
　Stockport SK2 ....124 A6
Canal Bank
　Appley Bridge WN6 ....35 C7
　Eccles M30 ....79 C3
Canal Bridge La WA3 ....83 E1
Canal Circ M30 ....80 A1
Canal Cotts WN3 ......150 B7
Canal Rd WA14 ....119 E8
Canal Row WN2 ....20 D1
Canal Side M32 ....79 C3
Canal St Adlington PR7 ..21 A6
　Droylsden M43 ....84 A1
　Dukinfield SK14 ......101 C3
　Heywood OL10 ....46 F8
　Leigh WN7 ....75 F4
　Littleborough OL15 ....16 B5
　Manchester M1 ......163 A8
　Manchester M5 ....81 C1
　Marple SK6 ....126 A6
　Oldham OL9 ....66 B3
　Rochdale OL11 ....31 A5
　Shevington WN6 ....36 F2

Canal St continued
　Stalybridge SK15 ......86 A1
　Stockport SK1 ....170 F8
　Wigan WN2 ....151 F6
Canal Terr WN1 ....151 E1
Canalside Ind Est OL16 ..31 B5
Canberra Rd Bramhall SK7 ..132 F5
　Shevington WN6 ....36 C1
Canberra St M11 ....83 C2
Candahar St BL3 ....42 A3
Candleford Pl SK2 .....124 E4
Candleford Rd M20 ....110 B6
Candlestick Pk BL9 .....28 D4
Canisp Cl OL9 ....48 A1
Canley Cl SK1 ....170 F8
Canmore Cl BL3 ....146 A3
Cann St BL3 ....26 D8
Cannel Fold M28 ....78 B7
Canning Dr BL1 ....143 E2
Canning St Bolton BL1 ..143 F2
　Bury BL9 ....140 F4
　Stockport SK4 ....169 E2
Cannock Dr SK4 ....168 A2
Cannon Cl M4 ....158 F2
Cannon Gr BL3 ....145 D5
Cannon St Atherton M46 ..58 D3
　Bolton BL3 ....145 D5
　Eccles M30 ....79 F1
　Hollingworth SK14 ...103 C5
　Manchester M4 ......158 D3
　Manchester M4 ......159 A2
　Oldham OL9 ....153 E7
　Radcliffe M26 ....43 F5
　Ramsbottom BL0 ......11 A4
Cannon St N BL3 .....145 D6
Cannon Wlk M34 .....100 E2
Canon Burrows
　CE Prim Sch OL7 .....85 A5
Canon Cl WN6 ....19 F2
Canon Dr WA14 ......119 B1
Canon Flynn Ct OL16 ..31 C7
Canon Green Ct M3 ..158 E2
Canon Green Dr M3 ..158 E2
Canon Hussey Ct M3 ..158 D1
Canon Johnson
　CE Prim Sch OL7 ....166 B4
Canon Slade Sch BL2 ..25 C4
Canon St Bury BL9 ....141 A4
　Rochdale OL16 ....15 B2
Canon Tighe Ct OL9 ..152 A7
Canon Williamson
　CE High Sch M30 ......78 F1
Canon's Cl BL1 ....142 B2
Canons Gr M40 ....157 E5
Canonsleigh Cl M8 ....155 E5
Canonsway M27 ....79 E8
Cansfield Gr WN4 ......73 A4
Cansfield High Sch WN4 ..73 A4
Canterbury WA3 ....74 D1
Canterbury
　Atherton M46 ....58 E4
　Dukinfield SK16 .....101 D6
　Rochdale OL11 ....30 A7
Canterbury Cres M24 ..47 D2
Canterbury Dr Bury BL8 ..140 D4
　Manchester M25 ....63 C2
Canterbury Gdns M30,M5 ..80 B2
Canterbury Gr BL3 ....147 D3
Canterbury Pk M20 ...109 F3
Canterbury Rd
　Altrincham WA15 ....120 C3
　Stockport SK1 ....112 B1
　Urmston M41 ....95 D3
Canterbury St OL16 ...166 C4
Canterfield Cl M43 .....84 D2
Cantley Wlk 6 M8 ....156 A6
Cantrell St M11 ....83 B2
Canute Rd M32 ....96 E3
Canute St M32 ....96 E3
Canute St 8 Bolton BL2 ..25 B3
　Radcliffe M26 ....43 E3
　Salford M6 ....81 B2
Cape St M14 ....110 C7
Capella Wlk M7 ....81 C4
Capenhurst Cl
　Poynton SK12 ....133 F4
　Sale M23 ....120 F4
Capesthorne Cl SK7 ...133 F8
Capesthorne Dr OL2 ....48 F7
Capesthorne Rd
　Altrincham WA15 ....120 D6
　Dukinfield SK16 .....101 D6
　Hazel Grove SK7 ....133 F8
　High Lane SK6 ......134 E7
　Wilmslow SK9 ....136 E5
Capesthorne Wlk M34 ..100 E2
Capital Quay M5 ......161 A2
Capital Rd M11 ....99 F7
Capitol Cl BL1 ....142 A3
Cappadocia Way BL5 ..57 D7
Capps St WN2 ....56 B3
Capricorn Way M6 ......81 C4
Capstan St M9 ....157 E8
Captain Clarke Rd SK14 ..101 C5
Captain Fold Rd M38 ..59 F6
Captain Lees Gdns BL5 ..58 A8
Captain Lees Rd BL5 ...40 A1
Captain St BL6 ....22 B4
Captain's Clough Rd BL1 ..142 B2
Captain's La WN4 ......73 C3
Car Bank Ave M46 ......58 D4
Car Bank Sq M46 ....58 D4
Car Bank St M46 ....58 D4
Car St WN2 ....56 B4
Caradoc Ave 12 M8 ...156 B6
Carawood Cl WN6 ......35 D7

Carberry Rd M18 ....99 D5
Cardale Wlk M9 ....157 D7
Carden Ave Swinton M27 ..79 D7
　Urmston M41 ....94 E2
Cardenbrook Gr 4 SK9 ..131 D2
Carder Cl M27 ....79 F7
Cardew Ave WN7 ....75 E4
Cardew Ave M22 ......121 F4
Cardiff Cl 1 OL8 ....66 B2
Cardiff St M7 ....155 E7
Cardiff Wlk 4 M34 ...100 F1
Cardigan Dr BL9 ....44 E7
Cardigan Rd OL8 ....66 B2
Cardigan St Radcliffe M26 ..43 F6
　Rochdale OL12 ....14 E3
　Royton OL2 ....48 E4
　2 Salford M6 ....154 E1
Cardigan Terr M14 ......97 F4
Cardinal Langley
　RC High Sch M24 .....47 B4
Cardinal Mews M24 .....46 D2
Cardinal St
　Manchester M8 ......156 B7
　10 Oldham OL1 ....67 A7
Carding Gr M3 ....158 E3
Cardroom Rd M4 .....159 C1
Cardus St M19 ....99 A1
Cardwell Gdns BL1 ...143 E2
Cardwell St OL8 ....66 F3
Cardwell St OL8 ....66 F3
Careless La WN2 ......151 F8
Carey Cl Manchester M7 ..158 D4
　Wigan WN3 ....54 D2
Carfax Manchester M8 ..156 A6
Carfax Fold OL12 ......14 B2
Carfax St M18 ....99 D5
Cargate Wlk 14 M8 ...155 F6
Carib St M15 ....162 F5
Carill Ave M40 ....165 A1
Carill Dr M14 ....110 D8
Carina Pl M7 ....81 C4
Cariocca Ent Pk M12 ..164 D6
Carisbrook Ave
　Prestwich M25,M45 ...63 A6
　Urmston M41 ....95 C2
Carisbrook Dr M27 .....80 A6
Carisbrook St M9 .....157 E7
Carisbrooke Ave SK7 ..124 D1
Carisbrooke Dr BL1 ...143 F3
Carisbrooke Rd WN2 ...76 D6
Carl St BL1 ....143 D2
Carlburn St M11 ....83 D2
Carleton Rd SK12 ....134 C4
Carlford Gr M25 ....64 B4
Carlford Gr M25 ....62 F3
Carlile St SK3 ....170 E8
Carlin Gate WA15 .....120 A6
Carling Dr M22 ....121 E2
Carlingford Cl SK3 ...170 E5
Carlisle Cl Little Lever BL3 ..43 A2
　Prestwich M45 ....63 B7
　Romiley SK6 ....113 A1
Carlisle Cres OL6 ....85 C7
Carlisle Dr Irlam M44 ...94 A2
　Sale WA14 ....119 E8
Carlisle PI PR6 ....21 A8
Carlisle St
　7 Alderley Edge SK9 ..137 A1
　Bolton BL7 ....25 A8
　Hindley WN2 ....56 B6
　Oldham OL9 ....152 C5
　Oldham OL9 ....66 C4
　Rochdale OL16 ....14 E3
　Swinton M27 ....61 F2
Carlisle Way Aspull WN2 ..38 D5
　8 Denton M34 ......100 F1
Carloon Dr M23 ....109 B1
Carloon Rd M23 ......109 B1
Carlow Dr M22 ....121 E2
Carlton Ave Bolton BL3 ..146 A4
　Bramhall SK7 ....132 D5
　Cheadle SK8 ....122 F3
　Handforth SK9 ......131 C2
　Manchester M14 ......98 B3
　Manchester M25 ....63 E2
　Oldham OL4 ....49 D1
　Orrell WN8 ....53 A7
　Romiley SK6 ....113 D2
　Whitefield M45 ....44 D1
Carlton Cl Ashton-in-M WN4 ..73 A5
　Blackrod BL6 ....21 D2
　Bolton BL2 ....42 E4
　Walkden M28 ....60 C1
Carlton Cres
　Stockport SK1 ....112 A2
　Urmston M41 ....95 D1
Carlton Ct
　Altrincham WA15 ....120 B1
　Manchester M25 ....63 A1
Carlton Dr Gatley SK8 ..122 A6
　Manchester M25,M8 ..156 B8
Carlton Gdns BL4 ......47 A2
Carlton Gr Hindley WN2 ..56 F4
　Manchester M14 ......98 B2
Carlton Grange M16 ....97 D3
Carlton Mans 4 M16 ...97 D3
Carlton PI Farnworth BL4 ..42 E7
　Hazel Grove SK7 ....125 A1
Carlton Range M18,M34 ..99 F4
Carlton Rd
　Altrincham WA15 ....120 B2
　Ashton-u-L OL6 ....85 D7
　Bolton BL1 ....144 A8
　Golborne WA3 ....91 A7
　Hyde SK14 ....102 A3
　Lymm WA13 ....117 B5

Carlton Rd continued
　Manchester M16 ....97 D3
　Manchester SK4 ......168 A2
　Sale M33 ....108 A6
　Salford M6 ....154 E4
　Urmston M41 ....95 D1
　Walkden M28 ....60 C1
Carlton St Bolton BL2 ..148 A6
　Bury BL9 ....44 F8
　Eccles M30 ....79 D3
　Farnworth BL4 ....42 D1
　Manchester M16 ....97 C4
　Salford M6 ....154 E4
Carlton Way Irlam M44 ..105 C5
　Oldham OL1,OL2 .....48 D2
Carlyle Cl M8 ....156 A6
Carlyle Gr WN7 ....75 C8
Carlyle St BL9 ....140 E2
Carlyn Ave M33 ......108 D4
Carmel Ave M5 ....161 C8
Carmel Cl M5 ....161 C8
Carmenna Dr SK7 ....132 F7
Carmichael Cl M31 ...105 E3
Carmichael St SK3 ...170 D8
Carmine Fold M24 .....46 F2
Carmona Dr M25 ....63 A4
Carmona Gdns M25,M7 ..63 C1
Carmoor Rd M13 .....163 C5
Carna Rd SK5 ....99 E2
Carnaby St M9 ....64 F1
Carnarvon St
　Manchester M7 ......158 F3
　Manchester M7 ......155 E7
　Oldham OL8 ....66 B2
　6 Stockport SK1 ....112 A1
Carnation Rd
　Farnworth BL4 ....42 A1
　Oldham OL4 ....67 E4
Carnegie Ave M19 .....99 B1
Carnegie Cl 1 M33 ...107 D3
Carnegie Dr WN4 ......73 A5
Carnforth Ave Hindley WN2 ..57 A5
　Middleton OL10 ....47 D7
　Oldham OL9 ....152 A6
Carnforth Dr
　Sale M33 ....108 A3
Carnforth Rd Cheadle SK8 ..123 C4
　Reddish SK4 ....111 D7
Carnforth Sq OL11 .....47 D7
Carnforth St M14 ......98 B3
Carnoustie BL3 ....146 A3
Carnoustie Cl
　Manchester M40 ....83 C7
　Wilmslow SK9 ....137 D8
Carnoustie Dr Gatley SK8 ..122 C1
　Ramsbottom BL0 ......13 B5
Carnwood Cl M40 ......83 D4
Carolina Ho M3 ......158 E3
Caroline Dr M4 ......159 C1
Caroline St
　Ashton-u-L OL6 .....166 C3
　Bolton BL3 ....147 D4
　Irlam M44 ....105 F8
　Manchester SK4 ......158 C4
　Stalybridge SK15 ......86 A1
　Stockport SK3 ....170 D7
　Wigan WN1 ....151 F8
　Wigan WN5 ....54 D2
Carpenters La M4 .....159 A2
Carpenters Wlk M43 ...83 F1
Carr Ave M25 ....62 F2
Carr Bank Ave
　Manchester M9 ....63 F3
　Ramsbottom BL0 ......11 A4
Carr Bank Dr BL0 ......11 A4
Carr Bank Rd BL0 .....11 A4
Carr Brook Dr M46 .....58 E4
Carr Brow SK6 ....135 A7
Carr Cl SK1 ....112 B1
Carr Common Rd WN2 ..57 D3
Carr Fold BL0 ....11 A4
Carr Gr OL16 ....32 A6
Carr House La WN6 ....18 F8
Carr House Rd OL4 ....67 A6
Carr La Alderley Edge SK9 ..136 D2
　Diggle OL3 ....51 C5
　Golborne WA3 ....91 A7
　Leigh WA3,WN7 ....91 E8
　Newhey OL16 ....32 C6
　Oldham OL3 ....69 B7
　Rawtenstall BB4 ....2 F7
　Wigan WN3 ....55 B3
Carr Mill Cres WN5 ....71 D4
Carr Mill Jun Sch WA11 ..71 C1
Carr Mill Mews SK9 ...131 B1
Carr Rd Altrincham WA15 ..120 B2
　Horwich BL6 ....22 B5
　Irlam M44 ....105 F8
Carr Rise SK15 ....86 F7
Carr St Ashton-u-L OL6 ..85 D5
　Hindley WN2 ....56 D6
　Leigh WN7 ....75 F3
　Ramsbottom BL0 ......11 A4
　Swinton M27 ....61 D1
Carr Wood Ave SK7 ...132 E6
Carr Wood Rd SK7 ....123 E1
Carradale Dr M33 ....107 C5
Carradale Wlk 8 M40 ..83 A6
Carradon Dr WN6 ......36 F2
Carrbrook Cl SK15 .....86 E6
Carrbrook Cres SK15 ..86 F6
Carrbrook Ind Est SK15 ..87 A6
Carrbrook Rd SK15 ....86 F7

Carrbrook Terr 6 M26 ..44 C4
Carrfield Ave
　Altrincham WA15 ....120 D6
　Stockport SK3 ....124 A4
　Walkden M38 ....59 E4
Carrfield Cl M38 ....59 E4
Carrfield Gr M38 ....59 E4
Carrgate Rd M34 .....101 B1
Carrgreen Cl M19 .....110 F5
Carrgreen La WA13 ...117 F6
Carrhill Quarry Cl OL5 ..68 C2
Carrhill Rd OL5 ....68 C2
Carrhouse La
　Hollingworth SK14 ...103 C4
　Mottram-in-L SK14 ...103 C2
Carriage Dr
　Littleborough OL15 ...16 B7
　Manchester M40 ....157 D5
Carriage Dr The SK13 ..103 F5
Carriage St M15 .....162 D5
Carriages The WA14 ..119 C4
Carrick Gdns
　Middleton M24 ....46 F4
　Wythenshawe M22 ..121 D4
Carrie St BL1 ....144 B8
Carrigart M25 ....63 B3
Carrill Gr M19 ....99 A1
Carrill Gr E M19 ....99 A1
Carrington Bsns Pk M31 ..106 C6
Carrington Cl OL16 .....15 D3
Carrington Dr BL3 ....145 F5
Carrington Field
　St SK1,SK2 ....124 A7
Carrington Gr WN7 ....75 F7
Carrington Ho M6 ......80 C7
Carrington La
　Sale M31,M33 ....107 C6
　Sale M33 ....107 C6
Carrington Rd
　Adlington PR7 ....20 F7
　Flixton M41 ....106 E8
　Manchester M14 ......98 F1
　Stockport SK1 ....112 B3
Carrington St Leigh WN7 ..75 F7
　Oldham OL9 ....66 B3
　Swinton M27 ....62 B1
Carrington Terr M27 ...62 D3
Carmel Cl OL3 ....50 F3
Carrock Wlk M24 ......46 D2
Carron Ave M9 ....64 F1
Carron Gr BL2 ....42 F7
Carrs Ave SK3,SK8 ...123 A6
Carrs Ct SK9 ....137 B7
Carrs Rd SK8 ....122 F6
Carrsfield Rd M22 ....121 E6
Carrslea Cl M26 ....43 E5
Carrsvale Ave M41 ....95 E3
Carrswood Rd M23 ...120 D8
Carruthers Cl OL10 ....29 F3
Carruthers St M4 ......160 D1
Carwood WN5 ....129 B7
Carrwood Hey BL0 .....11 A4
Carrwood Rd SK9 ....136 E4
Carsdale Rd M22 .....130 E8
Carslake Ave BL1 .....144 C8
Carslake Rd M40 .....157 D5
Carson Rd M19 ....111 A8
Carstairs Ave SK2 ....124 A4
Carstairs Cl M8 ......155 F7
Carswell Cl M29 ....59 C1
Carter Cl M34 ....100 F2
Carter St Bolton BL3 ...42 A4
　Dukinfield SK14 .....101 D5
　Farnworth BL4 ....60 E7
　Ince-in-M WN3 ......151 E6
　Manchester M7 ......155 D5
　Mossley OL5 ....68 D2
　Salford M5 ....80 C1
　Stalybridge SK15 ......86 B2
Carthage St OL8 ....67 A4
Carthorpe Arch M5 ...154 F1
Cartleach Gr M28 ......60 A2
Cartleach La M28 ......60 A2
Cartmel 6 OL12 ......139 F8
Cartmel Ave Milnrow OL16 ..31 F4
　Reddish SK4 ....111 C6
　Wigan WN1 ....37 B3
Cartmel Cl Bolton BL3 ..40 A4
　Gatley SK8 ....122 C3
　Hazel Grove SK7 ....124 C3
　Oldham OL8 ....66 D3
　Whitefield BL9 ....45 A3
Cartmel Cres Bolton BL2 ..25 C2
　Failsworth OL9 ....48 C2
Cartmel Gr M28 ....60 A4
Cartmel Wlk
　Manchester M24 ......46 F1
　Manchester M9 ....157 F7
Cartridge Cl M22 .....121 F3
Cartridge St BL10 ......29 C2
Cartwright Cl BL1 ....142 C1
Cartwright Gr WN7 ....75 D7
Cartwright Rd M21 ...109 A8
Cartwright St Denton M34 ..100 F4
　Dukinfield SK14 .....102 A5
Carver Ave M25 ....63 C5
Carver Cl M16 ....161 A6
Carver Dr SK6 ....125 E5
Carver Rd
　Altrincham WA15 ....119 E2
　Marple SK6 ....125 E5
Carver St M16 ....161 B5

Carver Wlk M15 . . . . .162 F5
Carville Rd M9 . . . . .65 B3
Carwood Gr BL6 . . . . .22 D1
Cascade Dr M7 . . . . .155 E5
Cash Gate Ct OL8 . . . . .66 D3
Cashmere Rd SK3 . . . . .123 C7
Cashmore Dr M7 . . . . .56 D4
Cashmore Wlk M12 . . . . .164 E6
Caspian Rd WA14 . . . . .119 A6
Cass Ave M5 . . . . .161 A8
Cassandra Ct M5 . . . . .161 C8
Cassidy Cl M4 . . . . .159 B2
Cassidy Ct M5 . . . . .96 E8
Cassidy Gdns M24 . . . . .46 D4
Casson Gate OL12 . . . . .14 E1
Casson St M35 . . . . .83 F7
Casterton Way M28 . . . . .78 A5
Castle Ave Denton M34 . . . . . .100 E2
  Rochdale OL11 . . . . .139 E6
Castle Cl M43 . . . . .84 B2
Castle Cres BL6 . . . . .22 C5
Castle Croft BL2 . . . . .25 E3
Castle Ct Ashton-u-L OL6 . . . . .85 B7
  Bolton BL2 . . . . .148 A7
Castle Dr PR7 . . . . .20 E6
Castle Edge Rd SK22 . . . . .127 B2
Castle Farm Dr SK2 . . . . .124 B5
Castle Farm La SK2 . . . . .124 C5
Castle Gr Leigh WN7 . . . . .76 D6
  Ramsbottom BL0 . . . . .11 A2
Castle Hall Cl SK15 . . . . .86 B1
Castle Hall Ct **1** SK15 . . . . . . .86 A1
Castle Hall View **10** SK15 . . .86 A1
Castle Hill Glossop SK13 . . . . .104 E2
  Newton-le-W WA12 . . . . .89 E4
Castle Hill Com Prim Sch
  BL2 . . . . .25 B2
Castle Hill Cres OL11 . . . . .139 E6
Castle Hill
  Mobile Home Pk SK6 . . . . . . .113 A6
Castle Hill Pk WN2 . . . . .56 F7
Castle Hill Rd Bury BL9 . . . . .28 D5
  Hindley WN2 . . . . .56 E6
  Manchester M25 . . . . .63 D2
Castle Hill Sch SK15 . . . . .112 C6
Castle Hill St Bolton BL2 . . . . . . .25 B2
  Bolton BL2 . . . . .25 B3
Castle Hill St Philip's
  CE Prim Sch WN2 . . . . .56 F6
Castle House La PR7 . . . . .20 E6
Castle Irwell
  Student Village M6,M7 . . . . . . .81 B5
Castle L Ctr BL9 . . . . .140 E2
Castle La OL5,SK15 . . . . .86 F8
Castle Mews BL4 . . . . .60 D7
Castle Mill La WA15 . . . . .129 B5
Castle Rd BL9 . . . . .45 C4
Castle Rise **4** WN2 . . . . .56 E5
Castle Shaw Rd SK2 . . . . .124 E5
Castle St Bolton BL2 . . . . .148 A7
  Bury BL9 . . . . .140 E2
  Eccles M30 . . . . .79 F2
  Farnworth BL4 . . . . .60 D7
  Hadfield SK13 . . . . .104 A4
  Hindley WN2 . . . . .56 E6
  Hyde SK14 . . . . .167 F3
  Manchester M3 . . . . .162 E8
  Middleton M24 . . . . .65 D7
  Ramsbottom BL0 . . . . .11 D2
  Stalybridge SK15 . . . . .86 A1
  Stockport SK3 . . . . .170 D7
  Stockport SK3 . . . . .170 E8
  Tyldesley M29 . . . . .58 F1
Castle Terr SK15 . . . . .86 F6
Castle Way M27 . . . . .62 A3
Castle Wlk OL6 . . . . .85 B7
Castle Yd SK1 . . . . .169 F2
Castlebrook Cl BL9 . . . . .45 B4
Castlebrook High Sch BL9 . . . . .45 C3
Castlecroft Ave BL6 . . . . .21 D2
Castlecroft Rd BL9 . . . . .140 E3
Castledene Ave M6 . . . . .154 E3
Castleford Ave M7 . . . . .155 E8
Castleford Visitor Ctr
  M3 . . . . .162 E8
Castleford Cl **1** BL1 . . . . . . .145 D8
Castleford St OL1 . . . . .48 C1
Castleford Wlk M21 . . . . .109 D7
Castlemere Dr OL2 . . . . .49 D8
Castlemere Rd M9 . . . . .64 C3
Castlemere St OL11 . . . . .139 E6
Castlemere Terr OL11 . . . . .139 F6
Castlemill St OL1 . . . . .67 B7
Castlemoor Ave M7 . . . . .81 B8
Castlerea Cl M30 . . . . .95 D8
Castlerigg Cl SK4 . . . . .111 D7
Castlerigg Dr
  Middleton M24 . . . . .46 C2
  Royton OL2 . . . . .48 C6
Castleton Ave M32 . . . . .96 B3
Castleton Bank **22** SK13 . . . .171 E1
Castleton Cres SK13 . . . . .171 E1
Castleton Ct
  16 Denton M34 . . . . .113 A8
  3 Tyldesley M29 . . . . .58 F1
Castleton Dr SK6 . . . . .134 F6
Castleton Gn **25** SK13 . . . . . .171 E1
Castleton Gr Ashton-u-L OL6 . .85 F6
  4 Gamesley SK13 . . . . .171 E1
Castleton Prim Sch OL11 . . . . . .30 D2
Castleton Rd
  Hazel Grove SK7 . . . . .124 E1
  Manchester M7 . . . . .155 E8
  11 Manchester M7 . . . . .63 E1
  Royton OL16,OL2 . . . . .48 D8

Castleton Rd S OL11 . . . . .30 D3
Castleton St
  Altrincham WA14 . . . . .119 C7
  Bolton BL2 . . . . .25 B2
  Oldham OL9 . . . . .152 C6
Castleton Sta OL11 . . . . .30 C2
Castleton Terr **2** SK13 . . . . .171 E1
Castleton Way
  14 Denton M34 . . . . .113 A8
  Wigan WN3 . . . . .54 C2
Castleton Wlk **2** M11 . . . . . .160 F1
Castleway
  Altrincham WA15 . . . . .129 C7
  Hindley WN2 . . . . .56 F5
  Hindley WN2 . . . . .57 A5
  Rochdale OL11 . . . . .30 B1
  Salford M6 . . . . .154 F2
Castlewood Gdns SK2 . . . . .124 C5
Castlewood Rd M7 . . . . .81 A8
Castlewood Sq **3** BL2 . . . . . . .25 C1
Catchdale Cl M9 . . . . .64 C5
Catches Cl OL11 . . . . .30 B8
Catches La OL11 . . . . .14 B1
Cateaton St **2** Bury BL9 . . . .140 F3
  Manchester M3,M4 . . . . .158 F2
Caterham St M4 . . . . .160 D1
Catesby Rd M16 . . . . .97 D3
Catfield Wlk M15 . . . . .162 D7
Catford Rd M23 . . . . .120 F5
Cathedral App M3 . . . . .158 F2
Cathedral Cl SK16 . . . . .101 D6
Cathedral Gates M4 . . . . .158 F2
Cathedral Rd OL9 . . . . .48 A1
Cathedral St M4 . . . . .158 F2
Catherine Ho SK4 . . . . .110 F2
Catherine Rd
  Altrincham WA14 . . . . .119 C3
  Manchester M8 . . . . .63 E1
  Romiley SK6 . . . . .112 F2
  Swinton M27 . . . . .79 C7
Catherine St Bolton BL3 . . . . . .146 B2
  Bury BL9 . . . . .44 E6
  Eccles M30 . . . . .79 E2
  Hazel Grove SK7 . . . . .167 D3
  Leigh WN7 . . . . .75 F6
  Manchester M11 . . . . .99 E7
  8 Oldham OL4 . . . . .67 F8
  Wigan WN1 . . . . .151 E8
Catherine St E **1** SK14 . . . . . .22 B4
Catherine St W BL6 . . . . .22 B5
Catherine Terr WN1 . . . . .151 E8
Catherton WA12 . . . . .89 B2
Catherston Cl **1** M16 . . . . .97 C3
Cathrine St M4 . . . . .100 D3
Cathrine St W M34 . . . . .100 D3
Catlow La **11** M4 . . . . .159 A2
Catlow St M7 . . . . .158 E4
Cato St M10 . . . . .11 A4
Caton Cl BL9 . . . . .44 E8
Caton St OL16 . . . . .139 F6
Catterall Cres BL2 . . . . .25 E6
Catterick Ave
  Manchester M20 . . . . .110 C3
  Sale M33 . . . . .107 C2
Catterick Dr BL3 . . . . .43 A3
Catterick Rd M20 . . . . .110 C3
Catterwood Dr SK6 . . . . .114 B2
Cattlin Way OL8 . . . . .66 C2
Caunce Ave
  Ashton-in-M WA12 . . . . .89 C1
  Golborne WA3 . . . . .90 A7
Caunce Rd WN1 . . . . .151 E8
Caunce St WN1 . . . . .151 E8
Causeway Head B84 . . . . .1 A8
Cavanagh Cl M13 . . . . .164 D6
Cavannah Ct OL1 . . . . .49 E3
Cavell St M1 . . . . .159 B1
Cavell Way M5 . . . . .81 A1
Cavendish Ave
  Manchester M20 . . . . .109 F6
  Swinton M27 . . . . .62 C3
Cavendish Ct
  Manchester M7 . . . . .63 D1
  Manchester M14 . . . . .110 F2
  Stretford M32 . . . . .96 E4
Cavendish Dr WN3 . . . . .54 D2
Cavendish Gdns
  Bolton BL3 . . . . .147 D3
  Manchester M20 . . . . .109 F6
Cavendish Gr M30 . . . . .79 E3
Cavendish Mews M9 . . . . .137 A6
Cavendish Mill OL6 . . . . .166 B2
Cavendish Pl
  Droylsden M11 . . . . .83 A2
  Pendlebury M27 . . . . .80 A8
Cavendish Rd
  Altrincham WA14 . . . . .119 C3
  Eccles M30 . . . . .79 E4
  Hazel Grove SK7 . . . . .133 E8
  Manchester M20 . . . . .109 F6
  Manchester M25,M7 . . . . .63 D1
  Manchester SK4 . . . . .110 F2
  Oldham OL9 . . . . .152 C6
  Stretford M32 . . . . .96 E4
  Swinton M28 . . . . .79 B6
  Urmston M41 . . . . .95 C2
Cavendish Road Prim Sch
  M20 . . . . .110 A5
Cavendish St
  Ashton-u-L OL6 . . . . .166 A2

Cavendish St continued
  Leigh WN7 . . . . .75 F7
  Manchester M15 . . . . .163 A6
  3 Oldham OL8 . . . . .153 E6
Cavendish Way OL1 . . . . .48 C2
Cavenham Gr **7** BL1 . . . . . . .144 C8
Cavenham Wlk M9 . . . . .156 C7
Caversham Dr M9 . . . . .157 E8
Cawdor Ave BL4 . . . . .42 B2
Cawdor Ct BL4 . . . . .42 C2
Cawdor Ho M30 . . . . .95 D8
Cawdor Pl **7** WA15 . . . . .120 C6
Cawdor Rd M14 . . . . .110 C8
Cawdor St Eccles M30 . . . . .79 C1
  Farnworth BL4 . . . . .42 C1
  Hindley WN2 . . . . .56 E5
  Leigh WN7 . . . . .75 F5
  Manchester M15 . . . . .162 D7
  Swinton M27 . . . . .79 D8
  Walkden M28 . . . . .60 E2
  2 Wigan WN5 . . . . .54 F6
Cawdor Wlk **6** BL4 . . . . .42 C2
Cawley Ave Culcheth WA3 . . . . .91 E4
  Prestwich M25 . . . . .62 F2
Cawley St M9 . . . . .64 A5
Cawood Sq SK5 . . . . .112 C6
Cawston Wlk **10** M8 . . . . . . .156 A6
Caxton Cl WN3 . . . . .54 F2
Caxton Rd M14 . . . . .110 B8
Caxton St Heywood OL10 . . . . . .29 D2
  Manchester M3 . . . . .158 E2
  Rochdale OL11 . . . . .30 C1
Caxton Way M5,M6 . . . . .81 B1
Caygill St M3 . . . . .158 E2
Cayley St OL16 . . . . .31 B7
Caythorpe St M14 . . . . .98 A3
Cayton St M12 . . . . .99 A3
CE Sch of the Resurrection
  M11 . . . . .160 F1
Ceal The SK6 . . . . .114 B2
Cecil Ave Sale M33 . . . . .107 F3
Cecil Ct SK3 . . . . .170 E2
Cecil Dr M41 . . . . .94 E2
Cecil Gr **10** M18 . . . . .99 D5
Cecil Rd Altrincham WA15 . . . .119 E2
  Eccles M30 . . . . .79 E1
  Manchester M9 . . . . .64 B5
  Stretford M32 . . . . .96 C1
Cecil St Ashton-u-L OL7 . . . . . .166 A1
  Ashton-u-L OL7 . . . . .84 F1
  Bolton BL2 . . . . .148 A7
  Bury BL9 . . . . .140 F1
  Ince-in-M WN3 . . . . .55 E4
  Leigh WN7 . . . . .76 A4
  Littleborough OL15 . . . . .15 F5
  Manchester M15 . . . . .163 B5
  Mossley OL5 . . . . .86 C8
  Oldham OL8 . . . . .153 E5
  Rochdale OL11 . . . . .139 F5
  Royton OL2 . . . . .48 C4
  Stalybridge SK15 . . . . .86 B1
  Wigan WN3 . . . . .151 E8
  Walkden M28 . . . . .60 F3
Cecil Walker Ho M31 . . . . .106 A3
Cecil Wlk **7** OL7 . . . . .166 A1
Cecilia St BL3 . . . . .42 A4
Cedar Ave
  Altrincham WA14 . . . . .119 C4
  Ashton-u-L OL6 . . . . .85 D5
  Atherton M46 . . . . .58 B4
  Golborne WA3 . . . . .90 F7
  Golborne WA3 . . . . .91 A7
  Hazel Grove SK7 . . . . .124 E2
  Heywood OL10 . . . . .29 C3
  Hindley WN2 . . . . .56 F3
  Horwich BL6 . . . . .22 E1
  Little Lever BL3 . . . . .43 B2
  Stalybridge SK15 . . . . .86 C3
  Standish WN6 . . . . .36 F8
  Westhoughton BL5 . . . . .62 F6
Cedar Bank Cl OL16 . . . . .31 D7
Cedar Cl Glossop SK13 . . . . . . .104 B2
  Stockport SK7 . . . . .133 E3
Cedar Cres
  Newton-le-W WA12 . . . . .89 D2
  Oldham OL9 . . . . .152 B8
  Ramsbottom BL0 . . . . .138 C7
Cedar Ct
  2 Altrincham WA15 . . . . . . .120 B5
  Culcheth WA3 . . . . .91 F1
  Manchester M14 . . . . .98 C1
Cedar Dr Droylsden M43 . . . . . . .84 C2
  Kearsley M27 . . . . .61 A8
  Manchester M41 . . . . .95 C1
  Wigan WN1 . . . . .37 D2
Cedar Gr Denton M34 . . . . .100 E3
  Downall Green WN4 . . . . .72 D5
  Farnworth BL4 . . . . .110 D8
  Manchester M14 . . . . .111 C5
  Orrell WN5 . . . . .53 F6
  Prestwich M25 . . . . .63 A6
  Royton OL2 . . . . .48 D6
  Shaw OL2 . . . . .48 F8
  Stalybridge SK16 . . . . .101 F8
  Westhoughton BL5 . . . . .57 E7
  Wigan WN7 . . . . .75 E8
Cedar Ho M14 . . . . .98 E4
Cedar La Newhey OL16 . . . . .32 A3
Cedar Lo M20 . . . . .110 A5
Cedar Lo SK7 . . . . .133 F7
Cedar Mews OL7 . . . . .85 B5
Cedar Pl M7 . . . . .81 C4
Cedar Rd Altrincham WA15 . . .119 E3
  Failsworth M35 . . . . .83 F6
  Gatley SK8 . . . . .122 A5
  Leigh WN7 . . . . .75 E8

Cedar Rd continued
  Marple SK6 . . . . .125 E4
  Middleton M24 . . . . .65 C8
  Partington M31 . . . . .105 E3
  Sale M33 . . . . .107 D6
  Stockport SK2 . . . . .124 B6
Cedar St Ashton-u-L OL6 . . . . . .85 D4
  Bury BL9 . . . . .141 A3
  Bury BL9 . . . . .141 B3
  Dukinfield SK16 . . . . .101 E5
  Newton-le-W WA12 . . . . .89 C2
  2 Oldham OL4 . . . . .67 C7
  Rochdale OL14 . . . . .14 F1
  Walsden OL14 . . . . .6 A8
Cedarfield Rd WA13 . . . . .117 B4
Cedars Rd M22 . . . . .121 D3
Cedarway BL6 . . . . .22 C5
Cedarwood Ave SK4 . . . . .168 A1
Cedric Rd Manchester M8 . . . . . .63 E2
  Oldham OL4 . . . . .67 C7
Cedric St M5 . . . . .154 E2
Celandine Cl OL6 . . . . .124 B6
Celandine Wlk WN3 . . . . .54 B4
Celia St M8 . . . . .156 C8
Cellini Sq BL1 . . . . .143 D1
Celtic St SK1 . . . . .124 A8
Cemetery La BL9 . . . . .45 E2
Cemetery Rd Bolton BL2 . . . . .148 B7
  Bolton BL3,BL4 . . . . .42 F1
  Denton M34 . . . . .100 F1
  Denton M34 . . . . .100 F6
  Droylsden M43 . . . . .83 F6
  Failsworth M35 . . . . .83 F6
  Glossop SK13 . . . . .104 C4
  Ince-in-M WN3 . . . . .151 E5
  Mossley OL5 . . . . .86 E8
  Radcliffe M26 . . . . .43 F4
  Ramsbottom BL0 . . . . .14 A4
  Royton OL2 . . . . .48 C5
  Salford M5 . . . . .154 E1
Cemetery Rd N M27 . . . . .61 E2
Cemetery Rd S M27 . . . . .61 E1
Cemetery St Middleton M24 . . .47 A1
  2 Westhoughton BL5 . . . . . . .39 E1
Cemetery View PR7 . . . . .21 A6
Cennick Cl **5** OL4 . . . . .67 C6
Centaur Cl M27 . . . . .61 F2
Centaur Way **8** M8 . . . . .155 F7
Centenary Circ M5 . . . . .80 B1
Centenary Ct BL3 . . . . .144 C8
Centenary Way M17 . . . . .96 B8
  Eccles M5 . . . . .80 A1
Central Ave Atherton M46 . . . . .58 E4
  Bury BL9 . . . . .45 B3
  Eccles M41 . . . . .95 E6
  Edenfield BL0 . . . . .1 D2
  Farnworth BL4 . . . . .60 B8
  Leigh WN7 . . . . .76 C3
  Littleborough OL15 . . . . .16 B6
  Manchester M19 . . . . .99 A1
  Manchester OL3 . . . . .69 B5
  Pendlebury M6 . . . . .80 C6
  Sale M33 . . . . .107 D1
  Salford M5 . . . . .154 E1
Central CE Prim Sch M29 . . . . .59 A1
Central Dr Bury BL9 . . . . .27 F8
  Gatley SK8 . . . . .131 D8
  Manchester M8 . . . . .64 A2
  Pendlebury M27 . . . . .80 B7
  Reddish SK5 . . . . .111 F5
  Romiley SK6 . . . . .113 C3
  Stockport SK7 . . . . .124 B2
  Urmston M41 . . . . .95 E2
  Westhoughton BL5 . . . . .39 F1
Central Flats WN7 . . . . .151 F7
Central Ho **17** M9 . . . . .64 E5
Central Park Est M17 . . . . .96 B6
Central Park Way WN1 . . . . .37 D1
Central Prim Sch
  Denton M34 . . . . .100 E3
  Leigh WN7 . . . . .75 F5
Central Rd
  Manchester M20 . . . . .110 A5
  Partington M31 . . . . .105 F3
Central Ret Pk M4 . . . . .159 C1
Central St Bolton BL1 . . . . .145 E7
  Manchester M2 . . . . .158 F1
  Ramsbottom BL0 . . . . .138 C6
Central Store **8** SK13 . . . . . .104 C1
Central Way
  Altrincham WA14 . . . . .119 D4
  Newton-le-W WA12 . . . . .89 E2
Centre Ct WN7 . . . . .75 B3
Centre Gdns BL1 . . . . .143 D1
Centre Park Rd BL1 . . . . .143 D1
Centre The WN7 . . . . .76 B6
Centre Vale Cl OL15 . . . . .16 C7
Centre Vale OL15 . . . . .16 C7
Centrepoint M17 . . . . .96 B5
Centurion Gr M7 . . . . .155 E6
Century Lo BL4 . . . . .60 C8
Century Park Ind Area
  WA14 . . . . .119 A6
Cestrian St BL3 . . . . .147 F3
Ceylon St Failsworth M40 . . . . . .83 A6
  Oldham OL4 . . . . .67 D5
Chadderton Dr BL9 . . . . .45 A2
Chadderton Hall
  Com Prim Sch OL9 . . . . .48 A2
Chadderton Hall Rd
  OL1,OL9 .47 F2
Chadderton Ind Est M24 . . . . . . .65 C5
Chadderton Park Rd OL9 . . . . . .47 F1
Chadderton Prec OL9 . . . . .47 F3
Chadderton St M4 . . . . .159 B2

Chadderton Way
  Oldham OL1,OL9 . . . . .153 D8
  Oldham OL1,OL9 . . . . .48 C1
Chaddesley Wlk M11 . . . . .165 A8
Chaddock La
  Boothstown M28 . . . . .77 F6
  Manchester M28,M29 . . . . .77 D6
Chaddock Level The M28 . . . . . .78 A5
Chadkirk SK6 . . . . .125 B8
Chadkirk Chap SK6 . . . . .113 C1
Chadkirk Rd SK6 . . . . .113 B1
Chadkirk St SK6 . . . . .122 C5
Chadwell Rd SK2 . . . . .124 E7
Chadwick Cl
  Handforth SK9 . . . . .131 C1
  12 Manchester M14 . . . . .98 B3
  Milnrow OL16 . . . . .32 A5
Chadwick Fold Bury BL9 . . . . . . .27 F7
  Heywood OL10 . . . . .29 F2
Chadwick Foundary
  Ind Est **9** BL1 . . . . .145 E8
Chadwick Hall Rd OL11 . . . . .30 B6
Chadwick La
  Rochdale OL10,OL11 . . . . .30 A2
  Rochdale OL16 . . . . .31 C2
Chadwick Rd Eccles M30 . . . . . .79 E2
  Urmston M41 . . . . .95 F2
Chadwick St Ashton-u-L OL6 . .85 E2
  Bolton BL2 . . . . .148 B6
  Bury BL9 . . . . .28 E4
  Glossop SK13 . . . . .116 B8
  2 Hindley WN2 . . . . .56 F6
  Leigh WN7 . . . . .75 F6
  Little Lever BL3 . . . . .43 B3
  Marple SK6 . . . . .125 F5
  Milnrow OL16 . . . . .31 D7
  Rochdale OL11 . . . . .139 D7
  Stockport SK1 . . . . .170 F8
  Swinton M27 . . . . .79 F8
  Wigan WN3 . . . . .150 B6
Chadwick Terr OL12 . . . . .14 D4
Chaffinch Cl Droylsden M43 . . .84 C3
  Oldham OL4 . . . . .67 D4
  Wythenshawe M22 . . . . .121 F5
Chaffinch Dr BL2 . . . . .141 C4
Chaffinch Gr SK15 . . . . .86 E7
Chain Bar La SK14 . . . . .102 F2
Chain Bar Way SK14 . . . . .102 F2
Chain Rd M9 . . . . .64 D5
Chain St M1 . . . . .159 A1
Chain Wlk **18** M9 . . . . .64 E5
Chainhurst Wlk **2** M13 . . . .163 C6
Chalbury Cl WN2 . . . . .56 D4
Chalcombe Grange **1**
  M12 . . . . .98 F4
Chale Cl M40 . . . . .160 D3
Chale Dr M24 . . . . .65 C6
Chale Gn BL2 . . . . .25 E3
Chalfont Ave **1** M41 . . . . .95 E2
Chalfont Cty Prim Sch
  BL1 . . . . .143 F2
Chalfont Dr
  Manchester M8 . . . . .156 A7
  Tyldesley M29 . . . . .77 A8
  Walkden M28 . . . . .78 E8
Chalfont Ho **2** M6 . . . . .154 F2
Chalfont St BL1 . . . . .143 F2
Chalford Rd M23 . . . . .121 A4
Challenge Way M45 . . . . .63 C8
Challenor Sq M12 . . . . .165 A6
Challum Dr OL9 . . . . .152 A8
Chamber Hall Cl OL8 . . . . .66 D4
Chamber House
  Dr OL11 .30 B3
Chamber House Farm
  OL11 . . . . .30 A3
Chamber Rd Oldham OL8 . . . . . .66 D4
  Shaw OL2 . . . . .149 A7
Chamberhall St BL9 . . . . .140 E3
Chamberlain Ho M22 . . . . .121 E4
Chamberlain Rd SK15 . . . . .86 C5
Chamberlain St BL3 . . . . .145 D6
Chambers Ct SK14 . . . . .103 A3
Chambers Field Ct
  8 Salford M5 . . . . .161 A8
  Salford M5 . . . . .81 A1
Champagnole Ct **26** SK16 . .166 B1
Champneys Wlk M9 . . . . .157 D6
Chancel Ave M5 . . . . .161 C8
Chancel Cl SK16 . . . . .101 C6
Chancel La SK9 . . . . .137 B8
Chancel Pl
  1 Manchester M1 . . . . .159 C1
  Rochdale OL16 . . . . .139 F7
Chancellor La M12 . . . . .164 D7
Chancery Cl M29 . . . . .77 B8
Chancery La Bolton BL1 . . . . . .145 F7
  16 Manchester M3 . . . . .158 F1
  Shaw OL2 . . . . .149 C7
Chancery Pl **11** M2 . . . . .158 F1
Chancery St Oldham OL4 . . . . . .67 A6
  Oldham OL9 . . . . .152 C8
Chancery Wlk **3** OL9 . . . . . .152 C8
Chandley Way WA3 . . . . .90 E8
Chandlers Row M28 . . . . .79 A5
Chandley Ct SK1 . . . . .124 B7
Chandley St SK1 . . . . .122 D6
Chandos Gr M5 . . . . .154 D2
Chandos Rd
  Manchester M21 . . . . .97 C1
  Manchester M25 . . . . .63 B2
  Manchester SK4 . . . . .111 C6
Chandos Rd S M21 . . . . .109 C2
Chandos St OL2 . . . . .149 C7
Change Way M3 . . . . .158 E3
Channing Ct **6** OL16 . . . . .31 B6
Channing Sq **4** OL16 . . . . . . .31 B6

Channing St OL16 . . . . 31 B6
Chanters Ave M46 . . . . 58 E3
Chanters The M28 . . . . 78 C7
Chantlers Ave BL8 . . . . 27 A1
Chantlers Prim Sch BL8 . . . 27 A2
Chantry Cl Disley SK12 . . . 135 E5
Reddish SK5 . . . . 111 E7
Westhoughton BL5 . . . . 57 F5
Chantry Fold SK12 . . . . . . 135 E6
Chantry Rd SK12 . . . . 135 E6
Chantry Wlk
Ashton-in-M WN4 . . . . 72 F5
Manchester M8 . . . . 155 F7
Chapel Alley 2 BL1 . . . . . 145 F7
Chapel Brow
Charlesworth SK13 . . . . . . 115 E6
Tintwistle SK13 . . . . 104 A7
Chapel Cl Dukinfield SK16 . 101 D8
Ince-in-M WN3 . . . . 151 D6
Whitefield BL9 . . . . 45 B4
Chapel Croft OL2 . . . . 48 D4
Chapel Ct
Altrincham WA14 . . . . 119 D4
Hyde SK14 . . . . 101 C1
5 Mossley OL5 . . . . 68 C1
Sale M33 . . . . 107 E6
Wilmslow SK9 . . . . 137 A6
Chapel Field Rd M34 . . . . 100 F3
Chapel Fields BL7 . . . . 9 C4
1 Marple SK6 . . . . 125 F5
Chapel Fields La WN2 . . . . 56 E5
Chapel Gate OL16 . . . . 31 F6
Chapel Gdns M34 . . . . . . 100 F6
Chapel Gn M34 . . . . 100 F3
Chapel Gr M27 . . . . 62 E7
Chapel Grange BL7 . . . . . . 9 C4
Chapel Green Rd WN2 . . . . 56 E5
Chapel Hill OL15 . . . . 16 B5
Chapel Hos SK6 . . . . 126 A5
Chapel La
Altrincham WA15 . . . . 129 C7
Coppull PR7 . . . . 19 F8
Hadfield SK13 . . . . 103 F5
Hollinfare WA3 . . . . 105 A2
Manchester M9 . . . . 64 C3
Partington M31 . . . . 105 F2
Ramsbottom BL8 . . . . 138 A6
Rochdale OL11 . . . . 29 C8
Royton OL2 . . . . 48 D4
Sale M33 . . . . 107 E6
Wigan WN3 . . . . 150 C7
Wilmslow SK9 . . . . 137 A6
Chapel Mdw M28 . . . . 78 B7
Chapel Pl Ashton-in-M WN4 . 73 B3
Bolton BL2,BL3 . . . . 148 C5
Eccles M41 . . . . 95 D8
Chapel Rd
Alderley Edge SK9 . . . . . . 137 A1
Irlam M44 . . . . 94 A2
Manchester M25 . . . . 63 A1
Oldham OL3 . . . . 69 A6
Oldham OL8 . . . . 66 C2
Sale M33 . . . . 108 B5
Swinton M27 . . . . 79 C7
Wythenshawe M22 . . . . . . 121 D8
Chapel St Adlington PM7 . 20 F6
6 Alderley Edge SK9 . . . . 137 A1
Ashton-in-M WN4 . . . . 73 B3
Ashton-u-L OL6 . . . . 166 C3
Aspull WN2 . . . . 38 A2
Atherton M46 . . . . 58 D3
14 Bacup OL13 . . . . 3 C8
Blackrod BL6 . . . . 21 D2
Bolton BL1 . . . . 145 F8
Bolton BL7 . . . . 8 D3
Boothstown M28 . . . . 77 F6
Bury BL8 . . . . 26 F7
Bury BL9 . . . . 140 F2
Cheadle SK8 . . . . 122 D5
Denton M34 . . . . 100 F6
Droylsden M43 . . . . 84 B1
Dukinfield SK16 . . . . 101 B8
3 Eccles M30 . . . . 79 C1
Farnworth BL4 . . . . 60 E8
Glossop SK13 . . . . 104 C1
Hazel Grove SK7 . . . . 124 E3
Heywood OL10 . . . . 29 D2
Hindley WN2 . . . . 56 D5
Horwich BL6 . . . . 22 C3
Hyde SK14 . . . . 167 D2
Ince-in-M WN3 . . . . 151 D6
Kearsley M26 . . . . 61 B8
Leigh WN2 . . . . 56 E1
Leigh WN7 . . . . 76 B4
Little Lever BL3 . . . . 43 B3
Littleborough OL12 . . . . . . 15 C7
Littleborough OL15 . . . . 6 D2
Manchester M19 . . . . 99 B1
Manchester M13 . . . . 158 E2
Manchester SK4 . . . . 110 D2
7 Middleton M24 . . . . 46 F1
4 Mossley OL5 . . . . 68 C1
Newton-le-W WA12 . . . . . . 89 B3
Oldham OL3 . . . . 69 B8
Oldham OL4 . . . . 67 E6
Platt Bridge WN2 . . . . 56 B2
Prestwich M25 . . . . 63 A4
16 Rochdale OL11 . . . . . . 31 A4
Romiley SK6 . . . . 113 B5
Rowarth SK22 . . . . 127 E7
Royton OL2 . . . . 48 D4
Shaw OL2 . . . . 149 B7
Stalybridge SK15 . . . . 86 A2
Swinton M27 . . . . 62 A1
Tyldesley M29 . . . . 77 A8

Chapel St continued
Whitworth OL12 . . . . 14 C8
Wigan WN3 . . . . 150 C7
Wigan WN5 . . . . 54 B5
Wigan WN6 . . . . 54 B5
Chapel Street Prim Sch
M19 . . . . 99 B1
Chapel Terr WA3 . . . . 91 B8
Chapel View SK16 . . . . . . 101 C8
Chapel Way PR7 . . . . 19 F8
Chapel Wlk 1 Eccles M30 . 79 F2
Golborne WN7 . . . . 75 B1
Hadfield SK13 . . . . 103 F5
Manchester M25 . . . . 62 F1
Middleton M24 . . . . 64 C7
Whitefield M45 . . . . 45 B1
Chapel Wlks Bramhall SK8 . 132 B6
Manchester M22 . . . . 158 F1
Sale M33 . . . . 108 B5
Chapelfield M26 . . . . 44 C1
Chapelfield Cl SK15 . . . . . 86 D4
Chapelfield Dr M28 . . . . . . 60 B3
Chapelfield Prim Sch M26 . 44 C1
Chapelfield Rd M12 . . . . . 163 C8
Chapelfield St BL1 . . . . . 143 E3
Chapelhill Dr M9 . . . . 64 C3
Chapels The SK8 . . . . 57 F5
Chapeltown Rd
Edgworth BL7 . . . . 9 C2
Radcliffe M26 . . . . 62 A8
Chapeltown St M1 . . . . . . 159 C1
Chapelway Gdns OL2 . . . . 48 D6
Chaplin Cl M6 . . . . 154 E4
Chapman Cl SK14 . . . . . . 102 D2
Chapman Mews M18 . . . . . 99 D5
Chapman Rd SK14 . . . . . . 102 E1
Chapman St Bolton BL1 . . 142 B1
Manchester M18 . . . . 99 D5
Chappell Rd M43 . . . . 84 A2
Chapter St M40 . . . . 160 F4
Charcoal Rd WA14 . . . . . . 118 F3
Charcoal Woods WA14 . . . 119 A3
Charcon Wlk 8 OL2 . . . . . 48 E4
Chard Dr M22 . . . . 121 D1
Chard St M20 . . . . 44 A3
Chardin Ave SK6 . . . . 126 C8
Charges St OL7 . . . . 84 F1
Chariot St M11 . . . . 99 D8
Charity St WN7 . . . . 75 C5
Charlbury Ave
Manchester M25 . . . . 63 E3
Reddish SK5 . . . . 111 F6
Charlbury Way OL2 . . . . . 149 A5
Charlecote Rd SK12 . . . . . 133 F4
Charles Ave
Droylsden M34 . . . . 100 A7
Marple SK6 . . . . 125 C7
Charles Barry Cres M15 . 162 E6
Charles Ct WA15 . . . . 120 B6
Charles Halle Rd M15 . . . 163 A5
Charles Holden St BL1 . . . 145 D6
Charles La Glossop SK13 . 104 E3
Milnrow OL16 . . . . 32 A5
Charles Mews OL16 . . . . . . 32 A5
Charles Morris Cl M35 . . . 84 B8
Charles Morris Ho M35 . . . 84 A7
Charles Shaw Cl 4 OL4 . . . 49 D1
Charles St Ashton-u-L OL7 . 166 B2
2 Bolton BL1 . . . . 148 A8
Bolton BL7 . . . . 8 D2
3 Bury BL9 . . . . 140 F3
Denton M34 . . . . 100 F5
Droylsden M43 . . . . 83 E1
Dukinfield SK16 . . . . 101 B8
3 Farnworth BL4 . . . . 42 E1
Farnworth BL4 . . . . 60 E7
Glossop SK13 . . . . 104 C1
Golborne WA3 . . . . 74 A1
Hazel Grove SK7 . . . . 124 D3
Heywood OL10 . . . . 46 D8
Hindley WN2 . . . . 56 E7
Ince-in-M WN2 . . . . 56 A7
Irlam M44 . . . . 105 E6
Leigh WN7 . . . . 76 A5
Leigh WN7 . . . . 76 B4
Littleborough OL15 . . . . . . 16 A5
Manchester M1 . . . . 163 A8
Manchester OL9 . . . . 152 C6
Royton OL2 . . . . 48 D4
Salford M6 . . . . 154 E4
Stockport SK1 . . . . 124 A7
Swinton M27 . . . . 61 D2
Tyldesley M29 . . . . 58 F1
Whitefield M45 . . . . 44 F1
2 Wigan WN1 . . . . 37 C1
Charles Whittaker St 2
OL12 . . . . 13 F1
Charles Wlk M45 . . . . 62 F7
Charleston Cl M33 . . . . . . 107 D2
Charleston Ct M29 . . . . . . 76 F8
Charleston Prim Sch M6 . . 81 B4
Charleston Sq M41 . . . . . . 95 B3
Charleston St OL8 . . . . 66 F4
Charlestown SK13 . . . . . . 116 C7
Charlestown Cl OL6 . . . . . 166 B3
Charlestown Ct OL6 . . . . . 166 B3
Charlestown Ind Est OL6 . 166 B4
Charlestown Prim Sch
M9 . . . . 65 B3
Charlestown Rd
Glossop SK13 . . . . 116 C7
Manchester M9 . . . . 64 E2
Charlestown Rd E SK2 . . . 124 A3
Charlestown Rd W SK3 . . 123 F3
Charlesworth Ave
Bolton BL3 . . . . 42 B3
Denton M34 . . . . 112 F8
Hindley WN2 . . . . 56 F4

Charlesworth Sch
Charlesworth SK13 . . . . . 115 C6
Charlesworth SK13 . . . . . 115 D6
Charlesworth St
Manchester M11 . . . . 164 F8
Stockport SK1,SK3 . . . . . 170 F7
Charley Ave M7 . . . . 158 D4
Charlock Ave BL5 . . . . 57 E6
Charlock Cl M7 . . . . 75 F3
Charlock Sq WA14 . . . . . . 119 B8
Charlock Wlk 6 M31 . . . . 105 F3
Charlotte La OL4 . . . . 68 E5
Charlotte St 5 Bolton BL1 . 143 E2
Cheadle SK8 . . . . 122 D5
Edgworth BL7 . . . . 9 C4
Manchester M1,M2 . . . . . 159 A1
Ramsbottom BL0 . . . . . . 138 B5
Rochdale OL16 . . . . 31 B3
Stockport SK1 . . . . 112 B3
Charlton Ave Eccles M30 . . 79 D1
Prestwich M25 . . . . 63 A4
Charlton Brook Ho SK8 . . 122 E6
Charlton Cl 2 M16 . . . . . . 97 C3
Charlton Dr Sale M33 . . . 108 C4
Swinton M27 . . . . 61 D2
Charlton Pl M12 . . . . 163 B7
Charlton Rd M19 . . . . 99 B1
Charlton Sh Ctr M21 . . . . . 97 B1
Charminster Dr M8 . . . . . 156 B8
Charmouth Wlk M22 . . . . 121 F3
Charnley Cl M40 . . . . 160 E3
Charnley St M45 . . . . 62 F8
Charnock Dr BL1 . . . . 143 E1
Charnock Rd WA3 . . . . 91 F3
Charnock St M28 . . . . 56 B1
Charnock's Yd 2 WN5 . . . . 54 B5
Charnville Rd SK8 . . . . . . 121 F5
Charnwood Ave M34 . . . . 100 B3
Charnwood Cl
Ashton-u-L OL6 . . . . 85 C7
Shaw OL2 . . . . 48 E8
Tyldesley M29 . . . . 77 B8
Walkden M28 . . . . 60 C2
Charnwood Cres SK7 . . . 133 D8
Charnwood Rd
Manchester M9 . . . . 64 D5
Romiley SK6 . . . . 113 C5
Charter M30 . . . . 79 F1
Charter Ave M26 . . . . 44 C2
Charter Cl 5 M33 . . . . . . 107 D3
Charter Ho M30 . . . . 79 F1
Charter Rd WA15 . . . . . . 119 E4
Charter St Manchester M3 . 158 F3
Oldham OL1 . . . . 67 A8
Rochdale OL16 . . . . 31 B4
Charterhouse Rd WN3 . . . 151 E6
Chartist Ho OL6 . . . . 166 B2
Chartwell Cl M5,M6 . . . . . 154 F2
Chartwell Dr M23 . . . . . . 120 E7
Chase St M4 . . . . 159 A4
Chase The M28 . . . . 79 A5
Chasefield WA14 . . . . 119 A2
Chaseley Rd
Rochdale OL12 . . . . 139 E8
Salford M6 . . . . 154 E4
Chasetown Cl 5 M23 . . . . 120 D6
Chassen Ave M41 . . . . 95 B2
Chassen Road Sta BL3 . . . 95 B1
Chassen Road Sta M41 . . . 95 B1
Chataway Rd M8 . . . . 156 C8
Chatburn Ave
Bolton BL3 . . . . 74 C1
Middleton OL11 . . . . 47 D8
Chatburn Ct Culcheth WA3 . 91 F2
Shaw OL2 . . . . 149 C8
Chatburn Gdns OL10 . . . . 28 F2
Chatburn Rd Bolton BL3 . . 23 F3
Manchester M21 . . . . 109 B8
Chatburn Sq OL11 . . . . . . 47 D8
Chatcombe Rd M22 . . . . . 121 A2
Chatfield Rd M21 . . . . . . 109 B8
Chatford Cl M7 . . . . 158 E4
Chatham Ct M20 . . . . 110 A6
Chatham Gdns BL3 . . . . . 145 D5
Chatham Gr M20 . . . . 110 A6
Chatham Ho 1 SK3 . . . . . 170 E8
Chatham Pl 2 BL3 . . . . . . 145 D5
Chatham Rd
Manchester M16 . . . . 97 C3
Reddish M18 . . . . 99 E3
Chatham St Hyde SK14 . . 113 E7
Ince-in-M WN2 . . . . 56 A8
Leigh WN7 . . . . 75 F7
Manchester M1 . . . . 159 B1
Stockport SK3 . . . . 170 D8
Wigan WN1 . . . . 151 E7
Chatley Rd M30 . . . . 78 F1
Chatley St M3,M4 . . . . . . 159 A4
Chatswood Ave SK2 . . . . 170 F6
Chatsworth Ave
Culcheth WA3 . . . . 91 F4
Ince-in-M WN3 . . . . 55 F4
Prestwich M25 . . . . 63 B4
Chatsworth Cl
Altrincham WA15 . . . . . . 120 C5
Ashton-in-M WN4 . . . . 72 F4
Droylsden M43 . . . . 83 E3
Shaw OL2 . . . . 49 D8
2 Urmston M41 . . . . 95 A5
Chatsworth Cres M32 . . . . 95 F3
Chatsworth Ct
Adlington PR6 . . . . 20 F8
Stockport SK2 . . . . 124 A6
Chatsworth Dr Leigh WN7 . 76 D7
Leigh WN7 . . . . 76 E7

Chatsworth Gr
Little Lever BL3 . . . . 43 A4
Manchester M16 . . . . 97 D2
Chatsworth Rd
Droylsden M43 . . . . 83 E2
Eccles M30 . . . . 79 F4
Hazel Grove SK7 . . . . 133 F8
High Lane SK6 . . . . 134 F6
Manchester M18 . . . . 165 C5
Radcliffe M26 . . . . 43 D5
Stretford M32 . . . . 96 A3
Swinton M28 . . . . 79 C5
Wilmslow SK9 . . . . 136 E4
Chatsworth St Oldham OL4 . 67 C5
Rochdale OL12 . . . . 14 E3
Wigan WN5 . . . . 54 C5
Chatteris Cl WN2 . . . . 56 E4
Chatterton BL0 . . . . 1 C2
Chatterton Cl M20 . . . . . . 110 C6
Chatterton La SK6 . . . . . . 127 B8
Chatterton Old La BL7 . . . . 1 C2
Chatterton Rd BL0 . . . . 1 C1
Chattock Cl M16 . . . . 97 E3
Chatton Cl BL8 . . . . 26 F2
Chatwell Cl OL16 . . . . 32 C4
Chatwood Rd M40 . . . . 65 D2
Chaucer Ave Denton M34 . 113 A7
Droylsden M43 . . . . 84 A1
Radcliffe M26 . . . . 43 E4
Reddish SK5 . . . . 99 D1
Chaucer Gr Atherton M46 . . 58 D5
Leigh WN7 . . . . 75 D8
Chaucer Mews SK1 . . . . . 112 B1
Chaucer Pl Abram WN2 . . . 56 B1
Wigan WN1 . . . . 37 C3
Chaucer Rd M24 . . . . 47 B2
Chaucer Rise SK16 . . . . . 102 A7
Chaucer St Bolton BL1 . . . 143 D2
Oldham OL1 . . . . 153 E6
Rochdale OL12 . . . . 30 C2
Royton OL2 . . . . 48 E5
Chaucer Wlk M13 . . . . . . 163 C6
Chaumont Way OL6 . . . . . 166 B3
Chauncy Rd M40 . . . . 83 E8
Chaytor Ave M40 . . . . 83 B7
Cheadle Ave M7 . . . . 81 A7
Cheadle Coll SK8 . . . . . . 132 B7
Cheadle Heath Jun
& Inf Sch SK3 . . . . 123 A7
Cheadle Hulme Sch SK8 . 132 A8
Cheadle Hulme Sta SK8 . 123 B2
Cheadle Old Rd SK3 . . . . 123 C7
Cheadle Prim Sch SK8 . . 122 C6
Cheadle RC Inf Sch SK8 . 122 C2
Cheadle RC Jun Sch SK8 . 122 C2
Cheadle Rd SK8 . . . . 122 F3
Cheadle Royal Hospl
SK8 . . . . 122 C2
Cheadle Sq BL1 . . . . 145 E7
Cheadle St M11 . . . . 99 D8
Cheadle Wood SK8 . . . . . 131 E8
Cheam Rd WA15 . . . . 119 F8
Cheap Side M24 . . . . 47 A2
Cheapside Hyde SK14 . . . 167 E3
Manchester M2 . . . . 158 F1
Oldham OL1 . . . . 153 E7
Cheapside Sq 8 BL1 . . . . 145 F7
Cheddar St 1 M18 . . . . . . 99 D5
Chedlee Dr SK8 . . . . 131 E8
Chedlin Dr M23 . . . . 121 A4
Chedworth Cres M38 . . . . 60 A6
Chedworth Dr M23 . . . . . 121 B6
Cheeryble St M11,M43 . . . 99 F7
Cheesden Wlk M45 . . . . . . 45 C1
Cheetham Ave M4 . . . . 47 B1
Cheetham CE Com
Sch M8 . . . . 155 F7
Cheetham Fold Rd SK14 . 113 D8
Cheetham Gdns 4 SK15 . . 86 B1
Cheetham Gr 1 WN3 . . . . . 54 F5
Cheetham Hill Shaw OL2 . 149 B6
Whitworth OL12 . . . . 4 D3
Cheetham Hill Rd
Dukinfield SK15,SK16 . . . 101 E7
Manchester M4 . . . . 159 A3
Manchester M8 . . . . 156 A6
Manchester M8 . . . . 155 F8
Cheetham Par M8 . . . . . . 156 B6
Cheetham Pl SK6 . . . . . . 112 F4
Cheetham Rd M27 . . . . 80 A7
Cheetham St
Failsworth M35 . . . . 84 A8
Manchester M40 . . . . 157 E5
Middleton M24 . . . . 64 F8
Oldham OL1 . . . . 67 B7
Radcliffe M26 . . . . 44 C4
Rochdale OL16 . . . . 139 F8
Shaw OL2 . . . . 149 C6
Cheetham's Cres OL2 . . . . 49 A4
Cheethams The BL6 . . . . . 38 E7
Cheetwood Rd M8 . . . . . . 155 F5
Cheetwood St M8 . . . . . . 158 E4
Chelbourne Dr 3 OL8 . . . . 66 B2
Chelburn Cl Leigh WN7 . . . 56 E1
Stockport SK2 . . . . 124 D5
Chelburn View OL15 . . . . . . 6 C1
Cheldon Wlk 8 M40 . . . . . 83 C6
Chelford Ave Bolton BL1 . . 24 E5
Golborne WA3 . . . . 90 D8
Chelford Cl
Altrincham WA15 . . . . . . 119 E6
Manchester M13 . . . . 164 D5
Wigan WN3 . . . . 54 F2
Chelford Ct 4 SK9 . . . . . 131 E5
Chelford Dr Swinton M27 . . 61 E2
Tyldesley M29 . . . . 77 C6

Chelford Gr SK3 . . . . 170 D5
Chelford Rd
Alderley Edge SK9 . . . . . . 136 E1
Handforth SK9 . . . . 131 D5
Manchester M16 . . . . 97 C3
Sale M33 . . . . 108 E2
Chell St M13 . . . . 98 F4
Chellow Ct OL5 . . . . 68 B1
Chellow Dene OL5 . . . . 68 B1
Chelmarsh Ave WN4 . . . . . 73 C3
Chelmer Cl BL5 . . . . 40 A1
Chelmer Gr OL10 . . . . 29 A3
Chelmorton Gr WN3 . . . . . 54 C2
Chelmsford Ave M40 . . . . . 83 A4
Chelmsford Dr WN3 . . . . . . 55 A4
Chelmsford Mews WN1 . . . 37 C2
Chelmsford Rd SK3 . . . . . 123 C8
Chelmsford St OL8 . . . . . 153 E5
Chelsea Ave M26 . . . . 43 D4
Chelsea Cl OL2 . . . . 149 B7
Chelsea Rd Bolton BL3 . . . 147 D3
Failsworth M40 . . . . 83 C5
Urmston M41 . . . . 94 C1
Chelsea St Bury BL9 . . . . . 44 F4
Rochdale OL11 . . . . 139 D5
Chelsfield Gr M21 . . . . . . 109 D8
Chelston Ave M40 . . . . 65 D2
Chelston Dr Gatley SK8 . . 131 C6
Haslingden BB4 . . . . 1 A7
Chelt Wlk M22 . . . . 121 B2
Cheltenham Ave WN3 . . . 151 D5
Cheltenham Cres M7 . . . . 155 E7
Cheltenham Dr
Newton-le-W WA3 . . . . 53 D2
Newton-le-W WA12 . . . . . . 89 C5
Sale M33 . . . . 108 C4
Cheltenham Gn M24 . . . . . 65 A6
Cheltenham Rd
Cheadle SK3 . . . . 123 A7
Manchester M21 . . . . 97 B2
Middleton M24 . . . . 65 A6
Cheltenham St
Oldham OL1 . . . . 49 B1
Rochdale OL11 . . . . 30 D4
1 Salford M6 . . . . 81 A2
3 Wigan WN2 . . . . 37 F2
Chelwood Cl BL1 . . . . 24 D7
Chelwood Dr M43 . . . . 83 F2
Chelwood Pk WA12 . . . . . . 73 A1
Chelworth Manor SK7 . . . 123 C1
Chemical St WA12 . . . . 89 B3
Chemist St BL1 . . . . 143 F1
Chendre Rd M9 . . . . 65 B3
Cheney Cl M11 . . . . 99 D7
Chepstow Ave M33 . . . . . 107 C3
Chepstow Cl OL11 . . . . 29 F8
Chepstow Dr
Hazel Grove SK7 . . . . 125 A2
Oldham OL1 . . . . 49 B1
Chepstow Gr WN7 . . . . 76 E7
Chepstow Rd
Manchester M21 . . . . 97 A1
Swinton M27 . . . . 62 A2
Chepstow St M1,M2 . . . . . 162 F8
Chepstow St N M1 . . . . . . 162 F8
Chequers Rd M21 . . . . . . 109 B8
Chequers St WN1 . . . . . . 150 B8
Cherington Cl
Handforth SK9 . . . . 131 F3
Wythenshawe M23 . . . . . 120 F5
Cherington Dr M29 . . . . . . 59 C1
Cherington Rd SK8 . . . . . 122 C4
Cheriton Ave M33 . . . . . . 108 C5
Cheriton Cl SK14 . . . . . . 102 D2
Cheriton Dr BL2 . . . . 42 E6
Cheriton Gdns BL6 . . . . . . 22 B5
Cheriton Rd M41 . . . . 94 D3
Cheriton Rise SK2 . . . . . . 125 A6
Cherrington Dr OL11 . . . . . 47 D8
Cherry Ave Ashton-u-L OL6 . 85 D2
Bury BL9 . . . . 141 C3
Oldham OL8 . . . . 67 C3
Cherry Cl Bury BL9 . . . . . . 45 A7
Stockport SK7 . . . . 124 E7
Cherry Cres BB4 . . . . 1 F8
Cherry Ct M33 . . . . 108 B4
Cherry Dr M27 . . . . 80 A8
Cherry Gr Leigh WN7 . . . . . 75 F8
Rochdale OL11 . . . . 30 A8
Royton OL2 . . . . 48 C6
Stalybridge SK15 . . . . . . 102 A8
Wigan WN6 . . . . 36 F3
Cherry Hall Dr OL2 . . . . . . 48 E7
Cherry Hinton OL1 . . . . . 153 D8
Cherry Holt Ave SK4 . . . . 110 F4
Cherry La
Dunham-Oil6,OL3 . . . . . . 33 B3
Sale M33 . . . . 108 C2
Cherry Manor Prim Sch
M33 . . . . 107 C2
Cherry Orchard Cl SK7 . . 123 D1
Cherry St M25 . . . . 63 C5
Cherry Tree Ave
Farnworth BL4 . . . . 60 A8
Poynton SK12 . . . . 133 F3
Cherry Tree Cl
1 Altrincham WA15 . . . . . 120 B5
Romiley SK6 . . . . 113 E2
Wilmslow SK9 . . . . 137 E8
Cherry Tree Cotts WA11 . . 71 A2
Cherry Tree Ct
8 Salford M6 . . . . 81 A2
Standish WN6 . . . . 19 D2
Cherry Tree Dr SK7 . . . . . 134 A8

Cherry Tree Gr
Atherton M46 ....58 C4
Leigh WN7 ....49 B2
Cherry Tree Hospl SK2 .....124 C5
Cherry Tree Jun Sch SK6 ..113 E2
Cherry Tree La
Billinge WA11 ....71 A2
Bury BL8 ....27 C1
Rawtenstall BB4 ....1 F8
Romiley SK6 ....113 E2
Stockport SK2 ....124 C5
Cherry Tree Prim Sch BL4 ..59 E8
Cherry Tree Rd
Cheadle SK8 ....123 A1
Golborne WA3 ....90 F8
Wythenshawe M23 ....108 F1
Cherry Tree Way
Bolton BL2 ....25 C5
Haslingden BB4 ....1 B7
🟥 Horwich BL6 ....22 E1
Cherry Tree Wlk
Mossley OL5 ....68 B1
Stretford M32 ....96 C1
Cherry Wlk Cheadle SK8 ...132 C8
Partington M31 ....105 D2
Cherrybrook Dr WN3 ....54 D1
Cherrycroft SK6 ....105 D2
Cherrton Wlk M13 ....163 C6
Cherrywood OL9 ....65 D7
Cherrywood Ave BL5 ....59 A7
Cherrywood Cl M28 ....60 B1
Chertsey Cl Droylsden M18 ..99 E5
Shaw OL2 ....149 B8
Chervil Cl M14 ....110 C8
Chervil Wlk WN3 ....54 C4
Cherwell Ave OL10 ....29 B3
Cherwell Cl Aspull WN2 ......38 C6
Cheadle SK8 ....132 A7
Oldham OL8 ....66 C1
Whitefield M45 ....63 A8
Cherwell Rd BL5 ....39 F2
Cheryl's Bank SK13 ....116 B8
Chesham Ave Bolton BL1 ...143 E2
Middleton OL11 ....47 D7
Urmston M41 ....94 E3
Wythenshawe M22 ....121 C4
Chesham Cl Hadfield SK13 .104 B5
Wilmslow SK9 ....136 F4
Chesham Cres BL9 ....141 A3
Chesham Fold Rd BL9 ....141 B4
Chesham Ho 🟥 M5 ....154 F1
Chesham Ind Est BL9 ....141 A4
Chesham Pl WA14 ....119 C2
Chesham Prim Sch BL9 ......28 A5
Chesham Rd Bury BL9 ....28 A6
Eccles M30 ....95 C8
🟥 Oldham OL4 ....67 C6
Wilmslow SK9 ....136 F4
Chesham St BL3 ....146 B2
Cheshill Ct M7 ....155 F6
Cheshire Cl
Newton-le-W WA12 ....89 E3
Stretford M32 ....96 B1
Cheshire Ct BL0 ....11 D6
Cheshire Gdns M14 ....48 A1
Cheshire Rd Mossley SK15 ..86 E5
Portington M31 ....105 D2
Cheshire Sq SK15 ....86 E5
Cheshire St OL5 ....86 D8
Cheshires The OL5 ....68 D1
Chesney Ave OL9 ....65 E2
Chesshyre Ave M4 ....160 D1
Chessington Rise M27 ....62 A3
Chester Ave
Altrincham WA15 ....119 F2
Dukinfield SK16 ....101 E7
Golborne WA3 ....90 D8
Little Lever BL3 ....43 B4
Rochdale OL11 ....30 A6
Sale M33 ....107 B1
Stalybridge SK15 ....86 D3
Urmston M41 ....95 E3
Whitefield M45 ....63 A7
Chester Cl Handforth SK9 ..131 E2
Irlam M44 ....105 D5
Little Lever BL3 ....43 B4
Chester Cres BB4 ....1 B8
Chester Dr
Ashton-in-M WN4 ....73 D2
Ramsbottom BL0 ....11 A4
🟥 Royton OL2 ....48 D4
Chester Rd
Hazel Grove SK7,SK12 ......124 D1
Manchester M15,M16 ....161 B5
Manchester M15,M16 ....161 B5
Poynton SK12 ....133 B4
Stretford M16,M32 ....96 E3
Tyldesley M29 ....77 D8
Woodford SK7 ....132 E2
Chester Sq OL7 ....166 A2
Chester St Bury BL9 ....141 A4
Denton M34 ....100 F2
Leigh WN7 ....75 D5
Manchester M1 ....163 A7
Manchester M1,M15 ....162 F7
Oldham OL9 ....152 C5
Prestwich M25 ....63 A5
Stockport SK3 ....169 D1
Swinton M27 ....79 F7
Tyldesley M46 ....58 E1
Chester Wlk 🟥 BL1 ....143 E2
Chester Wlks SK6 ....113 A1
Chesterfield Gr OL6 ....85 D3
Chesterfield Cl OL4 ....67 B6

Chesterfield Way 🟥 M34 ...113 A8
Chestergate SK1,SK3,SK4 ..169 E1
Chesterton Cl WN3 ....150 A5
Chesterton Dr BL3 ....40 E5
Chesterton Gr M43 ....84 A2
Chesterton Rd Oldham OL1 ..49 B2
Sale M23 ....120 D8
Chestnut Ave Atherton M46 ..58 C4
Bury BL8 ....27 A5
Bury BL9 ....27 C1
Cheadle SK8 ....122 E5
Droylsden M43 ....83 E3
Irlam M44 ....105 D5
Leigh WN7 ....75 F3
Manchester M21 ....109 B8
Walkden M28 ....60 D2
Whitefield M45 ....62 F7
Chestnut Cl Bolton BL3 ....146 B4
New Mills SK22 ....127 E1
Oldham OL4 ....67 D8
Stalybridge SK15 ....102 A8
Wilmslow SK9 ....137 E8
Chestnut Cres OL8 ....67 A2
Chestnut Ct
Manchester M19 ....111 B8
Stockport SK7 ....123 D2
Chestnut Dr Leigh WN7 ......75 F2
Poynton SK12 ....133 F3
Rawtenstall BB4 ....1 F8
Sale M33 ....107 D1
Westhoughton BL5 ....57 F7
Chestnut Dr S WN7 ....75 F1
Chestnut Fold M26 ....44 A4
Chestnut Gdns
Denton M34 ....100 E2
Heywood OL10 ....29 C1
Chestnut Gr
Ashton-in-M WN4 ....73 D4
Failsworth M35 ....83 F6
Golborne WA3 ....90 F8
Hindley WN2 ....57 A4
Radcliffe M26 ....62 A8
Chestnut La WN7 ....75 F2
Chestnut Rd Eccles M30 .....79 A4
Wigan WN1 ....37 E2
Chestnut St OL9 ....66 A3
Chestnut Villas SK4 ....168 C2
Chestnut Way OL15 ....15 F6
Chestnut Wlk
Partington M31 ....105 D2
🟥 Partington M31 ....105 E3
Chesworth Cl SK1 ....170 F8
Chesworth Ct M43 ....83 E1
Chesworth Fold SK1 ....170 F8
Chetham St M26 ....161 B7
Chetham's Sch of
Music M4 ....158 F2
Chetwode Ave WN4 ....73 F3
Chetwyn Ave Bolton BL7 .....25 A7
Royton OL2 ....48 C4
Chetwynd Ave 🟥 M41 ....95 C2
Chetwynd Cl M33 ....107 E6
Chevassut Prim Sch M15 ..162 E7
Chevassut St M15 ....162 E6
Chevin Gdns SK7 ....133 A7
Chevington Dr
Manchester M9 ....157 D6
Manchester SK4 ....110 D3
Chevington Gdns 🟥 BL1 ....143 E3
Cheviot Ave Cheadle SK8 ...122 F2
Oldham OL8 ....66 E3
Royton OL2 ....48 C3
Cheviot Cl Bolton BL1 ....24 D5
Bury BL8 ....27 A3
Horwich BL6 ....22 C5
Middleton M24 ....65 D8
Milnrow OL16 ....32 A7
Oldham OL9 ....152 A5
Ramsbottom BL0 ....11 C4
Salford M6 ....154 E3
Stockport SK4 ....169 D3
Wigan WN3 ....54 C2
Cheviot Ct OL8 ....66 E4
Cheviot Rd M41 ....158 F3
Cheviots Rd OL2 ....149 A8
Chevithorne Cl WA14 ....119 B5
Chevril Cl M15 ....163 A6
Chevron Cl Rochdale OL11 ...30 B3
🟥 Salford M5,M6 ....81 B2
Chevron Pl WA14 ....119 D7
Chew Brook Dr OL3 ....69 B5
Chew Moor La BL5,BL6 ......40 A2
Chew Rd OL3 ....79 A2
Chew Vale Dukinfield SK16 .101 F7
Oldham OL3 ....69 A5
Chew Valley Rd OL3 ....69 B5
Chicago Ave M90 ....130 B7
Chichester Cl WA14 ....119 B8
Chichester Cres M24 ....47 C3
Chichester Bsns Ctr OL16 ...31 A7
Chichester Cl
Littleborough OL15 ....15 F3
🟥 Sale M33 ....107 D3
Chichester Cres OL9 ....48 A1
Chichester Rd
Manchester M15 ....162 F5
Romiley SK6 ....113 C2
Chichester Rd S M15 ....162 E5
Chichester St OL16 ....31 B7
Chichester Way 🟥 M34 ....101 A1
Chidlow Ave M20 ....110 A7
Chidwall Rd M22 ....121 B2
Chief St OL4 ....67 A6
Chiffon Way M3 ....158 D3
Chigwell Cl M22 ....121 E5
Chilcombe Wlk 🟥 M9 ....64 E5
Chilcote Ave M33 ....107 E4
Childwall Cl BL3 ....147 E2

Chilgrove Ave BL6 ....21 D1
Chilham Rd Eccles M30 ......79 F4
Walkden M28 ....60 E2
Chilham St Bolton BL3 .....146 B2
Swinton M27 ....79 F6
Wigan WN5 ....54 B8
Chillingham Dr WN7 ....76 C4
Chillington Wlk M14 ....100 E1
Chilmark Dr M23 ....121 A6
Chiltern Ave Atherton M46 ..58 F5
Cheadle SK8 ....122 F2
Urmston M41 ....94 F3
Chiltern Cl
Ashton-in-M WN4 ....73 C2
Horwich BL6 ....22 C5
Ramsbottom BL0 ....11 C4
Shaw OL2 ....48 F8
Stockport SK7 ....124 B1
Walkden M28 ....78 E8
Chiltern Dr
Altrincham WA15 ....119 F2
Bolton BL2 ....148 C7
Bury BL8 ....27 B4
Royton OL2 ....48 C4
Stockport SK2 ....124 B4
Swinton M27 ....79 F6
Wigan WN3 ....54 D2
Chiltern Gdns M33 ....108 C1
Chiltern Rd Culcheth WA3 ...91 E4
Ramsbottom BL0 ....11 C4
Chiltern Way M29 ....77 B8
Chilton Ave OL9 ....152 A6
Chilton Cl WN7 ....75 F7
Chilton Dr M24 ....65 C7
Chilworth St M14 ....98 B2
Chime Bank M8 ....156 B6
Chimes Rd WN4 ....72 F6
China La 🟥 Bolton BL1 .....145 F8
Manchester M1 ....159 B1
Chingford Wlk 🟥 M13 ....98 F4
Chinley Ave
Manchester M40 ....83 A8
Stretford M32 ....96 A3
Chinley Cl Manchester SK4 .168 B3
Sale M33 ....108 D3
Stockport SK7 ....123 E3
Chinley St M6 ....81 A3
Chinnor Cl WN7 ....75 F7
Chinwell View 🟥 M19 ....99 A1
Chip Hill Rd BL3 ....146 A4
Chippendale Pl OL6 ....85 E5
Chippenham Ct M4 ....124 D7
Chippenham Cl M4 ....160 D1
Chippenham Rd M4 ....160 D2
Chipping Fold OL16 ....31 F5
Chipping Rd BL1 ....23 F2
Chipping Sq M12 ....99 A4
Chipstead Ave M12 ....164 E5
Chirmside St 🟥 BL8 ....27 B1
Chirton Wlk 🟥 M40 ....83 A7
Chisacre Dr WN6 ....35 D7
Chiseldon Ave M22 ....121 E2
Chiselhurst St M8 ....156 A7
Chisholm Ct WN6 ....35 C4
Chisholm Ct 🟥 M24 ....46 F1
Chisholm St M11 ....99 D7
Chisholme Cl BL8 ....10 E2
Chisledon Ave M7 ....155 F6
Chisledon Cl BL3 ....145 E5
Chislehurst Ave M41 ....95 D3
Chislehurst Cl BL8 ....27 B1
Chisnall Ave WN6 ....18 F6
Chisnall La Coppull PR7 .....19 C6
Wrightington Bar WN6 ....18 E2
Chiswell St WN5 ....54 C5
Chiswick Dr BL3 ....43 B5
Chiswick Rd M20 ....110 C3
Chisworth Cl Leigh WN7 .....75 E7
Stockport SK7 ....123 E3
Chisworth St BL2 ....25 B3
Chisworth Wlk 🟥 M34 ......113 A8
Choir St M7 ....158 E4
Chokeberry Cl WA14 ....119 B8
Cholmley Dr WN2 ....89 E2
Cholmondeley Ave WA14 ...119 E8
Cholmondeley Rd M6 ....80 C4
Chomlea WA14 ....119 B4
Chomlea Manor M6 ....80 C4
Choral Gr M7 ....155 D5
Chorley Cl BL8 ....27 B4
Chorley Hall Cl SK9 ....136 F1
Chorley Hall La SK9 ....137 A1
Chorley New Rd
Bolton BL1,BL6 ....40 C7
Horwich BL6 ....22 C2
Chorley New Rd Inf Sch
BL6 ....22 D2
Chorley New Rd Prim Sch
BL6 ....22 D2
Chorley Old Rd
Bolton BL1 ....142 B1
Bolton BL1,BL6 ....23 C3
Chorley Rd
Adlington BL6,PR7 ....21 B5
Adlington PR6 ....21 A8
Sale M33 ....108 E2
Standish WN1 ....20 C3
Swinton M27 ....79 F8
Westhoughton BL5,BL6 ......39 C4
Chorley St St Adlington PR6 .21 B8
Bolton BL1 ....145 E7
Ince-in-M WN3 ....151 E6
Stretford M32 ....96 F5
Chorley Wood Ave M19 ....110 F6
Chorlton CE Prim Sch
M21 ....109 A8
Chorlton Dr SK8 ....122 E6
Chorlton Fold M30 ....79 D4

Chorlton Gn M21 ....109 A8
Chorlton Gr SK1 ....124 B7
Chorlton Park Jun
& Inf Schs M21 ....109 C6
Chorlton Rd M15,M16 ......162 D6
Chorlton St
Manchester M1 ....163 A8
Manchester M1 ....161 C5
Chorlton Water Park
M21 ....109 C4
Chorlton Cl M46 ....58 E3
Chowbent Prim Sch M46 ....58 D3
Chretien Rd M22 ....109 E2
Christ Church (Patricroft)
CE Prim Sch
M30 ....79 D2
Christ Church Ainsworth
CE Prim Sch BL2 ....26 C1
Christ Church CE Prim Sch
Bury BL8 ....26 F4
Denshaw OL3 ....33 D1
Heywood OL10 ....31 C8
Oldham OL9 ....152 A6
Christ Church Cl BL2 ....25 F2
Christ Church La BL2 ....25 F3
Christ the King
RC Prim Sch Failsworth M40 83 C5
Walkden M28 ....60 E2
Christ's Church
CE Prim Sch BL2 ....25 F2
Christchurch Ave M5 ....81 B2
Christchurch Ct OL9 ....152 C5
Christchurch Rd M33 ....107 C5
Christie Hospl & Holt
Radium Inst M20 ....110 B6
Christie Rd M32 ....96 E2
Christine St OL4 ....67 A6
Christine St OL2 ....149 B7
Christleton WN6 ....36 B6
Christleton Ave M40 ....111 D5
Christleton Way 🟥 SK9 ....131 D5
Christopher Acre OL11 ......13 E1
Christopher St
Failsworth M40 ....83 D4
Ince-in-M WN3 ....151 F6
Salford M5 ....81 B1
Chronnell Dr BL2 ....42 E8
Chudleigh Cl
Altrincham WA14 ....119 B6
Stockport SK7 ....124 A3
Chudleigh Rd M8 ....64 A2
Chulsey Gate La BL6 ....40 A4
Chulsey St BL3 ....146 B4
Chunal La SK13 ....116 C6
Church Ave
Bickershaw WN2 ....74 F8
Bolton BL3 ....146 C4
Denton M34 ....100 F1
🟥 Failsworth M40 ....83 C5
Handforth SK9 ....131 A2
Hyde SK14 ....113 F8
Leigh WN7 ....75 A8
Middleton OL11 ....154 D2
Salford M6 ....154 E3
Church Bank BL1 ....148 A7
Church Brow
Altrincham WA14 ....119 B2
Hyde SK14 ....113 F8
Mottram-in-L SK14 ....103 A3
Church Cl Dukinfield M34 ..100 F7
Glossop SK13 ....104 E2
Handforth SK9 ....131 D3
Kearsley M26 ....61 B8
Ramsbottom BL0 ....138 B5
Church Croft BL9 ....45 C4
Church Ct
Altrincham WA14 ....119 E1
Dukinfield SK16 ....166 B1
Edenfield BL0 ....1 D4
Church Dr
Newton-le-W WA12 ....89 C1
Orrell WN5 ....53 D5
Prestwich M25 ....63 A4
Church Fields OL3 ....51 A2
Church Fold PR7 ....19 F8
Church Gn Lymm WA13 ....117 B8
Radcliffe M26 ....44 D4
Salford M6 ....154 F3
Church Grove SK4 ....124 E2
Church La
Alderley Edge SK9 ....137 A2
Culcheth WA3 ....91 F3
Edenfield BL0 ....1 D4
Golborne WA3 ....90 D7
Manchester M19 ....111 C8
Manchester M25,M7 ....63 C1
Manchester M40,M9 ....157 F7
Manchester M9 ....157 E8
Marple SK6 ....125 F5
Mossley OL5 ....68 C2
Oldham OL1 ....153 F7
Prestwich M25 ....63 A4
Rochdale OL16 ....139 F7
Sale M33 ....107 C6
Shevington WN6 ....36 A6
Westhoughton BL5 ....39 E3
Whitefield M45 ....44 E1
Woodford SK7 ....132 C2
Wrightington Bar WN6 ....18 D8
Church Lo SK4 ....110 E2
Church Manor SK4 ....168 B4
Church Mdw
Dukinfield SK14 ....101 C3
Whitefield BL9 ....45 C4
Church Mdws Bolton BL2 ....25 F3

Church Mdws continued
Uppermill OL3 ....68 E5
Church Meadow
Gdns SK14 ....101 C3
Church Mews Denton M34 .100 E3
🟥 Radcliffe M26 ....44 C1
Church Pl OL10 ....29 D2
Church Rd Bolton BL1 ......142 B2
Charlesworth SK13 ....115 C7
Cheadle SK8 ....132 B8
Eccles M30 ....79 D3
Farnworth BL4 ....60 E8
Gatley SK8 ....122 A5
Handforth SK9 ....131 D3
Hollingworth SK14 ....171 D4
Kearsley M26 ....61 B8
Middleton M24 ....65 D7
Moorend SK6 ....126 E6
Oldham OL3 ....69 C8
Platt Bridge WN2 ....56 B3
Ramsbottom BL0 ....11 B6
Sale M33 ....108 D4
Shaw OL2 ....149 B6
Stockport SK4 ....169 E2
Tyldesley M29 ....77 C6
Walkden M28 ....60 D3
Wilmslow SK9 ....136 E4
Wythenshawe M22 ....109 C1
Church Road
Com Prim Sch BL1 ....142 B2
Church St Adlington PR7 ...21 A7
Ashton-in-M OL6 ....26 D1
Altrincham WA14 ....119 D5
Ashton-u-L OL6 ....166 B2
Aspull WN2 ....38 B6
Atherton M46 ....58 D3
Bacup OL13 ....3 C8
Blackrod BL6 ....21 C2
Bolton BL2 ....25 D5
Bury BL8 ....26 F5
Bury BL9 ....141 A3
Cheadle SK8 ....122 D6
Delph OL3 ....50 E7
Dukinfield SK16 ....166 B1
Eccles M30 ....79 F2
Failsworth M35 ....83 F6
Farnworth BL4 ....60 E8
Glossop SK13 ....104 D2
Golborne WA3 ....74 B1
Hadfield SK13 ....104 A4
Heywood OL10 ....29 C2
Hindley WN2 ....56 D5
Horwich BL6 ....22 C3
Hyde SK14 ....167 D1
Ince-in-M WN3 ....75 F5
Leigh WN7 ....75 F5
Little Lever BL3 ....43 F3
Littleborough OL15 ....16 B5
Littleborough OL16 ....15 D3
Manchester M4 ....159 A2
🟥 Marple SK6 ....125 F6
Marple SK6 ....126 A5
Middleton M24 ....47 A2
Newhey OL16 ....32 B4
Newton-le-W WA12 ....89 E4
Oldham OL1 ....153 F8
Oldham OL4 ....67 E5
Orrell WN5 ....53 E5
Orrell WN5 ....53 C7
Pendlebury M27 ....80 B8
Radcliffe M26 ....44 B2
Rawtenstall BB4 ....1 B8
Rochdale OL12 ....139 E7
Romiley SK6 ....113 A5
Royton OL2 ....48 D4
Stalybridge SK15 ....86 E2
Standish WN6 ....19 E1
Stockport SK4 ....169 E3
Stretford M32 ....96 C1
Swinton M27 ....79 E8
Tintwistle SK13 ....84 A5
Westhoughton BL5 ....39 E2
Whitworth OL12 ....14 C8
Wigan WN1 ....150 C8
Wigan WN5 ....54 B6
Wilmslow SK9 ....137 B7
Church St E Oldham OL4 ...67 E8
Radcliffe M26 ....44 C3
Church St S M33 ....104 E2
Church St W M26 ....44 B3
Church Stile OL16 ....139 E7
Church Street Ind Est 🟥
M24 ....47 A2
Church Terr
Handforth SK9 ....131 D4
Milnrow OL16 ....32 A5
Oldham OL1 ....153 F7
Sale M33 ....108 A6
Church View
Handforth SK9 ....131 A2
Hyde SK14 ....167 D1
Irlam M44 ....105 D5
Lymm WA13 ....117 B4
Rochdale OL12 ....13 E2
Church Wlk Farnworth BL4 ..60 C8
Kearsley M26 ....61 F4
🟥 Royton OL2 ....48 A3
Stalybridge SK15 ....86 E2
Wilmslow SK9 ....136 F6
Churchbank SK15 ....86 D2

Churchdale Rd M9 64 B4
Churchfield
Manchester M21 109 A8
Shevington WN6 36 A5
Churchfield Cl M26 43 F1
Churchfield Rd 5 M6 80 D5
Churchfield Wlk M11 165 A8
Churchfields
Altrincham WA14 119 B1
Denton M34 100 E7
Sale M33 107 D6
Churchgate Bolton BL1 145 F7
Stockport SK1 169 F1
Urmston M41 95 E1
Churchgate Bldgs M1 163 C8
Churchill Ave
Ainsworth BL2 26 D1
Fowley Common WA3 92 B4
Manchester M16 97 D2
Churchill Cl OL10 46 E8
Churchill Cres
Marple SK6 125 D7
Reddish SK5 99 E1
Churchill Ct M6 154 F2
Churchill Dr BL3,M26 43 C3
Churchill Pl M30 79 C4
Churchill Rd WA14 119 D7
Churchill St 3 Bolton BL2 148 C7
Oldham OL4 67 A6
Rochdale OL11,OL12 14 C1
Stockport SK4 169 D3
Churchill St E OL4 67 A6
Churchill Way
Salford M5,M6 81 A2
Stretford M17 96 C7
Churchlands La WN6 19 F1
Churchley Cl SK3 123 A6
Churchley Rd SK3 123 A7
Churchside BL4 60 B7
Churchside Cl M9 64 D2
Churchstoke Wlk M23 120 E7
Churchston Ave SK7 124 A2
Churchtown Ave BL2 42 F7
Churchward Sq BL6 22 C2
Churchwood Rd M20 110 B3
Churnet St M40 157 D5
Churnett Cl BL5 39 F2
Churning Terr M44 94 B3
Churston Ave M9 64 E4
Churton Ave
Manchester M14 98 B2
Sale M33 107 F3
Churton Gr WN6 19 B2
Churton Rd M18 99 C3
Churwell Ave SK4 110 F4
Cicero St Manchester M9 157 F8
Oldham OL1 49 A1
Cinder Hill La M24,OL1,OL2 48 A3
Cinder St M4 159 C2
Cinnabar Dr M24 46 F2
Cinnamon Ave WN2 57 A4
Cinnamon Brow WN8 53 C6
Cinnamon Cl OL12 139 D8
Cinnamon St OL12 139 D8
Cipher St M4 159 C3
Circle Ct M41 95 F4
Circle S M17 96 E6
Circle The M32 95 F4
Circuit The
Alderley Edge SK9 137 B3
Bramhall SK8 132 A7
Manchester M20 110 B5
Stockport SK3 123 C6
Wilmslow SK9 136 D5
Circular Rd Denton M34 100 E1
Manchester M20 110 B5
Manchester M25 63 B2
Cirencester Cl M38 60 A6
Ciss La M41 95 E2
Citrus Way M6 81 A2
City Ave M34 100 E2
City Coll Manchester
Abraham Moss Ctr M8 156 B8
City Coll Manchester
Arden Ctr M23 109 C1
City Coll Manchester
Fielden Ctr M20 109 F4
City Course Trad Est
M11 165 A7
City Court Trad Est M4 159 C2
City Rd Boothstown M28 78 A8
Manchester M15 162 D6
Wigan WN5 54 B7
City Rd E M15 162 F7
City Wlk M27 80 B8
Civic Wlk 1 OL10 29 D2
Clacton Wlk M13 163 C6
Clague St M11 83 A2
Claife Ave M40 65 B2
Clammerclough Rd BL4 60 F8
Clandon Ave M30 79 B1
Clanwood Cl WN3 54 E2
Clap Gate La WN3 54 E3
Clapgate SK6 112 F1
Clapgate Rd OL11 13 E1
Clapham St M40 83 C8
Clara Gorton Ct 12 OL16 31 B6
Clara St Oldham OL9 66 C4
Rochdale OL11 139 F5
Whitworth OL12 4 D1
Clare Ave SK9 131 C3
Clare Cl BL8 27 D5
Clare Ct Farnworth BL4 147 F1
4 Stockport SK1 112 A1
Clare Rd Manchester M19 111 A8
Reddish SK5 169 F4
Clare St Denton M34 100 E4
Manchester M1 163 B7
Clare St *continued*
Manchester M5 81 C1
Clarebank BL1 40 F7
Claremont Ave
Altrincham WA14 119 E8
Hindley WN2 56 F5
Manchester M20 110 A5
Manchester SK4 111 C5
Marple SK6 125 C6
Claremont Ct 6 M20 110 A3
Claremont Dr
Altrincham WA14 119 E8
Walkden M38 60 B5
Claremont Gdns OL6 85 E5
Claremont Gr
Altrincham WA15 119 E3
Manchester M20 110 A3
Claremont Jun Sch M14 98 A3
Claremont Range M18,M34 99 F4
Claremont Rd Billinge WN5 71 E5
Cheadle SK8 132 A8
Culcheth WA3 91 D4
Manchester M14 98 B3
Manchester M16 97 F3
Milnrow OL16 31 F5
Rochdale OL11 30 C7
Sale M33 108 B5
Salford M6 80 D5
Stockport SK2 124 B4
Claremont Road Inf Sch
M14 98 A3
Claremont Sch M6 80 C5
Claremont St
Failsworth M35 83 F8
Oldham OL8 66 F2
Oldham OL9 48 C1
Claremont Terr OL14 6 D5
Clarence Arc OL6 166 B2
Clarence Ave Eccles M17 95 F7
Oldham OL8 66 D4
Whitefield M45 63 A7
Clarence Ct 15 Bolton BL1 145 E8
Newton-le-W WA12 89 A4
Wilmslow SK9 137 A6
Clarence Ho 1 SK15 101 F8
Clarence Rd
Altrincham WA15 119 F3
Ashton-u-L OL6 166 C4
Manchester M13 98 E4
Manchester SK4 111 C5
Swinton M27 79 C7
Clarence St
6 Ashton-in-M WN4 72 F5
Bolton BL1 145 F8
Farnworth BL4 42 E1
Golborne WA3 74 A1
Hyde SK14 167 E4
Ince-in-M WN2 56 A7
Leigh WN7 76 B4
15 Manchester M3 158 F1
Manchester M7 158 D4
Rochdale OL12 14 D2
Royton OL2 49 A3
Stalybridge SK15,SK16 85 E1
Tyldesley M46 58 E2
Clarence Yd WN1 150 C8
Clarendon Ave
Altrincham WA15 119 E5
Manchester SK4 168 B3
Clarendon Cres
Eccles M30 79 F3
Sale M33 108 D5
Clarendon Cty Prim Sch
BL3 145 E5
Clarendon Fields Prim Sch
SK16 101 B8
Clarendon Gr BL2 148 B6
Clarendon Ind Est SK14 167 E3
Clarendon Pl SK14 167 E2
Clarendon Rd Bolton BL2 148 C7
Denton M34 101 B2
Droylsden M34 100 B7
Eccles M30 79 F3
Hazel Grove SK7 124 F3
Hyde SK14 167 E3
Ince-in-M WN3 151 E5
Irlam M44 105 F7
Manchester M16 97 D2
Sale M33 108 D4
Swinton M27 79 F8
Urmston M41 94 E3
Clarendon Rd W M21 97 B2
Clarendon Recn Ctr M5 81 A2
Clarendon Road Prim Sch
M30 79 F3
Clarendon St Bolton BL3 145 E5
Bury BL9 141 A4
Dukinfield SK16 101 A8
Dukinfield SK16 101 B8
Hyde SK14 167 D3
Manchester M15 162 F6
Manchester M15 162 F7
Mossley OL5 86 D8
Reddish SK5 169 F3
Rochdale OL16 31 B4
Whitefield M45 62 F8
Claribel St M11 164 E8
Claridge Rd M21 97 A1
Clarington Gr WN1 151 E7
Clarington Pl WN2 151 F7
Clarion St M4 159 C3
Clark Ave M18 99 E5
Clark Way SK14 167 D3
Clark's Cross M25 63 D8
Clark's Hill M25 63 A4
Clarke Ave Culcheth WA3 92 A4
Salford M5 161 B7
Clarke Brow M24 47 A1
Clarke Cres
Altrincham WA15 120 B3
Walkden M38 59 E6
Clarke St Altrincham WA14 119 D7
Bolton BL1 144 C8
Dukinfield OL7 100 F8
Farnworth BL4 60 E7
Heywood OL10 29 D2
Leigh WN7 75 E4
Rochdale OL16 15 B2
Clarke's La OL12 139 D8
Clarkes Croft BL9 141 C3
Clarkethorn Terr SK5 169 E3
Clarksfield Jun & Inf Sch
OL4 67 C6
Clarksfield Rd OL4 67 C6
Clarksfield St OL4 67 C6
Clarkson Cl Denton M34 100 D2
Middleton M24 64 C7
Clarkwell Cl OL1 153 E8
Clatford Wlk 2 M9 157 D7
Claude Ave M27 79 D8
Claude Rd M21 109 B7
Claude St Eccles M30 79 B3
Manchester M8 64 A1
Swinton M27 79 D8
Wigan WN5 54 D6
Claudia Sq SK15 86 E5
Claughton Ave Bolton BL2 42 F7
Walkden M28 78 C8
Claughton Rd BL8 26 F5
Claverham Wlk 4 M23 120 E7
Claverton Rd M23 120 E5
Claxton Ave M9 64 D3
Clay Bank M43 83 F1
Clay Bank St OL10 29 C3
Clay Hall M5 154 F1
Clay La Altrincham WA15 120 D4
Handforth SK9 131 C5
Rochdale OL11 29 E8
Wilmslow SK9 136 C4
Wythenshawe M23 120 F4
Clay St Bolton BL7 25 A7
3 Littleborough OL15 15 F5
Oldham OL8 66 E4
Claybank Dr Bury BL8 26 D7
Bury BL8 26 E7
Claybank Terr OL5 68 E4
Claybar Dr M30 79 E3
Claybridge Cl WN5 36 B1
Claybrook Wlk M11 83 A1
Clayburn Rd M15 162 E6
Claycourt Ave M30 79 B4
Claydon Dr Ince-in-M WN3 151 F5
Little Lever BL3,M26 43 C5
Clayfield Dr OL11 29 F8
Claygate Dr M9 64 D5
Clayhill Gr WA3 91 B8
Clayhill Wlk M9 64 E1
Claylands Cl SK14 171 D4
Claymere Ave OL11 29 E8
Claymore OL1 153 E7
Claymore St Bolton BL3 147 F3
Droylsden M18 99 E6
Claypool Prim Sch BL6 22 F1
Claypool Rd BL6 22 E1
Claythorpe Wlk 2 M8 63 E2
Clayton Ave Bolton BL3 148 C5
Golborne WA3 90 E8
Manchester M20 110 B4
Rawtenstall BB4 1 E8
Clayton Brook Prim Sch
M11 99 D8
Clayton Cl Bury BL8 26 F1
Manchester M15 162 E5
Clayton Hall Rd M11 83 C2
Clayton Ho WN7 75 C5
Clayton La M11 83 B1
Clayton La S M11,M12 165 A7
Clayton St Bolton BL3 148 C5
Denton M34 100 F2
Droylsden M11 83 B2
5 Dukinfield SK16 101 D8
5 Failsworth M35 83 F7
Oldham OL9 66 A3
Rochdale OL12 15 B2
Wigan WN3 150 B7
Claytonbrook Rd M11 83 D1
Claytons Cl OL4 67 F7
Cleabarrow Dr M28 78 A5
Cleadon Ave M18 99 C4
Cleadon Dr S BL8 27 C5
Cleavley St M30 79 B2
Clee Ave M13 98 F2
Cleethorpes Ave M9 64 B3
Cleeve Rd 2 Oldham OL4 67 C6
Wythenshawe M23 109 A2
Cleeve Way SK8 132 B6
Clegg Hall Rd OL15,OL16 15 E1
Clegg Pl 2 OL6 85 D4
Clegg St 6 Bacup OL13 3 C8
Bolton BL2 148 C7
Bredbury SK6 112 F3
Droylsden M43 83 F1
Littleborough OL15 15 F7
Milnrow OL16 32 A5
Oldham OL4 153 F6
Oldham OL4 68 A6
Shaw OL2 48 F8
Tyldesley M29 77 A5
Whitefield M45 62 F7
Whitworth OL12 4 C2
Clegg's Bldgs BL1 145 E8
Clegg's Ct OL12 4 C2
Clegg's La M38 60 A5
Cleggswood Ave OL15 16 A3
Clelland St BL4 60 E7
Clematis Wlk M27 61 E2
Clement Ave M46 58 A2
Clement Ct
3 Droylsden M11 99 F7
13 Rochdale OL16 31 B6
Clement Rd SK6 126 C7
Clement Royds St OL12 139 E8
Clement Scott Cl M9 64 F4
Clement St Oldham OL9 66 B3
Stockport SK4 169 E3
Clementina St OL12 14 F1
Clementine Cl M6 81 B2
Clementine Ct M6 81 B2
Cleminson St M3 158 D2
Clemshaw Cl OL10 29 C1
Clerewood Ave SK8 131 B7
Clerke St BL9 140 F2
Clerks Ct M5 80 B2
Clevedon Ave M41 96 A2
Clevedon Dr WN3 54 D4
Clevedon Rd OL9 48 B1
Clevedon St M9 157 E7
Cleveland Ave Hyde SK14 101 C2
Manchester M19 99 B2
Salford M6 80 C3
Wigan WN3 54 C3
Cleveland Cl
Ramsbottom BL0 11 C3
Swinton M27 62 A2
Cleveland Dr
Ashton-in-M WN4 73 C4
Golborne WA3 74 D1
Milnrow OL16 32 A6
Cleveland Gdns BL3 146 B4
Cleveland Gr OL2 48 C3
Cleveland Rd
Altrincham WA15 119 F3
Manchester M8 64 B2
Manchester SK4 168 A4
Cleveland St 7 BL3 146 B4
Clevelands Prep Sch BL1 144 A7
Cleveleys Ave Bolton BL2 148 C8
Bury BL9 44 E7
Gatley SK8 122 B1
Manchester M21 109 C7
Rochdale OL16 31 B3
Cleveleys Gr M7 155 E7
Cleves Ct OL10 29 C1
Clevlands Cl OL2 149 A8
Cleworth Cl M29 77 C4
Cleworth Rd M24 46 F2
Cleworth St M15 162 D7
Cleworth Wlk M15 162 D7
Clibran St M8 156 B6
Clifden Dr M22 121 E2
Cliff Ave Bury BL8 26 E7
Manchester M7 81 C6
Ramsbottom BL9 11 C2
Cliff Cres M7 155 D7
Cliff Dale 3 SK15 101 F8
Cliff Gr SK4 168 B4
Cliff Grange M7 155 D7
Cliff Hill Rd OL2 32 D1
Cliff Mount BL0 138 B7
Cliff Rd Bury BL9 44 F5
Wilmslow SK9 137 B8
Cliff Side SK9 137 B8
Cliff St OL16 15 B1
Cliffbrook Gr 2 SK9 131 D2
Cliffdale Dr M8 64 A1
Cliffe Rd SK13 116 D8
Cliffe St OL15 6 D2
Cliffmere Cl SK8 122 F3
Clifford Ave
Altrincham WA15 120 B6
Denton M34 100 E5
Clifford Ct M15 162 E5
Clifford Lamb Ct M9 65 B2
Clifford Rd Bolton BL3 146 A2
Poynton SK12 133 D3
Wilmslow SK9 136 F6
Clifford St Eccles M30 95 B8
Leigh WN7 76 B4
Manchester M13 163 B6
Pendlebury M27 80 B8
Rochdale OL11 139 F5
Rochdale OL11 31 A5
Clifton Ave
Altrincham WA15 119 E5
Culcheth WA3 91 D3
Eccles M30 79 D3
Gatley SK8 122 A2
Manchester M14 110 D8
2 Oldham OL4 67 B5
Tyldesley M29 77 C6
Clifton Cl Heywood OL10 29 C1
Manchester M16 162 D5
Oldham OL4 67 B5
Clifton Cres Royton OL2 49 A3
Wigan WN1 37 C2
Clifton Ct 5 Farnworth BL4 42 B2
Swinton M27 61 F3
Clifton Ctry Pk M27 61 E5
Clifton Dr Blackrod BL6 21 C3
Gatley SK8 122 A2
Gatley SK8 122 A6
Marple SK6 125 F7
Swinton M27 61 D2
Swinton M27 62 C2
Wilmslow SK9 136 E4
Clifton Gr
Manchester M16 162 D5
Swinton M27 61 D2
Clifton Holm OL3 50 E5
Clifton House Rd M27 61 E4
Clifton Junction Sta M27 62 C2
Clifton Lo SK2 124 A5
Clifton Park Rd SK2 124 A5
Clifton Pl M25 63 A5
Clifton Prim Sch M27 61 F3
Clifton Rd Ashton-in-M WN4 72 F6
Billinge WN5 71 D4
Eccles M30 79 D3
Leigh WN7 75 E2
Manchester M21 109 C8
Manchester SK4 168 A4
Middleton OL11 47 D6
Prestwich M25 62 E4
Sale M33 108 B3
Urmston M41 95 A2
Clifton St
Alderley Edge SK9 137 A1
Ashton-u-L OL6 166 A3
Bolton BL1 145 E8
Bury BL9 140 F4
Failsworth M35 66 A1
Farnworth BL4 42 B2
Kearsley BL4 60 F7
Leigh WN7 75 D5
Manchester M16 162 D5
Manchester M40 160 F4
Milnrow OL16 31 F6
7 Rochdale OL11 31 A5
Tyldesley M29 77 E8
4 Wigan WN1 37 C1
Wigan WN3 55 A4
Clifton View M27 61 E4
Clifton Villas 5 M35 66 A1
Clifton Wlk M24 46 D3
Cliftonmill Mdw WA3 89 F8
Cliftonville Dr M6,M27 80 B6
Cliftonville Rd OL16 48 C8
Clinton Ave M14 98 A2
Clinton Gdns M14 98 A2
Clinton Ho 3 M5 154 F1
Clinton St 7 OL6 85 D4
Clinton Wlk 5 OL4 67 A6
Clippers Quay M5 161 A6
Clipsley Cres OL4 49 F4
Cliston Wlk SK7 124 A2
Clitheroe Cl OL10 29 D3
Clitheroe Dr BL8 26 F2
Clitheroe Rd M13 98 F3
Clito St M9 157 F8
Clive Ave M45 44 E1
Clive Rd Failsworth M35 83 E6
Westhoughton BL5 57 E6
Clive St Ashton-u-L OL7 85 A5
Bolton BL2 148 A7
Manchester M4 159 B3
3 Oldham OL8 66 D2
Clivedale Pl BL1 145 F7
Cliveley Wlk M27 80 B8
Clively Ave M27 62 C1
Clivewood Wlk M12 164 E6
Clivia Gr M7 155 D6
Cloak St M1 163 A7
Clock House Ave M43 83 E3
Clock St 11 OL9 66 B2
Clock Tower Cl
Hyde SK14 167 E1
3 Walkden M28 59 F3
Clockhouse Mews M43 83 E3
Clod La BB4 1 C8
Cloister Ave WN7 57 D1
Cloister Cl SK16 101 C6
Cloister Rd SK4 110 D2
Cloister St Bury BL1 142 C2
Manchester M9 157 F8
Cloisters The Cheadle SK8 123 A5
Rochdale OL16 15 B1
Sale M33 108 D4
Westhoughton BL5 57 E5
Clondberry Cl M29 59 E1
Close La Hindley WN2 56 E3
Leigh WN2 57 A1
Close St WN2 56 F6
Close The
Altrincham WA14 119 C5
Atherton M46 58 F5
Bolton BL2 25 B3
Bury BL8 27 C5
Denton M34 100 D4
Middleton M24 47 B3
Newton-le-W WA12 89 E1
Romiley SK6 114 B1
Stalybridge SK15 85 F4
Closebrook Rd WN5 54 D6
Closes Farm BL3 146 B2
Clothorn Rd M20 110 B4
Cloudberry Wlk M31 105 F3
Cloudstock Gr M38 59 E5
Clough Ave Handforth SK9 131 B2
Marple SK6 126 C6
Sale M33 107 D1
Westhoughton BL5 57 F7
Clough Bank
Littleborough OL15 16 A8
Manchester M9 64 D2
Clough Croft OL4 68 E6
Clough Dr M25 62 F4
Clough End Rd SK14 102 F1
Clough Fold Kearsley M26 61 B7
Westhoughton BL5 57 F8
Clough Fold Rd SK14 167 D1
Clough Gate Hyde SK14 113 F8
6 Oldham OL8 66 D2
Clough Gr Ashton-in-M WN4 72 F5
Whitefield M45 44 D2
Clough Ho M9 65 A2
Clough House Dr WN7 76 B5
Clough House La OL12 15 B6
Clough La Heywood OL10 29 C4
Prestwich M25 62 F4

Clough La *continued*
Uppermill M14 ....68 E6
Clough Mdw Bolton BL1 ....40 D6
  Romiley SK6 ....113 C5
Clough Meadow Rd M26 .....43 E3
Clough Park Ave OL4 ....68 E6
Clough Rd Droylsden M43 ....84 B2
  Failsworth M35 ....84 A6
  Littleborough OL15 ....16 A7
  Manchester M9 ....64 F1
  Middleton M24 ....47 A2
  Shaw OL2 ....49 D6
Clough Side Marple SK6 .....126 C7
  Oldham M9 ....64 F1
Clough St 8 Bacup OL13 ....3 D8
  Failsworth M40 ....83 C4
  Kearsley BL4 ....60 F7
  Littleborough OL12 ....15 C6
  Middleton M24 ....47 B2
  Radcliffe M26 ....44 C1
Clough Terr OL15 ....16 A7
Clough The
  Brinnington SK5 ....112 B6
  Garswood WN4 ....72 D4
Clough Top Rd M9 ....65 A2
Clough Wlk SK5 ....112 B6
Cloughbank M26 ....61 C7
Cloughfield Ave M5 ....161 B8
Cloughgate Ho 8 OL8 ....66 D2
Cloughs Ave OL9 ....65 D8
Cloughside SK12 ....135 E6
Cloughton Wlk M40 ....83 D5
Cloughwood Cres WN6 ....35 D6
Clovelly Ave Leigh WN7 ....75 F8
  Oldham OL8 ....66 C2
Clovelly Rd
  Manchester M21 ....109 C8
  Stockport SK2 ....124 C8
  Swinton M27 ....79 C6
Clovelly St Failsworth M40 ...83 D5
  Rochdale OL10 ....30 B3
Clover Ave SK3 ....170 D5
Clover Cres OL8 ....67 C3
Clover Croft M33 ....108 D1
Clover Hall Cres OL16 ....15 C1
Clover Rd
  Altrincham WA15 ....120 B5
  Romiley SK6 ....113 E3
Clover St Rochdale OL12 .....139 E8
  Wigan WN6 ....37 B2
Clover View OL16 ....31 C7
Cloverbank Ave M19 ....110 D4
Cloverdale Dr WN4 ....73 C2
Cloverdale Sq BL1 ....142 A1
Cloverfield Wlk M28 ....60 D3
Cloverlea Prim Sch
  WA15 ....120 B5
Cloverley M33 ....108 B2
Cloverley Dr WA15 ....120 A4
Clowes St Manchester M3 ..164 F6
  Manchester M3 ....158 E2
  Oldham OL9 ....66 B2
Club St Billinge WA11 ....71 A1
  Droylsden M11 ....99 F7
Clumber Cl SK12 ....133 E3
Clumber Rd Poynton SK12 .133 E3
  Reddish M18,M34 ....99 F4
Clunton Ave BL3 ....146 B4
Clutha Rd SK3 ....123 F4
Clwyd Ave SK3 ....170 D7
Clyde Ave M45 ....62 F6
Clyde Ct OL16 ....31 B6
Clyde St Bolton BL1 ....42 D3
  Dukinfield OL7 ....100 F8
  Leigh WN7 ....76 B4
  Oldham OL1 ....43 F5
Clyde Terr M26 ....43 F5
Clydesdale Gdns M11 ....83 A1
Clydesdale Rise OL3 ....51 D5
Clydesdale St OL8 ....66 E4
Clyne St M32 ....96 F4
Clyne St M32 ....96 F5
Clysbarton Ct SK7 ....123 D1
Co-operation St M35 ....83 F8
Co-operative St
  Hazel Grove SK7 ....124 E3
  8 Leigh WN7 ....75 D5
  12 Oldham OL3 ....69 B8
  Oldham OL4 ....67 F5
  3 Radcliffe M26 ....44 A4
  Salford M6 ....154 F2
  Shaw OL2 ....149 B7
  Walkden M38 ....59 E5
Coach House Dr WN6 ....36 B6
Coach La OL11 ....29 E5
Coach Rd
  Hollingworth SK14 ....103 B5
  Tyldesley M29 ....77 C6
Coach St M46 ....58 D3
Coal Pit La Atherton M46 .....58 B3
  Atherton M46 ....58 B4
  Leigh WN7 ....57 B1
  4 Leigh WN7 ....75 E8
  Oldham OL8 ....66 E1
  Oldham OL8 ....66 D4
Coal Pit Rd Rd BL1 ....23 D7
Coal Rd BL0 ....12 C5
Coalbrook Wlk M12 ....164 E8
Coalburn St M12 ....165 A6
Coalshaw Green Rd OL9 .....66 A3
Coatbridge St M11 ....83 C1

Cob Hall Rd 6 M32 ....96 C1
Cob Moor Ave WN5 ....53 C1
Cob Moor Rd WN5 ....53 D1
Cobal Ct SK2 ....124 A5
Cobalt Ave M41 ....95 F6
Cobb Cl M8 ....63 E3
Cobbett's Way SK9 ....136 F4
Cobble Bank M9 ....64 D3
Cobblestones OL3 ....50 F3
Cobden Ctr The M6 ....154 F1
Cobden St
  2 Ashton-u-L OL6 ....85 D2
  Bacup OL13 ....4 B8
  Bolton BL1 ....143 D3
  Bolton BL7 ....8 D2
  Bury BL9 ....141 A3
  Heywood OL10 ....29 D1
  Manchester M9 ....64 E2
  Manchester M9 ....89 D4
  Oldham OL4 ....49 D1
  Oldham OL9 ....152 B7
  Radcliffe M26 ....43 F6
  Salford M6 ....81 A4
  12 Tyldesley M29 ....59 A1
Coberley Ave M41 ....94 F4
Cobham Ave Bolton BL3 .....147 D3
  Manchester M40 ....65 C2
Coblers Hill OL3 ....50 F5
Cobourg St M1 ....163 B8
Coburg Ave M7 ....158 D4
Cochrane Ave M12 ....164 E5
Cochrane St BL3 ....145 F5
Cock Brow SK14 ....114 C7
Cock Clod St M26 ....44 D2
Cock Hall La OL12 ....14 C8
Cockcroft Rd M6 ....81 B2
Cockcroft St M9 ....64 D1
Cocker Hill SK15 ....86 B2
Cocker Mill La Royton OL2 ...48 F5
  Shaw OL2 ....149 A5
Cocker St M38 ....60 A4
Cockerell Springs 1 BL2 ....148 A6
Cockey Moor Rd BL2,BL8 ...26 E1
Cockhall La OL12 ....4 C1
Coconut Gr M6 ....81 B2
Codale Dr BL2 ....25 F1
Coddington Ave M11 ....99 E8
Cody La BL5 ....39 B4
Cody St M5 ....96 E8
Coe St BL3 ....145 F5
Coghlan Cl M11 ....83 B2
Coin St OL2 ....48 E4
Cojeton Ho M9 ....64 E4
Coke St M7 ....155 F8
Colborne Ave Eccles M30 ....79 B2
  Reddish SK5 ....99 F3
  Romiley SK6 ....113 C2
Colbourne Ave M8 ....63 F1
Colbourne Gr SK14 ....102 E3
Colbourne Way SK14 ....102 E3
Colburn St WN3 ....55 A2
Colby Rd WN3 ....55 B3
Colby Wlk M40 ....83 A7
Colchester Ave Bolton BL2 ..42 E8
  Manchester M25 ....63 C2
Colchester Cl M23 ....108 E1
Colchester Dr BL4 ....42 A1
Colchester Pl SK4 ....168 C3
Colchester St M40 ....160 D4
Colchester Wlk 1 SK1 ....153 F7
Colclough Cl M40 ....83 B6
Cold Greave Cl OL16 ....32 C4
Coldalhurst La M29 ....77 B5
Coldfield Dr M23 ....120 F6
Coldhurst St OL1 ....153 E8
Coldstone Dr WN4 ....72 D4
Coldstream Ave M9 ....64 D4
Cole Ave WA12 ....89 C4
Cole St M40 ....157 F8
Colebrook Dr M40 ....83 A6
Colebrook Rd WA15 ....120 A6
Coleby Ave
  Manchester M16 ....97 C4
  Wythenshawe M22 ....121 F1
Coleclough Pl WA3 ....91 F4
Coledale Dr M24 ....46 C2
Coleford Gr BL1 ....145 E6
Colemore Ave M20 ....110 D3
Colenso Ct OL8 ....67 C3
Colenso Rd BL8 ....42 D7
Colenso St OL8 ....66 D3
Coleport Cl SK8 ....123 A1
Coleridge Ave
  Middleton M24 ....47 C3
  Radcliffe M26 ....43 E4
  Wigan WN5 ....54 A6
Coleridge Cl SK5 ....99 E1
Coleridge Pl WN3 ....54 F3
Coleridge Rd
  Littleborough OL15 ....15 F2
  Longshaw WN5 ....53 D1
  Manchester M16 ....97 C3
  Oldham OL1 ....49 E4
  Ramsbottom BL8 ....65 E1
  Reddish SK5 ....99 E1
Coleridge Way SK5 ....99 E1
Colerne Way WN3 ....54 D2
Colesbourne Cl M38 ....60 A2
Coleshill Rise WN3 ....54 D2
Colesmere Wlk M40 ....65 D1
Colgate Cres M14 ....110 B8
Colgate La M5 ....161 A6
Colgrove Ave M40 ....65 C2
Colin Rd SK4 ....169 E4
Colin St WN1 ....37 D1

Colina Dr M7 ....155 E5
Colindale Ave M9 ....64 E3
Colindale Cl 7 BL3 ....144 C5
Colinton Cl BL1 ....143 D1
Collingwood Cl BL9 ....44 F3
Coll Dr M41 ....95 D5
Coll's La OL3 ....50 C8
Collard St M46 ....58 B4
College Ave Droylsden M43 .99 F8
  Oldham OL8 ....66 D3
  Wigan WN1 ....150 C8
College Cl Bolton BL3 ....145 E6
  Stockport SK2 ....124 A6
  Wilmslow SK9 ....136 F8
College Croft 10 M30 ....79 F2
College Dr M16 ....97 C2
College Ho
  Altrincham WA14 ....119 C1
  Manchester SK4 ....168 B4
College Land M3 ....158 E1
College Rd Manchester M16 .97 D2
  Oldham OL8 ....66 E4
  Orrell WN8 ....53 B8
  Orrell WN8 ....53 B8
  Rochdale OL12 ....139 E7
  Salford M30 ....80 A2
College St M7 ....76 A5
College Way SK8 ....145 E6
Collen Cres BL8 ....27 C6
Collett Cl WN1 ....151 E8
Collett St OL1 ....67 C8
Colley St Rochdale OL16 ......15 B1
  Stretford M32 ....96 F5
Collie Ave M6,M7 ....81 C5
Collier Cl SK14 ....102 E1
Collier Ct M19 ....99 A1
Collier Hill OL8 ....66 C3
Collier Hill Ave OL8 ....66 D3
Collier Cl Glossop SK13 ......116 C8
  3 Hindley WN2 ....56 D6
Collier St Manchester M3 ...158 E2
  Manchester M3 ....162 E8
  Manchester M6 ....80 F6
  Reddish SK5,M34 ....99 F4
Collier Wlk 4 SK14 ....102 E1
Collier's Row BL1 ....23 E5
Colliers Row Rd BL1 ....23 E5
Colliery La M46 ....58 A4
Colliery St Droylsden M11 ....83 A1
  Manchester M11 ....165 B8
Collin Ave M9 ....99 C4
Colling Cl M44 ....94 A1
Colling St BL8 ....138 B5
Collingburn Ave M5 ....161 B7
Collingham Ct M5 ....161 B7
Collingwood Ave M9 ....64 C8
Collinge St Bury BL8 ....42 B2
  Heywood OL10 ....62 E6
  Middleton M24 ....65 D7
  Platt Bridge WN2 ....56 A2
Collingwood Cl SK12 ....134 A3
Collingwood Dr M27 ....80 B7
Collingwood Rd
  Manchester M19 ....98 F1
  Newton-le-W WA12 ....89 B3
Collingwood St
  Middleton OL11 ....47 D8
  Standish WN6 ....19 E1
Collingwood Way
  Oldham OL1 ....153 F8
  Westhoughton BL5 ....39 E1
Collins La BL5 ....57 F6
Collins St BL8 ....26 F4
Collisdene Rd WN5 ....53 E6
Collop Dr BL9 ....45 B3
Collyhurst Ave 2 M28 ....60 E2
Collyhurst Rd M40 ....156 C5
Collyhurst St M40 ....161 B7
Colman Gdns M5 ....161 B7
Colmore Dr M9 ....65 A4
Colmore Gr BL2 ....25 B4
Colmore St BL2 ....25 B3
Colnbrook St M13 ....10 D1
Colne St OL11 ....30 D1
Colonial Rd SK3 ....124 A6
Colshaw Cl E M26 ....43 F4
Colshaw Cl S M26 ....43 F4
Colshaw Dr SK9 ....131 D2
Colshaw Rd M23 ....121 A4
Colshaw Wlk SK9 ....131 D1
Colson Dr M24 ....64 F7
Colsterdale Cl OL2 ....48 E5
Colt Hill La Oldham OL3 ....69 A6
Coltsfield Ho SK8 ....131 A8
Coltness Wlk 12 M40 ....83 C5
Coltsfoot Dr WA14 ....119 B8
Columbia Ave M18,M34 ....99 F4
Columbia Rd BL1 ....144 C8
Columbia St OL8 ....66 F4
Columbine Cl OL12 ....14 C3
Columbine St M11 ....99 D1
Columbine Wlk 8 M31 ....105 F3
Columbus St 2 WN4 ....72 E5
Columbus St OL8 ....27 B1
Colville Gr
  3 Altrincham WA15 ....120 B8
  Sale M33 ....107 E1
Colville Rd OL1 ....48 D1
Colwell Ave M32 ....96 B1
Colwell Wlk M9 ....64 B5

Colwick Ave WA14 ....119 E6
Colwith Ave BL2 ....25 E1
Colwood Wlk 18 M8 ....155 F6
Colwyn Ave
  Manchester M14 ....110 E8
  Middleton M24 ....65 A6
Colwyn Cres SK5 ....111 F5
Colwyn Dr WN2 ....57 C2
Colwyn Gr M46 ....58 C5
Colwyn Rd Bramhall SK7 ....132 F8
  Cheadle SK8 ....122 E1
  Swinton M27 ....79 C6
Colwyn St Ashton-u-L OL7 ...85 A6
  Oldham OL9 ....153 D7
  Rochdale OL11 ....30 B4
  Salford M6 ....154 F3
Colyton Wlk 7 M22 ....121 E1
Combe Cl M11 ....83 B3
Combermere Ave M20 ....110 A7
Combermere Cl SK8 ....122 F4
Combermere St SK16 ....166 C1
Combs Bank 9 SK13 ....171 D1
Combs Fold 45 SK13 ....171 D2
Combs Gdns 69 SK13 ....171 D1
Combs Lea 1 SK13 ....171 D1
Combs Mews SK13 ....171 D1
Combs Terr 3 SK13 ....171 D1
Combs Way 66 SK13 ....171 D2
Comer Terr M33 ....108 A4
Comet Rd WN5 ....54 C8
Comet St M1 ....159 B1
Commercial Ave SK8 ....131 F5
Commercial Brow SK14 .....167 E4
Commercial Rd
  Hazel Grove SK7 ....124 E3
  Oldham OL1 ....153 F6
Commercial St Bacup OL13 ...3 D8
  Hyde SK14 ....167 E3
  Manchester M15 ....162 F7
  Manchester M3 ....162 C6
Commodore Pl WN5 ....36 E1
Common End PR7 ....20 E5
Common La Culcheth WA3 ...91 E4
  Leigh WN7 ....75 B4
  Partington M31 ....106 B5
  Tyldesley M29 ....59 A1
Common Nook WN2 ....56 A6
Common Side Rd M28 ....77 F7
Common St BL5 ....57 B7
Common The PR7 ....20 E5
Commonwealth Cl WN7 ......76 B3
Comrie Wlk 7 M23 ....121 A5
Comus St M5 ....161 C8
Concert La M2 ....159 A1
Concord Ave WN3 ....55 B3
Concord Bsns Pk M22 ......121 E1
Concord Pl M6 ....81 A5
Concord Way 1 SK16 ....101 D8
Condor Cl M43 ....84 C3
Condor Pl M6 ....81 A5
Condor Wlk M13 ....163 B8
Conduit St Ashton-u-L OL6 ..166 C2
  Oldham OL1 ....49 E3
  Tintwistle SK13 ....103 F7
Conewood Wlk 9 M13 ....163 C6
Coney Gr M23 ....121 A7
Coney Green High Sch
  M26 ....44 B4
Congham Rd 6 SK3 ....123 C8
Congleton Ave M3 ....98 C2
Congou St M1 ....163 C8
Congreave St OL1 ....153 E8
Conham Rd WN7 ....75 D7
Conifer Wlk Leigh WN7 ......75 E5
  Partington M31 ....105 E3
Coningsby Dr M9 ....157 D8
Conisber Cl BL7 ....8 E1
Conisborough OL11 ....139 E6
Conisborough Pl M45 ....63 B8
Coniston Ave Adlington PR6 .21 B8
  Ashton-in-M WN4 ....73 B4
  Atherton M46 ....58 D5
  Dukinfield SK14 ....101 D8
  Farnworth BL4 ....59 F8
  Hindley WN2 ....56 C6
  Leigh WN7 ....75 D8
  Manchester M9 ....157 D8
  Oldham OL8 ....66 D4
  Rochdale OL11 ....30 C6
  Sale M33 ....108 C2
  Walkden M38 ....60 A4
  Whitefield M45 ....62 F8
  Wigan WN5 ....54 C8
Coniston Dr Abram WN2 ......74 B8
  Handforth SK9 ....131 C4
  Middleton M24 ....46 F2
  Stalybridge SK15 ....86 A3

Coniston Gr
  Ashton-u-L OL7 ....166 A4
  Heywood OL10 ....46 D8
  Royton OL2 ....48 D6
  Standish WN6 ....60 A4
Coniston Ho 6 M28 ....60 E2
Coniston Park Dr WN6 ....37 A6
Coniston Rd Blackrod BL6 ...21 D3
  Flixton M41 ....106 E8
  Gatley SK8 ....122 B5
  High Lane SK6 ....134 D8
  Hindley WN2 ....56 B4
  Partington M31 ....105 E4
  Reddish SK5 ....111 F6
  Stretford M32 ....96 C3
  Swinton M27 ....79 F7
  Urmston M41 ....95 B3
Coniston St Bolton BL1 ......143 F3
  8 Failsworth M40 ....83 C5
  Leigh WN7 ....75 E5
  Salford M6 ....81 B4
Coniston Wlk WA15 ....120 D5
Conmere Sq 9 M15 ....162 F7
Connaught Ave
  Manchester M19 ....110 F7
  Rochdale OL16 ....31 B3
  Whitefield M45 ....63 A7
Connaught Cl SK9 ....137 C8
Connaught Dr WA12 ....89 C2
Connaught Sq BL2 ....25 B2
Connaught St Bury BL8 ....27 B1
  4 Oldham OL8 ....153 E6
Connel Cl BL2 ....42 F6
Connell Rd M23 ....121 A6
Connell Way OL10 ....29 F3
Connery Cres OL6 ....85 D6
Connie St M11 ....165 C8
Conningsby Cl 10 BL7 ....27 F8
Connington Ave M9 ....64 D1
Connington Cl OL2 ....48 C4
Connor Way SK8 ....121 F4
Conquest Cl M12 ....165 A6
Conrad Cl Oldham OL1 ....49 E4
Conran Wy M9 ....150 A5
Conran St M9 ....157 E7
Consett Ave M23 ....121 A6
Consort Ave OL2 ....48 C6
Consort Ct 2 SK16 ....101 C6
Consort Pl WA14 ....119 B3
Constable Cl BL1 ....143 D1
Constable Dr Marple SK6 ...126 B8
  Wilmslow SK9 ....137 E8
Constable St M18 ....99 E6
Constable Wlk 18 M34 ......113 C4
Constance Gdns M5 ....154 F1
Constance Rd Bolton BL3 ..146 C4
  Partington M31 ....105 E3
Constance St M15 ....162 E7
Constantine Ct M5 ....155 F3
Constantine Rd OL16 ....139 F7
Constantine St OL4 ....67 A7
Consul St M22 ....109 E1
Convamore Rd SK7 ....132 D7
Convent St OL8 ....67 C4
Conway Ave Bolton BL1 .....142 A1
  Irlam M44 ....105 F8
  Swinton M27 ....62 B3
  Whitefield M45 ....62 F2
Conway Cl Heywood OL10 ...29 A3
  Leigh WN7 ....76 E7
  Manchester M16 ....97 A3
  Middleton M24 ....65 A7
  Ramsbottom BL0 ....138 B6
  Whitefield M45 ....62 F7
Conway Cres Billinge WN5 ..71 E6
  Ramsbottom BL8 ....10 F2
Conway Dr
  Altrincham WA15 ....120 C6
  Bury BL9 ....45 A8
  Billinge WN5 ....71 F5
  Hazel Grove SK7 ....124 C1
  Newton-le-W WA12 ....89 E3
  Stalybridge SK15 ....86 A3
  Wigan WN6 ....37 C3
Conway Rd
  Ashton-in-M WN4 ....73 E5
  Cheadle SK8 ....123 B3
  Hindley WN2 ....56 F4
  Sale M33 ....108 D3
  Urmston M41 ....95 D4
Conway St Farnworth BL4 ...60 D7
  Reddish SK5 ....169 E4
  Wigan WN5 ....54 C8
Conyngham Rd M14 ....98 D3
Cook St Abram WN2 ....56 B1
  Bury BL9 ....141 A2
  Denton M34 ....100 F6
  Eccles M30 ....79 F5
  Leigh WN7 ....76 B3
  Manchester M3 ....158 E2
  Oldham OL4 ....67 C7
  Stockport SK3 ....169 E1
Cook Terr
  20 Dukinfield SK16 ....166 B1
  Rochdale OL16 ....15 B1
Cooke St Ashton-in-M WN4 .72 F6
  Denton M34 ....100 F3
  Farnworth BL4 ....60 E7
  Failsworth M35 ....83 F8
  Farnworth BL4 ....60 E7
  Hazel Grove SK7 ....124 D4
  Horwich BL6 ....22 D4
Cooling La M29,WN7 ....76 E8
Coomassie St
  Heywood OL10 ....29 C1

Coomassie St continued
Radcliffe M26 ....44 A3
Salford M6 ....154 F3
Coombe Cl M29 ....77 B8
Coombes Ave Hyde SK14 ..167 F1
Marple SK6 ....125 F5
Coombes La SK13 ......115 C5
Coombes St SK2 ......124 B5
Coombes View SK14 ....114 F8
Coop St Bolton BL1 ....143 E4
[1] Manchester M4 ....159 B2
Wigan WN1 ....37 D1
Cooper Fold M24 ......47 A4
Cooper Ho M15 ......163 A6
Cooper La
Manchester M9 ......64 D5
Middleton M24 ......46 F3
Cooper St Bury BL9 ....140 E2
Dukinfield SK16 ......166 B1
Glossop SK13 ......104 B1
Hazel Grove SK7 ....124 F3
Horwich BL6 ....22 B4
Littleborough OL12 ..15 D4
Manchester M2 ......158 F1
Oldham OL4 ....68 A7
Stockport SK1 ......170 F7
Stretford M32 ......96 D1
Cooper Terr OL16 .....31 B8
Cooper's Fold SK8 ....131 F6
Cooper's La PR7 ......18 B8
Cooper's Row BL1 ....145 F7
Cooperative St OL14 ...6 A7
Coopers Glen WN2 ....56 A8
Coopers Row WN1 ....150 C8
Coopers Wlk OL16 ....15 C2
Cop Rd OL1 ....49 C4
Copage Dr SK6 ......113 A4
Cope Bank E BL1 ....142 C2
Cope Bank Mews BL1 ..142 C1
Cope Bank W BL1 ....142 B2
Cope Cl M11 ....99 E7
Cope St BL1 ....142 C1
Copeland Ave M27 ....62 C1
Copeland Cl M8 ......46 C1
Copeland Dr WN6 .....19 F1
Copeland Mews BL1 ..144 A7
Copeland St SK14 ....101 D5
Copeman Cl M13 ......163 C6
Copenhagen Sq **[20]** OL16 ..31 A8
Copenhagen St
Failsworth M40 ......83 A6
Rochdale OL16 ......31 A8
Copesthorne Cl WN2 ..38 C6
Copgrove Rd M21 ....109 B7
Copgrove Wlk M22 ....130 E7
Copley Ave SK15 .....86 C2
Copley High Sch SK15 ..86 D2
Copley Park Mews SK15 ..86 C2
Copley Rd M21 ......97 A2
Copley St OL2 ......149 C8
Coplow Dale WN2 .....56 E3
Copper Beech Dr SK13 ..171 E1
Copper Beech Manor
SK13 ....171 E1
Copper La M45 ......62 B7
Copperas La Aspull WN2 ..38 A6
Blackrod BL6 ....21 B1
Droylsden M43 ......99 E8
Copperas St M4 ......159 A2
Copperbeech M22 ....109 E1
Copperbeech Dr WN6 ..37 B7
Copperfield M M17 ....37 C2
Copperfield Rd
Bramhall SK8 ......132 B5
Poynton SK12 ......133 D2
Copperfields Bolton BL6 ..40 B3
Poynton SK12 ......133 D2
Wilmslow SK9 ......137 C8
Copperways M20 ....110 B5
Coppice Ave M33 ....107 D2
Coppice Cl
High Lane SK12 ....135 A6
Romiley SK6 ......113 B4
Coppice Dr
High Lane SK12 ....135 A6
Longshaw WN5 ......53 D2
Whitworth OL12 ....14 D7
Wigan WN3 ....54 F2
Wythenshawe M22 ..109 D1
Coppice Inf Sch OL8 ..66 E4
Coppice Jun Sch OL8 ..66 E4
Coppice La SK12 ....135 A5
Coppice Rd SK12 ....134 B3
Coppice St Bury BL9 ..141 C3
Oldham OL8 ....153 D5
Coppice The
Altrincham WA15 ....129 B8
Bolton BL2 ....25 D5
Middleton M25 ......65 B5
Prestwich M25 ......63 A4
Ramsbottom BL0 ....11 A4
Swinton M28 ......79 C5
Worsley M28 ....78 F8
Coppice Way SK9 ....131 E3
Coppice Wlk M34 ....100 D2
Copping St M12 ......164 F6
Coppingford Cl OL12 ..14 A2
Coppins The S SK9 ..136 E4
Coppleridge Dr M8 ....64 A2
Copplestone Ct M27 ..61 C1
Copplestone Dr M33 ..107 C5
Coppull Cross Rds PR7 ..19 F7
Coppull Hall La PR7 ..20 B8
Coppull La WN1 ......37 D2
Coppull Moor La PR7 ..19 E6
Copse Ave M22 ......121 E3
Copse Dr BL9 ....27 F6

Copse The
Altrincham WA15 ....129 D7
Edgworth BL7 ......9 C2
Marple SK6 ....126 C8
Newton-le-W WA12 ..89 B4
Wigan WN5 ....54 A6
Copse Wlk OL15 ....15 F5
Copson St M20 ......110 B7
Copster Ave M40 ....83 C6
Copster Hill Rd OL8 ..66 E4
Copster Pl M40 ......66 E3
Copthall La M8 ......63 F8
Copthorn Wlk BL8 ...26 F5
Copthorne Cl OL10 ...46 D8
Copthorne Cres WN3 ..98 E3
Copthorne Dr BL2 ....42 E6
Coptrod Head Cl OL12 ..14 E4
Coral Ave SK8 ......123 A1
Coral Cl M13 ....163 C8
Coral Gr WN7 ....75 E4
Coral St Manchester M13 ..163 C7
Wigan WN5 ....37 A3
Coralin Way WN4 ....72 F7
Coram St M18 ......99 F6
Corbar Rd SK2 ......124 B5
Corbett St OL16 .....56 E5
Corbett St Droylsden M11 ..83 A1
Rochdale OL16 ......31 B8
Corbridge Wlk **[7]** M8 ..156 B6
Corby St M12 ......165 A6
Corcoran Cl OL10 ....29 C3
Corcoran Dr SK6 ....113 F2
Corda Ave M22 ......121 D6
Corday La M25 ......63 D8
Cordingley Ave M43 ..99 F8
Cordova Ave M34 ....99 F3
Corelli St M40 ......160 F4
Corfe Cl Aspull WN2 ..38 D5
Urmston M41 ......94 C1
Corfe Cres WN7 ....124 D1
Corhampton Cres M46 ..58 E5
Corinth Wlk M28 ....60 D2
Corinthian Ave M7 ....81 C5
Cork St Ashton-u-L OL6 ..166 C2
Bury BL9 ....141 A2
Manchester M12 ....164 D8
Corkland Cl OL6 ....85 E2
Corkland Rd M21 ....109 C8
Corkland St OL6 .....85 E2
Corks La SK12 ......135 E5
Corley Ave SK3 ....122 F7
Cormallen Gr M35 ...84 A7
Cormorant Cl M28 ..60 C3
Cormorant Wlk M12 ..165 A6
Corn Cl M13 ....163 C5
Corn Hey Rd M33 ....107 C2
Corn Hill La M34 ....100 B5
Corn Mill La Garswood WN4 ..72 D4
Rochdale OL12 ......13 C8
Corn St Failsworth M35 ..83 C6
Glossop SK13 ......104 D1
Leigh WN7 ....75 D5
Oldham OL4 ....67 A7
Cornall St BL8 ......27 C3
Cornbrook Cl
Littleborough OL12 ..15 C6
Westhoughton BL5 ..57 D6
Cornbrook Ct M15 ...162 D6
Cornbrook Gr M16 ...162 D5
Cornbrook Park Rd M15 ..161 C6
Cornbrook Rd M15 ...161 C7
Cornbrook Sta M15 ..161 C6
Cornbrook St M16 ...162 D5
Cornbrook Way M16 ..162 D5
Cornelian Gr WN4 ....72 F5
Cornell St M4 ......159 B2
Corner Croft SK9 ....137 A4
Corner Ct SK8 ......122 F6
Corner La WN7 ......57 D3
Corner St OL6 ......166 C2
Cornergate BL5 .....57 E5
Cornet St M7 ......155 D5
Cornfield SK15 ......102 E7
Cornfield Dr Bury BL9 ..27 F7
[2] Sale M33 ......108 A1
Cornfield Dr M22 ...121 C3
Cornfield Rd SK6 ...113 E3
Cornfield St OL16 ...32 A5
Cornford Ave M18 ...99 B3
Cornhill Ave M41 ....95 B3
Cornhill Rd M41 ....95 B3
Cornhill St OL1 ......49 D2
Cornish Cl M22 .....130 D8
Cornish Way OL2 ....49 A4
Cornishway M22 ....130 D8
Cornishway Ind Est **[3]**
M22 ....130 D8
Cornlea Dr M28 ....78 C7
Cornwall Ave Atherton BL5 ..58 F8
Manchester M19 ....111 B8
Tyldesley M29 ......59 A3
Cornwall Cl SK6 ....134 E7
Cornwall Cres
Brinnington SK5 ....112 C6
Diggle SK3 ....51 B4
Shaw OL2 ....149 A8
Cornwall Ct **[2]** M46 ..99 D6
Cornwall Dr Bury BL9 ..45 A8
Hindley WN2 ......56 F6
Cornwall Ho M3 ....158 D1
Cornwall Pl WN5 .....54 D6
Cornwall Rd Droylsden M43 ..84 A3
Gatley SK8 ....131 B8
Irlam M44 ....105 D5
Cornwall St **[2]** Eccles M30 ..79 C1
Manchester M11,M18 ..99 D7
Oldham OL9 ......152 B5
Cornwallis Rd WN3 ..150 A5

Cornwell Cl SK9 .....137 D8
Cornwood Cl **[5]** M8 ..155 F7
Corona Ave Hyde SK14 ..167 E3
Oldham OL8 ....66 E3
Coronation Ave
Atherton M46 ......58 C5
Dukinfield SK16 ....101 F6
Glazebury WA3 ......92 C7
Heywood OL10 ......46 E8
Hyde SK14 ....167 E1
Coronation Dr
Ashton-in-M WA11 ..89 A7
Leigh WN7 ....76 E6
Newton-le-W WA12 ..89 E1
Coronation Gdns M26 ..43 E4
Coronation Rd
Ashton-u-L OL6 .....85 C6
Droylsden M43 ......83 F3
Failsworth M35 .....83 E6
Radcliffe M26 ......43 E4
Wigan WN6 ....36 D3
Coronation Sq
Little Lever BL3 .....43 B3
Manchester M11,M12 ..163 D8
Coronation St Bolton BL1 ..145 F7
Denton M34 ....100 D3
Downall Green WN4 ..72 D6
Ince-in-M WN3 ......52 S3
Manchester M5 .....165 C8
Manchester M3 .....162 E8
Reddish SK5 ....169 E4
Salford M5 ....161 B8
Swinton M27 ......62 A1
Wigan WN3 ....150 B6
Coronation Wlk
Billinge WN5 ....71 D4
Radcliffe M26 ......43 E5
Corporation Rd
Denton M34 ....100 D5
Eccles M30 ....79 F1
Rochdale OL11 .....139 D6
Rochdale OL11 .....139 D7
Corporation St Bolton BL1 ..145 F7
Hyde SK14 ....167 D4
Manchester M4 ....159 A2
Middleton M24 ......65 A8
Stalybridge SK15 ....86 A1
Stockport SK1 ......169 F2
Wigan WN3 ....150 B6
Corran Cl M30 ....79 F1
Corranstone Cl BL6 ..22 B3
Correction Brow SK12 ..134 C6
Corrie Cl M34 ......100 F1
Corrie Cres BL4 .....61 D4
Corrie Dr BL4 ....61 D5
Corrie Prim Sch M34 ..100 F1
Corrie Rd M27 ......62 A3
Corrie St M34 ......60 A4
Corrie Way SK6 ....112 F5
Corrigan St M18 .....99 E6
Corrin Rd BL2 ......148 B5
Corring Way BL1 ....25 B4
Corringham Rd M19 ..111 C7
Corriss Ave M9 .....64 A5
Corry St OL10 ......29 E2
Corsey Rd WN2 ......56 A4
Corsock Dr WN1 .....37 E1
Corson St BL4 ......42 D2
Corston Gr BL6 ......21 D1
Corston Wlk M40 ....83 B6
Corwen Ave M9 .....157 D6
Corwen Cl OL8 ......66 B2
Cosgrove Cres M35 ..83 E5
Cosgrove Rd M35 ....83 E5
Cosham Rd M22 ....121 F3
Costabeck Wlk M40 ..83 D4
Cotessey Way WN3 ..54 C3
Costobadie Cl SK14 ..102 F3
Costobadie Way SK14 ..102 F3
Cosworth Cl **[7]** WN7 ..76 B4
Cotaline Cl OL11 .....30 B3
Cote Green La SK6 ..114 B1
Cote Green Rd SK6 ..114 C1
Cote La Delph OL3 ....51 B7
Littleborough OL15 ..15 F6
Uppermill OL5 ......68 E3
Cotefield Ave BL3 ....147 E3
Cotefield Cl **[3]** SK14 ..125 F5
Cotefield Rd M22 ...121 C2
Cotford Rd BL1 ......24 F5
Cotman Dr SK6 .....126 C8
Cotswold Ave
Gollowne WA3 ......90 D6
Hazel Grove SK7 ....124 B1
Oldham OL9 ....152 A5
Shaw OL2 ....149 A8
Shaw OL2 ....48 B8
Urmston M41 ......94 F3
Wigan WN5 ....54 B5
Cotswold Cl Glossop SK13 ..116 A8
Prestwich M25 ......63 C5
Ramsbottom BL0 ....11 D6
Cotswold Cres Bury BL8 ..27 B3
Milnrow OL16 ......32 A7
Royton OL2 ....48 B3
Salford M6 ....154 D4
Cotswold Dr Horwich BL6 ..22 C5
Royton OL2 ....48 B3
Salford M6 ....154 D4

Cottage Wlk continued
Rochdale OL12 ....14 C4
Cottam Cres SK6 ....126 B7
Cottam Gr M27 ......80 A7
Cottam St Bury BL8 ..27 C3
Oldham OL1 ......153 D8
Cottenham La M3,M7 ..158 E4
Cottenham St M13 ..163 B6
Cotter St M12 ......163 C7
Cotterdale Cl M16 ...97 D2
Cotteril Cl M23 .....120 C3
Cotterill St M5,M6 ....81 B2
Cottesmore Dr M8 ..156 C8
Cottesmore Gdns WA15 ..129 C8
Cottingham Dr OL6 ..166 C3
Cottingham Rd M12 ..164 E6
Cottingley Cl BL1 ....24 D5
Cotton Cl SK14 ......167 E1
Cotton Fold OL16 ....31 C6
Cotton Hill M20 ....110 C5
Cotton La M20 ......110 C6
Cotton Mill Cres OL9 ..66 S3
Cotton St Bolton BL1 ..143 D2
Leigh WN7 ....75 D5
Manchester M4 ....159 B2
Cotton St E SK14 ....166 A2
Cotton Tree Cl OL4 ..67 E8
Cotton Tree St **[4]** SK5 ..169 E1
Cottonfield Rd M20 ..110 C6
Cottonwood Dr **[3]** M33 ..107 C5
Cottrell Rd WA15 ....129 D7
Coucill Sq BL4 ......60 E8
Coulsden Dr M9 ......64 D3
Coulthart St OL6 ....166 B3
Coulthurst St BL0 ...138 B6
Coultshead Ave WN5 ..71 E6
Council Ave WN4 ....73 B3
Councillor La SK8 ..123 A4
Councillor St M40 ..160 E1
Count St OL16 ......31 A5
Countess Ave SK8 ..131 E5
Countess Gr M7 ....158 D4
Countess La M26 ....43 D4
Countess Pl M25 ....63 C4
Countess Rd M20 ..110 B3
Countess St Ashton-u-L OL6 ..85 D2
Stockport SK2 ......124 A5
Counthill Com Sec Sch
OL4 ....49 D2
Counthill Dr M8 .....63 E2
Counthill Rd OL4 ....49 D2
Counting House Rd SK12 ..135 E5
County Ave SK8 ......124 A5
County Police St WN2 ..151 F7
County Rd M28 ......60 A4
County St Manchester M2 ..158 F1
Oldham OL8 ....66 E3
Courier St M18 ......99 F6
Courier Pl WN6 ......18 D5
Court St BL2 ....148 A6
Course View OL4 ....67 F3
Court Dr M40 ....83 E4
Court House Way **[4]** OL10 ..29 D2
Court St Bolton BL2 ..148 A7
Oldham OL4 ....69 B8
Courtfield Ave M9 ...64 D4
Courthill St SK1 ....124 A8
Courtney Gn SK9 ...131 D2
Courtney Pl WA14 ..119 A1
Courtyard Dr M28 ....60 A3
Courtyard The Bolton BL1 ..143 F1
Hollingworth SK14 ..103 D5
Newton-le-W WA12 ..89 E4
Cousin Fields BL7 ....25 C7
Covall Wlk **[4]** M8 ..156 B6
Cove The WA15 .....119 F3
Covell Rd SK12 .....133 C6
Covent Gdns SK1 ...169 F1
Coventry Ave SK3 ..122 F7
Coventry Gr OL9 ....48 A1
Coventry Rd M26 ....43 F5
Coventry St OL11 ..139 C6
Coverdale Ave Bolton BL1 ..144 A8
Royton OL2 ....48 C5
Coverdale Cl OL10 ...29 C1
Coverdale Cres M12 ..164 E6
Coverhill Rd OL4 ....68 B5
Covert Rd OL4 ......67 D3
Wythenshawe M22 ..121 E5
Coverts The M6 .....81 A6
Covington Pl SK9 ...137 B6
Cow La Ashley WA15 ..128 F6
Bolton BL3 ....146 B2
Failsworth M35 .....83 E7
Manchester M4 ....159 C2
Oldham OL4 ....68 A6
Sale M33 ....108 E5
Stockport SK2,SK7 ..124 D4
Cow Lees BL5 ......40 A1
Cowan St M40 ......160 D2
Cowbrook Ave SK13 ..104 F1
Cowburn Dr SK22 ...127 C1
Cowburn St Heywood OL10 ..29 E1
Hindley WN2 ......56 F6
[1] Leigh WN7 ....75 D5
Manchester M3 ....158 F3
Cowdals Rd BL6 .....40 B4

Cowesby St M14 .....98 A3
Cowhill La OL6 .....166 C3
Cowie St OL2 ......149 B8
Cowley Gr SK14 ....102 F3
Cowley Rd BL1 ......24 F5
Cowley St M40 ......83 C6
Cowling St Manchester M7 ..80 F8
Oldham OL8 ......66 F4
Wigan WN3 ....150 B6
Cowlishaw OL2 ......149 A5
Cowlishaw La WN2 ..149 A5
Cowlishaw Rd SK8 ..113 F4
Cown Park Way N OL12 ..4 D2
Cown Park Way S OL12 ..4 C1
Cowm St OL12 ......44 E6
Cown Top La OL11 ...30 E2
Cowpe Rd BB4 ......2 A5
Cowper Ave M46 ....58 D5
Cowper St Ashton-u-L OL6 ..166 C3
Leigh WN7 ....75 D5
Middleton M24 ......65 D8
Coxfield Wlk **[4]** M11 ..160 F1
Cox Green Cl **[4]** BL7 ..8 D3
Cox Green Rd
[2] Bolton BL7 ......24 F8
Bolton BL7 ....8 E2
Cox Way M46 ....58 D3
Coxton Rd M22 .....121 E1
Coxwold Gr BL3 ....146 C2
Crab Brow M46 .....58 B3
Crab Tree La M46 ...58 D2
Crab La M9 ....64 B4
Crabbe St M4 ......159 A3
Crabtree Ave
Altrincham WA15 ..129 D7
Disley SK12 ....135 E5
Crabtree Ct SK12 ..135 D6
Crabtree La M11 ...163 D1
Crabtree Rd Oldham OL1 ..67 B8
Wigan WN5 ....54 D7
Crabtree St BL9 ....141 B3
Craddock Rd M33 ..108 C2
Craddock St **[4]** OL5 ..68 C1
Cradley Ave M11 ....99 D8
Crag Ave BL9 ......11 D2
Crag Fold BL9 ......11 D2
Crag Gr WN4 ....71 B1
Crag La BL9 ....11 D2
Cragg Rd OL1 ......48 D2
Cragg St **[2]** M8 ...155 F5
Cragside Way SK9 ..137 C6
Craig Ave Bury BL9 ..27 B1
Urmston M41 ......95 A3
Craig Cl SK4 ....168 B1
Craig Rd Manchester M18 ..99 C4
Stockport SK4 ......168 B1
Craig Wlk OL8 ......153 E5
Craigend Dr M9 ....157 E7
Craighall Ave M19 ..110 F8
Craighall Rd BL1 ....24 E6
Craiglands OL11 ....31 B2
Craigmore Ave M20 ..109 E4
Craignair Ct M27 ....80 C7
Craigslands Ave M40 ..83 A6
Cragweil Ave M20 ..110 D3
Cragweil Rd M25 ..163 B7
Crail Pl OL10 ....28 F1
Cramer St M10,M40 ..157 F5
Crammond Cl M40 ..83 D6
Cramond Cl BL1 ....143 D1
Cramond Wlk **[1]** BL1 ..143 D1
Crampton Dr WA15 ..129 C8
Crampton La M31 ..106 D6
Cranage Rd M19 ...111 B8
Cranark Cl BL1 .....144 A7
Cranberry Ave **M** M33 ..163 B7
Cranberry Cl WA14 ..119 B8
Cranberry Dr BL3 ..147 E5
Cranberry St OL4 ....67 B6
Cranborne Cl Horwich BL6 ..22 F1
Standish WN6 ......19 D1
Cranbourne Ave SK8 ..123 B2
Cranbourne Cl
[1] Altrincham WA15 ..120 A6
Ashton-u-L OL7 ....166 A4
Cranbourne Ct SK4 ..168 B4
Cranbourne Rd
Ashton-u-L OL7 ....166 B4
Manchester M21 ....97 C4
Manchester M21 ....109 B8
Manchester SK4 ....168 B4
Rochdale OL16 ......31 A5
Cranbourne St **[2]** M5 ..81 C1
Cranbrook Cl BL1 ...143 F1
Cranbrook Dr M25 ..63 C2
Cranbrook Gdns OL7 ..166 B4
Cranbrook Rd Eccles M30 ..79 B4
Reddish M18 ......99 F3
Cranbrook St
Ashton-u-L OL7 ....166 B4
Oldham OL4 ....67 C6
Radcliffe M26 ......44 B4
Cranbrook Way WN1 ..37 B4
Cranbrook Wlk OL9 ..152 A6
Cranby St **[6]** WN2 ...56 D5
Crandon Ct M27 ....62 A1
Crandon Dr M20 ...122 C8
Crane St Bolton BL3 ..146 B3

Crane St continued
Coppull PR7 ...19 D6
Manchester M12 ...163 C8
Cranesbill Cl M22 ...121 C1
Cranfield Cl M40 ...160 D2
Cranfield Rd Horwich BL6 ...39 E7
Wigan WN3 ...55 A3
Cranford Ave
Manchester M20 ...110 D4
Sale M33 ...108 C6
Stretford M32 ...96 F3
Whitefield M45 ...44 E2
Cranford Cl Salford M27 ...80 B6
Whitefield M45 ...44 E2
Cranford Dr M44 ...93 F3
Cranford Gdns
Marple SK6 ...125 F8
Urmston M41 ...94 E3
Manchester M30 ...79 F3
Cranford Rd
Handforth SK9 ...131 A1
Urmston M41 ...94 E3
Cranford St BL3 ...146 C2
Cranham Ave WA3 ...90 E7
Cranham Cl Bury BL8 ...27 B3
Walkden M28 ...60 A6
Cranham Rd M22 ...121 A2
Crank Rd WA11,WN5 ...71 B8
Crankwood Rd WN2,WN7 ...74 D5
Cranleigh WN6 ...37 A8
Cranleigh Ave SK4 ...110 F4
Cranleigh Cl Blackrod BL6 ...21 D1
Oldham OL4 ...49 E1
Cranleigh Dr Cheadle SK8 ...122 F6
Hazel Grove SK7 ...134 A8
Sale M23,M33 ...108 C1
Sale M33 ...108 A5
Tyldesley M29 ...77 B8
Walkden M28 ...78 E8
Cramlington Dr M8 ...155 F6
Cranmer Ct OL10 ...29 C2
Cranmer Rd M20 ...110 B4
Cranmere Ave M19 ...99 C2
Cranmere Dr M33 ...107 D2
Cranshaw St M29 ...77 D8
Cranstal Dr WN2 ...57 A5
Cranston Dr
Manchester M20 ...122 B8
Sale M33 ...108 A3
Cranston Gr SK8 ...121 F5
Cranswick St M14 ...98 A3
Crantock Dr Gatley SK8 ...131 C8
Stalybridge SK15 ...86 D3
Crantock St M12 ...99 B3
Cranwell Ave WA3 ...91 F4
Cranwell Dr M19 ...110 E4
Cranworth Ave M7 ...77 A6
Cranworth St SK15 ...86 B1
Craston Rd M13 ...98 E2
Craunton M30 ...79 F2
Craven Ave Golborne WA3 ...90 E7
Salford M5 ...161 B8
Craven Ct BL6 ...22 D2
Craven Dr
Altrincham WA14 ...119 C8
Salford M5 ...161 A7
Craven Gdns OL11 ...139 E5
Craven Ho OL14 ...6 A8
Craven Pl Bolton BL1 ...23 E2
Droylsden M11 ...83 C2
Craven Rd
Altrincham WA14 ...119 C7
Reddish SK5 ...111 F6
Craven St Ashton-u-L OL6 ...85 D5
Bury BL9 ...141 C3
Manchester M45 ...81 C1
Oldham OL1 ...48 E1
Craven St E BL6 ...22 D2
Craven Terr M33 ...108 C4
Cravenhurst Ave M40 ...83 B4
Cravenwood Prim Sch M8 ...64 A1
Cravenwood Rd M8 ...156 A8
Crawford Ave
Adlington PR7 ...20 E5
Aspull WN2 ...38 C5
Bolton BL2 ...148 B6
Tyldesley M29 ...58 F2
Worsley M28 ...79 A8
Crawford Cl WN2 ...38 C5
Crawford Sq OL10 ...29 A1
Crawford St Ashton-u-L OL6 ...85 D2
Aspull WN2 ...38 C4
Bolton BL2 ...148 B6
Eccles M30 ...79 D3
Failsworth M40 ...83 C5
Rochdale OL16 ...31 B6
Walsden OL14 ...6 A8
Wigan WN1 ...150 C8
Crawley Ave Salford M30 ...80 A3
Wythenshawe M22 ...121 E3
Crawley Cl WN2 ...59 C1
Crawley Gr SK2 ...124 A6
Crawley Way OL9 ...152 A6
Cray The OL16 ...31 E6
Cray Wlk M13 ...163 B7
Craydon St M11 ...165 C8
Crayfield Rd M19 ...111 B8
Crayford Rd M40 ...83 B4
Creaton Way M24 ...46 D4
Creden Ave M22 ...121 F3
Crediton Cl
Altrincham WA14 ...119 B6
Manchester M15 ...162 F5
Crediton Dr Bolton BL2 ...42 A7
Platt Bridge WN2 ...56 A1

Crediton Ho M6 ...80 A3
Creel Cl M9 ...64 B4
Cremer M30 ...80 A2
Cresbury St M12 ...164 D8
Crescent M5 ...81 C2
Crescent Ave
Ashton-in-M WN4 ...73 A4
Atherton BL5 ...59 A8
Bolton BL1 ...145 D8
Farnworth BL4 ...60 C6
Manchester M25 ...63 B2
Manchester M8 ...156 A8
Prestwich M27 ...80 B8
Crescent Cl
Dukinfield SK16 ...166 C1
Stockport SK3 ...124 A5
Crescent Ct
Manchester M21 ...96 F1
Sale M33 ...108 B3
Crescent Dr Manchester M8 ...64 B1
Walkden M28 ...60 B5
Crescent Gr Cheadle SK8 ...122 C6
Manchester M19 ...99 A1
Manchester M25 ...63 B2
Crescent Pk SK4 ...168 C3
Crescent Range M14 ...98 C3
Crescent Rd
Alderley Edge SK9 ...137 B2
Altrincham WA14 ...119 A6
Altrincham WA15 ...119 E1
Bolton BL3 ...42 B3
Cheadle SK8 ...122 C6
Dukinfield SK16 ...166 C1
Failsworth OL9 ...65 C2
Horwich BL6 ...39 F8
Kearsley BL4 ...60 F6
Manchester M8 ...156 A8
Manchester M38 ...60 A4
Stockport SK1 ...112 B3
Crescent St M8 ...156 C8
Crescent The
Altrincham WA14 ...119 A5
Altrincham WA15 ...119 F7
Bolton BL2 ...25 F4
Bolton BL7 ...25 A7
Bredbury SK6 ...112 D4
Cheadle SK8 ...122 D6
Droylsden M43 ...83 F1
Eccles M28 ...79 A5
Horwich BL6 ...22 E1
Ince-in-M WN2 ...56 B7
Irlam M44 ...94 B3
Little Lever BL3 ...43 B2
Manchester M19 ...99 A1
Middleton M24 ...64 E4
Mossley OL5 ...68 B1
Prestwich M25 ...63 B4
Radcliffe M26 ...44 B3
Shaw OL2 ...149 A6
Stalybridge SK15 ...102 D6
Stockport SK4 ...124 A4
Urmston M41 ...94 F3
Westhoughton BL5 ...57 E7
Whitefield M45 ...62 A5
Wigan WN5 ...54 B6
Crescent View SK16 ...166 B1
Crescent Way SK3 ...124 A5
Cresgarth Ho SK3 ...124 A4
Cressell Pk WN6 ...19 B1
Cressfield Way M21 ...109 D7
Cressingham Rd
Bolton BL3 ...146 A4
Stretford M32 ...96 B2
Cressington Cl M5 ...154 E2
Cresswell Gr M20 ...110 A5
Crest Lo SK7 ...123 F2
Crest St M3 ...159 A3
Crest The M43 ...100 A7
Crestfield Gr M46 ...36 F2
Crestfield M38 ...60 A4
Crestwood Ave WN3 ...54 F3
Crestwood Wlk M40 ...156 C6
Creswick Cl WN2 ...56 C4
Crete St OL8 ...66 F4
Crewe Rd M23 ...120 E8
Crib Fold OL3 ...51 A2
Crib La OL3 ...51 A2
Criccieth Ave WN2 ...38 D5
Criccieth Rd SK3 ...123 A7
Criccieth St M16 ...97 F4
Cricket Gr The M21 ...109 B6
Cricket St Bolton BL3 ...145 D5
Dukinfield M34 ...101 A4
Wigan WN6 ...150 B8
Cricket View OL16 ...31 C5
Cricket's La OL6 ...85 D3
Cricketers Way BL5 ...57 F8
Cricketfield La M28 ...60 C3
Cricklewood Rd M22 ...121 C2
Crimble La OL10,OL11 ...29 F3
Crimble St OL12 ...139 D8
Crimbles St OL14 ...67 E8
Crime La OL8 ...84 D7
Crimsworth Ave M16 ...97 B2
Crinan Sq OL10 ...28 F1
Crinan Way BL2 ...42 A6
Crinan Wlk M40 ...160 D3
Cringle Barrow Cl M28 ...78 A5
Cringle Cl BL3 ...40 F4
Cringle Dr SK8 ...122 C3
Cringle Hall Rd M19 ...110 F8
Cringle Rd M19 ...111 C7
Cringleford Wlk M12 ...164 F5
Crippen St WN6 ...58 A1
Cripple Gate WN6 ...19 A2
Cripple Gate La OL11 ...30 E1
Crispin Rd M22 ...130 E8
Critchley Cl SK14 ...167 F1

Criterion St SK5 ...99 F2
Croal Ave WN2 ...56 A2
Croal St BL1 ...145 D6
Croal Wlk M45 ...45 B1
Croasdale Dr OL2 ...48 E5
Croasdale St BL1 ...143 F1
Crocker Wlk M9 ...157 E8
Crocus Dr OL2 ...149 A5
Crocus St BL1 ...143 F4
Crocus Wlk M7 ...155 D6
Croft Acres BL0 ...1 D2
Croft Ave Atherton M46 ...58 D2
Golborne WA3 ...73 F2
Middleton M25 ...63 F8
Croft Bank Manchester M18 ...99 E5
Manchester M7 ...81 C5
Stalybridge SK15 ...86 D6
Croft Brow OL8 ...66 E2
Croft Cl WA15 ...129 C6
Croft Dr BL8 ...26 E6
Croft Gate BL2 ...25 E4
Croft Gates Rd M24 ...64 D7
Croft Gr M38 ...59 F5
Croft Head OL2 ...48 D4
Croft Head Dr OL16 ...31 F7
Croft Hill Rd M40 ...65 A1
Croft Ind Est BL9 ...45 A5
Croft La Bolton BL3 ...148 B5
Radcliffe M26 ...44 C4
Whitefield BL9 ...45 A5
Croft Manor SK13 ...104 E1
Croft Pl M29 ...76 F8
Croft Rd Cheadle SK8 ...123 B2
Sale M33 ...108 D2
Wilmslow SK9 ...136 E4
Croft Side BL3 ...42 E5
Croft Sq OL12 ...15 C3
Croft St Bolton BL3 ...42 B4
Bury BL9 ...141 A2
Droylsden M11 ...83 B1
Failsworth M35 ...66 A1
Golborne WA3 ...90 A4
Hyde SK14 ...167 D2
Littleborough OL12 ...15 C3
Manchester M5,M7 ...81 C5
Stalybridge SK15 ...86 B2
Walkden M38 ...59 F5
Westhoughton BL5 ...39 E3
Croft The Hadfield SK13 ...104 A6
Oldham OL8 ...66 E2
Orrell WN5 ...53 D3
Stockport SK2 ...124 B6
Westhoughton BL5 ...39 E3
Whitefield BL9 ...45 A6
Crofters Brook M26 ...44 C4
Crofters Gn SK9 ...136 E5
Crofters Hall Wlk M40 ...83 B7
Crofters Wlk BL2 ...25 C6
Crofters'Yd WN1 ...150 C8
Crofthill Cl OL12 ...15 D4
Croftlands Orrell WN5 ...53 D4
Whitworth OL12 ...4 D3
Croftlands Rd M22 ...121 E4
Croftleigh Cl M45 ...44 E2
Crofton Ave WA15 ...120 A8
Crofton Gdns WA3 ...91 F3
Crofton St Manchester M14 ...98 B3
Manchester M16 ...97 D4
Oldham OL8 ...66 F3
Crofts OL2 ...49 E8
Crofts Bank Rd M41 ...95 D3
Croftside Ave M28 ...60 D3
Croftside Cl M28 ...60 D3
Croftside Gr M28 ...60 D3
Croftside Way SK9 ...137 C6
Croftwood Sq WN5 ...36 C2
Croichbank BL8 ...10 B2
Croichley Fold BL8 ...10 D2
Cromar Rd SK7 ...124 F3
Cromarty Ave OL9 ...66 A3
Cromarty Sq OL10 ...28 F1
Cromarty Wlk M11 ...160 F1
Crombie Ave M22 ...121 D7
Crombouke Dr WN7 ...57 E1
Cromdale Ave Bolton BL1 ...144 B8
Hazel Grove SK7 ...124 F3
Cromedale Cres WN6 ...37 A7
Cromer Ave Bolton BL2 ...25 C1
Manchester M20 ...110 B6
Reddish M34 ...100 A3
Cromer Dr M46 ...58 A2
Cromer Ind Est M24 ...47 B1
Cromer Rd Bury BL8 ...27 D5
Cheadle SK8 ...122 E6
Sale M33 ...108 C3
Wigan WN3 ...54 E3
Cromer St Droylsden M11 ...83 D1
Middleton M24 ...47 B1
Rochdale OL12 ...139 E8
Shaw OL2 ...149 B7
Stockport SK1 ...112 A2
Cromford Ave M32 ...96 B3
Cromford Bank SK13 ...171 D2
Cromford Bsns Ctr OL1 ...67 B8
Cromford Cl Bolton BL1 ...143 E1
Gamesley SK13 ...171 D2
Cromford Cts M19 ...159 A2
Cromford Dr WN5 ...36 E1
Cromford Fold SK13 ...171 D2
Cromford Gdns BL1 ...143 F2
Cromford Gr SK13 ...171 D2
Cromford La SK13 ...171 D2
Cromford Pl SK13 ...171 D2
Cromford St OL1 ...67 A8

Cromford Way SK13 ...171 D2
Cromhurst St M8 ...156 A8
Cromley Rd High Lane SK6 ...134 E6
Stockport SK2 ...124 A3
Crompton Ave Bolton BL2 ...42 E8
Rochdale OL16 ...31 B3
Crompton Cl Bolton BL1 ...25 A4
Marple SK6 ...125 F7
Radcliffe M26 ...62 B8
Crompton Ct BL3 ...43 C3
Crompton Fold Prim Sch
BL2 ...42 E7
Crompton Ho WN1 ...151 D8
Crompton House Sch OL2 ...48 F7
Crompton Pl Bolton BL1 ...145 F7
Radcliffe M26 ...44 B3
Crompton Rd Horwich BL6 ...39 F8
Kearsley M26 ...61 A8
Manchester M19 ...111 A7
Crompton St
Ashton-u-L OL6 ...85 E4
Bolton BL1 ...148 A8
Bury BL9 ...140 E2
Farnworth BL4 ...60 E7
Ince-in-M WN3 ...151 E8
Oldham OL1 ...153 E8
Oldham OL9 ...152 C7
Platt Bridge WN2 ...56 B3
Royton OL2 ...48 D3
Royton OL2 ...48 E3
Shaw OL2 ...149 B7
Swinton M27 ...80 B8
Walkden M38 ...59 D5
Wigan WN1 ...150 B8
Crompton Vale BL2 ...42 D8
Crompton Way Bolton BL2 ...25 C2
Shaw OL2 ...149 B7
Cromwell Ave Gatley SK8 ...122 A6
Manchester M16 ...97 C2
Marple SK6 ...125 D7
Cromwell Cl M42 ...89 A4
Cromwell Ct M44 ...105 E7
Cromwell Gr
Manchester M19 ...99 B1
Manchester M7 ...81 C5
Cromwell Range M14 ...98 D2
Cromwell Rd
Bramhall SK7 ...132 D6
Bredbury SK6 ...112 D6
Eccles M30 ...79 D2
Irlam M44 ...105 E7
Prestwich M25 ...63 C4
Royton OL2 ...48 D6
Salford M6 ...81 B5
Stretford M32 ...96 F2
Swinton M27 ...61 F5
Whitefield M45 ...44 E2
Wigan WN3 ...150 C7
Wigan WN5 ...54 B6
Cross The SK13 ...104 A5
Crossacres Cty Prim Sch
M22 ...121 E4
Crossacres Prim Sch
M22 ...121 E4
Crossacres Rd M22 ...121 E3
Crossbank Ave M44 ...67 F7
Crossbank Cl M13 ...164 D5
Crossbank St Oldham OL8 ...153 E5
Oldham OL8 ...153 E6
Crossbank Way M24 ...46 F1
Crossbridge Rd SK14 ...102 A2
Crossby Cl M9 ...64 F5
Crossdale Rd Bolton BL2 ...42 F8
Manchester M9 ...64 A3
Crossdale Way WA11 ...71 B1
Crossefield Rd SK8 ...123 A3
Crossen St BL3 ...148 C5
Crossfell Ave M9 ...64 C5
Crossfield Ave M12 ...91 F2
Crossfield Cl Denton M34 ...101 A2
Littleborough OL12 ...15 C6
Stalybridge SK15 ...86 A3
Crossfield Dr Radcliffe M26 ...43 E3
Swinton M27 ...61 E1
Worsley M28 ...78 F7
Crossfield Gr Romiley SK6 ...114 B1
Stockport SK2 ...124 B4
Crossfield Pl OL11 ...31 A5
Crossfield Rd
Altrincham WA15 ...120 B2
Handforth SK9 ...131 D4
Irlam M30,M44 ...94 C4
Littleborough OL12 ...15 C6
Crossfield St Bury BL9 ...44 F4
Crossfields BL7 ...25 C8
Crossford Dr BL3 ...40 E4
Crossford St M32 ...96 E2
Crossgate Ave M22 ...121 D6
Crossgate La SK13 ...103 F7
Crossgate Mews SK4 ...110 E2
Crossgates Prim Sch OL16 ...32 A7
Crossgates Rd OL16 ...32 A7
Crossgill M29 ...77 B5
Crosshill St M16 ...97 F4
Crosshill Wlk M45 ...40 E5
Crossings The WA12 ...89 C3
Crossland Rd
Droylsden M43 ...84 B2
Manchester M21 ...109 A8
Crosslands M25 ...63 A3
Crosslands Rd SK13 ...116 D8
Crosslands Rd M28 ...77 F6
Crossley Cty Prim Sch M9 ...64 F4
Crossley Cres OL6 ...85 E6
Crossley Rd
Manchester M19,SK4 ...111 A7
Sale M33 ...108 A6
Crossley St Little Lever BL3 ...43 A3
Manchester M18 ...165 B6
Milnrow OL16 ...31 E6
Oldham OL2 ...48 E2
Shaw OL2 ...149 C7
Stalybridge SK15 ...86 A2
Crossmead Dr M9 ...64 E5
Crossmoor Cres SK6 ...113 C1
Crossmoor Dr BL2 ...148 B8
Crossmoor Gr SK6 ...113 C2
Crosswaite Rd SK2 ...124 E6
Crossway Bramhall SK7 ...132 E5
Manchester M20 ...110 B3

Crossway continued
Stockport SK2 ....124 A4
Crossway CI WN4 ....73 E5
Crossway Rd ⓲ M20 ....110 B3
Crossway Rd M23 ....107 F1
Crossways Bramhall SK7 ..123 C1
 Oldham OL8 ....67 A1
Croston Ave PR6 ....21 A8
Croston CI SK4 ....137 C1
Croston Close Rd
 BL9,OL12 ....12 C4
Croston St Bolton BL3 ...146 C4
 Hindley WN2 ....56 C6
Croston Wlk M11 ....160 E1
Crostons Rd BL8 ....140 D3
Croton St SK4 ....110 E2
Croughton Cl M11 ....99 D7
Crow Hill SK15 ....86 E5
Crow Hill N M24 ....64 F7
Crow Hill S M24 ....64 F6
Crow Hill View OL4 ....67 C5
Crow La BL0 ....138 C6
Crow La E WA12 ....89 C4
Crow La W WA12 ....89 A4
Crow Orchard Rd WN6 .....19 A1
Crow Tree Ave BL3 ....3 B8
Crow Trees La BL7 ....9 C7
Crow Wood Rd
 Edenfield BB4 ....1 D6
 Golborne WA3 ....74 D1
Crow's Nest BL3 ....42 F5
Crow's Nest Cotts BL3 ....42 F5
Crowbank Wlk M40 ....83 A5
Crowborough CI BL6 ....22 F1
Crowborough Wlk M15 ...162 F5
Crowbrook Gr ⓲ SK9 ....131 D1
Crowcroft Park Prim Sch
 M12 ....99 A3
Crowcroft Rd M12,M13 ....99 A3
Crowden Rd M40 ....65 B2
Crowhill Rd OL7 ....84 F4
Crowhurst Dr WN1 ....37 B3
Crowhurst Wlk ⓶ M23 ...120 E7
Crowland Gdns SK8 ....132 B6
Crowland Rd Bolton BL2 ..25 C2
 Wythenshawe M23 ....120 F3
Crowley La OL4 ....49 D1
Crowley Rd
 Altrincham WA15 ....120 B6
 Manchester M9 ....157 F8
Crown Bsns Ctr M35 ....54 D5
Crown Ct SK7 ....124 D3
Crown Fields Cl WA12 .....89 B5
Crown Gdns Edgworth BL7 ..9 D6
 Newton-le-W M40 ....55 A1
 ⓲ Rochdale OL16 ....31 A5
Crown Gn WA3 ....117 B4
Crown Gr WN7 ....76 D6
Crown Hill OL5 ....86 D8
Crown Ind Est
 Altrincham WA14 ....119 E7
 Manchester M4 ....159 C2
Crown La Horwich BL6 ......22 A4
 Manchester M4 ....159 A3
Crown Mews SK2 ....124 C4
Crown Park Dr WA12 ....89 B5
Crown Passages WA15 ...119 E2
Crown Point BL7 ....9 D6
Crown Point Ave M40 ......83 C5
Crown Rd OL10 ....29 B2
Crown Royal Ind Pk SK1 ..124 A8
Crown Sq M3 ....158 E1
Crown St Ashton-u-L OL6 ..166 B2
 Atherton M46 ....58 B3
 Bolton BL1 ....145 F7
 Bredbury SK6 ....112 F4
 Denton M34 ....100 E4
 Failsworth M35 ....83 F8
 ⓲ Failsworth M40 ....83 C5
 Hindley WN2 ....56 C6
 Manchester M15 ....162 E7
 Manchester M3 ....158 E2
 Marple SK6 ....125 F3
 Newton-le-W WA12 ....89 A3
 Rochdale OL16 ....31 B5
 Shaw OL2 ....149 B7
 Wigan WN3 ....150 B6
Crowndale BL7 ....9 D7
Crowneast St OL11 ....30 C7
Crownhill Rd M43 ....84 A2
Crowsdale Rd SK2 ....124 E4
Crowshaw Dr OL12 ....14 E3
Crowswood Dr SK15 ....86 D6
Crowther Ave M5 ....161 A8
Crowther Ct ⓲ OL15 ......15 E4
Crowther St
 Littleborough OL15 ....15 E4
 Manchester M18 ....99 E5
 Rochdale OL16 ....31 B4
Crowthorn Dr M23 ....121 A2
Crowthorn Rd
 Ashton-u-L OL7 ....84 F1
 Edgworth BL7 ....10 B8
 Reddish SK4 ....111 D7
Croxton Ave M33 ....107 D2
Croxdale Cl OL7 ....84 E5
Croxdale Wlk M9 ....64 D5
Croxton Ave OL16 ....31 B8
Croxton Cl Marple SK6 ...125 E5
 Sale M33 ....107 D2
Croxton Wlk
 ⓲ Horwich BL6 ....22 B4
 Manchester M13 ....163 C6
Croyde Cl Bolton BL2 ......25 F3
 Wythenshawe M22 ....130 F7
Croydon Ave Leigh WN7 ...75 F8
 Middleton OL11 ....47 D8
 Royton OL2 ....48 C6

Croydon Ct M5 ....161 B8
Croydon Dr M40 ....83 C4
Croydon Sq OL11 ....47 D8
 Stockport SK5 ....123 C8
Crummock Dr
 Middleton M24 ....46 E3
 Wigan WN4 ....54 F3
Crummock Rd
 Farnworth BL4 ....59 E7
 Gatley SK8 ....122 B3
Crumpsall La M8 ....64 A1
Crumpsall Lane Prim Sch
 M8 ....64 A1
Crumpsall St BL1 ....143 E3
Crumpsall Sta M8 ....64 A1
Crumpsall Vale M9 ....64 C2
Crumpsall Way M9 ....64 B1
Crumsdale Rd ⓲ BL1 ......24 F6
Cruttenden Rd SK2 ....124 D4
Cryer St M43 ....84 C4
Cuba Ind Est BL0 ....138 C8
Cuba St WA13 ....65 C8
Cubley Rd M7 ....155 E8
Cuckoo Gr M25 ....63 B6
Cuckoo La Bury BL9 ......141 C2
 Bury BL9 ....141 C3
 Prestwich M25 ....63 B6
Cuddington Ave M20 .....110 A8
Cuddington Cres SK3 .....170 D6
Cuddington Way ⓷ SK9 .131 D3
Cudworth Rd M9 ....64 A5
Cuerden Wlk M22 ....121 E8
Culand St M12 ....164 E6
Culbert Ave M20 ....110 C3
Culcheth Ave SK6 ....125 F6
Culcheth Ave WN2 ....56 B1
Culcheth Cty High Sch
 WA3 ....92 A3
Culcheth Cty Prim Sch
 ....92 A3
Culcheth Hall Dr WA3 .....91 F4
Culcheth Hall Prep Sch
 WA14 ....119 D3
Culcheth La M40 ....83 C4
Culcheth Rd WA14 ....119 D3
Culcombe Wlk M13 ....163 C5
Culcross Ave WN3 ....54 C4
Culford Cl M12 ....164 E5
Culgaith Wlk M9 ....157 D7
Culham Cl BL1 ....143 D2
Cullen Cl WN2 ....56 A8
Cullen Gr M9 ....64 F3
Cullercoats Wlk ⓷ M11 ...99 B3
Culross Ave Bolton BL3 ...40 E6
 Failsworth M40 ....65 E1
Cuthill Wlk M40 ....83 D4
Cutland St ⓲ M40 ....83 A6
Cutland Way OL5 ....16 A4
Cutler Cres OL13 ....3 D7
Cutler Hill Rd M35 ....84 C7
Cutter Cl M5 ....161 A8
Cycle St M11 ....160 A8
Cyclone St M11 ....164 F8
Cygnet St WN3 ....150 B6
Cygnus Ave M7 ....81 C3
Cymbal Ct SK5 ....169 F3
Cynthia Dr SK6 ....125 F5
Cypress Ave OL9 ....152 B8
Cypress Cl SK3 ....123 C8
Cypress Gr Denton M34 ..101 A3
 Kearsley BL4 ....60 F7
Cypress Ho ⓲ M14 ....98 B7
Cypress Oaks SK15 ....86 D3
Cypress Rd Droylsden M43 ..84 A3
 Eccles M30 ....79 A4
 Oldham OL4 ....67 D8
 Leigh WN7 ....75 C5
Cypress St Manchester M9 ..157 D7
 Middleton M24 ....65 C8
Cypress Way SK6 ....135 A7
Cypress Wlk ⓶ M33 .....107 C6
Cyprus Cl Oldham OL4 .....67 D6
 Salford M5 ....154 F1
Cyprus Sq ⓲ M12 ....96 D2
Cyril St Bolton BL3 ....148 A5
 Manchester M14 ....98 B3
 Shaw OL2 ....149 C7
Cyrus St M40 ....160 E2

D
D'Olivera Ct ⓸ M24 ....46 E2
Daccamill Dr M27 ....79 F6
Dacre Ave M16 ....97 B2
Dacre Cl M24 ....46 A1
Dacre Rd OL11 ....30 F4
Dacres Dr OL3 ....68 E4
Dacres Dr OL3 ....68 E4
Dacres Rd OL3 ....68 E4
Daffodil Cl Haslingden BB4 ..1 A8
 Rochdale OL12 ....14 E3
Daffodil Rd BL4 ....42 E2
Daffodil St M8 ....24 F5
Dagenham Rd M14 ....98 C4
Dagnall Ave M21 ....109 B6
Dahlia Cl OL12 ....14 D3
Dailton Rd WN8 ....53 A7
Daimler St M8 ....156 B6
Dain Cl SK16 ....101 D8
Daine Ave M23 ....109 B1
Dainton St M12 ....99 A2
Daintry Cl M15 ....162 F6
Daintry Rd OL9 ....152 C7
Dairy House La SK7 ......132 B4
Dairy House Rd SK7 ......132 B5
Dairy House
 Small Holdings SK7 ......132 B4
Dairy St OL9 ....152 B7
Dairydale Cl ⓲ M44 ....94 B3
Dairyground Rd SK7 ......132 F7
Dairyhouse La WA14 .....119 B7

Daisy Ave Farnworth BL4 ..42 A1
 Manchester M13 ....98 E4
 Newton-le-W WA12 ....89 C2
Daisy Bank Failsworth M40 ..25 B3
 Hyde SK14 ....113 D8
Daisy Bank Ave M6,M27 ..80 C6
Daisy Bank La SK8 ....122 A1
Daisy Bank Mill Cl WA3 ...91 E3
Daisy Bank Rd M14 ....98 D4
Daisy Bank Rd WN5 ....57 E5
Daisy Hall Dr BL5 ....37 F5
Daisy Hill Cl OL4 ....57 F5
Daisy Hill Inf Sch PR6 .....21 A8
Daisy Hill Rd OL5 ....68 B3
Daisy Hill Sta BL5 ....57 F6
Daisy Mews SK3 ....123 D4
Daisy Nook Ctry Pk OL8 ..84 E6
Daisy Rd WN5 ....54 E6
Daisy St Bolton BL3 ......146 C4
 ⓵ Bury BL8 ....27 C2
 Oldham OL9 ....152 A8
 Oldham OL9 ....153 D7
 ⓸ Rochdale OL12 ....139 E8
 Stockport SK3,SK7 ....57 F5
Daisy Way SK6 ....134 F7
Daisybank Cl WN7 ....56 D5
Daisyfield Cl M22 ....121 C1
Daisyfield Ct BL8 ....27 C1
Daisyfield Wlk M28 ....60 D3
Daishhill Cl M33 ....108 E4
Daisyhill Ct BL5 ....57 F5
Dak Wlk M34 ....100 E6
Dakerwood Cl ⓷ M40 .....83 C5
Dakins Rd WN7 ....76 B3
Dakley St M11 ....163 C7
Dakota Ave M5 ....96 F8
Dakota S M5 ....96 F8
Dalbeatie Rise WN1 ....37 F1
Dalbeattie St M9 ....64 E1
Dalbury Dr M40 ....156 C5
Dalby Ave M27 ....79 E7
Dalby Gr SK1 ....112 A1
Dalby Rd WN2 ....57 B5
Dale Ave Bramhall SK7 ..132 F8
 Eccles M30 ....79 C3
 Uppermill OL5 ....83 E8
Dale Brook Ave SK16 ....101 D6
Dale Fields OL3 ....50 F4
Dale Gr Altrincham WA15 ..119 F7
 Ashton-u-L OL7 ....85 A5
 Irlam M44 ....105 E6
 Leigh WN7 ....75 C4
Dale Grove Sch OL7 ......85 A5
Dale Ho OL2 ....48 D6
Dale House Fold SK12 ...134 A4
Dale Ind Est M26 ....44 A2
Dale La OL3 ....50 F5
Dale Lee BL5 ....58 A8
Dale Prim Sch The SK6 ..125 D7
Dale Rd Golborne WA3 .....90 A7
 Marple SK6 ....125 E7
 Middleton M24 ....47 B2
 Ramsbottom BL0 ....1 C1
 Rochdale OL16 ....31 C7
Dale Sq OL2 ....48 F4
Dale St Ashton-u-L OL6 ..86 A6
 ⓲ Bacup OL13 ....2 C8
 Bury BL8 ....27 C4
 Farnworth BL4 ....42 E1
 Ince-in-M WN3 ....55 F3
 Leigh WN7 ....75 C5
 Manchester M1 ....159 A2
 Middleton M24 ....65 B7
 Milnrow OL16 ....31 F6
 Ramsbottom BL0 ....1 C1
 Rochdale OL16 ....31 C7
 Shaw OL2 ....149 C8
 Stalybridge SK15 ....85 F1
 Stockport SK3 ....170 D7
 Swinton M27 ....79 E6
 Westhoughton BL5 ....57 F5
 Whitefield M45 ....63 C2
Dale St E Ashton-u-L OL6 ..166 A2
Dale St W Ashton-u-L OL6 ..166 A2
Dale View Denton M34 ....113 A7

Daleswood Ave M45 ....44 D1
Dalham Ave M9 ....65 A2
Dalkeith Ave SK5 ....111 F7
Dalkeith Gr BL3 ....40 F5
Dalkeith Rd Hindley WN2 ..57 A5
 Reddish SK5 ....111 F7
Dalkeith Sq OL10 ....29 A1
Dalkeith St M18 ....165 B6
Dallas Ct M5 ....96 E8
Dalley Ave M7 ....158 D4
Dallimore Rd M22 ....120 E6
Dalmahoy Cl M40 ....83 C8
Dalmain Cl M8 ....155 F6
Dalmeny Terr OL11 ....30 F4
Dalmorton Rd M21 ....109 D8
Dalny St M19 ....99 B1
Dalrybrook Gr ⓸ SK9 ...131 E1
Dalston Ave M35 ....84 B8
Dalston Dr Billinge WA11 ..71 B1
 Bramhall SK7 ....132 C5
Dalston Gr SK3 ....123 F5
Dalton Ave Manchester M14 ..98 A2
 Milnrow OL16 ....31 D7
 Stretford M32 ....96 A4
 Swinton M27 ....63 C2
 Whitefield M45 ....63 C2
Dalton Cl Milnrow OL16 ...31 D7
 Ramsbottom BL0 ....11 A4
 Whitefield M45 ....54 B7
Dalton Ct M40 ....159 B4
Dalton Dr Pendlebury M27 ..80 B5
 Wigan WN3 ....54 E2
Dalton Fold BL5 ....57 F8
Dalton Gdns M41 ....95 B3
Dalton Gr Ashton-in-M WN4 ..73 A4
 Manchester M9 ....64 D4
Dalton Ho ⓲ M14 ....110 D8
Dalton Rd Manchester M9 ..64 D5
 Middleton M24 ....64 B7
Dalton St Bury BL8 ....27 B2
 Eccles M30 ....79 D3
 Failsworth M35 ....83 E8
 Manchester M4,M40 ......159 B4
 Oldham OL1 ....67 A6
 Sale M33 ....108 C6
 Shaw OL2 ....149 A8
Daltry St OL1 ....67 A8
Dalveen Ave M41 ....95 C4
Dalveen Dr WA15 ....119 F7
Dalwood Cl WN2 ....56 F4
Dalymount Cl BL2 ....25 B2
Dam Head Dr M9 ....64 E3
Dam Head La M43 ....105 A5
Damask Ave M3 ....158 D2
Dame Hollow SK8 ....131 C7
Dame St ⓳ OL9 ....153 D8
Damery Ct SK7 ....132 E8
Damery Rd SK7 ....132 E8
Dameral Cl M8 ....156 A6
Damery Rd SK7 ....132 E8
Damian Dr WA12 ....89 A3
Damien St M12 ....99 B2
Dams Head Fold BL5 ....39 F1
Damson Wlk M31 ....105 D3
Dan Bank SK6 ....125 C6
Dan Fold OL1 ....53 E7
Danby Wlk M9 ....157 D6
Danby Cl SK14 ....101 D5
Danby Ct ⓵ OL1 ....153 E8
Danby Pl SK14 ....101 D5
Danby Rd Bolton BL3 .....147 E3
 Hyde SK14 ....101 D5
Danby Wlk M9 ....64 E1
Dane Ave Cheadle SK3 ...123 A8
 Partington M31 ....105 F4
Dane Bank M24 ....65 B7
Dane Bank Dr SK12 ....133 C3
Dane Bank Prim Sch
 SK5 ....100 A2
Dane Ct SK5 ....123 D3
Dane Dr SK9 ....137 D6
Dane Hill Cl SK12 ....135 D5
Dane Mews M33 ....108 A4
Dane Rd Reddish M34 ....100 A2
 Sale M33 ....108 C5
Dane Road Sta M33 ......108 C5
Dane St Bolton BL3 ....146 C4
 ⓲ Manchester M11 ....99 E7
 Mossley OL5 ....68 D3
 ⓸ Rochdale OL11 ....139 E7
Danebank Mews M34 ....100 A2
Danebank Wlk ⓸ M13 ...163 B7
Danebridge Cl BL4 ....60 E8
Danebury Cl WN2 ....56 D4
Danecroft Cl M13 ....164 D5
Danefield Ct SK8 ....131 D8
Danefield Rd M33 ....108 C5
Daneholme Rd M19 ....110 E5
Danes Ave WN2 ....56 E6
Danes Brook Cl WN2 ......56 E6
Danes Brow OL7 ....85 A5
Danes Gr M10 ....60 F1
Danes Rd M14 ....98 D2
Danesbury Rd WN5 ....71 E4
Danesbury Rd BL2 ....25 B4
Danesmoor Dr BL9 ....44 F8
Danesmoor Rd M20 ......110 B5
Danesway Adlington PR7 ..20 F8
 Manchester M25 ....63 D2

Danesway continued
Pendlebury M27 . . . . .80 C6
Wigan WN1 . . . . .37 B3
Danesway Ct BL1 . . . . . . .143 D2
Daneswood Ave
Manchester M9 . . . . .64 F4
Whitworth OL12 . . . . .14 C8
Daneswood Cl OL12 . . . . .14 C8
Danett Cl M12 . . . . .165 B6
Danforth Gr M19 . . . . . . .111 B8
Daniel Adamson Ave
M31 . . . . .105 D3
Daniel Adamson Rd M5 . .154 D1
Daniel Ct M31 . . . . .105 F4
Daniel Fold OL12 . . . . .14 B2
Daniel St Hazel Grove SK7 . .124 E2
Heywood OL10 . . . . .29 B2
Oldham OL1 . . . . .67 C8
Royton OL2 . . . . .49 A3
Whitworth OL12 . . . . .4 D2
Daniel's La SK1 . . . . .169 F2
Danisher La OL8 . . . . .84 F8
Dannywood Cl SK14 . . . .113 C8
Danson St M40 . . . . .160 E3
Dantall Ave M9 . . . . .65 A3
Dante Cl M6,M30 . . . . .80 A4
Danty St 2 SK16 . . . . . . .166 B1
Dantzic St M4 . . . . .159 A3
Danwood Cl M34 . . . . . . .101 B1
Dapple Gr M11 . . . . .165 A8
Darbishire St BL1 . . . . . . .25 A1
Darby La WN2 . . . . .56 D6
Darby Rd M44 . . . . .106 A6
Darbyshire Cl BL1 . . . . . .144 C8
Darbyshire Ho WA15 . . . .120 C7
Darbyshire St M4 . . . . . . .159 B2
Darbyshire Wlk 1 M26 . . .44 B3
Darcy St BL2 . . . . .148 C5
Darcy Wlk M14 . . . . .98 A4
Darden Cl SK4 . . . . .110 E3
Darell Wlk M8 . . . . .156 B6
Daresbury Ave
Altrincham WA15 . . . . .119 E5
Urmston M41 . . . . .94 E4
Daresbury Cl Sale M33 . . .108 F3
Stockport SK3 . . . . .170 D5
Wilmslow SK9 . . . . .137 C8
Daresbury Rd M21 . . . . . . .96 F1
Daresbury St M8 . . . . . . .156 A7
Darfield Wlk M40 . . . . . . .160 D3
Dargai St M11 . . . . .83 D1
Dargle Rd M33 . . . . .108 B6
Darian Ave M22 . . . . .130 D8
Daric Cl WN7 . . . . .75 C1
Dark La Blackrod BL6 . . . . .21 B3
Delph OL3 . . . . .50 E6
Manchester M12 . . . . .164 D8
Mossley OL5 . . . . .68 D2
Oldham OL3 . . . . .69 A8
Darbeck Wlk M21 . . . . . .109 C5
Darley Ave Eccles M30 . . . .95 C8
Farnworth BL4 . . . . .42 E1
Gatley SK8 . . . . .122 B5
Manchester M21 . . . . .109 C5
Darley Gr BL4 . . . . .42 E1
Darley Ho 5 M5 . . . . .154 E1
Darley Rd Hazel Grove SK7 . .133 F7
Manchester M16 . . . . .97 C3
Rochdale OL11 . . . . .30 F4
Wigan WN3 . . . . .55 B3
Darley St Bolton BL1 . . . . .143 D1
Farnworth BL4 . . . . .60 E8
Horwich BL6 . . . . .22 B5
Manchester M11 . . . . .160 F1
Sale M33 . . . . .108 B4
Stretford M32 . . . . .96 E4
Darley Terr 7 BL1 . . . . . .143 D1
Darlington Cl BL8 . . . . . . .27 B5
Darlington Rd
Manchester M20 . . . . .110 A6
Rochdale OL11 . . . . .30 F3
Darlington St
Ince-in-M WN2 . . . . .56 A7
Tyldesley M29 . . . . .59 A1
Wigan WN1 . . . . .151 D7
Darlington St E
Tyldesley M29 . . . . .59 B1
Wigan WN1 . . . . .151 E7
Darliston Ave M9 . . . . .64 A5
Darlton Wlk 6 M9 . . . . . .157 A8
Darnall Ave M14 . . . . .110 A8
Darnbrook Dr 4 M22 . . .121 B1
Darncombe Cl M16 . . . . . . .97 F4
Darnhall St WN3 . . . . .55 F4
Darnhill Cty Prim Sch
OL10 . . . . .29 B2
Darnley Ave M28 . . . . .60 C1
Darnley St M16 . . . . .97 D4
Darnton Gdns OL6 . . . . . . .85 C3
Darnton Rd OL6,SK15 . . . . .85 E3
Darran Ave WN3 . . . . .54 F3
Darras Rd M18 . . . . .99 C3
Dart Cl OL9 . . . . .65 F8
Dartford Ave
Brinnington SK5 . . . . .112 B6
Eccles M30 . . . . .79 B2
Dartford Cl M12 . . . . .164 D6
Dartford Rd M41 . . . . .95 C1
Dartington Cl
Altrincham M23 . . . . .120 C6
Stockport SK7 . . . . .123 F2
Dartmouth Cl 4 OL8 . . . . .66 F4
Dartmouth Cres SK5 . . . .112 C5
Dartmouth Rd
Manchester M21 . . . . .109 C8

Dartmouth Rd continued
Whitefield M45 . . . . .63 A7
Dartnall Cl SK12 . . . . .135 A6
Darton Ave M40 . . . . .160 E3
Darul-Uloom Islamic Coll
BL8 . . . . .10 F4
Darvel Ave WN4 . . . . .72 C4
Darvel Cl BL2 . . . . .42 F6
Darwell Ave M30 . . . . .95 C8
Darwen Dr 1 WN2 . . . . . . .56 A2
Darwen Rd BL7 . . . . .25 A7
Darwen St M16 . . . . .161 C5
Darwin Gr SK7 . . . . .132 E6
Darwin St Bolton BL1 . . . .143 D2
Dukinfield SK14 . . . . .102 A5
Oldham OL4 . . . . .67 C5
Dashwood Rd M25 . . . . . . .62 F5
Dashwood Wlk M12 . . . . .165 A6
Datchett Terr OL11 . . . . . .30 F4
Dauntesy Ave M27 . . . . . . .80 D7
Davehall Ave SK9 . . . . . . .137 A7
Davenfield Ct M20 . . . . . .110 B3
Davenfield Ho 7 M20 . . .110 B3
Davenfield Rd 2 M20 . . . .110 B3
Davenham Rd
Handforth SK9 . . . . .131 D4
Reddish SK5 . . . . .99 F2
Sale M33 . . . . .107 F6
Davenhill Rd M19 . . . . . . .111 A8
Davenport Ave
Manchester M20 . . . . .110 B7
Radcliffe M26 . . . . .43 F6
Wilmslow SK9 . . . . .136 E4
Davenport Dr SK6 . . . . . . .113 B6
Davenport Fold BL2 . . . . . .26 A3
Davenport Fold Rd BL2 . . . .26 A4
Davenport Gdns 10 BL1 . .145 E8
Davenport La WA14 . . . . . .119 C7
Davenport Lo SK3 . . . . . . .170 F5
Davenport Park Rd SK2 . .124 A5
Davenport St Bolton BL1 . .145 E8
2 Denton M34 . . . . .100 E8
Droylsden M43 . . . . .83 E1
Davenport Sta SK3 . . . . . .170 F5
Daventry Rd
Manchester M21 . . . . .109 D8
Rochdale OL11 . . . . .30 F3
Davey La SK9 . . . . .137 B2
Davyhulme St OL12 . . . . . .15 B1
Daveylands Urmston M41 . . .94 F5
Wilmslow SK9 . . . . .137 D7
David Brow BL3 . . . . .146 A2
David Cl M34 . . . . .101 A1
David Lewis Cl OL16 . . . . .31 C6
David Mews M14 . . . . . . .110 C7
David Pegg Wlk M40 . . . . .83 A6
David St Bacup OL13 . . . . . . .3 D8
Bury BL8 . . . . .27 C4
Denton M34 . . . . .101 A2
2 Oldham OL1 . . . . .153 E6
Reddish SK5 . . . . .111 E8
15 Rochdale OL12 . . . . .14 F1
David St N 15 OL12 . . . . . .14 F1
David's Farm Cl M24 . . . . .65 C7
David's Rd M43 . . . . .83 E2
Davids La OL4 . . . . .67 F7
Davidson Dr M24 . . . . .65 B6
Davidson Wlk WN5 . . . . . . .54 E7
Davies Ave Gatley SK8 . . . .131 B6
Newton-le-W WA12 . . . . .89 C4
Davies Rd Bredbury SK6 . . .112 D3
Partington M31 . . . . .106 A3
Davies Sq M14 . . . . .98 A4
Davies St Ashton-u-L OL7 . . .84 F1
Kearsley BL4 . . . . .61 A7
Oldham OL1 . . . . .153 D8
Platt Bridge WN2 . . . . .56 A2
Davis St M30 . . . . .79 F1
Davy Ave M27 . . . . .62 D2
Davy St M40 . . . . .159 B4
Davyhulme Circ M41 . . . . .95 C4
Davyhulme Cty Jun & Inf Sch
M41 . . . . .95 D3
Davyhulme Rd
Stretford M32 . . . . .96 C3
Urmston M41 . . . . .94 F4
Urmston M41 . . . . .95 A3
Davyhulme Rd E M32 . . . . .96 D3
Daw Bank SK3 . . . . .169 E1
Dawber St WN4 . . . . .73 D4
Dawes St BL3 . . . . .145 F6
Dawley Cl Ashton-in-M WN4 . .73 A3
Bolton BL3 . . . . .144 C6
Dawlish Ave
Brinnington SK5 . . . . .112 C5
Chadderton OL9 . . . . .47 F1
Cheadle SK8 . . . . .131 F7
Droylsden M43 . . . . .83 E1
Dawlish Cl Bramhall SK7 . . .132 E7
Hattersley SK14 . . . . .102 E3
Hollinfare WA3 . . . . .105 B3
Dawlish Rd
Manchester M21 . . . . .109 C8
Sale M33 . . . . .107 E5
Dawlish Way WA3 . . . . .73 F1
Dawn St OL2 . . . . .149 B6
Dawnay St M11 . . . . .165 B7
Dawson Ave WN6 . . . . .37 A3
Dawson La BL1 . . . . .145 E7
Dawson Rd
Altrincham WA14 . . . . .119 D8
Gatley SK8 . . . . .131 D8
Dawson St Atherton M46 . . . .58 D7
Bury BL9 . . . . .141 A4
Heywood OL10 . . . . .29 C2
Hyde SK14 . . . . .167 E1
Manchester M3 . . . . .158 F2

Dawson St continued
Manchester M3,M15 . . . . . .162 D8
5 Oldham OL4 . . . . .67 D6
Oldham OL4 . . . . .67 E5
Pendlebury M27 . . . . .80 A8
Rochdale OL12 . . . . .139 F8
Stockport SK1 . . . . .112 B3
Day Dr M35 . . . . .83 F6
Day Gr SK14 . . . . .103 A3
Dayfield WN8 . . . . .35 D7
Daylesford Cl SK8 . . . . . . .122 D4
Daylesford Cres SK8 . . . .122 D4
Daylesford Rd SK8 . . . . . .122 D4
De La Salle Coll M6 . . . . . .80 C3
De Lacy Dr BL2 . . . . .25 B1
De Quincey Cl WA14 . . . . .107 D1
De Quincey Rd WA14 . . . .107 D1
De Trafford Dr WN2 . . . . . .56 B8
De Trafford Ho 15 M30 . . . .79 D1
De Trafford Mews 8
SK9 . . . . .131 D2
De Traffords The M44 . . . .94 B3
De-Massey Cl SK6 . . . . . .113 B6
Deacon Ave M27 . . . . .61 E1
Deacon Cl WA14 . . . . .119 E1
Deacon St OL16 . . . . .15 B1
Deacon Trad Est WA12 . . . .89 A2
Deacons Cl SK1 . . . . .112 A1
Deacons Cres BL8 . . . . . . .27 A5
Deacons Dr M6 . . . . .80 D6
Deakin St WN1 . . . . .151 E5
Deakins Bsns Pk BL7 . . . . .8 D1
Deal Ave SK5 . . . . .112 B6
Deal Cl M40 . . . . .83 D5
Deal Sq SK14 . . . . .167 E2
Deal St Bolton BL3 . . . . . . .147 F3
Bury BL9 . . . . .141 B2
Hyde SK14 . . . . .167 E2
Manchester M3 . . . . .158 E2
Deal Wlk OL9 . . . . .152 A6
Dealey Rd BL3 . . . . .146 A4
Dean Ave Failsworth M40 . . .83 B6
Manchester M16 . . . . .97 B3
Dean Bank Dr OL16 . . . . . .31 B1
Dean Bradley Rd M40 . . . .157 E6
Dean Cl Bolton BL4 . . . . . .147 F3
Dean Cl Billinge WN5 . . . . .71 D3
Edenfield BL0 . . . . .1 D3
Farnworth BL4 . . . . .59 F8
Handforth SK9 . . . . .131 C1
Orrell WN8 . . . . .53 C7
Partington M31 . . . . .105 F4
Whitefield M45 . . . . .62 D7
Dean Cres WN5 . . . . .54 B8
Dean Ct Bolton BL1 . . . . . .148 A8
11 Dukinfield SK16 . . . . . . .166 B1
Golborne WA3 . . . . .90 A4
Manchester M15 . . . . .162 D6
Rochdale OL11 . . . . .30 A6
Dean Dr Altrincham WA14 . .119 B1
Wilmslow SK9 . . . . .131 D2
Dean La Failsworth M40 . . . .83 B6
Hazel Grove SK7 . . . . .133 E8
Dean Lane Sta M40 . . . . . .83 B6
Dean Mdw WA12 . . . . .89 C4
Dean Moor Rd SK7 . . . . . .124 A1
Dean Rd Golborne WA3 . . . .90 A4
Handforth SK9 . . . . .131 E3
Irlam M44 . . . . .105 E6
Manchester M3 . . . . .158 E3
Reddish M18 . . . . .99 E4
Dean Row Ct 10 SK9 . . . .131 D1
Dean Row Cty Jun Sch
SK9 . . . . .131 E1
Dean Row Rd SK9 . . . . . . .137 F8
Dean St Ashton-u-L OL6 . . .166 A3
Failsworth M35 . . . . .83 E7
Manchester M1 . . . . .159 B1
Mossley OL5 . . . . .68 B1
Radcliffe M26 . . . . .43 F3
Rochdale OL16 . . . . .31 A4
Stalybridge SK15 . . . . .86 A1
Dean Villas OL6 . . . . .6 B7
Dean Wlk M24 . . . . .46 D2
Dean Wood Ave WN5 . . . . .53 E8
Deanbank Ave 2 M19 . . . .110 F8
Deane Ave
Altrincham WA15 . . . . .120 A5
Bolton BL3 . . . . .144 B5
Cheadle SK8 . . . . .122 F5
Deane Church La BL3 . . . .146 B4
Deane Com Sec Sch The
BL3 . . . . .146 C5
Deane Rd BL3 . . . . .145 D6
Deane Wlk BL3 . . . . .145 D6
Deanery CE High Sch
WN1 . . . . .150 B8
Deanery Gdns M7 . . . . . . .155 D8
Deanery Way SK1 . . . . . . .169 F2
Deanroyd Rd OL14 . . . . . . .4 B7
Deans Prim Sch The M27 . .79 E8
Deans Rd M27 . . . . .79 F7
Deanscourt Ave M27 . . . . .79 F8
Deansgate Bolton BL1 . . . .145 E7
Hindley WN2 . . . . .56 D4
Manchester M1,M2,M3 . . . .158 F1
Manchester M15 . . . . .162 E7
Radcliffe M26 . . . . .44 B3
Deansgate La
WA14,WA15 . . . . .119 E2
Deansgate Sta M3 . . . . . .162 E8
Deansgreave Rd OL13 . . . . .4 B7
Deanshut Rd OL8 . . . . .67 B4
Deansway M27 . . . . .79 E8
Deanswood Dr M9 . . . . . . .64 A5
Deanwater Cl M13 . . . . . .163 B7
Deanwater Ct Gatley SK8 . .131 D7

Deanwater Ct continued
Stretford M32 . . . . .108 C8
Deanway Handforth SK9 . . .131 C1
Manchester M40 . . . . .65 B4
Deanway Trad Est SK9 . . .131 D3
Dearden Ave M38 . . . . .60 A5
Dearden Clough BL0 . . . . . .1 E2
Dearden Fold BL0 . . . . .1 E2
Dearden St Little Lever BL3 . .43 A4
Littleborough OL15 . . . . .16 B6
Manchester M15 . . . . .162 E6
12 Stalybridge SK15 . . . . . . .86 A2
Deardens Fold BL8 . . . . . . .27 C1
Deardens St BL8 . . . . .27 C1
Dearmans Pl M3 . . . . .158 E2
Dearne Dr M32 . . . . .96 E2
Dearnley Cl OL15 . . . . .15 E4
Debdale La
Marsden M18,M34 . . . . .99 F4
Tyldesley M29 . . . . .76 F4
Deben Cl WN6 . . . . .19 D1
Debenham Ave M40 . . . . . .83 C4
Debenham Ct BL4 . . . . .60 D7
Debenham Rd M32 . . . . . . .96 C2
Dee Ave WA15 . . . . .120 D5
Dee Dr BL4 . . . . .61 B5
Dee Rd M29 . . . . .77 C7
Deep La Littleborough OL15 . .16 C1
Milnrow OL16,OL16 . . . . .32 B8
Deepcar St M19 . . . . .99 A1
Deepdale Leigh WN7 . . . . . .76 C3
Oldham OL4 . . . . .67 D6
Deepdale Ave
Billinge WN5 . . . . .71 C1
Manchester M14 . . . . .110 A8
Rochdale OL16 . . . . .31 C6
Royton OL2 . . . . .48 C8
Deepdale Cl 1 SK5 . . . . . .100 A1
Deepdale Ct M9 . . . . .65 B3
Deepdale Dr M27 . . . . .80 D7
Deepdale Rd BL2 . . . . .25 F1
Deepdene St M12 . . . . . . .164 F6
Deeping Ave M16 . . . . .97 D2
Deeplish Com Prim Sch
OL11 . . . . .31 A5
Deeplish Rd OL11 . . . . . . .139 F5
Deeplish St OL11 . . . . .139 F5
Deeply Vale La BL9 . . . . . . .12 C2
Deer St M1 . . . . .163 C8
Deeracre Ave SK2 . . . . . . .124 C6
Deerfold Cl 3 M18 . . . . . . .99 D5
Deerhurst Dr M8 . . . . .155 F6
Deeroak Cl M18 . . . . .165 B6
Deerpark Rd M16 . . . . .97 E3
Defence St BL3 . . . . .145 D6
Defiance St M46 . . . . .58 C5
Deganwy Gr SK5 . . . . .111 F5
Degas Cl M7 . . . . .81 B8
Deighton Ave M14 . . . . . . .110 A8
Delacourt Rd M14 . . . . . . .110 B8
Delafield Ave M12 . . . . . . .99 A2
Delaford Ave M28 . . . . .78 C8
Delaford Cl SK3 . . . . .123 E4
Delaford Wlk M40 . . . . .83 D4
Delahays Ln WA15 . . . . . . .120 B8
Delahays Dr WA15 . . . . . . .120 B2
Delahays Range M18,M34 . .99 F4
Delahays Rd WA15 . . . . . .120 B2
Delaine Rd M20 . . . . .110 C6
Delamer Rd WA14 . . . . . . .119 C3
Delamere Ave
Golborne WA3 . . . . .90 E6
Sale M33 . . . . .108 E3
Salford M6 . . . . .80 C6
Shaw OL2 . . . . .49 D8
Stretford M32 . . . . .96 D2
Swinton M27 . . . . .62 A2
Whitefield M45 . . . . .62 E8
Delamere Cl
Hazel Grove SK7 . . . . .125 A3
Mossley SK6 . . . . .86 E6
Delamere Gdns BL1 . . . . .143 D3
Delamere Ho M14 . . . . . . .110 C8
Delamere Lo SK7 . . . . .124 F2
Delamere Rd Gatley SK8 . .122 B5
Handforth SK9 . . . . .131 D3
Hazel Grove SK7 . . . . .125 A3
Manchester M19 . . . . .99 B1
Reddish M34 . . . . .100 B2
Rochdale OL16 . . . . .31 C4
Stockport SK2 . . . . .124 B4
Urmston M41 . . . . .94 D2
Delamere St
Ashton-u-L OL6 . . . . .166 B2
Bury BL9 . . . . .28 B4
Droylsden M11 . . . . .99 F7
6 Oldham OL8 . . . . .67 B5
Delanor Wlk WN8 . . . . .53 A7
Delaunays Rd
Manchester M8 . . . . .64 B2
Sale M33 . . . . .107 F4
Delaware Wlk M9 . . . . . . .157 D7
Delbooth Ave M41 . . . . . . .94 E4
Delegarte St WN3 . . . . . . .151 E6
Delfhaven Ct WN6 . . . . .37 A7
Delft Wlk M6 . . . . .81 A5
Delfur Rd SK7 . . . . .132 F7
Delhi Rd M44 . . . . .105 F8
Dell Ave Pendlebury M27 . . . .80 D7
Wigan WN6 . . . . .36 E3
Dell Cl OL4 . . . . .67 F5
Dell Gdns OL12 . . . . .14 C5
Dell Mdw OL12 . . . . .14 C5
Dell Rd OL12 . . . . .14 B3
Dell Side SK6 . . . . .112 E3

Dell Side Way OL12 . . . . . .14 C2
Dell St BL2 . . . . .25 C3
Dell The Appley Bridge WN6 . .35 D7
Orrell WN8 . . . . .53 B7
Dellar St OL12 . . . . .14 C1
Dellcot Cl Manchester M25 . .63 D2
Salford M6 . . . . .80 B5
Dellcot La M28 . . . . .78 F5
Dellhide Cl OL4 . . . . .68 A6
Dellside Cl WN4 . . . . .72 D5
Dellside Gr M28 . . . . .60 E3
Delph Ave BL7 . . . . .8 D2
Delph Brook Way BL7 . . . . . .8 D2
Delph Com Prim Sch OL3 . .50 E5
Delph Gr WN7 . . . . .57 D1
Delph Hill BL1 . . . . .23 E2
Delph Hill Cl BL1 . . . . .23 E2
Delph La Ainsworth BL2 . . . .26 C1
Delph OL3 . . . . .50 F5
Delph Lodge OL3 . . . . .50 F3
Delph New Rd OL3 . . . . . . .50 E2
Delph Rd OL3 . . . . .50 C8
Delph St Bolton BL3 . . . . . .145 D5
Milnrow OL16 . . . . .31 F6
Wigan WN6 . . . . .37 B3
Delphi Ave M28 . . . . .60 D2
Delphside Cl WN5 . . . . .53 D5
Delphside Rd WN5 . . . . . . .53 D5
Delside Ave M40 . . . . .83 A8
Delta Cl OL2 . . . . .48 D4
Delta Rd M34 . . . . .100 E7
Delta Wlk M40 . . . . .83 A7
Delvino Wlk M14 . . . . .98 A4
Delwood Gdns M22 . . . . .121 D3
Demesne Cl SK15 . . . . .86 C1
Demesne Cres SK15 . . . . . .86 C1
Demesne Dr SK15 . . . . .86 C1
Demesne Rd M16 . . . . .97 E2
Demmings Inf Sch SK8 . . .122 F5
Demmings Rd SK8 . . . . . . .122 F5
Dempsey Dr M45 . . . . .45 B2
Den Hill Dr OL4 . . . . .67 F6
Den La Oldham OL3 . . . . . . .69 B8
Oldham OL4 . . . . .67 F7
Denbigh Cl SK7 . . . . .133 C8
Denbigh Dr OL2 . . . . .48 C5
Denbigh Gr M46 . . . . .58 C5
Denbigh Pl M5 . . . . .81 A2
Denbigh Rd Bolton BL2 . . .148 B5
Denton M34 . . . . .100 F1
Swinton M27 . . . . .62 B2
Denbigh St Mossley OL5 . . .68 C2
Oldham OL8 . . . . .66 F3
Stockport SK4 . . . . .169 D3
Denbigh Wlk M15 . . . . . . .162 E5
Denbury Dr WA14 . . . . . . .119 D5
Denbury Gn SK7 . . . . .124 A1
Denbury Wlk M9 . . . . .156 C6
Denby La SK4 . . . . .169 D4
Denby Rd SK16 . . . . .101 C7
Denbydale Way OL2 . . . . . .48 C4
Dencombe St M12,M13 . . .98 F4
Dene Bank BL2 . . . . .25 C5
Dene Brow M34 . . . . .113 B8
Dene Ct SK4 . . . . .168 C2
Dene Dr M24 . . . . .64 F7
Dene Hollow SK5 . . . . .100 A1
Dene Ho SK4 . . . . .110 E1
Dene Manor M20 . . . . .110 A2
Dene Pk M20 . . . . .110 A3
Dene Rd M20 . . . . .109 F3
Dene Rd W M20 . . . . .109 F3
Dene St Bolton BL2 . . . . . . .25 C5
Leigh WN7 . . . . .75 B4
Denefield Cl SK6 . . . . .114 B1
Denefield Pl M30 . . . . .79 F3
Denefield Rd M40 . . . . .65 A2
Denehurst Rd OL11 . . . . . . .30 C8
Denehurst St M12 . . . . . . .164 F6
Denes The M5 . . . . .99 F1
Deneside Cres SK7 . . . . . .124 F3
Deneside Wlk 8 M9 . . . . .157 E8
Deneway M33 . . . . .107 E3
Deneway Bramhall SK7 . . . .132 D7
High Lane SK6 . . . . .134 F8
Stockport SK4 . . . . .168 C2
Deneway Cl SK4 . . . . .168 C2
Deneway Mews SK4 . . . . .168 C2
Denewell Cl M13 . . . . .164 D6
Denewood Ct 3 SK9 . . . . .137 A6
Denford Cl WN3 . . . . .54 F3
Denham Cl BL1 . . . . .25 A6
Denham Dr Bramhall SK7 . .132 D7
Irlam M44 . . . . .94 A1
Wigan WN3 . . . . .55 A3
Denham St
Manchester M13 . . . . .98 D4
Radcliffe M26 . . . . .43 F6
Denhill Rd M15 . . . . .162 F5
Denholm Rd M20 . . . . . . .122 C8
Denholme Rd OL11 . . . . . . .30 F4
Denhurst Rd OL15 . . . . . . .16 B5
Denison Ct 7 M14 . . . . . . .98 C3
Denison Rd
Hazel Grove SK7 . . . . .133 E8
Manchester M14 . . . . .98 C3
Denison St M14 . . . . .98 C3
Deniston Rd SK4 . . . . .111 B5
Denman Wlk 15 M8 . . . . .155 F6
Denmark Rd
Manchester M14,M15 . . . . . .98 A4
Salford M6 . . . . .81 A3
Denmark St
Altrincham WA14 . . . . .119 D4
Oldham OL4 . . . . .67 B7

Denmark St *continued*
Oldham OL9 . . . . .152 C8
Rochdale OL16 . . . . .31 A8
Denmark Way OL9 . . . . . .152 C8
Denmore Rd M40 . . . . .65 D3
Dennington Dr M41 . . . . . . .95 C4
Dennis Ho SK4 . . . . .168 B4
Dennison Ave M20 . . . . . .110 B7
Denshaw Ave SK8 . . . . . .132 B8
Denshaw Ave M14 . . . . . .100 D5
Denshaw Cl M19 . . . . .110 E3
Denshaw Rd OL3 . . . . .50 D5
Densmead Wlk 15 M40 . . .159 C3
Denstone St 6 M35 . . . . . . .83 F7
Denson Rd M41,L5 . . . . . .120 B8
Denstone Ave Eccles M30 . .79 E3
Sale M33 . . . . .107 E3
Urmston M41 . . . . .95 C3
Denstone Cres BL2 . . . . . . .25 D2
Denstone Rd Reddish SK5 . .99 F1
Salford M6 . . . . .80 D5
Urmston M41 . . . . .95 C3
Denstone Wlk 15 M9 . . . . .64 E3
Dent Cl SK5 . . . . .112 C6
Dental Hospl M13,M15 . . .163 A6
Dentdale Cl BL2 . . . . .40 D6
Dentdale Wlk M22 . . . . . . .130 C8
Denton Ct M34 . . . . .100 E5
Denton Gr WN5 . . . . .54 B8
Denton La OL9 . . . . .152 A5
Denton Rd Denton M34 . . .100 E6
Little Lever BL3 . . . . .43 B6
Denton St Bury BL9 . . . . . .140 F4
Heywood OL10 . . . . .29 C1
7 Rochdale OL12 . . . . .14 F1
Denton Sta M34 . . . . .100 C4
Denton West End
Prim Sch M34 . . . . .100 A3
Denver Ave M40 . . . . .160 D3
Denver Dr 8 WA15 . . . . . .120 A6
Denver Rd OL11 . . . . .30 F4
Denville Cres M22 . . . . . . .121 E3
Denyer Terr 22 SK16 . . . . .166 B1
Depleach Rd SK8 . . . . .122 D5
Deptford Ave M23 . . . . . . .121 A3
Deramore Cl OL6 . . . . .85 E3
Deramore St M14 . . . . .98 B3
Derby Ave M5 . . . . .154 E2
Derby Cl Irlam M44 . . . . . . .105 C5
Newton-le-W WA12 . . . . .89 B3
Derby Ct Oldham OL9 . . . . .152 C5
Sale M33 . . . . .108 C3
Derby Gr 2 M19 . . . . .99 B1
Derby High Sch The BL9 . .44 D8
Derby Ho WN1 . . . . .151 D8
Derby Pl PR6 . . . . .21 A8
Derby Range SK4 . . . . .168 B4
Derby Rd Ashton-u-L OL6 . .85 D3
Golborne WA3 . . . . .90 C8
Hyde SK14 . . . . .167 E4
Kearsley M26 . . . . .61 A8
Manchester M14,M20 . . . . . .110 D7
Manchester SK4 . . . . .168 C4
New Mills SK22 . . . . .127 D1
Prestwich M25,M45 . . . . .63 A6
Sale M33 . . . . .107 E6
Salford M5,M6 . . . . .154 E2
Urmston M41 . . . . .95 D3
Derby St Altrincham WA14 . .119 E5
Ashton-u-L OL7 . . . . .85 A5
Atherton M46 . . . . .58 C4
Bolton BL3 . . . . .145 E5
Bury BL9 . . . . .140 F2
Denton M34 . . . . .100 D3
Denton M34 . . . . .100 D4
1 Failsworth M35 . . . . .66 A1
Glossop SK13 . . . . .116 C8
Heywood OL10 . . . . .29 B2
Horwich BL6 . . . . .22 D1
Ince-in-M WN3 . . . . .55 F4
Leigh WN7 . . . . .76 A4
Manchester M8 . . . . .158 F4
8 Marple SK6 . . . . .125 F6
Mossley OL5 . . . . .86 D8
Newton-le-W WA12 . . . . .89 B3
Oldham OL9 . . . . .152 C5
Oldham OL9 . . . . .66 B8
Prestwich M25 . . . . .63 A4
Ramsbottom BL0 . . . . .11 C6
Rochdale OL11 . . . . .31 A5
Stockport SK3 . . . . .170 D8
15 Tyldesley M29 . . . . .59 F1
Westhoughton BL5 . . . . .39 F1
Derby St W WN7 . . . . .75 F4
Derby Terr M34 . . . . .100 E8
Derby Way 7 SK6 . . . . . . .125 F6
Derbyshire Ave M32 . . . . . .96 B3
Derbyshire Cres M32 . . . . .96 B3
Derbyshire Gn M32 . . . . . . .96 B3
Derbyshire Gr M32 . . . . . . .96 B3
Derbyshire La M32 . . . . . . .96 B2
Derbyshire La W M32 . . . . .96 B2
Derbyshire Level SK13 . . . .116 F6
Derbyshire Rd
Failsworth M40 . . . . .83 D4
High Lane SK12 . . . . .134 D5
Partington M31 . . . . .105 E2
Sale M33 . . . . .108 C4
Wigan WN3 . . . . .54 D1
Derbyshire Rd S M33 . . . .108 D2
Derbyshire Row BL1 . . . . .143 E3
Derbyshire St M11 . . . . . . .165 C7
Dereham Cl BL9 . . . . .27 D5
Dereham Way WN3 . . . . . . .54 D3
Derg St M6 . . . . .154 F1
Derker St OL1 . . . . .67 B8
Derker Sta OL1 . . . . .67 A8
Dermot Murphy Cl M20 . . .109 F6

Dernford Ave M19 . . . . . . .110 F5
Derngate Dr WN6 . . . . .37 A7
Derrick Walker Ct OL11 . .139 D5
Derry Ave M22 . . . . .121 E4
Derry St OL1 . . . . .153 F6
Derville Wlk 4 M9 . . . . . . .157 D8
Derwen Rd SK3 . . . . .170 E7
Derwent Ave
Altrincham WA15 . . . . .120 D5
Ashton-u-L OL7 . . . . .166 A4
Droylsden M43 . . . . .83 E1
Golborne WA3 . . . . .74 C1
Heywood OL10 . . . . .46 D8
Manchester M21 . . . . .109 D5
Milnrow OL16 . . . . .32 B6
Whitefield M45 . . . . .63 C8
Derwent Cl Culcheth WA3 . .92 A2
Glossop SK13 . . . . .116 F8
Horwich BL6 . . . . .22 C2
Leigh WN7 . . . . .75 E3
Little Lever BL3 . . . . .42 F4
Manchester M21 . . . . .109 D5
Partington M31 . . . . .105 F4
Reddish M34 . . . . .100 B2
Walkden M28 . . . . .60 B2
Whitefield M45 . . . . .63 B8
Derwent Dr Bramhall SK7 . .132 C5
Bury BL9 . . . . .44 D7
Chadderton OL9 . . . . .152 A7
Handforth SK9 . . . . .131 C5
Kearsley BL4 . . . . .61 B5
Littleborough OL15 . . . . .15 F2
Sale M33 . . . . .108 A2
Shaw OL2 . . . . .149 A8
Derwent Ind Area M5 . . . .162 D8
Derwent Pl WN5 . . . . .54 C7
Derwent Rd
Ashton-in-M WN4 . . . . .73 E5
Farnworth BL4 . . . . .59 F7
High Lane SK6 . . . . .134 E8
Hindley WN2 . . . . .56 E5
Middleton M24 . . . . .46 E3
Orrell WN5 . . . . .53 F8
Stretford M32 . . . . .96 B3
Urmston M41 . . . . .94 E2
Derwent St Droylsden M43 . .83 D1
Leigh WN7 . . . . .75 E3
Manchester M8 . . . . .156 C6
11 Rochdale OL12 . . . . .14 F1
Salford M5 . . . . .161 C8
Tyldesley M29 . . . . .77 A7
Derwent Terr SK15 . . . . . . .86 A4
Derwent Wlk Oldham OL4 . .67 F7
Whitefield M45 . . . . .63 B8
Desford Ave M16,M21 . . . . .97 C1
Design St BL3 . . . . .146 B4
Desmond Rd M22 . . . . .121 E4
Desmond St M46 . . . . .58 A2
Dettingen St M6 . . . . .80 D6
Deva Cl Hazel Grove SK7 . .124 D1
Poynton SK12 . . . . .163 A4
Deva Ctr M16 . . . . .161 C5
Deva Sq OL9 . . . . .152 C5
Devaney Wlk M34 . . . . . . .100 E1
Devas St M13,M15 . . . . . . .163 B5
Deverill Ave M18 . . . . .99 F4
Devine Cl Manchester M3 . .158 D2
Royton OL2 . . . . .48 F5
Devisdale Grange WA14 . .119 B3
Devisdale Rd WA14 . . . . . .119 B4
Devoke Ave Billinge WA11 . .71 A1
Walkden M28 . . . . .60 F2
Devoke Gr BL4 . . . . .59 E8
Devoke Rd M22 . . . . .121 B2
Devon Ave
Manchester M19 . . . . .110 F8
Whitefield M45 . . . . .44 E1
Devon Cl Aspull WN2 . . . . . .38 D5
Brinnington SK5 . . . . .112 C4
Little Lever BL3 . . . . .43 B4
Salford M6 . . . . .80 A3
Shaw OL2 . . . . .48 F7
Wigan WN5 . . . . .54 C6
Devon Cres BB4 . . . . .1 B8
Devon Dr Ainsworth BL2 . . . .26 D1
Diggle OL3 . . . . .51 C4
Standish WN1 . . . . .20 B1
Devon Mews 2 M45 . . . . . .64 E1
Devon Rd Droylsden M43 . . .84 A3
Failsworth M35 . . . . .83 E6
Irlam M44 . . . . .105 E2
Partington M31 . . . . .105 E2
Urmston M41 . . . . .94 E1
Devon St Bolton BL2 . . . . . .148 A7
Bury BL9 . . . . .44 F8
Farnworth BL4 . . . . .42 D2
Hindley WN2 . . . . .56 E5
Leigh WN7 . . . . .76 E4
Oldham OL9 . . . . .153 D6
Swinton M27 . . . . .62 C2
Devon Way OL8 . . . . .66 C2
Devonport Cres OL2 . . . . . .48 F4
Devonshire Cl
Heywood OL10 . . . . .29 A1
Urmston M41 . . . . .95 C2
Devonshire Ct
Manchester M7 . . . . .155 D8
Stockport SK2 . . . . .124 A5
Devonshire Dr
Alderley Edge SK9 . . . . .137 B2
Walkden M28 . . . . .77 F6
Devonshire Gdns WA12 . . .89 C2
Devonshire Park Rd SK2 . .124 A5
Devonshire Pl
Atherton M46 . . . . .58 D4

Devonshire Pl *continued*
Prestwich M25 . . . . .63 A5
Devonshire Rd
Altrincham WA14 . . . . .119 D6
Atherton M46 . . . . .58 C5
Bolton BL1 . . . . .144 B8
Eccles M30 . . . . .79 E2
Hazel Grove SK7 . . . . .133 F8
Manchester M21 . . . . .109 C8
Manchester SK4 . . . . .168 B3
Rochdale OL11 . . . . .30 F2
Salford M6 . . . . .80 A3
Walkden M28 . . . . .60 C6
Devonshire Road Cty
Prim Sch BL1 . . . . .144 B8
Devonshire St
Manchester M7 . . . . .164 D6
Manchester M7 . . . . .155 E6
Devonshire St E M35 . . . . . .83 E5
Devonshire St N M12 . . . . .164 D7
Devonshire St S M13 . . . . .164 D5
Dew Meadow Cl OL12 . . . . .14 E2
Dew Way OL9 . . . . .153 D7
Dewar Cl M11 . . . . .83 A1
Dewberry Cl Swinton M27 . .62 E1
Tyldesley M29 . . . . .59 E1
Dewberry Fields M8 . . . . . .53 B7
Dewes Ave M27 . . . . .62 B2
Dewey St M11 . . . . .99 D7
Dewhirst Rd OL12 . . . . .14 F4
Dewhirst Way OL12 . . . . . . .14 F4
Dewhurst Clough Rd BL7 . . .8 D2
Dewhurst Ct BL7 . . . . .8 D3
Dewhurst Rd BL2 . . . . .25 E3
Dewhurst St Heywood OL10 . .29 D2
Manchester M8 . . . . .158 F4
Dewint Ave SK6 . . . . .126 B8
Dewsnap Cl SK16 . . . . .101 C6
Dewsnap La
Dukinfield SK16 . . . . .101 D6
Mottram-in-L SK14 . . . . .103 A6
Dewsnap Way SK14 . . . . . .102 E2
Dexter Rd M9 . . . . .64 A5
Deyne Ave Manchester M14 . .98 C4
Prestwich M25 . . . . .63 A5
Deyne St 6 M6 . . . . .154 E2
Dial Ct BL4 . . . . .60 D8
Dial Park Prim Sch SK2 . . .124 D4
Dial Park Rd SK2 . . . . .124 D4
Dial Rd Altrincham WA15 . . .129 C8
Stockport SK2 . . . . .124 D5
Dialstone La SK1,SK2 . . . . .124 C6
Diamond Cl 9 OL6 . . . . .85 D4
Diamond St
8 Ashton-u-L OL6 . . . . .85 D4
Leigh WN7 . . . . .75 E4
Stockport SK2 . . . . .124 A6
Wigan WN6 . . . . .37 A3
Diamond Terr SK6 . . . . . . .125 F3
Diane Rd WN4 . . . . .73 E5
Dibben Wlk 8 M23 . . . . . . .121 A5
Dicconson Cres 6 WN1 . . .37 C1
Dicconson La Aspull BL5 . . . .39 B4
Aspull BL5,WN2 . . . . .39 A4
Dicconson Terr WN1 . . . . . .37 C1
Dicken Gn OL11 . . . . .30 D4
Dicken Green La OL11 . . . . .30 D4
Dickens Cl SK8 . . . . .132 B5
Dickens Dr WN2 . . . . .74 C8
Dickens La SK12 . . . . .133 E2
Dickens Pl WN3 . . . . .54 E2
Dickens Rd Coppull PR7 . . .19 E8
Eccles M30 . . . . .79 D1
Dickens St Heywood OL10 . .29 B2
Oldham OL1 . . . . .49 E4
Dickenson Rd M13,M14 . . .98 E3
Dickenson St WN2 . . . . .56 A2
Dickinson Cl 12 BL1 . . . . .143 E1
Dickinson Cl 1 BL1 . . . . . . .22 B4
Dickinson St Bolton BL1 . . .143 E1
Manchester M1 . . . . .163 A8
Oldham OL4 . . . . .67 B7
Dickinson St W BL6 . . . . . . .22 A4
Didcot Rd M22 . . . . .121 C1
Didley Sq M12 . . . . .165 A7
Didsbury CE Prim Sch
M20 . . . . .110 B3
Didsbury Pk M20 . . . . .110 B2
Didsbury Rd SK4 . . . . .168 B2
Didsbury Road Prim Sch
SK4 . . . . .110 C2
Dig Gate La OL16 . . . . .31 E3
Digby Lo M20 . . . . .110 B4
Digby Rd OL11 . . . . .30 F4
Digby Wlk 20 M11 . . . . . . .160 F1
Diggle Prim Sch OL3 . . . . . .51 C5
Diggle St Shaw OL2 . . . . . . .149 B6
Wigan WN6 . . . . .37 A1
Diggle Wlk SK15 . . . . .86 E6
Diggles La OL11 . . . . .29 F6
Diglands Ave SK22 . . . . . . .127 D1
Diglands Cl SK22 . . . . .127 D1
Diglea OL3 . . . . .51 D5
Dijon St BL3 . . . . .146 C4
Dilham Ct BL1 . . . . .144 C8
Dillicar Wlk M9 . . . . .157 D7
Dillmoss Wlk 15 M15 . . . . .162 D6
Dillon Dr M12 . . . . .164 E5
Dilston Cl M13 . . . . .163 C6
Dilworth Cl OL10 . . . . .29 A2
Dilworth Ct SK2 . . . . .124 E5
Dilworth St M13,M15 . . . . .163 B5

Dimple Pk BL7 . . . . .8 D3
Dimple Rd BL7 . . . . .8 C4
Dingle Ave
Alderley Edge SK9 . . . . .136 D3
Appley Bridge WN6 . . . . .35 E8
Denton M34 . . . . .101 B2
Orrell WN8 . . . . .53 C8
Shaw OL2 . . . . .32 C1
Dingle Bank Rd SK7 . . . . . .123 D1
Dingle Cl Glossop SK13 . . . .116 A8
Romiley SK6 . . . . .113 D2
Dingle Dr M43 . . . . .84 B3
Dingle Gr SK8 . . . . .121 F6
Dingle Rd Middleton M24 . . .64 F6
Orrell WN8 . . . . .53 D7
Dingle Terr OL6 . . . . .67 B2
Dingle The Bramhall SK7 . . .123 C1
Hyde SK14 . . . . .113 E7
Dingle Wlk 4 Bolton BL1 . .145 F8
Manchester M40 . . . . .83 B6
Dinglebrook Gr 6 SK9 . . . .131 D1
Dinglewood SK7 . . . . .123 C1
Dinmor Rd M22 . . . . .121 D1
Dinmore Ct SK2 . . . . .124 D5
Dinnington Dr M8 . . . . .155 F6
Dinorvic Cl M8 . . . . .156 B6
Dinsdale Cl M40 . . . . .160 D2
Dinsdale Dr BL3 . . . . .145 D5
Dinslow Wlk 18 M8 . . . . . .155 F7
Dinting Ave M20 . . . . .110 A7
Dinting CE Prim Sch
SK13 . . . . .104 A1
Dinting La SK13 . . . . .104 A1
Dinting Lane Trad Est
SK13 . . . . .104 A1
Dinting Lodge Ind Est
SK13 . . . . .171 F2
Dinting Rd SK13 . . . . .104 B2
Dinting Sta SK13 . . . . .104 A2
Dinting Vale SK13 . . . . .104 A1
Dinton St M15 . . . . .161 C7
Dipton Wlk M8 . . . . .156 C6
Dirty La Ashley WA14 . . . . . .128 A5
Delph OL3 . . . . .51 B8
Oldham OL4 . . . . .50 B1
Dirty Leech OL12 . . . . .14 F6
Disley Ave M20 . . . . .109 F6
Disley Cty Prim Sch
SK12 . . . . .135 D6
Disley Ho SK3 . . . . .170 E7
Disley St OL11 . . . . .30 C4
Disley Sta SK12 . . . . .135 C6
Disley Wlk M34 . . . . .101 A1
Distaff Rd SK12 . . . . .133 A4
District CE Prim Sch The
WA12 . . . . .89 A4
Ditton Mead Cl OL12 . . . . . .15 B2
Ditton Wlk 5 M23 . . . . . . .120 F6
Division St Bolton BL3 . . . .147 F4
Rochdale OL12 . . . . .15 B2
Dixey St 8 BL6 . . . . .22 B3
Dixon Ave Manchester M7 . .155 E6
Newton-le-W WA12 . . . . .89 C5
Shevington WN6 . . . . .36 A5
Dixon Cl Ashton-in-M WA11 . .89 A8
Sale M33 . . . . .108 D2
Dixon Closes OL11 . . . . .30 F3
Dixon Ct Cheadle SK8 . . . . .122 D5
Westhoughton BL5 . . . . .39 E3
Dixon Dr Kearsley M27 . . . . .61 E4
Shevington WN6 . . . . .36 A5
Dixon Green Dr 11 BL4 . . . .60 D8
Dixon Pl 8 WN2 . . . . .56 B1
Dixon Rd M34 . . . . .101 B1
Dixon St 15 Ashton-u-L OL6 . .85 D4
Failsworth M40 . . . . .83 B6
Horwich BL6 . . . . .22 B3
Irlam M44 . . . . .105 F8
Manchester M40 . . . . .65 C5
Middleton M24 . . . . .47 A2
Oldham OL4 . . . . .67 E8
Rochdale OL11 . . . . .30 C3
Westhoughton BL5 . . . . .39 E3
Dob Brook Cl M35,M40 . . . .83 C6
Dob Hedge Cl WA15 . . . . . .129 C6
Dobbin Dr OL11 . . . . .30 F3
Dobbinetts La M23,WA15 . .120 D4
Dobcross Cl M13 . . . . .98 F3
Dobcross New Rd OL3 . . . . .51 A1
Dobhill St BL4 . . . . .60 D8
Dobroyd Ho OL4 . . . . .67 E8
Dobroyd St M8 . . . . .156 A8
Dobson Cl
Appley Bridge WN6 . . . . .18 E2
Manchester M13 . . . . .164 D6
Dobson Ct M40 . . . . .83 B4
Dobson Pk Ind Est WN2 . . .56 C4
Dobson Rd BL1 . . . . .144 C7
Dobson St Bolton BL1 . . . . .143 D2
Ince-in-M WN2 . . . . .56 A6
Doctor Fold La OL10 . . . . . .46 C5
Doctor La OL4 . . . . .50 C1
Doctors La BL9 . . . . .140 D2
Dodd Croft OL16 . . . . .31 B3
Dodd La BL5 . . . . .39 B4
Dodd St M5 . . . . .154 D2
Dodd's Farm La WN2 . . . . . .58 A6
Doddington Cl M16 . . . . .97 F4
Doddington La M5 . . . . . . .161 A8
Doddington Wlk M34 . . . . .101 A1
Dodge Fold SK2 . . . . .124 E6
Dodge Hill SK4 . . . . .169 E2
Dodgson St OL16 . . . . .31 A6
Dodhurst Rd WN2 . . . . .56 F6
Doe Brow M27 . . . . .61 F8
Doe Hey Gr BL4 . . . . .42 B2
Doe Hey Rd BL3 . . . . .42 B2

Doefield Ave M28 . . . . .78 C8
Doeford Cl WA3 . . . . .91 E5
Doffcocker Brow BL1 . . . . .142 A1
Doffcocker La BL1 . . . . .23 F2
Dogford Rd OL2 . . . . .48 D5
Dolbey St M5 . . . . .154 E1
Dolefield M3 . . . . .158 E1
Dollond St M9 . . . . .64 E1
Dolman Wlk 4 M8 . . . . . . .155 F6
Dolphin Pl M12 . . . . .163 C7
Dolphin St M12 . . . . .163 C7
Dolwen Wlk M40 . . . . .83 B6
Doman St BL3 . . . . .145 F5
Dombey Rd SK12 . . . . .133 D2
Domestic App M90 . . . . . . .130 C6
Domett St M9 . . . . .64 C2
Dominic Cl M23 . . . . .120 C2
Don Ave M6 . . . . .80 C2
Don St Bolton BL3 . . . . .147 D3
Middleton M24 . . . . .47 C1
Dona St SK1 . . . . .124 A8
Donald Ave SK14 . . . . .167 F1
Donald St M1 . . . . .163 A7
Doncaster Ave M20 . . . . . .110 A7
Doncaster Cl BL3 . . . . .42 F3
Doncaster Wlk 4 OL1 . . . .153 F7
Donhead Wlk M13 . . . . . . .163 C6
Donington Gdns M28 . . . . . .60 A3
Donkey La SK9 . . . . .137 A5
Donleigh St M35 . . . . .83 D6
Donnington 6 OL11 . . . . . .139 E6
Donnington Ave SK8 . . . . . .122 F6
Donnington Cl WN7 . . . . . . .75 E1
Donnington Rd
Droylsden M18 . . . . .99 E5
Little Lever M26 . . . . .43 C5
Donnison St M12 . . . . .164 D4
Donovan St M40 . . . . .159 C4
Doodfield Prim Sch SK6 . .125 F2
Doodson Ave M44 . . . . .94 A2
Doodson Sq BL4 . . . . .60 D8
Dooley La SK2,SK6 . . . . . . .125 B7
Dooley's La SK9 . . . . .136 C2
Dootson St 4 Abram WN2 . .56 B1
Hindley WN2 . . . . .57 A6
Dora St BL0 . . . . .11 A4
Dorac Ave SK8 . . . . .131 C7
Dorchester Ave Bolton BL2 . .25 E5
Denton M34 . . . . .100 F1
Manchester M25 . . . . .63 C2
Urmston M41 . . . . .95 F3
Dorchester Cl
Altrincham WA15 . . . . .120 C3
Wilmslow SK9 . . . . .137 D8
Dorchester Ct
Bramhall SK8 . . . . .123 B1
Sale M33 . . . . .108 B2
Dorchester Dr Oldham OL2 .108 E2
Sale M23,M33 . . . . .108 E1
Dorchester Gr OL2 . . . . . . .108 E2
Dorchester Par SK7 . . . . . .124 B1
Dorchester Rd
Hazel Grove SK7 . . . . .124 B1
Orrell WN8 . . . . .53 C7
Swinton M27 . . . . .79 F6
Dorclyn Ave M41 . . . . .95 D2
Dorfield Cl SK6 . . . . .112 E3
Doric Ave SK6 . . . . .112 D2
Doric Cl M11 . . . . .160 F2
Doric Gn WN5 . . . . .53 D3
Doris Ave BL3 . . . . .147 E4
Doris Rd SK3 . . . . .123 C8
Doris St M24 . . . . .47 A2
Dorket Gr BL5 . . . . .57 D6
Dorking Ave M40 . . . . .83 C4
Dorking Cl Bolton BL1 . . . . .143 F2
Stockport SK1,SK2 . . . . .124 B7
Dorlan Ave M18 . . . . .99 F4
Dorland Gr SK2 . . . . .124 B7
Dorman St 8 M11 . . . . .99 D7
Dormer St BL1 . . . . .143 F3
Dorney St 8 M18 . . . . .99 D5
Dorning Rd M27 . . . . .80 A7
Dorning St Blackrod BL6 . . . .21 C3
Bury BL8 . . . . .27 F4
8 Eccles M30 . . . . .79 D1
Kearsley BL4 . . . . .60 F8
Leigh WN7 . . . . .75 E5
Tyldesley M29 . . . . .59 D8
Wigan WN1 . . . . .150 B8
Dornton Wlk M8 . . . . .155 F6
Dorothy Gr WN7 . . . . .75 E4
Dorothy Rd SK7 . . . . .124 F8
Dorothy St Manchester M8 . .155 F7
Ramsbottom BL0 . . . . .138 B5
Dorrian Mews BL1 . . . . .40 F7
Dorrington Rd
Cheadle SK3 . . . . .123 A7
Sale M33 . . . . .107 E4
Dorris St Bolton BL3 . . . . . .146 A3
Manchester M19 . . . . .111 B8
Dorrit Cl SK12 . . . . .133 C2
Dorset Ave Bramhall SK7 . .123 D1
Brinnington SK5 . . . . .112 C5
Cheadle SK8 . . . . .122 B3
Diggle OL3 . . . . .51 C4
Droylsden M34 . . . . .100 C8
Farnworth BL4 . . . . .60 C8
Manchester M14 . . . . .98 A2
Shaw OL2 . . . . .32 D1
Tyldesley M29 . . . . .59 B2
Dorset Cl Farnworth BL4 . . . .60 C8
Heywood OL10 . . . . .29 A1
Wigan WN5 . . . . .54 C6
Dorset Dr Bury BL9 . . . . .45 A8

Dorset Dr continued
Haslingden BB4 ....1 A8
Dorset Rd
Altrincham WA14 ....119 B5
Atherton M46 ....58 C5
Droylsden M43 ....83 F3
Failsworth M35 ....83 F6
Irlam M44 ....105 D5
Reddish M19 ....99 C1
Standish WN1 ....20 B1
Dorset St Ashton-u-L OL6 ..85 D2
Bolton BL2 ....148 A7
Hindley WN2 ....56 C6
Leigh WN7 ....76 D4
Oldham OL9 ....152 C5
Rochdale OL11 ....139 F6
Stretford M32 ....96 D1
Swinton M27 ....99 A3
Dorsey St M4 ....159 B2
Dorstone Cl Failsworth M40 .83 C4
Hindley WN2 ....57 B5
Dorwood Ave M9 ....64 C5
Dotterel Cl WN7 ....76 A6
Dougall Wlk M12 ....165 A6
Doughty Ave M30 ....79 F3
Dougill St BL1 ....142 B1
Douglas Ave Billinge WN5 ..71 D3
Bury BL8 ....27 B2
Horwich BL6 ....22 C5
Orrell WN8 ....53 B7
Stretford M32 ....96 D3
Douglas Bank Dr WN6 ......36 F2
Douglas Cl Horwich BL6 .....22 C5
Whitefield M45 ....45 C2
Douglas Dr Orrell WN5 ......53 F7
Shevington WN6 ....35 F5
Douglas Gn M6 ....81 A5
Douglas Ho M14 ....151 D7
Douglas Pk M46 ....58 E3
Douglas Rd Atherton M46 ...58 E2
Hazel Grove SK7 ....124 E3
Leigh WN7 ....75 C7
Shevington Moor WN6 ....19 B2
Stockport SK3 ....123 E4
Swinton M28 ....79 C7
Wigan WN1 ....37 D1
Douglas Sq OL10 ....28 F1
Douglas St Ashton-u-L OL6 ..85 D3
Atherton M46 ....58 E3
Bolton BL1 ....24 E5
Failsworth M35 ....84 A7
Hindley WN2 ....56 C4
Hyde SK14 ....167 E2
Manchester M40 ....83 A7
Manchester M7 ....155 D6
Oldham OL1 ....67 A8
Pendlebury M27 ....80 A7
Ramsbottom BL0 ....138 B6
Wigan WN5 ....150 A7
Douglas St Back BL0 ......138 B6
Douglas Way M45 ....45 C1
Douglas Wlk 2 Sale M33 ..107 C5
Whitefield M45 ....45 C2
Doulton St M40 ....83 C8
Dounby Ave M30 ....79 B3
Douro St M10,M40 ....157 F5
Douthwaite Dr SK6 ....113 E1
Dove Bank Rd BL3 ....43 A4
Irlam M44 ....94 A3
Dove Rd BL3 ....146 B4
Dove St Bolton BL1 ....143 E4
Golborne WA3 ....74 A2
Oldham OL4 ....67 C6
Rochdale OL11 ....139 D7
Dove Wlk Farnworth BL4 .....59 F8
Manchester M8 ....156 B5
Dovebrook Cl SK15 ....86 E7
Dovecote M43 ....84 D3
Dovecote Bsns & Tech Pk
M33 ....108 F4
Dovecote Cl BL7 ....25 B8
Dovecote La Oldham OL4 ....67 F8
Walkden M28 ....59 E3
Dovecote Mews M21 ....109 A8
Dovedale Ave
Droylsden M43 ....83 E2
Eccles M30 ....79 E3
Manchester M20 ....110 A7
Manchester M25 ....63 E3
Urmston M41 ....95 D3
Dovedale Cl SK6 ....134 E7
Dovedale Cres WN4 ....73 A8
Dovedale Ct Glossop SK13 ..104 F1
1 Middleton M24 ....46 E2
Dovedale Dr
Littleborough OL12 ....15 D6
Standish WN6 ....19 E2
Dovedale Rd
Ashton-in-M WN4 ....73 A8
Bolton BL2 ....25 F1
Stockport SK2 ....124 D7
Dovedale St M35 ....83 E7
Dovehouse Cl M45 ....62 D7
Doveleys Rd M6 ....154 D4
Dovenby Fold WN2 ....56 B7
Dover Cl BL8 ....11 A1
Dover Gr BL3 ....145 D5
Dover Pk M41 ....95 D4
Dover Rd M27 ....62 A2
Dover St Eccles M30 ....79 B2
Farnworth BL4 ....42 D2
Manchester M13 ....163 B6
Oldham OL9 ....152 C5

Dover St continued
1 Reddish SK5 ....111 E7
Rochdale OL16 ....15 B2
Dovercourt Ave SK4 ....110 F4
Doveston Rd M33 ....108 B6
Dovestone Cres SK16 ......101 F7
Doveston Wlk M40 ....65 E1
Dovey Cl M29 ....77 C7
Dow Fold BL8 ....26 F3
Dow La BL8 ....26 F3
Dow St SK14 ....101 D5
Dower St WN2 ....56 A3
Dowland Cl 3 M23 ....108 F2
Dowling Cl WN6 ....36 D3
Dowling St OL11 ....139 F6
Downal Green
RC dun Sch WN4 ....72 E6
Downall Green
RC Prim Sch WN4 ....72 E6
Downall Green Rd WN4 .....72 E6
Downbrook Way WN4 ....73 D5
Downesway SK9 ....136 F1
Downfield Cl BL0 ....138 B6
Downfields SK5 ....100 A1
Downgate Wlk 7 M8 ....156 A6
Downgreen Rd BL2 ....25 E3
Downhall Gn BL1 ....145 F8
Downham Ave Bolton BL2 ...148 C8
Culcheth WA3 ....91 F2
Downham Chase WA15 ......120 B6
Downham Cl OL1 ....48 D2
Downham Cres M25 ....63 E3
Downham Gdns M25 ....63 E3
Downham Gr M25 ....63 E3
Downham Rd
Heywood OL10 ....29 A2
Reddish SK4 ....111 D5
Downham Wlk
Longshaw WN5 ....53 D1
Sale M23 ....120 E8
Downhill Cl OL1 ....48 E1
Downing Cl Ashton-u-L OL7 ..84 F6
Platt Bridge WN2 ....56 A2
Downing St Ashton-u-L OL7 ..84 F5
5 Leigh WN7 ....75 F5
Manchester M1,M12,M13 ......163 B7
Downing Street Ind Est
M12 ....163 B7
Downley Cl OL12 ....14 B2
Downley Dr M4 ....159 C2
Downs Dr WA14 ....119 E8
Downs The
Altrincham WA14 ....119 D3
Cheadle SK8 ....122 D3
Middleton M24 ....65 B5
Prestwich M25 ....63 A2
Sale M33 ....107 F1
Downshaw Rd OL7 ....85 A6
Downton Ave WN2 ....56 D4
Dowry Rd OL4 ....67 F7
Dowry St OL8 ....67 A3
Dowson Cty Prim Sch
SK14 ....113 E8
Dowson Rd SK14 ....113 E8
Dowson St BL2 ....148 A7
Doyle Ave SK6 ....112 D3
Doyle Cl OL1 ....49 E4
Doyle Rd BL3 ....42 A4
Drake Ave Farnworth BL4 ...60 D7
Irlam M44 ....105 E6
Drake Cl OL1 ....153 F8
Drake Ct SK5 ....169 E4
Drake Hall BL5 ....57 E5
Drake Rd Altrincham WA14 ..119 B8
Littleborough OL15 ....6 C1
Drake St Manchester M4 ....58 C2
Rochdale OL11,OL16 ....139 F6
Draycott Cl WN2 ....56 C3
Draycott St BL1 ....143 E2
Draycott St E 10 BL1 ......143 F2
Drayfields M43 ....84 D2
Drayford Cl 2 M23 ....108 F2
Drayton Ave SK8 ....131 B7
Drayton Cl Bolton BL1 .....143 D2
Sale M33 ....107 D2
11 Handforth SK9 ....131 D1
Drayton Gr WA15 ....120 A5
Drayton Manor M20 ....122 B8
Drayton Wlk M16 ....162 D5
Dresden St M40 ....83 C8
Drewett St M40 ....160 E4
Dreyfus Ave M11 ....83 D2
Dreyfus St M40 ....160 E3
Driffield St Eccles M30 ....95 C8
Manchester M14 ....98 A3
Drill Wlk 8 M4 ....159 C1
Drinkwater Rd M25 ....62 F1
Driscoll St 1 M13 ....98 F3
Drive The
Altrincham WA14 ....129 D8
Bredbury SK6 ....112 C4
Brinnington SK5 ....112 C4
Broomedge WA13 ....117 D1
Bury BL9 ....25 F3
Cheadle SK8 ....123 C4
Edenfield BL0 ....1 D3
Leigh WN7 ....75 F3
Manchester M20 ....110 C4
Manchester M7 ....62 E3
Marple SK6 ....125 E6
Prestwich M25 ....63 B4
Sale M33 ....107 E1
Droitwich Rd M40 ....160 D4
Dronfield Rd Salford M6 ...154 D4
Wythenshawe M22 ....121 D8
Droughts La M25 ....63 E8
Drovers Wlk SK13 ....104 D1
Droxford Ct SK9 ....137 B6

Droxford Gr M46 ....58 E5
Droylsden High Sch M43 ....83 F2
Droylsden Rd
Droylsden M34 ....100 D8
Droylsden M34 ....84 C1
Failsworth M40 ....83 D5
Drs Green & Slater
Rest Hos** SK4 ....168 A3
Druid St WN4 ....73 C2
Druids Cl BL7 ....8 D3
Drummer's La WN4 ....72 E7
Drummond Sq WN5 ....54 E7
Drummond St BL1 ....143 E4
Drummond Way WN7 ....76 B5
Drury La OL9 ....66 B3
Drury St 8 M19 ....99 A1
Dryad Cl M27 ....61 F2
Drybrook Cl M13 ....164 E5
Dryburgh Ave BL1 ....143 D4
Dryclough Wlk OL2 ....48 E3
Dryden Ave
Ashton-in-M WN4 ....72 F6
Cheadle SK8 ....122 F6
Swinton M27 ....79 D7
Dryden Cl Dukinfield SK16 ..102 B7
Marple SK6 ....125 F4
Wigan WN3 ....150 A5
Dryden Rd 4 M16 ....97 C3
Dryden St M13 ....163 C6
Dryden Way M34 ....113 A8
Dryfield La BL6 ....22 A5
Drygate Wlk 9 M9 ....157 E7
Dryhurst Dr SK12 ....135 D6
Dryhurst La SK12 ....135 D6
Dryhurst Wlk M15 ....163 A6
Drymoss OL8 ....67 A1
Dryton Wlk M22 ....38 A2
Drywood Ave M28 ....79 A5
Ducal St M4 ....159 B4
Duchess Park Cl OL2 ......149 B8
Duchess Rd M8 ....156 B8
Duchess St OL2 ....149 B8
Duchess Wlk BL3 ....146 B4
Duchy Ave Atherton BL5 ....59 A8
Walkden M28 ....78 D8
Ducie Bank M6 ....80 D5
Ducie St Salford M6 ....154 F3
Stockport SK3 ....170 D7
Ducie Ave BL1 ....144 C7
Ducie Gr M13 ....163 C6
Ducie High Sch M15 ....98 B4
Ducie St Manchester M1 ...159 B1
Oldham OL6 ....66 F2
Radcliffe M26 ....43 F5
Whitefield M45 ....62 F8
Duckshaw La BL4 ....60 D8
Duckworth La BB4 ....1 E8
Duckworth Rd M25 ....62 F3
Duckworth St
3 Bury BL9 ....141 A4
Shaw OL2 ....149 C7
Duddon Ave BL2 ....25 F1
Duddon Cl M45 ....63 C8
Duddon Dr WN6 ....36 F7
Duddon St M44 ....46 E2
Dudley Ave Bolton BL2 .....25 C1
Whitefield M45 ....62 F8
Dudley Cl M16 ....162 E5
Dudley Ct 10 M16 ....97 D3
Dudley Rd Irlam M44 ....105 D4
Manchester M16 ....97 D3
Sale M33 ....108 A4
Sale M33 ....120 A5
Swinton M27 ....61 F1
Dudley St Ashton-in-M WN4 ..73 A5
Denton M34 ....100 E4
Eccles M30 ....79 C7
Manchester M7,M8 ....155 F6
6 Oldham OL4 ....67 D6
Dudlow Wlk 2 M15 ....162 D6
Dudwell Cl BL3 ....146 C2
Duerden St BL3 ....146 A2
Duffield Ct M15 ....163 A5
Duffield Gdns M9 ....64 F5
Duffield Rd Middleton M9 ....64 F5
Salford M6 ....80 D5
Duffins Cl OL12 ....14 D3
Dutton Wlk
8 Middleton M24 ....46 E2
Wythenshawe M22 ....130 E8
Dugdale Ave M9 ....64 E4
Dugie St BL0 ....149 E4
Duke Ave Cheadle SK8 ......131 F6
Glazebury WA3 ....92 C7
Duke Cl M16 ....162 D5
Duke of Norfolk's
CE Prim Sch** Glossop SK13 104 D1
Glossop SK13 ....104 E2
Duke Pl M3 ....162 E8
Duke Rd Ainsworth BL2 .....26 C1
Dukinfield SK14 ....101 F5
Duke St Alderley Edge SK9 ..137 B2
Ashton-in-M WN4 ....73 C2
Bolton BL1 ....166 B3
Bolton BL1 ....145 E8
Denton M34 ....100 E3
Eccles M30 ....79 C4
Farnworth BL4 ....145 E8
Golborne WA3 ....74 A1
Heywood OL10 ....29 B2
Leigh WN7 ....76 A4
Littleborough OL15 ....16 A5
Manchester M3 ....158 F2
Manchester M7 ....158 D2
Mossley OL5 ....68 E1

Duke St continued
Newton-le-W WA12 ....89 B3
Platt Bridge WN2 ....56 A3
Radcliffe M26 ....44 B2
Ramsbottom BL0 ....11 A4
Rawtenstall BB4 ....2 E8
Rochdale OL12 ....14 F1
Shaw OL2 ....149 C6
Stalybridge SK15 ....85 F1
Stockport SK1 ....169 F1
Tyldesley M29 ....77 C6
Walkden M28 ....61 A2
Walkden M38 ....60 A5
Wigan WN1 ....37 C2
Wigan WN3 ....150 B4
Duke St N BL1 ....145 E8
Duke's Terr 17 SK16 ....166 B1
Dukefield St M22 ....121 E8
Dukes Ave BL3 ....43 A4
Dukes Platting OL6 ....85 F5
Dukes St SK13 ....116 C8
Dukes Wharf M28 ....78 F5
Dukesgate Cty Prim Sch
M38 ....60 A5
Dukinfield Rd SK14 ....101 C4
Dukinfield St 6 WN7 ....76 A5
Dulford Wlk M13 ....163 C5
Dulgar St M11 ....165 B8
Dulverton Gdns BL3 ....43 B2
Dulverton St M40 ....83 B6
Dulwich Cl M33 ....107 D1
Dulwich St M4 ....159 B3
Dumbarton Cl SK5 ....111 F6
Dumbarton Dr OL10 ....46 A8
Dumbarton Gn WN6 ....36 E2
Dumbarton Rd
Heywood OL10 ....29 A1
Reddish SK5 ....111 F6
Dumbell St M27 ....61 F2
Dumber La M33 ....107 F6
Dumers Cl M26 ....44 D5
Dumers La BL9,M26 ....44 E5
Dumfries Ave OL3 ....33 C2
Dumfries Dr OL10 ....33 C2
Dumfries Hollow OL10 ....29 F3
Dumfries Wlk OL10 ....29 A1
Dumplington Circ M41 ....95 D7
Dun Cl M3 ....158 D2
Dunbar Ave M23 ....121 A3
Dunbar Dr BL3 ....147 E3
Dunbar Gr OL10 ....45 F8
Dunbar Rd SK16 ....153 E8
Dunblane Ave Bolton BL3 ...40 E5
Stockport SK4 ....169 D2
Dunblane Cl WN4 ....72 C4
Dunblane Gr OL10 ....46 A8
Duncan Ave WA12 ....89 C5
Duncan Edwards Ho 5
M6 ....154 F3
Duncan Pl WN5 ....54 E7
Duncan St Bolton BL1 ......145 F8
Dukinfield SK16 ....101 C6
Horwich BL6 ....22 C3
Manchester M7 ....81 C6
Salford M5 ....161 C8
Dunchurch Cl BL6 ....40 D6
Dunchurch Rd M33 ....107 E4
Duncombe Cl SK7 ....124 A3
Duncombe Dr M40 ....83 B7
Duncombe Rd BL3 ....147 E2
Duncombe St M7 ....155 E6
Duncote Gr OL2 ....149 A5
Dundee 3 M30 ....79 E2
Dundee Cl OL10 ....28 E1
Dundee La BL0 ....138 B6
Dundonald Rd
Cheadle SK8 ....132 A7
Manchester M20 ....110 C3
Dundonald St SK2 ....170 F6
Dundraw Cl M24 ....46 B1
Dundrennan Cl SK12 ....133 D5
Dunecroft M34 ....101 A4
Dunedin Dr M6 ....80 F6
Dunedin Rd BL8 ....10 F2
Dunelm Dr M33 ....108 D1
Dunham Ave WA3 ....73 F1
Dunham Cl BL5 ....57 D5
Dunham Gr M26 ....44 A3
Dunham Lawn WA14 ....119 B4
Dunham Massey Hall
WA14 ....118 D3
Dunham Pk WA14 ....118 D3
Dunham Rd
Altrincham WA14 ....118 F1
Altrincham WA14 ....119 F1
Dukinfield SK16 ....101 D6
Partington M31 ....106 D3
Partington WA13 ....117 E7
Dunham Rise WA14 ....119 C4
Dunkeld Gdns 2 M23 ....120 F6
Dunkeld Rd M23 ....120 F6
Dunkerley Ave M35 ....83 F7
Dunkerley St
Ashton-u-L OL7 ....85 A5
Oldham OL4 ....67 C7
Royton OL2 ....48 D4
Dunkerleys Cl M8 ....155 F8
Dunkery Rd M22 ....121 D1
Dunkirk Cl M34 ....100 A2
Dunkirk La SK14 ....101 B4
Dunkirk Rise OL12 ....13 F2
Dunkirk St M43 ....84 B1
Dunley Cl M12 ....165 A5
Dunlin Ave WA12 ....89 C4
Dunlin Cl Bolton BL2 ......148 A5

Dunlin Cl continued
Hazel Grove SK2 ....125 A5
Poynton SK12 ....133 A4
Rochdale OL11 ....29 F7
Dunlin Dr M44 ....94 A3
Dunlin Gr WN7 ....76 B5
Dunlop Ave OL11 ....130 E4
Dunlop St 2 M3 ....158 F1
Dunmail Cl WA11 ....71 C1
Dunmail Cl M29 ....77 C6
Dunmail Dr M24 ....46 E3
Dunmaston Ave M23 ....120 D7
Dunmere Wlk M9 ....156 C6
Dunmore Rd SK8 ....122 C4
Dunmow Ct SK2 ....124 E5
Dunmow Wlk M23 ....109 A2
Dunne La SK13 ....104 E2
Dunnerdale Wlk M18 ....165 C5
Dunnisher Rd M23 ....121 B5
Dunnock Cl SK2 ....124 F5
Dunollie Rd M23 ....108 E3
Dunoon Cl OL10 ....29 A1
Dunoon Dr BL1 ....24 C5
Dunoon Rd Aspull WN2 ......38 D5
Reddish SK5 ....111 F7
Dunoon Wlk M9 ....157 D7
Dunrobin Cl OL10 ....46 A8
Dunscar Cl M45 ....62 D7
Dunscar Ind Est BL7 ....24 E7
Dunscar Sq BL7 ....24 F8
Dunscore Rd WN3 ....54 E3
Dunsdale Dr WN3 ....73 C3
Dunsfold Dr M23 ....120 D8
Dunsford Ct OL4 ....67 F5
Dunsley Ave M40 ....65 D2
Dunsmore Cl M16 ....97 E4
Dunsop Dr BL1 ....23 F3
Dunstable 9 OL12 ....139 F8
Dunstable St M19 ....99 B1
Dunstall Rd M22 ....121 E5
Dunstan St M40 ....83 A8
Dunstar Ave M34 ....100 E7
Dunster Ave
Brinnington SK5 ....112 C5
Manchester M9 ....64 E4
Rochdale OL11 ....139 E5
Swinton M27 ....62 A3
Dunster Cl
Hazel Grove SK7 ....124 C1
Platt Bridge WN2 ....56 A1
Dunster Dr M41 ....94 C1
Dunster Pl M28 ....77 F7
Dunster Rd M28 ....77 F7
Dunsters Ave BL8 ....27 C5
Dunsterville Terr OL11 ....139 E5
Dunston St M11 ....165 C8
Dunton Gn SK5 ....112 B6
Dunton Towers SK5 ....112 B6
Dunvegan Rd SK7 ....124 F1
Dunwood Ct M22 ....149 C8
Dunwoods Park
Courts** OL2 ....32 C1
Dunworth St M14 ....98 B3
Durant St M4 ....159 B3
Durban Cl OL2 ....149 A6
Durban Rd 8 BL1 ....24 E5
Durban St Ashton-u-L OL7 ..84 E1
Atherton M46 ....58 A2
Golborne WN2,WN7 ....74 E4
Oldham OL8 ....66 C2
Durden Mews OL2 ....149 B6
Durham Ave M41 ....95 E3
Durham Cl
Dukinfield SK16 ....101 D6
Little Lever BL3 ....43 B4
Romiley SK6 ....113 A1
Swinton M27 ....61 F2
Tyldesley M29 ....59 A3
Durham Cres M35 ....84 A6
Durham Dr Ashton-u-L OL6 ..85 D8
Bury BL9 ....45 A8
Ramsbottom BL0 ....11 B3
Durham Ho 6 SK3 ....170 E8
Durham Rd Handforth SK9 ..131 D5
3 Hindley WN2 ....56 E5
Salford M6 ....80 C4
Durham St Bolton BL1 .....143 F2
Droylsden M43 ....100 A8
**17 Manchester M9 ....157 E7
Oldham OL9 ....66 C4
Radcliffe M26 ....44 C5
Reddish SK5 ....99 E2
Rochdale OL11 ....31 A5
Wigan WN1 ....150 C8
Durham Wlk
8 Denton M34 ....100 F1
Heywood OL10 ....29 A2
Durley Ave Manchester M8 ..156 B7
Sale M33 ....107 E3
Durling St M12 ....163 C7
Durn St OL15 ....16 C6
Durnford Ave M41 ....96 A1
Durnford Cl OL12 ....13 D2
Durnford St M24 ....46 F1
Durnford Wlk M22 ....121 B3
Durrell Way WA3 ....90 E8
Durrington Wlk M40 ....65 C3
Dursley Dr WN4 ....73 C2
Dutton Gr WN7 ....76 C2
Dutton St M3 ....158 F3
Duty St BL1 ....143 E3
Duxbury Ave Bolton BL2 .....25 E5
Little Lever BL3 ....43 A5
Duxbury Dr BL9 ....141 C2

Duxbury St BL1 .... 143 D2
Duxford Lo M8 .... 63 F2
Duxford Wlk M40 .... 65 C3
Dyche St M4 .... 159 B3
Dyche Street Trad Est
  M4 .... 159 B3
Dye House La
  New Mills SK22 .... 127 C1
  Rochdale OL16 .... 15 C3
Dye La SK6 .... 159 A2
Dyer St Golborne WA3 ... 73 F1
  Manchester M11 .... 165 A8
  Salford M5 .... 161 C7
Dyers Cl WA13 .... 117 A4
Dyers Ct OL15 .... 16 A6
Dyers La WA13 .... 117 A4
Dymchurch Ave M26 ...... 61 C7
Dymchurch St M40 .... 83 C4
Dysart St Ashton-u-L OL6 .. 85 D2
  Stockport SK2 .... 124 B5
Dysarts Cl OL15 .... 68 E3
Dyserth Gr SK5 .... 169 F4
Dyson Cl BL4 .... 60 D8
Dyson Ct OL4 .... 67 F8
Dyson St Farnworth BL4 .. 60 D7
  Mossley OL5 .... 68 B2
  Oldham OL1 .... 153 F6
Dystelegh Rd SK12 ...... 135 D6

E

Eades St M6 .... 81 A3
Eadington St M8 .... 64 A1
Eafield Ave OL16 .... 31 F7
Eafield Cl OL16 .... 31 A4
Eafield Rd
  Littleborough OL15 ... 15 E3
  Rochdale OL16 .... 15 C1
Eagar St M40 .... 83 C6
Eagle Cl Delph OL3 ..... 50 F5
  Salford M15 .... 162 E5
Eagle Dr M6 .... 81 A5
Eagle St Bolton BL2 .... 148 A7
  Manchester M4 .... 159 A2
  Oldham OL1 .... 153 E6
  Rochdale OL16 .... 31 A5
Eagle Tech Pk OL11 ..... 31 A4
Eagles Nest OL25 .... 63 A3
Eagley Bank OL12 .... 4 E6
Eagley Brook Way BL1 ... 25 A3
Eagley Brow BL1 .... 24 F7
Eagley Dr BL8 .... 27 A1
Eagley Ind Est BL7 ..... 24 F7
Eagley Jun Sch BL7 ..... 25 B8
Eagley Way BL1,BL7 ..... 24 F7
Ealees OL15 .... 16 C5
Ealees Rd OL15 .... 16 C5
Ealing Ave M14 .... 98 C2
Ealing Pl M19 .... 111 A6
Ealing Rd SK3 .... 170 D8
Eames Ave M26 .... 61 A8
Eamont Wlk M9 .... 157 D7
Earby Gr M9 .... 64 F3
Earl Rd Handforth SK8,SK9 .. 131 E5
  Manchester SK4 .... 168 C4
  Ramsbottom BL0 .... 138 B6
Earl St Atherton M46 ... 58 B2
  Bury BL9 .... 140 F2
  Heywood OL10 .... 29 C2
  Ince-in-M WN2 .... 56 A2
  Leigh WN7 .... 76 A4
  Manchester M7 .... 158 D4
  Middleton OL11 .... 47 D8
  Mossley OL5 .... 68 B1
  Prestwich M25 .... 63 A4
  Ramsbottom BL0 .... 11 D6
  Reddish M34 .... 100 A4
  Sale M33 .... 108 C5
  Stockport SK3 .... 170 D8
  Wigan WN1 .... 37 C1
Earl Terr SK16 .... 166 B1
Earl Wlk M12 .... 164 F5
Earl's Lo M35 .... 83 D6
Earle Rd SK7 .... 123 E3
Earle St Ashton-u-L OL7 .. 84 F2
  Newton-le-W WA12 ..... 89 A3
Earlesdon Cres M38 .... 60 A5
Earlestown Dist
  CE Jun Sch WA12 ...... 89 A3
Earlestown Sta WA12 ... 89 B3
Earls Way M35 .... 83 D6
Earlscliffe Ct WA14 ... 119 B4
Earlston Ave M34 ...... 100 A3
Earlsway SK13 .... 116 B8
Earlswood Rd OL8 ...... 66 E3
Earlswood Wlk Bolton BL1 .. 147 F4
  Manchester M18 .... 165 C6
Early Bank SK15 .... 102 C7
Early Bank Rd SK14,SK16 .. 102 B6
Earnshaw Ave
  Rochdale OL12 .... 14 E3
  Stockport SK1 .... 112 B1
Earnshaw Cl OL7 .... 84 F5
Earnshaw St Bolton BL3 .. 146 B3
  Hollingworth SK14 .... 171 F4
Easby Cl Bramhall SK8 .. 132 B6
  Poynton SK12 .... 133 A8
Easby Rd M24 .... 46 F3
Easedale Cl M41 .... 94 F3
Easedale Rd BL1 .... 144 A8
Easington Wlk M40 ..... 83 A6
Easingwold WA14 .... 119 C4
East Aisle Rd M17,M32 .. 96 C5
  Golborne WA3 .... 74 C1
  Leigh WN7 .... 76 C3

East Ave continued
  Manchester M19 .... 110 F7
  Stalybridge SK15 ..... 86 A3
  Whitefield M45 .... 44 E2
East Bond St WN7 ...... 76 A5
East Bridgewater St
  WN7 ....
East Central Dr M27 ... 80 B7
East Court Wlk M13 .... 163 C6
East Cres M24 .... 64 F7
East Crompton St George's
  CE Prim Sch
  OL2 .... 49 D7
East Didsbury Sta M20 .. 110 C1
East Downs Rd
  Altrincham WA14 ...... 119 C2
  Cheadle SK8 .... 122 F2
East Dr Marple SK6 .... 125 F3
  Pendlebury M27 .... 80 B7
  Whitefield M45 .... 80 E5
  Whitefield BL9 .... 45 B4
East Gate St OL16 ..... 139 F8
East Gr M13 .... 164 D5
East Grange M11 .... 83 C3
East Hill St OL1 ...... 67 A6
East Lancashire Rd
  Leigh WA3,WN7 .... 76 B1
  Newton-le-W WA11,WA12 .. 89 C7
  Pendlebury M6,M27 .... 80 B6
  Swinton M27,M28 ...... 79 D7
  Tyldesley M28,M29 .... 77 C5
  Worsley M28 .... 78 D7
East Lancashire Rly BL0 .. 138 C5
East Lancs Rly Bury BL0 .. 27 D6
  Heywood OL10 .... 29 C1
East Lea M31 .... 101 A2
East Lynn Dr M28 ...... 61 A3
East Meade Bolton BL3 .. 147 E2
  Manchester M21 .... 109 B7
  Manchester M25 .... 63 D2
  Swinton M27 .... 79 E6
East Moor M28 .... 78 A7
East Mount WN5 .... 53 F6
East Newton St M4 ..... 159 C3
East Ordsall La M3,M5 .. 158 D1
East Over SK6 .... 125 A8
East Philip St M3 ..... 158 E3
East Rd Eccles M41 .... 95 F6
  Manchester M18 .... 99 B4
  Mossley SK15 .... 86 E6
  Stretford M32 .... 96 B3
  Wythenshawe M90 ...... 130 C7
East St Ashton-in-M WN4 .. 73 D4
  Ashton-u-L OL6 .... 85 D4
  Bury BL9 .... 140 F1
  Dukinfield M34 .... 100 F7
  Haslingden BB4 .... 1 A7
  Hindley WN2 .... 57 B3
  Littleborough OL12 ... 15 C5
  Littleborough OL15 ... 16 C5
  Milnrow OL16 .... 31 D7
  Radcliffe M26 .... 44 B3
  Rochdale OL16 .... 31 A8
  Tyldesley M46 .... 58 F1
East Union St M16 ..... 161 C6
East Vale SK6 .... 126 A5
East View Middleton M24 .. 64 F8
  Ramsbottom BL0 .... 1 C1
  Ramsbottom BL9 .... 11 D1
East Ward Com Prim Sch
  BL9 .... 141 B2
East Way BL1 .... 25 B3
East Wlk BL7 .... 8 D2
Eastbank St BL1 .... 143 F2
Eastbourne Gr BL1 ..... 144 A8
Eastbourne St Oldham OL6 .. 67 B4
  Rochdale OL11 .... 139 F5
Eastbrook Ave M26 ..... 44 C4
Eastburn Ave M40 ...... 159 C3
Eastchurch Cl BL4 ..... 60 D7
Eastcombe Ave M7 ...... 81 B7
Eastcote Ave M11 ...... 99 E8
Eastcote Rd SK5 .... 111 F5
Eastcote Wlk BL4 ...... 42 E1
Eastdale Pl WA14 ...... 119 D7
Easterdale OL4 .... 67 C6
Eastern Ave M27 .... 62 D3
Eastern By-Pass
  Droylsden M11 .... 83 C2
  Manchester M11 .... 99 D8
Eastern Circ M19 ...... 111 A6
Eastern Terr WN1 ...... 154 E4
Eastfield Ave
  Manchester M40 .... 160 E3
  Middleton M24 .... 65 A7
Eastfields M26 .... 43 E5
Eastford Sq M40 .... 159 C4
Eastgate OL12 .... 14 C7
Eastgate St OL7 .... 166 A1
Eastgrove Ave BL1 ..... 24 E6
Eastham Ave Bury BL9 .. 27 F6
Eastham Way
  Handforth SK9 .... 131 D5
  Walkden M38 .... 60 B5
Eastleigh Ave M7 ...... 155 E8
Eastleigh Cres WN7 .... 76 B3

Eastleigh Dr M40 ...... 160 D3
Eastleigh Gr BL1 ...... 145 E8
Eastleigh Rd Gatley SK8 .. 122 B1
  Manchester M25 .... 63 E3
Eastmoor Dr M40 .... 83 D4
Eastmoor Gr BL3 ...... 146 B2
Eastnor Cl M15 .... 162 D6
Easton Cl Middleton M24 .. 65 C7
  Wigan WN5 .... 55 A2
Easton Dr SK8 .... 123 A5
Easton Rd M43 .... 83 E1
Eastpark Cl M13 ...... 163 C6
Eastry Ave SK5 .... 112 B6
Eastview M33 .... 108 B3
Eastville Gdns M19 ... 110 E5
Eastward Ave SK9 ..... 136 F6
Eastway Middleton M24 .. 46 F1
  Sale M33 .... 107 F1
  Shaw OL2 .... 149 B6
  Urmston M41 .... 94 E3
Eastwell Rd
  Ashton-in-M WN4 ..... 73 A3
  Wigan WN6 .... 36 F3
Eastwood M14 .... 98 C1
Eastwood Ave
  Droylsden M43 .... 83 E1
  Failsworth M40 ...... 65 F1
  Newton-le-W WA12 .... 89 F3
  Urmston M41 .... 95 D2
  Walkden M28 .... 60 A2
Eastwood Cl BL9 ...... 141 B2
Eastwood Dr BL3 ...... 146 A3
Eastwood Gr WN7 ...... 75 D5
Eastwood Rd M40 ...... 65 D1
Eastwood St Denton M34 .. 100 F7
  Littleborough OL15 .. 16 B5
Eastwood Terr BL1 .... 40 E8
Eatock Cty Prim Sch BL5 .. 57 E6
Eatock Way BL5 .... 57 D7
Eaton Cl Cheadle SK8 .. 122 F3
  Dukinfield SK16 ..... 101 C6
  Poynton SK12 .... 134 A3
  Swinton M27 .... 61 F2
Eaton Ct SK9 .... 137 A6
Eaton Dr Alderley Edge SK9 .. 136 F2
  Ashton-u-L OL7 ...... 84 F4
  Sale WA15 .... 120 A8
Eaton Rd Altrincham WA14 .. 119 C1
  Manchester M8 .... 63 F1
  Sale WA15 .... 120 A8
Eaton St WN2 .... 56 D3
Eaves Knoll Rd SK22 .. 127 A1
Eaves La OL9 .... 152 A5
Ebbdale Cl SK1 .... 124 A8
Ebberstone St M14 .... 98 A2
Eben St M11 .... 163 B8
Ebenezer St Glossop SK13 .. 116 D7
  Manchester M15 ...... 162 F7
Ebnal Wlk M14 .... 110 D7
Ebor Cl OL2 .... 149 A8
Ebor Rd M22 .... 96 F1
Ebor Rd M22 .... 121 E4
Ebor St OL15 .... 16 B5
Ebsworth St
  Manchester M40 ...... 157 F8
  Manchester M40 ...... 83 A8
Ebury St M26 .... 43 F3
Eccles Cl M11 .... 165 C8
Eccles Coll M30 ...... 79 F4
Eccles New Rd M5 ..... 80 C4
Eccles Old Rd M6,M30 .. 80 C3
Eccles Rd Swinton M27 .. 79 F6
  Wigan WN5 .... 54 D5
Eccles St BL0 .... 138 B6
Eccles Sta M30 ...... 79 F2
Ecclesbridge Rd SK6 .. 125 F4
Eccleshall St M11 .... 165 B8
Eccleston Ave
  Bolton BL2 .... 25 B1
  Manchester M14 ...... 98 B1
  Swinton M27 .... 79 D4
Eccleston Cl BL8 ..... 27 A1
Eccleston Pl M7 ...... 155 D8
Eccleston Rd SK3 ..... 123 E4
Eccleston St
  Failsworth M35 ...... 84 A8
  Wigan WN1 .... 37 C1
Eccleston Way SK9 .... 131 D4
Eccups La SK9 .... 136 C8
Echo St M1 .... 163 B8
Eckersley Cl M23 ..... 120 F6
Eckersley Fold La M46 .. 58 A1
Eckersley Rd BL1 ..... 143 E3
Eckersley St Bolton BL1 .. 145 F8
  Wigan WN1 .... 37 E1
Eckford St M8 .... 156 B6
Eclipse Cl OL16 ...... 31 A8
Edale Ave Denton M34 .. 100 D7
  Denton M34 .... 112 F8
  Manchester M40 ...... 83 A8
  Reddish M34 .... 100 C4
  Urmston M41 .... 95 B1
Edale Bank SK13 ...... 171 E1
Edale Cl Altrincham WA14 .. 119 B1
  Atherton M46 .... 58 C3
  Bramhall SK8 .... 132 B5
  Gatley SK8 .... 131 D2
  Hazel Grove SK7 ..... 124 E1
  Irlam M44 .... 94 A3
Edale Cres SK13 ...... 171 E1
Edale Dr Bury BL9 .... 27 F8
Edale Fold SK13 ...... 171 E2
Edale Gr Ashton-u-L OL6 .. 85 A8
  Sale M33 .... 107 E2
Edale Rd Bolton BL3 .. 146 A4
  Farnworth BL4 .... 60 C7

Edale Rd continued
  Leigh WN7 .... 76 C4
  Stretford M32 .... 96 B3
Edale St M6 .... 81 B5
Edbrook Wlk M13 ...... 164 D5
Edburton Ct WA3 ..... 90 A8
Edburton Ct WA3 ..... 90 A8
Eddie Colman Cl M40 .. 83 B5
Eddisbury Ave
  Manchester M20 ...... 109 F8
  Urmston M41 .... 94 D4
Eddisford Dr WA3 .... 91 D4
Edditch Gr BL2 ...... 148 C7
Eddleston St WN4 .... 72 F6
Eddystone Cl M5 ..... 81 A1
Eden Ave Bolton BL1 .. 143 E3
  Edenfield BL0 .... 1 D3
  Fowley Common WA3 ... 92 C4
  High Lane SK6 .... 134 E7
Eden Bank WN7 .... 76 B6
  Manchester M15 ...... 163 A6
  Stockport SK1 .... 124 A8
  Wilmslow SK9 .... 136 E5
Eden Ct Edenfield BL0 .. 1 D2
  Manchester M19 ...... 111 A8
Eden Gr Bolton BL1 .. 143 E3
  Leigh WN7 .... 75 C5
Eden Lo BL1 .... 143 E3
Eden Pl SK8 .... 122 D6
Eden Way OL2 .... 149 A8
Edenbridge Rd
  Cheadle SK8 .... 123 B4
  Failsworth M40 ...... 83 B4
Edendale Dr M22 ..... 121 D1
Edenfield Ave M21 ... 109 D4
Edenfield CE Prim Sch BL0 .. 1 D4
Edenfield La M28 .... 78 F4
Edenfield Rd
  Manchester M25,M8 ... 63 E2
  Rochdale OL11,OL12 .. 13 C2
Edenfield St OL11,OL12 .. 14 C1
Edenhall Ave M19 .... 110 F8
Edenhall Gr WN2 ..... 56 F3
Edenham Wlk M40 ..... 65 D2
Edenhurst Dr WA15 ... 120 B5
Edenhurst Rd SK2 .... 124 B6
Edensor Ct WN6 ...... 37 A4
Edensor Dr WA15 .... 120 C3
Edenvale M28 .... 78 A7
Edgar St Bolton BL3 .. 145 C6
  Ramsbottom BL0 ..... 138 B5
  Rochdale OL16 ...... 15 C2
Edgar St W BL0 ..... 138 B5
Edgbaston Dr M16 ... 97 A3
Edge Fold Cres M28 .. 78 D8
Edge Fold Rd M28 ... 60 D1
Edge Gn M28 .... 60 C1
Edge Green La WA3 .. 73 F2
Edge Green Rd WA3,WN4 .. 73 F4
Edge Green St WN4 .. 73 D4
Edge Hall Rd WN5 ... 53 E3
Edge Hill Ave OL2 .. 48 E3
Edge Hill Rd Bolton BL3 .. 146 A3
Edge La Bacup OL13 .. 4 C8
  Bolton BL1,BL6 ..... 23 C5
  Droylsden M11,M43 .. 83 D2
  Edgworth BL7 .... 9 A8
  Stalybridge SK14 ... 102 F4
  Stretford M21,M32 .. 96 E1
Edge La Rd OL1 ..... 67 A8
Edge Lane St OL2 ... 48 E4
Edge St M4 .... 159 A2
Edge View OL1 ...... 47 E1
Edge View La SK9 ... 136 B2
Edge Ware Gr WN3 ... 54 E3
Edgedale Ave M19 ... 110 E5
Edgefield Ave M9 ... 64 D4
Edgefold Ind Est BL4 .. 146 B1
Edgehill Cl M5 ..... 154 F2
Edgehill Ct SK14 ... 167 D3
Edgehill Rd M6 ..... 80 C2
Edgehill St M4 ..... 159 A2
Edgeley Fold SK3 ... 123 C7
Edgeley Park
  (Stockport County FC)
  SK3 .... 123 C8
Edgeley Rd Stockport SK3 .. 123 B7
  Urmston M41 .... 107 A8
Edgemoor WA14 ...... 119 A2
Edgemoor Cl Oldham OL4 .. 67 D5
  Radcliffe M26 ...... 43 E5
  Whitworth OL12 ..... 4 E5
Edgemoor Dr OL11 ... 29 F5
Edgerley Pl WN4 .... 73 A3
Edgerton Wlk M28 ... 60 D3
Edgeview Wlk M13 ... 163 B7
Edgeware Ave M25 ... 63 F5
Edgeware Rd Eccles M30 .. 79 A4
  Manchester M24 ..... 65 D3
Edgewater M5 .... 154 D2
Edgeway SK9 .... 137 B5
Edgeway Rd WN3 ..... 54 D2
Edgewood WN6 .... 36 A5
Edgeworth Ave BL2 .. 26 E6
Edgeworth Dr Bury BL8 .. 27 A1
  Manchester M14 ..... 110 D7
Edgeworth Rd
  Golborne WA3 .... 73 F1
  Hindley WN2 .... 57 A3

Edgmont Ave BL3 .... 147 D4
Edgware Rd M40 ..... 83 B4
Edgworth Cl OL10 ... 29 A2
Edgworth Prim Sch BL7 .. 9 D5
Edilom Rd M8 .... 63 E2
Edinburgh M30 ...... 79 D2
Edinburgh Cl Cheadle SK8 .. 122 F6
  Ince-in-M WN2 ...... 56 A8
  Sale M33 .... 107 D3
Edinburgh Dr Hindley WN2 .. 57 B3
  Romiley SK6 .... 113 C4
  Wigan WN5 .... 54 D5
Edinburgh Rd BL3 ... 43 A2
Edinburgh Sq M40 ... 160 E4
Edinburgh Way OL11 .. 30 D4
Edinburgh Wlk WN2 .. 38 D5
Edington OL12 ...... 139 F8
Edison Rd M30 ...... 95 B8
Edison St M11 ...... 99 E7
Edith Ave M14 ...... 98 A3
Edith Cavell Cl M11 .. 83 C1
Edith Cliff Wlk M40 .. 65 F1
Edith St Bolton BL3 .. 144 C6
  Farnworth BL4 ...... 60 D7
  Oldham OL8 .... 66 F3
  Ramsbottom BL0 ..... 11 E8
  Wigan WN5 .... 150 B7
Edlestone Gr SK9 ... 131 E1
Edlin Cl M12 .... 164 E5
Edlingham OL1 ...... 139 E6
Edlington Wlk M40 .. 83 C1
Edmonds St M24 ..... 47 B1
Edmonton Rd
  Failsworth M40 ..... 83 A4
  Stockport SK2,SK3 .. 124 A4
Edmund Cl SK4 ...... 169 F1
Edmund Dr M27 ...... 75 C5
Edmund Potter Hospl BL1 .. 40 F7
Edmund St Droylsden M43 .. 83 A1
  Failsworth M35 ..... 83 F8
  Manchester M3 ...... 158 E2
  Radcliffe M26 ...... 44 C4
  Rochdale OL12 ...... 139 D8
  Salford M6 .... 154 E3
  Shaw OL2 .... 149 C7
  Walsden OL14 .... 6 A8
Edmunds Fold OL15 .. 15 F6
Edna Rd WN7 .... 75 C7
Edna St WA14 .... 167 D2
Edridge Way WN2 .... 56 C4
Edson Rd M9 .... 64 E3
Edward Ave Bredbury SK6 .. 112 E3
  Littleborough OL15 .. 16 C5
  Manchester M21 ..... 109 B8
  Salford M5,M6 ...... 80 C3
Edward Charlton Rd
  M16,M21 .... 97 A2
Edward Dr WN4 ...... 73 B4
Edward Mews Ct M5 .. 154 E2
Edward Onyon Ct M5 .. 154 E2
Edward Rd Manchester M9 .. 64 D5
  Shaw OL2 .... 149 A6
Edward St Ashton-u-L OL6 .. 85 E2
  Bolton BL3 .... 145 F5
  Bury BL9 .... 140 F1
  Chadderton OL9 ..... 152 A8
  Denton M34 .... 100 F4
  Denton M34 .... 100 A8
  Droylsden M43 ...... 100 A8
  Dukinfield SK14 .... 101 C3
  Farnworth BL4 ...... 42 B2
  Glossop SK13 .... 104 C1
  Horwich BL6 .... 22 A1
  Kearsley M26 .... 61 B8
  Leigh WN7 .... 76 A4
  Littleborough OL15 .. 15 C4
  Manchester M7 ...... 158 D4
  Manchester M7 ...... 157 F8
  Middleton M24 ...... 47 A1
  Oldham OL9 .... 152 C6
  Prestwich M25 ...... 63 A5
  Radcliffe M26 ...... 44 B2
  Rochdale OL16 ...... 31 A8
  Romiley SK6 .... 114 B1
  Sale M33 .... 108 B5
  Stockport SK4 ...... 170 F8
  Westhoughton BL5 ... 57 E8
  Whitworth OL12 ..... 4 E2
  Wigan WN1 .... 151 F8
  Wigan WN1 .... 37 C2
Edward Sutcliffe Cl M14 .. 98 A2
Edwards Cl SK6 ..... 125 E5
Edwards Ct M22 ..... 121 D3
Edwards Dr M45 ..... 63 B8
Edwards Way SK6 .... 125 E5
Edwin Rd M11 .... 160 E1
Edwin St Bury BL9 .. 140 E2
  Stockport SK1 ...... 124 B8
Edwin Waugh Gdns OL12 .. 14 D3
Edzell Wlk M11 ..... 83 C1
Eeasbrook M41 ...... 95 D1
Egbert St M40 ...... 83 A7
Egerton Cl OL10 .... 117 C8
Egerton Cl OL10 .... 29 D3
Egerton Com Prim Sch BL7 .. 8 D3
Egerton Cres
  Heywood OL10 .... 110 B7
  Manchester M20 ..... 110 B7
  Hindley WN2 .... 56 E5
  Manchester M14 ..... 98 C4

Egerton Ct continued
Stockport SK3 ....124 A4
Stretford M21 ....108 F8
Egerton Dr
Altrincham WA15 ....120 A3
Sale M33 ....108 B5
Egerton Gr M28 ....60 D3
Egerton Ho ❸ M15 ....162 D7
Egerton Lo Bolton BL7 ....8 E1
Denton M34 ....101 A4
Egerton News
Droylsden M43 ....100 A8
Manchester M14 ....110 D8
Egerton Moss WA15 ...128 E5
Egerton Park Arts Coll
M34 ....100 E4
Egerton Pk M28 ....79 B7
Egerton Pl OL2 ....149 A6
Egerton Rd
Altrincham WA15 ....120 A2
Eccles M30 ....79 D4
Handforth SK9 ....131 B1
Manchester M14 ....110 D8
Stockport SK3 ....124 A4
Walkden M28 ....60 D3
Whitefield M45 ....62 F7
Egerton Rd N
Manchester M16,M21 ...97 C1
Manchester SK4 ....111 D8
Egerton Rd S
Manchester M21 ....109 C8
Manchester SK4 ....168 C4
Egerton Sch M41 ......95 E4
Egerton St
Abram Brow WN2 ....74 B7
Ashton-u-L OL6 ....166 C3
Denton M34 ....100 E5
Droylsden M43 ....84 B1
Eccles M30 ....79 B2
Farnworth BL4 ....42 C1
Heywood OL10 ....29 C1
Littleborough OL15 ....16 C5
Manchester M15 ......162 D7
Manchester M8 ....158 D1
Middleton M24 ....64 C7
Mossley OL5 ....68 C2
Oldham OL1 ....67 A8
Prestwich M25 ....63 C4
Egerton Terr M14 .....110 D7
Eggar Cl M29 ....77 B7
Eggington St M40 .....156 C5
Egham Ct ❶ BL2 ....25 B1
Egham Ho BL3 ....25 B1
Egmont St Manchester M8 ..156 A4
Mossley OL5 ....86 D8
Pendlebury M6 ....80 E6
Egremont Ave M20 ...110 A4
Egremont Cl M45 ......45 A1
Egremont Ct M7 ....81 C8
Egremont Gr ❷ SK3 ..123 B8
Egremont Rd OL16 ....31 F4
Egret Dr M44 ....94 A3
Egypt La M45 ....45 C1
Egyptian St BL1 ......143 F1
Ehlinger Ave SK13 ....104 A5
Eida Way M17 ....96 C8
Eight Acre M45 ....62 C7
Eighth Ave OL8 ....66 C4
Eighth St M17 ....96 D6
Eighth St W M17 ......96 D6
Eileen Gr M14 ....98 C2
Eileen Gr W M14 ......98 C2
Elaine Ave M9 ....64 A4
Elaine Cl WN4 ....73 D5
Elbain Wlk M40 ....83 C5
Elbe St M12 ....163 C8
Elberton Wlk 15 M8 ..155 F7
Elbow La OL11 ....31 A6
Elbow St M19 ....99 A1
Elbut La BL9 ....28 F5
Elcho Rd WA14 ....119 B3
Elcombe Ave WA3 .....90 E7
Elcot Cl M40 ....156 C5
Elder Cl SK2 ....124 D8
Elder Gr M40 ....65 F2
Elder Rd OL4 ....67 E6
Elder St OL16 ....31 B5
Elderberry Cl Diggle OL3 ..51 C5
Wigan WN3 ....37 B4
Elderberry Way SK9 ..137 E8
Elderberry Wlk M31 ..105 E3
Eldercot Gr BL3 ......146 A4
Eldercot Rd BL3 ......146 A4
Eldercroft Rd WA15 ..120 D5
Elderfield Dr SK6 .....112 F4
Eldermount Rd M9 ....64 D2
Elderwood OL9 ....65 E7
Eldon Cl M34 ....100 E7
Eldon Gdns WN4 ......73 A6
Eldon Pl M30 ....79 C1
Eldon Prec OL8 ......153 E5
Eldon Rd Irlam M44 ....94 A2
Stockport SK3 ....123 C7
Eldon St Bolton BL2 ...25 B2
Bury BL9 ....140 F4
Leigh WN7 ....153 F5
Oldham OL8 ....153 F5
Eldridge Dr M40 ....83 A6
Eleanor Rd
Manchester M21 ....109 A8
Oldham OL2 ....48 E3
Eleanor St Bolton BL1 ..25 A5
Oldham OL1 ....153 D8
Wigan WN3 ....150 A7
Electo St M11 ....99 E7

Elevator Rd M17 ....96 E6
Eleventh St M17 ....96 D6
Elf Mill Cl SK3 ....170 E6
Elford Gr M18 ....100 A4
Elgar St M12 ....99 A4
Elgin Ave Garswood WN4 ..72 D4
Manchester M20 ......110 D3
Elgin Cl WN2 ....56 A8
Elgin Dr M33 ....108 E3
Elgin Rd Dukinfield SK16 ..101 C6
Oldham OL4 ....67 C5
Elgin St Ashton-u-L OL7 ..166 A4
Bolton BL1 ....142 C2
Stalybridge SK15 ......86 B1
Elgol Cl SK3 ....170 F5
Elgol Ct OL10 ....29 A1
Elgol Dr BL3 ....40 E6
Elham Cl M26 ....61 C7
Eli St OL9 ....66 A3
Elim St OL15 ....16 C7
Elim Terr OL15 ....16 C7
Eliot Dr WN3 ....150 A5
Eliot Rd M30 ....79 D1
Elishaw Row M5 ......154 F1
Eliza Ann St ❺ Eccles M30 ..79 C1
Manchester M40 ......159 C4
Eliza St Manchester M15 ..162 E6
Ramsbottom BL0 ....11 D6
Elizabeth Ave Denton M34 ..100 E5
Disley SK12 ....135 D5
Leigh WN2 ....56 E1
Oldham OL9 ....66 A3
Royton OL2 ....48 D3
Elizabeth Ct ❶ Hindley WN2 ..56 E2
Stockport SK1 ....170 F8
Elizabeth Ct Edenfield BL0 ..1 D3
Manchester M14 ......110 D7
Reddish M18 ....99 F3
Stockport SK4 ....168 C2
Elizabeth Dr BB4 ....1 A8
Elizabeth Gr OL2 .....149 B7
Elizabeth Ho SK4 .....168 B2
Elizabeth Rd M31 .....105 F4
Elizabeth Slinger Rd
M20 ....109 F5
Elizabeth St
Ashton-u-L OL6 ....166 B4
Atherton M46 ....58 D3
Denton M34 ....100 D3
Edenfield BL0 ....1 D3
Heywood OL10 ....29 C2
Ince-in-M WN2 ....76 B3
Leigh WN7 ....76 B3
Manchester M8 ....155 F6
Manchester M8 ....156 A5
Prestwich M25 ....63 C4
❸ Radcliffe M26 ....44 A3
Rochdale OL11 ....30 C3
❶ Swinton M27 ....61 F1
Elizabethan Ct ❿ M29 ..58 F1
Elizabethan Dr WN3 ...55 E4
Elizabethan Way OL16 ..31 F5
Elizabethan Wlk ❶ WN2 ..56 A2
Elkanagh Gdns M6 ...154 F3
Elkstone Ave M38 ......60 A6
Elkstone Cl WN3 ....54 C2
Ellbourne Rd M9 ......64 A4
Ellen Brook Rd M22 ..130 D8
Ellen Gr BL4 ....61 C5
Ellen St ❺ Bolton BL1 ..142 C3
Droylsden M43 ....100 B8
Ince-in-M WN2 ....56 A7
Oldham OL9 ....153 D8
Stockport SK4 ....169 D3
Ellen Wilkinson Cres
M12 ....165 A5
Ellen Wilkinson High Sch
M12 ....164 D6
Ellenbrook Cl M12 ...165 B6
Ellenbrook Prim Sch M28 ..78 C8
Ellenbrook Rd M28 ....78 B7
Ellendale Grange M28 ..78 B8
Ellenhall Cl M9 ....157 D8
Ellenor Dr M29 ....77 C7
Ellenroad App OL16 ...32 A4
Ellenroad Engine Ho OL16 ..32 A4
Ellenroad St OL16 .....32 A4
Ellenror Cl OL12 ......14 A2
Ellenror Dr OL12 ......14 A2
Ellenshaw Cl OL12 ....14 A2
Elleray Cl BL3 ....43 C3
Elleray Rd Middleton M9 ..64 F5
Salford M6 ....80 D5
Ellerbeck Cl Bolton BL2 ..25 C5
Standish WN6 ....36 F7
Ellerbeck Cres M28 ...78 C8
Ellerby Ave M27 ....62 A3
Ellercroft SK22 ......127 C1
Ellesmere Ave
Ashton-u-L OL6 ....85 C7
Eccles M30 ....79 E2
Marple SK6 ....125 F6
Walkden M28 ....60 C3
Ellesmere Cl SK16 ...101 E8
Ellesmere Dr SK8 ....123 A5
Ellesmere Gdns BL3 ..147 D3
Ellesmere Rd
Altrincham WA14 .....119 E6

Ellesmere Rd continued
Ashton-in-M WN4 ......72 F4
Bolton BL3 ....146 C3
Cheadle SK3 ....123 A7
Eccles M30 ....91 E3
Eccles M30 ....79 E3
Manchester M21 ....97 D1
Wigan WN5 ....54 D6
Ellesmere Rd N SK4 ...111 C5
Ellesmere Rd S M21 ..109 C8
Ellesmere Ret Pk M28 ..60 D4
Ellesmere Sh Ctr M28 ..60 D3
Ellesmere St Bolton BL3 ..145 D6
❶❹ Eccles M30 ....79 D1
Failsworth M35 ....83 F8
Farnworth BL4 ....60 D8
Leigh WN7 ....75 F4
Manchester M15 ......162 D7
Rochdale OL11 ....139 F5
Swinton M27 ....62 A1
Swinton M27 ....62 B2
Tyldesley M29 ....59 A1
Tyldesley M29 ....77 C5
Walkden M38 ....60 C4
Ellesmere Terr M14 ...110 D7
Ellesmere Wlk ❸ BL4 ..60 D8
Ellingham Cl M11 ....160 F1
Elliot Sq ❶❶ OL1 ......67 A8
Elliot St Bury BL1 .....142 C3
Oldham OL4 ....67 E6
Elliot Wlk M24 ....47 C3
Elliott Ave Dukinfield SK14 ..101 D5
Golborne WA3 ....74 B1
Elliott Dr Hindley WN2 ..56 E2
Sale M33 ....107 E4
Elliott St Farnworth BL4 ..60 C7
Rochdale OL12 ....31 A8
Tyldesley M29 ....76 F8
Ellis Cres M28 ....60 B3
Ellis Dr M8 ....64 B1
Ellis Fold OL12 ....13 E2
Ellis La M40 ....64 B3
Ellis Rd WN5 ....71 D4
Ellis St Bolton BL3 ...145 D5
Bury BL8 ....27 B2
Hyde SK14 ....167 F2
Manchester M15 ......162 E6
Manchester M7 ....158 E4
Ramsbottom BL0 ......138 B5
Wigan WN1 ....37 C1
Ellisbank Wlk ❸ M13 ..163 B7
Ellisland Wlk ❶ M40 ..83 A6
Ellison Cl SK14 ....103 D5
Ellison Ho OL7 ....166 A1
Ellison St SK13 ....104 D1
Elliston Sq M12 ......165 A6
Ellor St Salford M5 ....81 B2
Salford M6 ....154 F3
Ellwood Rd SK1 ......112 B1
Elm Ave Downall Green WN4 ..72 D5
Atherton M46 ....44 A3
Newton-le-W WA12 .....89 C2
Radcliffe M26 ....61 F8
Whitefield M45 ....36 F6
Wigan WN5 ....54 F6
Elm Beds SK12 ....134 C2
Elm Cl Mottram-in-M SK14 ..103 A4
❷ Partington M31 .....105 F3
Poynton SK12 ....133 F3
Elm Cres
Alderley Edge SK9 ....137 B3
Swinton M28 ....79 A7
Elm Croft WN1 ....37 B4
Elm Ct SK1 ....124 B8
Elm Dr Billinge WN5 ...71 D5
Denton M34 ....100 E5
Stretford M32 ....108 C8
Elm Gr Alderley Edge SK9 ..137 B2
Ashton-u-L OL6 ....85 C5
Bolton BL7 ....25 A8
Denton M34 ....100 D5
Droylsden M43 ....83 D2
Farnworth BL4 ....60 B8
Glossop SK13 ....104 D2
Handforth SK9 ....131 C3
❻ Horwich BL6 ....22 C4
Hyde SK14 ....167 F2
Littleborough OL12 ....15 C6
Manchester M20 ......110 C3
Newhey OL16 ....32 A3
Oldham OL4 ....67 D6
Prestwich M25 ....63 A6
Rochdale OL11 ....139 E5
Sale M33 ....108 B6
Swinton M27 ....61 F2
Urmston M41 ....95 E2

Elm St continued
Platt Bridge WN2 ......56 A2
Ramsbottom BL0 ....11 D6
Royton OL2 ....48 D1
Tyldesley M29 ....59 A1
Whitworth OL12 ....4 D2
Elm Tree Cl Failsworth M35 ..84 B7
Stalybridge SK15 ....102 A8
Elm Tree Dr
Dukinfield SK16 ......101 F7
Wythenshawe M22 ....121 D3
Elm Tree Rd Bredbury SK6 ..112 C3
Golborne WA3 ....90 F8
Elm Wood Prim Sch M24 ..65 C8
Elmbank Ave M20 .....109 E4
Elmbank Rd M24 ......65 C8
Elmbridge Wlk
Bolton BL3 ....145 D5
❷ Manchester M40 ....83 A6
Elmdale Ave SK8 .....122 B2
Elmdale Wlk ❶ M15 ..163 A6
Elmfield M6 ....86 B6
Elmfield Ave Atherton M46 ..58 C4
Wythenshawe M22 ....121 E8
Elmfield Cl SK9 ......137 B2
Elmfield Dr SK6 ......125 E6
Elmfield Ho SK3 .....170 F5
Elmfield Rd
Alderley Edge SK9 ....137 B2
Droylsden M34 ....100 C8
Stockport SK3 ....170 F5
Wigan WN1 ....37 E1
Elmfield St Bolton BL1 ..143 F2
Manchester M8 ....156 A6
Elmgate Gr M19 ....99 A1
Elmham Wlk M40 .....159 C4
Elmhow Gr WN3 ....55 A2
Elmhurst Dr M19 .....110 F5
Elmley Cl SK2 ....125 A5
Elmore Wood OL15 ....15 E6
Elmpark Gate OL12 ...14 B3
Elmpark Gr OL12 ......14 B3
Elmpark Vale OL12 ....14 B3
Elmpark Way OL12 ....14 B3
Elmpark Way OL12 ....14 B3
Elmridge WA3 ....90 F8
Elmridge Dr
Bramhall SK7 ....132 E7
Hindley WN2 ....57 A4
Elmridge Prim Sch
WA15 ....129 C8
Elms Bank Com High Sch
M45 ....44 F2
Elms Cl M45 ....44 F2
Elms Farm ❸ M45 ......44 F2
Elms Rd Manchester SK4 ..111 B5
Stalybridge SK15 ......86 D3
Whitefield M45 ....44 F1
Elms The Golborne WA3 ..74 A1
Littleborough OL15 ....15 E4
Mossley OL5 ....68 B1
❹ Whitefield M45 .....44 F1
Elmsbury St ❶ WN4 ...72 F5
Elmscott Wlk M13 ....164 D5
Elmsdale Ave M9 ......64 D6
Elmsfield Ave OL11 ...13 E1
Elmsleigh Ct M30 .....79 F3
Elmsleigh Rd SK8 ....122 A2
Elmsmere Rd M20 ....110 D4
Elmstead Ave M20 ...110 A6
Elmsted Cl SK8 ......123 B3
Elmstone Gr BL1 .....143 F1
Elmsway Altrincham WA15 ..129 B8
Bramhall SK7 ....132 C7
High Lane SK6 ....126 A6
Elmswood Ave M14 ...97 F3
Elmswood Dr SK14 ...102 A3
Elmsworth Ave M19 ...99 B1
Elmton Rd M9 ....64 E3
Elmtree Dr SK14 .....167 A4
Elmsted Cl SK14 ......123 B3
Elmwood M33 ....107 C4
Elmwood Ave WN4 ....73 A2
Elmwood Cl BL5 ....40 A3
Elmwood Ct M32 .....108 C8
Elmwood Dr OL2 .....149 C8
Elmwood Gr Bolton BL1 ..144 C8
Farnworth BL4 ....60 C6
Manchester M9 ....157 F7
Elnup Ave M12 ....165 C8
Elnup Ave WN6 ....36 B6
Elnup Wood
Nature Reserve WN6 ..36 C6
Elsa Rd M19 ....99 C1
Elsdon Dr Atherton M46 ..58 E4
Manchester M18 ......165 C6
Elsdon Gdns ❽ BL2 ...25 B1
Elsdon Rd M13 ....98 F2
Elsfield Cl BL1 ....143 D2
Elsham Cl BL1 ....24 E5
Elsham Dr M28 ....60 B3
Elsham Gdns M18 .....99 B7
Elsie St Farnworth BL4 ..60 C7
Manchester M9 ....157 D8
Ramsbottom BL0 ....11 A4
Elsinore Ave M44 .....94 A1
Elsinore Cl M35 ....84 B6
Elsinore Rd M16 ......97 A4
Elsinore St BL2 ....42 D5
Elsma Rd M40 ....160 C4
Elson Dr SK14 ....167 E2
Elson St BL8 ....27 B4
Elstead Gdns M33 ....107 B1
Elstead Wlk M9 ....64 A3
Elsted Rd OL3 ....51 B4
Elston Ave M40 ....89 C5
Elstree Ave M40 ......83 B4

Elswick Ave Bolton BL3 ..144 B5
Bramhall SK7 ....132 E7
Manchester M21 ......109 D4
Elsworth Dr BL1 ......143 F4
Elsworth St M3 ....159 A4
Elterwater Cl BL8 .....27 B4
Elterwater Rd BL4 ....59 E7
Eltham Ave SK2 ......124 C5
Eltham Cl WN4 ....73 D3
Eltham Dr M41 ....95 C5
Eltham St ❻ M19 .....99 A1
Elton Ave Farnworth BL4 ..59 F8
Manchester M19 ......111 A8
Elton Bank ❽ SK13 ...171 D1
Elton Brook Cl BL8 ....27 C3
Elton Cl ❻ Gamesley SK13 ..171 D1
Golborne WA3 ....90 E7
Handforth SK9 ....131 E1
Whitefield M45 ....63 B8
Elton Com Prim Sch BL8 ..27 A4
Elton Dr SK7 ....133 D8
Elton High Sch The BL8 ..27 A4
Elton House WN5 ......54 C7
Elton Lea ❽ SK13 .....171 D1
Elton Pl ❷ SK13 ......171 D1
Elton Rd M33 ....107 E2
Elton St Bolton BL2 ...148 A7
Manchester M7 ....158 E3
Rochdale OL11 ....139 F4
❸ Stretford M32 ......96 F5
Elton Vale Rd BL8 .....27 B2
Elton's Yd M17 ....96 A5
Elvate Cres M8 ......155 F5
Elverston Cl M12 ....165 B5
Elverston St M22 ....109 E1
Elverston Way OL9 ...152 C8
Elvey St M10,M40 ....157 F5
Elvington Cl WN5 .....36 B1
Elvington Cres ❶ M28 ..78 C8
Elvira Cl M35 ....84 B7
Elway Rd WN4 ....73 C4
Elwick Cl ❻ M16 ......97 F3
Elworth Way ❻ SK9 ..131 D4
Elworthy Gr WN1 .....37 E2
Elwyn Ave M22 ......121 D7
Ely Ave M32 ....95 F3
Ely Cl M28 ....78 B8
Ely Cres M35 ....83 F5
Ely Dr Bury BL8 ......140 D4
Tyldesley M29 ....77 C7
Ely Gr BL1 ....143 E1
Ely St OL9 ....152 B5
Elysian St M11 ......165 C8
Embankment Rd BL7 ...9 C5
Embassy Wlk M18 .....99 D4
Ember St M11 ....83 D2
Embleton Cl BL2 .....145 D5
Embleton Cl BL2 ......25 E1
Embleton Wlk M18 ...165 C6
Embsay Cl BL1 ....143 E1
Emerald Ave WN7 .....75 E4
Emerald Cotts BL8 ....10 F3
Emerald Rd M22 .....130 F7
Emerald St ❽ Bolton BL1 ..143 F3
Denton M34 ....100 E7
Emerald Way M30 .....80 A3
Emerson Ave M30 .....80 A3
Emerson Dr M24 ......46 F1
Emerson St Salford M5 ..154 D2
Swinton M27 ....61 F1
Emery Ave M19 ......109 C6
Emery Cl Altrincham WA14 ..119 D7
Manchester SK4 ......168 A4
Emily Beavan Cl M11 ..83 B1
Emily Pl M43 ....99 E1
Emley St M19 ....99 B1
Emlyn Gr SK8 ....123 A6
Emlyn St Farnworth BL4 ..42 C1
❷ Hindley WN2 ....56 D5
Swinton M27 ....79 D8
Walkden M28 ....60 D3
Emma St Oldham OL8 ...66 F3
Rochdale OL12 ....139 E8
Emmanuel Cl BL3 ....145 D6
Emmanuel Ct OL6 ...166 B4
Emmanuel Holcombe
CE Prim Sch BL8 .....138 A6
Emmanuel Pl BL3 ...145 D6
Emmaus Wlk M6 ....154 F2
Emmett St E M40 ....157 F2
Emmott Cl OL10 ......29 C2
Emmott Cl OL1 ....153 F6
Emmous Wlk M6 ....154 F2
Empire Rd Bolton BL2 ..42 F2
Emsworth Cl ❻ BL2 ...25 B1
Emsworth Dr M33 ...108 A2
Ena Cres WN7 ....75 C8
Ena St Bolton BL3 ....42 A3
Oldham OL1 ....67 A5
Enbridge St M6 ......161 A8
Encombe Pl M3 ......158 E2
Endcott Cl M18 ......165 B6
Enderby Rd M40 ......65 C1
Ending Rake OL12 .....14 A2
Endon Dr M21 ....109 F8
Endon St BL1 ....142 B1

Endsleigh Gdns **1** WN7 . . . . .75 F5
Endsleigh Rd M20 . . . . .110 C6
Endsley Ave M28 . . . . .60 C1
Energy Cl M16 . . . . .97 F3
Energy St M40 . . . . .160 E3
Enfield Ave
  Manchester M19 . . . . .111 A6
  Oldham OL8 . . . . .66 E3
Enfield Cl Bolton BL1 . . . . . .143 E1
  Bury BL9 . . . . .44 F5
  Eccles M30 . . . . .95 D8
  Rochdale OL11 . . . . .29 E8
Enfield Dr **7** M11 . . . . .83 C2
Enfield Gr WN7 . . . . .76 B6
Enfield Ho M30 . . . . .95 D8
Enfield Rd Eccles M30 . . . . . .79 D4
  Swinton M27 . . . . .79 E6
Enfield St Hyde SK14 . . . . . .113 E7
  Walkden M28 . . . . .60 D5
  Wigan WN5 . . . . .54 C5
Enford Ave M22 . . . . .121 A2
Engell Cl M18 . . . . .99 D5
Engels Ho Eccles M30 . . . . . .95 D8
  Manchester M14 . . . . .110 D8
Engine Fold Rd M28 . . . . .60 A3
Engine La M29 . . . . .59 B4
Engine St OL9 . . . . .66 B4
Engineer St WN2 . . . . .56 A7
Engledene BL1 . . . . .24 B6
Englefield Gr **3** M18 . . . . . .99 D4
English Martyrs Sch M41 . . . .95 C2
English St WN7 . . . . .76 A4
Enid Cl M7 . . . . .155 D5
Enid Pl WN2 . . . . .73 F8
Ennerdale Ave
  Ashton-in-M WN4 . . . . .73 B5
  Billinge WA11 . . . . .71 B1
  4 Bolton BL2 . . . . .25 F1
  Manchester M21 . . . . .109 D4
  Royton OL2 . . . . .48 C7
  Swinton M27 . . . . .79 F6
Ennerdale Cl BL3 . . . . .42 F3
Ennerdale Dr Gatley SK8 . . .122 B3
  Sale M33 . . . . .107 E5
  Sale WA15 . . . . .120 A8
  Whitefield BL9 . . . . .45 A2
Ennerdale Gdns BL2 . . . . .25 E1
Ennerdale Gr
  Ashton-u-L OL7 . . . . .84 F5
  Farnworth BL4 . . . . .59 E8
  Manchester M24 . . . . .56 B8
Ennerdale Rd Hindley WN2 . . .56 E5
  Leigh WN7 . . . . .76 C4
  Middleton M24 . . . . .46 F2
  Partington M31 . . . . .105 E3
  Rochdale OL11 . . . . .30 B4
  Romiley SK6 . . . . .113 B4
  Stockport SK1 . . . . .124 B7
  Stretford M32 . . . . .96 C3
  Tyldesley M29 . . . . .77 B7
Ennerdale Terr SK15 . . . . .86 A3
Ennis Cl M23 . . . . .120 E5
Ennismore Ave M5,M30 . . . . .80 A2
Enstone Dr M40 . . . . .65 D5
Enstone Way M29 . . . . .59 C1
Enterprise Trad Est M31 . . . . .96 A8
Enterprise Way WA3 . . . . .91 A7
Enticott Rd M44 . . . . .105 C5
Entwisle Ave M41 . . . . .95 B4
Entwisle Rd OL16 . . . . .31 A8
Entwisle Row BL4 . . . . .60 D8
Entwisle St
  1 Farnworth BL4 . . . . . . .42 E1
  Milnrow OL16 . . . . .31 E6
  Swinton M27 . . . . .61 D1
Entwistle Gr WN7 . . . . .76 C3
Entwistle Hall La BL7 . . . . .9 B8
Entwistle St BL2 . . . . .148 B8
Entwistle Sta BL7 . . . . .9 B8
Enver Rd M8 . . . . .156 B8
Enville Rd
  Altrincham WA14 . . . . .119 C3
  Manchester M40 . . . . .65 B1
  Pendlebury M6 . . . . .80 E6
Enville St Ashton-u-L OL6 . . .166 C3
  Denton M34 . . . . .100 F7
  Manchester M9 . . . . .64 D3
Envoy Cl WN5 . . . . .36 E1
Enys Wlk M6 . . . . .81 A5
Ephraim's Fold WN2 . . . . .38 D6
Epping Cl Ashton-u-L OL6 . . . .85 C7
  Chadderton OL9 . . . . .65 E8
Epping Dr M33 . . . . .107 C5
Epping Rd M34 . . . . .100 B2
Epping St Manchester M15 . .162 F6
  Manchester M15 . . . . .163 A6
Epping Wlk M15 . . . . .163 A5
Eppleworth Rise M27 . . . . . . .62 A3
Epsley Cl M15 . . . . .163 A6
Epsom Ave
  Handforth SK8,SK9 . . . . . . .131 E4
  Manchester M19 . . . . .110 F6
  Sale M33 . . . . .107 C2
Epsom Cl Hazel Grove SK7 . .124 F2
  Rochdale OL11 . . . . .29 F8
Epsom Croft PR6 . . . . .21 B7
Epsom Dr WN2 . . . . .73 F2
Epsom Mews M7 . . . . .155 D6
Epsom Wlk OL9 . . . . .152 C6
Epworth Ct SK4 . . . . .168 B3
Epworth Gr **5** BL3 . . . . . .146 C3
Epworth St M40 . . . . .159 C1
Equitable St Milnrow OL16 . . .31 F5
  Oldham OL4 . . . . .67 D8
  3 Rochdale OL11 . . . . . . .31 A6
Era St Bolton BL2 . . . . .42 F7
  Sale M33 . . . . .108 B4
Ercall Ave M12 . . . . .164 E6

Eric Brook Cl **8** M14 . . . . . .98 A3
Eric Bullows Cl M22 . . . . . . .121 C1
Eric St Littleborough OL15 . . .16 A6
  Oldham OL4 . . . . .67 C6
Erica Ave OL4 . . . . .49 F4
Erica Cl **2** SK5 . . . . .100 A1
Erica Dr M19 . . . . .110 E4
Erica Wlk WN7 . . . . .75 B5
Erin St M11 . . . . .99 E7
Erindale Wlk M40 . . . . .156 C6
Erith Cl SK5 . . . . .112 B6
Erith Rd OL4 . . . . .67 C6
Erlesmere Ave M34 . . . . .101 A4
Erlesmere Cl OL4 . . . . .49 F4
Erlington Ave M16 . . . . .97 B2
Ermen Rd M30 . . . . .95 C8
Ermington Ct OL10 . . . . .29 C1
Ermington Dr M8 . . . . .155 F6
Erneley Cl M12 . . . . .99 B3
Ernest St Bacup OL13 . . . . .4 C8
  Bolton BL1 . . . . .145 D7
  Cheadle SK8 . . . . .122 C6
  Prestwich M25 . . . . .62 F4
  Stockport SK2 . . . . .124 A6
Ernest Terr OL12 . . . . .15 B1
Ernlouen Ave BL1 . . . . .144 A8
Ernocroft Gr **5** M18 . . . . . .99 E6
Ernocroft La SK6 . . . . .114 E3
Ernocroft Rd SK6 . . . . .114 D5
Erradale Cres WN3 . . . . .54 D2
Errington Cl SK2 . . . . .124 E6
Errington Cl BL3 . . . . .40 F5
Errington Dr M7 . . . . .158 D4
Errol Ave Manchester M9 . . . .64 A5
  Wythenshawe M22 . . . . . . .121 C4
Errwood Cres M19 . . . . .111 A8
Errwood Rd M19 . . . . .111 A7
Erskine Cl BL3 . . . . .40 E5
Erskine Pl WN2 . . . . .56 B1
Erskine Rd Manchester M9 . . .64 E1
  Partington M31 . . . . .105 F3
Erskine St
  Manchester M15 . . . . .162 D6
  Romiley SK6 . . . . .114 B3
Erwin St M40 . . . . .83 B6
Eryngo St SK1 . . . . .112 A1
Escott Wlk **1** M16 . . . . .97 F3
Esher Dr M23,M33 . . . . .108 C1
Esk Ave BL0 . . . . .1 D8
Esk Cl M41 . . . . .95 A4
Eskdale SK5 . . . . .112 A4
Eskdale Ave Blackrod BL6 . . . .38 E7
  Bolton BL2 . . . . .25 F2
  Bramhall SK7 . . . . .132 C5
  Manchester M20 . . . . .110 A7
  Oldham OL8 . . . . .69 B5
  Oldham OL8 . . . . .66 D4
  Rochdale OL11 . . . . .30 B4
  Royton OL2 . . . . .48 D7
  Wigan WN3 . . . . .37 B3
Eskdale Cl BL9 . . . . .45 A3
Eskdale Dr
  Altrincham WA15 . . . . .120 C7
  Middleton M24 . . . . .46 F3
Eskdale Gr BL4 . . . . .59 F8
Eskdale Ho **3** M13 . . . . .98 E4
Eskdale Mews OL3 . . . . .69 B5
Eskdale Rd
  Ashton-in-M WN4 . . . . .73 B4
  Hindley WN2 . . . . .56 E5
Eskdale Terr SK15 . . . . .86 A4
Eskrick St BL1 . . . . .143 D2
Eskrigge Cl M7 . . . . .155 F8
Esmond Rd M8 . . . . .156 A7
Esmont Dr M24 . . . . .46 E3
Esplanade The OL16 . . . . . . .139 E7
Essex Ave Droylsden M43 . . . .84 A3
  Heywood BL9 . . . . .28 B3
  Manchester M20 . . . . .110 B4
  Stockport SK3 . . . . .123 B8
Essex Cl Failsworth M35 . . . . .83 F5
  Shaw OL2 . . . . .48 F7
Essex Dr BL9 . . . . .45 A8
Essex Gdns M44 . . . . .105 C4
Essex Pl Swinton M27 . . . . . . .61 F2
  Tyldesley M29 . . . . .58 F3
Essex Rd Brinnington SK5 . . .112 C5
  Reddish M18 . . . . .99 F4
  Standish WN1 . . . . .37 B8
Essex St Horwich BL6 . . . . . . .22 D1
  Manchester M2 . . . . .158 F1
  Rochdale OL16 . . . . .139 F6
  Wigan WN1 . . . . .37 C1
Essex Way M15,M16 . . . . . . .162 D5
Essingdon St BL3 . . . . .147 D4
Essington Wlk M34 . . . . .100 E1
Est Bank Rd BL0 . . . . .11 A3
Estate St OL8 . . . . .66 F4
Estate St S **3** OL8 . . . . .66 F4
Estcourt Sch OL4 . . . . .49 F4
Esther Fold BL5 . . . . .57 E8
Esther St OL4 . . . . .67 D7
Esthwaite Dr M29 . . . . .77 A7
Eston St M13 . . . . .98 D4
Estonfield Dr M41 . . . . .95 F1
Eswick St M11 . . . . .83 C1
Etchell St M40 . . . . .156 C5
Etchells Prim Sch SK8 . . . . .122 C1
Etchells Rd SK8 . . . . .122 D1
Etchells St SK1 . . . . .169 F1
Ethel Ave Manchester M9 . . . .64 D5
  Pendlebury M27 . . . . .80 B8
Ethel St OL16 . . . . .31 B6
Ethel St Bolton BL3 . . . . .145 D6
  Oldham OL8 . . . . .66 F3
  Rochdale OL16 . . . . .31 B6
  Whitworth OL12 . . . . .4 D2

Ethel Terr M19 . . . . .99 A1
Etherley Cl **4** M44 . . . . .94 A2
Etherow Ave
  Failsworth M40 . . . . .65 F2
  Romiley SK6 . . . . .113 E2
Etherow Brow SK14 . . . . .115 B8
Etherow Ctry Pk SK6 . . . . . . .114 C4
Etherow Ctry Pk
  Visitors Ctr SK6 . . . . .114 B3
Etherow Way SK13 . . . . .103 E5
Etherstone St Leigh WN7 . . . .75 E4
  Manchester M9 . . . . .156 C8
Eton Ave OL8 . . . . .66 E3
Eton Cl Manchester M16 . . . .162 D5
  Rochdale OL11 . . . . .30 B6
Eton Ct M16 . . . . .162 D5
Eton Hill Ind Est M26 . . . . . . .44 C5
Eton Hill Rd M26 . . . . .44 C5
Eton St WN7 . . . . .75 F3
Eton Terr WN3 . . . . .53 F8
Etruria Cl M13 . . . . .99 D7
Etruscan Rd M13 . . . . .164 E5
Ettington Cl BL8 . . . . .27 A3
Ettrick Cl M11 . . . . .99 D7
Euclid Cl M11 . . . . .160 D1
Euro Ctr The M8 . . . . .158 E4
Europa Bsns Pk SK3 . . . . . .123 B6
Europa Gate M17 . . . . .96 D5
Europa Trad Est M26 . . . . . . .61 B7
Europa Way Cheadle SK3 . . .123 B6
  Kearsley M26 . . . . .61 B7
  Stretford M17 . . . . .96 D4
Euroterminal M17,M32 . . . . . .96 D4
Eustace St Bolton BL3 . . . . . . .42 A3
  Oldham OL9 . . . . .152 C8
Eustace Street
  Com Prim Sch OL9 . . . . . . .152 C8
Euston Ave M9 . . . . .65 A3
Euston Cl BL9 . . . . .27 A1
Eva Rd SK3 . . . . .123 A7
Eva St Leigh WN7 . . . . .75 C7
  Manchester M14 . . . . .98 C3
  Rochdale OL12 . . . . .15 A2
Evan St M40 . . . . .157 E5
Evans Cl M20 . . . . .110 A3
Evans Rd M30 . . . . .79 A1
Evans St Ashton-u-L OL6 . . . .85 D4
  Horwich BL6 . . . . .22 D4
  Leigh WN7 . . . . .75 F5
  Manchester M8 . . . . .158 E3
  Middleton M24 . . . . .65 B8
  Oldham OL1 . . . . .153 F8
Evanstone Cl BL6 . . . . .22 B3
Evanton Wlk **16** M9 . . . . . .157 E7
Eve St OL8 . . . . .66 F2
Evelyn St Manchester M14 . .110 D8
  Oldham OL4 . . . . .49 B1
Evening St M35 . . . . .83 E8
Evenley Cl **1** M18 . . . . .99 E6
Everard Cl M28 . . . . .78 C8
Everard St M5 . . . . .161 C7
Everbrom Rd BL3 . . . . .146 A3
Everdingen Wlk OL1 . . . . .49 A2
Everest Ave OL7 . . . . .85 B5
Everest Cl SK14 . . . . .102 A4
Everest Pl **4** WN1 . . . . .37 C2
Everest Rd Atherton M46 . . . .58 C5
  Hyde SK14 . . . . .102 A4
Everest St OL11 . . . . .31 A2
Everett Ct **3** M20 . . . . . . .110 B6
Everett Rd M20 . . . . .110 B6
Everglade OL8 . . . . .66 E1
Evergreen Wlk **3** M33 . . . .107 C6
Everleigh Cl BL2 . . . . .25 C5
Everleigh Dr M7 . . . . .155 F6
Eversden Ct M7 . . . . .158 E4
Eversley Ct M33 . . . . .108 B2
Eversley Rd M20 . . . . .110 A3
Everton Rd Oldham OL8 . . . . .66 F3
  Reddish SK5 . . . . .99 F2
Everton St
  Downall Green WN4 . . . . . . .72 D5
  Swinton M27 . . . . .79 E8
Every St Bury BL9 . . . . .140 F4
  Manchester M4 . . . . .160 D1
  Ramsbottom BL0 . . . . .11 D6
Evesham Ave
  Altrincham M23 . . . . .120 D7
  4 Hadfield SK13 . . . . . . .104 A5
  Manchester M14 . . . . .98 C3
Evesham Cl **16** Bolton BL3 .145 D6
  Leigh WN7 . . . . .75 E1
  Middleton M24 . . . . .65 B5
Evesham Dr
  Farnworth BL3,BL4 . . . . .42 B2
  Wilmslow SK9 . . . . .131 C2
Evesham Gdns M24 . . . . .65 A5
Evesham Gr Ashton-u-L OL6 . .85 C7
  Sale M33 . . . . .108 B4
Evesham Rd Cheadle SK8 . . .123 A4
  Manchester M9 . . . . .64 E2
  Middleton M24 . . . . .65 B5
Evesham Wlk
  5 Bolton BL3 . . . . .145 D6
  Middleton M24 . . . . .65 A5
  Oldham OL8 . . . . .153 E5
Eveside Cl SK8 . . . . .123 B4
Evington Ave M11 . . . . .100 A7
Ewan St M18 . . . . .99 D6
Ewart Ave M5 . . . . .81 A1
Ewart St BL1 . . . . .143 E2
Ewhurst Ave M27 . . . . .79 D6
Ewing Cl M8 . . . . .64 A1
Ewing Sch M20 . . . . .110 A5

Ewood **12** Eccles M30 . . . . . .79 F2
  Oldham OL8 . . . . .85 A8
Ewood Dr BL8 . . . . .44 A8
Ewood La BB4 . . . . .1 C7
Farnworth Rd M22 . . . . .121 C1
Exbridge Wlk M40 . . . . .83 D4
Exbury Cl M12 . . . . .139 E8
Exbury St M14 . . . . .110 D7
Excalibur Way M44 . . . . .105 F7
Excelsior Terr OL15 . . . . .15 F3
Exchange Quay M5 . . . . .161 A6
Exchange Quay Sta M5 . . . . .161 A6
Exchange St **9** Bolton BL1 .145 F7
  Edenfield BL0 . . . . .1 D3
  Manchester M2 . . . . .158 F1
  5 Oldham OL4 . . . . .67 B7
  Stockport SK3 . . . . .169 E1
Exeter Ave Bolton BL2 . . . . . . .25 B2
  Denton M34 . . . . .100 F1
  Farnworth M26 . . . . .59 F8
  Radcliffe M26 . . . . .43 E5
  Salford M30 . . . . .79 A2
Exeter Cl Cheadle SK8 . . . . .131 F8
  Dukinfield SK16 . . . . .101 D6
Exeter Ct Manchester M14 . .110 C7
  3 Middleton M24 . . . . . . .46 F1
Exeter Dr Ashton-u-L OL6 . . . .85 D7
  Aspull WN2 . . . . .38 D5
  Irlam M44 . . . . .94 B2
Exeter Gr OL11 . . . . .139 F5
Exeter Rd Brinnington SK5 . .112 C5
  Hindley WN2 . . . . .56 E6
  Urmston M41 . . . . .95 D4
Exeter St Rochdale OL11 . . . .139 F5
  Salford M6 . . . . .154 E2
Exeter Wlk SK7 . . . . .132 F7
Exford Ave WN3 . . . . .55 E2
Exford Cl Manchester M40 . . .160 D3
  Reddish SK5 . . . . .111 F6
Exford Dr BL2 . . . . .43 A6
Exhall Cl M38 . . . . .60 A6
Exit Rd W M90 . . . . .130 B7
Exmoor Cl OL6 . . . . .85 C7
Exmouth Ave SK5 . . . . .112 C5
Exmouth Pl OL11 . . . . .31 A4
Exmouth Rd M33 . . . . .107 D5
Exmouth Sq OL11 . . . . .31 A3
Exmouth St OL11 . . . . .31 A3
Exmouth Wlk **7** M16 . . . . . .97 F3
Eyam Cl **12** SK13 . . . . .171 D2
Eyam Fold **16** SK13 . . . . . .171 E2
Eyam Gdns **3** SK13 . . . . . .171 D2
Eyam Gn **3** SK13 . . . . .171 E2
Eyam Gr
  11 Gamesley SK13 . . . . .171 D2
  Stockport SK2 . . . . .124 D5
Eyam La **13** SK13 . . . . .171 E2
Eyam Lea **19** SK13 . . . . . . .171 E2
Eyam Mews SK13 . . . . .171 D2
Eyam Rd SK7 . . . . .124 E1
Eyebrook Rd WA14 . . . . .119 A2
Eyet St WN7 . . . . .75 B5
Eynford Ave SK5 . . . . .112 B6
Eyre St M15 . . . . .163 A5

F

Faber St M4 . . . . .159 A3
Factory Brow Blackrod BL6 . . .21 D3
  Middleton M24 . . . . .64 C7
Factory Hill BL6 . . . . .22 D4
Factory La Adlington PR6 . . . .21 B8
  Disley SK12 . . . . .135 E6
  Manchester M3 . . . . .158 D1
  Manchester M9 . . . . .157 D8
  Swinton M27 . . . . .62 A1
Factory St Middleton M24 . . . .64 F8
  Radcliffe M26 . . . . .44 B3
  Ramsbottom BL0 . . . . .138 C7
  Tyldesley M29 . . . . .58 F1
Factory St E M46 . . . . .58 C3
Factory St W M46 . . . . .58 C3
Faggy La WN3 . . . . .54 C2
Failsworth Ind Est **2** M40 . . .83 C6
Failsworth Rd M35 . . . . .84 C7
Failsworth Sch M35 . . . . .84 A7
Failsworth Sta M35 . . . . .83 E8
Fair Acres BL2 . . . . .25 E3
Fair Hill BB4 . . . . .1 A7
Fair Oak Rd M19 . . . . .110 F5
Fair St Bolton BL3 . . . . .146 C2
  Manchester M1 . . . . .159 C1
  Swinton M27 . . . . .62 A1
Fair View Bacup OL13 . . . . .4 C8
  Wilmslow SK9 . . . . .136 F4
Fair Way SK5,M35 . . . . .71 C6
Fair Way OL11 . . . . .30 B4
Fairacres WN6 . . . . .19 B1
Fairacres Rd SK6 . . . . .134 E8
Fairbairn St BL6 . . . . .22 B3
Fairbank M43 . . . . .99 F8
Fairbank Ave M14 . . . . .98 A3
Fairbank Dr M24 . . . . .46 D2
Fairbottom St OL1 . . . . .153 F7
Fairbottom Wlk **4** M43 . . . .100 A8
Fairbourne Ave
  Wigan WN3 . . . . .55 A4
  Wilmslow SK9 . . . . .136 F4
Fairbourne Cl SK9 . . . . .136 F4
Fairbourne Dr Sale WA15 . . .108 B1
  Wilmslow SK9 . . . . .136 F4
Fairbourne Rd
  Denton M34 . . . . .100 E2

Fairbourne Rd continued
  Reddish M19 . . . . .99 C1
Fairbrook Dr M6 . . . . .154 E2
Fairbrother St M5 . . . . .161 C7
Fairclough St Bolton BL3 . . . . .42 A4
  Droylsden M11 . . . . .83 A2
  Hindley WN2 . . . . .56 D6
  Newton-le-W WA12 . . . . . . .89 B3
  Wigan WN1 . . . . .151 D7
Fairfax Ave
  Altrincham WA15 . . . . .120 A6
  Manchester M20 . . . . .110 B4
Fairfax Cl SK6 . . . . .125 D7
Fairfax Dr
  Littleborough OL15 . . . . . . .15 F3
  Wilmslow SK9 . . . . .136 F4
Fairfax Rd M25 . . . . .63 A5
Fairfield OL6 . . . . .85 C8
Fairfield Ave Cheadle SK8 . . .122 F2
  Droylsden M43 . . . . .100 A7
  Platt Bridge WN2 . . . . .56 A3
  Romiley SK6 . . . . .113 A4
  Wigan WN5 . . . . .54 D5
Fairfield Ct M14 . . . . .98 D4
Fairfield Dr BL9 . . . . .28 D3
Fairfield General Hospl
  BL9 . . . . .28 E4
Fairfield High Sch
  for Girls M43 . . . . .100 A8
Fairfield Ho M43 . . . . .84 A1
Fairfield Rd
  Altrincham WA15 . . . . .120 C5
  Droylsden M11,M43 . . . . . . .99 F8
  Farnworth BL4 . . . . .42 A4
  Irlam M44 . . . . .105 C5
  Manchester M24 . . . . .46 E1
Fairfield Road Prim Sch
  M43 . . . . .99 F8
Fairfield Sq M43 . . . . .100 A8
Fairfield St
  Manchester M1,M12 . . . . . .163 C8
  Salford M6 . . . . .80 E5
  Wigan WN5 . . . . .54 D5
Fairfield View M34 . . . . .100 A7
Fairfields Bolton BL7 . . . . .24 F8
  Oldham OL8 . . . . .66 E2
Fairford Cl SK5 . . . . .111 F5
Fairford Dr BL3 . . . . .146 C4
Fairford Way Reddish SK5 . . .111 F5
  Wilmslow SK9 . . . . .137 D7
Fairham Wlk M12 . . . . .160 D1
Fairhaven Ave
  Manchester M21 . . . . .109 B8
  Westhoughton BL5 . . . . .58 B8
  Whitefield M45 . . . . .62 E7
Fairhaven Cl SK7 . . . . .132 F8
Fairhaven Rd BL1 . . . . .143 F3
Fairhaven St M12 . . . . .164 F6
Fairhill Terr BB4 . . . . .1 A7
Fairhills Ind Est M44 . . . . . . .105 F8
Fairhills Rd M44 . . . . .106 A8
Fairholme Ave
  Ashton-in-M WN4 . . . . .73 B4
  Urmston M41 . . . . .95 C1
Fairholme Cl
  Manchester M20 . . . . .110 C6
  Warton WA3 . . . . .168 C3
Fairhope Ave M6 . . . . .80 C3
Fairhurst Ave WN6 . . . . .19 D3
Fairhurst Dr M28 . . . . .59 F7
Fairhurst St Leigh WN7 . . . . . .75 E5
  Wigan WN5 . . . . .150 B8
Fairisle Cl M11 . . . . .160 F1
Fairlands Pl OL11 . . . . .31 B2
Fairlands Rd Bury BL9 . . . . . .27 F6
  Sale M33 . . . . .107 F2
Fairlands St OL11 . . . . .31 B2
Fairlands View OL11 . . . . .31 B2
Fairlawn SK4 . . . . .169 D3
Fairlawn Cl M14 . . . . .98 A4
Fairlea M34 . . . . .101 A2
Fairlea Ave M20 . . . . .110 C2
Fairleigh Ave M6 . . . . .80 C3
Fairless Rd M30 . . . . .79 D1
Fairlie Ave BL3 . . . . .40 F5
Fairlie Dr WA15 . . . . .120 B8
Fairlyn Cl BL5 . . . . .59 A7
Fairlyn Dr BL5 . . . . .59 A7
Fairman Cl M16 . . . . .97 C3
Fairmead Rd M23 . . . . .109 F1
Fairmile Dr M20 . . . . .122 C8
Fairmount Ave BL2 . . . . .42 E8
Fairmount Rd M27 . . . . .79 C6
Fairoak Ct BL3 . . . . .145 D5
Fairstead Wlk **4** M11 . . . . . .99 F7
Fairthorne Grange OL7 . . . . . .84 F6
Fairview Ave
  Manchester M19 . . . . .98 F2
  Reddish M34 . . . . .100 A1
Fairview Cl
  Ashton-in-M WN4 . . . . .73 B4
  Chadderton OL9 . . . . .65 F8
  Marple SK6 . . . . .125 F6
  Rochdale OL12 . . . . .13 C2
Fairview Dr SK6 . . . . .125 F7
Fairview Rd
  Altrincham WA15 . . . . .120 C5
  Denton M34 . . . . .100 A1
Fairway Bramhall SK7 . . . . . .132 A8
  Droylsden M43 . . . . .100 A8
  Gatley SK8 . . . . .122 B4

Fairway continued
Manchester M25 . . . . 63 D2
Milnrow OL16 . . . . 32 A6
Pendlebury M27 . . . . 80 C7
Whitworth OL12 . . . . 14 C7
Fairway Ave Bolton BL2 . . 26 A4
Sale M23 . . . . 120 C2
Fairway Cres OL2 . . . . 48 D6
Fairway Ct M34 . . . . 100 B4
Fairway Dr M33 . . . . 107 E2
Fairway Prim Sch SK2 . . . 124 E7
Fairway Rd Oldham OL4 . . 67 E4
Whitefield BL9 . . . . 45 A3
Fairway The Failsworth M40 . .83 C8
Stockport SK2 . . . . 124 D7
Fairways BL6 . . . . 22 C3
Fairways Cl SK13 . . . . 104 F1
Fairways The
Garswood WN4 . . . . 72 D2
Westhoughton BL5 . . . . 57 E8
Whitefield M45 . . . . 62 F6
Fairywood Rd M23 . . . . 120 D7
Fairy La Manchester M7,M8 . .155 E5
Wythenshawe M23 . . . . 109 A3
Fairy St BL8 . . . . 27 C2
Fairywell Cl SK9 . . . . 131 D1
Fairywell Dr M33 . . . . 108 A1
Fairywell Rd WA15 . . . . . . 120 C7
Faith St Bolton BL1 . . . . . . 142 A1
Leigh WN7 . . . . 75 C5
Falcon Ave M41 . . . . 95 E2
Falcon Bsns Ctr OL9 . . . . 152 C8
Falcon Cl Bury BL9 . . . . . . 141 B4
Leigh WN7 . . . . 76 B5
Rochdale OL12 . . . . 13 E2
Falcon Cres M27 . . . . 62 C2
Falcon Ct Manchester M15 . .162 E5
Manchester M7 . . . . 155 D8
Falcon Dr Irlam M44 . . . . . 94 B4
Middleton M24 . . . . 46 E3
Oldham OL9 . . . . 152 C8
Walkden M38 . . . . 60 A5
Falcon St Bolton BL1 . . . . 145 F8
Oldham OL8 . . . . 153 F5
Falconers Gn WN3 . . . . . . 150 B5
Falconwood Chase M28 . .78 C6
Falconwood Cl WN6 . . . . . 37 A1
Falfield Dr M8 . . . . 156 B5
Falinge Fold OL12 . . . . . . 14 D1
Falinge Mews OL12 . . . . . 139 E8
Falinge Park High Sch
OL12 . . . . 14 D1
Falinge Rd OL12 . . . . 14 E1
Falkirk Dr Bolton BL2 . . . 42 F6
Ince-in-M WN2 . . . . 56 A8
Falkirk St ■ OL4 . . . . 67 C7
Falkirk Wlk ■ M23 . . . . . . 121 A2
Falkland Ave
Manchester M40 . . . . 160 D4
Rochdale OL11 . . . . 30 C8
Falkland Cl OL4 . . . . 49 E4
Falkland Dr WN4 . . . . 72 C4
Falkland Ho M14 . . . . 98 C1
Falkland Rd BL2 . . . . 43 A7
Fall Bank SK4 . . . . 111 C6
Fall Birch Hospl BL6 . . . . 23 A1
Fall Birch Rd BL6 . . . . 39 F8
Fallons Rd M28 . . . . 61 C1
Fallow Cl BL5 . . . . 39 E2
Fallow Fields Dr SK5 . . . . 100 A1
Fallowfield Ave M5 . . . . . 161 B7
Fallowfield Dr OL12 . . . . . 14 D2
Fallowfield Sh Ctr M14 . .98 E1
Fallowfield Way M46 . . . . 58 E1
Fallows The OL9 . . . . 152 A5
Falls Gr SK8 . . . . 122 A3
Falmer Cl BL8 . . . . 27 C6
Falmer Dr M22 . . . . 121 D1
Falmer St M18 . . . . 99 F6
Falmouth Ave Sale M33 . .107 D5
Urmston M41 . . . . 94 E3
Falmouth Cres SK5 . . . . . 112 C5
Falmouth Rd M44 . . . . . . 94 B2
Falmouth St
Manchester M40 . . . . 160 F4
Oldham OL8 . . . . 66 F4
■ Rochdale OL11 . . . . . . 31 A5
Falsgrave Cl M40 . . . . 83 A5
Falshaw Dr BL0 . . . . 11 E1
Falside Wlk ■ M40 . . . . . 83 C5
Falstaff Mews SK13 . . . . 113 A3
Falston Ave M40 . . . . 65 D2
Falstone Ave BL0 . . . . . . 11 C4
Falstone Cl WN3 . . . . 54 E2
Falterley Rd M23 . . . . 120 F8
Fancroft Rd M22 . . . . 121 C5
Fane Wlk M9 . . . . 64 B2
Far Cromwell Rd SK6 . . . 112 D7
Far Hey Cl M26 . . . . 43 E3
Far La M18 . . . . 99 D4
Far Ridings M26 . . . . 113 D3
Far Woodseats La SK14 . .114 F5
Faraday Ave
Manchester M8 . . . . 156 A6
Swinton M27 . . . . 62 D2
Faraday Dr BL1 . . . . 143 E1
Faraday Rd M46 . . . . 150 A8
Faraday St M1 . . . . 159 B1
Farcroft Ave M26 . . . . . . 44 C6
Farcroft Cl M23 . . . . 120 F8
Fardale OL2 . . . . 149 B6
Farden Dr M23 . . . . 120 D8
Fardon Cl WN3 . . . . 54 F3
Farefield Ave WA3 . . . . . 73 F2

Fareham Ct M16 . . . . 162 D5
Farewell Cl ■ OL13 . . . . 30 C2
Farholme OL1 . . . . 48 C2
Farholme La OL13 . . . . . . 3 D8
Faringdon ■ OL11 . . . . . 139 E6
Faringdon Wlk BL3 . . . . 145 E5
Farland Pl BL3 . . . . 40 F5
Farlands Dr M20 . . . . 122 B7
Farlands Rise OL16 . . . . 31 C3
Farleigh Cl BL5 . . . . 40 A2
Farley Ave M18 . . . . 100 A4
Farley Ct SK8 . . . . 122 F3
Farley La WN8 . . . . 35 A3
Farley Rd M33 . . . . 108 C2
Farley Way SK5 . . . . 111 E7
Farm Ave Adlington PR6 . .21 A8
Stretford M32 . . . . 96 A4
Farm Cl Bury BL8 . . . . . . 26 F6
Reddish SK4 . . . . 111 C6
Farm La Aspull WN2 . . . . 38 A2
High Lane SK12 . . . . 135 A6
Hyde SK14 . . . . 113 D8
Middleton M25 . . . . 63 E8
Worsley M28 . . . . 78 F5
Farm Meadow Rd WN5 . .53 E5
Farm Rd OL8 . . . . 84 C8
Farm Side Pl ■ M40 . . . 99 E4
Farm St Failsworth M35 . .83 E6
Manchester M8 . . . . 155 F7
Haughton OL10,OL9 . . . . 48 B1
Farm Way WA12 . . . . 89 E1
Farm Wlk
Altrincham WA14 . . . . . . 118 E1
Littleborough OL15 . . . . 15 F5
Rochdale OL16 . . . . 31 C5
Farm Yd M19 . . . . 99 A1
Farman St BL3 . . . . 147 D3
Farmer St SK4 . . . . 169 E3
Farmers Cl M33 . . . . 109 A3
Farmfield M33 . . . . 107 B6
Farmfold SK9 . . . . 130 F3
Farmlands Wlk OL1 . . . . 49 C4
Farmside Ave M44 . . . . . 94 A3
Farmstead Cl M35 . . . . . 84 C6
Farmway M24 . . . . 65 A7
Farnan St SK4 . . . . 99 F2
Farnborough Ave OL4 . .67 D6
Farnborough Rd
Bolton BL1 . . . . 24 E6
Manchester M40 . . . . 160 D3
Farncombe Cl ■ M23 . .120 D7
Farndale Gr WN4 . . . . . . 73 C2
Farndale Sq M38 . . . . . . 60 C3
Farndale Wlk ■ M9 . . . 157 E8
Farndon Ave SK7 . . . . . . 124 A1
Farndon Cl M33 . . . . 108 E3
Farndon Dr WA15 . . . . . 120 A6
Farndon Rd SK5 . . . . 99 E2
Farnham Ave M9 . . . . . . 64 C3
Farnham Cl ■ Bolton BL1 . .143 E1
Cheadle SK8 . . . . 132 A7
Leigh WN7 . . . . 75 E6
Farnham Dr M44 . . . . . . 94 B1
Farnhill Wlk M23 . . . . . . 108 E1
Farnley Cl OL12 . . . . 13 F2
Farnsfield WN1 . . . . 37 F1
Farnsworth Ave OL7 . . 85 B5
Farnsworth Cl OL7 . . . . 85 B5
Farnworth Dr M14 . . . . . 98 C2
Farnworth St Bolton BL3 . .146 C4
■ Heywood OL10 . . . . . 29 C2
■ Leigh WN7 . . . . 76 B4
Farnworth Sta BL4 . . . . 42 E1
Farr Cl WN3 . . . . 54 F5
Farr St SK3 . . . . 170 D8
Farrand Rd OL8 . . . . 66 B2
Farrant Rd M12 . . . . 99 A4
Farrar Rd M43 . . . . 99 F8
Farrell St Manchester M7 . .158 D3
Wigan WN5 . . . . 54 C5
Farrer Rd M13 . . . . 98 F3
Farrier's Croft WN6 . . . 36 E3
Farriers La OL11 . . . . . . 30 B4
Farriers Ct M35 . . . . 83 F7
Farringdon St M6 . . . . . 154 E3
Farrington Ave M20 . . 110 A7
Farrow St OL2 . . . . 149 B6
Farrow St E OL2 . . . . . . 149 B6
Farrowdale Ave OL2 . . 149 B6
Farwood Cl M16 . . . . . . 161 C5
Fastnet St M11 . . . . 165 A8
Fatherford Cl OL3 . . . . . 51 D5
Faulkenhurst Mews OL1 . .48 C1
Faulkenhurst St OL1,OL9 . .48 C1
Faulkes Ho ■ M14 . . . . 110 D8
Faulkner Dr WA15 . . . . 120 B5
Faulkner Rd M32 . . . . . . 96 E2
Faulkner St Bolton BL3 . .145 E5
Manchester M1 . . . . 163 A8
Rochdale OL16 . . . . 139 F7
Fauvel Pl SK13 . . . . 104 C1
Fauvel Rd SK13 . . . . 104 C2
Faversham Brow ■ OL1 . .153 E8
Faversham St M40 . . . . 83 B7
Fawborough Rd M23 . .108 F1
Fawcett St ■ BL2 . . . . . 148 B7
Fawcetts Fold BL5 . . . . 39 C4
Fawley Ave SK14 . . . . . 167 D1
Fawley Gr M22 . . . . 121 D4
Fawns Keep
Stalybridge SK15 . . . . . 102 E6
Wilmslow SK9 . . . . 137 D7
Fay Ave M9 . . . . 65 A2
Fay Gdns SK13 . . . . 171 E4
Faywood Dr SK6 . . . . . . 126 A6
Fearn St OL10 . . . . 29 C2
Fearney Side BL3 . . . . . 42 F3

Fearnham Cl WN7 . . . . . 75 E1
Fearnhead Ave BL2 . . . 22 B5
Fearnhead Cl BL4 . . . . . 60 E8
Fearnhead St BL3 . . . . . 146 C4
Fearnley Way WA12 . . 89 C1
Fearns Moss OL13 . . . . 3 A8
Featherstall Brook View
OL15 . . . . 16 A5
Featherstall Ho OL9 . . . 152 C5
Featherstall Rd OL15 . . 16 A5
Featherstall Rd N
OL1,OL9 . . . . 153 D8
Featherstall Rd S OL9 . .153 D6
Fecit La BL0 . . . . 12 C8
Federation St
Manchester M4 . . . . 159 A2
Prestwich M25 . . . . 62 F5
Feldom Rd M23 . . . . 108 F2
Fell St Bury BL8 . . . . 27 C2
Leigh WN7 . . . . 75 B4
Fellbridge Cl BL5 . . . . . 40 B1
Fellbrigg Cl M18 . . . . . . 99 C3
Fellfoot Cl M28 . . . . 77 F5
Felling Wlk ■ M14 . . . . 98 B3
Fellpark Rd M23 . . . . . . 109 A2
Fells Gr M28 . . . . 60 F1
Fellside Bolton BL2 . . . 26 A3
Oldham OL1 . . . . 153 E7
Fellside Cl BL8 . . . . 10 F1
Fellside Gdns OL15 . . . 15 F7
Fellside Gdns SK15 . . . 86 A3
Felltop Dr SK5 . . . . 112 A8
Felskirk Rd M22 . . . . . . 130 C8
Felsted BL1 . . . . 40 E8
Felt Ct M34 . . . . 100 C2
Felthorpe Dr M8 . . . . . 155 F6
Felton Ave M22 . . . . . . 121 D3
Felton Cl BL9 . . . . 45 A5
Felton Wlk BL1 . . . . 143 E2
Fence St SK2 . . . . 124 D4
Fencegate Ave SK4 . . . 111 D5
Fenchurch Ave M40 . . 83 C4
Fencot Dr M12 . . . . 99 A4
Fenella St M13 . . . . 98 E4
Fenham Cl M40 . . . . 156 C5
Fenmore Ave M18 . . . . 99 B3
Fenn St M15 . . . . 162 E6
Fennel St M3,M4 . . . . . . 158 F2
Fenners Cl BL3 . . . . 147 D2
Fenney St M7 . . . . 155 D5
Fenney St E M7 . . . . 155 E6
Fenside Rd M22 . . . . . . 121 E5
Fenstock Wlk M40 . . . 83 D4
Fentewan Wlk SK14 . . 102 E3
Fenton Ave SK7 . . . . . . 124 D4
Fenton Mews OL11 . . . 139 F5
Fenton St Bury BL8 . . . 27 C3
Manchester M12 . . . . . . 165 A5
■ Oldham OL4 . . . . 67 B6
Stretford M15 . . . . 162 E5
Fenton Way WN2 . . . . . 56 F4
Fenwick Dr SK4 . . . . . . 110 E3
Fenwick St
Manchester M15 . . . . . . 163 A6
Rochdale OL12 . . . . 139 E7
Ferdinand St M40 . . . . 160 D4
Fereday St M28 . . . . 60 D4
Ferguson Cl M19 . . . . . 110 F8
Ferguson Gdns OL12 . .14 F3
Ferguson Rise WN5 . . 54 E8
Ferguson Way OL4 . . . 49 D1
Fern Ave
Newton-le-W WA12 . . . 89 D2
Urmston M41 . . . . 95 A2
Fern Banks Failsworth M40 . .83 C7
Stalybridge SK15 . . . . . 86 C1
Fern Bank Cl SK5 . . . . . 102 C8
Fern Bank Dr M23 . . . . 120 E8
Fern Bank St M34 . . . . 113 E8
Fern Cl Atherton M46 . . 58 C6
Marple SK6 . . . . 125 F6
Middleton M24 . . . . 65 F6
Oldham OL4 . . . . 67 F6
Shevington WN6 . . . . . . 36 A6
Fern Clough BL1 . . . . . 40 F7
Fern Common OL2 . . . . 149 B7
Fern Cres SK15 . . . . . . 86 C1
Fern Dene ■ OL12 . . . 14 B2
Fern Hill La OL12 . . . . 14 A3
Fern Isle Cl OL12 . . . . 14 B6
Fern Lea Gatley SK8 . . 122 B1
Hollingworth SK14 . . . 103 D5
Fern Lea Gr M38 . . . . . 59 F4
Fern Lea St B84 . . . . . 2 D8
Fern St Bolton BL3 . . . 145 E6
Bury BL9 . . . . 140 F3
Chadderton OL9 . . . . . 152 A8
Farnworth BL4 . . . . 42 E1
Littleborough OL12 . . 15 C4
Manchester M11 . . . . . 165 B8
Manchester M4,M8 . . 159 A4
Oldham OL8 . . . . 153 D5
Ramsbottom BL0 . . . . 11 D7
Rochdale OL11 . . . . . . 139 D6
Fern View WA15 . . . . 120 C5
Fernacre SK14 . . . . . . 108 C5
Fernally St SK14 . . . . 167 E2
Fernbank M26 . . . . . . 62 A8
Fernbray Ave M19 . . 57 A5
Fernbray Rd WN2 . . . 57 A5
Fernbrook Cl M13 . . 164 D5
Fernbrook Wlk ■ M8 . .155 F7
Ferncough Rd M9 . . . 157 D7
Ferndale Ave Royton OL16 . .48 C8
Stockport SK2 . . . . 124 B4
Whitefield M45 . . . . . . 62 C7

Ferndale Cl OL4 . . . . 67 D4
Ferndale Gdns M19 . . . 110 E6
Ferndale Rd M33 . . . . . 108 B2
Ferndale Wlk WN7 . . . 75 B5
Ferngrove BL9 . . . . 28 B5
Ferndene Gdns M20 . . 110 B5
Ferndene Rd
Manchester M20 . . . . . 110 B5
Prestwich M25,M45 . . 63 C7
Ferndown Ave
Chadderton OL9 . . . . . . 65 E7
Hazel Grove SK7 . . . . . 124 C1
Ferndown Dr M44 . . . . 94 A3
Ferndown Rd Bolton BL2 . .25 E3
Sale M23 . . . . 120 D8
Ferney Field
Com Specl Sch OL9 . . 65 F7
Ferney Field Rd OL9 . . 65 F7
Ferngate Dr M20 . . . . 110 B6
Ferngrove BL9 . . . . 28 B5
Fernhill SK6 . . . . 126 B6
Fernhill Ave Bacup OL13 . .3 E8
Bolton BL3 . . . . 146 A4
Fernhill Caravan Pk BL9 . .140 F4
Glossop SK13 . . . . 104 D3
Fernhill Cres ■ OL13 . .3 E8
Fernhill Dr Bacup OL13 . .3 E8
Manchester M18 . . . . . 99 B4
Fernhill Gr ■ OL13 . . . 3 E8
Fernhill Pk OL13 . . . . . 3 E8
Fernhill St BL9 . . . . 140 F3
Fernhill Way ■ OL13 . .3 E8
Fernhills 8 E2
Fernholme Ct OL8 . . . 66 C4
Fernhurst Cl WN3 . . . 151 F6
Fernhurst Gr BL1 . . . . 143 E1
Fernhurst Rd M20 . . . 110 C5
Fernhurst St OL1,OL9 . .48 C1
Fernie St M4 . . . . 159 A3
Fernilee Cl SK23 . . . . 127 C1
Fernlea Altrincham WA15 . .119 F1
Manchester SK4 . . . . . 111 C5
Fernlea Ave OL1 . . . . . 48 C1
Fernlea Cl Hadfield SK13 . .171 E4
■ Rochdale OL12 . . . 14 B2
Fernlea Cres M27 . . . 79 E7
Fernlea Gr WN4 . . . . . 72 D5
Fernleaf St M14 . . . . . 98 A4
Fernlea Lo BL4 . . . . . . 60 E7
Fernleaf St M14 . . . . . 98 A4
Fernleigh ■ OL12 . . . 14 A1
Fernleigh Ave M19 . . 99 C1
Fernleigh Dr M16 . . . 162 D5
Fernley Ave M34 . . . . 101 A2
Fernley Rd SK2 . . . . . . 124 B6
Ferns Gr BL1 . . . . 144 B7
Fernside M26 . . . . 61 C6
Fernside Ave M20 . . . 110 C5
Fernside Gr Walkden M28 . .60 E4
Wigan WN3 . . . . 54 D1
Fernside Way OL12 . . 14 A1
Fernstead BL3 . . . . . . 146 C4
Fernstone Cl BL6 . . . . 22 A3
Fernthorpe Ave SK15 . .85 C1
Fernview Dr BL0 . . . . 11 A1
Fernville Terr ■ OL8 . . 3 D8
Fernwood SK6 . . . . . . 126 A3
Fernwood Ave M18 . . 99 D3
Fernwood Gr SK9 . . . 137 C8
Ferrand Lodge OL15 . 16 C7
Ferrand Rd OL15 . . . . 16 B6
Ferrer St M44 . . . . 72 F6
Ferring Wlk OL9 . . . . 152 B6
Ferris St M11 . . . . 99 D8
Ferrous Way M44 . . . 105 F6
Ferry Rd M44 . . . . 94 B2
Ferry St M11 . . . . 164 E8
Ferryhill Rd M44 . . . . 94 A2
Fettler Cl M27 . . . . . . 79 F7
Fewston Cl BL1 . . . . . 24 E5
Fiddlers La M44 . . . . 94 B4
Fiddlers Lane Prim Sch
M44 . . . . 94 B4
Field Bank Gr M19 . . 99 C1
Field Cl Bramhall SK7 . .132 D4
Marple SK6 . . . . 125 D5
Field End Cl SK15 . . . 102 D8
Field House La SK6 . . 126 A6
Field La OL6 . . . . 85 D5
Field Pl ■ M20 . . . . . 110 B3
Field St Droylsden M43 . .84 A3
Failsworth M35 . . . . . 83 E7
Hindley WN2 . . . . 56 E4
Ince-in-M WN3 . . . . . 151 H4
Manchester M18 . . . . 99 F6
■ Rochdale OL11 . . . 31 A4
Romiley SK6 . . . . 113 A3
Salford M6 . . . . 154 F2
Wigan WN6 . . . . 150 B8
Field Vale Dr SK5 . . . 100 A1
Field View Wlk M16 . 97 F2
Field Wlk WA15 . . . . 119 F1
Fieldbrook Wlk BL5 . 40 A1
Fieldcroft OL11 . . . . . 30 A7
Fielden Ave M21 . . . . 97 B1
Fielden Ct M21 . . . . . 109 B8
Fielden St OL15 . . . . 16 B6
Fielders Way M27 . . 61 E4
Fieldfare Ave M40 . . 83 B4
Fieldfare Way OL7 . . 85 B7
Fieldhead Ave Bury BL8 . .27 C2
Rochdale OL11 . . . . . 30 B7
Tyldesley M27 . . . . . . 80 C7
Fieldhead Mews SK9 . .137 E8
Fieldhead Rd SK9 . . . 137 E8
Fieldhouse Ind Est OL12 . .14 F2

Fieldhouse Rd OL12 . . 14 F2
Fielding Ave SK12 . . . 133 E2
Fielding Pl PR6 . . . . . . 21 B8
Fielding St Eccles M30 . .79 C1
Middleton M24 . . . . . . 47 A2
Fields Cres SK14 . . . . 103 D6
Fields Ct SK14 . . . . . . 103 D6
Fields End Fold M30 . 94 C4
Fields Farm Cl SK14 . 102 D1
Fields Farm Rd SK14 .102 D1
Fields Farm Wlk ■ SK14 . .102 D2
Fields Gr SK14 . . . . . . 103 D5
Fields New Rd OL9 . . 152 B5
Fields The WN7 . . . . . 38 C4
Fieldsend Dr WN7 . . 91 C8
Fieldsway OL8 . . . . . . 66 E2
Fieldvale Rd M33 . . . 107 E1
Fieldview WN8 . . . . . 53 A7
Fieldway Platt Bridge WN2 . .56 B2
Rochdale OL16 . . . . . . 31 B3
Fife Ave OL9 . . . . 66 A4
Fifield Cl OL8 . . . . 67 A3
Fifth Ave Bolton BL1 . 144 B7
Bury BL9 . . . . 28 B4
Droylsden M11 . . . . . . 83 C2
Dukinfield SK16 . . . . 101 A8
Little Lever BL3 . . . . . 42 F4
Oldham OL8 . . . . 66 C2
Stretford M17 . . . . . . 96 C6
Fifth St Bolton BL1 . 23 F4
Stretford M17 . . . . . . 96 B6
Filbert St ■ OL1 . . . . 49 C1
Filby Wlk M40 . . . . . . 160 E4
Fildes St M34 . . . . 65 D7
Filey Ave Manchester M16 . .97 D2
Urmston M41 . . . . 95 A4
Filey Dr M6 . . . . 80 B5
Filey Rd Manchester M14 . .110 D8
Stockport SK2 . . . . . . 124 C7
Filey St OL16 . . . . 15 C3
Filton Ave ■ BL3 . . . 145 D5
Filton Wlk M9 . . . . . . 156 C6
Finance St OL15 . . . . 15 F4
Finborough Cl M16 . 97 E4
Finch Ave BL4 . . . . . . 59 F7
Finch La WN6 . . . . . . 18 B1
Finch Mill Ave WN6 . 35 D7
Finchale Dr WA15 . . 120 C1
Finchcroft OL1 . . . . . 49 D3
Finchdale Gdns WA3 .91 B8
Finchley Ave M40 . . 83 C4
Finchley Cres WN2 . 38 A2
Finchley Gr M40 . . . 65 A1
Finchley Rd
Altrincham WA15 . . . 119 E3
Manchester M14 . . . 110 B8
Findlay Cl WA12 . . . 89 C2
Findlay St WN7 . . . . 75 E5
Findon Rd M23 . . . . 121 A6
Finger Post BL3 . . . 43 A4
Fingerpost Rd WN2 . 95 B2
Finishing Wlk ■ M4 .159 C1
Finlan Rd M24 . . . . 47 E5
Finlay St Farnworth BL4 . .60 D8
Finlay Ct WN5 . . . . 54 E8
Finney Cl SK9 . . . . . 131 C2
Finney Dr Handforth SK9 . .131 C2
Manchester M21 . . . 109 A7
Finney La SK8 . . . . . 122 C1
Finney St ■ BL3 . . . 147 F4
Finningley Rd M9 . . 64 B5
Finny Bank Rd M33 . 108 A6
Finsbury Ave M40 . 83 C4
Finsbury Rd SK5 . . . 111 E8
Finsbury St OL11 . . 139 D5
Finstock Cl M30 . . 79 F8
Fintry Gr M30 . . . . 79 D1
Fir Ave SK7 . . . . . . 132 D8
Fir Bank Com Prim Sch
OL2 . . . . 48 D7
Fir Bank Rd OL2 . . 48 D6
Fir Cl SK12 . . . . . . 133 F3
Fir Gr Manchester M19 . .99 A1
Oldham OL9 . . . . . . 152 B8
Wigan WN6 . . . . . . 37 A3
Fir La OL2 . . . . 48 D6
Fir Rd Bramhall SK7 . .132 E8
Denton M34 . . . . . . 101 A3
Farnworth BL4 . . . . 60 B8
Marple SK6 . . . . . . 125 E5
Swinton M27 . . . . . 77 F7
Fir St Bolton BL1 . . 143 F2
Bury BL9 . . . . 141 A2
Eccles M30 . . . . . . 79 D1
Failsworth M35 . . . 83 E7
Heywood OL10 . . . 29 D2
■ Irlam M44 . . . . . 105 D6
Manchester M40 . . 160 D4
Radcliffe M26 . . . . 44 B2
Ramsbottom BL0 . . 138 B5
Royton OL2 . . . . . . 48 D5
Salford M6 . . . . . . 154 F2
Stockport SK4 . . . . 169 E2
Walsden OL14 . . . . 6 A8
Fir Tree Ave
Boothstown M28 . . 78 B5
Golborne WA3 . . . . 90 F8
Oldham OL8 . . . . . 67 A2
Fir Tree Cl SK16 . . 101 F8
Fir Tree Cres
Ince-in-M WN3 . . . 55 F3
Stalybridge SK16 . . 101 F8
Fir Tree Dr
Dukinfield SK14 . . 101 E5
Ince-in-M WN3 . . . 55 F3
Fir Tree Ho OL8 . . 67 A2

Fir Tree La SK16 ....101 F8
Fir Tree Prim Sch SK5 .....99 E2
Fir Tree St WN3 ....55 F4
Fir Tree Way 5 BL6 ....22 E1
Fir Tree Wlk WA3 ....90 F8
Firbank Rd Wigan WN3 .....55 B3
　Wythenshawe M23 ....121 B4
Firbarn Cl OL16 ....31 D7
Firbeck Dr M4 ....160 D2
Fircroft WN6 ....19 A2
Fircroft Cl 6 SK3 ....123 F4
Fircroft Rd OL8 ....67 A2
Firdale Ave M40 ....65 E1
Firdale Wlk OL9 ....152 C7
Firdon Wlk 17 M9 ....157 E7
Fire Station Sq M5 ....81 C2
Firecrest Cl M28 ....78 B8
Firefly Cl M3 ....158 D1
Firethorn Ave M19 ....110 F6
Firethorn Cl BL5 ....39 C2
Firethorn Dr SK14 ....102 A2
Firethorn Wlk 5 M33 .....107 C5
Firfield Gr M28 ....60 F3
Firgrove Ave OL16 ....31 D8
Firgrove Gdns OL16 ......31 D8
Firs Ave Ashton-u-L OL6 ...85 B5
　Failsworth M35 ....83 E7
Manchester M16 ....97 B2
Firs Cotts WN2 ....38 D1
Firs Ct SK8 ....122 A3
Firs Cty Prim Sch M33 ...107 D4
Firs Gr SK8 ....122 A4
Firs La WN7 ....75 C5
Firs Park Cres WN2 ....38 D1
Firs Rd Atherton BL5 .....59 A6
　Gatley SK8 ....122 A4
　Sale M33 ....107 D5
Firs The Altrincham WA14 ..119 B3
Manchester M14 ....98 D1
Wilmslow SK9 ....137 A5
Firs Way M33 ....107 C3
Firsby Ave SK6 ....112 F4
Firsby St 5 M19 ....99 A1
Firsdale Ind Est WN7 .....75 C6
First Ave Atherton M46 ...58 D4
　Bury BL8 ....26 F6
　Droylsden M11 ....83 D2
　11 Hindley WN2 ....56 D5
　Little Lever BL3 ....43 A4
　Mossley SK15 ....86 E5
　Oldham OL8 ....66 D2
　Poynton SK12 ....133 D1
　Stretford M17 ....96 D6
　Swinton M27 ....79 D5
　Tyldesley M29 ....77 C4
　Wigan WN6 ....37 A2
First St BL1 ....23 F4
Firsway WN7 ....75 B5
Firswood Dr Hyde SK14 ...102 A3
　Royton OL2 ....48 C6
　Swinton M27 ....79 E6
Firswood Mount SK8 .....122 A4
Firth Cl M7 ....155 D6
Firth St OL1 ....153 F6
Firtree Ave M33 ....107 C4
Firtree Ave Sk6 ....122 B1
Firvale Cl WN7 ....75 C5
Firwood Ave Farnworth BL4 ..60 C7
　Stretford M41 ....96 A2
Firwood Cl SK2 ....124 C8
Firwood Cres M26 ....44 B1
Firwood Gr
　Ashton-in-M WN4 ....73 A2
　Bolton BL2 ....25 B2
Firwood La BL2 ....25 C3
Firwood Pk OL9 ....65 E8
Firwood Spectl Sch BL2 ..25 C2
Firwood Stables BL2 .....25 C3
Fish Rake La BL0,BB4 .....1 E6
Fishbourne Sq 8 M14 ....98 C3
Fishbrook Ind Est BL4 ....61 A7
Fisher Ave WN2 ....74 C7
Fisher Cl WN4 ....54 F5
Fisher Dr WN5 ....53 E2
Fisher St OL1 ....153 F8
Fisherfield OL12 ....13 F1
Fishermore Rd M41 ....94 E2
Fishpool Inf Sch BL9 .....44 F8
Fishwick St OL16 ....31 A6
Fistral Ave SK8 ....131 C8
Fistral Cres SK15 ....86 D3
Fitchfield Wlk M18 ....60 D3
Fitton Ave M21 ....109 B6
Fitton Cres M27 ....61 F3
Fitton Hill Inf Sch OL8 ...67 B3
Fitton Hill Jun Sch OL8 ..67 A3
Fitton Hill Rd OL8 ....67 A4
Fitton St Bolton BL3 ......147 E4
　Rochdale OL16 ....31 A8
　Royton OL2 ....48 F4
　Shaw OL2 ....48 F7
Fitzadam St WN1 ....150 B8
Fitzalan St SK13 ....104 C1
Fitzgeorge St M40 ....156 C5
Fitzgerald Cl M25 ....62 F2
Fitzgerald Ct 11 M24 ....113 A8
Fitzgerald Way M6 ....154 F3
Fitzhugh St BL1 ....25 A5
Fitzroy St Ashton-u-L OL7 ..100 F8
　Droylsden M43 ....100 B8
　Stalybridge SK15 ....86 D4
Fitzwarren Cl M6 ....154 F2
Fitzwarren St M6 ....154 F2
Fitzwilliam St M7 ....158 D4
Five Fold Pk OL9 ....153 D6
Five Quarters M26 ....43 E5
Fiveways M43 ....84 A2
Fiveways Par SK7 ....133 E8

Flag St OL13 ....3 E8
Flagcroft Dr M23 ....121 B5
Flagg Wood Ave SK6 .....125 D7
Flagship Ave M5 ....161 B8
Flake La OL2 ....48 D5
Flamborough Wlk 7 M14 ..98 B3
Flamingo Cl M12 ....165 A6
Flamingo Villas M44 .....94 A3
Flamstead Ave M23 ......120 E6
Flannel St 4 OL12,OL16 ..31 A8
Flapper Fold La M46 .....58 C3
Flash Cotts OL4 ....68 A4
Flash St M40 ....83 C6
Flashfields M21 ....74 A1
Flatley Cl M15 ....163 A5
Flavion Wlk M11 ....165 B8
Flax Cl BB4 ....1 A8
Flax Moss Cl BB4 ....1 A8
Flax St Manchester M3 ...158 D3
　Ramsbottom BL0 ....11 A1
Flaxcroft Rd M22 ....121 B3
Flaxfield Ave SK15 ....86 D2
Flaxman Rise OL1 ....49 C4
Flaxpool Cl M16 ....97 E4
Flaxwood Wlk M22 ......121 B3
Fleece St 2 Oldham OL4 ..67 B7
　Rochdale OL16 ....139 F7
Fleeson St M14 ....98 C3
Fleet St Ashton-u-L OL6 ..166 B2
　Droylsden M18 ....99 F6
　Horwich BL6 ....22 D3
　Hyde SK14 ....167 E3
　Oldham OL4 ....67 C7
　Wigan WN5 ....54 B6
Fleetwood Rd M28 ....60 A3
Fleming Dr OL9 ....153 D6
Fleming Rd M22 ....121 D2
Flemish Rd M34 ....101 B2
Fletcher Ave
　Atherton M46 ....58 D5
　Swinton M27 ....62 A3
Fletcher Cl Heywood OL10 ..29 D2
　Oldham OL9 ....153 D6
Fletcher Dr
　Altrincham WA14 ....119 C1
　High Lane SK12 ....134 F6
Fletcher Fold Rd BL9 .....44 F6
Fletcher Moss Botanical
　& Parsonage Gdns
M20 ....110 B1
Fletcher Moss Mus
　& Art Gal M20 ....110 B1
Fletcher Sq 16 M1 ......159 C1
Fletcher St
　1 Ashton-u-L OL6 .....166 C3
　Atherton M46 ....58 C3
　Bolton BL3 ....145 E5
　Bury BL9 ....141 A2
　Farnworth BL4 ....60 D8
　Little Lever BL3 ....43 A4
　Manchester M10,M40 ...157 F5
　Radcliffe M26 ....44 C4
　Rochdale OL11 ....31 A5
　Stockport SK1 ....169 F1
Fletcher's Rd OL15 ....15 E3
Fletsand Rd SK9 ....137 D6
Flexbury Wlk M40 ....83 D4
Flint Cl Droylsden M11 ...83 B2
　Hazel Grove SK7 ....124 C1
Flint Gr M44 ....105 C6
Flint St Droylsden M43 ...84 B2
　Oldham OL1 ....67 C8
　Stockport SK3 ....170 E7
Flitcroft St BL3 ....147 F4
Flixton Girls' High Sch
M41 ....95 A2
Flixton Inf Sch M41 ......94 F3
Flixton Jun Sch M41 .....94 F2
Flixton Rd Flixton M41 ...106 E7
　Urmston M41 ....94 F1
Flixton Sta M41 ....94 F1
Flixton Wlk M13 ....164 D5
Floats Rd Altrincham M23 ..120 E6
　Altrincham M23 ....120 E6
Floatshall Rd M23 ....121 A6
Flockton Ave WN6 ....36 D4
Flockton Ct 7 BL6 ....22 B4
Flora Dr M7 ....158 D4
Flora St Ashton-in-M WN4 ..73 B2
　Bolton BL3 ....147 E4
　Manchester M9 ....64 C3
　Oldham OL1 ....153 E7
Floral Ct M7 ....155 D6
Florence Ave M3 ....24 F5
Florence Ct SK3 ....123 B6
Florence Nightingale
　Hospl BL8 ....27 C1
Florence Park Ct M20 ...110 C4
Florence St Bolton BL3 ...147 D4
　Droylsden M43 ....100 B8
　Eccles M30 ....79 F8
　Manchester M9 ....63 F8
　Sale M33 ....108 B6
　Stockport SK4 ....169 E2
　Wigan WN1 ....151 E8
Florence Way SK14 ......103 D5
Florian Ho OL1 ....153 F7
Florida St OL8 ....153 E5
Florist St SK3 ....170 E7
Flowery Bank OL8 ....67 B4
Flowery Field SK2 ....124 A3
Flowery Field Prim Sch
　SK14 ....167 D4
Flowery Field Sta SK14 ...101 D5
Floyd Ave M21 ....109 C5
Floyer Rd M9 ....64 E5

Foden La
　Alderley Edge SK9 ......136 C1
　Woodford SK7 ....132 D3
Foden Wlk 6 SK9 ....131 D2
Fog La M19,M20 ....110 C4
Fold Ave M43 ....84 B2
Fold Cres SK6 ....86 F6
Fold Gdns OL12 ....14 B4
Fold Gn OL9 ....152 A6
Fold Mews SK7 ....124 E3
Fold Rd M26 ....61 C7
Fold St Bolton BL1 ......145 F7
　Bury BL9 ....140 D2
　Golborne WA3 ....74 A1
　Heywood OL10 ....29 E3
　Manchester M40 ....83 A8
Fold The Manchester M9 ..64 E3
　Royton OL2 ....49 A4
　Urmston M41 ....95 A3
Fold View Bolton BL7 ....8 E1
　Oldham OL8 ....67 A2
Folds Rd BL1 ....21 C3
Folds Rd BL1,BL2 ....148 A8
Foleshill Ave M9 ....157 D7
Foley Gdns OL10 ....46 E7
Foley St 8 WN2 ....56 D5
Foley Wlk M22 ....130 E8
Foliage Cres SK5 ....112 B5
Foliage Rd SK5 ....112 C5
Foliage Rd SK5 ....112 B4
Folkestone Rd M11 ......83 D2
Folkestone Rd E M11 ....83 D2
Folkestone Rd W M11 ...83 D2
Follows St M18 ....99 D6
Folly Wlk 20 OL12 ....14 F1
Fonthill Gr M33 ....107 F1
Fontwell Cl
　3 Manchester M16 ....97 C3
　Standish WN6 ....19 F1
Fontwell La OL1 ....49 A1
Fontwell Rd BL3 ....43 A2
Fontwell Wlk 6 M40 ....65 D2
Foot Mill Cres OL12 .....14 D2
Foot Wood Cres OL12 ...14 D2
Footman Cl M29 ....77 B7
Forber Cres M18 ....99 D3
Forbes Cl Sale M33 ......108 D2
　Stockport SK1 ....124 B8
Forbes Pk SK7 ....124 D7
Forbes Rd SK1 ....112 B1
Forbes St M18 ....99 D6
Ford Gr SK14 ....103 A4
Ford La Manchester M20 ..110 A2
　Salford M6 ....80 A4
　Wythenshawe M22,M20 ..109 F1
Ford Lo M20 ....110 B2
Ford St Dukinfield SK16 ..101 C6
　Kearsley M26 ....61 A8
　Manchester M12 ....164 D7
　Manchester M3 ....158 D2
　Stockport SK3 ....169 D1
Ford Way SK14 ....103 A4
Ford's La SK7 ....131 C3
Fordbank Rd M20 ....110 A2
Fordham Gr BL1 ....144 C8
Fordland Cl WA3 ....74 E1
Fordoe La OL12 ....13 C4
Fordyce Way WN2 ....56 A8
Foreland Cl M40 ....157 D5
Forest Ave WN6 ....36 F3
Forest Cl SK16 ....101 C6
Forest Ct M41 ....94 D3
Forest Dr Altrincham WA15 ..119 F8
　Sale M33 ....107 E2
　Shevington Moor WN6 ...19 A2
　Westhoughton BL5 ......58 A8
Forest Gdns BL3 ....105 D3
Forest Range M19 ....99 A1
Forest Rd BL1 ....142 B3
Forest St Ashton-u-L OL6 ..166 C4
　Eccles M30 ....79 A4
　Oldham OL8 ....66 F7
Forest View OL12 ....14 D2
Forester Dr SK15 ....86 A1
Forester Hill Ave
　Bolton BL3 ....147 F3
　Bolton BL3 ....147 F3
Forester Hill Cl BL3 .....147 F3
Forfar St BL1 ....24 E6
Forge Ind Est OL4 ....67 B7
Forge La M11 ....160 F2
Forge St Oldham OL4 ....67 B7
Formby Ave M21 ....109 D7
Formby Dr SK8 ....131 B8
Formby Rd M6 ....80 E5
Forres Gr WN4 ....72 D4
Forrest Rd M34 ....101 B1
Forrester Dr OL2 ....49 D8
Forrester St M28 ....79 A8
Forshaw Ave M18 ....99 F6
Forshaw St M34 ....100 D4
Forster St WA3 ....90 A8
Forston Wlk M8 ....156 A6
Forsyth St OL12 ....13 E2
Forsythia Wlk 2 M31 ...105 E2
Forth Pl M26 ....43 F5
Forth Rd M26 ....43 F5
Fortescue Rd SK2 ....124 C7
Forth Pl M26 ....43 F5
Forton Ave BL2 ....42 E7
Forton Rd WN3 ....54 F2

Fortran Cl M5 ....81 A1
Fortrose Ave M9 ....64 B3
Fortuna Gr M19 ....110 F8
Fortune St BL3 ....148 B5
Fortyacre Dr Sk6 ....112 E3
Forum Gr M7 ....155 E5
Forum The SK6 ....113 C2
Fosbrook Ave M20 ......110 D4
Fossard Ave M23 ....121 B5
Fossgill Ave BL2 ....25 C5
Foster Ave WN3 ....151 E6
Foster Ct BL9 ....28 D4
Foster La BL2 ....25 F1
Foster St Denton M34 ...100 F3
　Oldham OL4 ....67 C7
　Radcliffe M26 ....43 F3
　Salford M5 ....154 D1
　6 Wigan WN6 ....37 A1
Foster Terr 1 BL1 ......143 E1
Fosters Bldgs WN6 .....150 B8
Fotherby Dr M9 ....64 C3
Fotherby Pl WN3 ....55 A3
Foul Clough Rd OL14 ....5 D8
Foulds Ave BL8 ....27 B2
Foundry La
　Manchester M4 ....159 B2
　Wigan WN3 ....54 D4
Foundry St Bolton BL3 ...145 F5
　Bury BL9 ....140 F2
　Dukinfield SK16 ....101 D8
　Heywood OL10 ....29 D2
　Leigh WN7 ....76 B4
　Little Lever BL3 ....43 A3
　Newton-le-W WA12 ......89 B3
　Oldham OL8 ....153 E6
　4 Radcliffe M26 ......44 A3
　Swinton M27 ....62 A1
Fountain Ave WA15 .....129 A2
Fountain Park 6 SK5 ....125 E4
Fountain St Poynton SK12 ..133 D4
　Whitefield M45 ....62 F7
Fountain St Ashton-u-L OL6 ..85 E4
　Bury BL8 ....27 C2
　Eccles M30 ....95 D8
　Hyde SK14 ....167 E3
　Manchester M2 ....159 A1
　Middleton M24 ....65 A8
　Oldham OL1 ....153 F6
Fountain St N BL9 ......141 A3
Fountain St S BL9 ....25 C1
Fountains Cl M29 ....77 C7
Fountains Rd
　Bramhall SK7,SK8 ......132 C6
　Stretford M32 ....95 F3
Fountains Wlk
　Dukinfield SK16 ....101 C6
　Golborne WA3 ....91 B8
　Oldham OL9 ....152 A5
Four Lane Ends BL2 .....25 E8
Four Lanes SK14 ....103 A4
Four Lanes End Rd OL13 ..3 B8
Four Lanes Way OL11 ...13 C2
Four Yards M2 ....158 F1
Fouracres WN2 ....56 F3
Fourways M17 ....96 A6
Fourth Ave
　Bolton BL1 ....144 B7
　Bury BL9 ....28 D4
　Droylsden M11 ....83 D1
　Mossley SK15 ....86 E6
　Oldham OL8 ....66 D2
　Stretford M17 ....96 D6
　Swinton M27 ....79 D5
　Trafford Park M17 ......96 A6
Fourways M17 ....96 A6
Fovant Cres SK5 ....111 E7
Fowey Wlk
　Hattersley SK14 ....102 E2
　5 Wythenshawe M23 ...121 A5
Fowler Ave M18 ....99 F6
Fowler Cl WN1 ....151 E8
Fowler Ind Pk BL6 ......22 C2
Fowler St OL8 ....66 F8
Fowley Common La WA3 ..92 C5
Fownhope Ave M33 ......107 F3
Foxall St 3 M24 ....65 C6
Fox Bank Ct SK3 ....170 E8
Fox Bench Cl SK7,SK8 ...132 C6
Fox Cl WA15 ....119 F6
Fox Hill OL2 ....48 E8
Fox Park Rd 5 OL8 ......66 C6
Fox Platt Rd OL5 ....68 B1
Fox Platt Terr OL5 ......86 C8
Fox St Bury BL9 ....140 F3
　Eccles M30 ....79 F2
　Heywood OL10 ....29 D2
　Horwich BL6 ....22 C2
　Milnrow OL16 ....31 E6
　Oldham OL8 ....66 C2
　Rochdale OL12 ....14 C2
　Stockport SK3 ....170 D8
Foxall Wlk M8 ....156 A6
Foxbank St M13 ....163 C6
Foxbench Wlk M21 ......109 D6
Foxcroft Cl 5 OL15 ......15 F3
Foxdale Ct 3 M41 ....83 C1
Foxdene Gr WN3 ....54 E3
Foxendale Wlk M5 ......161 A8
　Salford M5 ....161 A8
　Swinton M27 ....62 A1

Foxdenton Dr M32 ....95 F3
Foxdenton La M24,OL9 ...65 F6
Foxdenton Wlk M34 .....100 E1
Foxendale Wlk BL3 .....145 F5
Foxfield Cl BL8 ....27 B5
Foxfield Dr OL8 ....66 C1
Foxfield Gr WN6 ....36 B6
Foxfield Rd M23 ....121 A3
Foxford Wlk M22 ....121 E2
Foxglove Cl
　2 Golborne WA3 ....90 D8
　Standish WN6 ....19 D2
Foxglove Ct OL12 ....14 D3
Foxglove Dr
　Altrincham WA14 ....119 C8
　Bury BL9 ....28 D3
Foxglove La SK15 ....86 A3
Foxglove Wlk M31 ......105 E2
Foxhall Rd
　Altrincham WA15 ....119 F6
　Denton M34 ....100 D4
Foxham Wlk M7 ....155 E6
Foxhill WA14 ....119 A5
Foxhill Chase SK2 ....123 A6
Foxhill Dr SK15 ....102 C7
Foxhill Rd M30 ....78 F1
Foxholes Cl OL12 ....14 C3
Foxholes Rd Horwich BL6 ..22 D4
　Hyde SK14 ....113 C8
　Rochdale OL12 ....14 C2
Foxlair Ct M22 ....121 B3
Foxlair Rd M22 ....121 B3
Foxland Rd SK8 ....122 B4
Foxlea SK13 ....115 F8
Foxley Cl Droylsden M43 ..99 E8
　Lymm WA13 ....117 A2
Foxley Gr BL3 ....145 D6
Foxley Hall Mews WA14 ..117 A1
Foxley Wlk M12 ....165 A5
Foxton St M24 ....64 C7
Foxton Wlk 6 M23 .....121 A2
Foxwell Wlk 5 M8 ......156 A6
Foxwood Cl WN5 ....53 E5
Foxwood Dr SK15 ....68 D2
Foxwood Gdns M19 .....110 E5
Foy St WN4 ....73 B3
Foynes Cl M40 ....157 F8
Fram St Manchester M9 ..157 F8
　Salford M6 ....154 E2
Framingham Rd M33 ....108 B2
Framley Rd M20,M21 ...109 F7
Frampton Cl M24 ....65 B7
Frances Ave SK8 ....122 A2
Frances Ct 5 SK16 .....58 A2
Frances St Bolton BL1 ...143 D2
　Cheadle SK8 ....122 E6
　Denton M34 ....113 B8
　Dukinfield SK14 ....101 C3
　Irlam M44 ....105 C5
　Littleborough OL16 .....15 D4
　Manchester M13 ....163 B6
　Oldham OL1 ....49 B1
　7 Stockport SK1,SK3 ...170 E8
Frances St W SK14 .....101 C3
Francesca Wlk M18 .....99 E6
Francis Ave Eccles M30 ..79 E2
　Walkden M28 ....60 F2
Francis Rd Irlam M44 ...93 F1
　Manchester M20 ....110 C5
Francis St Eccles M30 ...79 F2
　Failsworth M35 ....83 F7
　Farnworth BL4 ....42 D1
　Hindley WN2 ....56 E5
　Leigh WN7 ....76 E5
　Manchester M3 ....158 D3
　Tyldesley M29 ....77 D8
Francis Terr 3 SK16 .....166 C1
Frandley Wlk 4 M13 ....158 D4
Frank Cowan Ct M7 .....158 D4
Frank Fold OL10 ....29 A2
Frank Perkins Way M44 ..105 F7
Frank St Bolton BL3 .....147 E4
　Bury BL9 ....140 F1
　Failsworth M35 ....83 E7
　Hyde SK14 ....167 E2
　3 Manchester M1 ......163 A7
　Salford M6 ....81 A4
Frank Swift Wlk 5 M14 ..98 A3
Frankby Cl M27 ....80 C7
Frankford Sq BL1 ....142 C2
Frankford Ave BL1 .....142 C2
Frankland Cl 1 Oldham OL11 ..160 A8
　Reddish M34 ....100 A2
Franklin St Eccles M30 ...79 D2
　Oldham OL11 ....160 A8
　Rochdale OL16 ....31 B5
Franklyn Ave M41 ....94 E2
Franklyn Rd M18 ....99 E6
Frankton Rd M45 ....62 F7
Franton Rd M11 ....83 B2
Fraser Ho BL1 ....143 D1
Fraser Pl M17 ....96 D5
Fraser Rd Manchester M8 ..63 F1
　Wigan WN5 ....54 B7
Fraser St Ashton-u-L OL6 ..166 C3
　Rochdale OL16 ....31 A4
　Swinton M27 ....62 A1
Fraternitas Terr M43 ....83 E3

Frawley Ave WA12 . . . . .89 C5
Freckleton Ave M21 . . . . . .109 C4
Freckleton Dr BL8 . . . . .43 F8
Freckleton St WN1 . . . . .37 C2
Fred Longworth High Sch
  M29 .58 E1
Fred Tilson Cl M14 . . . . .98 A3
Freda Wlk M11 . . . . .160 F1
Frederica Gdns WN2 . . . . . .56 A3
Frederick Ave OL2 . . . . . .149 B5
Frederick Ct BL4 . . . . .60 E8
Frederick Rd M6,M7 . . . . . .81 B4
Frederick St
  Ashton-in-M WN4 . . . . .73 A5
  Ashton-u-L OL6 . . . . .85 E2
  Denton M34 . . . . .100 F5
  Farnworth BL4 . . . . .60 D8
  Hindley WN2 . . . . .56 D5
  Ince-in-M WN3 . . . . .151 D6
  Littleborough OL15 . . . . . .16 A6
  Manchester M3 . . . . .158 E2
  Oldham OL8 . . . . .66 D4
  Oldham OL9 . . . . .152 B8
  Ramsbottom BL0 . . . . . . .138 B5
  Wigan WN1 . . . . .151 E8
Free La BB4 . . . . .1 A6
Freehold Com Prim Sch
  OL9 . . . . .152 C5
Freehold St OL11 . . . . .139 E5
Freeholds Rd OL12 . . . . .4 E6
Freeholds Terr OL12 . . . . . .4 E6
Freeland Wlk M11 . . . . . . .165 C8
Freelands M29 . . . . .59 C1
Freeman Ave OL6 . . . . .85 D3
Freeman Rd SK16 . . . . .101 C7
Freeman Sq M15 . . . . .163 A6
Freemantle St SK3 . . . . . . .170 D8
Freesia Ave 🟦 M20 . . . . . . .59 F3
Freestone Cl BL8 . . . . .140 D3
Freetown SK13 . . . . .116 C7
Freetown Cl M14 . . . . .98 A4
Freetrade St OL11 . . . . . . .139 E6
Freiston 🟦 OL12 . . . . .139 F8
Fremantle Ave M18 . . . . . . .99 D3
French Ave 🟦 Oldham OL1 . .49 C1
  Stalybridge SK15 . . . . .86 C1
French Barn La M9 . . . . . . .64 C2
French Gr BL3 . . . . .42 D5
French St Ashton-u-L OL6 . .85 D4
  Stalybridge SK15 . . . . .86 C1
Frenchwood Ct WN2 . . . . . .38 C1
Frensham Wlk M23 . . . . . .120 F4
Fresca Rd OL3 . . . . .49 D4
Fresh Ct SK13 . . . . .115 F7
Freshfield SK8 . . . . .131 B8
Freshfield Ave
  Atherton M46 . . . . .58 C4
  Bolton BL3 . . . . .147 D2
  Bolton BL3 . . . . .147 F2
  Hyde SK14 . . . . .167 D1
  Prestwich M25 . . . . .63 C6
Freshfield Cl
  Failsworth M35 . . . . .84 A6
  Romiley SK6 . . . . .114 B1
Freshfield Gr BL3 . . . . .147 F2
Freshfield Rd Hindley WN2 . .56 F5
  Manchester SK4 . . . . .110 F3
  Wigan WN2 . . . . .54 E3
Freshfields WN1 🔢 M11 . . .63 C2
Freshfields M26 . . . . .43 D5
Freshford Wlk 🟦 M22 . . . .121 B1
Freshville St M1 . . . . .163 B8
Freshwater Dr M34 . . . . . .113 B8
Freshwater St 🟦 M18 . . . . .99 E6
Freshwinds Ct OL4 . . . . . . .67 D4
Fresnel Cl SK14 . . . . .102 B6
Frew Cl M9 . . . . .65 B2
Frewland Ave SK3 . . . . . . .123 F4
Freya Gr M5 . . . . .161 C8
Friar's Cl SK9 . . . . .136 E8
Friar's Rd M33 . . . . .108 B4
Friarmere Rd OL3 . . . . .50 E5
Friars Cl Altrincham WA14 . .119 B1
  Tyldesley M29 . . . . .59 D6
Friars Cres OL11 . . . . .30 F2
Friars Ct M5 . . . . .80 A1
Friars Prim Sch The M3 . . .158 D3
Friendship Ave M18 . . . . . . .99 E4
Frieston Rd WA14 . . . . . . .119 E8
Friezland Cl SK15 . . . . .86 E6
Friezland La OL3 . . . . .69 A4
Friezland Prim Sch OL3 . . .68 E5
Frimley Gdns M22 . . . . . . .121 D3
Frinton Ave M40 . . . . .65 D3
Frinton Cl M33 . . . . .107 F1
Frinton Rd BL3 . . . . .146 B3
Frith Rd M20 . . . . .110 C5
Frith St WN6 . . . . .150 A7
Frobisher Cl M13 . . . . .164 D5
Frobisher Pl SK5 . . . . .169 E4
Frobisher Rd OL15 . . . . .6 C3
Frodsham Ave SK4 . . . . . . .168 C3
Frodsham Cl WN6 . . . . .36 D3
Frodsham Rd M33 . . . . . . .108 E2
Frodsham St 🟦 M14 . . . . . .98 B3
Frodsham Way SK9 . . . . . .131 E4
Frodsley Wlk M12 . . . . . . .164 F6
Frog La Wigan WN1,WN6 . .150 B8
  Wigan WN1 . . . . .37 A3
Frogley St BL2 . . . . .25 B3
Frogmore Ave SK14 . . . . . .115 A3
Frome Ave Stockport SK2 . .124 C5
  Urmston M41 . . . . .95 B1
Frome Cl M29 . . . . .77 C6
Frome Dr M8 . . . . .156 B7

Frome St OL4 . . . . .67 C6
Frost St Manchester M4 . . .160 D1
  Oldham OL8 . . . . .66 E4
Frostlands Rd 🔢 M16 . . . . .97 E4
Froxmer St M18 . . . . .165 C6
Fryent Cl BL6 . . . . .21 D2
Fulbeck Ave WN3 . . . . .55 A2
Fulbeck Wlk M8 . . . . .156 C5
Fulbrook Dr SK8 . . . . .132 A6
Fulbrook Way M29 . . . . . . .59 C1
Fulford St 🟦 M16 . . . . .97 C4
Fulham Ave M40 . . . . .83 B5
Fulham St OL4 . . . . .67 C6
Full Pot La OL11 . . . . .29 E8
Fullerton Rd SK4 . . . . .110 B6
Fulmar Cl Poynton SK12 . . .133 A4
  Westhoughton BL5 . . . . . . .57 B6
Fulmar Dr Hazel Grove SK2 .124 F5
  Sale M33 . . . . .107 C2
Fulmar Gdns OL11 . . . . . . .29 F7
Fulmards Cl SK9 . . . . .137 C7
Fulmead Wlk 🔢 M8 . . . . . .155 F6
Fulmer Dr M4 . . . . .159 C2
Fulmere Ct M27 . . . . .79 D6
Fulneck Sq 🟦 M43 . . . . . .100 A8
Fulshaw Ave SK9 . . . . .137 A6
Fulshaw CE Prim Sch
  SK9 . . . . .136 F6
Fulshaw Cross SK9 . . . . . .137 A5
Fulshaw Pk SK9 . . . . .137 A5
Fulshaw Pk S SK9 . . . . . . .137 A4
Fulshaw Wlk 🔢 M13 . . . . .163 B7
Fulstone Mews SK2 . . . . . .124 B6
Fulthorpe Wlk 🔢 M9 . . . . . .64 E5
Fulton Cl M15 . . . . .163 A5
Fulwell Ave M46 . . . . .76 E8
Fulwood Ave M9 . . . . .64 F4
Fulwood Cl BL8 . . . . .26 F1
Fulwood Rd M43 . . . . .90 E7
Furbarn La OL11 . . . . .29 D8
Furbarn Rd OL11 . . . . .29 D8
Furlong Cl WN2 . . . . .73 F7
Furlong Rd M22 . . . . .121 B3
Furnace St
  Dukinfield SK14 . . . . .101 C4
  Dukinfield SK16 . . . . .166 B2
Furness Ave
  Ashton-u-L OL7 . . . . .84 F5
  Bolton BL2 . . . . .25 D3
  Heywood OL10 . . . . .29 C3
  Littleborough OL15 . . . . . .16 A6
  Oldham OL8 . . . . .67 C3
  Whitefield M45 . . . . .63 A8
Furness Cl Glossop SK13 . .116 F8
  Milnrow OL16 . . . . .31 E6
  Poynton SK12 . . . . .133 D4
Furness Cres WN7 . . . . . . .57 D1
Furness Gr SK4 . . . . .168 A1
Furness Quay M5 . . . . . . .161 A7
Furness Rd Bolton BL1 . . . .144 B7
  Bramhall SK8 . . . . .132 C6
  Manchester M14 . . . . .98 C1
  Middleton M24 . . . . .47 A3
  Urmston M41 . . . . .95 D3
Furness Sq BL2 . . . . .25 B2
Furnival Cl M34 . . . . .100 A2
Furnival Rd M18 . . . . .165 C5
Furnival St Leigh WN7 . . . . .75 F7
  Reddish SK5 . . . . .99 F2
Furrow Com Prim Sch
  M24 . . . . .46 D2
Further Field OL11 . . . . . . .13 D1
Further Heights Rd 🔢
  OL12 . . . . .14 E8
Further Hey Cl OL4 . . . . . . .67 E7
Further La SK14 . . . . .102 E3
Further Pits OL11 . . . . .30 C7
Furtherwood Rd OL1 . . . . . .48 C1
Furze Ave BL5 . . . . .57 F7
Furze La OL4 . . . . .49 D1
Furze Wlk M31 . . . . .106 A3
Furzegate OL16 . . . . .31 C3
Fushia Gr M7 . . . . .155 D6
Fyfield Wlk 🔢 M8 . . . . . . .156 B6
Fylde Ave Bolton BL2 . . . . . .42 E7
  Gatley SK8 . . . . .131 C8
Fylde Cl M29 . . . . .108 C8
Fylde Rd SK4 . . . . .168 A2
Fylde St BL4 . . . . .42 D2
Fylde St E BL4 . . . . .42 D2

G

Gabbot St PR7 . . . . .21 A7
Gable Ave SK9 . . . . .137 A7
Gable Ct M34 . . . . .100 F2
Gable Dr M24 . . . . .46 E1
Gable St Bolton BL2 . . . . . . .25 D5
  Manchester M11 . . . . .164 F8
  Newton-le-W WA12 . . . . . . .89 B3
Gables The M33 . . . . .108 B3
Gabriel Wlk 🔢 M16 . . . . . . .97 F3
Gabriels Terr M24 . . . . .65 C7
Gabriels The OL2 . . . . .48 F7
Gadbury Ave M46 . . . . .58 B3
Gaddum Rd
  Altrincham WA14 . . . . . . .119 B1
  Manchester M20 . . . . .110 C3
Gadwell Cl M28 . . . . .78 D8
Gail Ave SK4 . . . . .169 D2
Gail Cl Alderley Edge SK9 . .137 B2
  Failsworth M35 . . . . .83 E5
Gainford Ave SK8 . . . . .122 B4
Gainford Gdns M40 . . . . . . .65 B1
Gainford Rd SK5 . . . . .99 F1
Gainford Wlk BL3 . . . . .147 E4

Gainsborough Ave
  Bolton BL3 . . . . .146 C3
  Manchester M20 . . . . .110 C5
  Marple SK6 . . . . .126 B8
  Oldham OL8 . . . . .66 E4
  Stretford M32 . . . . .96 F3
Gainsborough Cl
  Wigan WN3 . . . . .54 D3
  Wilmslow SK9 . . . . .137 D8
Gainsborough Dr
  Cheadle SK8 . . . . .122 F6
  Rochdale OL11 . . . . .30 E3
Gainsborough Rd
  Chadderton OL9 . . . . .47 E1
  Droylsden M34 . . . . .84 D1
  Ramsbottom BL0 . . . . .11 B1
Gainsborough St M7 . . . . .155 E7
Gainsborough Wlk
  Denton M34 . . . . .100 E1
  🟦 Dukinfield SK14 . . . . . .101 F5
Gair Rd SK5 . . . . .169 F4
Gair St SK14 . . . . .167 D4
Gairloch Ave M32 . . . . .96 B2
Gaitskell Cl M12 . . . . .160 E1
Galbraith Rd M20 . . . . . . .110 C3
Galbraith Way OL11 . . . . . . .29 E8
Gale Dr M24 . . . . .46 D2
Gale Rd M25 . . . . .62 F5
Gale St Heywood OL10 . . . .29 D2
  Rochdale OL12 . . . . .14 F3
Gales Terr OL11 . . . . .139 E5
Galgate Cl Bury BL8 . . . . . . .26 F1
  Manchester M15 . . . . .162 E7
Galindo St BL2 . . . . .25 C4
Galland St OL4 . . . . .67 D7
Galleria The 🔢 BL1 . . . . . .145 F7
Galleries The 🔢 WN1 . . . .150 C8
Galloway Cl Bolton BL3 . . . .40 E5
  Heywood OL10 . . . . .45 F8
Galloway Dr M27 . . . . .61 F5
Galloway Rd M27 . . . . .79 D6
Gallowsclough Rd SK15 . .102 E6
Galsworthy Ave M8 . . . . . .156 A6
Galvin Rd M9 . . . . .64 D3
Galway St OL1 . . . . .153 F6
Galway Wlk M23 . . . . .120 F2
Galwey Gr WN1 . . . . .37 C4
Gamble St WN7 . . . . .76 A5
Gambleside Cl M28 . . . . . . .78 B8
Gambrel Bank Rd OL6 . . . . .85 B6
Gambrel Gr OL6 . . . . .85 B6
Game St OL4 . . . . .67 C5
Games Wlk 🟦 M22 . . . . . .121 B1
Gamesley Cty Prim Sch
  SK13 . . . . .171 C2
Gamma Wlk M11 . . . . .83 B2
Gan Eden 🟦 M7 . . . . .63 E1
Gandy La OL12 . . . . .14 D4
Gantley Ave WN5 . . . . .53 D3
Gantley Cres WN5 . . . . .53 D3
Gantley Rd WN5 . . . . .53 D4
Gantock Wlk 🔢 M14 . . . . . .98 C3
Ganton Ave M45 . . . . .62 D7
Garbrook Ave M9 . . . . .64 C5
Garden Ave Droylsden M43 . .84 B2
  Stretford M32 . . . . .96 D3
Garden City BL0 . . . . .11 A2
Garden Cl OL15 . . . . .15 F2
Garden La
  Altrincham WA14 . . . . . . .119 D5
  Boothstown M28 . . . . .78 A6
  Manchester M3 . . . . .158 E2
  🟦 Manchester M3 . . . . . .158 F1
  🔢 Rochdale OL16 . . . . . . .31 A8
Garden Row Heywood OL10 . .29 C4
  Rochdale OL12 . . . . .14 D2
Garden St 🔢 Bacup OL13 . . . .3 C8
  Bury BL8 . . . . .26 F7
  Denton M34 . . . . .100 F6
  Eccles M30 . . . . .79 E1
  Farnworth BL4 . . . . .60 E8
  Heywood OL10 . . . . .29 D2
  Hyde SK14 . . . . .167 E4
  Manchester M4 . . . . .159 A2
  Newhey OL16 . . . . .32 B4
  Oldham OL8 . . . . .67 C7
  Ramsbottom BL0 . . . . .11 C3
  Stockport SK2 . . . . .124 C5
  Tyldesley M29 . . . . .77 A7
Garden Terr 🟦 OL2 . . . . . . .48 C7
Garden Wall Cl M5 . . . . . . .161 C8
Garden Way OL15 . . . . .15 F2
Garden Wlk
  Ashton-u-L OL6 . . . . .166 C4
  🔢 Denton M34 . . . . .101 A2
Gardens The Bolton BL1 . . .24 F6
  Salford M30 . . . . .80 A4
Gardner Grange SK5 . . . . .112 C4
Gardner Rd M30 . . . . .79 E2
Gardner Rd M25 . . . . .62 F4
Gardner St
  Manchester M12 . . . . .165 B6
  Salford M6 . . . . .81 A3
Garfield Ave M19 . . . . .99 B1
Garfield Cl OL11 . . . . .30 C7
Garfield Gr BL3 . . . . .145 D5
Garfield St Bolton BL3 . . . . .146 C3
  Stockport SK1 . . . . .112 A2
Garforth Ave M4 . . . . .159 C2
Garforth St OL9 . . . . .152 B8
Gargrave Ave BL1 . . . . .23 F2
Gargrave St Manchester M7 . .80 F8
  🟦 Oldham OL4 . . . . .67 B6
Garland Rd M22 . . . . .121 E3
Garlick St Hyde SK14 . . . . .167 F3
  Manchester M18 . . . . .99 D5

Garlick St continued
  Oldham OL9 . . . . .153 E6
Garnant Cl M9 . . . . .157 F8
Garner Ave WA15 . . . . .108 A1
Garner Cl WA14 . . . . .119 D2
Garner Dr Eccles M30 . . . . . .79 C3
  Salford M5 . . . . .154 D3
  Tyldesley M29 . . . . .77 B3
Garner's La SK3 . . . . .170 E5
Garnet St OL1 . . . . .67 B8
Garnett Cl SK14 . . . . .102 F3
Garnett Rd SK14 . . . . .102 F3
Garnett St Bolton BL1 . . . . .143 E3
  Ramsbottom BL0 . . . . . . .138 B5
  Stockport SK1 . . . . .169 F1
Garnett Way SK14 . . . . . . .102 F3
Garnham Wlk 🔢 M9 . . . . . .64 E5
Garratt Way M18 . . . . .165 C5
Garret Gr OL2 . . . . .149 C7
Garrett Hall Prim Sch
  M29 . . . . .77 D7
Garrett Hall Rd M28 . . . . . .77 E7
Garrett La M28,M29 . . . . . .77 D7
Garrett Wlk SK3 . . . . .123 C8
Garron Wlk 🔢 M22 . . . . . .121 A4
Garrowmore Wlk 🟦 M9 . . . .64 E3
Garsdale La BL1 . . . . .40 D7
Garside Ave M43 . . . . .84 C1
Garside Cl OL11 . . . . .142 C2
Garside Hey Rd BL8 . . . . . . .27 C6
Garside St Bolton BL1 . . . . .145 E7
  Denton M34 . . . . .100 F5
  Hyde SK14 . . . . .167 E1
Garstang Ave BL2 . . . . .42 F7
Garstang Dr BL8 . . . . .26 F1
Garston Cl Leigh WN7 . . . . .57 E1
  Manchester SK4 . . . . .168 A3
Garston St BL9 . . . . .141 A4
Garswood Cres WN5 . . . . . .71 E4
Garswood Cty Prim Sch
  WN4 . . . . .72 C4
Garswood Dr BL8 . . . . .27 B3
Garswood Old Rd
  WA11,WN4 . . . . .71 E1
Garswood Rd Billinge WN5 . .71 F4
  Bolton BL3 . . . . .147 E2
  Manchester M14 . . . . .98 C3
  Manchester M14 . . . . .98 B5
Garswood St WN4 . . . . .73 B3
Garswood Sta WN4 . . . . . . .73 B2
Garth Ave WA15 . . . . .119 E6
Garth Hts SK9 . . . . .137 C7
Garth Rd Marple SK6 . . . . .126 A6
  Stockport SK2 . . . . .124 C7
  Wythenshawe M22 . . . . . .121 D4
Garth The M5 . . . . .154 D2
Garthland Rd SK7 . . . . .124 F3
Garthmere Rd M46 . . . . .58 F5
Garthorne Cl M16 . . . . .97 D4
Garthorp Rd M23 . . . . .120 E7
Garthwaite Ave OL8 . . . . . .66 E4
Gartland Wlk M8 . . . . .156 C8
Garton Dr WA3 . . . . .74 E1
Gartside St 🔢 M9 . . . . .64 E5
Gartside Ave Ashton-u-L OL7 . .84 E1
  Delph OL3 . . . . .50 E4
Garton St SK5 . . . . .169 E4
  Oldham OL4 . . . . .67 D8
Garwick Rd BL1 . . . . .142 B3
Garwood St WN5 . . . . .162 F7
Gas St Adlington PR7 . . . . . .21 A6
  Ashton-u-L OL6 . . . . .166 B3
  Bolton BL1 . . . . .145 E7
  Farnworth BL4 . . . . .60 D8
  🔢 Heywood OL10 . . . . . . .29 D2
  Hollingworth SK14 . . . . . .103 D5
  Leigh WN7 . . . . .75 E3
  Platt Bridge WN2 . . . . .56 A2
  Rochdale OL11 . . . . .139 E7
  Stockport SK4 . . . . .169 E1
Gascoyne St M14 . . . . .98 B3
Gaskell Cl OL15 . . . . .16 A4
Gaskell Cty Prim Sch
  BL1 . . . . .145 E8
Gaskell Rd
  Altrincham WA14 . . . . . . .119 D6
  Eccles M30 . . . . .79 E1
Gaskell Rise OL1 . . . . .49 E5
Gaskell St 🔢 Bolton BL1 . . .145 E8
  🔢 Dukinfield SK16 . . . . . .166 B3
  Failsworth M40 . . . . .83 D6
  Hindley WN2 . . . . .56 E7
  Swinton M27 . . . . .61 F2
  Wigan WN3 . . . . .150 A8
Gaskell's Brow WN4 . . . . . .72 E5
Gaskill St OL10 . . . . .29 A2
Gaston Wlk M9 . . . . .157 E8
Gatcombe Mews 🔢 SK9 . .137 A6
Gatcombe Sq M14 . . . . .98 B3
Gate Ctte The SK6 . . . . . . .112 F6
Gate Field Cl M26 . . . . .43 F5
Gate Keeper Fold OL7 . . . . .85 A7
Gate Rd M23 . . . . .96 A4
Gate St Dukinfield SK16 . . .101 A6
  Manchester M11 . . . . .165 B8
  Rochdale OL11 . . . . .139 F5
Gate Stirrup M28 . . . . .77 A5
Gateacre Wlk M23 . . . . . . .120 E8
Gategill Gr WN5 . . . . .53 D3
Gatehead Croft OL3 . . . . . .50 F3
Gatehead Rd OL3 . . . . .50 F3
Gatehead Mews OL3 . . . . . .50 F3
Gatehead Rd OL3 . . . . .50 F3
Gatehouse Rd M28 . . . . . . .60 B3
Gatemere Cl M28 . . . . .78 B8
Gatesgarth Rd M24 . . . . . . .46 C2

Gateshead Cl M14 . . . . .98 B4
Gateside Wlk 🔢 M9 . . . . . .64 E5
Gateway Cres OL9 . . . . .65 E4
Gateway Ind Est M1 . . . . . .159 B1
Gateway Rd M18 . . . . .165 C6
Gateways The M27 . . . . .61 F1
Gathill Cl SK8 . . . . .122 F1
Gathurst La WN5,WN6 . . . .36 A4
Gathurst Rd Orrell WN5 . . . .53 C2
  Orrell WN5 . . . . .53 E8
Gathurst St M18 . . . . .99 E6
Gathurst Sta WN5 . . . . .36 A3
Gatley Ave M14 . . . . .98 A1
Gatley Brow OL1 . . . . .153 E8
Gatley Gn SK8 . . . . .122 A5
Gatley Prim Sch SK8 . . . . .122 A5
Gatley Rd Cheadle SK8 . . . .122 C5
  Sale M33 . . . . .108 B3
Gatley Sta SK8 . . . . .122 B5
Gatling Ave M12 . . . . .99 B2
Gatwick Ave M23 . . . . .121 B6
Gavel Wlk M24 . . . . .46 E1
Gavin Ave M5 . . . . .81 A1
Gawsworth Ave M20 . . . . .110 C1
Gawsworth Cl
  Altrincham M23,WA15 . . . .120 D6
  Bramhall SK7 . . . . .132 E6
  Hadfield SK13 . . . . .104 A5
  Poynton SK12 . . . . .133 F2
  Shaw OL2 . . . . .48 F7
  Stockport SK3 . . . . .170 D5
Gawsworth Mews SK8 . . . .122 B5
Gawsworth Pl M22 . . . . . . .121 F1
Gawsworth Rd
  Golborne WA3 . . . . .73 F1
  Sale M33 . . . . .108 A1
Gawsworth Way
  🔢 Denton M34 . . . . .101 A1
  Handforth SK9 . . . . .131 E4
Gawthorpe Cl BL9 . . . . .45 A5
Gaydon Rd M33 . . . . .107 D4
Gayford Wlk 🔢 M9 . . . . . . .64 E5
Gaythorn St M3,M5 . . . . . . .81 C1
Gaythorne Ave BL2 . . . . . . .25 E3
Gayton Cl WN3 . . . . .54 D3
Gayton Wlk 🔢 M40 . . . . . . .65 D2
Gaywood Wlk M40 . . . . . . .156 C6
Gee Cross Fold SK14 . . . . .113 E7
Gee Cross Holy Trinity
  CE Prim Sch SK14 . . . . . .113 E8
Gee La Eccles M30 . . . . .79 B3
  🔢 Oldham OL8 . . . . .66 B2
Gee St SK3 . . . . .170 D7
Geinsbury Cl OL8 . . . . .67 D4
Gelder Clough
  Residential Cvn Pk OL10 . .29 C5
Gellert Pl BL5 . . . . .57 E6
Gellert Rd BL5 . . . . .57 E6
Gellfield La OL3 . . . . .51 D1
Gemini Rd M6 . . . . .81 C4
Gencoyne Dr BL1 . . . . .24 D6
Gendre Rd BL7 . . . . .24 E8
Geneva Rd SK7 . . . . .123 E3
Geneva Terr OL11 . . . . .30 C8
Geneva Wlk
  🔢 Manchester M8 . . . . . .156 B6
  Oldham OL9 . . . . .152 C6
Genista Gr M7 . . . . .155 D6
Geo Hampson's Bldgs
  WA3 . . . . .92 C8
Geoff Bent Wlk M40 . . . . . . .83 A5
Geoffrey St Atherton BL5 . . .58 F8
  Bury BL9 . . . . .141 A4
  Ramsbottom BL0 . . . . .11 A4
George Barton St 🟦 BL2 . .25 B1
George Cl 🟦 SK16 . . . . . . .166 B1
George H Carnall
  Sports Ctr M41 . . . . .95 E4
George La SK6 . . . . .113 A4
George Leigh St M4 . . . . . .159 B2
George Mann Cl M22 . . . . .121 C1
George Rd BL0 . . . . .138 B5
George Richards Way
  WA14 . . . . .119 C7
George Sq OL1 . . . . .153 E6
George St
  Alderley Edge SK9 . . . . . .137 A1
  Altrincham WA14 . . . . . . .119 D4
  Ashton-in-M WN4 . . . . .73 C4
  Ashton-u-L OL6 . . . . .166 C3
  🟦 Atherton M46 . . . . .58 D3
  Bacup OL13 . . . . .3 C8
  Bury BL9 . . . . .140 F2
  Chadderton OL9 . . . . .152 A7
  Denton M34 . . . . .101 A3
  Eccles M30 . . . . .79 C2
  Failsworth M35 . . . . .83 F8
  Farnworth BL4 . . . . .60 D7
  Glossop SK13 . . . . .116 C8
  Heywood OL10 . . . . .29 B3
  Hindley WN2 . . . . .56 E6
  Horwich BL6 . . . . .22 C3
  Ince-in-M WN2 . . . . .151 F7
  Irlam M44 . . . . .94 B3
  🟦 Littleborough OL15 . . . .16 B5
  Littleborough OL16 . . . . . .15 F3
  Manchester M1 . . . . .163 A8
  Manchester M25 . . . . .63 B1
  Milnrow OL16 . . . . .31 F5
  Mossley OL5 . . . . .68 C1
  Newton-le-W WA12 . . . . . . .89 A4
  Oldham OL1 . . . . .153 E6
  Radcliffe M26 . . . . .44 D3
  Rochdale OL16 . . . . .15 B1
  Romiley SK6 . . . . .114 B2
  Shaw OL2 . . . . .149 C8
  🟦 Stalybridge SK15 . . . . . .86 A2
  Stockport SK1 . . . . .123 A2

George St *continued*
Urmston M41 95 E2
Westhoughton BL5 57 F8
Whitefield M45 44 E1
Whitworth OL12 14 C8
George St E SK1 124 B8
George St N M7 155 F8
George St S M7 155 F8
George St W SK1 124 B8
George Thomas Ct M9 157 D8
George Tomlinson Sch BL4 60 E6
George's Cl SK12 133 E3
George's La BL6 22 E5
George's Rd Sale M33 108 B3
Stockport SK4 169 D2
George's Rd E SK12 133 E3
George's Rd W SK12 133 E3
George's Row 2 BB4 2 F8
George's Terr WN5 53 D5
Georges La WN1 151 F8
Georgette Dr M3 158 E3
Georgian Ct 5 Leigh WN7 76 B4
12 Tyldesley M29 58 F1
Georgian Sq 2 WN2 56 A2
Georgiana St 2 Bury BL9 140 F1
3 Farnworth BL4 42 B2
Georgina Ct BL3 146 B3
Georgina St BL3 146 B3
Gerald Ave M8 156 A8
Gerald Rd M6,M7 81 B5
Gerard St WN4 73 B3
Germain Cl M9 64 C5
Gerrard Ave WA15 120 A8
Gerrard Cl WN2 38 D2
Gerrard Rd WN5 71 E5
Gerrard St Farnworth BL4 60 E8
Leigh WN7 75 F5
Rochdale OL11 31 A2
2 Salford M6 81 A3
Stalybridge SK15 86 B1
5 Westhoughton BL5 39 E1
Gerrards Cl M44 94 A2
Gerrards Gdns SK14 113 E7
Gerrards Hollow SK14 113 D7
Gerrardswood SK14 113 D7
Gertrude Cl M5 161 A8
Gertrude St OL12 4 E6
Gervis Cl M40 157 D5
Ghyll Gr Billinge WA11 71 B7
Walkden M28 60 E2
Giants Hall Rd WN6 36 E3
Gib Fold M46 58 D4
Gib La M23 121 C8
Gibb La SK6 126 E5
Gibb Rd M28 79 B7
Gibbon Ave M22 121 D2
Gibbon St Bolton BL3 145 D5
Droylsden M11 83 A2
Gibbon's Rd WN4 72 D3
Gibbs St M3 158 D1
Gibraltar La M34 113 B8
Gibraltar St Bolton BL3 145 D6
Oldham OL4 67 D5
Gibsmere Cl M23,WA15 120 D6
Gibson Ave M18 99 F6
Gibson Gr M28 60 A3
Gibson La M28 60 A3
Gibson Pl M4 159 A3
Gibson St Bolton BL2 25 C1
Leigh WN2 56 D1
Oldham OL4 67 C6
Rochdale OL16 31 C8
Gibson Terr OL7 166 A1
Gibson Way WA14 119 C8
Gibsons Rd SK4 168 B4
Gibwood Rd M22 121 C8
Gidlow Ave Adlington PR6 21 A7
Wigan WN6 37 A2
Gidlow La WN6 37 A2
Gidlow New Hos WN6 37 A4
Gidlow St 4 Hindley WN2 56 D6
Manchester M18 99 E6
Gifford Ave M9 64 F4
Gifford Pl WN2 56 F4
Gifford Wlk SK7 124 A2
Gigg La BL9 44 F8
Gilbert Rd WA15 119 E1
Gilbert St Eccles M30 95 B8
Hindley WN2 56 D5
Manchester M15 162 E7
Ramsbottom BL0 1 C1
Salford M6 154 F1
Walkden M28 60 D1
Gilbertbank SK6 113 B4
Gilbrook Way OL16 31 B2
Gilchrist Rd M44 105 F6
Gilda Brook Rd M30 80 A2
Gilda Cres M30 80 A3
Gilda Rd M28 77 F7
Gilded Hollins Prim Sch WN7 75 C1
Gilden Wlk 11 M9 64 E5
Gildenhall M35 84 A7
Gilderdale Cl OL2 149 B8
Gilderdale St 7 BL3 42 A4
Gildersdale Dr M9 64 C6
Gildridge Rd M16 97 E1
Giles St M12 99 A4
Gilesgate 3 M14 98 C3
Gill Ave WN6 36 B6
Gill St Manchester M9 64 F1
Stockport SK1 112 B3
Gillan Rd WN6 37 B3
Gillbent Rd SK8 132 A7
Gillbrook Rd M20 110 B2
Gillbrow Cres WN1 37 F1
Gillemere Gr OL2 149 C7
Gillers Gn M28 60 C3
Gillford Ave M9 157 F8
Gilliburns Wlk BL5 57 F5
Gillingham Rd M30 79 B2
Gillingham Sq M11 164 F8
Gillwood Dr SK6 112 F1
Gilman Cl M9 64 C2
Gilman St M9 64 C2
Gilmerton Dr 22 M40 83 C5
Gilmore Dr M25 63 B5
Gilmore St SK3 170 E7
Gilmour St M24 65 A8
Gilmour Terr M9 64 F1
Gilnow Cty Prim Sch BL1 144 C6
Gilnow Gdns BL1 144 C6
Gilnow Gr BL1 145 D6
Gilnow La BL3 145 D6
Gilnow Rd BL1 144 C6
Gilpin Pl WN2 55 F2
Gilpin Rd M41 95 F2
Gilpin Wlk M24 46 E1
Gilroy St WN1 151 D8
Giltbrook Ave M40 160 D4
Gilwell Dr M23 120 F4
Gilwood Gr M24 46 F4
Gin Croft La BL0 1 E4
Gingham Brow BL6 22 E4
Gingham Ct 7 M26 44 C4
Gingham Pk M26 43 E5
Gipsy La Stockport SK2 124 C6
Stockport SK2 124 D6
Girton Ave WN4 72 F4
Girton St Bolton BL2 42 D7
Manchester M7 158 E4
Girton Wlk M40 65 D1
Girvan Ave M40 65 D2
Girvan Cl BL3 146 C3
Girvan Cres WN4 72 D4
Girvan Wlk OL10 28 F1
Gisborn Dr M6 81 A5
Gisburn Ave Bolton BL1 23 E2
Golborne WA3 73 F2
Gisburn Dr BL8 26 E3
Gisburn Rd OL11 31 A3
Gisburne Ave M40 65 D2
Gissing Wlk M9 157 D6
Givendale Dr M8 64 A2
Givvons Fold 10 OL4 49 D1
Glabyn Ave BL6 39 F8
Gladden Hey Dr WN3 54 D1
Glade Brow OL4 68 A6
Glade St BL1 144 C7
Glade The Bolton BL1 143 D1
Shevington WN6 36 B6
Stockport SK4 168 A1
Gladeside Rd M22 121 C4
Gladewood Cl SK9 137 C8
Gladstone Cl
6 Bolton BL1 143 E2
Glossop SK13 116 D8
Gladstone Cres OL11 31 A3
Gladstone Ct
Farnworth BL4 42 C1
Manchester M15 97 E4
Manchester SK4 168 B3
Gladstone Gr SK4 168 A3
Gladstone Mews SK4 169 E3
Gladstone Pl BL4 42 C1
Gladstone Rd
Altrincham WA14 119 D6
Eccles M30 79 E2
Farnworth BL4 42 D1
Urmston M41 95 E2
Gladstone St Bolton BL1 143 E2
Bury BL9 141 B3
Glossop SK13 116 D8
Hadfield SK13 104 A4
Oldham OL4 67 B6
Pendlebury M27 80 B8
Stockport SK2 124 C4
Westhoughton BL5 39 E1
Gladstone Terrace Rd OL3 69 A4
Gladville Dr SK8 123 A6
Gladwyn Ave M20 109 E4
Gladys St 3 Farnworth BL4 42 D2
Manchester M16 97 C4
Glaisdale OL4 67 D6
Glaisdale Cl
Ashton-in-M WN4 73 C3
Bolton BL2 25 B2
Glaisdale St BL2 25 B2
Glaister La BL2 25 D1
Glamis Ave Droylsden M11 83 B3
Heywood OL10 46 F8
Stretford M32 96 A2
Glamis Cl WN7 76 D6
Glamorgan Pl OL9 152 C5
Glandon Dr SK8 132 C8
Glanford Ave M9 64 A3
Glanton Wlk M40 65 D1
Glanvor Rd SK3 123 C8
Glass St BL4 60 E7
Glassbrook St WN6 37 A1
Glasscroft Cl M14 97 F2
Glasshouse St 7 M4 159 C3
Glasson Wlk OL9 152 A6
Glastonbury 23 OL12 139 E8
Glastonbury Ave
Altrincham WA15 120 B2
Bramhall SK8 132 C6
Golborne WA3 91 C8
Glastonbury Dr SK12 133 D5
Glastonbury Gdns M26 43 E5
Glastonbury Rd
Tyldesley M29 77 B7
Urmston M32 95 F3
Glaswen Gr SK5 169 F4
Glaze Wlk M45 45 C2
Glazebrook Cl OL10 29 C1
Glazebrook La WA3 105 B5
Glazebrook Sta WA3 105 B5
Glazebury CE Prim Sch WA3 92 C7
Glazebury Dr
Westhoughton BL5 39 F2
Wythenshawe M23 121 B5
Glazedale Ave OL2 48 C5
Glaziers La WA3 91 D2
Gleave St 10 Bolton BL1 145 F8
Sale M33 108 B6
Gleaves Ave BL2 26 A4
Gleaves Rd M30 79 E1
Glebe Ave WN4 73 C2
Glebe Cl WN6 19 F1
Glebe End St WN6 150 B8
Glebe House M24 47 A2
Glebe House Sch OL16 139 E6
Glebe La OL1 49 E4
Glebe Rd Standish WN6 19 F1
Urmston M41 95 D2
Glebe St Ashton-u-L OL6 166 C3
Bolton BL2 148 A6
Hindley WN2 57 C2
Leigh WN7 75 F6
Oldham OL9 66 A3
Radcliffe M26 44 B3
Shaw OL2 149 B7
Stockport SK1 112 A1
Westhoughton BL5 39 E1
Glebeland WA3 91 E2
Glebeland Rd BL3 144 B5
Glebelands Rd
Prestwich M25 63 B5
Sale M33 108 A6
Wythenshawe M23 120 F6
Gleden St Manchester M40 160 E2
Manchester M40 160 E3
Gledhall St SK15 86 A2
Gledhill Ave M5 161 B7
Gledhill Cl OL2 32 A1
Gledhill St M20 110 B7
Gledhill Way BL7 9 A1
Glegg St WN2 151 F8
Glemsford Cl
Failsworth M40 83 B6
Wigan WN3 55 B3
Glen Ave Bolton BL3 144 B5
Kearsley BL4 61 B6
Manchester M9 64 F1
Sale M33 108 A6
Swinton M27 79 D8
Worsley M28 79 A8
Glen Bott St BL1 143 D2
Glen Cl WA3 105 B2
Glen Cres OL13 3 A8
Glen Dr WN6 35 E8
Glen Gdns OL12 14 F2
Glen Gr Middleton M24 65 C7
Royton OL2 48 D5
Glen Maye M33 108 C4
Glen Rd Oldham OL4 67 C6
Rawtenstall BB4 2 F8
Glen Rise WA15 120 A5
Glen Royd 1 OL12 14 C1
Glen St Bacup OL13 3 E8
Ramsbottom BL0 138 B7
Salford M5 161 A7
Glen The Bolton BL1 40 E7
Middleton M24 65 B6
Glen Trad Est OL4 67 D6
Glen View
Littleborough OL15 16 C7
Royton OL2 48 D5
Glenacre Gdns M18 99 E3
Glenarm Wlk M22 121 E2
Glenart M30 79 E3
Glenavon Dr
Rochdale OL12 14 D3
Shaw OL2 48 F8
Glenbarry Cl M13 163 B6
Glenbarry St M12 164 D8
Glenbeck Rd M45 44 E1
Glenboro Ave BL8 27 C2
Glenborough Ave OL13 3 C8
Glenbourne Pk SK7 132 D5
Glenbranter Ave WN2 56 A8
Glenbrook Gdns BL4 42 D2
Glenbrook Hill SK13 104 C2
Glenbrook Rd M9 64 A5
Glenburn St BL3 147 D3
Glenby Ave M22 121 F3
Glencar BL5 57 D7
Glencar Dr 8 M40 65 D2
Glencastle Rd M18 99 C4
Glencoe BL2 148 B7
Glencoe Cl OL10 28 F1
Glencoe Dr Bolton BL2 42 F6
Sale M33 107 C2
Glencoe Pl OL11 139 D7
Glencoe St 3 OL8 66 C2
Glencross Ave M21 97 A2
Glendale M27 62 B2
Glendale Ave
Ashton-in-M WN4 73 C4
Manchester M19 110 F6
Whitefield BL9 44 F3
Glendale Cl
Boothstown M28 77 F7
8 Heywood OL10 29 D2
Glendale Ct OL8 66 F4
Glendale Dr BL3 40 F6
Glendale Rd
Boothstown M28 77 F7
Salford M30 80 A3
Glenden Foot OL12 14 D2
Glendene Ave
Bramhall SK7 132 D5
Droylsden M43 84 C3
Glendevon Cl Bolton BL3 40 F5
Ince-in-M WN2 56 A8
Glendevon Pl M45 63 B7
Glendinning St M6 154 E2
Glendon Cres OL6 85 B7
Glendon Ct OL1 49 E4
Glendore M5 80 C2
Glendower Dr M40 156 C5
Gleneagles BL3 40 F3
Gleneagles Ave
10 Droylsden M11 83 C2
Heywood OL10 46 D8
Gleneagles Cl
Bramhall SK7 133 A7
Wilmslow SK9 137 D8
Gleneagles Rd Gatley SK8 122 C1
Urmston M41 94 F3
Gleneagles Way BL0 138 B5
Glenfield WA14 119 B4
Glenfield Cl OL4 67 D6
Glenfield Dr SK12 133 D3
Glenfield Rd SK4 169 D4
Glenfield Sq 2 BL4 42 B2
Glenfyne Rd M6 80 D5
Glengarth OL3 69 B7
Glengarth Dr BL1,BL6 40 C6
Glenham Ct 1 M15 97 E4
Glenhaven Ave M41 95 C2
Glenholme Rd SK7 132 D7
Glenhurst Rd M19 110 E5
Glenilla Ave M28 78 E7
Glenlea Dr M20 122 B8
Glenluce Wlk BL3 40 E5
Glenmaye Gr WN2 57 A5
Glenmere Cl M25 62 F6
Glenmere Rd M20 122 C8
Glenmoor Rd 2 SK1 112 A1
Glenmore Ave
Farnworth BL3,BL4 42 A2
Manchester M20 109 E4
Glenmore Bglws SK16 101 C7
Glenmore Cl Bolton BL3 40 E5
Rochdale OL11 29 E5
Glenmore Dr
Failsworth M35 84 B8
Manchester M8 156 B7
Glenmore Gr SK16 101 C8
Glenmore Rd BL0 10 F2
Glenmore St BL9 140 E1
Glenolden St M11 83 D2
Glenpark WN7 76 B6
Glenpark Wlk 5 M9 157 E7
Glenridding Cl OL1 49 A1
Glenridge Cl BL1 143 F2
Glenroy Wlk 15 M9 64 E5
Glensdale Dr M40 65 E1
Glenshee Dr BL3 40 F5
Glenside WN6 18 B2
Glenside Ave M18 99 D3
Glenside Dr Bolton BL3 147 F2
Romiley SK6 113 B5
Wilmslow SK9 137 C6
Glenside Gdns M35 84 B7
Glenside Gr M28 60 E3
Glent View SK15 86 A4
Glenthorn Gr M33 108 B3
Glenthorn Rd M9 64 D6
Glenthorne Dr OL7 166 A4
Glenthorne St 16 BL1 143 E1
Glentress Mews BL1 144 A8
Glentrool Mews BL1 144 A7
Glenvale Cl M26 44 B3
Glenville Way M34 101 A2
Glenville Wlk 13 SK15 86 A1
Glenwood Ave 2 SK14 101 D5
Glenwood Dr
Manchester M9 157 E7
Middleton M24 47 C1
Glenwood Gr SK2 124 B4
Glenwyn Ave M9 64 E4
Globe Cl M16 162 D5
Globe Ind Est M26 44 B3
Globe La Bolton BL7 8 D3
Dukinfield SK16 101 B7
Globe Lane Ind Est SK16 101 B8
Globe Lane Prim Sch SK16 101 B6
Globe Sq SK16 101 A7
Glodwick OL4 67 B5
Glodwick Inf Sch OL4 67 B5
Glodwick Rd OL4 67 B6
Glossop Brook Rd SK13 104 B1
Glossop Central Sta SK13 104 C1
Glossop Dale Com Coll
Glossop SK13 104 C2
Hadfield SK13 104 A4
Glossop Heritage Ctr SK13 104 C1
Glossop Rd
Charlesworth SK13 115 D7
Romiley SK14,SK6 114 D3
Rowarth SK13,SK22 116 C1
Glossop Way WN2 56 F4
Gloster St 5 BL2 148 A7
Gloucester Ave
Golborne WA3 90 B8
Heywood OL10 46 C8
Horwich BL6 22 D2
Littleborough OL12 15 D4
Manchester M19 111 B8
Marple SK6 125 F6
Whitefield M45 63 A8
Gloucester Cl OL6 85 D8
Gloucester Cres WN2 56 E6
Gloucester Ct BL6 22 D2
Gloucester Dr Diggle OL3 51 C4
Sale M33 107 D4
Gloucester Pl Atherton M46 58 D4
1 Salford M6 81 A3
Gloucester Rd
Droylsden M43 84 A3
Gatley SK8 131 C7
Hyde SK14 113 E8
Middleton M24 65 B6
Poynton SK12 133 D4
Reddish M34 100 A2
Salford M6 80 C4
Urmston M41 95 D1
Wigan WN5 54 C6
Gloucester Rise SK16 102 A7
Gloucester St Atherton M46 58 D3
1 Manchester M1 162 F7
Salford M5 161 C8
Salford M6 81 A4
Stockport SK3 170 D7
Gloucester St N OL9 152 C5
Gloucester Way SK13 116 F8
Glover Ave M8 156 B6
Glover Ct M7 155 F8
Glover Field M7 155 D6
Glover St Horwich BL6 22 B4
Leigh WN7 75 C8
Newton-le-W WA12 89 C3
Glyn Ave WA15 120 A2
Glyneath Cl M11 164 F8
Glyniss Cl SK3 170 F6
Glynn Gdns M20 109 D4
Glynne St BL4 60 C8
Glynrene Dr M27 61 C1
Glynwood Pk BL4 42 C1
GMB National Coll M16 97 D2
GMex Sta M1 162 F8
Goadsby St M4 159 A2
Goats Gate Terr M45 44 D2
Godbert Ave M21 109 C5
Goddard La Hadfield SK13 104 A6
Rowarth SK22 127 E7
Goddard Rd SK13 104 A4
Goddard St OL8 66 F4
Godfrey Ave M43 83 D3
Godfrey Ermen Meml CE Prim Sch M30 95 C8
Godfrey Range M18,M34 99 F4
Godfrey Rd M6 80 C5
Godlee Dr M27 79 E7
Godley Cl M11 165 C8
Godley Ct SK14 167 F2
Godley Hill SK14 102 B2
Godley Hill Rd SK14 102 B3
Godley Prim Sch SK14 167 F3
Godley St SK14 167 F4
Godley Sta SK14 102 A3
Godmond Hall Dr M28 77 F5
Godson St OL1 48 E1
Godward Rd SK22 127 B1
Godwin St M18 99 E6
Goit Pl OL16 139 F7
Golborne (All Saints) RC Prim Sch WA3 90 B8
Golborne Ave M20 109 F7
Golborne Cty Prim Sch WA3 90 A8
Golborne Dale Rd WA12 90 A5
Golborne Ent Pk WA3 74 A1
Golborne Gallery 9 WN1 150 C8
Golborne Ho 3 BL1 145 F8
Golborne Pl WN1 151 E8
Golborne Rd
Ashton-in-M WA3,WN4 73 E4
Golborne WA3 90 C8
Golborne St WA12 89 E4
Golbourne High Sch WA3 74 C1
Golbourne St Thomas' CE Jun & Inf Sch WA3 74 B1
Gold St M1 159 A1
Goldborne Ho OL2 149 B8
Goldbourne Dr OL2 149 B8
Goldbrook Cl 2 OL10 29 E1
Goldcraft Cl 4 OL10 29 E1
Goldcrest Cl
Boothstown M28 78 B7
Wythenshawe M22 121 F5
Golden St Eccles M30 79 D1
Shaw OL2 49 E8
Goldenhill Ave M11 83 C3
Goldenways WN1 37 C2
Goldfinch Dr BL9 141 C4
Goldfinch Way M43 84 C3
Goldie Ave M22 121 F2
Goldrill Ave BL2 42 F8
Goldrill Gdns BL2 42 F8
Goldsmith Ave Oldham OL1 49 E4
Salford M5 154 D2
Goldsmith Pl WN3 55 A4
Goldsmith Rd SK5 99 E1
Goldsmith St BL3 147 D4
Goldsmith Way 8 M34 113 A7
Goldstein Rd BL6 40 B4
Goldswcrthy Rd M41 94 E2
Goldwick Wlk M23 108 E1
Golf Rd Altrincham WA15 119 F3
Sale M33 108 F4
Golfview Dr M30 79 D4
Gooch Dr WA12 89 D2
Gooch St BL6 22 C2
Good Shepherd Cl OL16 31 B8
Goodacre SK14 102 B6

Gooden St OL10 .....29 E1
Goodier St
  Manchester M40 .....160 F4
  Sale M33 .....108 A4
Goodier View SK14 .....101 F5
Goodiers Dr M5 .....161 B8
Goodison Cl BL9 .....45 B3
Goodlad St BL8 .....27 B4
Goodman St M9 .....64 E1
Goodrich 3 OL11 .....139 E6
Goodridge Ave M22 .....121 C1
Goodrington Rd SK9 .....131 E3
Goodshaw Rd M28 .....78 C8
Goodwill Cl M27 .....79 F7
Goodwin Ct OL9 .....146 B4
Goodwin Sq M9 .....157 D7
Goodwin St BL1 .....148 A8
Goodwood Ave Sale M23 .....120 D7
  Sale M33 .....107 C4
Goodwood Cl BL3 .....42 F3
Goodwood Cres WA15 .....120 C6
Goodwood Ct M7 .....155 D6
Goodwood Dr Oldham OL1 .....49 B1
  Pendlebury M27 .....80 B7
Goodwood Lo 3 M16 .....97 D3
Goodworth Wlk M40 .....83 B7
Goole St M11 .....165 A8
Goose Cote Hill BL7 .....8 E1
Goose Gn WA14 .....119 D4
Goose La OL12 .....139 F8
Goosetrey Cl SK9 .....131 E1
Goostrey Ave M20 .....110 A8
Gorden St 11 OL13 .....3 C8
Gordon Ave Bolton BL3 .....144 C5
  Garswood WN4 .....72 E4
  Hazel Grove SK7 .....124 D3
  Manchester M19 .....111 B8
  Oldham OL4 .....67 C6
  Wigan OL9 .....66 A3
Gordon Cl WN5 .....54 E8
Gordon Pl M20 .....110 B5
Gordon Rd Eccles M30 .....79 D3
  Sale M33 .....108 B6
  Swinton M27 .....79 C6
Gordon St
  3 Ashton-u-L OL6 .....85 D4
  Bury BL9 .....140 E3
  Droylsden M18 .....99 E6
  Hyde SK14 .....167 E2
  Leigh WN7 .....75 F6
  Manchester M16 .....162 D5
  Manchester M7 .....158 D4
  Newhey OL16 .....32 B3
  Oldham OL4 .....68 A6
  Oldham OL1 .....65 F4
  8 Rochdale OL11 .....31 A5
  Shaw OL2 .....149 C7
  3 Stalybridge SK15 .....86 B1
  Stockport SK4 .....169 E3
  Wigan WN1 .....151 E7
Gordon Terr 2 SK15 .....86 A2
Gordon Way OL11 .....28 F1
Gordonstoun Cres WN5 .....53 F7
Gore Ave Failsworth M35 .....84 B7
  Salford M5 .....154 D2
Gore Cl BL9 .....141 C1
Gore Cres M5 .....154 D3
Gore Dr M5 .....154 D3
Gore La SK9 .....136 C3
Gore St Manchester M1 .....159 B1
  Manchester M3 .....158 E1
  Salford M6 .....81 A3
  Wigan WN5 .....54 B6
Gore's La WA11 .....71 A5
Gorebrook Ct M12 .....99 A4
Goredale Ave M18 .....99 E4
Gorelan Rd M18 .....99 D5
Goring Ave M18 .....99 D6
Gorman St 9 WN6 .....37 A1
Gorman Wlk WN3 .....54 F5
Gorrel St 4 OL11 .....31 A5
Gorrells Way OL11 .....30 D3
Gorrells Cl OL11 .....30 D3
Gorrells Way OL11 .....30 E3
Gorse Ave Droylsden M43 .....84 C2
  Marple SK6 .....125 E6
  Mossley OL5 .....68 C1
  Oldham OL8 .....67 C3
  Stretford M32 .....96 F3
Gorse Bank BL9 .....141 C3
Gorse Bank
  Com Speci Sch OL9 .....65 F5
Gorse Bank Rd WA15 .....129 C7
Gorse Cres M32 .....96 F3
Gorse Dr Stretford M32 .....96 F3
  Walkden M38 .....59 F6
Gorse Rd Bkbr 1 A8
Gorse Hall Cl SK16 .....101 F7
Gorse Hall Dr SK15 .....85 F1
Gorse Hall Prim Sch SK15 .....86 A1
Gorse Hall Rd SK16 .....101 F7
Gorse Hill Prim Sch M32 .....96 E4
Gorse La M32 .....96 E3
Gorse Rd Milnrow OL16 .....32 A6
  Swinton M27 .....79 E6
  Walkden M28 .....60 E2
Gorse Sq M11 .....105 D3
Gorse St Oldham OL9 .....65 F5
  Stretford M32 .....96 E3
Gorse The M44 .....128 B8
Gorse Way SK13 .....116 F7
Gorse Wlk WN7 .....75 B5
Gorsefield Cl M26 .....44 A4
Gorsefield Dr 11 M27 .....79 F7

Gorsefield Hey SK9 .....137 E8
Gorsefield Prim Sch M26 .....44 A4
Gorselands SK8 .....132 B5
Gorses Dr WN2 .....38 C6
Gorses Mount BL2 .....148 C5
Gorses Rd BL2,BL3 .....42 D5
Gorseway SK5 .....112 B4
Gorsey Ave M22 .....121 C4
Gorsey Bank Prim Sch
  SK9 .....136 F7
Gorsey Bank Rd SK3 .....123 B8
Gorsey Brow Billinge WN5 .....71 E5
  Mottram-in-L SK14 .....103 A1
  Romiley SK6 .....113 A2
  Stockport SK1 .....112 A1
Gorsey Brow Cl WN5 .....71 D5
Gorsey Clough Wlk BL8 .....26 F5
Gorsey Dr M22 .....121 C4
Gorsey Hey BL5 .....57 E7
Gorsey Hill St OL10 .....29 D1
Gorsey Intakes SK14 .....115 A8
Gorsey La
  Altrincham WA14 .....119 B5
  Ashton-u-L OL6 .....85 F6
  Partington WA13 .....118 B7
Gorsey Mount St SK1 .....112 A1
Gorsey Rd Wilmslow SK9 .....136 F8
  Wythenshawe M22 .....121 C4
Gorsey Way OL6 .....85 E6
Gorseyfields M43 .....100 A8
Gorsley Bank OL15 .....16 C7
Gorston Wlk M22 .....130 C8
Gort Cl M45 .....45 A1
Gorton Brook Fst Sch
  M12 .....165 A6
Gorton Cres M34 .....100 C2
Gorton Cross Ctr M18 .....99 D5
Gorton Fold BL6 .....22 C3
Gorton Gr M8 .....60 C5
Gorton Ind Est M18 .....165 C6
Gorton La M12,M18 .....165 B6
Gorton Mount Jun
  & Inf Schs M18 .....99 C3
Gorton Parks M18 .....165 C6
Gorton Rd
  Manchester M11,M12 .....164 F7
  Reddish SK5 .....99 F2
Gorton St Ashton-u-L OL7 .....84 F1
  Bolton BL2 .....148 B8
  Eccles M30 .....79 B1
  Farnworth BL4 .....60 B7
  Heywood OL10 .....29 E2
  Manchester M3 .....158 F2
  Oldham OL9 .....152 B6
Gorton Sta M18 .....99 D6
Gortonvilla Wlk M12 .....164 F6
Gosforth Cl Bury BL8 .....27 C5
  Oldham OL1 .....49 A1
Gosforth Wlk M23 .....108 F1
Goshen La BL9 .....44 F6
Goshen Sports Ctr BL9 .....45 A6
Gosling Cl 3 M16 .....97 F3
Gosport Sq M7 .....155 D5
Gosport Wlk M8 .....156 A6
Goss Hall St OL4 .....67 C6
Gotha Wlk M13,M13 .....163 C6
Gotherage Cl SK6 .....113 C2
Gotherage La SK6 .....113 E2
Gothic Cl SK6 .....113 C2
Gough St Heywood OL10 .....29 E2
  Stockport SK3 .....169 D1
Gould St Denton M34 .....100 E3
  Manchester M4 .....159 B3
  Oldham OL1 .....67 B8
Goulden Rd M20 .....110 A5
Goulden St
  Manchester M4 .....159 B2
  Salford M6 .....154 E2
Goulder Rd M18 .....99 F3
Gourham Dr SK8 .....122 F2
Govan St M22 .....109 E1
Gowan Dr M24 .....46 D1
Gowan Rd M16 .....97 E1
Gowanlock's St BL1 .....143 E2
Gower Ave SK7 .....124 C3
Gower Rd Hyde SK14 .....167 D1
  Reddish SK5 .....169 D4
Gower St Ashton-u-L OL6 .....166 C3
  Bolton BL1 .....145 D8
  Farnworth BL4 .....42 C1
  Leigh WN7 .....75 E4
  Oldham OL1 .....67 A7
  Swinton M27 .....62 A1
  Wigan WN5 .....150 A7
Gowerdale Rd SK5 .....112 C5
Gowers St OL16 .....31 B8
Gowran Pk 3 OL4 .....67 D6
Gowy Cl SK9 .....131 E1
Goya Rise OL1 .....49 D4
Goyt Ave SK6 .....125 F6
Goyt Cres Bredbury SK6 .....112 F3
  Stockport SK1 .....112 B3
Goyt Hey Ave WN5 .....71 E5
Goyt Rd Disley SK12 .....135 D5
  Marple SK6 .....125 F4
  Stockport SK1 .....112 B3
Goyt Valley Rd SK6 .....112 F3
Goyt Valley Wlk SK6 .....112 F3
Goyt Wlk M45 .....45 B2
Grace St Horwich BL6 .....22 B3
  Leigh WN7 .....75 C5
  Rochdale OL12 .....15 B2
Grace Wlk M4 .....160 D1
Gracie Ave 2 OL1 .....67 B8
Gradwell St SK3 .....170 D8
Graeme St 8 M14,M16 .....97 F3
Grafton Ave M30 .....80 A4

Grafton Ct
  Manchester M15 .....162 E5
  6 Rochdale OL16 .....31 B6
Grafton Mall 5 WA14 .....119 D4
Grafton St Adlington PR7 .....20 F6
  Altrincham WA14 .....119 D4
  Ashton-u-L OL6 .....85 D2
  Atherton M46 .....58 A1
  6 Bolton BL1 .....145 D8
  Bury BL9 .....44 F8
  Failsworth M35 .....84 A8
  Hyde SK14 .....167 D3
  Manchester M13 .....163 B5
  Newton-le-W WA12 .....89 B3
  Oldham OL1 .....49 E4
  Rochdale OL16 .....31 B6
  Stalybridge SK15 .....86 D3
  Manchester M3 .....158 D2
Grafton Wlk WN6 .....18 C2
Graham Cres M44 .....105 C3
Graham Dr SK12 .....135 C6
Graham Rd Salford M6 .....80 C4
  Stockport SK1 .....124 C8
Graham St Abram WN2 .....56 A1
  Ashton-u-L OL7 .....84 F1
  Bolton BL1 .....145 F8
  Manchester M11 .....165 A8
Grain View M5 .....161 A8
Grainger Ave M12 .....99 A3
Grains Rd Delph OL3,OL4 .....50 C4
  Shaw OL1,OL2 .....49 D7
Gralam Cl M33 .....108 C1
Grammar School Rd
  Lymm WA13 .....117 A2
  Oldham OL8 .....66 B2
Grampian Cl OL9 .....152 A5
Grampian Way
  Golborne WA3 .....74 D1
  6 Platt Bridge WN2 .....56 B2
  Shaw OL2 .....149 A8
Granada Mews M16 .....97 E1
Granada Rd M34 .....100 A3
Granada TV Ctr M3 .....158 E1
Granary La M28 .....78 F5
Granary Way M33 .....108 B2
Granby Rd Cheadle SK8 .....132 B8
  Sale WA15 .....108 A1
  Stockport SK2 .....124 B5
  Swinton M27 .....79 C7
Granby Row M1 .....163 A8
Granby St Bury BL8 .....26 F6
  Oldham OL9 .....66 A3
Grand Union Way M30 .....95 D8
Grandale St 8 M14 .....98 C3
Grandidge St OL11 .....139 E5
Granford Cl WA14 .....119 D7
Grange Ave
  Altrincham WA15 .....120 A2
  Cheadle SK8 .....122 F3
  Denton M34 .....101 B2
  Eccles M30 .....79 D4
  Little Lever BL3 .....43 C3
  Milnrow OL16 .....31 F4
  Oldham OL8 .....66 C4
  Reddish SK4 .....111 D5
  Sale WA15 .....120 B7
  Stretford M32 .....96 C2
  Urmston M41 .....94 E6
  Wigan WN5 .....150 B5
Grange Cl Golborne WA3 .....90 C6
  Hyde SK14 .....167 F1
Grange Com Sec Sch
  OL9 .....153 E7
Grange Cres M41 .....95 C1
Grange Ct
  Altrincham WA14 .....119 C1
  Oldham OL8 .....66 D4
Grange Dr Eccles M30 .....79 D4
  Manchester M9 .....64 F3
Grange Gr M45 .....62 F8
Grange La Delph OL3 .....50 F5
  Manchester M20 .....110 B2
Grange Mill Wlk M40 .....83 B7
Grange Park Ave
  Ashton-u-L OL6 .....85 F6
  Cheadle SK8 .....122 D5
  Wilmslow SK9 .....137 A8
Grange Park Rd Bolton BL7 .....25 C7
  Cheadle SK8 .....122 D5
Grange Pl M44 .....105 C5
Grange Rd
  Altrincham WA14 .....119 C1
  Ashton-in-WN4 .....72 F7
  Bolton BL3 .....144 B5
  Bolton BL7 .....25 C8
  Boothstown M28 .....77 E7
  Bury BL9 .....27 B2
  Eccles M30 .....79 A4
  Farnworth BL4 .....42 A1
  Leigh WN7 .....56 E1
  Manchester M21 .....97 A2
  Middleton OL11 .....47 D6
  Sale M33 .....108 A4
  Sale WA15 .....120 B7
  Stockport SK7 .....123 F3
  Urmston M41 .....95 C1
  Whitworth OL12 .....4 D3
Grange Rd W SK14 .....167 F2
Grange Rd S SK14 .....167 F1
Grange Sch M14 .....98 D3
Grange St Failsworth M35 .....83 D6
  Hindley WN2 .....56 E4
  Leigh WN7 .....75 E3
  Oldham OL8 .....153 E7
  Salford M6 .....154 E2

Grange The Hyde SK14 .....167 F1
  Manchester M14 .....98 C2
  Westhoughton BL5 .....57 D8
Grange Wlk M4 .....163 C8
Grangeforth Rd M8 .....155 F8
Grangepark Rd M9 .....65 A3
Grangethorpe Dr M19 .....110 F7
Grangethorpe Rd
  Manchester M14 .....98 C2
  Urmston M41 .....95 D1
Grangewood BL3 .....131 D4
Grangewood BL7 .....25 C7
Grangewood Dr M9 .....157 D7
Granite St 4 OL1 .....67 B8
Gransden Dr M8 .....156 C6
Granshaw St M40 .....160 E3
Gransmoor Ave M11 .....99 F7
Gransmoor Rd M11,M43 .....99 F7
Grant Cl M9 .....64 D2
Grant Mews BL0 .....138 B7
Grant Rd WN3 .....55 A3
Grant St Farnworth BL4 .....42 B2
  Rochdale OL11 .....30 D2
Grantchester Pl BL4 .....147 F1
Grantchester Way BL2 .....25 E1
Grantham Cl BL1 .....143 E1
Grantham Dr BL8 .....140 D4
Grantham Gr WN2 .....37 F2
Grantham Rd SK4 .....168 C2
Grantham St
  Manchester M14 .....98 B3
  Oldham OL4 .....67 A5
Grantley St WN4 .....73 A5
Grants La BL0 .....138 C6
Grantwood WN4 .....73 A5
Granville Ave
  Manchester M16 .....97 C2
  Manchester M7 .....155 E8
Granville Cl OL9 .....152 C7
Granville Ct
  Manchester M16 .....97 C3
  Newhey OL16 .....32 B3
Granville Gdns M20 .....110 A2
Granville Rd
  Altrincham WA15 .....120 C6
  Bolton BL3 .....146 C3
  Cheadle SK3,SK8 .....123 C5
  Droylsden M34 .....84 C1
  Manchester M14 .....110 C8
  Urmston M41 .....95 C3
  Wilmslow SK9 .....136 F5
Granville St Adlington PR6 .....21 A7
  Ashton-u-L OL6 .....85 D2
  Eccles M30 .....79 D3
  Farnworth BL4 .....42 D2
  Haslingden BB4 .....1 A7
  1 Hindley WN2 .....56 E5
  Leigh WN7 .....75 F7
  Oldham OL4 .....48 E1
  Oldham OL9 .....152 C8
  Swinton M27 .....79 C7
  Walkden M28 .....60 C6
Granville Terr 7 OL6 .....85 D2
Granville Wlk OL9 .....152 C8
Grasdene Ave 2 M9 .....64 E3
Grasmere Ave
  Farnworth BL4 .....59 F7
  Heywood OL10 .....46 D8
  Hindley WN2 .....56 E4
  Ince-in-M WN2 .....56 B3
  Little Lever BL3 .....43 A4
  Orrell WN5 .....53 F8
  Orrell WN8 .....53 B7
  Reddish SK4 .....111 E6
  Swinton M27 .....61 C2
  Urmston M41 .....94 E1
  Whitefield M45 .....62 C7
Grasmere Cl SK15 .....86 A4
Grasmere Cres
  Bramhall SK7 .....132 E8
  Eccles M30 .....79 B4
  High Lane SK6 .....125 E1
Grasmere Dr WN4 .....73 B5
Grasmere Gr
  Ashton-u-L OL7 .....166 A4
  Ashton-u-L OL7 .....84 F4
Grasmere Ho 6 M6 .....80 E2
Grasmere Rd
  Alderley Edge SK9 .....137 A1
  Altrincham WA15 .....120 C6
  Gatley SK8 .....122 B3
  Haslingden BB4 .....1 A6
  Oldham OL4 .....67 C7
  Partington M31 .....105 E3
  Royton OL2 .....48 D6
  Sale M33 .....108 B4
  Stretford M32 .....96 D3
  Swinton M27 .....79 F6
  Wigan WN5 .....54 C7
Grasmere St Bolton BL1 .....143 F2
  Leigh WN7 .....75 E3
  Manchester M12 .....164 F6
  10 Rochdale OL12 .....14 F1
Grasmere Terr WN7 .....74 B8
Grasmere Wlk M24 .....46 F2
Grason Ave SK9 .....131 C1
Grass Mead M34 .....113 B8
Grasscroft SK5 .....112 C6
Grasscroft Ind Sch OL4 .....68 C5
Grasscroft Rd Hindley WN2 .....57 A4
  Manchester M9 .....157 E6
Grassfield Ave M7 .....155 A8
Grassholme Dr SK2 .....125 A5
Grassholme Rd BL2 .....25 B1
Grassingham Gdns M6 .....154 F3
Grassington Ave M40 .....83 A5
Grassington Ct BL8 .....27 A3
Grassington Dr BL9 .....28 D1
Grassington Pl BL2 .....25 A1

Grassland Rise M38 .....59 E4
Grassmoor Cres SK13 .....171 D2
Grathie Ct BL1 .....142 B1
Grathome Wlk BL3 .....147 E3
Gratrix Ave M5 .....161 B7
Gratrix La M33 .....108 F3
Gratrix St M18 .....99 C4
Gratten Cl M28 .....60 C4
Gratten Ct M28 .....60 C4
Grave Oak La WN7 .....76 B1
Gravel Bank Rd SK6 .....113 B6
Gravel La Manchester M3 .....158 F2
  Wilmslow SK9 .....136 C5
Gravel Wlks 4 OL4 .....67 B7
Gravenmoor Dr M7 .....155 E6
Graver La Failsworth M40 .....83 D5
  Failsworth M40 .....83 E4
Graves St M26 .....43 F6
Graveyard La WA16 .....136 A5
Gray Cl Aspull WN2 .....38 A2
  Mottram-in-L SK14 .....102 F3
Gray St BL1 .....145 E8
Gray St N BL1 .....145 E8
Graymar Rd M38 .....60 A4
Graymarsh Dr SK12 .....133 C2
Grayrigg Wlk M9 .....157 D7
Graysands Rd WA15 .....119 F3
Grayson Ave M45 .....63 B8
Grayson Rd M38 .....60 B4
Grayson Way OL3 .....69 B6
Grayson's Cl WN1 .....37 C1
Grayston Ct SK6 .....126 B7
Graythorp Wlk 8 M14 .....98 B3
Graythorpe BL5 .....81 A1
Graythwaite Rd BL1 .....23 F2
Grazing Dr M44 .....94 B3
Greame St M14 .....98 A3
Great Acre WN1 .....37 D1
Great Ancoats St
  Manchester M4 .....159 B1
  Manchester M1,M4 .....159 B1
Great Arbor Way 12 M24 .....46 F1
Great Bank Rd BL5 .....39 D3
Great Bent Cl OL12 .....15 D4
Great Bridgewater St
  M1,M3 .....162 F8
Great Cheetham St E
  M7,M8 .....155 E7
Great Cheetham St W
  M6,M7 .....81 C5
Great Clowes St M7 .....155 D5
Great Ducie St M3 .....158 F3
Great Eaves Rd BL0 .....138 C7
Great Egerton St SK1,SK4 .....169 E2
Great Flatt OL12 .....14 B1
Great Gable Cl OL1 .....67 A8
Great Gates Cl OL11 .....31 A4
Great Gates Rd OL11 .....31 A3
Great George St
  Manchester M3 .....158 D2
  Rochdale OL16 .....139 F7
  Wigan WN3 .....150 B7
Great Hall Cl M26 .....44 A4
Great Heaton Cl M24 .....64 C7
Great Holme BL3 .....147 F4
Great Howarth OL12 .....4 F4
Great Jackson St M15 .....162 E7
Great John St M3 .....162 E8
Great Jones St M12 .....165 A6
Great Lee OL12 .....14 D3
Great Lee Wlk OL12 .....14 D2
Great Marlborough St
  M1 .....163 A7
Great Marld Cl BL1 .....23 F2
Great Mdw OL2 .....31 F1
Great Moor Prim Sch
  SK2 .....124 B4
Great Moor St Bolton BL1 .....145 F6
  Stockport SK2 .....124 B5
Great Moss Rd M29 .....77 C2
Great Newton St M40 .....83 C5
Great Norbury St SK14 .....167 D2
Great Portwood St SK1 .....169 F2
Great Southern St M14 .....98 B3
Great Stone Cl M26 .....43 D3
Great Stone Rd
  Manchester M16,M21,M32 .....97 A3
  Stretford M16,M32 .....96 F3
Great Stones Cl BL7 .....8 E2
Great Underbank SK1 .....169 F1
Great Western St M14 .....98 B3
Greater Manchester
  Visitor Ctr (GMex)
  M1,M2,M3 .....162 F8
Greatfield Rd M22 .....121 B4
Greave SK6 .....113 D4
Greave Ave OL11 .....30 B7
Greave Fold SK6 .....113 D4
Greave Ho OL11 .....30 B8
Greave Prim Sch SK6 .....113 D4
Greave Rd SK1,SK2 .....124 C8
Greaves Ave M35 .....83 F6
Greaves Cl WN6 .....35 F8
Greaves Rd SK9 .....136 E7
Greaves St Mossley OL5 .....68 C2
  Oldham OL1 .....153 F6
  Shaw OL2 .....149 C7
Grebe Cl Poynton SK12 .....133 B4
  Wigan WN3 .....54 B4
Grebe Wlk SK1 .....124 A4
Grecian Cres BL3 .....147 F4
Grecian St M5,M7 .....81 C1
Grecian St N M7 .....81 C1
Grecian Terr M7 .....81 C1
Gredle Cl M41 .....95 F2
Greeba Rd M23 .....120 E6
Greek St Manchester M1 .....163 B7
  Stockport SK1,SK3 .....170 E8

Green Acre BL5 .... 57 F7
Green Ave Bolton BL3 ..... 42 B3
Swinton M27 .... 79 F7
Tyldesley M29 .... 77 A4
Walkden M38 .... 59 E5
Green Bank Bacup OL13 .. 3 D8
Bolton BL2 .... 25 E3
Farnworth BL4 .... 42 C1
Glossop SK13 .... 115 F7
Reddish SK4 .... 111 D7
Green Booth Cl SK16 .... 101 F7
Green Bridge Cl OL11 .... 30 F4
Green Bridge N BB4 .... 2 E7
Green Bridge S BB4 .... 2 E7
Green Brook Cl BL9 ...... 141 A4
Green Cl Gatley SK8 ..... 122 A6
Tyldesley M46 .... 58 E1
Green Clough OL16 .... 16 C8
Green Common La BL5 ... 58 B7
Green Courts WA14 ...... 119 B3
Green Croft SK6 .... 113 E3
Green Ct WN7 .... 75 B1
Green Dr Altrincham WA15 . 120 A7
Bolton BL6 .... 40 C7
Handforth SK9 .... 131 D2
Manchester M19 .... 98 F1
Green End M34 .... 113 B8
Green End Jun Sch M19 . 110 F5
Green End Rd M19 .... 110 E5
Green Fold M18 .... 99 F6
Green Fold La BL5 .... 57 E7
Green Fold Sch BL4 .... 59 F8
Green Gables Cl SK8 .... 122 B1
Green Grove Bank OL16 .. 15 D3
Green Hall Cl M46 .... 58 F5
Green Hall Mews SK9 ... 137 B6
Green Hayes Ave WN1 .... 37 C3
Green Hill OL15 .... 16 A7
Green Hill Rd SK14 .... 102 A3
Green Hill St SK3 .... 170 D7
Green Hill Terr SK3 ...... 170 D7
Green La
Alderley Edge SK9 .... 136 F1
Altrincham WA15 .... 120 B4
Ashton-u-L OL6 .... 85 B5
Bolton BL3 .... 42 B2
Coppull PR7 .... 20 F6
Delph OL3 .... 50 F4
Disley SK12 .... 135 D4
Eccles M30 .... 79 C2
Failsworth M35 .... 83 D4
Glossop SK13 .... 115 F7
Golborne WA3 .... 75 A2
Hadfield SK14 .... 171 F4
Hazel Grove SK7 .... 124 D3
Heywood OL10 .... 29 F1
High Lane SK12 .... 134 C4
Hindley WN2 .... 57 B4
Hollingworth SK14 .... 103 D6
Horwich BL6 .... 22 B5
Hyde SK14 .... 102 A1
Hyde SK14 .... 102 A2
Irlam M44 .... 105 E5
Kearsley BL4 .... 61 A7
Leigh WN7 .... 76 C6
Manchester M18 .... 99 D6
Manchester SK4 .... 168 B3
Middleton M24 .... 47 C2
Middleton M24 .... 65 D7
Oldham OL4 .... 50 A2
Oldham OL8 .... 66 E2
Orrell WN5 .... 53 D3
1 Rochdale OL12 .... 139 E8
Romiley SK6 .... 113 B2
Sale M33 .... 107 E6
Standish WN6 .... 36 E8
Stockport SK4 .... 168 C2
Stockport SK4 .... 169 D1
Whitefield M45 .... 44 F1
Wilmslow SK9 .... 137 B7
Green La N WA15 .... 120 B3
Green Lane High Sch
WA15 .... 120 B3
Green Lane Ind Est
Stockport SK4 .... 168 C1
Stockport SK4 .... 168 C2
Green Mdw Golborne WA3 .. 90 E5
Marple SK6 .... 125 F7
Rochdale OL12 .... 14 C3
Green Mdws BL5 .... 57 D8
Green Meadows Dr SK6 . 125 F8
Green Meadows Wlk
M22 .... 121 E1
Green Pastures SK4 ...... 168 A5
Green Pine Rd BL6 .... 39 D8
Green Royde OL11 .... 139 E5
Green St Adlington PR6 .. 21 B8
3 Alderley Edge SK9 ... 137 A1
Bolton BL1 .... 145 F7
Bury BL8 .... 26 F4
Bury BL8 .... 27 B4
6 Eccles M30 .... 79 B1
Eccles M30 .... 95 B8
Edenfield BL0 .... 1 E3
Farnworth BL4 .... 42 C1
Hyde SK14 .... 167 E1
Manchester M14 .... 110 E7
Middleton M24 .... 47 C2
Oldham OL8 .... 153 D6
2 Platt Bridge WN2 ...... 56 B2
Radcliffe M26 .... 44 A3
Stockport SK3 .... 170 F6
Stretford M32 .... 108 C8
6 Tyldesley M29 .... 59 A1
Tyldesley M46 .... 58 E1
Wigan WN3 .... 150 C7
Green The Cheadle SK8 . 131 F8

Green The continued
Glossop SK13 .... 116 A7
Handforth SK9 .... 131 E3
Marple SK6 .... 126 A3
Oldham OL8 .... 67 A3
Partington M31 .... 105 F4
Ramsbottom BL8 .... 10 F1
Rochdale OL11 .... 30 C3
Sale M31 .... 120 C7
Stalybridge SK15 .... 86 E4
Stockport SK4 .... 168 C2
Swinton M27 .... 62 B2
Wigan WN5 .... 54 B6
Wigan WN5 .... 54 C7
Worsley M28 .... 78 F5
Green Tree Gdns SK6 ... 113 B2
Green View WA13 .... 117 B5
Green Villa Mk SK8 ...... 123 A4
Green Way Bolton BL1 ... 25 B4
8 Mottram-in-L SK14 ... 102 F2
Rochdale OL11 .... 30 B1
Green Way Cl BL1 .... 25 B4
Green Wlk
Altrincham WA14 .... 119 B3
Altrincham WA15 .... 120 A7
Gatley SK8 .... 122 A6
Manchester M16 .... 97 C2
7 Mottram-in-L SK14 .. 102 F2
Manchester M21 .... 109 E3
Stretford M32 .... 96 B7
Green Wlks M25 .... 63 C3
Greenacre WN1 .... 37 D1
Greenacre Cl BL0 .... 11 E7
Greenacre La M28 .... 78 F4
Greenacres Edgworth BL7 .. 9 E6
Lymm WA13 .... 117 A4
Greenacres Cl WA3 .... 91 B8
Greenacres Ct **5** OL12 . 15 D4
Greenacres Dr M19 ...... 110 E4
Greenacres Prim Sch OL4 . 67 C7
Greenacres Rd OL4 .... 67 D7
Greenall St WN4 .... 73 B5
Greenbank
Abram Brow WN2 .... 74 B7
Hadfield SK13 .... 103 F5
Hindley WN2 .... 57 B3
Heywood OL10 .... 22 D1
Whitworth OL12 .... 14 C1
Greenbank Ave
Gatley SK8 .... 122 A5
Manchester SK4 .... 110 E2
Orrell WN5 .... 53 D3
Swinton M27 .... 79 D6
Uppermill OL3 .... 51 C1
Greenbank Cres SK6 .... 125 F5
Greenbank Dr OL15 .... 15 F3
Greenbank Ind Est WN7 . 57 B3
Greenbank Rd Bolton BL3 . 144 B5
Bolton BL3 .... 146 B4
Radcliffe M26 .... 44 A5
Rochdale OL12 .... 14 F2
Rochdale OL12 .... 15 A2
Romiley SK6 .... 114 B1
Sale M33 .... 107 C5
Salford M6 .... 154 E3
Greenbank Sch
Cheadle SK8 .... 123 A1
Rochdale OL12 .... 14 F1
Greenbank Terr
Middleton M24 .... 47 C1
Stockport SK4 .... 169 E2
Greenbarn Way BL6 ...... 21 D1
Greenbeech Cl SK6 ..... 125 E7
Greenbooth Rd OL11,OL12 . 13 D2
Greenbridge La OL3 .... 69 B5
Greenbrow Par M23 ..... 121 A4
Greenbrow Prim Sch
M23 .... 120 F3
Greenbrow Rd M23 ...... 120 F3
Greenbrow Rd WA11 ..... 71 C1
Greenburn Dr BL2 .... 25 E2
Greenburn Dr M38 .... 59 F3
Greencourts Bsns Pk
M22 .... 131 A8
Greencroft Mdw OL2 ..... 48 F5
Greencroft Rd M30 .... 79 B4
Greendale M46 .... 58 E4
Greendale Cres WN7 ..... 76 C4
Greendale Dr M9 .... 64 E3
Greendale Gr Prim Sch
OL3 .... 69 B1
Greenfield Ave
Ashton-u-L OL6 .... 85 C6
Eccles M30 .... 95 A8
Irlam M30 .... 151 F7
Urmston M41 .... 95 D2
Greenfield Cl
Altrincham WA15 .... 120 C6
Bolton BL1 .... 24 E5
Newton-le-W WA12 .... 89 C4
Westhoughton BL5 .... 40 A1
Greenfield Ct **7** OL10 .. 29 D1
Greenfield La
Littleborough OL16 .... 15 D3
Rochdale OL11 .... 31 A4
Shaw OL2 .... 149 B6
Greenfield Prim Sch
SK14 .... 167 E2
Greenfield Rd
Adlington PR6 .... 21 A8
Atherton M46 .... 58 B2
Walkden M38 .... 59 F4
Greenfield St Denton M34 . 100 D7
Hadfield SK13 .... 104 A6

Greenfield St continued
Hyde SK14 .... 167 D2
Rochdale OL11 .... 31 A4
Greenfield Sta OL3 .... 69 A6
Greenfield View WN5 ..... 71 A4
Greenfields WN6 .... 37 A4
Greenfields Cl WN2 .... 56 B1
Greenfields Cres WN4 ... 73 B4
Greenfield Ave BL4 .... 60 B7
Greenfold Way M27 .... 76 A3
Greenford Cl Cheadle SK8 . 123 B4
Orrell WN5 .... 53 D6
Greenford Rd M8 .... 156 A7
Greengate
Altrincham WA15 .... 129 D7
Hyde SK14 .... 113 D8
Manchester M3 .... 158 F2
Middleton OL9,M24,M40 . 65 C5
Greengate Cl OL12 .... 15 D3
Greengate E M40 .... 65 D2
Greengate Ind Pk M24 ... 65 C5
Greengate La Bolton BL2 . 42 F8
Prestwich M25 .... 63 A4
Greengate Rd M34 .... 101 A4
Greengate St **6** OL4 .... 67 B6
Greengate W M3 .... 158 E3
Greenhalgh La PR6 .... 21 B8
Greenhalgh Moss La BL8 . 27 B5
Greenhalgh St
Failsworth M35 .... 83 C6
Stockport SK4 .... 169 E2
Greenhead M27 .... 108 F2
Greenhaven WN8 .... 53 B7
Greenhead Fold SK6 .... 113 A3
Greenhead Wlk BL3 ...... 147 E3
Greenhelgh Wlk **4** M44 . 159 C1
Greenheys BL2 .... 25 E3
Greenheys Bsns Ctr M15 . 163 A5
Greenheys Cres BL8 .... 10 F1
Greenheys La M15 .... 163 A5
Greenheys La W M15 .... 162 F5
Greenhill M25 .... 63 A4
Greenhill Ave Bolton BL3 . 144 B5
Farnworth BL4 .... 60 C6
Rochdale OL12 .... 139 E8
Sale M33 .... 108 A4
Shaw OL2 .... 31 E1
Greenhill Comm Sch OL4 . 67 A6
Greenhill Cotts OL5 .... 68 D2
Greenhill Cres WN5 .... 71 F5
Greenhill La BL3 .... 40 F4
Greenhill Pas **2** OL1 .. 67 A6
Greenhill Prim Sch BL8 . 26 F1
Greenhill Rd
Altrincham WA15 .... 120 C6
Billinge WN5 .... 71 F5
Bury BL8 .... 27 A1
Manchester M8 .... 156 A8
Middleton M24 .... 65 D7
Greenhill Terr
Middleton M24 .... 65 C7
6 Oldham OL1 .... 67 A6
Greenhill Wlk SK12 ...... 135 D6
Greenholm Ct M40 .... 65 D1
Greenhow St M43 .... 99 F8
Greenhurst Cres OL8 .... 67 A2
Greenhurst La OL8 .... 85 E6
Greenhurst Rd OL6 .... 85 D7
Greenhythe Rd SK8 ...... 131 C6
Greening Rd M19 .... 99 B2
Greenland Ave WN6 .... 19 E1
Greenland Cl M29 .... 77 B6
Greenland La PR6 .... 21 D5
Greenland Rd Bolton BL3 . 147 F2
Farnworth BL3,BL4 .... 42 A2
Tyldesley M29 .... 77 B6
Greenland St
Manchester M8 .... 155 F7
8 Salford M6 .... 154 E3
Greenlands Cl **3** SK8 . 131 E8
Greenlea Ave M18 .... 99 D3
Greenlea Cl WN5 .... 53 D6
Greenleach La M28 .... 79 A2
Greenleaf Cl M28 .... 77 F7
Greenlees St OL12 .... 139 F8
Greenmount Cl BL8 .... 10 F3
Greenmount Ct BL1 ...... 144 A8
Greenmount Dr
Heywood OL10 .... 46 F7
Ramsbottom BL8 .... 10 F3
Greenmount La BL1 ...... 144 A8
Greenmount Pk BL4 .... 61 A7
Greenmount Prim Sch
BL8 .... 10 F4
Greenoak M26 .... 61 C6
Greenoak Dr Sale M33 . 108 C1
Walkden M28 .... 60 E5
Greenock Cl BL3 .... 40 F5
Greenock Dr OL10 .... 28 E1
Greenough St
Atherton M46 .... 58 A1
Wigan WN1 .... 151 D8
Greenpark Cl BL0 .... 11 D7
Greenpark Rd M22 .... 109 D1
Greenpine Ind Pk BL6 .... 22 F3
Greenroyd Ave OL2 .... 32 B7
Greens Arms Rd BB3,BL7 . 8 E7
Greens La Bacup OL13 ..... 3 D7
Haslingden BB4 .... 1 C7
Greens The OL12 .... 14 D2
Greenshall La SK12 ...... 135 F5
Greenshank Cl Leigh WN7 . 76 B5

Greenshank Cl continued
Newton-le-W WA12 .... 89 C4
Rochdale OL11 .... 29 F7
Greenside Eccles M28 .... 79 A5
Farnworth BL4 .... 42 C1
Stockport SK4 .... 168 A1
Greenside Ave
Kearsley BL4 .... 60 F6
Oldham OL4 .... 49 E2
Greenside Cl
Ramsbottom BL8 .... 10 B3
Stalybridge SK15 .... 102 A8
Greenside Cres M43 ...... 83 F2
Greenside Ct M30 .... 79 D3
Greenside Dr
Altrincham WA14 .... 119 E1
Bury BL8 .... 26 F8
Irlam M44 .... 93 F1
Greenside La M43 .... 83 F3
Greenside Pl M34 .... 113 B8
Greenside Prim Sch M43 . 83 F2
Manchester M11 .... 165 C8
Greenside Way M40 .... 65 C5
Greenslate Ave WN6 ...... 35 E8
Greenslate Ct WN5 .... 53 E8
Greenslate Rd WN5 .... 53 E3
Greensmith Way BL5 ...... 39 E3
Greenson Dr M24 .... 64 F7
Greenstead Ave M8 ...... 156 A8
Greenstone Ave BL6 .... 22 B3
Greenstone Dr M6 .... 80 F5
Greensward Cl WN6 .... 19 B1
Greensway Ctr OL12 ..... 149 B7
Greenthorn Wlk M15 .... 162 F5
Greenthorne Ave BL7 .... 9 A4
Greenthorne Cl SK4 ..... 111 D7
Greenthorne Cl BL7 .... 9 A4
Greenvale Rochdale OL11 . 29 D8
Shevington WN6 .... 35 F4
Greenvale Dr SK8 .... 122 C6
Greenview Dr
Rochdale OL11 .... 30 A8
Wythenshawe M20 .... 122 C8
Greenwatch Cl **7** M30 . 79 C1
Greenway
Altrincham WA14 .... 119 A5
Ashton-in-M WN4 .... 73 A4
Bramhall SK7 .... 132 D6
Horwich BL6 .... 22 F3
Hyde SK14 .... 167 D1
Middleton M9 .... 64 F5
Poynton SK12 .... 133 E1
Shaw OL2 .... 31 F1
Wilmslow SK9 .... 137 B6
Wythenshawe M22 .... 121 E8
Greenway Ave **7** M19 . 99 B1
Greenway Cl Bury BL8 .... 27 B3
Sale M33 .... 107 E3
Greenway Dr OL5 .... 68 C2
Greenway Mews BL0 .... 1 A5
Greenway Rd Gatley SK8 . 131 C6
Sale WA15 .... 119 F8
Greenways
7 Ashton-u-L OL7 .... 85 A6
Failsworth M40 .... 65 D1
Leigh WN7 .... 76 B6
Orrell WN5 .... 53 D3
Standish WN6 .... 37 A8
Greenwich Cl
Failsworth M40 .... 83 D4
Rochdale OL11 .... 29 F6
Greenwood Ave
Ashton-u-L OL6 .... 85 C6
Horwich BL6 .... 22 D1
Stockport SK2 .... 124 C6
Swinton M27 .... 62 B1
Walkden M28 .... 60 C3
Wigan WN5 .... 54 C7
Greenwood Bsns Ctr **10**
M5 .... 81 A1
Greenwood Cl
Altrincham WA15 .... 119 D4
Boothstown M28 .... 77 E7
Culcheth WA3 .... 91 F1
Greenwood Dr
Newton-le-W WA12 .... 89 C4
Wilmslow SK9 .... 137 D8
Greenwood Gdns SK6 .. 112 F3
Greenwood La OL8 .... 66 E1
Greenwood Prim Sch M30 . 79 C4
Greenwood Rd
Standish WN6 .... 19 E2
Wythenshawe M22 .... 121 C3
Greenwood St
1 Altrincham WA14 .... 119 D4
Farnworth BL4 .... 60 F8
2 Littleborough OL15 ... 16 B5
Oldham OL4 .... 67 C8
Oldham OL8 .... 66 F1
Rochdale OL16 .... 139 F7
Salford M6 .... 154 F4
Salford M6 .... 154 F4
Greenwood Vale BL1 .... 143 E3
Greenwood Vale S **7**
BL1 .... 143 F3
Greenwoods La BL2 .... 25 F4
Greg Mews SK9 .... 131 B2
Greg St SK5 .... 111 E5
Gregge St Heywood OL10 . 29 F1
Heywood OL10 .... 46 E8
Gregory Ave Atherton M46 . 58 C3
Bolton BL2 .... 42 E8
Manchester M18 .... 99 C8
Gregory Fold BB4 .... 1 A7
Gregory St Dukinfield SK14 . 101 E5
Hindley WN2 .... 56 C6

Gregory St continued
Leigh WN7 .... 75 E4
Manchester M12 .... 164 F6
Oldham OL8 .... 66 C3
Westhoughton BL5 .... 57 A7
Gregory Way SK5 .... 111 F6
Gregorys Row WA3 .... 75 A1
Gregson Field BL3 .... 147 E4
Gregson Rd SK5 .... 111 E6
Gregson St **4** OL1 ...... 153 F6
Greily Wlk **3** M11 .... 98 C3
Grenaby Ave WN2 .... 57 B5
Grendale Ave
Hazel Grove SK7 .... 124 E1
Stockport SK1 .... 112 B1
Grendale Dr M16 .... 161 C5
Grendon Ave OL8 .... 66 E4
Grendon St BL3 .... 146 C3
Grendon Wlk M12 .... 165 A6
Grenfel Cl WN3 .... 150 A5
Grenfell Rd M20 .... 110 B3
Grenham Ave M15 .... 162 D6
Grenville Rd SK7 .... 132 F6
Grenville St
Dukinfield SK16 .... 101 C8
Stalybridge SK15 .... 86 D4
Stockport SK3 .... 170 D8
Gresford Cl M21 .... 109 A8
Gresham Cl M45 .... 62 D2
Gresham Dr OL9 .... 152 C7
Gresham St Bolton BL1 . 143 F3
Denton M34 .... 100 F4
Gresham Wlk SK4 .... 169 E2
Gresley Ave BL6 .... 22 F2
Gresley Cl WN1 .... 151 E8
Gresty Ave M22 .... 121 F1
Gresswell Prim Sch M34 . 100 F2
Greswell St M34 .... 100 F4
Greta Ave SK8 .... 131 C6
Greta Wlk WN2 .... 56 A2
Gretna Rd M46 .... 58 E2
Gretton Cl M13 .... 98 E4
Gretton Cl OL2 .... 48 F4
Greville St SK13 .... 104 A5
Grey Cl SK6 .... 113 A4
Grey Knotts M28 .... 78 A5
Grey Mare La M11 .... 83 A1
Grey St Ashton-u-L OL6 . 166 C2
Denton M34 .... 100 D3
Manchester M12 .... 164 E6
Middleton M24 .... 46 F1
Prestwich M25 .... 63 C4
Radcliffe M26 .... 44 B3
Stalybridge SK15 .... 86 C1
Greyfriars WN4 .... 72 F4
Greyfriars Ct M3 .... 158 E3
Greyfriars Rd M22 .... 121 B2
Greyhound Dr M6 .... 81 C5
Greylag Cres M28 .... 78 D8
Greylands Cl M33 .... 107 F4
Greylands Rd M20 .... 122 C8
Greymont Rd BL9 .... 27 F6
Greysham Ct M16 .... 97 E2
Greystoke Ave
Altrincham WA15 .... 120 D5
Reddish M19 .... 99 C1
Sale M33 .... 108 B3
Greystoke Cres M45 ...... 44 E2
Greystoke Dr
Alderley Edge SK9 .... 137 A2
Bolton BL1 .... 24 E6
Middleton M24 .... 46 D2
Greystoke La M35 .... 83 D6
Greystoke St SK1 .... 112 A1
Greystone Ave
Aspull WN2 .... 38 C5
Manchester M21 .... 109 F8
Greystone Wlk SK4 ...... 111 D7
Greyswood Ave **2** M8 . 155 F6
Greytown Cl M6 .... 80 F5
Greywood Ave BL9 .... 141 B2
Grid La SK6 .... 114 F1
Grierson St BL3 .... 143 E3
Grierson Wlk **8** M16 ... 97 E4
Griffe La BL9 .... 45 D4
Griffin Cl BL9 .... 141 B4
Griffin Ct M3 .... 158 E2
Griffin Gr M19 .... 111 A8
Griffin Rd M35 .... 83 D6
Griffin St M7 .... 81 C6
Griffiths Cl M7 .... 158 D4
Griffiths St **10** M40 ...... 83 C5
Grimes Cotts La BL6,PR6 . 21 C5
Grimes St OL12 .... 13 F1
Grimscott Cl **7** M9 .... 64 F3
Grimshaw Ave M35 .... 84 A8
Grimshaw Cl SK6 .... 113 A4
Grimshaw La
Manchester M40 .... 160 F4
Middleton M24 .... 65 C7
Grimshaw St
Failsworth M35 .... 83 E8
Leigh WN7 .... 75 E7
Golborne WA3 .... 74 C1
Stockport SK1 .... 112 A1
Grimstead Cl M23 .... 120 E6
Grindall Ave M40 .... 65 D1
Grindleton Ave M40 .... 65 A8
Grindleford Gdns **19**
SK13 .... 171 E2
Grindleford Gr **20** SK13 . 171 E2
Grindleford Lea **21** SK13 . 171 E2

Grindleford Wlk
Gamesley SK13 . . . . .171 E2
Manchester M21 . . . . .109 D5
Grindley Ave M21 . . . . . .109 D5
Grindlow St M13 . . . . . . .164 E5
Grindlow Wlk WN3 . . . . . .54 C2
Grindon Ave M7 . . . . .81 A7
Grindrod St M26 . . . . . . .44 A4
Grindsbrook Rd BL8,M26 . .43 F7
Grinton Ave M13 . . . . . . .98 F2
Grisbeck Way OL1 . . . . . .153 E7
Grisdale Dr M24 . . . . .46 E2
Grisdale Rd BL3 . . . . . . .144 C5
Grisedale Ave OL2 . . . . . .48 C8
Grisedale Ct M9 . . . . .65 A4
Grisedale Rd OL11 . . . . . .30 B4
Gristlehurst La BL9,OL10 . .29 A4
Gritley Wlk M22 . . . . . . .121 C1
Grizebeck Cl M18 . . . . . .165 C6
Grizedale Cl Bolton BL1 . . .23 F2
Mossley SK15 . . . . .86 F7
Grizedale Dr WN2 . . . . . . .56 A7
Grizedale Rd SK6 . . . . . .113 B4
Groby Ct WA14 . . . . .119 C4
Groby Pl WA14 . . . . .119 D5
Groby Rd Altrincham WA14 .119 C4
Denton M34 . . . . .100 E7
Manchester M21 . . . . .109 B8
Groby Rd N M34 . . . . . . .100 D8
Groby St Oldham OL8 . . . . .67 A3
Stalybridge SK15 . . . . .86 C1
Groom St M1 . . . . .163 B7
Grosvenor Ave
Golborne WA3 . . . . .90 D8
Whitefield M45 . . . . .44 E1
Grosvenor Cl Walkden M28 .60 C5
Wilmslow SK9 . . . . .137 A4
Grosvenor Cres SK14 . . . .101 C1
Grosvenor Ct
Ashton-u-L OL7 . . . . .166 A1
Cheadle SK8 . . . . .122 D6
Manchester M16 . . . . .97 E3
Manchester M7 . . . . .155 D8
Sale M33 . . . . .107 F5
Grosvenor Dr
Poynton SK12 . . . . .133 D3
Walkden M28 . . . . .60 C5
Grosvenor Gdns
Manchester M7 . . . . .158 D4
Newton-le-W WA12 . . . . . .89 C2
Stalybridge SK15 . . . . .86 A1
Wythenshawe M22 . . . . . .121 E6
Grosvenor Ho
Ashton-u-L OL7 . . . . .166 A1
Manchester M16 . . . . .97 E1
Stalybridge SK15 . . . . .86 A1
Grosvenor House Mews
M8 . . . . .63 F2
Grosvenor Pl OL7 . . . . . .166 A1
Grosvenor Rd
Altrincham WA14 . . . . .119 E5
Cheadle SK8 . . . . .123 C4
Eccles M30 . . . . .79 A3
Hyde SK14 . . . . .167 D1
Leigh WN7 . . . . .75 D6
Manchester M16 . . . . .97 D2
Manchester SK4 . . . . .168 B3
Marple SK6 . . . . .125 F7
Pendlebury M27 . . . . .80 E7
Sale M33 . . . . .107 F6
Urmston M41 . . . . .95 C2
Walkden M28 . . . . .60 C5
Whitefield M45 . . . . .44 E1
Grosvenor Rd
Cty Prim Sch M27 . . . . . .80 B7
Grosvenor Sq
Manchester M7 . . . . .158 D4
Oldham OL3 . . . . .69 B8
Sale M33 . . . . .108 A4
Grosvenor St
Ashton-u-L OL7 . . . . .166 A1
Ashton-u-L OL7 . . . . .84 F1
Bolton BL2 . . . . .48 F8
Bury BL9 . . . . .148 B6
Denton M34 . . . . .100 D4
Hazel Grove SK7 . . . . .124 D3
Heywood OL10 . . . . .29 C1
Hindley WN2 . . . . .56 D5
Kearsley BL4 . . . . .60 F7
Little Lever BL3 . . . . .43 B4
Manchester M1 . . . . .163 B7
Prestwich M25 . . . . .63 C4
Radcliffe M26 . . . . .43 F4
Rochdale OL11 . . . . .30 C1
Stalybridge SK15 . . . . .86 A1
Stockport SK1 . . . . .170 F8
Stretford M32 . . . . .96 D2
Swinton M27 . . . . .61 F2
Wigan WN5 . . . . .54 F6
Grosvenor Way
Horwich BL6 . . . . .22 C3
Oldham OL1,OL2 . . . . .48 D2
Grotton Hollow OL4 . . . . . .68 A6
Grotton Mdws OL4 . . . . . . .68 B5
Grouse St OL12 . . . . .14 F1
Grove OL15 . . . . .16 C8
Grove Arc SK9 . . . . .137 A2
Grove Ave Adlington PR6 . .21 A7
Failsworth M35 . . . . .53 E5
Wilmslow SK9 . . . . .137 B7
Grove Cl M14 . . . . .98 C2
Grove Cotts OL3 . . . . .51 D6
Grove Cres PR6 . . . . .21 A7
Grove Ct M33 . . . . .108 D4
Grove Hill M28 . . . . .77 F6

Grove La Altrincham WA15 .120 A6
Altrincham WA15 . . . . .120 B3
Bramhall SK7,SK8 . . . . . . .132 A6
Manchester M20 . . . . .110 B3
Standish WN6 . . . . .36 F8
Grove Pk M33 . . . . .107 F4
Grove Pl WN6 . . . . .36 F8
Grove Rd
Altrincham WA15 . . . . .119 E3
Middleton M24 . . . . .47 B2
Oldham OL3 . . . . .69 B7
Orrell WN8 . . . . .53 C8
Stalybridge SK15 . . . . .86 D4
Grove St
Ashton-in-M WN4 . . . . .73 A4
Ashton-u-L OL7 . . . . .84 E5
Bolton BL1 . . . . .143 D2
Bury BL9 . . . . .148 A3
Droylsden M43 . . . . .99 F8
Farnworth BL4 . . . . .60 E8
Hazel Grove SK7 . . . . .124 E3
Heywood OL10 . . . . .29 E2
Leigh WN7 . . . . .76 B4
Manchester M7 . . . . .155 E5
Oldham OL1 . . . . .67 B7
Oldham OL3 . . . . .69 B5
Rochdale OL11 . . . . .139 E5
Stalybridge SK16 . . . . .85 D1
Wilmslow SK9 . . . . .137 B7
Grove Terr OL4 . . . . .67 E8
Grove The
Appley Bridge WN6 . . . . . .18 C2
Bolton BL2 . . . . .148 B5
Bramhall SK8 . . . . .132 A6
Eccles M30 . . . . .79 F1
Golborne WA3 . . . . .74 D1
Hadfield SK14 . . . . .171 F4
Ince-in-M WN2 . . . . .151 F7
Little Lever BL3 . . . . .43 B3
Manchester M20 . . . . .110 B1
Sale M33 . . . . .108 B3
Shaw OL2 . . . . .149 A6
Stockport SK2 . . . . .170 E7
Uppermill OL3 . . . . .50 F1
Urmston M41 . . . . .94 F1
Grove Way SK9 . . . . .137 B7
Grovehurst M27 . . . . .79 C6
Grovewood Cl OL7 . . . . . . .84 E5
Grovewood Dr WN6 . . . . . .35 E8
Grundey St SK7 . . . . .124 E2
Grundy Ave M25 . . . . .62 F2
Grundy Rd BL4 . . . . .60 E2
Grundy St Bolton BL3 . . . .147 D4
Golborne WA3 . . . . .90 A7
Heywood OL10 . . . . .46 E8
Manchester SK4 . . . . .110 E2
Walkden M28 . . . . .60 E2
Westhoughton BL5 . . . . . . .39 E1
Grundy's Cl M29 . . . . .77 C7
Grundys Bldgs M29 . . . . . .77 A8
Guardian Angel's
RC Prim Sch BL8 . . . . . . .27 B3
Guardian Ct M33 . . . . . . .108 A5
Guernsey Cl M19 . . . . . . .111 A6
Guest Rd M23 . . . . .63 A6
Guest St WN7 . . . . .76 B5
Guide Bridge Mills Ind Est
OL7 . . . . .100 E8
Guide Bridge Sta M34 . . .100 F8
Guide La M34 . . . . .100 F7
Guide Post Sq M33 . . . . .164 D6
Guide St M5 . . . . .80 C1
Guido St Bolton BL1 . . . . .143 E2
Failsworth M35 . . . . .83 E7
Guild Ave M28 . . . . .60 E2
Guild St BL7 . . . . .25 B7
Guildford Ave SK8 . . . . . .132 A6
Guildford Cl M5 . . . . .124 B7
Guildford Cres M16 . . . . . .36 F3
Guildford Dr OL6 . . . . .85 C7
Guildford Gr M24 . . . . .47 C3
Guildford Rd Bolton BL1 . .142 B2
Dukinfield SK16 . . . . .102 A7
Salford M6 . . . . .80 B4
Urmston M41 . . . . .95 B4
Guildford St OL16 . . . . . . .31 A7
Guildhall Cl M15 . . . . . . .163 A5
Guilford Rd M30 . . . . .79 B1
Guinness Circ M17 . . . . . . .96 A8
Guinness Ho OL16 . . . . . . .31 A7
Guinness Rd M17 . . . . .96 A8
Guinness Road Trad Est
M17 . . . . .95 F8
Guiseley Cl BL9 . . . . .27 E8
Gull Cl SK12 . . . . .133 B3
Gullane Cl M40 . . . . .83 C7
Gulvain Pl OL9 . . . . .65 F8
Gun Rd SK13,SK6 . . . . . . .115 C2
Gun St M4 . . . . .159 B2
Gunson Ct M40 . . . . .159 C3
Gunson St M40 . . . . .159 C3
Gunters Ave BL5 . . . . .57 F6
Gurner Ave M5 . . . . .161 B7
Gurney St M4 . . . . .160 D1
Gutter La BL0 . . . . .138 B7
Guy Fawkes St M5 . . . . . .161 B7
Guy St M7 . . . . .155 F7
Guywood La SK6 . . . . . . .113 C3
Gwelo St M11 . . . . .83 A2
Gwenbury Ave SK1 . . . . . .112 B1
Gwendor Ave M8,M9 . . . . .63 F2
Gwladys St SK15 . . . . .86 E6
Gwynant Pl M20 . . . . .110 C7
Gylden Cl SK14 . . . . .102 B5
Gypsy La OL11 . . . . .30 C3
Gypsy Wlk SK2 . . . . .124 C6
Gyte's La M19 . . . . .99 C2

H

Habergham Cl M28 . . . . . . .78 C7
Hackberry Cl WA14 . . . . . .119 B8
Hacken Bridge Rd BL3 . . . .42 D4
Hacken La BL3 . . . . .42 C4
Hackford Ct Bolton BL1 . . .144 C8
Bury BL8 . . . . .27 D5
Hacking St Bury BL9 . . . . .141 A2
Manchester M7 . . . . .155 E6
Prestwich M25 . . . . .63 A4
Hackle St M11 . . . . .83 C2
Hackleton Cl M4 . . . . .160 D1
Hackness Rd M21 . . . . . . .108 F8
Hackney Ave M40 . . . . .83 C4
Hackney Cl M26 . . . . .44 A5
Hackwood Wlk M8 . . . . . .155 F7
Hackworth Cl M11 . . . . . .151 E8
Hadbutt La M29 . . . . .76 F4
Haddan Gn SK13 . . . . . . .171 D2
Haddan Lea SK13 . . . . . . .171 D2
Haddington Dr M9 . . . . . . .64 E3
Haddon Ave M40 . . . . .65 F1
Haddon Cl
Alderley Edge SK9 . . . . . . .136 F2
High Lane SK6 . . . . .134 E6
Whitefield BL9 . . . . .45 A5
Haddon Gr
Altrincham WA15 . . . . .119 F7
Reddish SK5 . . . . .111 E7
Sale M33 . . . . .108 A4
Haddon Hall Rd M43 . . . . .83 E2
Haddon Ho M5 . . . . .154 D3
Haddon Mews SK13 . . . . .171 D2
Haddon Rd Eccles M30 . . . .95 C8
Gatley SK8 . . . . .131 C7
Golborne WA3 . . . . .74 D2
Hazel Grove SK7 . . . . .124 E1
Manchester M21 . . . . .109 D5
Manchester M20 . . . . .79 C6
Wigan WN3 . . . . .54 E3
Haddon St
Ashton-in-M WN4 . . . . .72 F5
Rochdale OL11 . . . . .30 E4
Salford M6 . . . . .81 B5
Stretford M32 . . . . .96 D4
Haddon Way
Denton M34 . . . . .101 A1
Shaw OL2 . . . . .149 C8
Hadfield Ave OL9 . . . . .66 B4
Hadfield Cres OL6 . . . . . . .85 E5
Hadfield Cty Inf Sch
SK13 . . . . .103 F5
Hadfield Ind Est SK13 . . .103 F6
Hadfield Pl SK13 . . . . . . .116 C8
Hadfield Rd SK14 . . . . . . .171 F4
Hadfield Sq SK13 . . . . . . .116 C8
Hadfield St
Dukinfield SK16 . . . . .101 A7
Glossop SK13 . . . . .116 C8
Manchester M16 . . . . .161 C6
Manchester M7 . . . . .155 E6
Oldham OL8 . . . . .66 F3
Hadfield St Andrew's
CE Jun Sch SK14 . . . . . .171 F4
Hadfield Sta SK13 . . . . . .104 A5
Hadfields Ave SK14 . . . . .103 D5
Hadleigh Cl BL1 . . . . .25 A6
Hadley Ave M13 . . . . .98 E2
Hadley Cl SK8 . . . . .122 F1
Hadley St M6 . . . . .81 B5
Hadlow Gn SK5 . . . . .112 B6
Hadlow Wlk M40 . . . . .160 E3
Hadrian Ho OL1 . . . . .153 F7
Hadwin St BL3 . . . . .143 F1
Hafton Rd M7 . . . . .81 B6
Hag Bank La SK12 . . . . . .135 D7
Hag Fold Sta M46 . . . . . . .58 C5
Haggate OL2 . . . . .48 C3
Haggate Cres OL2 . . . . . . .48 C3
Hagley Rd M5 . . . . .161 A6
Hags The BL7 . . . . .45 A5
Hague Bar Prim Sch
SK22 . . . . .135 E8
Hague Bar Rd SK22 . . . . .135 F8
Hague Bush Cl WA3 . . . . . .74 E1
Hague Ct M20 . . . . .110 A5
Hague Fold Rd SK22 . . . . .135 F8
Hague Ho OL8 . . . . .153 F5
Hague Pl SK15 . . . . .86 A2
Hague Rd Manchester M20 110 A5
Mottram-in-L SK13,SK14 . .103 B1
Hague St Ashton-u-L OL6 . .85 D4
Glossop SK13 . . . . .116 D6
Manchester M10,M40 . . . .157 F5
Oldham OL4 . . . . .67 E8
Haig Ave M44 . . . . .105 C4
Haig Ct BL3 . . . . .27 B1
Haig Rd Aspull WN2 . . . . . .38 B7
Bury BL8 . . . . .27 B2
Stretford M32 . . . . .96 D3
Haig St WN3 . . . . .150 B7
Haigh Ave SK4 . . . . .111 E5
Haigh Ctry Pk WN2 . . . . . .37 F5
Haigh Hall Cl BL0 . . . . . . .11 B4
Haigh La M24,OL9 . . . . . . .47 E1
Haigh Lawn WA14 . . . . . .119 B3
Haigh Pk SK4 . . . . .111 E5
Haigh Rd WN2 . . . . .38 C6
Haigh St Bolton BL1 . . . . .145 F8
Rochdale OL1 . . . . .31 A6
Haigh View
Ince-in-M WN3 . . . . .151 E6
Wigan WN1 . . . . .37 D2
Hail St BL0 . . . . .12 A3
Haile Dr M28 . . . . .77 F6
Hailsham Cl BL8 . . . . .27 C7

Hailsham St M11 . . . . . . .160 F2
Hailwood St OL11 . . . . .30 E4
Halcyon Cl OL12 . . . . .14 B2
Haldene Wlk M8 . . . . .155 F6
Haldon Rd M20 . . . . .110 D5
Hale Ave SK12 . . . . .133 D2
Hale Dr WN7 . . . . .76 B2
Hale Ct WA14 . . . . .119 D7
Hale Gr WN4 . . . . .72 F5
Hale Green Ct WA15 . . . . .120 A3
Hale La M35,M40 . . . . .83 E8
Hale Low Rd WA15 . . . . . .119 F3
Hale Prep Sch WA15 . . . . .119 E3
Hale Rd
Altrincham WA15,WA14 . . .120 B1
Manchester SK4 . . . . .168 C3
Hale Sta WA14 . . . . .119 D2
Hale Wlk SK8 . . . . .122 F1
Halebank Ave M20 . . . . . .109 F7
Hales Cl M43 . . . . .83 D1
Halesden Rd SK4 . . . . . . .111 D5
Halesfield WN2 . . . . .72 F2
Halesworth Wlk M40 . . . .159 C4
Halewood Ave WA3 . . . . . .73 F1
Haley Cl SK5 . . . . .111 F8
Haley St M8 . . . . .156 B7
Half Acre M26 . . . . .43 F6
Half Acre Dr OL11 . . . . . . .30 C6
Half Acre La Blackrod BL6 .21 C2
Rochdale OL11 . . . . .30 B6
Half Acre Mews OL11 . . . .30 B6
Half Acre Rd OL11 . . . . . . .30 C6
Half Edge La M30 . . . . . . .79 F3
Half Moon La SK2 . . . . . . .124 E6
Half St Manchester M3 . . .158 E3
Middleton M24 . . . . .46 F1
Halfacre Rd M22 . . . . .121 C4
Halford Dr M40 . . . . .83 C8
Halfpenny Bridge Ind Est
OL11 . . . . .31 A6
Halifax Rd
Littleborough OL12 . . . . . .15 C3
Littleborough OL15 . . . . . .16 D7
Halifax St OL6 . . . . .166 B4
Haliwell St OL15 . . . . .16 C5
Hall Ave Altrincham WA15 .119 F7
Manchester M14 . . . . .98 D3
Sale M33 . . . . .107 E6
Halkyn Ave M14 . . . . .98 A3
Hall Bank M30 . . . . .79 C2
Hall Cl Mottram-in-L SK14 .103 A5
Shevington WN6 . . . . .36 B6
Hall Coppice The BL7 . . . . .8 E1
Hall Dr Middleton M24 . . . .64 F7
Mottram-in-L SK14 . . . . . .103 A5
Hall Farm Ave M41 . . . . . .95 B3
Hall Farm Cl SK7 . . . . . . .125 A3
Hall Fold OL12 . . . . .14 C8
Hall Gdns OL12 . . . . .14 C2
Hall Green Cl
Dukinfield SK16 . . . . .166 C1
Orrell WN8 . . . . .53 C8
Hall Green Rd SK16 . . . . .166 C1
Hall House La WN7 . . . . . .76 C4
Hall i' th' Wood La
Bolton BL1 . . . . .25 A4
Bolton BL1,BL2 . . . . .25 B3
Hall i' th' Wood (Mus) BL1 .25 A4
Hall La Appley Bridge WN6 .18 D2
Bolton BL3,BL4 . . . . .42 E3
Farnworth BL4 . . . . .42 D2
Horwich BL6 . . . . .39 E7
Orrell WN5 . . . . .53 E7
Partington M31 . . . . .105 F4
Pennington Green WN2 . . .38 D2
Romiley SK6 . . . . .113 B6
Wigan WN2 . . . . .37 D4
Wigan WN3,WN5 . . . . .54 A4
Wythenshawe M23 . . . . . .121 B6
Hall Lane Gr WN2 . . . . . . .56 D8
Hall Lee Dr BL5 . . . . .40 A1
Hall Meadow Rd SK13 . . .104 D2
Hall Moss La SK7 . . . . . . .132 C4
Hall Moss Rd M9 . . . . .65 A3
Hall Pool Dr SK2 . . . . .124 E7
Hall Rd Altrincham WA14 . .119 A8
Ashton-u-L OL6 . . . . .85 C5
Bramhall SK7 . . . . .123 D1
Handforth SK9 . . . . .131 E3
Manchester M14 . . . . .98 D3
Wilmslow SK9 . . . . .137 A7
Hall St Ashton-in-M WN2 . .73 E7
Ashton-u-L OL6 . . . . .85 E2
Bury BL8 . . . . .27 C4
Cheadle SK8 . . . . .122 D6
Denton SK14 . . . . .101 B3
Failsworth M35 . . . . .83 D6
Heywood OL10 . . . . .29 E2
Ince-in-M WN2 . . . . .151 F8
Manchester M1,M2 . . . . . .162 F8
Middleton M24 . . . . .47 A8
Oldham OL4 . . . . .67 B7
Radcliffe M26 . . . . .43 F6
Ramsbottom BL9 . . . . .11 C2
Royton OL2 . . . . .48 D4
Stockport SK1 . . . . .112 A2
Swinton M27 . . . . .61 F1
Whitworth OL12 . . . . .14 B8
Whitworth OL12 . . . . .14 B8
Wigan WN1 . . . . .151 D7
Hall Wood Ave WA11 . . . . .72 F1

Hall's Ct SK13 . . . . .104 C1
Hallam Rd M40 . . . . .83 B5
Hallam St Radcliffe M26 . . .44 D4
Stockport SK2 . . . . .124 A6
Hallas Gr M23 . . . . .109 B1
Hallbottom St SK14 . . . . .101 F5
Hallbridge Gdns WN8 . . . .53 B8
Hallcroft M31 . . . . .105 E4
Hallcroft Gdns OL6 . . . . . .85 C4
Hallgate Westhoughton BL5 .57 E5
Wigan WN1 . . . . .150 C8
Hallgate Dr SK8 . . . . .122 A2
Hallgate Rd SK1 . . . . .124 B8
Halliday Ct OL15 . . . . .15 E4
Halliday Rd M40 . . . . .83 B4
Halliford Rd M40 . . . . .83 A6
Hallington Cl BL3 . . . . . . .145 F5
Halliwell Ave OL8 . . . . .66 E3
Halliwell Ind Est BL1 . . . .143 D3
Halliwell La M8 . . . . .155 F7
Halliwell Rd Bolton BL1 . . .143 D2
Manchester M25 . . . . .62 F1
Halliwell St Bolton BL1 . . .143 D2
Manchester M14 . . . . .98 C1
Oldham OL9 . . . . .66 A2
Rochdale OL12 . . . . .139 E8
Halliwell St W M8 . . . . . . .155 F7
Halliwell Wlk M25 . . . . . . .65 D2
Hallkirk Wlk M40 . . . . . . .160 D6
Hallows Ave M21 . . . . . . .109 C5
Hallows Farm Ave OL12 . .14 D2
Hallroyd Brow OL1 . . . . . .153 E8
Hallstead Ave M38 . . . . . . .59 E4
Hallstead Gr M38 . . . . .59 E4
Hallsville Rd M19 . . . . .99 C1
Hallsworth Rd M30 . . . . . .79 A1
Hallwood Ave M6 . . . . .80 C5
Hallwood Rd
Wilmslow SK9 . . . . .131 D2
Wythenshawe M23 . . . . . .121 A6
Hallworth Ave M34 . . . . . .84 C1
Hallworth Rd M8 . . . . .156 B8
Hallworthy Cl WN7 . . . . . . .75 B1
Halmore Rd M40 . . . . .160 D2
Halsall Cl BL9 . . . . .27 F6
Halsall Dr BL3 . . . . .147 E2
Halsbury Cl M12 . . . . .164 E6
Halset Wlk SK7 . . . . .124 A2
Halsey Cl OL9 . . . . .65 E2
Halshaw La BL4 . . . . .60 F7
Halshaw La BL4 . . . . .60 F7
Halsmere Dr M9 . . . . .64 E3
Halstead Ave
Manchester M21 . . . . .109 A7
Salford M6 . . . . .94 B1
Halstead Dr M44 . . . . .94 B1
Halstead Gr Leigh WN7 . . .76 A6
Wythenshawe M22 . . . . . .121 F5
Halstead St Bolton BL2 . . .148 A7
Bury BL9 . . . . .141 A4
Halstead Wlk BL9 . . . . . . .28 A5
Halstock Wlk M40 . . . . . .157 D5
Halston Cl SK5 . . . . .169 F4
Halston St M15 . . . . .162 E6
Halstone Ave SK9 . . . . . . .136 C4
Halter Cl M26 . . . . .44 A5
Halton Cl OL10 . . . . .29 C2
Halton Bank M6 . . . . .154 F4
Halton Dr WA15 . . . . .108 B1
Halton Ho M5 . . . . .154 F1
Halton Rd M11 . . . . .83 C2
Halton St Bolton BL2 . . . .148 B7
Hyde SK14 . . . . .167 F3
Halvard Ave BL9 . . . . .27 F6
Halvard Ct BL9 . . . . .27 F6
Halvis Gr M16 . . . . .97 B3
Hambledon Cl BL3 . . . . . . .40 F5
Hambledon Dr M46 . . . . . .58 E5
Hambleton Cl BL8 . . . . . . .26 F6
Hambleton Dr Sale M33 . .107 D5
Wythenshawe M23 . . . . . .121 A8
Hamblett St WN7 . . . . .75 B5
Hambridge Cl M8 . . . . . . .156 A7
Hamel St Bolton BL3 . . . . .147 E3
Dukinfield SK14 . . . . .101 F5
Hamer Cl OL7 . . . . .166 A1
Hamer Com Prim Sch
OL16 . . . . .15 B2
Hamer Dr M16 . . . . .162 D5
Hamer Hall Cres OL12 . . .15 B1
Hamer Hill M9 . . . . .64 C3
Hamer La OL16 . . . . .15 B2
Hamer St Bolton BL2 . . . . .25 B3
Heywood OL10 . . . . .29 B2
Radcliffe M26 . . . . .44 C4
Ramsbottom BL9 . . . . .11 B2
Hamer's Bldg OL10 . . . . . .29 B2
Hamerton Rd M40 . . . . . .159 C4
Hamilcar Ave M30 . . . . . . .79 E2
Hamilton Ave Eccles M30 . .79 F1
Irlam M44 . . . . .105 D4
Royton OL2 . . . . .48 D3
Hamilton Cl Bury BL8 . . . . .27 D3
Prestwich M25 . . . . .63 A3
Hamilton Cres Sale M33 . .108 A6
Hamilton Ct Little Lever BL3 .43 B3
Sale M33 . . . . .54 E8
Hamilton Gr M16 . . . . .162 D5
Hamilton Lo M14 . . . . .98 C3
Hamilton Mews M30 . . . . .79 B3
Hamilton Rd
Garswood WN4 . . . . .72 D4
Hindley WN2 . . . . .56 F4
Manchester M13 . . . . .98 F3
Prestwich M25 . . . . .63 A3
Tyldesley M29 . . . . .77 D6

Hamilton Rd continued
Whitefield M45 62 E8
Hamilton Sq
Stockport SK4 169 E3
Wigan WN5 54 E8
Hamilton St Ashton-u-L OL7 84 F1
Atherton M46 58 C2
Bolton BL1 24 E5
Bury BL9 140 F4
Chadderton OL9 152 A7
Eccles M30 79 B3
Leigh WN7 75 D6
Manchester M16 162 D5
Manchester M7 155 D7
Oldham OL4 67 B7
Stalybridge SK15 85 F2
Swinton M27 61 D1
Hamilton Way OL10 28 E1
Hamlet Dr M33 107 E6
Hamlet The BL6 40 B8
Hammer Terr BL9 11 C3
Hammerstone Rd M18 165 C6
Hammett Rd M21 109 A8
Hammond 13 OL10 29 C2
Hammond Ave Bacup OL13 3 D8
Reddish SK4 111 E5
Hamnet Cl BL1 25 A5
Hamnett St
Droylsden M11,M43 83 D1
Hyde SK14 167 D3
Hamon Rd WA15 119 E4
Hampden Cres M18 165 C5
Hampden Gr M30 79 D2
Hampden Pl WN5 36 D1
Hampden Rd
Prestwich M25 63 C4
Sale M33 108 A3
Shaw OL2 49 D6
Hampden St Heywood OL10 29 D1
Rochdale OL11 139 F6
Hampshire Cl
Brinnington SK5 112 C5
Bury BL9 45 A8
Glossop SK13 116 F8
Hampshire Ho SK5 112 C5
Hampshire Rd
Brinnington SK5 112 C5
Droylsden M43 84 A3
Oldham OL9 152 B5
Partington M31 105 D2
Hampshire St M7 155 E7
Hampshire Wlk 6 M8 156 B6
Hampson Ave WA3 91 F3
Hampson Cl
Ashton-in-M WN4 73 B2
5 Eccles M30 79 B1
Hampson Cres SK9 131 C4
Hampson Fold M26 43 F4
Hampson Mill La BL9 44 F5
Hampson Pl OL6 85 E6
Hampson Rd
Ashton-u-L OL6 85 E6
Stretford M32 96 C2
Hampson Sq 5 M26 44 A4
Hampson St Atherton M46 58 C3
Droylsden M43 84 A2
Eccles M30 79 B1
Horwich BL6 22 B4
Manchester M3,M5 158 D1
Manchester M40 160 D4
Radcliffe M26 44 A3
Sale M33 108 D4
Stockport SK1 124 B8
Swinton M27 62 A1
Hampstead Ave M41 94 E1
Hampstead Dr SK2 124 C5
Hampstead La SK2 124 C5
Hampstead Rd WN6 19 D1
Hampton Gr Bury BL9 27 F6
Cheadle SK8 122 E2
Leigh WN7 76 E7
Sale WA14 107 F1
Hampton Mews 1 SK3 123 F4
Hampton Rd Bolton BL3 42 A3
Failsworth M35 84 B8
Irlam M44 105 D4
Stretford M21 96 F1
Urmston M41 95 D2
Hampton St OL8 66 D4
Hamsell Rd M13 163 C7
Hanborough Ct M29 76 F8
Hancock Cl M14 98 B3
Hancock St M32 108 D8
Hand La WN7 75 E1
Handel Ave M41 95 A2
Handel Mews M33 108 C4
Handel St Bolton BL1 143 D3
Whitworth OL12 14 B8
Handford Ho 5 M41 95 E2
Handforth Gr M13 98 E2
Handforth Hall
Cty Prim Sch SK9 131 D4
Handforth Rd
Handforth SK9 131 E1
Reddish SK5 111 F5
Handforth Sta SK9 131 D3
Handley Ave M14 98 B1
Handley Cl SK3 123 C5
Handley Rd SK7 123 E3
Handley St Bury BL9 44 F8
Rochdale OL12 139 D8
Hands La OL11 30 A7
Handsworth St M12 164 D7
Hanging Birch M24 64 B7
Hanging Chadder La OL2 48 C7
Hanging Ditch M4 158 F2
Hanging Lees Cl OL16 32 C4
Hani Ct M8 63 F1
Hankinson Cl M31 105 E2
Hankinson Way M6 81 A3
Hanley Cl Disley SK12 135 D5
Middleton M24 65 A5
Hanlith Mews M19 110 F8
Hanlon St Manchester M8 156 A8
Manchester M8 63 F1
Hanmer St WN2 56 D5
Hannah Baldwin Cl M11 164 F8
Hannah Lo M20 110 A4
Hannah St M12 99 A2
Hannerton Rd OL2 49 D7
Hannesburg Gdns M23 120 F4
Hannet Rd M22 121 D2
Hanover Bsns Pk WA14 119 B7
Hanover Cres M14 98 D4
Hanover Ct Bolton BL3 144 B5
Manchester M7 155 D7
Swinton M28 79 B6
Hanover Gdns M7 155 E8
Hanover Ho Bolton BL3 146 B2
10 Manchester M14 110 D8
Oldham OL8 153 D6
Hanover Rd
Altrincham WA14 119 B7
Hindley WN2 56 C6
Hanover St Bolton BL1 145 E7
Leigh WN7 76 A6
Littleborough OL15 16 A5
Manchester M4 159 A2
Mossley OL5 68 C1
Rochdale OL11 30 C2
Stalybridge SK15 85 F2
Hanover St N M34 100 E8
Hanover St S 4 M34 100 E8
Hanover Towers SK5 169 F3
Hansdon Cl M8 156 A6
Hansen Wlk 3 M22 121 C2
Hansham Wlk M23 108 E1
Hanslope Wlk 14 M9 157 E8
Hanson Cl M24 47 A1
Hanson Mews SK1 112 B2
Hanson Rd M40 83 B7
Hanson St Bury BL9 140 F4
Middleton M24 47 A1
Oldham OL4 67 C7
Hanstock Cl WN5 53 E5
Hanwell Cl WN7 75 E1
Hanworth Cl M13 163 B7
Hapsford Wlk M40 83 A5
Hapton Ave M32 96 D1
Hapton Pl SK4 169 E3
Hapton St M19 99 A1
Harbern Cl M30 79 D4
Harbern Dr WN7 57 D2
Harbord St M24 65 A8
Harboro Ct M33 107 F3
Harboro Gr M33 107 F4
Harboro Rd M33 107 E4
Harboro Way M33 107 F4
Harbour City Sta M5 96 F8
Harbour Farm Rd SK14 101 E5
Harbour La Edgworth BL7 9 D5
Milnrow OL16 31 F5
Harbour La N OL16 31 F6
Harbourne Ave M28 78 C8
Harbourne Cl M28 78 C8
Harburn Wlk M22 130 E8
Harbury Cl WN6 36 F2
Harbury Cres M22 121 C5
Harbury Wlk WN6 36 F2
Harcles Dr BL0 11 B2
Harcombe Rd M20 110 C6
Harcourt Ave M41 95 F1
Harcourt Cl M41 95 F1
Harcourt Ind Ctr M28 60 D5
Harcourt Mews 10 BL6 22 B4
Harcourt Rd
Altrincham WA14 119 D6
Sale M33 108 A6
Harcourt St Oldham OL1 67 B8
Reddish SK5 111 F8
Stretford M32 96 E3
Walkden M28 60 D5
Hard La OL12 15 A8
Hardacre St WN3 151 D6
Hardberry Pl SK2 124 E6
Hardcastle Ave M21 109 C6
Hardcastle Cl BL2 25 C6
Hardcastle Gdns BL2 25 C6
Hardcastle Rd SK3 170 D7
Hardcastle St Bolton BL1 143 F2
Oldham OL1 153 F7
7 Oldham OL1 67 A7
Harden Dr BL2 25 D2
Harden Hills OL2 49 D8
Harden Pk SK9 137 A3
Hardfield Rd M24 65 B5
Hardfield St OL10 29 D2
Hardicker St M19 111 B7
Hardie Ave BL4 60 B7
Harding St Adlington PR6 21 B8
Dukinfield SK14 101 D5
Manchester M3 158 F2
Manchester M4 160 D1
Salford M6 81 A4
Stockport SK1 112 B1
Hardman Ave
Manchester M25 63 D2
Rawtenstall BB4 2 A8
Romiley SK6 113 A3
Hardman Cl Radcliffe M26 43 F6
Rawtenstall BB4 2 F7
Hardman Dr BB4 2 F7
Hardman Fold BL3 42 B2
Hardman Fold Sch M35 83 D7
Hardman La M35 83 E8
Hardman Rd SK5 111 F8
Hardman St Bury BL9 140 F4
Failsworth M35 83 D7
Farnworth BL4 60 E7
Heywood OL10 29 D2
Manchester M3 158 E1
Milnrow OL16 32 A5
Oldham OL9 66 B3
Radcliffe M26 43 F6
Stockport SK3 169 D1
Stockport SK3 170 D8
Wigan WN3 150 B6
Hardman Terr OL13 3 D8
Hardman's La BL7 24 F8
Hardman's Mews M45 62 F6
Hardman's Rd M45 62 F6
Hardmans BL7 24 F7
Hardon Gr M13 98 F2
Hardrow Cl WN3 55 B2
Hardrush Fold M35 84 A6
Hardshaw Cl M13 163 B6
Hardsough La BL0 1 D5
Hardwick Cl
High Lane SK6 134 F6
Little Lever BL3 43 B5
Hardwick Rd
Ashton-in-M WN4 73 A5
Partington M31 106 A3
Hardwick St OL7 84 F2
Hardwicke Rd SK12 133 F4
Hardwicke St OL11 30 E4
Hardy Ave M21 109 A8
Hardy Cl Rochdale OL11 30 F3
Westhoughton BL5 39 E3
Hardy Dr Altrincham WA15 119 F7
Bramhall SK7 132 D7
Hardy Farm M21 109 B6
Hardy Gr Swinton M27 79 D5
Worsley M28 78 F8
Hardy La M21 109 B6
Hardy Mill Com Prim Sch
BL2 25 F4
Hardy Mill Rd Bolton BL2 25 F4
Bolton BL2 26 A3
Hardy St Ashton-u-L OL6 85 E6
Eccles M30 79 B1
Oldham OL4 67 A6
Wigan WN6 37 A1
Hardybutts Wigan WN1 151 D8
Wigan WN1 151 E8
Hardywood Rd 4 M34 113 A7
Hare Dr BL9 45 B4
Hare Hill Prim Sch SK14 102 C3
Hare Hill Rd
Hattersley SK14 102 C2
Littleborough OL15 16 B6
Hare Hill Wlk SK14 102 C3
Hare St 7 Manchester M4 159 A2
Rochdale OL11 139 F5
Rochdale OL11 31 A6
Harebell Ave 10 M28 59 F3
Harebell Cl OL12 14 D3
Haredale Dr M8 156 B6
Harefield Ave OL11 139 F5
Harefield Dr Heywood OL10 29 F2
Manchester M20 110 A2
Wilmslow SK9 137 B5
Harefield Rd SK9 131 E4
Hareford Wlk M9 156 C6
Harehill Cl 5 M13 163 B7
Hareshill Rd OL10 46 C7
Harewood Ave
Rochdale OL11 13 D2
Sale M33 107 D3
Harewood Cl OL11 13 D2
Harewood Ct M33 108 C3
Harewood Dr
Rochdale OL11 13 C2
Royton OL2 48 C5
Harewood Gr SK5 111 E8
Harewood Rd Hindley WN2 56 C5
Irlam M44 94 B2
Rochdale OL11 13 D2
Shaw OL2 49 D8
Harewood Way
Rochdale OL11 13 C2
Swinton M27 61 F2
Harewood Wlk 23 M34 101 A1
Harford Cl SK7 124 A1
Hargate Ave OL12 14 A2
Hargate Cl BL9 11 C2
Hargate Dr
Altrincham WA15 120 A1
Irlam M44 94 A3
Hargate Hill La SK13 115 E7
Hargrave Cl M9 64 C6
Hargreave's St M4 159 A3
Hargreaves Ho BL3 145 E6
Hargreaves Rd WA15 120 C6
Hargreaves St Bolton BL1 143 E2
Oldham OL1 153 F7
Oldham OL9 152 C6
Rochdale OL11 30 C4
Harkerside Cl M21 109 C8
Harkness St M12 164 D7
Harland Dr
Ashton-in-M WN4 73 C3
Manchester M8 156 B7
Harland Way OL12 14 B2
Harlea Ave WN2 57 A3
Harlech Ave Hindley WN2 57 B4
Prestwich M25,M45 63 B7
Harlech Dr SK7 124 D1
Harlech St WN4 72 F5
Harleen Gr SK2 124 D7
Harley Ave Ainsworth BL2 26 D1
Bolton BL2 25 E3
Manchester M14 98 E3
Harley Ct M24 46 F1
Harley Hall
Royal Northern Coll
of Music M16 97 E1
Harley Rd Middleton M24 46 F1
Sale M33 108 C5
Harley St Ashton-u-L OL6 166 B3
Manchester M11 99 D8
Harling Rd M22 121 E7
Harlington Cl 3 M23 120 D7
Harlock Ct M6 81 B3
Harlow Dr M18 99 D3
Harlyn Ave SK7 132 F7
Harmer Cl M40 83 B5
Harmol Gr OL7 84 F6
Harmony St OL4 67 A6
Harmsworth Dr SK4 111 B5
Harmsworth St M6 154 E2
Harmuir Cl WN6 36 E4
Harold Ave
Ashton-in-M WN4 73 A5
Dukinfield SK16 101 D8
Reddish M18 99 F4
Harold Lees OL10 29 F3
Harold Priestnall Cl M40 83 B6
Harold St Aspull WN2 38 D5
Bolton BL1 143 D2
Failsworth M35 83 E7
Manchester M16 161 C6
Middleton M24 46 E1
Oldham OL9 153 D7
Prestwich M25 62 F4
Rochdale OL16 15 C2
Stockport SK1,SK2 124 B8
Haroldene St BL2 25 B2
Harp Ind Est OL11 30 D2
Harp Rd M17 96 A8
Harp St M11 99 E7
Harp Trad Est M17 96 A8
Harper Ct SK3 170 E7
Harper Fold Rd M26 43 E3
Harper Green Rd BL3,BL4 42 B1
Harper Green Sch BL4 42 B1
Harper Ho M19 98 F1
Harper Pl OL6 166 C3
Harper Rd M22 121 E7
Harper Sq OL2 149 C7
Harper St Farnworth BL4 42 B2
Hindley WN2 56 C4
Oldham OL8 66 E4
Rochdale OL11 139 E5
Stockport SK3 170 E7
Wigan WN1 151 E7
Harper's La BL1 142 B2
Harpford Cl BL2 43 A5
Harpford Dr BL2 43 A5
Harptree Gr WN7 75 D7
Harpur Mount Prim Sch
M9 157 D8
Harpurhey Rd M8,M9 157 D8
Harridge Ave
Rochdale OL12 14 C3
Stalybridge SK15 86 D2
Harridge St OL12 14 C3
Harridge The OL12 14 C3
Harrier Cl Leigh WN7 76 B5
Worsley M28 78 D8
Harriet St Irlam M44 105 E5
Walkden M28 60 D3
Harriett St Manchester M4 159 C2
Rochdale OL16 31 A7
Harringay Rd M40 83 B5
Harrington Rd WA14 119 B5
Harrington St M18 99 E5
Harris Ave Reddish M34 100 B3
Urmston M41 95 D5
Harris Cl Heywood OL10 28 E1
Reddish M34 100 B3
Harris Dr Hyde SK14 102 A4
Whitefield BL9 45 B2
Harris Rd WN6 19 B3
Harris St Bolton BL3 145 E6
Manchester M8 158 E4
Harrison Ave M19 99 B2
Harrison Cl 1 OL12 13 F1
Harrison Cres BL6 21 C3
Harrison Rd PR7 21 A6
Harrison St Bacup OL13 4 B8
Eccles M30 95 B8
Hindley WN2 57 B3
Horwich BL6 22 B4
Hyde SK14 113 F8
Manchester M4 160 D1
Manchester M7 158 D4
1 Oldham OL1 153 F6
Ramsbottom BL0 138 C7
Stalybridge SK15 86 A2
Stockport SK1,SK2 170 F7
Walkden M38 60 A4
4 Wigan WN5 54 F6
Harrison Way WA12 89 C4
Harrison's Dr SK6 113 C5
Harrock La WN6 18 A5
Harrogate Ave M25 63 D2
Harrogate Cl M11 99 E7
Harrogate Dr SK5 111 E8
Harrogate Rd SK5 99 E1
Harrogate Sq BL8 26 F1
Harrogate St WN1 151 D7
Harrop Court Rd OL3 51 D5
Harrop Edge La OL3 51 B5
Harrop Edge Rd
SK14,SK15 102 E4
Harrop Fold OL8 67 A1
Harrop Green OL3 51 D5
Harrop Green La OL3 51 D5
Harrop Rd WA15 119 F2
Harrop St Bolton BL3 146 A4
Droylsden M18 99 F6
Harrop St continued
10 Stalybridge SK15 86 A2
Stockport SK1 124 A7
Walkden M28 60 B3
Harrow Ave
Manchester M19 111 A6
Oldham OL8 66 E3
Rochdale OL11 30 A6
Harrow Cl Bury BL9 44 F5
Orrell WN5 53 F8
Harrow Cres WN7 75 F3
Harrow Dr M33 108 A2
Harrow Mews OL2 149 B7
Harrow Pl WN3 55 F4
Harrow Rd Bolton BL1 144 B8
Sale M33 108 A2
Shevington WN5 36 D1
Harrow St Manchester M8 64 B1
Rochdale OL11 31 B2
Harrowby Ct BL4 60 B8
Harrowby Dr M40 157 D5
Harrowby Fold BL4 60 C8
Harrowby La BL4 60 C8
Harrowby Rd Bolton BL1 23 F2
Bolton BL3 146 A3
Swinton M27 79 E7
Harrowby St Farnworth BL4 60 C8
Wigan WN5 54 E6
Harrowdene Wlk 6 M9 157 D8
Harry Hall Gdns M7 81 C3
Harry Pigott Ave M40 83 A7
Harry Rd SK5 111 F8
Harry Rowley Cl 1 M22 121 C2
Harry St Oldham OL2 48 E2
Oldham OL9 152 C6
Rochdale OL11 30 B3
Harry Thorneycroft Wlk
M11 164 E8
Harry's Ct 3 WN7 75 D5
Harrycroft Rd SK6 113 B5
Harrytown SK6 113 A2
Harrytown RC High Sch
SK6 113 A2
Hart Ave Droylsden M43 84 B1
Sale M33 108 F3
Hart Ct OL5 68 B2
Hart Dr BL9 45 B4
Hart Hill Dr M5 154 D3
Hart Mill Cl OL5 68 B2
Hart Rd M14 98 B1
Hart St Altrincham WA14 119 E5
Droylsden M43 84 B1
Manchester M1 159 A1
Tyldesley M29 77 C8
Westhoughton BL5 57 B7
Hart's Houses BL6 22 D5
Harter St M1 163 A8
Hartfield Cl M13 163 C6
Hartfield Wlk BL2 148 C8
Hartford Ave
Heywood OL10 29 B3
Reddish SK4 111 D6
Wilmslow SK9 136 F5
Hartford Cl OL10 29 B3
Hartford Gdns WA15 120 D5
Hartford Rd Sale M33 107 D2
Urmston M41 95 E4
Westhoughton BL5 57 F6
Hartford Sq OL9 152 C6
Hartford St M34 100 E5
Harthill St M8 155 F5
Hartington Cl 4 M41 95 E2
Hartington Ct OL2 48 E4
Hartington Dr
Droylsden M11 83 B3
Hazel Grove SK7 133 E8
Standish WN6 36 F7
Hartington Rd
Altrincham WA14 119 D8
Bolton BL1 144 C8
Bramhall SK7 132 E6
Eccles M30 79 A3
Gatley SK8 131 D8
High Lane SK12,SK6 134 F7
Manchester M21 109 B8
Stockport SK2 124 D5
Hartington St M14 97 F3
Hartis Ave M7 155 E6
Hartland Ave M41 96 A2
Hartland Cl Poynton SK12 133 D5
Stockport SK2 124 C8
Tyldesley M29 77 B8
Hartland St OL10 29 D2
Hartlebury OL11 139 E6
Hartlepool Cl M14 98 B3
Hartley Ave
Manchester M25 63 D3
Wigan WN1 151 E7
Hartley Gr Irlam M44 94 B4
Wigan WN5 54 B7
Hartley Hall Gdns M16 97 E1
Hartley La OL11 30 E3
Hartley Rd
Altrincham WA14 119 C5
Manchester M21 97 A1
Hartley St Heywood OL10 29 D2
Horwich BL6 22 B3
Littleborough OL12 15 C6
Littleborough OL15 16 A5
Manchester M40 157 F8
Milnrow OL16 31 D7
Rochdale OL12 14 B1
Stalybridge SK15 86 D3
Stockport SK3 170 D8
13 Wigan WN5 54 B6

Hartley Terr
Ince-in-M WN3 . . . . .150 C7
Rochdale OL11 . . . . .30 E3
Harton Ave M18 . . . . .99 C3
Harton CI OL2 . . . . .149 A6
Harts Farm Mews WN7 . . . . .75 F7
Hartshead Ave
Ashton-u-L OL6 . . . . .85 C6
Stalybridge SK15 . . . . .86 A3
Hartshead CI M11 . . . . .100 A7
Hartshead Cres M35 . . . . .84 C6
Hartshead High Sch OL6 . . .85 E7
Hartshead Rd OL6 . . . . .85 C6
Hartshead St OL4 . . . . .67 F5
Hartshead View SK14 . . . . . .167 F1
Hartsop Dr M24 . . . . .46 C2
Hartswell CI WA3 . . . . .74 A2
Hartswood CI M34 . . . . .101 A4
Hartswood Rd M20 . . . . .110 D6
Hartwell CI Bolton BL2 . . . . . .25 C3
Manchester M11 . . . . .164 F8
Hartwell Gr 2 SK3 . . . . .123 F4
Harty Ho M30 . . . . .79 E2
Harvard CI SK4 . . . . .113 C5
Harvard St 18 OL11 . . . . .31 A4
Harvest CI Salford M6 . . . . . . .80 E5
Wythenshawe M23 . . . . .109 A3
Harvey CI M11 . . . . .165 A8
Harvey Ct WN7 . . . . .73 A1
Harvey La WA3 . . . . .73 F1
Harvey St Bolton BL1 . . . . . . .143 D3
Bury BL8 . . . . .27 C3
Ince-in-M WN3 . . . . .151 E6
Rochdale OL12 . . . . .15 B2
Stockport SK1 . . . . .169 F1
Harvin Gr M34 . . . . .101 A2
Harwich CI
Brinnington SK5 . . . . .112 C6
1 Manchester M19 . . . . .99 B1
Harwin CI OL12 . . . . .14 D3
Harwood Cres BL8 . . . . .26 E7
Harwood Ct
Manchester SK4 . . . . .110 E2
Salford M6 . . . . .81 B4
Harwood Dr BL8 . . . . .27 A1
Harwood Gdns OL10 . . . . . . .29 D1
Harwood Gr 22 BL2 . . . . .25 B1
Harwood Mdw BL2 . . . . .25 F3
Harwood Meadows
Com Prim Sch BL2 . . . . .25 F3
Harwood Park Prim Sch
OL10 .29 D1
Harwood Rd Bury BL2,BL8 . .26 C6
Manchester M19 . . . . .110 E6
Manchester SK4 . . . . .110 E2
Harwood St
Littleborough OL15 . . . . .15 F5
Stockport SK4 . . . . .169 E3
Harwood Vale BL2 . . . . .25 E3
Harwood Vale Ct BL2 . . . . . . .25 E3
Harwood Wlk BL8 . . . . .26 E7
Haseldine St WN4 . . . . .72 F6
Haseley CI Little Lever BL3 . . .43 B5
Poynton SK12 . . . . .133 E5
Haselhurst Wlk 7 M23 . . . .108 F2
Hasguard CI BL1 . . . . .40 F8
Haskoll St BL6 . . . . .22 D1
Haslam Brow BL0 . . . . .44 E8
Haslam Ct M7 . . . . .63 D1
Haslam Hey CI
Ainsworth BL2 . . . . .26 C1
Bury BL8 . . . . .26 F2
Haslam Park Cty Prim Sch
BL3 . . . . .144 B5
Haslam Rd SK3 . . . . .170 E6
Haslam St Bolton BL3 . . . . . .145 D5
Bury BL9 . . . . .141 A4
Middleton M24 . . . . .65 C7
Rochdale OL12 . . . . .139 D8
Haslemere Ave WA15 . . . . . .129 C6
Haslemere Dr SK8 . . . . .123 A1
Haslemere Ind Est
Ashton-in-M WN4 . . . . .72 F8
Ashton-in-M WN4 . . . . .73 A8
Haslemere Rd
Manchester M20 . . . . .110 D6
Urmston M41 . . . . .95 B1
Haslingden High Sch BB4 . . .1 B8
Haslington Rd M22 . . . . .121 E2
Hasper Ave M20 . . . . .110 A7
Hassal St BL9 . . . . .44 E5
Hassall Ave M20 . . . . .109 F7
Hassall St SK15 . . . . .86 B1
Hassall Way 7 SK9 . . . . .131 E5
Hassnes CI WN3 . . . . .55 B2
Hassop Ave M7 . . . . .81 A7
Hassop CI M11 . . . . .160 E1
Hassop Rd SK5 . . . . .100 A1
Hastings Ave
Manchester M21 . . . . .109 A8
Prestwich M45 . . . . .63 B7
Hastings CI Bramhall SK8 . . .123 C2
Prestwich M45 . . . . .63 B7
Stockport SK1,SK2 . . . . .124 B7
Hastings Dr M41 . . . . .94 E3
Hastings Rd Bolton BL1 . . . . .144 B8
Prestwich M45 . . . . .63 C5
Hastings St OL11 . . . . .139 F5
Hasty La Altrincham WA15 . .129 F8
Wythenshawe WA15 . . . . .129 F8
Wythenshawe M90 . . . . .130 A8
Hatchett Rd M22 . . . . .121 E1
Hatchmere CI WA15 . . . . .120 D6
Hatchmere Rd SK8 . . . . .122 F4

Hatfield Ave M19 . . . . .110 F6
Hatfield CI WN3 . . . . .55 F4
Hatfield Rd BL1 . . . . .142 C1
Hatford CI M29 . . . . .59 C1
Hathaway CI SK8 . . . . .131 B7
Hathaway Ct WN7 . . . . .76 B6
Hathaway Dr BL1 . . . . .25 A5
Hathaway Gdns SK6 . . . . . . .112 F3
Hathaway Rd BL9 . . . . .45 A3
Hathaway Wlk WN3 . . . . .55 F4
Hatherleigh Wlk BL2 . . . . .42 F6
Hatherley Rd M20 . . . . .110 D6
Hatherlow SK6 . . . . .113 A1
Hatherlow Hts SK6 . . . . .113 A1
Hatherlow La SK6 . . . . .124 D2
Hatherop CI M30 . . . . .79 B3
Hathersage Ave M5,M6 . . . .154 D3
Hathersage Cres SK13 . . . . .171 E2
Hathersage Dr SK13 . . . . . . .116 F8
Hathersage Rd M13 . . . . .98 D4
Hathersage St OL9 . . . . .152 C6
Hathersage Way 8 M34 . . .113 A8
Hathershaw OL8 . . . . .66 F3
Hathershaw Com High Sch
OL8 . . . . .66 F2
Hathershaw La OL8 . . . . .66 F3
Hatro Ct M41 . . . . .96 A1
Hatter St M4 . . . . .159 B2
Hattersley CI SK14 . . . . .102 D1
Hattersley Ctr The 2
SK14 . . . . .102 D2
Hattersley High Sch
SK14 . . . . .102 E2
Hattersley Rd E SK14 . . . . . .102 E2
Hattersley Rd W SK14 . . . . .102 C2
Hattersley St OL9 . . . . .153 A8
Hattersley Wlk SK14 . . . . . . .102 C3
Hatton Ave Atherton M46 . . . .58 D5
Manchester M7 . . . . .158 D3
Hatton Gr BL2 . . . . .25 A5
Hatton St Adlington PR7 . . . . .20 F6
Manchester M12 . . . . .99 A3
Stockport SK1 . . . . .169 E2
Hatton Terr 24 SK16 . . . . . . .166 B1
Hattonfold M33 . . . . .108 C1
Hattons Ct M32 . . . . .96 D2
Hattons Rd M17 . . . . .96 B6
Haugh Farm OL16 . . . . .32 C4
Haugh Fold OL16 . . . . .32 C4
Haugh Hill Rd OL4 . . . . .49 E3
Haugh La OL16 . . . . .32 C4
Haugh Sq OL16 . . . . .32 C4
Haughton CI SK6 . . . . .113 A6
Haughton Dr M22 . . . . .109 D1
Haughton Green Rd M34 . . .113 B8
Haughton Hall Rd M34 . . . . .101 A3
Haughton St Denton M34 . . .100 F5
Hyde SK14 . . . . .167 E1
Havana CI M11 . . . . .160 F1
Have Ct M6 . . . . .154 F4
Haveley Hey Prim Sch
M22 .121 C4
Haveley Rd M22 . . . . .121 C5
Havelock Dr M7 . . . . .158 D4
Havelock St OL8 . . . . .153 F5
Haven CI Hazel Grove SK7 . .124 C1
Radcliffe M26 . . . . .43 D5
Uppermill OL4 . . . . .68 D6
Haven Dr M43 . . . . .83 E2
Haven La OL4 . . . . .49 E3
Haven St M6 . . . . .154 E1
Haven The
Altrincham WA15 . . . . .119 F3
Littleborough OL15 . . . . .43 B3
Havenbrook Gr BL0 . . . . .11 A3
Havenscroft Ave M30 . . . . . . .95 D8
Havenwood Rd WN1 . . . . .37 B4
Havercroft CI WN3 . . . . .54 F3
Havercroft Pk BL1 . . . . .40 D8
Haverfield Rd M9 . . . . .64 E3
Haverford St M12 . . . . .164 F6
Havergate Wlks SK2 . . . . . . .124 D6
Haverhill Gr BL2 . . . . .25 B2
Haverton Dr M22 . . . . .121 B2
Haversham Rd M8 . . . . .63 E2
Haverton Dr M22 . . . . .121 B2
Haverty Prec WA12 . . . . .89 C1
Havisham CI BL6 . . . . .40 B4
Haw Clough La OL3 . . . . .69 C6
Hawarden CI WA12 . . . . .89 A4
Hawarden Ave M16 . . . . .97 C2
Hawarden Rd WA14 . . . . .119 D6
Hawarden St BL1 . . . . .24 E5
Hawdraw Gn SK2 . . . . .124 E6
Hawes Ave Farnworth BL4 . . .59 E8
Manchester M14 . . . . .110 E7
Swinton M27 . . . . .62 B3
Hawes CI Bury BL8 . . . . .27 B5
Stockport SK2 . . . . .124 A6
Hawes Cres WN4 . . . . .73 B5
Haweswater Ave
Ince-in-M WN2 . . . . .56 B7
Tyldesley M29 . . . . .77 B8
Haweswater CI M34 . . . . .100 A2
Haweswater Cres BL9 . . . . . . .45 A5
Haweswater Dr M24 . . . . .46 E2
Haweswater Mews 9 M46 . .46 E2
Hawfinch Gr M28 . . . . .78 B6
Hawick Gr OL10 . . . . .28 E1
Hawk CI BL9 . . . . .141 B4
Hawk Green Rd SK6 . . . . . . .126 A3
Hawk Rd M44 . . . . .94 A3
Hawk Yard La OL3 . . . . .69 D5
Hawke St SK15 . . . . .86 C1
Hawkedale Rd BL3 . . . . .147 D3
Hawkeshead Rd M8 . . . . .156 B6
Hawkhurst Rd M13 . . . . .98 F3
Hawkhurst St Leigh WN7 . . . .76 B4

Hawkhurst St continued
Leigh WN7 . . . . .76 C5
Hawkins St SK5 . . . . .169 E4
Hawkins Way OL15 . . . . .6 C1
Hawkley Ave WN3 . . . . .54 F2
Hawkley Brook Trad Est
WN3 . . . . .54 E2
Hawkley Hall High Sch
WN3 . . . . .55 B3
Hawkridge Dr M23 . . . . .108 F2
Hawkrigg CI WN6 . . . . .36 F7
Hawkshaw Ct WN2 . . . . .38 A3
Hawkshaw Ct Salford M5 . . .161 A8
9 Salford M5 . . . . .81 A1
Hawkshaw La BL8 . . . . .10 B5
Hawkshaw St BL6 . . . . .22 B3
Hawkshead Dr Bolton BL3 . .146 A3
Middleton M24 . . . . .46 E1
Royton OL2 . . . . .48 D6
Hawkshead Rd
Glossop SK13 . . . . .104 E3
Shaw OL2 . . . . .149 A8
Hawksheath CI BL7 . . . . .8 E1
Hawksley St Horwich BL6 . . . .22 D2
Oldham OL8 . . . . .66 C3
Hawksmoor Dr OL2 . . . . .149 B8
Hawkstone Ave
Droylsden M43 . . . . .83 E3
Whitefield M45 . . . . .62 D7
Hawkstone CI BL2 . . . . .25 F3
Hawkswick Dr M23 . . . . .109 A2
Hawksworth M29 . . . . .77 B5
Hawkyard Farm OL3 . . . . .69 D5
Hawley Dr WA15 . . . . .129 B8
Hawley Gn OL12 . . . . .14 D2
Hawley La WA15 . . . . .129 B8
Hawley St M19 . . . . .111 B8
Haworth Ave BL0 . . . . .11 A2
Haworth CI BL9 . . . . .44 F6
Haworth Dr Bacup OL13 . . . . .3 C8
Stretford M32 . . . . .96 A3
Haworth Rd M18 . . . . .99 D4
Haworth St Bury BL8 . . . . .26 F4
Edgworth BL7 . . . . .9 D5
Hindley WN2 . . . . .56 D6
Oldham OL1 . . . . .48 A6
Radcliffe M26 . . . . .44 B3
Hawsworth CI M15 . . . . .163 B5
Hawthorn Ave
Altrincham WA15 . . . . .119 F8
Bury BL8 . . . . .27 A4
Downall Green WN4 . . . . .72 D5
Eccles M30 . . . . .79 D3
Edenfield BL0 . . . . .1 D2
Hindley WN2 . . . . .57 A4
Marple SK6 . . . . .125 D6
Newton-le-W WA12 . . . . .89 D3
Orrell WN5 . . . . .53 F6
Ramsbottom BL0 . . . . .11 A2
Standish WN1 . . . . .36 B4
Urmston M41 . . . . .95 F1
Walkden M28 . . . . .60 E1
Wigan WN5 . . . . .54 D6
Wilmslow SK9 . . . . .137 A7
Hawthorn Bank
Bolton BL2 . . . . .25 E4
Hadfield SK14 . . . . .171 F4
Hawthorn CI
Altrincham WA15 . . . . .119 F7
Billinge WN5 . . . . .71 D5
Tyldesley M29 . . . . .59 A2
Hawthorn Cres Bury BL8 . . . .26 F7
Shaw OL2 . . . . .149 B6
Hawthorn Ct SK6 . . . . .112 D2
Hawthorn Dr Irlam M44 . . . . .105 D5
Pendlebury M27 . . . . .80 C7
Salford M6 . . . . .80 B4
Stalybridge SK15 . . . . .101 F8
Hawthorn Gn SK9 . . . . .137 A7
Hawthorn Gr
Bramhall SK7 . . . . .132 C6
Hollingworth SK14 . . . . .103 D6
Hyde SK14 . . . . .167 D1
Manchester SK4 . . . . .168 B3
Wilmslow SK9 . . . . .137 A7
Hawthorn La Sale M33 . . . . .108 D7
Stretford M21 . . . . .108 F8
Wilmslow SK9 . . . . .137 A7
Hawthorn Lo 3 SK3 . . . . . . .123 F4
Hawthorn Pk SK9 . . . . .137 A7
Hawthorn Rd
Altrincham WA15 . . . . .119 E3
Droylsden M43 . . . . .84 C2
Failsworth M40 . . . . .65 F1
Gatley SK8 . . . . .122 A5
Kearsley BL4 . . . . .60 E8
Manchester SK4 . . . . .110 F2
Oldham OL8 . . . . .66 B1
Reddish M34 . . . . .100 B6
Rochdale OL11 . . . . .29 E6
Stretford M21,M32 . . . . .108 E8
Hawthorn Rd S M43 . . . . .84 C2
Hawthorn St Denton M34 . . .100 F5
Manchester M18 . . . . .99 E5
Newhey OL16 . . . . .32 B3
Hawthorn Terr
Manchester SK4 . . . . .168 B3
8 Mossley OL5 . . . . .68 C2
Hawthorn View SK9 . . . . .137 A7
Hawthorn Wlk
Littleborough OL15 . . . . .15 F5
3 Partington M31 . . . . .105 E3
Hawthornden 1 M20 . . . . . .110 A3

Hawthorne Ave
Farnworth BL4 . . . . .60 B8
Fowley Common WA3 . . . . .92 C5
Horwich BL6 . . . . .22 B3
Hawthorne Cres OL8 . . . . .66 F2
Hawthorne Dr M28 . . . . .79 A7
Hawthorne Gr
Ashton-u-L OL7 . . . . .84 F1
Bredbury SK6 . . . . .112 E4
High Lane SK12 . . . . .134 C4
Leigh WN7 . . . . .75 E7
Oldham OL9 . . . . .152 B8
Hawthorne La OL16 . . . . .32 A4
Hawthorne Rd BL3 . . . . .146 D3
Hawthorne St BL3 . . . . .144 C5
Hawthorne View WA16 . . . . .136 B2
Hawthorns Com Sch
M34 . . . . .100 C5
Hawthorns The
6 Atherton M46 . . . . .58 D3
Denton M34 . . . . .100 D6
Hawthorpe Gr 7 OL3 . . . . . . .69 B8
Haxby Rd M18 . . . . .99 D3
Haxworth Wlk SK7 . . . . .124 A2
Hay Croft SK8 . . . . .131 E8
Hay Ho OL4 . . . . .67 E8
Hayburn Rd M23 . . . . .121 B7
Hayburn Rd SK2 . . . . .124 C8
Haycock CI SK15 . . . . .102 E7
Hayden Ct
4 Glossop SK13 . . . . .104 C1
Manchester M40 . . . . .157 D5
Hayden Fold SK13 . . . . .115 D7
Haydn Ave M14 . . . . .98 B4
Haydock Ave M33 . . . . .107 B2
Haydock Dr
Altrincham WA15 . . . . .120 B5
Boothstown M28 . . . . .78 B6
Hazel Grove SK7 . . . . .124 F2
Haydock La
Ashton-in-M WN4 . . . . .72 E1
Bolton BL7 . . . . .25 A8
Bolton BL7 . . . . .9 B1
Haydock Mews M7 . . . . .155 D6
Haydock Park Gdns WA12 . .73 B1
Haydock Park
Race Course WA12 . . . . .73 D1
Haydock St
Ashton-in-M WN4 . . . . .73 B2
Bolton BL1 . . . . .145 F8
Newton-le-W WA12 . . . . .89 A3
Haydock Wlk OL9 . . . . .152 C7
Haye's Rd M44 . . . . .105 E5
Hayes Row WA3 . . . . .75 A1
Hayes St Leigh WN7 . . . . .75 E4
Hayeswater Circ 7 M41 . . . . .95 C3
Hayeswater Rd M41 . . . . .95 C3
Hayfield Ave Romiley SK6 . .113 A4
Tyldesley M29 . . . . .77 C6
Hayfield CI
Manchester M12 . . . . .164 E7
Middleton M24 . . . . .47 C3
Oldham OL4 . . . . .49 F4
Ramsbottom BL0 . . . . .10 F1
Hayfield Rd
New Mills SK22 . . . . .127 E1
Romiley SK6 . . . . .113 A4
Salford M6 . . . . .80 B4
Hayfield St M33 . . . . .108 B5
Hayfield Wlk
Altrincham WA15 . . . . .120 C6
1 Denton M34 . . . . .113 A8
Haygrove Wlk 18 M9 . . . . . .157 D8
Hayle Rd OL1 . . . . .49 D4
Hayle Sr M12,M13 . . . . .98 E4
Hayling Rd M33 . . . . .107 E5
Haymaker Rise OL12 . . . . .15 D6
Hayman Ave WN7 . . . . .75 D2
Haymans Wlk M13 . . . . .163 B7
Haymarket CI M13 . . . . .163 C5
Haymarket St BL9 . . . . .140 E2
Haymarket The BL9 . . . . .140 F2
Haymill Ave M38 . . . . .60 A6
Haymond CI M6 . . . . .80 A5
Haynes St Bolton BL3 . . . . . .146 C3
Rochdale OL12 . . . . .139 F8
Hayour Wlk Bolton M28 . . . . .60 A4
Haysbrook CI OL7 . . . . .85 A4
Haysbrook Ave M38 . . . . .60 A4
Haythorp Ave M22 . . . . .121 E3
Hayward Ave BL3 . . . . .43 C3
Hayward Sch BL3 . . . . .146 D2
Hayward Sports Ctr BL3 . . .146 C2
Hayward St BL8 . . . . .27 C3
Hayward Way OL4 . . . . .68 A6
Haywards CI SK13 . . . . .104 C3
Haywood CI WA3 . . . . .74 E1
Haywood Gdns BL3 . . . . .147 E4
Haywood Park Way BL3 . . . .147 E4
Hazel Ave Ashton-u-L OL6 . . .85 F6
Bury BL9 . . . . .27 A5
Cheadle SK8 . . . . .122 E5
Kearsley M26 . . . . .61 A8
Manchester M16 . . . . .97 A3
Pendlebury M27 . . . . .80 A7
Ramsbottom BL0 . . . . .11 C4
Sale M33 . . . . .108 B6
Walkden M38 . . . . .59 D5
Westhoughton BL5 . . . . .57 F7
Wigan WN6 . . . . .37 A3
Hazel CI Droylsden M43 . . . . .84 C2
Marple SK6 . . . . .125 E4
Hazel Ct 12 M16 . . . . .97 D3

Hazel Dr Gatley M22 . . . . . . .131 A8
Poynton SK12 . . . . .133 F3
Stockport SK2 . . . . .124 B6
Hazel Gr Farnworth BL4 . . . . .60 B8
Golborne WA3 . . . . .90 B8
Leigh WN7 . . . . .75 E7
Oldham OL9 . . . . .152 B8
Radcliffe M26 . . . . .61 F8
Salford M5 . . . . .80 C2
Urmston M41 . . . . .95 E2
Hazel Grove High Sch
SK7 . . . . .133 C8
Hazel Grove Sta SK7 . . . . . .124 C2
Hazel Grove Prim Sch
SK7 . . . . .124 C3
Hazel Grove Sta SK7 . . . . . .124 D2
Hazel Hall La BL0 . . . . .11 B1
Hazel La OL8 . . . . .66 D2
Hazel Mount 1 . . . . .11 E2
Hazel Rd Altrincham WA14 . .119 D6
Atherton M46 . . . . .58 C4
Cheadle SK8 . . . . .123 B1
Middleton M24 . . . . .47 B2
Whitefield M45 . . . . .63 B8
Hazel St Denton M34 . . . . . . .100 E6
Hazel Grove SK7 . . . . .124 C3
Ramsbottom BL0 . . . . .11 A4
Hazel Terr M9 . . . . .64 D4
Hazel View SK6 . . . . .125 F3
Hazel Wlk M31 . . . . .105 E3
Hazel-Dene CI BL9 . . . . .44 F7
Hazelbadge CI SK12 . . . . . . .133 C4
Hazelbadge Rd SK12 . . . . . . .133 C4
Hazelbottom Rd
Manchester M8 . . . . .156 B7
Manchester M8 . . . . .156 C1
Hazeldean CI 16 SK9 . . . . . .131 E1
Hazeldene BL5 . . . . .57 D5
Hazeldene Rd M40 . . . . .65 E1
Hazelfields M28 . . . . .79 C7
Hazelhurst CI Bolton BL1 . . .143 E2
Ramsbottom BL0 . . . . .11 B4
Hazelhurst Dr M24 . . . . .46 F4
Hazelhurst Fold M28 . . . . .79 C7
Hazelhurst Prim Sch BL0 . . .11 A4
Hazelhurst Rd
Ashton-u-L OL6 . . . . .85 F6
Stalybridge SK15 . . . . .86 C1
Swinton M27,M28 . . . . .79 C7
Hazelmere Ave M30 . . . . .79 C4
Hazelmere CI M30 . . . . .95 E8
Hazelmere Gdns WN2 . . . . . . .56 E4
Hazelwell M33 . . . . .108 B3
Hazelwood OL9 . . . . .65 E8
Hazelwood Ave BL2 . . . . .25 E3
Hazelwood CI SK14 . . . . .102 A2
Hazelwood Ct M41 . . . . .95 D3
Denton M34 . . . . .100 F7
Hazelwood Rd
Altrincham WA15 . . . . .119 E2
Bolton BL1 . . . . .142 B2
Hazel Grove SK7 . . . . .124 A4
Stockport SK2 . . . . .124 A4
Wilmslow SK9 . . . . .137 D8
Hazlehurst Gr WN4 . . . . .73 C4
Headen Ave WN5 . . . . .53 E6
Headlands Dr M25 . . . . .63 A1
Headlands Rd SK7 . . . . .123 C1
Headlands St OL12 . . . . .14 E1
Headly Hill Rd OL10 . . . . .29 A2
Heady Hill Rd OL10 . . . . .29 A2
Heald Ave M14 . . . . .98 B3
Heald CI Altrincham WA14 . .119 C2
Littleborough OL15 . . . . .16 A3
Rochdale OL12 . . . . .14 C3
Heald Dr Altrincham WA14 . .119 C2
Rochdale OL12 . . . . .14 C3
Heald Gr Gatley SK8 . . . . . . .122 A1
Manchester M14 . . . . .98 B4
Heald Green Sta M22 . . . . . .131 A8
Heald La OL15 . . . . .16 A3
Heald PI M14 . . . . .98 B3
Heald Place Prim Sch
M14 . . . . .98 B3
Healds Gn OL1 . . . . .47 F3
Healdwood Rd SK6 . . . . .113 C4
Healey CI Manchester M7 . . . .81 C8
Wythenshawe M23 . . . . .109 A2
Healey Dell OL12 . . . . .14 D2
Healey Dell Cotts OL12 . . . . .14 B4
Healey Dell Nature Reserve
OL12 . . . . .14 B6
Healey Hall Farm OL12 . . . . .14 C5
Healey Hall Mews OL12 . . . .14 C4
Healey La OL12 . . . . .14 E3
Healey St 6 M24 . . . . .47 A1
Healey St OL16 . . . . .139 E6
Healey Stones OL12 . . . . .14 C4
Healing St BL9 . . . . .141 A4
Heap Bridge Cty Prim Sch
BL9 . . . . .28 D1
Heap Brow BL9 . . . . .28 D1
Heap Rd OL12 . . . . .13 B3
Heap St Bolton BL3 . . . . .147 E4
Heywood BL9 . . . . .28 D1

Heap St continued
Oldham OL4 ....67 C7
Radcliffe M26 ....44 B3
Whitefield M45 ....62 F7
Heape St OL11 ....30 C1
Heapfold 4 OL12 ....14 B2
Heaplands BL8 ....10 F1
Heaps Farm Ct SK15 ....102 D7
Heapworth Ave BL0 .....138 B6
Heapy Cl BL8 ....26 F1
Heardman Ave 1 WN6 ....37 A1
Hearlesden Cres 5 BL3 ..144 A3
Heath Ave Manchester M7 ..81 C4
  Ramsbottom BL0 ....11 B1
  Urmston M41 ....95 E3
Heath Cl BL3 ....146 B2
Heath Cres SK2 ....170 F5
Heath Farm La M31 .....106 B3
Heath Gdns WN7 ....57 C3
Heath Hill Dr OL13 ......3 C8
Heath La Culcheth WA3 ...91 A1
  Golborne WA3 ....90 F2
  Leigh WN7 ....75 B5
Heath Rd
  Altrincham WA14 ....119 D2
  Ashton-in-M WN4 ....73 C2
  Glossop SK13 ....104 D2
  Littleborough OL12 .....15 C6
  Sale WA15 ....119 F8
  Stockport SK2,SK3 .....170 F6
Heath St Ashton-in-M WN4 ..73 C2
  Golborne WA3 ....90 A8
  Manchester M8 ....155 F7
  Rochdale OL11 ....139 D6
Heath The Ashton-u-L OL7 ..85 A7
  Middleton M24 ....65 B6
Heath View M7 ....81 A8
Heathbank Rd
  Cheadle SK8 ....131 F8
  Manchester M9 ....64 C5
  Stockport SK3 ....123 B7
Heathbourne Rd OL13 .....3 C8
Heathcliffe Wlk 1 M13 ..163 C5
Heathcote Ave SK4 ......168 C3
Heathcote Gdns SK6 ....113 E1
Heathcote Rd M18 ....99 C4
Heather Ave Droylsden M43 ..84 C2
  Irlam M44 ....105 D6
  Shaw OL2 ....49 D8
Heather Bank Bury BL8 ...26 F7
  Littleborough OL15 .....16 D6
  Rawtenstall BL4 ....1 F4
Heather Bank Cl SK13 ...116 A7
Heather Brae WA12 ......89 A4
Heather Brow SK15 .....102 E7
Heather Cl Haslingden BB4 ..1 A8
  Heywood OL10 ....46 D8
  Horwich BL6 ....22 B4
  Oldham OL4 ....49 E1
Heather Ct SK4 ....111 D5
Heather Gr
  Ashton-in-M WN4 ....73 E4
  Droylsden M43 ....100 B8
  Hollingworth SK14 .....103 D6
  Leigh WN7 ....75 E7
  Wigan WN6 ....54 E6
Heather Lea M34 ....100 E4
Heather Rd WA14,WA15 ..119 E1
Heather St M11 ....83 B2
Heather Way Diggle OL3 ..51 D4
  Marple SK6 ....125 E6
  Heather Wlk M31 ....105 E3
Heatherdale Dr M8 .....156 A6
Heatherfield Bolton BL1 ..24 D5
  Edgworth BL7 ....9 E6
Heatherfield Ct SK9 ....137 E8
Heatherlands OL12 ....4 A3
Heatherlea Cl WN8 ....53 C7
Heathers The SK2 ......124 B4
Heatherside Reddish M34 ..100 A1
  Stalybridge SK15 ....86 D2
Heatherside Ave OL5 .....68 E1
Heatherside Rd BL0 ....138 C7
Heatherway
  Manchester M14 ....98 B4
  Sale M33 ....107 D5
Heathfield Bolton BL2 ....3 C8
  Farnworth BL4 ....42 E1
  Wilmslow SK9 ....137 A5
  Worsley M28 ....78 F5
Heathfield Ave Bacup OL13 ..3 C8
  Denton M34 ....100 D1
  Gatley SK8 ....122 B5
  Manchester SK4 ....111 C5
Heathfield Cl M33 ......108 F4
Heathfield Dr Bolton BL3 ..146 B2
  Pendlebury M27 ....80 A7
  Tyldesley M29 ....59 D1
Heathfield Flats Bolton BL3 ..146 A2
Heathfield Rd Bacup OL13 ..3 C8
  Stockport SK2 ....170 F6
  Wythenshawe M22 ....94 F3
Heathfield St M40 ....83 C5
Heathfields WA14 ....119 C3
Heathfields Rd OL3 ......69 C8
Heathfields Sq OL3 ......69 C8
Heathland Rd M25,M7 ....81 B8
Heathland Terr SK3 ....170 E7
Heathlands Dr M25 ......63 A1
Heathlea M29 ....57 C2
Heathmoor Ave WA3 ......90 D6
Heathside Gr M28 ....60 E3
Heathside Park Rd SK3 ..122 F7
Heathside Rd Cheadle SK3 ..123 A7
  Manchester M20 ....110 D6
Heathway Ave M11 ....83 D2
Heathwood OL3 ....69 C8
Heathwood Rd M19 ......110 E4

Heatley Cl Lymm WA13 ..117 A5
  Reddish M34 ....100 B2
Heatley St BL1 ....31 D6
Heatley Way 5 SK9 .....131 D4
Heaton Ave Bolton BL1 ...23 F1
  Bolton BL2 ....25 E5
  Farnworth BL4 ....60 C8
  Little Lever BL3 ....43 A4
  Stockport SK7 ....123 E3
Heaton Chapel Sta SK4 ..111 C5
Heaton Cl Manchester SK4 ..168 A3
  Orrell WN8 ....53 A7
  Whitefield BL9 ....45 A5
Heaton Court Gdns BL ...40 E7
Heaton Ct Manchester SK4 ..168 B4
  Prestwich M25 ....63 C3
Heaton Dr BL9 ....45 A5
Heaton Fold BL9 ....44 E8
Heaton Grange Dr BL1 ..144 A7
Heaton Hall M25 ....63 E5
Heaton La SK4 ....169 E1
Heaton Moor Rd SK4 ....168 B4
Heaton Mount BL1 ....23 F1
Heaton Park Rd M25 .....63 E5
Heaton Park Prim
  Sch M45 ....63 B6
Heaton Park Rd M9 ......64 B5
Heaton Park Rd N M25 ...63 E6
Heaton Park Sta M25 ....63 C4
Heaton Rd Bolton BL6 ....40 D6
  Little Lever BL3 ....43 B5
  Manchester M20 ....110 C6
Heaton Sch SK4 ....168 C3
Heaton Sch M45 ....63 B6
Heaton St Aspull WN2 ...38 D5
  Denton M34 ....100 D3
  Ince-in-M WN3 ....151 E6
  Manchester M7 ....155 E7
  Middleton M24 ....64 B8
  Milnrow OL16 ....32 A5
  Prestwich M25 ....63 C4
  Standish WN6 ....19 E1
  Wigan WN1 ....37 C2
Heaton Towers SK4 ......168 C3
Heatons Gr BL5 ....40 A2
Heaviley Gr Horwich BL6 ..22 A5
  Stockport SK2 ....124 A6
Hebble Butt Cl OL16 ....31 E6
Hebble Cl BL2 ....25 E5
Hebburn Dr BL8 ....27 C5
Hebden Ave
  Fowley Common WA3 .....92 B5
  Romiley SK6 ....113 A4
  Salford M5,M6 ....80 C3
Hebden Cl BL1 ....145 E8
Hebden Dr SK13 ....116 F8
Hebden Wlk M15 ....162 F5
Hebdon Cl WN4 ....73 A5
Heber Pl 2 OL15 ....16 B5
Heber St Ince-in-M WN2 ..151 F7
  Radcliffe M26 ....44 A3
Hebron St OL2 ....49 A3
Hector Ave OL16 ....31 B8
Hector Rd Manchester M13 ..98 F3
  Shevington WN6 ....36 D1
Heddles Ct WN7 ....75 E4
Heddon Cl SK4 ....110 E3
Heddon Wlk M8 ....156 C6
Hedge Rows OL12 ....4 C1
Hedgelands Wlk M3 ....107 C5
Hedgemead 4 WN6 ....37 A1
Hedgerows The SK14 ...102 A3
Hedges St M35 ....84 A8
Hedley St BL1 ....142 C2
Hedley Wlk 8 M8 ....155 F7
Heeley St WN1 ....37 A2
Heginbottom Cres OL6 ...85 C5
Height Barn La OL13 .....4 A8
Heights Ave OL12 ....14 E2
Heights Cl OL12 ....14 E2
Heights La Chadderton OL1 ..47 B2
  Delph OL3 ....50 E7
  Rochdale OL12 ....14 E1
Heights The BL6 ....22 D1
Helen St Ashton-in-M WN4 ..73 A4
  Eccles M30 ....95 B8
  Farnworth BL4 ....60 D7
  Golborne WA3 ....73 F1
  Manchester M7 ....81 C5
Helena St M6 ....80 C5
Helensville Ave M6 ......80 F5
Helga St M40 ....160 D4
Helias Cl M9 ....59 F3
Hell Nook WA3 ....73 F1
Helmclough Way M28 ....78 B8
Helmet St M1,M12 ......163 C8
Helmsdale M28 ....60 C2
Helmsdale Ave BL3 ......40 F6
Helmsdale Cl BL0 ....11 A4
Helmshore Ave OL4 ......49 E3
Helmshore Prim Sch BB4 ..1 A7
  Tyldesley M29 ....59 E1
Helmshore Rd
  Haslingden BB4 ....1 A7
  Ramsbottom BL0,BL8,BB4 ..1 A3
Helmshore Way OL12 ....149 B8
Helmsley Wlk M13 ......163 B7
Helmsman Way WN1 .....150 B5
Helsby Cl OL4 ....68 A6
Helsby Gdns BL1 ....143 F4
Helsby Rd M33 ....108 E2
Helsby Way
  4 Handforth SK9 ....131 D4
  Wigan WN3 ....54 C2
Helsby Wlk M12 ....164 E8
Helston Cl Bramhall SK7 ..132 F7
  Hattersley SK14 ....102 D1

Helston Cl continued
  Irlam M44 ....94 B2
Helston Dr OL2 ....48 F4
Helston Gr SK8 ....131 C8
Helston St M40 ....160 F4
Helston Way M29 ....77 C8
Helston Wlk SK14 ......102 D1
Helton Wlk M24 ....46 C1
Helvellyn Dr M24 ....65 B6
Helvellyn Rd WN5 ....54 B7
Helvellyn Wlk 2 OL1 ....49 A1
Hembury Ave M19 ....110 F6
Hembury Cl M24 ....47 B2
Hemfield Ct WN2 ....56 C8
Hemfield Rd WN2 ....56 C8
Hemley Cl BL5 ....57 E6
Hemlock Ave OL8 ....66 E3
Hemming Dr M30 ....79 E1
Hemmington Dr M9 .....157 D7
Hemmons Rd M12 ....99 B3
Hempcroft Rd WA15 ....120 D5
Hempsham La SK1,SK2 ..124 B1
Hemsby Cl BL3 ....146 A4
Hemsley St M9 ....64 E1
Hemsley St S M9 ....64 E1
Hemswell Cl M6 ....154 E4
Hemsworth Rd
  Bolton BL1 ....145 D8
  Manchester M18 ....99 D3
Hen Fold Rd M29 ....77 C7
Henbury Dr SK6 ....113 B6
Henbury La SK8 ....131 F6
Henbury Rd SK9 ....131 D4
Henbury St
  Manchester M14 ....98 A3
  Stockport SK2 ....124 C4
Henderson Ave 3 M27 ...61 F1
Henderson St
  Littleborough OL15 .....16 B8
  Manchester M19 ....111 B8
  Rochdale OL12 ....15 B2
Henderville St OL15 .....16 A6
Hendham Cl SK7 ....124 A2
Hendham Dr WA14 ......119 B5
Hendham Vale M9 ....156 D6
Hendon Dr Bury BL9 .....44 F5
  Cheadle SK3 ....123 A7
Hendon Gr WN7 ....75 F8
Hendon Rd Manchester M9 ..64 D4
  Wigan WN5 ....54 B8
Hendon St WN7 ....75 F8
Hendriff Pl 4 OL12 .....14 F1
Henfield Wlk M22 ......121 C3
Hengist St Bolton BL2 ..148 C7
  Manchester M18 ....99 D4
Henley Ave Cheadle SK8 ..122 F2
  Irlam M44 ....105 E6
  Manchester M16 ....97 B3
Henley Cl BL8 ....44 B8
Henley Dr
  Altrincham WA15 ....119 F7
  Ashton-u-L OL7 ....84 F4
Henley Gr BL3 ....147 D3
Henley Pl M19 ....111 A6
Henley St Aspull WN2 ...38 B6
  Oldham OL1 ....153 D8
  2 Rochdale OL12 ....66 A4
Henley Terr OL11 ....139 E5
Henlow Wlk 7 M40 ......65 D2
Henniker Rd BL3 ....146 A2
Henniker St M27 ....79 E6
Hennon St BL1 ....143 D1
Henrietta St
  Ashton-u-L OL6 ....166 B4
  Bolton BL3 ....146 B4
  Leigh WN7 ....75 F5
  Manchester M16 ....161 C5
Henry Herman St BL3 ..146 A3
Henry Lee St BL3 ......146 C3
Henry Park St WN1 .....151 E7
Henry St Aston-u-L OL6 ..166 C3
  Bolton BL2 ....148 A6
  Denton M34 ....113 B8
  Droylsden M43 ....84 A1
  Eccles M30 ....79 C1
  Failsworth M35 ....83 E7
  Glossop SK13 ....104 C1
  Hyde SK14 ....167 D2
  Ince-in-M WN3 ....55 E4
  Leigh WN7 ....76 A3
  Leigh WN7 ....76 A4
  Littleborough OL12 .....15 C7
  Littleborough OL15 .....16 C5
  Manchester M16 ....161 C5
  Manchester M4 ....159 B2
  Middleton M24 ....47 B7
  Prestwich M25 ....63 C5
  Ramsbottom BL0 ....11 D7
  Rochdale OL11 ....139 F6
  5 Tyldesley M29 ....59 E1
  6 Westhoughton BL5 ....39 E1
Henshaw Ct M16 ....97 B4
Henshaw La OL9 ....65 E2
Henshaw St Oldham OL1 ..153 E7
  Oldham OL1 ....153 F8
  Stretford M32 ....96 D2
Henshaw Wlk 10 M13 ...163 B7
Henson Gr WA15 ....120 A4
Henthorn St Oldham OL1 ..67 A8
  Shaw OL2 ....149 B8
Henton Wlk M40 ....65 D2
Henwick Hall Ave BL0 ...11 B4
Henwood Rd M20 ....110 C3
Hepley Rd SK12 ....134 A3
Hepple Cl SK4 ....110 F3

Hepple Wlk OL7 ....84 E5
Heppleton Rd M40 ....65 D2
Hepton St OL1 ....153 E8
Heptonstall Wlk M18 ...165 C5
Hepworth Cl WN3 ....73 E2
Hepworth St SK14 .....113 E1
Heraldic Ct M6 ....81 A4
Herbert St Bacup OL13 ...3 D8
  Droylsden M43 ....83 F1
  Dukinfield M34 ....101 A4
  Horwich BL6 ....22 B4
  Little Lever BL3 ....43 B3
  Manchester M8 ....155 F5
  Oldham OL4 ....49 D1
  Oldham OL9 ....152 B7
  Prestwich M25 ....62 F4
  Radcliffe M26 ....43 F5
  Stockport SK3 ....170 D7
  Stretford M32 ....96 D2
  Westhoughton BL5 ......39 E2
  Wigan WN3 ....150 B7
Hereford Ave WA3 ....90 B8
Hereford Cl
  Ashton-in-M WN4 ....73 C2
  Ashton-u-L OL6 ....85 D7
  Shaw OL2 ....48 F7
Hereford Cres BL3 ....43 A4
Hereford Ct SK5 ....112 C5
Hereford Dr Bury BL9 ....44 F8
  Handforth SK9 ....131 E3
  Manchester M25 ....63 C2
  Swinton M27 ....79 F6
Hereford Gr M41 ....95 C2
Hereford Rd Bolton BL1 ..144 B8
  Brinnington SK5 ....112 C5
  Cheadle SK8 ....123 A4
  Hindley WN2 ....56 F6
  Salford M30 ....80 A5
Hereford St Bolton BL1 ..143 F2
  Oldham OL9 ....152 C5
  5 Rochdale OL11 ....31 B5
  Sale M33 ....108 B4
Hereford Way
  Middleton M24 ....47 C2
  Stalybridge SK15 .....102 D7
Hereford Wlk
  6 Denton M34 ....100 F1
  Romiley SK6 ....113 A1
Hereward Grange M28 ...78 B7
Hereward Hall Dr BL1 ...84 B4
Heristone Ave M34 ....100 F3
Heritage Gdns M20 ....110 B2
Heritage Wharf OL7 ....166 A1
Herle Dr M22 ....121 C1
Hermitage Ave M6 ......153 F2
Hermitage Cl WN6 ......53 E7
Hermitage Ct WA15 ....120 A3
Hermitage Gdns SK6 ...113 F2
Hermitage Rd
  Altrincham WA15 ....120 A3
  Manchester M8 ....64 A1
Hermon Ave OL8 ....66 E4
Herne St M11 ....165 A8
Heron Ave Dukinfield SK16 ..101 E7
  Farnworth BL4 ....59 F7
Heron Ct Salford M6 ....80 B3
  Stockport SK3 ....170 E7
Heron Dr Droylsden M34 ..84 C1
  Irlam M44 ....94 A3
  Poynton SK12 ....133 A3
  Wigan WN3 ....54 E2
Heron Pl WN5 ....54 C8
Heron St Manchester SK5 ..162 E5
  Oldham OL8 ....66 D3
  Stockport SK3 ....170 D7
Heronfield Dr M11 ....99 D8
Herons Way BL3 ....147 D3
Heronville Dr M46 ......58 E5
Hersey St M6 ....154 E2
Hersham Wlk 9 M9 .....157 E8
Hertford Dr M29 ....59 A3
Hertford Gr M44 ....105 C6
Hertford Rd M9 ....64 D1
Hertford St OL7 ....166 A1
Hertfordshire Park Cl
  OL2 ....149 B8
Hesford Ave M9 ....157 F7
Hesketh Ave Bolton BL1 ..24 F5
  Manchester M20 ....110 A3
  Shaw OL2 ....149 B8
Hesketh Ct Atherton M46 ..58 C3
  5 Manchester SK5 ......99 E3
Hesketh Dr WN6 ....19 A2
Hesketh Fletcher
  CE High Sch M46 ....58 C2
Hesketh Manor M46 .....58 C3
Hesketh Meadow La
  WA3 ....91 A8
Hesketh Rd Rochdale OL16 ..31 C7
  Sale M33 ....107 F3
Hesketh St Atherton M46 ..58 F4
  Leigh WN7 ....75 D5
  Stockport SK4 ....169 E2
  Wigan WN5 ....54 F7
Hesketh Wlk
  5 Farnworth BL4 ....60 D8
  Middleton M24 ....46 E2
  Wythenshawe M22 ......94 D8
Hessel St M5 ....154 D1
Hester Wlk 2 M15 .....163 A5
Heston Ave M13 ....98 F3
Heston Dr M41 ....95 C3
Heswall Ave Culcheth WA3 ..91 A4
Heswall Ave continued
  Manchester M20 ....110 B7
Heswall Dr BL8 ....26 F5
Heswall Rd SK5 ....99 F1
Heswall St BL2 ....42 F7
Hetherington Wlk M12 ...99 A4
Hethorn St M40 ....83 C5
Hetton Ave M13 ....98 E2
Heversham Ave OL2 .....49 D7
Heversham Wlk M18 ...165 C5
Hewart Cl M40 ....159 C4
Hewart Dr BL9 ....141 C3
Hewitt Ave M34 ....99 F3
Hewitt Bsns Pk WN5 ....53 E4
Hewitt St M15 ....162 F7
Hewlett Rd M21 ....97 A2
Hewlett St Bolton BL2 ..148 A7
  Westhoughton BL5 ......57 B7
  Wigan WN1 ....150 C8
Hexham Ave Bolton BL1 ...23 C1
  Wigan WN3 ....54 A2
Hexham Cl Atherton M46 ..58 E4
  Oldham OL9 ....152 C7
  Sale M33 ....107 D3
  Stockport SK3 ....124 E5
Hexham Rd M18 ....99 C3
Hexon Cl M6 ....154 E3
Hey Bottom La OL12 .....14 A4
Hey Cres OL4 ....67 F7
Hey Croft M45 ....62 C7
Hey Head Ave BB4 ....3 A8
Hey Head La OL15 ....6 D1
Hey Hill Cl OL2 ....149 A5
Hey House Mews BL8 ....10 F4
Hey Shoot La WA3 ....92 C5
Hey St Ince-in-M WN3 ...55 F3
  Rochdale OL16 ....31 B8
  Wigan WN6 ....150 B8
Hey Top OL3 ....69 D3
Hey Willow BL7 ....25 C6
Hey with Zion
  CE/Methodist Prim Sch
  OL4 ....67 E7
Heybrook Cl M45 ....63 C8
Heybrook Prim Sch OL12 ..15 A1
Heybrook Rd M23 ......121 B5
Heybrook St OL16 ....31 B8
Heybrook Wlk M45 ......63 C8
Heybury Cl M11 ....164 F8
Heycrofts View BL0 ......1 E3
Heyden Bank 24 SK13 ..171 D2
Heyden Fold 22 SK13 ..171 D2
Heyden Terr 23 SK13 ...171 D2
Heyes Ave WA15 ....120 B7
Heyes Dr WA15 ....120 B7
Heyes La
  Alderley Edge SK9 ....137 B3
  Altrincham WA15 ......120 B8
Heyes Leigh WA15 .....120 B7
Heyes Rd WN5 ....53 C6
Heyes St WN6 ....35 C7
Heyford Ave M40 ....65 D2
Heyford Rd WN5 ....53 C6
Heyheads New Rd SK15 ..86 E7
Heyland Rd M23 ....121 A6
Heyridge Dr M22 ......109 D1
Heyrod St Manchester M1 ..163 C8
  Mossley SK15 ....86 D5
Heyrose Wlk 14 M15 ...162 D6
Heys Ave Romiley SK6 ..113 E3
  Swinton M27 ....61 D2
  Wythenshawe M23 .....109 A1
Heys Cl N M27 ....61 C2
Heys La Heywood OL10 ...29 A1
  Romiley SK6 ....113 E3
Heys Prim Sch The OL6 ..85 D3
Heys Rd Ashton-u-L OL6 ..85 D3
  Prestwich M25 ....63 B3
Heys St BL8 ....140 D2
Heys The Prestwich M25 ..63 B5
  Reddish M34 ....100 A1
Heys View M25 ....63 B4
Heysbank Rd SK12 .....135 D5
Heyscroft Rd
  Manchester M20 ....110 C6
  Manchester SK4 ....168 A2
Heysham Ave M20 ......109 F7
Heysham Rd WN5 ....54 D1
Heyshaw Wlk M23 .....108 F1
Heyside OL2 ....49 A3
Heyside Ave OL2 ....49 A3
Heyside Cl SK15 ....86 C6
Heywood Ave
  Golborne WA3 ....74 B1
  Oldham OL4 ....68 A8
  Swinton M27 ....62 B2
Heywood Cl SK9 ....137 E8
Heywood Com High Sch
  OL10 ....28 E1
Heywood Ct M25 ....64 A7
Heywood Distribution Pk
  BL9,OL10 ....45 F7
Heywood Fold Rd OL4 ...67 F7
Heywood Gdns
  Golborne WA3 ....74 B1
  Prestwich M25 ....63 B4
Heywood Gr M33 ....108 B5
Heywood Hall Rd OL10 ...29 D3
Heywood Ho 2 Atherton M46 ..58 C3
  Oldham OL8 ....153 E5
  Salford M6 ....80 C3
Heywood La OL4 ....68 A7
Heywood Old Rd
  M24,OL10 ....46 B3

Heywood Rd
Alderley Edge SK9 ....**137** B2
Prestwich M25 ....**63** C7
Rochdale OL11 ....**30** C1
Sale M33 ....**108** B3
Heywood St Bolton BL1 ....**145** F8
Bury BL9 ....**141** A2
Failsworth M35 ....**83** D7
Little Lever BL3 ....**43** B3
Manchester M8 ....**156** A6
Oldham OL4 ....**67** E8
Swinton M27 ....**79** E8
Heywood Sta OL10 ....**29** E1
Heywood Way M6 ....**154** F3
Heywood's Hollow BL1 ....**143** F3
Heyworth Ave SK6 ....**113** D3
Heyworth St M5 ....**154** E1
Hibbert Ave Denton M34 ...**100** E5
Hyde SK14 ....**167** E1
Hibbert Cres M35 ....**84** A6
Hibbert La SK6 ....**25** F5
Hibbert St Bolton BL1 .....**143** F2
Manchester M14 ....**98** C3
Oldham OL4 ....**67** E7
Reddish SK4,SK5 ....**111** E5
Hibernia St BL3 ....**144** C5
Hibernia Way M32 ....**96** A5
Hibson Ave OL12 ....**13** E2
Hibson Cl OL12 ....**15** C6
Hic Bibi La PR7 ....**19** E6
Hicken Pl SK14 ....**101** F5
Hickenfield Rd SK14 ....**101** F5
Hickton Dr WA14 ....**119** B6
Hieland Rd WN1 ....**37** E2
Higginshaw La OL1,OL2 ....**49** A2
Higginshaw Rd OL1 ....**67** A8
Higginson Rd SK5 ....**111** E8
Higginson St WN7 ....**76** A5
Higgs Cl OL4 ....**67** D7
High Ash Gr M34 ....**100** D7
High Ave BL2 ....**42** E7
High Bank
Altrincham WA14 ....**119** D5
Atherton M46 ....**59** A6
Bolton BL7 ....**24** F7
Manchester M18 ....**99** E5
High Bank Ave SK15 ....**102** D7
High Bank Cl M44 ....**105** D6
High Bank Cres M25 ....**63** C3
High Bank Gr M25 ....**63** C3
High Bank La BL6 ....**40** B8
High Bank Rd
Droylsden M43 ....**99** F8
Hyde SK14 ....**167** E1
Pendlebury M27 ....**80** B7
High Bank Side SK1 ......**169** F1
High Bank St BL2 ....**148** C7
High Barn Cl OL12 ....**139** E5
High Barn Com Prim Sch
OL2 ....**48** E4
High Barn La OL12 ....**4** C3
High Barn Rd
Middleton M24 ....**65** A7
Royton OL2 ....**48** F4
High Barn St OL2 ....**48** E4
High Beeches BL3 ....**43** B5
High Beeches Cres WN4 ...**73** A6
High Bent Ave SK8 ....**132** A6
High Birch Spect Sch
OL11 ....**30** B4
High Crest Ave SK8 ......**121** F5
High Croft Cl OL6 ....**102** A8
High Elm Dr WA15 ....**129** C8
High Elm Rd WA15 ....**129** D7
High Elms SK8 ....**132** B5
High Field WA14 ....**118** B2
High Gates M33 ....**108** E5
High Grove Rd
Cheadle SK8 ....**122** C5
Uppermill OL4 ....**68** E5
High Hill Rd SK22 ....**127** D1
High Hurst Cl M24 ....**64** C7
High Knowls OL4 ....**68** A4
High La Glossop SK13 ......**115** E7
Manchester M21 ....**109** B8
Romiley SK6 ....**113** E4
High Lane Prim Sch SK6 ..**134** F8
High Lawn Com Prim Sch
BL1 ....**24** E6
High Lea SK8 ....**122** C5
High Lee Ho M33 ....**108** D4
High Lee La OL4 ....**50** B4
High Legh Rd M11 ....**99** D8
High Level Rd OL11 ....**31** A6
High Mdw ☑ SK8 ....**131** E8
High Mdws Bolton BL7 ....**25** B8
Glossop SK13 ....**116** B7
Romiley SK6 ....**113** C3
High Moor Cres OL4 ....**49** F1
High Moor La WN6 ....**18** B4
High Moor View OL4 ....**49** E1
High Mount BL2 ....**25** E3
High Peak OL15 ....**16** F5
High Peak Rd
Ashton-u-L OL6 ....**86** A6
Whitworth OL12 ....**14** C6
High Peak St M40 ....**83** C6
High Pk WN6 ....**36** C6
High Rid La BL6 ....**23** B1
High St Altrincham WA14 ..**119** D4
Aspull WN2 ....**38** B6
Atherton M46 ....**58** D3
Bolton BL3 ....**147** E4
Bury BL8 ....**26** F4
Cheadle SK8 ....**122** D6

High St continued
Delph OL3 ....**50** F5
Droylsden M43 ....**84** B1
Edgworth BL7 ....**9** C4
Golborne WA3 ....**90** A8
Hazel Grove SK7 ....**124** F2
Heywood OL10 ....**29** B2
Horwich BL6 ....**22** B4
Hyde SK14 ....**167** F3
Ince-in-M WN3 ....**151** E6
Leigh WN7 ....**76** A5
Little Lever BL3 ....**43** B3
☑ Littleborough OL15 ....**15** F5
Manchester M1,M4 ....**159** A1
Manchester M4 ....**159** A2
Middleton M24 ....**47** A1
Middleton M24 ....**47** A2
Mossley OL5 ....**68** D2
Newton-le-W WA12 ....**89** D4
Oldham OL1 ....**153** F7
Rochdale OL12 ....**139** F8
Royton OL2 ....**48** D4
Shaw OL2 ....**149** B6
Stalybridge SK15 ....**85** F1
Stalybridge SK15 ....**86** A1
Standish WN6 ....**19** E1
Stockport SK1 ....**169** F1
Tyldesley M29 ....**58** F1
Tyldesley M29 ....**77** B5
Walkden M28 ....**60** D3
Wigan WN1 ....**37** D2
High St E SK13 ....**104** D1
High St W SK13 ....**104** B1
High Stile La OL4 ....**51** D2
High Stile St BL4 ....**60** E7
High View St
Bolton BL1 ....**24** E6
Bolton BL3 ....**146** C4
High Wood Fold SK6 ......**126** C8
Higham Cl OL2 ....**149** A5
Higham La SK14 ....**114** A7
Higham St SK8 ....**123** A1
Higham Way M6 ....**81** A3
Highbank SK13 ....**103** F7
Highbank Cres OL4 ....**68** E5
Highbank Dr M20 ....**122** B8
Highbank Private Hospl
BL8 ....**26** F4
Highbank Rd
Glossop SK13 ....**116** F7
Newhey OL16 ....**32** C4
Whitefield BL9 ....**44** F3
Highbridge Cl BL2 ....**43** A6
Highbrook Gr ☑ BL1 .....**143** E1
Highbury SK4 ....**110** F2
Highbury Ave Irlam M44 ...**94** A1
Urmston M41 ....**94** E2
Highbury Cl BL5 ....**57** D6
Highbury Rd
Manchester M16 ....**97** E1
Reddish SK4 ....**111** C6
Highbury Way OL2 ....**48** D6
Highclere Ave M7,M8 ....**155** F6
Highclere Rd M8 ....**63** F2
Highcliffe Ct WN6 ....**36** F7
Highcliffe Rd M9 ....**64** A3
Highclove La M28 ....**77** F5
Highcroft SK14 ....**102** A4
Highcroft Gr M29 ....**59** D1
Highcroft Rd SK6 ....**113** C3
Highcroft Way OL12 ......**14** F4
Highdales Rd M23 ....**121** B5
Highdown Wlk ☑ M9 ....**157** E8
Higher Ainsworth Rd
BL8,M26 ....**43** E7
Higher Ardwick M12 ......**163** C7
Higher Arthurs OL3 ....**69** B6
Higher Bank Rd OL15 ......**16** C5
Higher Barlow Row SK1 ..**170** F8
Higher Barn BL6 ....**22** F3
Higher Barn Rd SK14 ......**171** E8
Higher Bents La SK6 ......**113** A3
Higher Blue Bell Cotts
BL5 ....**39** C4
Higher Bridge St BL1 .....**145** F8
Higher Bury St SK4 ......**169** D2
Higher Calderbrook Rd
OL15 ....**6** C2
Higher Cambridge St
M15 ....**163** A6
Higher Carr La OL3 ....**51** A8
Higher Chatham St M15 ..**163** A6
Higher Cleggswood Ave
OL15 ....**16** A3
Higher Count Hill OL4 ......**49** E2
Higher Croft Eccles M30 ...**95** C8
Whitefield M45 ....**62** E8
Higher Cross La OL3 ....**69** C8
Higher Crossbank OL4 .....**67** F8
Higher Damshead BL5 .....**57** F8
Higher Darcy St BL2 ......**148** C5
Higher Dean St M26 ....**43** E3
Higher Dinting SK13 ......**104** A2
Higher Downs WA14 ......**119** C3
Higher Drake Mdw BL5 ....**57** E5
Higher Dunscar BL7 ....**8** E1
Higher Fold La BL0 ....**11** E7
Higher Folds Prim Sch
WN7 ....**76** D7
Higher Fullwood OL3 ......**49** D4
Higher Gamesley SK13 ...**104** C2
Higher Green La Ashton-u-L OL6 ..**166** C4
Salford M6 ....**154** F4
Higher Green La M29 ......**77** C6
Higher Henry St SK14 ....**167** E1

Higher Hillgate SK1,SK2 ..**170** F8
Higher House Cl OL9 ....**66** A4
Higher La Aspull WN2 ....**38** A4
Disley SK12 ....**135** E1
Lymm WA13 ....**117** B1
Orrell WN8 ....**53** C7
Whitefield M45 ....**62** E8
Higher Lane Cty Jun
& Inf Sch M45 ....**62** F7
Higher Lime Rd OL8 ....**84** C8
Higher Lo OL11 ....**13** D2
Higher Lomax La OL10 .....**29** A3
Higher Lydgate Pk OL4 ....**68** C6
Higher Market St BL4 ......**60** E8
Higher Moulding BL9 ......**28** E5
Higher Newtons OL5 ....**68** D2
Higher Noon Sun SK22 ...**127** F2
Higher Ormond St
M13,M15 ....**163** A6
Higher Oswald St ☑ M4 ..**159** A2
Higher Park OL2 ....**32** C2
Higher Pit La BL8 ....**43** E8
Higher Rd M41 ....**95** E2
Higher Ridings BL7 ....**24** F7
Higher Rise OL2 ....**32** A1
Higher Row BL9 ....**141** B3
Higher Shady La BL7 ......**25** C7
Higher Shore Rd OL15 .....**15** E7
Higher Southfield BL5 .....**57** E7
Higher Summerseat BL0 ...**11** B2
Higher Swan La BL3 ......**147** D3
Higher Tame St SK15 ......**86** B2
Higher Turf La OL4 ....**50** B1
Higher Turf Pk OL2 ....**48** E3
Higher Wharf St OL6,OL7 .**166** B2
Higher Wheat La OL16 .....**31** C8
Higher Wood St M24 ......**46** F1
Higher York St M13 ......**163** B6
Highfield Sale M33 ....**108** A3
Wigan WN3 ....**54** D4
Highfield Ave Atherton M46 ..**58** E5
Bolton BL2 ....**26** A3
Boothstown M28,M29 ....**77** F7
Bredbury SK6 ....**112** F2
Golborne WA3 ....**89** F8
Heywood OL10 ....**29** A2
Radcliffe M26 ....**43** F4
Higher Wlk M35 ....**83** B6
Highfield Cl Farnworth BL4 .**60** B7
Mottram-in-L SK14 ....**103** A4
Highfield Dr Eccles M30 ...**79** D3
Farnworth BL4 ....**60** A7
Middleton M24 ....**64** F7
Mossley OL5 ....**86** D8
Oldham OL2 ....**48** E2
Pendlebury M27 ....**80** C7
Standish WN6 ....**19** E1
☑ Urmston M41 ....**95** C3
Highfield Gdns
Hollingworth SK14 ....**103** D5
Hyde SK14 ....**167** F3
Highfield Glen OL6 ....**85** F7
Highfield Gr M30 ....**38** C5
Highfield Grange Ave
WN3 ....**54** D7
Highfield Ho SK3 ....**170** F5
Highfield La Golborne WA3 ..**90** C5
Whitefield M45 ....**44** F3
Highfield Park Rd SK6 ....**112** F3
Highfield Parkway SK7 ..**132** D8
Highfield Pk SK4 ....**110** F2
Highfield Pl Prestwich M25 ..**63** A5
Reddish M18 ....**99** F4
Highfield Private Hospl
OL11 ....**139** E5
Highfield Range M18 ......**99** F4
Highfield Rd Adlington PR6 ..**21** A7
Altrincham WA14 ....**120** A3
Altrincham WA15 ....**120** B5
Blackrod BL6 ....**21** D3
Bolton BL1 ....**142** B2
Cheadle SK8 ....**123** A5
Eccles M30 ....**79** D4
Edenfield BL0 ....**1** D3
Farnworth BL4 ....**60** A8
Glossop SK13 ....**116** D8
Hazel Grove SK7 ....**125** A2
Hawley WN2 ....**56** D7
☑ Marple SK6 ....**125** F6
Marple SK6 ....**134** B6
Milnrow OL16 ....**32** A6
Poynton SK12 ....**133** A4
Prestwich M25 ....**63** A5
Reddish M19 ....**99** C1
☑ Rochdale OL11 ....**31** A5
Salford M6 ....**154** E3
Stockport SK7 ....**123** F3
Stretford M32 ....**108** C8
Walkden M38 ....**59** F5
Highfield Rd N PR6 ....**21** A8
Highfield St Denton M34 ..**100** E5
Denton M34 ....**100** F6
Kearsley BL4 ....**61** A6
Manchester M7,M8 ....**155** F7
Middleton M24 ....**65** B1
Oldham OL9 ....**153** D7
☑ Stockport SK3 ....**123** C8

Highfield St Mathews
CE Prim Sch WN3 ....**54** C4
Highfield St W SK16 .....**166** B1
Highfield Terr
Ashton-u-L OL7 ....**85** A7
Manchester M9 ....**157** D8
Highfields Cty Prim Sch
BL4 ....**60** A8
Highgate BL3 ....**40** A2
Highgate Ave M41 ....**95** A4
Highgate Cres
Appley Bridge WN6 ....**35** E7
Manchester M18 ....**99** D3
Highgate Ctr ☑ SK6 ....**112** F3
Highgate Dr Royton OL2 ...**48** C7
Walkden M38 ....**59** E5
Highgate Ho ☑ OL8 ......**66** D2
Highgate La Walkden M38 ..**59** E5
Whitworth OL12 ....**14** B3
Highgate Rd
Altrincham WA14 ....**119** B4
Bolton BL1 ....**53** B7
Highgrove Cl BL1 ....**143** F3
Highgrove Mews ☑ SK9 ..**137** A6
Highgrove The BL1 ....**23** D1
Highland Ave SK6 ....**113** A2
Highland Lo WN6 ....**19** D1
Highland Rd Bolton BL7 ....**25** C8
Horwich BL6 ....**22** E1
Highland View ☑ OL5 ....**68** C2
Highland Wlk M35 ....**83** D6
Highlands
Littleborough OL15 ....**16** A3
Royton OL2 ....**48** C3
Highlands Dr SK2 ....**124** F6
Highlands Rd
Hazel Grove SK2 ....**124** F6
Rochdale OL11 ....**29** E5
Royton OL2 ....**48** C3
Shaw OL2 ....**149** A8
Highlands The ☑ OL5 ....**68** C1
Highmarsh Cres WA12 ....**89** B4
Highmead St M18 ....**99** D5
Highmead Wlk M16 ......**162** D5
Highmeadow Orrell WN8 ...**53** A6
Radcliffe M26 ....**43** F1
Highmore Dr M9 ....**64** E3
Highnam Wlk M22 ....**121** A1
Highover Ho M20 ....**109** F4
Highshore Dr BL9 ....**36** E4
Highstone Dr M8 ....**156** C6
Highthorne Gn OL2 ....**48** D8
Highview SK13 ....**116** A7
Highview Wlk M9 ....**64** E3
Highwood OL12 ....**14** A1
Highwood Cl ☑ Bolton BL2 ..**25** F1
Glossop SK13 ....**116** B8
Highwoods Cl WN4 ....**73** B3
Highworth Cl BL3 ....**145** E5
Highworth Dr M40 ....**65** D2
Hilary Ave Atherton M46 ...**58** C5
Gatley SK8 ....**131** D8
Oldham OL8 ....**74** D1
Oldham OL8 ....**84** F8
Hilary Cl SK4 ....**168** A2
Hilary Gr BL4 ....**60** D7
Hilary Rd M22 ....**121** C1
Hilary St OL11 ....**30** D1
Hilbre Ave OL8 ....**48** D2
Hilbury Ave M9 ....**64** D1
Hilda Ave Bury BL8 ....**26** F6
Cheadle SK8 ....**122** E5
Hilda Gr SK5 ....**169** F4
Hilda Rd SK14 ....**113** A8
Hilda St ☑ Bolton BL3 .....**42** A4
Heywood OL10 ....**29** D3
Leigh WN7 ....**76** D4
Oldham OL9 ....**153** D7
Reddish SK5 ....**169** F4
Hilden Ct M16 ....**97** D4
Hilden St Bolton BL2 ......**148** A6
☑ Leigh WN7 ....**75** F6
Hildyard St WN5 ....**54** B4
Hiley Rd M30 ....**79** A1
Hilgay Cl WN3 ....**54** E8
Hill ☑ WN6 ....**35** E8
Hill Cot Rd BL1 ....**24** F5
Hill Court Mews SK6 .....**113** B2
Hill Cres Leigh WN7 ....**75** C8
Manchester M9 ....**64** B4
Manchester SK4 ....**168** A4
Hill Crest Ave Leigh WN7 ..**75** C8
Manchester M19 ....**99** A1
Hill Dr SK9 ....**131** E3
Hill End Rd OL3 ....**50** F4
Hill Farm Cl OL8 ....**67** A6
Hill House Fold La WN6 ...**18** C5
Hill House La WN6 ....**18** C5
Hill La Blackrod BL6 ....**21** C2
Bolton BL2 ....**25** E4
Manchester M16 ....**102** A8
Hill Rise Altrincham WA14 ..**19** C4
Ramsbottom BL0 ....**11** A4
Romiley SK6 ....**113** B3
Hill Side BL1 ....**40** F7
Hill St Altrincham WA14 ...**119** C8
Ashton-u-L OL6,OL7 ....**166** B2
Bury BL9 ....**36** F8
Droylsden M43 ....**84** C1
Heywood OL10 ....**29** C2
Hindley WN2 ....**56** D6

Hill St continued
Leigh WN7 ....**75** E5
Manchester M20 ....**110** B7
Manchester M7 ....**155** D6
Oldham OL4 ....**67** B7
Oldham M24 ....**47** A3
Oldham OL8 ....**66** C4
Radcliffe OL16 ....**31** A7
Rochdale OL16 ....**31** A2
Shaw OL2 ....**149** C6
Wigan WN6 ....**37** B1
Hill Top Altrincham WA15 ..**120** A1
Atherton M46 ....**58** D1
Bolton BL1 ....**143** D3
Little Lever BL3 ....**43** A4
Romiley SK6 ....**113** B3
Hill Top Ave Cheadle SK8 ..**132** B8
Prestwich M25 ....**63** B4
Wilmslow SK9 ....**137** B8
Hill Top Com Prim Sch
OL3 ....**51** A1
Hill Top Com Specl Sch
SK8 ....**123** B1
Hill Top Dr
Altrincham WA15 ....**120** A1
Rochdale OL10 ....**30** F2
Hill Top Fold ☑ WN2 ......**56** E6
Hill Top Rd OL3 ....**50** C4
Hill View Delph OL3 ....**50** F4
Stalybridge SK15 ....**102** C6
Stalybridge SK15 ....**86** A4
Hill View Ct M24 ....**46** F3
Hill View Dr PR7 ....**19** D8
Hill's Ct ☑ BL8 ....**27** B4
Hillam Cl M41 ....**95** F1
Hillary Ave Ashton-u-L OL7 ..**85** B5
Wigan WN5 ....**54** D5
Hillary Rd SK14 ....**102** A5
Hillbank WN6 ....**37** A7
Hillbank Cl BL1 ....**142** C3
Hillbank St OL11 ....**47** D6
Hillbeck Cres WN4 ....**72** D4
Hillbre Ave WA11 ....**71** A1
Hillbre Way Handforth SK9 .**131** E4
☑ Wilmslow SK9 ....**131** D4
Hillbrook Ave M40 ....**65** B2
Hillbrook Rd
Bramhall SK7 ....**132** D6
Stockport SK1,SK2 ....**124** C8
Hillbrow Wlk ☑ M8 ....**155** F7
Hillbury Rd SK7 ....**123** F1
Hillcote Wlk M18 ....**165** B6
Hillcourt Rd
High Lane SK6 ....**134** F7
Romiley SK6 ....**113** C4
Hillcourt St M1 ....**163** A7
Hillcrest Hyde SK14 ....**113** F7
Middleton M24 ....**46** F3
Oldham OL8 ....**153** A5
Hillcrest Ave OL10 ....**29** A3
Hillcrest Cres OL10 ....**29** A3
Hillcrest Dr Denton M34 ..**101** B1
Reddish M19 ....**111** C7
Hillcrest Grammar Sch
SK3 ....**170** F6
Hillcrest Rd Prestwich M25 ..**63** C2
Rochdale OL11 ....**30** D1
Stockport SK2 ....**124** C7
Stockport SK2 ....**124** C7
Hillcroft Oldham OL8 ....**67** A1
Stockport SK6 ....**112** F1
Hillcroft Cl M8 ....**156** A8
Hillcroft Rd WA14 ....**64** E4
Hilldean WN6 ....**53** C8
Hillel Ho M15 ....**103** A1
Hillend SK14 ....**103** A1
Hillend La SK14 ....**103** A1
Hillend Rd M23 ....**109** A2
Hillfield M5 ....**154** E2
Hillfield Cl M13 ....**164** D5
Hillfield Dr Bolton BL2 .....**25** B1
Boothstown M28 ....**78** A6
Hillfield Wlk ☑ BL2 ....**25** B1
Hillfoot Wlk ☑ M15 ......**162** D6
Hillgate Ave M5 ....**161** B7
Hillgate St OL6 ....**85** B6
Hillhead Wlk M8 ....**156** A5
Hillhouse Ct OL12 ....**30** B3
Hillier St N M9 ....**157** E8
Hillingdon Cl OL8 ....**84** B8
Hillingdon Dr M9 ....**65** B2
Hillington Rd Sale M33 ...**108** C4
Stockport SK3 ....**123** C8
Hillkirk Dr OL12 ....**14** C3
Hillkirk St M11 ....**160** L1
Hillman Cl M40 ....**157** D5
Hillock The Bolton BL2 .....**25** B5
Tyldesley M29 ....**77** B5
Hillocks The M29 ....**77** B5
Hills La BL9 ....**45** B2
Hillsdale Gr BL2 ....**43** A2
Hillside WA13 ....**117** C1
Hillside Ave
Ashton-in-M WN4 ....**72** F8
Atherton M46 ....**58** E4
Bolton BL7 ....**25** C8
Diggle OL3 ....**51** C3

Hillside Ave continued
Farnworth BL4 ....60 C7
Horwich BL6 ....22 C4
Manchester M7 ....81 A8
Mossley SK15 ....86 F6
Oldham OL4 ....67 C7
Oldham OL4 ....68 B5
Romiley SK14 ....113 F6
Royton OL2 ....48 E5
Shaw OL2 ....49 D8
Walkden M28 ....60 C4
Whitefield M45 ....44 E2
Hillside Cl Billinge WN5 .71 D5
Bolton BL2 ....25 E5
Bolton BL3 ....40 D2
Bramhall SK7 ....133 A7
Disley SK12 ....135 E6
Hadfield SK14 ....171 E3
Manchester M40 ....65 A1
Wigan WN3 ....54 D3
Hillside Cres
Ashton-u-L OL6 ....85 F5
Bury BL9 ....27 F6
Horwich BL6 ....22 C4
Hillside Ct BL1 ....40 F7
Hillside Dr Middleton M24 .47 B1
Pendlebury M27 ....80 D6
Hillside Gr SK6 ....114 B1
Hillside Rd
Altrincham WA15 ....120 A3
Ramsbottom BL0 ....138 A5
Romiley SK14,SK6 ....113 D5
Stockport SK2 ....124 D7
Hillside St 6 BL3 ......145 D5
Hillside View Denton M34 .113 A7
Milnrow OL16 ....32 A6
Hillside Way OL12 ....4 C1
Hillstone Ave OL12 .....14 D4
Hillstone Cl BL3 ....10 F2
Hilltop OL12 ....14 C5
Hill Top Ave Manchester M9 .64 D3
Whitefield M45 ....63 B8
Hilltop Ct Manchester M14 ..98 D1
Manchester M8 ....63 F2
Hilltop Dr Bury BL9 ......26 E6
Haslingden BB4 ....1 C7
Marple SK6 ....125 C7
Oldham OL2 ....48 E2
Hilltop Gr M45 ....63 B8
Hilltop Rd SK13 ....104 B2
Hillview Cl BL1 ....143 E4
Hillview Rd Bolton BL1 ..143 E4
Reddish M34 ....100 A1
Hillwood Ave M8 ....63 F3
Hillwood Dr SK13 ....116 F8
Hilly Croft BL7 ....24 F8
Hillyard St 7 BL8 ....27 C3
Hilmarton Cl BL2 ....25 E5
Hilrose Ave M41 ....95 F2
Hilson Ct M43 ....84 A1
Hilton Arc OL1 ....153 F7
Hilton Ave Horwich BL6 ...22 C4
Urmston M41 ....95 D2
Hilton Bank M28 ....60 B3
Hilton Cl WN7 ....76 A5
Hilton Cres Ashton-u-L OL6 .85 C5
Boothstown M28 ....78 B6
Prestwich M25 ....63 B2
Hilton Ct SK3 ....123 C6
Hilton Dr Irlam M44 ....105 C5
Manchester M25 ....63 B2
Hilton Fold La M24 ....47 B1
Hilton Gr Poynton SK12 ..133 D4
Walkden M28 ....60 B2
Hilton La Prestwich M25 ...63 A2
Walkden M28 ....60 B2
Hilton Lo M25 ....63 B2
Hilton Pl WN2 ....38 C6
Hilton Rd Bury BL9 ......140 F2
Disley SK12 ....135 E6
High Lane SK12 ....134 C5
Stockport SK7 ....123 F1
Hilton Sq M27 ....62 A1
Hilton St
Ashton-in-M WN4 ....73 C3
Bolton BL2 ....148 C7
Bury BL9 ....37 B3
Dukinfield SK14 ....101 F5
Manchester M1 ....159 B1
Manchester M1,M4 ......159 B2
Manchester M7 ....155 D5
Stockport SK3 ....170 D8
Walkden M38 ....60 A4
Wigan WN1 ....37 D1
Hilton St W M7 ....155 D6
Hilton Wlk M24 ....64 C8
Hiltons Farm Cl M34 ....100 E6
Himley Rd M11 ....83 C3
Hincaster Wlk M18 ......165 C5
Hinchcombe Cl M38 ......60 A6
Hinchley Way M27 ....61 F2
Hinckley St M11 ....164 F8
Hind Hill St OL10 ....29 D1
Hind Rd WN5 ....54 D8
Hind St M12 ....148 C7
Hind's Head Ave WN6 ....18 F6
Hindburn Cl M45 ....45 B1
Hindburn Dr M28 ....78 A8
Hindburn Wlk M45 ....45 B1
Hindle St M40 ....83 D4
Hindell Terr OL3 ....50 F4
Hindhead Wlk M40 ....83 D4
Hindle Dr OL2 ....48 C3
Hindle St Bacup OL13 ......3 D8
Radcliffe M26 ....44 A3
Hindles Cl M46 ....58 A1

Hindley All Saints
CE Prim Sch WN2 ....56 E5
Hindley Ave M22 ....121 B2
Hindley Borsdane Brook
Com Specl Sch WN2 .....56 E4
Hindley Bsns Ctr 11 WN2 .56 D5
Hindley Cl OL7 ....84 F1
Hindley Green
Cty Prim Sch WN2 ....57 B3
Hindley Jun & Inf Sch
.........................56 E4
Hindley Mill La WN2 ......56 E7
Hindley Rd BL5,WN2 ....57 D5
Hindley St Ashton-u-L OL7 ..84 F1
Stockport SK1 ....170 F8
Hindley Sta WN2 ....56 D7
Hindley Tanfield Sch WN2 .56 E5
Hindley Wlk 1 WN1 ......150 C8
Hinds La Bury BL8 ....27 C1
Bury BL8,BL9 ....44 C7
Hindsford CE Prim Sch
M46 ....58 E1
Hindsford Cl M23 ....108 E1
Hindsford St M46 ....58 F1
Hinkler Ave BL3 ....147 E3
Hinstock Cres M18 ....99 D5
Hinton 2 OL12 ....139 E8
Hinton Cl OL11 ....29 E6
Hinton Gr SK14 ....114 A8
Hinton Mews M41 ....112 B1
Hinton St Manchester M4 ..159 B3
Oldham OL8 ....66 E3
Hipley Cl SK6 ....113 A5
Hirons La OL4 ....68 A5
Hirst Ave M28 ....60 C5
Hitchen Cl SK16 ....101 F7
Hitchen Dr SK16 ....101 F7
Hitchin Wlk M13 ....164 D5
Hive St OL8 ....66 E3
HM Prison Strangeways
.........................158 F4
HMS Bronington M17 ......96 E7
Hoad Wlk 3 M34 ....113 A7
Hoade St WN7 ....75 F5
Hob Hey La WA3 ....91 D3
Hob Hill 8 SK15 ....85 F1
Hob Hill Mdws SK13 ......116 D7
Hob La BL7 ....9 C7
Hob Mill Rise OL5 ....68 E4
Hobart Cl SK7 ....132 F4
Hobart St Bolton BL1 .....143 D2
Manchester M18 ....99 F5
Hobby Gr WN7 ....76 B5
Hobson Cres M34 ....100 E6
Hobson St M34 ....100 E6
Hobson Moor Rd
SK14,SK15 ....103 A7
Hobson St Droylsden M11 ..100 A7
Failsworth M35 ....83 D6
Oldham OL1 ....153 F6
Reddish SK5 ....99 F2
Hockenhull Cl M22 ......121 E2
Hockery View WN2 ....56 C4
Hockley Cl SK12 ....134 A3
Hockley Rd Poynton SK12 .134 A3
8 Wythenshawe M23 ....120 F6
Hodder Ave
Littleborough OL15 ....15 F6
Platt Bridge WN2 ....55 F2
Hodder Bank SK2 ....124 E5
Hodder Cl WN5 ....54 D7
Hodder Way M45 ....63 C8
Hoddesdon St M8 ....156 B7
Hodge Clough Inf Sch
OL1 ....49 D3
Hodge Clough Jun Sch
.........................49 D3
Hodge Clough Rd OL1 ......49 D3
Hodge La
Mottram-in-L SK14 ......114 F8
Salford M5,M6 ....154 F1
Hodge Rd Oldham OL1 ......49 D3
Walkden M28 ....60 D2
Hodge St M9 ....64 F1
Hodgson Dr WN6 ....37 A2
Hodgson Dr WA15 ....120 A8
Hodgson St
Ashton-u-L OL6 ....166 A2
Manchester M8 ....155 F5
Hodnet Dr WN4 ....73 C3
Hodnet Wlk M34 ....100 E1
Hodnett Ave M41 ....94 E1
Hodson Fold OL8 ....67 A1
Hodson Rd M27 ....61 E6
Hodson St Manchester M3 .158 E2
Wigan WN1 ....150 C2
Hogarth Rd Marple SK6 ...126 B8
Rochdale OL11 ....30 C1
Hogarth Rise OL1 ....49 D4
Hogarth Wlk M8 ....156 C6
Hoghton Ave OL13 ....4 A8
Holbeach Cl Bury BL8 .....27 D5
Manchester M18 ....99 D5
Holbeck M29 ....77 B5
Holbeck Ave OL12 ....14 D4
Holbeck Gr M14 ....98 E4
Holberton St M8 ....155 E5
Holbeton Cl SK7 ....124 A8
Holborn Ave
Failsworth M35 ....84 B7
Leigh WN7 ....75 F8
Radcliffe M26 ....43 D4
Holborn Dr M8 ....156 B5
Holborn Gdns OL11 ....139 D5
Holborn Sq OL11 ....139 D5
Holborn St OL11 ....139 D5
Holbrook Ave M38 ....60 A5

Holbrook St M1 ....163 A8
Holcombe Ave Bury BL8 ....27 B2
Golborne WA3 ....90 C8
Holcombe Brook
Prim Sch BL0 ....11 A2
Holcombe Cl Oldham OL4 ..
Altrincham WA14 ....119 B6
Kearsley BL4 ....61 A6
Oldham OL4 ....68 A7
Salford M6 ....81 A2
Holcombe Cres BL4 ....61 A6
Holcombe Ct BL0 ....10 F2
Holcombe Gdns M19 ......110 E5
Holcombe Lee BL0 ....11 A4
Holcombe Mews BL0 ....11 A4
Holcombe Old Rd BL8 ....138 A5
Holcombe Rd
Haslingden BB4 ....1 A6
Little Lever BL3 ....42 F3
Manchester M14 ....110 E7
Ramsbottom BL8 ....10 F2
Holcombe View Cl OL4 .....49 D2
Holcombe Wlk SK4 ....111 D7
Holcroft La WA3 ....92 D2
Holden Ave Bolton BL1 ....24 E6
Bury BL9 ....28 E4
Holden Brook Cl WN7 ......76 A5
Holden Clough Dr OL7 .....85 B7
Holden Clough
Prim & Com Sch OL6 ....85 D7
Holden Fold La OL1,OL2 ...48 D3
Holden Lea BL5 ....39 E3
Holden Rd Leigh WN7 ......76 B3
Manchester M25,M7 ....63 D1
Holden St Adlington PR7 ...20 F7
Ashton-u-L OL6 ....166 C4
Oldham OL8 ....66 F3
Rochdale OL12 ....15 A2
Holder Ave BL3 ....43 B5
Holdgate Cl M15 ....162 E5
Holding St WN2 ....56 D6
Holdsworth St M27 ....79 D7
Hole House Fold SK6 .....113 A2
Holebottom OL6 ....85 C6
Holford Ave M14 ....98 B2
Holford Ct M40 ....100 F3
Holford Rd M6 ....81 C4
Holford Way WA12 ....89 F3
Holford Wlk OL16 ....31 D7
Holgate Dr WN5 ....53 E6
Holgate Prim Sch WN5 ....53 E5
Holgate St OL4 ....49 E1
Holhouse La BL8 ....10 F2
Holiday La SK2 ....124 F7
Holker Cl
Manchester M13 ....164 D5
Poynton SK12 ....133 F4
Holker Way 21 M34 ......101 A1
Holkham Cl 9 M4 ....159 C2
Holland Ave SK15 ....86 A2
Holland Cl OL3 ....50 E4
Holland Ct Manchester M8 ..63 F2
Radcliffe M26 ....44 C4
Stockport SK1 ....124 A7
Holland Gr OL6 ....85 B6
Holland Rise 7 OL12 ....139 E8
Holland St Bolton BL1 ....143 F4
Denton M34 ....100 D4
Heywood OL10 ....29 D2
Littleborough OL16 ....15 D4
Manchester M40 ....160 D3
Radcliffe M26 ....44 C4
Rochdale OL12 ....139 E8
Salford M6 ....81 A5
Holland St E M34 ....100 E4
Holland St W M34 ....100 D4
Holland Wlk M6 ....81 A5
Hollands Cl SK14 ....103 B4
Hollies Dr SK6 ....126 A5
Hollies La SK9 ....137 F7
Hollies The
10 Atherton M46 ....58 D3
Bolton BL3 ....42 F8
Gatley SK8 ....122 B5
Manchester M20 ....109 F3
Manchester M45 ....168 B3
Pendlebury M27 ....80 D8
Salford M6 ....80 B3
Wigan WN1 ....37 D3
Hollin Acre BL5 ....57 F7
Hollin Bank SK4 ....111 D7
Hollin Cres OL4 ....68 A4
Hollin Cross La SK13 ....116 C8
Hollin Dr M24 ....46 F4
Hollin Hey Cl WN5 ....71 D3
Hollin Hey Rd BL1 ....23 E3
Hollin House M24 ....47 A3
Hollin La
Middleton M24,OL10 ......46 F4
Rochdale OL11 ....29 E6
Styal SK9 ....130 F5
Hollin Prim Sch M24 ......47 A3
Hollinbrook WN6 ....36 F2
Holliney Ave M22 ....121 F1
Holling Rd M22 ....121 E2
Hollington Way WN3 ....54 C2
Hollingwood Cl WN4 ....73 A3
Hollingworth Ave M40 .....65 F2
Hollingworth Cl 5 SK1 ..170 D8
Hollingworth Dr SK6 .....126 F3
Hollingworth High Sch
OL16 ....8 F3
Hollingworth La OL14 ......6 B8

Hollingworth Lake Ctry Pk
Visitor Ctr
OL15 ....16 C3
Hollingworth Lake Ctry Pk
OL15 ....16 B2
Hollingworth Lake
Water Sports Ctr OL15 ..16 B3
Hollingworth Prim Sch
SK14 ....103 C5
Hollingworth Rd
Bredbury SK6 ....112 E4
Littleborough OL15 ....16 B3
Hollingworth St OL9 ....66 B3
Hollinhall St OL4 ....67 C7
Hollinhey Terr SK14 .....103 C5
Hollinhurst Rd M26 ....40 C7
Hollinhurst Rd M26 ....44 C1
Hollins Ave
40 Gamesley SK13 ....171 D2
Hyde SK14 ....113 E7
Oldham OL4 ....67 B8
Hollins Bank 39 SK13 ....171 D2
Hollins Brook Cl BL9 ......45 B5
Hollins Brow SK13 ....44 F4
Hollins Cl
34 Gamesley SK13 ....171 D2
Garswood WN4 ....72 D4
Oldham OL4 ....67 B8
Whitefield BL9 ....45 B4
Hollins Cty Prim Sch
WN2 ....57 A5
Hollins Fold 38 SK13 ....171 D2
Hollins Gdns 59 SK13 ....171 D2
Hollins Gn M24 ....47 A3
Hollins Gr
37 Gamesley SK13 ....171 D2
Manchester M12 ....99 A3
Sale M33 ....108 C3
Hollins Green Rd SK6 ....125 F6
Hollins Grundy Prim
Sch BL9 ....45 B5
Hollins Ind Pk SK13 .....104 B5
Hollins La Edenfield BL0 ...1 E2
Gamesley SK13 ....171 D2
Marple SK6 ....125 F6
Marple SK6 ....126 C8
Mossley SK15 ....68 C3
Mossley SK6 ....69 D5
Oldham OL4 ....45 B4
Hollins Mews
Gamesley SK13 ....171 D2
Whitefield BL9 ....45 C4
Hollins Rd Hindley WN2 ...57 A5
Oldham OL4 ....67 F8
Oldham OL8 ....66 D2
Hollins St Bolton BL2 ....148 B6
6 Oldham OL4 ....67 F6
Stalybridge SK15 ....101 F8
Walsden OL14 ....6 B8
Hollins Terr 2 SK6 ......125 F6
Hollins The 4 SK6 ....125 F6
Hollins Way M22 ....121 E5
Hollins Wlk M22 ....121 E5
Hollinsciough Cl M22 ....121 E5
Hollinscroft Ave WA15 ...120 D5
Hollinshead M7 ....155 E6
Hollinsmoor Rd SK22 ....127 D7
Hollinswood Rd
Bolton BL2 ....148 B6
Boothstown M28 ....78 B6
Hollinwood Ave M40,OL9 ..65 E2
Hollinwood La SK6 .....126 B2
Hollinwood Rd SK12 ....135 D6
Hollinwood Sta OL9 .....66 A2
Hollow End M35 ....84 C3
Hollow Mdws M26 ....61 C6
Hollow The SK8 ....122 C1
Hollow Vale Dr SK5 ....112 A8
Hollow Vale Rd SK5 .....99 F1
Hollowbrook Way 4 OL12 .14 D2
Hollowell La BL6 ....22 D1
Hollowfield OL11 ....113 D1
Hollowgate M29 ....79 B6
Hollows The SK8 ....122 C1
Hollowspell OL12 ....15 C3
Holly Ave Cheadle SK8 ..122 D5
Newton-le-W WA12 ....89 D3
Walkden M38 ....60 C2
Holly Bank Ashton-u-L OL6 ..85 D2
Edgworth BL7 ....9 A7
Failsworth M40 ....83 C7
Hollingworth SK14 ......103 D5
2 Irlam M44 ....94 B3
7 Manchester M20 ......110 B6
Stockport SK3 ....170 E5
Holly Dene Dr BL6 ....40 F7
Holly Dr M33 ....108 A4
Holly Fold M45 ....44 F2
Holly Gr Bolton BL1 .....142 C1
Bolton BL6 ....40 B7
Chadderton OL9 ....152 B8
Denton M34 ....96 D4
Dukinfield SK15 ....101 E8
Farnworth BL4 ....60 D7
Leigh WN7 ....75 E7
Oldham OL4 ....67 C7
Sale M33 ....108 D4

Holly Grange
Altrincham WA14 ....119 D2
Stockport SK7 ....123 F3
Holly Heath Dr WN1 ....37 B4
Holly Heys 5 M33 ....108 D4
Holly House Dr M41 ....94 F2
Holly La Oldham OL8 ......66 C2
Wythenshawe SK9 ....130 E5
Holly Mill Cres BL1 .....143 F4
Holly Mount BB4 ....1 A7
Holly Mount RC Prim Sch
BL8 ....10 D1
Holly Oak Gdns OL10 ......29 C1
Holly Rd Aspull WN2 ....38 B5
Bramhall SK7 ....132 E5
Golborne WA3 ....90 C8
High Lane SK6 ....134 F7
Lymm WA13 ....117 B5
Poynton SK12 ....133 E3
Reddish SK4 ....111 C5
Swinton M27 ....79 D6
Wigan WN5 ....54 E6
Holly Rd N SK9 ....137 B6
Holly Rd S SK9 ....137 B5
Holly Royde Cl M20 ......110 B6
Holly St Bolton BL1 ......143 F4
Bury BL8 ....26 F6
Bury BL9 ....141 A2
Droylsden M43 ....83 D2
Littleborough OL12 ....16 C6
Manchester M11 ....164 E8
Ramsbottom BL9 ....11 C3
Stockport SK1 ....112 B1
Wigan WN2 ....37 F2
Holly Wlk M31 ....105 D3
Hollybank Rise SK16 .....101 F8
Hollybank St M26 ....143 F3
Hollybush Sq WA3 ....74 E1
Hollybush St M18 ....99 E6
Hollycroft Ave Bolton BL2 ..42 E5
Hollyedge Dr M25 ....121 D6
Hollyedge Dr M25 ....63 D1
Hollyhedge Court Rd
M22 ....121 E5
Hollyhedge Ct M22 ....121 E4
Hollyhedge Rd M22,M23 ..121 C5
Hollyhey Dr M23 ....109 C2
Hollyhurst M28 ....79 B6
Hollymount Ave SK2 .....124 C5
Hollymount Dr Oldham OL4 ..49 E3
Stockport SK2 ....124 C5
Hollymount Gdns SK2 ....124 D5
Hollymount Rd SK2 ......124 D5
Hollythorn Ave SK8 ......132 C7
Hollyway M22 ....121 E4
Hollywood
Altrincham WA14 ....119 D2
Bolton BL1 ....142 B2
Hollywood Rd Bolton BL1 .142 B2
Moorend SK6 ....126 F8
Hollywood Towers SK3 ...170 D8
Hollywood Way SK3,SK4 ..169 D1
Holm Cl M6 ....81 A3
Holmbrook M29 ....59 C1
Holmcroft Rd M18 ....99 D3
Holmdale Ave M19 ....110 E5
Holme Ave Bury BL8 ....27 C5
Wigan WN3 ....37 C2
Holme Ct 7 WN1 ....37 C2
Holme House St OL15 ......6 D1
Holme La Haslingden BB4 ...1 D8
Ramsbottom BB4 ....1 D8
Holme Park Way M35 ......84 B7
Holme Rd M20 ....110 A3
Holme St Bacup OL13 ......3 D8
Hyde SK14 ....167 D2
Holme Terr
Littleborough OL15 ....6 D1
Rawtenstall BB4 ....1 D8
Wigan WN1 ....37 B3
Holme Vale BB4 ....1 A6
Holmedale Cl M33 ....108 C4
Holmefield M33 ....108 B4
Holmepark Gdns M28 .....78 A5
Holmes Cotts BL1 ....142 C3
Holmes House Ave WN3 ...54 D3
Holmes Rd OL12 ....139 D7
Holmes St Bolton BL3 .....42 A4
Cheadle SK8 ....122 C6
Littleborough OL12 ......139 D7
Rochdale OL12 ....139 D7
Stockport SK3 ....170 E7
Holmes Way M34 ....113 F7
Holmeswood Cl SK9 ......137 C8
Holmeswood Pk BB4 ....1 E8
Holmeswood Rd BL3 ......147 D2
Holmfield Ave
Manchester M25 ....63 C3
Manchester M9 ....157 F7
Holmfield Ave W M9 ......157 F7
Holmfield Cl SK4 ....169 D3
Holmfield Dr Cheadle SK8 .132 B8
Whitefield M45 ....44 F4
Holmfield Gn BL3 ....40 F4
Holmfield Grove M46 .....157 D7
Holmfirth Rd SK13 ....104 C2
Holmlea Rd M43 ....83 E2
Holmleigh Ave M9 ....64 E1
Holmpark Rd M11 ....83 F2
Holmsfield Cl WN2 ....38 A2

Holmside Gdns M19 ....110 E4
Holmwood WA14 ....119 A3
Holmwood Cl WN4 ......73 A5
Holmwood Ct M20 ......110 B4
Holmwood Rd M20 .....110 B5
Holroyd St
　Manchester M11 ......165 A8
　Rochdale OL16 ....31 A7
Holset Dr WA14 ....119 B5
Holst Ave M8 ....156 A6
Holstein Ave OL12 .....14 D4
Holt Ave WN5 ....71 D4
Holt Cres WN5 ....71 D4
Holt Ho M20 ....110 B2
Holt La M35 ....84 B7
Holt Lane Mews M35 ...84 B7
Holt Mill Rd BB4 ....2 D8
Holt St Altrincham WA14 ..119 E8
　Ashton-u-L M34 ....100 E8
　Bolton BL3 ....145 D5
　Eccles M30 ....95 C8
　Hindley WN7 ....56 C5
　Leigh WN7 ....75 E7
　Littleborough OL15 ....6 D2
　Manchester M10,M40 ..157 F5
　Milnrow OL16 ....32 A5
　Oldham OL4 ....67 C8
　Orrell WN5 ....53 D5
　Ramsbottom BL0 ......11 A6
　Rawtenstall BB4 ....2 E8
　Shevington WN6 ......36 F2
　Stockport SK1 ....170 F8
　Swinton M27 ....61 F2
　Tyldesley M29 ....59 A1
　Whitworth OL12 ....4 C1
　Wigan WN1 ....151 F8
　Wigan WN3 ....55 A4
Holt St W BL0 ....138 B5
Holt Town M4,M40 ....160 E2
Holt's La SK9 ....130 F3
Holt's Terr OL12 ....14 E2
Holtby St M9 ....64 E1
Holthouse Rd BL8 .....26 F5
Holtown Ind Est M40 ..160 E2
Holts La OL4 ....67 D4
Holtswell Cl WA3 ......74 E1
Holwood Wlk SK5 .....112 C7
Holway Wlk M9 ....156 C7
Holwick Rd M23 ....108 F2
Holwood Dr M16 ......109 C8
Holy Cross & All Saints
　RC Sch N30 ....95 D8
Holy Cross Coll BL9 ...44 E8
Holy Family RC Inf Sch
　WN2 ....38 A2
Holy Family RC Prim Sch
　Boothstown M28 .....26 D4
　Oldham OL8 ....84 D8
　Platt Bridge WN2 .....56 A1
　Rochdale OL11 ....31 A2
　Sale M33 ....108 E4
Holy Harbour St BL1 ..142 C2
Holy Inf & St Anthony
　RC Prim Sch BL1 ....143 E4
Holy Name RC Prim Sch
　M15 ....163 A5
Holy Rosary RC Prim Sch
　OL8 ....66 F2
Holy St OL16 ....31 E2
Holy Trinity CE Dobcross
　Prim Sch OL3 ....50 F2
Holy Trinity CE Prim Sch
　Ashton-u-L OL6 ......166 A3
　Bury BL9 ....140 F1
　Littleborough OL15 ...16 B5
　Manchester M9 ....157 E8
Holy Trinity Stacksteads
　CE Prim Sch OL13 ...3 C8
Holybourne Wlk M23 ..120 D8
Holyhurst Wlk 8 BL1 .143 E2
Holyoak St M40 ....83 C6
Holyoake Rd M28 .....60 E2
Holyoake St M43 ......84 C2
Holyrood Cl Leigh WN7 ..76 E7
　Prestwich M25 ....63 C6
Holyrood Ct M25 .....63 C6
Holyrood Dr Prestwich M25 ..63 C6
　Swinton M27 ....79 D7
Holyrood Gr M25 .....63 C6
Holyrood Rd M25 .....63 C6
Holyrood St Failsworth M40 ..83 E4
　Oldham OL1 ....49 A1
Holywood St 1 M14 ...98 B3
Home Dr M24 ....64 F7
Home Farm Ave SK14 ..102 F1
Homebury Dr M11 .....83 B2
Homelands Cl M33 ....107 F2
Homelands Rd M33 ...107 F2
Homelands Wlk M9 ...157 D7
Homelaurel Ho M33 ..108 B2
Homer Dr SK6 ....126 B8
Homer St M26 ....43 E3
Homerton Rd M40 ....83 B4
Homestead Cl M31 ...106 A4
Homestead Cres M19 ..110 E4
Homestead Gdns OL12 ..15 D4
Homestead Rd SK12 ..135 C6
Homestead The M33 ..107 F5
Homewood Ave M22 ..109 D1
Homewood Rd M22 ...109 C1
Honduras St 1 OL4 ...67 B7
Hondwith Cl BL2 ......25 C5
Honey St M8 ....159 B4
Honeybourne Cl M29 ..59 C1
Honeysuckle Ave WN6 ..36 F3

Honeysuckle Cl
　Romiley SK6 ....113 A5
　Sale M23 ....108 D1
Honeysuckle Dr SK15 ..86 C2
Honeysuckle Way OL12 ..14 D3
Honeysuckle Wlk M33 ..107 D6
Honeywell La OL8 .....66 F3
Honeywood Cl BL0 ....11 A3
Honford Rd M22 .....121 C4
Hong Kong Ave M90 ..130 A8
Honister Dr M24 ......46 F2
Honister Rd
　Manchester M9 ......157 F7
　Wigan WN5 ....54 B6
Honister Way OL11 ....30 B4
Honiton Ave SK14 ....102 D2
Honiton Cl Chadderton OL9 ..47 E1
　Heywood OL10 ....46 C8
Honiton Ct SK14 .....102 D2
Honiton Dr BL2 ....43 A6
Honiton Gr M26 ......43 D4
Honiton Way M14 ....119 B6
Honiton Wlk 8 SK14 ..102 D2
Honor St M13 ....98 F3
Hood Cl M29 ....59 D1
Hood Gr WN7 ....76 B3
Hood Sq OL4 ....68 A5
Hood St M4 ....159 B2
Hook St WN7 ....151 F7
Hoole Cl SK8 ....123 A5
Hooley Bridge Ind Est
　OL10 ....29 C4
Hooley Range SK4 ...168 B3
Hooper St
　Manchester M12 ....164 D8
　9 Oldham OL4 ....67 A6
　Stockport SK1,SK4 ...169 E1
Hooten La WN7 ......76 C3
Hooton St Bolton BL3 ..146 C3
　Manchester M40 .....160 D1
Hooton Way 14 SK9 ..131 D5
Hopcroft Cl M9 ......64 B6
Hope Ave Bolton BL2 ..148 B6
　Bolton BL2 ....25 E5
　Handforth SK9 ......131 C3
　Stretford M32 ......96 B3
Hope Carr La WN7 ...76 B2
Hope Carr Rd Leigh WN7 ..76 A3
　Leigh WN7 ....76 B3
Hope Carr Way WN7 ..76 A3
Hope Cres WN6 .....36 B6
Hope Ct 5 OL12 .....139 F8
Hope Fold Ave M46 ..58 B2
Hope Green Way SK10 ..133 D2
Hope Hey La M38 ....59 F5
Hope High Sch M6 ...80 C4
Hope Hospl M6 ......80 B3
Hope La Leigh WA3,WN7 ..76 E2
　Poynton SK10 ......133 D1
　Poynton SK10 ......133 E1
Hope Park Cl M25 ...63 B3
Hope Park Rd M25 ...63 B3
Hope Pl OL11 ....30 C1
Hope Rd Manchester M14 ..98 D4
　Prestwich M25 ......63 A2
　Sale M33 ....108 B3
Hope St Adlington PR6 ..21 B8
　Ashton-in-M WN4 ...73 D5
　Ashton-u-L OL6 .....85 D4
　Aspull WN2 ....38 F3
　Blackrod BL6 ....38 E8
　Denton M34 ....100 F5
　Dukinfield SK16 .....101 B8
　Eccles M30 ....79 F2
　Glossop SK13 ......104 E2
　Hazel Grove SK7 ....124 D3
　Heywood OL10 .....56 F6
　Hindley WN2 ....56 C6
　Horwich BL6 ....22 B4
　Ince-in-M WN3 .....55 E4
　Leigh WN7 ....75 F6
　Manchester M1 .....159 A1
　Manchester M5 .....81 C1
　Newton-le-W WA12 ..89 B3
　Oldham OL1 ....67 B7
　Pendlebury M27 ....80 A8
　Ramsbottom BL0 ...138 B5
　Rochdale OL12 ......139 F8
　Shaw OL2 ....149 B7
　Stockport SK4 .....169 D1
　Swinton M27 ....79 F5
　Tyldesley M29 ......77 B5
　Walkden M38 ......60 A4
　Wigan WN1 ....150 C8
Hope St E SK10 .....22 B5
Hope Terr Stockport SK3 ..170 E8
　Dukinfield SK16 ....101 B8
Hopecourt Cl M6 ....80 B4
Hopedale Cl M11 ....160 F1
Hopedale Rd SK5 ....111 F6
Hopefield Rd WA13 ..117 B4
Hopefield St BL3 .....147 D4
Hopefold Dr M28 ....60 E2
Hopelea St M20 .....110 C5
Hopes Carr SK1 .....169 F2
Hopgarth Wlk M40 ..83 D5
Hopkin Ave OL1 .....67 D4
Hopkin Mill OL4 .....67 D4
Hopkin St OL1 ....153 F7
Hopkins Bldgs OL5 ..68 B3
Hopkins Field OL15 ..119 B1
Hopkins St 16 SK14 ..167 E4
　Manchester M12 ....166 A1
Hopkinson Ave M34 ..100 E5
Hopkinson Cl 4 OL3 ..69 B8

Hopkinson Rd M9 ....64 D5
Hoppet La M43 ......84 C2
Hopton Ave M22 ....121 F3
Hopton Ct M15 .....163 A6
Hopwood Ave Eccles M30 ..79 D3
　Heywood OL10 ......46 D8
　Horwich BL6 ....22 C4
Hopwood Cl
　5 Golborne WA3 ....90 F8
　Whitefield M45 ......44 F3
Hopwood Com Prim Sch
　OL10 ....46 E8
Hopwood Ct Heywood OL10 ..46 E8
　Middleton M24 ......47 F4
Hopwood Hall Coll OL12 ..139 E7
Hopwood M24 ....47 A4
Hopwood St Failsworth M40 ..83 B6
　Manchester M3 ....158 E2
　Pendlebury M27 ....80 A8
Horace Barnes Cl M14 ..98 A3
Horace Gr SK4 ......169 E4
Horace St BL1 ......143 D2
Horatio St 4 M18 ...99 F6
Horbury Ave M18 ...99 D3
Horbury Dr BL8 .....27 C2
Hordern Wlk 9 OL2 ..48 E4
Horeb St BL3 ....145 D5
Horest La OL3 ....50 B7
Horley Cl BL8 ....27 C7
Hornbeam Cl
　Altrincham WA15 ...120 E5
　Sale M33 ....107 C5
Hornbeam Cres WN4 ..73 B3
Hornbeam Ct M6 ....81 A3
Hornbeam Rd M19 ..99 B2
Hornby Ave M9 .....64 E5
Hornby Dr BL3 .....40 D3
Hornby Gr WN7 ....76 D7
Hornby Rd M16,M32 ..96 F4
Hornby St Bury BL9 ..140 F4
　Heywood OL10 .....29 D2
　Manchester M8 ....159 B4
　63 Radcliffe M26 ...65 A8
　Reddish SK5 ....111 E7
　Wigan WN1 ....37 C2
Horncastle Cl Bury BL8 ..27 D5
　4 Golborne WA3 ...90 F8
Horncastle Rd M40 ..65 B1
Hornchurch Ct 2 M15 ..162 F6
Hornchurch St M15 ..162 E6
Horncliffe Cl BB4 ...1 E8
Horncliffe View BB4 ..1 B8
Horne Dr M4 ....159 C2
Horne Gr Wigan WN3 ..150 A5
　Sale M33 ....54 F5
Hornet Cl OL11 .....31 A3
Horne St Bury BL8 ..26 F2
　Chadderton OL9 ....47 F1
Hornsea Rd SK2 ...125 A5
Hornsea Wlk M11 ...83 A1
Hornsey Gr WN3 ...54 D3
Horridge Ave WA12 ..89 C5
Horridge Fold BL7 ..8 E3
Horridge Fold Ave BL5 ..40 F2
Horrobin Fold BL7 ..27 B4
Horrobin La Adlington PR6 ..21 C8
　BL7 ....9 C2
Horrocks Fold BL1 ..24 C7
Horrocks Fold Ave BL1 ..24 D6
Horrocks Rd BL7 .....9 D6
Horrocks St Leigh WN7 ..75 A4
　Tyldesley M29 ......58 F1
　Tyldesley M46 .....58 E1
Horsa St 16 BL2 ....25 B5
Horsedge St OL1 ....153 F7
Horsefield Ave OL12 ..14 C6
Horsefield Cl M21 ..109 E7
Horseforth La OL3 ..69 A7
Horseshoe La
　Alderley Edge SK9 ..137 A2
　Bolton BL7 ....25 A8
　Oldham OL3 ....65 F6
Horsfield St BL3 ....144 A5
Horsfield Way SK6 ..112 F6
Horsham Ave SK7 ..124 C1
Horsham Cl Bury BL8 ..27 C7
　Westhoughton BL5 ..57 F6
Horsham Gr WN2 ...56 B3
Horsham St M6 ....154 E2
Horstead Wlk 8 M19 ..99 A2
Horton Ave BL1 ....24 E6
Horton Hill Prim Sch OL4 ..67 B6
Horton Rd M14 ....98 A2
Horton Sq OL2 ....149 B6
Horton St Stockport SK1 ..24 A7
　Wigan WN6 ....36 E3
Horton Rd M32 .....96 F2
Horwich Bsns Pk BL6 ..22 B2
Horwich L Ctr BL6 ..22 C3
Horwich Parish
　CE Prim Sch BL6 ..22 C3
Horwich Parkway Sta BL6 ..39 C7
Horwood Cres M20 ..110 D5
Hoscar Dr M19 .....110 F7
Hoskers Nook BL5 ..57 D7
Hoskers The BL5 ..57 D7
Hoskins Cl M12 ....165 A5
Hospital Ave M30 ..79 E2
Hospital Cotts M25 ..62 E5
Hospital Rd Bolton BL7 ..25 A8
　Pendlebury M27 ....80 B7
Hotel Rd M90 ....130 C7
Hotel St Bolton BL1 ..145 F7
　Newton-le-W WA12 ..89 B3
Hothersall Rd 4 SK5 ..111 F8

Hothersall St M7 .....158 E3
Hotspur Cl M14 ......110 A8
Hough Cl Oldham OL8 ..66 F3
Hough Ct OL7 ....67 A2
Hough End Ave M21 ..109 C6
Hough End Dr M21 ..109 E7
Hough Fold Way BL2 ..25 E4
Hough Gn WA15 ....128 E5
Hough Hall Rd M40 ..157 F8
Hough Hill Rd SK15 ..102 D8
Hough La Bolton BL7 ..24 F7
Houghend Cres M21 ..109 E8
Houghton Ave Oldham OL8 ..66 D2
Houghton WN5 ......36 E2
Houghton Cl
　Newton-le-W WA12 ..89 B3
　Rochdale OL16 ......31 C7
Houghton La
　Shevington WN6 ....35 F6
　Swinton M27 ....79 D5
Houghton Rd M8 ...64 A1
Houghton St Bolton BL3 ..145 E5
　Bury BL9 ....140 E1
　Leigh WN7 ....75 F6
　Newton-le-W WA12 ..89 B3
　Oldham OL8 ....48 E2
　Pendlebury M27 ....80 B6
Houghwood Grange WN4 ..72 F3
Houldsworth Ave M14 ..119 E7
Houldsworth Mill Ind Est
　SK4,SK5 ....111 F7
Houldsworth Sq 2 SK5 ..111 E7
Houldsworth St
　Manchester M1 .....159 B2
　8 Radcliffe M26 ....65 B5
　Reddish SK5 ....111 E7
Houseley Ave OL9 ..66 A3
Houseman Gr WN6 ..150 A5
Housley Cl WN3 ....150 A5
Huson St OL8 ......153 F5
Houston Pk M5 ....154 F1
Hove Cl BL8 ....10 F1
Hove Dr M14 ....110 E7
Hove St BL1 ....144 C5
Hove St N 8 BL3 ..144 C5
Howden St M8 .....158 F4
Hovey Cl M8 ......155 F7
Hovingham St OL16 ..31 B8
Hovis Gardens M19 ..110 E6
Hovis St M11 ......165 C8
How Clough Cl M28 ..60 F2
How Clough Dr M28 ..60 F2
How Lea Dr BL9 ....27 F6
Howard Ave Bolton BL3 ..146 A4
　Cheadle SK8 ....123 A1
　Kearsley M26 ......61 B7
　Walkden M43 ......117 B4
　Reddish SK4 ....111 C6
Howard Cl Glossop SK13 ..104 B2
　Romiley SK6 ....113 A2
Howard Ct OL6 .....166 C3
Howard Dr WA15 ...120 A1
Howard Hill BL9 ....45 A4
Howard La M40 .....100 F4
Howard Pl Hyde SK14 ..167 D2
　Rochdale OL16 .....139 F8
Howard Rd Culcheth WA3 ..92 A2
　Wythenshawe M22 ..109 D1
Howard Spring Wlk M8 ..155 F8
Howard St Ashton-u-L OL7 ..166 A4
　Bolton BL1 ....143 F1
　Denton M34 ....100 E5
　Glossop SK13 ......104 A3
　Manchester M8 ....158 F4
　Oldham OL4 ....49 E1
　Radcliffe M26 ......44 B3
　Rochdale OL12 ....139 F8
　Salford M5 ....161 A8
　Shaw OL2 ....149 A7
　Stalybridge SK15 ..86 D4
　Stockport SK1 .....169 F2
　Stretford M32 .....96 C2
　Wigan WN3 ....54 C5
Howarth Cross St OL16 ..15 B2
Howards La OL15 ..68 J1
Howards La WN5 ..53 F7
Howarth Ct 4 M26 ..44 B3
Howbridge Cl M28 ..78 C8
Howbro Dr OL7 ....84 B7
Howbrook Wlk 8 M15 ..162 F6
Howcroft Cl BL1 ...145 E8
Howcroft St BL3 ...145 E5
Howden Cl SK5 ....99 E2
Howden Dr WN3 ...55 B4

Howden Rd Manchester M9 ..64 C5
　New Mills SK22 .....127 C1
Howe Bridge Cl M46 ..58 A1
Howe Dr BL0 ....11 B2
Howe St Ashton-u-L OL7 ..100 F8
　Manchester M7 .....155 D7
Howell Croft N 7 BL1 ..145 F7
Howell Croft S BL1 ..145 F7
Howell's Yd 6 BL1 ..145 F7
Howells Ave M33 ...108 B5
Howgill La Bolton BL7 ..83 D1
Howsin Ave BL2 ....25 B4
Howton Cl M12 .....99 A4
Howty Cl SK9 ....131 D1
Hoxton Cl SK6 .....113 A4
Hoy Dr M41 ....95 D5
Hoylake Cl Failsworth M40 ..83 D8
　Leigh WN7 ....75 D2
Hoylake Rd Stockport SK3 ..123 B8
　Wythenshawe M33 ..108 F2
Hoyland Cl M12 ....164 F6
Hoyle Ave OL8 ......153 E5
Hoyle St Bacup OL13 ..3 E8
　3 Bolton BL1 ......143 E4
　Manchester M12 ...163 C8
　Radcliffe M26 ......44 C1
　Whitworth OL12 .....4 D3
Hoyle Street Ind Est M12 ..163 C7
Hoyle's Wlk M13 ...163 C6
Hoyle's Terr OL16 ..31 E6
Hubert Worthington Ho
　...................137 A1
Hucclecote Ave M22 ..121 C2
Hucklow Ave M23 ..121 A2
Hucklow Bank 5 SK13 ..171 D2
Hucklow Cl 28 SK13 ..171 D2
Hucklow Fold 22 SK13 ..171 D2
Hucklow Fold 22 SK13 ..171 D2
Hucklow Lanes 25 SK13 ..171 D2
Hudcar La BL9 .....141 A4
Huddart Cl M5 .....161 B8
Huddersfield Rd
　Diggle OL3 ....51 C7
　Diggle OL3 ....51 D5
　Newhey OL16,OL3 ..32 D5
　Oldham OL1,OL4 ...67 D8
　Stalybridge OL5,SK15 ..86 E4
　Uppermill OL3 .....90 E8
Hudson Gr WA3 ...74 D1
Hudson Rd Bolton BL3 ..146 B3
　Hyde SK14 ....113 E7
Hudson St OL9 ....66 A2
Hudsons Pas OL15 ..16 C7
Hudsons Wlk OL11 ..30 C7
Hudswell Cl WN5 ..62 E8
Hugh Lupus St BL1 ..25 A5
Hugh Oldham Dr M7 ..81 C6
Hugh St OL16 ......31 A8
Hughenden Ct BL8 ..26 F7
Hughes Ave BL6 ...22 A4
Hughes Cl BL9 .....141 A3
Hughes St Bolton BL1 ..142 C2
　Bolton BL3 ....148 A5
　Manchester M11 ..164 E8
Hughes Way M30 ..79 A1
Hughley Cl OL2 ....49 A4
Hughtrede St OL16 ..31 B3
Hugo St Farnworth BL4 ..42 A8
　Manchester M40 ....83 A7
　Rochdale OL11 .....30 C2
Hulbert St Bury BL8 ..27 C1
　Middleton M24 .....47 C1
Hull Mill La OL3 ....50 F5
Hull Sq M3 ....158 D2
Hullet Cl WN6 .....35 E8
Hully St 12 SK15 ...85 F3
Hulme Court Prep Sch
　...................66 D4
Hulme Ct M15 ......162 E7
Hulme Gr WN7 .....75 F6
Hulme Gram Sch
　for Boys The OL8 ..66 D4
Hulme Gram Sch
　for Girls The OL8 ..66 D4
Hulme Hall Cl SK8 ..132 B8
Hulme Hall Cl SK8 ..132 A8
Hulme Hall Cres SK8 ..132 A8
Hulme Hall La M40 ..160 E4
Hulme Hall Rd
　Cheadle SK8 ....123 A1
　Manchester M15 ..162 D7
Hulme Hall Schs SK8 ..123 A1
Hulme Pl M5 ....81 C2
Hulme St Ashton-u-L OL6 ..85 D4
　Bolton BL1 ....140 D3
　Bury BL8 ....140 D3
　Manchester M1,M15 ..81 C1
　Manchester M3,M45 ..81 C1
　Oldham OL8 ....153 D5
　Stockport SK1 .....124 B7
Hulme Wlk M15 ...162 F6
Hulme's Terr 9 BL2 ..25 B5
Hulmes Rd M35,M40 ..83 D6
Hulton Ave M28 ...60 A4
Hulton Cl BL3 ......146 A3
Hulton District Ctr M28 ..60 A4
Hulton Dr M16 .....97 D2
Hulton La BL3 .....146 A3
Hulton St Denton M34 ..100 F4
　Failsworth M35 .....83 E7
　Salford M5 ....161 A7

Humber Dr BL9 . . . . .27 F7
Humber Pl WN5 . . . . .54 C7
Humber Rd Milnrow OL16 . .32 A6
Tyldesley M29 . . . . .77 C7
Humber St Manchester M8 . .156 B7
Salford M5 . . . . .154 D1
Humberstone Ave OL5 . . . .156 B7
Hume St Manchester M19 . .111 B8
Rochdale OL16 . . . . .31 A5
Humphrey Booth Gdns
M6 . . . . .154 E3
Humphrey Cres M41 . . . . . . .96 A2
Humphrey La M41 . . . . .96 A2
Humphrey Park Sta M32 . . .96 A3
Humphrey Pk M41 . . . . .96 A2
Humphrey Rd M16 . . . . .161 B5
Humphrey St
Ince-in-M WN2 . . . . .56 A7
Manchester M8 . . . . .155 F8
Humphries Ct M40 . . . . .159 C4
Huncoat Ave SK4 . . . . .111 D5
Huncote Dr M9 . . . . .64 E1
Hunger Hill Ave BL3 . . . . . . .40 E2
Hungerford Wlk **5**
M23 .120 D7
Hunmanby Ave M15 . . . . . . .162 F7
Hunstanton Dr BL8 . . . . .27 D5
Hunston Rd M33 . . . . .107 F2
Hunt Ave OL7 . . . . .85 B5
Hunt Fold Dr BL8 . . . . .10 F1
Hunt La OL9 . . . . .152 A7
Hunt Rd SK14 . . . . .102 A5
Hunt St Atherton M46 . . . . . .58 D3
Manchester M9 . . . . .64 D1
Wigan WN1 . . . . .151 E7
Hunt's Bank
Manchester M3 . . . . .158 F2
Westhoughton BL5 . . . . .57 F6
Hunter Dr M26 . . . . .44 A5
Hunter Rd WN5 . . . . .36 E1
Hunter's La Oldham OL1 . . .153 F7
Rochdale OL12,OL16 . . . . . .139 F8
Hunter's View SK9 . . . . .131 C3
Hunters Chase WN5 . . . . . . .53 E1
Hunters Cl
6 Bredbury SK6 . . . . .112 F3
Wilmslow SK9 . . . . .131 F1
Hunters Ct SK15 . . . . .102 D8
Hunters Gn BL0 . . . . .10 F3
Hunters Hill BL9 . . . . .45 B8
Hunters Hill La OL3 . . . . .51 C6
Hunters La Glossop SK13 . .115 F8
Rochdale OL16 . . . . .139 F8
Hunters Mews Sale M33 . .108 A5
Wilmslow SK9 . . . . .137 C7
Hunterston Ave M30 . . . . . . .80 A2
Huntingdon Ave OL9 . . . . . .152 B5
Huntingdon Cres SK5 . . . . .112 C5
Huntingdon Way **7** M41 . . .95 A1
Huntingdon Wlk **1** BL1 . . .143 E2
Huntingdon Ave M20 . . . . . .110 A7
Huntley Mount Rd BL9 . . . .141 B3
Huntley Rd Cheadle SK3 . . .123 B7
Manchester M8 . . . . .63 E2
Huntley St BL9 . . . . .141 B3
Huntly Chase SK9 . . . . .137 C2
Huntly Way OL10 . . . . .28 E1
Huntroyde Ave **23** BL2 . . . .25 B1
Hunts Rd **2** M6 . . . . .80 D5
Huntsman Cl WA14 . . . . . . .119 B6
Huntsman Dr M44 . . . . .105 F7
Huntsworth Wlk M13 . . . . .164 D5
Hurdlow Ave M7 . . . . .81 A7
Hurdlow Gn **14** SK13 . . . . . .171 D1
Hurdlow Lea **8** SK13 . . . . . .171 D1
Hurdlow Mews SK13 . . . . . .171 D1
Hurdlow Way **10** SK13 . . . . .171 D1
Hurdlow Wlk M9 . . . . .157 D7
Hurdsfield Rd SK2 . . . . .124 D4
Hurford Ave M18 . . . . .99 D6
Hurlbote Cl SK9 . . . . .131 D5
Hurley Dr SK8 . . . . .122 E2
Hurlston Rd BL3 . . . . .147 D2
Hurst Ave Bramhall SK8 . . .132 D6
Sale M33 . . . . .107 C2
Hurst Bank Rd OL6 . . . . .85 E4
Hurst Brook Cl OL6 . . . . . . .166 C4
Hurst Cl BL5 . . . . .58 F7
Hurst Cross OL6 . . . . .85 E5
Hurst Ct Ashton-u-L OL6 . . .85 E5
Wythenshawe M23 . . . . . . .120 F4
Hurst Gr OL6 . . . . .85 E5
Hurst Green Cl BL8 . . . . .43 F8
Hurst Hall Dr OL6 . . . . .85 E5
Hurst Hill Cres OL6 . . . . . . .85 D5
Hurst Inf Sch OL6 . . . . .85 D5
Hurst Knoll Prim Sch
OL6 .166 C4
Hurst La WA3 . . . . .92 C7
Hurst Lea Ct SK9 . . . . .137 A2
Hurst Mdw OL16 . . . . .31 C3
Hurst Methodist Jun Sch
OL6 .85 D7
Hurst Mill La WA3 . . . . .92 C8
Hurst Rd BL3 . . . . .104 F1
Hurst St Bolton BL3 . . . . . . .146 C3
Bury BL9 . . . . .141 A2
Hindley WN2 . . . . .56 C6
Leigh WN7 . . . . .76 B3
Oldham OL9 . . . . .153 D7
Reddish SK5 . . . . .111 E7
Walkden M28 . . . . .61 A6
Hurst Wlk **4** M22 . . . . .121 A2
Hurstbank Ave M19 . . . . . . .110 D4
Hurstbourne Ave M11 . . . . .83 B2
Hurstbrook Cl SK13 . . . . . . .104 F1
Hurstbrook Dr M32 . . . . .95 F2

Hurstclough Prim Sch
SK14 . . . . .102 C1
Hurstead **2** OL12 . . . . .15 D4
Hurstead Gn **8** OL12 . . . . . .15 D4
Hurstead Rd OL16 . . . . .31 F6
Hursted Rd OL16 . . . . .31 F6
Hurstfield Ind Est
SK4,SK5 . . . . .111 E6
Hurstfield Rd M28 . . . . .78 B8
Hurstfold Ave M19 . . . . .110 D3
Hursthead Cty Jun Sch
SK8 .132 C7
Hursthead Inf Sch SK8 . . . .132 C6
Hursthead Rd SK8 . . . . .132 B7
Hursthead Wlk M13 . . . . . .163 B7
Hurstmead Terr M20 . . . . . .110 B2
Hurstvale Ave SK8 . . . . .122 B1
Hurstville Rd M21 . . . . .109 B6
Hurstway Dr **33** M9 . . . . . . .64 E3
Hurstwood BL1 . . . . .24 E5
Hurstwood Rd SK2 . . . . .124 F6
Hus St **1** M43 . . . . .100 A8
Husteads OL3 . . . . .50 E1
Husteads La OL3 . . . . .50 F1
Hutchins La OL4 . . . . .49 D1
Hutchinson Rd OL11 . . . . . . .13 D2
Hutchinson St
4 Radcliffe M26 . . . . .44 C4
Rochdale OL11 . . . . .30 C6
Hutchinson Way M6 . . . . . . .44 A3
Huttock End La OL13 . . . . . . .3 D8
Hutton Ave Ashton-u-L OL6 . .85 E3
Boothstown M28 . . . . .77 F6
Hutton Cl WA3 . . . . .91 E5
Hutton La M14 . . . . .110 C7
Hutton St WN2 . . . . .20 A3
Hutton Wlk **7** M13 . . . . . . .163 C6
Huxley Ave M8 . . . . .156 A6
Huxley Cl SK7 . . . . .132 E7
Huxley Dr SK7 . . . . .132 E7
Huxley Pl WN3 . . . . .150 A5
Huxley St
Altrincham WA14 . . . . .119 D7
Bolton BL1 . . . . .142 C2
6 Oldham OL4 . . . . .67 C6
Huxton Gn SK7 . . . . .124 A2
Huyton Rd PR6,PR7 . . . . . . .21 B6
Huyton Terr PR6 . . . . .21 B6
Hyacinth Cl SK3 . . . . .170 D5
Hyatt Cres WN6 . . . . .19 C3
Hyde Central Sta SK14 . . . .101 C2
Hyde Cl WN3 . . . . .150 A5
Hyde Dr M28 . . . . .60 C2
Hyde Fold Cl M19 . . . . .110 F6
Hyde Gr Manchester M13 . .163 C5
Sale M33 . . . . .108 B4
Walkden M28 . . . . .60 C2
Hyde Ho SK4 . . . . .111 C5
Hyde Hospl SK14 . . . . .167 F3
Hyde North Sta SK14 . . . . .101 C5
Hyde Rd Denton M34 . . . . . .101 A3
Manchester M12 . . . . .164 E6
Manchester M12,M18 . . . . . .99 D4
Oldham M24 . . . . .65 E6
Romiley SK14,SK6 . . . . .113 B5
Walkden M28 . . . . .60 C2
Hyde Sq M24 . . . . .46 E1
Hyde St Bolton BL3 . . . . . . .146 C3
Droylsden M43 . . . . .84 C4
Dukinfield SK16 . . . . .101 D8
Manchester M16 . . . . .162 D5
Hyde St Paul's
RC Prim Sch SK14 . . . . . . .167 D4
Hyde Tech Sch SK14 . . . . . .167 D4
Hyde's Cross M4 . . . . .159 A2
Hyde-Clarendon
Sixth Form Ctr SK14 . . . . .167 E4
Hydes Terr SK15 . . . . .86 D1
Hydon Brook Wlk OL11 . . . .30 C4
Hydrangea Cl **7** M33 . . . . .107 C6
Hyldavale Ave SK8 . . . . .122 B6
Hylton Dr Ashton-u-L OL7 . .84 F5
Cheadle SK8 . . . . .132 C8
Hyman Goldstone Wlk
M8 . . . . .155 F7
Hyndman Ct M5 . . . . .154 D2
Hypatia St BL2 . . . . .148 B7
Hythe Cl M14 . . . . .98 C3
Hythe Rd SK3 . . . . .123 B8
Hythe St BL3 . . . . .146 A4
Hythe Wlk OL9 . . . . .152 B6

I

Ibberton Wlk **8** M9 . . . . .64 F1
Ibsley **20** OL12 . . . . .139 E8
Ice House Cl **5** M28 . . . . . . .59 F3
Iceland St M6 . . . . .154 F2
Idonia St BL1 . . . . .143 D3
Ifco Ctr M14 . . . . .98 C3
Ilex Gr M7 . . . . .155 D6
Ilford St M11 . . . . .83 B2
Ilfracombe Rd SK2 . . . . .124 D8
Ilfracombe St M40 . . . . .83 B6
Ilk St M11 . . . . .83 B2
Ilkeston Dr WN2 . . . . .38 F3
Ilkeston Wlk
5 Denton M34 . . . . .113 A8
4 Manchester M40 . . . . . . .83 A6
Ilkley Cl Bolton BL2 . . . . . . .148 C7
Oldham OL9 . . . . .152 B6
Ilkley Cres WN5 . . . . .111 E8
Ilkley Dr M41 . . . . .94 D4
Ilkley St M40 . . . . .83 A7
Illingworth Ave SK15 . . . . . .86 C2
Ilona Dr M7 . . . . .81 A8

Ilminster OL11 . . . . .139 E6
Ilminster Wlk **2** M9 . . . . . . .64 E5
Ilthorpe Wlk **7** M40 . . . . . . .83 A6
Imex Bsns Pk M13 . . . . .98 F3
Imogen Ct M5 . . . . .161 C8
Imperial Dr WN7 . . . . .76 D6
Imperial Terr M33 . . . . .108 A4
Ina Ave BL1 . . . . .23 F1
Ince Cl Manchester M20 . . .110 B7
Stockport SK4 . . . . .169 E3
Ince Green La
Ince-in-M WN2 . . . . .56 A7
Ince-in-M WN2,WN3 . . . . . .151 F6
Ince Hall Ave
Ince-in-M WN2 . . . . .56 A8
Wigan WN2 . . . . .151 F8
Ince St SK4 . . . . .169 E3
Ince St Mary's
CE Prim Sch WN3 . . . . .55 F4
Ince Sta WN3 . . . . .151 F6
Ince Wlk WN1 . . . . .150 C8
Ince-in-Makerfield
CE Prim Sch WN2 . . . . .56 A7
Inchcape Dr M9 . . . . .64 B4
Inchfield Cl OL11 . . . . .29 E8
Inchfield Rd
Manchester M40 . . . . .65 B1
Walsden OL14 . . . . .6 A8
Inchley Rd M13 . . . . .163 B7
Inchwood Mews OL4 . . . . . .49 E4
Incline Rd OL8 . . . . .66 C2
Independent St BL3 . . . . . . .40 E4
India St BL9 . . . . .11 C3
Indigo St M6 . . . . .80 D5
Indigo Wlk M6 . . . . .80 F5
Industrial Cotts **13** BB4 . . . .2 F8
Industrial St Ramsbottom BL0 . .1 C1
Westhoughton BL5 . . . . .57 F7
Industry Rd OL8 . . . . .14 F1
Industry St
14 Littleborough OL15 . . . .16 B5
Oldham OL9 . . . . .66 A4
Rochdale OL11 . . . . .13 E1
Whitworth OL12 . . . . .4 D2
Infant St M25 . . . . .63 C4
Infirmary St **11** BL1 . . . . . . .145 F7
Ingersol Rd BL6 . . . . .22 E1
Ingham Ave WA12 . . . . .89 C1
Ingham Brow BL6 . . . . .22 F4
Ingham Rd WA14 . . . . .107 D1
Leigh WN7 . . . . .75 E8
8 Oldham OL1 . . . . .67 A7
Inghams La OL15 . . . . .16 B5
Inghamwood Cl M7 . . . . . . .155 F7
Ingle Dr SK2 . . . . .124 C7
Ingle Rd SK8 . . . . .123 A5
Ingleby Ave M9 . . . . .64 F4
Ingleby Cl Shaw OL2 . . . . . .149 A8
Standish WN6 . . . . .19 D2
Westhoughton BL5 . . . . .40 A3
Ingleby Ct M22 . . . . .96 E1
Ingleby Way OL2 . . . . .149 A8
Ingledene Ave M7 . . . . .63 E1
Ingledene Ct **8** M7 . . . . .63 E1
Ingledene Gr BL1 . . . . .142 A2
Inglefield OL11 . . . . .13 F1
Inglehead Cl M34 . . . . .101 A2
Ingles Fold M28 . . . . .78 B7
Inglesham Cl Leigh WN7 . . .75 E1
Wythenshawe M23 . . . . . . .121 B6
Ingleton Ave M8 . . . . .64 B2
Ingleton Cl Bolton BL2 . . . . .25 D4
Cheadle SK8 . . . . .122 C6
Newton-le-W WA12 . . . . .89 B4
Royton OL2 . . . . .48 D5
Ingleton Dr Oldham OL1 . . .71 B1
Ingleton Mews BL8 . . . . .27 B6
Ingleton Rd SK3 . . . . .123 C7
Inglewhite Ave WN1 . . . . . . .37 C2
Inglewhite Cl BL9 . . . . .44 D7
Inglewhite Cres **1** WN1 . . .37 C2
Inglewhite Pl **2** WN1 . . . . . .37 C2
Inglewood WA14 . . . . .119 B3
Inglewood Ave WN1 . . . . . .151 E7
Inglewood Cl
Ashton-u-L OL7 . . . . .84 F5
Partington M31 . . . . .105 F4
Inglewood Hollow SK15 . . .102 D8
Inglewood Rd M24 . . . . .47 E1
Inglewood Wlk M13 . . . . . .163 C6
Inglis St OL15 . . . . .16 B6
Ingoe Cl OL10 . . . . .29 E3
Ingoldsby Ave M13 . . . . .98 D4
Ingram Dr SK4 . . . . .110 E3
Ingram St Platt Bridge WN2 . .56 A3
Shevington WN6 . . . . .35 D7
Ings Ave OL12 . . . . .14 B2
Ings La OL12 . . . . .14 B2
Ink St OL16 . . . . .139 F7
Inkerman St Hyde SK14 . . .167 D4
Manchester M40 . . . . .157 D6
7 Rochdale OL2 . . . . .149 A8
Inman St Bury M26 . . . . .44 E8
Denton M34 . . . . .100 F3
Innes Cl OL12 . . . . .14 C1
Innes St M12 . . . . .99 B3
Innis Ave M40 . . . . .83 C5
Inst of Islamic H Ed BL7 . . .25 A8
Institute St BL1 . . . . .148 A7
Instow Cl Chadderton OL9 . .47 F1
Manchester M13 . . . . .164 D6
Intake Rd OL3 . . . . .51 C5
International App M90 . . . . .130 C7
Invar Rd M27 . . . . .61 D1
Inver Wlk **10** M40 . . . . .65 D2

Inverbeg Dr BL2 . . . . .43 A7
Invergarry Wlk **10** M11 . . . .83 C1
Inverlael Ave BL1 . . . . .144 B8
Inverness Ave M9 . . . . .65 A4
Inverness Cl WN2 . . . . .38 D5
Inverness Rd SK16 . . . . .101 C7
Inward Dr WN6 . . . . .36 A5
Inwood Wlk M8 . . . . .156 C6
Inworth Wlk **6** M8 . . . . . . .155 F7
Iona Pl BL2 . . . . .25 C2
Iona Way M41 . . . . .95 E5
Ionian Gdns **2** M7 . . . . .81 C5
Ipswich St OL11 . . . . .139 F5
Ipswich Way **10** M34 . . . . .101 A1
Ipswich Wlk M12 . . . . .164 D5
Iqbal Cl M12 . . . . .165 A5
Irby Wlk SK8 . . . . .123 A4
Iredy Cl M24 . . . . .46 D2
Iredale Cres WN6 . . . . .36 F7
Iredine St **8** M11 . . . . .83 C1
Irene Ave SK14 . . . . .101 E5
Iris Ave Farnworth BL4 . . . . .42 A1
Kearsley BL4 . . . . .60 F5
Manchester M11 . . . . .99 D8
Iris St Oldham OL8 . . . . .66 F3
Ramsbottom BL0 . . . . .138 B6
Iris Wlk **7** M31 . . . . .105 E2
Irk St M4 . . . . .159 A3
Irk Vale Dr OL1,OL9 . . . . . . .47 E1
Irk Wlk M45 . . . . .45 B2
Irkdale St M8 . . . . .156 C4
Irlam & Cadishead
Com High Sch M44 . . . . . . .105 C7
Irlam Ave M30 . . . . .79 D1
Irlam Endowed Prim Sch
M44 .94 A2
Irlam Prim Sch M44 . . . . . . .94 A1
Irlam Rd Sale M33 . . . . .108 C4
Urmston M41 . . . . .94 D2
Irlam Sq M6 . . . . .80 D5
Irlam St Bolton BL1 . . . . . . .143 E3
Manchester M40 . . . . .157 E5
8 Oldham OL4 . . . . .67 A7
Irlam Wharf Rd M44 . . . . . .106 A6
Irma St BL1 . . . . .143 F3
Irmass Ind Est M17 . . . . . . .96 D6
Iron St Denton M34 . . . . . . .100 F3
Manchester M40 . . . . .83 A6
Irvin Dr M22,SK8 . . . . .131 A8
Irvin St M40 . . . . .83 C6
Irvine Ave **6** M28 . . . . .78 A6
Irvine St WN7 . . . . .75 F6
Irving Cl SK2 . . . . .124 A3
Irving Ho BL1 . . . . .143 E2
Irving St Bolton BL1 . . . . . . .143 E2
Oldham M38 . . . . .66 B2
Walkden M38 . . . . .60 A6
Irwell Cl **1** M26 . . . . .44 B2
Irwell Gr M30 . . . . .79 F1
Irwell Ho **2** M15 . . . . .162 D7
Irwell Pl Eccles M30 . . . . . . .79 F1
Salford M5 . . . . .81 A2
Wigan WN5 . . . . .54 C6
Irwell Rd WN5 . . . . .53 F7
Irwell St Bury BL9 . . . . .140 E2
Kearsley M26 . . . . .61 A8
Manchester M3 . . . . .158 E1
Manchester M7,M8 . . . . . . .158 E4
Radcliffe M26 . . . . .44 B2
Ramsbottom BL0 . . . . .138 C6
Salford M6 . . . . .81 A6
Irwell Vale Rd BB4 . . . . .1 C6
Irwell Vale Sta BL0 . . . . .1 C5
Irwin Dr SK8 . . . . .131 C5
Irwin Rd WA14 . . . . .119 D8
Irwin St M34 . . . . .100 E3
Isa St BL0 . . . . .1 A4
Isaac Cl M5 . . . . .161 A8
Isaac St BL1 . . . . .144 C8
Isabella Cl M16 . . . . .97 C4
Isabella Sq WN1 . . . . .151 E8
Isabella St OL12 . . . . .15 A2
Isaiah St OL8 . . . . .66 F4
Isca St M11 . . . . .160 F1
Isel Wlk M40 . . . . .46 D2
Isherwood Dr SK6 . . . . .125 D6
Isherwood Fold BL7 . . . . .9 D7
Isherwood Rd M31 . . . . .106 F6
Isherwood St
Heywood OL10 . . . . .29 E1
Leigh WN7 . . . . .75 E8
7 Rochdale OL16 . . . . .31 A6
Isis Cl M7 . . . . .81 A6
Islamic Acad M13 . . . . .163 B6
Island Cotts BL9 . . . . .11 C2
Island Row WN2 . . . . .56 B7
Islington Rd SK2 . . . . .124 C4
Islington St M3 . . . . .94 D2
Islington Way M3 . . . . .158 D1
Isobel Cl Eccles M30 . . . . . .79 B1
7 Manchester M16 . . . . . . .97 F4
Isobel Wlk M13 . . . . .145 D5
Ivanhoe Ave WA3 . . . . .74 D1
Ivanhoe Ct BL3,BL4 . . . . . . .74 D1
Ivanhoe St
Farnworth BL3,BL4 . . . . .42 C2
Oldham OL1 . . . . .49 C1
Iveagh Ct BL3 . . . . .31 B6
Iver St OL11 . . . . .30 B3
Ivy Ave WA12 . . . . .89 C2
Ivy Bank Cl BL1 . . . . .24 E5
Ivy Bank Rd BL1 . . . . .24 E5
Ivy Cl Droylsden M43 . . . . . .83 F3
Shaw OL2 . . . . .149 A7
Ivy Cotts Denton M34 . . . . .113 A7

Ivy Cotts continued
Rawtenstall BB4 . . . . .2 F8
Ivy Dr M24 . . . . .64 F6
Ivy Gr Farnworth BL4 . . . . . . .60 B8
Kearsley BL4 . . . . .60 F7
Walkden M38 . . . . .59 F4
Ivy House Rd WA3 . . . . .74 D1
Ivy Rd Bolton BL1 . . . . .142 B1
Bury BL8 . . . . .27 B2
Golborne WA3 . . . . .90 B8
Poynton SK12 . . . . .133 C3
Westhoughton BL5 . . . . .57 F7
Ivy St Ashton-in-M WN4 . . . .73 B3
Bolton BL3 . . . . .146 C4
Eccles M30 . . . . .79 D1
Manchester M40 . . . . .83 A8
1 Rawtenstall BB4 . . . . .2 F8
Wigan WN1 . . . . .150 B8
Ivy Wlk M31 . . . . .105 D3
Ivybridge Cl M13 . . . . .164 D5
Ivycroft SK13 . . . . .171 E4
Ivydale Dr WN7 . . . . .76 C5
Ivygreen Dr OL4 . . . . .67 F6
Ivygreen Rd M21 . . . . .109 A8
Ivylea Rd M19 . . . . .110 E4
Ivyleaf Sq M7 . . . . .155 E6

J

Jack Brady Cl M23 . . . . .120 E4
Jack La Droylsden M43 . . . . .84 B2
Droylsden M43 . . . . .84 C2
Urmston M41 . . . . .95 E2
Jack McCann Ct M40 OL16 . .31 A8
Jack St **2** M27 . . . . .15 B1
Jack Taylor Ct OL12 . . . . . . .15 B1
Jack's La BL5 . . . . .57 A8
Jackdaw Rd BL8 . . . . .10 F2
Jackie Brown Wlk M40 . . . .157 D5
Jackman Ave OL10 . . . . .46 D7
Jackroom Dr M4 . . . . .159 C1
Jackson Ave Culcheth WA3 . .91 E3
3 Dukinfield SK16 . . . . . . .101 D8
Jackson Cres M15 . . . . .162 E7
Jackson Ct Manchester M21 . .96 F1
Urmston M41 . . . . .95 E2
Jackson Gdns M34 . . . . .100 D2
Jackson Mews OL4 . . . . .49 D1
Jackson Pit **8** OL1 . . . . . . .153 E6
Jackson Pl OL16 . . . . .15 E2
Jackson St Ashton-u-L OL6 . .166 B4
Cheadle SK8 . . . . .122 E6
Failsworth M35 . . . . .83 D6
Farnworth BL4 . . . . .60 D8
Glossop SK13 . . . . .104 C5
Hadfield SK13 . . . . .104 C5
Hyde SK14 . . . . .167 D2
Ince-in-M WN2 . . . . .56 A7
Kearsley BL4 . . . . .60 F7
Littleborough OL12 . . . . .15 C6
Middleton M24 . . . . .63 B8
Mottram-in-L SK14 . . . . . . .103 A3
Oldham OL4 . . . . .67 F6
Oldham OL4 . . . . .67 F6
Radcliffe M26 . . . . .44 B2
Rochdale OL16 . . . . .31 A6
Sale M33 . . . . .108 D5
Stretford M32 . . . . .96 C1
Walkden M28 . . . . .60 C4
Whitefield M45 . . . . .62 F7
Jackson's La SK7 . . . . .133 C8
Jackson's Row M2 . . . . .158 F1
Jacksons Edge Rd SK12 . . .135 B6
Jacob St WN2 . . . . .56 D6
Jacobite Cl M7 . . . . .63 C1
Jacobsen Ave SK14 . . . . . . .167 F4
Jaffrey St WN7 . . . . .75 E5
James Andrew St M24 . . . . .47 B1
James Bentley Wlk **4**
M40 .83 C5
James Brindley Basin
M1 . . . . .159 C1
James Brindley Prim Sch
M28 .60 C1
James Butterworth Ct **9**
OL16 .31 B6
James Butterworth St **9**
OL16 .31 B6
James Cl SK16 . . . . .101 E8
James Corbett Rd M5 . . . . .154 D1
James Dr Hyde SK14 . . . . . .167 E1
James Henry Ave M5 . . . . .161 B8
James Hilt St **13** OL15 . . . .16 B5
James Leech St SK1,SK3 . .170 E8
James Leigh St M1 . . . . . . .163 A8
James Pl Coppull PR7 . . . . . .19 E8
Standish WN6 . . . . .19 D2
James Rd OL2 . . . . .149 B7
James Sq WN6 . . . . .19 C3
James St Ashton-in-M WN2 . .73 E7
Bacup OL13 . . . . .3 D8
Bolton BL7 . . . . .8 D3
Bury BL9 . . . . .141 A1
Droylsden M43 . . . . .84 B2
Dukinfield M34 . . . . .101 A4
Dukinfield SK15,SK16 . . . . .101 E8
Failsworth M35 . . . . .84 A7
Glossop SK13 . . . . .116 C8
Heywood OL10 . . . . .29 D3
Horwich BL6 . . . . .21 F3
Ince-in-M WN3 . . . . .151 D6
Kearsley BL4 . . . . .60 F8

James St continued
Little Lever BL3 ....43 B3
Littleborough OL15 ....15 E4
Manchester M3 ....158 D1
🟦 Manchester M34 ....100 E8
Manchester M40 ....160 D3
Prestwich M25 ....63 A5
Radcliffe M26 ....44 B2
Rochdale OL12 ....15 C4
🟦 Rochdale OL12,OL16 ...31 A8
Romiley SK6 ....83 A3
Sale M33 ....108 D4
Shaw OL2 ....149 A5
Stockport SK3 ....170 E7
Tyldesley M29 ....79 F8
Tyldesley M46 ....58 E1
Westhoughton BL5 ....39 E2
Whitworth OL12 ....4 D2
James St S OL9 ....152 A7
James's St OL4 ....49 D1
Jameson St OL11 ....93 B8
Jammy La OL9 ....152 C6
Jane Barter Ho 🟦 BL4 .....60 D8
Jane St Oldham OL9 ......152 B6
Rochdale OL12 ....139 E8
Whitworth OL12 ....4 E6
Japan St M8 ....155 F7
Jarmain St M12 ....165 A7
Jarvis St 🟦 Oldham OL4 ...67 A6
Rochdale OL12 ....14 F1
Jasmine Ave M43 ....84 C2
Jasmine Cl M23 ....108 E1
Jasmine Rd WN5 ....54 D7
Jasmine Wlk M31 ....105 F2
Jason St M4 ....159 B3
Jasper Wlk 🟧 M16 ....97 E4
Jauncey St BL3 ....144 C5
Jaxons Ct WN1 ....150 C8
Jayton Ave M20 ....122 B8
Jean Ave WN7 ....75 E2
Jean Cl M19 ....99 A2
Jedburgh Ave BL1 ....144 B8
Jeff Joseph Sale Moor
Tech Coll M33 ....108 D2
Jefferson Way OL12 ....14 F3
Jeffrey St WN2 ....56 A8
Jeffrey Wlk OL10 ....29 A2
Jeffreys Dr SK16 ....110 D8
Jehlum Cl M8 ....156 B7
Jellicoe Ave M44 ....105 E6
Jenkinson St Hindley WN2 ..56 D6
Manchester M13,M15 .....163 A6
Jenkyn Wlk 🟧 M11 ....160 F1
Jennet Hey WN4 ....72 F6
Jennet's La WA3 ....76 C1
Jennings Ave M5 ....161 A8
Jennings Cl Hyde SK14 ...102 B5
Salford M5 ....161 A8
Jennings St SK3 ....170 D7
Jennison Cl M18 ....165 B6
Jenny Beck Gr BL3 ....147 E4
Jenny La SK7 ....132 E4
Jenny St OL8 ....66 C2
Jepheys Pl 🟧 OL12 ....14 F1
Jepheys St OL12 ....14 F1
Jepson St SK2 ....124 A6
Jericho Rd BL9 ....28 E4
Jermyn St OL12 ....31 A8
Jerrold St 🟦 OL15 ....16 B5
Jersey Cl M19 ....110 F7
Jersey Rd SK5 ....169 F4
Jersey St Ashton-u-L OL6 ..166 B4
Manchester M4 ....159 C2
Jerusalem Pl M2 ....158 E1
Jesmond Ave M25 ....63 B2
Jesmond Dr BL8 ....27 C5
Jesmond Gr SK8 ....132 B8
Jesmond Rd BL1 ....142 B4
Jesmond Wlk M9 ....64 D5
Jessperen St OL7 ....153 F7
Jessamine Ave M7 ....158 D4
Jessel Cl M13 ....163 C6
Jessica Way WN7 ....75 B4
Jessie St Bolton BL3 ....144 C5
Failsworth M40 ....83 A6
Jessop St M18 ....125 F8
Jessop St M18 ....99 D5
Jethro St Bolton BL2 ....148 C8
Bolton BL2 ....25 C4
Jetson St M18 ....99 F6
Jevington Wlk 🟧 M13 ......163 C6
Jimmy McMullen Wlk 🟧
M14 ....98 A3
Jinnah Cl M11 ....165 C8
Jo St M5 ....81 A1
Joan St M40 ....83 A7
Jobling St M11 ....164 F8
Jocelyn St M40 ....157 E5
Joddrell St M3 ....158 F1
Joe Connolly Way BB4 ....2 E8
Joel La SK14 ....113 F7
Johannesburg Gdns M23 .120 F4
John Ashworth St OL12 .....15 B1
John Atkinson Ct M5 ......154 D2
John Ave SK8 ....122 E5
John Beeley Ave M11 ....99 D8
John Booth St OL4 ....67 F5
John Boste Ct BL3 ....42 C3
John Brown St 🟦 BL1 .....145 E8
John Clynes Ave M40 .....159 C3
John Cross St BL3 ....147 E4
John Dalton St
Hadfield SK13 ....103 E5
Manchester M2 ....158 F1
John Foran Cl M40 ....83 B6

John Gilbert Way M17 ....96 E5
John Henry St OL12 ....4 D4
John Heywood St M11 ......83 B2
John Kemble Ct OL11 ....30 D4
John Kennedy Gdns SK14 .103 A3
John Kennedy Rd SK14 ....102 F3
John Knott St OL9 ....67 F6
John Lee Fold M24 ....47 A1
John Lloyd Ct M44 ....105 F8
John Nash Cres M15 ....162 E6
John Roberts Cl OL11 ......139 E5
John Robinson Wlk 🟦
M40 ....83 A7
John Shepley St SK14 .....167 E2
John Smeaton Ct 🟦 M1 ...159 C1
John St Altrincham WA14 ..119 D4
Ashton-in-M WN4 ....73 D5
Bolton BL7 ....25 A7
Bury BL9 ....140 F3
Denton M34 ....100 F4
Droylsden M43 ....83 F1
Eccles M30 ....79 B1
Failsworth M35 ....65 F1
Farnworth BL4 ....60 E8
Glossop SK13 ....9 F7
Golborne WA3 ....90 A8
Hazel Grove SK7 ....124 D3
Heywood OL10 ....29 D2
Heywood OL10 ....29 D2
Hindley WN2 ....57 B3
Hyde SK14 ....167 D3
Irlam M44 ....105 E5
Leigh WN7 ....75 F5
Little Lever BL3 ....43 B3
Littleborough OL15 ....15 C3
Manchester M3 ....158 E2
Manchester M4 ....159 A2
Manchester M7 ....158 D4
Marple SK6 ....126 A5
Middleton M25 ....63 E8
Oldham OL4 ....153 E6
Pendlebury M27 ....80 A8
Rochdale OL16,OL12 ......113 A4
Romiley SK6 ....113 C2
Romiley SK6 ....114 B3
Royton OL2 ....48 D4
Sale M33 ....108 B5
Shaw OL2 ....149 A5
Stalybridge SK15 ....86 C5
Stockport SK1 ....169 F1
🟦 Tyldesley M29 ....59 A1
Walkden M28 ....60 D4
Whitworth OL12 ....4 D2
Wigan WN1 ....151 D8
🟦 Wigan WN5 ....54 D5
John St E OL7 ....84 F1
John St W OL7 ....100 F8
John William St
Droylsden M11 ....83 C1
Reddish SK5 ....79 F2
John's Pl SK6 ....113 C2
Johnny King Cl M40 ....157 D5
Johns Ct OL16,OL12 ....15 F3
Johnson Ave Leigh WN7 ....56 E1
Newton-le-W WA12 ....89 B5
Johnson Cl WN7 ....75 B4
Johnson Fold Ave BL1 ......23 E2
Johnson Fold
Com Prim Sch BL1 ....23 F3
Johnson Gr M24 ....64 E8
Johnson St Atherton M46 ..58 A1
Bolton BL1 ....145 F6
Failsworth M35 ....162 D6
Manchester M3 ....158 E2
Pendlebury M27 ....80 A8
Radcliffe M26 ....44 B1
Tyldesley M29 ....79 A5
Wigan WN1 ....54 B6
Johnson Terr 🟦 SK16 .....166 B1
Johnson's Sq M40 ....160 D4
Johnsonbrook Rd
SK14,SK16 ....167 D4
Johnston 🟦 OL12 ....139 E8
Johnston Ave OL15 ....15 F3
Johnstone Ct M32 ....96 E1
Joicey St M19 ....110 E4
Joiner St Manchester M4 ...159 A1
Manchester M5 ....81 C1
Jolly Brows BL2 ....25 D3
Jolly Tar La PR7 ....20 B7
Jonas St Manchester M7 ...158 E3
Manchester M9 ....157 E6
Jonathan Cl BB4 ....1 A8
Jones St Bolton BL1 ....124 A7
Jones St Bolton BL1 ....145 F8
Hadfield SK13 ....104 A5
Horwich BL6 ....22 B4
Oldham OL1 ....67 A8
Oldham OL2 ....48 E2
Salford M6 ....154 F2
Jonquil Dr M28 ....78 F3
Jopson St M24 ....47 B1
Jordan Ave OL2 ....49 D8
Jordan St Glossop SK13 ....16 A7
Manchester M15 ....162 E2
Joseph Eastham High Sch
M28 ....60 B3
Joseph Jennings Ct OL7 ...85 A6
Joseph Johnson Mews
M22 ....109 E1
Joseph St Eccles M30 ....79 B1
Failsworth M35 ....83 E1

Joseph St continued
🟦 Farnworth BL4 ....42 D1
🟦 Littleborough OL15 ....16 B6
Marple SK6 ....126 A6
Middleton M24 ....46 F1
Radcliffe M26 ....44 B2
🟦 Rochdale OL12 ....14 D2
Josephine Dr M27 ....80 A7
Joshua La M24 ....65 D7
Josslyn Rd M5 ....154 D3
Joule St M9 ....64 E1
Joule St M9 ....64 E1
Joules Ct 🟦 SK1 ....170 F8
Jowett St Oldham OL1 ....49 C1
Reddish SK5 ....169 F4
Jowett's Wlk OL7 ....84 F2
Jowkin La OL11 ....29 D6
Joy Pl OL12 ....14 D2
Joy St Ramsbottom BL0 ...138 B6
Rochdale OL12 ....14 F2
Joyce St M40 ....83 B7
Joynson Ave M7 ....158 D4
Joynson St M33 ....108 B5
Jubilee OL2 ....32 C2
Jubilee Ave Orrell WN5 ....53 D4
Radcliffe M26 ....44 C1
Stalybridge SK16 ....85 E1
Jubilee Cl M30 ....79 D2
Jubilee Cotts M28 ....60 C3
Jubilee Ct Manchester M16 ..97 B4
Joyce St M40 ....99 F2
Jubilee Ho BL1 ....145 E6
Jubilee Ho BL1 ....145 E6
Jubilee St Bolton BL3 ......146 C3
Salford M6 ....154 F2
Leigh WN7 ....75 E5
Jubilee Terr M24 ....47 B2
Jubilee Way BL9 ....140 D2
Judith St OL12 ....14 C3
Judson Ave M21 ....109 C6
Judy St M9 ....157 F8
Julia Mews 🟦 BL6 ....22 B4
Julia St Horwich BL6 ....22 B4
Manchester M3 ....158 F3
Rochdale OL12 ....14 D3
Julian Ho OL1 ....153 F7
Julius St M19 ....111 B8
Jumbles Ctry Pk BL7 ....9 D2
Junction Alley OL16 ....113 A3
Junction La WA12 ....89 B3
Junction Rd Bolton BL3 ....144 A5
Bolton BL3 ....40 F5
Stockport SK1,SK2,SK3 ....170 F7
Junction Rd W BL6 ....40 D5
Junction St
Dukinfield SK14 ....101 C5
Middleton M24 ....101 C5
Oldham OL8 ....66 E4
Junction Terr WN3 ....151 E6
June Ave Leigh WN7 ....75 C6
June St OL7 ....166 A2
Juniper Bank SK5 ....112 A8
Juniper Cl Bolton BL1 ......143 E1
Oldham OL4 ....49 F4
Sale M33 ....108 A4
Sale M33 ....108 A4
Juniper Dr Hindley WN2 .....57 A3
Milnrow OL16 ....54 E2
Jupiter Gr WN3 ....54 B8
Jupiter Wlk M40 ....83 A5
Jura Cl SK14 ....101 D8
Jura Dr M41 ....95 E1
Jura Gr OL10 ....29 B1
Jurby Ave M9 ....64 E4
Jury St Leigh WN7 ....75 E7
Manchester M8 ....158 F4
Justin Cl M13 ....163 B7
Jutland Ave OL11 ....30 C8
Jutland Gr BL5 ....39 F1
Jutland St M1 ....159 B3

K

Kale St M13 ....163 B7
Kalima Gr M7 ....155 D6
Kane Ct WA3 ....75 A1
Kansas Ave M5 ....96 E8
Kara St M6 ....154 E1
Karen Rd WN1 ....151 F8
Kaskenmoor Sch OL8 ....66 B1
Kate St BL0 ....138 B6
Kathan Cl OL16 ....15 C1
Katherine Ct M16 ....161 C5
Katherine Rd SK2 ....124 C5
Katherine St M34 ....166 A2
Kathkin Ave M8 ....64 D2
Kathleen Gr M14 ....98 D2
Kathleen St OL12 ....14 D2
Kay Ave SK6 ....113 D3
Kay Brow Heywood OL10 ....29 D2
Ramsbottom BL0 ....138 B6
Kay Cl WN1 ....151 D8
Kay Garden Sh Ctr BL9 ...140 E2
Kay St Atherton M46 ....58 D8
Bolton BL1 ....145 F8
Bolton BL3 ....141 A3
Edgworth BL7 ....7 F4
Little Lever BL3 ....43 A3
Manchester M11 ....83 C1
Ramsbottom BL9 ....11 C3
Rochdale OL16 ....15 A3
Stalybridge SK15 ....86 A1
🟦 Stalybridge SK15 ....86 A1
Kay's Ave SK1 ....112 B1

Kaye Ave WA3 ....91 F3
Kayfields BL2 ....25 E4
Kayley Ind Est OL7 ....84 F3
Kays Gdns M3 ....158 D2
Kays Wood Rd SK6 ....125 D6
Keadby Cl M30 ....94 B4
Keal Dr M44 ....94 B4
Kean Pl M30 ....79 D1
Keane Cl M29 ....58 F1
Keane St M11 ....166 A3
Kearsley Dr BL3 ....42 B3
Kearsley Hall Rd M26 ....61 C7
Kearsley Mount Sh Prec
BL4 ....61 B6
Kearsley Rd Kearsley M26 ..61 D8
Manchester M8 ....64 A2
Kearsley St Eccles M30 .....79 B2
Leigh WN7 ....75 D5
Manchester M9 ....37 B1
Kearsley Sta BL4 ....61 A7
Kearsley Vale M26 ....61 B8
Kearsley West
Cty Prim Sch BL4 ....60 E7
Kearton Dr M30,M5 ....80 A1
Keary Cl M18 ....99 D6
Keaton Cl M6 ....154 E1
Keats Ave Denton M34 .....113 A8
Droylsden M43 ....84 A2
Longshaw WN5 ....53 D1
Rochdale OL12 ....15 A1
Wigan WN3 ....150 B5
Keats Cl M24 ....36 E3
Keats Cl M46 ....58 E5
Keats Cres M26 ....43 E4
Keats Fold OL12 ....102 B7
Keats Mews M23 ....120 C8
Keats Rd Eccles M30 ....49 B1
Ramsbottom BL0 ....10 F2
Keats St WN7 ....75 D7
Keats Way 🟦 M31 ....56 B1
Keats Wlk 🟦 BL1 ....56 A7
Ince-in-M WN2 ....56 A7
Ramsbottom BL0 ....11 A2
Stretford M32 ....96 D3
Keble Gr WN7 ....75 C8
Keble Rd M18 ....99 F6
Kedington Cl 🟧 M40 ....151 F7
Kedleston Ave M14 ....98 C4
Kedleston Grn SK2 ....124 D7
Kedleston Wlk M34 ....100 F1
Keele Cl SK2 ....124 B6
Keele Wlk M40 ....159 C3
Keeley Cl M40 ....13 E2
Keighley Ave M43 ....84 A3
Keighley Cl BL8 ....26 F2
Keighley St BL1 ....142 C2
Keilder Mews BL1 ....144 A7
Keilder Sq M5 ....154 F1
Keith Dr SK3 ....123 B7
Keith Wlk M40 ....160 D3
Kelboro Ave M34 ....100 D7
Kelbrook Ct SK2 ....126 A6
Kelbrook Rd M11 ....165 B8
Kelby Ave M23 ....121 B7
Keld Cl BL8 ....27 B5
Keld Wlk M18 ....165 C5
Kelday Wlk M8 ....156 C6
Kelfield Ave M23 ....109 A2
Kelfield Wlk M40 ....65 C1
Kellatt Cl WN3 ....151 E6
Kellaton Cl WN3 ....54 E3
Kellbank Rd WN3 ....54 E3
Kellbrook Cres
Whitefield M45 ....63 B1
Whitefield M45 ....81 A8
Kellet St Rochdale OL16 ....15 C2
Kellett Cl WN5 ....36 D1
Kellett St 🟦 Bolton BL1 ....24 F6
Rochdale OL16 ....31 B8
Kelling Wlk M15 ....162 D7
Kells Gr WN6 ....37 A2
Kelmarsh Cl 🟧 M11 ....99 D8
Kelsall Cres SK3 ....170 D6
Kelsall Dr
Altrincham WA15 ....120 C6
Droylsden M43 ....83 F3
Kelsall Rd SK8 ....123 A5
Kelsall St Manchester M12 .164 F6
Oldham OL9 ....66 D3
Rochdale OL16 ....31 B8
Sale M33 ....108 A4
Kelsall Way 🟦 SK9 ....131 D5
Kelsey Wlk M9 ....64 D2
Kelso Gr WN2 ....29 C2
Kelso Wlk M9 ....64 D2
Kelson Ave OL7 ....85 A6
Kelstern Ave M13 ....98 E3
Kelstern Sq M13 ....98 E3
Kelverlow St OL4 ....67 C6
Kelvin Ave Middleton M24 ...64 M6
Manchester M34 ....84 B8
Kelvin Cl WN4 ....72 D4
Kelvin Gr Manchester M8 ..156 A6
Wigan WN3 ....54 D8
Kelvin St Ashton-u-L OL7 ..100 F8
Manchester M4 ....159 A1
Kelvindale Dr WA15 ....120 C7
Kelvington Dr M9 ....157 E8
Kelway Terr WN1 ....37 D1
Kelwood Ave BL8 ....27 B5
Kemball 🟦 M30 ....80 A8
Kemble Ave M23 ....109 C1
Kemble Cl BL0 ....64 C8
Kemmel Ave M22 ....121 E5
Kemnay Wlk 🟦 M11 ....83 E1
Kemp Rd SK6 ....139 D5
Kemp St Hyde SK14 ....167 E4

Kemp St continued
Middleton M24 ....64 F8
Kempley Cl M12 ....164 F6
Kempnough Hall Rd M28 ...78 F7
Kempsey Cl OL9 ....152 C7
Kempsey St OL9 ....152 B7
Kempsey Wlk M40 ....65 D1
Kempsford Cl M23 ....121 B6
Kempster St M7 ....158 D4
Kempston Gdns 🟩 BL1 ....143 E2
Kempton Ave
Little Lever BL3 ....43 A2
Sale M33 ....107 D3
Kempton Cl Droylsden M43 ..84 C2
Hazel Grove SK7 ....125 A1
Newton-le-W WA12 ....89 D5
Kempton Rd M19 ....111 A8
Kempton Way OL9 ....152 C7
Kemsing Wlk 🟦 M5 ....65 D1
Kenchester Ave M11 ....99 D8
Kendal Ave Ashton-u-L OL7 ..84 F4
Sale M33 ....108 A2
Dukinfield SK14 ....101 C5
Rochdale OL12 ....13 E2
Sale M33 ....108 C3
Urmston M41 ....94 E4
Kendal Cl
Altrincham WA15 ....120 D5
Hadfield SK13 ....104 E8
Kendal Dr Bramhall SK7 ..132 C5
Bury BL9 ....28 C3
Gatley SK8 ....122 C4
Shaw OL2 ....49 D7
Kendal Gdns SK6 ....113 B4
Kendal Gr Ashton-in-M WN4 ..73 B4
Leigh WN7 ....75 D5
Walkden M28 ....60 F2
Whitefield M45 ....62 F8
Kendal Rd Bolton BL1 .....144 C8
Boothstown M28 ....78 E7
Hindley WN2 ....56 A7
Ince-in-M WN2 ....80 C5
Ramsbottom BL0 ....11 A2
Stretford M32 ....96 D3
Kendal Rd W BL0 ....10 F8
Kendal St WN6 ....150 B8
Kendal Terr 🟦 SK16 ....166 C1
Kendal Wlk M24 ....46 E1
Kendall Rd M9 ....63 F3
Kendon Gr M34 ....100 E3
Kendrew Rd BL3 ....146 A4
Kendrick Pl WN1 ....151 E8
Kenford Dr WN3 ....54 A4
Kenford Wlk M8 ....156 B7
Kenhall Rd WN7 ....76 C4
Kenilworth Ave
Manchester M11 🟧 OL11 ..139 D6
Cheadle SK8 ....123 B3
Handforth SK9 ....131 D3
Manchester M20 ....109 F5
Swinton M27 ....62 B3
Whitefield M45 ....94 E4
Kenilworth Cl Marple SK6 ..125 F8
Oldham OL4 ....67 F5
Radcliffe M26 ....44 C2
Kenilworth Dr
Hazel Grove SK7 ....133 D8
Hindley WN2 ....56 F4
Wigan WN7 ....76 E7
Kenilworth Gdns WA12 .....89 C1
Kenilworth Rd M34 ....100 C8
Kenilworth Rd
Cheadle SK3 ....122 F7
Golborne WA3 ....90 E7
Royton OL11,OL16 ....48 D8
Sale M33 ....107 C4
Urmston M41 ....94 C2
Kenion Rd OL11 ....142 B1
Kenion St M3 ....158 D1
Kenmay Ave BL3 ....40 E5
Kenmor Gr M40 ....65 B1
Kenmor Ave BL8 ....27 A1
Kenmore Gr M44 ....63 B8
Kenmore Gr WA15 ....120 B3
Kenmore Gr
Garswood WN4 ....72 D4
Irlam M44 ....105 D4
Kenmore Rd Sale M33 .....107 C1
Whitefield M45 ....63 B8
Manchester M23 ....121 D7
Kenmore Way M45 ....63 B8
Kennard Cl M9 ....64 F1
Kennard Pl WA14 ....119 E6
Kennedy Cl WN6 ....36 B4
Kennedy Dr Bury BL9 ....45 A3
Little Lever BL3 ....43 C3
Kennedy Rd Salford M5 .....80 C2
Tyldesley M29 ....77 D6
Kennedy St Bolton BL2 ....148 F1
Manchester M2 ....158 F1
Kennedy Way Denton M34 .100 D2
Stockport SK4 ....168 B4
Kennerley Ct SK2 ....124 A5
Kennerley Rd SK2 ....124 A5
Kennerley's La 🟦 SK9 ......137 A7
Kennet 🟧 OL16 ....139 D2
Kennet Cl Handforth SK9 ...131 D2
Kennet Way OL16 ....139 D2
Kenneth Ave WN7 ....75 F7
Kenneth Collis Ct M22 ....121 C3

Kenneth Gr WN7 . . . . .75 D6
Kenneth Sq M7 . . . . .155 E6
Kennett Rd M23 . . . . .121 A3
Kenninghall Rd M22 . . . . . . .121 D3
Kennington Ave M40 . . . . . . .83 B4
Kensington Fold BL3 . . . . . . .147 D3
Kenny Cl OL4 . . . . .67 D5
Kenside Wlk 2 M16 . . . . .97 F3
Kensington Ave
  Ashton-u-L OL6 . . . . .85 E4
  Chadderton OL9 . . . . .65 E8
  2 Hyde SK14 . . . . .167 E1
  Manchester M14 . . . . .98 D4
  Radcliffe M26 . . . . .43 D4
  Royton OL2 . . . . .48 C6
Kensington Cl
  Milnrow OL16 . . . . .32 A6
  Ramsbottom BL8 . . . . .11 A1
Kensington Ct Bolton BL1 . . .145 E7
  1 Hyde SK14 . . . . .167 E1
  Manchester M7 . . . . .81 C8
  Reddish M34 . . . . .100 B4
  Wilmslow SK9 . . . . .137 A6
Kensington Dr Bury BL8 . . . .44 A8
  Horwich BL6 . . . . .22 D3
  Leigh WN7 . . . . .76 E7
  Salford M5 . . . . .154 D3
Kensington Gdns
  Altrincham WA15 . . . . .119 F1
  Hyde SK14 . . . . .167 F1
Kensington Gr
  Reddish M34 . . . . .100 B4
  Sale WA14 . . . . .119 E8
  14 Stalybridge SK15 . . . . . . .86 A1
Kensington Rd
  Failsworth M35 . . . . .84 B8
  Manchester M21 . . . . .97 B2
  Oldham OL8 . . . . .66 D4
  Stockport SK3 . . . . .123 B7
  3 Wigan WN5 . . . . .54 D5
Kensington St Bolton BL1 . . .145 E7
  Hyde SK14 . . . . .167 E1
  Manchester M14 . . . . .98 A3
  Rochdale OL11 . . . . .30 E5
Kenslow Ave M8 . . . . .63 F2
Kensworth Cl
  6 Altrincham M23 . . . . .120 D6
  Bolton BL1 . . . . .143 D1
Kensworth Dr BL1 . . . . .143 D1
Kent Ave Cheadle SK8 . . . . . .123 C5
  Droylsden M43 . . . . .83 E1
  Oldham OL9 . . . . .152 B6
  Platt Bridge WN2 . . . . .56 A2
Kent Cl Diggle OL3 . . . . .51 C4
  Walkden M28 . . . . .60 B2
Kent Ct Bolton BL1 . . . . .145 E8
  Manchester M14 . . . . .98 C3
Kent Dr Bury BL9 . . . . .45 A8
  Kearsley BL4 . . . . .61 B6
Kent Rd Atherton M46 . . . . . .58 C4
  Failsworth M35 . . . . .83 E6
  Glossop SK13 . . . . .104 D1
  Irlam M44 . . . . .105 C5
  Partington M31 . . . . .105 E2
  Reddish M34 . . . . .100 A2
  Stockport SK3 . . . . .123 B8
  Wigan WN2 . . . . .59 A2
Kent Rd E M14 . . . . .98 D3
Kent Rd W M14 . . . . .98 D3
Kent St Bolton BL1 . . . . .145 E8
  Leigh WN7 . . . . .76 E4
  1 Manchester M2 . . . . .158 F1
  Manchester M7 . . . . .158 D4
  Oldham OL8 . . . . .66 F4
  Rochdale OL11 . . . . .139 F6
  Swinton M27 . . . . .61 F2
  Wigan WN1 . . . . .151 D7
Kent Way WA12 . . . . .89 C1
Kent Wlk Haslingden BB4 . . . .1 A8
  Heywood OL10 . . . . .29 A1
  Heywood OL10 . . . . .29 B2
Kentford Dr M40 . . . . .159 C4
Kentford Gr 2 BL4 . . . . .60 C8
Kentford Rd BL1 . . . . .143 F1
Kentmere Ave
  Billinge WA11 . . . . .71 C1
  Rochdale OL12 . . . . .15 B3
Kentmere Cl SK8 . . . . .122 B3
Kentmere Ct M9 . . . . .65 B4
Kentmere Dr
  Middleton M24 . . . . .46 E3
  Tyldesley M29 . . . . .77 B7
Kentmere Gr BL4 . . . . .59 F7
Kentmere Rd
  Altrincham M23, WA15 . . . . .120 D6
  Bolton BL2 . . . . .25 F1
Kentmore Cl SK4 . . . . .110 E2
Kenton Ave M18 . . . . .99 C3
Kenton Cl Bolton BL1 . . . . . .143 D1
  Denton M34 . . . . .100 D7
Kenton Rd Shaw OL2 . . . . . . .149 A7
  Shaw OL2 . . . . .48 F7
Kenton St OL8 . . . . .67 B5
Kentsford Dr BL3 . . . . .43 B5
Kentstone Ave SK4 . . . . .110 E3
Kentucky St OL4 . . . . .67 C6
Kentwell Cl SK16 . . . . .101 B7
Kenwick Dr M40 . . . . .65 E2
Kenwood Ave
  Altrincham WA15 . . . . .119 F2
  Bramhall SK7 . . . . .132 D5
  Gatley SK8 . . . . .122 A6
  Leigh WN7 . . . . .76 C5
  Manchester M19 . . . . .110 F6
Kenwood Cl Leigh WN7 . . . . .76 C5
  Stretford M32 . . . . .96 E2
Kenwood Ct M32 . . . . .96 E1
Kenwood La M28 . . . . .78 F5

Kenwood Rd Bolton BL1 . . . .142 B3
  Oldham OL1 . . . . .48 C1
  Reddish M18, SK5 . . . . .99 E2
  Stretford M32 . . . . .96 E1
Kenworthy Ave OL6 . . . . .85 E5
Kenworthy Cl SK14 . . . . .102 C2
Kenworthy Gdns OL3 . . . . . . .51 B1
Kenworthy La M22 . . . . .109 D1
Kenworthy St
  Rochdale OL16 . . . . .31 C7
  Stalybridge SK15 . . . . .102 A8
  3 Stalybridge SK15 . . . . . . .86 A1
Kenworthy Terr OL16 . . . . . . .31 C7
Kenwright St M4 . . . . .159 A2
Kenwyn St M40 . . . . .160 E3
Kenyon Ave
  Dukinfield SK16 . . . . .101 E7
  Oldham OL8 . . . . .66 F3
  Sale M33 . . . . .108 E2
Kenyon Cl SK14 . . . . .101 F5
Kenyon Fold OL11 . . . . .29 E5
Kenyon Gr M38 . . . . .59 C4
Kenyon La Culcheth WA3 . . . .91 A4
  Golborne WA3 . . . . .90 F3
  Golborne WA3 . . . . .90 F5
  Manchester M40 . . . . .83 A8
  Middleton M24 . . . . .65 C8
  Prestwich M25 . . . . .63 C4
Kenyon Rd Little Lever BL3 . . .43 B5
  Standish WN6 . . . . .19 D2
  Wigan WN1 . . . . .37 C2
Kenyon St Bacup OL13 . . . . . .4 B8
  Bury BL9 . . . . .141 A3
  Droylsden M18 . . . . .99 F6
  Dukinfield SK16 . . . . .101 B8
  Heywood OL10 . . . . .29 C2
  Leigh WN7 . . . . .75 D8
  Radcliffe M26 . . . . .44 B3
  Ramsbottom BL0 . . . . .138 C6
Kenyon Terr M38 . . . . .59 E3
Kenyon Way Bury BL8 . . . . . .26 F5
  Walkden M38 . . . . .59 E4
Keppel Rd M21 . . . . .97 B1
Keppel St OL6 . . . . .166 C3
Kepplecove Mdw M28 . . . . . .77 F5
Kepwick Dr M22 . . . . .121 E1
Kerans Dr BL5 . . . . .39 E1
Kerenhappuch St BL0 . . . . .138 B6
Kerfield Wlk 13 M13 . . . . . . .163 B7
Kerfoot Cl M22 . . . . .121 E8
Kerfoot St WN7 . . . . .76 C4
Kermishaw Nook M29 . . . . . .77 B6
Kernan Ave BL1 . . . . .24 E6
Kerne Gr M23 . . . . .109 A1
Kerr St M9 . . . . .64 D3
Kerrera Dr M5 . . . . .154 D1
Kerridge Dr M6 . . . . .112 F4
Kerridge Wlk 8 M16 . . . . . . .97 F3
Kerrier Cl M30 . . . . .80 A2
Kerry Gr BL2 . . . . .148 B8
Kerry Wlk M23 . . . . .120 F3
Kersal Ave Pendlebury M27 . . .80 C8
  Walkden M38 . . . . .60 B4
Kersal Bank M7 . . . . .81 C8
Kersal Bar M7 . . . . .63 C1
Kersal Cl Prestwich M25 . . . . .63 A1
  Prestwich M7 . . . . .63 C1
Kersal Crag M25, M7 . . . . .63 C1
Kersal Dr WA15 . . . . .120 C7
Kersal Hall Ave M7 . . . . .81 A8
Kersal High Sch M7 . . . . .81 A8
Kersal Rd M25, M7 . . . . .63 A1
Kersal Vale Ct M7 . . . . .81 A8
Kersal Vale Rd M7, M25 . . . . . .80 F8
Kersal Way M7 . . . . .81 B7
Kerscott Rd M23 . . . . .108 F2
Kersh Ave M19 . . . . .111 B8
Kershaw Ave
  Little Lever BL3 . . . . .43 A4
  Prestwich M25 . . . . .62 F2
  Sale M33 . . . . .108 E2
Kershaw Dr OL9 . . . . .65 D3
Kershaw La M34 . . . . .100 C8
Kershaw Rd M35 . . . . .83 F7
Kershaw St Bolton BL2 . . . . . .25 C5
  Bolton BL3 . . . . .145 D5
  Bury BL9 . . . . .141 A2
  Droylsden M43 . . . . .83 F1
  Dukinfield OL7 . . . . .100 F8
  Glossop SK13 . . . . .116 C8
  Heywood OL10 . . . . .29 B2
  2 Rochdale OL12 . . . . .139 F8
  Royton OL2 . . . . .48 D5
  Shaw OL2 . . . . .149 B7
  Tyldesley M29 . . . . .59 A1
  Wigan WN5 . . . . .54 B6
Kershaw St E OL2 . . . . .149 B7
Kershaw Way WA12 . . . . .89 C5
Kershaw Wlk M12 . . . . .164 D6
Kershope Gr M5 . . . . .161 A8
Kersley St OL4 . . . . .67 B6
Kerswell Wlk M40 . . . . .83 A6
Kerwin Wlk M11 . . . . .165 A8
Kesteven Rd M9 . . . . .157 D7
Keston Ave Droylsden M43 . . .83 E1
  Manchester M9 . . . . .65 A3
  Keston Cres SK5 . . . . .112 B6
Keston Rd 4 OL1 . . . . .49 C1
Kestor St BL2 . . . . .148 B7
Kestrel Ave Droylsden M34 . . .84 C1
  Farnworth BL4 . . . . .59 F7
  Oldham OL4 . . . . .67 C5
  Walkden M28 . . . . .60 A5
Kestrel Dr Marple SK6 . . . . . .126 A3
  Prestwich M25 . . . . .63 B6

Kestrel Dr Ashton-in-M WN4 . .73 C6
  Bury BL9 . . . . .141 B4
  Irlam M44 . . . . .94 A3
Kestrel Rd M17 . . . . .95 F8
Kestrel St 3 BL1 . . . . .148 A8
Kestrel Wlk M12 . . . . .165 A6
Keswick Ave Ashton-u-L OL7 . .84 F5
  Chadderton OL9 . . . . .152 A7
  Denton M34 . . . . .100 D4
  Dukinfield SK14 . . . . .101 C4
  Gatley SK8 . . . . .122 B4
  Oldham OL8 . . . . .67 A3
  Urmston M41 . . . . .94 E1
Keswick Cl Irlam M44 . . . . . .105 D4
  Manchester M13 . . . . .164 D5
  Middleton M24 . . . . .46 D2
  Stalybridge SK15 . . . . .86 A4
Keswick Ct 3 M24 . . . . .46 D2
Keswick Dr Bramhall SK7 . . .132 C5
  Bury BL9 . . . . .44 D7
Keswick Gr M6 . . . . .154 F2
Keswick Pl WN2 . . . . .56 A7
Keswick Rd
  Altrincham WA15 . . . . .120 D6
  High Lane SK6 . . . . .134 E8
  Reddish SK4 . . . . .111 D7
  Stretford M32 . . . . .96 C3
  Walkden M28 . . . . .60 B2
Keswick St Bolton BL1 . . . . . .143 F2
  Rochdale OL11 . . . . .30 C2
Ketley Wlk 1 M22 . . . . .121 F3
Kettering Rd M19 . . . . .99 B2
Kettleshulme Way SK12 . . . .134 A3
Kettleshulme Wlk 4 SK9 . . .131 E1
Kettlewell Wlk M13 . . . . .165 C5
Ketton Cl M11 . . . . .99 E7
Keverlow La OL8 . . . . .67 C2
Kevin Ave OL2 . . . . .48 F4
Kevin St M19 . . . . .111 B8
Kew Ave SK14 . . . . .167 E1
Kew Dr Cheadle SK8 . . . . . . .122 E2
  Urmston M41 . . . . .95 A4
Kew Gdns M40 . . . . .65 A1
Kew Rd Failsworth M35 . . . . . .84 A8
  Oldham OL4 . . . . .67 C6
  Rochdale OL11 . . . . .31 A3
Key Ct M34 . . . . .113 A8
Key West Cl M11 . . . . .160 F1
Keyhaven Wlk M40 . . . . .157 D5
Keymer St M11 . . . . .160 E2
Keynsham Rd M11 . . . . .83 B3
Keystone Cl M6 . . . . .154 E4
Keyworth Wlk M40 . . . . .160 E4
Khartoum St
  Droylsden M11 . . . . .83 D2
  Manchester M16 . . . . .97 D4
Kibbles Brow BL7 . . . . .25 B8
Kibboth Crew BL0 . . . . .138 B7
Kibworth Cl M45 . . . . .62 E8
Kibworth Wlk 7 M9 . . . . .64 E5
Kid St 4 M24 . . . . .46 F1
Kidacre Wlk 2 M40 . . . . .83 A7
Kidd Rd SK13 . . . . .116 E6
Kidderminster Way OL9 . . . . .47 F1
Kidwall Wlk 9 M9 . . . . .64 F1
Kiel Cl M30 . . . . .95 E8
Kielder Hill M24 . . . . .46 F4
Kilbride Ave BL2 . . . . .42 F6
Kilbuck La WA11 . . . . .89 A8
Kilburn Ave
  Ashton-in-M WN4 . . . . .73 D4
  Manchester M9 . . . . .64 D5
Kilburn Cl Gratley SK8 . . . . . .131 B7
  Leigh WN7 . . . . .57 D1
Kilburn Dr WN5 . . . . .36 B7
Kilburn Gr WN3 . . . . .54 D3
Kilburn Rd Orrell WN5 . . . . . .53 C5
  Radcliffe M26 . . . . .43 E4
  Stockport SK3 . . . . .123 C7
Kilburn St 2 OL1 . . . . .49 C1
Kildale Cl BL3 . . . . .40 E4
Kildare Cres OL11 . . . . .30 E7
Kildare Grange WN2 . . . . .56 C5
Kildare Rd
  Manchester M21 . . . . .109 D8
  Swinton M27 . . . . .79 E6
Kildare St Farnworth BL4 . . . .60 C7
  Hindley WN2 . . . . .56 C5
  Wigan WN3, WN5 . . . . .54 F6
  Middleton M24 . . . . .47 A1
  Mossley OL5 . . . . .68 D1
  Mottram-in-L SK14 . . . . .115 A8
  Newton-le-W WA12 . . . . .89 B3
  Oldham OL8 . . . . .153 E6
  Radcliffe M26 . . . . .44 B2
  Ramsbottom BL0 . . . . .138 C6
  Rawtenstall BB4 . . . . .2 E8
  Rochdale OL16 . . . . .139 F7
  Salford M6 . . . . .80 D5
  8 Stalybridge SK15 . . . . . . .86 A2
  Stretford M32 . . . . .96 D1
  Westhoughton BL5 . . . . .39 F4
  Whitworth OL12 . . . . .4 D3
  Wigan WN1 . . . . .150 C7
King Sq 5 OL8 . . . . .153 E6
King St Bolton BL1 . . . . .145 E7
  Bolton BL2 . . . . .25 D5
  5 Bolton BL7 . . . . .24 F8
  Delph OL3 . . . . .50 F4
  Denton M34 . . . . .100 F3
  Droylsden M43 . . . . .100 A8
  Dukinfield SK16 . . . . .101 C7
  Eccles M30 . . . . .79 F1
  Failsworth M35 . . . . .84 B6
  Farnworth BL4 . . . . .60 D8
  Glossop SK13 . . . . .116 C8
  Heywood OL10 . . . . .29 D1
  Hindley WN2 . . . . .56 D6
  Hollingworth SK14 . . . . .103 D5
  Horwich BL6 . . . . .22 A4
  Hyde SK14 . . . . .167 D3
  Ince-in-M WN2 . . . . .56 A7
  Leigh WN7 . . . . .75 F4
  Manchester M2 . . . . .158 E2
  Manchester M7 . . . . .155 E7
  Milnrow OL16 . . . . .31 F6
  Newton-le-W WA12 . . . . .89 B3

Kilnsley Wlk M18 . . . . .165 C5
Kilnwick Cl M18 . . . . .99 B3
Kilphin The BL6 . . . . .40 B8
Kilrush Ave M30 . . . . .95 D8
Kilsby Cl Bolton BL6 . . . . .40 D6
  Farnworth BL4 . . . . .42 C2
Kilsby Wlk M40 . . . . .160 D4
Kilshaw St WN5 . . . . .54 C5
Kilton Wlk M40 . . . . .159 C4
Kilvert Dr M33 . . . . .107 F5
Kilworth Ave M33 . . . . .107 F3
Kilworth Dr BL6 . . . . .40 D6
Kilworth St OL11 . . . . .139 D5
Kimberley Ave SK6 . . . . .113 C2
Kimberley Pl WN4 . . . . .73 B3
Kimberley Rd BL1 . . . . .24 E5
Kimberley St Bacup OL13 . . . .3 A7
  Manchester M7 . . . . .155 E7
  Oldham OL8 . . . . .66 C3
  Stockport SK3 . . . . .170 E7
Kimberley Wlk M15 . . . . . . .162 D7
Kimberly St WN6 . . . . .37 A1
Kimble Cl BL8 . . . . .10 F2
Kimbolton Cl M12 . . . . .165 A6
Kinburn Rd M19 . . . . .110 D2
Kinbury Wlk M40 . . . . .159 C4
Kincardine Rd M13 . . . . .163 B6
Kincraig Cl Bolton BL2 . . . . . .40 E4
  Manchester M11 . . . . .83 C2
Kinder Ave Ashton-u-L OL6 . . .86 A6
  Oldham OL4 . . . . .67 D5
Kinder Cl SK13 . . . . .116 A8
Kinder Dr SK6 . . . . .126 A6
Kinder Fold SK15 . . . . .102 D6
Kinder Gr Ashton-in-M WN4 . .72 F6
  Romiley SK6 . . . . .113 E2
  Walkden M38 . . . . .60 B5
Kinder Mews OL3 . . . . .69 B5
Kinder St Stalybridge SK15 . . .86 A2
  Stockport SK3 . . . . .170 E7
Kinder Way Middleton M24 . . .46 F2
  Mottram-in-L SK14 . . . . .102 F3
Kinders Cres OL3 . . . . .69 B5
Kinders Fold OL15 . . . . .15 F7
Kinders La OL3 . . . . .69 B6
Kinderton Ave M20 . . . . .110 B7
Kineton Wlk 13 M13 . . . . . . .163 C6
King Albert St OL2 . . . . .149 B7
King Charles Ct SK13 . . . . . .116 D7
King David High Sch M8 . . . .63 F1
King David Jun
  & Inf Schs M8 . . . . .63 F1
King Edward Ave SK13 . . . . .104 D1
King Edward Rd SK14 . . . . . .113 E8
King Edward St Eccles M30 . . .79 C2
  4 Manchester M19 . . . . .99 B1
  Salford M5 . . . . .161 B8
King Edward's Bldgs M7 . . . .155 F8
King George Cl WN4 . . . . .73 B3
King George Rd
  Hindley WN2 . . . . .56 D6
  Hollingworth SK14 . . . . .103 D5
  Horwich BL6 . . . . .22 A4
  Hyde SK14 . . . . .167 D3

Ken-Kin 219

King's Dr continued
  Marple SK6 . . . . .125 E7
  Middleton M24 . . . . .64 D8
King's Gdns WN7 . . . . .76 C5
King's Lynn Cl 3 M20 . . . . . .110 B3
King's Rd Ashton-in-M WN4 . .73 A5
  Ashton-u-L OL6 . . . . .85 E5
  Manchester M25 . . . . .63 C2
  Oldham OL8 . . . . .153 F5
  Reddish M34 . . . . .100 B6
  Rochdale OL16 . . . . .31 B5
  Romiley SK6 . . . . .113 A3
  Wilmslow SK9 . . . . .136 E8
King's Terr 14 SK16 . . . . .166 B1
Kingcombe Wlk 12 M9 . . . . .157 E8
Kingfisher Ave M34 . . . . .84 C1
Kingfisher Cl M12 . . . . .164 E5
Kingfisher Ct
  Ashton-in-M WN4 . . . . .73 B6
  Rochdale OL12 . . . . .15 C4
  10 Wigan WN6 . . . . .37 A1
Kingfisher Dr Bury BL9 . . . . .141 B4
  Farnworth BL4 . . . . .59 F7
Kingfisher Mews SK6 . . . . . .126 A6
Kingfisher Rd SK2 . . . . .124 F5
Kingham Dr M4 . . . . .159 C2
Kinghom Gdns BL1 . . . . .143 D1
Kingmoor Ave M26 . . . . .44 B4
Kings Acre WA14 . . . . .119 A1
Kings Ave Gatley SK8 . . . . . .122 A4
  Manchester M8 . . . . .156 B8
  Whitefield M45 . . . . .44 E2
Kings Cl Prestwich M25 . . . . . .63 C5
  Wilmslow SK9 . . . . .137 A6
Kings Cres M16 . . . . .97 B3
Kings Ct Stockport SK5 . . . . .169 F3
  11 Tyldesley M29 . . . . .58 F1
Kings Dr SK8 . . . . .123 A3
Kings Gr Rochdale OL12 . . . . .15 C4
  Stretford M32 . . . . .96 F3
Kings La M32 . . . . .96 F3
Kings Rd Cheadle SK8 . . . . . .123 A3
  Failsworth OL9 . . . . .65 E3
  Golborne WA3 . . . . .90 A7
  Hazel Grove SK7 . . . . .124 E3
  Irlam M44 . . . . .105 E6
  Manchester M16 . . . . .97 B3
  Manchester M21 . . . . .109 D8
  Sale M33 . . . . .107 F4
  Shaw OL2 . . . . .149 A6
  Stretford M32 . . . . .96 E2
Kings Road Prim Sch M16 . . .97 A3
Kings Terr M22 . . . . .96 F3
Kings Wlk M43 . . . . .100 A8
Kings'Wlk OL6 . . . . .85 D5

Kingsbridge Ave 26 D1
  Hattersley SK14 . . . . .102 C2
Kingsbridge Cl SK6 . . . . .125 E7
Kingsbridge Ct M9 . . . . .157 D7
Kingsbridge Dr SK16 . . . . . . .101 B7
Kingsbridge Rd
  Manchester M9 . . . . .157 D7
  6 Oldham OL8 . . . . .67 B5
Kingsbrook Rd M16, M21 . . . .109 E8
Kingsbury Ave BL1 . . . . .142 A1
Kingsbury Ct BL1 . . . . .142 A1
Kingsbury Ct Lo BL1 . . . . . . .142 A1
Kingsbury Rd M11 . . . . .83 C2
Kingscliffe St M9 . . . . .157 E8
Kingscourt Ave BL1 . . . . .142 C2
Kingscroft Ct WN1 . . . . .151 D7
Kingsdale Rd M18 . . . . .100 A4
Kingsdown Cres WN1 . . . . . . .37 C4
Kingsdown Dr BL1 . . . . .143 F1
Kingsdown Gdns 8 BL1 . . . .143 F1
Kingsdown Rd
  Abram Brow WN2 . . . . .74 B7
  Wythenshawe M22 . . . . .121 C1
Kingsdown Wlk SK5 . . . . . . .112 B5
Kingsfield Way M29 . . . . .77 B8
Kingsfold Ave M40 . . . . .159 C4
Kingsfold Cl BL2 . . . . .42 E6
Kingsford St M5 . . . . .154 D2
Kingsgate BL1 . . . . .142 C2
Kingsgate Rd M22 . . . . .121 C1
Kingshill Ct WN6 . . . . .36 F7
Kingshill Rd M21 . . . . .109 A8
Kingsholme Rd M22 . . . . . . .121 C2
Kingsland Cl M40 . . . . .160 D3
Kingsland Rd
  Cheadle SK3 . . . . .123 A7
  Farnworth BL4 . . . . .42 A1
  Rochdale OL11 . . . . .30 B3
Kingslea Rd M20 . . . . .110 C5
Kingsleigh Rd SK4 . . . . .110 F4
Kingsley Ave
  Handforth SK9 . . . . .131 C2
  Manchester M9 . . . . .64 D5
  Prestwich M25 . . . . .157 F7
  Stockport SK4 . . . . .169 E4
  Stretford M33 . . . . .108 A3
  Urmston M41 . . . . .95 B2
  Whitefield M45 . . . . .63 A8
Kingsley Cl Ashton-u-L OL6 . . .86 A5
  Denton M34 . . . . .100 D1
Kingsley Dr Cheadle SK8 . . . .123 A3
  Oldham OL4 . . . . .67 C7
Kingsley Gr M34 . . . . .100 C8

Kingsley Rd
Altrincham WA15 ....120 B7
Hindley WN2 ....56 F5
Middleton M24 ....47 B2
Oldham OL4 ....67 C6
Swinton M27 ....61 D1
Walkden M28 ....60 C4
Wythenshawe M22 ....121 D8
Kingsley St Bolton BL1 .....143 D2
  Bury BL8 ....27 B2
  Leigh WN7 ....75 C7
Kingsmead Mews M9 ....64 C5
Kingsmede WN1 ....37 D3
Kingsmere Ave M19 ....98 F1
Kingsmill Ave M19 ....111 B8
Kingsmoor Fields SK13 ...104 D3
Kingsmoor Rd SK13 ....104 D2
Kingsneath Ave M11 ....83 B3
Kingsnorth Cl 5 BL1 ......143 F1
Kingsnorth Rd M14 ....94 E4
Kingsoak Cl WN1 ....151 D8
Kingston Arc 6 SK14 .....102 E2
Kingston Ave Bolton BL2 ....25 C1
  Manchester M20 ....110 B1
  6 Oldham OL1 ....49 B1
  Oldham OL9 ....66 A4
Kingston Cl
  Hattersley SK14 ....102 E2
  Manchester M7 ....155 D8
  Sale M33 ....107 D2
  Shaw OL2 ....149 B8
  Wigan WN3 ....55 B3
Kingston Cres BB4 ....1 A7
Kingston Ct
  14 Manchester M9 ....131 E1
  Manchester M20 ....110 B1
Kingston Dr Royton OL2 .....48 C6
  Sale M33 ....108 D5
  Urmston M41 ....107 B8
Kingston Gdns SK14 ....101 B3
Kingston Gr M9 ....64 F4
Kingston Hill SK8 ....122 D4
Kingston Pl SK8 ....122 E2
Kingston Rd Failsworth M35 ..84 B7
  Handforth SK9 ....131 D5
  Manchester M20 ....110 B1
  Radcliffe BL9 ....44 C6
Kingston St SK3 ....169 D1
Kingsway
  Altrincham WA14 ....119 D5
  Bredbury SK6 ....112 E3
  Cheadle M20,SK8 ....122 C6
  Dukinfield SK16 ....101 E7
  Ince-in-M WN2 ....151 F7
  Kearsley BL4 ....61 D5
  Manchester M14,M19, M20 ..110 D4
  Manchester M19 ....98 F1
  Middleton M24 ....65 B6
  Newton-le-W WA12 ....89 C2
  Pendlebury M27 ....80 C6
  Rochdale OL16 ....31 C5
  Stockport SK7 ....123 F2
  Stretford M32 ....96 C1
  Walkden M28 ....78 D8
  Wigan WN1 ....37 D2
Kingsway Ave M19 ....98 F1
Kingsway Bldgs M19 ....110 E5
Kingsway Cl OL8 ....153 E5
Kingsway Cres M19 ....110 E5
Kingsway Pk M41 ....95 D4
Kingsway Prim Sch M41 ....95 E4
Kingsway Sec SchThe
  SK8 ....122 C4
Kingswear Dr BL1 ....142 C1
Kingswood Gr SK5 ....99 F1
Kingswood Rd Eccles M30 ...79 B4
  Manchester M14 ....110 E8
  Middleton M24 ....46 F3
  Prestwich M25 ....62 F5
Kingthorpe Gdns BL3 ....147 F4
Kingwood Ave BL1 ....40 F8
Kingwood Cres WN5 ....54 D6
Kinlet Rd WN3 ....54 C4
Kinlett Wlk 7 M40 ....65 D2
Kinley Cl M12 ....164 F6
Kinloch Dr BL1 ....144 B7
Kinloch St Droylsden M11 ...83 A2
  Oldham OL8 ....67 A4
Kinmel Ave SK5 ....112 C4
Kinmel Wlk 4 M23 ....120 F6
Kinmount Wlk M9 ....157 D6
Kinnaird Cres SK1 ....124 B8
Kinnaird Rd M20 ....110 C5
Kinnerly Gr M28 ....60 A1
Kinniside Cl WN3 ....55 A2
Kinross Ave Garswood WN4 ..72 C4
  Stockport SK2 ....124 A3
Kinross Dr BL3 ....40 F5
Kinross Rd M14 ....98 E3
Kinsale Wlk M23 ....120 F3
Kinsey Ave M23 ....120 E7
Kinsley Dr M28 ....60 C2
Kintbury St WN2 ....73 F7
Kintore Ave SK7 ....124 F3
Kintore Wlk 5 M40 ....156 C5
Kintyre Ave M5 ....154 E1
Kintyre Cl 8 M11 ....83 C1
Kintyre Dr BL3 ....40 E5
Kinver Cl BL3 ....146 C3
Kinver Rd M40 ....65 C2
Kipling Ave Denton M34 ....113 A7
  Droylsden M43 ....84 A3
Kipling Cl SK2 ....124 E7

Kipling Gr WN7 ....75 D7
Kipling Rd OL1 ....49 B2
Kipling St M7 ....155 D6
Kippax St M14 ....98 B3
Kirby Ave Atherton M46 .....58 C5
  Failsworth OL9 ....65 D3
  Swinton M27 ....79 D5
Kirby Rd WN7 ....75 E5
Kirby Wlk
  6 Manchester M4 ....159 C2
  Oldham OL2 ....149 B8
Kiribati Way WN7 ....75 E6
Kirk Rd M19 ....111 B7
Kirk St M18 ....99 D5
Kirkbank St Oldham OL9 ...153 D7
  Oldham OL9 ....153 D8
Kirkbeck WN7 ....76 C3
Kirkburn View BL8 ....27 C5
Kirkby Ave Manchester M40 ..83 B7
  Sale M33 ....64 E7
Kirkby Cl BL9 ....45 F5
Kirkby Dr M33 ....108 D2
Kirkby Rd Bolton BL1 ....144 B8
  Culcheth WA3 ....91 F3
Kirkdale Ave M40 ....65 D2
Kirkdale Dr OL2 ....48 D6
Kirkdale Gdns WN8 ....53 A7
Kirkebrok Rd BL3 ....146 A4
Kirkfell Dr High Lane SK6 ..134 E8
  Tyldesley M29 ....77 B7
Kirkfell Wlk OL1 ....48 F1
Kirkgate Cl 4 M40 ....159 C3
Kirkhall La Bolton BL1 ....144 C8
  Leigh WN7 ....75 F6
Kirkhall Wkshp The BL1 ...144 C8
Kirkham Ave Golborne WA3 ..90 E6
  Manchester M18 ....99 D6
Kirkham Cl M34 ....100 F3
Kirkham Rd Gatley SK8 .....131 C8
  Leigh WN7 ....75 D2
Kirkham St Abram WN2 .....74 B8
  Bolton BL2 ....25 C1
  Oldham OL9 ....153 E7
  Salford M5 ....154 E1
  Walkden M38 ....60 A5
Kirkhaven Sq M40 ....160 E4
Kirkhill Wlk 11 M40 ....65 D2
Kirkhill Wlk 11 M40 ....64 E3
Kirkhope Dr BL1 ....143 D1
Kirkhope Wlk BL1 ....143 D1
Kirklands Bolton BL2 ....25 D2
  Sale M33 ....108 A2
Kirklee Ave OL9 ....48 A1
Kirklee Rd OL11 ....30 D2
Kirklees St Bury BL8 ....26 F7
  Wigan WN1 ....151 E8
Kirklees Wlk M45 ....63 A8
Kirkless La WN2 ....38 B1
Kirkless St WN2 ....38 A3
Kirkless Villas WN2 ....38 A2
Kirkley St SK14 ....167 E1
Kirklinton Dr M9 ....157 D6
Kirkman Ave M30 ....95 C8
Kirkman Cl M18 ....99 D4
Kirkman St BL9 ....44 F3
Kirkmanshulme La
  M12,M18 ....165 B5
Kirkpatrick St WN2 ....57 B3
Kirkstall 2 OL12 ....139 E8
Kirkstall Ave Heywood OL10 ..29 C3
  Littleborough OL15 ....16 A7
Kirkstall Cl SK12 ....133 D4
Kirkstall Gdns M26 ....43 E5
Kirkstall Rd Middleton M24 ..46 F3
  Urmston M41 ....95 E3
Kirkstall Sq M13 ....163 C6
Kirkstead Cl M11 ....165 A8
Kirkstead Rd SK8 ....132 C6
Kirkstile Cres WN3 ....54 E2
Kirkstile Pl M27 ....61 E4
Kirkstone M43 ....54 C7
Kirkstone Ave M28 ....60 F1
Kirkstone Cl OL1 ....48 F1
Kirkstone Dr
  Middleton M24 ....46 E2
  Royton OL2 ....48 D6
Kirkstone Rd
  Dukinfield SK14 ....101 C5
  Failsworth M40 ....65 C2
Kirktown Wlk M11 ....165 C8
Kirkwall Dr BL2 ....148 B5
Kirkway Manchester M9 ......65 A4
  Middleton M24 ....65 A7
  Rochdale OL11 ....30 D2
Kirkwood Dr M40 ....159 C4
Kirtley Ave M30 ....79 D3
Kirtlington Cl OL2 ....149 A5
Kirton Cl WN5 ....63 C4
Kirton Wlk M9 ....64 C5
Kirtton St 10 OL16 ....31 A8
Kitchener Ave M44 ....105 C4
Kitchener St Bolton BL3 ......42 B3
  Bury BL9 ....27 B1
Kite Gr WN7 ....75 E6
Kitepool St M30 ....79 A3
Kites Nest La WN6 ....54 C8
Kitt's Moss La SK7 ....132 D6
Kitter St OL12 ....15 C3
Kittiwake Cl M27 ....77 A7
Kitty Wheeldon Gdns
  M33 ....108 A5
Kiveton Cl M28 ....60 C2
Kiveton Dr WN4 ....73 C2
Knacks La OL12 ....14 A5
Knaresborough Cl SK5 ....99 F1
Knaresborough Rd WN2 ....56 E4
Knarr Barn La OL3 ....50 D3
Knarr La OL3 ....50 E2

Kneller Wlk OL1 ....49 D4
Knight Cres M24 ....46 D3
Knight St Ashton-u-L OL7 ...84 F2
  Bolton BL1 ....145 F8
  Bury BL8 ....27 C2
  Hyde SK14 ....167 E1
  Manchester M20 ....110 B2
Knight's Cl M25 ....63 B5
Knightley Wlk M40 ....157 D5
Knights Cl M5 ....80 A2
Knightsbridge SK1 ....169 F2
Knightsbridge Cl
  12 Handforth SK9 ....131 D1
  Manchester M7 ....155 D8
Knightscliffe Cres WN6 .....35 D6
Knightshill Cres WN6 ....37 A1
Knightswood BL3 ....40 F3
Kniveton Rd M12 ....164 F6
Kniveton St SK14 ....167 F3
Knob Hall Gdns M23 ....120 F3
Knole Ave SK12 ....133 F4
Knoll St Manchester M7 .....155 D7
  Rochdale OL11 ....30 C2
Knoll The Mossley OL5 ....68 B1
  Shaw OL2 ....149 C6
Knott Fold SK14 ....167 D1
Knott Hill La OL3 ....50 E3
Knott Hill St OL12 ....4 E6
Knott La Bolton BL1 ....23 F2
  Hyde SK14 ....113 E8
Knott Lanes OL8 ....84 F8
Knott's Hos
  Golborne WN7 ....91 C8
  Golborne WN7 ....91 B8
Knotts Brow BL7 ....9 F4
Knowe Ave 8 M22 ....121 D1
Knowl Cl Ramsbottom BL0 ....11 C4
  Reddish M34 ....100 B2
Knowl Hill Dr OL12 ....13 E2
Knowl La OL12 ....13 B5
Knowl Mdw BB4 ....1 A6
Knowl Rd Milnrow OL16 ....31 D6
  Shaw OL2 ....149 C6
Knowldale Way M12 ....164 E5
Knowle Ave OL7 ....166 A4
Knowle Gn SK9 ....131 C3
Knowle Pk SK9 ....131 C3
Knowle Rd SK6 ....126 D6
Knowle Way SK14 ....113 C8
Knowles Ave WN3 ....54 F4
Knowles Ct M6 ....80 B3
Knowles Edge St BL1 ....142 C2
Knowles Pl
  1 Manchester M15 ....162 F6
  Wigan WN1 ....151 E8
Knowles St Bolton BL1 ....25 A1
  Ince-in-M WN3 ....151 D6
  Radcliffe M26 ....44 A4
Knowles The OL8 ....66 C1
Knowls La OL4 ....67 F5
Knowsley Grange BL1 ....40 D7
Knowsley Ave 68 A7
  Atherton M46 ....58 C4
  Golborne WA3 ....90 B6
  Oldham OL8 ....68 A7
  Salford M5 ....161 B8
  Urmston M41 ....95 C4
Knowsley Cres
  Stockport SK5 ....124 B8
  Whitworth OL12 ....4 E6
Knowsley Dr Leigh WN7 ....75 E2
  Oldham OL8 ....68 A7
  Swinton M27 ....79 D5
Knowsley Gn Oldham OL4 ....68 A7
  Salford M5 ....161 B8
Knowsley Gr BL6 ....22 D1
Knowsley Jun Sch OL4 ....68 A7
Knowsley Park Way BB4 ......1 B8
Knowsley Rd
  Ainsworth BL2 ....26 C1
  Bolton BL1 ....142 B2
  Haslingden BB4 ....1 B8
  Hazel Grove SK7 ....133 F8
  Stockport SK5 ....124 B8
  Whitefield M45 ....62 F8
  Wigan WN6 ....37 A3
Knowsley Rd Ind Est BB4 ...1 B8
Knowsley St Bolton BL1 ....145 F7
  Bury BL9 ....140 E1
  Leigh WN7 ....75 D5
  Manchester M8 ....159 A4
  Rochdale OL12 ....139 E8
Knowsley Terr OL4 ....68 A7
Knutsford Ave
  Manchester M16 ....97 D3
  Reddish SK4 ....111 D7
  Sale M33 ....108 E4
Knutsford Rd
  Manchester M18 ....99 C4
  Wilmslow SK9,M14,M16 .....136 D3
Knutsford St M6 ....81 A3
Knutsford View WA15 ....129 C8
Knutshaw Cres BL3 ....40 E2
Knypersley Ave SK2 ....124 C7
Kranj Way OL1 ....153 F7
Krester Ct M20 ....110 A3
Krokus Sq OL2 ....152 A7
Kyle Rd SK7 ....124 F1
Kylemore Ave BL3 ....144 B5
Kynder St M34 ....100 F3

L

Labrador Quay M5 ....96 F7
Labtec St M27 ....62 B1
Laburnum Ave
  Ashton-u-L OL6 ....85 C6
  Atherton M46 ....58 E3
  Bury BL9 ....27 F8
  Droylsden M43 ....84 C1
  Eccles M30 ....95 A8
  Failsworth M35 ....83 F6
  Hyde SK14 ....113 D8
  Ince-in-M WN3 ....151 F6
  Leigh WN7 ....75 E8
  Oldham OL9 ....48 C1
  Shaw OL2 ....149 B6
  Stalybridge SK15,SK16 ....101 F8
  Swinton M27 ....62 A7
  Whitefield M45 ....62 F7
Laburnum Cl 4 WA15 ....120 B5
Laburnum Ct BL8 ....26 F7
Laburnum Dr
  Whitefield BL9 ....45 A1
  Wigan WN6 ....37 A4
Laburnum Gr Horwich BL6 ....22 E1
  Prestwich M25 ....62 E5
  Tyldesley M29 ....59 D1
Laburnum La
  Altrincham WA15 ....128 E8
  Milnrow OL16 ....32 A3
Laburnum Pk BL2 ....25 B5
Laburnum Rd
  Farnworth BL4 ....60 B8
  Manchester M18 ....99 F7
  Haslingden BB4 ....1 A7
  Irlam M44 ....105 D5
  Manchester M18 ....99 D4
  Middleton M24 ....65 C8
  Oldham OL8 ....84 D8
  Urmston M41 ....95 A4
  Walkden M28 ....60 E1
Laburnum St
  Ashton-in-M WN4 ....73 B2
  Bolton BL1 ....58 E3
  7 Bolton BL1 ....145 D8
  Salford M6 ....154 F2
Laburnum Terr OL11 ....30 E4
Laburnum Villas OL8 ....67 A1
Laburnum Way
  Littleborough OL15 ....15 F5
  Stockport SK3 ....123 B8
Laburnum Wlk 11 M33 ......107 C5
Lacey Ave SK9 ....131 B1
Lacey Ct SK9 ....131 B1
Lacey Gr SK9 ....131 C1
Lacey Green
  Cty Prim Sch** SK9 ....131 B1
Lackford Dr M40 ....159 C4
Lacrosse Ave OL8 ....66 C4
Lacy Ct SK9 ....131 B1
Lacy St M32 ....96 D1
Lacy St Stockport SK1 ....170 F8
  Stretford M32 ....96 D1
Lacy Wlk M12 ....164 E8
Ladbrooke Cl OL6 ....166 C4
Ladbrooke Rd OL6 ....85 C5
Ladcastle Rd OL3 ....69 A7
Ladhill La OL3 ....69 B5
Ladies La WN2 ....56 A7
Lady Barn House Sch
  SK8 ....122 D3
Lady Bridge Brow BL1 ....40 F7
Lady Bridge La BL1,BL3 ....40 F7
Lady Bridge La BL1 ....40 F7
Lady Kelvin Rd WA14 ....119 C6
Lady La Culcheth WA3 ....91 C1
  Wigan WN3 ....54 E3
Lady Rd OL4 ....67 E6
Ladybarn Ave WA3 ....89 F7
Ladybarn Cres
  Bramhall SK7 ....132 F6
  Manchester M14 ....110 D7
Ladybarn Ho 1 M14 ....110 D8
Ladybarn La M14 ....110 D8
Ladybarn Manor SK7 ....132 F8
Ladybarn Mews 8 M14 .....110 D8
Ladybarn Prim Sch M20 ...110 D6
Ladybarn Rd M14 ....110 D7
Ladybower SK8 ....123 C4
Ladybridge Ave M28 ....78 C8
Ladybridge Com Prim Sch
  BL3 ....40 F5
Ladybridge Prim Sch
  SK8 ....123 B4
Ladybridge Rd SK8 ....123 B3
Ladybridge Rise SK8 ....123 C3
Ladybrook Ave WA15 ....120 B8
Ladybrook Gr 6 SK9 ....131 D2
Ladybrook Prim Sch SK7 ...132 F7
Ladybrook Rd SK7 ....123 E3
Ladyfield St SK9 ....137 B7
Ladyfield Terr SK9 ....137 C7
Ladyhill View M28 ....78 C8
Ladyhouse Cl OL16 ....32 A5
Ladyhouse La OL16 ....32 A5
Ladylands Ave 11 M11 ....67 F8
Ladymere Dr M28 ....78 B8
Ladys Cl SK12 ....133 E4
Ladyshore Cl M16 ....154 F1
Ladyshore Rd BL3 ....43 C2
Ladysmith Ave
  Ashton-in-M WN4 ....73 C3
  Bury BL9 ....28 A5
Ladysmith Rd
  Ashton-u-L OL6 ....85 F5

Ladysmith Rd continued
  Manchester M20 ....110 C3
  Stockport SK5 ....86 A4
Ladysmith Sh Ctr OL6 ....166 B3
Ladysmith St Oldham OL6 ....66 C3
  Stockport SK3 ....170 E7
Ladysmith The OL6 ....85 F5
Ladythorn Ave SK6 ....112 F6
Ladythorn Cres SK7 ....132 F6
Ladythorn Ct M25 ....63 A2
Ladythorn Gr SK7 ....132 F6
Ladythorn Rd SK7 ....132 E6
Ladythorne Ave M25 ....63 A2
Ladythorne Dr M25 ....63 A2
Ladywell Ave M38 ....60 A5
Ladywell Cl SK7 ....124 A2
Ladywell Gr M38 ....60 A5
Lafford La Orrell WN8 ....53 C3
  Shaw OL2 ....53 C8
Lagos Cl M14 ....98 A4
Laindon Rd M13,M14 ....98 E4
Lainton St 6 SK4 ....123 C8
Laithwaite Rd WN5 ....54 F2
Lake Bank OL15 ....16 A3
Lake Dr M24 ....64 F7
Lake Rd Denton M34 ....100 F4
  Stalybridge SK15 ....84 F1
  Stretford M17 ....96 C7
Lake Side Leigh WN7 ....75 D6
  Littleborough OL15 ....16 A2
Lake Side Cotts WN1 ....20 C1
Lainton St 6 SK3 ....123 C8
Lake St Bolton BL3 ....145 F5
Lake WN7 ....76 A6
  Stockport SK2 ....124 B5
Lake View M9 ....65 A2
Lake View WN5 ....54 B7
Lakeland Ave WN4 ....73 C4
Lakeland Cres BL9 ....44 E6
Lakeland Ct 1 M24 ....46 D2
Lakeland Dr OL2 ....48 C8
Lakelands Dr BL3 ....40 F5
Lakenheath Cl 10 BL1 ....24 F6
Lakenheath Dr BL1 ....25 A6
Lakes Dr WN5 ....53 E6
Lakes Rd Dukinfield SK16 ...101 C8
  Marple SK6 ....126 B5
Lakes Terr WN2 ....56 A7
Lakeside Bury BL9 ....44 F5
  Gatley SK8 ....122 C3
  Hadfield SK13 ....104 A6
  Prestwich M7 ....63 D1
Lakeside Ave
  Ashton-u-L OL7 ....84 F4
  Bolton BL3 ....42 A2
  Orrell WN5 ....53 E3
  Walkden M28 ....60 D5
Lakeside Cl M18 ....99 F6
Lakeside Dr SK12 ....133 E5
Lakeside Gn SK2 ....124 C6
Lakeside Way BL9 ....140 F1
Lakin St M40 ....83 A7
Laleham Gn SK7 ....123 D3
Lamb Cl M12 ....164 F5
Lamb La M3 ....158 E2
Lamb La Ashley WA14 ....128 E2
  Manchester M3 ....158 E2
Lamb St WN1 ....37 E1
Lamb Wlk 11 M34 ....113 A7
Lamberhead Ind Est WN5 ....54 B5
Lamberhead Rd WN5 ....54 C6
Lambert Dr M33 ....107 E5
Lambert St OL7 ....100 F8
Lamberton Dr M23 ....120 E6
Lambeth Ave M35 ....84 B8
Lambeth Cl BL6 ....22 D3
Lambeth Gr SK6 ....126 A3
Lambeth Rd Failsworth M40 ..83 C4
  Reddish SK5 ....111 F7
Lambeth St M46 ....58 B3
Lambgates SK13 ....104 A5
Lambley Cl WN7 ....75 D8
Lambourn Cl Bolton BL3 .....145 E5
  Poynton SK12 ....133 D4
Lambourn Rd M41 ....94 D4
Lambourne Cl M22 ....121 D8
Lambourne Gr OL16 ....31 F5
Lambrook Wlk M40 ....83 D4
Lambs Fold SK4 ....111 D5
Lambton Rd
  Manchester M21 ....109 D8
  Worsley M28 ....79 C7
Lambton St Bolton BL3 ......146 C2
  Eccles M30 ....79 B3
  Wigan WN3 ....54 C5
Lamburn Ave M40 ....65 D2
Lamerton Way SK9 ....131 E2
Lamonna Cl M7 ....81 B2
Lamport Cl M1 ....163 B7
Lamport Ct M1 ....163 B7
Lampson St M8 ....158 E4
Lamsholme Cl M19 ....99 A2
Lanark Ave M22 ....121 E8
Lanark Cl Hazel Grove SK7 ..125 A2
  Heywood OL10 ....28 F1
Lanbury Dr M8 ....155 F7
Lancanshire Cotts OL5 ....68 D2
Lancashire Cricket Club
  Mus** M22 ....96 F4
Lancashire Ct OL9 ....52 C5
Lancashire City
  & Manchester Cricket Gd**
  M16 ....97 A4
Lancashire Fusiliers
  Regimental Mus** BL8 ....27 B1
Lancashire Hill
  SK1,SK4,SK5 ....169 E3

Lancashire Rd M31 ....105 E2
Lancashire St M10,M40 ....157 F5
Lancaster Ave
Atherton M46 ....58 E2
Failsworth M35 ....83 E7
Golborne WA3 ....90 C8
Haslingden BB4 ....1 B8
Horwich BL6 ....22 D2
Middleton M24 ....65 C7
Ramsbottom BL0 ....11 A4
Stalybridge SK15 ....86 A3
Tyldesley M29 ....59 A3
Urmston M41 ....95 E3
Whitefield M45 ....63 A7
Lancaster Cl Adlington PR6 ..21 B7
Bolton BL2 ....148 A7
Hazel Grove SK7 ....133 D8
Romiley SK6 ....113 A1
Lancaster Ct
Failsworth M40 ....83 C4
4 Leigh WN7 ....76 B4
3 Manchester M19 ....110 F8
Lancaster Dr Bury BL9 ......27 F8
Little Lever BL3 ....43 B4
Manchester M25 ....63 C2
Lancaster Ho Royton OL2 ....48 D5
5 Stockport SK3 ....170 E8
Lancaster Pl PR6 ....21 A8
Lancaster Rd Denton M34 ..100 F1
Droylsden M43 ....83 F3
Handforth SK9 ....131 E1
Hindley WN2 ....56 F5
Irlam M44 ....105 D5
Manchester M20 ....110 A3
Salford M6 ....80 B4
Shevington WN5 ....36 D1
Lancaster Sq OL2 ....48 D5
Lancaster St
Ince-in-M WN3 ....151 D6
Mossley OL5 ....68 B1
Oldham OL9 ....66 A3
Radcliffe M26 ....43 E3
Stockport SK1 ....112 A2
Lancaster Terr
24 Bolton BL1 ....143 E2
Rochdale OL11 ....13 D2
Lancaster Way BL5 ....39 D2
Lancaster Wlk
22 Bolton BL1 ....143 E2
Shevington WN5 ....36 D1
Lancasterian Sch M20 ....109 E4
Lance Wood Pl WN5 ....54 D6
Lancelot Rd M22 ....121 F2
Lancelyn Dr SK9 ....137 D8
Lanchester Dr BL3 ....145 D5
Lanchester St M40 ....160 E3
Lancing Ave M20 ....110 D3
Lancing Wlk OL9 ....152 A6
Land Gate OL12 ....4 F5
Land Gate La WN4 ....73 B8
Land La SK9 ....137 C6
Land St WN6 ....150 B8
Landcross Rd M14 ....98 C1
Landedmans BL5 ....58 A7
Landells Wlk M40 ....83 A5
Lander Gr M9 ....64 F3
Landgate Ind Est
Ashton-in-M WN4 ....72 F8
Ashton-in-M WN4 ....73 A8
Landkey Cl 1 M23 ....108 F2
Landor Cl WA3 ....90 E8
Landor Ct M34 ....99 F3
Landore Cl M26 ....44 B4
Landos Ct 16 M40 ....159 C3
Landos Rd M40 ....159 C3
Landrace Dr M28 ....78 B6
Lands End Rd M24 ....64 B7
Landsberg Rd M35 ....84 B8
Landsberg Terr M35 ....84 B8
Landseer Dr SK6 ....126 B7
Landseer St OL4 ....67 A5
Landside WN7 ....75 F2
Lane Brow OL4 ....68 B5
Lane Dr OL4 ....68 B5
Lane End Eccles M30 ....79 F1
Heywood OL10 ....46 F8
Lane End Cl M35 ....84 A6
Lane End Prim Sch SK8 ...123 C2
Lane End Rd Bacup OL13 ......4 A8
Manchester M19,SK4 ....110 E4
Lane Ends Romiley SK6 ....113 D3
5 Wigan WN5 ....54 D5
Lane Head Ave WA3 ....90 F8
Lane Head Rd
Mossley OL4,OL5 ....68 A3
Oldham OL4 ....67 F4
Lane Mdw OL2 ....149 A6
Lane The BL1 ....40 D7
Lanegate SK14 ....113 D8
Lanesfield Wlk M8 ....156 C8
Laneside Ave OL2 ....49 D7
Laneside Cl OL15 ....16 A6
Laneside Dr SK7 ....124 A1
Laneside Rd
Manchester M20 ....122 C8
Rowarth SK22 ....127 E6
Laneside Wlk OL16 ....31 F7
Lanfield Dr M8 ....155 F7
Langcliff Wlk 12 BL1 ......143 F2
Langcliffe Cl WA3 ....91 E3
Langcliffe Wlk M18 ....165 C5
Langcroft Dr 16 M40 ....83 C5
Langdale Ave
Golborne WA3 ....74 C1
Ince-in-M WN2 ....56 B8
Manchester M19 ....111 B8
Oldham OL8 ....66 D4
Royton OL11,OL16 ....48 C8
Langdale Ave *continued*
Wigan WN1 ....37 B3
Langdale Cl
Altrincham WA15 ....119 E5
Denton M34 ....100 E1
Gatley SK8 ....122 C3
High Lane SK6 ....134 E8
Langdale Cres Abram WN2 ..74 B8
Wigan WN5 ....54 B8
Langdale Ct M8 ....156 B6
Langdale Dr Middleton M24 ..46 F3
Walkden M28 ....60 F1
Whitefield BL9 ....45 A3
Langdale Gr WN2 ....56 B2
Langdale Rd Bramhall SK7 .132 C5
Hindley WN2 ....56 E5
Manchester M14 ....98 D4
Partington M31 ....105 E3
Reddish SK4 ....111 C6
Romiley SK6 ....113 B4
Sale M33 ....107 E1
Stretford M32 ....96 C3
Wigan WN5 ....54 B7
Langdale St Bolton BL3 ....147 E3
Farnworth BL4 ....60 C7
Leigh WN7 ....75 E5
Langdale Terr SK15 ....86 A4
Langden Cl Culcheth WA3 ...91 D4
Shaw OL2 ....149 A8
Langdon Cl BL1 ....143 D1
Langdon Coll M7 ....63 F1
Langfield WA3 ....90 E7
Langfield Ave M16 ....97 D3
Langfield Cres M43 ....84 C2
Langford Dr Irlam M44 ......94 A1
Leigh WN7 ....75 E2
Langford Rd
Manchester M20 ....110 A6
Manchester SK4 ....168 C4
Langford St M34 ....100 F3
Langham Cl BL1 ....25 A5
Langham Ct
Manchester M20 ....109 F4
Stretford M32 ....96 A4
Langham Gr WA15 ....120 B8
Langham Ho SK4 ....168 B2
Langham Rd
Altrincham WA14 ....119 C2
Oldham OL8 ....66 E4
Salford M6 ....154 F2
Standish WN6 ....19 D1
Stockport SK4 ....168 B1
Langham St OL7 ....85 A5
Langholm Cl WN3 ....54 D3
Langholm Dr BL2 ....42 F6
Langholm Rd WN4 ....72 C4
Langholme Cl M15 ....162 D7
Langholme Pl M30 ....79 B2
Langholme Way OL10 ....28 F1
Langland Cl
Manchester M19 ....99 D2
Manchester M9 ....64 E4
Langland Dr M30 ....95 C7
Langley Ave
Hazel Grove SK7 ....124 B1
Middleton M24 ....46 E4
Newton-le-W WA12 ....89 C1
Oldham OL4 ....68 B5
Prestwich M25 ....63 B6
Langley Cl Golborne WA3 ....74 C1
Standish WN6 ....19 E2
Urmston M41 ....95 E2
Langley Cres M25 ....63 B6
Langley Ct Hadfield SK13 ...104 A5
9 Manchester M7 ....63 E1
Langley Dr 3 Bolton BL3 ...144 C5
Boothstown M28 ....77 F6
Glossop SK13 ....116 F8
Handforth SK9 ....131 E3
Langley Gdns M25 ....63 B6
Langley Gr M25 ....63 B6
Langley Grange M25 ....63 B6
Langley Hall Rd M25 ....63 B6
Langley La M24,OL10 ....46 D4
Langley Platt La
M29,M46 ....76 D8
Langley Prim Sch M24 ......46 E2
Langley Rd
Manchester M14 ....98 D1
Manchester M6,M27 ....80 F7
Prestwich M25 ....63 A5
Sale M33 ....107 E4
Langley Rd S M6,M27 ....81 A5
Langley St WN5 ....54 D6
Langness St 2 M11 ....83 C1
Lango St 1 M16 ....97 C4
Langport Ave M12 ....164 E6
Langroyd Wlk 11 M8 ....155 F7
Langset Ave 2 WN2 ....56 D6
Langsett Ave
24 Gamesley SK13 ....171 D1
Salford M6 ....80 C3
Langsett Gn 22 SK13 ....171 D1
Langsett Gr 23 SK13 ....171 D1
Langsett La SK13 ....171 D1
Langsett Terr 21 SK13 .....171 D1
Langshaw Rd BL3 ....144 C5
Langshaw St
Manchester M16 ....97 C4
Salford M5,M6 ....154 F1
Langshaw Wlk BL3 ....144 C5
Langside Ave M9 ....64 E4
Langside Dr BL3 ....40 E4
Langston St M3 ....158 F3
Langstone Cl BL6 ....22 B3
Langthorne St M19 ....111 B8
Langthorne Wlk BL3 ....145 D5
Langton Ave WN6 ....19 E1
Langton Cl
Newton-le-W WA12 ....89 A4
Oldham M35 ....84 C8
Langton Gn SK7 ....124 A1
Langton Pl WN6 ....19 E1
Langton St Heywood OL10 ...29 D3
Middleton M24 ....65 A8
Salford M6 ....154 E2
Langton Terr OL11 ....30 E4
Langtree Cl M28 ....78 B8
Langtree La WN6 ....19 D3
Langworthy Ave M38 ....60 B4
Langworthy Rd
Manchester M40 ....83 A7
Salford M6 ....154 F3
Langworthy Road Sch
M6 ....154 F3
Lanhill Dr M8 ....156 C6
Lankro Way M30,M17 ....79 F1
Lanreath Wlk 10 M8 ....156 B6
Lansbury Ho 2 M16 ....97 D3
Lansbury St WN5 ....54 A6
Lansdale Gdns M19 ....110 E5
Lansdale St Eccles M30 .....95 A8
Walkden M28 ....60 D5
Lansdown Cl SK7,SK8 .....132 C7
Lansdowne WA3 ....91 E2
Lansdowne Ave
Droylsden M34 ....84 C1
Romiley SK6 ....113 D2
Lansdowne Cl 11 BL2 ....25 B1
Lansdowne Ct OL9 ....152 B6
Lansdowne Dr M28 ....60 C1
Lansdowne Ho M20 ....110 B2
Lansdowne Rd
Altrincham WA14 ....119 D6
Atherton M46 ....58 F5
Bolton BL2 ....25 B2
Eccles M30 ....79 D3
Flixton M41 ....106 E8
Manchester M8 ....64 A1
Oldham OL9 ....152 C6
Sale M33 ....108 A6
Lansdowne Rd N M41 ....94 E1
Lansdowne St OL11 ....30 C7
Lanstead Dr M40 ....160 E2
Lantern View SK22 ....127 B1
Lapwing Cl
Newton-le-W WA12 ....89 C3
Rochdale OL11 ....29 E7
Stalybridge SK15 ....86 A4
Lapwing Ct 4 M20 ....110 A5
Lapwing La
Brinnington SK5 ....112 C6
Manchester M20 ....110 A5
Larch Ave Cheadle SK8 .....123 A1
Newton-le-W WA12 ....89 C2
Radcliffe M26 ....44 B1
Stretford M32 ....96 D1
Swinton M27 ....79 C6
Wigan WN5 ....54 D6
Larch Cl Billinge WN5 ....71 D5
Failsworth M35 ....83 F6
Golborne WA3 ....90 F6
Marple SK6 ....125 E5
Poynton SK12 ....133 F3
Rawtenstall BB4 ....1 F8
Sale M23 ....120 C8
Larch Gr Atherton M46 ......58 C4
Oldham OL4 ....67 E8
Oldham OL9 ....152 B8
Swinton M27 ....61 B2
Larch Rd Denton M34 ......101 A3
Eccles M30 ....79 A4
Leigh WN7 ....75 E8
Partington M31 ....105 E3
Larch St Bury BL9 ....141 B2
Oldham OL8,OL9 ....153 D6
Larch Way SK13 ....116 F8
Larches The OL5 ....68 E1
Larchview Rd M24 ....65 C8
Larchway Bramhall SK7 ....132 C7
High Lane SK6 ....134 F7
Milnrow OL16 ....31 D7
Larchwood Chadderton OL9 ..65 E8
Cheadle SK8 ....122 D6
Larchwood Ave M9 ....157 F7
Larchwood Cl M33 ....107 C4
Larchwood Dr Wigan WN1 ...37 B4
Wilmslow SK9 ....137 E8
Larchwood St BL1 ....143 F2
Larden Wlk 1 M8 ....155 F6
Largs Wlk 7 M23 ....120 F6
Lark Hill Farnworth BL4 ......60 E7
Stalybridge SK15 ....86 A4
Lark Hill Ct M24 ....65 A8
Lark Hill La OL3 ....51 A4
Lark Hill Pl OL12 ....14 E1
Lark Hill Prim Sch SK3 ....123 C8
Lark Hill Rd Stockport SK3 ..123 C8
Uppermill OL3 ....51 A3
Lark St Bolton BL1 ....145 F8
Farnworth BL4 ....60 D7
Oldham OL1 ....49 D3
Larkfield Ave Walkden M38 ..59 F5
Wigan WN1 ....37 B4
Larkfield Cl Ashton-u-L OL7 ..85 F7
Ramsbottom BL8 ....10 F1
Larkfield Gr Bolton BL2 ....148 B8
Walkden M38 ....59 F5
Larkhill Ave WN6 ....36 F8
Larkhill Cl WA15 ....120 B6
Larkhill Rd SK8 ....123 C5
Larkhill Wlk 2 M8 ....156 B6
Larks Rise M43 ....84 D3
Larkside Ave M28 ....60 E3
Larkspur Cl WN7 ....75 F3
Larkswood Dr SK2 ....124 F5
Larkwood Cl SK15 ....86 E7
Larmuth Ave M21 ....109 C6
Larne Ave Stockport SK3 ....123 B7
Stretford M32 ....96 C2
Larne St M11 ....165 A8
Larwood Ave SK4 ....168 B1
Lascar Ave M5 ....161 A8
Lashbrook Cl M40 ....160 D4
Lassell Fold SK14 ....102 B6
Lassell St M11 ....99 F7
Lassington Ave M11 ....99 D8
Last Drop Village The BL7 ....9 A1
Lastingham St M40 ....83 C6
Latchford St OL7 ....166 A4
Latchmere Rd M14 ....110 C8
Latham Ave WA12 ....89 C4
Latham Cl SK6 ....112 F5
Latham Ho WA12 ....89 B4
Latham La WN5 ....54 A8
Latham Rd BL6 ....21 C3
Latham St Bolton BL1 ......143 F2
Droylsden M11 ....99 F7
Lathbury Rd M40,M9 ....157 D6
Lathom Gr M33 ....108 E3
Lathom Hall Ave OL4 ....68 A7
Lathom Rd Irlam M44 ....105 F8
Manchester M20 ....110 D7
Lathom St 8 BL9 ....141 A4
Latimer Cl 2 WN5 ....53 F7
Latimer St OL4 ....67 A6
Latrigg Cres M24 ....46 C2
Latrobe St M43 ....100 A8
Lauderdale Cres M13 ......163 C6
Launceston Dr SK7 ....132 F7
Launceston Rd
Hindley WN2 ....57 C3
Radcliffe M26 ....43 D5
Laundry St M6 ....154 F4
Laura St BL9 ....11 C2
Laureate's Pl OL4 ....68 B7
Laurel Ave Chadderton OL9 ...65 E8
Cheadle SK8 ....122 D5
Manchester M14 ....98 A2
Newton-le-W WA12 ....89 D3
Laurel Bank Hyde SK14 .....113 C8
Stalybridge SK15 ....102 B8
Laurel Bank Gdns M9 ....64 D3
Laurel Cres WN2 ....57 A3
Laurel Ct 18 OL16 ....31 B6
Laurel Dr Altrincham WA15 ..120 B4
Walkden M38 ....60 A4
Laurel End La SK4 ....168 A3
Laurel Gn M34 ....101 A2
Laurel Gr Ashton-in-M WN4 ...73 B4
Golborne WA3 ....90 D8
Leigh WN7 ....75 E8
Salford M5 ....80 C2
Laurel Ho SK4 ....168 B4
Laurel Rd SK4 ....168 B4
Laurel St Bolton BL1 ....144 C7
Bury BL8 ....26 F6
Bury BL9 ....141 B2
Middleton M24 ....65 D8
Stockport SK4 ....169 E2
Wigan WN5 ....54 F7
Laurel Way SK8 ....132 C8
Laurel Wlk M31 ....105 E2
Laurels Dr OL15 ....15 F2
Laurels The OL5 ....68 D1
Laurence Cl M12 ....165 B6
Laurence Lowry Ct 2 M27 .61 F1
Lauria Terr BL2 ....26 D1
Laurie Pl 2 OL12 ....14 F1
Laurieston Ct SK8 ....122 C5
Lausanne Rd
Manchester M20 ....110 B7
Stockport SK7 ....123 E3
Lavender Cl Sale M23 ......108 E1
Sale M33 ....107 C5
Lavender Hill BB4 ....1 F8
Lavender Rd Farnworth BL4 ..42 A1
Oldham OL4 ....67 E4
Wigan WN6 ....36 F3
Lavender St M26 ....43 D3
Lavender Wlk
Downall Green WN4 ....72 D5
Partington M31 ....105 E2
Lavenders Brow SK1 ....169 F1
Lavenham Ave M11 ....83 D1
Lavenham Cl
Hazel Grove SK7 ....133 E8
Whitefield M45 ....44 F3
Laverton Cl BL9 ....28 E1
Lavington Ave SK8 ....123 A6
Lavington Gr M18 ....99 D4
Lavinia St M30 ....79 B2
Lavister Ave M19 ....110 E3
Law St Rochdale OL11 ....30 C4
Walsden OL14 ....6 B7
Lawefield Cres M27 ....61 D4
Lawers Ave OL9 ....152 A8
Lawflat OL12 ....15 C5
Lawler Ave M5 ....161 B6
Lawn Cl OL8 ....67 C3
Lawn Dr Altrincham WA15 ...119 E6
Swinton M27 ....79 E7
Lawn St BL1 ....143 D1
Lawnbank Cl M24 ....46 E1
Lawnfield Ct SK7 ....123 D2
Lawnfold SK13 ....171 E4
Lawngreen Ave M21 ....109 A7
Lawnhurst Trad Est
SK3,SK8 ....123 B5
Lawns Ave WN5 ....53 C5
Lawns The
Altrincham WA14 ....119 C3
Hindley WN2 ....56 C5
Lawnside Mews M20 ....110 A5
Lawnswood OL11 ....30 C3
Lawnswood Dr
Pendlebury M27 ....80 B6
Tyldesley M29 ....59 D1
Lawnswood Park Rd M27 ...80 B6
Lawrence Cl OL12 ....14 A1
Lawrence Ct WN2 ....74 B8
Lawrence Pl SK12 ....133 D2
Lawrence Rd
Altrincham WA14 ....119 C6
Hazel Grove SK7 ....124 E3
Urmston M41 ....94 E2
Lawrence St Bury BL9 ....44 F4
Stockport SK1 ....169 E1
Lawrie Ave BL0 ....138 B5
Lawson Ave Gatley SK8 ....122 B5
Leigh WN7 ....57 E1
Lawson Cl Middleton M24 ....47 A4
Swinton M28 ....79 C7
Lawson Dr WA15 ....120 A6
Lawson Gr M33 ....108 A6
Lawson Rd Bolton BL1 ......142 C2
Horwich BL6 ....22 C4
Lawson St 2 Bolton BL1 ...143 E4
Manchester M9 ....64 C2
Lawson Wlk M34 ....112 F8
Lawton Ave SK7 ....132 E8
Lawton Cl Culcheth WA3 .....91 E3
Romiley SK6 ....112 F1
Lawton Fold OL4 ....68 B7
Lawton Moor Rd M23 .....109 A1
Lawton Rd SK4 ....168 C4
Lawton Sq OL3 ....50 F4
Lawton St Delph OL3 ....50 F4
Droylsden M43 ....84 B2
Hyde SK14 ....167 E3
Manchester M11 ....99 D7
Rochdale OL12 ....15 A1
1 Stalybridge SK15 ....86 B1
Laxey Ave M46 ....58 E2
Laxey Cres WN7 ....75 C7
Laxey St M40 ....83 B7
Laxfield Dr M41 ....94 D3
Laxford Gr BL3 ....40 E6
Layard St OL6 ....166 A3
Laycock Ave Bolton BL2 .....25 B3
Stalybridge SK15 ....86 E4
Laycock Cres 4 M35 ....83 F7
Laycock Dr SK16 ....102 A7
Laycock Gr M35 ....83 F7
Laycock St OL16 ....15 D3
Laycock Way M34 ....112 F8
Layfield Cl BL8 ....26 D7
Layland Ave WA3 ....91 E4
Layland St WN3 ....150 B8
Laystall St M1 ....159 B1
Laythe Barn Cl OL16 ....31 E6
Layton Ave SK14 ....101 C2
Layton Cl SK1 ....124 A8
Layton Dr Kearsley BL4 ......60 F6
Romiley SK6 ....113 C3
Layton St M40 ....160 D2
Lazenby Cres WN4 ....72 F3
Lazonby Ave WN2 ....38 F3
Lazonby Wlk 7 M13 ....98 F4
Le Bas Ho M20 ....109 F6
Le Gendre St 1 BL2 ....25 B2
Le Mans Cres BL1 ....145 F7
Lea Ct Failsworth M35 ....83 E7
Manchester SK4 ....168 B4
Lea Dr M9 ....64 F3
Lea Gate Cl Bolton BL2 ......25 D5
Wigan WN3 ....54 E3
Lea Mount Dr BL9 ....28 D4
Lea Rd Gatley SK8 ....122 B1
Manchester SK4 ....168 C4
Lea St WN3 ....150 A7
Lea Vale Cl M38 ....59 F4
Lea View Royton OL2 ....48 C3
Wigan WN1 ....37 F1
Leabank St 5 M19 ....99 A2
Leabrook Dr M40 ....83 E8
Leaburn Dr M19 ....110 E4
Leach Cl OL16 ....15 C2
Leach St Bolton BL3 ....145 E5
4 Farnworth BL4 ....42 E1
Manchester M18 ....165 B6
Milnrow OL16 ....31 F5
Prestwich M25 ....62 F4
Rochdale OL16 ....31 B6
Shaw OL2 ....149 C6
Leach Wlk OL4 ....67 E8
Leaches Rd BL0 ....11 D8
Leaconfield Dr M28 ....78 F7
Leacroft WN4 ....72 F6
Leacroft Ave BL2 ....42 D5
Leacroft Rd M21 ....109 D5
Leadale Cl WN6 ....19 D1
Leadale Rise OL4 ....68 A6
Leader St Wigan WN1 ......151 E8
Wigan WN5 ....54 C6
Leader Williams Rd M44 ...93 F1
Leaf St Bolton BL3 ....148 C5
Manchester M15 ....162 F6
Reddish SK5 ....111 E7
Leafield M29 ....59 C1
Leafield Ave M20 ....110 D4
Leafield Cl M26 ....43 E3
Leafield Dr Boothstown M28 .78 A6
Cheadle SK8 ....131 F6
Leafield Rd SK12 ....135 C6
Leaford Ave M34 ....100 D4
Leaford Cl M34 ....100 D4
Leagate M41 ....95 E1
League St OL16 ....31 A5

Leaht St **3** OL15 ......16 B5
Leaholme Cl M40 ......83 D5
Leak St M16 ......161 C6
Leal Holme Ave WN2 ......38 A3
Leam St OL6 ......85 D4
Leamington Ave Bury BL9 ......27 E8
Manchester M20 ......109 F4
Newton-le-W WA12 ......89 C1
Leamington Ct **3** SK5 ......111 E7
Leamington Rd Eccles M30 ......79 B3
Reddish SK5 ......111 E7
Urmston M41 ......95 C3
Leamington St
Manchester M11 ......99 D7
Oldham OL4 ......67 D8
Rochdale OL12 ......139 E8
Leamore Wlk **9** M9 ......64 E3
Leander Cl M9 ......64 E2
Leander Dr OL11 ......30 D1
Leas The WA15 ......120 C3
Leaside Ave OL1 ......48 B2
Leaside Cl OL12 ......14 D2
Leaside Dr M20 ......110 D5
Leaside Gr M28 ......60 E3
Leaside Way SK9 ......137 C6
Leaton Ave M23 ......121 A6
Leavengreave Ct OL12 ......4 D4
Leaway Ince-in-m WN2 ......151 F7
Littleborough OL12 ......15 C6
Lecester Rd M8 ......156 B6
Leckenby Cl **7** M28 ......78 A6
Leconfield Dr M9 ......64 E4
Leconfield Rd M30 ......78 F4
Lecturers Cl BL3 ......145 F5
Ledbrooke Cl M5 ......161 B8
Ledburn Ct M15 ......162 D6
Ledburn Ct M15 ......162 D6
Ledbury Ave M41 ......95 C3
Ledbury Cl M24 ......65 A6
Ledbury Rd M35 ......83 E4
Ledbury St Leigh WN7 ......75 F6
Leigh WN7 ......75 F7
Ledbury Wlk M9 ......64 C3
Leddy Wlk **1** M16 ......97 F4
Ledge Ley SK8 ......131 E8
Ledmore Gr WN4 ......72 D3
Ledsham Ave M9 ......64 A5
Ledson Rd M23 ......120 F5
Ledward La WA14 ......119 C7
Bolton BL3 ......147 D3
Lee Bank BL5 ......58 B8
Lee Cl M44 ......93 F2
Lee Cres M32 ......96 E2
Lee Ct M22 ......121 E8
Lee Dale Cl M34 ......101 A2
Lee Fold M29 ......77 C7
Lee Gate BL2 ......25 D5
Lee Gr BL4 ......59 F8
Lee Head SK13 ......115 C5
Lee Ho M22 ......121 E8
Lee La La Abram WN2 ......74 B8
Horwich BL6 ......22 B4
Lee Mount SK13 ......116 C7
Lee Rd Bacup OL13 ......3 E8
Manchester M9 ......157 D8
Lee Side OL3 ......51 D4
Lee St Atherton M46 ......58 D2
Bury BL9 ......27 F8
Littleborough OL15 ......16 B6
Middleton M24 ......46 F3
Oldham OL3 ......69 B8
Oldham OL8 ......153 E5
Stockport SK1 ......169 F1
Lee Vale Dr SK13 ......115 D7
Lee's St OL13 ......4 C8
Leech Ave OL6 ......85 E5
Leech Brook Ave M34 ......100 E5
Leech Brook Cl M34 ......100 E6
Leech St Hyde SK14 ......167 F2
Stalybridge SK15 ......86 A1
Leedale St M12 ......99 A2
Leeds Cl BL9 ......45 B3
Leeds St WN3 ......150 B7
Leeds St Ind Est WN3 ......150 B7
Leefields Cl OL3 ......69 B8
Leegate Cl SK4 ......110 F4
Leegate Dr M9 ......64 F4
Leegate Gdns SK4 ......168 A4
Leegate Rd SK4 ......168 A4
Leegrange Rd M9 ......64 E1
Leek St M26 ......43 E3
Leemans Hill St BL8 ......27 A5
Lees Ave M34 ......100 E3
Lees Cotts BL7 ......9 C2
Lees Gr OL4 ......67 D5
Lees Hall Cres M41 ......110 D8
Lees Hall Ct **6** M14 ......110 D8
Lees La WN6 ......35 B6
Lees New Rd OL4,OL6 ......67 D2
Lees Park Ave M43 ......84 C2
Lees Park Way M43 ......84 C2
Lees Rd Adlington PR6 ......21 B8
Ashton-u-L OL6 ......85 D7
Bramhall SK7 ......132 D5
Oldham OL4 ......67 C6
Lees Row SK13 ......104 D5
Lees Sq OL6 ......166 C3
Lees St Ashton-u-L OL6 ......166 B4
Droylsden M43 ......84 B2
Manchester M11,M18 ......99 E6
Middleton M24 ......65 D7
2 Mossley OL5 ......68 C2
Oldham OL8 ......85 A8

Lees St continued
Shaw OL2 ......149 B7
6 Stalybridge SK15 ......86 A2
Swinton M27 ......61 F1
Lees St E OL2 ......149 C7
Leesfield OL6 ......166 B4
Leeside SK4 ......168 A1
Leestone Rd M22 ......121 E6
Leesway OL4 ......67 E5
Leesway Dr M34 ......101 A2
Leeswood Ave M21 ......109 C6
Leewood M27 ......61 D4
Leewood Ct SK4 ......168 B3
Left Bank M3 ......158 E1
Legh Ct M33 ......108 E3
Legh Dr Droylsden M34 ......84 B1
Romiley SK6 ......113 B6
Legh Rd High Lane SK12 ......135 A6
Manchester M7 ......155 D8
Sale M33 ......108 E3
Legh St Ashton-in-M WN4 ......73 B2
Eccles M30 ......79 C1
Golborne WA3 ......90 A8
Manchester M7 ......155 D7
Newton-le-W WA12 ......89 A3
Leghorn Wlk **14** M11 ......160 F1
Legion Gr M7 ......155 C6
Legwood Ct M41 ......95 C2
Leicester Ave Denton M34 ......100 F1
Droylsden M43 ......83 F3
Hindley WN2 ......56 F6
Horwich BL6 ......22 A2
Leicester Ct M7 ......155 F8
Manchester M7 ......155 D8
Sale WA15 ......120 A8
Leicester Ct M7 ......63 F1
Leicester Dr SK13 ......116 F8
Leicester Rd
Altrincham WA15 ......119 F2
Failsworth M35 ......84 A6
Manchester M7 ......155 E7
Sale M33 ......108 B5
Tyldesley M29 ......59 A2
Whitefield M45 ......44 D1
Leicester St
Ashton-u-L OL7 ......166 B4
Oldham OL4 ......67 B6
Reddish SK5 ......99 F2
Rochdale OL11 ......31 A5
Leicester Wlk M7 ......155 E6
Leigh Arr **27** WN1 ......150 C8
Leigh Ave Marple SK6 ......125 E6
Swinton M27 ......79 D5
Leigh Bsns Pk WN7 ......75 F5
Leigh CE Inf Sch WN7 ......75 E5
Leigh CE Jun Sch WN7 ......75 F5
Leigh Cl BL8 ......26 E7
Leigh Commerce Pk WN7 ......76 B2
Leigh Common BL5 ......39 C1
Leigh Infmy WN7 ......76 A6
Leigh La BL8 ......27 B3
Leigh Prim Sch SK14 ......167 E2
Leigh Rd Atherton WA15 ......119 E2
Atherton M46 ......58 B3
Hindley WN2 ......57 B2
Leigh WN7 ......75 F7
Westhoughton BL5 ......57 F7
Westhoughton BL5 ......57 F8
Wilmslow SK9 ......136 B8
Worsley M28 ......78 C6
Leigh St Aspull WN2 ......38 F3
Bury BL8 ......26 F4
Farnworth BL4 ......60 D8
Heywood OL10 ......29 D2
2 Leigh WN7 ......75 F6
Leigh WN7 ......57 B1
Leigh WN7 ......75 C5
Leigh WN7 ......75 F5
Milnrow OL16 ......31 D7
Westhoughton BL5 ......39 E1
Wigan WN1 ......151 D7
Leighbrook Rd M14 ......110 B8
Leighs Cotts WA15 ......120 C4
Leighton Ave Atherton M46 ......58 B3
Bolton BL1 ......144 B8
Littleborough OL15 ......15 F2
Leighton Dr Golborne WN7 ......75 B1
Marple SK6 ......126 C8
Leighton Rd M16 ......97 C4
Leighton St Atherton M46 ......58 B3
Manchester M40 ......83 A8
Leinster Rd M27 ......79 E7
Leinster St BL4 ......60 C7
Leith Ave M33 ......108 E4
Leith Rd M33 ......108 E4
Lemnos St OL1 ......67 A7
Lemon St M29 ......76 F8
Lemonpark Ind Est OL10 ......46 E8
Len Cox Wlk **3** M4 ......159 B2
Lena St Bury BL4 ......143 E1
Manchester M1 ......159 B1
Lench Rd BB4 ......2 D8
Lench St BB4 ......2 F8
Leng Rd M40 ......83 D5
Lenham Ave M30 ......79 D4
Lenham Cl SK5 ......112 B6
Lenham Gdns BL2 ......42 E6
Lenham Towers SK5 ......112 B6
Lenham Wlk M22 ......130 D8
Lennox Gdns BL3 ......40 F5
Lennox St OL6 ......66 C2
Lennox Wlk OL10 ......28 F1
Lenora St BL3 ......146 B4
Lenten Gr OL10 ......46 E7
Lenthall Wlk **20** M8 ......155 F7
Lentmead Dr M40 ......65 A1
Lenton Gdns M22 ......121 E5
Leominster Dr M22 ......121 F2

Leominster Rd M24 ......65 B6
Leonard Ct WN7 ......75 B4
Leonard St Bolton BL3 ......147 E3
Rochdale OL11 ......30 C1
Leonardin Cl OL2 ......48 F8
Leopold Ave M20 ......110 A5
Leopold St Rochdale OL11 ......139 D7
Wigan WN5 ......54 B5
Wigan WN5 ......54 C5
Lepp Cres BL8 ......27 C5
Leryn Dr SK7 ......123 D1
Lesley Rd M32 ......96 A1
Leslie Ave Oldham OL9 ......66 B3
Whitefield BL9 ......44 F3
Leslie Gr WA15 ......120 A6
Leslie Hough Way M6 ......81 B4
Leslie St Bolton BL2 ......25 B1
Manchester M14 ......98 B3
Lessingham Ave WN1 ......37 B3
Lester Rd M38 ......59 E5
Lester St M32 ......96 D2
Letchworth Ave **2** OL11 ......31 A5
Letchworth St M14 ......98 B3
Letcombe Cl WN7 ......75 F7
Letham St OL8 ......66 E3
Letitia St BL6 ......22 A3
Levedale Rd M9 ......64 E4
Leven Cl BL4 ......61 B5
Leven Wlk Whitefield M45 ......63 C8
2 Wythenshawe M23 ......121 A5
Levenhurst Rd M8 ......155 F7
Levens Cl SK8 ......122 B4
Levens Dr BL2 ......25 E1
Levens Pl Ince-in-M WN2 ......56 A8
Wigan WN5 ......54 C5
Levens Rd SK7 ......124 C2
Levens St Manchester M40 ......83 A7
Salford M6 ......81 B5
Levens Wlk Oldham OL9 ......152 A5
Wigan WN5 ......54 C5
Levenshulme High Sch
 for Girls M19 ......111 A7
Levenshulme Rd M18 ......99 D4
Levenshulme Sta M19 ......99 A1
Levenshulme Terr **8** M19 ......99 A1
Levenshulme Trad Est
 M19 ......99 C2
Lever Ave M27 ......62 B2
Lever Bridge Pl BL3 ......42 D5
Lever Cl **7** M29 ......58 F1
Lever Dr BL3 ......147 F4
Lever Edge La BL3 ......147 E3
Lever Edge Prim Sch
 BL3 ......147 E2
Lever Gr BL2 ......148 A5
Lever Hall Rd BL2 ......42 D7
Lever Park Ave BL6 ......22 B5
Lever Park Sch BL6 ......22 C3
Lever St Bolton BL3 ......147 F4
Hazel Grove SK7 ......124 D3
Heywood OL10 ......29 D3
Little Lever BL3 ......43 A4
Manchester M1 ......159 B1
Middleton M24 ......47 A1
Radcliffe M26 ......43 F5
Ramsbottom BL0 ......138 C6
Tyldesley M29 ......58 F1
Westhoughton BL5 ......39 E3
Lever Wlk M24 ......64 F7
Leverett Cl M14 ......119 A5
Leverhulme Ave BL3 ......42 A3
Levi St BL1 ......23 F1
Levington Dr OL8 ......66 F4
Lewes Ave M34 ......100 F1
Lewes Wlk OL9 ......152 B6
Lewis Ave Manchester M9 ......64 C1
Urmston M41 ......95 D5
Lewis Cl Adlington PR7 ......20 E6
Wigan WN3 ......150 A5
Lewis Dr OL10 ......28 F1
Lewis Rd Droylsden M43 ......83 E2
Reddish SK5 ......99 F1
Lewis St Eccles M30 ......29 E3
Heywood OL10 ......29 D3
Manchester M40 ......160 D3
Shaw OL2 ......149 B5
Lewis Street Prim Sch
 M30 ......79 D1
Lewisham Ave M40 ......83 B4
Lewisham Cl OL2 ......48 C6
Lewtas St M30 ......79 E1
Lexton Ave M8 ......64 B2
Ley Cres M29 ......77 D6
Ley Dr OL10 ......46 E7
Ley Hey Ave SK6 ......125 F7
Ley Hey Ct SK6 ......125 F7
Ley Hey Rd SK6 ......125 F7
Ley La M23 ......126 D8
Ley Rd M29 ......77 A2
Leybourne Ave M19 ......99 B2
Leybourne St BL1 ......143 E2
Leybrook Rd M22 ......121 C3
Leyburn Ave Royton OL2 ......48 D4
Stretford M32 ......96 B2
Urmston M41 ......95 B1
Leyburn Cl Whitefield M45 ......62 E8
Wigan WN1 ......151 F8
Leyburn Gr
2 Farnworth BL4 ......42 D1
Romiley SK6 ......113 C2
Leyburn Ho **2** M13 ......98 E4
Leyburn Rd M22 ......65 C2
Leyburne Rd SK2 ......124 B6
Leycett Dr M23 ......109 A1
Leycroft St Manchester M1 ......159 B1
Manchester M1 ......163 B8

Leyden Wlk M23 ......121 A4
Leyfield Ave SK6 ......113 C2
Leyfield Rd OL16 ......31 E6
Leygate View SK22 ......127 B1
Leyland Ave Gatley SK8 ......122 B6
Hindley WN2 ......56 E3
Irlam M44 ......94 B4
Manchester M20 ......110 D3
Leyland Green Rd WN4 ......72 C5
Leyland Mill La WN1 ......37 C3
Leyland St Abram WN2 ......56 B1
Bury BL9 ......44 F4
Hindley WN2 ......56 C4
Stockport SK1 ......169 E1
Leylands La SK14 ......114 F7
Leys Rd WA14 ......119 E8
Leyton Ave M40 ......83 B7
Leyton Cl Farnworth BL4 ......147 F1
2 Wigan WN5 ......54 D5
Leyton Dr BL9 ......44 F5
Leyton St **2** OL12 ......15 A2
Leywell Dr OL1 ......49 D3
Libra St BL1 ......143 D2
Library La OL9 ......153 D8
Library St
Westhoughton BL5 ......57 F8
Wigan WN1 ......150 C8
Lichens Cres OL8 ......67 A3
Lichfield Ave
Altrincham WA15 ......120 C3
Ashton-u-L OL6 ......85 B8
Bolton BL2 ......25 B2
Oldham OL8 ......90 D8
Reddish SK5 ......111 E8
Tyldesley M29 ......77 C7
Lichfield Cl Farnworth BL4 ......60 A8
Radcliffe M26 ......43 D5
Lichfield Dr Bury BL8 ......140 D4
Chadderton OL9 ......48 A1
Manchester M25 ......63 C2
Manchester M8 ......156 B7
Swinton M27 ......79 B6
Lichfield Gr WN4 ......73 C2
Lichfield Rd Eccles M30 ......79 F4
Radcliffe M26 ......43 D5
Urmston M41 ......95 D3
Lichfield St Salford M6 ......81 A3
Wigan WN5 ......54 C5
Lichfield Terr OL16 ......31 C4
Lidbrook Wlk M12 ......164 E5
Liddington Hall Dr BL0 ......11 B4
Lidgate Cl **7** Farnworth BL4 ......60 C8
4 Manchester M20 ......110 A3
Lidgett Cl M38 ......60 C5
Lidgett La BL8 ......64 A1
Lido Ho OL4 ......68 A6
Liffey Ave M22 ......121 E3
Lifton Ave M40 ......160 E4
Light Alders La SK12 ......135 A6
Light Oaks Inf & Jun Sch
 M6 ......80 B4
Light Oaks Rd
Fowley Common WA3 ......92 C6
Salford M6 ......80 C4
Lightbourne Rd M33 ......107 E4
Lightbounds Rd BL1 ......23 F3
Lightbourne Ave **5** M27 ......79 F7
Lightbowne Rd M40 ......65 C2
Lightburn Ave OL15 ......15 E4
Lightburne Ave
 Bolton BL1 ......144 B7
Leigh WN7 ......75 E3
Lightfoot Wlk **6** M11 ......160 F1
Lighthorne Gr SK4 ......122 F7
Lighthorne Rd SK4 ......122 F7
Lighthouse OL15 ......6 C1
Lightowlers La OL15 ......16 D7
Lightshaw La WA3 ......74 B4
Lightwood M38 ......78 B8
Lignum Avenue Cl **7** BL4 ......60 C8
Lignum Ave OL9 ......152 B8
Lila St M9 ......157 F7
Lilac Ave Bury BL9 ......44 D7
Downall Green WN4 ......72 D5
Hyde SK14 ......113 D8
Leigh WN7 ......75 E7
Newhey OL16 ......32 A3
Pendlebury M27 ......80 A8
Wigan WN6 ......37 A3
Lilac Cl **16** M6 ......81 A2
Lilac Gr Billinge WN5 ......71 D4
Manchester M40 ......65 A1
Oldham OL9 ......152 B8
Prestwich M25 ......63 A4
Lilac La OL8 ......66 D2
Lilac Rd Altrincham WA15 ......120 A3
Golborne WA3 ......74 A1
Hollinfare WA3 ......105 C3
Lilac St SK2 ......124 B6
Lilac View Cl OL2 ......49 D6
Lilac Wlk M31 ......105 E3
Lilburn Cl BL0 ......11 C4
Liley St OL16 ......31 A7
Lilford Cl M12 ......165 A6
Lilford St Atherton M46 ......58 B2
Leigh WN7 ......75 F6
Lilian St BL1 ......144 B8
Lilian St M16 ......97 C4
Lilley St M16 ......97 C4
Lily Ave BL4 ......60 C7
Lilly St Bolton BL1 ......145 D8
Hyde SK14 ......113 F8
Lilmore Ave M40 ......83 C6

Lilstock Wlk **10** M9 ......64 E3
Lily Ave Farnworth BL4 ......42 B1
Newton-le-W WA12 ......89 D2
Lily Cl SK3 ......170 D5
Lily Hill St M45 ......44 E2
Lily La Ashton-in-M WN2 ......73 F7
Manchester M40,M9 ......157 F8
Manchester M9,M40 ......83 A8
Platt Bridge WN2 ......56 A1
Lily Lane Jun & Inf Sch
 M40 ......83 A8
Lily Lanes OL6 ......85 E8
Lily Pl WN4 ......73 C2
Lily St Ashton-in-M WN4 ......73 E5
Eccles M30 ......79 B1
Middleton M24 ......65 C8
Milnrow OL16 ......31 F6
Oldham OL1 ......48 E1
Royton OL2 ......48 F4
Lily Thomas Ct **3** M11 ......99 D7
Lima St BL9 ......141 B3
Limbert Circ M8 ......64 C1
Lime Ave Leigh WN7 ......75 E8
New Mills SK22 ......127 D1
Swinton M27 ......79 C6
Urmston M41 ......95 E3
Whitefield M45 ......62 F7
Lime Bank St M12 ......164 D8
Lime Cl Abram Brow WN2 ......74 C7
Dukinfield SK16 ......101 D6
Hollinfare WA3 ......105 C3
Salford M6 ......81 A3
Lime Cres M16 ......97 B4
Lime Ct M6 ......81 A3
Lime Gate OL8 ......66 C2
Lime Gdns Dukinfield SK16 ......101 D6
Middleton M24 ......64 E8
Lime Gn OL8 ......66 D1
Lime Gr Altrincham WA15 ......120 B7
Ashton-u-L OL6 ......85 C5
Bury BL9 ......27 F7
Cheadle SK8 ......122 D6
Denton M34 ......100 F4
Dukinfield SK15 ......101 E8
Golborne WA3 ......90 E6
Heywood OL10 ......29 C2
Hindley WN2 ......56 F3
Littleborough OL15 ......15 F6
Manchester M16 ......97 B4
Prestwich M25 ......63 A6
Ramsbottom BL0 ......11 D7
Royton OL2 ......48 E6
Walkden M28 ......60 D1
Lime Green Rd OL8 ......84 D8
Lime Kiln La SK6 ......126 A5
Lime La M35 ......84 C7
Lime Pl SK16 ......101 D6
Lime Rd M32 ......96 D1
Lime St Atherton M46 ......57 F3
Bredbury SK6 ......112 E4
Bury BL9 ......27 F6
Dukinfield SK16 ......101 D6
Eccles M30 ......79 D1
Farnworth BL4 ......60 E8
Oldham OL1 ......48 C1
Rochdale OL11 ......30 C4
Tyldesley M29 ......58 F1
Lime Tree Cl M41 ......95 E1
Lime Tree Gr M35 ......84 B7
Lime Trees Prim
 Sch M33 ......108 E3
Lime Vale WN3 ......55 F4
Lime Vale Rd WA11,WN5 ......71 C3
Lime Wlk
6 Handforth SK9 ......131 D1
8 Handforth SK9 ......131 D1
Partington M31 ......105 D3
Limebrook Cl M11 ......99 F7
Limeditch Rd M35 ......84 A8
Limefield Middleton M24 ......64 E8
Milnrow OL16 ......31 E7
Mossley OL5 ......68 B8
1 Wigan WN1 ......151 D8
Limefield Ave BL4 ......42 D1
Limefield Brow BL9 ......27 F7
Limefield Cl BL1 ......142 B4
Limefield Ct M7 ......63 E3
Limefield Rd Bolton BL2 ......142 B4
Bury BL9 ......27 F7
Manchester M7 ......63 D1
Radcliffe M26 ......43 E3
Limefield Terr M19 ......99 A1
Limehurst Ave
3 Ashton-u-L OL7 ......85 A6
Manchester M20 ......109 F8
Limehurst Prim Sch OL8 ......84 D8
Limehurst Rd OL7 ......85 A6
Limekiln La M12 ......14 F5
Limes Gate OL12 ......14 F5
Limerston Dr M40 ......83 A5
Limes Ave WN6 ......37 B6
Limes The Culcheth WA3 ......91 D4
Mossley OL5 ......90 D6
Wigan WN3 ......54 D1
Mossley OL5 ......68 B1
Standish WN6 ......37 A6
Limesdale Cl BL3 ......42 E6
Limeside Com Prim Sch
 OL8 ......66 D1
Limeside Rd OL8 ......66 D1
Limestead Ave M8 ......156 A8
Limetree Wlk M11 ......160 F1
Limetrees Rd M24 ......64 E8
Limley Gr M21 ......109 C6
Linacre Ave BL3 ......147 E2
Linacre Way SK13 ......116 F7
Linbeck Gr WA3 ......74 E1

Linby St M15 ....162 E7
Lincoln Ave Denton M34 ....100 F1
 Droylsden M43 ....84 A3
 Gatley SK8 ....131 B7
 Golborne WA3 ....74 D1
 Irlam M44 ....105 C4
 Little Lever BL3 ....43 A2
 Manchester M19 ....99 B1
 Urmston M32 ....95 F3
Lincoln Cl Ashton-u-L OL6 ...85 D8
 Golborne WN7 ....91 C8
 Rochdale OL11 ....31 A6
 Tyldesley M29 ....59 A2
Lincoln Close Ind Est 2
 OL1 ....31 A6
Lincoln Ct Failsworth M40 ...83 B4
 12 Manchester M7 ....63 E1
Lincoln Dr
 Altrincham WA15 ....120 B5
 Ashton-in-M WN4 ....73 D2
 Aspull WN2 ....38 D5
 7 Bury BL9 ....44 F8
 Littleborough OL15 ....16 A3
 Manchester M25 ....63 C2
Lincoln Gn SK5 ....112 C6
Lincoln Gr Atherton M46 .....58 B3
 Bolton BL2 ....25 F4
 Manchester M13 ....163 C5
 Sale M33 ....108 E4
Lincoln Leach Ct OL11 ....139 F5
Lincoln Mill (Ent Ctr)
 BL3 ....144 C6
Lincoln Minshull Cl 12
 M23 ....108 F2
Lincoln Pl WN5 ....36 C1
Lincoln Rd Bolton BL1 ....144 B8
 Failsworth M35 ....84 A6
 Handforth SK9 ....131 E1
 Hindley WN2 ....56 E5
 Middleton M24 ....65 C5
 7 Swinton M27 ....79 F7
Lincoln Rise SK6 ....113 A1
Lincoln St Eccles M30 ....79 C1
 Manchester M13 ....98 F4
 Oldham OL9 ....152 C5
 Rochdale OL11 ....31 A6
Lincoln Way SK13 ....116 F8
Lincoln Wlk OL10 ....29 A2
Lincombe Rd M22 ....130 D8
Lincroft Rd WN2 ....57 A3
Lind St M40 ....160 E2
Linda Dr SK7 ....124 D2
Lindale SK14 ....101 C5
Lindale Ave Bolton BL1 ....40 F8
 Failsworth M40 ....65 D2
 Oldham OL9 ....152 A6
 Royton OL2 ....48 C8
 Urmston M41 ....94 F3
 Whitefield BL9 ....45 A3
Lindale Cl M28 ....77 E7
Lindale Dr M24 ....46 E3
Lindale Rd M43 ....77 E7
Lindale Rise OL2 ....49 D7
Lindbury Ave SK2 ....124 C7
Linden Ave
 Altrincham WA15 ....119 E5
 Ashton-in-M WN4 ....72 F5
 Atherton M46 ....58 B2
 Denton M34 ....100 D7
 Little Lever BL3 ....43 A5
 Oldham OL4 ....67 D8
 Orrell WN5 ....53 E6
 Pendlebury M6 ....80 E6
 Ramsbottom BL0 ....11 D6
 Sale M33 ....107 F4
 Swinton M27 ....79 D7
Linden Cl Denton M34 ....101 A3
 Edenfield BL0 ....1 D2
 Lymm WA13 ....117 A4
Linden Ct WN5 ....53 E6
Linden Dr M5 ....161 A8
Linden Gr
 Billinge WA11,WN5 ....71 C3
 Bramhall SK7 ....132 D4
 Leigh WN7 ....75 E7
 Manchester M14 ....110 D8
 Orrell WN5 ....53 E6
 Stockport SK2 ....124 B4
Linden Lea Rawtenstall BB4 ..1 F8
 Sale M33 ....108 B2
Linden Mews M28 ....77 F6
Linden Pk M19 ....111 A8
Linden Rd Boothstown M28 ...77 F6
 Cheadle SK8 ....123 A3
 Denton M34 ....101 A3
 Hindley WN2 ....56 E7
 Manchester M20 ....110 A4
 Stalybridge SK15 ....102 D7
Linden Road Prim Sch
 M34 ....101 A3
Linden St WN5 ....54 C5
Linden Way SK6 ....135 A7
Linden Wlk Bolton BL2 ....25 B5
 Orrell WN5 ....53 E6
Lindenwood OL9 ....65 E8
Lindeth Ave M18 ....99 D4
Lindfield Dr BL1 ....143 E1
Lindfield Est N SK9 ....137 A6
Lindfield Est S SK9 ....136 F6
Lindfield Rd SK5 ....99 F1
Lindinis Ave M5,M6 ....81 B2
Lindisfarne **17** OL12 .....139 E8
Lindisfarne Ave WA3 ....91 C8
Lindisfarne Cl M33 ....108 B2
Lindisfarne Dr SK12 ....133 D4
Lindisfarne Pl BL2 ....25 C2
Lindisfarne Rd OL7 ....84 E5
Lindley Ave WN5 ....53 C5

Lindley Gr SK3 ....170 D5
Lindley St Kearsley BL4 ......61 B6
 Little Lever BL3 ....43 B3
Lindleywood Rd M14 ....110 E8
Lindon Park Rd BB4 ....1 C7
Lindon Way M43 ....99 E8
Lindop Rd WA15 ....119 F1
Lindow Cl BL8 ....27 B6
Lindow Ct Bredbury SK6 .....112 D3
 Sale M33 ....108 F3
Lindow Fold Dr SK9 ....136 D5
Lindow La SK9 ....136 E6
Lindow Par SK9 ....136 F6
Lindow Prim Sch SK9 ....136 D3
Lindow Rd M16 ....97 C2
Lindow St Leigh WN7 ....75 D6
 Sale M33 ....108 F3
Lindrick Ave M45 ....62 D6
Lindrick Cl M40 ....83 C7
Lindrick Terr BL3 ....145 D5
Lindsay Ave Bramhall SK8 ...123 B1
 Manchester M19 ....98 F1
 Swinton M27 ....79 E7
Lindsay Cl OL4 ....49 D2
Lindsay Rd M19 ....110 E8
Lindsay St Horwich BL6 ......22 D1
 Stalybridge SK15 ....86 B1
Lindsay Terr M27 ....38 B5
Lindsell Rd WA14 ....119 C8
Lindsgate Dr WA15 ....120 B7
Lindside Wlk **18** M9 ......64 E3
Lindum Ave M16 ....97 C4
Lindum St M14 ....98 B3
Lindwall Cl M23 ....109 B2
Linear View WA12 ....89 C1
Linehan Cl SK4 ....110 D2
Lineholme OL1 ....48 C2
Linen Ct M3 ....158 D3
Lines Rd Droylsden M43 ......84 B1
 Irlam M44 ....105 F8
Linfield Cl BL2 ....25 D4
Linfield St M11 ....83 B1
Linford Ave M40 ....65 C2
Ling Dr M46 ....58 D2
Lingard Cl M34 ....100 C8
Lingard La SK6 ....112 D5
Lingard Rd M22 ....109 D1
Lingard St Leigh WN7 ....76 B4
 Reddish SK5 ....111 F8
Lingard Terr M34 ....100 C8
Lingards Dr M29 ....77 A4
Lingards La M29 ....77 A4
Lingcrest Rd M19 ....111 C7
Lingdale Rd SK8 ....122 F2
Lingdale Wlk M40 ....83 A7
Lingfield Ave
 Hazel Grove SK7 ....124 F2
 Sale M33 ....107 B2
Lingfield Cl Bury BL8 ....27 C7
 Farnworth BL4 ....60 C7
Lingfield Cres WN6 ....36 E3
Lingfield Rd M11 ....83 C2
Lingfield Wlk **9** OL9 .....152 C7
Lingholme Dr M24 ....46 C2
Lingmell Ave WA11 ....71 C1
Lingmell Cl Bolton BL1 ......40 F8
 Middleton M24 ....46 A1
 Urmston M41 ....95 A4
Lingmoor Cl Middleton M24 ..46 C2
 Wigan WN3 ....55 A1
Lingmoor Dr M29 ....77 B7
Lingmoor Rd BL1 ....23 F1
Lingmoor Wlk M15 ....162 F5
Lings Wlk M22 ....121 E1
Linhope Cl SK4 ....110 E3
Link Ave M41 ....96 A1
Link La OL8 ....66 E2
Link Rd Oldham OL4 ....67 F7
 Sale M33 ....107 D2
Link The Brinnington SK5 ...112 C6
 Handforth SK9 ....131 D3
 Shaw OL2 ....48 F8
Link Wlk M31 ....105 D2
Linkfield Dr M28 ....77 F6
Links Ave M35 ....83 F5
Links Cres M25 ....63 D2
Links Dr BL6 ....40 B7
Links Pl OL6 ....85 E6
Links Rd Bolton BL2 ....26 A3
 Bolton BL6 ....40 B8
 Heywood OL10 ....46 D8
 Marple SK6 ....125 F4
 Romiley SK6 ....113 D2
 Wilmslow SK9 ....136 E4
Links Rise M41 ....95 A4
Links The M40 ....83 C7
Links View Manchester M25 ..63 A1
 Rochdale OL11 ....30 B6
Links Way OL9 ....152 C8
Linksfield M34 ....100 F5
Linkside Ave OL2 ....48 D5
Linksview Ct M45 ....62 D7
Linksway Gatley SK8 ....122 A4
 Manchester M25 ....63 D2
 Pendlebury M27 ....80 A6
Linksway Cl SK4 ....111 A5
Linksway Dr BL9 ....45 B3
Linkway Ave M46 ....73 E5
Linkway The BL6 ....39 D8
Linley Ave BL9 ....44 F5
Linley Cl WN6 ....36 C4
Linley Dr OL4 ....67 D4
Linley Gr Bolton BL4 ....60 E7
Linley Rd Cheadle SK8 ......132 B8
 Sale M33 ....108 B5
Linn St M8 ....64 A1
Linnell Dr OL11 ....29 E8

Linnet Cl Droylsden M34 .....84 C1
 Hazel Grove SK7 ....124 F5
Linnet Dr Bury BL9 ....141 B4
 Irlam M44 ....94 A3
 Leigh WN7 ....76 B5
Linnet Hill OL11 ....30 C6
Linnet's Wood Mews M28 .....60 E3
Linney La OL2 ....49 C7
Linney Rd SK7 ....123 D2
Linney Sq WN1 ....151 E8
Linslade Gdns BL3 ....145 E5
Linslade Ho **10** M6 ....154 F1
Linslade Wlk **7** M9 ....160 E7
Linstead Dr M8 ....155 F6
Linstock Way M46 ....58 B3
Linthorpe Wlk BL3 ....146 B4
Linton Ave Bury BL9 ....27 F5
 Golborne WA3 ....73 F2
 Reddish SK4 ....100 A3
Linton Cl M4 ....164 D8
Linton Rd M33 ....108 C6
Linton Vale M26 ....61 B8
Linton Wlk M7 ....80 F8
Linwood Cl WN2 ....56 D4
Linwood Gr M12 ....99 A2
Linwood St M35,M40 ....83 C6
Lion Brow M9 ....64 D3
Lion Fold La M9 ....64 D3
Lion La BL6 ....21 C2
Lion St M9 ....64 D2
Lions Dr M27 ....80 A7
Liptrot St WN5 ....54 F7
Lisbon St **12** OL12 ....14 C1
Lisburn Ave
 Manchester M16,M21 ....97 C1
 Sale M33 ....108 A3
Lisburn Rd M40 ....83 A8
Lisburne Ave SK2 ....124 D7
Lisburne Cl SK2 ....124 D6
Lisburne La SK2 ....124 D6
Lisburne Sch SK2 ....124 E6
Liscard Ave M14 ....98 B1
Liscard St M46 ....58 B3
Lisetto Ave **8** OL4 ....67 B5
Liskeard Ave OL2 ....48 F4
Liskeard Cl OL16 ....15 C1
Liskeard Dr SK7 ....132 F7
Lisle St **3** OL12 ....31 A8
Lismore WA15 ....119 F2
Lismore Ave Bolton BL3 ......40 F5
 Stockport SK3 ....123 B8
Lismore Rd SK16 ....101 D7
Lismore Way M41 ....95 E5
Lismore Wlk M22 ....121 B1
Lissadel St M6 ....81 B4
Lisson Gr WA15 ....119 E2
Lister Rd M24 ....64 B6
Lister St BL3 ....146 B3
Liston St SK16 ....101 E8
Litcham Cl M1 ....163 B7
Litchfield Cl OL13 ....33 C2
Litchfield Ct M24 ....64 C7
Litchfield Gr M28 ....79 A7
Litherland Ave M22 ....121 E2
Litherland Rd Bolton BL3 ...147 E2
 Sale M33 ....108 A3
Little Ancoats St M1,M4 .159 B2
Little Bank St **1** OL4 .....67 B6
Little Bollington
 CE Prim Sch WA14 ....118 B2
Little Brook Rd M33 ....107 D3
Little Brow BL7 ....25 A7
Little Church St **3** WN5 ...54 B6
Little Clegg Rd OL15 ....15 F2
Little David St M1 ....163 A8
Little Ees La SK13 ....57 A2
Little Egerton St SK1 ....169 E2
Little Factory St M29 ....58 F1
Little Flatt OL12 ....14 B1
Little Harwood Lee BL2 ......25 F3
Little Heath La WA14 ....118 D3
Little Holme St M4 ....99 E3
Little Hoolme Wlk BL3 ......147 F4
Little Howarth Way **1**
 OL12 ....14 B1
Little Hulton Com Sch
 M28 ....60 A4
Little John St M3 ....158 E1
Little La WN3,WN5 ....54 E4
Little Lever Sch BL3 ....42 F3
Little Lever St
 8 Manchester M1,M4 .....159 B2
Little Meadow Rd WA14 ......119 B1
Little Moor Clough BL7 ....8 E2
Little Moor La OL4 ....67 F5
Little Moss La M27 ....61 F2
Little Nelson St M4 ....159 A3
Little Oak Cl OL4 ....67 E6
Little Pasture WN7 ....75 D7
Little Peter St M15 ....162 F7
Little Pit St M1 ....159 B1
Little Quay St M3 ....158 E1
Little Scotland BL6 ....21 B2
Little St SK1 ....169 F2
Little Stones Rd BL7 ....9 D2
Little Town OL8 ....66 C4
Little Underbank SK1 ....169 F1
Littleborough
 Com Prim Sch OL15 ......16 B7

Littleborough Sta OL15 .....16 B5
Littleborough Wlk BL1 ......25 A6
Littlebrook Cl
 Cheadle SK8 ....123 C4
 Hadfield SK13 ....104 A4
Littledale St OL12 ....139 E8
Littlefields SK14 ....103 A4
Littlegate BL5 ....57 E5
Littlegreen Gdns M6 ....154 F3
Littleham Wlk M18 ....165 C5
Littlehaven Cl M12 ....164 E5
Littlehills Cl M24 ....46 E1
Littlemoor Cotts SK1 ....124 B8
Littlemoor Ho **1** OL4 .....67 A6
Littlemoor La OL3 ....51 B4
Littlemoor Prim Sch OL4 ....67 C8
Littlemoor Rd OL4 ....103 A2
Littlemoss Bsns Pk M43 .....84 C3
Littlemoss High Sch
 for Boys M43 ....84 C3
Littlemoss Rd M43 ....84 C3
Litter Ave M21 ....109 C5
Littlers Point M17 ....96 D5
Littleton Gr WN6 ....19 E2
Littleton Rd M6,M7,M25 .....81 A6
Littlewood OL2 ....49 A4
Littlewood Ave **8** BL9 .....27 F5
Littlewood Rd M22 ....121 D4
Littlewood St M6 ....154 E2
Litton Bank **15** SK13 .....171 E1
Litton Fold SK13 ....171 E1
Litton Gdns **11** SK13 .....171 E1
Litton Mews SK13 ....171 E1
Littondale Cl OL2 ....48 E5
Liverpool Cl SK5 ....111 E7
Liverpool Rd
 Ashton-in-M WN4 ....73 A3
 Eccles M30 ....79 C1
 Eccles M30 ....95 A8
 Garswood WA11,WN4 ....72 D2
 Irlam M30,M44 ....94 A8
 Irlam M44 M43 ....105 D4
 Manchester M3 ....162 E8
 Platt Bridge WN2 ....56 C3
Liverpool St
 7 Reddish SK5 ....111 E7
 Salford M6,M5 ....81 B1
Liverstudd Ave SK5 ....111 F8
Liverton Ct M9 ....64 B5
Livesey St
 8 Ashton-in-M WN4 ......73 A5
 Oldham OL4 ....67 C5
 Oldham OL4 ....68 A6
Livsey La OL10 ....29 A2
Livsey St Rochdale OL16 .....14 A4
 Whitefield M45 ....62 E8
Liza St WN7 ....75 E8
Lizard St M1 ....159 B1
Lizmar Terr
 4 Manchester M40,M9 ....83 A8
 Manchester M40,M9 ....157 F8
Llanberis Rd SK8 ....122 E1
Llanfair Rd **7** SK3 ....123 C8
Lloyd Ave SK8 ....122 A6
Lloyd Ct M12 ....164 F6
Lloyd Gdns WA14 ....119 D3
Lloyd Rd M19 ....111 B7
Lloyd Sq **6** WA14 ....119 D4
Lloyd St
 Altrincham WA14,WA15 ......119 D4
 Heywood OL10 ....29 D1
 Manchester M2 ....158 F1
 Rochdale OL11 ....139 D5
 Stockport SK4 ....169 D3
 Whitworth OL12 ....4 C1
Lloyd St N M14,M15 ....163 A5
Lloyd St S M14 ....110 A7
Lloyd's Ct WA14 ....119 D4
Lobden Cres OL12 ....14 D8
Lobelia Ave BL4 ....42 A1
Lobelia Wlk **5** M31 ....105 E2
Lobley Cl OL12 ....15 B2
Local Board St WN2 ....151 F7
Loch St WN5 ....54 B6
Lochawe Cl OL10 ....29 A1
Lochinver Gr OL10 ....29 A1
Lochmaddy Cl SK7 ....133 C1
Lock Cl OL10 ....46 E8
Lock Flight Bldgs WN3 ......54 D7
Lock La Bolton BL3,BL6 ......40 D3
Lockton Cl Manchester M1 ..163 B7
 Reddish SK5 ....111 E6

Lockton Ct M1 ....163 B7
Lockwood St **7** M12 ....99 B3
Locomotion Ind Est Bolton BL6 ..22 B2
Lodden Wlk **21** M9 ....157 E8
Lodge Ave M41 ....95 E2
Lodge Bank SK13 ....104 A6
Lodge Bank Rd OL15 ....15 F3
Lodge Brow M26 ....44 B2
Lodge Cl Dukinfield SK16 ...101 E7
Lymm WA13 ....117 B4
Lodge Ct Manchester SK4 ...110 F2
 Mottram-in-L SK14 ....103 A3
 Wythenshawe M22 ....121 C5
Lodge Dr Culcheth WA3 ....91 F3
 Tyldesley M29 ....77 B6
Lodge Farm Cl SK7 ....123 E2
Lodge Fold M43 ....84 B2
Lodge Gn SK16 ....101 E7
Lodge Gr M46 ....58 E1
Lodge La Atherton M46 ....58 D1
 Delph OL3 ....50 E5
 Dukinfield SK16 ....101 E8
 Hyde SK14 ....167 D4
 Leigh WN7 ....76 E4
 Newton-le-W
 WA11,WA12,WN4 ....89 B8
Lodge Mill La BL0 ....2 A1
Lodge Rd Orrell WN5 ....53 E4
 Radcliffe M26 ....44 B2
 Tyldesley M46 ....58 E1
Lodge Rise M43 ....43 B2
Lodge St Ashton-u-L OL7 ....84 F1
 Dukinfield SK14 ....101 E5
 Littleborough OL12 ....15 C6
 Littleborough OL15 ....16 B5
 Manchester M40 ....157 C5
 Middleton M24 ....47 A1
 Ramsbottom BL0 ....11 E8
 Ramsbottom BL0 ....18 C6
Lodge The SK13 ....104 A6
Lodgepole Cl M30 ....94 F8
Lodgeside Cl M43 ....84 B2
Loeminster Pl WN2 ....151 F7
Loen Cres BL1 ....24 C3
Logan St BL1 ....24 F5
Logan Wlk M22 ....121 F2
Loganberry Ave M46 ....81 A3
Logwood Ave Bury BL8 ......140 D3
 Wigan WN5 ....54 F7
Logwood Ho WN5 ....54 E8
Logwood Pl WN5 ....54 E8
Loire Dr WN5 ....54 F8
Loisine Cl OL11 ....30 B3
Lomas Cl M19 ....110 E4
Lomas La BL8 ....1 F8
Lomas St Failsworth M35 ....66 A1
 Middleton M24 ....47 B1
 Stockport SK3 ....170 D7
 Swinton St Bolton BL1 ......143 E2
 Bury BL9 ....141 A3
 7 Farnworth BL4 ....42 C2
 Manchester M1,M4 ....159 C1
 4 Platt Bridge WN2 .....56 B2
 Radcliffe M26 ....44 A2
 Ramsbottom BL8 ....10 F1
 Rochdale OL12 ....14 E2
 Whitefield M45 ....44 E2
Lomax's Bldgs BL2 ....145 F6
Lombard Cl SK6 ....112 F4
Lombard Gr M14 ....110 C8
Lombard St Atherton M46 ....58 B3
 Oldham OL1 ....153 E7
 Rochdale OL12 ....139 D8
Lombardy Ct **9** M6 ....81 A3
Lomond Ave
 Altrincham WA15 ....120 A3
 Stretford M32 ....96 D3
Lomond Cl SK2 ....124 A3
Lomond Dr BL8 ....27 B4
Lomond Pl BL3 ....40 D6
Lomond Rd M22,SK8 ....121 F2
Lomond Terr OL16 ....31 C4
London Cl WN5 ....54 E8
London Fields WN5 ....71 E5
London Pl SK1 ....169 F2
London Rd
 Alderley Edge SK9 ....137 A1
 Hazel Grove SK2,SK7 ....124 D3
 Manchester M1 ....163 B8
 Oldham OL1 ....49 B1
 Poynton SK10,SK12 ....133 C1
London Rd N SK12 ....133 C5
London Rd S SK12 ....133 D3
London Sq SK1 ....169 F1
London St Bolton BL3 ....147 E4
 Salford M6 ....81 B4
London Mkts 62 F7
Long Croft La SK8 ....122 F1
Long Cswy Farnworth BL4 ....60 D7
 Leigh M46 ....76 B8
Long Grain PI SK2 ....124 D5
Long Hey WA15 ....120 A3
Long Heys or Back La
 WN8 ....35 A6
Long Hill M11 ....30 D4
Long La Bolton BL2,BL3 .....42 E6
 Bury BL9 ....27 E2
 Charlesworth SK13 ....115 C7
 Hindley WN2 ....56 B7
 Oldham OL3 ....65 F3
Uppermill OL3 ....51 A3
 Westhoughton BL5 ....39 D2
Long Marl Dr SK9 ....131 F4
Long Mdw Bolton BL2 ....25 C7

Long Mdw continued
Dukinfield SK14 ....101 F6
Long Meadow Pas SK14 .167 D3
Long Millgate
Manchester M3,M4 ......159 A2
Manchester M4 ....158 F2
Long Row SK15 ....86 F7
Long Rushes OL2 ....48 F8
Long St Manchester M18 .99 E6
Middleton M24 ....47 A1
Swinton M27 ....79 F7
Long Wlk M31 ....105 D3
Longacre St M1,M4 ......159 C1
Longacres La OL12 ......4 D2
Longacres Rd WA15 .....129 C7
Longbow Ct M7 ....155 D5
Longbridge Rd M17 .....96 A6
Longbrook No M6 ....36 B7
Longbutt La WA13 ......117 A2
Longclough Dr SK13 ....116 A8
Longcrag Wlk ■ M15 ....163 A5
Longcroft M29 ....76 E4
Longcroft Cotts BL9 ....11 F1
Longcroft Dr WA14 .....119 B4
Longcroft Gr
Droylsden M34 ....100 B8
Wythenshawe M23 ......120 F7
Longdale Cl OL2 ....48 C4
Longdale St SK14 ....103 A3
Longdale Gdns SK14 ....103 A3
Longdell Wlk ■ M9 .....157 E8
Longden Ave OL4 ....49 E3
Longden Ct SK7 ....132 E5
Longden Rd
Ashton-in-M WN4 ....73 A3
Manchester M19 ....99 B2
Longden St ■ BL1 ......144 C8
Longdendale High Sch
SK14 ....103 C5
Longdendale Recn Ctr
SK14 ....102 F3
Longdale Rd WN6 ....36 E8
Longfellow Ave BL3 ....146 B3
Longfellow Cl WN3 .....150 A5
Longfellow Cres OL1 ....49 D4
Longfellow St M6 ....81 C4
Longfellow Wlk ■ M34 .113 A7
Longfield Ave
Altrincham WA15 ....120 C6
Gatley SK8 ....131 C7
Urmston M41 ....95 C1
Longfield Cl SK14 ......101 E6
Longfield Cres OL4 .....67 D8
Longfield Dr M41 ....95 B2
Longfield La ■ OL4 .....49 D1
Longfield Pk OL2 ....149 A6
Longfield Rd Bolton BL3 .146 B3
Rochdale OL11 ....30 C8
Shaw OL2 ....149 A6
Wythenshawe M23 ......120 F8
Longfield Sh Ctr M25 ...63 A5
Longfield St ■ WN2 ....37 F2
Longford Ave Bolton BL1 .142 C2
Stretford M32 ....96 E2
Longford Ct M32 ....96 E3
Longford Cotts M32 ....96 F2
Longford Gdns BL3 .....147 E4
Longford Ho ■ M21 ....96 F1
Longford Park Sch M32 .96 F2
Longford Pl M14 ....98 E4
Longford Rd
Manchester M21 ....97 A1
Manchester M35 ....99 F1
Stretford M32 ....96 E3
Longford Rd W SK5 .....99 E1
Longford St Heywood OL10 .29 D2
Manchester M18 ....99 D6
Longford Trad Est M32 .96 D3
Longham Cl ■ Bramhall SK7 .123 D1
Manchester M11 ....160 E1
Longhey Rd M22 ....121 D5
Longhill Wlk ■ M40 ....83 A6
Longhurst Cl OL1 ......142 B3
Longhope Rd M22 .....121 C2
Longhurst La SK6 ......126 C6
Longhurst Rd Hindley WN2 .57 A4
Manchester M9 ....64 B5
Longlevens Rd M22 ....121 C3
Longley Dr M28 ....79 B6
Longley La M22 ....121 E7
Longley Rd M28 ....60 D2
Longley St Oldham OL1 .153 F6
Shaw OL2 ....149 B5
Longmead Ave
Ashton-in-M WN4 .....73 C4
Hazel Grove SK7 ......124 D1
Longmead Rd M6 ......154 D4
Longmead Way M24 ...47 B1
Longmeade Gdns SK9 .137 C6
Longmeadow SK8 .....132 C7
Longmeadow Gr M34 ..100 E2
Longmere Ave M22 ...121 D3
Longmoor Rd SK13 ....116 A7
Longnor Rd Gatley SK8 .131 D8
Hazel Grove SK7 ......133 E7
Longnor Way ■ SK13 ...171 D2
Longport Ave M20 ....110 A7
Longridge BL7 ....25 C8
Longridge Ave
Stalybridge SK15 .....86 A4
Standish WN6 ....36 F8
Longridge Cres BL1 ....23 F2
Longridge Dr ■ Bury BL8 .44 A8

Longridge Dr continued
Heywood OL10 ....28 F2
Longridge Way WN6 ...36 F8
Longshaw Ave
Longshaw WN5 ....53 E1
Swinton M27 ....61 F1
Longshaw Cl WN5 .....53 E1
Longshaw Comm
Billinge WN5 ....71 E8
Longshaw WN5 ....53 E1
Longshaw Dr M28 .....60 A4
Longshaw Ford Rd BL1 .23 F5
Longshaw Old Rd WN5 .53 E1
Longshoot Cl WN1 ....37 D1
Longshut La SK1,SK2 ..170 F7
Longshut La W SK2 ....170 F7
Longsides Rd WA15 ...129 C7
Longsight BL2 ....25 E5
Longsight Com Prim Sch
BL2 ....25 E4
Longsight La Bolton BL2 .25 D4
Cheadle SK8 ....131 F6
Longsight Park Sch M12 .164 E5
Longsight Rd
Manchester M18 ....99 B3
Ramsbottom BL0,BL8 ..11 A2
Longson St BL1 ....25 A1
Longsons The SK5 .....169 F3
Longthwaite Cl M24 ...46 D2
Longton Ave Golborne WA3 .90 C7
Manchester M20 ......110 A5
Longton Rd Manchester M9 .64 C4
Pendlebury M6 ....80 A5
Longton St Bury BL9 ..44 F4
Hindley WN2 ....56 C4
Longtown Gdns ■ BL1 .143 E2
Longview Dr M27 .....61 C1
Longwall Ave M28 ....78 C8
Longwood Ave SK2 ...124 B6
Longwood Cl SK6 .....113 E3
Longwood Rd
Stretford M17 ....96 B6
Wythenshawe M22 ....121 C3
Longworth Ave BL6 ...21 C3
Longworth Cl M41 ....94 E1
Longworth Clough BL7 .8 D2
Longworth La BL7 .....8 C2
Longworth Rd Bolton BL7 .8 B3
Rochdale OL12 ....14 A5
Longworth St Bolton BL2 .148 C7
Manchester M3 ....162 E8
Lonsdale Ave Leigh WN7 .75 D2
Reddish SK5 ....99 F3
Rochdale OL16 ....31 B5
Swinton M27 ....79 D5
Urmston M41 ....95 A4
Lonsdale Gr ■ BL4 ....60 C8
Lonsdale Rd Bolton BL1 .144 B8
Manchester M19 ......99 B2
Oldham OL8 ....66 B2
Lonsdale St ■ Bury BL8 .27 C2
Failsworth M40 ....83 C6
Lonsdale Wlk WN5 ....54 B8
Loom St M4 ....160 A2
Loonies Ct ■ SK1 ....170 F8
Lord Ave Bacup OL13 .3 C8
■ Tyldesley M46 .....58 F1
Lord Byron Sq M5 ....154 F1
Lord Derby Rd SK14 ..113 E7
Lord Gr ■ M46 ....58 F1
Lord Kitchener Ct M33 .108 B5
Lord La M35 ....83 F6
Lord Lane Mews M35 ..83 F6
Lord Napier Dr M5 ....161 B7
Lord North St M40 ...160 F4
Lord St Ashton-in-M WN4 .73 D4
Ashton-u-L OL6 ......166 B4
Bury BL9 ....140 F2
Bury BL9 ....141 C1
Farnworth BL4 ....147 E2
Glossop SK13 ....104 D1
Hindley WN2 ....56 D4
Hollingworth SK14 ...171 D4
Horwich BL6 ....22 B4
Ince-in-M WN2 ....57 A6
Leigh WN7 ....75 F5
Little Lever BL3 ......43 B3
Manchester M3,M4 ...159 A3
Manchester M5,M7 ...81 C4
Middleton M24 ....47 A2
Newton-le-W WA12 ..153 F7
Oldham OL1 ....153 F6
Radcliffe M26 ....44 A3
Reddish M34 ....100 A4
Stalybridge SK15,SK16 ..101 F8
Stockport SK1 ....169 F1
Tyldesley M29 ....76 F6
Tyldesley M46 ....58 E1
Westhoughton BL5 ...39 E1
Wigan WN1 ....37 C1
Lord St S WN7 ....76 A4
Lord Street Prim Sch BL4 .147 E2
Lord's Ave M5 ....154 D2
Lord's St M44 ....105 C5
Lord's Stile La BL7 ...25 B2
Lords Coll BL2 ....148 A6
Lordsfields Ave OL7 ..166 B4
Lordship Cl M9 ....64 F1
Lordsmead St M15 ...162 D6
Lordy Cl WN6 ....37 B7
Loreto Coll M15 .....162 E5
Loreto Convent Gram Sch
WA14 ....119 C5
Loreto Convent Prep Sch
WA14 ....119 C5
Loretto Rd M41 .....95 F1
Lorgill Cl SK3 ....123 F4
Loring St M40 ....83 C5

Lorland Rd SK3 ....123 B7
Lorna Gr SK8 ....121 F6
Lorna Rd SK8 ....123 B2
Lorne Ave OL3 ....48 B3
Lorne Gr Stockport SK3 .170 E6
Urmston M41 ....95 C2
Lorne Rd M14 ....110 C8
Lorne St Bolton BL1 ..145 F7
Eccles M30 ....95 B8
Farnworth BL3,BL4 ...42 C2
Heywood OL10 ....29 A4
Manchester M13 .....163 C5
Mossley OL5 ....68 C1
Oldham OL8 ....66 E4
Rochdale OL12 ......15 B3
Wigan WN1 ....151 E8
Lorne Way OL10 .....28 F1
Lorraine Cl OL10 ....46 E8
Lorraine Rd WA15 ...120 B5
Lorton Cl Boothstown M28 .77 F6
Middleton M24 ......46 C2
Lorton Gr BL2 ....42 F8
Lostock Ave
Hazel Grove SK7 ....124 B1
■ Manchester M19 ...99 B1
Poynton SK12 ....133 B4
Sale M33 ....108 E4
Lostock Cir Billinge WN5 .71 E5
Heywood OL10 ......29 B3
Lostock Com Prim Sch
BL6 ....40 C6
Lostock Ct Handforth SK9 .131 D4
Urmston M32 ....95 F4
Lostock Dr BL9 .....27 F6
Lostock Gr M32 .....96 B3
Lostock Hall Cty Prim Sch
SK12 ....133 B3
Lostock Hall Rd SK12 .133 B3
Lostock High Sch M32 .96 A3
Lostock Ind Est BL6 ..39 E7
Lostock Junction La BL6 .40 C7
Lostock La BL5,BL6 ..39 C6
Lostock Park Dr BL6 .40 A7
Lostock Park Sch BL6 .40 C5
Lostock Rd Poynton SK12 .133 D2
Salford M5 ....154 E2
Lostock St M40 .....160 D3
Lostock Sta BL6 ....40 C6
Lostock Way SK9 ...131 D4
Lostock Wlk Leigh WN7 .75 D6
Whitefield M45 .....11 G3
Lothian Ave M30 ....79 B3
Lottery Row BL1 ....145 F7
Lottery St SK3 ......169 D1
Lottie St M27 ....80 A8
Loughborough Cl ■
M23 ....107 D3
Loughrigg Ave
Billinge WN5 ....71 B1
Royton OL2 ....48 C8
Loughrigg Cl M29 ...77 B7
Louis Ave BL9 ......140 F4
Louis St BL0 ....1 D5
Louisa St Bolton BL1 ..143 E2
Manchester M11 ....99 D6
Walkden M28 ....60 D4
Louise Cl OL12 .....15 C3
Louise Gdns Rochdale OL12 .15 C3
Westhoughton BL5 ..57 F6
Louise St OL12 .....15 C3
Louvaine Ave BL1 ...23 F4
Louvoine Cl M18 ....99 E5
Lovalle St BL1 ......142 C1
Lovat Rd BL2 ....43 A7
Love La Edenfield BL0 ..1 C5
Stockport SK1 ......169 E2
Loveless Ho M46 ....58 D4
Lovell Ct M8 ....63 F2
Lovell Dr SK14 .....167 F4
Lovers La Atherton M46 .58 B1
Uppermill OL4 ......48 D6
Lovett Wlk M22 ....121 E8
Low Bank OL3 ......15 C3
Low Bank Rd WN4 ...72 F4
Low Crompton Rd OL2 .48 E6
Low Gate La OL3 ....34 A6
Low Gn M35 ....58 F5
Low Grove La OL3 ..68 E5
Low Hall Com Prim Sch
WN2 ....56 A3
Low Hall Gdns WN2 .56 A3
Low Hill OL12 ....15 C3
Low Lea Rd SK6 ....126 B6
Low Mdws OL2 .....48 D6
Low Wood Cl SK7 ..123 C1
Low Wood Rd M34 ..100 A4
Lowcock St M7 .....81 C4
Lowcroft Cres OL9 ..65 F8
Lowcross Rd M40 ...83 A6
Lowe Ave M46 .....58 C5
Lowe Gn OL2 ....48 D6
Lowe Mill La WN2 ..56 D5
Lowe St Denton M34 ..101 B3
Golborne WA3 ......90 A8
Radcliffe M26 ....44 A3
Stockport SK1 ......169 F1
Lower Albion St M1 ..163 B8
Lower Alma St SK16 ..101 F8
Lower Bamford Cl M24 .47 A2
Lower Bank SK13 ...116 D8
Lower Bank Cl SK13 .116 D8
Lower Bank St BL9 ..140 E2
Lowerlea SK12 .....135 C6
Lower Barn Rd SK13 .171 E4

Lower Bennett St SK14 .101 C5
Lower Bents La SK6 ..112 F4
Lower Blue Bell Cotts BL5 .39 C4
Lower Bridgeman St BL2 .148 A6
Lower Broadacre SK15 ..102 E6
Lower Brook La M28 ..79 A5
Lower Brook St M1 ...163 B8
Lower Brooklands Par ■
M8 ....63 E2
Lower Broughton Rd
Manchester M7 ......158 D4
Manchester M7 ......81 C6
Lower Bury St SK4 ..169 D2
Lower Byrom St M3 ..162 E8
Lower Calderbrook OL15 ..6 C1
Lower Carr La OL3 ...69 B6
Lower Carrs SK1 .....169 F1
Lower Chatham St M1 .163 A7
Lower Clowes BB4 ...1 E8
Lower Clowes Rd BB4 .1 E8
Lower Count Hill OL4 .49 D2
Lower Crimble OL11 .29 F4
Lower Croft M45 ....62 C6
Lower Crossbank OL4 .67 F8
Lower Darcy St BL2 ..148 C5
Lower Dingle OL1 ...49 C4
Lower Drake Fold BL5 .57 E5
Lower Edge Ave OL1 .153 E8
Lower Falinge OL12 .139 E8
Lower Fields OL3 ...51 A1
Lower Fold Bolton BL2 .25 F4
Denton M34 ....101 A2
Marple SK6 ....126 B8
Lower Frenches Dr OL3 .69 A5
Lower Gates OL16 ..139 F7
Lower Goodwin Cl BL2 .25 E2
Lower Green La M29 ..77 C3
Lower Greenshall La
SK12 ....135 F6
Lower Hague SK22 ...135 E8
Lower Hardman St M3 .158 E1
Lower Hey La OL5 ...68 E3
Lower Higham Visitors Ctr
BL2 ....134 C8
Lower Hillgate SK1 ..169 F1
Lower House Dr BL6 ..40 C7
Lower House La OL12 ..15 B7
Lower House St ■ OL1 .67 B8
Lower House Wlk BL7 .25 A8
Lower Hyde Green Farm
SK15 ....86 E4
Lower Jowkin La OL11 .29 D7
Lower Kersall Prim Sch
M7 ....81 B6
Lower Knoll Rd OL3 ..51 C5
Lower La OL16 ......31 D4
Lower Landedmans BL5 .57 F7
Lower Leigh Rd BL5 ..57 F5
Lower Lime Rd OL8 ..84 C8
Lower Longshoot WN1 .150 B8
Lower Lyndon Ave WN6 .36 A6
Lower Makinson Fold BL6 .22 D1
Lower Marlands BL7 ..24 F8
Lower Mead BL7 ....9 D6
Lower Meadow Rd SK9 .131 E4
Lower Moat Cl SK4 ..169 E3
Lower Monton Rd M30 .79 F2
Lower Mosley St M1,M2 .162 F8
Lower Moss La
Manchester M15 ...162 D7
Whitefield M45 .....62 F8
Lower New Row M28 ..60 A1
Lower Ormond St M13 .163 A7
Lower Park Cres SK12 .133 C6
Lower Park Prim Sch
SK12 ....133 C4
Lower Park Rd
Manchester M14 ....98 C3
Poynton SK12 ......133 B5
Lower Rawson St BL4 .60 E8
Lower Rd BL0 ....11 E8
Lower Seedley Rd M6 .154 E3
Lower Sheriff St OL12 .139 E8
Lower Southfield BL5 ..57 E7
Lower Sq SK13 .....104 A7
Lower St Farnworth BL4 .60 C7
■ Rochdale OL11 ...30 A6
Lower St Stephen St ■
WN6 ....37 A1
Lower Stones OL3 ..50 E3
Lower Strines Rd SK6 .126 A5
Lower Sutherland St M27 .79 E8
Lower Tenterfield OL11 ..13 D2
Lower Tong BL7 ....24 F7
Lower Turf La OL4 ..49 F3
Lower Tweedale St OL11 .139 F6
Lower Vickers St M40 .160 D3
Lower Victoria St OL9 .152 B7
Lower Wharf St OL6 ..166 C2
Lower Wheat End OL16 .31 B8
Lower Woodhill Rd BL8 .140 E4
Lowerbank M34 .....100 F5
Lowercroft Prim Sch BL8 .26 F2
Lowercroft Rd BL8 ..26 E2
Lowerfield Dr SK2 ...124 F5
Lowerfields OL8 .....84 B6
Lowerfields Rise OL2 .149 B8
Lowerfold Cl OL12 ..14 C4
Lowerfold Cres OL12 .14 C4
Lowerfold Dr OL12 ..14 C4
Lowerfold Way OL12 .14 C4
Lowerford Ave ■ OL2 .49 A4
Lowerlea SK12 ......135 C6
Lower Market St SK14 .115 B8

Lowerplace Com Prim Sch
OL16 ....31 B4
Lowerwood La ■ BL2 ...25 B1
Lowes Rd BL9 ....28 A6
Lowes The WA14 ...119 B1
Lowestead Rd ■ M11 .83 C2
Lowestoft St M14 ...98 B2
Loweswater Ave M29 .77 A7
Loweswater Rd
Farnworth BL4 ......59 E7
Gratley SK8 ....122 B3
Loweswater Terr SK15 .86 A4
Lowfell Wlk M18 ....99 D3
Lowfield Ave
Ashton-u-L OL6 .....85 F5
Droylsden M34 .....83 F3
Lowfield Gdns WA3 ..92 C7
Lowfield Gr SK2 ....170 F7
Lowfield Rd SK3,SK3 .170 E7
Lowfield Wlk ■ M9 ..64 E3
Lowick Ave BL3 ....42 A3
Lowick Cl SK7 ......124 D2
Lowick Gn SK6 .....112 F5
Lowland Gr OL7 ....85 A6
Lowland Rd SK2 ...124 B4
Lowlands Cl M24 ...65 C5
Lowndes Cl SK2 ...124 B7
Lowndes La SK1,SK2 .124 B7
Lowndes St BL1 ...142 B1
Lowndes Wlk ■ M13 .163 C6
Lownorth Rd M22 ..130 E8
Lowood Ave M41 ...94 F4
Lowood Cl OL16 ...31 F6
Lowood St WN7 ....75 D5
Lowrey Wlk ■ M9 ..157 E7
Lowry Ct SK14 .....103 A4
Lowry Dr Marple SK6 .126 B8
Swinton M27 ......61 F1
Lowry Gr SK14 ....102 F3
Lowry High Sch M7 ..155 D5
Lowry Ho Eccles M30 ..79 E2
■ Manchester M14 ..110 D8
Lowry The M5 ......96 F7
Lowry Wlk BL1 .....143 D1
Lows The OL4 .....67 B5
Lowside Ave Bolton BL1 .40 C6
Romiley SK6 ....113 C5
Lowside Dr OL4 ....67 B5
Lowstern Cl BL7 ...8 E1
Lowther Ave
Altrincham WA15 ..120 A6
Culcheth WA3 ......91 F4
Manchester M18 ...99 B3
Royton OL2 ....48 C8
Lowther Cl M25 ...63 A3
Lowther Cres M24 ..46 C6
Lowther Ct M25 ...63 C3
Lowther Dr WN7 ...76 E7
Lowther Gdns M41 .94 D3
Lowther Rd Manchester M8 .64 A1
Prestwich M25 .....62 F3
Rochdale OL11 ....30 C8
Lowther St BL3 ....42 A3
Lowther Terr WN6 ..35 C8
Lowthorpe St M14 ..98 A2
Lowton Ave M9 ...157 F7
Lowton Bsns Pk WA3 .91 A7
Lowton Gdns WA3 ..90 B5
Lowton High Sch WA3 .91 B8
Lowton Jun & Inf Sch
WA3 ....91 A7
Lowton Rd Golborne WA3 .74 C1
Sale M33 ....107 D2
Lowton St M26 .....44 A4
Lowton St Mary's
CE Prim Sch WA3 ..91 A8
Lowton West Cty Prim Sch
WA3 ....90 D8
Loxford St M15 ....162 F6
Loxford St M15 ....162 F6
Loxham St BL4 ....42 D2
Loxley Wlk M40 ...160 A8
Loxton Cres WN3 ..55 B3
Loynd St OL10 ....11 C6
Lubeck St M9 .....157 E8
Lucas Rd BL4 .....60 A7
Lucas St Bury BL9 ..141 A3
Oldham OL4 ....67 B7
Lucas Wlk M11 ...164 F8
Lucerne Cl OL9 ...152 C6
Lucerne Rd SK7 ...123 E3
Lucien Cl M12 ....164 E5
Luciol Cl M29 .....59 D1
Lucknow St OL11 ..139 F5
Lucy St Bolton BL1 .142 A1
Manchester M15 ..162 D6
Manchester M7 ...155 D5
Stockport SK3 .....170 E7
Ludford Gr M33 ...107 F1
Ludgate Hill M4 ...159 B2
Ludgate Rd Failsworth M40 .83 C4
Rochdale OL11 ....31 A2
Ludgate St M4 ....159 B2
Ludlow Ave ■ Leigh WN7 .76 C5
Prestwich M25,M45 .62 F3
Swinton M27 ......62 A2
Ludlow Dr ■ M7 ..76 E7
Ludlow Pk ■ OL4 ..67 B8
Ludlow Rd SK2 ...124 C8
Ludlow St WN6 ...19 D3
Ludovic Terr WN1 ..37 C4
Ludwell Wlk ■ M8 .156 A6
Ludworth Prim Sch SK6 .126 B8
Lugano Rd SK7 ....123 E2
Luke Kirby St M7 ..63 F1
Luke Rd M43 ....84 B1
Luke St Ashton-in-M WN4 .73 D5

Luke St continued
🔟 Bacup OL13 . . . . 3 C8
Luke Wlk M8 . . . . 156 B6
Lullington Cl M22 . . . . .121 C1
Lullington Rd M6 . . . . .154 D4
Lulworth Ave M41 . . . . .94 F2
Lulworth Cl BL8 . . . . .27 C6
Lulworth Cres M35 . . . . .84 B8
Lulworth Dr WN7 . . . . .57 A4
Lulworth Gdns M23 . . . . . . .120 F8
Lulworth Rd Bolton BL3 . . . .146 A3
  Eccles M30 . . . . .79 C3
  Middleton M24 . . . . .47 A2
Lum Head Prim Sch SK8 . .122 E3
Lum St BL1 . . . . .148 A8
Lumb Carr Ave BL0 . . . . .11 A4
Lumb Carr Rd BL0,BL8 . . . . .11 A4
Lumb Cl SK7 . . . . .132 E6
Lumb Cotts BL0 . . . . 1 B4
Lumb Flats BL0 . . . . 1 B4
Lumb Holes La M48 . . . . 2 E7
Lumb La Bramhall SK7 . . . . .132 E6
  Droylsden M34 . . . . .100 C8
  Droylsden M34 . . . . .84 C1
  Droylsden M34, M43, OL7 . . . 84 D4
  Droylsden M43 . . . . .84 C3
Lumber La M28 . . . . .78 E8
Lumley Cl M14 . . . . .98 B4
Lumn Hollow SK14 . . . . .167 E2
Lumn Rd SK14 . . . . .167 E2
Lumn St BL9 . . . . .27 F8
Lumn's La M27 . . . . .62 C1
Lumsden St BL3 . . . . .145 E5
Lumwood BL1 . . . . .142 B3
Luna St M4 . . . . .159 B2
Lund Ave M26 . . . . .62 B8
Lundale Wlk M40 . . . . .83 A6
Lundy Ave M21 . . . . .109 C5
Lune Cl M45 . . . . .45 A1
Lune Dr M45 . . . . .63 A8
Lune Gr Heywood OL10 . . . . .29 B3
  Leigh WN7 . . . . .75 C5
Lune Rd M41 . . . . .56 A2
Lune St Oldham OL8 . . . . .66 C4
  Tyldesley M29 . . . . .76 F8
Lune Way SK5 . . . . .111 F5
Lunedale Wlk Droylsden M43 .100 B8
  Whitefield M45 . . . . .63 A8
Lunedale 🔟 WN2 . . . . .56 B2
Lunedale Gr M24 . . . . .124 E6
Lunehurst 🔢 WA3 . . . . .90 E8
Lunn Ave M18 . . . . .99 F6
Lupin Ave BL4 . . . . .42 A1
Lupton St Denton M34 . . . . .100 F4
  Manchester M3 . . . . .158 D2
Lurden Wlk OL9 . . . . .66 B4
Lurdin La WN1,WN6 . . . . .37 B7
Lurgan Ave M33 . . . . .108 C3
Lutener Ave WA14 . . . . .119 C8
Luton Dr M23 . . . . .121 A4
Luton Gr M46 . . . . .58 B3
Luton Rd SK5 . . . . .111 F8
Luton St Bolton BL3 . . . . .42 A4
  🔢 Bury BL8 . . . . .27 B1
Luxor Gr M34 . . . . .99 F3
Luzley Brook Rd OL2 . . . . . .149 A5
Luzley Rd OL5,OL6 . . . . .86 B7
Lyceum Pas OL16 . . . . .139 F7
Lyceum Pl M15 . . . . .163 A7
Lychgate WN5 . . . . .54 E5
Lychgate Cl OL4 . . . . .67 E4
Lychgate Mews SK4 . . . . . . .110 E2
Lychwood 🔟 SK6 . . . . .125 F6
Lydbrook Cl BL1 . . . . .145 E6
Lydden Ave M11 . . . . .83 D3
Lydford OL11 . . . . .139 E6
Lydford Gdns BL2 . . . . .42 F6
Lydford Gn WN6 . . . . .36 F8
Lydford St M6 . . . . .81 B4
Lydford Wlk M13 . . . . .163 C6
Lydgate Ave BL2 . . . . .42 F6
Lydgate Cl Denton M34 . . . . .101 B1
  Mossley SK15 . . . . .86 E6
  Whitefield M45 . . . . .45 A1
Lydgate Dr OL4 . . . . .67 D5
Lydgate Fold OL4 . . . . .68 C5
Lydgate Prim Sch OL4 . . . . . .68 C6
Lydgate Rd Droylsden M43 . . .83 E2
  Sale M33 . . . . .108 C2
Lydgate The OL16 . . . . .16 E6
Lydgate Wlk M45 . . . . .45 A1
Lydiat La SK9 . . . . .137 A1
Lydney Ave SK8 . . . . .131 C7
Lydney Rd M41 . . . . .94 D3
Lyefield Ave WN7 . . . . .37 F1
Lyefield Wlk 🔟 OL16 . . . . . . .31 B6
Lymbridge Dr BL6 . . . . .21 D1
Lyme Ave SK9 . . . . .131 B1
Lyme Clough Way M24 . . . . . .46 F4
Lyme Gr Altrincham WA14 . . .119 C4
  Droylsden M43 . . . . .99 C4
  Marple SK6 . . . . .125 F5
  Romiley SK6 . . . . .113 D2
  Stockport SK2 . . . . .170 F7
Lyme Hall SK12 . . . . .135 B1
Lyme Park Ctry Pk SK12 . . . .135 B2
Lyme Rd Disley SK12 . . . . . .134 C3
  Hazel Grove SK7 . . . . .124 E1
  High Lane SK12 . . . . .135 A6
Lyme St Hazel Grove SK7 . . .124 D3
  Manchester SK4 . . . . .110 F2
Lyme Terr 🔟 SK16 . . . . .166 B1
Lymefield Dr M28 . . . . .78 A7
Lymefield Gr SK2 . . . . .124 B6
Lymefield Terr SK14 . . . . . . .102 A1
Lymewood Dr Disley SK12 . . .135 C6
  Wilmslow SK9 . . . . .137 E8
Lymington Cl M24 . . . . .65 B5

Lymington Dr M23 . . . . .108 D1
Lymm Cl Stockport SK3 . . . .170 D6
  Walkden M28 . . . . .60 A3
Lymm High Sch WA13 . . . . . .117 B3
Lymm Rd WA14 . . . . .118 B1
Lymn Ave WA14 . . . . .123 A5
Lymn St WN2 . . . . .56 B3
Lyn Gr OL10 . . . . .29 A3
Lyncombe Cl SK8 . . . . .132 B6
Lyndale Ave Reddish SK5 . . . .99 F3
  Swinton M27 . . . . .79 D6
Lyndale Dr OL15 . . . . .16 A6
Lyndene Ave M28 . . . . .79 A8
Lyndene Ct OL10 . . . . .29 C3
Lyndene Gdns SK8 . . . . .122 B6
Lyndene Rd M22 . . . . .121 D5
Lyndhurst Ave
  Ashton-u-L OL6 . . . . .85 B5
  Bredbury SK6 . . . . .112 F4
  Denton M34 . . . . .100 E3
  Hazel Grove SK7 . . . . .124 C1
  Irlam M44 . . . . .94 B3
  Manchester M25 . . . . .63 E3
  Middleton OL11 . . . . .47 D8
  Oldham OL9 . . . . .65 F5
  Sale M33 . . . . .107 F3
  Urmston M41 . . . . .95 C4
Lyndhurst Cl SK9 . . . . .136 D5
Lyndhurst Com Prim Sch
  OL8 .66 D3
Lyndhurst Dr WA15 . . . . . . .120 A2
Lyndhurst Prim Sch
  SK16 . . . . .166 C1
Lyndhurst Rd
  Manchester M20 . . . . .110 B5
  Oldham OL8 . . . . .66 D3
  Reddish SK5 . . . . .99 E2
  Stretford M32 . . . . .96 B3
Lyndhurst St M5,M6 . . . . . . .154 E2
Lyndhurst View SK16 . . . . . .166 C1
Lyndon Ave WN6 . . . . .36 A7
Lyndon Cl Bury BL8 . . . . .26 F6
  Oldham OL8 . . . . .66 D3
Lyndon Croft OL8 . . . . .66 C4
Lyndon Rd M44 . . . . .93 F2
Lyne Ave SK13 . . . . .116 A8
Lyne Edge Cres SK16 . . . . . .101 F7
Lyne Edge Rd SK16 . . . . .102 A7
Lyne View SK14 . . . . .101 F6
Lyneham Wlk
  Manchester M7 . . . . .155 F6
  🔟 Manchester M9 . . . . .64 E5
Lyngard Cl SK9 . . . . .131 E1
Lyngarth Ho 🔟 WA14 . . . . . .119 C6
Lyngate Cl SK1 . . . . .124 A8
Lynham Dr OL10 . . . . .46 D8
Lynmouth Ave
  Manchester M20 . . . . .110 A6
  Oldham OL8 . . . . .66 F3
  🔟 Reddish SK5 . . . . .111 E7
  Royton OL2 . . . . .48 C3
  Urmston M41 . . . . .107 B8
Lynmouth Cl
  Chadderton OL9 . . . . .47 E1
  Radcliffe M26 . . . . .44 C4
  Whitefield M45 . . . . .37 A2
Lynmouth Ct M25 . . . . .62 F3
Lynmouth Gr M25 . . . . .62 F3
Lynn Ave M33 . . . . .108 D6
Lynn Dr M43 . . . . .83 E2
Lynn St OL9 . . . . .66 C4
Lynne Cl SK13 . . . . .116 F8
Lynnwood Dr OL11 . . . . .30 B8
Lynnwood Rd M19 . . . . .110 D2
Lynroyle Way OL11 . . . . .30 D3
Lynside Wlk M22 . . . . .130 E8
Lynsted Ave BL3 . . . . .42 A3
Lynstock Way BL6 . . . . .39 E6
Lynthorpe Ave M44 . . . . . . .105 D6
Lynthorpe Rd M40 . . . . .65 D2
Lynton Ave
  Hattersley SK14 . . . . .102 C2
  Irlam M44 . . . . .105 E6
  Oldham OL8 . . . . .66 C2
  Rochdale OL11 . . . . .30 B3
  Royton OL2 . . . . .48 C3
  Swinton M27 . . . . .61 F1
  Urmston M41 . . . . .94 C2
  Wigan WN5 . . . . .37 A3
Lynton Cl OL9 . . . . .47 F1
Lynton Cres M28 . . . . .78 D8
Lynton Dr High Lane SK6 . . .134 E8
  Manchester M19 . . . . .110 F7
  Prestwich M25 . . . . .63 C6
Lynton Gr WA15 . . . . .119 F5
Lynton La SK9 . . . . .137 A2
Lynton Lee M26 . . . . .44 C4
Lynton Park Rd SK8 . . . . . . .131 F8
Lynton Rd Bolton BL3 . . . . . .146 C2
  Cheadle SK8 . . . . .122 C5
  Hindley WN2 . . . . .56 F6
  Manchester M21 . . . . .97 A1
  Manchester M21 . . . . .97 A1
  Swinton M27 . . . . .61 F1
  Tyldesley M29 . . . . .77 D8
Lynton St Leigh WN7 . . . . . . .75 D5
  Manchester M14 . . . . .98 B2
Lynton Wlk SK14 . . . . .102 C2
Lyntonvale Ave SK8 . . . . . . .122 B6
Lynway Dr M20 . . . . .110 B5
Lynway Gr M24 . . . . .47 B2
Lynwell Rd M30 . . . . .79 D2
Lynwood Altrincham WA15 . .129 A8
  Wilmslow SK9 . . . . .137 A6
Lynwood Ave Bolton BL3 . . . .42 B2
  Eccles M30 . . . . .79 C2
  Golborne WA3 . . . . .90 B8
  Manchester M16 . . . . .97 C2

Lynwood Cl OL7 . . . . .85 A7
Lynwood Ct M8 . . . . .63 F2
Lynwood Dr OL4 . . . . .67 E8
Lynwood Gr Atherton M46 . . .58 B3
  Bolton BL2 . . . . .25 D4
  Droylsden M34 . . . . .84 C1
  Reddish SK4 . . . . .111 C6
  Sale M33 . . . . .108 C5
Lyon Gr M28 . . . . .79 A8
Lyon Ind Est WA14 . . . . .119 B7
Lyon Rd Altrincham WA14 . . .119 C7
  Kearsley BL4 . . . . .60 E6
  Wigan WN6 . . . . .37 A2
Lyon St Ashton-in-M WN4 . . . .72 F7
  Shaw OL2 . . . . .149 B7
  Swinton M27 . . . . .79 E7
  Swinton M27 . . . . .79 E7
Lyons Dr BL8 . . . . .27 A1
Lyons Fold M33 . . . . .108 B6
Lyons Rd M17 . . . . .96 A7
Lysander Cl M14 . . . . .110 B8
Lyth St M14 . . . . .110 D7
Lytham Ave M21 . . . . .109 C7
Lytham Cl OL6 . . . . .85 E6
Lytham Dr Bramhall SK7 . . . .133 A7
  Heywood OL10 . . . . .29 C1
Lytham Rd
  Ashton-in-M WN4 . . . . .72 F5
  Gatley SK8 . . . . .122 B1
  Manchester M14,M19 . . . . . .98 F1
  Urmston M41 . . . . .94 C2
Lytham St Rochdale OL12 . . .14 E3
  Stockport SK4 . . . . .170 F6
  Stretford M32 . . . . .96 E1
Lytherton Ave M44 . . . . .105 D4
Lytton Ave M8 . . . . .156 A6
Lytton Rd M43 . . . . .84 A2
Lytton St BL1 . . . . .143 D2

M

Mab's Cross Prim Sch
  WN1 . . . . .37 D1
Mabel Ave Bolton BL3 . . . . . . .42 A3
  Manchester M28 . . . . .79 A7
Mabel Rd M35 . . . . .84 A6
Mabel St 🔟 Bolton BL1 . . . .144 C8
  Failsworth M40 . . . . .83 D5
  Westhoughton BL5 . . . . .57 F6
  Wigan WN5 . . . . .54 E6
Mabel's Brow BL4 . . . . .60 E7
Maberry Cl WN6 . . . . .35 D7
Mabfield Rd M14 . . . . .98 C1
Mabledon Cl SK8 . . . . .131 D8
Mableden Cl SK8 . . . . .131 D8
Mabs Ct OL6 . . . . .166 C3
Macaulay St Rochdale OL11 . .30 D2
  Royton OL2 . . . . .48 E4
Macaulay Way 🔽 M34 . . . . .113 A8
Macauley Cl SK16 . . . . .102 A7
Macauley Pl WN3 . . . . .54 F4
Macauley Rd
  Manchester M16 . . . . .97 B2
  Reddish SK5 . . . . .99 E1
Macclesfield Cl M14 . . . . .98 C3
Macclesfield Rd
  Alderley Edge SK9 . . . . .137 B1
  Hazel Grove SK7 . . . . .133 F8
  Wilmslow SK9 . . . . .137 D6
Macdonald Ave
  Farnworth BL4 . . . . .60 B7
  Wigan WN3 . . . . .55 A3
Macdonald Rd M44 . . . . .105 E8
Macdonald St Oldham OL8 . . .66 F4
  Wigan WN5 . . . . .54 B6
Macefin Ave M21 . . . . .109 D4
Macfarren St M12 . . . . .99 A3
Macintosh Way M11 . . . . . . .153 F7
Mackenzie Ave WN3 . . . . .55 A3
Mackeson Dr OL6 . . . . .85 E4
Mackeson Rd OL6 . . . . .85 E4
Maclaren Dr M8 . . . . .63 E1
Maclure Rd OL11 . . . . .139 F6
Macnair Ct SK6 . . . . .126 A5
Macnair Mews SK6 . . . . .126 A5
Madams Wood Rd M28 . . . . . .60 A3
Maddison Rd M43 . . . . .99 F8
Madeira Pl Eccles M30 . . . . . .79 B1
  Eccles M30 . . . . .79 C2
Madeley Cl
  Altrincham WA14 . . . . .128 E8
  Wigan WN3 . . . . .54 E3
Madeley Dr SK8 . . . . .131 B6
Madeley Gdns Bolton BL1 . . .143 E2
  Rochdale OL12 . . . . .14 C1
Maden St M27 . . . . .76 F6
Maden Wlk OL9 . . . . .152 B8
Maden's Sq 🔟 OL15 . . . . . . .16 B5
Madison Ave Cheadle SK8 . .123 A2
  Droylsden M34 . . . . .100 C8
Madison Gdns M35 . . . . .83 E7
Madison St M18 . . . . .99 F6
Madras Rd SK3 . . . . .123 C7
Maesbrook Dr M29 . . . . .77 A8
Mafeking Ave BL3 . . . . .28 A5
Mafeking Pl WN4 . . . . .73 C3
Mafeking Rd BL2 . . . . .42 E7
Mafeking St OL8 . . . . .66 F3
Magda Rd SK2 . . . . .124 D5
Magdala St Heywood OL10 . .46 F8
  Oldham OL4 . . . . .153 E8

Magdalen Dr WN4 . . . . .72 F4
Magenta Ave M44 . . . . .105 E6
Magna Carta Ct M6,M27 . . . .80 B6
Magnolia Cl
  🔟 Partington M31 . . . . .105 E2
  Sale M33 . . . . .107 C6
Magnolia Ct 🔢 Sale M33 . . .107 C6
  🔢 Salford M6 . . . . .81 A2
Magnolia Dr M8 . . . . .156 A6
Magpie Cl M43 . . . . .84 C3
Magpie La OL4 . . . . .67 E4
Magpie Wlk 🔟 M11 . . . . . . .160 F1
Maguire Ave SK13 . . . . .104 A6
Maher Gdns M15 . . . . .97 E4
Mahogany Wlk 🔟 M33 . . . . .107 C5
Mahood St SK3 . . . . .170 D7
Maida St M12 . . . . .99 B2
Maiden Cl 🔽 OL7 . . . . .85 A6
Maiden Mews 🔢 M27 . . . . . .79 F7
Maidford Cl
  Manchester M4 . . . . .160 D1
  Stretford M32 . . . . .96 E2
Maidstone Ave M21 . . . . .97 A1
Maidstone Cl SK8 . . . . .131 B7
Maidstone Mews 🔢 M21 . . . .97 A1
Maidstone Rd M19 . . . . .110 D3
Maidstone Wlk M34 . . . . .101 A1
Main Ave Manchester M19 . .110 F7
  Stretford M17,M32 . . . . .96 A5
Main La WA3 . . . . .90 F3
Main Rd Oldham OL9 . . . . . . .152 C7
  Swinton M27 . . . . .62 C3
Main St Billinge WN5 . . . . . . .71 E5
  Hattersley SK14 . . . . .102 E8
  Hyde SK14 . . . . .167 D4
Maine Rd M14 . . . . .98 A3
Mainhill Wlk M40 . . . . .83 C5
Mainprice Cl M6 . . . . .154 F4
Mains Ave WN2 . . . . .73 F7
Mainwaring Dr SK9 . . . . .137 D8
Mainwaring Terr M23 . . . . . .109 A2
Mainway M24 . . . . .64 F6
Mainway E M24 . . . . .65 C6
Mainwood Rd WA15 . . . . . . .120 C5
Maismore Rd M22 . . . . .121 B1
Maitland Ave M21 . . . . .109 C5
Maitland Cl 🔟 OL12 . . . . . . .15 C3
  Walsden OL14 . . . . .6 A8
Maitland St Stockport SK1 . .124 B7
  Walsden OL14 . . . . .6 A8
Maitland Wlk OL9 . . . . .152 B8
Maizefield Cl M33 . . . . .108 F4
Major St Manchester M1 . . . .163 A8
  Milnrow OL16 . . . . .31 F6
  Ramsbottom BL0 . . . . .138 B6
  Wigan WN5 . . . . .54 C6
Makants Cl M46 . . . . .58 F5
Makepeace Wlk M8 . . . . .63 E2
Makerfield Dr WA12 . . . . .89 A5
Makerfield Way M29 . . . . .56 E7
Makin Ct OL10 . . . . .29 D1
Makin St M1 . . . . .163 A7
Makinson Arc 🔟 WN1 . . . . . .150 C6
Makinson Ave Hindley WN2 . .56 C7
  Horwich BL6 . . . . .22 C1
Makinson La BL6 . . . . .22 F4
Makkah Cl M40 . . . . .83 A5
Malaga Ave M90 . . . . .130 B7
Malakoff St SK15 . . . . .85 E1
Malbrook Wlk 🔢 M13 . . . . .163 C6
Malby St OL1 . . . . .153 D8
Malcolm Ave M27 . . . . .62 A3
Malcolm Dr M27 . . . . .62 A2
Malcolm St OL11 . . . . .30 D3
Malden Gr M23 . . . . .121 A7
Maldon Cl
  Hazel Grove SK2 . . . . .125 A6
  Wigan WN2 . . . . .37 F2
Maldon Cres M27 . . . . .79 F6
Maldon Dr M30 . . . . .79 E4
Maldon Rd WN6 . . . . .36 F8
Maldon St OL11 . . . . .139 F5
Maldwyn Ave Bolton BL3 . . . .146 A2
  Manchester M8 . . . . .64 A2
Maleham St M7 . . . . .155 E6
Malgam Dr M20 . . . . .122 B8
Malham Ave WN3 . . . . .55 A2
Malham Cl Leigh WN7 . . . . . . .75 C5
  Whitefield M45 . . . . .63 A8
Malham Ct 🔟 SK2 . . . . .124 D5
Malham Dr M45 . . . . .63 A8
Malia Rd SK4 . . . . .168 A4
Malik St 🔢 M40 . . . . .160 D3
Malkins St 🔟 M40 . . . . .160 D3
Mall The Bury BL9 . . . . .140 F2
  🔽 Eccles M30 . . . . .79 C2
Mallaig Wlk M11 . . . . .165 C8
Mallard Cl Dukinfield SK16 . .101 C8
  Hazel Grove SK2 . . . . .125 A5
  🔟 Oldham OL8 . . . . .66 D2
Mallard Cres SK12 . . . . .133 A4
Mallard Ct Oldham OL8 . . . . .153 B8
  🔟 Salford M5 . . . . .22 A3
Mallard Gn WA14 . . . . .119 B8
Mallard St M1 . . . . .163 A7
Mallards Reach SK6 . . . . . . .113 A2
Mallet Cres BL1 . . . . .23 D3
Malley Wlk 🔢 M9 . . . . .64 E3
Malling Rd M23 . . . . .121 B5
Mallison St BL1 . . . . .143 F3
Mallory Ave OL7 . . . . .85 B5
Mallory Ct WA14 . . . . .119 C3
Mallory Dr WN7 . . . . .76 C5
Mallory Rd SK14 . . . . .102 A4
Mallory Wlk M23 . . . . .120 D8

Mallow Croft OL16 . . . . .31 C4
Mallow St M15 . . . . .162 E6
Mallow Wlk M31 . . . . .105 F2
Mallowdale M28 . . . . .78 B8
Mallowdale Cl BL1 . . . . .40 D7
Mallowdale Rd SK2 . . . . .124 E5
Mally Gdns OL5 . . . . .86 D8
Malmesbury Cl SK12 . . . . . . .133 D4
Malmesbury Rd SK8 . . . . . . .132 B6
Malpas Ave WN1 . . . . .37 E1
Malpas Cl Cheadle SK8 . . . . .123 A4
  Handforth SK9 . . . . .131 E1
Malpas Dr WA14 . . . . .107 E1
Malpas St Manchester M12 . .165 A6
  Oldham OL1 . . . . .153 F7
Malpas Wlk M16 . . . . .162 D5
Malsham Rd M23 . . . . .108 F2
Malt St M15 . . . . .162 D7
Malta Cl M24 . . . . .65 C8
Malta St Manchester M4 . . . .160 D1
  Oldham OL4 . . . . .67 D6
Maltby Dr BL3 . . . . .146 C3
Maltby Rd M23 . . . . .120 F6
Malton Ave Bolton BL3 . . . . .146 A4
  Golborne WA3 . . . . .90 E7
  Manchester M21 . . . . .109 B8
  Whitefield M45 . . . . .44 F2
Malton Cl Chadderton OL9 . . .47 F1
  Leigh WN7 . . . . .75 C6
  🔟 Whitefield M45 . . . . .44 F2
Malton Dr
  Altrincham WA14 . . . . .119 A6
  Hazel Grove SK7 . . . . .133 A8
Malton Rd Boothstown M28 . .77 E7
  Manchester SK4 . . . . .168 A4
  Manchester SK4 . . . . .153 D5
Malus Ct M6 . . . . .81 A3
Malverley Dr M7 . . . . .155 D6
Malvern Ave Ashton-u-L OL6 .85 C7
  Atherton M46 . . . . .58 F5
  Bolton BL1 . . . . .23 F3
  Bury BL9 . . . . .27 F5
  Droylsden M43 . . . . .84 C2
  Hindley WN2 . . . . .57 A4
  Urmston M41 . . . . .95 B2
  Wythenshawe SK8 . . . . .121 F5
Malvern Cl
  Ashton-in-M WN4 . . . . .73 B4
  🔢 Farnworth BL4 . . . . .59 F8
  Horwich BL6 . . . . .22 C5
  Milnrow OL16 . . . . .32 A7
  Pendlebury M27 . . . . .80 C8
  Prestwich M25 . . . . .63 C5
  Royton OL2 . . . . .48 C3
  Shaw OL2 . . . . .48 F8
  Stockport SK4 . . . . .169 D3
  Wigan WN3 . . . . .54 C3
Malvern Cres WN3 . . . . .55 F4
Malvern Dr
  Altrincham WA14 . . . . .119 B5
  Pendlebury M27 . . . . .80 C8
Malvern Gr
  Manchester M20 . . . . .110 A6
  Salford M6 . . . . .80 C3
  Walkden M28 . . . . .60 D3
Malvern Rd M24 . . . . .65 A5
Malvern Rise SK13 . . . . .104 A5
Malvern Row 🔟 M15 . . . . . .162 D6
Malvern St
  Manchester M15 . . . . .162 D6
  Oldham OL8 . . . . .153 D5
  Standish WN6 . . . . .19 D3
Malvern St E OL11 . . . . .30 C7
Malvern St W OL11 . . . . .30 C7
Malvern Terr WN7 . . . . .75 F3
Malvern Way BB4 . . . . .1 A7
Manchester Utd FC
  (Old Trafford) M17 . . . . .96 F5
Manby Rd M18 . . . . .99 B4
Manby Sq M18 . . . . .99 B4
Mancentral Trad Est M3 . . . .158 D1
Manchester Airport
  M90 . . . . .130 A2
Manchester Airport Sta
  M90 . . . . .130 B7
Manchester Bsns Sch
  M15 . . . . .163 A8
Manchester Cath (CE)
  M3 .158 F2
Manchester Cath (RC)
  M3 .158 D2
Manchester Chambers
  OL1 . . . . .153 F7
Manchester City Coll
  (Wythenshawe Ctr)
  M23 . . . . .120 F8
Manchester City FC
  (Maine Rd) M14 . . . . .98 A2
Manchester Coll of Art
  & Tech M3 . . . . .158 E1
Manchester Coll of Arts
  & Tech (Openshaw Ctr)
  M11 . . . . .165 B7
Manchester Gram Sch
  M13 .98 C2
Manchester High Sch
  for Girls M14 . . . . .98 C1
Manchester Islamic
  High Sch for Girls M21 . . . .109 A8
Manchester Jewish Mus
  M8 .159 A4
Manchester Jun Girls Sch
  M7 . . . . .63 E1

Manchester Met Univ
Hollings Bldg M14 ....98 D2
Manchester Met Univ The
Manchester M1 ....163 B8
Manchester M1,M13,M15 ..163 A7
Manchester M20 ....110 B2
**Manchester Met Univ The
(John Dalton Bldg)**
M1,M15 ....162 F7
**Manchester Met Univ,
Elizabeth Gaskell Campus**
M13,M14 ....98 C4
Manchester Mus The
M13 ....163 B6
Manchester New Rd
Middleton M24,M9 ....64 F6
Partington M31 ....105 F3
**Manchester Northern
Hospl** M8 ....156 A7
Manchester Old Rd
Bury BL9 ....140 E1
Middleton M24 ....64 D7
Manchester Rd
Altrincham WA14 ....119 D7
Ashton-u-L M34, M43, OL7 ..84 E1
Blackrod BL6 ....38 E8
Bolton BL3 ....42 B4
Bury BL9 ....140 E1
Bury BL9 ....140 E2
Bury BL9,M45 ....44 F5
Carrington M31 ....106 B6
Denton M34 ....100 E3
Diggle HD7,OL3 ....52 A8
Droylsden M34 ....100 B8
Dukinfield SK14 ....101 C3
Handforth SK9 ....131 C2
Haslingden BB4 ....1 D7
Heywood OL10 ....46 D7
Hollinfare WA3 ....105 A2
Hollinfare WA3 ....105 B3
Ince-in-M WN2,WN1 ....56 A7
Kearsley BL4,M27 ....61 D4
Leigh M29,WN7 ....76 C4
Manchester M16,M21 ....97 B1
Manchester M21 ....109 A8
Mossley OL3,OL5,SK15 .....68 D3
Oldham OL8 ....6 D4
Pendlebury M27 ....80 B7
Ramsbottom BL0,BL9 ....11 E4
Reddish M34 ....100 B4
Rochdale OL11 ....30 C4
Shaw OL2 ....54 A5
Stockport SK4 ....169 E4
Swinton M27,M28 ....61 C2
Tintwistle SK13 ....103 E7
Tintwistle SK13 ....104 A7
Tyldesley M29 ....77 C8
Walkden M28 ....60 E2
Westhoughton BL5 ....40 B1
Manchester Rd E M38 ....60 B4
Manchester Rd N M34 ...100 D4
Manchester Rd S M34 ...100 D3
Manchester Rd W M38 ...59 E5
Manchester Road
Cty Prim Sch M43 ....83 E1
Manchester Royal Infmy
M13 ....163 C5
Manchester St
Heywood OL10 ....29 E1
Manchester M16 ....161 C5
Oldham OL8,OL9 ....153 D6
Manchester Yeshivah Coll
M8 ....63 F1
Manchet St OL11 ....30 B1
Mancroft Ave BL3 ....147 D4
Mancroft Terr BL3 ......147 D4
Mancroft Wlk 1 M1 .....163 B7
Mancunian Rd M34 ......113 A8
Mancunian Way
M1,M12,M15 ....163 B7
Mandalay Gdns SK6 .....125 D7
Mandarin Gn WA14 ......119 B8
Mandarin Wlk 3 M6 .....81 A3
Mandeville Cl WN3 ......54 D2
Mandeville St M19 .....111 B8
Mandeville Terr BL8 ....10 B2
Mandley Ave M40 ....65 D2
Mandley Cl BL3 ....43 A5
Mandley Park Ave M7 ..155 E7
Mandley Park Sch M7 ..155 D7
Mandon Cl M26 ....43 E5
Manesty Cl M24 ....46 C2
Manet Cl M7 ....81 B8
Mangle St M1 ....159 B1
Mango Pl M6 ....81 A2
Manifold Dr SK6 ....134 F6
Manifold St M6 ....81 B5
Manilla Wlk 1 M11 ....160 F1
Manipur St M11 ....99 E8
Manley Ave Golborne WA3 .73 F2
Kearsley M27 ....61 E4
Manley Cl Leigh WN7 ....75 D8
Ramsbottom BL9 ....11 C2
Manley Cres BL5 ....44 A1
Manley Gr Bramhall SK7 .132 E6
Mottram-in-L SK14 ......102 F3
Manley Park Inf Sch M16 ..97 F2
Manley Park Jun Sch M16 .97 C3
Manley Rd
Manchester M16,M21 ....97 D1
Oldham OL8 ....66 E4
Rochdale OL11 ....30 C4
Sale M33 ....107 F1
Manley St Ince-in-M WN3 .151 E6

Manley St continued
Manchester M7 ....155 D6
Manley Terr BL1 ....143 E4
Manley Units M16 ....97 E3
Manley Way SK14 ....103 A3
Manning Ave WN6 ....37 A2
Manningham Rd BL3 .....144 B5
Mannington Dr M9 ......156 C7
Mannion Ho WN1 ....151 D8
Mannock St OL8 ....153 D6
Manor OL3 ....68 F5
Manor Ave Golborne WA3 .90 C8
Little Lever BL3 ....43 C3
Manchester M16 ....97 D2
Sale M33 ....107 D4
Urmston M41 ....95 D1
Manor Cl Cheadle SK8 ..123 C1
Denton M34 ....101 B2
Garswood WN4 ....72 C3
Oldham OL9 ....152 C8
Uppermill OL4 ....68 E5
Wilmslow SK9 ....136 F8
Manor Ct Golborne WA3 ..90 C8
Sale M33 ....107 D4
5 Stockport SK1 ....112 A1
Stretford M32 ....96 B1
Manor Dr Manchester M21 .109 D4
Royton OL2 ....48 E3
Manor Farm Cl OL4 ......84 F5
Manor Farm Rise OL4 ....67 D7
Manor Gate Rd BL2 ......43 A8
Manor Gdns SK9 ....137 D7
Manor Gr Aspull WN2 ....38 B5
Leigh WN7 ....76 C3
Wigan WN5 ....54 B8
Manor Green Prim Sch
M34 ....113 A8
Manor Hill Rd SK6 .....125 F7
Manor House Cl WA11 ....71 B1
Manor La OL3 ....51 E8
Manor Lo Bramhall SK8 .123 C1
Pendlebury M27 ....80 D8
Manor Park Rd SK13 ....104 E1
Manor Pk M41 ....95 D1
Manor Pl WN3 ....151 F6
Manor Rd
Altrincham WA15 ....119 E4
Bramhall SK7,SK8 ....123 C1
Brinnington SK5 ....112 C4
Denton M34 ....101 B1
Droylsden M34 ....101 A2
Droylsden M43 ....83 F1
Dukinfield SK14 ....101 F5
Hindley WN2 ....56 F5
Horwich BL6 ....22 D4
Manchester M19 ....99 B2
Marple SK6 ....125 F7
Middleton M24 ....65 A6
Oldham OL4 ....67 C4
Romiley SK6 ....113 B5
Sale M33 ....108 B4
Salford M6 ....154 D4
Shaw OL2 ....149 A6
Shevington WN6 ....36 A6
Stretford M32 ....96 B2
Swinton M27 ....79 F6
Tyldesley M29 ....77 C6
Wilmslow SK9 ....136 E8
Manor St Bolton BL1 ....145 F7
Bury BL9 ....141 A2
Dukinfield BL4 ....100 F7
Farnworth BL4 ....60 C7
Glossop SK13 ....104 D1
Golborne WA3 ....74 B1
Kearsley BL4 ....61 B5
Manchester M12 ....163 C7
Middleton M24 ....47 A2
Mossley OL5 ....68 C2
Oldham OL2 ....49 A2
Ramsbottom BL0 ....138 B7
Wigan WN5 ....54 F6
Manor View SK6 ....113 B5
Walkden M28 ....100 F7
Manordale Wlk M40 .....156 C6
Manorfield Cl BL1 .....142 A1
Manorial Dr M38 ....59 E5
Mansart Cl WN4 ....73 D3
Manse Ave WN4 ....18 F5
Manse Gdns WA12 ....89 D4
Manse The OL5 ....86 C8
Mansell Way BL6 ....39 E8
Mansfield Ave
Denton M34 ....100 D5
Manchester M9 ....64 D4
Ramsbottom BL0 ....11 B2
Mansfield Cl Ashton-u-L OL7 .84 F1
Denton M34 ....100 D5
Mansfield Cres M34 ....100 D4
Mansfield Dr M9 ....64 E4
Mansfield Gr BL1 ....142 B1
Mansfield Grange OL11 ..30 C6
Mansfield Rd Hyde SK14 .167 F1
Manchester M9 ....64 D4
Mossley OL5 ....68 E1
7 Oldham OL8 ....67 B5
Rochdale OL11 ....29 E7
Urmston M41 ....95 B1
Mansfield St Ashton-u-L OL7 .84 F1
Golborne WA3 ....73 F1
Mansfield View OL5 ......68 E1
Mansford Dr M10,M40 ...157 F5
Manshaw Cres M34 ......100 A7
Manshaw Rd M11,M34 ...100 A7
Manson Ave M15 ....162 D7
Manstead Wlk M40 ......160 E2
Manston Dr SK8 ....123 A2
Manswood Dr M8 ....156 A7

Mantell Wlk M40 ....83 A5
Mantley La OL1,OL3 ......50 A7
Manton Ave Manchester M9 .65 B2
Reddish M34 ....100 A3
Manton Cl M7 ....155 F6
Manvers St SK5 ....169 E3
Manwaring St M35 ....83 E8
Maple Ave
Altrincham WA15 ....120 E5
Atherton M46 ....58 B4
Bolton BL1 ....142 B1
Bury BL9 ....141 B2
Cheadle SK8 ....122 F2
Denton M34 ....100 C3
Droylsden M34 ....86 B1
Eccles M30 ....79 A4
Golborne WA3 ....90 F7
Hindley WN2 ....56 F3
Horwich BL6 ....22 E1
Ince-in-M WN2 ....151 A6
Manchester M21 ....109 B8
Marple SK6 ....125 F4
Newton-le-W WA12 ....89 D2
Poynton SK12 ....133 F3
Stalybridge SK15 ....101 F8
Stretford M32 ....96 D1
Whitefield M45 ....62 F6
Maple Cl Billinge WN5 ...71 D5
Kearsley BL4 ....60 F5
Middleton M24 ....65 D6
Oldham OL9 ....48 B1
Sale M33 ....107 C4
Salford M6 ....154 F3
Shaw OL2 ....48 F8
Stockport SK2 ....124 B6
Maple Cres WN7 ....75 F7
Maple Ct SK4 ....168 C4
Maple Dr WN2 ....74 B7
Maple Gr Bury BL8 ....27 A5
Failsworth M35 ....83 E5
Failsworth M40 ....83 C5
Manchester M40 ....65 C3
Prestwich M25 ....63 A6
Ramsbottom BL0 ....11 D6
Walkden M28 ....78 D8
Wigan WN6 ....37 A3
Maple M23 ....120 C8
Maple Rd
Alderley Edge SK9 ....137 B3
Bramhall SK7 ....132 E6
Farnworth BL4 ....60 A8
Oldham OL9 ....48 B1
Partington M31 ....105 E3
Sale M23 ....108 C1
Swinton M27 ....79 E6
Maple Rd W M23 ....120 C8
Maple St Ashton-in-M WN4 .73 A6
Bolton BL2 ....25 C5
Bolton BL3 ....145 D5
Oldham OL8 ....66 C3
Rochdale OL11 ....139 D6
Walsden OL14 ....6 A7
Maple Wlk M23 ....120 C8
Maplecroft SK1 ....124 B8
Mapledon Rd M9 ....157 F8
Maplefield Dr M28 ......78 B7
Maplewood Cl OL16 ......31 A6
Maplewood Gdns BL1 ...143 F2
Maplewood Ho BL1 ......143 E1
Maplewood Rd SK9 .....137 E8
Mapley Ave M22 ....121 D8
Maplin Cl M13 ....163 C7
Maplin Dr SK2 ....125 A5
Mapperton Wlk 6 M16 ..97 E3
Marble St Manchester M2 .159 A1
Oldham OL1 ....67 B8
Marbury Ave M14 ....98 B1
Marbury Cl M41 ....94 D3
Marbury Dr WA14 ....107 E1
Marbury Gr WN6 ....36 E8
Marbury Rd Handforth SK9 .131 B1
Reddish SK4 ....111 D7
Marcer Rd M40 ....160 D2
March Ave SK4 ....168 B2
March Dr BL8 ....27 D5
March St OL16 ....31 A7
Marchbank WN2 ....38 A2
Marchbank Dr SK8 ......122 C6
Marchioness St 6 M18 ..99 F6
Marchmont Cl M13 ......164 D6
Marchwood Ave M21 ......97 D1
Marcliff Gr SK4 ....168 B2
Marcliffe Dr Reddish M19 .99 C1
Rochdale OL11 ....30 B6
Marcliffe Ind Est SK7 .124 E1
Marcroft Pl 8 OL11 .....31 A4
Marcus Garvey Ct M16 ...97 E2
Marcus Gr M14 ....98 C3
Mardale Ave BL3 ....142 B1
Mardale Ave
Manchester M20 ....110 C5
Royton OL16,OL2 ....48 C8
Swinton M27 ....61 C2
Urmston M41 ....95 C4
Mardale Cl Atherton M46 .58 C5
Bolton BL2 ....25 F1
Prestwich M45 ....63 C7
Stalybridge SK15 ....86 A3
Mardale Dr 1 Bolton BL2 ..25 F1
Gatley SK8 ....122 B6
Middleton M24 ....46 E1
Swinton M27 ....62 A1
Tyldesley M29 ....58 F1
Mardyke OL12 ....139 E8
Marfield Ave M22 ....121 B5
Marfield St M9 ....64 E1
Marford Cl M22 ....121 D6
Marford Cres M33 ......107 F2
Margaret Ashton Cl M9 .157 F7

Margaret Ave
Rochdale OL16 ....31 C7
Wigan WN6 ....36 C4
Margaret Ho 5 OL6 ......66 A2
Margaret Rd Droylsden M43 .83 E2
Dukinfield M34 ....101 A4
Margaret St
Ashton-u-L OL6 ....166 A2
Manchester M11 ....165 A8
3 Bury BL9 ....140 F1
Heywood OL10 ....29 B2
Hindley WN2 ....56 D6
Oldham OL8 ....66 B2
Reddish SK5 ....111 E7
Shaw OL2 ....149 B6
Wigan WN6 ....37 A1
Margaret Terr OL6 .....166 A2
Margate Ave M40 ....83 B5
Margate Rd SK5 ....111 F7
Margrove Cl M35 ....84 C7
Margrove Rd M6 ....80 C4
Margroy Cl OL12 ....15 A2
Marguerita Rd M40 .....83 D4
Marham Cl
Dukinfield SK14 ....101 D6
Manchester M21 ....109 E6
Maria St BL1 ....143 E2
Marie Cl M34 ....100 F2
Marie St M7 ....155 E7
Marigold St
Rochdale OL11 ....139 F5
Wigan WN5 ....54 D7
Marigold Terr M24 ......65 D7
Mariman Dr M8 ....64 A2
Marina Ave M34 ....101 A1
Marina Cl SK9 ....131 D5
Marina Cres M11 ....83 B3
Marina Dr Marple SK6 ..125 C7
Wigan WN5 ....54 D5
Marina Rd Bredbury SK6 .112 A3
Droylsden M43 ....84 B2
Manchester M19 ....99 A2
Marion St WN2 ....73 F8
Marion St Farnworth BL3 .42 C2
Oldham OL8 ....66 F3
Maritime Cl WA12 ....89 C5
Maritime Cl 5 M33 ....107 F4
Marjorie Cl M18 ....165 B6
Mark Ave M6 ....81 B4
Mark Jones Wlk M40 .....83 B5
Mark La OL2 ....49 D6
Mark St Bacup OL13 ......3 C8
Boothstown M28 ....77 F7
Droylsden M43 ....153 D7
Rochdale OL12 ....15 B1
Markenfield Dr OL2 ......48 F7
Market App WN4 ....73 B3
Market Ave OL6 ....166 B3
Market Par BL9 ....140 F2
Market Pl Adlington PR7 ..21 A7
Ashton-u-L OL6 ....166 B3
Bury BL9 ....140 E2
Edenfield BL0 ....1 D3
Farnworth BL4 ....60 D8
Heywood OL10 ....29 D2
Hyde SK14 ....167 D2
Middleton M24 ....47 A1
Mottram-in-L SK14 ......103 A3
Oldham OL1 ....153 E7
Ramsbottom BL0 ....138 C7
Standish WN6 ....19 E1
Stockport SK1 ....169 F2
Wigan WN1 ....150 C8
Market Pl The BL1 .....145 F8
Market Prec BL4 ....60 D8
Market Sq OL2 ....48 D4
Market St Adlington PR7 ..21 A6
Altrincham WA14 ....119 D4
Atherton M46 ....58 C3
Bolton BL1 ....145 F8
8 Bury BL9 ....26 F6
Bury BL9 ....140 F1
Bury BL9 ....44 F8
Denton M34 ....100 F3
Disley SK12 ....195 D6
Droylsden M43 ....84 B1
Edenfield BL0 ....1 D4
Farnworth BL4 ....42 D1
7 Glossop SK13 ....104 C1
Heywood OL10 ....29 C2
Hindley WN2 ....56 D5
Hollingworth SK14 ......103 D5
Hyde SK14 ....167 D2
Kearsley M26 ....61 B8
Leigh WN7 ....75 F5
Little Lever BL3 ....43 B3
Manchester M1 ....159 A1
Manchester M4 ....158 F2
Manchester M46 ....125 F6
4 Middleton M24 ....46 F1
Mossley OL5 ....68 C1
Mottram-in-L SK14 ......115 A8
Newton-le-W WA12 ....89 A3
5 Rawtenstall BB4 ....2 F8
Shaw OL2 ....149 C8
Stalybridge SK15 ....86 A2
Standish WN6 ....19 E1
Swinton M27 ....62 A1
Tyldesley M29 ....58 F1
Westhoughton BL5 ....57 E8
Whitworth OL12,OL13 ....14 C7
Wigan WN1 ....150 C8
Market Street Sta M1 ..159 A1
Market Way
Rochdale OL16 ....139 F8

Market Way continued
Salford M6 ....154 F3
Market Wlk M33 ....108 B4
Marketgate WN1 ....150 C8
Marketside WN7 ....150 C8
Markfield Ave M13 .....164 D5
Markham Cl M12 ....164 E8
Markham St SK14 ....101 D5
Markington St M14 ......98 A3
Marks St M26 ....44 B3
Markland Cl M46 ....153 A8
Markland Hill BL1 ......40 E8
Markland Hill Cl BL1 ...23 F1
Markland Hill
Com Prim Sch BL1 ....40 F8
Markland Hill La BL1 ....23 F1
Markland St 8 Bolton BL3 .145 F6
Hyde SK14 ....167 E1
Ramsbottom BL0 ....138 C6
Wigan WN1 ....151 E8
Marklands Rd Horwich BL6 .22 E5
Tyldesley M29 ....77 A4
Marks St M26 ....44 A3
Markwood OL3 ....50 F4
Marl Gr WN5 ....53 D4
Marland Ave Cheadle SK8 .122 F2
Oldham OL8 ....67 A1
Rochdale OL11 ....30 A6
Marland Cl OL11 ....30 B5
Marland Cres SK5 ......111 F8
Marland Fold OL11 ......30 B5
Marland Fold La OL8 .....67 A1
Marland Fold Sch OL8 ...67 A1
Marland Gn OL11 ....30 B4
Marland Hill
Com Prim Sch OL11 ....30 C5
Marland Hill Rd OL11 ...30 B4
Marland Old Rd OL11 ....30 B4
Marland St OL9 ....66 A3
Marlands Sq 15 M29 ....58 F1
Marlborough Ave
Alderley Edge SK9 ....137 B2
Bramhall SK8 ....123 C2
Ince-in-M WN3 ....55 F4
Manchester M16 ....97 C2
Marlborough Cl
Ashton-u-L OL7 ....100 E8
Denton M34 ....100 F3
Marple SK6 ....125 D7
Ramsbottom BL0 ....11 C3
Whitworth OL12 ....14 C7
Marlborough Dr
Failsworth M35 ....83 E6
Reddish SK4 ....169 D4
Marlborough Gdns 3 BL4 .59 F8
Marlborough Gr M43 .....84 C2
Marlborough Rd
Altrincham WA14 ....119 D2
Atherton M46 ....58 F4
Hyde SK14 ....113 E8
Irlam M44 ....94 B3
Manchester M7 ....155 F7
Manchester M7,M8 ....155 F6
Oldham OL12 ....48 E2
Sale M33 ....108 B4
Salford M30 ....80 A4
Stretford M32 ....96 C3
Urmston M41 ....94 F2
Marlborough Rd
Prim Sch M7 ....155 F6
Marlborough St
Ashton-u-L OL7 ....166 A1
Bolton BL1 ....145 E8
Heywood OL10 ....46 E8
Oldham OL4 ....67 A6
14 Rochdale OL12 ....14 C1
Marlbrook Dr BL5 ....57 E5
Marlbrook Wlk BL3 .....147 F4
Marlcroft Ave SK4 .....168 B2
Marld Cres BL1 ....23 F2
Marle Ave OL5 ....68 E1
Marle Croft M45 ....62 C6
Marle Rise OL5 ....68 E1
Marled Hey BL7 ....9 D5
Marler Rd SK14 ....167 E4
Marley Cl WA15 ....119 F7
Marley Dr M33 ....108 A6
Marley Rd
Manchester M19 ....111 B8
Poynton SK12 ....133 E2
Marleyer Cl M40 ....83 C7
Marleyer Rise SK6 .....125 A8
Marlfield Rd
Altrincham WA15 ....129 D7
Shaw OL2 ....48 E8
Marlhill Cl SK2 ....124 E5
Marlinford Dr M40 ......83 C5
Marlor Cl OL10 ....29 B2
Marlor St M34 ....100 E8
Marlow Brow SK13 ......104 A4
Marlow Cl Bolton BL2 ...25 F1
Cheadle SK8 ....122 F2
Urmston M41 ....95 A4
Marlow Dr
Altrincham WA14 ....118 F2
Handforth SK9 ....131 C5
Irlam M44 ....94 A3
Swinton M27 ....79 E6
Marlow Ho 9 M5 ....154 F1
Marlowe Cl WN3 ....150 A5
Marlowe Dr M20 ....110 B4
Marlowe Wlk 15 M34 ....113 A7
Marlowe Wlks SK6 ....96 F1
Marlton Wlk M9 ....64 E4
Marlwood Cl OL12 ....48 C2
Marlwood Rd BL1 ....23 F2
Marmion Cl WA3 ....74 E1
Marmion Dr M21 ....109 A8

Marne Ave Ashton-u-L OL6 . . .85 F5
Wythenshawe M22 . . . . .121 E5
Marne Cres SL11 . . . . .30 C7
Marnland Gr BL3 . . . . .40 E4
Marnock CI WN4 . . . . .74 F8
Maroon Rd M22 . . . . .130 F7
Marple Ave BL1 . . . . .25 A4
Marple CI Oldham OL8 . . . . .66 D2
Shevington Moor WN6 . . . . .19 B2
Marple Ct SK1 . . . . .124 A7
Marple Gr M32 . . . . .96 C3
Marple Hall Dr SK6 . . . . .125 C7
Marple Hall Sch SK6 . . . . .125 C7
Marple Old Rd SK2 . . . . .125 A6
Marple Rd
  Charlesworth SK13 . . . . .115 B5
  Stockport SK2,SK6 . . . . .124 E6
Marple Sta SK6 . . . . .125 B6
Marquis Ave BL9 . . . . .140 E4
Marquis Dr SK8 . . . . .131 D7
Marquis St M19 . . . . .99 D1
Marrick Ave SK8 . . . . .122 C5
Marriott's OL3 . . . . .55 A2
Marriott St
  Manchester M20 . . . . .110 B6
  Stockport SK1 . . . . .170 F8
Marriott's St M1 . . . . .159 A1
Marron PI M2 . . . . .162 F7
Marryat Ct M12 . . . . .164 F6
Mars Ave BL3 . . . . .146 C3
Mars St Edgworth BL7 . . . . .9 E6
  Oldham OL9 . . . . .152 C7
Marsden CI Ashton-u-L OL7 . . . .84 F5
  Newhey OL5 . . . . .68 B1
  Royton OL16 . . . . .48 C8
Marsden Dr WA15 . . . . .120 C6
Marsden Rd Bolton BL1 . . . . . . .145 F7
  Romiley SK6 . . . . .113 C3
Marsden St
  Boothstown M28 . . . . .77 F6
  Bury BL9 . . . . .140 F3
  Eccles M30 . . . . .79 C3
  Hadfield SK13 . . . . .104 A4
  Ince-in-M WN3 . . . . .55 A6
  [M] Manchester M2 . . . . .158 F1
  Middleton M24 . . . . .65 C7
  Walkden M28 . . . . .61 B2
  Westhoughton BL5 . . . . .57 E8
  Wigan WN1 . . . . .150 C8
  Wigan WN5 . . . . .54 F6
Marsett CI OL12 . . . . .14 A1
Marsett Wlk [9] WN3 . . . . .108 F2
Marsh Brook Fold BL5 . . . . .57 A7
Marsh CI SK3 . . . . .170 D6
Marsh Fold La BL1 . . . . .144 C8
Marsh Gn WN5 . . . . .36 D1
Marsh Green Prim Sch
  WN5 . . . . .54 D8
Marsh Hey CI M38 . . . . .59 F6
Marsh La Ashley WA16 . . . . . . .128 A4
  Farnworth BL4 . . . . .60 A8
  Little Lever BL3 . . . . .43 B4
  Wigan WN1 . . . . .150 C8
Marsh Rd Little Lever BL3 . . . . . .43 B4
  Walkden M38 . . . . .60 B4
Marsh Row WN2 . . . . .57 A4
Marsh St [2] Bolton BL1 . . . . . . .143 E2
  Horwich BL6 . . . . .22 A4
  Walkden M28 . . . . .60 F2
  Westhoughton BL5 . . . . .39 E1
  Wigan WN3 . . . . .55 A4
Marshall CI
  [6] Ashton-u-L OL6 . . . . .85 D2
  [J] Oldham OL1 . . . . .153 E8
Marshall Rd M19 . . . . .99 A1
Marshall St Denton M34 . . . . . .100 E4
  Leigh WN7 . . . . .75 E4
  Manchester M12 . . . . .163 C6
  Manchester M4 . . . . .159 B2
  Rochdale OL16 . . . . .31 C7
Marshall Stevens Way
  M17 . . . . .96 B5
Marsham CI
  [7] Manchester M13 . . . . .98 E4
  Oldham OL4 . . . . .68 B5
Marsham Dr SK6 . . . . .126 A5
Marsham Rd
  Hazel Grove SK7 . . . . .124 C1
  Westhoughton BL5 . . . . .57 F6
Marshbank [4] BL5 . . . . .39 E1
Marshbrook CI WN2 . . . . .57 A6
Marshbrook Rd [4] M41 . . . . . . .95 C3
Marshdale Rd BL1 . . . . .40 E8
Marshfield Rd WA15 . . . . .120 E6
Marshfield Wlk [8] M13 . . . . . . .163 C6
Marsland Ave WA15 . . . . .120 B6
Marsland CI M34 . . . . .63 C8
Marsland Green La M29 . . . . . . .76 E3
Marsland Rd
  Altrincham WA15 . . . . .120 B6
  Sale M33 . . . . .125 D7
  Sale M33 . . . . .108 B3
Marsland St
  Hazel Grove SK7 . . . . .124 D2
  Stockport SK1 . . . . .169 F2
Marsland St N M7,M8 . . . . .155 F7
Marsland St S M7,M8 . . . . .155 F7
Marsland Terr SK1 . . . . .124 B8
Marslands OL3 . . . . .51 B3
Marston CI Failsworth M35 . . . . .84 C6
  Horwich BL6 . . . . .39 F8
  Whitefield M45 . . . . .63 C8
Marston Dr M44 . . . . .94 B1
Marston Ho [6] M5 . . . . .154 F1
Marston Rd
  Manchester M7 . . . . .155 C8
  Stretford M32 . . . . .96 F2
Marston St M40 . . . . .157 D5

Marston Way SK14 . . . . .102 F3
Marsworth Dr M4 . . . . .159 C2
Martens Rd M44 . . . . .105 E5
Martha St [8] Bolton BL3 . . . . . .147 D4
  Oldham OL1 . . . . .153 D8
Martha's Terr OL16 . . . . .15 C3
Marthall Dr M33 . . . . .108 E1
Marthall Way [8] SK9 . . . . .131 E5
Martham Dr SK2 . . . . .125 A6
Martin Ave Farnworth BL4 . . . . . .59 F7
  Little Lever BL3 . . . . .43 C3
  Newton-le-W WA12 . . . . .89 C5
  [8] Oldham OL4 . . . . .67 C6
Martin Ct Denton M34 . . . . .100 F5
  Marple SK2 . . . . .124 F5
Martin Dr M44 . . . . .94 A4
Martin Gr BL4 . . . . .60 F7
Martin Ho M14 . . . . .98 D3
Martin La OL12 . . . . .14 B1
Martin Rd M27 . . . . .62 B2
Martin St [8] Atherton M46 . . . . .58 D3
  Bury BL9 . . . . .28 D3
  Dukinfield M34 . . . . .100 F7
  Edgworth BL7 . . . . .9 D4
  Hyde SK14 . . . . .167 E2
  Salford M5 . . . . .154 E2
Martindale CI OL2 . . . . .48 E5
Martindale Cres
  Manchester M12 . . . . .164 E5
  Middleton M24 . . . . .46 D3
  Wigan WN5 . . . . .54 F6
Martindale Gdns BL1 . . . . .143 E2
Martindale Rd WA11 . . . . .71 C2
Martingale CI M26 . . . . .44 A5
Martingale Way M43 . . . . .84 D2
Martins Ct WN2 . . . . .57 A6
Martins Field OL12 . . . . .13 F1
Martinsclough BL6 . . . . .40 C6
Martinscroft Rd M23 . . . . .121 B5
Martland Ave
  Golborne WA3 . . . . .90 E7
  Shevington WN6 . . . . .35 F5
Martland Cres WN6 . . . . .36 E3
Martland Mill La WN5 . . . . .36 D2
Martlesham Wlk [4] M44 . . . . . .159 A2
Martlet Ave Disley SK12 . . . . . .135 C6
  Rochdale OL11 . . . . .29 F7
Martlet CI M14 . . . . .98 B1
Martlew Dr M29 . . . . .58 F4
Martock Ave M22 . . . . .121 B3
Marton Ave Bolton BL2 . . . . . . .148 C8
  Manchester M20 . . . . .110 C2
Marton Dr WA3 . . . . .91 E4
Marton Dr M46 . . . . .58 E4
Marton Gn SK2 . . . . .124 E6
Marton Gr SK4 . . . . .111 E6
Marton Grange M25 . . . . .63 E3
Marton PI M33 . . . . .108 A4
Marton St WN1 . . . . .37 C1
Marton Way [4] SK9 . . . . .131 E5
Marus Ave WN3 . . . . .54 C2
Marus Bridge Prim Sch
  WN3 . . . . .54 E2
Marvic Ct M13 . . . . .98 E3
Marwick CI WN6 . . . . .19 D2
Marwood CI
  Altrincham WA14 . . . . .119 B6
  Kearsley M26 . . . . .61 A8
Marwood Dr M23 . . . . .120 F3
Mary France St M15 . . . . .162 E6
Mary Hulton Ct BL5 . . . . .58 A8
Mary St Cheadle SK8 . . . . .122 D6
  Droylsden M43 . . . . .84 B1
  Dukinfield M34 . . . . .101 A4
  Dukinfield SK16 . . . . .166 B1
  Farnworth BL4 . . . . .60 D7
  Heywood OL10 . . . . .29 C2
  Hyde SK14 . . . . .167 D3
  Littleborough OL16 . . . . .15 D4
  Manchester M3 . . . . .158 F3
  Ramsbottom BL0 . . . . .138 B5
  Stockport SK1 . . . . .112 A2
  Tyldesley M29 . . . . .77 A8
Mary St E BL6 . . . . .22 B4
Mary St W BL6 . . . . .22 A4
Mayfield CI WA3 . . . . .90 A4
Maryland Ave BL2 . . . . .42 D7
Marylebone Ct WN1 . . . . .37 D3
Marylebone PI WN1 . . . . .37 D3
Marylon Dr M22 . . . . .121 E8
Masboro St M8 . . . . .155 F7
Masbury CI BL1 . . . . .24 F6
Masefield Ave Leigh WN7 . . . . . .75 D7
  Prestwich M25 . . . . .62 F3
  Radcliffe M26 . . . . .43 E4
  Wigan WN5 . . . . .54 A6
Masefield CI SK16 . . . . .102 B7
Masefield Com Prim Sch
  BL3 . . . . .43 B4
Masefield Cres M43 . . . . .84 A1
Masefield Dr Farnworth BL4 . . . .60 B7
  [4] Wigan WN3 . . . . .54 F5
Masefield Gr SK5 . . . . .99 E1
Masefield Rd
  Droylsden M43 . . . . .84 A1
  Little Lever BL3 . . . . .43 B4
  Oldham OL1 . . . . .49 B2
Mason CI WN4 . . . . .73 D4
Mason Gdns BL3 . . . . .145 E6
Mason La M46 . . . . .58 E2
Mason Row BL7 . . . . .8 A4
Mason St [5] Abram WN2 . . . . . .74 B8
  Bolton BL7 . . . . .8 B3
  Bury BL9 . . . . .141 A2
  Heywood OL10 . . . . .29 B2
  Horwich BL6 . . . . .22 B3
  Manchester M3 . . . . .158 D1

Mason St continued
  Manchester M4 . . . . .159 B2
  Rochdale OL16 . . . . .139 F7
Mason's Row [2] BL6 . . . . .21 C3
Mason St Ind Est WN3 . . . . .150 B7
Masons Gr SK13 . . . . .104 A6
Massey Ave Ashton-u-L OL6 . . . .85 C6
  Failsworth M35 . . . . .84 B8
Massey Croft OL12 . . . . .14 C8
Massey Rd
  Altrincham WA15 . . . . .119 E4
  Sale M33 . . . . .108 E4
Massey St
  [4] Alderley Edge SK9 . . . . .137 A1
  Bury BL9 . . . . .141 B3
  Failsworth M35 . . . . .81 C1
  Stockport SK1 . . . . .169 F1
Massey Wlk M22 . . . . .121 F1
Massie St SK8 . . . . .122 D6
Matchmoor La BL6 . . . . .23 A4
Matham Wlk M15 . . . . .163 A7
Mather Ave Eccles M30 . . . . .79 E2
  Golborne WA3 . . . . .90 E6
  Manchester M25 . . . . .63 C1
  Whitefield M45 . . . . .44 F1
Mather Ct WN5 . . . . .44 F1
Mather Fold Rd M28 . . . . .60 B1
Mather La WN7 . . . . .76 A4
Mather Rd Bury BL9 . . . . .27 F7
  Eccles M30 . . . . .79 E2
Mather St [2] Atherton M46 . . . .58 D3
  Bolton BL3 . . . . .145 E6
  Failsworth M35 . . . . .83 E7
  Kearsley M26 . . . . .61 B8
  Radcliffe M26 . . . . .44 A3
Mather Street Prim Sch
  M35 . . . . .83 D7
Mather Way [4] M6 . . . . .81 A3
Matheson Dr WN5 . . . . .54 E8
Matisse Way M7 . . . . .81 B4
Matley Ct SK14 . . . . .102 B5
Matley Gn SK5 . . . . .112 C6
Matley La SK14,SK15 . . . . .102 D6
Matley Park La WA15 . . . . .120 B5
Matlock Ave Ashton-u-L OL6 . . .85 C6
  Manchester M20 . . . . .109 F6
  Manchester M7 . . . . .81 A7
  Urmston M41 . . . . .107 B8
Matlock Bank [18] SK3 . . . . .171 E1
Matlock CI Atherton M46 . . . . . . .58 D3
  Farnworth BL4 . . . . .42 E1
  Sale M33 . . . . .108 C4
Matlock Dr SK7 . . . . .133 E8
Matlock Gdns [18] SK3 . . . . .171 E1
Matlock La [18] SK13 . . . . .171 E1
Matlock Mews M14 . . . . .119 E5
Matlock PI [14] SK13 . . . . .171 E1
Matlock Rd Gatley SK8 . . . . . . .131 C7
  Reddish SK5 . . . . .100 A1
Matlock St M30 . . . . .95 C8
Matson Wlk [3] M22 . . . . .121 A2
Matt Busby CI M27 . . . . .80 B7
Matterdale Terr SK15 . . . . .86 A4
Matthew CI SK13 . . . . .103 F7
Matthew Moss High Sch
  OL11 . . . . .30 B4
Matthew Moss La OL11 . . . . .30 B4
Matthew's St M12 . . . . .164 F7
Matthews Ave BL4 . . . . .60 F7
Matthews La M12,M19 . . . . .99 B2
Matthias Ct M3 . . . . .158 D3
Mattison St M11 . . . . .99 E7
Maud St Bolton BL2 . . . . .25 C5
  Rochdale OL12 . . . . .15 A2
Maudsley St BL9 . . . . .140 E1
Mauldeth CI SK4 . . . . .168 A3
Mauldeth Rd
  Manchester M4,M19,M20 . . . . .110 D7
  Manchester M19,SK4 . . . . .110 F6
  Manchester M20,M21 . . . . .109 D8
Mauldeth Road Prim Sch
  M20 . . . . .110 C7
Mauldeth Road Sta M20 . . . . . .110 E7
Maunby Gdns M38 . . . . .60 C3
Maureen Ave M8 . . . . .156 A8
Maureen St OL12 . . . . .15 A2
Maurice CI SK16 . . . . .101 E8
Maurice Dr M6 . . . . .154 F4
Maurice Pariser Wlk M8 . . . . . .155 F7
Maurice St M6 . . . . .154 F4
Maveen Gr SK2 . . . . .124 A4
Mavis Gr OL16 . . . . .32 A6
Mavis St OL11 . . . . .30 C1
Mawdsley Dr M8 . . . . .156 C8
Mawdsley St BL1 . . . . .145 F7
Max Woosnam Wlk [3]
  M14 . . . . .98 A3
Maxwell Ave SK2 . . . . .124 C5
Maxwell St Bolton BL1 . . . . .143 E4
  Bury BL9 . . . . .141 B3
May Ave Abram Brow WN2 . . . . .74 C7
  Bramhall SK8 . . . . .132 B6
  Leigh WN7 . . . . .75 E7
  Stockport SK4 . . . . .168 C2
May Ct [8] M16 . . . . .97 D3
May Dr M19 . . . . .110 F6
May Gr M19 . . . . .111 B8
May PI [8] OL11 . . . . .31 A6
May Rd Bramhall SK8 . . . . .132 B6
  Manchester M16 . . . . .97 D3
  Pendlebury M27 . . . . .80 B6
May St Bolton BL2 . . . . .148 A7
  Eccles M30 . . . . .79 C4

May St continued
  Edgworth BL7 . . . . .9 E6
  Failsworth M40 . . . . .83 C5
  Golborne WA3 . . . . .74 B2
  Heywood OL10 . . . . .29 B2
  Leigh WN7 . . . . .75 C5
  Oldham OL8 . . . . .66 C4
  Radcliffe M26 . . . . .44 A3
May Tree Dr WN1 . . . . .37 B4
May Wlk [2] M31 . . . . .105 E3
Mayall St OL5 . . . . .68 C1
Mayall St E [9] OL4 . . . . .67 C7
Mayan Ave M3 . . . . .158 D2
Maybank St BL3 . . . . .145 D5
Mayberth Ave M8 . . . . .64 A2
Maybreck CI BL3 . . . . .144 C5
Maybrook Wlk [11] M9 . . . . . . .157 D8
Mayburn CI M22 . . . . .65 C5
Maybury St M18 . . . . .99 F6
Maycroft SK5 . . . . .112 B6
Maycroft Ave M20 . . . . .110 C5
Maycroft Inf Sch SK5 . . . . .112 C6
Maycroft Prim Sch SK5 . . . . . . .112 C6
Mayer St [2] SK2 . . . . .124 C7
Mayes Gdns M4 . . . . .160 D1
Mayes St M4 . . . . .159 A2
Mayfair Horwich BL6 . . . . .22 D3
  Manchester M7 . . . . .63 C1
Mayfair Ave Radcliffe M26 . . . . .43 D4
  Salford M6 . . . . .80 B3
  Urmston M41 . . . . .95 B2
  Whitefield M45 . . . . .62 F7
Mayfair CI Haslingden BB4 . . . . . .1 A7
  Poynton SK12 . . . . .133 E4
  Stalybridge SK16 . . . . .101 F8
  Stockport SK2 . . . . .124 A4
Mayfair Cotts WN1 . . . . .20 C1
Mayfair Cres M35 . . . . .84 B8
Mayfair Ct
  Altrincham WA15 . . . . .120 B7
  Manchester M20 . . . . .110 A5
Mayfair Dr Atherton M46 . . . . . . .58 E4
  Irlam M44 . . . . .94 A2
  Oldham OL2 . . . . .48 D2
  Pennington Green WN2 . . . . .38 D2
  Sale M33 . . . . .108 B1
  Wigan WN3 . . . . .54 F2
Mayfair Gdns OL11 . . . . .139 D5
Mayfair Gr M45 . . . . .62 F7
Mayfair Rd M22 . . . . .121 E4
Mayfield Bolton BL2 . . . . .42 B3
  [7] Denton M34 . . . . .113 A7
  Farnworth BL4 . . . . .60 C7
  Reddish SK5 . . . . .111 F5
  Sale M33 . . . . .108 E4
  Stretford M32 . . . . .96 B1
  Walkden M28 . . . . .79 C6
Mayfield CI
  Altrincham WA15 . . . . .120 B6
  Ramsbottom BL0 . . . . .11 A2
Mayfield Com Prim Sch
  SK10 . . . . .134 B1
Mayfield Ct Wigan WN6 . . . . .36 B1
  Wigan WN5 . . . . .54 B8
Mayfield Dr WA3,WN7 . . . . .91 C8
Mayfield Gr Reddish M18 . . . . . . .99 F3
  Reddish SK5 . . . . .111 F5
  Wilmslow SK9 . . . . .136 E5
Mayfield Ind Est M44 . . . . .94 C3
Mayfield Mans M16 . . . . .97 E3
Mayfield Rd
  Altrincham WA15 . . . . .120 B6
  Bramhall SK7 . . . . .132 E4
  Manchester M16 . . . . .97 E3
  Manchester M25 . . . . .63 C1
  Orrell WN8 . . . . .53 B7
  Ramsbottom BL0 . . . . .11 A2
  Romiley SK6 . . . . .114 B1
  Wigan WN5 . . . . .54 B8
Mayfield St
  Ashton-in-M WN4 . . . . .73 A3
  Atherton M46 . . . . .58 C3
  Denton M34 . . . . .100 E5
  Rochdale OL16 . . . . .15 B1
Mayfield Terr OL16 . . . . .15 B1
Mayflower Ave M5 . . . . .161 B8
Mayflower Cotts WN1 . . . . .37 C8
Mayford Rd M19 . . . . .99 A1
Maygate OL9 . . . . .153 D8
Mayhill Dr Salford M6 . . . . .80 A4
  Worsley M28 . . . . .79 A8
Mayhurst Ave M21 . . . . .109 E8
Maylo St M12 . . . . .164 D8
Mayor St Bolton BL1 . . . . .145 D6
  Bury BL8 . . . . .27 C3
  Oldham OL9 . . . . .152 C7
Mayor's Rd WA15 . . . . .119 E4
Mayorlowe Ave SK5 . . . . .112 C5
Maypole Ind Est WN2 . . . . .74 C7
Maypool Dr SK5 . . . . .111 F6
Maysmith Mews M7 . . . . .155 D6
Mayton St M11 . . . . .165 A8
Mayville Dr M20 . . . . .110 B5
Maywood Ave M20 . . . . .122 B8
Maze St BL3 . . . . .148 A5
Mc Naught St [20] OL16 . . . . . . .31 B6
McCall Wlk M11 . . . . .83 B2
McConnell Rd M40 . . . . .83 B7
McCormack Dr WN1 . . . . .151 D8
McCready Dr M5 . . . . .161 B8
McDonna St BL1 . . . . .142 C3
McDonough CI OL8 . . . . .67 A3

May St continued
  Edgworth BL7 . . . . .9 E6
McEvoy St [8] BL1 . . . . .143 F2
McKean St BL3 . . . . .42 A4
Mckie CI OL8 . . . . .67 A3
McLaren Ct M21 . . . . .97 A1
McLean Dr M44 . . . . .94 B4
Meachin Ave M21 . . . . .109 C5
Mead The Manchester M21 . . . .109 B7
  Salford M5 . . . . .154 D2
Mead Way M34 . . . . .112 F8
Meade CI M41 . . . . .95 C2
Meade Gr M13 . . . . .98 F3
Meade Hill Rd M8,M25 . . . . .63 E3
Meade Hill Sch M8 . . . . .63 F4
Meade Manor M21 . . . . .109 B7
Meade The Bolton BL3 . . . . .147 E2
  Wilmslow SK9 . . . . .137 C8
Meadfoot Ave M25 . . . . .63 C3
Meadfoot Rd M18 . . . . .99 D6
Meadland Gr BL1 . . . . .143 F4
Meadow Ave
  Altrincham WA15 . . . . .120 B3
  Swinton M27 . . . . .62 B1
Meadow Bank
  Altrincham WA15 . . . . .120 A7
  Bredbury SK6 . . . . .112 F3
  Glossop SK13 . . . . .115 F7
  Hollingworth SK14 . . . . .103 D6
  Manchester M21 . . . . .109 A7
  Stockport SK4 . . . . .168 B3
Meadow Bank CI OL4 . . . . .67 E4
Meadow Bank Ct M32 . . . . .96 B3
Meadow Brow SK9 . . . . .137 A2
Meadow CI
  Altrincham WA15 . . . . .120 B3
  Denton M34 . . . . .113 A7
  Heywood OL10 . . . . .29 C2
  High Lane SK6 . . . . .134 F8
  Leigh WN7 . . . . .75 E2
  Little Lever BL3 . . . . .43 A2
  Romiley SK6 . . . . .113 A5
  Stretford M32 . . . . .96 E1
  Uppermill SL3 . . . . .68 E3
  Wilmslow SK9 . . . . .136 E4
Meadow Cotts OL12 . . . . .4 D3
Meadow Croft
  Hazel Grove SK7 . . . . .124 E4
  Whitefield M45 . . . . .62 C6
Meadow Ct
  [2] Altrincham WA15 . . . . .120 D6
  Salford M6 . . . . .80 B3
  Stretford M21 . . . . .108 F8
  [7] Wigan WN6 . . . . .37 A1
Meadow Fold OL3 . . . . .69 C8
Meadow Head Ave OL12 . . . . . . .14 D6
Meadow Ind Est SK1 . . . . .169 F3
Meadow La Bolton BL2 . . . . .43 A7
  Denton M34 . . . . .113 A7
  Disley SK12 . . . . .135 D6
  Dukinfield SK16 . . . . .101 D8
  Oldham OL8 . . . . .66 E2
  Worsley M28 . . . . .78 F5
Meadow Pit La WN2 . . . . .37 F8
Meadow Pk BL0 . . . . .1 C4
Meadow Rd
  Manchester M24 . . . . .64 C6
  Manchester M7 . . . . .81 C3
  Urmston M41 . . . . .95 D1
Meadow Rise
  Glossop SK13 . . . . .115 F7
  Shaw OL2 . . . . .32 A1
Meadow St Adlington PR7 . . . . . .21 A6
  Hyde SK14 . . . . .167 E1
  Stockport SK2 . . . . .124 C5
Meadow The BL6 . . . . .40 C7
Meadow View OL12 . . . . .14 A1
Meadow Way
  Altrincham WA15 . . . . .120 B3
  Blackrod BL6 . . . . .21 E1
  Bury BL8 . . . . .26 E6
  Coppull PR7 . . . . .19 D8
  Edgworth BL7 . . . . .7 B8
  Manchester M40 . . . . .65 A1
  Wilmslow SK9 . . . . .136 E4
Meadow Wlk
  Bredbury SK6 . . . . .112 F3
  Farnworth BL4 . . . . .60 A8
  Littleborough OL15 . . . . .15 F5
Meadowbank [2] BL3 . . . . .145 D5
Meadowbank Ave M46 . . . . .58 E5
Meadowbank CI M35 . . . . .84 A6
Meadow Bank Cty Prim Sch
  M46 . . . . .58 D4
Meadowbank Gdns WA3 . . . . . . .92 C7
Meadowbank Rd BL3 . . . . .146 B2
Meadowbrook CI
  Bolton BL6 . . . . .40 B3
  Bolton BL7 . . . . .141 C4
Meadowbrook Nook M30 . . . . . . .79 B4
Meadowcroft
  Ashton-in-M WN4 . . . . .72 F6
  Mottram-in-L SK14 . . . . .103 A4
  Radcliffe M26 . . . . .43 F5
  Westhoughton BL5 . . . . .57 F7
Meadowcroft La
  [1] Oldham OL1 . . . . .49 B1
  Rochdale OL11 . . . . .31 B3
Meadowfield Bolton BL6 . . . . .40 C7
  Orrell WN8 . . . . .53 A7
  Rochdale OL16 . . . . .31 B3
Meadowfield CI SK13 . . . . .171 F3
Meadowfield Ct SK14 . . . . .167 D4
Meadowfield Dr M28 . . . . .78 B6
Meadowgate Urmston M41 . . . . .95 D1
  Worsley M28 . . . . .78 F8
Meadowgate Rd M6 . . . . .80 C3

Meadows OL3 ....69 B7
Meadows Cl 4 WN2 ....56 D5
Meadows La BL2 ....25 F3
Meadows Rd Cheadle SK8 .131 F8
 Gatley SK8 ....122 B1
 Reddish SK4 ....111 C6
 Sale M33 ....108 C6
Meadows St WN6 ....37 A1
Meadows The Irlam M44 ...105 E6
 Middleton M24 ....65 B6
 Oldham OL4 ....68 A6
 Prestwich M25 ....63 C3
 Romiley SK6 ....113 B4
 Whitworth OL12 ....4 C1
Meadowside
 Bramhall SK7 ....123 C2
 Newhey OL16 ....32 C3
Meadowside Ave
 Ashton-in-M WN4 ....73 A8
 Bolton BL2 ....148 C2
 Irlam M44 ....94 A2
 Walkden M28 ....60 E4
 Wythenshawe M22 ....121 E4
Meadowside Cl M26 ....44 A5
Meadowside Gr M28 ....60 E3
Meadowside Rd WN2 ....57 A4
Meadowvale Dr WN5 ....54 C6
Meads Gr Farnworth BL4 ...59 E8
 Tyldesley M29 ....77 C6
Meads The OL9 ....152 A6
Meadscroft Dr SK9 ....136 F1
Meadway Bramhall SK7 ....132 E5
 Bury BL9 ....44 F6
 Dukinfield SK16 ....101 E7
 Failsworth OL9 ....65 E2
 Golborne WA3 ....90 D8
 High Lane SK6 ....134 F8
 Ince-in-M WN2 ....151 F7
 Poynton SK12 ....133 B4
 Ramsbottom BL0 ....1 C1
 Rochdale OL11 ....30 C4
 Sale M33 ....107 E2
 Stalybridge SK15 ....102 E6
 Tyldesley M29 ....59 D1
Meadway Cl Horwich BL6 ...22 D3
 Sale M33 ....107 E2
Meadway Rd SK8 ....123 B3
Meal St M4 ....169 E3
Mealhouse Brow SK1 .....169 F1
Mealhouse Ct M46 ....58 C3
Mealhouse La
 Atherton M46 ....58 C3
 Bolton BL1 ....145 F7
Meanley Rd M29,WN7 ......76 F7
Meanley St M12 ....59 A1
Meanwood Brow M9 OL12 ..14 C1
Meanwood Fold OL12 .....139 D8
Meanwood Prim Sch
 OL12 ....14 C1
Measham Mews M1 ....163 A7
Meburn Wlk M14 ....98 B4
Mechinah L'Yeshivah Sch
 M7 ....63 E1
Medina Cl SK15 ....106 D1
Medina Cl SK8 ....123 B4
Mediar Way WN4 ....72 F5
Medley St OL12 ....14 F1
Medlock Cl BL4 ....60 B8
Medlock City Inf Sch M13 ..163 C7
Medlock City Prim Sch
 M13 ....163 C7
Medlock Dr OL6 ....85 A8
Medlock Ho 1 M15 ....162 D7
Medlock Rd M35 ....84 B5
Medlock Sports Ctr M43 ...84 B2
Medlock St Droylsden M43 ..84 B2
 Manchester M15 ....162 F7
Medlock Vale M35 ....84 E6
Medlock Valley High Sch
 M11 ....160 E1
Medlock Valley Visitor Ctr
 OL6 ....67 C2
Medlock Way Oldham OL4 ..67 E6
 Platt Bridge WN2 ....56 A2
 Whitefield M45 ....63 C8
Medowcroft Wlk M8 ....64 B2
Medway Cl
 Ashton-in-M WN4 ....72 F6
 Golborne WN7 ....91 C8
 Handforth SK9 ....131 D2
 Oldham OL8 ....66 C3
 Salford M5 ....154 D3
Medway Cres WA14 ....119 C6
Medway Dr Horwich BL6 ....22 D3
 Kearsley BL4 ....61 B5
Medway Pl WN5 ....54 D7
Medway Rd Culcheth WA3 ..92 A2
 Oldham OL8 ....66 C3
 Shaw OL2 ....149 B8
 Walkden M28 ....78 B8
Medway Wlk
 Manchester M40 ....160 D3
 Wigan WN5 ....54 D7
Mee's Sq M30 ....95 D8
Meech St M11 ....165 C8
Meek St OL1,OL2 ....49 A2
Meerbrook Rd SK3 ....123 A8
Megfield BL5 ....57 E6
Melandra Castle Rd
 SK13 ....171 D2
Melandra Cres SK14 ......102 E2
Melandra Rd SK13 ....171 E3
Melanie Cl SK13 ....116 A8

Melanie Dr SK5 ....111 F8
Melba St M11 ....99 E8
Melbecks Wlk 5 M23 ....108 F2
Melbourne Ave
 Oldham OL9 ....152 B7
 Stretford M32 ....96 D2
 Wythenshawe M90 ....130 A8
Melbourne Cl Horwich BL6 ..22 C3
 Rochdale OL11 ....31 B2
Melbourne Gr BL6 ....22 C3
Melbourne Mews M7 .....155 E5
Melbourne Rd Bolton BL3 ..148 B5
 Bramhall SK7 ....132 F5
 Rochdale OL11 ....31 A2
Melbourne St Denton M34 ..100 E2
 Manchester M15 ....162 E7
 Manchester M9 ....155 E5
 Manchester M9 ....157 E8
 Oldham OL9 ....152 B7
 Pendlebury M27 ....80 B8
 Reddish SK5 ....111 F8
 Stalybridge SK15 ....86 A1
Melbourne St N OL6 ....166 C4
Melbourne St S OL6 ......166 C3
Melbourne Wlk M5 ....161 B8
Melbury Ave M20 ....110 D4
Melbury Dr BL6 ....39 F8
Melbury Rd SK8 ....132 B6
Meldon Rd M13 ....98 E2
Meldreth Dr M12 ....98 F4
Meldrum St Oldham OL8 ...66 F4
Meldrum Wlk OL8 ....67 A4
Melford Ave M40 ....65 E1
Melford Dr
 Ashton-in-M WN4 ....73 A4
 Orrell WN5 ....53 D3
Melford Gr OL4 ....67 D6
Melford Rd SK7 ....124 F1
Melfort Ave M32 ....96 E1
Meliden Cres Bolton BL1 ...142 B1
 Wythenshawe M22 ....121 C3
Melksham Cl 4 M5,M6 ....81 B2
Mellalieu St Middleton M24 ..46 F1
 Oldham OL2 ....48 E2
Melland Ave M21 ....109 C5
Melland Rd M18 ....99 C3
Melland Sch M18 ....99 D2
Meller Rd M13 ....98 F2
Melling Ave
 Chadderton OL9 ....47 E1
 Reddish SK4 ....111 E6
Melling Cl WN7 ....75 F1
Melling Rd OL4 ....67 C6
Melling St Manchester M12 ..99 A4
 Wigan WN5 ....54 E5
Melling Way WN5 ....54 D1
Mellings Ave WN5 ....53 E1
Mellington Ave M20 ....122 C8
Mellodew Dr OL1 ....49 D4
Mellor Brook Dr WN2 ....56 A2
Mellor Brow OL10 ....29 C2
Mellor Cl Ashton-u-L OL6 ...85 E2
 Standish WN6 ....19 E2
Mellor Ct SK2 ....124 E6
Mellor Dr Bury BL9 ....44 D7
 Walkden M28 ....60 C1
Mellor Gr BL1 ....142 B1
Mellor Prim Sch SK6 .....126 C6
Mellor Rd Ashton-u-L OL6 ...85 E3
 Ashton-u-L OL6 ....85 F4
 Cheadle SK8 ....123 B1
 New Mills SK22 ....127 C3
Mellor St Droylsden M43 ...83 F1
 Eccles M30 ....79 D1
 Failsworth M35 ....83 D6
 Manchester M12 ....163 C8
 Manchester M40 ....160 D3
 Oldham OL4 ....67 E6
 Prestwich M25 ....62 F4
 2 Radcliffe M26 ....44 B2
 Rochdale OL11,OL12 .....139 D7
 Royton OL2 ....48 D5
 Stretford M32 ....96 E4
Mellor Way OL9 ....66 B8
Mellors Rd M17 ....96 B7
Mellowstone Dr M21 ......109 F8
Melloy Pl M8 ....159 A4
Melmerby Cl WN4 ....72 F3
Melmerby Ct M5 ....154 F1
Melon Pl M6 ....81 B2
Melrose 10 OL12 ....139 E8
Melrose Ave Bolton BL1 ...142 A1
 Bury BL8 ....27 C3
 Cheadle SK3 ....122 E7
 Eccles M30 ....79 B4
 Heywood OL10 ....29 C3
 Leigh WN7 ....57 D1
 Littleborough OL15 ....16 A7
 Manchester M20 ....110 D4
 Sale M33 ....108 B4
Melrose Cl 4 M45 ....104 F2
Melrose Cres
 Altrincham WA15 ....120 B1
 Garswood WN4 ....72 C3
 High Lane SK12 ....134 D5
 Stockport SK3 ....123 D4
Melrose Ct
 15 Handforth SK9 ....131 E1
 Oldham OL9 ....66 A4
Melrose Dr WN3 ....54 D2
Melrose Gdns M26 ....43 E5
Melrose Rd Little Lever BL3 ...42 F3
 Radcliffe M26 ....43 E5
Melrose St Failsworth M40 ..83 C5
 3 Oldham OL1 ....49 B1
 Ramsbottom BL9 ....11 B2
 Rochdale OL11 ....139 D7
Melsomby Rd M23 ....109 A2

Meltham Ave M20 ....110 A6
Meltham Cl SK4 ....110 E1
Meltham Pl 7 BL3 ....147 D4
Meltham Rd SK4 ....110 E1
Melton Ave Reddish M34 ..100 A3
 Urmston M41 ....94 D3
Melton Cl Heywood OL10 ...29 B1
 Tyldesley M29 ....77 B8
 Walkden M28 ....60 C2
Melton Dr BL9 ....45 A5
Melton Rd M8 ....63 E1
Melton Row M26 ....43 F4
Melton St Heywood OL10 ...29 B1
 Manchester M9 ....64 F1
 Radcliffe M26 ....43 F4
 Reddish SK5 ....169 F4
Melton Way M26 ....43 F4
Melverley Rd M9 ....64 A5
Melverley St WN3 ....150 A7
Melville Cl M11 ....99 E7
Melville Ct 3 M20 ....110 A2
Melville Rd Irlam M44 .....105 C5
 Kearsley BL4 ....60 F6
 Stretford M32 ....96 B3
Melville St Ashton-u-L OL6 ..166 B3
 Bolton BL3 ....42 A4
 Manchester M3 ....158 D2
 Oldham OL4 ....67 E5
 Rochdale OL11 ....30 D1
Melvin Ave M22 ....121 E4
Melyncourt Rd SK14 ......102 E3
Memorial Rd M28 ....60 D2
Menai Gr SK8 ....123 A6
Menai Rd SK3 ....170 E6
Menai St BL3 ....34 A8
Mendip Ave Wigan WN3 ...54 C3
 Wythenshawe M22 ....121 F4
Mendip Cl Bolton BL2 ......43 A7
 Gatley SK8 ....131 B7
 Horwich BL6 ....23 C2
 Oldham OL9 ....152 A5
 Royton OL2 ....48 C3
 Stockport SK4 ....169 E3
Mendip Cres BL8 ....27 B3
Mendip Ct Platt Bridge WN2 ..56 B3
 Stockport SK4 ....169 E3
Mendip Dr Bolton BL2 ......43 A6
 Milnrow OL16 ....32 A7
Mendip Rd OL8 ....66 D3
Mendips Cl OL2 ....48 F8
Menston Ave M40 ....65 F1
Mentmore Rd OL16 ....31 D8
Mentone Cres M22 ....121 E4
Mentor St M13 ....98 F3
Menzies St M17 ....97 B1
Mercer Cres BR4 ....1 A8
Mercer La OL11 ....29 E8
Mercer St M19 ....99 D5
Mercer St Droylsden M43 ..84 B2
 Manchester M19 ....99 D4
 Newton-le-W WA12 ....89 C4
Mercer's Rd OL10 ....46 D7
Merchants Cres WA3 ....74 E1
Merchants Quay M5 ....161 A6
Mercia St BL3 ....144 C5
Mercian Dr SK8 ....166 B8
Mercian Way SK3 ....170 E7
Mercury Bsns Pk M41 .....95 F6
Mercury Way M41 ....95 F6
Mere Ave Droylsden M43 ...99 E8
 Leigh WN7 ....75 C5
 Middleton M24 ....65 A6
 Salford M6 ....154 E2
Mere Bank Cl M28 ....60 C3
Mere Cl Reddish M34 ......100 B2
 Sale M33 ....108 A6
 Whitefield BL9 ....45 B5
Mere Dr Manchester M20 ..110 B4
 Swinton M27 ....62 A2
Mere Fold M28 ....60 B3
Mere Gdns BL1 ....145 F8
 Gee M WA11 ....71 B1
 Mere Ho SK4 ....110 E1
Mere La OL11 ....139 F5
 Mere Oaks Sch WN1 ....37 B5
 Mere Rd Ashton-in-M WN4 ..73 C4
 Newton-le-W WA12 ....89 E4
 Mere Side SK15 ....85 F4
Mere St 7 Leigh WN7 .....75 D5
 Rochdale OL11 ....139 F6
 Wigan WN5 ....54 F6
Mere The Ashton-u-L OL6 ...66 A6
 Cheadle SK8 ....123 A4
Mere Wlk BL1 ....145 E8
Merebank Cl OL11 ....29 E8
Mereclough Ave M28 ......60 F1
Meredew Ave M27 ....79 F6
Meredith St 6 M14 ....163 A6
Meredith St Bolton BL3 ...147 F3
 Manchester M14 ....110 D7
Merefield Ave OL11 ....139 E5
Merefield Rd WA15 ....120 C5
Merefield St OL11 ....139 E5
Merefield Terr OL11 ....139 E5
Merefold BL5 ....21 F3
Merehall Cl BL1 ....145 E8
Merehall Dr BL1 ....145 E8
Merehall St BL1 ....143 E1
Mereland Ave M20 ....110 C4
Mereland Cl WN5 ....53 E6
Meremanor M28 ....60 E1
Merepool Cl SK6 ....112 C1
Mereside Cl SK3 ....123 C4
Mereside Gr M28 ....60 E3
Mereside Wlk 15 M15 ....162 D6
Merewood Ave M22 ....121 D6
Melsomby Rd M23 ....109 A2

Meriden Cl M26 ....43 F6
Meriden Gr BL6 ....40 D6
Meridian Pl M20 ....110 A4
Merinall Cl OL16 ....31 C7
Meriton Rd SK9 ....131 D4
Meriton Wlk M18 ....99 B4
Merlewood BL0 ....1 E3
Merlewood Ave
 6 Droylsden M34 ....84 B1
 Oldham OL3 ....69 B8
 Reddish M19 ....111 C7
Merlewood Dr
 Swinton M27 ....79 C6
 Tyldesley M29 ....77 B8
Merlin Cl Hazel Grove SK2 ..125 A6
 Littleborough OL15 ....16 A2
 Oldham OL8 ....85 A8
Merlin Gr BL1 ....142 B1
Merlin Rd Irlam M44 ....94 A4
 Milnrow OL16 ....31 C6
Merlyn Ave Denton M34 ...100 E2
 Manchester M20 ....110 C4
 Sale M33 ....108 C6
Merlyn Ct M20 ....110 C4
Merrick Ave M22 ....121 E4
Merrick St Oldham OL9 ....29 E1
Merridale The M15 ....129 A8
Merridge Wlk 3 M8 ....155 F6
Merrill St M4 ....160 D1
Merriman St M16 ....97 E4
Merrow Ct SK4 ....84 F9
Merrow Wlk M1 ....163 B7
Merrybent Cl SK2 ....124 D4
Merrybower Rd M7 ....155 E8
Merrydale Ave M30 ....79 E4
Merryman Hall OL16 ....15 B2
Mersey Bank Rd SK14 ....171 F4
Mersey Cl Hindley WN2 ....57 C3
 Whitefield M45 ....45 B1
Mersey Cres M20 ....109 D3
Mersey Dr Partington M31 ..106 A4
 Whitefield M45 ....45 B1
Mersey Drive Com Sch
 M45 ....45 C2
Mersey Ind Est
 Manchester SK4 ....110 E1
 Oldham M35 ....66 B1
Mersey Mdws M20 ....109 F3
Mersey Rd
 Manchester M20 ....110 F2
 Manchester SK4 ....110 E1
 Orrell WN5 ....53 F7
 Platt Bridge WN2 ....55 F2
 Sale M33 ....108 B6
Mersey Rd N M35 ....66 B1
Mersey Sq Stockport SK1 ..169 E1
 Leigh WN7 ....75 C5
 Stockport SK1 ....112 A2
Mersey Vale Prim Sch
 SK4 ....168 A1
Merseybank Ave M21 .....109 D4
Merseyway SK1 ....169 E2
Merston Dr M20 ....122 C8
Merton Ave
 Hazel Grove SK7 ....133 F8
 Oldham OL8 ....66 D3
 Romiley SK6 ....113 A4
 Merton Dr M43 ....83 E1
Merton Gr
 Altrincham WA15 ....120 B6
 Failsworth OL9 ....65 D3
 Tyldesley M29 ....77 C6
Merton Rd Prestwich M25 ..63 C5
 Sale M33 ....108 A6
 3 Stockport SK3 ....123 B8
 Wigan WN6 ....54 C4
Merton St BL8 ....140 D3
Merton Wlk 14 M9 ....157 E7
Merville Ave M40 ....64 F1
 Merryn Pl WN3 ....55 B4
 Meryn Rd M7 ....81 B6
 Merwell Rd M41 ....94 E1
 Merwood Ave SK8 ....131 D8
 Merwood Gr M14 ....98 E4
 Mesne Lea Gr M28 ....78 B8
 Mesne Lea Rd M28 ....60 E1
 Mesne Lea Sch M28 ....60 E1
 Mesnefield Rd M7 ....81 A8
 Mesnes Ave WN3 ....150 A5
 Mesnes Park Terr 2 WN1 ..37 C1
 Mesnes Rd Wigan WN1 ...150 C8
 Wigan WN1 ....37 C3
 Mesnes Terr WN1 ....37 C1
 Metal Box Way BL5 ....40 A2
 Metcalf Mews 3 OL3 ....69 B8
 Metcalf Terr BL2 ....26 D1
 Metcalfe Ct M38 ....59 F4
 Metfield Pl 8 BL1 ....144 C8
 Metfield Wlk 19 M40 ....65 D2
 Methodist Cotts BL5 ....39 D3
 Methuen St 8 M12 ....99 B3
 Methwold St BL3 ....146 C4
 Metron Rd SK12 ....133 B4
 Metroplex Bsns Ctr M5 ....96 D8
 Mevagissey Wlk 3 OL4 ....67 C8
 Mews The Bolton BL1 .....144 B8
 Gatley SK8 ....122 B5
 12 Hindley WN2 ....56 D5
 Manchester M10,M40 ....160 E3
 Prestwich M25 ....63 B3
 Sale M33 ....108 A6
 Whitefield M45 ....62 D8
 Willowlow SK9 ....130 D4
 Worsley M28 ....78 E6

Meyer St SK2,SK3 ....170 F6

Meynell Dr WN7 ....75 F2
Meyrick Rd M6 ....81 A3
Meyrick St WN5 ....54 F6
Miall St OL11 ....139 F6
Micawber Rd SK12 ....133 E2
Michael Cl M19 ....110 D2
Michael St 3 M24 ....64 F8
Michael Wife La
 Edenfield BL0 ....1 F2
 Edenfield BL0 ....1 F3
Michaels Hey Par M23 ....120 C8
Michigan Ave M5 ....96 F8
Mickleby Wlk M40 ....160 D3
Micklehurst All Saints'
 CE Prim Sch OL5 ....68 E1
Micklehurst Ave M20 .....109 E4
Micklehurst Gn SK2 ......124 E5
Micklehurst Rd OL5 ....68 E1
Mickleton M46 ....58 E4
Midbrook Wlk 8 M22 .....121 B1
Middle Field OL11 ....13 E1
Middle Gate OL8 ....66 E2
Middle Gn OL6 ....166 C4
Middle Hill OL12 ....14 F4
Middle Hillgate SK1 ....170 F8
Middle Newgate OL15 .....16 B8
Middle Rd M41 ....95 F6
Middle St 4 ....4 D1
Middle Wood La OL15 .....15 E6
Middlebourne St M6 ....154 E2
Middlebrook Dr BL6 ....40 D6
Middlefield OL8 ....85 A8
Middlefields SK8 ....123 B4
Middlegate M40 ....65 D3
Middleham St M14 ....98 A2
Middlesex Dr 3 BL9 ....44 F8
Middlesex Rd
 Brinnington SK5 ....112 C6
 Manchester M9 ....64 D2
Middlesex Wlk OL9 ....153 D6
Middlestone Dr M9 ....157 D7
Middleton Ave M35 ....83 F7
Middleton Central Ind Est
 M24 ....64 F8
Middleton Cl BL8 ....43 F7
Middleton Dr BL9,M45 .....44 F3
Middleton Old Rd M9 ......64 D2
Middleton Parish
 CE Prim Sch M24 ....46 F2
Middleton Rd
 Chadderton M24,OL9 ....47 E1
 Heywood OL10 ....46 E7
 Manchester M7,M8,M9 ....63 F3
 Middleton M24 ....64 A6
 Oldham OL9 ....152 C7
 Reddish SK5 ....99 F2
 Sale M33 ....108 A6
Middleton Rd W OL9 ....65 F8
Middleton Tech Sch M24 ...65 C8
Middleton View M24 ....65 B8
Middleton Way M24 ....64 F8
Middleton Wlk OL4 ....68 B5
Middlewich Wlk M18 ......165 C5
Middlewood Ct M33 ....90 E8
Middlewood Ct OL9 ....152 A8
Middlewood Dr SK4 ....168 A1
Middlewood Rd
 High Lane SK12,SK7 ......134 C7
 High Lane SK6 ....134 D7
 Poynton SK12 ....134 B4
Middlewood St M5 ....158 D1
Middlewood Sta (Lower)
 SK6 ....134 D6
Middlewood Wlk M9 ......154 D7
Midford Ave M30 ....79 B2
Midford Dr BL1 ....24 E7
Midford Wlk 14 M8 ....156 A6
Midge Hall Dr OL11 ....30 A6
Midge Hill M6 ....99 E6
Midgley Ave M18 ....99 E6
Midgley Cres OL6 ....85 C2
Midgley Dr OL16 ....31 C2
Midgley St M27 ....79 D6
Midgrove OL3 ....50 F3
Midgrove La OL3 ....50 F4
Midhurst Ave M40 ....83 B4
Midhurst Cl 1 Bolton BL1 ..143 F8
 Cheadle SK8 ....131 F8
Midhurst St OL11 ....139 F5
Midhurst Way OL9 ....152 B6
Midland Cl WN7 ....75 C6
Midland St M12 ....164 D7
Midland Wlk SK7 ....123 E3
Midlothian St M11 ....83 B2
Midmoor Wlk 6 M9 ....64 A3
Midville Rd M11 ....83 C3
Midway SK8 ....132 B5
Midway St M12 ....99 A2
Milan St M7 ....155 E7
Milbourne Rd BL9 ....27 F6
Milburn Ave M23 ....109 A2
Milburn Dr BL2 ....42 F8
Milburn Rd OL15 ....16 A2
Milden Cl M20 ....110 C4
Mildred Ave
 Manchester M25 ....63 C1
 Oldham OL8 ....48 E2
 Oldham OL4 ....68 B5
Mildred St M7 ....81 C5
Mile End La SK2 ....124 B6
Mile La OL8 ....26 F5
Miles Ave OL13 ....3 D8
Miles La Appley Bridge WN6 ...35 E6
 Shevington M9 ....36 A6
Miles St 5 Bolton BL1 .....143 D2

Miles St continued
Farnworth BL4 ....60 C8
Hyde SK14 ....167 F2
Manchester M12 ....165 A7
Oldham OL1 ....67 B8
Milford Ave 2 OL8 ....66 C2
Milford Brow OL4 ....67 E7
Milford Cres OL15 ....16 B6
Milford Dr M19 ....111 C7
Milford Gr SK2 ....124 C7
Milford Rd Bolton BL2 ...25 F4
 Bolton BL3 ....147 E3
 4 Wigan WN2 ....37 F2
Milford St Ince-in-M WN3 .151 E6
 Manchester M9 ....64 B4
 6 Rochdale OL12 ....14 F1
 Salford M6 ....154 E2
Milk St Hyde SK14 ....167 D2
Manchester M2 ....159 A1
 2 Oldham OL4 ....67 C7
 Ramsbottom BL0 ....138 B5
 Rochdale OL11 ....139 F6
 Tyldesley M29 ....59 A1
Wigan WN3 ....150 C7
Milkstone Pl OL11 ....139 F6
Milkstone Rd OL11 ....139 F6
Milkwood Gr 3 M18 ......99 D4
Mill Bank
 Appley Bridge WN6 ....35 D7
 Bolton M26 ....44 B2
Mill Beck Gr BL3 ....147 E4
Mill Brook Ind Est M23 .120 E6
Mill Brow Chadderton OL1 .48 A2
 Manchester M9 ....64 C2
 Mottram-in-L SK14 ....115 A8
 Oldham OL6,OL8 ....67 C2
 Worsley M28 ....78 F6
Mill Brow Rd SK6 ....126 E8
Mill Croft Bolton BL1 ...145 D8
 Shaw OL2 ....149 C6
Mill Croft Cl OL12 ......13 C2
Mill Ct M41 ....95 E1
Mill Fold Rd M24 ....64 F8
Mill Gate Oldham OL8 ....66 D2
 Rochdale OL16 ....15 C2
Mill Green Spec Sch
 WA12 ....89 E3
Mill Green St M12 ....164 D8
Mill Hill M38 ....59 E6
Mill Hill Ave SK12 ......133 D7
Mill Hill Gr SK14 ....102 F2
Mill Hill Hollow SK12 ...133 D7
Mill Hill St BL2 ....148 A8
Mill Hill Way 3 SK14 ...102 F2
Mill House Cl OL12 ......15 D4
Mill House View WN6 .....53 C7
Mill La Altrincham WA15 .129 E4
 Appley Bridge WN6 ....35 D7
 Ashton-u-L OL6 ....166 B2
 Aspull WN2 ....38 F3
 4 Bury BL8 ....27 B4
 Cheadle SK8 ....122 D6
 Cheadle SK8 ....123 B3
 Denton M34,SK14 ....101 B2
 Droylsden SK5 ....99 F1
 Failsworth M35 ....63 C7
 Hazel Grove SK6 ....125 B7
 Hazel Grove SK7 ....133 F8
 Horwich BL6 ....22 D4
 Leigh WN7 ....76 B4
 Lymm WA13 ....117 C4
 Mossley OL5 ....68 C2
 Newton-le-W WA12 ....89 C3
 Oldham OL9 ....66 C4
 Orrell WN8 ....53 A8
 Reddish SK5 ....142 B6
 Romiley SK6 ....113 A5
 Royton OL2 ....48 C4
 Uppermill OL4 ....50 D1
 Westhoughton BL5 ....57 E5
 Wythenshawe M22 ....109 E1
Mill New Ince-in-M WN1 ..151 D7
 Newton-le-W WA12 ....89 E3
Mill Rd Bury BL9 ....27 F8
 Orrell WN8 ....53 D5
Mill St Adlington PR6 ...21 B8
 Altrincham WA14 ....119 E5
 Ashton-in-M WN4 ....73 C2
 Bolton BL1 ....148 A8
 3 Bolton BL7 ....24 F8
 Boothstown M28 ....78 A6
 Bury BL8 ....26 F8
 Dukinfield SK14 ....101 E5
 Failsworth M35 ....83 D7
 Farnworth BL4 ....60 C8
 Glossop SK13 ....104 D1
 Golborne WA3 ....90 A8
 Hazel Grove SK7 ....124 D3
 Hindley WN2 ....56 D5
 Leigh WN7 ....76 A4
 Manchester M11 ....165 A8
 Mossley OL5 ....56 D8
 Oldham OL3 ....69 B8
 Radcliffe M26 ....44 B2
 Ramsbottom BL0 ....11 A4
 Royton OL2 ....48 D4
 Salford M6 ....81 A4
 Stalybridge SK15 ....86 D1
 Tyldesley M46 ....58 E1
 Westhoughton BL5 ....57 F8
 Wigan WN3 ....150 B7
 Wilmslow SK9 ....137 B7
 Wigan WN2 ....141 A3
Millais St M40 ....83 A8
Millam Cl OL16 ....15 C1
Millar Barn La BB4 .....2 F8
Millard St 3 M18 ......152 A7
Millard Wlk 4 M18 .....99 D4

Millbank Ct OL10 ....29 B2
Millbank St Heywood OL10 .29 B2
 Manchester M1,M4 ....159 C1
Millbeck Cres WN5 ......54 D5
Millbeck Cl M24 ....46 D2
Millbeck Gr WA11 ....71 B2
Millbeck Rd M24 ....46 D2
Millbeck St 4 M15 .....163 A6
Millbrae Gdns OL2 .....48 F7
Millbrook SK14 ....103 E6
Millbrook Ave
 Atherton M46 ....58 E5
 Denton M34 ....100 D1
Millbrook Bank OL11 ....13 D1
Millbrook Cl OL2 ....49 D6
Millbrook Gr 1 SK9 ....131 D1
Millbrook Ho BL4 ....60 E8
Millbrook Prim Sch
 Mossley SK15 ....88 E5
 Shevington WN6 ....35 D6
Millbrook Rd M23 ....121 A4
Millbrook St SK1 ....170 F8
Millcrest Cl M28 ....77 F5
Millcroft Ave WN5 .....53 D5
Millcroft La OL3 ....51 A7
Milldale Cl M46 ....58 C3
Milldale Rd M7 ....75 B1
Miller Meadow Cl OL2 ..149 C8
Miller Rd OL8 ....67 A1
Miller St Ashton-u-L OL6 .166 C4
 Blackrod BL6 ....38 E7
 Bolton BL1 ....146 E4
 Heywood OL10 ....29 D2
 Manchester M4 ....159 A2
 Radcliffe M26 ....43 F6
 Ramsbottom BL9 ....11 C2
Miller's La Atherton M46 .58 D1
 Platt Bridge WN2 ....56 A2
Millers Brook Cl OL10 .29 D3
Millers Cl M23 ....109 A3
Millers Ct M15 ....80 A2
Millers La WA13 ....117 B5
Millers St M30 ....79 C2
Millers Stile Cl SK13 ..104 F1
Millet Terr BL9 ....28 E7
Millett St Bury BL9 ....140 D2
Ramsbottom BL0 ....11 D7
Millfield St WA15 ......119 F2
Millfield Dr M28 ....78 B6
Millfield Gr OL16 ......31 B6
Millfield La WN4,WA11 ..72 E1
Millfield Rd BL2 ....43 A7
Millfield Wlk 2 M40 ...65 C2
Millfold OL12 ....4 D2
Millford Ave M41 ......94 F2
Millford Gdns M41 .....94 E2
Millgate Bolton BL7 ...8 D2
 Delph OL3 ....50 F4
 Stockport SK1 ....169 F2
 Wigan WN1 ....150 C8
Millgate La M20 ....110 B1
Millgate Terr OL12 ....4 E5
Millhall Cl M15 ....162 E5
Millhead Ave M40 .....160 E2
Millhouse Ave M23 ....121 A4
Millhouse St M22 ......121 C4
Millhouse St BL0 ......11 E8
Milling St M1 ....162 F8
Millingford Ave WA3 ...73 F2
Millingford Gr WN4 ....73 B3
Millingford Ind Est WA3 .90 A8
Millington Wlk 1 M15 .162 D6
Millom Ave M23 ....109 B1
Millom Dr BL9 ....45 A2
Millom Pl SK8 ....122 B3
Millow St M4 ....159 A3
Millpool Wlk 1 M9 ....157 D8
Millrise OL1 ....153 E8
Mills Farm Cl OL8 .....67 A1
Mills Hill Com Prim Sch
 OL9 ....65 E8
Mills Hill Rd M24 .....65 D8
Mills Hill Sta M24 ....47 D1
Mills St Heywood OL10 .29 B2
 Whitworth OL12 ....4 D1
Millstone Cl SK12 .....133 C6
Millstone Rd BL1 ......23 F1
Millstream La M40 .....83 E4
Milltown SK13 ....104 D1
Milltown Cl 3 M26 ....44 B2
Milltown St M26 ....44 B3
Millwall Cl M19 ....99 C5
Millway WA15 ....129 C7
Millway 10 M40 ....83 C5
Millwell La 5 BL1 ....145 F7
Millwood
 Ashton-in-M WN4 ....73 A5
 4 Cheadle SK8 ....131 E8
Millwood Cls BL9 .....44 F6
Millwood Prim Sch BL9 .44 F6
Millwood Terr 3 M9 ...167 D2
Millwright St M40 .....83 C5
Milne St Chadderton OL9 .152 C8
 Oldham OL1 ....49 A2
 Oldham OL3 ....152 B7
 Oldham OL9 ....153 D2
 Oldham OL9 ....48 C1
 Rochdale OL11 ....30 C2
 Shaw OL2 ....149 B6

Milnes Ave WN7 ....75 F2
Milngate Cl OL16 ......31 C3
Milnholme BL1 ....142 B3
Milnrow Cl M13 ....163 B7
Milnrow Parish
 CE Prim Sch OL16 ......31 F6
Milnrow Rd
 Littleborough OL15 ....16 A2
 Rochdale OL1,OL16 .....31 B7
 Shaw OL16,OL2 ....32 C2
 Shaw OL2 ....149 B7
 Shaw OL2 ....149 C8
Milnrow Sta OL16 ......31 F5
Milnthorpe Rd BL2 ....42 F8
Milnthorpe St M6 .....81 B5
Milnthorpe Way M12 ...164 E6
Milo St M9 ....64 B3
Milsom Ave BL3 ....146 C3
Milstead Wlk M40 .....83 A5
Milston Wlk M8 ....156 A6
Milton Ave Bolton BL3 .146 B4
 Droylsden M43 ....84 A1
 Irlam M44 ....105 E6
 Little Lever BL3 ......43 B4
 Newton-le-W WA12 ......89 B3
 Salford M6 ....154 D2
 Stalybridge SK15 ......86 C1
Milton Cl Atherton M46 .58 D5
 Dukinfield SK16 ....102 B7
 Haslingden BB4 ....1 A7
 Marple SK6 ....125 F4
 Stretford M32 ....96 E3
Milton Cres Cheadle SK8 .122 C5
 Farnworth BL4 ....60 B6
Milton Ct Bramhall SK7 .132 F6
 Manchester M19 ....110 E4
 5 Manchester M7 ......63 E1
Milton Dr Oldham OL9 ..152 A6
 Poynton SK12 ....133 D4
 Sale M33 ....108 B6
 Sale WA15 ....108 A1
Milton Gr Longshaw WN5 .53 D1
 Manchester M9 ....97 C2
 Sale WA15 ....98 D4
 Sale M33 ....108 A6
 Wigan WN1 ....37 C3
 Wigan WN5 ....54 A6
Milton La Prim Sch M28 .60 B3
Milton Lo WN1 ....37 C2
Milton Mount 1 M18 ...99 D4
Milton Pl M6 ....81 B3
Milton Rd Bramhall SK7 .132 E7
 Coppull PR7 ....19 E8
 Droylsden M34 ....84 D1
 Golborne WA3 ....90 D7
 Prestwich M25 ....63 C5
 Radcliffe M26 ....43 E4
 Stretford M32 ....96 E3
 Swinton M27 ....61 D1
Milton St Denton M34 ..100 E4
 Eccles M30 ....79 D2
 Hyde SK14 ....167 D4
 Leigh WN7 ....75 E5
 Manchester M7 ....158 E4
 Middleton M24 ....46 F1
 Mossley SK15 ....68 C2
 Ramsbottom BL0 ....138 B6
 Rochdale OL16 ....139 F7
 Royton OL2 ....48 E4
Milton St John's
 CE Prim Sch OL5 ......68 C2
Milton Street Day Hospl
 ....68 C2
Milton View OL5 ......68 D2
Milverton Ave SK14 ...102 C2
Milverton Cl BL1 .....40 C5
Milverton Dr SK7 .....132 B5
Milverton Rd M14 .....98 D3
Milverton Wlk SK14 ...102 C2
Milwain Dr SK4 ....111 C6
Milwain Rd
 Manchester M19 ....111 A8
 Stretford M32 ....96 C1
Mimosa Dr M27 ....61 F2
Mincing St 2 M4 ......159 A3
Minden Cl Bury BL8 ...27 B2
 Manchester M20 ....110 D4
Minden Par BL9 ....140 F2
Minden St M6 ....80 E6
Mine St OL10 ....29 D4
Minehead Ave
 Hindley WN7 ....57 D2
 Manchester M20 ....109 F6
 Urmston M41 ....107 B8
Minerva Rd
 Ashton-u-L SK16,SK16 .166 C2
 Farnworth BL4 ....42 A2
Minford Cl M40 ....83 B6
Minnie St Bolton BL3 .146 B3
 Whitworth OL12 ....4 D2
Minoan Gdns M7 ....81 C5
Minor St Failsworth M35 .66 A1
 Oldham OL1 ....30 C1
 Rochdale OL11 ....139 F6
Minorca Ave M11 .....83 D2
Minorca Cl OL11 .....29 E8
Minorca St BL3 ....147 E4
Minshull St N M1 .....163 B8
Minshull St S M1 .....163 B8
Minsmere Cl 5 M8 ....156 A6
Minsmere Wlks SK2 ...124 F4
Minstead Cl SK14 ....102 A1
Minstead Wlk M22 ....121 B2
Minster Cl Bury BL8 ...27 B2
 Dukinfield SK16 ....101 D6
Minster Dr
 Altrincham WA14 ......128 A8
 Cheadle SK8 ....123 A5
Minster Gr M29 ....77 B7

Minster Rd Bolton BL2 .25 C2
 Manchester M9 ....157 F8
Minster Way OL9 ......48 A1
Minsterley Par M22 ...121 C1
Minstrel Cl WN2 ......74 B7
Mint St BL0 ....1 C2
Minto St OL7 ....166 A2
Minton St Failsworth M40 .83 C8
 Oldham OL4 ....67 A5
Mintridge Cl 9 M11 ...99 E7
Mirabel St M3 ....158 F3
Miranda Ct M5 ....161 C8
Mirfield Ave
 Manchester M9 ....64 D4
 Oldham OL8 ....66 E4
 Stockport SK4 ....168 B2
Mirfield Cl WA3 ......90 E4
Mirfield Dr Eccles M30 .79 D4
 Middleton M24 ....46 F1
 Urmston M41 ....95 C4
Mirfield Rd M9 ....74 A4
Miriam St 6 Bolton BL3 .146 B4
 Failsworth M35 ....83 D5
Miry La Westhoughton BL5 .57 E6
 Wigan WN3,WN6 ....150 A8
Missenden Ho 12 M5 ...154 F1
Mission St M9 ....97 C2
Missouri Ave M5 ......154 E1
Mistletoe Gr M3 .....158 D3
Mistral Ct M30 ....79 E3
Mitcham Ave M9 ......65 A3
Mitchell Cl SK8 ......121 F6
Mitchell Gdns M22 ...121 E4
Mitchell Hey OL12 ...139 E7
Mitchell Rd WN5 .....71 E5
Mitchell St
 Ashton-in-M WN4 ......73 C2
 Bury BL8 ....27 C4
 Eccles M30 ....79 C3
 Failsworth M40 ....83 B5
 Glossop SK13 ....90 A8
 Ince-in-M WN2 ....56 A7
 Leigh WN7 ....75 B6
 Littleborough OL15 ...15 C3
 Manchester M11 ......164 F8
 Middleton M24 ....46 F1
 Oldham OL1 ....153 E8
 Rochdale OL12 ....139 E8
 Wigan WN5 ....54 E6
Mitchells Quay M35 ..83 E7
Mitcheson Gdns M6 ...154 F1
Mitford Rd M14 ......110 C7
Mitford St M32 ......96 C3
Mitre Rd M12,M13 ....98 F4
Mitre St Bolton BL1 ..143 E4
 Failsworth M35 ....83 F8
Mitton Cl Bury BL8 ...26 F2
 Culcheth WA3 ....91 E5
Mizpah Gr BL8 ....27 B2
Mizzy Rd OL12 ....14 F1
Moadlock SK6 ....113 C4
Moat Ave M22 ....121 C5
Moat Gdns M22 ....121 C4
Moat Hall Ave M30 ...95 A8
Moat Hall Sports Ctr M30 .79 A1
Moat House St WN2 ...56 A7
Moat Rd M22 ....121 C4
Moat St OL9 ....153 C7
Mobberley Cl M19 ....110 E4
Mobberley Rd
 Ashley WA14,WA15,WA16 .128 E3
 Bolton BL2 ....42 E8
 Wilmslow SK9 ....110 D3
Mocha Par M7 ....158 D3
Modbury Cl SK7 ......124 A1
Modbury Wlk 14 M8 ...156 A6
Mode Hill La M45 ....45 C1
Mode Hill Wlk M45 ...63 C8
Mode Wheel Cir M5 ...161 A4
Mode Wheel Rd M5 ...154 D1
Mode Wheel Rd S M5 .154 D1
Mode Wheel Wkshp M5 .96 D8
Modwen Rd M5 ....161 B6
Moffat Cl BL2 ....42 F6
Moggie La SK10 ......133 F1
Moisant St BL3 ......147 D3
Mold St Bolton BL1 ..143 E3
 Oldham OL1 ....153 D7
Molesworth St OL16 ..31 A7
Mollets Wood M34 ....101 A5
Mollington Rd M22 ...130 E8
Molyneux Rd Reddish M19 .99 C1
 Westhoughton BL5 .....40 B1
Molyneux St
 Rochdale OL12 ....139 D8
 Wigan WN1 ....151 D8
Mona Ave Cheadle SK8 .122 D1
 Stretford M32 ....96 C3
Mona St N Hyde SK14 .167 A4
 Salford M6 ....81 A4
 Wigan WN1 ....150 B8
Monaco Dr M22 ......109 F1
Monarch Cl Irlam M44 .105 E6
 Oldham OL8 ....67 C7
Monart Rd M9 ....64 E1
Moncliffe St Bolton BL3 .145 F6
 Bolton BL3 ....148 A5
Mond Rd M44 ....94 B4
Monde Trad Est M17 ..96 A6
Money Ash Rd WA15 ..119 E3
Monfa Ave SK2 ....124 A4
Monica Ave M8 ....63 F2
Monica Gr M19 ......110 F8
Monica Terr WN4 .....73 B2
Monks Cl Manchester M8 .64 B2

Monks Cl continued
 Milnrow OL16 ....31 E6
Monks Ct M5 ....80 B2
Monks Hall Gr M30 ...79 F2
Monks La BL2 ....25 D2
Monks' Rd SK13 ......116 A3
Monksdale Ave M41 ...95 B2
Monkswood OL1 ....153 E7
Monkton Ave M18 .....99 C5
Monkwood Dr 1 M9 ...157 E8
Monmouth Ave Bury BL9 .27 F5
 Sale M33 ....107 F5
Monmouth Cres WN4 ..73 D2
Monmouth Rd SK8 ....123 B1
Monmouth St
 2 Manchester M18 ....99 E6
 Middleton M24 ....65 C8
 Oldham OL9 ....152 C5
 Oldham OL9 ....139 F6
 Rochdale OL11 ....154 E6
Monroe Cl Salford M6 .154 E4
 Wigan WN3 ....55 A3
Mons Ave OL11 ......30 C8
Monsal Ave Manchester M7 .81 A7
 Stockport SK2 ....124 A7
Monsall Cl BL9 ....45 A2
Monsall Rd M40,M9 ...157 E6
Monsall St
 Manchester M40 ......157 D5
 Oldham OL8 ....66 E3
Montagu Rd SK2 .....124 D8
Montague Ho 5 SK3 ..170 D8
Montague Rd
 Ashton-u-L 85 D3
 Manchester M16 ......161 A5
 Sale M33 ....108 B4
Montague St BL3 .....146 B3
Montague Way SK15 ..86 A2
Montana Sq M11 .....99 E7
Montcliffe Cres M16 .97 F2
Monteagle St M9 ....64 B4
Montford Rise WN2 ..38 A2
Montford St M5 ......96 F8
Montfort Cl BL5 ....57 D6
Montgomery OL11 ....139 E6
Montgomery Dr BL9 ..45 B2
Montgomery Ho OL8 ..66 B1
Montgomery Rd M13 .98 F2
Montgomery St
 Oldham OL8 ....66 B1
 Rochdale OL11 ....66 B1
Montgomery Way BL3,M26 .43 C5
Monton Ave M30 .....79 E3
Monton Bridge Ct M30 .79 C4
Monton Gn M30 ......79 D4
Monton Green Prim Sch
 ....79 C4
 Eccles M30 ....79 C4
Monton Ho M5 ....112 B4
Monton La M30 ......79 E2
Monton Mews 4 WN1 ..37 B3
Monton Prep Sch M30 .79 D3
Monton Rd
 Brinnington SK5 ......112 C4
 Eccles M30 ....79 D3
Monton St Bolton BL3 .147 E3
 Manchester M14 ......98 A4
 Oldham OL9 ....43 E3
Montondale M30 .....79 C3
Montonfields Rd M30 .79 C3
Montonmill Gdns M30 .79 C3
Montpellier Rd M22 ..121 D2
Montreal St
 Abram Brow WN2 ......74 E4
 3 Manchester M19 ....99 B1
 Oldham OL8 ....66 F4
Montrey Cres WN4 ...72 E2
Montrose 2 M30 .....79 E2
Montrose Ave Bolton BL2 .25 C1
 Dukinfield SK16 ......101 C7
 2 Manchester M20 ...110 A5
 Ramsbottom BL0 ......11 A2
 Stockport SK2 ......124 A6
 Stretford M32 ....96 B2
 Wigan WN5 ....54 D7
Montrose Ct 3 M19 ..99 A1
Montrose Dr BL7 .....25 B7
Montrose Gdns OL2 ..48 F8
Montrose Sch M5 ....54 D7
Montrose St OL11 ...30 C1
Montserrat Brow BL1 .23 D2
Montserrat Rd BL1 ..23 E2
Monument Mansions 6
 WN1 ....37 C2
Monument Rd WN1 ...37 D2
Monyash Ct 10 SK13 .171 D1
Monyash Gr SK13 ....171 D1
Monyash Lea SK13 ...171 D1
Monyash Mews SK13 .171 D1
Monyash Pl SK13 ....171 D1
Monyash View SK13 ..171 D1
Monyash Way 18 SK13 .171 E1
Moody St WN6 ....19 D2
Moon Gr M14 ....98 C3
Moon St CB 152 C7
Moor Allerton Sch M20 .109 F4
Moor Ave WN6 ....35 E8
Moor Bank La OL16 ..31 E3
Moor Cl M26 ....43 E5
Moor Cres OL3 ......51 B3
Moor Edge Rd OL5,SK15 .86 F8
Moor End M22 ....121 D8
Moor End Ave M7 ....81 C8
Moor End Ct M7 .....81 C8
Moor End Rd SK6 ....127 A5

Moor Gate SK4 . . . . .25 D5
Moor Gate La OL15 . . . . .15 E7
Moor Hill OL11 . . . . .29 F8
Moor La Bolton BL1,BL3 . . . .145 E6
Leigh WN7 . . . . .75 E8
Manchester M25,M7 . . . . . .81 B8
Manchester M7 . . . . .63 C1
Uppermill OL3 . . . . .51 C2
Urmston M41 . . . . .95 A3
Wilmslow SK9 . . . . .136 D5
Wilmslow SK9 . . . . .136 D5
Woodford SK7 . . . . .132 E3
Wythenshawe M23 . . . . . . .109 A2
Moor Lo SK4 . . . . .168 B4
Moor Nook M33 . . . . .108 D3
Moor Park Ave OL11 . . . . . . .30 B2
Moor Park Rd M20 . . . . . . .122 C8
Moor Platt M33 . . . . .108 D3
Moor Platt Cl BL6 . . . . .22 F3
Moor Rd Haslingden BB4 . . . .1 A5
Littleborough OL15 . . . . .6 C1
Orrell WN5 . . . . .53 E6
Ramsbottom BL8 . . . . .138 A6
Wythenshawe M23 . . . . . . .120 E8
Moor Side La BL0 . . . . .12 A7
Moor St Bury BL9 . . . . .140 F3
Eccles M30 . . . . .79 B1
Heywood OL10 . . . . .29 B2
Oldham OL1 . . . . .67 B7
Shaw OL2 . . . . .149 A6
Swinton M27 . . . . .79 F7
Moor Top Pl SK4 . . . . .168 B3
Moor View Bacup OL13 . . . . .3 B7
Rawtenstall BB4 . . . . .2 F6
Moor View Cl OL12 . . . . . . .13 F2
Moor Way BL8 . . . . .10 C3
Moorbottom Rd BL8 . . . . . .10 E5
Moorby Ave M19 . . . . .110 E4
Moorby St 7 OL1 . . . . .67 A8
Moorby Wlk BL3 . . . . .145 F5
Moorclose St M24 . . . . .65 C8
Moorcock Ave M27 . . . . .80 B8
Moorcot Cl M23 . . . . .120 F7
Moorcroft Edenfield BL0 . . . . .1 D2
Rochdale OL11 . . . . .30 F3
Moorcroft Dr M19 . . . . .110 F4
Moorcroft Rd M23,M33 . . .108 F1
Moorcroft Sq SK14 . . . . . . .101 E6
Moorcroft St
 1 Droylsden M43 . . . . .84 B1
Oldham OL4 . . . . .66 C2
Moorcroft Wlk M19 . . . . . .110 F4
Moordale Ave OL4 . . . . .49 E1
Moordown Cl M8 . . . . .156 B6
Moore Dr BL4 . . . . .60 D7
Moore Gr WA13 . . . . .117 B5
Moore Ho M30 . . . . .95 D8
Moore St Rochdale OL16 . . .139 F7
Wigan WN1 . . . . .37 E1
Moore St E WN1 . . . . .37 E1
Moore Wlk 10 M34 . . . . . . .113 A7
Moore's Ct 5 BL1 . . . . .144 C8
Mooredge Terr OL2 . . . . .48 E2
Moores La WN6 . . . . .19 D2
Moorfield Boothstown M28 . .77 F6
Edgworth BL7 . . . . .9 D6
Manchester M7 . . . . .63 C1
Radcliffe M26 . . . . .43 E4
Worsley M28 . . . . .78 F8
Moorfield Ave
Denton M34 . . . . .101 A2
Littleborough OL15 . . . . .16 A7
Manchester M14 . . . . .110 C7
Swinton M27 . . . . .102 D7
Moorfield Chase BL4 . . . . . .60 D7
Moorfield Cl 3 Eccles M30 .79 D1
Irlam M44 . . . . .94 B3
Swinton M27 . . . . .79 D6
Moorfield Cres WA3 . . . . . . .91 A7
Moorfield Dr
Dukinfield SK14 . . . . .101 E5
Wilmslow SK9 . . . . .136 E5
Moorfield Gr Bolton BL2 . . . .25 B1
Manchester SK4 . . . . .168 B4
Sale M33 . . . . .108 D3
Moorfield Hamlet OL2 . . . . .48 F7
Moorfield Hts SK15 . . . . . . .86 E7
Moorfield Inf Sch SK7 . . . .124 C1
Moorfield Jun Sch SK7 . . .124 C1
Moorfield Mews OL2 . . . . .149 B7
Moorfield Par M44 . . . . .94 B3
Moorfield Pl 3 OL10 . . . . .14 F1
Moorfield Prec SK14 . . . . .103 D5
Moorfield Prim Sch M44 . . .94 A3
Moorfield Rd Irlam M44 . . . .94 A3
Manchester M20 . . . . .109 F4
 1 Oldham OL8 . . . . .66 B2
Salford M6 . . . . .80 D5
Swinton M27 . . . . .79 C6
Moorfield St
Hollingworth SK14 . . . . .103 D5
 1 Manchester M20 . . . . . .110 B7
Platt Bridge WN2 . . . . .56 B3
Moorfield Terr
Hollingworth SK14 . . . . .103 D5
Stalybridge SK15 . . . . .86 E7
Moorfield Wlk M41 . . . . . . .95 D2
Moorgate BL9 . . . . .141 A3
Moorgate Ave
Manchester M20 . . . . .109 F6
Rochdale OL11 . . . . .30 A7
Moorgate Ct BL2 . . . . .25 B1
Moorgate Dr Mossley SK15 . .86 E7
Tyldesley M29 . . . . .77 C5
Moorgate Mews SK15 . . . . .86 E7

Moorgate Prim Sch BL2 . . .148 B8
Moorgate Rd Bury BL8 . . . . .43 F8
Mossley SK15 . . . . .86 E7
Moorgate Ret Pk BL9 . . . . .140 F3
Moorgate St OL3 . . . . .69 B8
Moorhead St M4 . . . . .159 B3
Moorhey Rd M38 . . . . .59 F6
Moorhey St OL4 . . . . .67 B6
Moorhill Ct M7 . . . . .63 C1
Moorhouse Com Prim Sch
OL16 .31 E6
Moorhouse Farm OL16 . . . .31 E6
Moorhouse Fold OL16 . . . .31 E6
Moorings Cl WN1 . . . . .151 F8
Moorings Rd M17 . . . . .96 B8
Moorings The Disley SK12 . .135 E6
Eccles M28 . . . . .79 A5
Uppermill OL5 . . . . .68 E3
Moorland Ave
Droylsden M43 . . . . .83 E1
Manchester M8 . . . . .63 F2
Milnrow OL16 . . . . .32 A6
Rochdale OL11 . . . . .29 F8
Sale M33 . . . . .108 C3
Uppermill OL3 . . . . .50 F2
Whitworth OL12 . . . . .14 C7
Moorland Cres OL12 . . . . . .14 C7
Moorland Dr Cheadle SK8 . .131 F8
Horwich BL6 . . . . .22 F3
Walkden M38 . . . . .60 A6
Moorland Gr BL1 . . . . .142 A2
Moorland Rd
Ashton-in-M WN4 . . . . .73 E5
Hindley WN2 . . . . .56 C5
Manchester M20 . . . . .110 B3
Mossley SK15 . . . . .86 E5
Stockport SK2 . . . . .124 B4
Moorland St
Littleborough OL15 . . . . .16 C7
Rochdale OL11 . . . . .30 C2
Moorland Terr OL12 . . . . . . .14 A1
Moorlands Ave Leigh WN7 . .75 F3
Urmston M41 . . . . .95 B3
Moorlands Cres OL15 . . . . .68 D1
Moorlands Dr OL5 . . . . .68 E3
Moorlands Jun Sch M33 . .108 E5
Moorlands St OL2 . . . . .149 C7
Moorlands View
Bolton BL3 . . . . .146 A2
Edenfield BL0 . . . . .1 D5
Moorlea M35 . . . . .83 F8
Moorsbrook Gr 9 SK9 . . .131 E1
Moorsholme Ave 8 M40 . .83 A7
Moorside
Littleborough OL15 . . . . .16 D6
Rochdale OL11 . . . . .30 F3
Moorside & Wardley Sta
M27 .61 D1
Moorside Ave
Ainsworth BL2 . . . . .26 D1
Bolton BL1 . . . . .142 A1
Droylsden M43 . . . . .84 D2
Farnworth BL4 . . . . .60 B7
Horwich BL6 . . . . .22 C4
Oldham OL4 . . . . .49 F4
Moorside Cl SK13 . . . . .116 B7
Moorside Cres M43 . . . . . . .84 C2
Moorside Ct
Dukinfield M34 . . . . .101 A4
Sale M33 . . . . .108 B4
Moorside High Sch M27 . . .79 D7
Moorside Ho WN5 . . . . .120 C7
Moorside La M34 . . . . .101 A4
Moorside Lo M27 . . . . .79 D8
Moorside Prim Sch
Droylsden M43 . . . . .84 B1
Swinton M27 . . . . .79 D7
Moorside Rd Bury BL8 . . . . .26 E5
Manchester M25,M7 . . . . . .81 C8
Manchester M8 . . . . .64 A1
Manchester SK4 . . . . .168 A2
Mossley OL5 . . . . .68 E1
Swinton M27 . . . . .79 D8
Urmston M41 . . . . .94 E3
Urmston M41 . . . . .95 B3
Moorside St M43 . . . . .84 C2
Moorside View OL2 . . . . . .149 C8
Moorside Wlk WN5 . . . . . . .54 B8
Moorsley Dr M9 . . . . .64 F4
Moorsview BL0 . . . . .138 B6
Moorton Ave M19 . . . . .110 F7
Moorton Pk M19 . . . . .110 F7
Moortop Cl M9 . . . . .64 C6
Moorville Rd M6 . . . . .80 C5
Moorway M9 . . . . .136 D5
Moorway Dr M9 . . . . .65 A4
Moorwood Dr Oldham OL8 . .67 C4
Sale M33 . . . . .107 E3
Mora Ave OL9 . . . . .48 B1
Mora St M9 . . . . .157 F8
Moran Cl SK7 . . . . .131 E2
Moran Wlk 3 M15 . . . . . .162 F6
Morar Dr BL2 . . . . .43 A7
Morar Rd SK16 . . . . .101 D7
Moravian Cl SK16 . . . . .101 D7
Moravian Field 3 M43 . . .100 A8
Moray Cl BL0 . . . . .11 A4
Moray Rd OL9 . . . . .66 A4
Morbourne Cl M12 . . . . . . .164 E6
Morden Ave
Ashton-in-M WN4 . . . . .73 B3
 1 Droylsden M11 . . . . .83 C2
Morecambe Cl M40 . . . . . . .83 B6
Morely St OL4 . . . . .49 E1
Moresby Cl WN7 . . . . .75 D5
Moresby Dr M20 . . . . .122 B8
Moreton Ave
Bramhall SK7 . . . . .132 E5

Moreton Ave continued
Sale M33 . . . . .107 F3
Stretford M32 . . . . .96 D2
Whitefield M45 . . . . .44 F1
Moreton Cl
Dukinfield SK16 . . . . .101 D6
Golborne WA3 . . . . .89 E3
Moreton Dr Bury BL8 . . . . . .27 B3
Handforth SK9 . . . . .131 E3
Leigh WN7 . . . . .75 E1
Poynton SK12 . . . . .133 F4
Moreton La SK2 . . . . .124 C7
Moreton St OL9 . . . . .65 F8
Moreton Wlk SK2 . . . . .124 D7
Morestead Wlk M40 . . . . .160 D3
Morgan St M5 . . . . .169 F4
Morgan St OL15 . . . . .16 B5
Morillon Rd M44 . . . . .94 A4
Morland Rd M16 . . . . .97 C4
Morley Ave
Manchester M14 . . . . .98 A1
Manchester M19 . . . . .79 E6
Morley Gn SK9 . . . . .130 C1
Morley Rd M26 . . . . .43 D4
Morley St Atherton M46 . . .58 C2
Bolton BL3 . . . . .145 D6
Bury BL9 . . . . .44 F8
Glossop SK13 . . . . .116 D8
Rochdale OL16 . . . . .15 B1
Whitefield M45 . . . . .62 F8
Morley Way OL3 . . . . .69 B5
Morley's La M29 . . . . .76 F3
Morna Wlk M12 . . . . .164 D8
Morningside Cl
Droylsden M43 . . . . .100 A7
 22 Rochdale OL16 . . . . . . .31 B6
Morningside Dr M20 . . . . .122 C8
Mornington Ave SK8 . . . . .122 D4
Mornington Cres M14 . . . .110 B8
Mornington Cres OL11 . . . .30 D2
Mornington Rd
Bolton BL1 . . . . .144 B8
Cheadle SK8 . . . . .122 D4
Hindley WN2 . . . . .56 D5
Rochdale OL11 . . . . .31 A3
Sale M33 . . . . .108 D5
Morpeth Cl Ashton-u-L OL7 .84 F4
Manchester M12 . . . . .164 E5
Morpeth St M12 . . . . .79 E6
Morrell Rd M22 . . . . .121 E8
Morris Fold Dr BL6 . . . . .40 C6
Morris Gn BL3 . . . . .146 C2
Morris Green St BL3 . . . . .146 C2
Morris Green Bsns Pk
BL3 .146 C4
Morris Green La BL3 . . . . .146 C3
Morris Green St BL3 . . . . .146 C2
Morris Ho WN1 . . . . .151 D8
Morris St Bolton BL1 . . . . .148 A7
 1 Hindley WN2 . . . . .56 D5
Inc-in-M WN3 . . . . .55 E4
Manchester M20 . . . . .110 B7
Oldham OL4 . . . . .67 A5
Radcliffe BL9 . . . . .44 E5
Tyldesley M29 . . . . .58 F1
Wigan WN1 . . . . .151 D8
Morrison St BL3 . . . . .147 E3
Morrison Wlk M40 . . . . .83 A5
Morrowfield Ave M8 . . . . .155 F7
Morse Rd M40 . . . . .83 A6
Mort Fold M38 . . . . .60 A5
Mort La M28,M29,M38 . . . .59 E2
Mort St Farnworth BL4 . . . . .60 B8
Hindley WN2 . . . . .57 A5
Horwich BL6 . . . . .22 B4
Leigh WN7 . . . . .75 B5
 8 Tyldesley M29 . . . . .58 F1
Wigan WN6 . . . . .37 A1
Mortar St Oldham OL4 . . . . .67 C7
Oldham OL4 . . . . .67 D7
Mortfield Gdns BL1 . . . . . .145 D8
Mortfield La BL1 . . . . .145 D8
Mortimer Ave M9 . . . . .64 E4
Mortimer St OL1 . . . . .67 A8
Mortlake Cl M29 . . . . .76 F8
Mortlake Dr M40 . . . . .83 B5
Morton Ave WN3 . . . . .150 B5
Morton Cl WN3 . . . . .54 C2
Morton St Failsworth M35 . .83 C6
Middleton M24 . . . . .47 A1
Radcliffe M26 . . . . .44 C3
Stockport SK4 . . . . .169 E4
Morton Terr
 11 Denton M34 . . . . .101 A1
Romiley SK6 . . . . .113 B5
Mortons The BL5 . . . . .58 B4
Morven Ave SK7 . . . . .124 F3
Morven Dr M23 . . . . .121 A5
Morven Gr BL2 . . . . .42 F7
Morville Dr WN3 . . . . .54 D5
Morville Rd M21 . . . . .97 D1
Morville St M1 . . . . .163 C8
Moschatel Wlk M31 . . . . . .106 A3
Moscow Rd SK3 . . . . .170 D7
Moscow Rd E SK3 . . . . . . .170 D7
Mosedale Ave WA11 . . . . . .71 B1
Mosedale Cl
Altrincham M23 . . . . .120 E6
Tyldesley M29 . . . . .77 C6
Mosedale Rd M24 . . . . .46 E2
Moseldene Rd SK2 . . . . . .124 D5
Moseley Ct M19 . . . . .98 F1
Moseley Grange SK8 . . . . .122 F3
Moseley Rd Cheadle SK8 . .122 F3

Moseley Rd continued
Manchester M14 . . . . .110 E8
Manchester SK3 . . . . .170 E8
Moses Gate Ctry Pk BL3 . .42 D4
Moses Gate Sta BL4 . . . . . .42 A2
Moses Gate Wkshp 2 BL4 .42 D2
Mosley Ave Bury BL9 . . . . . .27 F5
Ramsbottom BL0 . . . . .11 B2
Mosley Cl WA15 . . . . .119 F7
Mosley Common Rd
Boothstown M28 . . . . .78 A7
Boothstown M28,M29 . . . . .77 F7
Mosley Rd
Altrincham WA15 . . . . .120 B6
Manchester M17 . . . . .96 C6
Mosley St
Manchester M1,M2 . . . . . . .159 A1
Radcliffe M26 . . . . .44 B1
Mosley Street Sta M1 . . . .159 A1
Moss Ave Leigh WN7 . . . . . .76 B5
Orrell WN5 . . . . .53 D3
Rochdale OL16 . . . . .31 C6
Moss Bank
Bramhall SK7,SK8 . . . . .132 C5
Manchester M8 . . . . .156 A8
Moss Bank Ave M43 . . . . . .84 C2
Moss Bank Cl BL1 . . . . .143 E4
Moss Bank Ct M43 . . . . . . .84 C2
Moss Bank Gr M27 . . . . .61 D2
Moss Bank Ho BL1 . . . . . . .142 A3
Moss Bank Rd
Billinge WA11 . . . . .71 B2
Swinton M27 . . . . .61 D2
Moss Bank Way
Bolton BL1 . . . . .142 B3
Bolton BL1 . . . . .23 C5
Moss Bridge Rd OL16 . . . . .31 C5
Moss Brook Rd M9 . . . . . . .157 E7
Moss Cl Haslingden BB4 . . . .1 A8
Radcliffe M26 . . . . .43 D5
Moss Colliery Rd M27 . . . . .61 E4
Moss Croft Cl M41 . . . . .94 F3
Moss Cty Prim Sch The
BL3 . . . . .42 F6
Moss Dr BL6 . . . . .22 F3
Moss Farm Cl M24 . . . . .65 B6
Moss Field Com Sch OL10 . .29 C3
Moss Fold M27 . . . . .79 F7
Moss Gate Rd OL2 . . . . .32 A1
Moss Gn M31 . . . . .106 F6
Moss Gr Lymm WA13 . . . . .117 B4
 3 Shaw OL2 . . . . .149 A7
Moss Grange Ave M16 . . . . .97 D4
Moss Grove Ct 2 M15 . . . .97 E4
Moss Hall Rd BL9,OL10 . . . .45 F7
Moss Hey Dr M23 . . . . .109 B1
Moss Hey Prim Sch SK7 . .132 C5
Moss Hey St OL2 . . . . .149 C6
Moss House La M28 . . . . . . .78 A5
Moss House Terr M9 . . . . . .64 C1
Moss Ind Est Golborne WN7 .75 B1
Moss La Alderley Edge SK9 .137 B1
Altrincham WA14,WA15 . . .119 C1
Altrincham WA15 . . . . .119 F7
Altrincham WA15 . . . . .120 A5
Appley Bridge WN6 . . . . . . .18 E3
Ashton-u-L OL7 . . . . .84 E2
Blackrod BL6 . . . . .21 F2
Bolton BL1 . . . . .142 B3
Bramhall SK7 . . . . .132 D5
Fowley Common WA3 . . . . . .92 D5
Golborne WA3 . . . . .89 D8
Irlam M44 . . . . .105 D5
Kearsley BL4 . . . . .61 B5
Middleton M9 . . . . .64 F5
Mottram-in-L SK14 . . . . . . .114 F8
Partington M31 . . . . .105 F3
Partington M31,WA13,WA14
M31,WA13,WA14 . . . . .106 A2
Platt Bridge WN2 . . . . .56 A3
Rochdale OL16 . . . . .31 A6
Royton OL2 . . . . .49 A3
Sale M33 . . . . .107 B3
Sale M33 . . . . .107 E4
Swinton M27 . . . . .61 D2
Tyldesley M29 . . . . .77 A1
Urmston M41 . . . . .95 E5
Walkden M28 . . . . .60 C3
Whitefield M45 . . . . .62 D6
Wilmslow WA16 . . . . .136 A4
Wythenshawe SK9 . . . . . . .130 C6
Moss La E M14,M16 . . . . . . .98 A4
Moss La W M15,M16 . . . . . .97 E4
Moss Lea BL1 . . . . .143 D4
Moss Lodge La OL7 . . . . . . .84 E1
Moss Manor M33 . . . . .107 E3
Moss Mdw BL5 . . . . .39 E2
Moss Meadow Rd M6 . . . . .80 C4
Moss Mill St OL16 . . . . .31 B5
Moss Park Jun & Inf Sch
M32 . . . . .96 B2
Moss Pk Rd M32 . . . . .96 B2
Moss Pl 5 BL9 . . . . .44 B1
Moss Rd Alderley Edge SK9 .137 C2
Irlam M44 . . . . .105 C7
Kearsley BL4 . . . . .60 F6
Orrell WN5 . . . . .53 D3
Sale M33 . . . . .107 B3
Stretford M32 . . . . .96 C3
Moss Rose SK9 . . . . .137 B2
Moss Row Bury BL9 . . . . . .140 F1
Rochdale OL11 . . . . .13 D1
Moss Shaw Way M26 . . . . .43 E5
Moss Side La
Hollinfare WA3 . . . . .105 A2

Moss Side La continued
Rochdale OL16 . . . . .31 C5
Moss Side Rd M44 . . . . . . .105 E6
Moss Side St OL12 . . . . .4 E5
Moss St Bury BL9 . . . . .140 E2
Droylsden M34 . . . . .84 B1
Droylsden M43 . . . . .84 B2
 2 Farnworth BL4 . . . . .42 E1
 8 Heywood OL10 . . . . . . .29 C2
Hollingworth SK14 . . . . .103 D5
Ince-in-M WN3 . . . . .55 F3
Manchester M7 . . . . .155 D5
Oldham OL4 . . . . .67 E8
Platt Bridge WN2 . . . . .56 A3
Ramsbottom BL9 . . . . .11 D2
Rochdale OL16 . . . . .31 B6
 12 Wigan WN5 . . . . .54 B6
Wigan WN6 . . . . .37 A1
Moss St E OL6 . . . . .166 B3
Moss St W OL7 . . . . .84 F2
Moss Terr Ashton-u-L OL6 . .166 A2
Rochdale OL16 . . . . .31 B6
 3 Wigan WN5 . . . . .54 B5
Wilmslow SK9 . . . . .137 F8
Moss The M24 . . . . .65 B6
Moss Vale Cres M32 . . . . . .95 F3
Moss Vale Rd M41 . . . . .95 E2
Moss View Prim Sch
M31 .106 A3
Moss View Rd Bolton BL2 . . .42 E8
Partington M31 . . . . .106 A3
Mossack Ave M22 . . . . .121 D1
Mossbank Cl SK13 . . . . . . .171 E4
Mossbank Gr OL10 . . . . .29 C3
Mossbray Ave M19 . . . . . . .110 D4
Mossbrook Ct M40 . . . . . . .159 C4
Mossbrook Dr M38 . . . . .59 C6
Mossclough Ct M9 . . . . . . .157 E7
Mosscot Wlk M13 . . . . .163 B7
Mossdale Ave BL1 . . . . .40 D7
Mossdale Rd
Ashton-in-M WN4 . . . . .73 A8
Sale M31 . . . . .107 F1
Wythenshawe M23 . . . . . . .108 F1
Mossdown Rd OL2 . . . . .49 A3
Mossfield Cl Bury BL9 . . . .141 B4
Stockport SK4 . . . . .168 B2
Mossfield Ct BL1 . . . . .145 E8
Mossfield Dr M9 . . . . .65 A4
Mossfield Gn M30 . . . . .94 C4
Mossfield Prim Sch M27 . .61 F1
Mossfield Rd
Altrincham WA15 . . . . .120 D6
Farnworth BL4 . . . . .60 B8
Kearsley BL4 . . . . .60 F5
Swinton M27 . . . . .61 F2
Mossgrove Rd WA15 . . . . .119 F6
Mossgrove St 8 OL6 . . . . .85 C5
Mosshall Cl M15 . . . . .162 D6
Mossland Cl OL10 . . . . .46 D8
Mossland Gr BL3 . . . . .40 E8
Mosslea Ave M8 . . . . .63 F3
Mossley CE Prim Sch OL5 . .68 E1
Mossley Hollins High Sch
OL5 . . . . .68 E1
Mossley Rd
Ashton-u-L OL6 . . . . .166 C3
Ashton-u-L OL6 . . . . .85 E4
Ashton-u-L OL6,8 . . . . .86 A7
Uppermill OL4 . . . . .68 D5
Mossley Sta OL5 . . . . .68 C1
Mossmere Rd SK8 . . . . . . .123 A4
Mossway M24,M9 . . . . .64 F5
Mosswood Pk M20 . . . . . . .122 B8
Mosswood Rd SK9 . . . . . . .131 E1
Mossy Lea Fold WN6 . . . . . .19 A3
Mossy Lea Rd WN6 . . . . . . .18 F5
Moston Bank Ave M9 . . . . .157 F7
Moston Brook High Sch
M40 .157 F6
Moston Fields Prim Sch
M40 . . . . .65 A1
Moston La Manchester M40 . .65 B2
Manchester M9,M40 . . . . . .157 F8
Moston Lane Prim Sch
M40 .157 F8
Moston Rd M24 . . . . .65 D5
Moston St Manchester M7 . .158 F7
Reddish SK5 . . . . .111 F8
Moston Sta M40 . . . . .65 D2
Mostyn Ave Bury BL9 . . . . . .27 F5
Cheadle SK8 . . . . .122 E1
Manchester M14 . . . . .110 E8
Mostyn Rd SK7 . . . . .124 C1
Mostyn St SK15,SK16 . . . .101 F8
Motcombe Farm Rd SK8 . .122 B1
Motcombe Gr SK8 . . . . . . .122 A3
Motcombe Rd SK8 . . . . . . .122 A2
Mother Street Prim Sch
M35 .83 D7
Motherwell Ave 2 M19 . . . .99 A1
Mottershead Ave BL3 . . . . .43 A4
Mottershead Rd M22 . . . . .121 C4
Mottram Ave M22 . . . . .109 C5
Mottram CE Prim Sch
SK14 .103 A3
Mottram Cl SK8 . . . . .123 A5
Mottram Dr
Altrincham WA15 . . . . .120 A5
Wigan WN3 . . . . .150 B5
Mottram Fold 6 SK14 . . .170 F8
Mottram Moor SK14 . . . . .103 B4
Mottram Old Rd
Hyde SK14 . . . . .114 B8
Stalybridge SK15 . . . . .102 D7

Mottram Rd
Alderley Edge SK9 ....137 D1
Hattersley SK14 ....102 C3
Mottram-in-L SK14 ....115 A8
Sale M33 ....108 F3
Stalybridge SK14,SK15 ....102 D7
Mottram St Horwich BL6 .....22 B4
■ Stockport SK1 ....170 F8
Mough La OL9 ....65 E3
Mouldsworth Ave
Manchester M20 ....110 A7
Reddish SK4 ....111 D6
Moulton St M8 ....158 E4
Moulton St Prec M8 ....158 E4
Mouncey St M1 ....163 A7
Mount Ave
Littleborough OL12 ....15 E4
Littleborough OL15 ....16 A7
Rawtenstall BB4 ....2 F8
Mount Carmel Cres M5 .....161 C7
Mount Carmel Ct M5 ....161 C7
Mount Carmel RC Jun Sch
M9 ....64 D2
Mount Cl ■ OL7 ....166 A1
Mount Cres WN5 ....53 F6
Mount Dr Marple SK6 ......125 F5
Urmston M41 ....95 F2
Mount Fold M24 ....65 B7
Mount Sk8 SK8 ....121 F6
Mount La OL3 ....50 E1
Mount Pleasant
Adlington PR6 ....21 A8
■ Bacup OL13 ....3 C8
Bolton BL3 ....148 C5
Edgworth BL7 ....9 D5
Hazel Grove SK7 ....124 D3
Middleton M24 ....64 C8
Middleton M25 ....63 F8
Ramsbottom BL9 ....11 F3
Wilmslow SK9 ....137 B8
Mount Pleasant Rd
Denton M34 ....100 F2
Farnworth BL4 ....59 F8
Mount Pleasant St
Ashton-u-L OL6 ....166 C3
Dukinfield M34 ....100 F7
Horwich BL6 ....22 D1
Oldham OL4 ....67 B7
Mount Pleasant Trad Est
OL6 ....166 C4
Mount Pleasant Wlk M26 ...44 A4
Mount Rd
Manchester M18,M19 ....99 C3
Manchester M20 ....65 A7
Prestwich M25 ....63 E3
Romiley SK14 ....114 A6
Stockport SK4 ....168 C2
Mount Sion Rd M26 ....43 E2
Mount Skip La M38 ....60 A4
Mount St Bolton BL1 ......143 E1
Denton M34 ....101 B1
Eccles M30 ....95 C8
Glossop SK13 ....116 C8
Heywood OL10 ....29 D1
Horwich BL6 ....22 D3
Hyde SK14 ....167 E2
Leigh WN7 ....75 C4
Manchester M2 ....162 F8
Manchester M3 ....158 D3
Oldham OL2 ....48 E3
Ramsbottom BL0 ....138 B6
Rochdale OL11 ....30 C1
Rochdale OL12 ....139 E8
Swinton M27 ....79 F7
Mount St Joseph Sch BL4 ..42 A2
Mount St Joseph's Rd
BL3 ....144 B5
Mount Terr M43 ....83 E3
Mount The
Altrincham WA14 ....119 D5
Altrincham WA15 ....129 C8
Ashton-u-L OL6 ....85 D3
Brinnington SK5 ....112 B4
Mount View
Ince-in-M WN3 ....151 D5
Oldham OL3 ....69 B8
Mount View Rd OL12 ....49 D6
Mount Zion Rd BL9 ....44 F5
Mountain Ash OL12 ....14 B3
Mountain Ash Cl
■ Sale M33 ....107 C5
Mountain Ash Cotts OL3 ....33 D1
Mountain Gr M28 ....60 C4
Mountain Rd PR7 ....19 E8
Mountain St
Failsworth M40 ....83 D4
Mossley OL5 ....68 C1
Stockport SK1 ....112 A2
Walkden M28 ....60 C4
Mountbatten Ave SK16 .....101 F6
Mountbatten Cl BL0 ....45 C2
Mountbatten St M18 ....165 C5
Mountfield M25 ....63 B4
Mountfield Ct WN5 ....53 F7
Mountfield Rd
Bramhall SK7 ....132 E5
Stockport SK3 ....123 C7
Mountfield Wlk
■ Bolton BL1 ....143 E1
■ Manchester M11 ....160 F1
Mountford Ave M8 ....63 F2
Mountheath Ind Pk M25,M2 .63 C3
Mountmorres Ct BL5 ....59 A7
Mountroyal Cl SK14 ....102 A5
Mountside Cl OL12 ....14 F2
Mountside Cres M25 ....62 F4
Mousell St M8 ....159 A4

Mouselow Cl SK13 ....171 F3
Mow Halls La OL3 ....51 A1
Mowat Ct M41 ....110 D8
Mowbray Ave
Manchester M25 ....63 C1
Sale M33 ....108 C3
Mowbray St
Ashton-u-L OL7 ....166 A2
Bolton BL1 ....142 B1
■ Oldham OL1 ....153 F6
Rochdale OL11 ....30 B3
Stockport SK1 ....170 F8
Mowbray Wlk ■ M24 ....46 E2
Moxley Rd M8 ....63 F1
Moxon Way WN4 ....73 D4
Moyse Ave BL8 ....26 F5
Mozart Cl M4 ....159 C2
Mudhurst La SK12 ....135 E3
Muirfield Ave M40 ....105 C3
Muirfield Cl Bolton BL3 ...40 F3
Failsworth M40 ....83 C7
Heywood OL10 ....29 D1
Prestwich M25 ....63 B5
Wilmslow SK9 ....137 D8
Muirfield Dr M29 ....77 C7
Muirhead Ct M6 ....81 A5
Mulberry Ave WA3 ....90 F7
Mulberry Cl Gatley SK8 ...131 C7
Rochdale OL11 ....139 E5
Wigan WN5 ....54 D6
Mulberry Ct
Altrincham WA14 ....119 D6
■ Salford M6 ....81 A3
Mulberry Mews SK4 ....169 E2
Mulberry Mount St SK3 ...170 E8
Mulberry Rd M6 ....81 A3
Mulberry St ■
Ashton-u-L OL6 ....166 C3
Manchester M2 ....158 F1
Mulberry Wlk
Droylsden M43 ....99 E8
Sale M33 ....107 D6
Mule St BL2 ....148 A7
Mulgrave Rd M28 ....79 A8
Mulgrave St Bolton BL3 ...146 C2
Swinton M27 ....61 D1
Mulgrove Wlk ■ M9 ....64 E3
Mull Ave M12 ....164 F5
Mullacre Rd M22 ....121 D6
Mullein Cl ■ BL1 ....143 F1
Mullineux St ■ M28 ....60 D2
Mullins Ave WA12 ....89 C5
Mullion Cl M19 ....99 D2
Mullion Dr WA15 ....119 E6
Mullion Wlk M8 ....156 B6
Mulmount Cl OL8 ....66 C3
Mumps OL1 ....67 A7
Mumps Sta OL4 ....67 A6
Munday St M4 ....160 D1
Munford Wlk M40 ....65 C5
Municipal Cl ■ OL10 ......29 D2
Munn Rd M9 ....64 C5
Munro Ave Orrell WN5 .....53 E6
Wythenshawe M22 ....121 F2
Munslow Wlk M9 ....64 F3
Munster St M4 ....159 A3
Muriel St Heywood OL10 ...29 E2
Manchester M7 ....155 D5
Rochdale OL11 ....31 B5
Murieston Rd WA15 ....119 E7
Murphy Cl WN3 ....150 A5
Murray Rd BL9 ....140 F2
Murray St Atherton M46 ...58 B2
Manchester M4 ....159 C2
Manchester M7 ....155 D6
Murrayfield OL11 ....29 E6
Murrow Wlk ■ M9 ....157 D8
Murton Terr BL1 ....143 F4
Mus of Science & Ind
M3 ....162 E8
Mus of Science & Ind
(Air & Space Gal) M3 ...162 E8
Musbury Ave SK8 ....123 B2
Musden Ave BB4 ....1 A7
Musden Wlk M40 ....111 D7
Museum of the
Manchesters The OL6 ....166 B3
Museum of Transport
M8 ....156 B6
Museum St M2 ....162 F8
Musgrave Gdns BL1 ....144 C8
Musgrave Rd Bolton BL1 ..144 C8
Wythenshawe M22 ....121 D3
Muslin St BL5 .... .81 C1
Mustard La WA3 ....91 B1
Muter Ave M22 ....121 F2
Mutual St OL10 ....29 E2
My St M5 ....154 E1
Mycroft Cl WN7 ....75 E8
Myerscroft Cl M40 ....65 E1
Myrrh St BL1 ....143 E2
Myrtle Ave
Ashton-in-W WN4 ....72 F6
Leigh WN7 ....75 E7
Newton-le-W WA12 ....89 C2
Myrtle Bank M25 ....63 A1
Myrtle Gdns BL9 ....141 B2
Myrtle Gr Billinge WN5 ...71 D4
Droylsden M43 ....84 C2
Manchester M25 ....63 B2
Reddish M34 ....99 F3
Whitefield M45 ....44 D2
Myrtle Pl M7 ....81 C4
Myrtle Rd Middleton M24 ..47 C2
Partington M31 ....105 D3
Myrtle St Bolton BL1 .....145 D8
Manchester M11 ....164 F8

Myrtle St continued
■ Manchester M16 ....97 C4
Stockport SK3 ....123 B8
Wigan WN1 ....150 B8
Myrtle St N BL9 ....141 B2
Myrtle St S BL9 ....141 B2
Myrtleleaf Gr M5 ....154 D2
Mytham Com Prim Sch
BL3 ....43 B3
Mytham Gdns BL3 ....43 B2
Mytham Rd BL3 ....43 B2
Mythorn Wlk M40 ....83 B5
Mythorne Ave M44 ....105 C3
Mytton Rd BL1 ....142 B4
Mytton St M15 ....162 F5

N

Nabbs Fold BL8 ....10 F3
Nabbs Way BL8 ....11 A1
Naburn Cl SK5 ....112 C6
Naburn St M13 ....98 D4
Nada Lo M8 ....156 C6
Nada Rd M8 ....63 F1
Naden Wlk M45 ....63 A8
Nadin St OL8 ....66 D3
Nadine St M6 ....154 E3
Nailgate OL16 ....31 C2
Nailsworth Wlk ■ M13 ...163 C5
Nairn Cl WN6 ....19 D1
Nairn Wlk M40 ....160 E3
Nall St Manchester M19 ..111 B7
Marple OL16 ....31 C6
Nameplate Cl M30 ....79 B2
Nan Nook Rd M23 ....108 F1
Nancy St M15 ....162 D6
Nandywell BL3 ....43 B3
Nangreave Rd SK1,SK2 ...124 B6
Nangreave St M5 ....158 D1
Nangreaves St WN7 ....75 C5
Nansen Ave M30 ....79 C3
Nansen Cl M32 ....96 E4
Nansen St Bolton BL3 .....42 A4
Nansen St Sk8 ....122 A4
Nansen St
Manchester M11 ....164 E8
Salford M6 ....154 E2
Stretford M32 ....96 E4
Nansmoss La SK9 ....130 D1
Nantes Ct BL1 ....143 D2
Nantwich Ave OL12 ....14 F3
Nantwich Cl SK8 ....123 A5
Nantwich Rd M14 ....98 A1
Nantwich Way ■ SK9 .....131 E5
Napier Ave M20 ....109 A4
Napier Cl OL8 ....67 A6
Napier Ct Manchester M15 .161 C6
Manchester M16 ....168 B3
Napier Gn M5 ....161 B7
Napier Ho OL16 ....6 A8
Napier Rd Eccles M30 .....79 C3
Manchester M20 ....109 B8
Manchester M21 ....97 A8
Napier St Hazel Grove SK7 .124 D3
Hyde SK14 ....167 E1
Shaw OL2 ....49 B8
Swinton M27 ....79 D7
Napier St E OL8 ....153 D5
Napier St W OL8 ....153 D5
Naples Rd SK3 ....123 B7
Naples St M4 ....159 A3
Narbonne Ave M30 ....80 A4
Narborough Cl WN2 ....56 E4
Narbuth Dr M8 ....155 F7
Narcissus Ave BB4 ....1 A8
Narcissus Wlk ■ M28 .....59 F3
Narrow La SK10 ....133 A1
Narrows The WA14 ....119 C4
Naseby Ave M9 ....64 F4
Naseby Cl SK5 ....63 C5
Naseby Pl M25 ....63 C5
Naseby Wlk M45 ....63 C8
Nash Rd M17 ....95 F8
Nash St M15 ....162 E6
Nasmyth Ave M34 ....101 A4
Nasmyth Bsns Ctr M30 ....79 C2
Nasmyth Rd M30 ....95 C8
Nasmyth St Horwich BL6 ..22 C3
Manchester M8 ....156 C5
Nately Rd M16 ....97 A2
Nathan Dr M3 ....158 F3
Nathaniel Ct WN2 ....56 B3
Nathans Rd M22 ....121 C4
National Cycling Ctr M11 .83 A2
National Dr M5 ....161 A8
Naunton Ave M47 ....75 C5
Naunton Rd M24 ....65 B7
Naunton Wlk ■ M9 ....157 E8
Naval St M4 ....159 C2
Navenby Ave M16 ....97 C4
Navenby Rd WN3 ....55 A2
Navigation Cl WN7 ....75 E4
Navigation Prim Sch
WA14 ....119 D6
Navigation Rd
WA14,WA15 ....119 D6
Navigation Road Sta
WA14 ....119 D6
Naylor Ave WA3 ....90 B8
Naylor Ct ■ M40 ....159 C3
Naylor St Atherton M46 ...58 C2
Manchester M40 ....160 D3
Oldham OL1 ....153 E7
Naylorfarm Ave WN6 ......35 F5
Nazarene Theological Coll
The M20 ....110 A3
Naze Ct ■ OL1 ....153 E8
Naze Wlk SK5 ....112 C6

Nazeby Wlk OL9 ....152 C5
Neal Ave Ashton-u-L OL6 ..85 D3
Gatley SK8 ....122 A1
Neale Ave OL3 ....69 B5
Neale Rd M21 ....109 B7
Near Birches Par OL4 .....67 E4
Near Hey Cl M26 ....43 E3
Nearbrook Rd M22 ....121 C4
Nearcroft Rd M23 ....121 B7
Nearmaker Ave M22 ......121 C4
Nearmaker Rd M22 ....121 C4
Neary Way M41 ....95 C5
Neasden Gr ■ BL3 ....144 C5
Neath Ave M22 ....121 D7
Neath Cl Poynton SK12 ...133 D5
Prestwich M25 ....63 C7
Neath Fold BL3 ....147 D3
Neath St OL9 ....153 D7
Nebo St BL3 ....147 D4
Nebraska St BL1 ....143 E1
Neden Cl M11 ....165 B8
Needham Ave M21 ....109 B8
Needwood Cl M40 ....157 D5
Needwood Rd SK6 ....113 C5
Neenton Sq M12 ....165 A7
Neild Gdns WN7 ....75 E4
Neild St Manchester M1 ..163 B8
Oldham OL8 ....66 F4
Neill St M7 ....155 D8
Neilson Cl M24 ....65 C7
Neilson Ct M23 ....121 A6
Neilston Ave M40 ....83 B7
Nel Pan La WN7 ....75 D8
Nell Carrs BL0 ....11 E8
Nell La M20,M21 ....109 D6
Nell St BL1 ....143 F4
Nellie St OL10 ....29 B2
Nelson Ave Eccles M30 ...79 D3
Poynton SK12 ....134 A3
Nelson Cl SK12 ....134 A3
Nelson Ct Manchester M15 .97 E4
Manchester M40 ....160 D4
Nelson Dr Droylsden M43 ..83 E2
Irlam M44 ....56 A8
Nelson Fold ■ 105 E6
Nelson Mandela Ct ■
M16 ....97 E3
Nelson Rd M9 ....64 B1
Nelson St ■ BL3 ....145 F7
Nelson St Atherton M46 ...58 B3
Atherton M46 ....58 B4
Bacup OL13 ....4 C8
Bolton BL3 ....148 A5
■ Bury BL9 ....44 F8
Denton M34 ....100 F4
Denton M34 ....100 F6
Eccles M30 ....79 D2
Farnworth BL4 ....60 E8
Hazel Grove SK7 ....124 D3
Heywood OL10 ....29 D1
■ Hindley WN2 ....56 D6
Horwich BL6 ....22 D3
Hyde SK14 ....167 E2
Little Lever BL3 ....43 B3
■ Littleborough OL15 .....16 B5
Manchester M13 ....163 B5
Manchester M40 ....160 E4
Manchester M40 ....155 D5
Middleton M24 ....65 A3
Newton-le-W WA12 ....89 A3
Oldham OL4 ....67 E5
Rochdale OL16 ....139 F7
Salford M5 ....154 E1
Stretford M32 ....154 E1
77 B8 Stockport SK5 ....111 B5
Nelson Way OL9 ....152 B7
Nelstrop Cres SK4 ....111 D6
Nelstrop Rd SK4 ....111 D6
Nelstrop Rd N M19,SK4,SK5 .111 C8
Nelstrop Wlk SK4 ....111 C6
Nepaul Rd M9 ....64 E1
Neptune Gdns ■ M7 ......81 C5
Nesbit St BL2 ....25 B3
Nesfield Rd M23 ....108 F2
Neston Ave Bolton BL1 ....24 F5
Manchester M20 ....110 A6
Sale M33 ....108 E2
Neston Gr SK3 ....170 D5
Neston Rd Bury BL8 ....26 F5
Rochdale OL16 ....31 C4
Neston St M11 ....99 F7
Neston Way ■ SK9 ....131 E1
Neswick Wlk ■ M23 .....108 F2
Nether Hey St OL8 ....67 B4
Nether St Hyde SK14 ....113 F8
Manchester M12 ....163 C8
Netherbury Cl M18 ....99 C3
Netherby Rd WN6 ....36 E3
Nethercote Ave M23 .....121 B6
Nethercott Ct M29 ....58 E1
Nethercroft
Altrincham WA14 ....119 C5
Altrincham WA14 ....120 C5
Nethercroft Rd WA15 ....120 C5
Netherfield Cl OL8 ....66 C4
Netherfield Rd BL3 ......147 E2
Netherfields WN7 ....75 D7
Netherhouse Rd OL2 ......48 F4
Netherland St M5 ....161 A8
Netherlees OL4 ....67 D5
Netherley Rd PR7 ....19 E8
Netherlow Ct SK14 ......167 E2
Netherton Gr BL4 ....42 B2

Netherton Rd M14 ....98 A1
Nethervale Dr M9 ....157 E7
Netherwood Ct WN6 ....36 A6
Netherwood Rd M22 .....121 C7
Netley Ave OL12 ....14 F3
Netley Gdns M26 ....43 E5
Netley Gr OL8 ....67 C4
Netley Rd M23 ....121 A4
Nettlebarn Rd M22 ....121 C5
Nettleford Rd M16 ....109 E8
Nettleton Gr M9 ....64 F1
Nevada St ■ BL1 ....143 E1
Nevendon Dr M23 ....120 F4
Nevern Cl BL1 ....40 F8
Nevile Ct M7 ....81 B8
Nevile Rd M7 ....81 B8
Nevill St M7 ....123 E2
Nevill Road Inf Sch SK7 .123 E2
Nevill Road Jun Sch SK7 .123 E2
Neville Cardus Wlk ■
M14 ....98 C3
Neville Cl BL1 ....145 E8
Neville Dr M44 ....94 A4
Neville St Hazel Grove SK7 .124 D3
Newton-le-W WA12 ....89 A3
Oldham OL9 ....152 C7
Platt Bridge WN2 ....56 A3
Nevin Ave SK8 ....122 E1
Nevin Cl Bramhall SK7 ...133 A7
Oldham OL8 ....66 B2
Nevin Rd M40 ....65 A5
Nevis Gr BL1 ....24 D5
Nevis St OL11 ....31 A2
Nevy Fold Ave BL6 ....22 F3
New Allen St M4,M40 ....159 C3
New Bailey St M3 ....158 E1
New Bank St
■ Hadfield SK13 ....104 A5
Hadfield SK13 ....104 A5
Manchester M12 ....164 F5
Tyldesley M29 ....77 A8
New Barn BB4 ....1 B6
New Barn Ave WN4 ....73 C3
New Barn Jun Sch OL2 ..149 A6
New Barn La Leigh WN7 ..75 E2
Rawtenstall BB4 ....2 A8
Rochdale OL11 ....30 E4
New Barn Rd OL8 ....67 A2
New Barn St Bolton BL1 ..142 B1
■ Rochdale OL11 ....31 A5
Shaw OL2 ....49 E4
New Barton St M6 ....80 C5
New Beech Rd SK4 ....110 E2
New Bridge La SK1 ....112 A2
New Bridge St M3 ....158 F3
New Briggs Fold BL7 ......8 E2
New Broad La OL16 ....31 C3
New Broadcasting House
(BBC) M16 ....163 A7
New Brook Sch M20 .....109 F5
New Brunswick St ■ M13 .98 F4
New Buildings Pl ■
OL16 ....139 F8
New Cathedral St M1 ....158 F2
New Chapel La BL6 ....22 F2
New Church Cl M26 ....44 C2
New Church Ct M45 ....63 B1
New Church Rd BL1 ....23 F2
New Church St M26 ....44 B3
New City Rd M28 ....78 A8
New Collier's Row BL1 ....23 E6
New Court Dr BL7 ....8 E3
New Croft High Sch M6 ..154 F3
New Cross M4 ....159 B2
New Cross St
Pendlebury M27 ....80 A7
Salford M5 ....80 C2
New Drake Gn BL5 ....57 E5
New Earth St Mossley OL5 .68 D2
Oldham OL4 ....67 C5
New Elizabeth St M8 .....156 A5
New Ellesmere App M28 ..60 D3
New Elm Rd M3 ....162 D8
New Field Cl Radcliffe M26 .43 E3
Rochdale OL16 ....31 B8
New Fold WN5 ....53 C4
New Forest Rd M23 .....120 D8
New Gate BL5 ....146 A1
New George St ■ BL8 ....27 C3
New Hall Ave Eccles M30 ..95 A8
Gatley SK8 ....123 B3
New Hall Ave
Manchester M7 ....155 D8
New Hall La Bolton BL1 ..144 A8
Culcheth WA3 ....91 E1
Culcheth WA3 ....92 A2
New Hall Mews BL1 ......23 D1
New Hall Pl BL1 ....144 A8
New Hall Rd Bury BL9 ....27 E6
New Hall Rd SK3 ....123 C7
New Hall Rd Bury BL9 .....28 E4
New Hall Rd Sale M33 ...108 F4
New Herbert St M6 ....80 C5
New Hey Rd Cheadle SK8 .122 E6
Denshaw M27 ....34 F8
New Heys Way BL2 ....25 B6
New Ho OL4 ....68 C8
New Holder St BL1 ....145 E7
New Islington M4 ....159 C2
New Kings Head Yd M3 ..158 F2
New La Bolton BL2 ....25 E2
Eccles M30 ....79 B1
Middleton M24 ....47 A1
Royton OL2 ....48 D4
New Lane Ct BL2 ....25 E2

New Lawns SK5 ....100 A1
New Lees St OL6 ....85 D5
New Lester Way M38 ......59 E4
New Line OL13 ....4 B8
New Lodge WN1 ....37 D2
New Market M2 ....158 F1
New Market La M1,M2 ....159 A1
New Market St WN1 ......150 C8
New Mdw Rd Bolton BL2 ....40 C7
New Miles La WN6 ....35 F5
New Mill St OL15 ....16 A5
New Mills Rd M43 ....115 B4
New Moor La SK7 ....124 D3
New Moss Rd M44 ....105 D6
New Moston Prim Sch
  M40 ....65 E2
New Mount St ⓼ M4 .....159 A3
New Park Rd M5 ....161 B7
New Quay St M3 ....158 E1
New Radcliffe St OL1 .....153 E7
New Raven Ct BL3 ....43 A3
New Rd Adlington PR6 .....21 D8
  Aspull WN2 ....38 A5
  Littleborough OL15 ....15 F5
  Oldham OL8 ....66 E4
  Radcliffe M26 ....44 B2
  Tintwistle SK13 ....104 A7
  Whitworth OL12 ....4 B1
New Ridd Rise SK14 ....113 D8
New Rock BL7 ....57 F5
New Royd Ave OL4 ....67 F8
New Smithfield Mkt M18 ..165 C7
New Springs BL1 ....142 B3
New St Altrincham WA14 ..119 D4
  Ashton-in-M WN4 ....73 C4
  Blackrod BL6 ....21 D2
  Bolton BL1 ....145 E6
  Bury BL8 ....26 F6
  Droylsden M43 ....100 A8
  Eccles M30 ....79 C1
  Littleborough OL15 ....15 F4
  Manchester M40 ....160 E4
  Milnrow OL16 ....32 A5
  Mottram-in-L SK14 ....115 A8
  Oldham OL3 ....69 B8
  Oldham OL4 ....67 E6
  Platt Bridge WN2 ....56 A2
  Radcliffe M26 ....44 B2
  Rochdale OL12 ....14 E2
  Stalybridge SK15 ....102 A8
  Swinton M27 ....62 A1
  Wigan WN5 ....54 B5
New Summerseat House
  Specl Sch BL0 ....11 B2
New Tame OL3 ....50 C7
New Tempest Rd BL6 ....40 C4
New Terr SK14 ....101 F5
New Thomas St M6 ....81 A4
New Tong Field BL7 ....24 F7
New Union St M4 ....159 C2
New Vernon St ⓬ BL9 ....140 F4
New Viaduct St M11,M40 ..160 E2
New Vine St M15 ....162 F6
New Wakefield St M1 ......163 A7
New Way OL13 ....4 C1
New Welcome St M15 .....162 F6
New York BL10 ....29 B2
New Zealand Rd SK1 ......112 B2
Newall Gr WN7 ....75 F6
Newall Green High Sch
  M23 ....120 F3
Newall Green Prim Sch
  M23 ....121 B4
Newall Rd M23 ....120 F3
Newall St
  Littleborough OL15 ....16 B6
  Oldham OL9 ....66 B2
  Walsden OL14 ....6 A8
Newark Ave
  Little Lever M26 ....43 C5
  ⓷ Manchester M14 ....98 B3
Newark Park Way OL2 .....48 C6
Newark Rd Handley WN2 ..54 C4
  Reddish SK5 ....111 F5
  Rochdale OL12 ....14 F3
  Swinton M27 ....62 B2
Newark Sq OL12 ....14 F3
Newark St WN6 ....36 F1
Newbank Chase OL9 ......152 A8
Newbank Towers M3 ......158 E3
Newbarn Cl OL2 ....149 A7
Newbeck St ⓷ M4 ....159 A2
Newberry Gr SK3 ....170 D5
Newbold Mews OL16 ....31 B8
Newbold St Bury BL8 ......27 C2
  Rochdale OL16 ....31 C7
Newboult Rd SK8 ....122 E6
Newbourne Cl SK7 ....124 D3
Newbreak Cl ⓷ OL4 ....67 D8
Newbreak St ⓷ OL4 ....67 D8
Newbridge OL5 ....86 D8
Newbridge Cl WN4 ....72 D3
Newbridge Gdns BL2 ......25 E4
Newbrook Ave M21 ....109 D4
Newbrook Rd BL5,M46 .....58 F6
Newburn Ave M9 ....64 F4
Newburn Ave M43 ....100 C7
Newbury Cl SK8 ....132 A6
Newbury Ct SK7 ....137 A6
Newbury Dr Eccles M30 ...79 B3
  Urmston M41 ....95 C5
Newbury Gr OL10 ....46 C8

Newbury Pl M7 ....155 D7
Newbury Rd Gatley SK8 ..131 C7
  Little Lever BL3 ....42 F3
Newbury Wlk Bolton BL1 ..143 E1
  Manchester M9 ....157 D6
  Oldham OL9 ....152 C7
Newby Dr
  Altrincham WA14 ....119 D6
  Gatley SK8 ....122 A6
  Middleton M24 ....46 F3
  Sale M33 ....108 E3
Newby Rd Bolton BL2 ......25 F2
  Hazel Grove SK7 ....124 D2
  Stockport SK4 ....168 C2
Newby Road Ind Est SK7 ..124 D2
Newby Sq WN5 ....54 B5
Newcastle St ⓷ M15 .....162 F7
Newcastle Wlk ⓶ M34 ..101 A1
Newchurch OL8 ....85 A8
Newchurch Cl ⓶ M26 .....44 B3
Newchurch Cty Prim Sch
  WA3 ....91 E2
Newchurch La WA3 ....91 F2
Newchurch Rd OL13 ....3 C8
Newchurch St
  Manchester M11 ....164 F8
  Rochdale OL11 ....30 B1
Newchurch Wlk ⓶ M26 ...44 B3
Newcliffe Rd M9 ....64 F4
Newcombe Cl M11 ....160 F1
Newcombe Ct ⓶ M33 ....107 F4
Newcombe Dr M38 ....59 F6
Newcombe Rd BL0 ....11 B2
Newcombe St M3 ....158 F3
Newcroft M35 ....84 B6
Newcroft Cres M41 ....95 F1
Newcroft Dr
  Stockport SK3 ....170 D6
  Stretford M41 ....96 A1
Newcroft Rd M41 ....95 F1
Newdale Rd M22 ....99 B2
Newearth Rd M28 ....78 B8
Newenden Rd WN1 ....37 B4
Newfield Ct WA14 ....112 B5
Newfield Head La OL16 ....32 B5
Newfield View OL16 ....32 A6
Newgate Rochdale OL16 ..139 F7
  Wilmslow SK9 ....136 D7
Newgate Ave WN6 ....35 E8
Newgate Dr M38 ....60 A6
Newgate Rd M23 ....107 C1
Newgate St M44 ....159 A2
Newhall Ave BL3 ....43 B6
Newhall Dr M23 ....109 B2
Newhall Rd SK5 ....100 A2
Newham Ave M11 ....83 B2
Newhart Gr M28 ....60 C2
Newhaven Ave
  Droylsden M11 ....99 F7
  Leigh WN7 ....75 F8
Newhaven Bsns Pk M30 ..79 F1
Newhaven Cl
  Bramhall SK8 ....123 C2
  Bury BL8 ....27 C7
Newhaven Wlk ⓳ BL2 ....25 B1
Newhey Ave M22 ....121 D5
Newhey Com Prim Sch
  OL16 ....32 A4
Newhey Rd Milnrow OL16 ..32 A5
  Wythenshawe M22 ....121 D5
Newhey Sta OL16 ....32 B3
Newholme Ct
  Manchester M20 ....110 C6
  Stretford M32 ....96 E2
Newholme Gdns M28 ....60 C3
Newholme Rd M20 ....109 F5
Newhouse Cl OL12 ....15 C6
Newhouse Cres OL16 ......29 E8
Newhouse Rd OL10 ....46 D8
Newhouse St OL12 ....15 C6
Newick Wlk ⓺ M9 ....64 E3
Newington Ave M8 ....63 F4
Newington Dr WN4 ....119 B3
Newington Dr Bolton BL1 ..143 F1
  Bury BL8 ....27 A1
Newington Wlk ⓺ BL1 ....143 F1
Newland Ave WN5 ....54 D5
Newland Dr BL5 ....58 B8
Newland Mews WA3 ....91 E5
Newlands M35 ....84 B1
Newlands Ave Bolton BL2 ..25 F1
  Bramhall SK7 ....132 A7
  Cheadle SK8 ....132 A7
  Irlam M44 ....94 A2
  Rochdale OL16 ....14 F3
Newlands Cl Cheadle SK8 ..132 A7
  Rochdale OL16 ....14 F3
Newlands Dr Blackrod BL6 ..38 E7
  Hazel Grove SK7 ....124 D3
  Hadfield SK13 ....171 F4
  Manchester M20 ....122 C8
  Pendlebury M27 ....80 C6
  Prestwich M25 ....63 A5
  Wilmslow SK9 ....136 E5
Newlands Rd Cheadle SK8 ..122 D6
  Leigh WN7 ....75 F3
  Wythenshawe M23 ....120 F8
Newlands Wlk M24 ....46 E3
Newlyn Ave SK15 ....86 D3
Newlyn Cl SK7 ....124 D2
Newlyn Dr Ashton-in-M WN4 ..73 B1
  Romiley SK6 ....113 A3
  Sale M33 ....108 C1
Newlyn St M14 ....98 B2

Newman Ave WN6 ....37 A2
Newman Cl WN2 ....56 C6
Newman St
  Ashton-u-L OL6 ....166 A3
  Hyde SK14 ....167 E3
  Rochdale OL16 ....15 C3
  Wigan WN1 ....37 E2
Newmarket Cl M33 ....107 B2
Newmarket Gr OL7 ....84 E5
Newmarket Mews M7 .....155 D6
Newmarket Rd
  Ashton-u-L OL7 ....84 F5
  Little Lever BL3 ....43 A2
Newmill Wlk ⓶ M8 ....156 A6
Newnham St BL1 ....143 D3
Newpark Wlk ⓺ M8 ....156 A6
Newport Ave SK5 ....111 E7
Newport Mews BL4 ....60 D7
Newport Rd Bolton BL3 ....42 A3
  Denton M34 ....113 B8
  Droylsden M43 ....84 A1
Newport St Bolton BL1,BL3 ..145 F6
  Bury BL8 ....27 A5
  Farnworth BL4 ....60 D7
  Manchester M14 ....98 B3
  Middleton M24 ....47 C1
  Oldham OL8 ....153 D5
  Salford M6 ....154 E2
Newquay Ave
  Ainsworth BL2 ....26 D1
  Reddish SK5 ....111 E7
Newquay Dr SK7 ....132 F7
Newry Rd M30 ....95 E8
Newry St BL1 ....143 D3
Newry Wlk M9 ....64 B3
Newsham Cl BL3 ....145 D5
Newsham Wlk
  ⓶ Manchester M12 ....99 B3
  Shevington WN6 ....36 F1
Newshaw La SK13 ....171 F4
Newsholme Cl WA3 ....91 F3
Newsholme St M8 ....155 F7
Newstead ⓾ OL12 ....139 E8
Newstead Ave
  Ashton-u-L OL6 ....85 C7
  Manchester M20 ....110 C6
Newstead Cl SK12 ....133 D5
Newstead Dr BL3 ....146 A2
Newstead Gr SK6 ....112 F3
Newstead Rd Urmston M41 ..95 E3
  Wigan WN1 ....54 F3
Newstead Terr WA15 ......119 F7
Newton Ave
  Manchester M12 ....98 F4
  Manchester M20 ....110 A6
Newton Bank Sch WA12 ..89 E4
Newton Bsns Pk SK14 ....102 A5
Newton Cl WN1 ....37 D2
Newton Comm Hospl
  WA12 ....89 B2
Newton Cts Prim Sch
  WA12 ....89 D3
Newton Dr Bolton BL1 ....11 A1
Newton Gn SK14 ....101 F5
Newton Hall Cl SK14 ......101 C5
Newton Hall Rd SK14 .....101 C5
Newton Heath Upper Sch
  M40 ....157 F5
Newton Ho M14 ....110 D8
Newton La WA12 ....89 E6
Newton Moor Ind Est
  SK14 ....101 E5
Newton Park Dr WA12 .....89 F7
Newton Rd
  Altrincham WA14 ....119 E2
  Billinge WN5,WA9,WN4 ....71 F6
  Failsworth M35 ....83 E6
  Golborne WA12,WA3 ....90 D5
  Golborne WA3,WN7 ....91 A8
  Handforth SK9 ....131 A1
  Manchester M24 ....64 B6
  Manchester M40 ....157 C6
⓶ Newton St Ashton-u-L OL6 ..166 C3
  Bolton BL1 ....143 E2
  Bury BL9 ....27 F6
  Droylsden M43 ....84 C3
  Hyde SK14 ....167 D4
  Leigh WN7 ....75 F5
  Manchester M1 ....159 B1
  Newton-le-W WA11 ....83 B1
  Newton Ave M34 ....100 F2
Newtown Cl
  Manchester M11 ....165 B8
  Swinton M27 ....61 F2
Newtown Ct
  Manchester M40 ....159 C4
  Prestwich M25 ....63 C4
Newtown St Prestwich M25 ..63 C4

Newtown St continued
  Shaw OL2 ....149 B6
Newville Dr M20 ....110 D5
Ney St OL7 ....84 F6
Neyland Cl BL1 ....84 F7
Niagara St SK2 ....124 A6
Nicholas Croft M4 ....159 A2
Nicholas Owen Cl M11 ...165 C8
Nicholas Rd OL8 ....66 E4
Nicholas St Bolton BL2 ...148 A8
  Manchester M1,M2 ....159 A1
Nicholas Varley
  Com Sch M40 ....160 E4
Nicholls St M12 ....164 D7
Nichols St M6 ....81 A3
Nicholson Rd SK14 ....101 C5
Nicholson Sq SK14 ....101 B8
Nicholson St Oldham OL4 ..67 E6
  Rochdale OL11 ....139 F5
  Stockport SK4 ....169 D3
Nickleby Rd SK12 ....133 E3
Nicol Mere Dr WN4 ....73 A5
Nicol Rd WN4 ....73 B5
Nicola St BL4 ....24 E8
Nicolas Rd M21 ....97 A1
Nield Rd M34 ....113 A8
Nield St OL5 ....68 B2
Nield's Brow WA14 ....119 C2
Nields Way SK6 ....126 D4
Nigel Rd M9 ....157 F7
Nigher Moss Ave OL16 .....31 C6
Nightingale Cl SK9 ....131 B1
Nightingale Ct M7 ....37 A1
Nightingale Dr M34 ....84 C1
Nightingale Gdns M23 ...109 A1
Nightingale Rd BL6 ....21 C8
Nightingale St M6 ....21 A8
Nightingales Wlk ⓷ BL3 ..147 F3
Nile St Bolton BL3 ....145 F5
  Dukinfield OL7 ....100 F8
  Oldham OL1 ....153 E8
  Rochdale OL16 ....31 A5
Nile Terr M7 ....155 D5
Nimble Nook OL9 ....152 A5
Nina Dr M40 ....65 C3
Nine Acre Ct M5 ....161 B7
Nine Acre Dr M5 ....161 B7
Ninehouse La BL3 ....147 F4
Ninfield Rd M23 ....121 B4
Ninian Ct ⓶ M24 ....46 F1
Ninian Gdns M28 ....60 D3
Ninth Ave OL8 ....66 D1
Nipper La M45 ....44 E2
Nisbet Ave M12 ....121 E3
Niven St M12 ....163 C7
Nixon Rd BL3 ....146 C3
Nixon Rd S M35 ....146 D5
Nixon St Failsworth M35 ...83 E7
  Rochdale OL11 ....30 B3
  Stockport SK3 ....170 E8
No 11 Pass M20 ....109 F5
No 2 Pass SK3 ....169 D1
Noahs Ark La WA14 ....136 A1
Noble Mdw OL12 ....15 D4
Noble St Bolton BL3 ......145 E5
  ⓻ Leigh WN7 ....76 A5
  Oldham OL8 ....153 F6
Noel Dr M33 ....108 D4
Noel St BL1 ....145 E7
Nolan St M9 ....157 E8
Nona St M6 ....154 E3
Nook Farm Ave OL12 ......14 F3
Nook Fields BL2 ....25 F2
Nook La Ashton-u-L OL6 ....85 E6
  Golborne WA3 ....90 B8
  Tyldesley M29 ....77 D2
Nook Terr ⓵ OL12 ....14 F3
Nook The
  Appley Bridge WN6 ....35 E7
  Bramhall SK7 ....132 D5
  Eccles M30 ....79 A4
Noon Ct WA12 ....89 B1
Noon Sun Cl OL3 ....69 A4
Noon Sun St OL12 ....14 F1
Norbet Wlk ⓼ M9 ....157 E7
Norbreck Ave
  Cheadle SK8 ....123 A6
  Manchester M14 ....110 C7
Norbreck Cres WN6 ....37 A2
Norbreck Gdns BL2 ....148 C8
Norbreck St BL2 ....148 C8
Norburn Rd M13 ....98 F2
Norbury Ave Billinge WN5 ..71 D6
  Hyde SK14 ....167 D3
  Marple SK6 ....125 E6
  Sale M33 ....107 F4
  ⓶ Salford M6 ....80 D5
  Uppermill OL3 ....68 C6
Norbury Cl M40 ....160 D4
Norbury Cres SK7 ....124 D2
Norbury Dr SK6 ....125 F6
Norbury Gr Bolton BL1 .....25 A4
  Hazel Grove SK7 ....124 E2
  Swinton M27 ....61 F1
Norbury Hall Prim Sch
  SK7 ....124 E1
Norbury Ho OL4 ....67 B5
Norbury Hollow Rd SK7 ..134 B8
Norbury La OL8 ....66 D2
Norbury Mews SK6 ....125 E6
Norbury St Leigh WN7 ......75 D5
  Manchester M7 ....155 E6
  Rochdale OL16 ....31 B4
  Stockport SK1 ....169 F3
Norbury Way ⓷ SK9 ......131 D5
Norcliffe Wlk ⓲ M18 ....99 B4
Norcot Wlk ⓯ M15 ....162 D6
Norcross Cl SK2 ....124 D5

Nordale Pk OL12 ....13 D2
Nordek Cl OL2 ....48 D5
Nordek Dr OL2 ....48 D5
Norden Ave M20 ....110 A6
Norden Cl OL11 ....13 C2
Norden Com Prim Sch
  OL12 ....13 F2
Norden Ct BL3 ....147 E4
Norden Rd OL11 ....29 E6
Norden Way OL11 ....13 C2
Nordens Dr OL9 ....47 F1
Nordens Rd OL9 ....65 F8
Nordens St OL9 ....152 A8
Noreen Ave M25 ....63 C5
Norfield Cl SK16 ....101 C8
Norfolk Ave Droylsden M43 ..83 F3
  Heywood OL10 ....29 A2
  Manchester M18 ....99 C4
  Reddish M34 ....99 F3
  Reddish SK4 ....111 C6
  Whitefield M45 ....63 A8
Norfolk Cl Hindley WN2 ....57 A6
  Irlam M44 ....105 C5
  Little Lever BL3 ....43 B4
  Littleborough OL15 ....6 C1
  Shaw OL2 ....148 F7
Norfolk Cres M35 ....83 E6
Norfolk Dr BL4 ....42 D1
Norfolk Gdns M41 ....94 D3
Norfolk Ho
  ⓮ Manchester M7 ....63 E1
  ⓼ Sale M33 ....108 D4
Norfolk Rd Atherton M46 ..58 C5
  Longshaw WN5 ....53 E1
  Manchester M18 ....99 C4
Norfolk St Glossop SK13 ..104 D1
  Hyde SK14 ....167 D2
  ⓾ Manchester M2 ....158 F1
  Manchester M7 ....159 A1
  Oldham OL9 ....66 C4
  Rochdale OL16 ....139 F6
  Salford M6 ....81 A3
  Walkden M28 ....60 D6
  ⓽ Wigan WN5 ....54 F6
  Wigan WN6 ....37 A2
Norford Way OL11 ....13 B3
Norgate St M20 ....110 B3
Norlan Ave M34 ....100 E7
Norland Wlk M40 ....83 A5
Norleigh Rd M22 ....121 D8
Norley Ave M32 ....96 E3
Norley Cl OL1 ....48 B2
Norley Dr Manchester M19 ..99 C2
  Sale M33 ....108 E4
Norley Hall Ave WN5 ....54 C6
Norley Rd Leigh WN7 ....75 B4
Norley St WN5 ....54 C7
Norman Ave
  Ashton-in-M WA11 ....89 A7
  Hazel Grove SK7 ....124 C3
  Newton-le-W WA12 ....89 E3
Norman Cl M24 ....47 C1
Norman Gr ⓶ Manchester M12 ..98 F4
  Manchester M12 ....99 A4
  Reddish SK5 ....111 E7
Norman House Prep Sch
  M40 ....165 D3
Norman Rd
  Altrincham WA14 ....119 C6
  Ashton-u-L OL6 ....85 C6
  Manchester M14 ....98 D2
  Rochdale OL11 ....139 D6
  Sale M33 ....108 B3
  Stalybridge SK15 ....85 F2
Norman Rd W M9 ....157 E7
Norman St ⓹ Bury BL9 ....141 B4
  Failsworth M35 ....66 A1
  Hyde SK14 ....167 E2
  Manchester M12 ....165 B5
  Manchester M24 ....47 B1
  Oldham OL1 ....153 D8
  Radcliffe M26 ....44 D4
Norman Weall Ct ⓷ M24 ..47 A2
Normanby Chase WA14 ..119 B4
Normanby Gr M27 ....61 E2
Normanby Rd M28 ....60 C1
Normanby St Bolton BL3 ..146 C2
  Manchester M14 ....98 A4
  Swinton M27 ....61 E1
  Wigan WN5 ....54 B6
Normandale Ave BL1 ......142 A1
Normandy Cres M26 ....43 F3
Normanton Ave M6 ....80 C3
Normanton Cl WN6 ....36 E4
Normanton Dr M9 ....64 B4
Normanton Rd SK3,SK8 ..123 A6
Normington St ⓵ OL4 ......67 C7
Norreys Ave M16 ....94 E3
Norreys St OL16 ....31 A8
Norris Ave SK4 ....168 C1
Norris Bank Prim Sch
  SK4 ....168 B3
Norris Bank Terr SK4 .....168 B3
Norris Hill Dr SK4 ....168 C2
Norris Rd M33 ....108 B5
Norris St Bolton BL3 ....145 E5
  Farnworth BL4 ....60 D7
  Little Lever BL3 ....43 A3
  Tyldesley M29 ....77 A8
Norris Towers SK1 ....169 E2
North Area Coml Sch 18 B3
North Ave Eccles M41 ......95 E6
  Golborne WN7 ....74 F4

North Ave continued
Leigh WN7 ...76 C3
Manchester M19 ...110 F7
Oldham OL3 ...69 B5
Ramsbottom BL8 ...10 F1
Stalybridge SK15 ...86 A3
Whitefield B3 ...45 B4
North Back Rock BL9 ...140 F2
North Blackfield La M7 ...81 C8
North Bolton
 Sixth Form Coll BL1 ...142 C4
North Brook Rd SK13 ...171 E4
North Broughton St M3 ...158 E2
North Butts St WN7 ...76 B3
North Cestrian Gram Sch
 WA14 ...119 C5
North Chadderton
 Comp Sch OL9 ...152 A8
North Chadderton Sch
 OL9 ...48 A2
North Cheshire
 Jewish Prim Sch SK8 ...122 C2
North Circ M45 ...63 A6
North Cl SK13 ...103 F7
North Clifden La M7 ...155 E6
North Cres Droylsden M11 ...83 D3
 Failsworth M40 ...65 C1
North Croft OL3 ...67 A3
North Dean St M27 ...62 A1
North Downs Rd SK8 ...122 F3
North Dr Appley Bridge WN6 ...18 C2
 Droylsden M34 ...84 C1
 Pendlebury M27 ...80 B7
North Edge WN7 ...76 B6
North End Rd SK15 ...86 B2
North Gate OL8 ...66 E2
North George St M3 ...158 D2
North Gr Manchester M13 ...164 D5
 Urmston M41 ...95 C2
 Walkden M28 ...60 C3
North Grecian Street
 Prim Sch M7 ...81 C5
North Harvey St SK14 ...169 F1
North Heaton Prim Sch
 SK4 ...111 C6
North Hill St M3 ...158 D3
North La Rochdale OL12 ...139 F8
 Tyldesley M29 ...77 A6
North Lonsdale St M32 ...96 E4
North Manchester
 General Hospl M8 ...64 B1
North Manchester High Sch
 for Boys (Lower)
 M9 ...65 B3
North Manchester High Sch
 for Girls M40 ...65 A1
North Mead M21 ...109 B7
North Nook OL4 ...67 F8
North Par Newhey OL16 ...32 C4
 Sale M33 ...108 D2
North Park Rd SK7 ...123 E3
North Phoebe St M5 ...161 B8
North Pl SK1 ...169 F1
North Quarry Bsns Pk
 WN6 ...18 D2
North Rd Altrincham WA15 ...129 A8
 Atherton M46 ...58 B5
 Carrington M31 ...106 E4
 Droylsden M11 ...83 C2
 Droylsden M34 ...84 D1
 Glossop SK13 ...104 C3
 Prestwich M25 ...62 F5
 Stretford M17 ...96 C5
 Stretford M32 ...96 B4
North Reddish Jun
 & Inf Schs SK5 ...99 F1
North Rise OL3 ...69 B5
North St Ashton-in-M WN4 ...73 D5
 Ashton-u-L OL6 ...166 A2
 Atherton M46 ...58 E3
 Heywood OL10 ...29 B2
 Leigh WN7 ...76 B4
 Manchester M8 ...159 A4
 Middleton M24 ...47 A2
 Radcliffe M26 ...44 C4
 Ramsbottom BL0 ...1 C2
 Rochdale OL16 ...31 A8
 Royton OL2 ...48 D3
 1 Royton OL2 ...48 E4
 Whitworth OL12 ...4 C1
North Stage M5 ...96 F8
North Star Dr M3 ...158 D1
North Trafford Coll of F Ed
 M32 ...96 F4
North Vale Rd WA15 ...119 F6
North View M45 ...44 C4
North View Mossley OL5 ...68 E1
 Ramsbottom BL0 ...11 B2
 Ramsbottom BL9 ...11 B2
North View Cl OL4 ...68 C5
North Walkden Prim Sch
 M28 ...60 C5
North Way Bolton BL1 ...25 B4
 Brinnington SK5 ...112 C6
 Hyde SK14 ...167 E2
North Western St
 Manchester M1,M12 ...163 C8
 Manchester M12 ...164 D7
 Manchester M12 ...164 D7
North Woodley 6 M26 ...44 C1
Northallerton Rd M7 ...81 B6
Northampton Rd
 Manchester M40 ...157 F6
 Manchester M40 ...83 A6
Northampton Wlk 1
 M34 ...101 A1
Northavon Cl WN4 ...80 A1
Northbank Gdns M19 ...110 E6

Northbank Ind Pk M44 ...105 F7
Northbank Wlk M20 ...109 D3
Northbourne St M6 ...154 E2
Northbrook Ave WN7 ...63 F4
Northcliffe Rd SK2 ...124 C8
Northcombe Rd SK3 ...170 E5
Northcote Rd SK7 ...132 F7
Northcroft WN1 ...37 F1
Northdale Rd M9 ...64 B5
Northdene Dr OL11 ...29 F6
Northdown Ave
 Manchester M15 ...162 D6
 Romiley SK6 ...113 C5
Northdowns Rd OL2 ...48 F8
Northen Gr M20 ...109 F4
Northenden Prim Sch
 M22 ...109 D1
Northenden Rd
 Gatley SK8 ...122 A6
 Sale M33 ...108 C3
 Sale M33 ...108 C4
Northenden View M20 ...110 B2
Northern Ave M27 ...62 C3
Northern Gr BL1 ...142 C1
Northfield Ave M40 ...65 F2
Northfield Cl WN3 ...74 C1
Northfield Dr SK9 ...137 D8
Northfield Rd Bury BL9 ...27 F6
 Failsworth M40 ...65 F2
Northfield St BL3 ...144 C5
Northfleet Rd M30 ...94 F8
Northgate OL12 ...14 C7
Northgate La OL1 ...49 E3
Northgate Rd SK3 ...123 C8
Northland Rd Bolton BL1 ...24 F6
 Manchester M9 ...64 E3
Northleigh Dr M25 ...63 D2
Northleach Cl BL8 ...27 B3
Northleigh Ho 1 M16 ...97 B2
Northleigh Rd M16 ...97 B3
Northmoor Rd M12 ...99 A3
Northolme Gdns M19 ...110 E5
Northolt Ave WN7 ...75 F8
Northolt Ct M11 ...83 D2
Northolt Dr BL3 ...147 F4
Northolt Rd M23 ...108 F1
Northridge Rd M9 ...64 D6
Northside Ave M41 ...94 F1
Northstead Ave M34 ...101 B2
Northumberland Ave
 OL7 ...166 A4
Northumberland Cl M16 ...161 C5
Northumberland Cres
 M16 ...161 C5
Northumberland Rd
 Brinnington SK5 ...112 B6
 Manchester M16 ...161 C5
 Partington M31 ...105 E2
Northumberland St
 Manchester M7 ...155 E7
 Wigan WN1 ...37 E1
Northumbria St 8 BL3 ...144 C5
Northurst Dr M8 ...63 F3
Northward Rd SK9 ...136 F6
Northway
 Altrincham WA14 ...119 E6
 Droylsden M43 ...100 A8
 2 Eccles M30 ...79 F2
 Wigan WN1 ...37 C1
Northways WN6 ...19 D2
Northwell St 7 WN7 ...75 E8
Northwold Dr 1 M9 ...64 D3
Northwold Dr Bolton BL1 ...40 E8
 Manchester M9 ...64 D3
Northwood BL2 ...25 D4
Northwood Ave WA12 ...89 F3
Northwood Cres BL3 ...144 C5
Northwood Gr M33 ...108 B4
Norton Ave
 Manchester M12 ...99 B3
 Reddish M34 ...100 A3
 Sale M33 ...107 D6
 Urmston M41 ...95 D4
Norton Gr SK4 ...168 B1
Norton Grange M25 ...63 D3
Norton Rd Boothstown M28 ...77 E7
 Rochdale OL12 ...143 F3
Norton St Bolton BL1 ...143 F1
 3 Manchester M1 ...159 C1
 Manchester M16 ...97 D4
 Manchester M40 ...160 E4
Norville Ave M40,M9 ...65 E3
Norway Gr SK5 ...169 F4
Norway St Bolton BL1 ...143 D2
 Manchester M11 ...164 E8
 Salford M6 ...154 E2
 Stretford M32 ...96 E3
Norweb Way WN7 ...76 B3
Norwell Rd M22 ...121 E5
Norwich Ave
 Ashton-in-M WN4 ...73 D3
 Chadderton OL9 ...48 A1
 Denton M34 ...100 F1
 Golborne WA3 ...90 D8
 Rochdale OL11 ...30 B7
Norwich Cl Ashton-u-L OL6 ...85 D8
 Dukinfield SK16 ...102 A7
Norwich Dr BL8 ...140 D3
Norwich Rd M32 ...95 F3
Norwich St OL11 ...31 A5
Norwood Cl BL3 ...40 E4
Norwood M25 ...63 B2
Norwood Ave
 Ashton-in-M WN4 ...72 F6

Norwood Ave continued
 Bramhall SK7 ...132 D5
 Cheadle SK8 ...123 A3
 Golborne WA3 ...90 F7
 High Lane SK6 ...134 D7
 Manchester M20 ...110 D4
 Manchester M7 ...81 B8
 Tyldesley M29 ...77 B6
 Wigan WN6 ...37 A3
Norwood Cl Adlington PR6 ...21 A8
 Shaw OL2 ...149 A8
 Walkden M28 ...78 E8
Norwood Cres OL2 ...48 E2
Norwood Ct M32 ...96 E1
Norwood Dr
 Altrincham WA15 ...120 D5
 Swinton M27 ...79 D7
Norwood Gr Bolton BL1 ...144 C8
 Oldham OL2 ...48 E2
Norwood Lo M7 ...81 B8
Norwood Rd Gatley SK8 ...122 B6
 Stockport SK2 ...124 B4
 Stretford M32 ...96 E2
Noseby Ct M25 ...63 C5
Nostell Rd WN4 ...73 A5
Nottingham Ave SK5 ...112 C6
Nottingham Cl SK5 ...112 C5
Nottingham Dr
 Ashton-u-L OL6 ...85 B7
 Bolton BL1 ...143 E1
 Failsworth M40 ...65 A3
Nottingham Pl M1 ...37 E1
Nottingham Way 3 M34 ...101 A1
Nowell Ct M24 ...47 A3
Nowell House M24 ...47 A3
Nowell Rd M24 ...47 A3
Nudger Cl OL3 ...50 F2
Nudger Gn OL3 ...51 A2
Nuffield Rd M22 ...121 E4
Nugent House Sch WN5 ...71 D4
Nugent Rd BL3 ...147 E3
Nugget St OL4 ...67 B6
Nuneaton Dr M40 ...160 D3
Nuneham Ave M20 ...110 C7
Nunfield Cl M40 ...65 B2
Nunnery Rd BL3 ...146 B4
Nunthorpe Dr M8 ...156 C6
Nursery Ave WA15 ...128 E8
Nursery Cl Glossop SK13 ...116 C8
 Sale M33 ...108 C4
 Stockport SK2 ...124 D7
Nursery Dr SK12 ...133 E4
Nursery La Cheadle SK13 ...123 A7
 Wilmslow SK9 ...136 F5
Nursery Rd Cheadle SK8 ...123 A1
 Failsworth M35 ...84 A7
 Prestwich M25 ...63 A4
 Stockport SK4 ...168 C2
 Urmston M41 ...95 A3
Nursery St Manchester M16 ...97 F3
 Salford M6 ...154 F3
Nuthatch Ave M28 ...78 D8
Nuthurst Rd M40 ...65 D1
Nutsford Vale M12,M18 ...99 B4
Nutt La M25 ...63 E8
Nutt St WN1 ...37 E2
Nuttal Sq BL9 ...44 F5
Nuttall Ave Horwich BL6 ...22 A3
 Little Lever BL3 ...43 C3
 Whitefield M45 ...62 F8
Nuttall Cl BL0 ...138 C5
Nuttall Hall Cotts BL0 ...11 D5
Nuttall Hall Rd BL0 ...11 D5
Nuttall La M45 ...138 B5
Nuttall Mews M45 ...62 F8
Nuttall Rd BL0 ...11 D4
Nuttall St Atherton M46 ...58 C3
 Bury M25 ...141 A1
 Irlam M44 ...105 D4
 Manchester M11 ...165 A4
 Manchester M16 ...161 C5
 Oldham OL8 ...67 B4

O

O'Kane Ho 10 M30 ...79 D1
Oadby Cl M12 ...99 A4
Oak Ave Abram Brow WN2 ...74 A2
 Cheadle SK8 ...123 A2
 Golborne WA3 ...90 B8
 High Lane SK6 ...134 D7
 7 Horwich BL6 ...22 E1
 Irlam M44 ...105 D5
 Little Lever BL3 ...43 B3
 Manchester M21 ...109 B8
 Manchester SK4 ...168 B3
 Middleton M24 ...65 A7
 Newton-le-W WA12 ...89 D3
 Ramsbottom BL0 ...11 A2
 Reddish M34 ...99 F4
 Romiley SK6 ...113 C2
 Royton OL2 ...48 D6
 Standish WN6 ...36 F8
 Whitefield M45 ...62 F7
 Wilmslow SK9 ...136 F6
Oak Bank Manchester M9 ...158 D7
 Prestwich M25 ...62 F1
 Prestwich M25 ...62 F1
Oak Bank Ave M9 ...64 F1
Oak Bank Cl M45 ...63 B8
Oak Brow Cotts SK9 ...130 E4
Oak Cl Mottram-in-L SK14 ...103 A4
 Whitworth OL12 ...4 D4
 Wilmslow SK9 ...136 F6
Oak Coppice BL1 ...144 A7

Oak Cotts SK9 ...130 E4
Oak Ct SK6 ...113 A5
Oak Dr Bramhall SK7 ...132 C7
 Manchester M14 ...98 D1
 Marple SK6 ...125 D6
 Reddish M34 ...100 A4
Oak Gates BL7 ...8 E1
Oak Gr Ashton-u-L OL6 ...85 D6
 Cheadle SK8 ...122 E5
 Eccles M30 ...79 B1
 Poynton SK12 ...133 D4
 Urmston M41 ...95 E2
Oak Hill OL15 ...15 F5
Oak Hill Cl WN1 ...37 B4
Oak La Whitefield M45 ...63 B8
Oak Lea Ave SK9 ...137 A5
Oak Lo SK7 ...132 F7
Oak Mews SK9 ...131 C1
Oak Rd Altrincham WA15 ...119 E3
 Cheadle SK8 ...122 E5
 Failsworth M35 ...83 F6
 Manchester M20 ...110 B5
 Manchester M7 ...81 C5
 Oldham OL8 ...66 D2
 Partington M31 ...105 D2
 Sale M33 ...108 D4
Oak St Atherton M46 ...58 A1
 Denton M34 ...100 F6
 Eccles M30 ...79 D1
 Glossop SK13 ...104 C1
 Hazel Grove SK7 ...124 D3
 Heywood OL10 ...29 B3
 Hyde SK14 ...167 E4
 Leigh WN7 ...75 F3
 Littleborough OL15 ...16 C5
 Manchester M4 ...159 A2
 2 Manchester M4 ...159 B2
 Middleton M24 ...65 D7
 Newhey OL16 ...32 B4
 Radcliffe M26 ...44 B2
 Ramsbottom BL0 ...138 B5
 Rochdale OL16 ...139 F7
 Shaw OL2 ...149 C2
 Stockport SK3 ...123 B8
 Swinton M27 ...62 A1
 Tyldesley M29 ...59 A1
 Whitworth OL12 ...4 D1
 Wigan WN1 ...151 E7
Oak Terr OL15 ...6 D2
Oak Tree Cl Atherton M46 ...58 A1
Oak Tree Cres SK15 ...102 B8
Oak Tree Dr SK16 ...101 F7
Oak View OL12 ...4 D4
Oak View Rd OL3 ...69 B5
Oak Wood View OL5 ...86 C6
Oakbank WN2 ...56 B3
Oakbank Ave OL9 ...65 F8
Oakbank Dr BL1 ...24 D6
Oakcliffe Rd OL12 ...15 D4
Oakcroft SK15 ...102 E8
Oakdale BL2 ...25 E4
Oakdale Cl M45 ...62 D8
Oakdale Ct
 Altrincham WA14 ...119 C5
 Delph OL3 ...50 E3
 Stalybridge SK15 ...86 B2
Oakdale Dr Gatley SK8 ...122 B2
 Manchester M20 ...110 C1
 Tyldesley M29 ...77 C6
Oakdale Sch M16 ...101 E6
Oakdene M27 ...79 B6
Oakdene Ave Gatley SK8 ...131 C7
 Reddish SK4 ...111 D5
Oakdene Cres SK6 ...125 F7
Oakdene Gdns SK6 ...125 F7
Oakdene Rd Marple SK6 ...125 F7
 Middleton M24 ...65 C8
 Sale WA15 ...120 B8
Oakdene St M9 ...157 F8
Oaken Bank Rd M24 ...47 A5
Oaken Clough Dr OL7 ...84 F5
Oaken Clough Dr 1 OL7 ...84 F5
Oaken Clough Terr OL7 ...84 F6
Oaken St 2 OL7 ...84 F6
Oakenbottom Rd BL2 ...42 D7
Oakenclough 1 SK9 ...131 D2
Oakenclough Dr BL1 ...23 F2
Oakenclough Prim Sch
 SK9 ...131 D1
Oakenden Cl WN4 ...73 A6
Oakengates WN6 ...19 F1
Oakenrod Hill OL11 ...30 C6
Oakenrod Prim Sch
 OL11 ...139 D7
Oakenshaw Ave OL12 ...14 C6
Oakenshaw View OL12 ...14 C6
Oaker Ave M20 ...109 E4
Oaker Pl M20 ...109 E4
Oakes St BL4 ...60 F7
Oakes The SK13 ...116 A7
Oakfield Dukinfield SK16 ...101 E6
 Manchester M25 ...63 D3
 Sale M33 ...108 D4
Oakfield Ave Atherton M46 ...58 C4
 Cheadle SK8 ...122 E6
 Droylsden M43 ...73 F1
 Manchester M14 ...98 C4
 Manchester M16 ...97 D3
 Mossley SK15 ...86 E6
Oakfield Cl
 Bramhall SK7 ...137 B3
 Bramhall SK7 ...132 E4
 Horwich BL6 ...22 F2
Oakfield Cres WN2 ...38 C5

Oakwood Ave *continued*
Failsworth M40 . . . . .65 D1
Gatley SK8 . . . . .122 B5
Kearsley M27 . . . . .61 E4
Shevington WN6 . . . . .35 F5
Crosskey M28 . . . . .60 B7
Wilmslow SK9 . . . . .136 E6
Oakwood Cl BL8 . . . . .27 B3
Oakwood Com Prim Sch
M31 .105 D3
Oakwood Ct WA14 . . . . .128 B8
Oakwood Dr Bolton BL1 . . . .40 F8
Leigh WN7 . . . . .75 E1
Salford M6 . . . . .80 B5
Walkden M28 . . . . .60 F2
Oakwood Est M5 . . . . .154 D1
Oakwood High Sch M21 . . .109 C5
Oakwood High Sch
(Upper Sch) M21 . . . . .109 C7
Oakwood La WA14 . . . . .119 B1
Oakwood Rd Disley SK12 . .135 D6
Romiley SK6 . . . . .113 C2
Oakworth Croft OL4 . . . . . . .49 F4
Oakworth Dr BL1 . . . . .24 D5
Oakworth St M9 . . . . .64 C3
Oat St SK1 . . . . .124 B2
Oatlands Rd M22 . . . . .121 C2
Oban Ave OL1 . . . . .49 B1
Oban Cres SK4 . . . . .123 D4
Oban Dr Garswood WN4 . . . .72 C4
Sale M33 . . . . .108 E3
Oban Gr BL1 . . . . .24 E5
Oban St BL1 . . . . .143 D3
Oban Way WN2 . . . . .38 D5
Oberlin St Oldham OL4 . . . . .67 D7
Rochdale OL11 . . . . .139 D5
Oberon Cl M30 . . . . .79 D2
Occlestone Cl M33 . . . . .108 E1
Ocean St WA14 . . . . .119 B6
Ocean Street Trad Est
WA14 . . . . .119 B6
Ocean Wlk M15 . . . . .162 F5
Ockendon Dr M9 . . . . .157 E7
Octavia Dr M40 . . . . .83 C4
Odell St M11 . . . . .165 B7
Odessa Ave M6 . . . . .80 B4
Odette St M18 . . . . .99 C4
Off Grove Rd SK15 . . . . .86 D4
Off Ridge Hill La 2 SK15 . .85 F2
Off Stamford St SK15 . . . . . .86 D4
Offerton Dr SK2 . . . . .124 D6
Offerton Fold SK2 . . . . .124 C7
Offerton Gn SK2 . . . . .124 F6
Offerton Hall Prim Sch
SK2 .124 E6
Offerton High Sch SK2 . . . .124 E8
Offerton Ind Est SK1,SK2 . .124 C7
Offerton La SK2 . . . . .124 D7
Offerton Rd SK2,SK7 . . . . . .125 A4
Offerton St Horwich BL6 . . . .22 A3
Stockport SK1 . . . . .112 B2
Ogbourne Wlk 11 M13 . . . .163 C6
Ogden Cl Haslingden BB4 . . .1 A7
Heywood OL10 . . . . .29 A2
Whitefield M45 . . . . .45 A1
Ogden Ct SK14 . . . . .167 E2
Ogden Dr BB4 . . . . .1 A7
Ogden Gdns SK16 . . . . .101 E8
Ogden Gr SK8 . . . . .121 F4
Ogden La Manchester M11 . . .99 D7
Newhey OL16 . . . . .32 D5
Ogden Rd Bramhall SK7 . . . .132 D5
Failsworth M35 . . . . .83 F6
Ogden Sq SK16 . . . . .101 B8
Ogden St
4 Manchester M20 . . . . . . .110 B3
Middleton M24 . . . . .65 A8
Mottram-in-L SK14 . . . . .115 B8
9 Oldham OL4 . . . . .67 D6
Oldham OL9 . . . . .152 C8
Prestwich M25 . . . . .63 C4
Rochdale OL11 . . . . .30 C2
Swinton M27 . . . . .79 F7
Ogden Wlk M45 . . . . .63 A8
Ogmore Wlk M40 . . . . .65 C2
Ogwen Dr M25 . . . . .63 B5
Ohio Ave M5 . . . . .96 F8
Okehampton Cl M26 . . . . . . .43 C5
Okehampton Cres M33 . . . .107 D5
Okell Gr WN7 . . . . .75 D6
Okeover Rd M7 . . . . .155 D8
Olaf St 18 BL2 . . . . .25 B1
Old Bank Cl SK6 . . . . .113 A3
Old Bank St M2 . . . . .158 F1
Old Bank View OL1 . . . . .49 C4
Old Barn Pl BL7 . . . . .25 A8
Old Barton Rd M41 . . . . .95 C7
Old Bedions Sports Ctr
M20 .122 A8
Old Bent La OL4 . . . . .15 A7
Old Birley St M15 . . . . .162 F5
Old Boston WA11 . . . . .89 A7
Old Boston Trad Est WA11 .89 B8
Old Broadway M20 . . . . .110 B5
Old Brook Cl OL2 . . . . .49 D8
Old Brow OL5 . . . . .68 C1
Old Brow La OL16 . . . . .15 C3
Old Brown Ct OL5 . . . . .86 C8
Old Chapel St SK3 . . . . .170 D7
Old Church Mews 2
SK16 . . . . .101 E8
Old Church St
Failsworth M40 . . . . .83 C6
Oldham OL1 . . . . .153 F7
Old Clay Dr OL12 . . . . .15 D4

Old Clough La
Walkden M28 . . . . .60 F1
Worsley M28 . . . . .78 F8
Old Colliery Yd WN4 . . . . . . .72 C3
Old Crofts Bank SK1 . . . . . .124 B7
Old Crofts Bank M41 . . . . . . .95 C3
Old Cross St OL6 . . . . .166 C3
Old Ctyd The M22 . . . . .121 F5
Old Dairy Mews SK14 . . . . .101 C5
Old Delph Rd OL11 . . . . .13 F1
Old Doctors St BL8 . . . . .26 F7
Old Eagley Mews BL1 . . . . . .24 F6
Old Edge La OL2 . . . . .48 E2
Old Elm St M12,M13 . . . . . . .163 C6
Old Engine La BL0 . . . . .11 D6
Old Farm Cres M43 . . . . .99 F8
Old Farm Dr SK2 . . . . .124 F6
Old Fold Eccles M30 . . . . . . .79 C4
7 Wigan WN5 . . . . .54 B6
Old Fold Rd Aspull WN2 . . . .38 D5
Westhoughton BL5 . . . . .57 C7
Old Garden The WA15 . . . . .120 B7
Old Gardens St 3 SK1 . . . .170 F8
Old Gn BL2 . . . . .25 E6
Old Green BL8 . . . . .10 F1
Old Greenwood La BL6 . . . . .22 D1
Old Ground St BL0 . . . . .138 C6
Old Hall Cl Bury BL8 . . . . . . .27 B7
Glossop SK13 . . . . .104 D2
Old Hall Clough BL6 . . . . . . .40 C7
Old Hall Cres SK9 . . . . .131 E3
Old Hall Ct Sale M33 . . . . . .108 E4
Whitefield M45 . . . . .62 C7
Old Hall Dr
Ashton-in-M WN4 . . . . .73 A2
Manchester M18 . . . . .99 D4
Stockport SK2 . . . . .124 E6
Old Hall Farm BL3 . . . . .42 E4
Old Hall La Bolton BL1,BL6 . .23 C1
Manchester M13,M14,M19 . . .98 E2
Manchester M25 . . . . .64 A6
Marple SK6 . . . . .126 C5
Mottram-in-L SK14 . . . . .103 A5
Westhoughton BL5 . . . . .57 E5
Whitefield M45 . . . . .62 C6
Woodford SK7 . . . . .132 D1
Worsley M28 . . . . .78 E7
Old Hall Mill La M46 . . . . . . .76 A8
Old Hall Prim Sch BL8 . . . . .27 B7
Old Hall Rd Failsworth M40 . .83 B7
Gatley SK8 . . . . .122 A6
Manchester M7 . . . . .63 D1
Sale M33 . . . . .108 E4
Stretford M32 . . . . .96 A4
Whitefield M45 . . . . .62 C7
Old Hall Sq 2 SK13 . . . . . . .104 A5
Old Hall St Dukinfield SK16 .101 A7
Farnworth BL4 . . . . .60 E7
Ince-in-M WN3 . . . . .150 A8
3 Manchester M11 . . . . .99 E7
Middleton M24 . . . . .47 A1
Old Hall St N BL1 . . . . .145 F7
Old Hey Wlk WA12 . . . . .89 C1
Old Heyes Rd WA15 . . . . . . .120 B8
Old House Terrs OL6 . . . . . . .85 E5
Old Kiln OL3 . . . . .3 D8
Old Kiln La Bolton BL1 . . . . . .23 D1
Mossley OL4 . . . . .68 B4
Old La Bury BL9 . . . . .27 F8
Glossop SK13 . . . . .116 A7
Horwich BL6 . . . . .22 F2
Manchester M11 . . . . .99 D7
Oldham OL4 . . . . .68 A8
Oldham OL9 . . . . .66 B4
Shevington WN6 . . . . .36 B6
Uppermill OL3 . . . . .51 B2
Uppermill OL4 . . . . .68 E6
Walkden M38 . . . . .59 F6
Westhoughton BL5 . . . . .57 D8
Worsworth OL12,OL13 . . . . . .4 C6
Wigan WN1 . . . . .37 B4
Old Lansdowne Rd M20 . . . .110 A4
Old Lees St OL6 . . . . .85 D5
Old Lord's Cres BL6 . . . . . . .22 B5
Old Manor Pk M46 . . . . .58 A2
Old Market Pl WA14 . . . . . . .119 D5
Old Market St M9 . . . . .64 D2
Old Meadow Dr M34 . . . . . . .100 F5
Old Meadow La WA15 . . . . .120 B3
Old Mill Cl M27 . . . . .162 E8
Old Mill Ct M27 . . . . .80 B8
Old Mill Ho OL4 . . . . .68 A5
Old Mill La
Hazel Grove SK7 . . . . .134 A8
Oldham OL4 . . . . .68 A5
Old Mill St M4 . . . . .159 C1
Old Mills Hill M24 . . . . .47 D1
Old Moat Jun & Inf Sch
M20 .110 A7
Old Moat La M20 . . . . .110 B7
Old Moss La WA3 . . . . .92 E6
Old Mount St M4 . . . . .159 B3
Old Nans La BL2 . . . . .25 F2
Old Nursery Fold BL2 . . . . . .25 E4
Old Oak Cl BL2 . . . . .43 B5
Old Oak Dr M34 . . . . .101 A1
Old Oak St M20 . . . . .110 B3
Old Oake Cl M28 . . . . .60 E2
Old Orch The WA15 . . . . . . .120 B8
Old Orchard SK9 . . . . .137 A7
Old Pack Horse Rd OL4 . . . .51 E6
Old Packhorse Rd OL15 . . . .16 F6
Old Parrin La M30 . . . . .79 B3
Old Pasture Cl SK2 . . . . .124 E7
Old Pepper La WN6 . . . . .19 B2
Old Quarry La BL7 . . . . .8 F1

Old Rake BL6 . . . . .22 E5
Old Rd Ashton-in-M WN4 . . . .73 A4
Ashton-u-L OL6 . . . . .86 A6
Bolton BL1 . . . . .143 E3
Cheadle SK8 . . . . .122 F6
Dukinfield SK16 . . . . .166 C1
Failsworth M35 . . . . .83 E8
Handforth SK9 . . . . .131 D3
Hyde SK14 . . . . .167 D8
Littleborough OL16 . . . . .15 E4
Manchester M9 . . . . .64 D2
Stalybridge SK14 . . . . .102 F5
Stalybridge SK15 . . . . .102 C8
Stockport SK4 . . . . .169 E3
Tintwistle SK13 . . . . .104 A7
Wilmslow SK9 . . . . .137 B8
Old Rectory Gdns SK8 . . . . .122 D5
Old River Cl M44 . . . . .94 A2
Old School Ct Eccles M30 . . .79 C4
Manchester M9 . . . . .64 C2
Old School Dr M9 . . . . .64 C2
Old School House The
OL15 .15 F6
Old School La PR7 . . . . .20 E5
Old School Mews
12 Bacup OL13 . . . . .3 C8
1 Dukinfield SK15,SK16 . . .101 E8
Old School Pl WN4 . . . . .73 A2
Old Shaw St M5 . . . . .161 B8
Old Sirs BL5 . . . . .57 F5
Old St Oldham OL4 . . . . .166 C3
Old St Ashton-u-L OL6 . . . . . .166 B3
Mottram-in-L SK14 . . . . .115 A8
Oldham OL4 . . . . .67 D5
Old Station St 3 M30 . . . . . . .79 C1
Old Swan Cl BL7 . . . . .8 E2
Old Swan Cotts BL7 . . . . .8 E2
Old Thorn La OL3 . . . . .69 D6
Old Towns Cl BL8 . . . . .26 F7
Old Trafford Jun Sch
M16 .161 C5
Old Trafford Prim Sch
M15 .161 C6
Old Trafford Sta M16 . . . . . . .97 A4
Old Vicarage BL5 . . . . .57 E5
Old Vicarage Gdns M28 . . . .60 D3
Old Vicarage Mews BL5 . . . .57 E5
Old Vicarage Rd BL6 . . . . . . .22 F3
Old Wargrave Rd WA12 . . . . .89 C3
Old Well Wlk M33 . . . . .107 D2
Old Wellington Rd M30 . . . . .79 E2
Old Wells Cl M38 . . . . .60 A6
Old Will's La BL6 . . . . .22 B6
Old Wool La SK8 . . . . .122 F4
Old York St M15 . . . . .162 E6
Oldbridge Dr WN2 . . . . .56 D6
Oldbrook Fold WA15 . . . . . . .120 B4
Oldbury Cl Heywood OL10 . . .46 D7
Manchester M40 . . . . .160 D3
Oldcastle Ave M20 . . . . .110 A8
Oldcott Cl M28 . . . . .77 F5
Oldcroft OL4 . . . . .68 A6
Oldershaw Dr M9 . . . . .157 D6

Oldfield Brow Prim Sch
WA14 . . . . .119 A5
Oldfield Cl BL5 . . . . .57 F8
Oldfield Dr WA15 . . . . .119 F6
Oldfield Gr M33 . . . . .108 C5
Oldfield La WA14 . . . . .118 F4
Oldfield Mews WA14 . . . . . .119 C5
Oldfield Rd
Altrincham WA14 . . . . .119 B5
Manchester M30 . . . . .81 C1
Prestwich M25 . . . . .63 C7
Sale M33 . . . . .108 C5
Salford M5 . . . . .161 C8
Oldfield St M11 . . . . .83 C1
Oldgate Wlk 17 M15 . . . . . .162 E6
Oldham Art Gal & Mus
OL1 .153 F6
Oldham Athletic AFC
(Boundary Pk) OL1 . . . . . . .48 D2
Oldham Ave SK1 . . . . .112 B1
Oldham Coll OL9 . . . . .153 E7
Oldham Ct 15 M40 . . . . .159 C3
Oldham Dr SK5 . . . . .113 B4
Oldham Rd Ashton-u-L OL7 . .85 A5
Delph OL3,OL4 . . . . .50 D2
Failsworth M35,M40 . . . . .83 D6
Middleton M24 . . . . .65 A8
Rochdale OL11,OL16,OL12 . . .31 A3
Royton OL1,OL2 . . . . .48 E3
Shaw OL1,OL4 . . . . .50 B7
Shaw OL2 . . . . .149 B5
Uppermill OL3,OL4 . . . . .51 C6
Oldham Sixth Form Coll
OL4 .153 E6
Oldham St Denton M34 . . . . .100 C3
Droylsden M43 . . . . .84 B2
Hyde SK14 . . . . .167 D2
Manchester M1,M4 . . . . .159 B2
Manchester M5 . . . . .158 D1
8 Reddish SK5 . . . . .111 E7
Oldham Study Ctr
& Natural History Mus
OL1 .153 D5
Oldham Way
OL1,OL4,OL8,OL9 . . . . .153 E6
Oldhams Com Prim Sch
BL1 . . . . .24 C5
Oldhams La BL1 . . . . .143 D4
Oldhams Terr BL1 . . . . .143 D4
Oldknow Rd SK6 . . . . .126 A6
Oldmill St OL12 . . . . .139 F8
Oldmoor Rd SK6 . . . . .112 E5
Oldstead Gr BL3 . . . . .40 F3
Oldstead Wlk M9 . . . . .157 D6

Oldway Wlk M40 . . . . .83 B5
Oldwood Inf Sch M22 . . . . . .121 B2
Oldwood Jun Sch M22 . . . . .121 B2
Oldwood Rd M23 . . . . .121 A3
Olga St BL1 . . . . .143 D2
Olivant St Bury BL9 . . . . .140 E1
Bury BL9 . . . . .44 E8
Olive Bank BL8 . . . . .27 B4
Olive Gr WN6 . . . . .36 F3
Olive Rd WA15 . . . . .120 A8
Olive Shapley Ave M20 . . . .110 B3
Olive St Bacup OL13 . . . . .3 E8
Bolton BL3 . . . . .147 D4
Bury BL8 . . . . .140 D2
Failsworth M35 . . . . .83 E8
Heywood OL10 . . . . .29 E2
Radcliffe M26 . . . . .44 C3
Rochdale OL11 . . . . .30 C1
Oliver Cl M35 . . . . .161 C8
Olivia Gr M14 . . . . .98 D3
Ollerbarrow Rd WA15 . . . . . .119 E2
Ollerbrook Ct 11 BL1 . . . . .143 F2
Ollersett Ave SK22 . . . . .127 D1
Ollersett La SK22 . . . . .127 E1
Ollerton 10 OL12 . . . . .139 E8
Ollerton Ave
Manchester M16 . . . . .97 C3
Sale M33 . . . . .107 D5
Ollerton Cl WN2 . . . . .38 A2
Ollerton Dr M35 . . . . .83 F6
Ollerton Rd SK9 . . . . .131 E5
Ollerton St Adlington PR6 . . .21 A8
Bolton BL1 . . . . .24 F6
Ollier Ave M12 . . . . .99 B2
Olney OL11 . . . . .139 E6
Olney Ave M22 . . . . .121 B6
Olney St M13 . . . . .98 D4
Olsberg Cl M26 . . . . .44 C4
Olwen Ave M12 . . . . .165 A5
Olwen Cres SK5 . . . . .111 F8
Olympia Ct 2 M44 . . . . .94 A2
Olympic St M11 . . . . .165 A6
Omer Ave M13 . . . . .98 F2
Omer Dr M19 . . . . .110 E7
Onchan Ave OL4 . . . . .67 B6
One Ash Cl OL12 . . . . .14 F2
One Oak Ct SK7 . . . . .132 F6
One Oak La SK9 . . . . .137 F7
Ongar Wlk M9 . . . . .64 B3
Onslow Ave M40 . . . . .65 E1
Onslow Cl OL1 . . . . .153 F8
Onslow Rd SK3 . . . . .123 C8
Onslow St OL11 . . . . .30 C4
Onward St SK14 . . . . .167 D2
Oozewood Rd M24,OL2 . . . . .48 B5
Opal Ct 5 M14 . . . . .110 D8
Opal Gdns M14 . . . . .98 D4
Opal Gr WN7 . . . . .75 E4
Opal St M19 . . . . .111 B8
Openshaw Fold Rd BL9 . . . . .44 D8
Openshaw La M44 . . . . .105 E6
Openshaw Pl BL4 . . . . .60 B8
Openshaw St BL9 . . . . .141 A1
Openshaw Wlk 19 M11 . . . . .83 C1
Oracle Ct M28 . . . . .60 D2
Oram St BL9 . . . . .141 A4
Orama Ave M6 . . . . .80 A4
Orange Hill Rd M25 . . . . .63 C5
Orange St M6 . . . . .81 A3
Orchard Ave Bolton BL3 . . . .143 F3
Boothstown M28 . . . . .78 B7
Partington M31 . . . . .105 F4
Reddish M8 . . . . .99 E4
Orchard Brow WA3 . . . . .105 A2
Orchard Cl Bramhall SK8 . . .132 C7
Leigh WN7 . . . . .75 F7
Poynton SK12 . . . . .133 C3
Shevington WN6 . . . . .36 A7
Wilmslow SK9 . . . . .136 F5
Orchard Ct SK2 . . . . .124 D6
Orchard Dr
Altrincham WA15 . . . . .119 E5
Failsworth M35 . . . . .83 F7
Lymm WA13 . . . . .117 B5
Romiley SK6 . . . . .114 B2
Orchard Gdns BL2 . . . . .42 D5
Orchard Gn SK9 . . . . .137 B1
Orchard Gr
Manchester M20 . . . . .109 F5
Shaw OL2 . . . . .149 A7
Orchard Ind Est M6 . . . . .81 A5
Orchard La WN7 . . . . .76 A7
Orchard Pl Poynton SK12 . . .133 D4
3 Sale M33 . . . . .120 B7
8 Sale M33 . . . . .108 B5

Orchard The Disley SK12 . . .135 D6
Oldham OL4 . . . . .67 C3
4 Westhoughton BL5 . . . . . .39 E1
Orchard Trad Est M6 . . . . . . .80 F5
Orchard Vale SK3 . . . . .123 C6
Orchard Way BL3 . . . . .10 F1
Orchards The OL10 . . . . .29 E2
Orchid Ave BL4 . . . . .42 B1
Orchid Cl Irlam M44 . . . . . . .105 E8
Oldham OL1 . . . . .48 D1
Orrell WN8 . . . . .53 B6
Orchid Dr BL9 . . . . .45 A7
Orchid St M9 . . . . .157 D7
Orchid Way OL12 . . . . .14 D3
Ordell Wlk 1 M9 . . . . .64 E3
Ordsall Ave M38 . . . . .59 F5
Ordsall District Ctr M5 . . . .161 B8
Ordsall Hall (Mus) M5 . . . . .161 B7
Ordsall La M5 . . . . .161 A6
Oregon Ave OL1 . . . . .48 E1
Oregon Cl M13 . . . . .163 C6
Orford Ave SK12 . . . . .135 D6
Orford Cl SK6 . . . . .134 E7
Orford Rd Failsworth M40 . . . .83 C5
Prestwich M25 . . . . .63 B5
Organ St Hindley WN2 . . . . . .57 B3
Leigh WN7 . . . . .75 E5
Oriel Ave OL8 . . . . .66 E3
Oriel Bank High Sch SK3 . .170 F5
Oriel Cl Oldham OL9 . . . . . . .152 A5
Stockport SK2 . . . . .124 B6
Oriel Rd Ashton-in-M WN4 . . .72 F4
Manchester M20 . . . . .110 A4
Oriel St Bolton BL3 . . . . .144 C5
Rochdale OL11 . . . . .139 F5
Orient Rd M6 . . . . .80 B4
Orient St M7,M8 . . . . .155 F7
Oriole Cl M28 . . . . .78 B8
Orion Bsns Pk SK3,SK8 . . . .123 B5
Orion Pl M7 . . . . .155 E7
Orkney Cl Radcliffe M26 . . . . .44 B4
Manchester M23 . . . . .121 A4
Orkney Dr M41 . . . . .95 D5
Orlanda Ave M6 . . . . .80 B4
Orlanda Dr M7 . . . . .155 E6
Orlando St BL3 . . . . .148 A5
Orleans Way OL1 . . . . .153 F7
Orley Wlk OL1 . . . . .49 D4
Orme Ave Middleton M24 . . . .65 A7
Salford M6 . . . . .80 C4
Orme Cl Manchester M11 . . .160 E1
Urmston M41 . . . . .95 F2
Orme St Alderley Edge SK9 . .137 A1
Oldham OL4 . . . . .67 A5
Ormerod Ave OL2 . . . . .48 E7
Ormerod Cl SK6 . . . . .113 A1
Ormerod St Bolton BL3 . . . . .42 D5
Bury BL9 . . . . .141 A3
Ormonde Ave M6 . . . . .80 B4
Ormonde Cl OL6 . . . . .166 C4
Ormonde St OL6 . . . . .166 C4
Ormrod St Bolton BL2 . . . . . .25 C4
Bolton BL3 . . . . .145 E6
Bury BL9 . . . . .141 A2
8 Farnworth BL4 . . . . .60 E8
Ormrods The BL9 . . . . .28 F5
Orms Gill Pl SK2 . . . . .124 E6
Ormsby Cl Standish WN6 . . . .19 E2
Ormsgill Ct M15 . . . . .162 F6
Ormsgill Cl M15 . . . . .162 F6
Ormside Cl WN2 . . . . .57 C4
Ormskirk Ave M20 . . . . .109 F6
Ormskirk Cl BL8 . . . . .44 A8
Ormskirk Rd Orrell WN8 . . . . .53 E7
2 Reddish SK5 . . . . .111 F6
Wigan WN5 . . . . .54 D6
Ormston Ave BL6 . . . . .22 C5
Ormston Gr WN7 . . . . .75 F7
Ornatus St BL1 . . . . .24 F5
Ornsey Wlk 81 M11 . . . . .83 C1
Oronsay Gr M5 . . . . .154 E1
Orphanage St SK4 . . . . .169 E3
Orpington St WN5 . . . . .54 C6
Orpington Rd 2 M9 . . . . . . .157 E7
Orpington St WN5 . . . . .54 C6
Orrel St M5,M6 . . . . .154 E2
Orrell Arc 3 WN1 . . . . .150 C8
Orrell Gdns WN5 . . . . .53 F6
Orrell Hall Cl WN5 . . . . .54 B8
Orrell Lamberhead Green
Cty Jun Sch WN5 . . . . .54 A7
Orrell Newfold
Cty Prim Sch WN5 . . . . .53 D4
Orrell St Bury BL8 . . . . .140 D3
Manchester M11 . . . . .99 D7
Wigan WN1 . . . . .151 D7
Orrel Wks WN5 . . . . .53 E4
Orrel Water Pk WN5 . . . . .53 F4
Orrishmere Prim Sch
SK8 .123 A3
Orrishmere Rd SK8 . . . . .122 F3
Orsett Cl M40 . . . . .159 C3
Orthes Gr SK4 . . . . .111 D5
Orton Ave M23 . . . . .109 A1
Orton Rd M23 . . . . .109 A1
Orton Way WN3 . . . . .54 D1
Ortonbrook Prim Sch
M31 .105 E2
Orvietto Ave M6 . . . . .80 B4
Orville Dr M19 . . . . .110 F7
Orwell Ave Reddish M34 . . . .100 A3

Orwell Ave continued
Wythenshawe M22 .... 121 D6
Orwell Cl Bury BL8 .... 140 D4
Handforth SK9 .... 131 D2
Orwell Rd BL1 .... 142 B2
Osborne Cl BL8 .... 44 B8
Osborne Dr M27 .... 80 C7
Osborne Gr Bolton BL1 .... 142 C1
Gatley SK8 .... 122 A3
Leigh WN7 .... 74 D6
Osborne Ho M30 .... 79 C2
Osborne Pl SK13 .... 104 A5
Osborne Rd
Althancham-M WN15 .... 119 E5
Ashton-in-M WN4 .... 73 A4
Denton M34 .... 100 F4
Golborne WA3 .... 90 E7
Hyde SK14 .... 167 E1
Manchester M19 .... 99 A1
3 Manchester M9 .... 157 E7
Oldham OL8 .... 153 D5
Salford M6 .... 80 A2
Stockport SK2 .... 170 F7
Osborne St Bredbury SK6 ... 112 D3
Heywood OL10 .... 29 D1
Manchester M20 .... 110 A3
Manchester M40 .... 159 C4
Oldham OL9 .... 152 C8
Rochdale OL11 .... 139 F5
Salford M6 .... 154 F2
Shaw OL2 .... 149 C6
Osborne Terr Bacup OL13 ...... 3 D8
Sale M33 .... 108 B4
Osbourne Cl Farnworth BL4 .. 42 D1
Wilmslow SK9 .... 137 D6
Osbourne Ct M46 .... 58 C3
Osbourne Pl **7** WA14 ..... 119 D4
Osbourne Wlk M20 .... 43 E3
Oscar St Bolton BL1 .... 142 C2
Manchester M40 .... 83 A7
Oscott Ave M38 .... 60 A6
Oscroft Cl M8 .... 155 F6
Oscroft Wlk M14 .... 110 D7
Osmond St OL4 .... 67 C7
Osmund Ave BL2 .... 42 D7
Osprey Ave BL5 .... 57 D6
Osprey Cl Dukinfield SK16 .. 101 E7
Manchester M15 .... 162 E5
Osprey Ct M15 .... 162 E5
Osprey Dr Droylsden M43 ..... 84 C3
Irlam M44 .... 94 A3
Wilmslow SK9 .... 137 D6
Osprey Wlk M13 .... 163 C6
Ospreys The WN3 .... 54 C4
Ossington Ct M23 .... 109 A3
Ossington Wlk M23 .... 109 A2
Ossory St M14 .... 98 B3
Osterley Rd M9 .... 65 A3
Ostlers Gate M43 .... 84 D2
Ostrich La M25 .... 63 C3
Oswald Cl M6 .... 81 A5
Oswald Rd M21 .... 97 B1
Oswald Rd M21 .... 97 A1
Oswald Road Prim Sch
M21 .... 97 A1
Oswald St Bolton BL3 .... 146 C4
Manchester M4 .... 159 A3
Manchester M4 .... 160 D1
Oldham OL9 .... 153 D8
Reddish SK5 .... 99 F3
Rochdale OL16 .... 31 B8
Shaw OL2 .... 149 C8
Oswestry Cl BL8 .... 26 F8
Otago St **9** OL4 .... 49 C1
Othello Dr M30 .... 79 D2
Otley Ave M6 .... 80 C3
Otley Cl OL9 .... 152 B6
Otley Ct M23 .... 123 D4
Otmoor Way OL2 .... 49 A4
Otranto Ave M6 .... 80 B4
Otter Dr Manchester M8 .... 155 E5
Whitefield BL9 .... 45 B4
Otterburn Pl SK2 .... 124 E6
Otterbury Cl BL8 .... 26 F2
Otterham Wlk M40 .... 83 D5
Otterspool Rd SK6 .... 125 B8
Otterwood Sq WN5 .... 36 C2
Ottery Cl WN4 .... 65 D2
Ottowa Cl M23 .... 120 F4
Oughtrington Cres WA13 ... 117 B4
Oughtrington La WA13 .... 117 A2
Oughtrington Prim Sch
WA13 .... 117 B4
Oughtrington View
WA13 .... 117 B4
Oulder Hill OL11 .... 30 B7
Oulder Hill Com Sch
OL11 .... 30 B7
Oulder Hill Dr OL11 .... 30 B7
Ouldfield Cl **22** OL16 ...... 31 B6
Oulton Ave WA3 .... 108 E5
Oulton Cl **5** WN7 .... 76 A4
Oulton St BL1 .... 25 A5
Oulton Wlk M40 .... 160 D3
Oundle Cl M14 .... 98 C3
Our Lady & St Paul
RC Prim Sch OL10 .... 28 F1
Our Lady
& the Lancashire Martyrs
RC Prim Sch M28 .... 60 A3
Our Lady Mount Carmel
RC High Sch M6 .... 80 C3
Our Lady of Grace
RC Prim Sch M25 .... 63 A6
Our Lady of Lourdes
RC Prim Sch Bury BL8 .. 27 C6
Farnworth BL4 .... 60 A8
Partington M31 .... 105 E3

Our Lady of Mount Carmel
Inf Sch M9 .... 64 D1
Our Lady of the Rosary
RC Prim Sch Leigh WN7 ... 75 B5
Urmston M41 .... 95 C4
Our Lady's RC Comp Sch
OL2 .... 48 D3
Our Lady's RC High Sch
M9 .... 64 D5
Our Lady's RC Prim Sch
Asgull WN2 .... 38 C5
Manchester M16 .... 97 D3
Oldham OL4 .... 49 E3
Stockport SK3 .... 170 E8
Ouse St M5 .... 80 C1
Outham Mews OL3 .... 51 B1
Outram Cl SK6 .... 125 F4
Outram Rd SK14,SK16 ..... 101 B6
Outram Sq M43 .... 100 A8
Outrington Dr M11 .... 165 A8
Outterside St PR7 .... 21 A6
Outwood Ave M27 .... 61 D4
Outwood Dr SK8 .... 131 A8
Outwood Gr BL1 .... 24 E5
Outwood La WN0 .... 130 C7
Outwood La M W90 .... 130 B8
Outwood Prim Sch SK8 .... 131 D7
Outwood Rd Gatley SK8 ... 131 B7
Radcliffe M26 .... 44 A1
Oval Dr SK16 .... 101 B7
Oval The Gatley SK8 .... 131 B8
Shevington WN6 .... 35 F5
Over Hos BL7 .... 9 B6
Over Town La
Rochdale OL12 .... 13 A3
Rochdale OL12 .... 13 C3
Overbeck Cl WN6 .... 37 A4
Overbridge Rd M7,M8 ...... 158 E4
Overbrook Ave M40 .... 156 C5
Overbrook Dr M25 .... 63 B3
Overcombe Wlk **4** M40 .. 156 C5
Overdale **3** Marple SK6 . 125 F6
Pendlebury M27 .... 80 A6
Overdale Cl OL1 .... 48 E1
Overdale Cres M41 .... 94 F2
Overdale Dr BL1 .... 144 A7
Overdale Rd
New Mills SK12 .... 135 F6
Romiley SK6 .... 125 A8
Wythenshawe M22 .... 121 D5
Overdell Dr OL12 .... 14 C4
Overdene Cl BL6 .... 40 C6
Overens St OL4 .... 67 B7
Overfield Way OL12 .... 14 F2
Overgreen BL2 .... 25 E3
Overhill Dr SK9 .... 137 E7
Overhill La SK9 .... 137 E7
Overhill Rd Chadderton OL9 . 65 F8
Wilmslow SK9 .... 137 D7
Overhill Way WN3 .... 54 D3
Overlea Dr M19 .... 110 E5
Overlinks Dr M6 .... 80 B5
Overshores Rd BL7 .... 9 B8
Overstone Dr M8 .... 155 F7
Overt St OL11 .... 139 F5
Overton Ave M22 .... 121 D5
Overton Cres
Hazel Grove SK7 .... 124 E4
Sale M33 .... 107 D1
Overton Rd M22 .... 121 D5
Overton St WN7 .... 75 E4
Overton Way **2** SK9 ..... 131 D5
Overwood Rd M22 .... 121 D8
Ovington Wlk **1** M40 .... 156 C5
Owen Fold OL4 .... 67 F7
Owen St Eccles M30 .... 79 B1
2 Leigh WN7 .... 75 D5
Oldham OL1 .... 49 A3
Salford M6 .... 81 A5
Stockport SK3 .... 169 D1
Owen's Row BL6 .... 22 C3
Owenington Gr M38 .... 60 A5
Owens Cl OL9 .... 65 E8
Owens Farm Dr SK2 .... 124 E7
Owler La OL9 .... 65 E3
Owlerbarrow Rd BL8 .... 27 A3
Owlwood Cl M38 .... 59 E3
Owlwood Dr M38 .... 59 E3
Ox Gate BL2 .... 25 D5
Ox Hey Cl BL6 .... 39 E8
Ox Hey La Denshaw OL3 .... 33 E1
Horwich BL6 .... 39 F7
Oxbow Rd M9 .... 64 C6
Oxbow Way M45 .... 63 A8
Oxbridge **3** M33 .... 107 D3
Oxburgh Rd WN3 .... 55 F4
Oxendale Dr M24 .... 46 D1
Oxendon Ave M11 .... 83 B3
Oxenhurst Gn SK2 .... 124 E6
Oxford Ave Droylsden M43 . 83 F3
Rochdale OL11 .... 30 A6
Sale M33 .... 107 D4
Whitefield M45 .... 44 D3
Oxford Cl BL4 .... 59 E8
Oxford Ct Manchester M16 162 D5
Manchester M2 .... 162 F8
Wigan WN1 .... 37 D1
Oxford Dr Middleton M24 .. 47 C2
Romiley SK6 .... 113 D1
Oxford Dr Bolton BL1 ...... 142 C1
Irlam M44 .... 105 C6
Oxford Grove
Com Prim Sch BL1 .... 142 C1
Oxford Ho OL9 .... 152 C6
Oxford Pl **7** Manchester M14 98 C4
16 Rochdale OL11 .... 31 A5
Oxford Rd
Altrincham WA14 .... 119 D3

Oxford Rd continued
Atherton M46 .... 58 B5
Dukinfield SK16 .... 101 D8
Horwich BL6 .... 39 F8
Hyde SK14 .... 113 E8
Little Lever BL3 .... 42 F3
Manchester M1,M13 .... 163 B6
Orrell WN5 .... 53 F8
Salford M6 .... 80 B4
Oxford Road Sta M1 ...... 163 A7
Oxford St Adlington PR7 ..... 21 A6
Bolton BL1 .... 145 F7
Bury BL9 .... 141 A1
Eccles M30 .... 79 E1
Hindley WN2 .... 56 F7
Leigh WN7 .... 75 F6
Manchester M1,M60,M2 ... 163 A8
Manchester M16 .... 162 D5
Newton-le-W WA12 .... 89 B3
Oldham OL4 .... 153 C5
Shaw OL2 .... 149 B7
Stalybridge SK15 .... 86 C1
Stalybridge SK15 .... 86 D4
Oxford St E OL7 .... 166 A1
Oxford St W OL7 .... 100 F8
Oxford Way Rochdale OL12 . 14 E2
Stockport SK6 .... 169 D3
Oxford Wlk **4** M34 .... 101 A1
Oxhill Wlk **17** M40 .... 65 D2
Oxhouse Rd WN5 .... 53 D4
Oxlea Gr BL5 .... 57 E7
Oxney Rd M14 .... 98 C4
Oxted Wlk **8** M8 .... 156 A6
Oxton Ave M22 .... 121 C4
Oxton St M11 .... 99 F7
Ozanam Ct M7 .... 155 D7

P

Pacific Rd WA14 .... 119 A6
Pacific Way M5 .... 96 C8
Pack Horse Yd OL16 .... 139 F7
Packer St **1** Bolton BL1 . 142 C2
Rochdale OL16 .... 139 F7
Packwood Chase OL9 .... 65 F8
Padbury Cl M41 .... 94 D3
Padbury Ho **7** M6 .... 154 F1
Padbury Way BL2 .... 25 E1
Padbury Wlk M40 .... 157 F5
Padden Brook SK6 .... 113 B2
Padden Brook Mews
SK6 .... 113 B2
Paddington Ave M40 .... 83 B5
Paddington Cl M6 .... 81 A2
Paddison St **2** M27 .... 79 E7
Paddock Chase SK12 .... 133 C6
Paddock Cl M46 .... 58 E5
Paddock Hill La WA16 ...... 136 A3
Paddock La Failsworth M35 . 83 F5
Lymm WA13 .... 117 C2
Partington WA13,WA14 ... 118 B5
Paddock Rd SK14 .... 113 D8
Paddock Rise WN6 .... 36 E3
Paddock St M12 .... 163 C7
Paddock The
Altrincham WA15 .... 120 B4
Ashton-in-M WN4 .... 72 F6
Bramhall SK7 .... 123 D1
Cheadle SK8 .... 122 E5
Hadfield SK13 .... 103 F5
Handforth SK9 .... 131 D4
Hollingworth SK14 .... 103 E5
Lymm WA13 .... 117 C4
Ramsbottom BL0 .... 138 B7
Uppermill OL3 .... 68 F4
Worsley M28 .... 78 E7
Paddocks The SK3 .... 124 A4
Paderborn Ct BL1 .... 145 E6
Padfield Cty Prim Sch
SK13 .... 104 B5
Padfield Gate SK13 .... 116 D7
Padfield Main Rd SK13 ... 104 C5
Padiham Cl Bury BL9 .... 44 D7
Leigh WN7 .... 76 A5
Padstow Cl SK14 .... 102 D3
Padstow Dr SK7 .... 132 F7
Padstow St M40 .... 160 D3
Padstow Wlk SK14 .... 102 D3
Padworth Wlk M23 .... 120 D8
Pagan St OL16 .... 139 F8
Pagefield Cl **15** WN6 ...... 37 A1
Pagefield Ind Est WN6 ...... 36 F1
Pagefield St WN6 .... 37 A1
Paget St M40 .... 157 D5
Pagnall Ct OL9 .... 152 B5
Paignton Ave
Hattersley SK14 .... 102 D2
Manchester M19 .... 71 E8
Paignton Cl WN5 .... 71 D8
Paignton Dr M33 .... 107 D5
Paignton Gr SK5 .... 111 E7
Paignton Wlk SK14 .... 102 C2
Pailin Dr M43 .... 84 A3
Pailton Cl BL6 .... 40 D6
Painswick Rd M22 .... 121 B1
Paiton St BL1 .... 144 C7
Palace Arc WN4 .... 73 B3
Palace Gdns OL1 .... 48 D2
Palace Gr WN7 .... 76 D6
Palace Rd Ashton-u-L OL6 .. 85 E5
Sale M33 .... 108 A5
Palace St Bolton BL1 .... 145 F8
Bury BL9 .... 141 A2
Oldham OL9 .... 152 B8
Palatine Ave
Manchester M20 .... 110 B6
Rochdale OL11 .... 30 A8

Palatine Cl Irlam M44 .... 93 F1
Wigan WN3 .... 54 E4
Palatine Cres M20 .... 110 B5
Palatine Dr BL9 .... 27 F8
Palatine Ho **4** SK3 .... 170 E8
Palatine Rd
Manchester M20 .... 110 B6
Rochdale OL11 .... 30 A8
Wythenshawe M20,M22 ... 109 E2
Palatine Sq WN7 .... 75 B5
Palatine St **4** Bolton BL1 145 F7
Denton M34 .... 100 E4
Ramsbottom BL0 .... 138 C6
Rochdale OL16 .... 31 C7
Palewood Cl WN1 .... 37 C1
Paley St BL1 .... 145 F7
Palfrey Pl M12 .... 163 C7
Palgrave Ave M40 .... 157 D5
Palin St WN3 .... 57 B3
Palin Wood Rd OL3 .... 50 F5
Pall Mall M2 .... 158 F1
Pallotine Wlk OL11 .... 139 D5
Palm Ave WN4 .... 72 D5
Palm Bsns Ctr OL9 .... 152 B7
Palm Cl M33 .... 107 D5
Palm St Oldham OL9 .... 152 B8
Wigan WN5 .... 54 D6
Palm St Bolton BL1 .... 143 F3
Droylsden M43 .... 83 E2
Manchester M13 .... 98 F3
Oldham OL4 .... 67 C8
Palma Ave WN0 .... 130 B8
Palmer Ave SK8 .... 122 F6
Palmer Cl Manchester M25 . 63 D2
Oldham OL8 .... 66 F4
21 Rochdale OL12 .... 14 F1
Palmer Gr WN7 .... 57 E1
Palmer St Dukinfield SK16 166 B1
Manchester M7 .... 81 C5
Sale M33 .... 108 A4
Palmerston Ave M16 .... 97 D2
Palmerston Cl
Ramsbottom BL0 .... 11 C4
Reddish M34 .... 100 B3
Palmerston Rd
Reddish M34 .... 100 B3
Stockport SK2 .... 124 C6
Palmerston St M12 .... 160 E1
Pandora St M20 .... 110 A5
Panfield Rd M22 .... 121 D4
Pangbourne Ave M41 .... 95 E3
Pangbourne Cl SK3 .... 123 C6
Pankhurst Wlk **11** M14 .. 98 B3
Panmure St OL8 .... 66 F4
Pansy Rd BL4 .... 60 A8
Panton St BL6 .... 22 D1
Paper Mill Rd BL7 .... 25 A7
Parade Rd M90 .... 130 C7
Parade The
1 Alderley Edge SK9 .... 137 A1
Romiley SK6 .... 113 A1
Swinton M27 .... 79 F8
2 Whitefield M45 .... 44 E2
Paradise St Dukinfield M34 100 F7
Hadfield SK13 .... 104 A5
Ramsbottom BL0 .... 138 C7
Parbold Ave M20 .... 110 A6
Parbrook Cl M40 .... 157 D5
Parbrook La WN6 .... 36 B7
Parchments The WN2 .... 89 D4
Parham Wlk **3** M9 .... 64 E3
Paris Ave Salford M5 .... 161 B7
Wigan WN3 .... 54 C3
Paris St BL3 .... 146 B4
Parish Church
CE Jun Sch The OL1 ..... 153 F8
Parish View M5 .... 161 B8
Park Ave Altrincham WA14 119 F1
Altrincham WA15 .... 119 F1
Bolton BL1 .... 143 E4
Bramhall SK7 .... 132 D5
Chadderton OL9 .... 48 B1
Cheadle SK3 .... 122 F1
Cheadle SK8 .... 122 F1
Failsworth M35 .... 83 D8
Golborne WA3 .... 73 F2
Hyde SK14 .... 167 D4
Longshaw WN5 .... 53 B1
Manchester M16 .... 161 C5
Manchester M19 .... 99 A1
Manchester M7 .... 155 F8
Pendlebury M27 .... 80 A7
Poynton SK12 .... 133 E4
Prestwich M25 .... 63 A6
Ramsbottom BL0 .... 11 D6
Romiley SK6 .... 113 C2
Sale M33 .... 108 A6
Shevington WN6 .... 36 B7
Urmston M41 .... 95 D2
Whitefield M45 .... 62 D7
Whitefield M45 .... 63 E2
Park Cl Chadderton OL9 ..... 48 B1
Glossop SK13 .... 104 D2
Sale WA14 .... 119 F8
Stalybridge SK15 .... 85 F3
Stalybridge SK15,SK16 ...... 85 D1
Standish WN6 .... 36 E8
Stretford M17,M32 .... 96 C6
Walkden M38 .... 60 D1
Westhoughton BL5 .... 58 A8
Wigan WN5 .... 54 B6

Park Cres continued
Chadderton OL9 .... 47 F1
Glossop SK13 .... 104 B3
Handforth SK9 .... 131 B1
Manchester M14 .... 98 C3
Wigan WN1 .... 37 B1
Park Cres W WN1 .... 37 B1
Park Ct Manchester M25 .... 63 E2
Rochdale OL11 .... 139 F6
Sale M33 .... 108 A5
Wythenshawe M22 .... 121 D3
Park Dean Sch OL8 .... 67 A4
Park Dene Dr SK13 .... 104 C2
Park Dr Altrincham WA15 .. 119 F1
Altrincham WA15 .... 120 A7
Eccles M30 .... 79 D4
Hyde SK14 .... 167 D4
Manchester M16 .... 97 C2
Stockport SK4 .... 168 B2
Park Edge BL5 .... 58 A7
Park Field Rd OL4 .... 68 E6
Park Gate Ave M20 .... 110 B6
Park Gate Cl SK6 .... 112 E5
Park Gates Ave SK8 .... 123 C1
Park Gates Dr SK8 .... 123 C1
Park Gr Manchester M19 .... 99 A2
Manchester M44 .... 168 B4
Radcliffe M26 .... 43 F4
Walkden M28 .... 78 D8
Park Hey Dr WN6 .... 35 E7
Park Hill Manchester M25 .. 63 D2
21 Rochdale OL12 .... 14 F1
Park Hill Cl SK22 .... 127 C1
Park Hill Dr M45 .... 62 E8
Park Hill Rd WA15 .... 120 A1
Park Hill St BL1 .... 145 D8
Park Ho Manchester M19 .... 99 A1
Manchester M20 .... 110 A4
Sale WA14 .... 120 C7
Droylsden M43 .... 100 A8
Park House Bridge Rd M6 . 80 E6
Park Ind Est WN4 .... 72 E3
Park La Altrincham WA15 .. 120 A1
Dukinfield SK16 .... 101 D8
Golborne WN2,WN7 .... 74 D6
Horwich BL6 .... 22 D3
Leigh WN7 .... 76 C4
Little Bollington WA14 ..... 118 B2
Manchester M7 .... 155 D8
Oldham OL3 .... 69 C5
Oldham OL8 .... 66 F2
Pendlebury M27 .... 80 D6
Pendlebury M6 .... 80 C5
Poynton SK12 .... 133 E3
Radcliffe M26 .... 44 D4
Rochdale OL16 .... 139 F8
Royton OL2 .... 48 D4
Royton OL2 .... 48 D5
Royton OL2 .... 48 E5
Stockport SK1 .... 124 B8
Whitefield M45 .... 62 D7
Park La W M7 .... 80 D7
Park Lane Ct M7 .... 155 D8
Park Lane Jun Inf Sch WN4 72 F7
Park Lo **6** M19 .... 99 A1
Park Lodge Cl SK8 .... 122 E4
Park Mdw BL5 .... 58 A8
Park Mews M16 .... 97 C2
Park Mount SK8 .... 122 A5
Park Par Ashton-u-L OL6 .. 166 B2
Shaw OL2 .... 32 C1
Park Par Ind Est OL6 ...... 166 A2
Park Pl Manchester M4 ... 159 A3
Prestwich M25 .... 63 D5
Salford M6 .... 80 A3
Park Range M14 .... 98 D3
Park Rd Adlington PR7 ...... 20 F6
Altrincham WA14 .... 119 A2
Altrincham WA15 .... 119 A2
Altrincham WA15 .... 120 A7
Bolton BL1 .... 144 C7
Bramhall SK8 .... 123 C1
Bury BL9 .... 140 E4
Cheadle SK8 .... 122 E4
Denton M34 .... 100 E3
Droylsden M34 .... 100 D8
Eccles M30 .... 79 D4
Edgworth BL7 .... 9 E5
Golborne WA3 .... 90 A7
Hadfield SK13 .... 104 B4
High Lane SK12 .... 134 F6
Hindley WN2 .... 56 E3
Hyde SK14 .... 167 D4
Little Lever BL3 .... 42 F4
Longsight WN5 .... 53 A2
Manchester M25,M7,M8 .... 63 E2
Manchester M14 .... 98 C3
Middleton M24 .... 65 A8
Oldham OL4,OL8 .... 67 A5
Oldham OL8 .... 153 F8
Partington M31 .... 106 A3
Partington M31 .... 117 C8
Ramsbottom BL0 .... 10 F3
Rochdale OL12 .... 15 A1
Romiley SK6 .... 113 C3
Sale M33 .... 108 A6
Sale WA15,SK,M14 .... 120 B7
Salford M6 .... 80 A3
Stalybridge SK15,SK16 .... 85 D1
Standish WN6 .... 36 E8
Stretford M17,M32 .... 96 B6
Walkden M25 .... 60 D1
Westhoughton BL5 .... 58 A8
Wigan WN5 .... 54 B6

Park Rd continued
Wigan WN6 ....37 A1
Wilmslow SK9 ....136 F7
Wythenshawe SK8 ......121 F5
Park Rd N
Newton-le-W WA12 ......89 E4
Urmston M41 ....95 C2
Park Rd S
Newton-le-W WA12 ......89 D2
Urmston M41 ....95 C2
Park Rise SK6 ....113 C3
Park Road Prim Sch
Sale M33 ....108 A6
Sale M14 ....119 E8
Park Row 🖪 Bolton BL1 ...24 F6
Manchester M14 ....110 F2
Park Seventeen M45 .....44 F1
Park Side Ave OL2 ......149 C8
Park Sq Ashton-u-L OL6 ...85 E4
Manchester M16 ....97 A2
Park St Ashton-u-L OL7 ...166 A1
Ashton-u-L OL7 ....166 B2
Atherton M46 ....58 E4
Bolton BL1 ....145 D8
Bradbury SK6 ....112 F3
Denton M34 ....100 D3
Droylsden M43 ....84 C2
Farnworth BL4 ....40 D1
Heywood OL10 ....46 E8
Manchester M3 ....158 D1
Manchester M3 ....158 F3
Manchester M7 ....155 D8
Mossley OL5 ....86 C8
Oldham OL8 ....153 E5
Oldham OL8 ....153 E6
Pendlebury M27 ....80 A7
Prestwich M25 ....63 C4
Radcliffe M26 ....44 C4
Rochdale OL16 ....139 F6
Royton OL2 ....48 E4
Shaw OL2 ....149 C7
Stalybridge SK15 ....86 B1
Stockport SK1 ....169 F2
🖪 Tyldesley M29 ....59 A1
Wigan WN3 ....150 B6
Park Sta M40 ....83 A4
Park Terr Heywood OL10 ...29 D3
Mossley OL5 ....86 C8
Prestwich M45 ....62 D7
Westhoughton BL5 ......39 F1
Park The Oldham OL3 ....69 C5
Uppermill OL4 ....68 D6
Park View Abram WN2 ...56 B1
Abram WN2 ....74 B8
Ashton-in-M WN4 ....73 B2
🖪 Bolton BL1 ....24 F6
Bredbury SK6 ....112 C3
Chadderton OL9 ....48 B1
Cheadle SK3 ....122 F7
Droylsden M34 ....100 D8
Farnworth BL4 ....42 D1
Gatley SK8 ....122 A6
High Lane SK7 ....134 B8
Kearsley BL4 ....60 F7
Little Bollington WA14 ...118 B2
Littleborough OL15 ......16 B6
Manchester M14 ....110 E7
🖪 Manchester M21 ......96 F1
Manchester M9 ....156 C6
Newton-le-W WA12 .....89 E3
Stockport SK1 ....124 B7
Park View Ct
Poynton SK12 ....133 E4
Prestwich M25 ....63 B3
Romiley SK6 ....113 C2
Park View Prim Sch M25 ...63 B3
Park View Rd Bolton BL3 ...146 C4
Prestwich M25 ....63 B3
Park View Rise SK22 .....127 C1
Park Way Eccles M17,M41 ...96 A6
Eccles M32,M41 ....95 F5
Parkbridge Wlk M13 ....163 B6
Parkbrook Rd M23 .....121 B7
Parkdale Chadderton OL9 ...48 B1
Tyldesley M29 ....77 B5
Parkdale Ave Denton M34 ...100 D7
Manchester M18 ....165 C5
Parkdale Rd BL2 ....25 C1
Parkdene Cl BL2 ....25 D4
Parkend Dr WN7 ....75 D2
Parkend Rd M23 ....121 A5
Parker St Bury BL9 ......141 A2
Manchester M1 ....159 A1
Parkes Field Prim Sch
M27 ....80 A7
Parkfield Chadderton OL9 ...48 B1
🖪 Middleton M24 ....64 F8
Salford M5 ....154 D2
Shevington WN6 ....36 B7
Parkfield Ave
Farnworth BL4 ....60 C7
Manchester M14 ....98 B3
Manchester M25 ....63 D3
Marple SK6 ....125 F6
Oldham OL8 ....66 B2
Tyldesley M29 ....77 B6
Urmston M41 ....95 B1
Parkfield Cl Leigh WN7 ...76 A7
Tyldesley M29 ....77 B6
Parkfield Ct M14 ....119 C4
Parkfield Dr Middleton M24 ...64 E8
Tyldesley M29 ....59 D1
Parkfield Ind Est M24 ...64 F8
Parkfield Lo M20 ....110 A4
Parkfield Prim Sch M24 ...46 E1

Parkfield Rd
Altrincham WA14 ....119 C4
Bolton BL3 ....147 F3
Cheadle SK8 ....122 F1
Parkfield Rd N M40 ....65 F1
Parkfield Rd S M20 ....110 A4
Parkfield St
Manchester M14 ....98 B3
Manchester M14 ....98 B4
Rochdale OL16 ....31 B2
Parkfields
Abram Brow WN2 ....74 C6
Stalybridge SK15 ....86 D3
Parkgate Altrincham WA14 ...119 B4
Bury BL8 ....26 F5
Chadderton OL9 ....48 B1
Parkgate Dr Bolton BL1 ...25 A5
Pendlebury M27 ....80 A7
Stockport SK2 ....124 B4
Parkgate Way
🖪 Handforth SK9 ....131 D4
Shaw OL2 ....49 D7
Parkhill Ave M8 ....64 B2
Parkhills Rd BL9 ....44 F8
Parkhouse St M11 .....165 B8
Parkhurst Ave M40 ....65 E1
Parkin Cl SK16 ....101 C8
Parkin St M12 ....99 A3
Parkinson St Bolton BL3 ...144 C5
Bury BL9 ....27 F5
Parklake Ave M7 ......155 E8
Parkland Ave SK22 .....127 C1
Parklands Royton OL2 ...48 C7
Sale M33 ....108 C5
Shaw OL2 ....49 D8
Whitefield M45 ....62 E8
Parklands Dr Aspull WN2 ...38 C6
Sale M33 ....107 D2
Parklands High Sch M22 ...121 C3
Parklands Rd M23 .....120 F7
Parklands The M44 .....169 E4
Parklands Way OL2 .....133 E4
Parklea Ct 🖪 M7 ....63 E1
Parklee Cty Prim Sch M46 ...58 D2
Parkleigh Dr M40 ......65 E2
Parkmount Rd M9 ......64 E1
Parks Nook BL4 ....60 C7
Parks The WA12 ....73 B1
Parks Yd BL9 ....140 E2
Parkside High Lane SK6 ...134 D8
Hindley WN2 ....56 E6
Middleton M24 ....64 F6
Parkside Ave
Ashton-in-M WN4 ....72 F8
Eccles M30 ....79 C2
Failsworth M35 ....83 F5
Manchester M7 ....155 E8
Walkden M28 ....60 D1
Parkside Cl High Lane SK6 ...134 D8
Radcliffe M26 ....44 D4
Parkside Cres WN5 ....53 E6
Parkside Ind Est OL2 ...48 E4
Parkside La SK6 ....126 C6
Parkside Rd
Golborne WA12,WA2 ....90 B2
Manchester M14 ....98 A2
Sale M33 ....108 D3
Parkside St 🖪 BL2 ......25 C1
Parkside Wlk Bury BL9 ...140 F1
Stockport SK7 ....123 E3
Parkstead Dr M9 ....157 D6
Parkstone Ave
Droylsden M18 ....99 F6
Whitefield M45 ....62 D6
Parkstone Cl BL8 ....26 F2
Parkstone Dr M27 .....80 B6
Parkstone La M28 .....78 F4
Parkstone Rd M44 .....94 A3
Parksway Manchester M25 ...63 C2
Pendlebury M27 ....80 C6
Parkview Cl M32 ....96 E1
Parkview Pk WA13 .....117 E7
Parkville Rd
Manchester M20 ....110 C5
Prestwich M25 ....63 D4
Parkway Chadderton OL9 ...48 A1
Cheadle SK3 ....122 F7
New Mills SK22 ....127 C1
Rochdale OL11 ....30 B8
Shevington Moor WN6 ...19 A2
Stockport SK7 ....123 E2
Walkden M38 ....59 F4
Westhoughton BL5 ......57 D6
Wilmslow SK9 ....137 B6
Parkway Bsns Ctr M14 ...97 F2
Parkway Circ M17 ......96 F6
Parkway Four Ind Est M17 ...96 A6
Parkway Gr M38 ....59 E4
Parkway Ind Est M17 ...96 A6
Parkway Trad Est M32 ...96 A5
Parkwood BL7 ....8 D2
Parkwood Cl WN3 .....151 E6
Parkwood Dr BL5 .....148 F7
Parkwood Rd M23 .....121 C7
Parlane St M4 ....159 B3
Parliament Pl BL9 .....140 E1
Parliament St Bury BL9 ...140 E1
Ince-in-M WN3 ....151 D6
Orrell WN8 ....53 C7
Parndon Dr SK2 ....124 C2
Parnell Ave M22 ....121 D8
Parnham Cl BL3 ....43 B5
Parr Cl BL4 ....60 B8
Parr Fold M45 ....45 B2
Parr Fold Ave M28 .....60 C1
Parr Ho OL8 ....153 F5

Parr La BL9,M45 ....45 B2
Parr St Droylsden M11 ...99 E7
Eccles M30 ....79 C3
Tyldesley M29 ....76 F8
Parrbrook Cl M45 ......45 A1
Parrbrook Wlk M45 ....45 B1
Parrenthorn High Sch
M25 ....63 D7
Parrenthorn Rd M25 ...63 C7
Parrfield Rd M28 ....79 A7
Parrin La M30 ....79 C3
Parrot St Bolton BL3 ...145 E5
Droylsden M11 ....83 C1
Parrs Ct M44 ....93 F2
Parrs Mount Mews SK4 ...110 F2
Parrs Wood Ave M20 ...110 C2
Parrs Wood High Sch
M20 ....110 D1
Parrs Wood La
M19,M20,SK4 ....110 D2
Parrs Wood Rd
Manchester M20 ....110 D4
Manchester M20 ....122 B8
Parry Mead SK6 ....113 A4
Parry Rd M12 ....99 A4
Parry Wlk 🖪 OL6 ....85 D4
Parslow Ave M8 ....156 A8
Parson's La BL9 ....140 F3
Parson's Wlk WN1 .....37 B1
Parsonage M3 ....158 F1
Parsonage Brow WN8 ...53 A8
Parsonage Ct Bury BL9 ...141 A3
Orrell WN8 ....53 A7
Salford M5 ....161 C8
Parsonage Ct
🖪 Manchester M20 .....110 B6
Manchester SK4 ....168 B4
Parsonage Dr M28 .....60 C2
Parsonage Gdns SK6 ...126 A4
Parsonage La M3 ....158 F2
Parsonage Rd
Kearsley M26 ....61 C7
Manchester M20 ....110 C7
Manchester SK4 ....168 C4
Urmston M41 ....94 D3
Walkden M28 ....60 C2
Parsonage St Bury BL9 ...141 A3
Manchester M15 ....162 E5
Manchester M8 ....64 A4
Radcliffe M26 ....44 A3
Stockport SK4 ....169 E2
Parsonage Way
Cheadle SK8 ....123 B5
Leigh WN7 ....75 E6
Parsonage Wlk OL16 ...31 F7
Parsons Dr M24 ....46 F2
Parsons Field M27 .....81 A5
Parsons St OL9 ....152 C6
Part St BL5 ....39 E2
Partington Ct
Farnworth BL4 ....42 C1
Glossop SK13 ....104 F1
Partington La M27 .....79 E7
Partington Pk SK13 ....104 C3
Partington Pl 🖪 M33 ...108 B5
Partington Prim Sch
M31 ....105 F3
Partington St Bolton BL3 ...146 C2
Failsworth M35 ....83 F7
Heywood OL10 ....29 A2
Manchester M10,M40 ...157 F5
🖪 Oldham OL1 ....67 A7
Rochdale OL11 ....30 A8
Swinton M28 ....79 C8
Wigan WN5 ....54 E8
Partridge Ave M23 .....121 C6
Partridge Cl Irlam M44 ...94 A4
Rochdale OL11 ....29 F7
Partridge Rd M35 ......84 C6
Partridge Rise M43 ....84 D3
Partridge St M32 ......96 F5
Partridge Way OL9 .....65 E8
Parvet Ave M43 ....83 F3
Pascal St M19 ....111 A8
Pass Ct SK8 ....153 D6
Pass The OL16 ....31 A8
Passmonds Cres
OL11,OL12 ....14 B1
Passmonds Way OL11 ...30 B8
Pasture Cl OL4 ....67 A8
Pasture Ct Ashton-in-M WN4 ...72 E6
Pasture Field Rd M22 ...121 F1
Pasturefield Cl 🖪 M33 ...108 F3
Pasturegreen Way M44 ...94 B3
Pastures La OL4 ....68 B8
Patch Croft Rd M22 ...121 F1
Patch La SK7 ....132 D5
Patchett St
Manchester M12 ....164 F6
🖪 Tyldesley M29 ....59 A1
Pateley Sq 🖪 WN6 .....37 B3
Patey St M12 ....99 B3
Pathfield Wlk 🖪 M9 ...157 D8
Patience St 🖪 OL12 ...14 C1
Patmos St BL0 ....11 D6
Paton Ave BL3 ....42 A3
Paton Ct M7 ....81 C4
Paton Mews 🖪 BL3 .....44 A1
Paton St Manchester M1 ...159 B1
Rochdale OL12 ....14 D3
Patricia Dr M28 ....60 D2
Patrick Roddy Ct M18 ...165 C5
Patricroft Rd M30 .....79 A2
Patricroft Sta M30 ....79 C2

Patten St M20 ....110 B6
Patterdale Ave
Ashton-u-L OL7 ....84 F5
Urmston M41 ....95 B4
Patterdale Cl Oldham OL1 ...49 A1
Rochdale OL11 ....30 B3
Stalybridge SK15 ....86 A3
Patterdale Dr Bury BL9 ...44 E7
Middleton M24 ....46 E2
Patterdale Pl WN2 .....56 A7
Patterdale Rd
Ashton-in-M WN4 ......73 A8
Ashton-u-L OL7 ....84 F5
Bolton BL2 ....25 F4
Leigh WN7 ....76 C4
Partington M31 ....105 E3
Romiley SK6 ....113 B4
Stockport SK1,SK2 .....124 B7
Wythenshawe M22 .....121 E8
Patterdale Wlk WA15 ...120 D5
Patterson Ave M21 .....97 A1
Patterson St Bolton BL3 ...146 A4
Denton M34 ....100 F4
Westhoughton BL5 .....39 B3
Pattishall Cl M4 ....160 D1
Pattison Cl OL12 ....14 D3
Pattison Ct BL9 ....45 B2
Paul Ct SK1 ....112 A1
Paul Row OL15 ....6 C1
Paulden Ave Oldham OL4 ...49 E1
Wythenshawe M23 .....121 B6
Paulden Dr M35 ....84 A7
Paulette St BL1 ....143 E2
Paulhan Rd M20 ....110 D4
Paulhan St BL3 ....147 E3
Pauline St WN2 ....57 B1
Pavilion Cl OL12 ....14 F2
Pavilion Dr OL6 ....85 D5
Pavilion Ho M20 ......110 A4
Pavilion Wlk M26 ......43 F3
Pavilions The M20 .....110 B4
Paxford Pl SK9 ....137 A5
Paythorne Cl WA3 .....91 F3
Paythorne Gn SK2 .....124 E5
Peabody St BL3 ....147 E4
Peace St Atherton M46 ...58 E3
Bolton BL3 ....145 D5
🖪 Failsworth M35 ......66 A1
Tyldesley M29 ....76 F2
Peacefield SK6 ....125 E5
Peacefield Prim Sch SK6 ...125 E5
Peacehaven Ave 🖪 M11 ...83 C2
Peaceville Rd M19 .....98 F1
Peach Bank M24 ......65 A8
Peach Bank Ho M24 ...65 A8
Peach Rd OL4 ....49 D1
Peach St M25 ....63 C5
Peach Tree Cl M7 .....155 F6
Peach Tree Ct M6 .....81 A2
Peacock Ave Gatley SK8 ...122 B1
🖪 Salford M6 ....80 D5
Peacock Cl Hadfield SK13 ...171 E4
Manchester M18 ......165 C6
Peacock Fold WN7 .....75 D6
Peacock Gr M18 ....99 C4
Peacock Way 🖪 SK9 ...131 D5
Peak Ave M46 ....58 D5
Peak Bank M24 ....113 B3
Peak Cl OL4 ....49 F4
Peak Dr BL4 ....59 E7
Peak St Bolton BL1 ....159 B1
Manchester M1 ....159 B1
Oldham OL9 ....152 C6
Stockport SK1 ....112 A2
Peakdale Ave Gatley SK8 ...122 B1
Manchester M8 ....64 A2
Peakdale Rd Droylsden M43 ...83 E3
Hadfield SK13 ....171 E3
Marple SK6 ....126 A4
Peaknaze Cl Glossop SK13 ...116 B8
Pendlebury M27 ....80 B6
Pear Ave BL9 ....141 C3
Pear Cl M24 ....65 B6
Pear New Mill Ind Est
SK6 ....112 C2
Pear Tree Cl
Hadfield SK13 ....171 E4
Marple SK6 ....126 B8
Salford M6 ....81 A2
Pear Tree Ct 🖪 M6 ....81 A2
Pear Tree Dr SK15 .....86 B2
Pear Tree Gr M29 .....59 C1
Pear Tree Wlk 🖪 M33 ...107 C5
Pearl Ave M7 ....63 E1
Pearl Brook Ind Est BL6 ...22 B3
Pearl Mill Cl OL8 ......67 B4
Pearl St Denton M34 ...100 E3
Hazel Grove SK7 ......124 E4
Rochdale OL11 ....30 C8
Wigan WN6 ....37 B3
Pearl Way M44 ....103 A2
Pearly Bank OL1 ....49 D4
Pearn Ave M19 ....110 F5
Pearn Rd M19 ....110 F5
Pearson Cl Milnrow OL16 ...31 F7
Partington M31 ....106 A3
Pearson Gr 🖪 OL4 .....67 A7
Pearson St Bury BL9 ...140 F4
Denton M34 ....101 C6
Rochdale OL16 ....139 F8
Reddish SK5 ....169 F3
Stockport SK5 ....169 F3
Peart Ave SK6 ....113 C6
Peart St M34 ....100 E3
Peartree Wlk M22 .....121 B2
Peary St M4 ....159 B3
Peaslake Cl SK6 ....113 D2

Peatfield Ave M27 .....61 E2
Peatfield Wlk M15 ....162 F5
Pebble Cl SK15 ....86 A4
Pebworth Cl M24,M9 ...64 F5
Peckford Dr M40 ......83 A5
Peckforton Cl SK8 ....122 A5
Peckforton Wlk 🖪 SK9 ...131 E1
Peckmill Cl SK9 ....131 E2
Pedder St BL1 ....142 C1
Pedler Brow La OL12 ...15 E6
Pedley Wlk M13 ......163 B7
Peebles Cl WN4 ....72 C4
Peebles Dr M40 ....83 D4
Peel Ave Altrincham WA14 ...119 D2
Ramsbottom BL0 ......138 A5
Peel Brow BL0 ....11 D6
Peel Brow Prim Sch BL0 ...11 D6
Peel Cl M46 ....58 E3
Peel Cotts CW7 ....48 F1
Peel Cott St OL4 ....6 A8
Peel Cottage Rd OL14 ...6 A8
Peel Cross Rd M5 ......81 A1
Peel Ctr The
Stockport SK1 ....112 A2
Stockport SK1 ....169 F2
Peel Dr Sale M33 .....108 C4
Walkden M38 ....59 F4
Peel Gr Manchester M12 ...99 A4
Worsley M28 ....78 F8
Peel Green Rd M30 ...95 C8
Peel Hall Prim Sch
Walkden M38 ....59 F3
Wythenshawe M22 ....121 F3
Peel Hall Rd
Ramsbottom BL0,BL9 ...11 B2
Wythenshawe M22 ....121 F2
Peel La Heywood OL10 ...29 B3
Manchester M8 ....159 B4
Tyldesley M29 ....77 B4
Walkden M28,M38 ....59 F3
Peel Moat Ct SK4 .....111 B5
Peel Moat Rd SK4 ....111 B5
Peel Moat Sports Ctr
SK4 ....111 B5
Peel Mount
Ramsbottom BL0 ....11 A4
Salford M6 ....81 B3
Peel Park Cres M38 ...59 F4
Peel Rd WA15 ....119 E3
Peel Sq M18 ....99 D5
Peel St Adlington PR6 ...21 B8
Ashton-u-L OL6 ....166 B3
Denton M34 ....100 E4
Denton M34 ....100 E6
Droylsden M43 ....99 F8
Dukinfield SK16 ......166 C1
Eccles M30 ....79 F2
Failsworth M35 ....83 D6
Farnworth BL4 ....60 E8
Hadfield SK13 ....104 C5
Heywood OL10 ....29 D2
Hyde SK14 ....167 F1
Leigh WN7 ....75 E5
Littleborough OL15 ....16 B5
Newton-le-W WA12 ....89 A3
Oldham OL9 ....152 B7
Platt Bridge WN2 ......56 A2
🖪 Radcliffe M26 ....44 B2
Rochdale OL12 ....139 E8
Stalybridge SK15 ......85 F1
Stockport SK2 ....170 F6
Westhoughton BL5 ....39 E1
Peel Terr 🖪 SK16 .....166 B1
Peel Twr BL8 ....10 F5
Peel View BL8 ....27 A6
Peel Way BL9 ....140 E2
Peelgate Dr SK8 ......122 E2
Peels Ave OL4 ....68 A7
Peelwood Ave M38 ....60 A4
Peelwood Gr M46 .....58 E2
Peerglow Pk Est WA14 ...119 E8
Peers Cl M41 ....94 D4
Peers St BL3 ....27 C2
Pegamoid St BL2 .....25 B1
Pegasus Ct Rochdale OL11 ...30 C6
Sale M33 ....108 D5
Pegasus Sq M7 ....81 C3
Pegwell Dr M7,M8 ....155 F5
Pekin St OL6 ....166 C4
Pelham Pl M8 ....64 B2
Pelham St Ashton-u-L OL7 ...84 E1
Bolton BL3 ....146 C3
Oldham OL8 ....66 E2
Pellowe Rd OL8 ....66 E4
Pelton Ave M27 ....61 D2
Pelton Wlk M40 ....157 D5
Pemberley Rd WN2 ....38 D3
Pemberton
Com High Sch WN5 ...54 C7
Pemberton Ho OL2 ...149 B8
Pemberton Prim Sch
WN5 ....54 C6
Pemberton Rd
Garswood WN3,WN5 ...72 A8
Wigan WN3,WN5 ......54 B2
Pemberton St Bolton BL1 ...143 E4
Manchester M16 ......97 C4
🖪 Rochdale OL11 ......30 C4
Walkden M38 ....60 B4
Pemberton Sta WN3 ...54 D4
Pemberton Way OL2 ...149 B8
Pembridge Fold M24 ...65 C8
Pembridge Rd M9 .....64 F4
Pembroke Ave Eccles M30 ...79 D2
Sale M33 ....108 D5
Pembroke Cl
Horwich BL6 ....22 A4
Manchester M13 ......164 D6

Pembroke Ct
Bredbury SK6 ....112 F2
Hazel Grove SK7 ....124 E2
Pendlebury M27 ....80 B8
 Rochdale OL12 ....14 F1
Pembroke Dr Bury BL9 ....44 E7
Oldham OL4 ....49 E4
Pembroke Gr M44 ....105 C6
Pembroke Ho 6 SK3 ....170 E8
Pembroke Rd Hindley WN2 ..57 C3
Shevington WN5 ....36 D1
Pembroke St Bolton BL1 ..145 D8
Littleborough OL15 ....16 B6
Manchester M7 ....155 E6
Oldham OL8 ....153 D6
 Salford M6 ....154 E1
Pembroke Way 6 M34 ...101 A1
Pembry Cl SK5 ....112 B5
Pembury Cl M22 ....121 C3
Penarth Rd Bolton BL3 ..146 B4
Wythenshawe M22 ....121 D8
Penbury Rd M11 ....37 B5
Pencarrow Cl M20 ......109 F3
Pencombe Cl M12 ......165 A5
Pencroft Way M15 ......163 A5
Pendeen Cl M29 ....77 A7
Pendennis 2 OL11 ......139 E6
Pendennis Ave BL6 ......40 D5
Pendennis Cl M26 ......43 C5
Pendennis Cres WN2 ....57 A3
Pendennis Rd SK4 ......168 C3
Pendle Ave BL1 ....24 E6
Pendle Cl Bury BL8 ......27 B3
Wigan WN5 ....54 D5
Pendle Ct BL1 ....143 D3
Pendle Dr BL8 ....22 C5
Pendle Gdns WA3 ....91 E2
Pendle Gr OL2 ....48 C3
Pendle Rd Denton M34 ..100 F2
Golborne WA3 ....74 C1
Pendle Wlk SK5 ....112 A4
Pendlebury Cl M25 ......62 F2
Pendlebury Fold BL3 ....40 D2
Pendlebury La WN2,M27 ..37 D6
Pendlebury Rd Gatley SK8 122 B6
Swinton M27 ....79 F8
Pendlebury St BL1 ......143 F3
Pendlebury Towers SK5 ..169 F3
Pendlebury Way M27 ....80 C7
Pendlegreen Cl M11 ....164 F8
Pendleton Coll M6 ......154 D4
Pendleton Gn 6 M6 .....154 F3
Pendleton Sta M6 ....81 A4
Pendleton Way M6 ......154 F3
Pendleway M27 ....62 A1
Pendragon Pl M35 ....84 A7
Pendrell Wlk 35 M9 .....64 E3
Penelope Rd 4 M6 ......80 D5
Penerly Dr M9 ....157 D6
Penfair Cl M11 ....83 A1
Penfield Cl M1 ....163 B7
Penfold Wlk M12 ....164 F6
Pengarth Rd BL6 ....22 C4
Pengham Wlk M23 ......109 A1
Pengwern Ave 2 BL3 ...146 B4
Penhale Mews SK7 ......132 F7
Penhall Wlk M40 ....83 A5
Peninsula M7 ....81 B7
Penistone Ave
Manchester M9 ....65 A3
Rochdale OL16 ....31 C6
Salford M6 ....80 C3
Penketh Ave
Manchester M18 ....99 B4
Tyldesley M29 ....77 B6
Penketh St WN6 ....37 B2
Penleach Ave WN7 ......76 B5
Penmere Gr M33 ....107 E1
Penmoor Chase SK7 ....124 B1
Penmore Cl OL2 ....49 D7
Penn Gn SK8 ....123 B1
Penn House Cl SK7 .....132 E8
Penn St Farnworth BL4 ..60 C8
Heywood OL10 ....29 D1
Horwich BL6 ....22 C3
Manchester M40 ....157 F8
Oldham OL8 ....153 D5
Rochdale OL16 ....139 F8
Pennant Dr M25 ....63 A5
Pennant St OL1 ....67 B8
Pennant Street Ind Est
OL1 ....67 B8
Pennell Dr 8 WN1 ......54 F5
Pennell St M11 ....83 D1
Pennine Ave Oldham OL9 152 A5
Wigan WN5 ....54 C2
Pennine Cl Bury BL8 .....27 B3
Horwich BL6 ....22 C5
Manchester M9 ....64 F4
Pennine Cl 3 Oldham OL4 ..47 A6
Stalybridge SK15 ....86 D3
Swinton M27 ....62 A1
Pennine Dr
Altrincham WA14 ....119 B5
Ashton-u-L OL6 ....85 E4
Littleborough OL12 ....15 C6
Milnrow OL16 ....32 A6
Pennine Gr Ashton-u-L OL6 ..85 E6
Leigh WN7 ....75 C8
Pennine La WA3 ....74 C1
Pennine Prec OL16 ......31 F5
Pennine Rd Glossop SK13 116 A8
Horwich BL6 ....22 C5
Romiley SK6 ....113 C6
Stockport SK7 ....124 B1
Pennine Terr 2 SK16 ...166 C1
Pennine Vale OL2 ....149 C8

Pennine View Denton M34 .100 E5
Littleborough OL15 ....6 D2
Mossley OL5 ....68 D1
Stockport SK1 ....169 F2
Stalybridge SK15 ....86 C4
Pennine Wlk WN2 ....56 B2
Pennington Ave M7 ......75 E3
Pennington Green
Pennington Cl M44 ....38 E2
Walkden M28 ....59 E4
Pennington Ct WN7 ......75 B1
Pennington Flash Ctry Pk
Golborne WA3 ....74 F4
Leigh WN7 ....75 B3
Pennington Gdns WN7 ...75 E3
Pennington Green La
WN2 ....38 E2
Pennington La
Ince-in-M WN2 ....56 A8
Standish WN2 ....37 E8
Pennington Mews WN7 ...75 E2
Pennington Rd Bolton BL3 147 F3
Leigh WN7 ....75 F3
Pennington St Bury BL8 ...26 F4
 Hindley WN2 ....56 D6
Manchester M12 ....99 A2
Oldham OL9 ....66 B3
 Walkden M28 ....60 E2
Penny Black Chambers
M28 ....78 F5
Penny Bridge La M41 ....95 A2
Penny Brook Fold SK7 ..124 F3
Penny La Ashton-in-M M41 ..89 A7
Stockport SK5 ....169 F3
Penny Mdw OL6 ....166 C3
Pennygate Cl WN2 ......56 D6
Pennyhurst St WN3 .....150 B7
Pennymoor Dr WA14 ....119 B6
Penrhos Ave SK8 ....121 F4
Penrhyn Ave Cheadle SK8 122 C1
Middleton M24 ....65 A7
Penrhyn Cres SK7 ......133 C8
Penrhyn Dr
Hazel Grove SK7 ....124 D1
Prestwich M25 ....63 B4
Penrhyn Gr M46 ....58 C5
Penrhyn Rd SK3 ....123 C8
Penrice Cl M26 ....43 D5
Penrice Fold M28 ....78 B7
Penrith Ave Ashton-u-L OL7 84 F1
Bolton BL1 ....142 A1
Droylsden M11 ....83 B3
Oldham OL8 ....66 C4
Prestwich M45 ....63 B7
Reddish SK5 ....99 E2
Walkden M28 ....60 F2
Penrith Cl M31 ....105 E4
Penrith Cres WN4 ....73 B4
Penroll Pl M6 ....81 B4
Penrose Gdns M24 ....47 B1
Penrose St BL2 ....148 C7
Penrose Wlk M24 ....47 A4
Penroy Ave M20 ....109 D3
Penroyson Cl M12 ......164 F6
Penruddock Wlk 4 M13 ..98 F4
Penry Ave M44 ....105 E6
Penryn Ave Royton OL2 ..48 F3
Sale M33 ....108 C1
Penry Ct M7 ....63 D1
Pensarn Ave M14 ....110 E8
Pensarn Gr SK5 ....169 F4
Pensby Cl M27 ....80 C7
Pensford Ct BL2 ....25 E6
Pensford Rd M23 ....120 F3
Penshaw Ave WN3 ......55 B3
Penshurst St SK5 ....112 B6
Penshurst Wlk 20 M34 ..101 A1
Penson St WN1 ....37 D2
Penthorpe Dr OL2 ....49 E7
Pentland Ave M40 ......65 C2
Pentland Cl SK7 ....124 B1
Pentland Terr BL1 ......143 E1
Pentland Way SK14 ....102 B6
Pentlands Ave M7 ......155 D5
Penton Wlk 5 M8 ....97 F3
Pentwyn Gr M23 ....121 B7
Penzance St M40 ....160 E3
Peover Ave M33 ....108 C4
Peover Rd SK9 ....131 E5
Peover Wlk SK8 ....123 A5
Pepler Ave M23 ....109 B2
Peploe Wlk M23 ....108 D1
Pepper Cl SK9 ....137 A6
Pepper La WN6 ....19 B3
Pepper Mill Bsns
Pk WN1 ....151 D7
Pepper Mill La WN1 ....151 D7
Pepper Rd SK7 ....124 B2
Pepperhill Rd M16 ......97 F4
Peppermint Cl OL16 ....32 C4
Pepys Pl WN3 ....55 A4
Perch St 4 WN1 ....37 E1
Perch Wlk 7 M4 ....159 C3
Percival Cl M8 ....155 F6
Percival Rd M43 ....84 B1
Percival Wlk OL2 ....48 E3
Percy Dr M5 ....161 B7
Percy Rd M34 ....100 E2
Percy St Bolton BL3 ....145 E6
Bury BL9 ....143 B3
Farnworth BL4 ....60 E7
Manchester M15 ....162 D6
Oldham OL4 ....67 C7
Ramsbottom BL0 ....138 B5

Percy St *continued*
Rochdale OL16 ....31 B5
Stalybridge SK15 ....86 B2
Stockport SK3 ....169 F2
Whitworth OL12 ....4 E6
Peregrine Dr WN7 ....76 B5
Peregrine Cres M43 .....84 C3
Peregrine Dr M44 ....94 A3
Peregrine Rd SK2 ......125 A4
Peregrine St M15,M16 ..162 F5
Periton Wlk 8 M9 ......64 E3
Perivale Dr OL8 ....67 B4
Perkins Ave M7 ....155 E5
Perran Cl SK14 ....50 D4
Perrin St SK14 ....167 D2
Perry Ave SK14 ....102 A4
Perry Brook
Com Prim Sch WN4 .....73 A7
Perry Cl OL11 ....139 D5
Perry Rd WA15 ....120 B6
Perrybrook Wlk WN4 ....73 D4
Perrygate Ave M20 .....110 A6
Perrymead M25 ....63 C6
Perryn Pl WN6 ....19 F1
Pershore 6 OL12 ....139 E8
Pershore Rd M24 ....47 A3
Perth 6 M30 ....79 E2
Perth Ave Ince-in-M WN2 ..56 A8
Oldham OL8 ....66 D4
Perth Cl SK7 ....132 F5
Perth Rd OL11 ....31 B2
Perth St Bolton BL3 ....146 C3
Royton OL2 ....49 A4
Swinton M27 ....79 D7
Peru St M3 ....158 D2
Peter Martin St 2 BL2 ..22 B4
Peter Moss Way M19 ....99 C1
Peter St Altrincham WA14 ..119 D3
Ashton-in-M WN4 ....73 C3
Bury BL9 ....140 F3
Denton M34 ....101 A3
Eccles M30 ....79 D1
Golborne WA3 ....90 A8
Hadfield SK13 ....104 A6
Hazel Grove SK7 ....124 D3
Hindley WN2 ....56 D5
Leigh WN7 ....76 B4
Manchester M2,M3 ......162 F8
Oldham OL1 ....153 F6
Stockport SK1 ....169 F2
 Tyldesley M29 ....58 F1
Westhoughton BL5 ....57 A7
Wigan WN5 ....54 B8
Peterborough Cl OL6 .....85 B6
Peterborough Dr 17 BL1 143 E1
Peterborough St 8 M18 ..99 F6
Peterborough Wlk BL1 ...143 E1
Peterchurch Wlk M11 ...165 C8
Peterhead Cl BL1 ....143 D1
Peterhead Wlk 4 M5 ....81 A1
Peterhouse Gdns SK6 ..113 C4
Peterhouse Wlk WN4 ....72 F3
Peterloo Ct 6 M5 ......154 E2
Peterloo Terr 8 M24 ....47 A2
Peters Ct WA15 ....120 D5
Petersburg Rd SK3 .....170 D6
Petersfield Dr M23 .....120 D7
Petersfield Gdns WA3 ...91 E4
Petersfield Wlk 1 BL1 ..145 E8
Peterswood Cl M22 ....121 B3
Petherige Dr 9 M22 ....121 B1
Petrel Ave SK12 ....133 B4
Petrel Cl Droylsden M43 ..84 C3
Rochdale OL11 ....29 F7
Stockport SK3 ....170 D6
Petrie Ct M6 ....81 B4
Petrie St OL12 ....139 F8
Petrock Wlk 5 M40 .....83 C5
Petticoat La M9 ....56 B7
Petts Cres OL15 ....16 A6
Petunia Wlk 8 M28 .....59 F3
Petworth Ave WN3 ......54 D2
Petworth Cl M22 ....121 E5
Petworth Rd OL9 ....152 B6
Pevensey Ct M9 ....64 D3
Pevensey Rd M6 ....80 E5
Pevensey Wlk OL9 ......152 B6
Peveril Ave SK22 ......127 C1
Peveril Cl M25,M45 .....63 C7
Peveril Cres M21 ....97 A2
Peveril Ct SK13 ....116 F8
Peveril Dr SK7 ....133 F8
Peveril Rd
Altrincham WA14 ....119 C7
Oldham OL1 ....49 C1
Salford M5 ....154 C3
Peveril St BL3 ....146 C3
Peveril Terr SK14 ......113 F8
Pewfist Gn BL5 ....57 E6
Pewfist Spinney The BL5 ..57 D7
Pewfist The BL5 ....57 E6
Pewsey Rd M22 ....121 F3
Pexhill Ct SK4 ....168 A2
Pexwood OL1 ....47 E1
Pheasant Cl M28 ....78 B6
Pheasant Dr M21 ......109 D7
Pheasant Rise WA14 ...119 E1
Phelan Cl M40 ....156 C5
Phethean St Bolton BL2 ..148 A7
Farnworth BL4 ....42 C2
Philip Arnold Ct 2 BL4 ..60 C8
Philip Dr M33 ....108 B2
Philip Cl 13 WN5 ....54 D5
Philip Dr M33 ....108 B2
Philip Howard Rd SK13 116 C8
Philip St Bolton BL3 ....145 D5
Eccles M30 ....79 D1

Philip St *continued*
Oldham OL4 ....67 C8
Rochdale OL11 ....139 F5
Philips Ave BL4 ....60 D7
Philips Dr M45 ....62 D6
Philips High Sch M45 ...62 E8
Philips Park Rd
Manchester M11 ....160 E2
Whitefield M45 ....62 D6
Whitefield M45 ....62 F6
Phillimore St OL4 ....67 E5
Phillip Way 1 SK14 ....102 E1
Phillips Pl M45 ....62 E7
Phillips St M3 ....159 A3
Philton Wlk M9 ....75 E8
Phipps St M28 ....60 C4
Phoebe St 5 Bolton BL3 ..146 C4
Salford M5 ....161 B8
Phoenix Cl OL10 ....29 F1
Phoenix Park Ind Est OL12 29 F1
Phoenix Pl OL4 ....67 F7
Phoenix St Bolton BL1 ..148 A8
Bury BL9 ....140 E2
Farnworth BL4 ....60 D7
Littleborough OL15 ......16 B6
Manchester M2 ....159 A1
Oldham OL1 ....153 F6
Oldham OL4 ....67 F7
Rochdale OL12 ....14 C1
Phoenix Way Eccles M41 ..95 E6
Radcliffe M26 ....44 A2
Phyllis St Middleton M24 ..65 C7
Rochdale OL12 ....14 B1
Picadilly WN5 ....71 E5
Piccadilly Manchester M1 ..159 B1
Stockport SK1 ....169 F1
Piccadilly Gardens Sta
M1 ....159 A1
Piccadilly Plaza M1 .....159 A1
Piccadilly Sta 6 M1 ....163 B8
Piccadilly Trad Est M1 ..163 C8
Piccadilly Village M1 ...159 C1
Pickering Cl
Altrincham WA15 ....120 A7
Bury BL8 ....27 B5
Kearsley M26 ....61 A8
Urmston M41 ....95 B2
Pickford Ave BL3 ......43 C3
Pickford Ct M15 ....162 E5
Pickford La SK16 ......101 C8
Pickford Mews SK16 ....101 C8
Pickford St M4 ....159 B2
Pickford Wlk OL2 ....48 E3
Pickford's Brow SK1 ....169 F1
Pickhill La OL3 ....69 B8
Pickhill Mews 3 OL3 ....69 B8
Pickley Gn WN7 ....57 E1
Pickmere Ave M20 ....110 B8
Pickmere Cl
 Droylsden M43 ....84 B1
Stockport SK3 ....123 C6
Westhoughton M33 .....108 F2
Pickmere Ct 10 SK9 ...131 D5
Pickmere Gdns SK8 ....122 F4
Pickmere Mews 2 OL3 ..69 B8
Pickmere Rd SK9 ......131 D5
Pickmere Terr 9 SK16 ..166 B1
Pickley St WN7 ....76 B4
Pickthorn Cl WN2 ......56 B3
Pickup St Ince-in-M WN2 ..151 F7
Rochdale OL16 ....31 A7
Pickwick Rd SK12 .....133 D3
Picton Cl M3 ....158 E2
Picton Dr SK9 ....131 E2
Picton Sq 4 OL4 ....67 A6
Picton St Ashton-u-L OL7 ..84 A6
Manchester M7 ....158 D3
Picton Wlk 3 M16 ......97 F3
Pierce St OL1 ....49 C1
Piercy Ave M7 ....158 D4
Piercy St Failsworth M35 ..83 C2
Manchester M4 ....160 D2
Pierpoint St WA3 ....90 A7
Piethorne Cl OL16 ......32 C4
Pigeon St M1 ....159 B1
Piggott St BL4 ....60 C7
Pike Ave Atherton M46 ..58 A2
Failsworth M35 ....84 C6
Pike Fold La M9 ....64 C3
Pike Fold Prim Sch M9 ..64 C3
Pike Nook Wkshp BL3 ..145 D5
Pike Rd BL3 ....147 D4
Pike St OL11 ....139 F5
Pike View BL6 ....22 D4
Pike View Cl OL4 ......67 B5
Pike's La SK13 ....116 B8
Pikehouse Cotts OL15 ..16 D7
Pikes Lane Prim Sch
BL3 ....145 D6
Pilgrim Dr M11 ....160 F1
Pilgrims Way WN6 ......37 A2
Pilkington Cl M45 ......45 B2
Pilkington Rd Kearsley BL4 ..60 F6
Manchester M9 ....65 A3
Radcliffe M26 ....43 F4
Pilkington St Bolton BL3 145 E5
Hindley WN2 ....56 D6
Middleton M24 ....47 C1
Ramsbottom BL0 ....138 B5
Pilkington Way M26 ....44 A2
Pilling Field BL7 ....8 E1
Pilling St Bury BL8 .....27 C2
Denton M34 ....100 F3
Leigh WN7 ....75 D5
Manchester M10,M40 ...157 F5
 Rawtenstall BB4 ....2 F8
Rochdale OL12 ....139 D8

Pilling Wlk OL9 ....152 A6
Pilning St BL3 ....42 A4
Pilot Ind Est BL3 ....42 B4
Pilot St BL9 ....140 F1
Pilsley Ct WN5 ....36 A1
Pilsworth Cotts BL9 ....45 C5
Pilsworth Rd
Heywood BL9,OL10 .....45 C7
Heywood OL10 ....46 A8
Pilsworth Way BL9 ......45 A6
Pimblett St Golborne WA3 ..90 A7
Manchester M3 ....158 F3
Pimbo La WN8 ....53 A4
Pimhole Rd BL9 ....141 A2
Pimlico Cl M7 ....155 D6
Pimlott Gr Dukinfield SK14 ..101 D5
Prestwich M25 ....62 F2
Pimlott Rd BL1 ....25 B3
Pimmcroft Way M33 ...109 A3
Pin Mill Brow M12 ....164 D8
Pincher Wlk 11 M11 ....83 C1
Pinder Wlk 4 M15 .....162 F6
Pine Ave
Newton-le-W WA12 ......89 D2
Whitefield M45 ....62 F6
Pine Cl Denton M34 .....68 A6
Marple SK6 ....125 E4
Pine Ct Manchester M20 ..110 A4
Stockport SK7 ....123 D2
Pine Gr Denton M34 .....101 A3
Eccles M30 ....79 E4
Farnworth BL4 ....60 B8
Golborne WA3 ....90 C8
Manchester M13,M14 ...98 E4
Prestwich M45 ....63 A6
Royton OL2 ....48 D6
Sale M33 ....54 E6
Stalybridge SK16 ....101 F8
Swinton M27 ....79 D7
Westhoughton BL5 ....57 E7
Worsley M28 ....78 E8
Pine Lo SK7 ....132 E7
Pine Mdw M26 ....61 C6
Pine Rd Bramhall SK7 ..132 F8
Dukinfield SK15 ....101 E8
Manchester M20 ....110 B4
Poynton SK12 ....133 C3
Wigan WN5 ....54 E6
Pine St Ashton-u-L OL6 ..166 B4
Bolton BL1 ....143 F2
Bury BL9 ....141 B2
Chadderton OL9 ....152 A8
Dukinfield SK14 ....101 D5
Heywood OL10 ....29 D2
Littleborough OL15 ......16 B6
Manchester M1 ....159 A1
Middleton M24 ....65 C7
Oldham OL9 ....48 D4
Radcliffe M26 ....44 B4
Romiley SK6 ....113 B5
 Tyldesley M29 ....59 A1
Pine St N BL9 ....141 B2
Pine Tree Rd OL8 ....66 D1
Pine View WN3 ....54 B1
Pine Wlk 1 M31 ....105 E3
Pineapple St SK7 ......124 E2
Pinecroft Marple M40 ...157 E1
Orrell WN5 ....53 C6
Ramsbottom BL0 ....11 B2
Pinewood Ct
Altrincham WA14 ....119 E1
Sale M33 ....108 D5
Pinewood Rd
Manchester M21 ....109 A7
Wilmslow SK9 ....137 E8
Pinewoods The SK6 ....113 A5
Hadfield Hadfield SK13 ..171 E4
Rochdale OL11 ....139 E6
Pinfold Ave M9 ....65 A2
Pinfold Cl
Altrincham WA15 ....129 D7
Westhoughton BL5 ....57 D5
Pinfold Ct 3 M32 ....96 C1
Pinfold Dr Cheadle SK8 ..123 A1
Prestwich M25 ....62 F5
Pinfold La Romiley SK6 ..113 E4
Westhoughton BL5 ....57 D5
Wythenshawe M9,M45,M18 ..129 F6
Pinfold Prim Sch SK14 ..102 E1
Pinfold Rd M28 ....60 D1
Pinfold St WN2 ....56 A7
Pingate Dr SK8 ....132 A6
Pingate La SK8 ....132 A6
Pingate La S SK8 ......132 A6
Pingle La OL3 ....50 E5
Pingot OL2 ....32 D1
Pingot Ave M23 ....109 B1

Pingot Ct 6 WN7 . . . . .75 D5
Pingot La SK14 . . . . .103 B1
Pingot Rd WN5 . . . . .71 E5
Pingot The Irlam M44 . . . .94 B3
  Leigh WN7 . . . . .75 D5
Pingot La 4 SK13 . . . .104 A5
Pink Bank La M12 . . . . .99 A4
Pinnacle Dr BL7 . . . . .8 E2
Pinner Pl M19 . . . . .111 A6
Pinners Ctl BL0 . . . . .138 B7
Pinnington La M32 . . . . .96 D2
Pinnington Rd M18 . . . . .99 D6
Pintail Ave SK3 . . . . .170 D6
Pintail Cl 5 OL12 . . . . .14 B2
Pinwood Cl 8 SK9 . . . .131 E1
Pioneer Rd M27 . . . . .62 D2
Pioneer St Droylsden M11 . .83 B2
  Horwich BL6 . . . . .22 C4
  4 Littleborough OL15 . . .16 B5
  Walsden OL14 . . . . .6 A7
Pioneers St 4 OL11 . . . .31 A6
Pioneers Villa OL16 . . . .32 E4
Piper Hill High Sch M23 . .109 B2
Piperhill Ave M22 . . . .109 D2
Pipers Cl OL11 . . . . .29 D8
Pipers The WA3 . . . . .90 F8
Pipewell Ave M18 . . . .165 C5
Pipit Ave WA12 . . . . .89 C3
Pipit Cl M34 . . . . .84 C2
Pirie Wlk 4 M40 . . . . .83 C6
Pit La OL16,OL12 . . . . .31 D1
Pit St Denton M34 . . . .100 F3
  Oldham OL9 . . . . .66 B4
Pitcairn Ho 12 M30 . . . .79 D1
Pitchcombe Rd M22 . . . .121 B2
Pitcombe Cl BL1 . . . . .24 D7
Pitfield Gdns M23 . . . .120 F7
Pitfield La BL2 . . . . .25 F4
Pitfield St BL2 . . . . .148 B7
Pitman Cl M11 . . . . .165 A8
Pitmore Wlk 3 M40 . . . .65 D2
Pits Farm Ave OL11 . . . .30 C7
Pitsford Rd M40 . . . .157 E5
Pitshouse OL12 . . . . .13 E2
Pitshouse La OL12 . . . .13 E2
Pitt St Denton M34 . . . .100 F6
  Heywood OL10 . . . . .29 C2
  Hyde SK14 . . . . .167 A3
  Ince-in-M WN3 . . . .151 D6
  Oldham OL4 . . . . .67 A5
  Radcliffe M26 . . . . .43 E3
  Rochdale OL12 . . . .139 F8
  Stockport SK3 . . . .170 D8
  Wigan WN3 . . . .150 B7
Pitt St E OL4 . . . . .67 B5
Pittbrook St M12 . . . .164 D7
Pixmore Ave BL1 . . . . .25 B4
Place Rd M14 . . . . .91 A3
Plain Pit St SK14 . . . .101 C5
Plainsfield Cl M16 . . . .97 F4
Plane Ave WN5 . . . . .54 E7
Plane Ct 4 M44 . . . . .81 A2
Plane Rd M35 . . . . .83 F5
Plane St OL4 . . . . .67 C7
Plane Tree Cl SK6 . . . .125 D5
Plane Tree Gr WA11 . . . .89 A7
Plane Tree Rd M31 . . . .105 D3
Plane Way M34 . . . .100 E5
Planetree Rd M14/15 . . .120 A2
Planetree Wlk M23 . . . .120 C8
Plank La WN7 . . . . .75 B4
Plant Cl M33 . . . . .108 A5
Plant Hill High Sch M9 . . .64 C4
Plant Hill Rd M9 . . . . .64 D4
Plant St M1 . . . . .159 B1
Plantagenet Wlk M40 . . .83 D4
Plantation Ave M28 . . . .60 C4
Plantation Gates WN1 . . .37 E2
Plantation Gr BL9 . . . . .45 C4
Plantation Ind Est
  Ashton-u-L OL6 . . . . .85 D2
  Dukinfield OL6 . . . .166 C2
Plantation Rd BL7 . . . . .9 F7
Plantation St
  Ashton-u-L OL6 . . . . .85 D2
  Bacup OL13 . . . . .3 C8
  Manchester M18 . . . .99 E5
Plantation View BL9 . . . .11 C3
Plasden Cl M23 . . . .121 A5
Plate St OL1 . . . .153 F7
Plato St OL9 . . . .153 D7
Platt Ave OL6 . . . . .85 C6
Platt Cl OL16 . . . . .32 A5
Platt Croft WN7 . . . . .76 C2
Platt Ct M14 . . . . .98 C2
Platt Fold Rd WN7 . . . .76 A6
Platt Fold St WN7 . . . .76 A5
Platt Hall Art Gall
& Gallery of
English Costume M14 . . .3 C2
Platt Hill Ave BL3 . . . .146 A4
Platt La Atherton BL5 . . .58 B7
  Hindley WN2 . . . . .56 D5
  Manchester M14 . . . .98 B2
  Standish WN1 . . . . .20 F2
  Uppermill OL3 . . . .50 F2
  Wigan WN1 . . . . .37 E1
Platt St Cheadle SK8 . . .122 E6
  Dukinfield SK16 . . . .101 A7
  Hadfield SK13 . . . .104 B5
  Leigh WN7 . . . . .75 F6
  8 Oldham OL4 . . . .67 F6
Platt Wlk M34 . . . .100 E1
Plattbrook Cl M14 . . . .98 B1

Platting La OL11 . . . . .31 A4
Platting Rd OL4 . . . . .68 C7
Platts Br M44 . . . . .94 A2
Plattwood Wlk 10 M15 . .162 D6
Playfair Cl OL10 . . . . .46 E7
Playfair St Bolton BL1 . . .24 F6
  Manchester M14 . . . . .98 B4
Pleachway SK4 . . . .110 F2
Pleasance Way WA12 . . .89 D4
Pleasant Ct 6 BL1 . . . . .30 C2
Pleasant Gdns BL1 . . . .145 E8
Pleasant Rd M30 . . . . .79 E1
Pleasant St Bury BL8 . . .26 F4
  Heywood OL10 . . . . .29 C4
  Manchester M9 . . . .157 D7
  Rochdale OL1 . . . . .30 C2
Pleasant Terr 8 SK16 . .166 C1
Pleasant View Bacup OL13 . .3 F7
  Radcliffe M26 . . . . .62 B8
Pleasant Way SK7,SK8 . .132 C6
Pleasington Dr Bury BL8 . .26 E2
  Failsworth M40 . . . . .65 C2
Plevna St BL2 . . . .148 A7
Plodder La BL4,BL5 . . . .59 D8
Plodder La Prim Sch BL4 . .60 A8
Plough Cl M41 . . . . .94 C1
Plough Fields M28 . . . .78 A5
Plough St 6 SK16 . . . .101 D8
Ploughbank Dr M21 . . . .109 D7
Ploughfields BL5 . . . . .39 E3
Plover Cl
  Newton-le-W WA12 . . . .89 C3
  Rochdale OL11 . . . . .29 F7
Plover Dr
  Altrincham WA14 . . . .119 B8
  Bury BL9 . . . . .141 B4
  Irlam M44 . . . . .94 A4
Plover Way WA3 . . . . .90 E8
Plowden Ave BL3 . . . .146 C3
Plowden Rd M22 . . . .121 B2
Plowley Cl M20 . . . .110 B2
Plucksbridge Rd SK6 . . .126 B3
Plum St OL8 . . . .153 D5
Plum Tree Ct 2 M5 . . . .81 A2
Plumbley Dr M16 . . . . .97 F3
Plumbley St 11 M11 . . . .99 F7
Plumley Cl SK3 . . . .170 F5
Plumley Rd WA3 . . . .131 D5
Plummer Ave M21 . . . .109 B6
Plumpton Cl OL1,OL2 . . .48 E1
Plumpton Dr BL9 . . . . .27 E8
Plumpton Rd OL11 . . . . .48 C8
Plumpton Wlk 6 M13 . . .98 F4
Plunge Rd BL0 . . . . .1 E3
Pluto Cl M6 . . . . .81 C4
Pobgreen La OL3 . . . . .51 D1
Pochard Dr
  Altrincham WA14 . . . .119 B7
  Poynton SK12 . . . .133 A4
Pochin St M40 . . . .160 E3
Pocket Nook La WA3 . . .91 B7
Pocket Nook Rd BL6 . . . .40 B3
Pocket Wkshp The BL3 . .144 C6
Pocklington Dr M23 . . .120 F7
Podnor La SK6 . . . .127 A6
Podsmead Rd M22 . . . .121 B2
Poet's Nook WN7 . . . . .75 E4
Poise Brook Dr SK2 . . .124 F5
Poise Brook Rd SK2 . . .124 F5
Poise Cl SK7 . . . .125 A3
Poke St 8 WN5 . . . . .54 B6
Poland St
  8 Ashton-u-L M34 . . . .100 E8
  Manchester M4 . . . .159 C2
Poland Street Ind Est
  M4 . . . .159 C2
Polden Wlk 1 M9 . . . . .64 F1
Polding St WN3 . . . . .55 E4
Pole La Failsworth M35 . . .83 F8
  Whitefield BL9,M45 . . . .45 C2
  Whitefield M45 . . . . .45 C1
Pole St Ashton-u-L OL7 . .166 B4
  Bolton BL2 . . . . .25 B1
  Standish WN6 . . . . .19 E1
Poleacre La SK6 . . . .113 C6
Polebrook Ave M12 . . . .164 D6
Polefield App M25 . . . . .63 B6
Polefield Circ M25 . . . . .63 B6
Polefield Gdns M25 . . . .63 B6
Polefield Grange M25 . . .63 B6
Polefield Hall Rd M25 . . .63 B6
Polefield Rd
  Manchester M9 . . . . .64 E2
  Prestwich M25 . . . . .63 C6
Polegate Dr WN2 . . . . .57 D2
Polesworth Cl M12 . . . .165 A6
Police St
  1 Altrincham WA14 . . .119 D5
  Eccles M30 . . . . .79 C2
  Manchester M2 . . . .158 F1

Pollard Ct 4 OL1 . . . .153 E8
Pollard Gr OL15 . . . . .16 C8
Pollard Ho BL3 . . . .146 B2
Pollard Sq M31 . . . .106 A3
Pollard St M4 . . . .160 D1
Pollard St E M4,M40 . . .160 D2
Pollards La BL9 . . . . .11 C2
Polldean Ho SK8 . . . .122 D3
Pollen Cl M33 . . . .108 D1
Pollen Rd M14 . . . .119 C6
Polletts Ave SK5 . . . .112 C6
Pollit Croft SK6 . . . .112 F1
Pollitt Ave OL6 . . . . .85 C5
Pollitt Cl M12 . . . .164 F6
Pollitt St M26 . . . . .44 C3
Pollitts Cl M30 . . . . .79 B2
Polly Gn OL12 . . . . .14 F3
Polonia Ct OL8 . . . . .66 C3
Polperro Wlk SK14 . . . .102 D3
Polruan Rd M21 . . . . .97 A2
Polruan Wlk SK14 . . . .102 E3
Polworth Rd M9 . . . . .64 E1
Polygon Ave M12,M13 . .163 C6
Polygon Rd M8 . . . . .63 F1
Polygon St M13 . . . .163 C7
Polygon The
  Manchester M7 . . . . .81 C5
  Salford M30 . . . . .80 A2
Pomfret St M6 . . . . .80 C5
Pomona Cres M5 . . . .161 B7
Pomona St OL11 . . . .139 F5
Pomona St M5,M16 . . . .161 B6
Pomona Strand
  Salford M15 . . . .161 C7
  Salford M16,M5 . . . .161 B6
Pond St WA3 . . . . .91 A8
Ponds Cl M21 . . . . .97 B1
Pondwater Cl M28 . . . .60 A3
Pondwater Wlk 6 M16 . .97 C3
Ponsford Ave M9 . . . . .64 F5
Ponsonby Rd M32 . . . .96 D3
Pontefract Cl M27 . . . . .80 B7
Pool Bank St M24 . . . . .64 B7
Pool Fold M35 . . . . .84 A6
Pool House Rd SK12 . . .134 D5
Pool Rd WA3 . . . . .105 A3
Pool St Bolton BL1 . . . .145 E7
  Bolton BL1 . . . .145 E8
  Hindley WN2 . . . . .56 D4
  Oldham OL8 . . . . .66 A4
  Wigan WN3 . . . . .150 B6
Pool Terr BL1 . . . . .142 A2
Poolcroft M33 . . . .108 F3
Poole Cl SK7 . . . .123 D1
Pooley Cl M24 . . . . .46 B4
Poolfield Cl M26 . . . . .43 E3
Poolstock WN3 . . . .150 B6
Poolstock La WN3 . . . . .55 A4
Poolton Rd M9 . . . . .64 B4
Poot Hall OL12 . . . . .14 F3
Pope John Paul II
  RC High Sch M6 . . . . .81 A5
Pope Way 9 M34 . . . .113 A8
Poplar Ave
  Altrincham WA14 . . . .119 E6
  Bolton BL1 . . . . .24 F5
  Bolton BL2 . . . . .25 C6
  Bury BL9 . . . . .141 B3
  Culcheth WA3 . . . . .91 F3
  Downall Green WN4 . . . .72 D5
  Horwich BL6 . . . . .22 C4
  Manchester M19 . . . .111 B7
  New Mills SK22 . . . .127 D1
  Newton-le-W WA12 . . .89 D3
  Oldham OL8 . . . . .66 D2
  4 Rochdale OL12 . . . .14 C1
  Uppermill OL4 . . . . .68 C4
  Wigan WN5 . . . . .54 E6
  Wilmslow SK9 . . . .136 F5
Poplar Cl SK8 . . . .122 B5
Poplar Ct Dukinfield M34 . .100 F7
  Manchester M14 . . . . .98 D1
Poplar Dr M25 . . . . .63 A2
Poplar Gr Ashton-u-L OL6 . .85 C5
  Hindley WN2 . . . . .57 B3
  Irlam M44 . . . .105 D4
  Manchester M18 . . . . .99 D4
  Ramsbottom BL0 . . . .11 D7
  Sale M33 . . . .108 B3
  Stockport SK2 . . . .124 C4
  Tyldesley M29 . . . . .77 A4
  4 Urmston M41 . . . . .95 C2
  Westhoughton BL5 . . . .57 E8
Poplar Rd Dukinfield M34 .101 F7
  Eccles M30 . . . . .79 E4
  Manchester M19 . . . .110 D3
  Salford M27 . . . . .80 B8
  Swinton M27 . . . . .79 D7
  Walkden M28 . . . . .60 E1
Poplar St Dukinfield M34 .100 F7
  Failsworth M35 . . . . .83 D6
  Manchester M19 . . . . .111 A8
  Leigh WN7 . . . . .75 F4
  Manchester M11 . . . .164 E8
  Manchester M24 . . . .116 A2
  Middleton M24 . . . . .65 D7
  Tyldesley M29 . . . . .59 A1
Poplar St Prim Sch M34 .100 E6
Poplar Way SK6 . . . .135 A7
Poplar Wlk
  Chadderton OL9 . . . .152 B8
  Partington M31 . . . .105 D3
Poplars Rd SK15 . . . . .86 D3
Poplars The Adlington PR7 . .20 F6
  Golborne WA3 . . . . .74 B1
  Golborne WN7 . . . . .91 C8
  Mossley OL5 . . . . .68 E1

Poplin Dr M3 . . . .158 E3
Poppy Cl Chadderton OL9 . .65 E7
  Sale M33 . . . .108 E1
Poppythorn La M25 . . . .63 A5
Porchester Dr M26 . . . . .43 C5
Porchfield Sq M3 . . . .162 E8
Porlock Ave
  Droylsden M34 . . . .100 C8
  Hattersley SK14 . . . .102 E1
Porlock Cl Part Bridge WN2 . .56 A2
  Stockport SK1 . . . .124 C8
Porlock Rd Urmston M41 . .107 B8
  Wythenshawe M23 . . . .121 B6
Porlock Wlk SK14 . . . .102 C2
Porritt Cl OL11 . . . . .29 E6
Porritt St Bury BL9 . . . .141 A4
  Bury BL9 . . . . .141 B4
Porritt Way BL0 . . . .138 C7
Port Soderick Ave M5 . . .81 A1
Port St Manchester M1 . .159 B1
  Oldham OL8 . . . . .66 F4
  Stockport SK1 . . . .169 E2
Portal Ct M24 . . . . .65 C8
Portal Gr M34 . . . .101 B1
Portal Wlk 8 M9 . . . .157 D8
Porter Ave WA12 . . . . .89 C5
Porter St Bury BL9 . . . .140 F4
  Oldham OL9 . . . .152 C5
Porters Wood Cl WN5 . . .54 B7
Portfield Cl M40 . . . . .83 A6
Portfield Wlk 8 M40 . . .83 A6
Portgate Wlk M13 . . . .164 D5
Porthleven Cres M29 . . .77 C8
Porthleven Dr M23 . . . .120 E6
Porthtowan Wlk SK14 . .102 E3
Portinscale OL18 . . . . .27 B3
Portland Basin Mus OL7 .166 A1
Portland Cl Abram WN2 . .74 A8
  Hazel Grove SK7 . . . .124 B1
  Platt Bridge WN2 . . . .56 B2
Portland Cres M13 . . . .164 D5
Portland Ct M20 . . . .110 B3
Portland Gr SK4 . . . .168 B4
Portland Ho
  3 Ashton-u-L OL6 . . .166 A2
  Salford M6 . . . . .80 A3
  Marple SK6 . . . .125 E5
Portland Ind Est 10 BL9 .141 A4
Portland Pl OL7 . . . .166 A2
Portland Rd
  Altrincham WA14 . . . .119 D3
  Manchester M13 . . . . .98 F3
  New Mills SK22 . . . .127 D1
  Pendlebury M27 . . . . .80 B7
  Salford M30 . . . . .80 A4
  Stretford M32 . . . . .96 D2
  Walkden M28 . . . . .60 C5
Portland St Bolton BL3 . .143 E2
  6 Leigh WN7 . . . . .75 F5
  Manchester M1 . . . .163 A8
  Manchester M1 . . . .163 A8
  Rochdale OL16 . . . .139 F8
  Wigan WN6 . . . . .54 E6
Portland St N OL6 . . . .166 A3
Portland St S OL6,OL7 . .166 A2
Portland Terr OL6 . . . .166 A2
Portloe Rd SK8 . . . .131 B7
Portman Cl M16 . . . . .97 E3
Portman St OL5 . . . . .68 C1
Porton Wlk 1 M22 . . . .121 B1
Portrea Cl SK3 . . . .170 F5
Portree Cl M30 . . . . .79 B2
Portrush Rd M22 . . . .121 B2
Portside Cl M28 . . . . .78 B5
Portslade Wlk
  Wythenshawe M23 . . . .120 F4
  10 Wythenshawe M23 . .121 A5
Portsmouth Cl M7 . . . .155 D5
Portsmouth St M13 . . .163 B5
Portstone Cl M16 . . . . .97 E4
Portugal Rd M25 . . . . .63 C2
Portugal St Ashton-u-L OL7 . .84 F1
  Bolton BL2 . . . .148 B7
  Manchester M4 . . . .159 C2
  10 Manchester M4 . . .159 C3
Portugal St E M1 . . . .163 A8
Portville Rd M19 . . . . .99 A2
Portway M22 . . . .121 C1
Portwood Ind Est SK1 . .112 B2
Portwood Pl SK1 . . . .169 F2
Portwood Wlk 9 M9 . . .157 D7
Posnett St SK3 . . . . .123 C8
Post Office St WA14 . . .119 D5
Post St SK13 . . . .104 B5
Postal St M1 . . . .159 B1
Postbridge Cl M13 . . . .163 C6
Pot Gn BL0 . . . . .1 A3
Pot Hill OL6 . . . .166 C4
Pot Hill Sq OL6 . . . .166 C4
Potato Wharf M3 . . . .162 D8
Pott St M27 . . . . .61 F2
Potter Ho OL8 . . . .153 F5
Potter St Bury BL9 . . . .141 A3
  Radcliffe M26 . . . . .44 D4
Potterdale Cl OL11 . . . .49 A1
Potters La M9 . . . .157 F7
Pottery La M11,M12 . . .165 A7
Pottery Rd WN3 . . . .150 B7
Pottery Terr WN3 . . . .150 B7
Pottinger St Ashton-u-L . .84 F1
  Dukinfield OL7 . . . .100 F8
Poulton Ave BL2 . . . . .42 E7
Poulton Dr 7 WN4 . . . .72 F7
Poulton St M11 . . . . .99 E7
Poundswick Cty Prim Sch
  M22 . . . .121 C2
Poundswick La M22 . . .121 D3

Powell Ave SK14 . . . .167 E3
Powell Dr WN5 . . . . .71 D3
Powell St Abram WN2 . . .56 B1
  Bury BL8 . . . . .27 B1
  Droylsden M11 . . . . .83 D2
  Manchester M16 . . . . .97 C4
  10 Wigan WN1 . . . . .37 C1
Powicke Dr SK6 . . . .112 F1
Powicke Wlk SK6 . . . .113 A1
Powis Rd M41 . . . . .94 C1
Pownall Ave Bramhall SK7 .132 F7
  4 Manchester M20 . . .110 A8
Pownall Ct SK9 . . . .136 E8
Pownall Green Prim Sch
  SK7 . . . .132 E7
Pownall Hall Sch SK9 . .136 F8
Pownall Rd
  Altrincham WA14 . . . .119 D3
  Cheadle SK8 . . . .123 A1
  Wilmslow SK9 . . . .136 F8
Pownall St
  Hazel Grove SK7 . . . .124 D3
  Leigh WN7 . . . . .76 A5
Powys St M44 . . . . .58 E1
Poynings Dr M22 . . . .121 C2
Poynt Chase M28 . . . .78 B6
Poynter St M40 . . . . .65 C1
Poynter Wlk M11 . . . . .49 D4
Poynton High Sch SK12 .133 F2
Poynton St Bury BL9 . . .141 A1
  Manchester M15 . . . .162 F6
Poynton Sta SK12 . . . .133 C4
Poynton Worth Prim Sch
  SK12 . . . .133 F2
Praed Rd M17 . . . . .96 C6
Pratt Wlk 18 M11 . . . .160 F1
Precinct The Cheadle SK8 .123 A2
  Ramsbottom BL0 . . . . .10 F3
  Rochdale OL11 . . . . .29 E7
  Stockport SK2 . . . .124 D6
Preece Cl SK14 . . . .102 A4
Preesall Ave SK8 . . . .131 B8
Preesall Cl BL8 . . . . .26 F1
Prefect Pl WN5 . . . . .54 C8
Premier Rd M8 . . . .158 F4
Premier St M16 . . . . .97 C4
Prentice Wlk M11 . . . . .83 A1
Prenton St M11 . . . . .99 E8
Prenton Way M11 . . . . .26 F5
Presall St 2 BL2 . . . .148 C8
Presbury Cl 4 M20 . . .110 A2
Presbyterian Fold 1 WN2 . .56 D6
Prescot Ave Atherton M46 . .58 E5
  Tyldesley M29 . . . . .59 D1
Prescot Cl BL9 . . . . .141 A1
Prescot Rd
  Altrincham WA15 . . . .119 F2
  Manchester M9 . . . .157 D7
Prescott Ave WA3 . . . . .73 F2
Prescott La WN5 . . . . .54 B8
Prescott Rd SK9 . . . .131 E1
Prescott St Bolton BL3 . .146 C4
  Golborne WA3 . . . . .74 A1
  Hindley WN2 . . . . .56 D5
  Leigh WN7 . . . . .75 F6
  Rochdale OL16 . . . . .15 C2
  Walkden M28 . . . . .60 B3
  Wigan WN3,WN5,WN6 . .150 B8
  Walkden M34 . . . .101 B1
Press St M11 . . . . .99 D7
Prestage St
  Manchester M12 . . . . .99 B2
  Manchester M16 . . . . .97 D4
Prestbury Ave
  Altrincham WA15 . . . .119 E6
  Manchester M14 . . . . .97 F1
  Wigan WN3 . . . . .54 E2
Prestbury Cl Bury BL9 . .141 A1
  Stockport SK2 . . . .124 D4
Prestbury Dr
  Bredbury SK6 . . . .112 E3
  OL7 . . . .166 A3
Prestbury Rd Bolton BL1 . .25 A5
  Wilmslow SK10,SK9 . . .137 E5
Prestfield Rd M45 . . . . .63 A7
Presto Gdns BL3 . . . .146 B4
Preston Cl St Bolton BL3 . .146 B4
  Farnworth BL4 . . . . .60 E8
Prestolee Prim Sch M26 . .61 B8
Prestolee Rd Kearsley M26 . .43 B1
  Little Lever BL3 . . . . .43 A1
Preston Ave Irlam M44 . .105 F7
  Salford M30 . . . . .80 A3
Preston Cl M30 . . . . .80 A3
Preston Rd
  Manchester M19 . . . .111 A8
  Standish PR7,WN6 . . . .19 D5
Preston St 2 Bolton BL3 . .42 B4
  Manchester M18 . . . .165 C6
  Middleton M24 . . . . .65 A8
  Oldham OL4 . . . . .67 A6
  10 Rochdale OL12 . . . .14 C1
Prestwich Ave
  Culcheth WA3 . . . . .91 E3
  Leigh WN7 . . . . .76 B5
Prestwich Cl SK4 . . . .168 A4
Prestwich Com High Sch
  M25 . . . .63 B5
Prestwich Hills M25 . . . .63 A2
Prestwich Hospl M25 . . .62 D3
Prestwich Park Rd S M25 . .63 A3
Prestwich Prep Sch M25 . .63 C5
Prestwich St Denton M34 . .58 B3
  Denton M34 . . . .100 E4
Prestwich Sta M25 . . . .63 A5
Prestwich Wlk 1 M40 . . .65 C2

Prestwood Cl BL1 ....143 D1
Prestwood Dr BL1 ....143 D1
Prestwood Rd
  Farnworth BL4 ....42 A1
  Salford M6 ....80 C4
Pretoria Rd
  Ashton-in-M WN4 ....73 B4
  Bolton BL2 ....42 E8
  Oldham OL8 ....66 C3
Pretoria St 2 OL12 ....14 C1
Price St Bury BL9 ....141 A1
  Dukinfield SK16 ....101 C8
  Farnworth BL4 ....42 D1
  Manchester M4 ....160 D1
Prichard St M32 ....96 D2
Prickshaw OL12 ....14 B6
Prickshaw La OL12 ....14 B6
Pridmouth Rd M20 ....110 C6
Priest Ave SK8 ....122 A4
Priest St SK1 ....170 F7
Priestley Rd M27,M28 ....79 C8
Priestley Way OL2 ....49 D7
Priestnall Ct SK4 ....110 F3
Priestnall Rd SK4 ....110 F3
Priestnall Rec Ctr SK4 ....110 F3
Priestnall Sch SK4 ....110 F3
Priestners Way WN7 ....75 E6
Priestwood Ave OL4 ....49 F4
Primley Wlk 8 M9 ....157 E8

Primrose Ave
  Farnworth BL4 ....42 A1
  Hyde SK14 ....113 D8
  Marple SK6 ....125 E6
  Uppermill OL3 ....51 C1
  Urmston M41 ....95 D2
  Walkden M28 ....60 B2
Primrose Bank
  Altrincham WA14 ....119 C1
  1 Bacup OL13 ....3 C8
  Bury BL8 ....26 E7
  Oldham OL3 ....66 A5
  Oldham OL8 ....153 E5
  Walkden M28 ....60 B2
Primrose Cl Bolton BL2 ....26 A4
  Salford M6 ....154 F2
Primrose Cotts WA14 ....119 C1
Primrose Cres
  Glossop SK13 ....116 B8
  Hyde SK14 ....113 D8
Primrose Dr Bury BL9 ....28 D4
  Droylsden M43 ....84 C3
Primrose Gr WN5 ....54 E7
Primrose Hill SK13 ....116 B8
Primrose La Glossop SK13 ....116 B8
  New Mills SK6,SK22 ....127 A3
  Standish WN6 ....19 D2
Primrose St 9 Bacup OL13 ....3 C8
  Bolton BL1 ....143 F4
  Farnworth BL4 ....60 E7
  4 Leigh WN7 ....75 D5
  Manchester M4 ....159 B2
  Rochdale OL12 ....139 D8
  Tyldesley M29 ....59 A1
Primrose St N M29 ....59 A1
Primrose St S M29 ....77 A8
Primrose Terr
  Glossop SK13 ....116 B8
  Urmston M41 ....95 C6
Primrose View WN4 ....73 C2
Primrose Wlk Marple SK6 ....125 E6
  Oldham OL8 ....153 E5
Primula Dr WA3 ....90 D8
Primula St BL1 ....24 F5
Prince Albert Ave 4 M19 ....99 A2
Prince Charlie St OL1 ....67 C8
Prince Edward Ave
  Denton M34 ....100 F2
  8 Oldham OL4 ....67 C7
Prince George St OL1 ....49 C1
Prince of Wales Bsns Pk
  OL1 ....67 C8
Prince Rd SK12 ....134 C5
Prince St Ashton-in-M WN4 ....73 A5
  Bacup OL13 ....4 D7
  Bolton BL1 ....145 E8
  Heywood OL10 ....29 D2
  6 Oldham OL1 ....67 A7
  Ramsbottom BL0 ....138 C6
  Rochdale OL16 ....31 B5
Prince Way OL2 ....48 C6
Prince's Ave
  Little Lever BL3 ....43 B4
  Manchester M20 ....110 C4
  Romiley SK6 ....113 A3
  Tyldesley M29 ....77 B6
Prince's Bridge M3 ....162 D8
Prince's Dr SK6 ....125 E7
Prince's Pk WN6 ....35 F4
Prince's Rd SK6 ....113 A3
Prince's St SK1 ....169 E2
Princedom St M9 ....157 E8
Princes Ave M44 ....94 C3
Princes Ct M20 ....110 B3
Princes Dr M33 ....108 B5
Princes Gdns WN7 ....76 C5
Princes Rd
  Altrincham WA14 ....119 D6
  Sale M33 ....108 D3
Princess Ave
  Ashton-in-M WN11 ....89 A7
  Ashton-in-M WN4 ....73 C3
  Atherton M46 ....58 D5
  Cheadle SK8 ....123 A3
  Denton M34 ....100 E3
  Kearsley BL4 ....60 F6
  Manchester M25 ....63 C2

Princess Ave continued
  Rochdale OL12 ....15 C4
Princess Christian Coll
  M14 ....98 C1
Princess Cl
  Dukinfield SK16 ....101 D8
  Heywood OL10 ....29 D1
  Mossley OL5 ....86 E8
Princess Ct M15 ....162 E8
Princess Dr M24 ....64 E8
Princess Par BL9 ....60 D8
Princess Par BL9 ....140 F2
Princess Parkway
  Wythenshawe
  M20,M22,M23 ....109 C2
Wythenshawe M22 ....121 C8
Princess Rd Adlington PR6 ....21 B8
  Ashton-in-M WN4 ....73 C3
  Bolton BL6 ....40 B8
  Failsworth OL9 ....65 E3
  Manchester M14,M16 ....97 F4
  Manchester
    M14,M20,M21,M15 ....109 C6
  Milnrow OL16 ....31 D7
  Prestwich M25 ....63 C2
  Shaw OL2 ....149 A6
  Urmston M41 ....95 B2
  Wigan WN6 ....36 C4
  Wilmslow SK9 ....136 F5
Princess St
  Altrincham WA14 ....119 C8
  Ashton-u-L OL6 ....85 D4
  Bolton BL1 ....145 F7
  Eccles M30 ....79 C2
  Failsworth M35 ....83 E7
  Glossop SK13 ....116 C8
  Hindley WN2 ....56 C5
  Hyde SK14 ....167 E2
  6 Leigh WN7 ....76 A5
  Manchester M1,M60,M2 ....163 A8
  Manchester M15 ....162 D6
  Oldham OL4 ....67 E6
  Pendlebury M27 ....80 A7
  Radcliffe M26 ....43 C3
  Rochdale OL12 ....14 F1
  Salford M6 ....81 A4
  Whitworth OL12 ....14 C8
  Wigan WN3 ....150 C7
Princess Wlk SK7 ....133 A7
Princethorpe Cl BL6 ....40 D6
Prinknash Rd M22 ....121 D1
Printer St Droylsden M11 ....99 D8
  Oldham OL1 ....153 F7
Printers Fold SK14 ....103 D5
Printers La BL2,BL7 ....25 C6
Printers Pk SK14 ....103 E5
Printon Ave M9 ....64 B3
Printshop La M46 ....58 E1
Printworks La M19 ....99 C1
Printworks Rd SK15 ....86 C3
Prior St OL8 ....67 B5
Priorsleigh SK4 ....110 F2
Priory Ave Leigh WN7 ....57 D1
  Manchester M21 ....109 B8
  Manchester M7 ....81 C6
Priory Cl Dukinfield SK16 ....101 D6
  Oldham OL8 ....66 D3
  Sale M33 ....108 D8
  1 Wigan WN5 ....54 B5
Priory Ct Eccles M30 ....79 E2
  Reddish SK5 ....111 E8
Priory Gdns M20 ....110 B4
Priory Gr Manchester M7 ....81 C6
  Oldham OL9 ....66 A4
Priory La SK5 ....111 E8
Priory Nook WN8 ....53 C7
Priory Pl Bolton BL2 ....25 C2
  Manchester M7 ....81 C6
Priory Rd Altrincham WA14 ....128 B8
  Ashton-in-M WN4 ....72 F5
  Cheadle SK8 ....123 A5
  Orrell WN8 ....53 C7
  Sale M33 ....108 D5
  Swinton M27 ....79 E8
  Wilmslow SK9 ....136 F6
Priory Sch M33 ....108 A4
Priory St WA14 ....119 C1
Private La BB4 ....2 C8
Privet St OL4 ....49 D1
Proctor Cl WN5 ....36 E1
Proctor St BL8 ....27 C1
Proctor Way M30 ....94 F7
Prodesse Ct WN2 ....56 D6
Proe's Ct WN1 ....150 B8
Progress Ave M30 ....100 F6
Progress St
  Ashton-u-L OL6 ....166 A3
  Bolton BL1 ....143 F1
  Hindley WN2 ....56 D5
  Rochdale OL11 ....30 C1
Promenade St OL10 ....29 E2
Props Hall Dr M35 ....83 E6
Props Prim Sch M35 ....83 E6
Prospect Ave
  Farnworth BL4 ....60 C7
  Irlam M44 ....105 E6
Prospect Cotts WN2 ....38 A6
Prospect Ct BL8 ....26 F7
Prospect Dr
  Atrincham WA15 ....129 D8
  Failsworth M35 ....83 F5
Prospect Hill BL2 ....25 F4
Prospect Ho M9 ....157 E7
Prospect Pl 4 OL10 ....29 E2
Prospect Rd Ashton-u-L OL6 ....85 D5
  Farnworth BL4 ....60 C7

Prospect Pl continued
  Heywood OL10 ....29 D3
Prospect Rd Ashton-u-L OL6 ....85 E5
  Dukinfield SK16 ....101 D8
  Irlam M44 ....105 E6
  Oldham OL9 ....152 C7
  Standish WN6 ....36 C7
Prospect St Bolton BL1 ....143 F1
  Heywood OL10 ....46 E8
  Hindley WN2 ....56 D5
  Littleborough OL15 ....16 B6
  Rochdale OL11 ....30 E4
  Tyldesley M29 ....58 F1
Prospect Terr Bacup OL13 ....3 E7
  Bury BL8 ....140 D4
Prospect Vale SK8 ....122 E1
Prospect Vale Prim Sch
  SK8 ....122 B1
Prospect View M27 ....80 A7
Prosperity View 1 M40 ....64 F1
Prosperity M29 ....77 D8
Prosser Ave M46 ....58 A2
Protector Way M44 ....105 F8
Prout St M12 ....99 A3
Providence Ho OL4 ....67 E8
Providence St
  4 Ashton-u-L OL6 ....85 D1
  Bolton BL3 ....145 F5
  Dukinfield SK16 ....100 F7
  Manchester M4 ....160 D1
  Walsden OL14 ....6 A7
Provident Ave M19 ....99 C1
Provident St OL2 ....149 B7
Provident Way WA15 ....120 A7
Provis Rd M21 ....109 B7
Prubella Ave M44 ....105 E6
Pryce Ave WN2 ....151 F7
Pryce St BL1 ....143 D1
Pryme St M15 ....162 E7
Pudding La SK14 ....102 C3
Puddiford La SK14 ....133 B4
Puffingate Cl SK15 ....86 E7
Pugin Wlk M9 ....157 D6
Pulborough Cl BL3 ....27 B7
Pulford Ave M21 ....109 D4
Pulford Rd M33 ....108 D2
Pullman Cl M19 ....111 B8
Pullman Dr M32 ....95 F3
Pullman St 1 WN3 ....150 C7
Pulman St BL3 ....148 A5
Pump House (Mus) The
  M3 ....158 E1
Pump St 10 Hindley WN2 ....56 D5
  Manchester M40,M12 ....160 E2
  8 Oldham OL9 ....66 B2
Punch La BL3 ....40 D2
Punch St BL3 ....145 D6
Pungle The BL5 ....57 D5
Purbeck Cl M22 ....121 C1
Purbeck Dr Bury BL8 ....27 C6
  Manchester M16 ....39 F8
Purbeck Way M29 ....77 B7
Purcell Cl BL1 ....143 D1
Purcell St M12 ....99 A3
Purdon St BL9 ....27 F6
Purdy Ho OL8 ....66 D3
Puritan Wlk 7 M40 ....156 C5
Purley Ave M23 ....109 B1
Purley Dr M44 ....105 C5
Purple St BL1 ....145 F7
Purslow Cl M12 ....160 E1
Purton Wlk 9 M9 ....157 E7
Putney Cl OL1 ....48 E1
Puzzletree Ct SK2 ....124 C7
Pye Cl WA11 ....89 B8
Pyegreave Cl SK13 ....104 E1
Pyegreave Rd SK13 ....104 E1
Pyke St WN1 ....37 D1
Pym St Eccles M30 ....79 D2
  Heywood OL10 ....29 D1
  Manchester M40 ....157 F8
Pymgate Dr SK8 ....122 A2
Pyramid Ct M7 ....155 D6
Pyrus Cl SK9 ....94 F8
Pytha Fold Rd M20 ....110 D5

Q

Quadrant The
  Droylsden M43 ....83 F1
  Manchester M9 ....157 E7
  Manchester SK6 ....113 A2
  Stockport SK1 ....112 B1
  Stockport SK1 ....169 C4
Quail St OL4 ....67 C6
Quainton Ho 6 M5 ....154 F1
Quakerfields BL5 ....57 D7
Quakers Field BL8 ....26 F8
Quakers Terr WN6 ....19 C3
Quakers' Pl WN6 ....19 E1
Quantock Cl
  7 Manchester M16 ....97 E4
  Stockport SK4 ....169 E2
  Wigan WN5 ....54 C2
Quariton Dr BL8 ....10 B3
Quarmby Rd M18 ....99 F4
Quarry Bank Mill Sk9 ....130 F1
Quarry Bank Rd SK9 ....130 F3
Quarry Cl SK13 ....104 D1
Quarry Clough SK15 ....102 D8
Quarry Hill OL12 ....14 E3
Quarry Hts 4 SK15 ....101 F8
Quarry Pl WN1 ....151 E8
Quarry Pond Rd M28 ....59 F3
Quarry Rd Kearsley BL4 ....61 A3
  New Mills SK22 ....127 F2
  Romiley SK6 ....113 B2

Quarry Rise Romiley SK6 ....113 B3
  Staly-B SK15,SK16 ....101 F8
Quarry St Radcliffe M26 ....44 B3
  Ramsbottom BL0 ....11 D6
  Rochdale OL16 ....14 E1
  Romiley Sk6 ....113 B5
  Stalybridge SK15 ....85 F1
  Whitworth OL12 ....4 E6
Quarry Wlk 7 M11 ....160 F1
Quay St Heywood OL10 ....29 E1
  Manchester M3 ....162 F8
  Manchester M3 ....158 E2
Quay View M5 ....161 A8
Quays The M5 ....96 E7
Quayside WN7 ....75 E4
Quayside Cl M28 ....78 B5
Quebec Pl BL3 ....145 D5
Quebec St
  Abram Brow WN2,WN7 ....74 F5
  Bolton BL3 ....145 D5
  Denton M34 ....100 E4
  Oldham OL8 ....67 A5
  Orrell WN5 ....53 C5
  Sale M33 ....107 F5
Queen Alexandra Cl M5 ....161 C8
Queen Ann Cl BL9 ....45 C4
Queen Ann Dr M28 ....78 B7
Queen Anne Ct WN9 ....137 C6
Queen Elizabeth Sch The
  M24 ....45 E1
Queen Sq OL6 ....85 C4
Queen St Ashton-u-L OL6 ....166 C3
  Bacup OL13 ....3 C8
  Bolton BL1 ....145 E7
  Bury BL8 ....27 A5
  Bury BL9 ....141 A2
  Cheadle SK8 ....122 F6
  Denton M34 ....100 E4
  Denton M34 ....100 F6
  Dukinfield SK16 ....166 B1
  Eccles M30 ....79 F1
  Failsworth M35 ....83 E7
  Farnworth BL4 ....60 D8
  Glossop SK13 ....116 B8
  Hadfield SK13 ....104 A4
  Heywood OL10 ....29 D2
  6 Hindley WN2 ....56 D5
  Horwich BL6 ....22 B3
  Hyde SK14 ....167 E1
  Leigh WN7 ....76 A5
  Leigh WN7 ....76 D6
  Littleborough OL15 ....16 B5
  Manchester M2 ....158 F1
  Manchester M3 ....158 E2
  Middleton M24 ....65 C8
  Mossley OL5 ....68 C1
  Newton-le-W WA12 ....89 B3
  Oldham OL1 ....153 F6
  Oldham OL4 ....67 E6
  Platt Bridge WN2 ....56 A2
  Radcliffe M26 ....44 C2
  Ramsbottom BL0 ....138 B6
  Royton OL2 ....48 D4
  Salford M6 ....80 D5
  Shaw OL2 ....149 B6
  Stalybridge SK15 ....86 A2
  Stockport SK1 ....112 A2
  Walkden M38 ....60 A3
  Westhoughton BL5 ....57 E8
  Wigan WN3 ....150 C7
  Wigan WN5 ....54 D5
Queen St Prim Sch BL4 ....60 D8
Queen St W M20 ....110 B7
Queen Victoria St
  Eccles M30 ....79 C2
  Rochdale OL11 ....31 A4
Queen's Ave
  Ashton-in-M WN4 ....73 B3
  Atherton M46 ....58 C5
  Bolton BL7 ....25 A7
  Glazebury WA3 ....90 C8
  Little Lever BL3 ....43 A4
  Romiley SK6 ....113 A3
Queen's Ct
  Manchester M20 ....110 A4
  3 Manchester M21 ....97 B2
Queen's Dr Glossop SK13 ....104 F1
  Manchester M25 ....63 C2
  Manchester SK4 ....168 A2
Queen's Gdns SK8 ....122 E6
Queen's Gr M12 ....97 E4
Queen's Park Rd OL10 ....29 D3
Queen's Rd
  Altrincham WA15 ....119 F3
  Ashton-in-M WN4 ....73 B4
  Cheadle SK8 ....123 B3
  Cheadle SK8 ....122 F4
  Cheadle SK8 ....123 A3
  Hazel Grove SK7 ....124 C3
  12 Littleborough OL15 ....16 B5
  Romiley SK6 ....113 A3
  Urmston M41 ....95 D1
  Wilmslow SK9 ....137 A6
Queen's Terr 3 Bacup OL13 ....3 E8
  4 Dukinfield SK16 ....166 B1
Queenhill Dr M12 ....102 A1
Queenhill Rd M22 ....109 E1
Queens Ave
  Manchester M18 ....165 B5
  Rochdale OL12 ....15 C4
Queens Cl Boothstown M28 ....77 F7
  Hyde SK14 ....113 E7
Queens Ct
  Manchester M40 ....157 D5
  Manchester SK4 ....168 A3

Queens Ct continued
  Urmston M41 ....94 E2
Queens Dr Cheadle SK8 ....123 A2
  Golborne WA3 ....90 C8
  Hyde SK14 ....113 F7
  Newton-le-W WA12 ....89 C5
  Rochdale OL11 ....30 E3
Queens Gdns WN7 ....76 C5
Queens Pl BL9 ....11 C2
Queens Rd
  Ashton-in-M WA11 ....89 A7
  Bolton BL3 ....146 B4
  Chadderton OL9 ....152 A7
  Manchester M40 ....160 E4
  Manchester M40,M9 ....157 D5
  Manchester M8 ....156 A5
  Manchester M8,M9 ....156 A5
  Oldham OL8 ....67 A5
  Orrell WN5 ....53 C5
  Sale M33 ....107 F5
Queens Road Prim Sch
  SK8 ....123 A3
Queens Terr SK9 ....131 D3
Queens View OL15 ....16 A3
Queens Wlk M43 ....84 A1
Queensbank BL1 ....145 E7
Queensbury Cl Bolton BL1 ....24 D5
  14 Handforth SK9 ....131 D1
Queensbury Par M40 ....160 E3
Queenscroft M30 ....79 F3
Queensferry St M40 ....83 C6
Queensgate Bolton BL1 ....144 C8
  Bramhall SK7 ....132 E5
Queensgate Dr M29 ....59 A1
Queensgate Prim Sch
  SK7 ....132 E4
Queensland Rd M18 ....165 B5
Queenston Rd M20 ....110 A4
Queensway
  Dukinfield SK16 ....101 F7
  Gatley SK8 ....131 C8
  Ince-in-M WN2 ....56 A8
  Irlam M44 ....93 F2
  Kearsley BL4 ....60 F5
  Leigh WN7 ....76 D6
  Manchester M19 ....110 D2
  Mossley OL5 ....86 D8
  Poynton SK12 ....133 D1
  Poynton SK12 ....30 E3
  Shevington WN6 ....35 F4
  Swinton M27 ....62 A2
  Urmston M41 ....95 E4
  Walkden M28 ....78 C8
  Wigan WN3 ....37 B2
Queensway Com Prim Sch
  OL11 ....30 F3
Quenby St M15 ....162 D7
Quendon Ave M7 ....158 E4
Quick Edge La OL4 ....68 B8
Quick View OL5 ....68 E3
Quickedge Rd OL4,OL5 ....68 C3
Quickwood OL5 ....68 D2
Quilt Ct M44 ....105 E6
Quilter Gr M9 ....64 C2
Quinn St M11 ....83 A1
Quinney Cres M16 ....97 F4
Quinton 10 OL12 ....139 E8
Quinton Wlk M13 ....163 B6
Quintrell Brow BL7 ....25 A8

R

Rabbit La SK14 ....103 A6
Raby St M14,M16 ....97 F4
Race The SK9 ....131 D2
Racecourse Pk SK9 ....136 E6
Racecourse Rd SK9 ....136 E6
Racecourse Wlk M26 ....43 F4
Racefield Hamlet OL2 ....48 A4
Racefield Rd WA14 ....119 C4
Rachel Rosing Wlk M8 ....155 F8
Rachel St M12 ....163 C8
Rackhouse Prim Sch
  M23 ....109 A1
Rackhouse Rd M23 ....109 A1
Radbourne Cl M12 ....165 A6
Radcliffe Ave WA3 ....91 E3
Radcliffe New Rd M26 ....75 F7
Radcliffe Hall
  CE/Meth Prim Sch M26 ....44 D4
Radcliffe High Sch M26 ....44 A3
Radcliffe Inf Sch M26 ....43 E4
Radcliffe Moor Rd
  BL2,BL3,M26 ....43 C5
Radcliffe New Rd
  M45,M26 ....44 D2
Radcliffe Park Cres M6 ....80 C5
Radcliffe Park Rd M6 ....80 C5
Radcliffe Rd Bolton BL2 ....148 B7
  Bolton BL2,BL3 ....42 D5
  Bury BL9 ....44 A6
  Oldham OL4 ....49 D2
Radcliffe St Oldham OL1 ....153 F8
  Oldham OL1 ....153 F8
  Royton OL2 ....48 E4
Radcliffe Sta M26 ....44 B2
Radcliffe View M5 ....161 B7
Radcliffe Com Sec Sch
  (Upper) The OL9 ....65 F7

Radclyffe Prim Sch M5 . . . . .**161** A7
Radclyffe Sch (Lower)
　The OL9 . . . .**152** A6
Radclyffe St Middleton M24 . .**47** A2
　Oldham OL9 . . . .**152** C8
Radclyffe Terr M24 . . . .**47** A2
Radelan Gr M26 . . . .**43** D4
Radford Cl SK2 . . . .**124** E7
Radford Dr Irlam M44 . . . .**94** A3
　2 Manchester M9 . . . .**157** E8
Radford Ho SK2 . . . .**124** E7
Radford St M7 . . . .**81** C8
Radium St M4 . . . .**159** C2
Radlet Dr WA15 . . . .**120** A8
Radlett Wlk **3** M13 . . . .**163** C5
Radley Cl Bolton BL1 . . . .**142** A1
　7 Sale M33 . . . .**107** D3
Radley St M43 . . . .**99** E8
Radley Wlk **1** M16 . . . .**97** F3
Radnor Ave M34 . . . .**100** B3
Radnor Cl WN2 . . . .**57** A3
Radnor Dr WN7 . . . .**75** C5
Radnor St Manchester M15 . . .**97** F4
　Manchester M18 . . . .**99** C4
　Oldham OL9 . . . .**152** C5
Radstock Cl Bolton BL1 . . . . . .**24** E7
　Manchester M14 . . . .**98** B1
Radstock Rd M32 . . . .**96** C2
Raglan Ave Prestwich M25,M45 . .**63** B7
　Swinton M27 . . . .**62** B2
Raglan Cl M11 . . . .**160** F1
Raglan Dr WA14 . . . .**119** E8
Raglan Rd Sale M33 . . . .**108** A3
　Stretford M32 . . . .**96** B3
Raglan St Bolton BL1 . . . .**143** D2
　Denton SK14 . . . .**101** C2
　Rochdale OL11 . . . .**30** C1
Raglan Wlk **5** M15 . . . .**162** F6
Ragley Cl SK12 . . . .**133** F4
Raikes Clough Ind Est
　BL3 . . . .**42** C4
Raikes La BL3 . . . .**42** B4
Raikes Lane Ind Est BL3 . . . . .**42** C4
Raikes Rd BL3 . . . .**42** D5
Raikes Way BL3 . . . .**42** D5
Railgate OL13 . . . .**4** C8
Railside Terr M30 . . . .**80** A2
Railton Ave M16 . . . .**97** D3
Railton Terr M9 . . . .**157** F7
Railway App **2** OL11 . . . .**30** C2
Railway Bank SK14 . . . .**101** C2
Railway Brow OL11 . . . .**30** C1
Railway Cotts
　Bredbury SK6 . . . .**112** F4
　Hollinfare WA3 . . . .**105** B5
Railway Rd
　Adlington PR6,PR7 . . . .**21** A7
　Golborne WA3 . . . .**74** B1
　Leigh WN7 . . . .**75** E5
　Oldham OL9 . . . .**153** D6
　Oldham OL9 . . . .**66** A2
　Stockport SK1,SK3 . . . .**170** E8
　Stretford M32 . . . .**96** F5
　Urmston M41 . . . .**95** E2
Railway St
　Altrincham WA14 . . . .**119** D4
　Atherton M46 . . . .**58** B4
　Bacup OL13 . . . .**3** B8
　Dukinfield SK16 . . . .**166** B1
　Farnworth BL4 . . . .**42** E1
　Glossop SK13 . . . .**104** C1
　Hadfield SK13 . . . .**104** A5
　Heywood OL10 . . . .**29** E1
　Hindley WN2 . . . .**56** F7
　Littleborough OL15 . . . .**16** B5
　Manchester M18 . . . .**99** D6
　Newhey OL16 . . . .**32** B4
　Newton-le-W WA12 . . . .**89** B3
　Radcliffe M26 . . . .**44** A3
　Ramsbottom BL0 . . . .**138** C6
　Ramsbottom BL9 . . . .**11** C2
　Rochdale OL16 . . . .**31** A6
　Stockport SK4 . . . .**169** E2
　Wigan WN6 . . . .**37** A1
Railway Street Ind Est
　M18 . . . .**99** D6
Railway Terr Bury BL8 . . . .**27** C1
　Disley SK12 . . . .**135** D6
　Edgworth BL7 . . . .**9** B8
　5 Manchester M21 . . . .**97** B2
Railway View
　3 Oldham OL4 . . . .**67** F6
　Shaw OL2 . . . .**149** C8
Raimond St BL1 . . . .**142** C3
Rainbow Cl M21 . . . .**109** B7
Rainbow Dr M46 . . . .**58** D5
Raincliff Ave M13 . . . .**98** F2
Raines Crest OL16 . . . .**32** A6
Rainford Ave
　Altrincham WA15 . . . .**120** A6
　Manchester M20 . . . .**110** A8
Rainford Ho **2** BL1 . . . .**145** F8
Rainford Rd WA11,WN5 . . . . . .**71** C5
Rainford St BL2 . . . .**25** C1
Rainforth St M13 . . . .**98** F3
Rainham Dr Bolton BL1 . . . . .**143** E1
　Manchester M8 . . . .**156** A4
Rainham Gr **2** BL1 . . . .**143** E1

Rainham Way
　Brinnington SK5 . . . .**112** B6
　Oldham OL9 . . . .**152** B6
Rainhill Wlk M40 . . . .**83** D4
Rainow Ave M43 . . . .**83** E1
Rainow Rd SK3 . . . .**123** C6
Rainow Way **10** SK9 . . . .**131** E1
Rainshaw St Bolton BL1 . . . .**143** F4
　8 Oldham OL4 . . . .**67** D8
　Royton OL2 . . . .**48** D4
Rainsough Ave M25 . . . .**63** A1
Rainsough Brow M25 . . . .**62** F1
Rainsough Cl M25 . . . .**63** A1
Rainton Wlk **8** M40 . . . .**65** D2
Rainwood OL9 . . . .**65** E8
Raithby Dr WN3 . . . .**55** A3
Raja Cl M8 . . . .**156** B7
Rake OL11 . . . .**30** A8
Rake Fold Rd BL8 . . . .**138** A6
Rake Head Barn La OL14 . . . . .**6** A8
Rake La M27 . . . .**62** B2
Rake St BL9 . . . .**140** F4
Rake Terr OL15 . . . .**16** D6
Rakehead La OL13 . . . .**3** B8
Rakehead Wlk M15 . . . .**162** F5
Rakewood Dr OL4 . . . .**49** E4
Rakewood Rd OL15 . . . .**16** C2
Raleigh Cl
　Manchester M20 . . . .**110** A5
　Oldham OL1 . . . .**153** F8
Raleigh Gdns OL15 . . . .**6** C1
Raleigh St Reddish SK5 . . . . .**169** E4
　Stretford M32 . . . .**96** E2
Ralli Courts M3 . . . .**158** E1
Ralph Ave SK14 . . . .**113** E7
Ralph Green St OL9 . . . .**66** B3
Ralph Sherwin Ct OL12 . . . . . .**15** D4
Ralph St Bolton BL1 . . . .**143** D2
　Droysden M11 . . . .**83** D1
　Rochdale OL12 . . . .**15** A1
Ralphs La SK16 . . . .**101** C7
Ralston St M7 . . . .**155** F8
Ralstone Ave OL8 . . . .**66** F4
Ram St M38 . . . .**59** F5
Ramage Wlk M12 . . . .**160** E1
Ramillies Ave SK8 . . . .**123** C1
Ramillies Hall Sch SK8 . . . . .**123** C2
Ramp Rd E M90 . . . .**130** C7
Ramp Rd S M90 . . . .**130** C7
Ramp Rd W M90 . . . .**130** B7
Ramsay Ave BL4 . . . .**60** B7
Ramsay Pl OL16 . . . .**31** A8
Ramsay St Bolton BL1 . . . . . .**143** E4
　Rochdale OL16 . . . .**31** A8
Ramsay Terr **7** OL16 . . . .**31** A8
Ramsbottom
　Cottage Hospl BL0 . . . .**138** C5
Ramsbottom
　Heritage Ctr Mus BL0 . . . . .**138** C7
Ramsbottom La BL0 . . . .**138** C7
Ramsbottom Rd
　Horwich BL6 . . . .**22** C3
　Ramsbottom BL8,BL7 . . . .**10** A3
Ramsbottom Sta BL0 . . . .**138** C6
Ramsbury Dr M40 . . . .**65** D2
Ramsdale Rd SK7 . . . .**132** E8
Ramsdale St OL9 . . . .**152** A7
Ramsden Cl Glossop SK13 . . .**104** D2
　Oldham OL1 . . . .**153** E7
　Wigan WN3 . . . .**150** A5
Ramsden Cres OL1 . . . .**153** E8
Ramsden Fold M27 . . . .**61** F2
Ramsden La OL14 . . . .**5** F7
Ramsden Rd OL12 . . . .**15** C6
Ramsden St
　Ashton-u-L OL6 . . . .**166** B4
　Bolton BL1 . . . .**42** D5
　Oldham OL1 . . . .**153** E7
　Walsden OL14 . . . .**6** A7
Ramsden Wood Rd OL14 . . . . . .**6** A7
Ramsey Ave M19 . . . .**99** D1
Ramsey Cl Ashton-in-M WN4 . .**73** B2
　Atherton M46 . . . .**58** E2
Ramsey Gr BL8 . . . .**27** B2
Ramsey St **3** Leigh WN7 . . . .**76** A4
　Manchester M40 . . . .**83** B7
　Oldham OL1 . . . .**67** B8
　Oldham OL9 . . . .**152** B5
Ramsgate Rd
　Failsworth M40 . . . .**83** C4
　Reddish SK5 . . . .**111** F7
Ramsgate St M7,M8 . . . .**155** E5
Ramsgill Cl M23 . . . .**108** F2
Ramsgreave Cl BL9 . . . .**44** D7
Ramwell Gdns BL3 . . . .**145** D5
Ramwells Brow BL7 . . . .**25** A8
Ranby Ave M9 . . . .**64** F1
Rand St **1** OL1 . . . .**49** D1
Randal St BL3 . . . .**146** C4
Randale Dr BL9 . . . .**45** A2
Randall Ave WN6 . . . .**36** A5
Randall Wlk **2** M11 . . . .**83** D1
Randall Wlk **22** M11 . . . .**160** F1
Randerson St M12 . . . .**163** C7
Randle St **1** WN2 . . . .**56** D6
Randlesham St M25 . . . .**63** C4
Randolph Pl SK3 . . . .**170** E7
Randolph Rd BL4 . . . .**60** D7
Randolph St Bolton BL3 . . . . .**145** D6
　Manchester M19 . . . .**99** B2
　Oldham OL8 . . . .**66** C4
Rands Clough Dr M28 . . . .**78** B6
Ranford Rd M19 . . . .**111** A8
Range Dr SK6 . . . .**113** C6
Range Hall Ct **7** SK1 . . . . . .**112** A1

Range La OL3 . . . .**33** D1
Range Rd Dukinfield SK16 . . .**102** B7
　Manchester M16 . . . .**97** E3
　Stalybridge SK15 . . . .**102** B8
　Stockport SK3 . . . .**170** E7
Range St Bolton BL3 . . . .**147** D4
　Manchester M11 . . . .**165** C8
Rangemore Ave M22 . . . .**121** D8
Ranicar Steet WN2 . . . .**57** C3
Rankine Terr BL3 . . . .**145** D5
Ranmore Ave
　Droylsden M11 . . . .**99** D8
　Garswood WN4 . . . .**72** E5
Rannoch Rd BL2 . . . .**43** A7
Ransfield Rd M21 . . . .**97** B1
Ranulph Ct **1** M6 . . . .**80** D5
Ranworth Ave SK4 . . . .**110** F2
Ranworth Cl Bolton BL1 . . . . . .**25** A6
　Manchester M11 . . . .**165** A8
Raper St OL4 . . . .**67** C8
Rapes Highway OL3 . . . .**33** F5
Raphael St BL1 . . . .**143** D2
Rappax Rd WA15 . . . .**129** A8
Rassbottom St BL3 . . . .**145** E5
Raspberry La M44 . . . .**94** A5
Rassbottom Brow **5** SK15 . . .**85** F2
Rassbottom Ind Est SK15 . . . .**85** F2
Rassbottom St SK15 . . . .**85** F2
Rassey Cl WN6 . . . .**37** A7
Rastell Wlk **8** M9 . . . .**64** E3
Ratcliffe Ave M44 . . . .**94** A2
Ratcliffe Rd WN2 . . . .**38** C6
Ratcliffe St Leigh WN7 . . . .**75** F6
　Manchester M19 . . . .**99** B1
　Tyldesley M29 . . . .**59** B1
　Wigan WN6 . . . .**37** A1
Ratcliffe Terr OL5 . . . .**86** C8
Rath Wlk **7** M40 . . . .**83** C5
Rathan Rd M41 . . . .**95** A3
Rathbone St OL16 . . . .**31** C7
Rathbourne Ave M9 . . . .**64** D4
Rathen Ave WN2 . . . .**56** A8
Rathen Rd M20 . . . .**110** C5
Rathmel Rd M23 . . . .**120** F8
Rathmell Cl WA3 . . . .**91** E3
Rathmore Ave M40 . . . .**157** E5
Rathvale Dr M22 . . . .**130** C8
Rattenbury Ct M6 . . . .**80** C5
Raveden Cl BL1 . . . .**142** C3
Raveley Ave M14 . . . .**110** D8
Ravelston Dr M9 . . . .**157** D7
Raven Ave Haslingden BB4 . . . .**1** A7
　Oldham OL9 . . . .**152** A5
Raven Cl M43 . . . .**84** C3
Raven Croft BB4 . . . .**1** B8
Raven Dr M44 . . . .**94** A3
Raven Ho M6 . . . .**81** A5
Raven Pk BB4 . . . .**1** B8
Raven Rd Bolton BL1 . . . .**146** A4
　Sale WA15 . . . .**128** B8
Raven St Bury BL9 . . . .**140** F4
　Manchester M12 . . . .**163** C8
　Rochdale OL16 . . . .**13** E1
Raven Way Salford M6 . . . . . .**154** F3
　8 Salford M6 . . . .**81** A3
Ravendale Cl OL12 . . . .**14** A1
Ravenfield Gr **10** BL1 . . . . . .**145** D8
Ravenhead Cl **18** M14 . . . . .**110** D8
Ravenhead Sq WN8 . . . .**53** A7
Ravenhead Sq SK15 . . . .**86** E5
Ravenhurst **4** M7 . . . .**81** B5
Ravenhurst Dr BL1 . . . .**40** D6
Ravenna Ave M23 . . . .**120** D7
Ravenoak Ave M19 . . . .**111** C8
Ravenoak Dr M35 . . . .**84** A8
Ravenoak Park Rd SK8 . . . . . .**132** B8
Ravenoak Rd Cheadle SK8 . . .**132** B8
　Stockport SK2 . . . .**124** A4
Ravenoak St M25,M8 . . . .**63** E2
Ravens Holme BL1 . . . .**40** E7
Ravens Wood BL1 . . . .**40** E7
Ravensbury Cty Prim Sch
　M11 . . . .**83** B2
Ravensbury St M11 . . . .**83** B2
Ravenscar Cres M22 . . . .**130** D8
Ravenscar Wlk BL4 . . . .**60** D7
Ravenscraig Rd M38 . . . .**60** B6
Ravensdale Gdns M30 . . . .**79** E3
Ravensdale Rd BL2 . . . .**40** D7
Ravensdale St **1** M14 . . . . . .**98** C3
Ravensfield Ind Est SK16 . . . .**166** B1
Ravenside Pk OL9 . . . .**152** A5
Ravenside Ret Pk BL2 . . . . . .**148** A6
Ravenstone Dr Diggle OL3 . . . .**51** C3
　Sale M33 . . . .**108** E5
Ravenstonedale Dr OL2 . . . . . .**48** E5
Ravensway M25,M8 . . . .**63** D2
Ravenswood M20 . . . .**109** F4
Ravenswood Ave
　Stockport SK4 . . . .**168** A1
　Wigan WN3 . . . .**54** D3
Ravenswood Cl **6** SK3 . . . . .**123** F4
Ravenswood Dr Bolton BL1 . . .**40** D4
　Cheadle SK8 . . . .**132** B8
　Hindley WN2 . . . .**56** E7
　Manchester M9 . . . .**64** E4
Ravenswood Rd
　Stretford M32 . . . .**96** F4
　Wilmslow SK9 . . . .**136** E4
Ravenwood Dr
　Altrincham WA15 . . . .**129** D7
　Denton M34 . . . .**100** E6
Ravine Ave M9 . . . .**157** F7
Rawcliffe Ave BL2 . . . .**42** F7
Rawcliffe St M14 . . . .**98** B3

Rawdon Cl **9** M19 . . . .**99** B1
Rawkin Cl M15 . . . .**162** E5
Rawlinson St **8** BL6 . . . .**22** B4
Rawlyn Rd BL1 . . . .**142** A2
Rawpool Gdns M23 . . . .**121** A7
Rawson Ave BL4 . . . .**42** E1
Rawson Rd BL1 . . . .**142** C1
Rawson St BL4 . . . .**42** E1
Rawsons Rake BL0,BL8 . . . . .**138** A6
Rawsthorne Ave BL0 . . . .**1** D2
Rawsthorne St Bolton BL1 . . .**143** E2
　Tyldesley M29 . . . .**77** D8
Rawstron St OL12 . . . .**4** C1
Rawthey Pl WN2 . . . .**55** F2
Rayburn Way M8 . . . .**156** A5
Raycroft Ave M9 . . . .**65** A2
Raydale Cl WA3 . . . .**74** E1
Rayden Cres BL5 . . . .**57** E6
Raydon Ave M40 . . . .**157** D5
Rayleigh Ave M11 . . . .**99** D8
Raymond Ave Bury BL9 . . . . . .**27** F5
　Oldham OL9 . . . .**66** B4
Raymond Rd M23 . . . .**109** B2
Raymond St M27 . . . .**61** F1
Rayner Ave WN2 . . . .**56** E3
Rayner La M34, M43, OL7 . . . . .**84** C2
Rayner St SK1 . . . .**124** B8
Rayners Cl SK15 . . . .**85** F1
Raynham Ave M20 . . . .**110** B4
Raynham St OL6 . . . .**166** C3
Rayson Hill Dr M9 . . . .**64** C2
Rayson St M9 . . . .**64** C2
Reabrook Ave M12 . . . .**164** F6
Reach The M28 . . . .**60** E2
Read Cl BL9 . . . .**44** D7
Read St SK14 . . . .**101** C3
Read St W SK14 . . . .**101** C3
Reade Ave M41 . . . .**94** F1
Reading Cl M11 . . . .**160** F1
Reading Dr M33 . . . .**107** D4
Reading St M6 . . . .**81** B5
Reading Wlk **1** M34 . . . .**100** F1
Readitt Wlk M11 . . . .**83** B2
Reaney Wlk M12 . . . .**165** A6
Reather Wlk M40 . . . .**159** C3
Rebecca St M8 . . . .**156** A8
Recreation Ave WN4 . . . .**73** D4
Recreation Dr WN5 . . . .**71** E5
Recreation Rd M35 . . . .**83** A6
Recreation St Bolton BL2 . . . . .**25** E5
　Bolton BL3 . . . .**147** E4
　Prestwich M25 . . . .**63** C4
Rectory Ave Golborne WA3 . . .**90** D8
　Manchester M8 . . . .**64** A1
　Prestwich M25 . . . .**63** B4
Rectory CE Prim Sch
　WN4 . . . .**72** D5
Rectory Ct Denton M34 . . . . . .**101** A2
　Radcliffe M26 . . . .**44** D4
Rectory Fields SK1 . . . .**125** F5
Rectory Fields SK1 . . . .**112** A1
Rectory Gdns
　Prestwich M25 . . . .**63** B4
　Westhoughton BL5 . . . .**57** E5
Rectory Gn Prestwich M25 . . . .**63** B4
　Stockport SK1 . . . .**112** A1
Rectory Gr M25 . . . .**63** B3
Rectory La Bury BL9 . . . .**28** A6
　Prestwich M25 . . . .**63** A4
　Standish WN1,WN6 . . . .**20** A1
Rectory Rd
　Downall Green WN4 . . . .**72** D5
　Manchester M8 . . . .**63** F1
Rectory St M24 . . . .**46** F1
Red Bank M4 . . . .**159** A3
Red Bank Ave WA12 . . . .**89** F1
Red Bank Rd M26 . . . .**43** F5
Red Barn Rd WN5 . . . .**71** C6
Red Bridge BL2 . . . .**26** A1
Red Brook Cl OL11 . . . .**139** D7
Red Gables OL7 . . . .**166** A4
Red Hall St **4** OL4 . . . .**67** C6
Red Hill Way WN2 . . . .**56** D6
Red Houe La WA14 . . . .**118** C8
Red La Bolton BL2 . . . .**25** F5
　Disley SK12 . . . .**135** C5
　Rochdale OL12 . . . .**13** C8
Red Lane Com Prim Sch
　BL2 . . . .**25** F1
Red Lion St M4 . . . .**159** A2
Red Lumb St OL12 . . . .**13** A3
Red Pike Wlk **2** OL1 . . . .**67** A8
Red Rock Brow WN1 . . . .**37** C8
Red Rock La Kearsley M26 . . . .**61** E6
　Standish WN1,WN2 . . . .**37** D8
Red Rose Cres M19 . . . .**111** C7
Red Rose Ct M33 . . . .**108** B6
Red Rose Gdns M38 . . . .**60** A4
Red Rose Ret Pk M5 . . . .**161** B8
Red Row M27 . . . .**53** E8
Red St M46 . . . .**58** E8
Red Waters WN7 . . . .**76** A6
Redacre St **3** M7 . . . .**133** F6
Redacre Rd M18 . . . .**99** E5
Redbarn Cl SK6 . . . .**112** F4
Redbourne Dr M41 . . . .**94** F4
Redbrick Ct **8** OL7 . . . .**166** A1
Redbridge Gr M21 . . . .**109** A8
Redbrook Ave M40 . . . .**157** E5
Redbrook Cl **6** BL4 . . . .**42** E1
Redbrook Gr **6** SK9 . . . .**131** D1
Redbrook Rd
　Altrincham WA15 . . . .**120** D5
　Partington M31 . . . .**105** E2
　Wigan WN3 . . . .**151** E6
Redburn Cl WN3 . . . .**150** B6

Redburn Rd M23 . . . .**121** B7
Redby St M11 . . . .**165** B7
Redcar Ave
　Manchester M20 . . . .**110** B6
　Urmston M41 . . . .**95** A4
Redcar Cl SK7 . . . .**125** A3
Redcar Rd Bolton BL1 . . . . . .**142** B4
　Little Lever BL3 . . . .**43** A3
　Pendlebury M27 . . . .**80** C7
Redcar St OL12 . . . .**139** E8
Redcliffe Ct M25 . . . .**63** B2
Redclyffe Ave M14 . . . .**98** C4
Redclyffe Rd Eccles M41 . . . . .**95** D7
　Manchester M20 . . . .**110** A5
Redcot Cl M45 . . . .**62** C7
Redcote St M40 . . . .**83** A8
Redcourt Ave M20 . . . .**110** B4
Redcroft Gdns **2** M19 . . . . .**110** E4
Redcroft Rd M33 . . . .**107** C6
Redcross St
　Rochdale OL12 . . . .**139** F8
　Rochdale OL12 . . . .**14** F1
Redcross St N OL12 . . . .**14** F1
Reddaway Cl M6 . . . .**81** A5
Reddish Cl BL2 . . . .**25** E6
Reddish La Lymm WA13 . . . . .**117** A5
　Reddish M18,M34 . . . .**99** E4
Reddish North SK5 . . . .**99** F2
Reddish Rd SK5 . . . .**111** E6
Reddish South Sta SK5 . . . . .**111** F7
Reddish Vale Ctry Pk
　SK5 . . . .**112** B7
Reddish Vale Rd SK5 . . . .**112** A4
Reddish Vale Sch SK5 . . . . . .**111** F7
Reddy La WA14 . . . .**118** B5
Reddyshore Brow OL15 . . . . . .**16** C8
Reddyshore Scout Gate
　OL14 . . . .**6** C5
Redesmere Cl
　Altrincham WA15 . . . .**120** D6
　Droylsden M43 . . . .**84** B1
Redesmere Dr
　Alderley Edge SK9 . . . .**137** A1
　Cheadle SK8 . . . .**122** F4
Redesmere Pk M41 . . . .**107** B8
Redesmere Rd SK9 . . . .**131** D5
Redfearn Wood OL12 . . . .**14** B2
Redfern Ave M33 . . . .**108** E3
Redfern Cl SK13 . . . .**104** A6
Redfern Cotts OL11 . . . .**30** C5
Redfern Ho SK6 . . . .**113** A2
Redfern St M4 . . . .**159** A2
Redfern Way OL11 . . . .**13** D1
Redfield Cl M11 . . . .**160** F1
Redford Cl WN7 . . . .**76** A4
Redford Dr SK7 . . . .**124** A2
Redford Rd M9 . . . .**88** F8
Redgate Hadfield SK13 . . . . . .**104** C4
　Hyde SK14 . . . .**113** D8
Redgate La
　Manchester M12 . . . .**164** F5
　Manchester M12 . . . .**99** A4
Redgate Rd WN4 . . . .**73** B6
Redgate Way BL4 . . . .**147** F1
Redgrave Pas OL4 . . . .**67** D8
Redgrave Rise WN3 . . . .**54** D3
Redgrave St OL4 . . . .**67** D8
Redgrave Wlk M19 . . . .**99** C1
Redhill Dr SK6 . . . .**112** E3
Redhill Gr BL1 . . . .**143** E1
Redhill St M4 . . . .**159** B2
Redhouse La Disley SK12 . . . .**135** E7
　Romiley SK6 . . . .**113** A4
Redington Cl M28 . . . .**78** A5
Redmere Gr M14 . . . .**110** C8
Redmere Dr BL8 . . . .**10** F3
Redmire Mews SK16 . . . .**101** F7
Redmires **7** M5 . . . .**81** A1
Redmond Cl M34 . . . .**100** E7
Redmoor Sq **3** M13 . . . .**163** B7
Rednal Wlk WN3 . . . .**150** B6
Redpol Ave WN7 . . . .**76** B5
Redpoll Cl M28 . . . .**78** B7
Redruth St M14 . . . .**98** B2
Redscar Wlk M24 . . . .**46** E1
Redshank Cl WA12 . . . .**89** C4
Redshank Gr WN7 . . . .**76** A6
Redshaw Ave BL2 . . . .**26** A3
Redshaw Cl M14 . . . .**98** D1
Redstart Cl **7** WA3 . . . .**90** E8
Redstart Gr M28 . . . .**78** D8
Redstock Cl BL5 . . . .**40** B1
Redstone Rd M19 . . . .**110** E3
Redthorn Ave **3** M19 . . . . . .**110** F7
Redvale Wlk M7 . . . .**155** E6
Redvales Rd BL9 . . . .**44** E7
Redvers
　Manchester M11 . . . .**164** E8
　Oldham OL1 . . . .**153** D8
Redwater Cl **9** M28 . . . .**78** A6
Redwing Rd BL8 . . . .**10** F2
Redwood Chadderton OL9 . . . .**65** D7
　Sale M33 . . . .**107** D4
　Shevington WN6 . . . .**36** B6
　Westhoughton BL5 . . . .**57** D6
Redwood Ave Wigan WN5 . . . .**54** A6
　Wigan WN6 . . . .**36** F3
Redwood Cl OL12 . . . .**14** B3

Redwood Dr Bredbury SK6 .112 F3
Denton M34 ....100 E6
Manchester M8 ....156 B5
Rawtenstall BB4 ....1 FB
Redwood Ho M22 ....109 E1
Redwood La OL4 ....67 E7
Redwood Park Gr OL16 ... 31 D7
Redwood Rd OL3 ....69 C7
Redwood St M6 ....81 A4
Reece Cl 4 SK16 ....101 D8
Reed Cres WN3 ....55 A4
Reed Ct 2 OL1 ....153 E8
Reed Hill OL16 ....139 F8
Reed St Manchester M18 ...99 D6
  8 Oldham OL1 ....67 A7
Reedbank M26 ....62 A8
Reedham Cl BL1 ....144 C8
Reedham Wlk
Manchester M40 ....160 D4
Oldham OL9 ....66 C4
Reedley Dr M28 ....78 C8
Reedmace Cl M28 ....60 E1
Reedshaw Bank SK2 ....124 D5
Reedshaw Rd M9 ....156 C6
Reedsmere Cl WN5 ....54 F6
Reeman Cl SK6 ....113 A4
Reeman Ct SK9 ....131 B2
Reepham Cl WN3 ....54 D3
Reeve Cl SK2 ....124 F5
Reeve St WA3 ....91 B8
Reeves Ct M5 ....80 A2
Reeves Rd M21 ....109 B7
Reeves St WN7 ....75 F6
Reevey Ave SK7 ....124 C2
Reform St OL12 ....14 F1
Reform Wlk M11 ....165 B8
Refuge St OL2 ....149 B6
Regaby Gr WN2 ....57 A5
Regal Cl M45 ....63 B8
Regal Wlk 11 M40 ....83 C6
Regan Ave M21 ....109 D7
Regan St Bolton BL1 ....143 D3
  8 Radcliffe M26 ....44 B2
Regatta Cl OL9 ....66 A3
Regatta St M6 ....30 F6
Regency Chambers BL9 ...140 E2
Regency Cl Glossop SK13 .104 D1
  Manchester M40 ....157 D5
  Oldham OL8 ....66 D4
Regency Ct Cheadle SK8 ...123 A2
  Rochdale OL11 ....29 F7
  Wigan WN1 ....151 D8
Regency Gdns SK8 ....131 E8
Regency Lo M25 ....63 A3
Regency Pk SK4 ....136 F5
Regency Wharf WN7 ....76 C4
Regent Ave
  Ashton-in-M WN4 ....72 F5
  Manchester M14 ....98 A2
  Walkden M38 ....60 C4
Regent Bank SK9 ....136 F5
Regent Cl 11 Bramhall SK7 .132 D4
  Cheadle SK8 ....123 C4
  Wilmslow SK9 ....138 F5
Regent Cres Failsworth M35 .83 E6
  Oldham OL1,OL2 ....48 D2
Regent Ct
  Altrincham WA14 ....119 D4
  Manchester M7 ....63 D1
  Manchester SK4 ....111 C5
Regent Dr Bolton BL6 ....80 B7
  Denton M34 ....100 D1
  Leigh WN7 ....76 D7
Regent Ho M14 ....98 D3
Regent Pl M14 ....98 C4
Regent Rd
  Altrincham WA14 ....119 D4
  Bolton BL6 ....40 B6
  Platt Bridge WN2 ....56 A3
  Salford M15,M5 ....161 C8
  Salford M5 ....81 A1
  Stockport SK2 ....124 A6
Regent Road Ind Est M5 .162 D8
Regent Sq M5 ....161 B8
Regent St Bury BL9 ....140 F4
  Eccles M30 ....79 F2
  Failsworth M40 ....83 D5
  Glossop SK13 ....104 D1
  Hadfield SK13 ....104 B5
  Heywood OL10 ....29 B2
  8 Hindley WN2 ....56 D5
  Littleborough OL15 ....16 B5
  Middleton M24 ....46 F2
  Newton-le-W WA12 ....89 A3
  Oldham OL1 ....67 A7
  Ramsbottom BL0 ....11 A4
  2 Rochdale OL12,OL16 ....15 A1
  8 Rochdale OL16 ....31 A8
  Shaw OL2 ....149 B7
  Tyldesley M46 ....58 E2
Regent Trad Est M5 ....158 D1
Regent Wlk BL4 ....60 D8
Regents Dr OL5 ....86 D8
Regina Ave SK15 ....86 A2
Regina Cres WN7 ....76 E6
Regina St M6 ....80 A3
Reginald Latham Ct M40 ..160 D3
Reginald St Bolton BL3 ....146 A2
  2 Droylsden M11 ....99 F7
  Eccles M30 ....95 A8
  Swinton M27 ....61 D1
Reigate Cl M14 ....113 A8
Reigate Cl BL0 ....27 B1
Reigate Rd M41 ....106 E8
Reilly St M15 ....162 F6
Reins Lee Ave OL8 ....67 A2
Reins Lee Rd OL7 ....85 A6
Reliance St M40 ....83 C6

Reliance Street Ent Pk
  M40 ....83 C6
Reliance Street Trad Est
  M40 ....83 C6
Rembrandt Wlk OL11 ....49 D4
Rena Cl SK4 ....169 D3
Rena Ct SK4 ....169 D3
Rendel Cl
  Newton-le-W WA12 ....89 D2
  Stretford M32 ....99 D2
Renfrew Cl WN3 ....55 A3
Renfrew Dr BL3 ....40 F3
Renfrew Rd WN2 ....38 D5
Rennie Cl M32 ....96 E2
Renshaw Ave M30 ....79 D1
Renshaw Dr BL9 ....141 C3
Renshaw St
  Altrincham WA14 ....119 E5
  Manchester M46 ....79 D1
Renton Rd Bolton BL3 ......146 B3
  Stretford M32 ....96 E3
  Wythenshawe M22 ....121 D4
Renwick Gr BL3 ....146 C3
Renwick Sq WN4 ....72 F3
Repton Ave Droylsden M43 .83 D3
  Failsworth M40 ....65 E1
  Hyde SK14 ....167 E3
  Ince-in-M WN3 ....55 F4
  Oldham OL8 ....66 D3
  Reddish M34 ....100 A3
  Urmston M41 ....94 D2
Repton Cl 6 M33 ....107 D3
Reservoir Rd SK3 ....170 D7
Reservoir St Aspull WN2 .....38 F3
  Ince-in-M WN2 ....56 A8
  Manchester M3 ....158 E3
  Rochdale OL16 ....15 C1
  Salford M6 ....154 F2
Restormel Ave WN2 ....38 D5
Retford Ave OL16 ....31 B4
Retford Cl BL8 ....27 E5
Retford St OL4 ....67 B5
Retiro St OL1 ....153 F6
Retreat The SK6 ....113 C1
Reuben St SK4 ....169 E4
Revers St BL8 ....140 D3
Reveton Gn SK7 ....124 A2
Rex Bldgs SK9 ....137 B6
Reynard Ct 5 M14 ....98 E4
Reynard Rd M21 ....109 B7
Reynard St SK14 ....167 D3
Reynell Rd M13 ....98 F2
Reyner St Ashton-u-L OL6 ..85 E2
  Manchester M1 ....163 A8
  Reynold St SK14 ....100 F5
Reynolds Cl BL5 ....58 F6
Reynolds Dr Atherton BL5 ...58 F7
  Manchester M18 ....99 D6
  Marple SK6 ....126 B8
Reynolds Mews SK9 ....137 E8
Reynolds Rd M16 ....97 C4
Rhine Cl BL8 ....26 F7
Rhine Dr M8 ....155 E5
Rhiwlas Dr BL9 ....44 F8
Rhode Hos SK6 ....125 F3
Rhode St BL8 ....26 F6
Rhodes Ave Haslingden BB4 .1 A7
  Oldham OL4 ....67 F5
  Uppermill OL3 ....51 C1
Rhodes Bank OL1 ....67 A6
Rhodes Cres OL11 ....30 F3
Rhodes Dr BL9 ....45 A2
Rhodes Hill OL4 ....67 E8
Rhodes St Dukinfield SK14 .101 C3
  Hadfield SK13 ....104 B5
  Oldham OL1 ....67 A7
  Oldham OL4 ....67 F7
  Rochdale OL12 ....15 B3
  Royton OL2 ....49 A3
Rhodes St N SK14 ....101 C3
Rhodeswood Dr SK13 ....106 A6
Rhos Ave Cheadle SK8 ....122 E1
  Manchester M14 ....110 E8
  Middleton M24 ....65 A7
Rhos Dr SK7 ....124 A1
Rhosleigh Ave BL1 ....143 E4
Rialto Gdns M7 ....155 E6
Ribbesford Rd WN3 ....54 C4
Ribble Ave Bolton BL2 ....42 E7
  Chadderton OL9 ....47 F1
  Littleborough OL15 ....15 F6
Ribble Cl WA3 ....92 E1
Ribble Cres WN5 ....71 C3
Ribble Dr Boothstown M28 ..77 F6
  Bury BL9 ....27 F8
  Kearsley BL4 ....61 B5
  Walkden M45 ....54 C7
  Wigan WN5 ....53 D4
Ribble Drive Com Prim Sch
  M45 ....45 A1
Ribble Gr Heywood OL10 .....29 A3
Ribble Pl WN5 ....53 D4
Ribble Rd Oldham OL8 ....66 C3
  Platt Bridge WN2 ....56 A2
  Shevington Moor WN6 ....19 B2
Ribble St Bacup OL13 ....4 A8
Ribble Wlk M43 ....100 A8
Ribblesdale Cl OL10 ....46 E7
Ribblesdale Dr M40 ....156 C5
Ribblesdale Rd BL3 ....147 D4
Ribbleton Cl BL8 ....26 F1
Ribchester Dr M9 ....157 F8
Ribchester Gdns WA3 ....92 A3
Ribchester Gr BL2 ....25 E1
Riber Bank SK13 ....171 E1
Riber Cl 25 SK13 ....171 E1
Riber Fold 27 SK13 ....171 E1

Riber Gn 26 SK13 ....171 E1
Ribston St M15 ....162 E6
Rice St M3 ....162 E8
Richard Burch St 3 BL9 ...140 F3
Richard Gwyn Cl BL5 ....57 D6
Richard Reynolds Ct
  M44 ....105 E6
Richard St Failsworth M35 ...83 F7
  Manchester M13 ....151 D6
  Radcliffe M26 ....43 F3
  Ramsbottom BL0 ....11 E7
  Rochdale OL11 ....139 F6
  Stockport SK1 ....124 B2
Richards Rd WN6 ....19 B3
Richardson Cl M45 ....44 F1
Richardson Rd M30 ....79 F2
Richardson St
  8 Manchester M11 ....99 E7
  Stockport SK1 ....124 A7
Richbell Cl M44 ....105 F7
Richborough Cl M7 ....155 E5
Richelieu St BL3 ....42 A4
Richmond Ave
  Handforth SK9 ....131 D4
  Manchester M25 ....63 C1
  Oldham OL9 ....68 A4
  Royton OL2 ....48 D4
  Urmston M41 ....95 E2
Richmond Cl Bury BL8 ....26 F6
  Cheadle SK8 ....122 A3
  Dukinfield SK16 ....101 D6
  Hadfield SK13 ....104 A5
  Lymm WA13 ....117 B4
  Mossley OL5 ....86 E8
  Rochdale OL16 ....31 C3
  Sale M33 ....108 F3
  Shaw OL2 ....149 B5
  Stalybridge SK15 ....86 A1
  Standish WN1 ....37 B7
  Whitefield M45 ....62 D7
Richmond Cres OL5 ....86 E8
Richmond Ct
  Altrincham WA14 ....119 B2
  Cheadle SK8 ....122 C5
  Sale M33 ....108 A4
  Stockport SK2 ....124 D5
Richmond Dr Leigh WN7 .....76 D7
  Lymm WA13 ....117 B4
  Swinton M28 ....79 C8
Richmond Gdns Bolton BL3 .42 B3
  Newton-le-W WA12 ....89 C2
Richmond Gn WA14 ....119 B2
Richmond Gr Cheadle SK8 .122 F1
  Eccles M30 ....79 E3
  Manchester M13 ....98 F4
  Leigh WN7 ....76 E6
  Manchester M13 ....98 F4
Richmond Gr E M12 ....164 E5
Richmond Hill Hyde SK14 .167 F1
  Wigan WN5 ....54 D6
Richmond Hill Rd SK8 ......122 C6
Richmond Inf Sch OL9 ....68 A4
Richmond Jun Sch OL9 ....153 D6
Richmond Pk M14 ....98 D1
Richmond Rd
  Altrincham WA14 ....119 C2
  Altrincham WA14 ....119 D5
  Ashton-in-M WN4 ....72 F5
  Boothstown M28 ....77 E7
  Dukinfield SK16 ....101 D6
  Eccles M17 ....96 A7
  Failsworth M35 ....84 B8
  Hindley WN2 ....57 A3
  Manchester M14 ....98 D1
  Reddish M34 ....100 A3
  Romiley SK6 ....113 C3
Richmond St
  Ashton-u-L OL7 ....84 F3
  Atherton M46 ....58 C2
  Bury BL9 ....44 E8
  Denton M34 ....100 F6
  Droylsden M43 ....84 C2
  Horwich BL6 ....22 B3
  Hyde SK14 ....167 E2
  Manchester M1 ....163 A7
  Manchester M3 ....158 E3
  Stalybridge SK15 ....86 C2
  Wigan WN1 ....150 A8
  Wigan WN3 ....150 A5
Richmond Terr SK6 ....113 C3
Richmond Wlk
  Oldham OL9 ....153 D6
  Radcliffe M26 ....43 E6
Ricroft Rd SK6 ....114 B3
Riddell Ct M23 ....121 E3
Ridding Cl SK2 ....124 D6
Riddings Ct WA15 ....119 F8
Riddings Rd
  Altrincham WA14 ....119 F2
  Sale WA15 ....119 A5
  Sale WA15 ....119 A5
Riddle Ct M5 ....80 C2

Ridge Ave
  Altrincham WA14 ....129 D6
  Marple SK6 ....125 F5
  Standish WN1 ....37 B7
Ridge Cl Hadfield SK14 .....171 E1
  Romiley SK6 ....113 F2
Ridge Cres Marple SK6 .....126 A3
  Whitefield M45 ....63 B8
Ridge Danyers Coll
  Cheadle SK8 ....122 F3
  Marple SK6 ....125 F5
  Marple SK6 ....125 E5
Ridge End Fold SK6 ....126 A2
Ridge Gr M45 ....63 B8

Ridge Hill La SK15 ....86 A3
Ridge La OL3 ....51 D5
Ridge Pk SK7 ....132 D6
Ridge Rd SK6 ....126 A3
Ridge The SK6 ....126 A3
Ridge Wlk M9 ....64 D3
Ridgecroft OL7 ....85 B6
Ridgedale Ctr 3 SK6 ....125 F6
Ridgedales The OL1 ....49 E4
Ridgefield M2 ....158 F1
Ridgefield St M35 ....83 E6
Ridgegreen M28 ....78 A5
Ridgemont Ave SK4 ....168 B2
Ridgemont Wlk 11 M23 ....120 E7
Ridgeway Golborne WA3 .....90 E7
  Swinton M27 ....62 B2
  Wilmslow SK9 ....137 F7
Ridgeway Gates 3 BL1 ....145 F7
Ridgeway Rd WA15 ....120 C5
Ridgeway The SK12 ....135 C6
Ridgewood Ave M45 ....90 D8
Ridgewood Ave
  Manchester M40 ....157 D5
  Oldham OL9 ....65 E8
Ridgmont Cl BL6 ....22 F3
Ridgmont Dr
  Boothstown M28 ....77 F6
  Horwich BL6 ....22 F3
Ridgway St M40 ....160 D2
Ridgway The SK6 ....113 A1
Riding Cl M27 ....62 B4
Riding Fold M43 ....84 D3
Riding Fold La M28 ....79 A5
Riding Gate BL2 ....25 E6
Riding Gate Mews BL2 ....25 E6
Riding Head La BL0 ....11 F8
Riding La WN4 ....73 F5
Riding St M3 ....162 D7
Riding's Ct SK13 ....51 A2
Ridings Rd SK13 ....103 F5
Ridings St
  Manchester M10,M40 ....157 F5
  Manchester M11 ....165 B8
Ridley Dr WA14 ....107 E1
Ridley Gr M33 ....108 F3
Ridley St OL4 ....67 A6
Ridling La Hyde SK14 ....167 F3
Ridling La SK14 ....167 E2
Ridsdale Ave M20 ....110 A6
Ridsdale Way M6 ....81 A5
Ridyard St Platt Bridge WN2 ..56 B3
  Walkden M38 ....60 C6
  Wigan WN5 ....54 E7
Riefield BL1 ....142 B3
Rifle Rd M21,M33 ....100 F5
Rifle St OL1 ....153 F8
Riga Rd M14 ....98 B4
Riga St M4 ....159 A2
Rigby Ave Blackrod BL6 ......21 C2
Rigby Cl 7 WN3 ....54 A6
Rigby Ct Bolton BL3 ....147 F4
  Rochdale OL12 ....13 E2
Rigby Gr M38 ....59 E4
Rigby La BL2 ....25 C5
Rigby St Altrincham WA14 .119 D3
  Ashton-in-M WN4 ....73 A3
  Bolton BL3 ....90 A8
  Hindley WN2 ....56 E6
  Manchester M7 ....155 E6
  Salford M7 ....81 B2
  Tyldesley M29 ....77 C6
Rigel Pl M7 ....81 C3
Rigel St M4 ....159 C3
Rigton Cl M12 ....165 A6
Riley Cl M33 ....107 B1
Riley Ct 3 BL1 ....143 F1
Riley La WN2 ....38 B7
Riley St WN4 ....73 A3
Riley Wood Cl SK6 ....112 F1
Rilldene Wlk OL11 ....29 D8
Rimington Ave WA3 ....73 D1
Rimington Cl WA3 ....91 E3
Rimington Fold M24 ....46 D3
Rimmer Cl M11 ....160 E1
Rimmington Cl M9 ....64 E4
Rimsdale Cl SK8 ....122 A3
Rimsworth Dr M40 ....83 A6
Rindle Rd M29 ....93 C8
Ring Lows La OL12 ....15 A4
Ring-o-Bells La SK12 ....135 D6
Ringcroft Gdns M40 ....65 B1
Ringfield Cl M16 ....97 E4
Ringford Wlk M40 ....157 E5
Ringley Ave WA3 ....73 F1
Ringley Chase M45 ....62 D8
Ringley Cl M45 ....62 D8
Ringley Dr M45 ....62 C7
Ringley Gr BL1 ....143 E2
Ringley Hey M45 ....62 C8
Ringley Meadows M26 ....61 C7
Ringley Old Brow M26 ....61 C7
Ringley Pk M45 ....62 D8
Ringley Rd Kearsley M26 .....61 C5
  Kearsley M26 ....62 A1
  Whitefield M45 ....62 C8
Ringley Rd W M26 ....62 E8
Ringlow Ave M27 ....79 C7
Ringlow Park Rd M27 ....79 C7
Ringmer Dr 4 M22 ....121 C1
Ringmere Ct 7 OL1 ....153 E8

Ringmore Rd SK7 ....124 A2
Rings Cl M35 ....83 F6
Ringstead Cl SK9 ....131 D1
Ringstead Dr
  Manchester M40 ....159 C3
  3 Handforth SK9 ....131 D1
Ringstone M25 ....63 A3
Ringway Ave WN7 ....75 F8
Ringway Gr M33 ....108 E2
Ringway Rd M22,M90 ....130 D8
Ringway Rd W M22,M90 ...130 D8
Ringway Trad Est M22 ....130 E8
Ringwood Ave
  Droylsden M34 ....84 C1
  Grove Karse SK7 ....124 B1
  Hyde SK14 ....102 A1
  Manchester M12 ....99 B3
  Radcliffe M26 ....44 B1
  Ramsbottom BL0 ....11 A4
Ringwood Way OL9 ....152 D7
Rink St M14 ....110 D7
Ripley Ave Bramhall SK8 ...132 B5
  Stockport SK2 ....124 B4
Ripley Cl Hazel Grove SK7 .133 E8
  Manchester M4 ....164 D8
Ripley Cres M41 ....94 F5
Ripley Dr Leigh WN7 ....75 A6
Ripley St WN3 ....54 C4
Ripley St BL2 ....25 B4
Ripley Way M34 ....112 F8
Ripon Ave Bolton BL1 ....23 F1
  Golborne WA3 ....90 C8
Ripon Cl Altrincham WA15 .120 C1
  Little Lever BL3 ....42 F3
  Newton-le-W WA12 ....89 C5
  Oldham OL9 ....65 B3
  Radcliffe BL9 ....44 D5
  5 Whitefield M45 ....44 F2
Ripon Cres M32 ....95 F3
Ripon Dr
  Bolton BL1 ....23 F1
Ripon Gr M33 ....107 F6
Ripon Hall Ave M26 ....11 B4
Ripon Ho M14 ....98 E4
Ripon Rd M32 ....95 F3
Ripon St Ashton-u-L OL6 ...166 C2
  Manchester M15 ....163 A5
  Oldham OL1 ....153 D8
Ripon Wlk SK6 ....113 A1
Rippenden Ave M21 ....97 A2
Rippingham Rd M20 ....110 B7
Rippingham Rd M22 ....121 E4
Rippondeen Rd
  Denshaw OL3 ....33 D3
  Oldham OL1,OL4 ....49 C1
Rippon Wlk M40 ....84 C6
Risbury Wlk 8 M40 ....83 C6
Rise The Oldham OL4 ....67 F7
  Wigan WN6 ....36 C3
Rises The SK13 ....103 F5
Rishton Ave BL3 ....147 F2
Rishton La BL3 ....147 F3
Rishworth Dr M40 ....83 E8
Rishworth Rise OL2 ....32 A1
Rising La OL8 ....66 E2
Rising Lane Cl OL8 ....66 E2
Risley Ave M9 ....64 D1
Risley St OL1 ....153 F8
Rissington Ave M23 ....121 B6
Rita Ave 8 M14 ....98 B3
Ritson Cl M18 ....165 B6
Riva Rd M19 ....110 E3
River La M31 ....105 F4
River Pl Manchester M15 ..162 E7
  Rochdale OL16 ....31 F6
River St Bolton BL2 ....148 A6
  Heywood OL10 ....29 D3
  Manchester M12 ....163 C8
  Manchester M15 ....162 F7
  Radcliffe M26 ....44 B3
  Stockport SK1 ....123 B3
  Swinton M27 ....137 B8
River View SK5 ....112 A7
  Whitefield M45 ....62 F7
River Way WN1 ....150 C8
Riverbank OL3 ....50 F1
Riverbank Dr BL8 ....140 D3
Riverbank Lawns M3 ....158 E3
Riverbank The M26 ....62 A4
Riverbank Tower M3 ....158 E3
Riverbank Wlk M20 ....116 F7
Riverbank Wlk M20 ....109 E4
Riverdale Cl WN6 ....36 D4
Riverdale Rd M9 ....64 B4
Rivermead Ave WA15 ....129 C7
Rivermead Cl M34 ....113 A7
Rivermead Rd M34 ....113 A7
Rivermead Way M45 ....63 B8
Riverpark Rd M40 ....83 B3
Rivers La M41 ....95 C5
Riversdale Ct M25 ....63 A1
Riversdale Dr OL8 ....67 A1
Riversdale Rd SK8 ....122 C5
Riversdale View SK15 ....101 A3
Riversdale Ct M25 ....63 A3
Rivershill M33 ....108 A6
Rivershill Dr OL10 ....29 B1
Rivershill Gdns WA15 ....129 C7
Riverside Bolton BL1 ....25 A2

Riverside continued
Chadderton OL1 .....47 E1
Dukinfield SK16 .....166 C1
Manchester M7 .....158 D3
Riverside Ave Irlam M44 .....94 B1
Manchester M21 .....109 D3
Wigan WN1 .....37 D1
Riverside Bsns Pk SK9 .....137 B7
Riverside Cl SK13 .....104 D1
Riverside Ct
Manchester M20 .....109 F3
Whitworth OL12 .....4 D4
Riverside Dr Kearsley M26 .....61 B8
Ramsbottom BL9 .....11 B2
Rochdale OL16 .....15 C2
Urmston M41 .....107 B8
Riverside Mews M15 .....162 E7
Riverside Rd M26 .....44 D4
Riverside Wlk BB4 .....1 A7
Riverleigh Cl BL1 .....23 C7
Riversmeade Bolton BL7 .....25 C7
Leigh WN7 .....76 A6
Riverstone Bridge OL15 .....16 B5
Riverstone Dr M23 .....120 D7
Riverton Rd M20 .....122 B8
Riverview Cotts SK13 .....116 C7
Riverview Ct M7 .....81 C8
Riviera Ct OL12 .....13 C2
Rivington M6 .....80 C4
Rivington & Blackrod Coll
 Horwich Campus
BL6 .....22 D2
Rivington & Blackrod
 High Sch BL6 .....22 B6
Rivington & Blackrod
 High Sch (Annexe) BL6 .....22 B4
Rivington Ave
Adlington PR6 .....21 B7
Golborne WA3 .....74 C1
Pendlebury M27 .....80 C8
Platt Bridge WN2 .....56 B2
Wigan WN1 .....37 D1
Rivington Cres M27 .....80 C7
Rivington Ctry Pk BL6 .....22 A8
Rivington Dr
Bickershaw WN2 .....74 F8
Bury BL8 .....27 A1
Orrell WN8 .....53 C7
Shaw OL2 .....49 D7
Rivington Gr
Droylsden M34 .....100 C8
Irlam M44 .....105 D6
Rivington Hall Cl BL0 .....11 C4
Rivington La Adlington PR6 .....21 D6
Horwich BL6 .....22 A7
Rivington Pl PR7 .....19 C6
Rivington Rd
Altrincham WA15 .....119 F2
Oldham OL4 .....68 A7
Salford M6 .....80 C4
Rivington St Atherton M46 .....58 E3
Blackrod BL6 .....21 D2
Oldham OL1 .....48 F1
Rochdale OL12 .....15 A2
Rivington Way WN6 .....36 F8
Rivington Wlk M12 .....164 F5
Rix St BL1 .....143 E2
Rixson St OL4 .....49 D2
Rixton Ct M16 .....97 B3
Rixton Dr M29 .....77 B8
RL Hughes
 Cty Prim Sch WN4 .....73 A3
Roach Ct M40 .....159 C4
Roach Gn WN1 .....37 E1
Roach Pl BL1 .....31 A8
Roach St Bury BL9 .....141 C2
 Bury BL9 .....44 F4
Roach Vale OL16 .....15 C2
Roaches Mews OL5 .....68 D3
Roaches Way OL5 .....68 E3
Roachill Cl WA14 .....119 B5
Roachwood Cl OL9 .....65 E7
Road La OL12 .....14 D4
Roading Brook Rd BL2 .....26 B3
Roads Ford La OL16 .....31 F7
Roadside Ct WA3 .....90 C8
Roaring Gate La WA15 .....120 E2
Rob La WA12 .....89 E5
Robe Wlk [5] M18 .....99 D6
Robert Hall St M15 .....161 B8
Robert Lawrence Ct M41 .....95 A1
Robert Malcolm Cl M40 .....157 D5
Robert Owen Gdns M22 .....121 D8
Robert Owen St M43 .....84 C2
Robert Salt Ct WA14 .....119 E6
Robert Saville Ct OL11 .....30 C6
Robert St Bolton BL2 .....25 E5
 Bury BL8 .....27 C3
 Dukinfield SK14 .....101 C3
 Dukinfield SK16 .....101 B8
 [6] Failsworth M35 .....66 A1
 Heywood OL10 .....46 E8
 Manchester M10,M40 .....157 F5
 Manchester M3 .....158 F3
 Manchester M8 .....158 F4
 Oldham OL8 .....66 D3
 Platt Bridge WN2 .....56 A3
 Prestwich M25 .....63 C4
 Radcliffe M26 .....44 A4
 Ramsbottom BL0 .....1 C1
 [15] Rochdale OL16 .....31 A8
 Sale M33 .....108 E4
 Tyldesley M46 .....58 E1
Roberts Ave M14 .....98 B4

Roberts St M30 .....79 D1
Robertscroft Cl M22 .....121 C3
Robertshaw Ave M21 .....109 B6
Robertshaw St WN7 .....75 E7
Robertson St Ramsbottom BL0 .....11 E7
Robeson Way M22,SK8 .....121 F6
Robin Cl BL4 .....59 F7
Robin Croft SK6 .....112 D3
Robin Dr M44 .....94 A3
Robin Hill Dr WN6 .....19 B2
Robin Hill La WN6 .....19 C3
Robin Hood La WN6 .....18 B3
Robin Hood St M40 .....159 B6
Robin Park Rd WN5 .....54 F7
Robin Rd BL9 .....11 B2
Robin St OL1 .....153 E8
Robin's La Billinge WA11 .....71 A8
 Bramhall SK7 .....132 D7
Robinia Cl M30 .....94 F8
Robins Cl Bramhall SK7 .....132 E7
 Droylsden M43 .....84 C3
Robins La WA3 .....91 D2
Robinsbay Rd M22 .....130 E8
Robinson St
 Ashton-u-L OL6 .....166 B4
 Dukinfield SK15 .....101 E8
 [8] Horwich BL6 .....22 B4
 Hyde SK14 .....167 F3
 Leigh WN7 .....76 A4
 Oldham OL9 .....152 B6
 Rochdale OL16 .....31 A7
 Stockport SK3 .....170 D7
 [6] Tyldesley M29 .....59 A1
Robinsway WA14 .....119 C1
Robinswood Rd M22 .....121 D2
Robinwood Lo SK13 .....171 E1
Robson Ave M41 .....95 E7
Robson Pl WN2 .....74 B8
Robson St Oldham OL1 .....153 F6
 Oldham OL1 .....67 A8
Robson Way [3] WA3 .....90 F8
Roby Mill WN8 .....35 B3
Roby Mill CE Prim Sch
 WN8 .....35 B3
Roby Rd M30 .....95 C8
Roby St M1 .....159 B1
Roby Well Way WN5 .....71 D5
Roch Ave OL10 .....29 A2
Roch Ct M45 .....45 E1
Roch Cres M45 .....45 C1
Roch Mills Cres OL11 .....30 C5
Roch Mills Gdns OL11 .....139 D5
Roch Pl WN2 .....56 D8
Roch St OL16 .....15 B1
Roch Valley Way OL11 .....30 C5
Roch Wlk M45 .....45 B1
Roch Wlk M45 .....45 B1
Rochbury Cl OL11 .....29 F6
Rochdale AFC
 (Spotland Stadium) OL11 .....30 C8
Rochdale Ho M15 .....162 E7
Rochdale Ind Ctr OL11 .....139 D6
Rochdale Infmy OL12 .....14 F1
Rochdale La Heywood OL10 .....29 D2
 Royton OL2 .....48 F5
Rochdale Old Rd BL9 .....28 D4
Rochdale Pioneers Mus
 OL12 .....139 F8
Rochdale Rd Bacup OL13 .....4 B8
 Bury BL9 .....141 B2
 Denshaw OL3 .....33 C3
 Edenfield BL0 .....1 F2
 Heywood OL10 .....29 D2
 Littleborough HX6,OL15 .....7 E1
 Manchester M40,M8,M9 .....157 D6
 Manchester M9 .....64 D3
 Middleton M24 &OL11 .....47 C4
 Milnrow OL16 .....31 F7
 Oldham OL1 .....153 E8
 Oldham OL1 .....48 E1
 Ramsbottom BL0,BL9 .....12 B7
 Royton OL2 .....48 D6
 Shaw OL2 .....149 B7
 Shaw OL2,OL16 .....48 F8
 Walsden OL14,OL15 .....6 B5
Rochdale Rd E OL10 .....29 F3
Rochdale Sta OL11 .....139 F6
Roche Gdns SK8 .....132 B6
Roche Rd OL3 .....50 E5
Rochester Ave Bolton BL2 .....25 E1
 Manchester M25 .....63 A1
 Walkden M28 .....60 C1
Rochester Cl
 Ashton-u-L OL6 .....85 C7
 Dukinfield SK16 .....102 A7
 Golborne WA3 .....90 A8
Rochester Dr WA14 .....107 E1
Rochester Gr SK7 .....124 E3
Rochester Rd M41 .....95 D4
Rochester Way OL9 .....152 B6
Rochford Ave
 Whitefield M45 .....62 D7
 Wythenshawe M22 .....130 D8
Rochford Cl M45 .....62 D7
Rochford Mo M34 .....100 E6
Rochford Rd M30 .....94 F8
Rock Ave BL1 .....142 C2
Rock Fold BL7 .....8 F1
Rock Gdns SK14 .....113 E7
Rock Nook OL15 .....16 D1
Rock Rd Boothstown M28 .....78 B2
 Urmston M41 .....95 F2
Rock St Ashton-u-L OL7 .....85 A5
 Droylsden M11 .....99 E8
 Golborne WA3 .....74 D2
 [3] Heywood OL10 .....29 E1
 Horwich BL6 .....22 B3
 Hyde SK14 .....113 E7

Rock St continued
 Manchester M7 .....155 D6
 Oldham OL1 .....153 F7
 Radcliffe M26 .....44 B2
 Ramsbottom BL0 .....11 E7
Rock Terr Bolton BL7 .....8 F1
 Mossley OL5 .....68 D3
Rock The Bury BL9 .....140 E2
 Bury BL9 .....140 F3
Rockall Ave M11 .....160 F1
Rockbourne Cl WN2 .....56 D4
Rockcliffe Villas OL13 .....3 C8
Rockdove Ave M15 .....162 F7
Rocket Way M3 .....158 D1
Rockfield Dr [5] M9 .....157 E8
Rockhampton St M18 .....99 E5
Rockhaven Ave BL6 .....22 C4
Rockhouse Cl M30 .....95 C8
Rockingham Cl
 Manchester M12 .....164 D6
 Shaw OL2 .....48 E8
Rockland Wlk [6] M40 .....65 C2
Rockley Gdns M6 .....81 B4
Rocklyn Ave M40 .....65 C2
Rocklynes M5 .....113 B2
Rockmead Dr M9 .....64 E3
Rocky Bank Terr M43 .....151 E5
Rocky La M27,M30 .....79 D4
Roda St M7 .....157 F7
Rodborough Rd M23 .....121 A3
Rodehaath Cl SK9 .....137 D7
Rodenhurst Dr [7] M40 .....65 C2
Rodepool Cl SK9 .....131 D2
Rodgers Cl BL5 .....57 E6
Rodgers Way BL5 .....57 E6
Rodmell Ave M40 .....157 D5
Rodmell Cl BL7 .....24 F7
Rodmill Ct M14 .....98 C1
Rodmill Dr SK8 .....122 A4
Rodney Ct [8] M4 .....159 C3
Rodney Dr SK6 .....113 A5
Rodney St Ashton-u-L OL6 .....85 D4
 Atherton M46 .....58 C2
 Manchester M3 .....158 D1
 Manchester M4 .....159 C2
 Rochdale OL11 .....30 B2
 Wigan WN1 .....150 C7
Roe Cross Gn SK14 .....102 F5
Roe Cross Ind Est SK14 .....103 A5
Roe Cross Rd SK14,SK15 .....102 F5
Roe Gn M28 .....79 A8
Roe Green Ave M28 .....79 A8
Roe La OL4 .....67 D5
Roe St Manchester M4 .....159 C3
 Rochdale OL12 .....14 C1
Roeacre St OL10 .....29 E2
Roebuck La Oldham OL4 .....50 A3
 Sale M33 .....108 A4
Roebuck St WN2 .....57 C3
Roeburn Wlk M45 .....63 C8
Roecliffe Cl WN3 .....150 B6
Roedean Gdns M41 .....94 D2
Rogate Dr M23 .....121 A5
Roger Byrne Cl M40 .....83 B5
Roger Cl SK6 .....112 F2
Roger Hay SK8 .....123 A2
Rogerstead BL3 .....144 C5
Rogerton Cl WN7 .....76 D5
Rokeby Ave Golborne WA3 .....74 D1
 Manchester M32 .....96 D1
Rokeden WA12 .....89 D4
Roker Ave M13 .....98 F2
Roker Ind Est OL1 .....67 B7
Roker Park Ave M34 .....100 D7
Roland Rd [2] Bolton BL3 .....146 C4
 Reddish SK5 .....111 E8
Rolla St M3 .....158 E2
Rollesby Cl BL4 .....27 D5
Rolleston Ave M40 .....160 D2
Rollins La M45 .....114 A1
Rolls Cres M15 .....162 E5
Rollswood Dr M40 .....83 A6
Roman Cl
 Newton-le-W WA12 .....89 C2
 Wigan WN3 .....54 F4
Roman Ct M7 .....155 D5
Roman Rd Ashton-in-M WN4 .....73 A5
 Manchester M25 .....63 B1
 Oldham M35,OL8 .....66 B1
 Royton OL2 .....48 E3
 Stockport SK4 .....169 E2
Roman St Manchester M4 .....159 A2
 Mossley OL5 .....68 D3
 Radcliffe M26 .....43 E3
Rome Rd M40 .....159 C3
Romer Ave M40 .....65 E1
Romer St BL2 .....148 C7
Romford Ave
 Dukinfield M34 .....101 A4
 Leigh WN7 .....75 F6
Romford Cl OL8 .....153 E5
Romford Pl WN2 .....56 A4
Romford Rd M33 .....107 D6
Romford Wy [1] SK1 .....56 C5
Romiley Cres BL2 .....42 D8
Romiley Dr Bolton BL2 .....148 B8
 Bolton BL2 .....42 D8
Romiley Prec SK6 .....113 C2
Romiley Prim Sch SK6 .....113 C2
Romiley Sq WN6 .....36 E8
Romiley St Salford M6 .....80 D5
 Stockport SK1 .....112 B3
Romiley Sta SK6 .....113 C2
Romley Rd M41 .....95 D4
Romney Ave OL11 .....30 F2

Romney Rd BL1 .....23 E2
Romney St Ashton-u-L OL6 .....166 C3
 Manchester M40 .....83 A8
 Salford M6 .....81 B5
Romney Towers SK5 .....112 B6
Romney Way
 Brinnington SK5 .....112 B6
 Wigan WN1 .....37 B3
Romney Wlk OL9 .....152 B6
Romney Sq [2] OL12 .....139 E8
Romsey Ave M24 .....46 F3
Romsey Dr SK8 .....132 C6
Romsey Gdns M23 .....121 A6
Romsey Gr WN3 .....54 D2
Romsley Cl M12 .....165 A6
Romsley Dr Bolton BL3 .....146 C3
Rona Wlk M12 .....164 F5
Ronald St
 Droylsden M11,M43 .....83 D1
 Oldham OL4 .....67 C7
 Rochdale OL11 .....30 C1
Ronaldsay Gdns M5 .....154 E1
Rondin Cl M12 .....164 E2
Rondin Rd M12 .....164 E8
Ronnis Mount OL7 .....85 A7
Ronton Wlk M8 .....156 C8
Roocroft Ct BL1 .....143 D1
Roocroft Sq BL6 .....21 C2
Rooden Ct M25 .....63 C4
Roods La OL11 .....13 A5
Rook St Manchester M15 .....162 E5
 Oldham OL4 .....67 C5
 Ramsbottom BL0 .....138 C6
Rooke St M30 .....95 A8
Rookery Ave
 Appley Bridge WN6 .....35 E8
 Ashton-in-M WN4 .....73 B2
 Droylsden M18 .....99 F6
Rookery Cl SK15 .....102 E7
Rookery The M12,M13 .....89 D4
Rookerypool Cl SK9 .....131 D2
Rookfield Ave M33 .....108 C5
Rookley Wlk [11] M14 .....98 C3
Rookswood Dr OL11 .....30 B3
Rookway M24 .....65 A7
Rookwood OL1,OL9 .....47 E1
Rookwood Ave M23 .....120 F7
Rookwood Hill SK7 .....123 E1
Roogate Cl M14 .....97 F3
Roseahay Ave M44 .....100 F2
Rosehill Cl M6 .....154 F2
Rosehill Ct Oldham OL4 .....67 E8
 Salford M6 .....154 F2
Rosehill Rd M27 .....61 E2
Roseland Ave M20 .....110 B4
Roseland Dr M25 .....63 C6
Roselands Ave M33 .....107 F2
Roseleigh Ave M19 .....110 F8
Rosemary Cres WN1 .....37 D2
Rosemary Dr Hyde SK14 .....113 D7
 Littleborough OL15 .....15 F6
 Newton-le-W WA12 .....89 F1
Rosemary Gr M7 .....81 C5
Rosemary La Atherton BL5 .....59 B6
 Stockport SK1 .....112 A1
Rosemary Wlk M31 .....105 F2
Rosemount Cl [5] SK5 .....111 F6
Rosemount M24 .....101 D5
Rosemount Cres M14 .....101 D5
Rosen Sq OL9 .....152 B7
Roseneath SK7 .....123 D1
Roseneath Ave M19 .....99 C1
Roseneath Gr BL3 .....147 D3
Roseneath Rd Bolton BL3 .....147 D3
 Urmston M41 .....95 C2
Rosette Wlk [3] M27 .....79 F7
Rosevale Ave M19 .....110 E5
Roseway SK7 .....123 F2
Rosewell Cl M40 .....160 D4
Rosewood Rochdale OL13 .....3 E1
 Westhoughton BL5 .....57 D6
Rosewood Ave Bury BL8 .....27 A6
 Droylsden M43 .....84 C3
 Stockport SK4 .....168 A1
Rosewood Cl
 [6] Sale M33 .....108 F3
 Wythenshawe SK8 .....121 F6
Rosewood Wlk M23 .....120 C8
Rosford Ave M14 .....98 B2
Rosgill Cl SK4 .....110 E2
Rosgill Wlk M18 .....165 C5
Rosina Cl WN4 .....72 F6
Rosina St M11 .....99 F7
Rosley Rd WN3 .....55 B3
Roslin Gdns BL1 .....142 C3
Roslin St M11 .....83 D2
Roslyn Ave M41 .....94 E1
Roslyn Rd SK4 .....170 E5
Ross Ave Manchester M19 .....98 F1
 Oldham OL9 .....65 F4
 Stockport SK3 .....170 E5
Ross Cl Billinge WN5 .....71 E6
 Wigan WN2 .....37 F2
Ross Dr M27 .....61 E4
Ross Lave La M34 .....100 C1
Ross St OL8 .....153 D5
Rossall Ave
 [5] Radcliffe M26 .....44 C1
 Stretford M32 .....96 C3
Rossall Cl BL2 .....148 C7
Rossall Cres WN7 .....76 A3
Rossall Dr SK7 .....132 E6

Rossall Rd Bolton BL2 148 C8
Rochdale OL12 15 A2
Rossall St 1 BL2 148 C8
Rossall Way M6 81 A3
Rossdale Gr WN6 131 D6
Rossenclough Rd SK9 131 D1
Rossendale Ave 6 M9 64 F1
Rossendale Cl OL2 49 D7
Rossendale Rd SK8 131 C8
Rossendale Sch BL0 12 A7
Rossendale Way OL2 149 B8
Rossett Ave Sale WA15 120 A8
1 Wythenshawe M22 130 D8
Rossett Cl WN3 54 D2
Rossett Dr M41 95 A4
Rossetti Wlk 2 M34 113 A7
Rosshill Wlk 26 M15 162 D6
Rossington St M40 83 D5
Rossini St BL1 143 D3
Rosslare Rd M22 121 E2
Rosslove Wlk SK5 112 C7
Rosslyn Gr WA15 120 A6
Rosslyn Rd Cheadle SK8 122 D1
Manchester M16 97 A2
Manchester M40 65 A1
Rossmere Ave OL11 30 C6
Rossmill La WA15 129 B7
Rostherne Ave
Golborne WA3 90 D8
High Lane SK6 134 E8
Manchester M14 98 A1
Manchester M16 97 C3
Rostherne Ct WA14 119 D3
Rostherne Gdns BL3 146 B4
Rostherne Rd Sale M33 108 F3
Stockport SK3 170 E5
Wilmslow SK9 136 F4
Rostherne St
1 Altrincham WA14 119 D3
1 Salford M6 154 E1
Rosthernmere Rd SK8 122 F4
Rosthwaite Cl
Middleton M24 46 C1
Wigan WN3 55 A2
Rosthwaite Gr WA11 71 B1
Roston Ct M7 155 E8
Roston Rd M7 155 E8
Rostrevor Rd SK3 170 E5
Rostron Ave M12 164 E6
Rostron Rd BL0 138 B6
Rostron St 6 M19 99 B1
Rothay Cl BL2 25 F1
Rothay Dr Middleton M24 46 E3
Reddish SK5 111 F8
Rothay St WN7 76 B4
Rothbury Ave OL7 84 E5
Rothbury Cl BL8 26 F2
Rothbury Ct BL3 146 B3
Rotherby Rd M22 121 E5
Rotherdale Ave WA15 120 D5
Rotherhead Cl BL6 21 F2
Rothermere Wlk 5 M23 120 E7
Rotherwood Ave M32 96 E3
Rotherwood Rd SK9 136 D6
Rothesay Ave SK16 101 C7
Rothesay Cres M33 107 C2
Rothesay Rd Bolton BL3 146 B3
Manchester M8 63 E2
Oldham OL1 49 C1
Pendlebury M27 80 C7
Rothesay Terr OL16 31 C4
Rothiemay Rd M41 94 E2
Rothley Ave M22 121 D5
Rothman Cl M40 83 C6
Rothwell Cres M38 59 E5
Rothwell La M38 59 E5
Rothwell Rd Adlington PR6 21 B7
Golborne WA3 74 C1
Rothwell St Bolton BL3 145 E5
Failsworth M35 83 F7
Failsworth M40 83 C6
Ramsbottom BL0 138 B6
Rochdale OL12 15 B1
Royton OL2 48 D3
Walkden M28 60 F3
Rottingdene Dr 3 M22 121 C1
Rough Hill La BL9 28 E4
Roughey Gdns M22 121 D4
Roughlea Ave WA3 91 D4
Roughlee Ave M27 79 D7
Roughtown Rd OL5 68 D2
Round Hey OL5 86 C8
Round Hill Cl SK13 171 F3
Round House Ave WN1 37 E1
Round Thorn Rd M24 65 B7
Roundcroft SK6 113 E3
Roundham Wlk 27 M9 157 E8
Roundhey SK8 131 C8
Roundhill Way OL4 49 E1
Roundmoor Rd WN6 37 A7
Roundthorn Bsns Pk
M23 120 E5
Roundthorn Ct M23 120 F7
Roundthorn Ind Est M23 120 E6
Roundthorn La BL5 57 E7
Roundthorn Prim Sch
OL4 67 C5
Roundthorn Rd
Oldham OL4 67 C5
Wythenshawe M23 120 F6
Roundthorn Wlk 9 M23 120 F6
Roundthorne Ind Est
M23 120 E4
Roundway SK7 132 D6
Roundwood High Sch
M22 121 D7
Roundwood Rd M22 121 D7
Rousdon Cl M40 157 D5
Rouse Cl M11 160 F1
Rouse St OL11 30 C4
Routledge Wlk M9 157 E8
Rowan Ave Golborne WA3 90 F7
2 Horwich BL6 22 E1
Manchester M16 97 D3
Sale M33 108 C2
Urmston M41 95 D3
Wigan WN6 36 F3
Rowan Cl Failsworth M35 83 F6
Rochdale OL12 14 B3
6 Salford M6 81 A2
Rowan Cres SK16 101 F7
Rowan Ct Hyde SK14 167 E1
Wilmslow SK9 137 B7
Rowan Dr SK8 132 C8
Rowan Lo SK7 132 F7
Rowan Pl M25 63 B3
Rowan St SK14 167 F1
Rowan Tree Dr M33 108 B1
Rowan Tree Rd OL8 66 D1
Rowan Wlk Hadfield SK13 171 E4
Partington M31 105 E2
Rowanhill WN1 37 D1
Rowans St BL8 27 C4
Rowans The Bolton BL1 40 F7
Mossley OL5 68 D1
Rowanside Dr SK9 137 E8
Rowanswood Dr SK14 102 A3
Rowanwood OL9 65 E7
Rowany Cl M25 63 A2
Rowarth Ave Denton M34 113 A8
10 Gamesley SK13 171 D2
Rowarth Bank 5 SK13 171 D2
Rowarth Cl 6 SK13 171 D2
Rowarth Fold 9 SK13 171 D2
Rowarth Rd
Wythenshawe M23 120 F2
Wythenshawe M23 121 A2
Rowarth Way 8 SK13 171 D2
Rowbotham St SK14 113 E8
Rowbottom Sq WN1 150 C8
Rowbottom Wlk OL8 153 E5
Rowcon Cl M34 100 E6
Rowdell Wlk M23 109 B2
Rowden Rd OL4 67 E4
Rowe Gn M34 100 F2
Rowe St M29 77 B8
Rowell Sq M3 158 D2
Rowell St M3 158 D2
Rowena St BL3 42 C2
Rowendale St M1,M15 162 F8
Rowfield Dr M23 120 F3
Rowland Ave M41 95 E3
Rowland Ct 17 OL16 31 B6
Rowland St Atherton M46 58 D3
16 Rochdale OL16 31 B6
Salford M5 161 A8
Rowland St S M46 58 D2
Rowland Way OL4 67 E7
Rowlands Rd BL9 11 D2
Rowlandsway M22 121 D2
Rowley Rd SK7 133 E8
Rowley St OL6 85 D6
Rowood Ave
Manchester M8 156 B6
Reddish SK5 99 F2
Rowrah Cres M24 46 C1
Rowsley Ave Bolton BL1 142 A1
Manchester M20 109 E4
Rowsley Cl 27 SK13 171 E2
Rowsley Gn 29 SK13 171 E2
Rowsley Gr
30 Gamesley SK13 171 E2
Reddish SK5 111 E7
Rowsley Mews SK13 171 E2
Rowsley Rd Eccles M30 95 C8
Stretford M32 96 A3
Rowsley St
Manchester M11 160 F1
Salford M6 81 B5
Rowsley Wlk 28 SK13 171 E2
Rowson Dr M44 105 D6
Rowton Rise WN1 37 B8
Rowton St BL2 25 B3
Roxalina St BL3 147 E4
Roxburgh St 5 M18 99 D5
Roxbury Ave OL4 67 D5
Roxby Cl M28 60 B3
Roxby Dr 18 M40 65 D2
Roxholme Wlk M22 130 C8
Roxton Cl BL6 22 B5
Roxton Rd SK4 111 C6
Roxwell Wlk 8 M9 157 D8
Roy Grainger Ct 10 M16 97 E3
Roy Ho OL2 48 D6
Roy St Bolton BL3 146 B4
Royton OL2 48 D4
Royal Arc 5 WN1 150 C8
Royal Ave Bury BL9 27 F5
Droylsden M43 84 B2
Heywood OL10 29 D1
Manchester M21 109 A8
Urmston M41 95 D2
Royal Bolton Hospl BL4 147 F1
Royal Dr WN7 76 E6
Royal Eye Hospl M13 163 B5
Royal Gdns WA14 118 F2
Royal George Cotts OL3 68 E5
Royal George St SK1,SK3 170 F8
Royal Manchester
Children's Hospl M27 80 C7
Royal Northern Coll
of Music M13 163 A6
Royal Oak Prim Sch
M23 121 A7
Royal Oak Rd M23 121 A7
Royal Oak Yd SK1 169 F1
Royal Oldham Hospl The
OL1 48 D1
Royal Rd SK12 135 D5
Royal School
for the Deaf The SK8 131 D6
Royal St OL16 15 C3
Royalthorn Ave M22 121 D6
Royalthorn Dr M22 121 C6
Royalthorn Rd M22 121 D6
Royce Ave WA15 119 E5
Royce Ct 22 M15 162 D6
Royce Prim Sch M15 162 E5
Royce Rd M15 162 E6
Royce Trad Est M17 95 F7
Royd St OL8 66 C4
Roydale St M40 160 E3
Royden Ave Irlam M44 105 F8
Manchester M9 64 D5
Wigan WN3 55 A2
Royden Cres WN5 71 E5
Royden Rd WN5 71 E5
Roydes St M24 47 B2
Royds Cl Bury BL8 27 A5
Manchester M13 164 D5
Royds Pl 15 OL16 31 A5
Royds Rd OL13 3 A7
Royds St Bury BL8 26 F7
Bury BL9 28 D4
Littleborough OL15 16 C5
Milnrow OL16 32 A5
Rochdale OL16 31 B5
Royds St W OL11,OL16 31 A5
Royland Ave BL3 42 A3
Royland Ct BL3 147 F3
Royle Ave SK13 104 D1
Royle Barn Rd OL11 30 C2
Royle Cl Oldham OL8 66 F3
Stockport SK2 124 A5
Royle Green Rd M22 121 E8
Royle Pennine Trad Est
OL11 30 D3
Royle Rd OL11 30 D3
Royle St Denton M34 100 F5
Manchester M14 110 D7
Salford M6 154 F1
Stockport SK1 170 F7
Walkden M28 60 D2
Roylelands Bglws OL11 30 C3
Royley OL2 48 C3
Royley Carr Flats SK6 113 A3
Royley Cres OL2 48 C3
Royley House OL2 48 C3
Royley Rd OL8 66 E4
Royley Way OL2 48 C3
Roynton Rd BL6 22 B7
Royon Dr SK3 123 B7
Royston Ave Bolton BL2 148 C8
Manchester M16 97 D3
Reddish M34 100 A3
Royston Cl
2 Golborne WA3 90 E8
Ramsbottom BL8 10 F1
Royston Ct 5 M16 97 D3
Royston Rd
Manchester M16 97 B3
Urmston M41 95 E3
Royton & Crompton
Com Sec Sch OL2 49 A4
Royton Ave M33 108 E2
Royton Hall Wlk OL2 48 E4
Rozel Sq M3 162 E8
Ruabon Cres WN2 57 A4
Ruabon Rd M20 110 C2
Rubens Cl SK6 126 C8
Ruby Gr WN7 75 E4
Ruby St Bolton BL1 143 F3
Denton M34 100 E3
Manchester M15 163 A6
Ramsbottom BL9 11 C3
Rudcroft Cl M13 163 B6
Rudd St M40 83 A7
Rudding St OL2 49 A2
Ruddpark Rd M22 121 D1
Rudford Gdns BL3 147 F4
Rudgwick Dr BL8 27 C7
Rudheath Ave M20 110 A7
Rudman Dr M5 161 C8
Rudman St OL12 14 E2
Rudolph St BL3 147 F3
Rudston Ave M40 65 B2
Rudyard Ave Middleton M24 47 C3
Standish WN6 19 E2
Rudyard Gr Reddish SK4 111 D6
Rochdale OL11 30 F2
Sale M33 107 E2
Rudyard Rd M6 80 C5
Rudyard St M7 155 D6
Rufford Ave Hyde SK14 167 F2
Rochdale OL11 30 D4
Rufford Cl Ashton-u-L OL6 85 C7
Shaw OL2 48 F7
Whitefield BL9 45 A2
Rufford Dr Bolton BL3 147 D2
Whitefield M45 44 F2
Rufford Gr BL3 147 D2
Rufford Pl Reddish M18 99 F4
Tyldesley M29 76 F4
Rufford Rd M16 97 D3
Rufford St 4 WN4 72 F5
Rufus St M14 110 E7
Rugby Dr Orrell WN5 53 F8
Sale M33 108 A2
Rugby Rd Leigh WN7 75 F3
Rochdale OL12,OL16 15 A1
Salford M6 80 A3
Rugby Rd Ind Est OL16 15 A1
Rugby St M7,M8 158 E4
Rugeley St M6 81 B5
Ruins La BL2 25 E4
Ruislip Ave M40 157 E5
Ruislip Cl OL8 67 B4
Rumbles La OL3 50 F4
Rumbold St 6 M18 99 E6
Rumworth Rd BL6 40 C6
Rumworth St BL3 147 D4
Runcorn St M15 161 C7
Runger La M90,WA15 129 F8
Runhall Cl M12 165 A6
Running Hill Farm OL3 51 D2
Running Hill Gate OL3 51 D1
Running Hill La OL3 51 D2
Runnymeade M6,M27 80 B5
Runnymede Cl SK3 123 C6
Runnymede Ct Bolton BL3 145 D5
Royton OL2 48 E4
Stockport SK3 123 C6
Runshaw Ave WN6 35 E8
Rupert St Bolton BL3 147 F3
Failsworth M40 83 E4
Radcliffe M26 44 B1
Reddish SK5 111 E7
Rochdale OL12 14 C1
Wigan WN1 151 E7
Rupert Terr 5 SK5 111 E7
Ruscombe Fold M24 46 D3
Rush Acre Cl M26 43 E3
Rush Bank OL2 48 F8
Rush Gr OL3 69 B7
Rush Hill Rd OL3 69 B7
Rush Mount Shaw OL2 149 A8
Shaw OL2 48 F8
Rush St SK16 101 F8
Rushall Wlk M23 120 F2
Rushbrooke Ave 1 M11 83 C2
Rushbury Dr OL2 49 A4
Rushcroft Com Prim Sch
OL2 149 B8
Rushcroft Ct M9 65 A2
Rushcroft Rd OL2 48 F8
Rushden Rd M19 99 B2
Rushdene WN3 55 B4
Rushen St 4 M11 83 C1
Rushes The SK14 171 F4
Rushey Ave M22 121 C6
Rushey Cl WA15 129 D7
Rushey Field BL7 24 F8
Rushey Fold Ct 24 BL1 143 D2
Rushey Fold La BL1 143 D2
Rushey Rd M22 121 C6
Rusheylea Cl BL1 142 C2
Rushfield Dr M13 98 F3
Rushfield Rd SK8 132 A6
Rushford Ave M19 99 A2
Rushford Ct 1 M19 99 A2
Rushford Gr BL1 143 F4
Rushford St M12 99 A3
Rushgreen Rd WA13 117 A4
Rushill Terr OL3 69 B7
Rushlake Dr BL1 143 E1
Rushley Ave M7 81 B7
Rushmere OL6 85 E6
Rushmere Ave M19 99 B1
Rushmere Dr BL8 27 C5
Rushmere Wlk M16 162 D5
Rushmoor Ave WN4 73 E4
Rushmoor Cl M44 94 A2
Rusholme Gdns 3 M14 98 C2
Rusholme Gr M14 98 C3
Rusholme Pl M14 98 C4
Rushside Rd SK8 132 A6
Rushton Ave Leigh WN7 75 D8
Newton-le-W WA12 89 B4
Rushton Cl SK6 126 A5
Rushton Dr Marple SK6 125 F5
Romiley SK6 113 C3
Stockport SK7 123 D3
Rushton Gdns SK7 123 D2
Rushton Gr
Manchester M11 99 E7
Oldham OL4 49 E3
Rushton Rd Bolton BL1 142 B1
Cheadle SK8 132 A6
Stockport SK3 123 B7
Rushton St 5 Bacup OL13 3 E8
Manchester M20 110 B2
Walkden M28 60 D2
Rushwick Ave M40 157 E5
Rushworth Bldgs OL13 3 C8
Rushworth Ct SK4 111 C5
Rushy Hill View OL12 14 C1
Rushy View WA12 89 A4
Rushycroft SK14 103 A4
Rushyfield Cres SK6 113 D3
Ruskin Ave Denton M34 100 E1
Droylsden M34 100 C7
Kearsley BL4 60 F7
Manchester M14 98 B4
Newton-le-W WA12 89 C4
Oldham OL9 65 F3
Wigan WN3 54 F3
Ruskin Cres Abram WN2 56 B1
Prestwich M25 62 F3
Ruskin Gdns SK6 113 A3
Ruskin Gr SK6 113 A3
Ruskin Rd Droylsden M43 84 A2
Little Lever BL3 43 B4
Manchester M16 97 C3
Prestwich M25 62 F3
Reddish SK5 99 E1
Rochdale OL11 30 F2
Ruskin St Oldham OL1 153 D8
Radcliffe M26 44 C4
Ruskington Dr M9 157 D7
Rusland Ct Manchester M9 65 A3
Sale M33 108 A5
Rusland Dr BL2 25 E2
Rusland Wlk 8 M22 121 C2
Russel St OL11 139 E5
Russeldene Rd WN3 54 E3
Russell Ave High Lane SK6 134 E7
Manchester M16 97 D2
Sale M33 108 D5
Russell Cl BL1 144 C8
Russell Ct Farnworth BL4 60 E7
Manchester M16 97 C3
Walkden M38 60 C3
Russell Dr M44 94 A2
Russell Gdns SK4 168 B1
Russell Rd Manchester M16 97 D3
Partington M31 106 A3
Salford M6 80 B5
Russell Scott Prim Sch
M34 100 E4
Russell St
6 Ashton-u-L OL6 85 D4
Atherton M46 58 C3
Bolton BL1 145 D8
5 Bury BL9 140 F4
Denton M34 100 F3
Dukinfield SK16 101 C8
Eccles M30 79 F2
Farnworth BL4 60 E8
Heywood OL10 29 E1
Hindley WN2 57 C2
Hyde SK14 167 D3
Ince-in-M WN2 56 A8
Manchester M16 97 F3
Manchester M8 158 F4
Mossley OL5 68 C1
Oldham OL9 152 B7
Prestwich M25 63 C4
Stockport SK2 124 A6
Walkden M38 60 C3
Russet Rd M9 64 D1
Russet Wlk BL1 143 E4
Rustons Wlk 2 M40 65 E1
Ruth Ave M40 65 E1
Ruth St Bolton BL1 145 E8
10 Bury BL9 140 F4
Edenfield BL0 1 D2
Manchester M18 99 D3
Oldham OL1 153 F8
Whitworth OL12 4 D1
Ruthen La M16 97 B4
Rutherford Ave 2 M14 98 B3
Rutherford Cl SK14 167 D2
Rutherford Dr BL5 58 F7
Rutherford Way SK14 167 D2
Rutherglade Cl M40 156 C6
Rutherglen Dr BL3 40 F6
Rutherglen Wlk M40 157 E5
Ruthin Ave Cheadle SK8 122 E2
Manchester M9 64 C5
Middleton M24 65 A6
Ruthin Cl Oldham OL8 66 B2
Salford M6 81 A2
Ruthin Ct M6 81 A2
Rutland OL11 139 E6
Rutland Ave Atherton M46 58 F5
Denton M34 101 B2
Golborne WA3 90 D7
Manchester M16 97 A3
Manchester M20 110 A6
Swinton M27 61 F2
Urmston M41 95 E3
Rutland Cl
5 Ashton-u-L OL6 85 D2
Gatley SK8 122 B6
Little Lever BL3 43 B4
Rutland Cres SK5 112 D6
Rutland Ct SK2 124 A5
Rutland Dr
Ashton-in-M WN4 73 C4
Bury BL9 45 A8
Manchester M7 63 D1
Rutland Gr Bolton BL1 142 C1
Farnworth BL4 60 C7
Rutland La M33 108 F4
Rutland Rd
Altrincham WA14 119 D6
Droylsden M43 83 E2
Eccles M30 79 F3
Hazel Grove SK7 133 E8
Hindley WN2 56 F6
Irlam M44 105 D5
Partington M31 105 E2
Tyldesley M29 58 F2
Walkden M28 60 D1
Rutland St Ashton-u-L OL6 85 D2
Bolton BL3 147 D4
Droylsden M43 100 B8
Dukinfield SK14 101 D5
Failsworth M35 83 F8
Heywood OL10 29 D3
Leigh WN7 76 E4
4 Manchester M18 99 E6
Oldham OL9 152 C5
Swinton M27 61 E1
Rutland Way OL2 149 C7
Rutland Wlk BB4 1 A8
Rutter's La SK7 124 C2
Ryall Ave M5 161 B8
Ryall Ave S M5 161 B8
Ryan St M11 99 E7
Ryburn Sq OL11 29 E6
Rydal Ave Chadderton OL9 47 F1
Droylsden M43 83 E1
Dukinfield SK14 101 C5
Eccles M30 79 B4
Hazel Grove SK7 124 C3
High Lane SK6 134 E8

Rydal Ave continued
Hindley WN2 . . . . .56 E5
Middleton M24 . . . . .64 F6
Orrell WN5 . . . . .53 F7
Royton OL2 . . . . .48 C8
Sale M33 . . . . .107 F5
Urmston M41 . . . . .107 A8
Rydal Cl Ashton-in-M WN4 . . .73 C4
Blackrod BL6 . . . . .21 C3
Bury BL9 . . . . .44 E7
Gatley SK8 . . . . .122 B4
Reddish M34 . . . . .100 B2
Tyldesley M29 . . . . .77 A7
Rydal Cres Swinton M27 . . . .79 F7
Walkden M28 . . . . .60 E1
Rydal Dr WA15 . . . . .129 D8
Rydal Gr Ashton-u-L OL7 . .166 A4
Farnworth BL4 . . . . .59 F7
Heywood OL10 . . . . .46 D8
Whitefield M45 . . . . .63 A8
Rydal Ho ■ M28 . . . . .60 E2
Rydal Mount SK5 . . . . .99 F2
Rydal Pl Abram WN2 . . . . . .74 B8
Ince-in-M WN2 . . . . .56 B8
Rydal Rd Bolton BL1 . . . . .144 A8
Haslingden BB4 . . . . .1 C8
Little Lever BL3 . . . . .43 A3
Stretford M32 . . . . .96 D3
Rydal St Leigh WN7 . . . . . .75 E5
Newton-le-W WA12 . . . . . .89 C3
Rydal Wlk Stalybridge SK15 . .86 A3
Wigan WN5 . . . . .54 C7
Ryde Ave Denton M34 . . . .113 B8
Manchester SK4 . . . . .168 B2
Ryde St Bolton BL3 . . . . . .146 A4
Wigan WN5 . . . . .54 E6
Ryder Ave WA14 . . . . .119 E7
Ryder Brow M18 . . . . .99 D4
Ryder Brow Sta M18 . . . . .99 D4
Ryder Gr WN7 . . . . .76 C2
Ryder St Bolton BL1 . . . . .142 C2
Heywood OL10 . . . . .29 D2
Manchester M40 . . . . .160 D4
Ryderbrow Rd M18 . . . . . .99 D4
Rydings La OL12 . . . . .15 A5
Rydings Rd OL12 . . . . .15 B4
Rydings Specl Sch OL12 . .15 B4
Rydley St BL2 . . . . .148 B6
Rye Bank Rd M16 . . . . . . .97 B3
Rye Croft M45 . . . . .62 C7
Rye Croft Ave M6 . . . . . . .80 C3
Rye Hill BL5 . . . . .57 F8
Rye St OL10 . . . . .29 E3
Rye Wlk Chadderton OL9 . .152 A6
Manchester M13 . . . . .163 C5
Ryebank Gr OL6 . . . . .85 D5
Ryebank Mews ■ M21 . . . .96 F1
Ryebank Rd M21 . . . . .96 F1
Ryeburn Ave M22 . . . . . . .121 D3
Ryeburn Dr BL2 . . . . .25 B5
Ryeburn Wlk M41 . . . . . . .94 F4
Ryeburne St OL4 . . . . .67 C7
Ryecroft Ave Bury BL8 . . . .26 F6
Golborne WA3 . . . . .74 E1
Heywood OL10 . . . . .29 E2
Ryecroft Cl OL9 . . . . .65 F1
Ryecroft Dr BL5 . . . . .39 D3
Ryecroft Gr M23 . . . . .121 A7
Ryecroft Ho ■ OL7 . . . . . .166 A1
Ryecroft La Dukinfield M34 .100 F7
Worsley M28 . . . . .78 F4
Ryecroft Rd M32 . . . . .96 C1
Ryecroft St OL7 . . . . .84 F1
Ryecroft View M34 . . . . . .100 C8
Ryedale Ave M40 . . . . . . .157 D5
Ryedale Ct M24 . . . . .168 B3
Ryefield M6 . . . . .80 D6
Ryefield Cl WA15 . . . . . . .120 C5
Ryefield Rd M33 . . . . .107 C2
Ryefield St BL1 . . . . .25 A1
Ryefields ■ OL12 . . . . . . .15 D4
Ryefields Dr OL3 . . . . .51 B1
Ryeford Cl WN3 . . . . .151 F6
Ryeland Cl OL16 . . . . .31 B4
Ryelands BL5 . . . . .57 F8
Ryelands Ct BL5 . . . . .57 F8
Rygate Wlk ■ M8 . . . . . . .155 F6
Rylance Rd WN3 . . . . .54 D1
Rylance St M11 . . . . .164 E8
Ryland Cl SK5 . . . . .99 F1
Rylands Ave WN6 . . . . . . .37 A2
Rylands Ct ■ BL5 . . . . . . .162 D6
Rylands Ho ■ M14 . . . . . .110 D8
Rylands St M18 . . . . .99 E6
Rylane Wlk M40 . . . . .157 D5
Rylatt St M33 . . . . .107 F5
Ryley Ave BL3 . . . . .144 B5
Ryley St ■ BL3 . . . . .144 C6
Rylstone St SK9 . . . . .136 F1
Ryleys Sch The SK9 . . . . .136 F1
Rylstone Ave M21 . . . . . . .109 D3
Ryther Gr WN9 . . . . .64 B5
Ryton Ave M18 . . . . .99 C3
Ryton Cl WN2 . . . . .150 B6

S

Sabden Brook Dr WN2 . . . .55 F2
Sabden Cl Bury BL9 . . . . . .27 F7
Heywood OL10 . . . . .29 A2
Manchester M40 . . . . .160 E3
Sabden Rd BL1 . . . . .23 E2
Sabrina St M7 . . . . .81 C8
Sack St ■ SK14 . . . . .101 D5

Sackville Cl OL2 . . . . .32 A1
Sackville St
Ashton-u-L OL6 . . . . .166 B3
■ Bolton BL2 . . . . .148 C7
Manchester M1 . . . . .163 A8
Manchester M3 . . . . .158 E2
■ Rochdale OL11 . . . . . . .30 C2
Sacred Heart RC Inf Sch
M18 . . . . .99 D4
Sacred Heart RC Jun Sch
M18 . . . . .99 D4
Sacred Heart RC Prim Sch
Hindley WN2 . . . . .57 B3
Leigh WN7 . . . . .75 E5
Oldham OL1 . . . . .49 C2
Rochdale OL16 . . . . .31 C6
Westhoughton BL5 . . . . . . .39 F1
Wigan WN6 . . . . .36 F2
Wythenshawe M23 . . . . . .120 F6
Saddle Cl ■ WN5 . . . . .54 F6
Saddle Gr M43 . . . . .84 D3
Saddle St BL2 . . . . .25 B2
Saddleback Cl ■ M28 . . . . .78 B6
Saddleback Cres WN5 . . . .54 B6
Saddleback Rd WN5 . . . . . .54 B7
Saddleworth Bsns Pk OL3 . .50 F4
Saddleworth Mus OL3 . . . .69 B8
Saddleworth Prep Sch
OL4 . . . . .68 C8
Saddleworth Sch OL3 . . . . .51 B1
Sadie Ave M32 . . . . .96 A4
Sadler St Bolton BL3 . . . . .42 A4
Manchester M24 . . . . .46 F1
■ Middleton M24 . . . . . . .47 A1
Saffron Cl WA3 . . . . .90 E8
Saffron Dr OL4 . . . . .49 D2
Saffron Wlk
Partington M31 . . . . .105 F2
■ Wythenshawe M22 . . . .121 D1
Sagar St M8 . . . . .158 E4
Sagars Rd Handforth SK9 . .131 B4
Handforth SK9 . . . . .131 C3
St Aelred's RC High Sch
WA12 . . . . .89 B4
St Agnes CE Prim Sch
Manchester M13 . . . . .98 F3
Oldham OL4 . . . . .68 A4
St Agnes Rd M13 . . . . . . .98 F2
St Agnes St SK5 . . . . .99 F3
St Aidan's Cl Billinge WN5 . .71 E6
Rochdale OL11 . . . . .139 D5
St Aidan's Gr M7 . . . . .81 B6
St Aidans RC Prim Sch
M23 . . . . .109 B1
St Alban's Cl M26 . . . . .44 A1
St Alban's St SK4 . . . . . . .111 C5
St Alban's Ct OL11 . . . . . .139 E6
St Alban's St OL16 . . . . . .139 E6
St Alban's Terr
Manchester M8 . . . . .155 F5
Rochdale OL11 . . . . .139 E6
St Albans Ave
Ashton-in-M WA11 . . . . . . .89 A7
Oldham OL8 . . . . .66 F4
St Albans Cres WA14 . . . .119 C8
St Albans RC High Sch
Manchester M40 . . . . .83 A7
St Aldates SK6 . . . . .112 F2
St Aldwyn's Rd M20 . . . . .110 B5
St Alphonsus RC Prim Sch
M16 . . . . .162 D5
St Ambrose Barlow
RC High Sch M27 . . . . . .79 F7
St Ambrose Barlow
RC Prim Sch M29 . . . . .77 A6
St Ambrose Coll WA15 . . .129 B8
St Ambrose Gdns M6 . . . .154 F2
St Ambrose RC Prim Sch
Manchester M21 . . . . .109 D4
Stockport SK3 . . . . .170 E5
St Ambrose Rd
Oldham OL1 . . . . .49 C1
Tyldesley M29 . . . . .77 A5
St Andrew's Ave
Altrincham WA14 . . . . . . .119 F7
Droylsden M43 . . . . .83 E1
St Andrew's CE Prim Sch
Boothstown M28 . . . . .78 A6
Eccles M30 . . . . .79 E1
Littleborough OL12 . . . . . .15 E4
Ramsbottom BL0 . . . . . . .11 B8
Ramsbottom BL0 . . . . . . .138 B5
Shevington WN6 . . . . .36 F3
St Andrew's Cl
Ramsbottom BL0 . . . . . . .138 C5
Romiley SK6 . . . . .113 B1
St Andrew's Cres WN2 . . . .56 D5
St Andrew's Dr
Heywood OL10 . . . . .29 D1
Shevington WN6 . . . . .36 F2
St Andrew's RC Prim Sch
BL2 . . . . .42 E8
St Andrew's Rd
Radcliffe M26 . . . . .43 F6
Stretford M32 . . . . .96 B2
St Andrew's Sq M1 . . . . . .163 C8
St Andrew's St
Manchester M1 . . . . .163 C8
Radcliffe M26 . . . . .43 F6
St Andrew's View M26 . . . .43 F6
St Andrews Ave M30 . . . . .79 E1

St Andrews Cl
Manchester SK4 . . . . .168 B4
Sale M33 . . . . .107 C1
St Andrews Ct
Altrincham WA15 . . . . . . .119 F3
Stockport SK1 . . . . .112 A1
St Andrews Dr
Heywood OL10 . . . . .46 D8
Leigh WN7 . . . . .76 C5
St Andrews Meth Prim Sch
M28 . . . . .60 D3
St Andrews Over Hulton
CE Prim Sch BL5 . . . . . . .59 A8
St Andrews Rd Bolton BL6 . .40 B7
Gatley SK8 . . . . .122 C1
Manchester SK4 . . . . .168 B4
St Ann St Bolton BL1 . . . . .143 E1
Manchester M2 . . . . .158 F1
St Ann's Pas M2 . . . . .158 F1
St Ann's RC Inf Sch M32 . .96 D2
St Ann's RC Jun Sch M32 . .96 D2
St Ann's RC Prim Sch
OL6 . . . . .166 A3
St Ann's Rd
Hazel Grove SK7 . . . . . . .124 C1
Prestwich M25 . . . . .63 A3
Rochdale OL16 . . . . .31 D8
St Ann's Rd N SK8 . . . . . .122 B2
St Ann's Sq SK8 . . . . .131 C8
St Ann's Sq Gatley SK8 . . .131 C8
Manchester M2 . . . . .158 F1
St Ann's St M27 . . . . .79 E8
St Anne's Ave Oldham OL2 . .48 E3
Salford M6 . . . . .154 E3
St Anne's Cl M7 . . . . .81 A8
St Anne's CE Prim Sch
Oldham OL2 . . . . .48 E3
Sale M33 . . . . .108 D4
Wigan WN6 . . . . .36 D3
St Anne's Cres OL4 . . . . . .68 D5
St Anne's Ct Denton M34 . .100 E6
Sale M33 . . . . .108 C4
Shevington WN6 . . . . .35 F5
St Anne's Dr
Dukinfield M34 . . . . .101 A4
Shevington WN6 . . . . .36 A5
St Anne's Gdns OL10 . . . . .29 F2
St Anne's Hospl WA14 . . .119 A7
St Anne's Prim Sch M34 . .101 A4
St Anne's RC Prim Sch
Droylsden M34 . . . . .100 A7
Manchester M8 . . . . .160 D1
Manchester M8 . . . . .156 A8
Oldham OL4 . . . . .67 C7
St Anne's Rd M34 . . . . . . .101 A4
St Anne's St Bolton BL2 . . .148 A7
Manchester M10,M40 . . . .157 F5
St Annes Mdw BL8 . . . . . . .10 F3
St Annes RC High Sch
M34 . . . . .169 D4
St Annes Rd Denton M34 . .100 F6
Horwich BL6 . . . . .22 C4
St Annes Sq OL3 . . . . .50 F4
St Annes St SK14 . . . . . . .115 A8
St Anns Cl M25 . . . . .63 A3
St Anns St M33 . . . . .108 D4
St Anselm's RC Prim Sch
OL12 . . . . .4 D2
St Anthony's RC Prim Sch
M22 . . . . .121 D1
St Antony's RC High Sch
M41 . . . . .95 F2
St Asaph's Dr M7 . . . . . . .155 F8
St Asaphs Dr OL6 . . . . . . .85 B6
St Aubin's Rd BL2 . . . . . .148 B6
St Aubyn's Rd WN1 . . . . . .37 C4
St Augustine Barlow
RC Sec Sch
OL8 . . . . .66 D3
St Augustine St
Bolton BL1 . . . . .143 D2
Manchester M40 . . . . . . .157 E5
St Augustine's CE Prim
Sch Manchester M40 . . . .80 B8
Pendlebury M27 . . . . .80 B8
St Augustine's Ct ■ SK2 . .25 E1
St Augustine's Rd SK3 . . .123 B8
St Austell Ave M27 . . . . . .77 C8
St Austell Dr Gatley SK8 . .131 B8
Ramsbottom BL8 . . . . .10 F2
St Austell Rd M16 . . . . . . .97 E1
St Austell Rd M16 . . . . . . .97 E1
St Austell's Dr M27 . . . . . .80 C7
St Austells Dr M25 . . . . . .63 B5
St Barnabas CE Prim Sch
M11 . . . . .165 B8
St Barnabas Sq M11 . . . . .165 B8
St Barnabas's Dr OL15 . . .16 A6
St Bartholomew St ■
BL3 . . . . .42 A4
St Bartholomew's
CE Prim Sch OL2 . . . . . .48 E3
St Bartholomew's Dr M5 . .161 C8
St Bede CE Prim Sch
BL3 . . . . .146 C2
St Bede's Ave BL3 . . . . . .146 B2
St Bede's Coll
Development Trust M16 . .97 E3
St Bees Cl Gatley SK8 . . . .122 B3
Manchester M14 . . . . .98 A4
St Bees Rd BL2 . . . . .25 C2
St Bees Wlk ■ M24 . . . . . .46 E2
St Benedict's RC Prim Sch
SK9 . . . . .137 A8
St Benedict's Sq M12 . . . .164 F6
St Benedicts RC Prim Sch
WN2 . . . . .56 C6

St Bernadett's
RC Prim Sch WN6 . . . . . .36 A6
St Bernadette's RC Prim
Sch Brinnington SK5 . . . .112 B4
Whitefield M45 . . . . .44 F2
St Bernard RC Prim Sch
BL3 . . . . .40 E5
St Bernard's RC Inf Sch
M6,M7 . . . . .81 C5
St Bernard's RC Prim Sch
M19 . . . . .110 F6
St Boniface RC Prim Sch
M7 . . . . .81 C4
St Boniface Rd M7 . . . . . . .81 C4
St Brannock's Rd M21 . . . .97 C1
St Brannocks Rd SK8 . . . .132 B7
St Brelades Dr M7 . . . . . .155 F8
St Brendan's RC Prim Sch
BL2 . . . . .25 C7
St Brendan's Rd M20 . . . .110 B7
St Brendan's Rd N M20 . . .110 B7
St Bride St M16 . . . . .162 D5
St Brides Cl BL6 . . . . .22 A4
St Brides Way M16 . . . . . .162 D5
St Brigid's RC Prim Sch
(Jun & Inf) M11 . . . . . . .165 A8
St Catherine's CE Prim Sch
Horwich BL6 . . . . .22 B3
Wigan WN1 . . . . .151 E8
St Catherine's RC Prim Sch
Golborne WA3 . . . . .90 E7
Manchester M20 . . . . .110 C2
St Catherine's Rd M20 . . .110 B7
St Catherines Prep Sch
SK6 . . . . .113 C2
St Chad's Ave SK6 . . . . . .113 C2
St Chad's CE Jun Sch BL9 . .44 F8
St Chad's CE
Saddleworth Prim Sch
OL3 . . . . .69 C8
St Chad's Cl OL16 . . . . . .139 F7
St Chad's Ct OL16 . . . . . .139 F7
St Chad's Gr SK6 . . . . . . .113 C2
St Chad's Rd M20 . . . . . . .110 D7
St Chad's St M4,M8 . . . . .159 A4
St Chads Cres Oldham OL3 . .69 C8
Oldham OL8 . . . . .66 D1
St Chads RC Prim Sch
M8 . . . . .156 A5
St Charles Cl SK13 . . . . . .103 F5
St Charles RC Prim Sch
SK13 . . . . .103 E5
St Charles's RC Prim Sch
M27 . . . . .79 D8
St Christopher's Ave OL6 . .85 E6
St Christopher's Dr SK6 . .113 A2
St Christopher's RC Prim
Sch Ashton-u-L OL6 . . . .85 E6
Romiley SK6 . . . . .113 A2
St Christophers Cl M20 . . .109 F6
St Chrysostoms
CE Prim Sch M13 . . . . . .164 D5
St Clair Rd BL8 . . . . .11 A6
St Clare Terr BL6 . . . . .39 F8
St Clare's RC Inf Sch M9 . .64 C5
St Clare's RC Prim Sch M9 . .64 C5
St Clement's (Egerton)
CE Prim Sch M11 . . . . .161 B7
St Clement's CE Prim Sch
M11 . . . . .99 E7
St Clement's Ct ■
■ Irlam M44 . . . . .94 B3
Oldham OL8 . . . . .153 F5
Prestwich M25 . . . . .63 C4
Wigan WN3 . . . . .150 A5
St Clement's Dr M5 . . . . . .161 B7
St Clement's Rd
Manchester M21 . . . . .109 A8
Wigan WN1 . . . . .37 C4
St Clements St WN3 . . . . . .55 F4
St Clements Fold M41 . . . .95 E2
St Columbo's RC Prim Sch
BL2 . . . . .25 B4
St Cuthbert's RC High Sch
OL16 . . . . .31 B1
St Cuthbert's RC Jun
& Inf Sch WN5 . . . . . . .54 D6
St Cuthbert's RC Prim Sch
M20 . . . . .110 C6
St Cuthberts Fold OL8 . . . .67 A1
St Damian's RC High Sch
M24 . . . . .65 E7
St David's CE Prim Sch
M40 . . . . .38 B7
St David's Cl OL6 . . . . .85 D7
St David's Cres WN2 . . . . .38 B5
St David's Rd SK7 . . . . . .124 C1
St David's Rd M22 . . . . . . .96 A2
St Davids Cl M33 . . . . . . .108 A3
St Davids Rd SK8 . . . . . . .123 A6
St Domingo St OL9 . . . . . .153 E8
St Dominics Mews BL3 . . .146 C3
St Dominics Way M24 . . . .65 A7
St Dunstan's RC Prim Sch
M40 . . . . .83 A8
St Dunston Wlk ■ M40 . . .83 A6
St Edmund Arrowsmith
RC High Sch WN4 . . . . . .73 A2
St Edmund Hall Cl BL0 . . . .11 C4
St Edmund St BL1 . . . . . .145 E7
St Edmund's RC Sch M30 . .80 A4
St Edmund's Rd M40 . . . .157 E6
St Edmunds Dr M24 . . . . . .65 E7

St Edward's RC Prim Sch
Manchester M14 . . . . .98 B2
Oldham OL4 . . . . .67 E7
Wigan WN5 . . . . .54 F7
St Edwards CE Prim Sch
OL11 . . . . .30 C2
St Elisabeth's CE Prim Sch
SK5 . . . . .111 E8
St Elisabeth's Way SK5 . . .111 E8
St Elizabeth Pk M34 . . . . .100 D3
St Elizabeth's
RC Prim Sch M22 . . . . .121 E2
St Elmo Ave SK12 . . . . . . .38 B5
St Elmo Ave SK12 . . . . . .124 D7
St Elmo Pk SK12 . . . . . . .134 C4
St Ethelbert's Ave BL3 . . .144 B5
St Ethelbert's
RC Prim Sch BL3 . . . . .144 B5
St Francis' RC Prim Sch
M12 . . . . .165 B6
St Gabriel Cl WN8 . . . . . . .35 C3
St Gabriel's RC Prim Sch
M24 . . . . .65 D7
St Gabriel's Cl OL11 . . . . . .30 D1
St Gabriel's RC High Sch
BL9 . . . . .1 C4
St Gabriel's Rd Leigh WN7 . .76 E7
Rochdale OL11 . . . . .30 D1
St George's Ave M15 . . . .162 D7
St George's Ave
Sale M33 . . . . .120 A8
Westhoughton BL5 . . . . . . .57 E6
St George's CE Inf Sch
Atherton M46 . . . . .58 B4
Stockport SK2 . . . . .170 F6
St George's CE Jun Sch
SK2 . . . . .170 F6
St George's Cl
Hyde SK14 . . . . .167 D1
Salford M6 . . . . .81 A5
Tyldesley M29 . . . . .76 F8
St George's Cres
Sale M33 . . . . .120 B8
Salford M6 . . . . .80 A3
Walkden M28 . . . . .60 D2
St George's Ct
Altrincham WA14 . . . . . . .119 B7
■ Bolton BL1 . . . . .145 E8
■ Bolton BL1 . . . . .145 F8
Eccles M30 . . . . .96 C1
■ Stretford M32 . . . . .96 C1
Whitefield BL9 . . . . .45 C3
St George's Dr M40 . . . . . .83 B7
St George's Gdns M34 . . .101 A1
St George's Pl
Atherton M46 . . . . .58 B4
Salford M6 . . . . .81 A5
St George's RC High Sch
M28 . . . . .60 C2
St George's Rd
Bolton BL1 . . . . .145 E8
Carrington M31 . . . . .106 D6
Droylsden M43 . . . . .83 F3
Rochdale OL11 . . . . .29 F8
St George's Sq
■ Bolton BL1 . . . . .145 F8
Failsworth OL9 . . . . .65 E3
St George's St Bolton BL1 . .145 F8
Stalybridge SK15 . . . . .86 A3
Tyldesley M29 . . . . .76 F8
St George's Terr BB4 . . . . . .3 A6
St George's Way M6 . . . . . .81 A4
St Georges Dr SK14 . . . . .167 D1
St Georges Rd
Stretford M32 . . . . .96 C1
Whitefield BL9 . . . . .45 C3
St Germain St BL4 . . . . . . .60 C8
St Gilbert's RC Prim Sch
M29 . . . . .79 B2
St Giles Dr SK14 . . . . .167 F2
St Gregory's RC High Sch
M11 . . . . .99 E8
St Gregory's RC Prim Sch
BL4 . . . . .60 E8
St Gregorys Cl BL4 . . . . . .60 E8
St Helen's Coll
Newton Campus WA12 . .89 B4
St Helena Rd BL1 . . . . . . .145 E7
St Helens Cl WA3 . . . . . . .105 B3
St Helens Rd
Bolton BL3,BL5 . . . . .146 B3
Leigh WN7 . . . . .75 C2
St Helier Sq WN9 . . . . . . .110 F5
St Helier's St M7,M8 . . . . .155 F8
St Heliers St BL3 . . . . . . .147 D4
St Herberts Ct OL9 . . . . . .152 B7
St Hilary Gr OL9 . . . . .152 A7
St Hilda's CE Prim Sch
Oldham OL1 . . . . .153 D8
Prestwich M25 . . . . .63 C4
St Hilda's Dr OL1 . . . . . . .109 E1
St Hilda's Rd OL1 . . . . . . .153 D8
St Hilda's Rd Denton M34 . .100 F6
Manchester M16 . . . . .161 C5
Wythenshawe M22 . . . . . .109 D1
St Hilda's View M34 . . . . .100 E5

St Hugh of Lincoln
RC Prim Sch M32 ....95 F3
St Hugh's CE Prim Sch
OL4 ....67 E3
St Hugh's CI WA14 ....119 E8
St Hugh's RC Prim Sch
WA15 ....119 F8
St Ignatius Prim Sch
M13 ....163 C6
St Ignatius Wlk M5 ....161 B8
St Ives Ave SK8 ....123 A6
St Ives Cres M33 ....108 A1
St Ives Rd M14 ....98 B2
St James's Ct OL16,OL2 ....48 C8
St James Ave BL2 ....42 E7
St James CE Prim Sch
Farnworth BL4 ....60 C7
Littleborough OL12 ....15 C6
Manchester M14 ....98 D2
St James CE Sch OL2 ....149 B7
St James CI Glossop SK13 ....116 C7
Salford M6 ....80 B3
St James Cres WN7 ....74 F8
St James Ct
Altrincham WA15 ....119 E4
Cheadle SK8 ....131 F6
Manchester M20 ....122 B8
■ Oldham OL4 ....67 C8
Standish WN6 ....19 D2
St James Dr M33 ....108 A3
St James Gr WN3 ....150 B6
St James Lo SK3 ....124 A4
St James Rd SK4 ....111 B5
St James St Ashton-u-L OL6 ....85 D2
Eccles M30 ....79 E2
Farnworth BL4 ....60 B7
Heywood OL10 ....29 C2
Manchester M1 ....163 A8
Milnrow OL16 ....31 F6
Shaw OL2 ....149 B7
Westhoughton BL5 ....57 F5
St James' Ave BL8 ....27 B4
St James' CE Prim Sch
Ashton-u-L OL6 ....166 C3
Manchester M18 ....99 D5
Wigan WN1 ....54 F5
St James' Ct
■ Hattersley SK14 ....102 D2
Salford M6 ....80 B3
St James' Dr SK9 ....137 A6
St James' Gr ■ OL10 ....29 C2
St James' RC High School
SK8 ....131 F6
St James' Sch
Hattersley SK14 ....102 D2
Orrell WN5 ....53 D4
St James' Rd WN5 ....53 D4
St James' St BB4 ....2 E8
St James' Way SK8 ....131 F6
St James's CE Sch BL4 ....60 A8
St James's Rd WA14 ....107 F1
St James's RC Prim Sch
M6 ....154 F3
St James's Rd M7 ....155 E6
St James's Sq ■ M2 ....158 F1
St James's Terr OL10 ....29 C2
St John Bosco
RC Prim Sch M9 ....65 A3
St John Fisher
& St Thomas More
RC Prim Sch M22 ....121 D4
St John Fisher
RC High Sch WN6 ....36 F2
St John Fisher
RC Prim Sch Denton M34 ....101 B1
Manchester M20 ....47 B3
St John Rigby
RC Sixth Form Coll WN5 ....35 F2
St John Southworth
RC Prim Sch WN4 ....73 D4
St John St Atherton M46 ....58 D3
Dukinfield SK16 ....101 E8
■ Eccles M30 ....79 D1
Horwich BL6 ....22 B3
Irlam M44 ....94 A2
Newton-le-W WA12 ....162 E8
■ Oldham OL4 ....67 E6
St John the Baptist CE Sch
WN2 ....73 D4
St John the Evangelist
RC Prim Sch BL7 ....24 F8
St John Vianney Lower Sch
SK4 ....168 B2
St John Vianney Upper Sch
M16 ....97 B2
St John with St Michael
CE Prim Sch OL12 ....4 E5
St John's (Wingates)
CE Prim Sch BL5 ....39 E3
St John's Ave
Droylsden M43 ....84 B2
Westhoughton BL5 ....39 D3
St John's CE Inf Sch
Failsworth M35 ....83 F8
Leigh WN7 ....75 F6
St John's CE Jun Sch WA5 ....84 A7
St John's CE Mosley
Common Prim Sch M28 ....77 F7
St John's CE Prim Sch
BL9 ....140 F4
Coppull PR7 ....19 D6

St John's CE Prim Sch *continued*
Dukinfield SK16 ....101 E8
Farnworth BL4 ....60 E8
Hindley WN2 ....57 B3
Manchester M13 ....98 E4
Manchester SK4 ....110 E2
Middleton M24 ....47 E6
Radcliffe M26 ....44 B1
Wigan WN5 ....54 B6
St John's CI
Dukinfield SK16 ....101 E8
Romiley SK6 ....113 B2
St John's Ct ■ Abram WN2 ....56 B1
Altrincham WA14 ....119 D3
Hyde SK14 ....167 E1
Manchester M7 ....155 D6
Radcliffe M26 ....44 C2
■ Rochdale OL16 ....31 B6
St John's Dr Hyde SK14 ....167 F3
■ Rochdale OL16 ....31 B6
St John's Gdns OL5 ....68 D2
St John's Ind Est OL4 ....67 E6
St John's PI SK4 ....110 E2
St John's Rd
Altrincham WA14 ....119 D3
Aspull WN2 ....38 B5
Bolton BL6 ....40 B8
Boothstown M28,M29 ....77 E7
Denton M34 ....100 F5
Hazel Grove SK7 ....124 B1
Manchester M13 ....98 F4
Manchester M16 ....97 C4
■ Manchester SK4 ....110 E2
Wilmslow SK9 ....136 E3
St John's St Abram WN2 ....74 B8
Farnworth BL4 ....60 E8
Manchester M7 ....155 D6
Oldham OL9 ....152 C6
Radcliffe M26 ....44 B2
Rawtenstall BB4 ....2 F8
St John's Wlk OL9 ....152 C6
St Johns CE Prim Sch
Rochdale OL12 ....15 B4
Salford M6 ....80 C6
St Johns Ct OL4 ....67 F7
St Johns Sq M3 ....158 D2
St Johns Wlk SK3 ....123 B8
St Johns Wood BL6 ....40 B4
St Joseph & St Bede
RC Prim Sch BL9 ....141 B4
St Joseph St ■ BL1 ....143 D2
St Joseph's Con Ctr
WN8 ....35 B2
St Joseph's Dr
Rochdale OL16 ....31 B4
Salford M5 ....161 B8
St Joseph's RC High School
OL11 ....29 C1
St Joseph's RC Inf Sch
SK5 ....111 E8
St Joseph's RC Jun Sch
Manchester M13 ....98 E4
Reddish SK5 ....111 E8
St Joseph's RC Prim Sch
Adlington PR6 ....21 B8
Bacup OL13 ....3 D8
Bolton BL1 ....142 C1
Heywood OL10 ....29 C1
Irlam M44 ....94 A3
Leigh WN7 ....76 A4
Mossley OL5 ....68 C1
Ramsbottom BL0 ....138 B6
Sale M33 ....108 B4
Salford M5 ....161 B8
Shaw OL2 ....149 B5
Walkden M38 ....60 A5
St Joseph's RC Sch
Horwich BL6 ....22 E1
Reddish SK5 ....111 E8
St Joseph's Wrightington
RC Prim Sch WN6 ....19 A3
St Josephs Ave M45 ....54 F5
St Jude's Jun & Inf Schs
WN3 ....54 F5
St Katherines Rd BL6 ....21 C3
St Kentigern's RC Prim Sch
M14 ....98 A1
St Kilda Ave BL4 ....60 F6
St Kilda's Ave M43 ....83 F3
St Kilda's Dr M7 ....155 C8
St Lawrence Quay M5 ....96 F7
St Lawrence Rd M34 ....101 A3
St Leonard's Ave BL4 ....22 F1
St Leonard's Ct ■ M33 ....107 F4
St Leonard's Sq M24 ....47 A1
St Leonard's St M24 ....47 A1
St Leonards Dr WA15 ....119 F6
St Lesmo Ct SK3 ....123 C7
St Lesmo Rd SK3 ....123 C7
St Lewis RC Prim Sch
WA3 ....91 B1
St Luke St OL11 ....139 F5
St Luke with All Saints
CE Prim Sch M5 ....154 D1
St Luke's Ave WA3 ....90 D8
St Luke's CE Prim Sch
Glossop SK13 ....104 C1
Golborne WA3 ....90 E7
Heywood OL10 ....29 C2
Manchester M14 ....164 D5
St Luke's Dr WN5 ....53 E4
St Luke's Rd Prim Sch M6 ....80 C5
St Luke's Sch M5,M6 ....154 E2

St Lukes CE Prim Sch
OL9 ....152 A7
St Lukes Ct Bolton BL1 ....144 C8
Chadderton OL9 ....152 A7
St Lukes Wlk ■ M40 ....83 A6
St Malachy's RC Prim Sch
M40 ....156 C5
St Malo Rd WN1 ....37 C4
St Margaret Mary's
RC Prim Sch M40 ....65 D3
St Margaret Ward
RC Prim Sch M33 ....107 C2
St Margaret's CE Prim Sch
Heywood OL10 ....29 A1
Manchester M16 ....97 D2
Oldham OL4 ....66 B2
Prestwich M25 ....63 D7
St Margaret's CI
Altrincham WA14 ....119 C4
Bolton BL1 ....144 B8
Prestwich M25 ....63 C6
St Margaret's Gdns OL8 ....66 C2
St Margaret's Rd
Altrincham WA14 ....119 C4
Bolton BL1 ....144 B8
Cheadle SK8 ....123 A6
Failsworth M24,M40 ....65 D3
Prestwich M25 ....63 C6
St Margarets RC Prim Sch
SK13 ....115 D8
St Marie's RC Prim Sch
BL9 ....140 F1
St Mark St SK16 ....166 B1
St Mark's Ave
Altrincham WA14 ....119 A5
Royton OL2 ....49 A4
Wigan WN5 ....54 F7
St Mark's CE Prim Sch
Bury BL9 ....141 A4
Manchester M40 ....160 D3
Romiley SK6 ....113 A4
Worsley M28 ....78 F6
St Mark's Ct OL2 ....49 A4
St Mark's Cres M28 ....60 D1
St Mark's Ct OL9 ....152 B8
St Mark's La M7,M8 ....155 F8
St Mark's RC Prim Sch
M27 ....62 A2
St Mark's Sq ■ BL1 ....140 F4
St Mark's St Bolton BL3 ....145 F5
Reddish M19 ....99 C1
Romiley SK6 ....113 A4
St Mark's View BL3 ....145 F5
St Mark's Wlk BL3 ....147 E4
St Marks CE Prim Sch
WN5 ....54 F6
St Mark's Ave SK4 ....168 C2
St Martin's CE Prim Sch
OL8 ....67 B2
St Martin's Ct
Droylsden M43 ....83 F3
Hyde SK14 ....167 D2
St Martin's Dr M7,M8 ....155 F8
St Martin's Rd
Marple SK6 ....126 A6
Oldham OL8 ....67 B2
St Martin's Sch M33 ....107 E5
St Martin's St OL11 ....30 D1
St Martins Rd M43 ....107 E6
St Mary & St John
RC Prim Sch WN1 ....37 D1
St Mary's Ave Billinge WN5 ....71 C4
Bolton BL3 ....144 B5
Denton M34 ....113 A8
St Mary's CE Prim Sch
Bolton BL3 ....146 A4
Droylsden M43 ....84 B1
Failsworth M40 ....65 C1
Irlam M44 ....105 C5
Manchester M16 ....97 E4
Oldham OL3 ....69 C4
Prestwich M25 ....63 A4
Ramsbottom BL8 ....10 C2
Reddish SK5 ....112 A6
Rochdale OL11 ....31 A4
Sale M33 ....108 A4
Shaw OL2 ....48 F8
Urmston M41 ....95 B4
St Mary's CI Aspull WN2 ....38 B5
Atherton M46 ....58 C2
Rochdale OL16 ....31 B4
Stockport SK1 ....112 A1
St Mary's Crest OL3 ....69 C5
St Mary's Ct Failsworth M40 ....83 B8
Manchester M8 ....63 F1
Prestwich M25 ....63 A4
St Mary's Dr Cheadle SK8 ....122 F6
Oldham OL3 ....69 C5
Reddish SK5 ....111 F6
St Mary's Gate
Manchester M3 ....158 F2
Oldham OL1 ....69 B8
Rochdale OL12,OL16 ....139 E8
Shaw OL2 ....149 B7
St Mary's Hall Rd M8 ....63 F1
St Mary's Hospl M13 ....98 C4
St Mary's Parsonage M3 ....158 F1
St Mary's PI BL9 ....140 E2
St Mary's RC Prim Sch M35 ....83 E6
St Mary's RC High Sch
M29 ....77 A7
St Mary's RC Inf Sch
WA12 ....89 C4
St Mary's RC Jun Sch
WA12 ....89 B3

St Mary's RC Prim Sch
Ashton-u-L OL6 ....85 D4
Denton M34 ....100 E3
Dukinfield SK16 ....101 E6
Glossop SK13 ....116 D8
Horwich BL6 ....22 B4
Horwich BL6 ....22 D2
Littleborough OL15 ....16 A5
Manchester M19 ....111 A8
Marple SK6 ....125 E5
Middleton M24 ....46 E2
Radcliffe M26 ....44 A4
Stockport SK4 ....169 E2
Swinton M27 ....79 F8
St Mary's RC Sch M30 ....79 E1
St Mary's Rd
Altrincham WA14 ....119 C3
Aspull WN2 ....38 C5
Disley SK12 ....135 D5
Dukinfield SK14 ....101 F5
■ Eccles M30 ....79 F2
Failsworth M40 ....83 B7
■ Glossop SK13 ....104 C1
Glossop SK13 ....116 C8
Prestwich M25 ....63 B4
Sale M33 ....107 F5
Walkden M28 ....60 C5
St Mary's St
Manchester M15 ....162 E5
Manchester M3 ....158 F1
St Mary's Way
■ Leigh WN7 ....75 F5
Oldham OL1 ....153 F7
Stockport SK1 ....112 A2
St Marys Cl M25 ....63 A4
St Marys St OL1 ....153 F8
St Matthew's CE Prim Sch
Bolton BL1 ....143 E1
Little Lever BL3 ....43 A3
Stockport SK3 ....170 E8
St Matthew's CE Sch M24 ....47 F2
St Matthew's Ct WN3 ....54 C4
St Matthew's Dr OL1 ....48 A2
St Matthew's RC High Sch
Failsworth M40 ....65 C2
Manchester M9 ....64 D3
St Matthew's Rd SK3 ....170 D8
St Matthew's Terr ■ BL1 ....143 E1
St Matthew's Terr BL1 ....170 D8
St Matthew's Wlk BL1 ....143 E1
St Matthews CE Prim Sch
M32 ....108 C8
St Matthews Ct ■ M32 ....96 C1
St Mawes Ct M26 ....43 C5
St Maxentius CE Prim Sch
BL2 ....25 D5
St Michael's Ave
Atherton M46 ....58 A1
Bolton BL3 ....42 B2
Bramhall SK7 ....132 E8
St Michael's Bamford
CE Prim Sch OL11 ....29 D5
St Michael's CE Prim Sch
Atherton M46 ....58 B2
Bolton BL3 ....42 C3
Middleton M24 ....65 A5
Urmston M41 ....94 F1
St Michael's Ct Eccles M30 ....95 A8
■ Wigan WN1 ....37 E1
St Michael's RC Prim Sch
M45 ....45 B1
St Michael's Rd SK14 ....102 A2
St Michael's Sq
■ Ashton-u-L OL6 ....166 C3
■ Manchester M4 ....159 A3
St Michaels Cl BL3 ....43 F8
St Michaels Gdns M45 ....45 B1
St Modwen Rd M32 ....96 A5
St Monica's RC High Sch
M45 ....63 C3
St Nathaniel's CE Prim Sch
WN2 ....56 B3
St Nicholas Rd WA3 ....75 A1
St Osmund's Dr BL2 ....42 E7
St Osmund's Gr BL2 ....42 E7
St Osmund's RC Prim Sch
BL2 ....42 E7
St Oswald's Rd M19 ....99 B2
St Oswalds Rd M19 ....99 C1
St Ouen Ctr M20 ....60 D3
St Patrick St WN1 ....151 D8
St Patrick's RC High Sch
M4 ....159 C3
St Patrick's RC Prim Sch
Manchester M4,M40 ....159 C3
Rochdale OL16 ....15 A1
Wigan WN1 ....151 D8
St Patricks RC Prim Sch
OL16 ....153 D6
St Patricks Way WN1 ....151 D7
St Paul's Ave WN3 ....54 F4
St Paul's
Catholic High Sch M23 ....121 B4
St Paul's CE Prim Sch
Adlington PR6 ....21 A7
Bolton BL1 ....143 F3
Brinnington SK5 ....112 B4
Bury BL9 ....141 B4
Manchester M20 ....110 B6
Ramsbottom BL0 ....138 C6
Royton OL2 ....48 C3
Stalybridge SK15 ....86 C2
Walkden M28 ....60 F2

St Paul's CE Prim Sch *continued*
Wigan WN3 ....54 F3
St Paul's Ct PR6 ....21 A8
St Paul's Ct M26 ....44 A1
St Paul's Gdns SK14 ....167 E3
St Paul's Hill SK14 ....102 A3
St Paul's Hill Rd SK14 ....167 F2
St Paul's PI ■ BL1 ....142 C3
St Paul's Rd
Manchester M20 ....110 C6
Manchester M25 ....63 C1
Manchester SK4 ....168 B4
St Paul's Sch Bury BL9 ....141 A3
Hyde SK14 ....167 E3
Ramsbottom BL0 ....138 C6
Stalybridge SK15 ....86 C2
Stockport SK1 ....112 A3
St Paul's Villas BL9 ....141 A3
St Pauls CE Prim Sch
Salford M6 ....81 B1
Walkden M28 ....60 E1
St Pauls Ct SK15 ....86 C2
St Pauls Ct Prestwich M25 ....63 C1
Walkden M28 ....60 C5
St Pauls Peel CE Prim Sch
M38 ....59 F5
St Pauls RC Prim Sch
SK12 ....133 E2
St Pauls Rd M28 ....60 E2
St Pauls Trad Est SK15 ....86 C2
St Peter & St Paul's
Prim Sch BL3 ....145 E5
St Peter Smithills Dean
CE Prim Sch BL1 ....142 B4
St Peter's Ave BL1 ....142 A2
St Peter's CE Prim Sch
Ashton-in-M WN4 ....72 F6
Bury BL9 ....141 A4
Farnworth BL4 ....60 D7
Hindley WN2 ....56 C5
Newton-le-W WA12 ....89 E4
Rochdale OL16 ....31 B5
St Peter's CI WA14 ....117 A4
St Peter's Ct M32 ....96 E3
St Peter's Dr SK14 ....167 F2
St Peter's Gate OL14 ....6 B8
St Peter's RC High Sch
WN5 ....53 F7
St Peter's Rd
Hazel Grove SK7 ....124 D1
Middleton M24 ....65 A7
Stalybridge SK15 ....86 A1
Wythenshawe M22 ....121 A3
St Peter's Rd Bury BL9 ....44 F6
Swinton M27 ....79 E8
St Peter's Sq
■ Ashton-u-L OL6 ....166 C3
Rochdale OL16 ....31 B6
St Peter's Terr BL4 ....60 C7
St Peter's Way Bolton BL1 ....145 F8
Bolton BL1,BL2,BL3,BL4 ....142 B4
St Peters CE Jun Sch
WN1 ....75 C5
St Petersgate SK1 ....169 F1
St Philip Howard RC Sch
SK13 ....116 B8
St Philip's Ave BL3 ....147 D4
St Philip's CE Prim Sch
M46 ....58 D2
St Philip's PI M3 ....158 D2
St Philips CE Prim Sch
Manchester M7 ....63 C1
Stockport SK2 ....124 E6
St Phil's Rd M18 ....99 D4
St Philips CE Prim Sch
Manchester M15 ....162 F6
Manchester M7 ....158 D2
St Philips Sq M3 ....158 D2
St Phillip's Dr OL1,OL2 ....48 E1
St Raphael's RC Prim Sch
SK15 ....86 A4
St Richard's RC Jun
& Inf Sch M46 ....58 C4
St Richard's RC Prim Sch
M22 ....99 B3
St Robert's RC Prim Sch
M13 ....98 F3
St Saviour's Com Prim Sch
OL3 ....4 A8
St Saviour's Cty Prim Sch
OL13 ....3 F8
St Saviour's Rd SK2 ....124 C5
St Saviours CE Prim Sch
M26 ....61 C7
St Sebastian's
RC Prim Sch M6 ....81 A5
St Simon St M3 ....158 E3
St Simon's RC Prim Sch
SK7 ....124 E3
St Simons CI SK2 ....124 E3
St Stephen & All
Martyrs CE Inf Sch OL1 ....153 F8
St Stephen & All Martyrs'
CE Prim Sch
BL2 ....148 C5
St Stephen CE Prim Sch
BL4 ....61 A6
St Stephen
Manchester M3 ....158 E2

St Stephen St continued
🟦 Oldham OL1 ....67 A8
St Stephen's Ave
Denton M34 ....100 E8
Wigan WN1 ....37 E2
St Stephen's CE Prim Sch
Bury BL8 ....27 B1
Hazel Grove SK2 ....124 F4
Tyldesley M29 ....77 B6
Wigan WN1 ....37 E2
St Stephen's Cl
Bolton BL2 ....148 C5
Manchester M13 ....164 D5
St Stephen's Gdns
Kearsley BL4 ....61 A6
🔟 Middleton M24 ....47 A2
St Stephen's RC Prim Sch
M43 ....84 A2
St Stephen's Rd WN6 ....19 C1
St Stephens Cl M29 ......77 A5
St Stephens View M43 ....84 A2
St Teresa's RC Prim Sch
Irlam M44 ....105 E8
Little Lever BL3 ....43 A3
Manchester M16 ....97 A3
Orrell WN8 ....35 B1
St Teresa's Rd M16 ....97 A3
**St Thomas (Chequerbent)
CE Prim Sch**
BL5 ....40 B1
**St Thomas Aquinas
RC High Sch** M16 ......97 E1
**St Thomas Aquinas
RC High Sch (Upper Sch)**
M21 ....109 D7
**St Thomas CE Jun
& Inf Sch** WN4 ....73 C3
**St Thomas CE Leesfield
Prim Sch** OL4 ....67 E5
**St Thomas CE Moorside
Prim Sch** OL1 ....49 A6
St Thomas CE Prim Sch
Leigh WN7 ....76 B4
Newton-le-W WN12 ....32 B4
St Thomas CE BB4 ....1 A7
St Thomas Hospl SK3 ...170 E8
**St Thomas More
RC High Sch** Denton M34 .100 F2
Wigan WN5 ....54 F7
**St Thomas More
RC Prim Sch** M24 ......65 A5
**St Thomas of Canterbury
RC Prim Sch**
Bolton BL1 ....144 A8
Manchester M7 ....155 E6
St Thomas Par OL4 ....67 E6
St Thomas St Bolton BL1 .143 D2
Wigan WN1 ....150 C7
🟥 St Thomas St N OL8 ....153 D5
St Thomas St S OL8 ......153 C5
**St Thomas the Martyr
CE Prim Sch** WN8 ....53 B7
**St Thomas'
CE Parochial Sch** SK4 ..111 C6
St Thomas' CE Prim Sch
BL9 ....141 B1
St Thomas' Cl M26 ....44 A3
St Thomas' Cty Prim Sch
M8 ....156 C8
St Thomas' Pl M8 ....159 A4
St Thomas'CE Prim Sch
SK1 ....170 E8
St Thomas's CE Prim Sch
Bolton BL1 ....143 D2
Oldham OL8 ....153 D5
St Thomas's Circ OL8 ...153 D5
St Thomas's Ct WN8 .....53 C7
St Thomas's Pl SK1 .....170 F8
St Veronica's RC Prim Sch
BB4 ....1 B7
**St Vincent de Paul
RC High Sch** M14 ......98 D3
St Vincent St
Altrincham WA14,WA15 ..119 E4
Manchester M4 ....159 C2
St Vincent's RC Inf Sch
WA15 ....119 E5
St Vincent's RC Jun Sch
WA15 ....119 E5
St Vincent's RC Prim Sch
OL12 ....14 A1
St Werburgh's Rd
M21,M16 ....109 C8
**St Wilfred's CE Jun
& Inf Schs** WN6 ....19 F1
St Wilfred's CE Prim Sch
M40 ....83 D5
St Wilfred's Dr OL12 ....14 D4
St Wilfrid's RC Prim Sch
M15 ....162 E6
🟦 St Wilfrid's Rd WN6 ....19 F1
St Wilfrid's Way WN6 ....19 E1
St Wilfrids CE Prim Sch
M22 ....121 E8
St Wilfrids St M15 .....162 E6
St William's RC Prim Sch
WN2 ....151 F7
St Williams Ave BL3 ....147 E3
St Williams' RC Prim Sch
BL3 ....147 E3
**St Willibrord's
RC Prim Sch** M11 ....83 C3
**St Winifred's
RC Prim Sch** SK4 ......168 A2

**SS Aidan & Oswald's
RC Prim Sch** OL2 ....48 E3
**SS Peter & John
RC Prim Sch** M3 ....158 D2
**SS Simon & Jude's
CE Prim Sch** BL3 ....42 A3
Saintsbridge Rd M22 ...121 C2
Salcombe Ave BL2 ....26 D1
Salcombe Cl Sale M33 ..107 E5
Wigan WN1 ....37 E2
Salcombe Gr BL2 ....42 F6
Salcombe Rd
Droylsden M11,M43 ....99 D8
Stockport SK2 ....124 C8
Salcot Wlk 🟩 M40 ......159 C3
Sale Gram Sch M33 .....108 C3
Sale Heys Rd M33 ....107 F3
Sale La M29 ....77 D8
Sale Rd M23 ....109 B2
Sale St OL15 ....16 C6
Sale Sta M33 ....108 B4
Sale Water Pk M33 .....108 E7
Sale West Cty Sec Sch
M33 ....107 D5
Salem Gr OL4 ....67 C6
Sales's La BL9 ....12 B3
Salisbury Way WN3 ......55 A3
Salford App M3 ....158 F2
Salford Art Gall & Mus
M6 ....81 C2
Salford Central Sta M3 .158 E1
**Salford Coll
(Wardley Campus)** M27 ..61 C2
**Salford Coll
(Worsley Campus)** M28 ..60 D1
Salford Crescent Sta M6 .81 B2
Salford Foyer M6 ....154 F3
Salford Quays M5 ....96 F7
Salford Quays Sta M5 ..161 A7
Salford Rd BL5 ....59 C7
Salford St Bury BL9 ....141 A4
Oldham OL4 ....67 C5
Salik Gdns OL11 ....139 F5
Salisbury Ave
Heywood OL10 ....46 C8
Hindley WN2 ....56 E6
Salisbury Cres OL6 ....85 D7
Salisbury Dr
Dukinfield SK16 ....102 A7
Manchester M25 ....63 C2
Salisbury House M3 ....158 E2
Salisbury Rd
Altrincham WA14 ....119 D7
🟥 Ashton-in-M WN4 ......73 A5
Horwich BL6 ....22 F1
Manchester M21 ....97 C1
Manchester M6 ....80 B6
Radcliffe M26 ....43 E5
Salford M30 ....80 A4
Swinton M27 ....79 E7
Urmston M41 ....95 D4
Whitefield M45 ....62 F3
Salisbury St Bolton BL3 .145 D6
Golborne WA3 ....90 A8
Hadfield SK13 ....104 A5
Manchester M14 ....98 A4
Manchester M40 ....47 B1
Reddish SK5 ....111 F8
Shaw OL2 ....48 F8
Salisbury Terr BL3 ....43 C3
Salisbury Way M29 ....77 B8
Salix Ct M6 ....81 A3
Salkeld Ave WN4 ....72 F3
Salkeld St OL11 ....139 F5
Salley St OL15 ....6 C2
Sallowfields WN5 ....53 D5
Salmon Fields OL2 ....48 F3
Salmon St Manchester M4 .159 A2
🟥 Wigan WN1 ....37 E1
Salmsbury Hall Cl BL0 ...11 C4
Salop St Bolton BL2 ....148 A6
Salford M6 ....81 A4
Salop St M40 ....159 C2
Salsted Gr OL10 ....46 E7
Salthill Ave OL10 ....46 E7
Salthill Dr M22 ....121 E1
Saltire Gdns M7 ....155 E8
Saltney Ave M20 ....109 F7
Saltram Cl BL3,M26 ....43 C5
Saltram Rd WN3 ....54 A4
Saltrush Rd M22 ....121 D1
Salts Dr OL15 ....16 A6
Salts St OL2 ....149 B7
Saltwood Gr BL1 ....143 F1
Salutation St 🟥 M15 ...162 F6
Salvin Cl WN4 ....73 D3
Sam Cowan Cl M14 ....98 A3
Sam Rd OL3 ....51 C5
Sam Swire St M15 ......162 F5
Samian Gdns M7 ....81 C5
Samlesbury Cl
Manchester M20 ....109 F3
Shaw OL2 ....48 F7
Sammy Cookson Cl M14 ..98 A3
Samouth Cl M40 ....160 D3

Sampson Sq M14 ....98 A4
Samson St OL16 ....31 C8
Samuel La OL2 ....48 E8
Samuel Laycock Specl Sch
SK15 ....85 F4
Samuel Ogden St M1 ....163 A8
Samuel St Bury BL9 .....141 A3
Failsworth M35 ....83 F8
Hollingworth SK14 ......103 C4
Manchester M19 ....111 B8
Middleton M24 ....47 A2
Rochdale OL11 ....30 C2
Stockport SK4 ....169 D3
Tyldesley M46 ....58 F1
Samwoods Ho WN4 ....73 A5
Sanby Ave M18 ....99 C4
Sanby Rd M18 ....99 C4
Sanctuary Cl M15 ....163 B5
Sanctuary The M15 .....162 E6
Sand Banks BL1 ....24 F6
Sand Beds La BL8,BB4 .....2 B5
Sand Hole La
Rochdale OL11 ....29 E5
Rochdale OL11 ....30 F1
Sand Hole Rd BL4 ....61 A6
Sand St Manchester M40 .159 C4
Stalybridge SK15 ....101 F8
Sandacre Rd M23 ....121 B7
Sandal Ct M40 ....160 E3
Sandal St M40 ....160 E3
Sandbach M30 ....36 F3
Sandbach Dr WN6 ....36 F3
Sandbach Ave M14 ......109 H8
Sandbach Rd Reddish SK5 .99 E2
Sale M33 ....108 F3
Sandbach Wlk SK8 ......123 A4
Sandbank Gdns OL12 ......4 C2
Sandbed La Delph OL3 ....51 A5
Mossley OL5 ....68 C2
Sandbrook Gdns WN5 .....53 D5
Sandbrook Rd WN5 ....53 D5
Sandbrook Way M34 .....101 A5
Sandby Dr SK6 ....126 B8
Sanderling Cl BL5 ....57 D6
Sanderling Dr WN7 ....76 A6
Sanderling Rd
Hazel Grove SK2 ....125 A4
Newton-le-W WA12 ....89 C4
Sanderson Ave M40 .....157 E5
Sanderson Cl M28 ....79 B7
Sanderson Ct M40 ......157 E5
Sanderson La PR7 ....18 A8
Sanderson St Bury BL9 ..141 A3
Leigh WN7 ....75 D5
Manchester M40 ....157 E5
Sanderson's Croft WN7 ...76 A4
Sandersead Dr M9 ....64 E3
Sandfield Cl 🟥 WA3 ....90 E8
Sandfield Cres WA3 ....92 C7
Sandfield Dr BL6 ....40 C6
Sandfield Rd OL16 ....31 B5
Sandford Ave M18 ....99 C4
Sandford Cl 🟥 M18 ....99 D6
Sandford Rd Orrell WN5 ...53 C5
Sale M33 ....108 F3
Sandford St M26 ....44 D4
Sandford Station La SK5 ..99 D2
Sandgate Ave
Droylsden M11 ....83 D2
Kearsley M26 ....61 C7
Sandgate Cl WN7 ....75 F6
Sandgate Dr M41 ....95 C4
Sandgate Rd Oldham OL9 .152 B6
Prestwich M45 ....63 B7
Sandham St BL3 ....147 F4
Sandham Wlk BL3 ....147 F4
Sandheys Gr M18 ....100 F5
Sandheys M34 ....100 E4
Sandhey Gr M18 ....99 E4
Sandhill Cl BL3 ....147 F4
Sandhill La SK6 ....114 E1
Sandhill St SK14 ....102 B1
Sandhill Wlk M22 ....121 B2
Sandhurst Ave M20 ......110 A6
Sandhurst Cl BL8 ....27 B3
Sandhurst Ct BL2 ....42 E6
Sandhurst Dr
Farnworth BL2 ....42 E6
Wigan WN3 ....137 C8
Sandhurst Rd
Manchester M20 ....110 C2
Stockport SK2 ....124 B5
Sandhurston Rd M9 ....64 D1
Sandiacre WN6 ....36 F4
Sandilands Prim
Sch M33 ....120 D8
Sandilands Rd M23 ......120 D7
Sandilea Cl M7 ....63 A1
Sandileigh Ave
Altrincham WA15 ....119 F3
Brinnington SK5 ....112 B4
Cheadle SK8 ....123 A6
Manchester M20 ....110 B4
Sandileigh Dr WA15 .....119 F3
Sandiness Ct 🟥 M33 ...107 F4
Sandiway Bredbury SK6 ..112 F3
Glossop SK13 ....116 F7
Heywood OL10 ....29 E2
Irlam M44 ....94 C2
Stockport SK7 ....123 E2
Sandiway Cl SK6 ....125 F8
Sandiway Dr M20 ....110 A3
Sandiway Pl WA14 ....119 D5
Sandiway Rd
Altrincham WA14 ....119 D6
Handforth SK9 ....131 D5
Sale M33 ....107 F4
Sandling Dr WA3 ....74 A2

Sandmere Wlk 🟩 M9 ......64 E3
Sandon St BL3 ....147 D4
Sandown Ave M5,M6 .....154 E2
Sandown Cl Culcheth WA3 .91 F4
Oldham OL1 ....49 A1
Wilmslow SK9 ....137 D8
Sandown Cres
Little Lever BL3 ....43 A2
Manchester M18 ....99 D3
Sandown Dr
Altrincham WA15 ....129 D6
Denton M34 ....113 B8
Sale M33 ....107 E3
Sandown Gdns M41 ....95 A2
Sandown Rd Bolton BL2 ...25 E3
Hazel Grove SK7 ....125 A2
Stockport SK3 ....123 B8
Whitefield BL9 ....44 F3
Whitefield BL9 ....45 A2
Wigan WN6 ....36 E3
Sandown St M18 ....99 F6
Sandpiper Cl
Dukinfield SK16 ....101 E7
Farnworth BL4 ....59 F7
Newton-le-W WA12 ....89 C4
Rochdale OL11 ....29 F7
Sandpiper Dr SK3 ....170 D6
Sandpiper Rd WN3 ....54 B4
Sandra Dr WA12 ....89 E3
Sandray Cl BL3 ....40 F5
Sandray Gr M5 ....154 E1
Sandridge Cl BL4 ....60 E8
Sandridge Wlk M12 .....164 E6
Sandringham Ave
Denton M34 ....100 B8
Reddish M34 ....100 A3
Stalybridge SK15 ....86 A3
Sandringham Cl
Adlington PR7 ....20 E6
Altrincham WA14 ....118 F1
Wigan WN5 ....54 E5
Sandringham Ct 🟩 SK9 .137 A6
Sandringham Dr
Dukinfield SK16 ....101 F7
Leigh WN7 ....76 E7
Milnrow OL16 ....32 A6
Poynton SK12 ....133 D3
Ramsbottom BL8 ....11 A1
Stockport SK4 ....168 A1
Sandringham Grange M25 .63 E3
Sandringham Rd
Boothstown M28 ....78 A6
Bredbury SK6 ....112 D3
Cheadle SK8 ....123 A3
Hazel Grove SK7 ....124 F2
Hindley WN2 ....56 E4
Hyde SK14 ....113 E7
Sandringham St M18 ......99 C4
Sandringham Way
Royton OL2 ....48 C6
🟥 Wilmslow SK9 ....137 A6
Sands Ave M24,OL9 ....47 D1
Sands Cl SK14 ....102 D1
Sands Wlk SK14 ....102 D1
Sandsend Cl M8 ....155 E5
Sandsend Rd M41 ....95 C3
Sandstone Rd
Milnrow OL16 ....31 F7
Wigan WN4 ....54 E2
Sandstone Way M21 .....109 D6
Sandway WN6 ....36 F4
Sandwell Dr M33 ....108 B6
Sandwich Rd M30 ....79 F3
Sandwich St M28 ....60 D2
Sandwick Cres BL3 ......145 D5
Sandwith Cl WN3 ....55 B2
Sandwood Ave BL3 ....40 E6
Sandy Acre OL5 ....86 C8
Sandy Bank Ave SK14 ...102 D1
Sandy Bank Ct SK14 ....102 D1
Sandy Bank Rd
Edgworth BL7 ....9 D5
Manchester M8 ....155 F8
Sandy Bank Wlk SK14 ...102 D1
Sandy Brow M9 ....64 D2
Sandy Cl BL9 ....44 F4
Sandy Gr Salford M6 ......80 C5
Swinton M27 ....79 A1
Sandy Haven Cl SK14 ...102 D1
Sandy Haven Wlk SK14 ..102 D1
Sandy La Adlington PR7 ...20 F6
Altrincham M23 ....120 E7
Charlesworth SK13 ......115 A4
Dobcross OL3 ....50 F3
Droylsden M43 ....84 C2
Dukinfield SK16 ....101 D8
Golborne WA3 ....75 A1
Golborne WA3 ....89 F8
Irlam M44 ....94 A2
Lymm WA13 ....117 B4
Manchester M21 ....109 C8
Middleton M24 ....64 B6
Orrell WN5 ....53 D4
Prestwich M25 ....63 A2
Reddish SK4,SK5 ....169 E3
Rochdale OL11 ....30 C7
Romiley SK6 ....113 D3
Royton OL2 ....48 D4
Stretford M32 ....96 C1
Tyldesley M29 ....77 A4
Tyldesley M29 ....77 B1
Uppermill OL3 ....51 B2

Sandy La continued
Wilmslow SK9 ....136 E8
Sandy Meade M25 ....63 A3
Sandy Pk WN2 ....57 A6
Sandy Way WN2 ....56 F6
Sandy Wlk 🟥 OL2 ....48 D4
Sandyacre Cl BL5 ....59 A6
Sandybank Cl SK13 ......171 E4
Sandybrook Cl BL8 ....26 F6
Sandycroft Ave 🟩 WN1 ...37 C1
Sandygate Cl M27 ....79 E7
Sandyhill Rd M9 ....64 B3
Sandylands Dr M25 ....63 A1
Sandywob Wlk 🟩 M22 ...121 F3
Sandyway M25 ....63 A3
Sandywell Cl M11 ....99 D7
Sandywell St M11 ....99 D8
Sanfold La M19 ....99 C2
Sangster Ct M5 ....161 A8
Sankey Gr M9 ....64 B3
Sankey St Bury BL9 ......140 D2
Sanky Rd Bolton BL3 ......90 A8
Newton-le-W WA12 ....89 A3
Sankey Valley Ind Est
WA12 ....89 A2
Santiago St M14 ....98 B3
Santley St M12 ....99 A3
Santon Ave M14 ....110 E8
Santon Dr WA3 ....90 E8
Sapling Rd Bolton BL3 ...146 C2
Swinton M27 ....79 D5
Sarah Butterworth Ct 🟥
OL16 ....31 B6
Sarah Butterworth St 🟩
OL16 ....31 B6
Sarah St Bacup OL13 ......4 C8
🟥 Eccles M30 ....79 B1
Edenfield BL0 ....1 E3
Hindley WN2 ....52 B2
Manchester M11 ....164 F8
Middleton M24 ....64 F8
🟥 Oldham OL8 ....66 D2
🟩 Rochdale OL11 ....31 A6
Swinton M27 ....79 B2
Sarah La WN4 ....73 F7
Sargent Dr M16 ....97 E4
Sargent Rd SK6 ....112 D2
Sark Rd M21 ....97 A2
Sarn Ave M22 ....121 D4
Sarnesfield Cl M12 ....99 A4
Sarnia Ct M7 ....155 D7
Sarsfield Ave 🟥 WA3 .....90 D8
Satinwood Cl WN4 ....72 F2
Saturn Gr M6 ....81 C4
Saunton Ave BL2 ....25 F3
Saunton Rd M11 ....99 D8
Sautridge Cl OL11 ....47 D7
Savernake Rd SK6 ....113 C5
Radcliffe BL8 ....42 F7
Saville St Bolton BL2 ....148 A6
Middleton M24 ....65 D7
Savio Way M24 ....65 A6
Saviour CE Prim Sch
M40 ....156 C5
Saviours Terr BL3 ....144 C5
Savoy Ct M45 ....44 E2
Savoy Dr OL2 ....48 D2
Savoy St Oldham OL4 .....67 B5
Rochdale OL11 ....30 C8
Saw St BL1 ....143 E2
Sawley Ave Golborne WA3 .74 D1
Littleborough OL15 ....16 A7
Oldham OL4 ....67 D4
Shevington WN6 ....36 B2
Whitefield M45 ....44 F2
Sawley Cl WA3 ....92 A2
Sawley Dr SK8 ....132 C6
Sawley Rd M40 ....160 E4
Sawpit Brow WA14 ....118 A6
Sawston Wlk M40 ....65 C3
Sawyer Brow SK14 ....167 F4
Sawyer St Bury BL8 ....27 B4
🟩 Rochdale OL12 ....14 F1
Saxbrook Wlk 🟩 M22 ...121 F3
Saxby Ave BL7 ....24 F8
Saxby St M6 ....80 C5
Saxelby Dr M8 ....156 B7
Saxfield Dr M23 ....121 C6
Saxholme Wlk 🟥 M22 ..121 C2
Saxon Ave Dukinfield SK16 .101 D8
Manchester M8 ....64 A2
Saxon Cl BL8 ....27 B2
Saxon Dr Chadderton OL9 .65 E8
Denton M34 ....100 E7
Saxon Hall La Ctr OL16 ...31 C8
🟥 Saxon Ho M16 ....97 D3
Saxon Rd OL5 ....68 D3
Saxon St Denton M34 ....100 F3
Droylsden M43 ....84 E3
Manchester M40 ....160 E3
Middleton M24 ....65 B8
Oldham OL4 ....67 C7
Radcliffe M26 ....43 F3
Saxonholme Rd OL11 .....47 C7
Saxthorpe Cl Sale M33 ..107 D5
Wigan WN3 ....137 C8
Saxthorpe Wlk M12 .....164 E5
Saxwood Ave M9 ....64 D1
Saxwood Cl OL12 ....13 F1
Saxon Fold WA3 ....90 E8
Scafell Cl High Lane SK6 .134 E8
Oldham OL1 ....48 F1
Scafell Dr WN5 ....54 B6
Scafell Gr WN5 ....54 B6

Scalby Wlk **2** M22 . . . . .121 D1
Scale St M5 . . . . .81 A1
Scarcroft Bd M17 . . . . .165 A5
Scardale Ave BL1 . . . . .142 A1
Scarfield Dr OL11 . . . . .13 E1
Scargill Cl M14 . . . . .110 C8
Scargill Rd BL3 . . . . .146 A4
Scarisbrick Ave M20 . . . . . . .110 D3
Scarisbrick Rd M19 . . . . . . .110 F8
Scarisbrick St **3** WN1 . . . . .37 C1
Scarr Ave M26 . . . . .44 C2
Scarr Dr OL12 . . . . .14 F3
Scarr La OL2 . . . . .49 D7
Scarsdale Rd M14 . . . . .98 E4
Scarsdale St M6 . . . . .81 B3
Scarthwood Cl BL2 . . . . .25 E5
Scawfell Ave BL2 . . . . .25 B2
Scawton Wlk M9 . . . . .64 B5
Sceptre Cl WA12 . . . . .89 A3
Schofield Gdns WN7 . . . . . . .75 E3
Schofield Hall Rd OL15 . . . . .16 C1
Schofield La M46 . . . . .57 F3
Schofield Rd
  Droylsden M43 . . . . .84 B1
  Eccles M30 . . . . .79 F2
Schofield St Droylsden M11 . .83 C2
  Failsworth M35 . . . . .83 F8
  Haslingden BB4 . . . . .1 A6
  Heywood OL10 . . . . .29 D1
  Leigh WN7 . . . . .75 E4
  Littleborough OL15 . . . . .16 C6
  Littleborough OL15 . . . . .6 D2
  Manchester M3 . . . . .158 D1
  Milnrow OL16 . . . . .32 A5
  Oldham OL8 . . . . .66 F3
  Radcliffe M26 . . . . .44 B4
  Rawtenstall BB4 . . . . .2 E8
  Rochdale OL11 . . . . .31 A4
  Royton OL2 . . . . .48 D5
Scholars Dr M20 . . . . .110 A7
Scholars Way **15** M24 . . . . .46 F1
Scholefield La WN1 . . . . . . .151 E8
Scholes WN1 . . . . .151 D8
Scholes Bank BL6 . . . . .22 A5
Scholes Cl M7 . . . . .155 F8
Scholes Dr M40 . . . . .65 E2
Scholes La M25 . . . . .63 C3
Scholes St Bury BL8 . . . . .27 C3
  Failsworth M35 . . . . .66 A1
  11 Oldham OL1 . . . . .67 A7
  Oldham OL9 . . . . .66 A4
  Pendlebury M27 . . . . .80 A8
  Rochdale OL11 . . . . .30 C1
Scholes Wlk M25 . . . . .63 B3
Scholey St BL2 . . . . .148 A5
Scholfield Ave M41 . . . . .95 F1
School Ave Ashton-u-L OL6 . .85 D6
  Stretford M32 . . . . .96 F3
  Wigan WN1 . . . . .37 E1
School Brow Billinge WN5 . . .71 E5
  Bury BL9 . . . . .140 E3
  Bury BL9 . . . . .140 F2
  Romiley SK6 . . . . .113 A2
  Worsley M28 . . . . .78 F6
School Cl SK12 . . . . .133 E3
School Court No 1 M4 . . . . . .159 B3
School Cres SK15 . . . . .86 A4
School Ct Bolton BL7 . . . . .8 E2
  Manchester M4 . . . . .159 C2
  Ramsbottom BL0 . . . . .1 D2
  Stockport SK3 . . . . .170 F6
School Dr WN5 . . . . .71 E5
School Gr
  Manchester M20 . . . . .110 D6
  Prestwich M25 . . . . .63 A2
School Gr W M20 . . . . .110 C6
School Hill BL1 . . . . .145 E8
School House Flats **1**
  OL8 .66 C2
School La Aspull WN2 . . . . . . .37 E7
  Bury BL9 . . . . .27 E8
  Carrington M31 . . . . .106 E6
  Cheadle SK8 . . . . .132 A8
  Edgworth BL7 . . . . .9 D8
  Garswood WN4 . . . . .72 C3
  Hollinfare WA3 . . . . .105 A2
  Hyde SK14 . . . . .113 E7
  Irlam M44 . . . . .105 D5
  Irlam M44 . . . . .93 F2
  Manchester M19,M20 . . . . .110 C3
  Manchester M9 . . . . .64 C2
  Mossley SK15 . . . . .86 E7
  Orrell WN5,WN8 . . . . .53 C7
  Orrell WN8 . . . . .35 B3
  Partington WA14 . . . . .118 D5
  Poynton SK12 . . . . .133 F4
  Reddish SK4 . . . . .111 C5
  Rochdale OL16 . . . . .29 C8
  Rochdale OL16 . . . . .139 F7
  Romiley SK6 . . . . .114 B4
  Standish WN6 . . . . .19 D1
  Wigan WN1 . . . . .151 D8
School Mews
  Bramhall SK7 . . . . .132 E7
  Newhey OL16 . . . . .32 B4
School Rd
  Altrincham WA15 . . . . .119 F3
  Eccles M30 . . . . .95 C8
  Failsworth M35 . . . . .83 F7
  Handforth SK9 . . . . .131 D4
  Oldham OL8 . . . . .66 B2
  Sale M33 . . . . .108 A5
  Sale M33 . . . . .108 B5
  Stretford M32 . . . . .96 E3
School St Ashton-in-M WN4 . .73 D5
  Atherton M46 . . . . .58 B2
  Bacup OL13 . . . . .3 B8

School St continued
  Bolton BL7 . . . . .24 F7
  Bury BL9 . . . . .141 B1
  Eccles M30 . . . . .79 B3
  Golborne WA3 . . . . .90 A8
  Hazel Grove SK7 . . . . .124 E2
  Heywood OL10 . . . . .29 C2
  Horwich BL6 . . . . .22 C3
  Ince-in-M WN2 . . . . .151 F7
  Leigh WN7 . . . . .75 E8
  Little Lever BL3 . . . . .43 B3
  Littleborough OL15 . . . . .15 E5
  Manchester M4 . . . . .159 B3
  Manchester M7 . . . . .158 E4
  Newton-le-W WA12 . . . . .89 B3
  Oldham OL3 . . . . .69 B8
  Oldham OL4 . . . . .68 A6
  Oldham OL8 . . . . .153 D5
  Radcliffe M26 . . . . .44 B3
  Ramsbottom BL0 . . . . .138 B5
  Rochdale OL12 . . . . .139 F8
  Tyldesley M29 . . . . .76 F7
  Tyldesley M29 . . . . .76 F8
  Westhoughton BL5 . . . . .57 E8
  Wigan WN1 . . . . .151 D8
School Street Ind Est
  SK7 . . . . .124 E2
School Terr Golborne WA3 . . .90 A8
  Whitworth OL12 . . . . .4 F2
School View BL7 . . . . .9 D8
School Way WN5 . . . . .54 C6
School Wlk M16 . . . . .162 D5
Schoolhouse M17 . . . . .96 D5
Schools Hill SK8 . . . . .122 D3
Schools Rd M18 . . . . .99 E5
Schoolside La M24 . . . . .64 C7
Schwabe St M24 . . . . .64 C8
Scobell St BL8 . . . . .27 A5
Scoles Prec WN1 . . . . .151 D8
Score St M11 . . . . .83 A1
Scorton Ave BL2 . . . . .42 F7
Scorton St **15** BL1 . . . . . . .144 C8
Scorton Wlk **28** M40 . . . . .65 D2
Scot La Aspull BL6,WN2 . . . . .38 E6
  Shevington WN5,WN6 . . . . . .36 E1
  Wigan WN5 . . . . .54 F7
Scot Lane End CE Prim Sch
  BL6 .38 E4
Scot Lane Prim Sch WN5 . . . .54 F7
Scotforth Cl M15 . . . . .162 E7
Scotia Wlk **1** WA3 . . . . .90 F8
Scotland M4 . . . . .159 A3
Scotland Hall Rd M40 . . . . . . .83 C4
Scotland La BL9 . . . . .28 D8
Scotland Pl BL0 . . . . .138 C6
Scotland St
  Ashton-u-L OL6 . . . . .166 C2
  Failsworth M40 . . . . .83 C5
Scott Ave Bury BL9 . . . . .44 F6
  Eccles M30 . . . . .79 C3
  Hindley WN2 . . . . .56 A6
  Manchester M21 . . . . .97 B2
Scott Cl SK5 . . . . .169 F4
Scott Dr SK6 . . . . .126 B8
Scott Gate M34 . . . . .100 E7
Scott Ho Manchester M19 . . . .99 A2
  Walsden OL14 . . . . .6 A8
Scott House
  (Childrens Orthopaedic)
  Hospl OL11 . . . . .29 D8
Scott Rd Denton M34 . . . . . .100 E1
  Droylsden M43 . . . . .84 B1
  Golborne WA3 . . . . .74 D2
  Prestwich M25 . . . . .62 F3
Scott St Kearsley M26 . . . . . . .61 D7
  Leigh WN7 . . . . .75 D8
  Oldham OL8 . . . . .153 F5
  Salford M6 . . . . .81 C4
  Tyldesley M29 . . . . .77 C4
  Walsden OL14 . . . . .6 A8
  Wigan WN6 . . . . .37 B1
Scott Wlk WA12 . . . . .89 C1
Scottfield OL8 . . . . .153 F5
Scottfield Rd OL8 . . . . .153 F5
Scottia Rd M30 . . . . .95 C8
Scotts Ind Est OL16 . . . . .31 A6
Scout Dr M23 . . . . .120 F4
Scout Rd Bolton BL1,BL7 . . . .24 B7
  Edenfield BL0 . . . . .2 A2
Scout View BL8 . . . . .27 A6
Scovell St M7 . . . . .155 D6
Scowcroft La OL2 . . . . .149 A6
Scowcroft St **21** BL2 . . . . . .25 B1
Scroggins La M31 . . . . .105 F4
Scropton St M40 . . . . .157 D6
Seabright Wlk **17** M11 . . . .160 F1
Seabrook Cres M41 . . . . .95 D4
Seabrook Rd M40 . . . . .83 C4
Seacombe Ave M14 . . . . .98 A1
Seacombe Gr SK3 . . . . .123 B8
Seaford Rd Bolton BL2 . . . . . .25 E6
  Salford M6 . . . . .81 B4
Seaford Wlk
  Manchester M9 . . . . .64 C3
  Oldham OL9 . . . . .152 B6
Seaforth Ave M46 . . . . .58 A3
Seaforth Rd BL1 . . . . .24 E5
Seaham Dr BL8 . . . . .27 C5
Seaham Wlk **5** M14 . . . . . . .98 B3
Seal Rd SK7 . . . . .133 A7
Sealand Cl M33 . . . . .108 E2
Sealand Dr M30 . . . . .95 A8
Sealand Ho M6 . . . . .63 C5
Sealand Rd M23 . . . . .108 E2
Sealand Way SK9 . . . . .131 D4
Seale Ave M34 . . . . .100 D7
Sealey Wlk M40 . . . . .160 E4

Seaman Way WN2 . . . . .56 A6
Seamon's Dr WA14 . . . . .119 A6
Seamon's Rd WA14 . . . . .119 A6
Seamons Wlk WA14 . . . . .119 B5
Searby Rd M18 . . . . .99 B4
Searness Rd M24 . . . . .46 D2
Seascale Ave M11 . . . . .83 B3
Seascale Cres WN1 . . . . .37 C3
Seascales Wlk **6** WN7 . . . . .46 E2
Seathwaite Cl M29 . . . . .77 A7
Seathwaite Rd BL4 . . . . .59 F7
Seathwaite Wlk M18 . . . . . . .165 C5
Seatoller Cl OL2 . . . . .48 E4
Seatoller Dr M24 . . . . .46 C1
Seatoller Pl WN5 . . . . .54 B7
Seaton Cl SK7 . . . . .124 D1
Seaton Mews OL7 . . . . .84 F4
Seaton Rd BL1 . . . . .142 C2
Seaton Way M14 . . . . .98 A4
Sebastopol Wlk **2** M4 . . . .159 C2
Second Ave Atherton M46 . . . .58 D4
  Bolton BL1 . . . . .144 B7
  Bury BL9 . . . . .28 D4
  Droylsden M11 . . . . .83 E8
  Little Lever BL3 . . . . .42 F4
  Mossley SK15 . . . . .86 E5
  Oldham OL8 . . . . .66 D1
  Poynton SK12 . . . . .133 D1
  Stretford M27 . . . . .96 D5
  Swinton M27 . . . . .79 D6
  Tyldesley M29 . . . . .77 B4
  Wigan WN6 . . . . .37 A2
Second St BL1 . . . . .23 F4
Section St **6** BL3 . . . . .145 F6
Sedan Cl M5 . . . . .161 A8
Seddon Cl M46 . . . . .58 C3
Seddon Gdns M26 . . . . .61 A8
Seddon House Dr WN6 . . . . . .36 E1
Seddon La M26 . . . . .61 A8
Seddon Rd M44 . . . . .105 D7
Seddon St Little Lever BL3 . . .43 B3
  Manchester M12 . . . . .99 B2
  Radcliffe M26 . . . . .44 A3
  Walkden M38 . . . . .59 F5
  Westhoughton BL5 . . . . .39 E3
Seddons Ave BL8 . . . . .44 A8
Sedge Ct SK5 . . . . .112 A8
Sedgeborough Rd M16 . . . . . .97 F3
Sedgefield Cl BL1 . . . . .142 B3
Sedgefield Dr Bolton BL1 . . .142 B3
  Wigan WN6 . . . . .36 E5
Sedgefield Pk **4** OL4 . . . . .67 D6
Sedgefield Rd M26 . . . . .43 F1
Sedgefield Wlk **8** M23 . . . .108 F2
Sedgeford Cl SK9 . . . . .131 D1
Sedgeford Rd M40 . . . . .157 D5
Sedgely Wn2 . . . . .150 C7
Sedgemoor Cl SK8 . . . . .123 B2
Sedgemoor Vale BL2 . . . . .25 F2
Sedgemoor Way OL1 . . . . . . .153 E7
Sedgley Ave
  Manchester M25 . . . . .63 C2
  Prestwich M25 . . . . .62 F5
  Rochdale OL16 . . . . .31 B4
Sedgley Cl M24 . . . . .65 C7
Sedgley Dr BL5 . . . . .57 E5
Sedgley Park
  Com Prim Sch M25 . . . . .63 C2
Sedgley Park Rd M25 . . . . . . .63 C2
Sedgley Park Trad Est
  M25 .63 B1
Sedgley Rd M8 . . . . .156 A8
Sedgley St M24 . . . . .64 F8
Sedgwick Cl M46 . . . . .58 E3
Sedwyn St **7** WN1 . . . . .37 E1
Seed St BL1 . . . . .144 C7
Seedley Ave M38 . . . . .60 B5
Seedley Park Rd M6 . . . . . . .154 E2
Seedley Prim Sch M6 . . . . . .154 E2
Seedley Rd M6 . . . . .154 F3
Seedley St M14 . . . . .98 B3
Seedley Terr M6 . . . . .154 E3
Seedley View Rd M6 . . . . . . .154 E2
Seel St M15 . . . . .162 F5
Sefton Ave Atherton M46 . . . .58 C5
  Orrell WN5 . . . . .53 D5
Sefton Cl Manchester M13 . .163 B6
  Middleton M24 . . . . .64 E8
  Orrell WN5 . . . . .53 D5
Sefton Cres M33 . . . . .108 B6
Sefton Ct BL1 . . . . .145 E8
Sefton Dr Bury BL9 . . . . .28 A6
  Eccles M30 . . . . .79 A6
  Handforth SK9 . . . . .131 C2
  Swinton M27 . . . . .79 D6
  Tyldesley M29 . . . . .77 A6
Sefton Fold Gdns WN5 . . . . . .71 D5
Sefton La M33 . . . . .22 D1
Sefton Rd Ashton-in-M WN4 . .72 F6
  Bolton BL1 . . . . .142 B2
  Manchester M21 . . . . .109 B8
  Middleton M24 . . . . .64 E8
  Orrell WN5 . . . . .53 D5
  Sale M33 . . . . .108 B5
  Swinton M27 . . . . .61 F1
  Wigan WN3 . . . . .54 F4
Sefton St Bury BL9 . . . . .27 F6
  Glossop SK13 . . . . .116 C8
  Heywood OL10 . . . . .29 E1
  Leigh WN7 . . . . .75 F5
  Manchester M8 . . . . .156 A8
  Oldham OL9 . . . . .66 B2

Sefton St continued
  Radcliffe M26 . . . . .44 C1
  Rochdale OL11 . . . . .139 F5
  Whitefield M45 . . . . .62 F7
Sefton View WN5 . . . . .53 D5
Selborne Rd M21 . . . . .97 B2
Selbourne Cl Bolton BL5 . . . . .40 A1
  Reddish SK5 . . . . .99 E2
Selbourne St WN7 . . . . .75 F7
Selby Ave Chadderton OL9 . . .47 F1
  Whitefield M45 . . . . .44 F2
Selby Cl Milnrow OL16 . . . . . .31 E6
  Poynton SK12 . . . . .133 D5
  Radcliffe BL9 . . . . .44 D5
  Stretford M32 . . . . .96 A3
Selby Dr Salford M6 . . . . .80 B3
  Urmston M41 . . . . .94 F5
  Urmston M41 . . . . .95 A5
  Wigan WN3 . . . . .54 E4
Selby Gdns SK8 . . . . .132 C6
Selby Rd Middleton M24 . . . . .46 F3
  Stretford M32 . . . . .96 A3
Selby St Manchester M11 . . .165 A8
  Reddish SK4 . . . . .169 D4
  Rochdale OL16 . . . . .31 B8
Selby Wlk BL8 . . . . .26 F1
Selden St OL8 . . . . .153 D5
Selham Wlk M13 . . . . .163 C7
Selhurst Ave M11 . . . . .83 C2
Selkirk Ave Garswood WN4 . . .72 D4
  Oldham OL8 . . . . .66 D4
Selkirk Dr M9 . . . . .64 F3
Selkirk Gr WN5 . . . . .54 C8
Selkirk Pl OL10 . . . . .29 A1
Selkirk Rd Bolton BL1 . . . . . . .24 D5
  Oldham OL9 . . . . .66 A4
Sellars Sq M43 . . . . .100 A8
Sellers Way OL9 . . . . .66 A3
Selsby Ave M30 . . . . .79 B2
Selsey Ave Cheadle SK3 . . . .122 F7
  Sale M33 . . . . .107 F3
Selsey Dr M20 . . . . .122 C8
Selside WN3 . . . . .55 B2
Selside Wlk M14 . . . . .110 C8
Selstead Rd M22 . . . . .121 C1
Selston Rd M9 . . . . .64 B5
Selwood Wlk **8** M9 . . . . . .157 D7
Selworth Ave M33 . . . . .108 E4
Selworth Cl **5** WA15 . . . . .119 E6
Selworthy Rd M16 . . . . .97 E4
Selwyn Ave
  Manchester M9 . . . . .157 D8
  Manchester M9 . . . . .64 D1
Selwyn Cl
  Newton-le-W WA12 . . . . .89 B3
  Oldham OL8 . . . . .153 E5
Selwyn Dr SK8 . . . . .132 C7
Selwyn St Bolton BL2 . . . . . .148 A6
  Leigh WN7 . . . . .75 F6
  Oldham OL8 . . . . .153 E5
Senecar Cl WN2 . . . . .38 B2
Senior Ave M14 . . . . .110 E7
Senior Rd Eccles M30 . . . . . . .94 F8
  Eccles M30 . . . . .95 A8
Senior St M3 . . . . .158 E3
Sennicar La Aspull WN2 . . . . .37 C5
  Wigan WN1 . . . . .37 C5
Sepal Cl SK5 . . . . .100 A1
Sephton Ave WA3 . . . . .91 E3
Sephton St WN3 . . . . .151 F6
Sepia Gr M24 . . . . .46 F1
Sequoia St M9 . . . . .157 E8
Sergeants La M45 . . . . .62 F6
Serin Cl Hazel Grove SK2 . . .124 F5
  Newton-le-W WA12 . . . . .89 C3
Service St SK3 . . . . .123 B8
Set St SK15 . . . . .85 E1
Settle Cl BL8 . . . . .26 F2
Settle St Bolton BL3 . . . . . . .147 E3
  Little Lever BL3 . . . . .43 C3
Settstones La OL3 . . . . .51 D1
Seven Acres La OL12 . . . . . . .14 C4
Seven Oaks WN7 . . . . .76 A6
Seven Stars Rd WN3 . . . . . . .150 A7
Seven Stiles Dr SK6 . . . . .125 E7
Sevenacres OL3 . . . . .50 F5
Sevenoaks Ave
  Manchester SK4 . . . . .111 A5
  Urmston M41 . . . . .95 D4
Sevenoaks Dr Bolton BL3 . . .147 E3
  Pendlebury M27 . . . . .80 A6
Sevenoaks Rd SK8 . . . . .122 B4
Sevenoaks Wlk **1** M13 . . .163 B6
Sevenside Trad Est M17 . . . . .96 B5
Seventh Ave OL8 . . . . .66 D1
Severn Cl
  Altrincham WA14 . . . . .119 C6
  Billinge WN5 . . . . .71 D3
  Bury BL9 . . . . .27 F7
Severn Dr Bramhall SK7 . . . .132 C6
  Hindley WN2 . . . . .57 C3
  Milnrow OL16 . . . . .32 A6
Severn Rd Ashton-in-M WN4 . .73 E5
  Chadderton OL9 . . . . .65 F8
  Culcheth WA3 . . . . .91 F2
  Oldham OL8 . . . . .66 C3
  Wigan WN5 . . . . .54 D6
Severn St M11 . . . . .99 D8
Severn Way Kearsley BL4 . . . .61 B8
  Reddish SK5 . . . . .111 F5
Seville St Oldham OL2 . . . . . . .48 E2
  Shaw OL2 . . . . .149 A5
Seville's Bldgs OL15 . . . . .16 C5
Sewerby St M16 . . . . .97 F4
Sexa St M11 . . . . .99 D8
Sexton St Heywood OL10 . . . .29 C2
  Tintwistle SK13 . . . . .103 F7

Seymour Ave M11 . . . . .83 D2
Seymour Cl M16 . . . . .161 C5
Seymour Ct
  Manchester M7 . . . . .155 F8
  Manchester M7 . . . . .110 E2
  2 Radcliffe M26 . . . . .44 B3
Seymour Dr BL2 . . . . .25 C6
Seymour Gr
  Altrincham WA15 . . . . .120 A5
  Farnworth BL4 . . . . .42 A1
  Manchester M16 . . . . .97 B3
  Marple SK6 . . . . .125 E6
  Rochdale OL16 . . . . .31 B3
  Sale M33 . . . . .108 B4
Seymour Ho **10** SK9 . . . . .131 E1
Seymour Park Jun Sch
  M16 .97 B4
Seymour Park Prim Sch
  M16 .97 B4
Seymour Rd Bolton BL1 . . . . .143 F3
  Cheadle SK8 . . . . .132 A8
  Manchester M7,M8 . . . . .63 F1
  Stockport SK2 . . . . .124 B5
Seymour Rd S M11 . . . . .83 D2
Seymour Road Inf Sch
  M11 .83 D1
Seymour Road Jun Sch
  M11 .83 D1
Seymour St Bolton BL2 . . . . . .25 C6
  Denton M34 . . . . .100 D4
  Heywood OL10 . . . . .29 C1
  Manchester M18 . . . . .99 D6
  Radcliffe M26 . . . . .44 B3
Seymour Wlk **4** M26 . . . . . .44 B3
Shackleton Cl M40 . . . . .83 C4
Shackleton Gr BL1 . . . . .23 E2
Shackleton St M30 . . . . .79 C3
Shackliffe Rd M40 . . . . .65 B2
Shaddock Ave OL12 . . . . .13 F1
Shade Ave OL4 . . . . .67 F5
Shade Terr SK6 . . . . .134 F7
Shadowmoss Rd M22 . . . . . .130 E8
Shadows La OL3 . . . . .68 E4
Shadows Mews OL5 . . . . .68 E4
Shadwell Gr WN7 . . . . .75 C8
Shadwell St E OL10 . . . . .29 E3
Shadwell St W OL10 . . . . .29 D3
Shady La Altrincham M23 . . .120 D7
  Bolton BL7 . . . . .25 B7
Shady Oak Rd SK2 . . . . .124 F6
Shaftesbury Ave
  Altrincham M23,WA15 . . . . .120 C6
  Bramhall SK8 . . . . .123 C1
  Eccles M30 . . . . .95 C8
  Horwich BL6 . . . . .39 F8
  Littleborough OL15 . . . . .15 F3
Shaftesbury Cl BL6 . . . . .39 F8
Shaftesbury Dr OL12 . . . . . . .15 D6
Shaftesbury Gdns M41 . . . . . .94 F6
Shaftesbury Ho **4** M6 . . . .154 F3
Shaftesbury Rd
  Cheadle SK3 . . . . .123 B6
  Manchester M8 . . . . .156 A7
  Swinton M27 . . . . .79 F8
Shafton Wlk **22** M40 . . . . . .65 D2
Shaftsbury Cl **20** BL1 . . . .143 E1
Shaftsbury Ct **11** M15 . . . .120 D6
Shaftsbury Dr OL12 . . . . .15 D6
Shaftsbury Gdns M41 . . . . . . .94 F6
Shaftsbury Rd WN6 . . . . .36 F3
Shakerley CE Prim Sch
  M29 .58 F4
Shakerley Rd M29 . . . . .58 F4
Shakespeare Ave Bury BL9 . . .44 F6
  Denton M34 . . . . .112 F8
  Radcliffe M26 . . . . .43 E4
  Stalybridge SK15 . . . . .86 E4
Shakespeare Cres
  Droylsden M43 . . . . .84 A2
  Eccles M30 . . . . .79 D2
Shakespeare Dr SK8 . . . . . . .122 F6
Shakespeare Gr WN3 . . . . . . .55 A4
Shakespeare Rd
  Bredbury SK6 . . . . .112 F2
  Droylsden M43 . . . . .84 A2
  Oldham OL1 . . . . .49 C2
  Prestwich M25 . . . . .62 F2
  Swinton M27 . . . . .79 E8
Shakespeare Wlk M13 . . . . .163 C6
Shakleton Ave M9 . . . . .65 A3
Shalbourne Rd M28 . . . . .60 D3
Shaldon Dr M40 . . . . .83 B8
Shalfleet Cl BL2 . . . . .25 E5
Shalford Dr M22 . . . . .130 D8
Shandon Ave M22 . . . . .109 D1
Shanklin Ave **3** M41 . . . . . .95 C2
Shanklin Cl Denton M34 . . . .113 B8
  Manchester M21 . . . . .97 A1
Shanklin Ho **4** M21 . . . . . . .97 A1
Shanklin Wlk BL3 . . . . .148 C5
Shanley Ct OL9 . . . . .152 B8
Shannon Cl OL10 . . . . .29 A3
Shannon Rd M22 . . . . .121 E4
Shap Ave WA15 . . . . .120 D5
Shap Cres M28 . . . . .60 F1
Shap Dr M28 . . . . .60 F1
Shap Gate WN5 . . . . .54 B7
Shapwick Cl **9** M9 . . . . . . .157 D8
Sharcott Cl **9** M16 . . . . . . .97 F4
Sharcott Wlk **3** M16 . . . . . .97 F4
Shardlow Cl M40 . . . . .160 D4
Shared St WN1 . . . . .151 D7

Shargate CI SK9 .....131 C1
Sharman St BL3 .....148 B5
Sharnbrook Wlk
 [9] Bolton BL2 .....25 B1
 [4] Manchester M8 .....63 E2
Sharnford CI BL2 .....148 A6
Sharnford Sq M12 .....165 A6
Sharon Ave OL4 .....68 E5
Sharon CI OL7 .....84 E1
Sharon Sq WN2 .....73 F8
Sharp St Bury BL8 .....27 B4
 Ince-in-M WN3 .....151 E6
 Manchester M4 .....159 B3
 Middleton M24 .....65 A8
 Prestwich M25 .....63 A4
 Walkden M28 .....60 E3
Sharples Ave BL1 .....24 E6
Sharples Com Prim Sch
 BL1 .....25 A5
Sharples Com Sec Sch
 BL1 .....24 F5
Sharples Dr BL8 .....27 A3
Sharples Gn BL7 .....9 D6
Sharples Hall [9] BL1 .....24 F6
Sharples Hall Dr BL1 .....24 F6
Sharples Hall Fold BL1 .....24 E5
Sharples Hall Mews BL1 .....24 F6
Sharples Hall St OL4 .....67 D8
Sharples Mdw BL7 .....9 D6
Sharples Pk BL1 .....143 D4
Sharples St SK4 .....169 E3
Sharraw Wlk M9 .....157 E7
Sharrington Dr M23 .....120 E6
Sharrow Wlk M9 .....157 D7
Sharston Ind Area M22 .....121 E7
Sharston Rd M22 .....121 E7
Shaving La M28 .....60 D1
Shaw & Crompton Sta
 OL2 .....149 C6
Shaw Ave SK14 .....113 F8
Shaw Hall Ave SK14 .....102 B5
Shaw Hall Bank Rd BL3 .....68 F5
Shaw Hall CI OL3 .....68 F5
Shaw Head Dr M35 .....83 F6
Shaw Heath SK2,SK3 .....170 E7
Shaw Ho Atherton M46 .....58 D4
 Farnworth BL4 .....60 D7
Shaw La Hadfield SK13 .....171 F3
 Littleborough OL15,OL16 .....16 A1
Shaw Moor Ave SK15 .....86 C1
Shaw Rd Horwich BL6 .....22 B5
 Manchester SK4 .....168 B4
 Newhey OL16 .....32 B3
 Oldham OL1 .....67 A8
 Royton OL16 .....31 B1
 Royton OL2 .....48 F4
Shaw Rd S SK3 .....170 E6
Shaw St Ashton-in-M WN4 .....73 B5
 Ashton-u-L OL6 .....85 D3
 Bolton BL3 .....145 E5
 Bury BL9 .....141 B3
 Culcheth WA3 .....92 A3
 Farnworth BL4 .....42 D2
 Glossop SK13 .....116 C8
 Manchester M3 .....158 F3
 Mottram-in-L SK14 .....103 A4
 Oldham OL1 .....153 F8
 Oldham OL3 .....69 B6
 Oldham OL4 .....68 A6
 Rochdale OL12 .....15 B2
 Royton OL2 .....48 E4
 Wigan WN1 .....37 C1
Shaw Terr [8] SK16 .....166 C1
Shaw The SK13 .....171 F3
Shaw's Rd WA14 .....119 D4
Shawbrook Ave M28 .....78 B8
Shawbrook Rd M19 .....111 A5
Shawbury CI BL6 .....21 D1
Shawbury Gr M33 .....107 F2
Shawbury Rd M23 .....121 B4
Shawbury St M24 .....65 C7
Shawclough CI OL12 .....14 D3
Shawclough Com Prim Sch
 OL12 .....14 E3
Shawclough Dr OL12 .....14 D3
Shawclough Rd OL12 .....14 D3
Shawclough Way OL12 .....14 D3
Shawcroft CI OL2 .....149 A5
Shawcross Fold SK1 .....169 F2
Shawcross La M22 .....121 E8
Shawcross St Hyde SK14 .....113 F8
 Salford M6 .....154 F1
 Stockport SK1 .....124 A8
Shawdene Rd M22 .....121 D8
Shawe Hall Ave M41 .....107 A8
Shawe Hall Cres M41 .....107 A8
Shawe Rd M41 .....95 A2
Shawe View M41 .....95 A2
Shawes Dr PR6 .....21 C7
Shawfield CI M14 .....110 A8
Shawfield CI SK2 .....124 D5
Shawfield La Rochdale OL12 .....13 F2
 Rochdale OL12 .....14 A2
Shawfield Rd SK13 .....171 F3
Shawfields SK15 .....86 D3
Shawfold OL2 .....149 B7
Shawford Cres M40 .....65 C2
Shawford Rd M40 .....65 C2
Shawgreen CI M15 .....162 D6
Shawgrove Sch M20 .....110 B5
Shawheath CI M15 .....162 D6
Shawhill Wlk M40 .....160 E2
Shawlea Ave M19 .....110 E6
Shaws Fold SK9 .....130 F3
Shaws La OL3 .....69 C7

Shay Ave WA15 .....120 E1
Shay La WA15 .....120 D1
Shayfield Ave
 Chadderton OL9 .....65 E8
 Wythenshawe M22 .....121 D5
Shayfield Dr M22 .....121 D6
Shayfield Rd M22 .....121 D5
Sheader Dr M5 .....80 C2
Sheaf Field Wlk M26 .....44 A4
Sheard Ave OL6 .....85 D6
Sheardhall Ave SK12 .....135 E5
Shearer Way M6,M27 .....80 E7
Shearing Ave OL12 .....13 F1
Shearsby CI M15 .....162 E5
Shearwater Ave M29 .....77 A8
Shearwater Dr
 Walkden M28 .....60 C3
 Westhoughton BL5 .....57 D6
Shearwater Gdns M30 .....95 A8
Shearwater Rd SK2 .....125 A5
Shed St OL12 .....4 D1
Sheddings The BL3 .....42 A4
Sheep Gap OL12 .....14 B1
Sheep Gate Dr BL8 .....26 E5
Sheepfoot La
 Manchester M25,M8 .....63 E3
 Oldham OL1 .....48 D1
Sheerness St M18 .....99 D5
Sheffield Rd Glossop SK13 .....104 F1
 Hyde SK14 .....102 A3
 Hyde SK14 .....167 F4
Sheffield St
 Manchester M1 .....163 C8
 Stockport SK4 .....169 E3
Shefford CI M11 .....164 F8
Shefford Cres WN3 .....54 C2
Sheiling Ct WA14 .....119 C4
Sheilings The WA3 .....90 F8
Shelbourne Ave BL1 .....142 B1
Shelden Mews SK13 .....171 D1
Shelderton CI [8] M40 .....83 A7
Sheldon Ave Standish WN6 .....19 E2
 Urmston M41 .....95 B2
Sheldon CI Farnworth BL4 .....42 B2
 [8] Gamesley SK13 .....171 D1
 Partington M31 .....105 E3
Sheldon CI OL7 .....85 B5
Sheldon Fold [9] SK13 .....171 D1
Sheldon Pl [8] SK13 .....171 D1
Sheldon Rd Disley SK12 .....134 C2
 Hazel Grove SK7 .....133 E8
Sheldon St M11 .....83 B2
Sheldrake CI SK16 .....101 E7
Sheldrake Rd WA14 .....119 B8
Sheldwich CI WN7 .....75 F3
Shelfield CI L1 .....13 F1
Shelfield CI OL11 .....13 F1
Shelfield La OL11 .....13 F1
Shelford Ave M18 .....99 B4
Shellbrook Gr [8] SK9 .....131 D1
Shelley Ave M24 .....47 B3
Shelley CI PR7 .....19 F8
Shelley Ct SK3 .....123 A1
Shelley Dr Abram WN2 .....56 B1
 Wigan WN5 .....54 A6
Shelley Gr Droylsden M43 .....84 A1
 Dukinfield SK14 .....101 D5
 Stalybridge SK15 .....86 E4
Shelley Rd [9] Oldham OL1 .....49 C1
 Oldham OL9 .....65 F3
 Prestwich M25 .....62 F3
 Reddish SK5 .....99 E1
 Swinton M27 .....79 E8
 Walkden M28 .....60 A5
Shelley Rise SK16 .....102 B7
Shelley St Failsworth M40 .....83 C8
 Leigh WN7 .....75 D7
Shelley Way M34 .....112 F8
Shelley Wlk Atherton M46 .....58 D5
 [9] Bolton BL1 .....143 D1
 Bolton BL1 .....143 D1
Shellingford CI WN6 .....35 D7
Shelmerdine CI [8] SK14 .....102 F2
Shelmerdine Gdns M6 .....80 C4
Shelton Ave M33 .....107 D4
Shena Simon Coll M1 .....163 A8
Shenfield Wlk M40 .....160 D3
Shenhurst CI SK9 .....136 E4
Shenton Park Ave M33 .....107 C2
Shenton St SK14 .....101 C4
Shentonfield Rd M22 .....121 E6
Shepherd Cross St BL1 .....142 C1
Shepherd Cross St Ind Est
 BL1 .....143 D2
Shepherd CI [8] OL16 .....31 B6
Shepherd St Bury BL8 .....26 F8
 Bury BL9 .....140 F1
 Heywood OL10 .....29 C2
 Manchester M9 .....64 E1
 Rochdale OL11 .....13 D1
 Rochdale OL12 .....139 F8
 Royton OL2 .....48 E4
Shepherd's Brow WA14 .....119 A3
Shepherd's Dr BL6 .....23 A3
Shepherds CI Blackrod BL6 .....21 C2
 Barrowshaw BL8 .....10 F1
Shepherds Gn OL3 .....69 D5
Shepherds Way OL16 .....31 F5
Shepley Ave [3] .....
Shepley [2] .....
 [2] Dukinfield SK16 .....101 D8
 Hazel Grove SK7 .....133 D8
Shepley Dr SK7 .....124 E1
Shepley La Marple SK6 .....125 F3
 Marple SK6 .....125 F4

Shepley North Ind Est
 M34 .....101 A7
Shepley Rd M34,SK16 .....100 F6
Shepley South Ind Est
 M34 .....101 A6
Shepley St Dukinfield M34 .....100 F7
 Failsworth M35 .....66 A1
 Glossop SK13 .....104 F2
 Hadfield SK13 .....171 E3
 Hyde SK14 .....167 E2
 Manchester M1 .....163 B8
 [4] Oldham OL4 .....67 E6
 [11] Stalybridge SK15 .....86 A2
Shepton Ave WN2 .....56 A1
Shepton CI BL1 .....24 D7
Shepton Dr M23 .....121 A2
Sheraton CI WN5 .....36 B1
Sheraton Rd OL8 .....66 E4
Sherborne Ave WN2 .....57 A5
Sherborne House M24 .....47 A3
Sherborne Rd
 Cheadle SK3 .....123 A7
 Middleton M24 .....47 A3
 Urmston M41 .....95 E3
Sherborne St M3,M8 .....158 F4
Sherborne St W M3,M7 .....158 E3
Sherborne Trad Est M8 .....156 A5
Sherbourne CI
 Bramhall SK8 .....132 B6
 Oldham OL8 .....67 C4
 Radcliffe M26 .....43 D5
Sherbourne Ct M25 .....63 A4
Sherbourne Dr OL10 .....29 A3
Sherbourne Pl WN3 .....151 E5
Sherbourne Rd BL1 .....142 A1
Sherbourne St M25 .....63 A4
Sherbrook CI M33 .....107 F3
Sherbrook Rise SK9 .....137 C6
Sherbrooke Ave OL3 .....51 C1
Sherbrooke Rd SK12 .....135 D6
Sherdley Ct M8 .....64 A1
Sherdley Rd M8 .....64 A1
Sherford CI SK7 .....124 A2
Sheri Dr WA12 .....89 E2
Sheridan Ave M40 .....90 D7
Sheridan Ct M40 .....157 E5
Sheridan Way
 Chadderton OL9 .....65 E8
 Denton M34 .....112 F8
Sheriff St Bolton BL2 .....25 B1
 Milnrow OL16 .....32 A5
 Rochdale OL12 .....139 E8
 Rochdale OL12 .....14 E1
Sheriffs Dr M29 .....59 D1
Sheringham Dr Bury BL8 .....27 B5
 Hyde SK14 .....102 A3
 Swinton M27 .....79 F6
Sheringham Pl BL3 .....145 D5
Sheringham Rd M14 .....110 D7
Sherlock St M14 .....110 D7
Sherratt St M4 .....159 B2
Sherrington St M12 .....99 A3
Sherway Dr WA15 .....120 C6
Sherwell Rd M9 .....64 B3
Sherwin Way OL11 .....30 D1
Sherwood Ave
 Ashton-in-M WN4 .....73 C4
 Bury BL8 .....43 F8
 Cheadle SK8 .....122 F2
 Droylsden M43 .....84 C2
 Manchester M14 .....110 C8
 Manchester M7 .....81 B7
 Sale M33 .....108 D5
 Stockport SK4 .....168 A1
 Tyldesley M29 .....77 A6
Sherwood Bsns Pk OL11 .....30 D2
Sherwood CI
 Ashton-u-L OL6 .....85 C7
 Bury BL8 .....26 F7
 Marple SK6 .....125 F4
 Salford M5 .....154 D3
Sherwood Cres
 Platt Bridge WN2 .....56 A2
 Wigan WN5 .....54 D7
Sherwood Dr
 Pendlebury M27 .....80 B7
 Wigan WN5 .....54 D6
Sherwood Fold SK13 .....115 D7
Sherwood Gr Leigh WN7 .....76 B2
 Wigan WN5 .....54 D7
Sherwood Ind Pk OL11 .....30 D2
Sherwood Rd
 Reddish M34 .....100 B3
 Romiley SK6 .....113 B5
Sherwood St Bolton BL1 .....143 F3
 Manchester M14 .....110 C8
 Oldham OL1 .....153 D8
 Rochdale OL11 .....30 D2
Sherwood Way OL2 .....48 E8
Shetland Rd M40 .....160 D3
Shetland Way
 Radcliffe M26 .....44 A5
 Urmston M41 .....95 D5
Shevington Com Prim Sch
 WN6 .....35 F6
Shevington Gdns M23 .....109 B1
Shevington High Sch
 WN6 .....36 B7
Shevington La WN6 .....36 B7
Shevington Moor WN6 .....19 A2
Shevington Vale Prim Sch
 WN6 .....35 E8
Shiel St WN6 .....36 D3
Shield CI OL8 .....153 E6
Shield Dr M28 .....79 C8
Shield St SK3 .....170 E8
Shieldborn Dr M9 .....157 E7

Shields View M5 .....161 B7
Shiers Dr SK8 .....122 E4
Shiffnall St BL2 .....148 A6
Shildon CI WN2 .....37 F2
Shilford Dr M4 .....159 C3
Shillingford Rd BL4 .....60 C8
Shillingstone CI BL2 .....26 A3
Shillington CI [1] M28 .....59 F3
Shiloh La OL4 .....50 B3
Shiloh Rd OL4 .....50 B3
Shilton Gdns BL3 .....145 E5
Shilton St BL0 .....138 B5
Shilton Wlk [2] M40 .....65 D2
Ship Canal Ho M15 .....162 E8
Ship La OL3,OL4 .....50 B5
Ship Yd WN1 .....150 C8
Shipgates BL1 .....145 F7
Shipham CI WN7 .....75 D8
Shipla CI OL9 .....153 E7
Shipley Ave M6 .....80 C3
Shipley View M41 .....94 F5
Shipper Bottom La BL0 .....11 D5
Shippey St M14 .....110 D7
Shipston CI BL8 .....27 B3
Shipton St BL1 .....142 B1
Shirburn [8] OL11 .....139 E6
Shire Gdns M26 .....43 F4
Shire Hill Hospl SK13 .....104 E3
Shire Way SK13 .....104 E3
Shirebrook Dr
 Glossop SK13 .....116 F8
 Radcliffe M26 .....44 B4
Shireburn Ave BL2 .....148 C8
Shiredale CI SK8 .....123 B4
Shiredale Dr M9 .....157 D7
Shiregreen Ave M40 .....156 C5
Shirehills M25 .....63 A3
Shireoak Rd M20 .....110 D7
Shires The Droylsden M43 .....84 D3
 Radcliffe M26 .....44 A5
Shires CI SK8 .....131 A1
Shires Dr SK7 .....124 C2
Shirley Ave
 Denton M34 .....100 E6
 Eccles M30 .....95 A5
 Failsworth OL9 .....65 E2
 Gatley SK8 .....131 C6
 Manchester M7 .....81 A7
 Marple SK6 .....125 E6
 Pendlebury M27 .....80 C7
 Stretford M32 .....96 F3
Shirley CI SK7 .....124 C2
Shirley Ct SK13 .....170 E6
Shirley Gr SK3 .....170 E6
Shirley Rd M8 .....156 A7
Shirley St OL11 .....30 C2
Shoecroft Ave M34 .....100 E2
Shoemaker Gdns WN2 .....38 C5
Sholver Hill CI OL1 .....49 E4
Sholver La OL1 .....49 D4
Shone Ave M22 .....121 F2
Shore Ave OL2 .....32 C1
Shore Fold OL15 .....15 F6
Shore Hill OL15 .....16 C6
Shore La OL15 .....15 F6
Shore Mount OL15 .....15 F6
Shore Rd OL15 .....15 F7
Shore St Milnrow OL16 .....31 F6
 Oldham OL1 .....67 A7
Shoredicth CI SK4 .....111 B5
Shorefield CI OL16 .....31 F7
Shorefield Mount BL7 .....24 E8
Shoreham CI [3] M16 .....97 F4
Shoreham Wlk OL9 .....152 A6
Shoreswood BL1 .....24 D5
Shorland St M27 .....79 C7
Shorrocks St BL8 .....26 F6
Short Ave M43 .....99 F8
Short St Bacup OL13 .....3 B8
 Golborne WA3 .....74 B1
 Hazel Grove SK7 .....124 D3
 Heywood OL10 .....29 B1
 Manchester M1 .....159 A1
 Manchester M7 .....158 E3
 Stockport SK4 .....169 E3
Short St E SK4 .....169 E3
Shortcroft St M15 .....162 F7
Shortland Cres M19 .....110 D3
Shortland Pl WN2 .....75 A8
Shortlands Ave BL9 .....44 F8
Shortwood CI [8] M40 .....83 A6
Shorton Wlks SK6 .....112 F3
Shotton CI WN7 .....76 B2
Shotton Wlk [4] M14 .....98 C3
Shrewsbury CI WN2 .....56 F6
Shrewsbury Ct M16 .....162 D5
Shrewsbury Rd
 Bolton BL1 .....144 B8
 Droylsden M43 .....84 A3
 Prestwich M25 .....63 A3
 Sale M33 .....108 A2
Shrewsbury St
 Glossop SK13 .....104 C1
 Manchester M16 .....162 D5
 Oldham OL4 .....67 C8
Shrewsbury Way [7] M34 .....101 C1
Shrigley CI SK9 .....131 D1
Shrigley Rd SK10,SK12 .....134 C2
Shrigley Rd N SK12 .....134 D3
Shrivenham Wlk M23 .....120 C6
Shropshire Ave SK5 .....112 C6
Shropshire CI SK13 .....116 F8
Shropshire Rd M35 .....84 A6
Shropshire Sq M12 .....164 F6
Shrowbridge Wlk M12 .....165 A6
Shrub St BL3 .....146 C2

Shudehill M4 .....159 A2
Shudehill Rd M28 .....60 A1
Shurdington Rd BL5,M46 .....58 F6
Shurmer St BL3 .....146 C4
Shuttle St OL3 .....50 F2
Shuttle Hillock Rd WN2 .....74 F7
Shuttle St [8] Eccles M30 .....79 F2
 Hindley WN2 .....56 E6
 Radcliffe M26 .....44 C1
 Tyldesley M29 .....59 A1
Shuttleworth CI M21 .....109 E8
Shutts La SK15 .....102 D8
Siam St M11 .....164 F8
Sibley Ave WN4 .....73 D4
Sibley Rd SK4 .....168 B3
Sibley St M18 .....99 D5
Sibles Wlk [7] M22 .....121 B1
Sibson Ct [3] M21 .....97 A1
Sibson Rd Manchester M21 .....97 A1
 Sale M33 .....108 B4
Sickle St
 Manchester M1,M2 .....159 A1
 Oldham OL4 .....67 A5
Sidbrook St WN2 .....56 C5
Sidbury Rd M21 .....109 C8
Sidcup Rd M23 .....120 F5
Siddal Moor Sports Coll
 OL10 .....46 D7
Siddall St Heywood OL10 .....46 E8
 Manchester M12 .....164 F6
 Oldham OL1 .....153 F8
 [2] Radcliffe M26 .....44 A4
 Shaw OL2 .....149 B7
Siddeley St WN7 .....75 D5
Siddington Ave
 Manchester M20 .....110 A7
 Stockport SK3 .....170 D6
Siddington Rd
 Handforth SK9 .....131 D5
 Poynton SK12 .....133 F2
Side Ave WA14 .....119 C1
Side St Droylsden M11 .....83 B2
 Oldham OL8 .....66 C2
Sidebotham St Sk6 .....112 F4
Sidebottom St
 Droylsden M43 .....83 F1
 [8] Oldham OL4 .....67 E8
 Stalybridge SK15 .....86 A2
Sidford CI BL3 .....42 D5
Siding St OL13 .....2 D8
Sidings The Bacup OL13 .....4 A8
 Eccles M28 .....79 A5
Sidley Ave M9 .....64 F4
Sidley Pl SK14 .....167 F3
Sidley St SK14 .....167 F3
Sidmouth Ave M41 .....94 E3
Sidmouth Dr M9 .....64 D2
Sidmouth Gr [8] Cheadle SK8 .....131 F7
 Wigan WN3 .....54 E3
Sidmouth Rd M33 .....108 D7
Sidmouth St Denton M34 .....100 D2
 Oldham OL9 .....152 B5
Sidney Rd M9 .....64 D1
Sidney St Bolton BL3 .....145 F5
 Leigh WN7 .....76 A5
 Manchester M1 .....163 A7
 Manchester M3 .....158 F1
 [6] Manchester M3 .....158 F1
 Oldham OL1 .....49 A1
Sidwell Wlk M4 .....160 D1
Siemens Rd Irlam M44 .....105 E5
 Manchester M20 .....109 E5
Siemens St BL6 .....22 C2
Sienna CI M44 .....105 E6
Signhill Wlk M9 .....157 D8
Signal CI M30 .....79 D2
Signet Wlk [8] M8 .....156 B5
Silas St M5 .....85 D5
Silburn Way M24,M9 .....64 D7
Silbury Wlk M8 .....155 F5
Silchester Dr M40 .....157 D6
Silchester Way BL2 .....25 E1
Silchester Wlk [3] OL1 .....153 F7
Silcock St WA3 .....74 A1
Silfield CI M11 .....160 E1
Silk St Eccles M30 .....79 F1
 Failsworth M40 .....83 C5
 Glossop SK13 .....104 E1
 Leigh WN7 .....75 F5
Silkstone St M11 .....165 C7
Sillavan Way M3 .....158 E2
Sillitoe Dr WN6 .....37 A1
Silsbury Gr WN6 .....37 A8
Silsden Ave Golborne WA3 .....91 B8
 Manchester M9 .....64 B5
Silsden Wlk M7 .....80 F8
Silton St M9 .....157 F8
Silver Birch Gr
 Ashton-in-M WN4 .....73 A5
 Manchester M7 .....80 B6
Silver Birch Mews SK16 .....101 E7
Silver CI SK16 .....101 E7
Silver CI [3] M45 .....44 E1
Silver Hill OL16 .....31 F7
Silver Hill Rd SK14 .....167 E1
Silver Springs [4] M44 .....159 B2
Silver Spring SK14 .....113 F8
Silver St Bury BL9 .....140 E2
 Irlam M44 .....94 B4

Silver St *continued*
Manchester M1 ...159 A1
Manchester M1 ...163 A8
Oldham OL1 ...153 E6
5 Platt Bridge WN2 ...56 B2
Ramsbottom BL0 ...138 C6
Rochdale OL12 ...139 D8
Walsden OL14 ...6 A7
Whitefield M45 ...44 E1
Silver Terr WN1 ...151 D7
Silverbirch Cl M33 ...107 D2
Silverbirch Way 3 M35 ...83 F7
Silvercroft St M15 ...162 E7
Silverdale
Altrincham WA14 ...119 C4
5 Bredbury SK6 ...112 F3
Swinton M27 ...62 A2
Wigan WN1 ...37 C2
Silverdale Ave
Denton M34 ...101 A2
Ince-in-M WN2 ...56 A8
Irlam M44 ...94 B3
Manchester M25 ...63 E2
Oldham OL9 ...152 A6
Walkden M38 ...60 A5
Silverdale Cl SK6 ...134 E8
Silverdale Ct WN1 ...151 D8
Silverdale Dr Oldham OL4 ...67 F6
Wilmslow SK9 ...137 A4
Silverdale Prim Sch M27 ...62 B1
Silverdale Rd
Bolton BL1 ...144 C7
Farnworth BL4 ...42 A1
Gatley SK8 ...122 B4
Hindley WN2 ...56 F5
Manchester M21 ...97 C1
Manchester SK4 ...168 C4
Newton-le-W WA12 ...89 B4
Wigan WN5 ...54 B8
Silverdale St M11 ...99 F8
Silverlea Dr M9 ...64 C2
Silvermere OL6 ...85 E6
Silverstone Dr M40 ...83 D4
Silverthorne Cl 12 SK15 ...86 A1
Silverton Cl SK14 ...102 E2
Silverton Gr Bolton BL1 ...143 F4
Middleton M24 ...46 D4
Silverton Ho M6 ...80 A3
Silverwell La BL1,BL2 ...145 F7
Silverwell St Bolton BL1 ...145 F7
Failsworth M40 ...83 D5
Horwich BL6 ...22 B4
Silverwood OL9 ...65 E7
Silverwood Ave M21 ...109 B8
Silvester St BL6 ...21 D2
Silvington Way WN2 ...38 A2
Simeon St Manchester M4 ...159 B3
Milnrow OL16 ...31 F6
Walsden OL14 ...6 A8
Simfield Cl WN6 ...19 D1
Simister Dr BL9 ...45 A2
Simister Gn M25 ...63 E8
Simister La
Middleton M24,M25 ...46 A1
Middleton M25 ...63 E8
Simister Rd M35 ...83 F7
Simister St 10 M9 ...157 E8
Simm's Sq WN2 ...38 D4
Simmondley Cty Prim Sch
SK13 ...116 A8
Simmondley Gr SK13 ...116 A8
Simmondley La SK13 ...116 A8
Simmondley New Rd
SK13 ...116 A7
Simms Cl M3 ...158 D2
Simon Cl M33 ...108 A3
Simon Freeman Cl
M19,SK4 ...111 C6
Simon La M24 ...46 A2
Simonbury Cl BL8 ...26 F2
Simons Cl SK13 ...116 A7
Simons Wlk SK13 ...116 A8
Simonsway M22,M23,SK8 ...121 D2
Simpkin St Abram WN2 ...56 B1
Abram WN2 ...74 C8
Simpson Ave M27 ...62 C2
Simpson Gr M28 ...78 A6
Simpson Hill Cl OL10 ...29 F3
Simpson Rd M28 ...78 A6
Simpson Sq OL9 ...65 C6
Simpson St Droylsden M11 ...83 A1
Hyde SK14 ...167 D2
Manchester M4 ...159 B3
Oldham OL9 ...66 B4
Wilmslow SK9 ...136 F6
Sinclair Pl WN5 ...54 E8
Sinclair St OL11 ...30 D3
Sinderland La
Partington WA14 ...106 D1
Partington WA14 ...118 E8
Sinderland Rd
Altrincham WA14 ...119 C8
Partington M31,WA14 ...106 C2
Sindsley Ct M27 ...61 D1
Sindsley Gr BL3 ...147 E3
Sindsley Rd M27 ...61 D2
Singapore Ave M90 ...130 A8
Singleton Ave Bolton BL2 ...42 F7
Horwich BL6 ...22 C5
Singleton Cl M7 ...63 C1
Singleton Gr BL5 ...40 B1
Singleton Lo M7 ...63 D1
Singleton Rd
Manchester M7,M8 ...63 D1
Manchester SK4 ...168 B4
Singleton St M26 ...43 D4
Sion St M26 ...44 A2
Sir Matt Busby Way M17 ...96 F5
Sir Richard Fairey Rd
SK4 ...111 B7
Sirdar St M11 ...99 F8
Sirius Pl M7 ...158 D3
Siskin Cl Leigh WN7 ...76 B5
Newton-le-W WA12 ...89 C3
Siskin Rd SK2 ...124 F5
Sisley Cl M7 ...81 B8
Sisson St M35 ...83 E7
Sisters' St M43 ...100 A8
Sitch La SK22 ...127 F3
Sittingbourne Rd WN1 ...37 C4
Sixpools Gr 6 M28 ...78 C8
Sixth Ave Bolton BL1 ...144 B7
Bury BL9 ...28 D4
Little Lever BL3 ...42 F4
Oldham OL8 ...66 C1
Sixth St M17 ...96 D5
Size House Pl 7 WN7 ...76 A4
Size St OL12 ...4 D1
Skagen BL1 ...143 E1
Skagen Ct BL1 ...143 E1
Skaife Rd M33 ...108 E4
Skarratt Cl M12 ...164 F6
Skegness Cl BL8 ...27 D5
Skellorn Green La SK10 ...133 F1
Skelton Gr Bolton BL2 ...42 F8
Manchester M13 ...98 F2
Skelton Rd
Altrincham WA14 ...119 E7
Stretford M32 ...96 D3
Skelton St WN4 ...72 F6
Skelwith Ave BL3 ...147 F2
Skelwith Cl M41 ...95 A4
Skerry Cl M13 ...163 B7
Skerton Rd M16 ...97 B4
Skiddaw Pl WN5 ...54 C6
Skilgate Wlk 10 M40 ...83 C6
Skip Pl M3,M4 ...159 A3
Skipton Ave
Chadderton OL9 ...47 F1
Failsworth M40 ...65 D1
Hindley WN2 ...57 A4
Skipton Cl Bury BL8 ...26 F2
Hazel Grove SK7 ...133 C8
Reddish SK5 ...111 E8
Skipton Dr M41 ...94 F5
Skipton St Bolton BL2 ...148 C8
Oldham OL8 ...67 B4
Skipton Wlk BL2 ...148 C7
Skull House La WN6 ...35 D8
Skye Cl OL10 ...28 F1
Skye Croft SK6 ...113 D3
Skye Rd M41 ...95 D5
Skye Wlk M23 ...121 A4
Skyes Cres WN3 ...54 C1
Skyes Ct 8 OL16 ...31 B6
Slack Fold La BL4 ...147 D1
Slack Gate OL12 ...14 F8
Slack Gate La OL3 ...50 D8
Slack Hall OL4 ...67 F8
Slack La Bolton BL2 ...25 E7
Delph OL3 ...50 D6
Swinton M27 ...62 A1
Westhoughton BL5 ...39 F3
Slack Rd M9 ...64 D1
Slack St Hyde SK14 ...167 F4
Rochdale OL16 ...139 F7
Slackcote OL3 ...50 C7
Slackcote La OL3 ...50 C7
Slackey Brow BL4 ...61 C6
Slackey Fold WN2 ...57 B1
Slade Gr M13 ...98 F3
Slade Hall Rd M12 ...99 A2
Slade La M13,M19 ...98 F2
Slade Mount M19 ...110 F8
Slade St BL3 ...43 A3
Sladen Fold OL15 ...16 D8
Sladen St OL12 ...14 F1
Slades View Cl OL3 ...51 C5
Slag La Golborne WA3 ...74 F2
Golborne WA3 ...90 D8
Slaidburn Ave BL2 ...42 F6
Slaidburn Cl Milnrow OL16 ...31 F5
Wigan WN3 ...55 A3
Slaidburn Cres WA3 ...73 F2
Slaidburn Dr BL8 ...26 F3
Slaithwaite Dr 5 M11 ...83 C2
Slant Cl SK13 ...116 E8
Slate Ave 10 M4 ...159 C1
Slate La Ashton-u-L OL7 ...84 E1
Droylsden M34 ...100 C8
Droylsden OL7 ...100 E8
Slate Wharf M15 ...162 D7
Slateacre Rd SK14 ...113 F7
Slatelands Ave SK13 ...116 B8
Slatelands Rd SK13 ...116 B8
Slater Ave BL6 ...22 C4
Slater La Bolton BL1 ...148 A8
Bolton BL1 ...25 A1
Slater St Bolton BL1 ...143 F1
Eccles M30 ...79 B2
Failsworth M35 ...65 F1
Farnworth BL4 ...60 D8
Oldham OL8,OL9 ...153 E6
Slater St N WN7 ...75 D5
Slater Way 2 SK14 ...102 F2
Slater's Nook 10 BL5 ...39 E1
Slaterfield BL3 ...145 E5
Slaunt Bank OL12 ...13 D2
Slawson Way OL10 ...29 F3
Sleaford Cl Bury BL8 ...27 D5
Manchester M40 ...160 D3
Sledbrook St WN5 ...54 C5
Sleddale Cl SK2 ...124 D5
Sledmere Cl Bolton BL1 ...143 F2
Droylsden M11 ...83 A1
Sledmoor Rd M23 ...108 F1
Slimbridge Cl BL2 ...26 A1
Sloane Ave OL4 ...67 F8
Sloane St
5 Ashton-u-L OL6 ...166 C3
Bolton BL3 ...146 B3
Droylsden M11 ...83 A2
Slough Ind Est M5 ...161 C8
Smallbridge Cl 5 M28 ...78 C8
Smallbridge Prim Sch
OL12 ...15 B3
Smallbrook La WN7 ...57 E3
Smallbrook Rd OL2 ...32 C1
Smalldale Ave M16 ...97 F3
Smalley St Rochdale OL11 ...30 C2
Standish WN6 ...19 E1
Smallfield Dr M9 ...157 D8
Smallridge Cl M40 ...160 D3
Smallshaw Cl WN4 ...73 A2
Smallshaw La OL6 ...85 C5
Smallshaw Rd OL12 ...14 A4
Smallshaw Sq OL6 ...85 B5
Smallwood St M40 ...83 C6
Smart St M12 ...99 A3
Smeaton Cl M32 ...96 E2
Smeaton St Horwich BL6 ...22 C2
Manchester M8 ...156 C6
Smedley Ave Bolton BL3 ...42 A3
Manchester M8 ...156 C6
Smedley La
Manchester M8 ...156 B6
Manchester M8,M9 ...156 B7
Smedley Rd M40,M8 ...156 C6
Smedley St M8 ...156 B6
Smethurst Hall Pk WN5 ...53 C2
Smethurst Hall Rd BL9 ...28 F4
Smethurst La
Bolton BL3,BL4 ...146 B2
Wigan WN5 ...54 C5
Smethurst Rd WN5 ...53 C2
Smethurst St 7 Bury BL8 ...27 C4
Heywood OL10 ...29 B2
Manchester M9 ...64 D1
Middleton M24 ...65 D7
Wigan WN5 ...54 C5
Smith Ave WN5 ...54 B8
Smith Brow BL6 ...21 C3
Smith Fold La M28 ...60 A3
Smith Hill OL16 ...32 A6
Smith La Ashley WA16 ...128 E1
Bolton BL7 ...8 F1
Smith St Adlington PR7 ...20 F6
Ashton-u-L OL7 ...84 F1
Aspull WN2 ...38 C5
Atherton M46 ...58 C3
Bury BL9 ...141 A3
Cheadle SK8 ...122 F6
Denton M34 ...100 F2
Dukinfield SK14 ...101 D5
Dukinfield SK16 ...101 A8
7 Heywood OL10 ...29 D2
Leigh WN7 ...76 A5
6 Littleborough OL15 ...16 B5
Manchester M16 ...161 C6
Mossley OL5 ...68 B2
Oldham OL4 ...67 E8
Ramsbottom BL0 ...138 B5
Rochdale OL16 ...139 F7
Walkden M28 ...60 D3
Smith's La WN2 ...75 B8
Smith's Pl 11 M46 ...58 D3
Smith's Rd BL3 ...42 D3
Smithies Ave M24 ...47 A2
Smithies St OL10 ...29 E2
Smithill's Hall (Mus) BL1 ...142 B4
Smithills Croft Rd BL1 ...142 B3
Smithills Dean Rd BL1 ...142 B4
Smithills Dr BL1 ...23 F2
Smithills Hall Cl BL0 ...138 C5
Smithills Sch BL1 ...142 C4
Smiths Lawn SK9 ...137 A5
Smithwood Ave WN2 ...56 F6
Smithy Bridge Prim Sch
OL15 ...15 F3
Smithy Bridge Rd
OL15,OL16 ...15 F3
Smithy Bridge Sta OL15 ...15 F3
Smithy Brow WN6 ...18 C8
Smithy Cl SK13 ...104 D1
Smithy Croft BL7 ...24 F8
Smithy Fold Glossop SK13 ...104 D1
Rochdale OL12 ...14 C1
Smithy Fold Rd 3 SK14 ...167 E1
Smithy Gn Cheadle SK8 ...132 A8
Newhey OL16 ...32 E4
Romiley SK6 ...113 B5
Smithy Gr OL6 ...166 C4
Smithy Hill BL3 ...146 A4
Smithy La
Altrincham WA14 ...118 D3
Flixton SK6 ...114 F1
Hyde SK14 ...167 E1
4 Manchester M3 ...158 F1
Oldham OL3 ...69 B8
Partington M31 ...105 F3
Smithy Nook OL15 ...6 C1
Smithy St Hazel Grove SK7 ...124 D3
Leigh WN7 ...75 F4
Ramsbottom BL0 ...138 C6
Westhoughton BL5 ...39 E3
Smock La WN4 ...72 C4
Smyrna St Heywood OL10 ...29 C1
7 Oldham OL4 ...67 C6
Radcliffe M26 ...43 F4
Salford M5 ...154 E1
Smyrna Wlk M26 ...43 F4
Snape St M26 ...43 F6
Snapebrook Wlk 6 SK9 ...131 E1
Snell St M4 ...160 D1
Snipe Ave OL11 ...29 F7
Snipe Cl SK12 ...133 A4
Snipe Rd OL8 ...67 B2
Snipe Ret Pk OL7 ...100 D8
Snipe St BL3 ...147 F4
Snipe Way OL7 ...100 D8
Snow Hill Rd BL3 ...42 D5
Snowberry Wlk M31 ...105 E3
Snowden Ave
Urmston M41 ...107 B8
Wigan WN3 ...55 A4
Snowden St Bolton BL1 ...145 E8
Heywood OL10 ...46 E8
1 Oldham OL8 ...66 F4
Snowden Wlk 4 M40 ...65 C2
Snowdon Dr BL6 ...22 C5
Snowdon Rd M30 ...80 A3
Snowdon St OL11 ...31 A2
Snowdrop Cl BB4 ...1 A8
Snowdrop Wlk M7 ...155 D6
Snowshill Dr WN3 ...54 C4
Snydale Cl BL5 ...40 B2
Snydale Way BL3,BL5 ...40 C1
Soane Cl WN4 ...73 D3
Soap St M4 ...159 A2
Society St OL2 ...149 B7
Sofa St BL1 ...142 B1
Soham Cl WN2 ...56 E4
Soho St Bolton BL3 ...145 F6
Oldham OL4 ...67 B7
Wigan WN5 ...54 F7
Sole St WN1 ...37 E1
Solent Ave M8 ...64 A2
Solent Dr BL3 ...42 D5
Solness St BL9 ...27 F6
Solway Cl Ashton-in-M WN4 ...73 A4
Bolton BL3 ...147 D3
Kearsley M27 ...61 E4
Oldham OL8 ...153 E5
Solway Rd M22 ...121 E4
Somerby Dr M22 ...121 C1
Somerdale Ave BL1 ...144 A7
Somerfield Rd M9 ...64 D1
Somerford Ave M20 ...110 A8
Somerford Rd SK5 ...99 F2
Somerford Way 3 SK9 ...131 E5
Somers Rd SK5 ...99 F1
Somers Wlk M9 ...64 B3
Somersby Dr BL7 ...24 F8
Somersby Wlk BL3 ...145 F5
Somerset Ave Shaw OL2 ...48 F7
Tyldesley M29 ...58 F3
Somerset Cl
Brinnington SK5 ...112 C4
Irlam M44 ...105 D6
Somerset Dr BL9 ...44 F8
Somerset Gr OL11 ...30 A8
Somerset Pl M33 ...108 B6
Somerset Rd
Altrincham WA14 ...119 D6
Atherton M46 ...58 C5
Bolton BL1 ...144 B8
Droylsden M43 ...84 A3
Failsworth M35 ...83 E6
Salford M30 ...80 A4
Wigan WN5 ...54 C7
Somerset St OL4 ...67 C6
Somerset Wlk BB4 ...1 B8
Somerton Ave Sale M33 ...108 C3
Wythenshawe M22 ...121 C3
Somerton Ct M9 ...65 A3
Somerton Rd BL2 ...43 A6
Somerville Gdns WA15 ...119 F7
Somerville Rd WN1 ...37 C3
Somerville Sq BL1 ...142 C3
Somerville St BL1 ...142 C3
Somerwood Wlk M12 ...164 F6
Sommerville Ct M7 ...155 D8
Sonning Dr BL3 ...146 A2
Sonning Wlk M8 ...156 B6
Sopwith Dr M14 ...98 B1
Sorby Rd M44 ...106 A7
Sorrel Bank M6 ...154 F4
Sorrel Dr OL15 ...15 F6
Sorrel St M15 ...162 E6
Sorrel Way OL4 ...49 E2
Sorrell Bank SK5 ...100 A1
Sorton St M1 ...163 A7
Soudan Rd SK2 ...124 A6
Soudan St M24 ...47 C1
Sougher's La WN4 ...72 F7
Sougher's Lane End WN4 ...72 E6
Sound The OL3 ...50 F4
Souracre Fold SK15 ...86 B3
South Acre Dr SK9 ...131 D3
South Ave Eccles M41 ...95 E6
Golborne WN7 ...74 F4
Heywood OL10 ...29 B2
Kearsley BL4 ...60 F6
Leigh WN7 ...76 C3
Manchester M19 ...110 F7
Oldham OL3 ...69 B6
Swinton M27 ...79 D5
Whitefield M45 ...44 E1
South Back Rock 1 BL9 ...140 F2
South Bank Cl SK9 ...137 B2
South Bank Rd BL9 ...140 E1
South Bolton
Sixth Form Coll BL3 ...146 C2
South Chadderton
Com Sec Sch OL9 ...65 F3
South Cl Tintwistle SK13 ...103 F7
Whitefield BL9 ...45 A3
Wilmslow SK9 ...136 F6
South Cliffe St 1 M11 ...99 F7
South Cres Droylsden M11 ...83 D2
Failsworth M40 ...65 D3
South Croft OL8 ...67 B3
South Cross St Bury BL9 ...140 F2
Bury BL9 ...141 A1
South Croston St M16 ...97 D4
South Ct OL16 ...31 A8
South Downs Dr WA14 ...119 D1
South Downs Rd WA14 ...119 D1
South Dr Altrincham WA15 ...120 A7
Appley Bridge WN6 ...18 C2
Bolton BL2 ...25 E3
Gatley SK8 ...122 A4
Manchester M21 ...109 B6
South Failsworth
Cty Prim Sch M35 ...83 F5
South Field Ind Est M17 ...96 C6
South Gr
Alderley Edge SK9 ...137 A1
Manchester M13 ...164 D5
Sale M33 ...108 B3
Walkden M28 ...60 C2
South Hall St M5 ...161 C8
South Hey WN7 ...75 C5
South Hill OL4 ...67 F5
South Hill St OL4 ...67 A6
South King St Eccles M30 ...79 B2
Manchester M2 ...158 F1
South La M29 ...77 A5
South Lancashire Ind Est
WN4 ...73 B6
South Langworthy Rd
Salford M5 ...154 F1
Salford M5 ...96 E8
South Lonsdale St M32 ...96 E3
South Manchester
High Sch M22 ...121 D3
South Marlow St SK13 ...104 A4
South Mead SK12 ...133 B5
South Meade
Altrincham WA15 ...120 A7
Manchester M21 ...109 B7
Manchester M25 ...63 D2
Swinton M27 ...79 E6
South Meadway SK6 ...134 F7
South Mesnefield Rd M7 ...81 A8
South Oak La SK9 ...136 F5
South Par Rochdale OL16 ...139 F7
Stockport SK7 ...123 F2
South Park Dr SK12 ...133 E5
South Park Rd SK8 ...122 B6
South Pine St BL9 ...141 B2
South Pl 11 OL16 ...31 A8
South Pump St M1 ...163 B8
South Radford St M7 ...81 A7
South Rd Altrincham WA14 ...119 C2
Altrincham WA14 ...128 E8
Manchester M20 ...110 B2
Stretford M17,M32 ...96 C4
Stretford M32 ...96 B4
Swinton M27 ...62 D2
South Ridge M34 ...100 F5
South Row M25 ...62 F1
South Royd St BL8 ...26 F7
South Side SK14 ...113 F8
South St Alderley Edge SK9 ...137 A1
Ashton-u-L OL7 ...100 E8
Bolton BL3 ...147 E3
Heywood OL10 ...29 B2
Manchester M11 ...165 C7
Manchester M12 ...164 E5
Oldham OL8 ...66 B2
Ramsbottom BL0 ...11 D6
Rochdale OL16 ...31 A8
Tyldesley M46 ...58 E1
South Terr Bury BL9 ...44 D7
Ramsbottom BL0 ...1 C2
South Terrace Ct 12 OL16 ...31 A5
South Trafford Coll
WA14 ...119 D8
South Vale Cres WA15 ...119 F5
South View Atherton M46 ...58 C3
2 Manchester M14 ...98 C2
Mossley SK15 ...86 F6
Reddish SK5 ...99 F3
Rochdale OL11 ...29 E6
Romiley SK6 ...113 C6
South View Gdns SK8 ...122 C3
South View Rd OL12 ...15 E3
South View St BL2 ...148 C7
South View Terr OL16 ...15 E4
South Way OL8 ...66 E2
South William St M3 ...158 D1
Southall St M3,M8 ...158 F4
Southam St M7,M8 ...155 F7
Southampton Cl M7 ...155 D5
Southbank Rd M19 ...110 D5
Southbourne Ave M41 ...95 F2
Southbourne St M6 ...154 E2
Southbrook Ave M9 ...63 F3
Southbrook Cl SK13 ...171 E4
Southbrook Gr BL3 ...147 F3
Southchurch Par M40 ...159 C4
Southcliffe Rd 3 SK5 ...111 F6
Southcombe Wlk M15 ...97 F4
Southcourt WN7 ...76 B6
Southcross Rd M18 ...99 D3
Southdene Ave M20 ...109 E4
Southdown Cl
Rochdale OL11 ...30 C5
Stockport SK4 ...169 E2
Southdown Cres
Cheadle SK8 ...131 F8
Manchester M9 ...65 A2
Southdown Dr M28 ...77 F6
Southdowns Cl Shaw OL2 ...149 A8
Shaw OL2 ...48 F8
Southend Ave M15 ...162 D6

250 Sou–Sta

Southend St BL3 ...... 146 C3
Southern App M27 ...... 62 C2
Southern Cl Denton M34 ...112 F8
Stockport SK7 ...... 123 F1
Southern Cres SK7 ...... 123 F1
Southern Ho 4 BL1 ...... 143 D1
Southern Rd M33 ...... 108 A6
Southern St
Manchester M3 ...... 162 E8
Salford M6 ...... 154 E2
Walkden M28 ...... 60 D5
Wigan WN5 ...... 54 D5
Southern's Fold WN2 ...... 38 A3
Southeroy Cl 8 M13 ...... 98 F4
Southery Ave WN3 ...... 54 D3
Southey Cl OL15 ...... 15 F2
Southey Ct 12 M34 ...... 113 A8
Southey Wlk 6 M34 ...... 113 A7
Southfield WN2 ...... 56 B2
Southfield Ave BL9 ...... 27 F6
Southfield Cl
Dukinfield SK16 ...... 101 D6
Handforth SK9 ...... 131 C3
Southfield Dr BL5 ...... 57 E7
Southfield Rd BL0 ...... 11 A2
Southfield St 6 BL3 ...... 42 A4
Southfields Ave 2 M11 ...... 83 C2
Southfields Dr WA15 ...... 120 B7
Southgarth Rd M6 ...... 154 E3
Southgate Bolton BL2 ...... 25 E4
Manchester M21 ...... 109 B7
Manchester M3 ...... 158 F1
Manchester SK4 ...... 111 C5
Uppermill OL3 ...... 51 A2
Urmston M41 ...... 107 B8
Whitworth OL12 ...... 14 C7
Southgate Ave M40 ...... 83 A4
Southgate Ct M33 ...... 108 C5
Southgate Ind Pk OL10 ...... 29 E1
Southgate Rd
Failsworth OL9 ...... 65 E3
Whitefield BL9 ...... 44 F3
Southgate St OL1 ...... 153 F6
Southgate Way 5 OL7 ...... 166 A1
Southgrove Ave BL1 ...... 24 C6
Southlands Ave Eccles M30 ...95 A8
Standish WN6 ...... 36 E8
Southlawn SK9 ...... 137 A5
Southlea Rd M19,M20 ...... 110 D5
Southleigh Dr BL2 ...... 43 A6
Southlink OL4 ...... 67 A6
Southlink Bsns Pk OL4 ...67 A6
Southlink Wkshp OL4 ...... 67 A6
Southmere Cl M40 ...... 65 C3
Southmill St M2 ...... 162 F8
Southmoor Rd M23 ...... 120 F6
Southmoor Wlk BL3 ...... 145 E5
Southover BL5 ...... 57 E6
Southpoint SK4 ...... 168 A2
Southpool Cl SK7 ...... 124 A2
Southsea St M11 ...... 99 D7
Southside SK6 ...... 112 E6
Southview Rd SK13 ...... 116 F7
Southview Wlk OL4 ...... 49 E1
Southward Rd WA11 ...... 89 A7
Southwark Dr SK16 ...... 101 D6
Southway
Altrincham WA14 ...... 119 E6
Ashton-u-L OL7 ...... 85 B6
Droylsden M43 ...... 100 A8
7 Eccles M30 ...... 79 F2
Failsworth OL9 ...... 65 E3
Southwell Cl
18 Bolton BL1 ...... 145 D8
Golborne WA3 ...... 90 C8
Romiley SK6 ...... 113 A1
Southwell 6 4 M32 ...96 C1
Southwell Gdns OL6 ...... 85 B7
Southwell St M9 ...... 157 E7
Southwick Rd M23 ...... 109 A2
Southwood Cl M19 ...... 99 C1
Southwood Cl BL3 ...... 147 F3
Southwood Dr M9 ...... 64 A3
Southwood Rd SK2 ...... 124 B4
Southworth Ct M33 ...... 108 D3
Southworth Rd WA12 ...89 F4
Southyard St M19 ...... 111 B8
Sovereign Ent Pk M5 ...... 161 A7
Sovereign Fold Rd WN7 ...57 E1
Sovereign Rd WN1 ...... 151 D7
Sovereign St M6 ...... 81 A4
Sowerby Cl BL8 ...... 26 F2
Sowerby Wlk M9 ...... 64 B4
Spa Cl SK5 ...... 111 E8
Spa Cres M38 ...... 60 A6
Spa Gr M38 ...... 60 A6
Spa La Oldham OL4 ...... 67 E5
Walkden M38 ...... 60 A6
Spa Rd Atherton M46 ...58 D5
Bolton BL1 ...... 145 D7
Spa St M13,M15 ...... 163 B5
Spadden Wlk M45 ...... 45 C1
Spalding Dr M23 ...... 121 A2
Spark Rd M23 ...... 120 F7
Sparkford Ave M23 ...... 108 D1
Sparkle St M1 ...... 163 B8
Sparrow Cl SK5 ...... 99 F1
Sparrow Hill
Appley Bridge WN6,WN8 ...18 A2
Rochdale OL16 ...... 139 F7
Sparrow Hill
Com Prim Sch OL16 ...139 F7
Sparrow Hill Com Prim
Sch (Annexe) OL16 ...139 F6
Sparrow St OL2 ...... 48 E2

Sparrowfield Cl SK15 ...... 86 E7
Sparta Ave M28 ...... 60 D2
Sparta Wlk M11 ...... 165 A8
Sparth Bottoms Rd OL11 ...139 D6
Sparth Ct SK4 ...... 169 D3
Sparth Hall SK4 ...... 169 D3
Sparth La SK4 ...... 169 D3
Sparth Rd M40 ...... 83 D5
Sparthfield Ave OL11 ...... 139 E5
Sparthfield Rd SK4 ...... 169 D3
Spath Holme 2 M20 ...... 110 A3
Spath La SK8 ...... 131 F5
Spath La E SK8 ...... 132 B5
Spath Rd M20 ...... 110 A3
Spath Wlk SK8 ...... 132 B5
Spathfield Ct SK4 ...... 169 D3
Spaw St M3 ...... 158 E2
Spawell Cl WA3 ...... 90 E8
Speakman Ave Leigh WN7 ...76 B5
Newton-le-W WA12 ...... 89 C5
Speakmans Dr WN6 ...... 35 C6
Spean Wlk 8 M11 ...... 83 C1
Spear St M1,M4 ...... 159 B2
Spectator St M4 ...... 160 D2
Specton Wlk 5 M12 ...... 99 B3
Speedwell SK13 ...... 103 F7
Speedwell Cl
11 Golborne WA3 ...... 90 E8
Tintwistle SK13 ...... 103 F7
Speke Wlk M34 ...... 100 E1
Spelding Dr WN6 ...... 36 E4
Spen Fold Bury BL8 ...... 44 A8
Littleborough OL15 ...... 16 A4
Spencer Ave
1 Dukinfield SK14 ...... 101 D5
Little Lever BL3 ...... 43 C3
Manchester M16 ...... 97 C2
Whitefield M45 ...... 44 E2
Spencer La OL11 ...... 29 E5
Spencer Rd WN1 ...... 37 C3
Spencer Rd W WN6 ...... 37 A3
Spencer St Bury BL8 ...... 27 C3
Dukinfield SK16 ...... 101 C8
Eccles M30 ...... 79 C1
Littleborough OL15 ...... 16 C6
Mossley OL5 ...... 68 B1
Oldham OL1 ...... 67 A8
Oldham OL4 ...... 66 C4
Radcliffe M26 ...... 44 C4
Ramsbottom BL0 ...... 138 B5
Reddish SK5 ...... 111 F8
Spencer's La WN5 ...... 53 D7
Spender Ave M8 ...... 156 A6
Spendmore La PR7 ...... 19 D8
Spenleach La BL8 ...... 10 D3
Spenlow WN7 ...... 76 C3
Spenlow Cl SK12 ...... 133 E1
Spennithorne Rd M41 ...... 95 B2
Spenser Ave Denton M34 ...113 A8
Radcliffe M26 ...... 43 E4
Spenwood Rd OL15 ...... 15 E5
Spey Cl Altrincham WA14 ...119 C6
Standish WN6 ...... 19 D1
Spey Ho SK5 ...... 99 F2
Speyside Cl M45 ...... 63 A8
Spilsby Sq WN3 ...... 55 A2
Spindle Ave SK15 ...... 86 C3
Spindle Croft BL4 ...... 60 D8
Spindle Ct OL2 ...... 48 E4
Spindle Hillock WN4 ...... 72 D4
Spindle Point Prim Sch
BL4 ...... 61 B5
Spindle Wlk BL5 ...... 57 D3
Spindlepoint Dr 4 M28 ...78 C8
Spindles Sh Ctr The OL1 ...153 E6
Spindles The OL5 ...... 86 D8
Spinks St M4 ...... 67 B5
Spinnerbottom SK22 ...... 127 F2
Spinnerette Cl WN7 ...... 76 A5
Spinners Gdns OL12 ...... 15 C4
Spinners Gn OL12 ...... 14 F2
Spinners La SK12 ...... 133 C4
Spinners Mews BL1 ...... 145 F8
Spinners Way OL4 ...... 49 E4
Spinney Cl Glossop SK13 ...104 C2
Handforth SK9 ...... 131 C3
Spinney Dr Bury BL9 ...... 27 E6
Sale M33 ...... 107 D2
Spinney Gr M34 ...... 100 F5
Spinney Nook BL2 ...... 25 D2
Spinney Rd M23 ...... 121 B7
Spinney The Bolton BL1 ...144 B7
Cheadle SK8 ...... 122 E3
Edgworth BL7 ...... 9 C2
Oldham OL4 ...... 68 A8
Oldham OL4 ...... 24 D3
Urmston M41 ...... 95 A2
Whitefield M45 ...... 62 E7
Wigan WN5 ...... 54 E5
Spinning Gate Sh Ctr WN7 ...75 F4
Spinning Jenny Way WN7 ...75 F4
Spinning Jenny Wlk 5
M4 ...... 159 C2
Spinning Mdw BL1 ...... 145 D8
Spinningdale M38 ...... 59 D6
Spinningfield W3 ...... 158 E1
Spinningfield Way OL10 ...46 D7
Spinningfields BL1 ...... 145 D8
Spinnings The BL9 ...... 11 C3
Spion Kop WN4 ...... 73 A3
Spire Hollin SK13 ...... 104 C2
Spire Wlk M12 ...... 164 D8
Spiredale Dr M9 ...... 19 F2
Spirewood Gdns SK6 ...... 113 A2
Spod Rd OL12 ...... 14 D1
Spodden Cotts OL12 ...... 4 D2

Spodden Fold OL12 ...... 14 C8
Spodden St OL12 ...... 139 D8
Spodegreen La WA14 ...... 118 C1
Spokeshave Way OL16 ...15 C2
Spooner Rd 6 M30 ...... 79 C1
Sportside Ave M28 ...... 60 E4
Sportside Gn M28 ...... 60 E4
Sportside Gr M28 ...... 60 E4
Sportsman St WN7 ...... 75 D5
Sportsmans Dr OL8 ...... 67 A3
Spotland Bridge Ind Ctr
OL11 ...... 139 D8
Spotland Prim Sch OL12 ...139 D8
Spotland Rd OL12 ...... 139 E8
Spotland Tops OL12 ...14 B1
Spreadbury St 7 M40 ...83 A7
Spring Ave Hyde SK14 ...113 F8
Whitefield M45 ...... 44 E2
Spring Bank
Altrincham WA14 ...... 119 D3
Appley Bridge WN6 ...... 35 C8
Marple SK6 ...... 126 C6
Salford M6 ...... 154 E3
Stalybridge SK15 ...... 102 B8
Stalybridge SK15 ...... 86 B1
Spring Bank Ave
Ashton-u-L OL6 ...... 85 B5
Denton M34 ...... 100 D7
Spring Bank La
Rochdale OL11 ...... 29 E8
Stalybridge SK15 ...... 86 C5
Spring Bank PI SK15 ...... 170 E8
Spring Bank Rd SK22 ...... 127 C1
Spring Bank St OL8 ...... 66 D4
Spring Bank Terr M34 ...100 C7
Spring Bottom OL14 ...... 5 F7
Spring Bridge Rd M16 ...97 F1
Spring Clough BL8 ...... 26 E6
Oldham OL4 ...... 67 D5
Ramsbottom BL0 ...... 138 D6
Spring Clough M28 ...... 79 B6
Spring Clough Ave M28 ...60 F2
Spring Clough Dr
Oldham OL4 ...... 67 C4
Walkden M28 ...... 60 F2
Spring Gardens 8 4 BB4 ...2 F8
Spring Gdns
Altrincham WA15 ...... 120 C5
11 Atherton M46 ...... 58 D3
Bolton BL2 ...... 25 F4
Hadfield SK13 ...... 104 A5
Hazel Grove SK7 ...... 124 D3
12 Heywood BL6 ...... 22 B4
Hyde SK14 ...... 167 D4
Manchester M1,M2 ...... 159 A1
Middleton M24 ...... 47 A1
Rawtenstall BB4 ...... 2 F6
8 Royton OL2 ...... 48 D6
Salford M6 ...... 154 F3
Stockport SK1 ...... 112 A1
Wigan WN1 ...... 150 B8
Spring Gr Oldham OL3 ...69 B5
Bolton BL2 ...... 25 F4
Spring Grove M45 ...... 44 E2
Spring Hall Rise OL4 ...... 49 F4
Spring Hill Ct 5 OL4 ...67 D8
Spring Hill High Sch OL16 ...31 B5
Spring La Lymm WA13 ...... 117 F3
Oldham OL4 ...... 67 C5
Radcliffe M26 ...... 44 B3
Spring Meadow La OL3 ...69 C8
Spring Mill Cl 4 BL3 ...147 C4
Spring Mill Wlk OL16 ...15 C2
Spring Rd
Altrincham WA14 ...... 119 D2
Orrell WN5 ...... 53 F8
Poynton SK12 ...... 133 F2
Wigan WN4 ...... 36 A1
Spring Rise Glossop SK13 ...115 F7
Shaw OL2 ...... 32 A1
Spring Side Rawtenstall BB4 ...2 F6
Whitworth OL12 ...... 4 D4
Spring Side Cotts BL7 ...... 8 A2
Spring St Bolton BL3 ...... 145 F5
Bury BL8 ...... 26 F4
Bury BL9 ...... 140 F1
Farnworth BL4 ...... 42 D1
Glossop SK13 ...... 104 B1
Hollingworth SK14 ...... 103 C5
Horwich BL6 ...... 22 B4
Ince-in-M WN3 ...... 55 E4
Manchester M12 ...... 99 A2
Mossley OL5 ...... 68 C2
Mottram-in-L SK14 ...... 115 A8
Oldham OL3 ...... 69 B8
Oldham OL4 ...... 67 C8
Oldham OL4 ...... 68 A6
Ramsbottom BL0 ...... 138 B6
Stalybridge SK15 ...... 86 B2
Wigan WN1 ...... 151 D7
Wilmslow SK9 ...... 136 F8
Spring Terr 4 Bacup OL13 ...3 D8
Bury BL8 ...... 26 F7
Chadderton OL9 ...... 152 A7
Newhey OL16 ...... 32 B3
Rochdale OL16 ...... 14 A1
Spring Vale
Hazel Grove SK7 ...... 124 E2
Middleton M24 ...... 64 E2
Prestwich M25 ...... 63 A2
Spring Vale Dr BL8 ...... 26 E6
Spring Vale St BL8 ...... 26 F6
Spring Vale Way OL2 ...149 A5

Spring Wood St BL0 ...... 138 B7
Springbank
Chadderton OL9 ...... 152 A7
Hadfield SK13 ...... 103 F5
Springbank Cl SK6 ...... 113 C6
Springbank Ct
Manchester M8 ...... 63 F1
Romiley SK6 ...... 113 B5
Springbank Ind Est WN2 ...56 B3
Springbank Rd SK6 ...... 113 C6
Springbourne WN6 ...... 36 F2
Springbourn 6 1 M28 ...78 A6
Springdale Gdns M20 ...110 A3
Springfield
Charlesworth SK13 ...... 115 C6
Kearsley M26 ...... 61 C6
1 Urmston M41 ...... 95 C2
Springfield Ave
Golborne WA3 ...... 89 F8
Hazel Grove SK7 ...... 124 D3
Littleborough OL15 ...... 16 A7
Lymm WA13 ...... 117 B5
9 Marple SK6 ...... 125 F6
Reddish SK5 ...... 111 E7
Springfield Cl
Failsworth M35 ...... 83 F8
Hadfield SK13 ...... 171 E4
6 Heywood OL10 ...... 29 E1
Springfield Dr SK9 ...... 136 D6
Springfield Gdns BL4 ...61 A6
Springfield La Irlam M44 ...93 F2
Littleborough OL16 ...... 15 D3
Manchester M3 ...... 158 E3
Royton OL2 ...... 48 C7
Springfield Prim Sch
M33 ...... 108 B4
Springfield Rd
Adlington PR6 ...... 21 A8
Altrincham WA14 ...... 119 D5
Atherton M46 ...... 58 E4
Bolton BL1 ...... 24 E7
Coppull PR7 ...... 19 E8
Droylsden M43 ...... 83 F3
Farnworth BL4 ...... 42 A1
Gatley SK8 ...... 122 B5
Hindley WN2 ...... 56 C6
Horwich BL6 ...... 22 D1
Kearsley BL4 ...... 60 F6
Middleton M24 ...... 46 F2
Ramsbottom BL0 ...... 11 A2
Sale M33 ...... 108 B4
Wigan WN6 ...... 37 A2
Springfield Rd N PR7 ...19 E8
Springfield St
Ashton-u-L OL6 ...... 85 E5
18 Bolton BL3 ...... 42 A4
Denton M34 ...... 100 F6
Heywood OL10 ...... 29 A2
Wigan WN1 ...... 37 D2
Springhead Ave
Manchester M20 ...... 110 A7
Oldham OL4 ...... 68 A5
Springhead Inf Sch OL4 ...68 A6
Springhill OL2 ...... 48 D4
Springhill Ave OL13 ...... 3 D8
Springhill Villas OL13 ...... 3 D8
Springlawn BL1 ...... 40 F8
Springlees Ct 7 OL4 ...67 E6
Springmeadow WA13 ...... 117 D7
Springmount WA3 ...... 90 E7
Springpool WN3 ...... 54 B2
Springs Brow PR7 ...... 19 D5
Springs La SK15 ...... 85 F3
Springs Rd M24,OL9 ...... 65 E6
Springs The
Altrincham WA14 ...... 119 B2
Rochdale OL11 ...... 29 E7
Springside Ave M28 ...... 60 E3
Springside Cl M28 ...... 60 E3
Springside Gr M28 ...... 60 E3
Springside Prim Sch BL9 ...27 E7
Springside Rd BL9 ...... 27 E8
Springvale 2 M24 ...... 47 C7
Springvale Ho 8 M15 ...162 D6
Springvale Cl OL7 ...... 84 F5
Springvale La M45 ...... 44 E2
Springvale Ave M9 ...... 157 F7
Springwater Ave BL0 ...... 11 A2
Springwater Cl BL2 ...... 25 E3
Springwater La M45 ...... 44 E2
Springwell Cl 1 M6 ...154 E3
Springwell Gdns SK14 ...102 E1
Springwood 8 SK14 ...102 E1
Springwood Delph OL3 ...50 E8
Glossop SK13 ...... 115 F8
Springwood Prim Sch
M22 ...... 85 A3
Springwood Ave OL7 ...... 85 A6
Sprodley Dr WN6 ...... 18 B2
Spruce Ave BL9 ...... 141 B2
Spruce Cl WA3 ...... 90 F7
Spruce Ct 18 M6 ...... 81 A2
Spruce Lo SK8 ...... 122 D6
Spruce Rd WN6 ...... 53 A4
Spruce St Manchester M15 ...162 E6
Ramsbottom BL0 ...... 138 B6
Rochdale OL16 ...... 31 B6
Spruce Wlk 6 Sale M33 ...107 C6

Sprucewood OL9 ...... 65 D8
Spur The OL8 ...... 67 A3
Spur Wlk M8 ...... 155 F7
Spurley Hey High Sch
M18 ...... 99 C3
Spurn La OL3 ...... 51 B4
Square Rd OL14 ...... 6 A8
Square St BL0 ...... 138 C6
Square The
Altrincham WA15 ...... 129 C8
Bury BL9 ...... 140 F2
Hyde SK14 ...... 167 D2
Stockport SK4 ...... 168 C3
Swinton M27 ...... 79 E5
Uppermill OL3 ...... 51 A2
Square View OL14 ...... 6 B8
Squire Rd M8 ...... 155 F7
Squires Ct M45 ...... 80 A2
Squires La M46 ...... 76 E8
Squirrel Dr WA14 ...... 119 C8
Squirrel La BL6 ...... 22 A4
Squirrel's Jump SK9 ...... 137 C1
Stable Fold M26 ...... 44 A4
Stable St OL9 ...... 66 A2
Stablefold Eccles M28 ...79 A5
Mossley OL5 ...... 86 B4
Stableford Ave M30 ...... 79 C4
Stables The Droylsden M43 ...84 D3
Prestwich M25 ...... 63 C3
Stablings The SK9 ...... 137 A5
Stack La OL13 ...... 4 B8
Stadium Way WN5 ...... 36 E1
Stafford Cl SK13 ...... 116 F8
Stafford Ct 8 OL16 ...15 E4
Stafford Rd Eccles M30 ...79 C2
Failsworth M35 ...... 84 A5
Swinton M27 ...... 79 F8
Walkden M28 ...... 60 C1
Stafford St Bury BL8 ...... 140 D4
Hindley WN2 ...... 56 C5
Ince-in-M WN3 ...... 55 E4
Leigh WN7 ...... 76 D4
New Mills SK22 ...... 127 C1
Oldham OL9 ...... 66 C4
Stafford View M5 ...... 161 B7
Stafford Way 12 M34 ...101 A1
Stag Ind Est WA14 ...... 119 B6
Stag Pasture Rd OL8 ...66 D1
Stage La WA13 ...... 117 C4
Stainburn Cl WN6 ...... 35 C6
Stainburn Rd M11 ...... 165 B8
Stainburne Rd SK2 ...... 124 D6
Staindale OL4 ...... 67 D6
Stainer St M12 ...... 99 A3
Stainforth Cl BL8 ...... 26 F3
Stainforth St M11 ...... 164 F8
Stainmoor Ct SK2 ...... 124 D6
Stainmore Ave OL6 ...... 85 D7
Stainsbury St BL3 ...... 146 C4
Stainton Ave M18 ...... 99 E4
Stainton Cl M26 ...... 43 F5
Stainton Dr M24 ...... 46 D3
Stainton Rd M26 ...... 43 F5
Stairgate WN1 ...... 150 D8
Staithes Rd M22 ...... 130 D8
Stakeford Dr M8 ...... 156 C8
Stakehill Ind Est M24 ...47 D4
Stakehill La M24 ...... 47 E5
Staley Cl SK15 ...... 86 C2
Staley Hall Cres SK15 ...86 C3
Staley Rd OL5 ...... 86 B3
Staley St Oldham OL4 ...67 B6
18 Oldham OL4 ...... 67 B8
Stalham Cl M40 ...... 160 D3
Stalmine Ave SK8 ...... 131 B8
Staly Hall Rd SK15 ...... 86 C2
Stalybridge Ridge Hill
Cty Inf Sch SK15 ...... 85 F3
Stalybridge Ridge Hill
Jun Sch SK15 ...... 85 F3
Stalybridge Sta SK15 ...85 F3
Stalyhill Dr SK15 ...... 102 E2
Stalyhill Inf Sch SK15 ...102 E2
Stalyhill Jun Sch SK15 ...102 F2
Stamford Ave
Altrincham WA14 ...... 119 A5
Ashton-u-L SK15 ...... 85 E2
Stamford Cl SK15 ...... 85 F3
Stamford Ct
3 Ashton-u-L OL6 ...... 85 D2
Manchester M13 ...... 98 E3
Stamford Dr
Failsworth M35 ...... 84 B6
Stalybridge SK15 ...... 85 F2
Stamford Grange 1
WA14 ...... 119 C4
Stamford High Sch OL6 ...85 E4
Stamford New Rd WA14 ...119 D4
Stamford Park Inf Sch
WA15 ...... 119 C3
Stamford Park Jun Sch
WA15 ...... 119 C3
Stamford Pl M33 ...... 108 D3
Stamford Rd
Alderley Edge SK9 ...... 137 B1
Altrincham WA14 ...... 119 C8
Carrington M31 ...... 106 C6
Denton M34 ...... 100 C6
Dukinfield SK14 ...... 101 A1
Little Bollington WA14 ...118 B2
Manchester M7 ...... 81 B6
Mossley OL5 ...... 68 C2
Urmston M41 ...... 95 B2

Stamford Sq
- [3] Altrincham WA14 ....119 D5
- Ashton-u-L OL6 ....85 D2

Stamford St
- Altrincham WA14 ....119 A2
- Atherton M46 ....58 E4
- Heywood OL10 ....29 E1
- Manchester M16 ....161 C5
- Manchester M16 ....97 D4
- Mossley OL5 ....68 B1
- [10] Oldham OL4 ....67 E6
- Rochdale OL16 ....31 B6
- Sale M33 ....108 A6
- Stalybridge OL6,SK15 ...85 F2
- Stalybridge SK15 ....86 A2
- Stalybridge SK15 ....86 A2
- Swinton M27 ....62 A1

Stamford St Central OL6 ..166 B2
Stamford St E OL6 ....85 D2
Stamford St W OL6 ....166 A2
Stamford Way [2] WA14 ....119 D5
Stampstone St OL1 ....67 B8
Stan Jolly Wlk M11 ....165 C8
Stanage Ave M9 ....44 F4
Stanbank St SK4 ....169 E4
Stanbridge Cl BL1 ....143 F4
Stanbridge Cl SK4 ....169 E2
Stanbrook St M19 ....111 C8
Stanbury Cl BL9 ....28 D1
Stanbury Dr SK16 ....101 D8
Stanbury Wlk M40 ....160 D3
Stancliffe Gr WN2 ....38 C6
Stancliffe Rd M22 ....121 E5
Stancross Rd M23 ....120 C8
Stand Ave M45 ....44 E1
Stand Cl M45 ....62 C8
Stand La M26,M45 ....44 C1
Stand Rise M45 ....62 B8
Standedge Foot Rd OL3 ....51 D8
Standedge Rd OL3 ....51 C5
Standedge Wlk SK15 ....86 E6
Standell Wlk M9 ....64 E1
Standfield Ctr [2] M28 ...78 A6
Standfield Dr M28 ....78 A7
Standish Ave WN5 ....74 E5

Standish Com High Sch
- 97 E4

Standish Gallery [10] WN1 .150 C8
Standish Rd M14 ....110 D8
Standish St M29 ....77 A8
Standish Wlk M34 ....100 E2
Standishgate WN1 ....150 C8
Standmoor Rd M45 ....62 D7
Standon Wlk [20] M40 .....65 D2
Standring Ave BL8 ....44 A8
Stanedge Cl BL0 ....11 C4
Stanedge Gr WN3 ....55 B2
Stanford Cl M26 ....61 C7
Stanford Hall Cres BL0 ...11 E4
Stanhope Ave Denton M34 .100 E5
- Prestwich M25 ....63 A5
Stanhope Cl Denton M34 ..100 E5
- Wilmslow SK9 ....137 D8
Stanhope Ct M25 ....63 A5

Stanhope Rd
- Altrincham WA14 ....119 A2
- Salford M6 ....80 E5

Stanhope St Ashton-u-L OL6 .85 D4
- Denton M34 ....100 E5
- Leigh WN7 ....75 D6
- Manchester M19 ....99 B1
- Mossley OL5 ....86 C8
- Reddish SK5 ....111 E7
- Rochdale OL11 ....139 F5
Stanhope Way M35 ....83 E8
Stanhorne Ave M8 ....64 A2
Stanier Ave M30 ....79 D3
Stanier Pl BL6 ....22 C2
Stanion Gr SK16 ....101 D8
Stanlaw M30 ....79 E1

Stanley Ave
- Hazel Grove SK7 ....124 D3
- Hyde SK14 ....167 E4
- Manchester M14 ....98 D3
- Marple SK6 ....125 D7
Stanley Ave N M25 ....63 A6
Stanley Ave S M25 ....63 A6

Stanley Cl
- Manchester M16 ....161 C5
- Westhoughton BL5 ....57 F7
- Whitefield M45 ....44 F1
Stanley Ct M16 ....161 C5

Stanley Dr
- Altrincham WA15 ......120 A5
- Gatley SK8,SK9 ....131 D6
- Leigh WN7 ....75 D8
- Whitefield M45 ....44 F1

Stanley Gr Horwich BL6 ...22 D1
- Manchester M12 ....98 F4
- Manchester M12,M18 ....99 B4
- Manchester M21 ....109 A8
- Manchester SK4 ....168 B4
- Urmston M41 ....95 D2

Stanley Green Ind Est
- SK8 ....131 E5

Stanley Green Ret Pk
- SK8 ....131 F6

Stanley Grove Jun & Inf Sch M12 ....99 A4
Stanley Hall La SK12 ....135 D6
Stanley Ho M16 ....97 E2
Stanley La WN2 ....38 C7
Stanley Mews M32 ....42 D7
Stanley Mount M23 ......108 A3
Stanley Park Wlk BL2 ...148 C8
Stanley Pl Rochdale OL12 .139 E8
- Wigan WN1 ....151 E8

Stanley Rd Aspull WN2 ....38 C6
Bolton BL1 ....142 B1
Eccles M30 ....95 C8
Farnworth BL4 ....59 E8
Handforth SK8,SK9 ......131 E6
Manchester M16 ....161 C5
Manchester M16 ....97 E2
Manchester M7 ....155 E8
Manchester SK4 ....168 B3
Oldham OL9 ....66 B4
Orrell WN8 ....53 B7
Pendlebury M27 ....80 A8
Platt Bridge WN2 ....56 A3
Radcliffe M26 ....43 E6
Reddish M34 ....100 B3
Walkden M28 ....60 D2
Whitefield M45 ....44 F1

Stanley Road Jun & Inf Sch
- OL9 ....66 B4

Stanley Sq SK15 ....85 F1
Stanley St Atherton M46 ..58 C3
Heywood OL10 ....29 D2
Manchester M10,M40 ....157 F5
Manchester M11 ....99 E7
Manchester M3 ....158 E1
Manchester M8 ....159 A4
Manchester M9 ....157 E8
Newton-le-W WA12 ......89 A3
Oldham OL4 ....67 E5
Oldham OL4 ....68 A6
Oldham OL9 ....152 B8
Prestwich M25 ....63 C4
Ramsbottom BL0 ....138 B5
Rochdale OL12 ....139 E8
[3] Stalybridge SK15 ...85 F1
Stanley St S BL3 ....145 E6
Stanmoor Dr WN2 ....38 C6
Stanmore Ave M32 ......96 B2
Stanmore Dr BL3 ....144 C5
Stannard Rd M30 ....79 A1
Stanney Cl OL16 ....31 E5
Stanney Rd OL16 ....31 E6
Stanneybrook Cl OL16 ...31 B8
Stanneylands Cl SK9 ...131 C2
Stanneylands Dr SK9 ...131 B2
Stanneylands Rd SK9 ...131 B2
Stanrose Cl BL7 ....8 E1
Stansbury Pl SK2 ......124 E6
Stansby Gdns M12 ......164 E6
Stansfield Cl WN7 ......76 C2
Stansfield Dr OL11 .....13 F1
Stansfield Hall OL5 .....6 C1

Stansfield Hall CE/Free Church Prim Sch OL15 ..16 D8

Stansfield Rd
Failsworth M35 ....84 A8
Hyde SK14 ....167 E4
Rawtenstall BB4 ....2 E8

Stansfield Road Jun & Inf Schs M35 ......84 A8
Stansfield St [2] Bacup OL13 .3 C8
Droylsden M11 ....99 D8
Failsworth M40 ....83 D4
Oldham OL1 ....153 E8
Oldham OL9 ....152 B5
Stanstead Cl WN2 ......37 F2
Stansted Wlk M23 ......108 D1
Stanthorne Ave M20 ...110 A7

Stanton Ave
- Manchester M20 ....109 E4
- Manchester M7 ....81 B7
Stanton Cl WN3 ....55 B3
Stanton Ct M32 ....96 D4

Stanton Gdns
- Manchester SK4 ....168 A4
- Stockport SK4 ....168 A1
Stanton St Droylsden M11 .83 C2
- Oldham OL9 ....66 B3
- Manchester M32 ....96 D4
Stanway Ave BL3 ....145 D6
[3] Stanway Cl [2] Bolton BL3 .145 D6
- Middleton M24 ....65 B6
Stanway Dr WA15 ......119 F3
Stanway Rd M45 ....63 B8

Stanway St
- Manchester M9 ....157 E8
- Stretford M32 ....96 D4
Stanwell Rd Failsworth M40 .65 C1
- Swinton M27 ....79 F7
Stanwick Ave M9 ......64 A5
Stanworth Ave BL2 ....42 E6
Stanworth Cl [3] M16 ..97 E1
Stanyard Ct M5 ....161 A8
Stanyforth St SK13 ...104 A4
Stapleford Cl Bolton BL1 .23 E1
Stapleford Cl Atherton BL5 .59 A6
- Sale M33 ....108 C5
- Wythenshawe M23 ......120 F4
Stapleford Gr BL8 ....27 A2
Stapleford Wlk M34 ...100 E1
Staplehurst Cl WN7 ...57 C2
Staplehurst Rd M40 ...83 A4
Staplers Wlk [9] M14 ..98 F2
Stapleton Ave BL3 ....40 E8
Stapleton Rd M6 ......80 C5
Stapleton St M6 ......56 A2
Star Bank OL13 ....3 D7
Star Gr M7 ....155 E6
Star Ind Est OL8 .....153 F5
Star La BL6 ....23 C8
Starbeck Cl BL4 ......26 F2
Starcliffe St BL3,BL4 .42 D2
Starcross Wlk M40 ....83 B6

Starfield Ave OL15 .....15 F2
Starkey St OL10 ....29 D3
Starkie Rd BL2 ....25 B1
Starkie St M28 ....79 A8
Starkies BL9 ....44 E7
Starling Cl M43 ....84 D3
Starling Dr BL4 ....59 F7
Starling Rd BL4 ....43 E8
Starmoor Dr M8 ....156 A6
Starmount Cl BL2 .....43 B6
Starring La OL15 .....15 E5
Starring Way OL15 ....15 E5
Startham Ave WN5 .....71 D3
Starting Chair OL4 ...68 C8
Stash Gr M23 ....121 B7
Statford Ave M30 .....95 C8
Statham Fold SK14 ...102 A4
Statham St M6 ....81 B2
Statham Wlk [5] M13 ..163 B7

Station App
- Manchester M1 ....163 A8
- Manchester M1 ....163 B8
- Manchester M20 ......110 C1

Station Approach Bsns Ctr
- OL11 ....139 F6

Station Ave Leigh WN7 ..76 C2
- Orrell WN5 ....53 D5
Station Bridge M41 ....95 D2
Station Cl [1] SK14 ...167 D2
Station Cotts SK8 ....123 B2
Station La OL4 ....68 B5
Station Mews WN4 .....72 D3
Station Rd Adlington PR7 .21 A6
Blackrod BL6 ....21 E1
Cheadle SK8 ....123 B1
Diggle OL3 ....51 D5
Eccles M30 ....79 D1
Edgworth BL7 ....9 C4
Garswood WN4 ....72 C3
Hadfield SK13 ....104 A5
Handforth SK9 ....131 A4
Handforth SK9 ....131 D3
Haslingden BB4 ....1 A7
Hazel Grove SK7 ......169 F4
Irlam M44 ....105 E7
Kearsley BL4 ....61 A7
[9] Littleborough OL15 .16 B5
Manchester M8 ....64 A1
Manchester SK4 ....110 E1
Marple SK6 ....125 F6
Marple SK6,SK22 .....126 D1
Mossley OL5 ....86 C8
Mossley OL5 ....68 D1
Oldham OL4 ....69 B8
Partington WA14 ......118 B5
Ramsbottom BL0 ......138 F6
Reddish SK5 ....99 E2
Rochdale OL11 ....139 F6
Romiley SK6 ....113 B5
Stockport SK1 ....169 E1
Stockport SK6 ....113 C8
Stretford M32 ....96 D3
Swinton M27 ....61 F1
Urmston M41 ....95 D2
Whitworth OL12 ......14 C5
Whitworth OL12 ....4 D3
Wigan WN1 ....150 C8
Wilmslow SK9 ....137 B7
Station St Bolton BL3 ..145 F6
Dukinfield SK16 .....166 B1
Glossop SK13 ....104 D1
Hazel Grove SK7 ....124 D2
Oldham OL4 ....67 A5
Station View [11] M19 .99 A1
Stationers Entry OL16 .139 F7
Staton Ave BL2 ......148 C8
Staton St M11 ....165 C8
Statter St BL9 ......45 A4
Staveleigh Mall SK14 .166 B3
Staveley Ave Bolton BL1 .24 A6
Stalybridge SK15 ....86 A3
Staveley Cl Middleton M24 .46 E2
Shaw OL2 ....49 D6
Stavely Wlk OL2 ....48 E4
Staverton Cl M13 ...163 C7
Stavesacre WN7 .....75 F3
Staveton Cl SK7 ....124 A3
Stavordale [10] OL12 .139 E8
Stayley Dr SK15 ....86 C2
Stayley Rd OL5 .....86 D8
Stead St BL0 ....138 C6
Steadway OL3 ....69 E5
Stedman Cl M11 ....160 E1
Steele Gdns BL2 ....42 E5
Steeles Ave SK14 ...167 E3
Steeple Dr M5 .....161 A8
Steeple View OL2 ..48 D4
Stein Ave WA3 .....90 E8

Stelfox Ave
- Manchester M14 ....98 A1
- Sale WA15 ....120 C7
Stelfox St Eccles M30 .79 F2

Stella Maris RC Jun Sch
- SK4 ....110 E2

Stella St M9 ....64 B4
Stelling St M18 ...99 D5
Stenbury Cl M14 ...98 C3
Stenner La M20 ...110 B1
Stenson Sq [1] M11 .99 D7
Stephen [7] BL8 ...27 C2
Stephen Lowry Wlk [5] M40 .83 A7
Stephen St Bury BL8 .27 C2
- Manchester M3 ....158 F4

Stephen St continued
- Platt Bridge WN2 ...56 A2
- Stockport SK1 .....124 B8
- Urmston M41 ......95 E2
Stephen St S BL8 ..27 C1
Stephen Wlk SK1 ..124 B8
Stephen's Way WN3 .54 E5

Stephens Rd
- Manchester M20 ...110 D6
- Stalybridge SK15 ..85 F4
Stephens St BL2 ...42 D8
Stephens Terr [5] M20 .110 B3
Stephenson Ave M43 .84 A1

Stephenson Rd
- Newton-le-W WA12 .89 D2
- Stretford M32 ....96 E3
Stephenson Sq OL12 .15 C3
Stephenson St Abram WN2 .74 B8
- Failsworth M35 ...66 A6
- Horwich BL6 ......22 B2
- [4] Oldham OL4 ...67 B6
Stepping Hill Hospl SK2 .124 C4
Steps Mdw OL12 ....15 D4
Sterling [6] M30 ..79 E2
Sterling Pl OL10 ..28 F1
Stern Ave M5 .....161 A8
Sterndale Ave WN6 .19 E2

Sterndale Rd
- Boothstown M28 ...77 F6
- Romiley SK6 .....113 B1
- Stockport SK3 ...170 E5
Sterratt St BL1 ..145 D6
Stetchworth Dr M28 .78 B7
Steven Ct M21 ....109 C8
Stevens St SK9 ...137 A1
Stevenson Dr WN3 .150 B5
Stevenson Cl OL1 .49 E4
Stevenson Pl M1 ..159 B1
Stevenson Rd M27 .61 E1
Stevenson Sq M1 ..159 B1

Stevenson St
- Manchester M3 ...158 D1
- Walkden M28 .....60 B3
Stewart Ave M46 ..60 B7
Stewart Rd WN3 ...55 A3
Stewart St Ashton-u-L OL7 .84 F2
- Bolton BL1 ......143 E2
- Bury BL8 ....27 B3
- Bury BL8 ....27 C4
- Newhey OL16 .....32 B3
Stewerton Cl WA3 .73 E2
Steynton Cl BL1 ..40 F8
Stile Cl M41 .....94 C2
Stiles Ave SK6 ...123 C3
Stiles Cl SK13 ...103 E5
Stilton Dr M11 ...165 A8

Stirling Ave
- Hazel Grove SK7 .124 D1
- Irlam-M M20 .....109 F8
- Manchester M20 ..109 F8
- [6] Marple SK6 ..125 F5
Stirling Cl Leigh WN7 .76 D6
- Stockport SK3 ...123 C6
Stirling Dr Garswood WN4 .72 D4
- Stalybridge SK15 .86 A3
Stirling Gr M45 ..63 A8
Stirling Rd Bolton BL1 .24 E5
- Hindley WN2 .....56 F4
- Oldham OL9 ......65 F8
Stirling St Oldham OL9 .152 C7
- Wigan WN1 ....54 C7
Stirrup Brook Gr M28 .77 F5
Stitch La SK4 .....169 D3
Stitch-Mi-Lane BL2 .25 F3
Stiups La OL16 ...31 B4
Stobart Ave M25 ..63 C2
Stock Gr OL16 ....31 F7
Stock La OL9 .....152 B6
Stock St BL8 .....27 E5
Stockburn Dr M35 .84 C7
Stockbury Cl [6] BL1 .143 F1
Stockdale Ave SK3 .170 F5
Stockdale Gr BL2 .25 F1
Stockdale Rd M9 ..64 E4
Stockfield Mount OL9 .152 B6
Stockfield Rd OL9 .152 B7
Stockholm Rd SK3 .170 E6
Stockland Cl M13 .163 B7
Stockley Ave BL2 .25 F2
Stockley Gr WN6 ..35 E8
Stockley Wlk [20] M15 .162 D6

Stockport Air Raid Shelters Mus SK1 ..169 E1

Stockport Coll of F & H Ed
- SK1 ....170 D8

Stockport Gram Sch
- SK2 ....124 C8

Stockport Hat Mus SK4 .169 E1
Stockport Infmy SK3 ..170 E8

Stockport Rd
- Altrincham M23,WA15 .120 B6
- Altrincham WA15 ..119 F5
- Cheadle SK3 .....123 A7
- Cheadle SK8 .....122 E6
- Denton M34 ......100 E8
- Dukinfield OL7 ...100 F8
- Hattersley SK14 ..102 E2
- Hyde SK14 ....113 D7
- Manchester M12,M13,M19 .164 D5
- Marple SK6 ......125 A6
- Mossley OL5 .....68 C2
- Romiley SK6 .....113 B2
- Uppermill OL3 ...68 C5
Stockport Rd E SK6 .112 F4
Stockport Rd W SK6 .112 D3
Stockport Sta SK3 ..170 E8

Stockport Trad Est
- Stockport SK3 ...168 B1
- Stockport SK4 ...123 B8
Stocks Gdns SK15 ..86 C1
Stocks La SK15 ....86 C1
Stocks Park Dr BL6 .22 C3

Stocks St
- Manchester M4,M8 .159 A4
- Rochdale OL11 ...30 B2
Stocks St E M4,M8 .159 A4
Stocks The SK13 ..104 A7

Stocksfield Dr
- Manchester M9 ...64 E3
- Walkden M28 .....59 F5
Stocksgate OL12 ..14 B2
Stockton Ave [4] SK3 .123 B8
Stockton Dr BL8 ..27 B5
Stockton Pk OL4 ..67 D6

Stockton Rd
- Manchester M21 ..109 A8
- Wilmslow SK9 ....136 F4
Stockton St Farnworth BL4 .42 C2
- Littleborough OL15 .16 A5
- [4] Manchester M16 .97 E4
- [5] Swinton M27 .79 E7
Stockwell Cl WN3 .54 D3
Stockwood Wlk M9 .157 D7
Stoke Abbott Cl SK7 .132 E7
Stoke St OL16 ....31 B6
Stokes St M11 ....83 D2
Stokesay Cl Bury BL9 .44 F5
- Royton OL2 ......49 A4
Stokesay Dr SK7 ..124 C1
Stokesay Rd M33 ..107 E5
Stokesley Wlk BL3 .147 E3
Stokoe Ave WA14 ..119 A6
Stonall Ave M15 ..162 D7
Stone Breaks Rd OL4 .68 B7
Stone Cl BL0 .....11 A4
Stone Cross La W A3 .90 C7
Stone Cross La S WA3 .90 C6
Stone Cross Park WA3 .90 B7
Stone Gdns WN7 ...76 A5
Stone Hall La WN8 .35 A5
Stone Haven WN3 ..54 D2
Stone Hall La OL12 .14 A2
Stone Hill Rd BL4 .60 D6
Stone House Rd WN5 .36 D2
Stone Mead SK13 ..113 E3
Stone Mead Ave WA15 .129 C7
Stone Pale M45 ...62 F7
Stone Pit La OL3 ..74 F1
Stone Pit La WA3 ..90 F2
Stone Pits BL0 ....1 E3
Stone Pl M14 .....98 C3
Stone Row SK6 ....126 A6
Stone St Bolton BL2 .25 B1
- Manchester M3 ...162 E8
- Milnrow OL16 ....31 F5
- Rawtenstall BB4 ..2 E8
Stoneacre BL6 ....39 F8
Stoneacre Ct M27 .79 F7
Stoneacre Rd M22 .121 C2
Stonebeck Rd M23 .120 F5
Stonebridge Cl BL6 .40 C6

Stonechat Cl
- Boothstown M28 ..78 B8
- Droylsden M43 ...84 C3
- [10] Golborne WA3 .90 E8
Stonechurch BL3 ..145 D5
Stonecliffe Ave SK15 .86 A2
Stonecliffe Terr SK15 .86 A2
Stoneclough Rd BL4,M26 .61 A7
Stonecroft [2] OL1 .153 E7
Stonecroft M27 ...110 A4
Stonecrop WN6 ...18 D2
Stonedelph Cl BL2 .26 D1
Stonefield M29 ...59 C1
Stonefield Dr M8 ..155 F5
Stonefield St OL16 .31 F5
Stoneflat Ct OL12 .139 D8
Stonehaven BL3 ...40 F3
Stonehead St M9 ..157 F7
Stoneheuer St M26 .44 B2
Stonehill Cres OL12 .14 A2
Stonehill Dr OL12 .14 B3
Stonehill Rd OL12 .14 A2
Stonehouse [1] M23 .120 E7
Stonehouse Wlk [1] M23 .120 E7
Stonehurst Cl M12 .165 A6
Stonelands Way OL4 .68 A4
Stoneleigh Ave M33 .107 E6

Stoneleigh Com Prim Sch
- OL1 ....49 B2
Stoneleigh Dr M26 .61 B7
Stoneleigh Rd OL4 .68 A7
Stoneleigh St OL1 .67 B8
Stonelow Cl M15 ..162 F6
Stonely Dr OL14 ...6 A7
Stonemead Cl BL3 .147 F4
Stonemill Terr SK5 .169 F3
Stonepail Cl SK8 ..121 F5
Stonepail Rd SK8 ..122 A5
Stoner Rd PR7 ....20 F7
Stoneridge SK13 ..103 F5
Stones Bank Rd BL7 .8 F4
Stonesby Cl M16 ..97 D4
Stonesdale Cl OL2 .48 E5
Stonesteads Dr BL7 .25 A8
Stonesteads Way BL7 .25 A8
Stoneswood Dr OL3 .68 D2
Stoneswood Rd OL3 .50 F4
Stonethwaite Cl WN3 .55 A2
Stoney Bank M26 ..61 C7
Stoney Brow WN8 ..35 B1

Stratton Rd continued

Stockport SK2	124 C8
Swinton M27	61 F1
Strawberry Bank M6	81 B3
Strawberry Cl WA14	119 B7
Strawberry Hill M6	81 B3
Strawberry Hill Rd BL2	148 B5

Strawberry La

Uppermill OL5	68 C4
Wilmslow SK9	136 E6
Strawberry Rd M6	81 B3
Stray St M11	99 E8
Stray The BL1	25 B4
Stream Terr SK1	112 B1
Streamside Cl WA15	120 B4
Street Bridge Rd OL1,OL2	48 A2
Street La BL8	43 F8
Street Lodge OL11	30 B1
Streetgate M38	59 F5
Streethouse La OL3	50 F1
Stretford Gram Sch M32	96 E1
Stretford High Sch M32	96 F4
Stretford Ho 7 M32	96 C1

Stretford Meml Hospl

M16	97 B3

Stretford Motorway Est

M32	96 A5

Stretford Rd

Manchester M15,M16	161 C5
Urmston M41	95 E1
Stretford Sta M32	96 D1
Stretton Ave Billinge WN5	71 F5
Golborne WA3	90 E7
Manchester M20	110 A3
Sale M33	107 E4
Stretford M32	96 A3

Stretton Cl

Bolton BL2	157 D5
Standish WN6	36 E8
Stretton Rd Bolton BL3	146 B4
Ramsbottom BL0	11 A2
Stretton Way 3 SK9	131 D5
Striding Edge Wlk 1 OL1	49 A1
Strines Cl WA14	56 D6
Strines Ct SK14	167 E4
Strines Rd Marple SK6	126 B3
New Mills SK6	135 D8
Strines St OL14	6 A7
Strines Sta SK22	126 D1
Stringer Ave SK14	102 F2
Stringer Cl SK14	102 F2
Stringer St Leigh WN7	75 F5
Stockport SK1	112 A2
Stringer Way SK14	102 F2
Stroma Gdns M41	95 C5
Stromness Gr OL10	29 B1
Strong St M7	158 E4
Strongstry Rd BL0	1 C2
Strontian Wlk 5 M11	83 C1
Stroud Ave M30	79 A3
Stroud Cl Middleton M24	65 A5
Wigan WN2	37 F2
Stuart Ave Bacup OL13	3 D8
Hindley WN2	57 C3
Irlam M44	93 F2
Stuart Cres WN5	71 E5
Stuart Dr SK6	125 C7

Stuart Hampson Ct 1

M31	105 F3
Stuart Ho M43	100 A8
Stuart Rd Bredbury SK6	112 D6
Stretford M32	96 D3
Stuart St Droylsden M11	83 A2
Manchester M11	160 F2
Middleton M24	65 C8
Oldham OL8	153 E5
Rochdale OL16	31 A6
Rochdale OL16	31 A6
Wigan WN1	151 D8
Stuart St E M11	83 A2
Stuart Wlk M24	64 F7
Stubbins Cl M23	108 E1
Stubbins La BL0	138 C8
Stubbins Prim Sch BL0	1 D1
Stubbins Rd M6	80 D8
Stubbins Vale Rd BL0	1 C1
Stubbins Vale Terr BL0	1 B1
Stubley La OL3	51 A7
Stubbylee La OL13	3 F8
Stubley Gdns OL15	16 A5
Stubley La OL15	15 F4

Stubley Mill Rd

Littleborough OL15	15 F4
Littleborough OL15	16 A5
Stubworth Wlk 3 M15	163 A5
Studland Rd M22	121 F3
Studley Cl M29	77 A7
Studley Ct M29	58 F1
Sturton Ave WN3	54 E3
Styal Ave Reddish SK5	111 F6
Stretford M32	96 A6
Styal Ctry Pk SK9	130 C4
Styal Cty Prim Sch SK9	130 E4
Styal Gn SK9	130 F3
Styal Gr SK8	122 A3

Styal Rd

Gatley M22,SK8,& SK9	122 A3
Manchester SK8	137 B8
Wythenshawe M22	130 F7
Styal St BL1	144 B8
Styal Sta SK9	131 A4
Styal View SK9	131 B2
Styhead Dr M24	46 D3
Style St M4	159 A3
Styperson Way SK12	133 E3
Sudbrook Cl WA3	90 E8

Sudbury Cl

Manchester M16	161 C5

Sudbury Cl continued

Wigan WN3	55 B2
Sudbury Dr Bolton BL6	40 C6
Gatley SK8	131 C8
Sudbury Rd SK7	133 E8
Sudden Cl OL11	30 C4
Sudell St M4,M40	159 B3
Sudell Street Ind Est M4	159 B3
Sudley Rd OL11	139 D5
Sudlow St OL16	15 B2
Sudren St BL8	26 F3
Sue Patterson Wlk M40	156 C5
Suez St WA12	89 B3
Suffield St M24	65 A8
Suffield Wlk 1 M22	121 D1
Suffolk Ave M43	84 A3
Suffolk Cl Little Lever BL3	43 B5
Standish WN1	37 B7
Suffolk Dr Brinnington SK5	112 C6
Handforth SK9	131 C1
Suffolk Gr WN7	75 C5
Suffolk Rd WA14	119 B5
Suffolk St Oldham OL9	66 B4
Rochdale OL11	139 F6
Salford M6	81 A5
Sugar La OL3	51 A2
Sugden Sports Ctr M1	163 A7
Sugden St OL6	85 D3
Sulby Ave M41	96 B2
Sulby St Kearsley M26	61 B2
Manchester M40	83 A8
Sulgrave Ave SK12	133 F4
Sullivan St M12	99 A3
Sullivan Way WN1	37 D1
Sultan St BL9	44 F8
Sulway Cl M27	80 A7
Sumac St M11	83 D2
Sumbland Ho M27	62 B2
Summer Ave M41	95 E2

Summer Castle

Rochdale OL16	139 F7
Rochdale OL16	31 A7
Summer Pl 1 M14	98 C2
Summer St Horwich BL6	22 B4
Rochdale OL16	31 A7
Summerbottom SK14	115 A8
Summercroft OL9	65 E4
Summerdale Dr BL0	11 B2
Summerfield Ave M43	83 E3
Summerfield Ct 2 M21	96 F1
Summerfield Dr 7	
Middleton M24	47 C1
Tyldesley M29	77 B8
Summerfield Pl SK9	137 A5

Summerfield Rd

Bolton BL3	42 B4
Worsley M28	79 A8
Wythenshawe M22	121 C2
Summerfields PR7	19 F7
Summerfields Ctr SK9	67 C1
Summerfields View OL8	67 C3
Summerlea SK8	132 B8
Summers Ave SK15	86 D2
Summers St OL9	152 C7

Summersales Ind Est

WN3	54 C4

Summerseat Cl

Oldham OL4	68 A7
Salford M5	161 A8
Summerseat La BL0	11 A2

Summerseat

Meth Prim Sch BL9	11 D2
Summerseat Sta BL0	11 C2
Summersgill Cl OL10	29 E1
Summershades La OL4	68 D6
Summershades Rise OL4	68 D6
Summerton Ho 3 M5	81 A1
Summerville Ave M9	157 F7

Summerville Prim Sch

M6	80 D5
Summerville Rd M6	80 D5
Summit St BL9	28 F4
Sumner Ave BL2	26 D1
Sumner Rd M6	80 D5
Sumner St Aspull WN2	38 C5
Atherton M46	58 C3
Bolton BL3	146 B2
Glossop SK13	116 C8
Shaw OL2	149 B5
Sumner Way M41	95 D2
Summers Pl SK13	104 B1
Sun Gate OL15	15 F1
Sun Inn Mews OL3	33 D3
Sun St Mossley OL5	68 C1
Ramsbottom BL0	138 B7
Sun Vale Ave OL14	6 B7
Sunadale Cl BL3	144 B5
Sunbank Cl OL12	14 D2
Sunbank La WA15	129 E2
Sunbeam St WA12	89 C3
Sunbury Cl Handforth SK9	131 E2
Stalybridge SK16	101 F8
Sunbury Dr M40	83 A8
Sundance Ct M5	96 E8
Sunderland Ho OL6	166 C4
Sunderland Pl WN5	36 D1
Sunderton Wlk M12	164 E6
Sundew Pl M24	65 D7
Sundial Cl SK14	102 D3
Sundial Rd SK2	124 D7
Sundial Wlk SK14	102 D3
Sundridge Cl BL3	146 A3
Sunfield SK6	125 F6
Sunfield Ave OL4	49 E4
Sunfield Cres OL2	48 E3
Sunfield Dr OL2	48 F3

Sunfield Est OL3	51 C4
Sunfield La OL3	51 C4
Sunfield Rd OL1	153 E8
Sunfield Way OL4	67 E7
Sunflower Mdw M44	94 B3
Sunhill Cl OL16	31 B2
Sunk La M24	65 A7
Sunkhurst Cl WA3	116 B8
Sunleigh Rd WN2	56 E6
Sunlight Rd BL1	144 C7
Sunning Hill Cty Prim Sch	
BL3	147 D4
Sunning Hill St 10 BL3	147 D4
Sunningdale Ave	
Droylsden M11	83 B2
Radcliffe M26	43 D4
Sale M33	108 E3
Whitefield M45	62 C2
Sunningdale Cl Bury BL8	44 A8
Dukinfield SK14	101 F5

Sunningdale Ct

Reddish M34	100 B4
Sale M33	108 E3

Sunningdale Dr

Bramhall SK7	133 A7
Glossop SK13	104 E1
Heywood OL10	46 D8
Irlam M44	93 F3
Prestwich M25	63 B5
Salford M6	80 B5
Sunningdale Gr WN7	76 D7

Sunningdale Rd

Denton M34	101 B1
Urmston M41	95 B1
Sunningdale Wlk 1 BL3	145 D5
Sunninghey Ct SK9	136 F2
Sunny Ave BL9	27 F5
Sunny Bank Kearsley M26	61 A8
Oldham OL4	67 E5
Whitworth OL12	136 D4
Wilmslow SK9	137 A8
Sunny Bank Ave M43	83 F1
Sunny Bank Cl BB4	1 A6
Sunny Bank Prim Sch BL9	45 A3
Sunny Bank Rd	
Altrincham WA14	128 C8
Droylsden M43	83 F1
Haslingden BB4	1 A6
Manchester M13	98 E3
Whitefield BL9	45 A3
Sunny Banks SK13	116 B8
Sunny Bower St BL8	26 F6

Sunny Brow Rd

Manchester M18	99 C4
Middleton M24	64 E8
Sunny Dr Orrell WN5	53 F6
Prestwich M25	62 F4
Sunny Garth BL5	57 E8
Sunny Lea Mews SK9	137 A6
Sunny Side M32	96 D2
Sunnybank Ave Eccles M30	79 F3
Manchester SK4	110 F4
Sunnybank Cl WA12	89 C4
Sunnybank Rd BL1	142 C2
Tyldesley M29	77 B6
Sunnybank Rd	
Manchester SK4	110 F3
Prestwich M25,M45	63 C7
Sunnyfields WN3	54 C2
Sunnylea Ave M19	110 E5
Sunnymead Ave BL1	143 F4
Sunnymede Vale BL0	11 A3
Sunny Side OL7	84 F5
Sunnyside Ave M43	83 F4
Sunnyside Cres 8 OL6	85 D2

Sunnyside Ct

Droylsden M43	83 F3
Manchester M20	110 C3
Sunnyside Gr OL6	85 D2

Sunnyside Rd

Ashton-in-M WN4	72 F7
Bolton BL1	142 C2
Droylsden M43	84 A3
Sunnywood Dr BL8	27 A6
Sunnywood La BL8	27 A6
Sunset Ave M22	109 D2
Sunwell Terr SK6	125 F3
Surbiton Rd M40	83 C6
Surma Cl Oldham OL9	153 D7
Rochdale OL16	31 B5
Surrey Ave Droylsden M43	83 F4
Leigh WN7	76 E4
Shaw OL2	48 F7
Surrey Cl BL3	43 B9
Surrey Dr BL9	44 F8
Surrey Park Cl OL2	149 B8
Surrey Rd M9	64 D3
Surrey St Ashton-u-L OL6	85 D5
Glossop SK13	104 C1
Manchester M9	64 D3
Oldham OL9	152 C5
Rochdale OL12	14 C3
Surtees Rd M23	109 A2
Sussex Ave Heywood OL10	28 E1
Manchester M20	110 B4
Sussex Cl Hindley WN2	57 A5
Oldham OL9	65 E8
Standish WN1	37 B3
Swinton M27	62 A2
Sussex Dr Bury BL9	44 F8
Droylsden M43	84 A3
Sussex Pl SK14	102 D3
Sussex Rd Irlam M44	105 C6
Partington M31	105 D3
Stockport SK3	123 B8
Sussex St Leigh WN7	76 E4
12 Manchester M2	158 F1

Sussex St continued

Manchester M7	158 D4
Rochdale OL11	139 F6
Sutch La WA13	117 A3
Sutcliffe Ave M12	99 B2
Sutcliffe St Ashton-u-L OL7	84 F1
Bacup OL13	4 C8
Bolton BL1	143 E2
Littleborough OL15	16 B6
Middleton M24	65 C8
Oldham OL8	153 E5
Royton OL2	49 A3
Sutcliffes Pl 3 OL11	31 A4
Sutherland Cl OL8	66 C3
Sutherland Gr BL4	60 C8
Sutherland Rd Bolton BL1	142 A1
Heywood OL10	28 F1
Manchester M16	97 A3
Wigan WN3	55 A3

Sutherland St

Ashton-u-L OL6	85 E3
Eccles M30	79 B3
3 Farnworth BL4	60 C8
Hindley WN2	56 C5
Swinton M27	61 E1
1 Wigan WN5	54 F6
Suthers St Oldham OL9	152 C6
Radcliffe M26	44 C1
Sutton Ave WA3	91 F4
Sutton Dr M43	83 E3
Sutton Ho M3	158 E6
Sutton La PR6	21 B8
Sutton Manor 1 M21	97 A1

Sutton Rd

Alderley Edge SK9	136 F2
Bolton BL3	40 A4
Manchester M18	99 C3
Poynton SK12	134 A2
Sutton Way Hadfield SK13	104 A5
9 Handforth SK9	131 E5
Salford M6	154 F3
Suttons La SK6	126 A5
Swailes St 3 OL4	67 B6
Swain St OL12	14 C1
Swaindrod La OL15	16 C5
Swaine St SK3	169 E1
Swainsthorpe Dr 18 M9	157 E8
Swale Cl SK9	131 E2
Swalecliff Ave M23	108 D1
Swaledale Cl OL2	48 E5
Swallow Bank Dr OL11	30 B3
Swallow Cl SK15	86 F7
Swallow Ct SK1	169 E4
Swallow Dr Bury BL9	141 B4
Irlam M44	94 A3
Rochdale OL11	30 B3
Swallow La SK15	86 F6

Swallow St

Manchester M11	160 F1
Manchester M12	99 A2
Oldham OL8	66 D2
Stockport SK1	170 F7
Swallowfield WN7	76 A5
Swan Cl SK12	133 B4
Swan Ct OL2	149 B6
Swan La Bolton BL3	147 D4
Hindley WN2	57 B4
Swan Meadow Rd WN3	150 B7
Swan Rd Ramsbottom BL8	10 F2
Sale WA15	108 A1
Swan St Ashton-u-L OL6	166 C3
Manchester M4	159 B3
Radcliffe M26	44 C2
Wilmslow SK9	137 B7
Swanage Ave Sale M23	108 D1
Stockport SK2	124 D6
Swanage Cl BL8	27 C6
Swanage Rd M30	79 B3
Swanbourne Gdns SK3	123 C6
Swanhill Cl M18	99 F6
Swanley Ave M40	157 E5
Swann Gr SK8	123 B1
Swann La SK8	123 B1
Swann St WN3	150 B7
Swansea St OL8	67 B4
Swanton Wlk 17 M8	155 F6
Swarbrick Dr M25	62 F2
Swayfield Ave M13	98 F3
Swaylands Dr M33	108 B1
Swedenborg Sq 5 BL3	41 C5
Sweet Briar Cl OL12	14 E2
Sweet Briar La OL12	14 E2
Sweetbriar Cl OL2	149 B8
Sweetloves Gr BL1	24 E5
Sweetloves La BL1	24 E5
Sweetnam Dr M11	83 B2
Swettenham Rd SK9	131 D5
Swift Cl SK6	112 C5
Swift Rd Oldham OL1	49 E5
Rochdale OL11	29 F7
Swift St Ashton-u-L OL6	166 C3
Wigan WN5	150 A7
Swift Wlk 2 M40	83 B2
Swiftsure Ave M3	158 D1
Swinbourne Gr M20	110 C7
Swinburn Gr WN5	53 D1
Swinburn St 2 M9	64 F1
Swinburne Ave M43	84 A3
Swinburne Gn SK5	99 D1
Swinburne Way 12 M34	113 A7
Swindell's St 6 M11	99 E7
Swindells St Heyside OL2	48 F5
Swindon Cl M18	99 F6
Swinfield Ave M21	108 F8
Swinford Gr OL2	149 A5
Swinford Wlk 14 M9	64 E3

Swinley Chase SK9 131 F1
Swinley La WN1 37 C2
Swinley Rd WN1 37 C2
Swinley St WN1 37 C2
Swinside WN1 37 F1
Swinside Cl M24 46 C2
Swinside Rd BL2 42 F8
Swinstead Ave M40 157 E5
Swinton Cres M45 45 A1
Swinton Gr M13 163 C5
Swinton Hall Rd M27 80 A8
Swinton High Sch The M27 61 F1
Swinton Park Rd M6 80 B8
Swinton St Bolton BL2 42 E7
  Oldham OL4 67 C5
Swinton Sta M27 61 F1
Swiss Hill SK9 137 B1
Swithenby St BL4 22 A4
Swithin Rd M22 130 E8
Swythamley Cl SK3 123 A8
Swythamley Rd SK3 123 A8
Sybil St OL15 16 A6
Sycamore Ave
  Altrincham WA14 119 A5
  Denton M34 100 F2
  Golborne WA3 74 A1
  Heywood OL10 46 E8
  Hindley WN2 56 C6
  Newhey OL16 32 A3
  Newton-le-W WA12 89 C3
  Oldham OL4 67 D8
  Oldham OL9 65 F3
  Radcliffe M26 61 F8
  Tyldesley M29 59 D1
  Wigan WN6 36 F3
Sycamore Cl
  Ashton-u-L OL6 85 E2
  Handforth SK9 131 B2
  Littleborough OL15 15 F5
  Manchester M20 110 C7
  New Mills SK22 127 E1
  Stalybridge SK16 101 E6
Sycamore Cotts OL3 50 F1
Sycamore Cres
  Ashton-u-L OL6 85 C5
  Hollinfare WA3 105 B2
Sycamore Ct
  ▪ Manchester M16 97 D3
  Manchester M40 160 E3
  ▪ Salford M6 81 A3
Sycamore Dr Radcliffe M26 44 A5
  Wigan WN3 54 C2
Sycamore Gr M35 84 B7
Sycamore Pl M45 62 F6
Sycamore Rd Atherton M46 58 E3
  Bury BL8 27 A5
  Eccles M30 79 A4
  New Mills SK22 127 F2
  Partington M31 105 E3
  Romiley SK6 113 A4
Sycamore St Sale M33 108 E4
  Stockport SK3 123 B8
Sycamore Wlk
  Cheadle SK8 122 D6
  ▪ Horwich BL6 22 E1
Sycamores The
  Hadfield SK13 171 F3
  Kearsley M26 61 B6
  Mossley OL5 68 E1
  Oldham OL4 67 E8
  Stalybridge SK15 102 B8
Sydall St M34 100 F3
Syddal Cl SK7 132 D5
Syddal Cres SK7 132 D5
Syddal Gn SK7 132 D5
Syddal Park Prep Sch SK7 132 D5
Syddal Park Sch SK7 132 D5
Syddal Rd SK7 132 D5
Syddall Ave SK8 131 D8
Syddall St SK14 167 D2
Sydenham St ▪ OL1 49 B1
Sydenham Terr OL12 14 D3
Syderstone Cl WN2 56 E4
Sydney Ave Eccles M30 79 D2
  Leigh WN7 75 D2
  Wythenshawe M90 130 A8
Sydney Gdns OL15 6 C1
Sydney Jones Ct M40 65 C1
Sydney Rd SK7 132 F5
Sydney St Failsworth M35 83 E7
  Mossley OL5 86 D8
  Platt Bridge WN2 56 A3
  Salford M6 154 E2
  Stockport SK2 124 C7
  Stretford M32 96 E2
  Swinton M27 79 D7
Syke La OL12 14 F4
Syke Rd Littleborough OL15 16 C2
  Rochdale OL12 15 A3
Sykes Ave BL9 45 B4
Sykes Cl OL3 69 B5
Sykes Mdw SK3 170 D6
Sykes St Bury BL9 141 A3
  ▪ Rochdale OL12 14 C1
  Newhey OL16 32 A5
  Reddish SK5 111 F8
  ▪ Rochdale OL16 31 B6
Sykes Wlk ▪ SK5 111 F8
Sylvan Ave Failsworth M35 83 E5
  Manchester M16 97 D3
  Sale M33 108 C3
  Urmston M41 95 D3
  Wythenshawe M22 136 F5
Sylvan Cl M24 46 D2

Sylvan Gr WA14 119 D5
Sylvan St OL9 152 C7
Sylvandale Ave M19 99 A1
Sylvester Ave SK1,SK2 124 B7
Sylvester Cl SK14 102 E2
Sylvester Way
  ▪ Denton M34 113 A7
  ▪ Hattersley SK14 102 E2
Sylvia Gr ▪ SK5 111 E7
Symms St M6 81 B4
Symond Rd M9 64 E5
Symons Rd M33 108 B5
Symons St M7 155 E7
Syndall Ave M12 164 D6
Syndall St M12 164 D6
Synergy Ho M15 163 A5
Syresham St ▪ WN2 56 B2

T

Taberner Cl WN6 19 F1
Taberner St ▪ WN2 56 B2
Tabley Ave M14 98 B2
Tabley Gdns
  ▪ Droylsden M43 84 B1
  Marple SK6 126 A4
Tabley Gr Manchester M13 98 F2
  Reddish SK5 111 B7
  Sale WA15 120 A8
Tabley Mere Gdns SK8 122 F3
Tabley Rd Bolton BL3 146 B4
  Handforth SK9 131 D5
  Sale M33 108 E2
Tabley St Dukinfield SK16 101 E8
  Mossley OL5 86 D8
  Salford M6 81 B5
Tabor St M24 46 F2
Tackler Cl M27 79 F7
Tadcaster Wlk OL1 153 F7
Taddington Pl ▪ SK13 171 E1
Tadlow Wlk ▪ M40 159 C3
Tadman Gr WA14 119 F4
Tadmor Cl M38 59 F4
Tagore Cl M13 98 E4
Tahir Cl M8 156 B7
Tait Mews SK4 110 F2
Talavera St M7 155 D5
Talbenny Cl BL1 40 F8
Talbot Ave BL3 43 A4
Talbot Cl Oldham OL4 67 C8
  Rawtenstall BB4 1 E8
Talbot Ct BL3 143 F4
Talbot Gr BL9 28 A6
Talbot Pl M16 161 B5
Talbot Rd
  Alderley Edge SK9 137 B1
  Altrincham WA14 119 B2
  Dukinfield SK14 103 C2
  Glossop SK13 104 C2
  Manchester M14 110 E7
  Sale M33 108 E4
  Stretford M16,M32,M15 96 F3
Talbot St Ashton-in-M WN4 73 D4
  Ashton-u-L OL6 166 A3
  Eccles M30 79 E1
  Glossop SK13 104 C1
Talford Gr M20 110 A5
Talgarth Rd M40 159 C4
Talkin Dr M24 46 E3
Tall Trees M7 63 D1
Tall Trees Cl OL2 48 A1
Tall Trees Pl SK2 124 C6
Talland Wlk M13 164 D5
Tallarn Cl M20 110 C7
Tallis St M12 99 A3
Talman Gr WN4 73 D3
Talmine Ave M40 157 E5
Tamar Cl BL4 61 B5
Tamar Ct ▪ M15 162 D6
Tamar Dr M23 121 A4
Tamar Way OL10 29 A3
Tamarin Cl M27 79 C8
Tame La OL3 50 D7
Tame St Denton M34 100 C4
  Dukinfield M34 101 A7
  Manchester M4 160 D1
  Oldham OL3 69 B8
  Stalybridge SK15,SK16 85 F1
  Uppermill OL3 69 B4
Tame Valley Prim Sch SK5 112 C2
Tame Water Villas OL3 50 F1
Tame Wlk ▪ SK9 131 D2
Tame Wlk ▪ M34 101 A7
Tamebank OL5 68 D3
Tamer Gr WN7 75 C8
Tamerton Dr M8 156 A6
Tameside Coll
  (The Hyde Ctr) SK14 113 D7
Tameside Coll of Tech
  Ashton-u-L OL6 166 B2
  Ashton-u-L OL6 85 D3
  Hyde SK14 167 E2
Tameside Ct
  Dukinfield SK16 101 B8
  ▪ Hattersley SK14 102 E2
Tameside General Hospl OL6 85 E4
Tamworth Ave
  Prestwich M45 63 B7

Tamworth Ave continued
  Salford M5 161 A8
Tamworth Ave W M5 161 A8
Tamworth Cl
  Hazel Grove SK7 133 D8
  Manchester M15 162 E5
Tamworth Ct M15 162 E5
Tamworth Dr Bury BL8 27 C5
Tamworth Gn SK1 112 B2
Tamworth St
  Manchester M15 97 E4
  Newton-le-W WA12 89 A3
  Oldham OL9 152 C5
  Stockport SK1 112 B2
Tamworth Wlk M5 161 B8
Tan House Dr WA3 54 C2
Tan House La WN3 54 C2
Tan Pit Cotts WN8 35 C4
Tan Pits Cl M29 77 C7
Tan Yard Brow M18 99 E5
Tandis Ct M6 80 A4
Tandle Hill Ctry Pk OL2 48 A6
Tandle Hill Rd OL2 48 B6
Tandlewood Mews ▪ M40 83 C5
Tandlewood Pk OL2 48 B6
Tanfield Dr M26 61 B7
Tanfield Rd M20 122 B8
Tang The SK6 113 B1
Tangmere Cl M40 65 C3
Tangmere Ct M16 97 D3
Tanhill Cl SK2 67 A2
Tanhouse Ave M29 77 D7
Tanhouse Rd M41 94 D3
Tanner Brook Cl BL3 146 C4
Tanner St M13 167 D3
Tanner's La WA3 90 B8
Tanners Croft BL0 138 B6
Tanners Fold OL8 67 A2
Tanners Gn ▪ M6 154 F3
Tanners St Droylsden M18 99 E5
  Ramsbottom BL0 138 B6
Tannery Way WA14 119 E7
Tannock Rd SK7 124 F1
Tanpit Wlk ▪ M22 121 C2
Tanpits Rd BL9 140 F3
Tansey Gr M7 155 F7
Tansley Ave PR7 19 D8
Tansley Rd M8 64 B2
Tansley Sq WN5 53 C6
Tanworth Wlk ▪ BL1 143 E2
Tanyard Dr WA15 129 C6
Tanyard Gn SK5 111 F5
Tanyard La WA15 129 A5
Tape St BL0 138 B6
Taper St BL0 138 B6
Tapley Ave SK12 133 E2
Taplin Dr M18 165 C5
Taplow Gr SK8 122 F2
Tarbet Dr BL2 42 F8
Tarbet Rd SK16 101 C7
Tarbet Wlk M8 156 B6
Tarbolton Cres WA15 120 C3
Tarbrook Gr ▪ SK9 131 D2
Tariff St M1 159 A1
Tarland Wlk ▪ M11 83 C1
Tarleton Ave M46 58 B5
Tarleton Cl BL8 26 F1
Tarleton Pl BL3 146 A3
Tarleton Wlk M13 164 D6
Tarn Cl WN4 73 A4
Tarn Gr WN4 44 E6
Tarn Gr M28 60 F1
Tarnbrook Cl M45 63 C8
Tarnbrook Dr WN2 38 B5
Tarnbrook Wlk M15 163 A5
Tarnrigg Cl WN3 54 E1
Tarporley Ave M14 110 A8
Tarporley Cl SK3 170 D5
Tarporley Wlk SK9 131 E2
Tarran Gr M34 101 B1
Tarran Pl WA14 119 E6
Tarrant Cl WN3 54 D2
Tarrington Cl M12 165 A5
Tartan St M11 83 B2
Tarves Wlk M11 83 B1
Tarvin Ave
  Manchester M20 110 A7
  Reddish SK4 111 D7
Tarvin Cl SK3 112 E4
Tarvin Dr SK6 112 E4
Tarvin Rd SK8 123 A4
Tarvin Way ▪ SK5 131 D5
Tarvin Wlk BL1 143 E2
Tarvington Cl M40 156 C6
Tasle Alley M2 158 F1
Tatchbury Rd M35 84 A2
Tate St OL8 67 A2
Tatham Cl ▪ M13 98 F3
Tatham Gr WN3 54 D1
Tatham St M9 31 A7
Tatland Dr M22 121 E3
Tatlock Cl WN5 71 E5
Tattenhall Wlk ▪ M14 110 D8
Tattersall Ave BL1 23 F7
Tattersall St OL9 153 D6
Tatton Cl Cheadle SK8 123 A4

Tatton Cl continued
  Hazel Grove SK7 124 F4
Tatton Ct
  ▪ Handforth SK9 131 E5
  ▪ Manchester M14 110 D8
  Manchester M40 168 C4
Tatton Dr WN4 72 F4
Tatton Fold M22 109 E1
Tatton Gdns SK6 113 D5
Tatton Gr M20 110 B6
Tatton Mere Dr M43 84 B1
Tatton Pl Manchester M13 98 E4
  Sale M33 108 B5
Tatton Rd Denton M34 101 A1
  Handforth SK9 131 E5
  Sale M33 108 B5
Tatton Rd N SK4 111 C5
Tatton Rd S SK4 168 C4
Tatton St Hyde SK14 113 E7
  Manchester M15 162 D7
  Salford M5 161 B8
  Stalybridge SK15 86 B1
  Stockport SK1 169 F1
Tatton Terr SK16 166 B1
Tatton View ▪ M20 110 B6
Tattonmere Gdns SK8 123 A4
Taunton Ave
  Ashton-u-L OL7 166 A4
  Brinnington SK5 112 C5
  Eccles M30 79 B3
  Hindley WN7 57 D2
  Rochdale OL11 30 B7
  Urmston M41 107 B8
Taunton Brook La OL7 84 E5
Taunton Cl Bolton BL1 142 C1
  Hazel Grove SK7 125 A2
Taunton Dr BL4 147 D1
Taunton Gr OL7 84 F5
Taunton Hall Cl OL7 84 F5
Taunton Lawns OL7 85 A5
Taunton Pl OL7 84 F5
Taunton Rd
  Ashton-u-L OL7 166 A4
  Chadderton OL9 48 A1
  Sale M33 107 D4
Taunton Sq M11 160 D1
Taunton St M4 160 D1
Taurus St OL4 67 C8
Tavern Court Ave M35 84 B7
Tavern Ct M35 84 B7
Tavery Cl ▪ M4 159 C2
Tavistock Cl SK14 103 C5
Tavistock Dr OL9 47 F1
Tavistock Rd Bolton BL1 145 D6
  Hindley WN2 57 A4
  Rochdale OL11 30 F2
  Sale M33 108 D4
  Wigan WN3 150 D4
Tavistock Sq M9 157 D7
Tavistock St M6 58 B4
Tawton Ave SK14 102 E3
Taxi Rd M90 130 B7
Tay Cl OL8 153 E5
Tayfield Rd M22 121 C2
Taylor Ave OL11 29 F8
Taylor Bldgs BL4 61 B8
Taylor Gr WN2 57 C3
Taylor Green Way OL4 67 E7
Taylor Ho BL3 27 C5
Taylor Holme Ind Est OL13 3 B8
Taylor Ind Est WA3 91 F1
Taylor La M34 100 D4
Taylor Rd
  Altrincham WA14 119 A5
  Eccles M41 95 E7
  Hindley WN2 57 C3
Taylor St ▪ Bolton BL3 145 F6
  Bury BL9 141 A3
  Chadderton OL9 152 A7
  Denton M34 100 F4
  Droylsden M43 84 A1
  Golborne WN3 74 C1
  Heywood OL10 29 C2
  Middleton M24 47 B1
  Oldham OL1 67 A7

Tealby Rd M18 99 B4
Teasdale Cl OL9 65 E3
Tebbutt St M4 159 B3
Ted Jackson Wlk M11 164 F8
Tedburn Wlk ▪ M40 65 D2
Tedder Cl BL9 45 B2
Tedder Dr M22 130 F7
Teddington Rd M40 65 C1
Teer St M1 160 D2
Tees St OL16 31 B6
Tees Wlk OL8 153 E5
Teesdale Ave M41 95 A4
Teesdale Cl SK2 124 E6
Teesdale Dr WN7 76 C5
Teesdale Wlk ▪ M9 64 E3
Teignmouth Ave M40 159 C4
Teignmouth St M40 159 C4
Telfer Ave M13 98 E2
Telfer Rd M13 98 E2
Telford Cres WN7 75 D8
Telford Mews ▪ OL3 69 B8
Telford Rd SK6 126 A4
Telford Sch M9 64 C4
Telford St Atherton M46 58 A2
  Horwich BL6 22 D2
  Manchester M8 156 C5
Telford Way OL11 31 A2
Telford Wlk ▪ M16 97 D4
Tell St OL12 139 D7
Tellers Cl M46 58 D3
Tellson Cl M6 80 D6
Tellson Cres M6 80 D6
Telryn Wlk M8 156 C8
Temperance Sq SK14 103 A4
Temperance St
  Bolton BL3 145 E5
  Manchester M12 163 C8
  Manchester M12 164 D7
  Mottram-in-L SK14 115 A8
Tempest Chase BL6 40 C4
Tempest Rd
  Alderley Edge SK9 137 C1
  Bolton BL6 40 C4
Temple Cl OL4 67 E8
Temple Dr Bolton BL1 142 C3
  Pendlebury M27 80 B7
Temple Inf & Jun Sch M8 156 A6
Temple La OL15 6 D1
Temple Moor Inf Sch 108 E4
Temple Rd Bolton BL1 142 C3
  Sale M33 108 D4
Temple Sq M8 156 B6
Temple St Hadfield SK13 104 C5
  Heywood OL10 29 D2
  Middleton M24 47 B1
  Oldham OL1 67 A7
Templecombe Dr BL1 24 E7
Templegate Cl WN6 19 F2
Templeton Cl
  Altrincham WA14 119 B6
  Westhoughton BL5 56 B2
Templeton Rd WN2 56 B2
Tembsbury Wlk M40 157 E5
Ten Acre Ct M45 62 D7
Ten Acre Dr M45 62 D7
Ten Acres La M40 83 A4
Ten Foot Cl SK13 104 B2
Ten Ho OL4 67 C2
Tenax Circ M17 96 B8
Tenax Rd M17 96 B8
Tenbury Cl M6 154 F3
Tenbury Dr
  Ashton-in-M WN4 73 A4
  Middleton M24 65 A5
Tenby Ave Bolton BL3 142 A1
  Manchester M20 110 B6
  Stretford M32 96 E4
Tenby Ct M15 161 C6
Tenby Dr Cheadle SK8 123 B1
  Pendlebury M6 80 D5
Tenby Gr ▪ OL12 14 C1
Tenby Rd Oldham OL8 66 B2
  Stockport SK3 123 B7
Tenby St OL12 14 C1
Tenchill La SK7,SK8 123 C3
Tenement St WN7 56 B1
Tenerife St M7 155 D5
Tenham Wlk ▪ M9 64 E3
Tennis St Bolton BL1 143 D3
  Manchester M16 97 D3
Tennyson Ave Bury BL9 44 F6
  Denton M34 113 A7
  Dukinfield SK16 102 B7
  Leigh WN7 75 C8
  Radcliffe M26 43 E4
Tennyson Cl SK4 168 B2
Tennyson Dr
  Longshaw WN5 37 C3
Tennyson Gdns M25 62 F3
Tennyson Rd Cheadle SK8 122 F6
  Droylsden M43 83 F2
  Farnworth BL4 60 B6
  Middleton M24 47 B2
  Reddish SK5 99 D1
  Swinton M27 79 D8
Tennyson St Bolton BL1 143 D3
  Manchester M13 163 C5
  Oldham OL1 49 C1
  ▪ Rochdale OL11 31 A5

Tennyson St continued
Salford M6 ....81 C4
Tennyson Wik 8 BL1 .....143 E2
Tensing Ave Ashton-u-L OL7 .85 B5
  Atherton M46 ....58 C5
Tensing St OL8 ....85 A8
Tenter Dr WN6 ....37 B7
Tentercroft Oldham OL1 ...153 E7
  Rochdale OL12 ....139 E7
Tenterden St BL9 ....140 D2
Tenterden Wik M22 ....121 C3
Tenterfield St 6 BB4 ....2 F8
Tenterheads 2 F7
Tenterhill La OL11 ....13 D2
Tenters St BL9 ....140 D2
Tenth St M17 ....96 D6
Terence St M40 ....83 D5
Terling Wik M40 ....157 E5
Terminal Rd E M90 ....130 C7
Terminal Rd N M90 ....130 B7
Terminal Rd S M90 ....130 B7
Tern Ave BL4 ....59 F8
Tern Cl Altrincham WA14 ..119 B8
  Dukinfield SK16 ....101 E7
  Rochdale OL11 ....29 F7
Tern Dr SK12 ....133 B4
Ternhill Ct BL4 ....60 D8
Terrace St OL4 ....67 B7
Terrace The M25 ....63 B3
Terrington Cl M21 ....109 E7
Tetbury Dr BL2 ....43 A8
Tetbury Rd M22 ....121 B1
Tetlow Gr M30 ....79 C1
Tetlow La M7,M8 ....155 E8
Tetlow St Dukinfield SK14 ..101 E5
  Failsworth M40 ....83 D5
  Middleton M24 ....65 A8
  Oldham OL9 ....153 D6
Tetsworth Wik M40 ....65 D2
Teviot St 8 M13 ....98 E4
Tewkesbury Ave
  Altrincham WA15 ....120 C3
  Ashton-u-L OL6 ....85 C7
  Chadderton OL9 ....48 A2
  Droylsden M43 ....84 A3
  Middleton M24 ....46 F3
  Urmston M41 ....95 D4
Tewkesbury Cl
  Bramhall SK8 ....132 B6
  Poynton SK12 ....133 D4
Tewkesbury Dr M25 ....63 C2
Tewkesbury Rd
  Cheadle SK3 ....123 B6
  Golborne WA3 ....90 B8
  Manchester M40 ....160 D3
Texas St OL6 ....166 C2
Textile St M12 ....165 A7
Textilose Rd M17 ....96 B5
Teynham Wik 5 M22 ....121 C1
Thackeray Cl M8 ....156 A6
Thackeray Gr M43 ....84 A2
Thackeray Pl WN3 ....150 A5
Thackeray Rd OL1 ....49 C1
Thames Ave WN7 ....75 F1
Thames Cl Bury BL9 ....27 F7
  Manchester M11 ....165 B8
Thames Dr 2 M15 ....162 D6
Thames Dr WN5 ....53 F7
Thames Ind Est M12 ....164 D7
Thames Rd Culcheth WA3 ..92 A2
  Milnrow OL16 ....32 B6
Thames St OL1 ....67 A8
Thames Steet OL16 ....31 B6
Thames Trad Ctr M44 ......105 F7
Thanet Cl M7 ....155 E5
Thanet Gr WN7 ....76 A5
Thankerton Ave M34 ....84 D1
Thatch Leach OL9 ....65 F5
  Thatch Leach La M45 ....63 A7
Thatcher Cl WA14 ....119 C1
Thatcher St OL8 ....67 A4
Thaxmead Dr M40 ....83 D4
Thaxted Cl SK2 ....125 A5
Thaxted Dr SK2 ....125 A5
Thaxted Pl BL1 ....144 C8
Thaxted Wik M22 ....130 C8
Theatre St OL1 ....153 F7
Thekla St OL9 ....153 D8
Thelma St OL0 ....138 B6
Thelwall Ave Bolton BL2 ...42 DB
  Manchester M14 ....110 D8
Thelwall Cl
  8 Altrincham WA15 ....119 E6
  Leigh WN7 ....75 B4
Thelwall Ct M14 ....110 AB
Thelwall Rd M33 ....108 E3
Theobald Rd WA14 ....119 D1
Theta Cl M11 ....83 B2
Thetford 2 OL12 ....139 EB
Thetford Cl Bury BL8 ....27 D5
  Hindley WN2 ....56 E4
Thetford Dr M8 ....156 B7
Thicketford Brow BL2 ......25 D1
Thicketford Cl BL2 ....25 C2
Thicketford Rd BL2 ....25 C1
Thicknesse Ave WN6 ....36 F3
Thimble Cl OL12 ....15 D4
Thimbles The OL12 ....15 D4
Third Ave Bolton BL1 ....144 B7
  Bury BL9 ....28 D4
  Droylsden M11 ....99 E8
  Little Lever BL3 ....42 F4
  Mossley SK15 ....86 D6
  Oldham OL8 ....66 D1
  Poynton SK12 ....133 D1

Third Ave continued
  Stretford M17 ....96 D6
  Swinton M27 ....79 E5
  Tyldesley M29 ....77 B4
  Wigan WN6 ....37 A2
Third St BL1 ....23 F4
Thirkhill Pl 2 M30 ....79 F2
Thirlby Dr M22 ....121 D1
Thirlemere Rd SK1 ....124 B7
Thirlmere Ave Abram WN2 ..74 B8
  Ashton-in-M WN4 ....73 C4
  Ashton-u-L OL7 ....84 F4
  Haslingden BB4 ....1 C8
  Horwich BL6 ....22 C2
  Ince-in-M WN2 ....56 B7
  8 Orrell WN5 ....53 F7
  Orrell WN8 ....53 B7
  Pendlebury M27 ....80 A7
  Standish WN6 ....37 A7
  Stretford M32 ....96 C3
  Tyldesley M29 ....77 A7
Thirlmere Cl Adlington PR6 ..21 B8
  Alderley Edge SK9 ....136 F1
  Stalybridge SK15 ....86 A4
Thirlmere Dr Bury BL9 ....44 E7
  Middleton M24 ....46 E2
  Walkden M38 ....60 A5
Thirlmere Gr
  Farnworth BL4 ....59 E8
  Royton OL2 ....48 D6
Thirlmere Mews M24 ....46 E2
Thirlmere Rd Atherton BL5 ..58 F7
  Blackrod BL6 ....21 C3
  Gatley SK8 ....131 B8
  Hindley WN2 ....56 E5
  Partington M31 ....105 E4
  Rochdale OL11 ....30 B4
  Urmston M41 ....94 E3
  Wigan WN5 ....54 D6
  Wythenshawe M22 ....121 B1
Thirlmere St WN7 ....75 E5
Thirlspot Cl BL1 ....24 E6
Thirlstone Ave OL4 ....49 F4
Thirlswood Dr 8 M11 ....83 C2
Thirsk Ave Chadderton OL9 ..47 F1
  Sale M33 ....107 C3
Thirsk Cl BL8 ....27 B5
Thirsk Mews M7 ....155 D6
Thirsk Rd BL3 ....43 A2
Thirsk St M12 ....163 C7
Thistle Cl SK15 ....102 E7
Thistle Sq M31 ....105 E2
Thistle Way OL4 ....49 D2
Thistle Wik 4 M31 ....105 E2
Thistledown Cl Eccles M30 ..95 D8
  Wigan WN6 ....37 A2
Thistleton Rd BL3 ....40 F3
Thistlewood Dr SK9 ....137 D8
Thomas Cl M34 ....101 A4
Thomas Dr BL3 ....145 D5
Thomas Garnet Cl 8 BL4 ...60 C8
Thomas Gibbon Cl 5 M32 ..96 C1
Thomas Henshaw Ct OL11 ..30 C4
Thomas Holden St BL1 ......145 E8
Thomas Holden St BL1 ......145 E8
Thomas Johnson Cl 4
  M30 ....79 C1
Thomas More Cl
  Kearsley BL4 ....60 F6
  Kearsley BL4 ....61 A6
Thomas Regan Ct 4 M48 ..99 D6
Thomas St
  Altrincham WA15 ....119 E4
  Aspull WN2 ....38 B6
  Atherton M46 ....58 D3
  Bolton BL3 ....145 D5
  Farnworth BL4 ....60 E7
  Farnworth BL4 ....60 E8
  Glossop SK13 ....104 E1
  Golborne WA3 ....90 A8
  Hindley WN2 ....57 B3
  Littleborough OL15 ....15 E4
  Manchester M8 ....159 A2
  Manchester M8 ....155 F8
  Oldham OL4 ....67 E5
  Radcliffe M26 ....44 B3
  6 Rochdale OL16 ....31 A8
  Romiley SK6 ....113 A3
  Romiley SK6 ....114 B2
  Royton OL2 ....49 A3
  Shaw OL2 ....149 C6
  Stockport SK1 ....170 F7
  Stretford M32 ....96 D3
  Westhoughton BL5 ....39 E3
  Whitworth OL12 ....4 D2
  7 Shaw St SK1,SK2 ....170 F7
Thomas Telford Basin
  M1 ....159 C1
Thomason Fold BL7 ....9 D6
Thomasson Cl BL1 ....143 E1
Thomasson Memorial Sch
  BL1 ....144 B7
Thompson Ave
  Ainsworth BL2 ....26 D1
  Culcheth WA3 ....91 E3
  Whitefield M45 ....63 A7
Thompson Cl
  Newton-le-W WA12 ....89 C1
Thompson St
  Reddish M34 ....100 B3
  Stalybridge SK15 ....85 F2
Thompson Dr BL9 ....141 C3
Thompson Fold SK15 ....85 F2
Thompson Ho M46 ....58 C3
Thompson La OL9 ....66 A4
Thompson Rd Bolton BL1 ..142 B1

Thompson Rd continued
  Eccles M17 ....95 EB
  Reddish M34 ....100 B3
Thompson St
  Ashton-in-M WN4 ....73 D4
  Bolton BL3 ....145 F5
  Horwich BL6 ....22 A3
  Leigh WN7 ....75 B5
  Manchester M10,M40 ....157 F5
  Manchester M3 ....158 F3
  Manchester M4 ....159 B2
  Wigan WN1 ....37 E1
  Wigan WN3 ....55 A4
Thomson Rd M18 ....99 C4
Thomson St
  Manchester M13 ....163 C6
  Stockport SK3 ....170 EB
Thor Gr M5 ....161 C8
Thoralby Cl M12 ....165 A5
Thorburn Dr OL12 ....14 B7
Thorburn Ho WN5 ....54 C7
Thorburn La WN5 ....54 DB
Thorburn Rd WN5 ....54 DB
Thoresby Cl
  Little Lever BL3 ....43 C5
  Wigan WN3 ....54 E3
Thoresway Rd
  Manchester M13 ....98 E3
  Wilmslow SK9 ....136 E5
Thorgill Wik M40 ....83 A7
Thorlby Rd WA3 ....91 F3
Thorley Cl OL9 ....65 E2
Thorley Dr
  Altrincham WA15 ....120 B5
  Urmston M41 ....95 D2
Thorley La
  Altrincham WA15 ....120 B4
  Wythenshawe M22,WA15 ....121 A1
Thorley Mews SK7 ....132 F7
Thorley St M35 ....83 F6
Thorn Ave M35 ....83 F6
Thorn Cl OL10 ....29 B3
Thorn Ct 2 M6 ....81 B2
Thorn Dr M22 ....131 A8
Thorn Gr Altrincham WA15 ..119 F3
  Bramhall SK8 ....132 A7
  Manchester M14 ....110 DB
  Sale M33 ....108 B4
Thorn Grove Prim Sch
  SK8 ....132 A7
Thorn Lea Atherton M46 ....58 A7
  Bolton BL2 ....25 D4
Thorn Lea Cl BL1 ....40 F7
Thorn Rd Bramhall SK7 .....132 E5
  Oldham OL8 ....67 C3
  Swinton M27 ....79 B7
Thorn St Bolton BL1 ....143 F2
  Hindley WN2 ....56 D4
  Ramsbottom BL0 ....11 C3
Thorn View BL9 ....141 C3
Thorn Well BL5 ....57 A7
Thorn Wik M31 ....105 E2
Thornaby Wik M9 ....157 D6
Thornage Dr M40 ....159 C4
Thornbank BL3 ....144 C6
Thornbank Cl OL10 ....46 F7
Thornbeck Dr BL1 ....23 F1
Thornbeck Rd BL1 ....23 F1
Thornbridge Ave M21 ......109 B8
Thornbury 9 OL11 ....139 E6
Thornbury Ave
  Golborne WA3 ....90 E7
  Hattersley SK14 ....102 E2
Thornbury Cl
  8 Bolton BL1 ....145 E8
Thornbury Rd M32 ....96 E4
Thornbury Way M18 ....165 C5
Thornbush OL16 ....74 E1
Thornby Wik 8 M23 ....121 A5
Thorncliff Ave
  Dukinfield SK16 ....101 C7
  Royton OL2 ....48 C6
Thorncliffe Gr M19 ....99 C1
Thorncliffe Pk OL2 ....48 C6
Thorncliffe Rd Bolton BL1 ..24 E5
  Hadfield SK14 ....171 F4
Thorncombe Rd 1 M16 .....97 F3
Thorncross Cl M15 ....161 C7
Thorndale Cl OL2 ....48 E5
Thorndale Gr WA15 ....120 A5
Thornden Rd M40 ....160 D4
Thorne Ave M41 ....95 A3
Thorne Ho M14 ....98 B3
Thorne St BL4 ....42 C1
Thorneside M34 ....100 E3
Thorney Dr SK7,SK8 ....132 C6
Thorney Hill Cl OL4 ....67 A6
Thorneycroft WN7 ....76 C5
Thorneycroft Ave M21 .....109 B6
Thorneycroft Cl WA15 .....120 B5
Thorneycroft Rd WA15 .....120 B5
Thorneyholme Cl BL6 ....40 C6
Thorneylea OL12 ....4 D1
Thornfield Ave 8 BB4 ....2 F8
Thornfield Cl WA3 ....90 C8
Thornfield Cres M38 ....59 F5
Thornfield Ct SK4 ....111 C6
Thornfield Ct 4 M27 ....79 E7
Thornfield Gr
  Cheadle SK8 ....123 A2
  Walkden M38 ....59 F5
Thornfield Hey SK9 ....137 E8
Thornfield Rd Bury BL9 .....26 F7
  Manchester M19 ....110 E5

Thornfield Rd continued
  Manchester Sch SK4 ....168 A3
  Stretford M5 ....154 D1
Thornfield Terr OL6 ....166 C2
Thornford Wik M40 ....65 D2
Thorngate Rd M8 ....156 A5
Thorngrove Ave 1 M23 ....120 D7
Thorngrove Dr SK9 ....137 C6
Thorngrove Hill SK9 ....137 C6
Thorngrove Ho 4 M23 ......120 D7
Thorngrove Rd SK9 ....137 C6
Thornham Cl BL8 ....27 C6
Thornham Ct OL16 ....48 C8
Thornham Dr BL1 ....25 A6
Thornham La
  Middleton M24,OL11,OL2 ...47 E6
  Royton OL16,OL12 ....48 C8
Thornham New Rd
  OL11,OL16 ....47 EB
Thornham Old Rd OL2 ....48 B7
Thornham Rd Sale M33 .....107 F3
  Shaw OL2 ....48 EB
Thornham St James'
  CE Prim Sch OL2 ....48 C8
Thornhill Cl Bolton BL1 .....142 C3
  Reddish M34 ....100 A2
Thornhill Dr M28 ....60 E1
Thornhill Rd Droylsden M43 ..84 B2
  Garswood WN4 ....72 C4
  Manchester SK4 ....110 F2
  Ramsbottom BL0 ....11 A1
Thornholme Cl M18 ....99 B3
Thornholme Rd SK6 ....125 F4
Thorniley Brow M4 ....159 A2
Thornleigh Rd M14 ....98 B3
Thornlea Ave Oldham OL8 ..66 C1
  Swinton M27 ....79 D6
Thornlea Dr OL12 ....14 B2
Thornlee Cl OL4 ....68 B5
Thornleigh Rd M14 ....98 B3
Thornleigh Salesian Coll
  BL1 ....143 D4
Thornley Ave BL1 ....142 C2
Thornley Cl OL4 ....68 A5
Thornley Cres Oldham OL4 ..68 A5
  Romiley SK6 ....113 A4
Thornley La OL4 ....68 A5
Thornley La N M34,SK5 .....99 F3
Thornley La S M34,SK5 .....100 A2
Thornley Mews BL1 ....142 C2
Thornley Park Rd OL4 ......68 A5
Thornley Rd
  Dukinfield M34 ....101 A4
  Prestwich M25 ....63 C7
Thornley St Hyde SK14 .....167 E1
  Middleton M24 ....47 B1
  Radcliffe M26 ....44 B2
Thornmere Cl M27 ....61 C2
Thorns Ave BL1 ....143 D3
Thorns Cl BL1 ....143 D3
Thorns Clough OL3 ....51 C5
Thorns Rd BL1 ....143 D3
Thornsett M26 ....122 C2
Thornsett Cl M9 ....157 E8
Thornset Cty Prim Sch
  SK22 ....127 E3
Thornsgreen Rd M22 ....130 DB
Thornton Ave Bolton BL1 ...23 F1
  Dukinfield M34 ....100 C8
  Urmston M41 ....95 A2
Thornton Cl
  Ashton-in-M WN4 ....72 C4
  Boothstown M28 ....77 E7
  Farnworth BL4 ....60 B7
  Golborne WA3 ....75 A1
  Horwich BL6 ....22 F8
  Little Lever BL3 ....43 C3
Thornton Cres M25 ....62 F5
Thornton Ct M16 ....161 C5
Thornton Dr SK9 ....131 D3
Thornton Gate SK8 ....122 A6
Thornton Pl SK4 ....168 B4
Thornton Rd
  Boothstown M28 ....78 A8
  Gatley SK8 ....131 C8
  Manchester M14 ....98 A1
  Wigan WN5 ....36 A1
Thornton St 1 Bolton BL2 ..148 A7
  Manchester M40 ....160 D4
  Oldham OL4 ....153 F5
  Rochdale OL11 ....139 F5
Thorntree Cl M9 ....157 D7
Thorntree Pl 2 OL12 ....139 F8
Thornvale WN2 ....74 C7
Thornway Boothstown M28 ..78 A8
  Bramhall SK7 ....132 C7
  High Lane SK6 ....114 E8
Thornycroft OL8 ....66 D4
Thornydyke Ave BL1 ....24 E5
Thorold Gr M33 ....108 E4
Thorp Ave BL9 ....44 E5
Thorp Com Prim Sch OL2 ..48 C5
Thorp Rd Manchester M40 ..83 A8
  Royton OL2 ....48 DB
Thorp St Eccles M30 ....95 B8
  Whitefield M45 ....44 E1
Thorpe Ave M27 ....61 E1
Thorpe Cl Denton M34 ......100 F4
  Oldham OL8 ....66 A4
Thorpe Gr SK4 ....111 D6
Thorpe Hall Gr SK14 ....100 F4

Thorpe St Bolton BL1 ......143 D2
  Glossop SK13 ....104 E2
  Manchester M16 ....97 C4
  Middleton M24 ....64 C7
  Ramsbottom BL0 ....138 B5
  Walkden M26 ....60 D4
Thorpe View M5 ....161 C7
Thorpebrook Rd M40 ....83 A6
Thorpeness Sq M18 ....99 D6
Thorsby Cl BL9 ....167 F2
Thorsby Ct Bolton BL7 ......24 F8
  Droylsden M18 ....99 D6
Thorsby Rd WA15 ....119 E5
Thorsby Way 10 M34 ....101 A1
Thorverton Sq M40 ....83 C8
Thrapston Ave M34 ....84 D1
Threaphurst La SK7 ....125 C1
Threapwood Rd M22 ....121 E1
Three Acre Ave OL2 ....49 A4
Three Acres Dr SK5 ....111 E5
Three Lane Ends OL10 ......45 F7
Three Sisters Rd WA3 ......73 B7
Three Sisters Recn Area
  WN4 ....73 C7
Threlkeld Cl M24 ....46 C1
Threlkeld Rd Bolton BL1 ....24 D6
  Middleton M24 ....46 C1
Thresher Cl 3 M33 ....108 F3
Threshfield Cl BL9 ....27 F7
Threshfield Dr WA15 ....120 C7
Throstle Bank St SK14 .....101 C4
Throstle Ct 8 OL2 ....48 D4
Throstle Gr Bury BL8 ....27 C5
  Marple SK6 ....125 E5
Throstle Hall Ct 1 M24 ....46 F1
Throstle Nest Ave WN6 ....37 A2
Throstle St OL4 ....6 B6
Throstles Cl M43 ....84 C3
Thrum Fold OL12 ....14 D3
Thrum Hall La
  Rochdale OL12 ....14 D3
  Rochdale OL12 ....14 E3
Thrush Ave BL4 ....59 FB
Thrush Dr BL9 ....141 B4
Thrush Ho M6 ....81 A5
Thrush St OL12 ....14 C1
Thruxton Cl 4 M16 ....97 E3
Thurland Rd OL4 ....67 C6
Thurland St OL9 ....65 EB
Thurlby Ave M9 ....64 E5
Thurlby Cl WN4 ....73 D4
Thurlby St M13 ....98 F2
Thurleigh Rd M20 ....110 B4
Thurlestone Ave BL2 ....26 D1
Thurlestone Dr
  Stockport SK7 ....124 B2
  3 Urmston M41 ....95 C3
Thurlestone Rd WA14 ......119 B6
Thurloe St M14 ....98 C3
Thurlow WA3 ....90 E7
Thurlow St Salford M5 ......154 F1
  Stretford M5 ....96 FB
Thurlston Cres M8 ....156 B7
Thurlwood Ave M20 ....110 A7
Thurnham St BL3 ....146 C3
Thurnley Wik M8 ....155 F5
Thursby Ave M20 ....110 A6
Thursby Ho WN5 ....54 A4
Thursby Wik M24 ....46 C2
Thursfield St M6 ....81 B5
Thursford Gr BL6 ....21 D1
Thurstan St WV3 ....55 E4
Thurstane St BL1 ....142 C2
Thurston Ave WN3 ....55 B3
Thurston Cl BL9 ....45 A2
Thurston Clough Rd
  OL3,OL4 ....50 D2
Thurston Gn SK9 ....137 A1
Thurstons OL3 ....51 D6
Thynne St Bolton BL3 ......145 F5
  Farnworth BL4 ....42 C2
Tib La M2 ....158 F1
Tib St Denton M34 ....100 E2
  Manchester M4,M1 ....159 A2
  Ramsbottom BL0 ....138 B5
Tiber Ave OL8 ....66 A4
Tideswell Ave
  Manchester M40 ....160 D3
  Wigan WN5 ....36 A1
Tideswell Bank 8 SK13 ....171 E1
Tideswell Rd
  Droylsden M43 ....83 E3
  Hazel Grove SK7 ....133 EB
Tideswell Way M34 ....113 A8
Tideswell Wik 7 SK13 ......171 E1
Tideway Cl M7 ....80 F8
Tidworth Ave M4 ....160 D2
Tiefield Wik M21 ....109 E8
Tiernan Lo 4 WN6 ....37 A1
Tiflis St OL12 ....14 C3
Tig Fold Rd BL4 ....59 EB
Tilbury Gr WN6 ....35 D7
Tilbury St OL1 ....153 EB
Tilbury Wik M40 ....160 D3
Tilby Cl M41 ....94 E2
Tildsley St BL3 ....147 E4
Tile St BL3 ....140 F3
Tilehurst Ct M7 ....81 B7
Tilgate Wik 17 M9 ....64 E3
Tillard Ave SK3 ....123 B8
Tillhey Rd M22 ....121 D2
Tillington Cl BL1 ....143 E3
Tilney Ave M32 ....96 C1
Tilshead Wik M13 ....163 C6
Tilson Rd M23 ....120 E8
Tilstock Wik M23 ....120 E8
Tilston Wik 5 SK9 ....131 E1

Tilton St OL1 .... 49 C1
Timberbottom BL2 ...... 25 C4
Timbercliffe OL15 ...... 6 D1
Timberhurst BL9 .... 28 D2
Timbersbrook Gr 🟦 SK9 .131 D2
Times Ret Pk OL10 ..... 29 C2
Times St M24 .... 65 B8
Timothy Cl M6 .... 80 B3
Timperley Cl OL8 ...... 67 B2
Timperley Fold OL6 .... 85 C6
Timperley Heyes Lane
  Prim Sch WA15 ...... 120 B8
Timperley La WN7 ...... 76 B2
Timperley Rd OL6 ..... 85 C6
Timperley St M11 ..... 165 C8
Timperley Sta WA15 ... 119 F8
Timpson Rd M23 ...... 120 E7
Timsbury Cl BL2 .... 42 F5
Timson St 🟦 M33 ...... 81 E7
Tin St BL3 .... 145 E5
Tindall St Eccles M30 ... 95 B8
  Reddish SK5 .... 99 F3
Tindle St M28 .... 60 F3
Tinkersfield WN7 ...... 75 D7
Tinline St BL9 .... 141 A2
Tinningham Ct 🟦 M11 ..99 E7
Tinsdale Wlk M24 ...... 46 C1
Tinshill Cl M12 .... 165 A5
Tinsley Cl M40 .... 160 E2
Tinsley Gr BL2 .... 148 B8
Tintagel Ct Bolton M26 ..43 C5
  Stalybridge SK15 ...... 85 F2
Tintagel Rd WN2 ...... 57 A4
Tintagel Wlk SK14 .... 102 E3
Tintern Ave
  Ashton-in-M WN4 ..... 73 D3
  Bolton BL2 .... 25 B2
  Heywood OL10 .... 29 C4
  Littleborough OL15 .... 15 A4
  Manchester M20 ...... 109 F5
  Rochdale OL12 .... 14 E2
  Tyldesley M29 .... 77 C7
  Urmston M41 .... 107 A8
  Whitefield M45 .... 44 F1
Tintern Cl SK12 .... 133 D5
Tintern Ct M20 .... 109 F5
Tintern Dr WA15 ...... 120 C2
Tintern Gr SK1 .... 112 B1
Tintern Pl OL10 .... 29 C2
Tintern Rd Bramhall SK8 .132 B6
  Middleton M24 .... 47 A4
Tintern St M14 .... 98 B2
Tintwistle CE Prim Sch
  SK13 .... 104 A7
Tinwald Pl WN1 .... 37 F1
Tipperary St SK15 ..... 86 E5
Tipping St
  Altrincham WA14 ..... 119 D3
  Wigan WN3 .... 150 B6
Tipton Cl Cheadle SK8 ..123 B4
  Radcliffe M26 .... 43 D5
Tipton Dr M23 .... 109 B2
Tiptree Wlk 🟦 M9 .... 157 E8
Tiree Cl SK7 .... 124 F1
Tirza Ave M19 .... 110 F8
Tissington Bank 🟦 SK13 .171 D1
Tissington Terr 🟦 SK13 .171 D1
Titanian Rise OL1 ..... 49 P5
Titchfield Rd OL8 ..... 67 C4
Tithe Barn Cl OL22 .... 15 D4
Tithe Barn Cres BL1 ... 25 B4
Tithe Barn Ct SK4 .... 110 F4
Tithe Barn Prim Sch SK4 .168 A3
Tithe Barn Rd
  Garswood WN4 .... 72 C2
  Manchester SK4 ...... 110 F4
Tithe Barn St 🟦 BL5 ...39 E1
Tithebarn Rd
  Altrincham WA15 ..... 129 C8
  Garswood WN4 .... 72 D2
Tithebarn St 🟦 Bury BL9 .140 F2
  Orrell WN8 .... 53 B7
  Radcliffe M26 .... 44 D4
Titian Rise OL1 .... 49 D3
Titterington Ave M11 ..97 B2
Tiverton Ave Hindley WN7 ..57 D2
  Sale M33 .... 107 E3
Tiverton Cl OL8 Little Lever M26 ..43 C5
  Tyldesley M29 .... 77 D7
Tiverton Dr M33 ...... 107 F3
Tiverton Ho M6 .... 80 A3
Tiverton Pl OL7 .... 85 A5
Tiverton Rd M41 ..... 95 E3
Tiverton Wlk BL1 ..... 142 C1
Tiviot Dale SK1 .... 169 F2
Tiviot Way SK1,SK4,SK5 .169 F3
Tivoli St SK1 .... 158 E1
Tixall Wlk 🟦 M8 ...... 63 E2
Toad La OL12 .... 139 F8
Tobermory Cl M11 .... 83 D2
Tobermory Rd SK8 .... 122 C1
Todd St Bury BL9 ..... 140 F4
  Glossop SK13 .... 116 D8
  Heywood OL10 .... 29 A2
  Manchester M3 .... 159 A2
  Manchester M7 .... 155 D6
  Rochdale OL16 .... 31 B3
Todd's Pl M9 .... 64 C1
Toddington La WN2 ... 38 B8
Todmorden Rd OL15 ... 16 C7
Toft Rd M18 .... 99 C4
Toft Way SK9 .... 131 E4
Toledo St M11 .... 83 D1
Toll Bar Bsns Pk OL13 ..3 C8
Toll Bar St M12 ...... 164 E6
Toll Gate Cl M13 ..... 98 E4
Toll St Platt Bridge WN2 ..56 A1

Toll St continued
  Radcliffe M26 .... 43 D4
Tolland La WA15 ...... 128 F8
Tollard Ave M40 ...... 157 D5
Tollard Cl SK8 .... 132 B6
Tollbar St SK1 .... 170 F8
Tollemache Cl SK14 ... 103 A5
Tollemache Rd SK14 ... 103 A5
Tollesbury Cl M40 .... 160 D4
Tollgate Way OL16 .... 31 C8
Tollworth Dr M8 ...... 156 A4
Tom Lomas Wlk M11 ...83 B2
Tom Shepley St SK14 ..167 E2
Tomcroft La M34 ..... 100 D2
Tomlin Sq 🟦 BL2 .... 148 C7
Tomlinson Cl OL8 .... 153 E5
Tomlinson St Horwich BL6 ..22 B3
Tommy Browell Cl 🟦 M14 .98 A3
Tommy Johnson Wlk 🟦
  M14 .... 98 A3
Tommy Taylor Cl 🟦 M40 ..83 C5
Tomwood Rise SK13 ...115 C6
Tonacliffe Cty Prim Sch
  OL12 .... 14 C6
Tonacliffe Rd OL12 ... 14 C6
Tonacliffe Terr OL12 .. 14 C7
Tonacliffe Way OL12 .. 14 C6
Tonbridge Cl BL8 ..... 27 C7
Tonbridge Pl 🟦 BL2 .. 25 B1
Tonbridge Rd
  Manchester M19 ..... 111 B8
  Reddish SK5 .... 111 F8
Tong End OL12 .... 4 C2
Tong Head Ave BL1 ... 25 B4
Tong La Bacup OL13 ... 4 C8
  Whitworth OL12 ...... 4 D1
Tong Rd BL3 .... 43 A3
Tong St BL4 .... 61 C5
Tonge Bridge Way BL2 ..148 B8
Tonge Cl M45 .... 45 B1
Tonge Clough BL7 .... 24 F8
Tonge Ct M24 .... 65 B8
Tonge Fold Rd BL2 ... 148 C7
Tonge Gn SK15 .... 102 E6
Tonge Hall Cl M24 .... 65 B8
Tonge Moor Com Prim Sch
  BL2 .... 25 B1
Tonge Moor Rd BL2 ... 25 B2
Tonge Old Rd BL2 .... 25 B2
Tonge Park Ave BL2 .. 25 C1
Tonge Roughs M24 ... 65 D8
Tonge St Heywood OL10 ..29 D2
  Manchester M12 ..... 164 D7
  Oldham M24 .... 65 E6
  Rochdale OL11,OL16 ...31 A6
Tongfields BL7 .... 24 F8
Tongley Wlk 🟦 M40 .. 65 D2
Tonman St M3 .... 162 E8
Tontine WN5 .... 53 C5
Tontine Rd WN5,WN8 ..53 C6
Toogood La WN6 ..... 18 D6
Tooley Ho M30 .... 95 D8
Toon Cres BL8 .... 27 C6
Tootal Dr M5,M6 ..... 80 C3
Tootal Drive Prim Sch M6 ..80 C3
Tootal Gr M5 .... 80 C2
Tootal Rd M5 .... 154 D2
Toothill Cl WN4 ...... 73 C6
Top o' th' Brow
  Com Prim Sch BL2 ...25 E2
Top o' th' Gn OL9 .... 66 C4
Top o' th' La BL2 ..... 42 D5
Top o' th' Meadows La
  OL4 .... 50 A1
Top O'Th' Close Rd OL14 ..6 C6
Top Of Heap OL10 .... 28 F2
Top of Wallsuches BL6 ..22 F4
Top Schwabe St M24 ..64 E8
Top St Middleton M24 ..46 F1
  Oldham OL4 .... 67 D8
  Walsden OL14 .... 5 F7
Topcliffe St WN2 ..... 56 F6
Topcroft Cl M22 ..... 121 E8
Topfield Rd M22 ..... 121 C4
Topham St Bury BL9 .. 141 A1
  Bury BL9 .... 45 A8
Topley St M40 .... 157 D6
Topp St BL4 .... 60 E7
Topp Way BL1 .... 145 E8
Topping Fold Rd BL9 . 141 C3
Topping St Bolton BL1 .143 E1
  Bury BL9 .... 141 A3
Toppings Gn BL7 ..... 25 A7
Toppings The Sk6 .... 113 A3
Topsham Wlk M40 ... 83 D5
Tor Ave BL8 .... 10 F2
Tor End Rd BB4 ...... 1 A6
Tor View Sch Valley Site
  BB4 .... 1 D8
Torah St M8 .... 159 A4
Torbay Cl 🟦 BL3 .... 144 C5
Torbay Dr SK2 ...... 124 B7
Torbay Rd
  Manchester M21 .... 109 C8
  Urmston M41 .... 95 E1
Torcross Rd M9 ...... 64 B5
Torkington Ave M27 .. 61 F1
Torkington La SK6,SK7 ..125 E3
Torkington Prim Sch
  SK7 .... 125 A2
Torkington Rd Gatley SK8 ..122 B5
  Hazel Grove SK7 ..... 124 F2
  Hazel Grove SK7 ..... 125 A3
  Wilmslow SK9 .... 137 D6
Torkington St SK14 ... 170 D8
Torksey Wlk M9 ...... 64 C5

Torness Wlk M11 ..... 83 B1
Toronto Ave M90 .... 130 B7
Toronto Rd SK2 ...... 124 A6
Toronto St BL2 .... 42 E8
Torpoint Wlk M40 .... 65 C1
Torquay Cl 🟦 M13 ... 163 C5
Torquay Dr WN5 ..... 71 E8
Torquay Gr SK2 ..... 124 B4
Torra Barn Cl BL7 .... 8 E3
Torrax Cl M6 .... 80 B6
Torre Cl M24 .... 47 A3
Torrens St M6 .... 80 D5
Torridon Cl WN6 ..... 37 B7
Torridon Rd BL2 ..... 148 C7
Torridon Wlk 🟦 M22 .121 C1
Torrin Cl SK3 .... 170 F5
Torrington Ave
  Bolton BL1 .... 143 E3
  Manchester M9 ...... 65 A2
Torrington Dr SK14 .. 102 E2
Torrington Rd M27 ... 80 B6
Torrington St OL10 ... 46 E8
Torside CT WN2 ...... 56 D6
Torside Way SK13 ... 104 A5
Torver Cl WN3 .... 55 A2
Torver Dr Bolton BL2 ..42 F8
  Middleton M24 ...... 46 F1
Torver Wlk M22 ..... 121 B2
Torwood Rd OL9 ..... 47 E1
Totland Cl M12 ...... 99 B3
Totley Ave 🟦🟦 SK13 ..171 D1
Totley Cl 🟦 SK13 ... 171 D1
Totley Gdns 🟦 SK13 .171 D1
Totley Gn 🟦 SK13 ... 171 D1
Totley Lanes 🟦 SK13 .171 D1
Totley Mews 🟦 SK13 .171 D1
Totley Pl 🟦 SK13 ... 171 D1
Totnes Ave Chadderton OL9 ..47 F1
  Stockport SK7 ...... 124 A2
Totnes Rd
  Manchester M21 .... 109 C8
  Sale M33 .... 107 D5
Totridge Cl SK2 ..... 124 D5
Tottenham Dr M23 .. 120 E7
Tottington Ave OL4 .. 67 F7
Tottington High Sch BL8 ..26 F5
Tottington La M27 ... 62 F5
Tottington Prim Sch BL8 ..26 F5
Tottington Rd Bolton BL2 ..25 F3
  Bolton BL7,BL8 .... 9 F2
  Bury BL8 .... 27 C4
Totton Ho BL1 ...... 144 C7
Totton Rd M35 ...... 83 F7
Touchet Hall Rd M24 ..47 D4
Toulston Rd WN6 .... 36 F2
Tours Ave M23 ...... 109 A2
Towcester Cl M4 .... 160 D1
Tower Ave BL10 ..... 138 A5
Tower Gr WN7 .... 76 D6
Tower Grange M27 .. 155 D8
Tower Hill Rd WN8 ... 53 B8
Tower Rd M29 .... 53 A5
Tower Sq M13 ...... 163 C6
Tower St Edgworth BL7 ..9 C4
  Heywood OL10 ...... 29 C2
  Hyde SK14 .... 167 D1
Radcliffe M26 .... 44 B4
  Stalybridge SK15 .... 85 D1
Tower View BL6 ...... 21 C3
Towers Ave BL3 ..... 146 A4
Towers Cl SK12 ..... 133 F5
Towers Rd SK12 .... 133 F5
Towers St 🟦 OL4 .... 49 D1
Towey Cl M18 .... 99 D6
Town Fields Cl BL7 .. 140 F1
Town Fold SK6 ...... 126 B7
Town Gate Dr M41 ... 94 D2
Town Hall La M2 .... 158 F1
Town Hall Sq OL16 .. 139 F7
Town House Rd OL15 ..16 B6
Town La
  Charlesworth SK13 ...115 D6
  Coppull PR7 .... 19 B8
  Dukinfield SK16 ..... 101 C8
Town Mill Brow OL12 .139 E7
Town Sq M3 .... 108 B4
Town Sq Sh Ctr OL11 .153 F6
Town Sq Sk6 .... 126 B7
Town's View SK15 .... 86 B1
Towncliffe Wlk 🟦 M15 .162 D6
Towncroft M34 ...... 101 A4
Towncroft La BL1 .... 40 B8
Townend SK14 ...... 167 E2
Townfield M41 ...... 95 B1
Townfield Ave BB4 ... 2 F8
Townfield Gdns WA14 .119 D5
Townfield La WA13 .. 117 B7
Townfield Rd WA14 .. 119 D5
Townfield St 🟦 OL4 ..67 B7
Townfields WN3 ..... 73 A3
Townley Fold SK14 .. 102 B6
Townley Rd OL16 .... 32 A6
Townley St
  Manchester M11 .... 164 F8
  Manchester M8 ...... 156 A6
  Middleton M24 ...... 65 A8
Townrow St OL10 .... 29 A3
Townscliffe La SK6 .. 126 C6
Townsend Rd M27 ... 61 F1
Townsend St BB4 ..... 2 F8
Townsfield Rd BL5 ... 57 F7
Townside Row M4 ... 140 F1

Townsley Gr OL6 ..... 85 E5
Townson Dr WN7 .... 75 F1
Towton St M9 .... 157 E8
Towyn Ave M5 ...... 81 A2
Toxhead Cl BL6 ...... 22 A3
Toxteth St M11 ...... 99 F7
Tracey St M8 .... 64 A1
Tracks La WN5 ...... 53 D3
Tracy Dr WA13 ...... 89 E3
Traders Ave M41 .... 95 E6
Trafalgar Ave Denton M34 ..100 C7
  Poynton SK12 .... 134 A3
Trafalgar Bsns Pk M7,M8 ..158 E4
Trafalgar Cl SK12 .... 134 A3
Trafalgar Ct M16 .... 97 E2
Trafalgar Gr M7 ..... 155 D5
Trafalgar Ho M34 ... 100 C7
Trafalgar Pl M20 ... 110 A4
Trafalgar Rd Hindley WN2 ..56 D1
  Sale M33 .... 108 C6
  Salford M6 .... 80 A3
  Wigan WN1 .... 37 C1
Trafalgar Sq OL7 .... 84 F1
Trafalgar St Ashton-u-l OL7 ..84 F1
  Manchester M7 ..... 155 E5
  Oldham OL1 .... 153 E8
  Rochdale OL16 .... 31 A8
Trafalgar Wlk
  Manchester M11 .... 165 B8
  Manchester M15 .... 162 E5
Trafford Ave M41 .... 95 E3
Trafford Bank Rd M16 .161 C5
Trafford Bar Sta M16 .161 B5
Trafford Ct 🟦 M15 .. 162 D6
Trafford Ctr The M41 .95 A6
Trafford Dr Sale WA15 ..120 B8
  Walkden M38 .... 60 B5
Trafford General Hospl
  M41 .... 95 A5
Trafford Gr Farnworth BL4 ..42 C1
  Stretford M32 .... 96 C3
Trafford Mans 🟦 M16 .97 B2
Trafford Park Rd M17 .96 C6
Trafford Park Sta M32 .96 C3
Trafford Pl M15 ..... 162 D6
Trafford Rd
  Alderley Edge SK9 .. 137 B1
  Eccles M30 .... 79 D1
  Eccles M30 .... 79 C8
  Handforth SK9 ...... 131 B1
  Hindley WN2 .... 56 D1
  Salford M5 &M16,M17 .161 A7
Trafford Ret Pk M41 ..95 C5
Trafford St Farnworth BL4 ..42 D1
  Manchester M1,M3 .. 162 F8
  Oldham OL8 .... 153 E5
  Rochdale OL11 ...... 139 E5
Trafford Wharf Rd M17 ..96 E6
Tragan Cl SK2 ...... 124 D6
Tragan Dr SK2 ...... 124 D6
Trail St M6 .... 154 E2
Trajan Ho OL1 ...... 153 F7
Tram St Manchester M11 ..165 C8
  Platt Bridge WN2 .... 56 A1
Tramore Wlk M22 ... 121 C2
Tramway Rd M44 ... 105 F7
Tranby Cl M22 ...... 121 F4
Tranmere Cl M18 ... 165 B5
Tranmere Dr SK9 ... 131 E2
Tranmere Rd 🟦 SK3 .123 B8
Transpennine Trad Est
  OL11 .... 30 D3
Transvaal St M11 .... 83 D1
Travers St M6 .... 22 D1
Travis Brow SK4 .... 169 D1
Travis Cl OL2 .... 48 E4
Travis Ho OL14 .... 6 A7
Travis St Hyde SK14 .167 E2
  Manchester M1 ..... 163 C8
  Newhey OL16 .... 32 B8
  Shaw OL2 .... 149 C7
Trawden Ave BL1 ... 142 C2
Trawden Dr BL9 ..... 27 E8
Trawden Gn SK2 ... 124 D4
Traylen Way OL12 ... 14 F1
Trecastell Cl WN1 ... 37 B3
Tredcroft St SK13 ... 116 B8
Tredgold St BL6 ..... 22 C2
Tree Ave M43 .... 84 A3
Tree Cl OL4 .... 67 D8
Tree House Ave 🟦 OL7 ..85 A6
Tree Tops BL7 ...... 25 C6
Tree Wlk M32 ...... 96 C1
Treelands Wlk M5 ... 161 B6
Treen Rd M29 .... 77 C8
Treetop Cl OL3 ...... 50 F1
Treetops Ave BL0 ... 11 A3
Trefoil Way OL15 .... 15 F6
Tregaer Fold M24 ... 65 C8
Tregaron Gr WN2 ... 57 A3
Tremain Wlk 🟦 M9 .157 D7
Trenam Pl M5 .... 81 B2
Trenant Rd M6 ..... 154 D4
Trenchard Ct M11,M43 ..83 D2
Trenchard Dr M22 .. 130 F7
Trencherbone M26 .. 43 E5
Trengrove St 🟦 OL12 ..14 C1
Trent Ave Chadderton OL9 ..65 F8
  Heywood OL10 .... 29 A3
  Milnrow OL16 .... 32 A6
Trent Bridge Wlk M16 ..97 D4
Trent Cl Bramhall SK7 .132 C6
  Ermington SK5 ...... 99 F1
Trent Dr Bury BL9 ... 27 F8
  Hindley WN2 .... 57 B3
  Walkden M28 .... 60 B2

Trent Gr WN7 .... 75 C4
Trent Rd Ashton-in-M WN4 ..73 E5
  Billinge WN5 .... 71 D3
  Shaw OL2 .... 149 A8
  Wigan WN5 .... 54 C7
Trent St OL16 .... 31 B6
Trent Way BL4 .... 61 B5
Trentham Ave
  Farnworth BL4 ...... 42 C1
  Manchester SK4 ..... 110 F4
Trentham Cl BL4 .... 42 C1
Trentham Gr M40 ... 65 A1
Trentham Lawns M6 ..81 B4
Trentham Rd M16 ... 97 A3
Trentham St Farnworth BL4 ..42 C1
  Salford M15 .... 81 A1
  Swinton M27 .... 61 E1
Tresco Ave M32 ..... 96 E1
Trescott Mews WN6 ..36 F8
Treverick Ct Horwich BL6 ..22 F2
  🟦 Oldham OL4 ...... 67 C8
Trevelyan Dr WN5 ... 53 D1
Trevelyan St M30 ... 80 A2
Trevor Ave Bolton BL3 .147 D3
  Sale M33 .... 107 F2
Trevor Gr SK1 ...... 124 A8
Trevor Rd Eccles M30 ..79 B3
  Swinton M27 .... 79 E6
  Urmston M41 .... 94 F2
  Urmston M41 .... 95 A2
Trevor St Manchester M11 ..99 F7
  Rochdale OL11 ...... 30 B3
Triangle The WA15 .. 120 B7
Tribune Ave WA14 .. 119 B7
Trident Rd M30 ..... 94 F7
Trillo Ave BL2 ...... 148 B6
Trimdon Cl M11 ..... 83 B2
Trimingham Dr BL8 .. 27 D5
Trimley Ave M40 ... 157 E5
Tring Wlk M9 .... 64 B3
Trinity Ave M33 .... 108 D4
Trinity Bldgs OL6 ... 85 D2
Trinity CE High Sch M15 .163 A6
Trinity Cl SK16 ..... 101 E8
Trinity Cres SK2 .... 60 E3
Trinity Ct M13 ...... 158 D2
Trinity Gdns
  Ashton-in-M WN4 .... 72 F4
  Manchester M3 ..... 158 D2
  Stockport SK3 ...... 123 F3
Trinity Pl 🟦 SK15 ... 85 F1
Trinity St 🟦 Bacup OL13 ..3 C8
  Bolton BL3 .... 140 F1
  Marple SK6 .... 125 F6
  🟦 Middleton M24 ... 64 F8
  Oldham OL1 .... 153 E8
  Rochdale OL12 ...... 86 A1
Trinity Way M3 ...... 158 D2
Trinity Wlk 🟦 M14 .. 98 B3
Tripper Rd M30 ..... 95 B8
Tripps Mews M20 .. 109 F4
Triscombe Way M16 ..97 E3
Tristam Cl M13 ..... 163 C7
Trojan Gdns M7 .... 81 C5
Trongate Wlk 🟦 M9 .157 C7
Troon Cl Bolton BL3 ..40 F3
  Bramhall SK7 .... 133 A7
Troon Dr SK8 .... 122 C1
Troon Rd M23 ...... 120 E6
Trough Gate OL8 ... 66 D2
Troutbeck Ave M4 .. 160 D2
Troutbeck Cl BL8 .... 10 E2
Troutbeck Dr
  Ramsbottom BL0 .. 138 C7
  🟦 Rossendale OL13 ..77 A7
Troutbeck Gr WA11 ..71 B1
Troutbeck Rd
  Altrincham WA15 .. 120 D5
  Ashton-in-M WN4 .... 73 C5
Troutbeck Rise WN5 .54 B6
Troutbeck Wlk 🟦 OL2 .48 E4
Trowbridge Dr M40 .. 65 C1
Trowbridge Rd M34 .101 A1
Trows La OL11 ...... 30 D1
Trowtree Ave M12 .. 164 E6
Troy Wlk M5 .... 161 B7
Troydale Dr M40 ... 83 B6
Trumpet St M1 ..... 162 F8
Truro Ave Ashton-u-l OL6 ..85 D7
  Brinnington SK5 .... 112 C5
  Stretford M32 ...... 96 E3
Truro Cl Bramhall SK7 .132 F7
  Bury BL9 .... 140 D3
Truro Dr M33 .... 107 D4
Truro Rd Chadderton OL9 ..48 A1
  Tyldesley M29 ...... 77 C8
Truro Wlk M34 ..... 100 F1
Trust Rd M18 .... 99 C3
Tucker's Hill Brow WN2 ..21 B1
Tudbury Way M3 ... 158 D2
Tudor Ave Bolton BL1 .144 B7
  Failsworth BL4 ..... 65 D3
  Manchester M9 ..... 64 E1
  Stalybridge SK15 .... 86 D3
Tudor Cl OL5 .... 68 E1

Tudor Ct Bolton BL1 . . . . .145 E8
Manchester M16 . . . . .161 C5
Manchester M25 . . . . .63 C3
Rochdale OL12 . . . . .15 B1
Tudor Gn SK9 . . . . .131 E1
Tudor Gr Middleton M24 . . . .46 D3
Wigan WN3 . . . . .54 E2
Tudor Hall St OL11 . . . . .30 C2
Tudor Hey SK5 . . . . .111 E7
Tudor Ind Est SK16 . . . . .101 A7
Tudor Rd Altrincham WA14 ..119 B7
Handforth SK9 . . . . .131 E1
Tudor St █ Bolton BL3 . . . .146 C4
Middleton M24 . . . . .65 B8
Oldham OL8 . . . . .153 D5
Oldham OL8 . . . . .153 E5
Shaw OL2 . . . . .149 B7
Tuer St M13 . . . . .163 A6
Tuffley Rd M23 . . . . .121 A3
Tufton Wlk M9 . . . . .157 D7
Tugford Cl M16 . . . . .97 E4
Tuley St M11 . . . . .164 F7
Tulip Ave Farnworth BL4 . . . . .42 A1
Kearsley BL4 . . . . .60 F5
Tulip Cl Chadderton OL9 . . . . .65 E7
Sale M33 . . . . .107 C4
Stockport SK3 . . . . .170 D5
Tulip Dr Altrincham WA15 . . .119 F6
Wigan WN6 . . . . .36 F3
Tulip Gr OL12 . . . . .14 C8
Tulip Rd M31 . . . . .105 E2

Tulketh Street Ind Est
M40 . . . . .83 A8
Tulle Ct M25 . . . . .63 A4
Tully St M7 . . . . .155 E7
Tully St S M7 . . . . .155 E6
Tulpen Sq OL9 . . . . .152 B7
Tulworth Rd SK12 . . . . .133 D4
Tumblewood Dr SK8 . . . . . . .122 E4
Tumbling Bank Terr OL4 . . . . .67 F5
Tumbling Wlk M9 . . . . .64 D3
Tunbridge Sq M5 . . . . .81 A2
Tunicliffe's New Row
WN7 . . . . .75 C5
Tunley La WN6 . . . . .18 E5
Tunley Moss WN6 . . . . .18 E4
Tuns Rd OL8 . . . . .67 B2
Tunshill Gr OL16 . . . . .32 A6
Tunshill La OL16 . . . . .32 C7
Tunshill Rd M23, M33 . . . . . .108 E1
Tunstall La WN5 . . . . .54 D5
Tunstall Rd OL4 . . . . .67 C6
Tunstall St
█ Manchester M11 . . . . .99 E7
Stockport SK4 . . . . .169 E2
Tunstead Ave M20 . . . . .109 F6
Tunstead La Bacup OL13 . . . . .3 B8
Oldham OL3 . . . . .69 C5
Tunstead Mill Terr █ OL13 . . .3 B8
Tunstead Rd OL13 . . . . .3 C8
Turbory Wlk OL16 . . . . .31 D6
Turf Cl OL2 . . . . .48 E3
Turf Hill Rd OL16 . . . . .31 C4
Turf House Cl OL15 . . . . .15 F7
Turf La Oldham OL9 . . . . .66 A3
Royton OL2 . . . . .48 F3
Turf Lea Rd SK6 . . . . .126 B1
Turf Park Rd OL2 . . . . .48 F3
Turf Pit La OL4 . . . . .49 F4
Turf St M20 . . . . .43 F3
Turf Terr OL15 . . . . .16 A6
Turfland Ave OL2 . . . . .48 F3
Turfton Rd OL2 . . . . .48 F3
Turk St █ BL1 . . . . .144 C8
Turks Rd M26 . . . . .43 E5
Turley St M8 . . . . .156 B6
Turn Moss Rd M21, M32 . . . . .96 F1
Turn St M8 . . . . .11 E8
Turn St OL6 . . . . .85 D4
Turnberry BL3 . . . . .40 F3
Turnberry Cl M29 . . . . .77 C8
Turnberry Dr SK9 . . . . .137 D8
Turnberry Rd SK8 . . . . .122 C1
Turnbull Ave M18 . . . . .156 C8
Turnbull Ave M25 . . . . .63 C7
Turnbull Rd
Manchester M13 . . . . .98 F2
Reddish M18 . . . . .99 F4
Turnbull St OL12 . . . . .108 B6
Turnbury Rd M22 . . . . .121 E5
Turncliff Cres SK6 . . . . .125 D7
Turncroft La SK1 . . . . .112 B1
Turncroft Way M28 . . . . .77 F6
Turnditch Cl WN6 . . . . .37 A4
Turnell Way M28 . . . . .79 A5
Turner Ave Failsworth M35 . . .83 E6
Irlam M44 . . . . .94 A3
Leigh WN2 . . . . .56 E1
Turner Bridge Rd BL2 . . . . . .148 C8
Turner Dr M41 . . . . .95 F2
Turner Gdns SK14 . . . . .167 E4
Turner La Ashton-u-L OL6 . .166 B4
Bredbury SK6 . . . . .112 F6
Hyde SK14 . . . . .167 F4
Turner Rd SK6 . . . . .113 B4
Turner St Ashton-u-L OL6 . . .166 B4
█ Bacup OL13 . . . . .3 C8
Bolton BL1 . . . . .148 A8
Denton M34 . . . . .100 E5
Droylsden M11 . . . . .83 C1
Hindley WN2 . . . . .56 F1
Leigh WN7 . . . . .76 A4
Manchester M16 . . . . .161 C6
Manchester M18 . . . . .99 D5
Manchester M4 . . . . .159 A2

Turner St continued
Manchester M7 . . . . .155 E7
Oldham OL4 . . . . .67 E8
Rochdale OL12 . . . . .14 E1
Westhoughton BL5 . . . . .57 E5
Wigan WN1 . . . . .37 D1
Turner's Pl OL12 . . . . .14 E3
Turnerford Cl BL7 . . . . .8 E1
Turnfield Cl OL16 . . . . .15 D3
Turnfield Ho SK8 . . . . .122 D3
Turnfield Rd SK8 . . . . .122 D3
Turnhill Rd OL16 . . . . .31 B3
Turnill Dr WN4 . . . . .73 B2
Turnlee Cl SK13 . . . . .116 C7
Turnlee Dr SK13 . . . . .116 C7
Turnlee Rd SK13 . . . . .116 C7
Turnough Rd OL16 . . . . .31 F7
Turnpike Cl OL3 . . . . .51 C5
Turnpike Ct █ M16 . . . . .97 D3
Turnpike Gn █ M6 . . . . .154 F3
Turnpike The SK6 . . . . .125 D7
Turnpike Wlk M11 . . . . .160 F1
Turnstone Ave WA12 . . . . .89 C4
Turnstone Cl WN7 . . . . .76 A6
Turnstone Rd
█ Bolton BL2 . . . . .148 A6
Hazel Grove SK2 . . . . .125 A5
Turret Hall Dr █ WA3 . . . . . . .90 E8
Turriff Gr WN2 . . . . .56 A8
Turton Ave █ BL3 . . . . .43 A4
Turton Cl Bury BL8 . . . . .44 A8
Heywood OL10 . . . . .29 A2
Turton High Sch BL7 . . . . .25 B7
Turton Ho █ BL1 . . . . .148 A8
Turton Hts BL2 . . . . .25 B6
Turton La M25 . . . . .62 F5
Turton Rd Bolton BL2,BL7 . . . .25 C5
Bury BL8 . . . . .26 D8
Turton St Bolton BL1 . . . . . . .148 A8
Golborne WA3 . . . . .90 A8
Manchester M11 . . . . .99 D7
Turton Tower BL7 . . . . .9 C3
Turves Rd SK8 . . . . .122 F1
Turville Ho SK9 . . . . .131 D2
Tuscan Rd HX6,OL15 . . . . .7 D2
Tuscan Rd M22 . . . . .122 B8
Tuscany View M7 . . . . .81 B8
Tutbury St M4 . . . . .160 D1
Tutor Bank Dr WN3 . . . . .89 D3
Tuxford Wlk M40 . . . . .157 D7
Tweed Cl Altrincham WA14 .119 C6
Oldham OL8 . . . . .153 E5
Tweed St WN7 . . . . .76 B4
Tweedale Ave M9 . . . . .64 C4
Tweedale St OL11 . . . . .30 C3
Tweedale Way OL9 . . . . .66 A1
Tweedle Hill Rd M9 . . . . .64 C4
Tweesdale Cl M45 . . . . .45 B1
Tweenbrook Ave M23 . . . . . .121 A3
Twelve Apostles
RC Prim Sch WN7 . . . . .75 D8
Twelve Yards Rd
Irlam M30 . . . . .94 B6
Irlam M44 . . . . .93 D4
Twigworth Rd M22 . . . . .121 C2
Twillbrook Dr M3 . . . . .158 E3
Twin St OL10 . . . . .29 E1
Twinegate OL12 . . . . .14 E3
Twining Brook Rd SK8 . . . . .123 B4
Twinnies Ct SK9 . . . . .131 B1
Twinnies Rd SK9 . . . . .131 B1
Twirl Hill Rd OL6 . . . . .85 E8
Twiss Green Cty Prim Sch
WA3 . . . . .91 E4
Twiss Green Dr WA3 . . . . .91 E4
Twiss Green La WA3 . . . . .91 E4
Twisse Rd BL2 . . . . .42 F7
Twist Ave WA3 . . . . .90 C8
Twist La WN7 . . . . .75 E5
Two Acre Dr OL2 . . . . .48 F7
Two Acre La OL4 . . . . .50 A8
Two Bridges Rd OL16 . . . . . . .32 C3
Two Brooks La BL8 . . . . .10 B2
Two Porches Specl Sch
M46 . . . . .58 D4
Two Trees Com High Sch
M34 .101 A1
Two Trees La M34 . . . . .101 A1
Twoacre Ave M22 . . . . .121 C5
Twyford Cl OL11 . . . . .109 F3
Tyberne Cl M28 . . . . .77 F7
Tydden St OL8 . . . . .66 F3
Tydeman Wlk OL16 . . . . .32 A5
Tydesley Arc █ WN1 . . . . . .150 C8
Tyersall Cl M30 . . . . .79 E4
Tyldesley Cty Prim Sch
M29 . . . . .76 F8
Tyldesley Highfield Sch
M28 . . . . .77 C7
Tyldesley Old Rd M46 . . . . . . .58 E2
Tyldesley Pas █ M29 . . . . . . .58 F1
Tyldesley Prim Sch M29 . . . . .77 B7
Tyldesley Rd M46 . . . . .58 E2
Tyldesley St M14 . . . . .98 A3
Tyler St SK9 . . . . .137 A1
Tyler Wlk █ WA3 . . . . .90 F8
Tymm St M40 . . . . .83 C8
Tyndall Ave M40 . . . . .65 A1
Tyndall St OL4 . . . . .67 C6
Tyne Ct M28 . . . . .60 C3
Tyne St █ OL4 . . . . .67 C7
Tynedale Cl SK5 . . . . .111 F5
Tynesbank M28 . . . . .60 C3
Tynesbank Cotts M28 . . . . . . .60 C3
Tyntesfield Cty Prim Sch
M33 .107 E1
Tynwald St OL4 . . . . .67 C7

Tynwald Wlk █ M40 . . . . . . .156 C5
Tyrer Ave WN3 . . . . .54 F5
Tyrer Rd WA12 . . . . .89 C1
Tyrol Wlk M11 . . . . .164 F8
Tyrone Dr M23 . . . . .120 D8
Tyrone Dr OL11 . . . . .29 F5
Tyrrel Rd SK5 . . . . .99 F1
Tyrrell Gr SK14 . . . . .102 A1
Tysoe Gdns M3 . . . . .158 D2
Tyson St M8 . . . . .155 F8
Tytherington Dr M19 . . . . .99 D1

Uganda St BL3 . . . . .146 C2
Ukraine Rd M7 . . . . .81 B6
Uldale Dr M24 . . . . .46 E1
Ullesthorpe █ OL12 . . . . . . .139 E8
Ulleswater Cl BL3 . . . . .42 F3
Ulleswater St BL3 . . . . .143 F2
Ullock Wlk M24 . . . . .46 D2
Ullswater Ave
Ashton-in-M WN4 . . . . .73 B5
Ashton-u-L OL7 . . . . .166 A4
Orrell WN5 . . . . .53 F7
Rochdale OL12 . . . . .14 C1
Royton OL2 . . . . .48 D7
Ullswater Ct WA3 . . . . .74 C1
Ullswater Dr Bury BL9 . . . . . . .44 E7
Farnworth BL4 . . . . .59 E7
Ince-in-M WN2 . . . . .56 B7
Middleton M24 . . . . .46 F2
Ullswater Gr OL10 . . . . .46 D8
Ullswater Rd Golborne WA3 . .74 C1
Manchester M20 . . . . .110 C4
Stockport SK1 . . . . .124 B7
Tyldesley M29 . . . . .77 B6
Urmston M41 . . . . .94 E3
Wythenshawe M22 . . . . .121 C2
Ullswater St █ M17 . . . . .75 E5
Ullswater Terr SK15 . . . . .86 A4
Ullswater Wlk █ M9 . . . . .64 E3
Ulster Ave OL11 . . . . .139 E5
Ulundi St M26 . . . . .44 A3
Ulverston Ave
Manchester M20 . . . . .109 F7
Oldham OL9 . . . . .152 A6
Ulverston Rd WN3 . . . . .54 F3
Umberton Rd BL5 . . . . .58 F7
Uncouth Rd OL16 . . . . .31 E7
Under La Oldham OL4,OL5 . . .68 B4
Oldham OL4 . . . . .68 A5
Underhill SK6 . . . . .113 C2
Underhill Rd OL11 . . . . .48 E1
Underhill Wlk █ M40 . . . . .83 B4
Underwood OL12 . . . . .139 E7
Underwood Cl M18 . . . . .99 F6
Underwood Ct SK14 . . . . . . .102 D2
Underwood Rd
Alderley Edge SK9 . . . . .137 C1
Hattersley SK14 . . . . .102 D2
Underwood St SK16 . . . . . . .101 B8
Underwood Villas OL15 . . . . . .15 E4
Underwood Way █ OL2 . . . . . .49 DB
Underwood Wlk █
SK14 . . . . .102 D2
Undsworth Ct █ OL10 . . . . . .29 D2
Unicorn St M30 . . . . .95 B8
Union Arc BL9 . . . . .140 F2
Union Bldgs BL2 . . . . .145 F6
Union Ct █ BL1 . . . . .145 F8
Union Rd Ashton-u-L OL6 . . .166 C4
Bolton BL1,BL2 . . . . .25 A1
Littleborough OL12 . . . . .15 E4
Marple SK6 . . . . .125 F6
Union St Ashton-u-L OL6 . . .166 C3
Bacup OL13 . . . . .3 C8
Bolton BL1 . . . . .145 F8
Bolton BL7 . . . . .8 D2
Bury BL9 . . . . .140 F2
Dukinfield SK16 . . . . .101 B8
Hyde SK14 . . . . .167 E2
Ince-in-M WN2 . . . . .56 A8
Leigh WN7 . . . . .75 F5
Manchester M12 . . . . .163 C7
Manchester M14 . . . . .98 B3
Manchester M16 . . . . .99 E6
Manchester M4 . . . . .159 A2
Middleton M24 . . . . .47 A1
Oldham OL1 . . . . .153 F6
Oldham OL1 . . . . .6 A7
Oldham OL8 . . . . .66 F4
Oldham OL9 . . . . .66 B6
Ramsbottom BL0 . . . . .138 C6
Rochdale OL12,OL16 . . . . . . .139 F8
Royton OL2 . . . . .48 D3
Salford M6 . . . . .81 A4
Stockport SK1 . . . . .170 F8
Swinton M27 . . . . .62 A3
Swinton M27 . . . . .79 EB
Whitworth OL12 . . . . .14 CB
Union St W OL8 . . . . .153 G6
Union Terr M7 . . . . .155 F8
United Rd M17 . . . . .96 F5
United Trad Est M17 . . . . .96 F5
Unity Cl OL10 . . . . .29 B1
Unity Cres OL10 . . . . .29 B1
Unity Dr M7 . . . . .155 F6
Unity St Heywood OL10 . . . . . .29 B1
Skelmersdale OL14 . . . . .6 A8
Unity Way SK1 . . . . .124 A8
Unity Wlk SK13 . . . . .116 C7
Univ of Manchester (Lab)
M30 . . . . .94 D6
Univ of Manchester Inst
of Science & Tech M1 . .163 B8

Univ of Manchester The
Manchester M15 . . . . .163 A5
Manchester M13 . . . . .163 B6
Univ of Salford
Manchester M3 . . . . .158 D2
Salford M6 . . . . .81 B3
University Rd
Salford M5,M6 . . . . .81 B2
Salford M5,M6 . . . . .81 B3
University Rd W M5,M6 . . . .81 B2
Unsworth Ave
Golborne WA3 . . . . .74 E1
Tyldesley M29 . . . . .77 B6
Unsworth Prim Sch BL9 . . . .45 A2
Unsworth St Bacup OL13 . . . .3 D7
█ Hindley WN2 . . . . .56 D4
Leigh WN7 . . . . .75 E7
Radcliffe M26 . . . . .43 F1
Tyldesley M29 . . . . .59 B1
Unsworth Terr WN2 . . . . .56 C5
Unsworth Way █ OL1 . . . . . .153 E8
Unwin Ave M18 . . . . .99 D4
Up Holland High Sch
WN5 . . . . .53 C4
Upavon Ct M8 . . . . .155 F6
Upavon Rd M22 . . . . .121 F3
Upcast La SK9 . . . . .136 E3
Upholland Rd WN5 . . . . .53 D2
Upland Dr Ashton-in-M WN4 . .73 D4
Walkden M38 . . . . .59 F6
Upland Rd OL8 . . . . .66 E4
Uplands M41 . . . . .65 A7
Uplands Ave M20 . . . . .44 E1
Uplands Ave Flixton M41 . . .106 E8
Glossop SK13 . . . . .116 D8
Romiley SK14 . . . . .114 A6
Uplands The OL5 . . . . .68 D1
Upper Brook St
Manchester M13 . . . . .163 B6
Stockport SK1 . . . . .112 A1
Upper Broom Way BL5 . . . . . .40 A2
Upper Camp St M7 . . . . .155 D5
Upper Chorlton Rd M16 . . . . .97 C3
Upper Cliff Hill OL2 . . . . .32 C1
Upper Conran St M9 . . . . .157 E8
Upper Cyrus St M40 . . . . . . .160 E2
Upper Dicconson St WN1 . . .37 C1
Upper Downs WA14 . . . . .119 C3
Upper George St
█ Rochdale OL12 . . . . .14 F1
Tyldesley M29 . . . . .77 A8
Upper Gloucester St M6 . . . .81 A3
Upper Hayes Cl OL16 . . . . . . .31 CB
Upper Helena St M40 . . . . . .160 E2
Upper Hibbert La Sk6 . . . . . .125 F4
Upper Kent Rd M14 . . . . .98 B3
Upper Kirby St M4 . . . . .159 C1
Upper Lees Dr BL5 . . . . .40 A1
Upper Lloyd St M14 . . . . .98 A3
Upper Mead BL7 . . . . .8 F1
Upper Medlock St M15 . . . . .162 F6
Upper Monsall St M40 . . . . .157 E6
Upper Moss La M15 . . . . .162 E6
Upper Park Rd
Manchester M14 . . . . .98 C4
Manchester M7 . . . . .63 E1
Upper Passmonds Gr
OL11 . . . . .30 B8
Upper St Stephen St
WN6 .150 B8
Upper Stone Dr OL16 . . . . . . .31 D6
Upper West Gr M13 . . . . .164 D5
Upper Wharf St M3,M5 . . . . . .81 C1
Upper Wilton St M25 . . . . . . .63 C4
Uppermill Dr M19 . . . . .110 E3
Uppingham Dr BL0 . . . . .138 B7
Upton Cl Golborne WA3 . . . . . .90 D8
Uppton St Ashton-u-L OL6 . .166 A3
Manchester SK4 . . . . .110 E4
Upton Cl Golborne WA3 . . . . . .90 D8
Manchester M24 . . . . .65 A5
Upton Dr WA14 . . . . .119 E8
Upton La M29 . . . . .77 C8
Upton Rd M46 . . . . .58 E4
Upton St M1 . . . . .159 B1
Upton Way Bury BL8 . . . . .26 F5
Unsworth Sch SK13 . . . . .131 D5
Uranus Dr OL11 . . . . .139 E6
Urban Ave WA15 . . . . .119 E4
Urban Dr WA15 . . . . .119 E4
Urban Rd Altrincham WA15 . .119 E4
Sale M33 . . . . .108 A4
Urmson St OL8 . . . . .66 D2
Urmston Ave WA12 . . . . .89 B5
Urmston Gram Sch M41 . . . . .95 C2
Urmston Inf Sch M41 . . . . . . .95 C2
Urmston Jun Sch M41 . . . . . .95 C2
Urmston La M32,M41 . . . . . . .96 B1
Urmston Pk M41 . . . . .95 C2
Urmston St WN7 . . . . .75 D5
Urmston Sta M41 . . . . .95 D2
Urwick Rd SK6 . . . . .113 B2
Usk Cl M45 . . . . .63 C7
Uttley St Bolton BL1 . . . . . . .143 D2
Rochdale OL11 . . . . .30 C4
Uvedale Ho █ M40 . . . . .79 D1
Uxbridge Ave █ M11 . . . . . .83 C2
Uxbridge St OL6 . . . . .166 A3

Vaal St OL8 . . . . .66 C3
Valance Cl M12 . . . . .165 A6
Valdene Cl BL4 . . . . .60 D7
Valdene Dr Farnworth BL4 . . .60 D7

Valdene Dr continued
Walkden M28 . . . . .78 D8
Vale Ave Bury BL9 . . . . .44 D7
Horwich BL6 . . . . .22 A3
Hyde SK14 . . . . .102 A3
Kearsley M26 . . . . .61 C7
Sale M33 . . . . .108 E5
Swinton M27 . . . . .62 A1
Urmston M41 . . . . .94 E1
Vale Cl Apsley Bridge WN6 . . .35 E8
Hazel Grove SK7 . . . . .124 E4
Manchester SK4 . . . . .110 F2
Romiley SK6 . . . . .113 F2
Vale Coppice Horwich BL6 . . .22 A3
Ramsbottom BL0 . . . . .11 C3
Vale Cotts Horwich BL6 . . . . .21 F2
Littleborough OL15 . . . . .16 A5
Vale Cres SK8 . . . . .122 F2
Vale Dr Oldham OL9 . . . . .153 D6
Prestwich M25 . . . . .63 A2
Vale Edge M26 . . . . .44 A5
Vale Head SK4 . . . . .131 D2
Vale House Dr SK13 . . . . .104 A5
Vale La M35 . . . . .84 A4
Vale Park Ind Est M8 . . . . . . .156 C7
Vale Rd Altrincham WA14 . . .119 B1
Altrincham WA15 . . . . .120 B5
Droylsden M43 . . . . .84 B3
Manchester SK4 . . . . .110 F1
Mossley SK15 . . . . .86 E6
Stockport SK7 . . . . .125 B8
Shaw OL2 . . . . .49 D6
Wilmslow SK9 . . . . .136 E8
Vale Side OL5 . . . . .86 C8
Vale St Ashton-u-L OL7 . . . . . .85 A6
Bolton BL2 . . . . .43 A7
Droylsden M11 . . . . .99 E2
Heywood OL10 . . . . .29 E2
Middleton M24 . . . . .65 B8
Vale The Appley Bridge WN6 . .35 D8
Mossley SK15 . . . . .86 C8
Vale Top Ave M9 . . . . .157 F7
Vale View M7 . . . . .24 F7
Valencia Rd M7 . . . . .81 B6
Valentia Rd M9 . . . . .64 D4
Valentine St Failsworth M35 . .83 F7
Oldham OL4 . . . . .67 C6
Valentines Rd M46 . . . . .58 A1
Valerie Wlk █ M15 . . . . .162 F7
Valetta Cl M14 . . . . .110 B8
Valewood Ave SK4 . . . . .168 A1
Valiant Rd WN5 . . . . .54 D8
Valiant Wlk █ M40 . . . . .65 E1
Valletts La BL1 . . . . .142 C1
Valletts S BL1 . . . . .142 C1
Valley Ave BL8 . . . . .27 B4
Valley Cl █ Cheadle SK8 . . .122 E3
Mossley OL5 . . . . .68 B2
Valley Cotts OL3 . . . . .69 C4
Valley Dr SK9 . . . . .131 C3
Valley Gdns SK14 . . . . .114 E8
Valley Gr M34 . . . . .101 B2
Valley Mew Rd OL2 . . . . .48 E3
Valley Rd Bramhall SK7 . . . . .123 F1
Bredbury SK6 . . . . .113 A2
Cheadle SK8 . . . . .122 E3
Glossop SK13 . . . . .115 F8
Hattersley SK14 . . . . .114 E8
Middleton M24 . . . . .47 B2
Oldham OL2 . . . . .48 E3
Stockport SK4 . . . . .168 A1
Urmston M41 . . . . .94 D4
Wigan WN5 . . . . .54 D5
Valley Rd S M41 . . . . .94 D4
Valley Rise █ OL2 . . . . .32 A1
Valley SK SK7 . . . . .132 C5
Valley Sch SK7 . . . . .132 C5
Valley The M46 . . . . .58 E3
Valley View Bolton BL7 . . . . . .25 A7
Hyde SK14 . . . . .102 A4
Newton-le-W WA12 . . . . .89 B1
Whitworth OL12 . . . . .4 D4
Valley Way SK15 . . . . .86 C1
Valley Wlk M11 . . . . .160 F1
Valpy Ave BL2 . . . . .42 D3
Vanbrugh Gr WN3 . . . . .54 F4
Vancouver Quay M5 . . . . .96 F7
Vandyke Ave M6 . . . . .80 B3
Vandyke St █ OL12 . . . . .13 F1
Vane St █ M30 . . . . .79 D2
Vanguard Cl M30 . . . . .94 F7
Vannes Gr SK14 . . . . .102 F3
Vantomme St BL1 . . . . .143 E4
Varden Gr SK3 . . . . .170 D5
Varden Rd SK12 . . . . .133 C3
Vardon Dr SK9 . . . . .137 D6
Varey St M18 . . . . .99 D5
Varley Rd BL3 . . . . .146 A4
Varley St M40 . . . . .160 D3
Varna St M11 . . . . .99 E7
Varna Street Prim Sch
M11 . . . . .99 D6
Vauban Dr M6 . . . . .80 B3
Vaughan St Eccles M30 . . . . .79 B3
Manchester M12 . . . . .164 F7
Royton OL2 . . . . .48 E3
Vauxhall Ct M40 . . . . .159 C4

Vauxhall Ind Est SK5 . . . . . . .111 E6
Vauxhall Rd WN1 . . . . .151 D8
Vauxhall St M40 . . . . .159 B4
Vauze Ave BL6 . . . . .21 D1
Vauze House Cl BL6 . . . . .21 D2
Vavasour Ct 5 OL16 . . . . .31 B6
Vavasour St OL16 . . . . .31 B6
Vawdrey Dr 6 M23 . . . . .108 F2
Vaynor 8 OL12 . . . . .139 E8
Vega St M8 . . . . .158 E4
Vela Wlk M6 . . . . .81 C3
Velmere Ave M9 . . . . .64 A5
Velour Cl M13 . . . . .158 D3
Velvet Cl M1 . . . . .163 A8
Vendale Ave M27 . . . . .79 D6
Venesta Ave M6 . . . . .80 B4
Venetia St M40 . . . . .83 C5
Venice St Bolton BL3 . . . . . . .146 C4
Manchester M1 . . . . .163 A8
Venlow Gdns SK8 . . . . .123 B1
Ventnor Ave Bolton BL1 . . . . .143 F3
Manchester M19 . . . . .111 C8
Sale M33 . . . . .108 B6
Whitefield BL9 . . . . .45 A3
Ventnor Cl M34 . . . . .113 B8
Ventnor Rd
Manchester M20 . . . . .110 C3
Manchester SK4 . . . . .168 A2
Ventnor St Manchester M9 .157 E8
Rochdale OL11 . . . . .139 F5
Salford M6 . . . . .81 B4
Ventor St M9 . . . . .157 D8
Ventura Cl M14 . . . . .98 A1
Ventura Ct SK22 . . . . .127 D1
Venture Scout Way M8 . . . . .155 F6
Venture Way SK12 . . . . .133 F3
Venwood Rd M25 . . . . .62 F2
Verbena Ave BL4 . . . . .42 A1
Verbena Cl M31 . . . . .105 F3
Verda St WN2 . . . . .74 B8
Verdant La Eccles M30 . . . . . .94 F8
Eccles M30 . . . . .95 A8
Verdon St M4 . . . . .159 A3
Verdun Ave M6 . . . . .80 B3
Verdun Cres OL11 . . . . .30 C8
Verdun Rd M30 . . . . .79 B4
Verdure Ave Bolton BL1 . . . . .40 E8
Sale M33 . . . . .108 C1
Verdure Cl M35 . . . . .84 B7
Vere St M5 . . . . .154 F1
Verity Cl 5 Manchester M20 .110 C6
Royton OL2 . . . . .48 D3
Verity Wlk M9 . . . . .64 B3
Vermont St BL1 . . . . .145 D8
Verne Ave M27 . . . . .79 E8
Verne Dr OL1 . . . . .49 F3
Verney Rd OL2 . . . . .48 E2
Vernham Wlk BL3 . . . . .147 E4
Vernon Ave Eccles M30 . . . . . .79 F2
Stockport SK1 . . . . .112 B2
Stretford M32 . . . . .96 D1
Vernon Ct Cheadle SK8 . . . . .122 E1
Poynton SK12 . . . . .133 D2
Vernon Ct M7 . . . . .63 C1
Vernon Dr Marple SK6 . . . . . .125 D7
Prestwich M25 . . . . .63 A2
Vernon St Ashton-u-L OL6 . . .85 D3
Vernon Jun & Inf Schs
The SK12 . . . . .133 E3
Vernon Park Prim Sch
SK1 . . . . .112 A1
Vernon Pk WA15 . . . . .120 A7
Vernon Rd Bredbury SK6 . . . .112 E3
Droylsden M43 . . . . .83 E2
Manchester M7 . . . . .63 C1
Poynton SK12 . . . . .133 E2
Ramsbottom BL8 . . . . .11 A1
Vernon St Ashton-u-L OL6 . . .166 C4
Bolton BL1 . . . . .145 E8
Bury BL9 . . . . .140 F4
Farnworth BL4 . . . . .42 E1
Grasscroft SK7 . . . . .124 B8
Hyde SK14 . . . . .167 E2
Leigh WN7 . . . . .75 F5
Manchester M16 . . . . .162 D5
Manchester M7 . . . . .155 D5
Mossley OL5 . . . . .68 C2
Stockport SK1 . . . . .169 F2
Vernon View 3 SK6 . . . . . . .112 F3
Vernon Wlk 5 Bolton BL1 . . .145 E8
Stockport SK1 . . . . .169 F2
Vernon Dr M40 . . . . .83 C4
Veronica Rd M20 . . . . .110 C3
Verrill Ave M23 . . . . .109 C1
Verwood Wlk 3 M23 . . . . . . .121 A5
Vesper St M35 . . . . .84 A8
Vesta St Manchester M4 . . . .159 C1
Ramsbottom BL0 . . . . .138 B6
Vestris Dr M6 . . . . .80 B3
Vetch Cl WA3 . . . . .105 B5
Viaduct St
Manchester M12 . . . . .164 E8
Manchester M3 . . . . .158 F2
Newton-le-W WA12 . . . . .89 A3
Stockport SK3 . . . . .169 E1
Vicar's Dr OL16 . . . . .139 F6
Vicar's Gate OL16 . . . . .139 F7
Vicarage Ave SK8 . . . . .132 B7
Vicarage Cl Adlington PR6 . . .21 A8
Dukinfield SK16 . . . . .101 E8
Oldham OL4 . . . . .67 F7
Platt Bridge WN2 . . . . .56 A2
Salford M6 . . . . .80 B3
Vicarage Cres OL6 . . . . .85 D5
Vicarage Ct 3 M23 . . . . .120 D6
Vicarage Dr
Dukinfield SK16 . . . . .101 E8

Vicarage Dr continued
Littleborough OL12,OL16 . . . .15 C3
Vicarage Gdns SK14 . . . . . . .167 F2
Vicarage Gr M30 . . . . .79 F2
Vicarage La
Altrincham WA14 . . . . .119 C1
Middleton M24 . . . . .65 D7
Poynton SK12 . . . . .133 E5
Shevington WN6 . . . . .36 A5
Vicarage Rd Abram WN2 . . . .56 B1
Ashton-in-M WN4 . . . . .73 B2
Ashton-u-L OL7 . . . . .85 B5
Blackrod BL6 . . . . .21 D2
Golborne WN2 . . . . .74 A1
Irlam M44 . . . . .94 A2
Orrell WN5 . . . . .53 D4
Stockport SK3 . . . . .170 E6
Swinton M27 . . . . .79 E8
Urmston M41 . . . . .95 B8
Walkden M28 . . . . .60 C4
Vicarage Rd N OL11 . . . . .30 D1
Vicarage Rd S OL11 . . . . .30 C1
Vicarage Rd W BL6 . . . . .21 C2
Vicarage Sq WN7 . . . . .75 F5
Vicarage St Bolton BL3 . . . . .145 E5
Oldham OL8 . . . . .66 C3
1 Radcliffe M26 . . . . .44 A3
Shaw OL2 . . . . .149 B7
Vicarage View OL11 . . . . .30 D1
Vicarage Way OL2 . . . . .149 A6
Vicars Hall Gdns M28 . . . . . . .77 F5
Vicars Hall La M28 . . . . .77 F4
Vicars Rd M21 . . . . .109 A8
Vicars St M30 . . . . .79 F2
Viceroy Ct M20 . . . . .110 B2
Vicker Cl M27 . . . . .61 F2
Vicker Gr M20 . . . . .109 F5
Vickerman St BL1 . . . . .143 D2
Vickers Row BL4 . . . . .60 B8
Vickers St Bolton BL3 . . . . . .145 E5
Manchester M40 . . . . .160 E4
Victor Ave BL9 . . . . .140 E4
Victor Cl WN5 . . . . .54 D8
Victor Mann St M11 . . . . . . .100 A7
Victor St Heywood OL10 . . . . .46 E8
Manchester M3 . . . . .158 D2
Manchester M40 . . . . .159 C4
Victoria Ave
Altrincham WA15 . . . . .119 F7
7 Bredbury SK6 . . . . .112 F3
Cheadle SK8 . . . . .123 A2
Eccles M30 . . . . .79 F3
Hadfield SK13 . . . . .104 A5
Hazel Grove SK7 . . . . .124 E3
Leigh WN2 . . . . .56 E1
Manchester M19 . . . . .111 A8
Manchester M20 . . . . .110 A3
Manchester M9 . . . . .64 C5
Pendlebury M27 . . . . .80 A8
Whitefield M45 . . . . .44 A1
Wigan WN6 . . . . .37 A1
Victoria Ave E M24,M40,M9 . .65 B4
Victoria Avenue Prim Sch
M9 . . . . .64 D5
Victoria Bridge St M3 . . . . . .158 F2
Victoria Cl Aspull WN2 . . . . . .38 B6
5 Boothstown M28 . . . . .78 A6
Bramhall SK7 . . . . .132 D6
Stockport SK3 . . . . .170 E7
Victoria Cres Eccles M30 . . . .79 F3
Standish WN6 . . . . .36 E8
Victoria Ct
5 Ashton-u-L OL7 . . . . .166 A1
Farnworth BL4 . . . . .42 C2
Horwich BL6 . . . . .22 C3
Manchester M11 . . . . .165 C8
Manchester M20 . . . . .110 A3
Stretford M32 . . . . .96 C2
Victoria Dr M33 . . . . .108 D3
Victoria Gdns Hyde SK14 . . .167 F4
Shaw OL2 . . . . .149 B7
Victoria Gr Bolton BL1 . . . . .142 C1
Manchester M14 . . . . .110 C7
Reddish SK4 . . . . .111 D5
Victoria Grange M20 . . . . . .110 A4
Victoria Ho
Manchester M11 . . . . .165 C8
Salford M6 . . . . .80 A4
Victoria Ind Est The M4 . . . .160 D1
Victoria La Swinton M27 . . . . .79 D8
Whitefield M45 . . . . .62 F7
Victoria Lo M7 . . . . .81 C5
Victoria Mews
1 Dukinfield SK16 . . . . .101 C6
Whitefield BL9 . . . . .45 B2
Victoria Mkt SK15 . . . . .86 A1
Victoria Par Rawtenstall BB4 . .2 B8
Urmston M41 . . . . .95 D2
Victoria Park Prim Sch
M32 . . . . .96 D2
Victoria Pk SK1 . . . . .124 B8
Victoria Rd
Altrincham WA15 . . . . .119 D3
Altrincham WA15 . . . . .120 A6
Bolton BL1 . . . . .40 D8
Dukinfield SK16 . . . . .101 C6
Eccles M30 . . . . .79 E3
Garswood WN4 . . . . .72 C2
Horwich BL6 . . . . .22 C2
Irlam M44 . . . . .93 F1
Kearsley BL4 . . . . .61 A6
Manchester M14 . . . . .110 B8
Manchester M7 . . . . .81 C5
Manchester M19 . . . . .98 F1
Newton-le-W WA12 . . . . .89 C3
Platt Bridge WN2 . . . . .56 A2
Sale M33 . . . . .108 D3
Salford M6 . . . . .80 A4

Victoria Rd continued
Stockport SK1 . . . . .112 B1
Stretford M32 . . . . .96 D2
Urmston M41 . . . . .95 B2
Wilmslow SK9 . . . . .137 A6
Wythenshawe M22 . . . . .121 D8
Victoria Sq Bolton BL1 . . . . .145 F7
Manchester M4 . . . . .159 B2
Walkden M28 . . . . .60 D3
Victoria St
Altrincham WA14 . . . . .119 D5
Ashton-u-L OL7 . . . . .166 A1
Bacup OL13 . . . . .3 D8
Blackrod BL6 . . . . .21 D7
Boothstown M28 . . . . .78 A6
Bury BL8 . . . . .140 D2
Bury BL8 . . . . .140 D3
Bury BL8 . . . . .26 E7
Bury BL9 . . . . .140 F3
Dukinfield SK14 . . . . .102 A5
Dukinfield SK16 . . . . .101 D8
Failsworth M35 . . . . .83 D6
4 Farnworth BL4 . . . . .42 B2
Glossop SK13 . . . . .116 C8
Heywood OL10 . . . . .29 E1
Leigh WN7 . . . . .75 E6
Littleborough OL15 . . . . .16 B5
Manchester M3 . . . . .158 F2
Manchester M24 . . . . .65 A8
Oldham OL4 . . . . .67 A6
Oldham OL8 . . . . .67 E6
Oldham OL8 . . . . .84 F8
Oldham OL9 . . . . .152 C8
Platt Bridge WN2 . . . . .56 A2
4 Radcliffe M26 . . . . .44 A3
Ramsbottom BL0 . . . . .138 B6
Rawtenstall BB4 . . . . .2 E8
22 Rochdale OL12 . . . . .14 F1
Shaw OL2 . . . . .149 B6
1 Stalybridge SK15 . . . . . . .85 F2
Stalybridge SK15 . . . . .86 D4
Westhoughton BL5 . . . . .57 F8
Whitworth OL12 . . . . .14 C8
Wigan WN3 . . . . .150 B8
Victoria St E OL7 . . . . .166 A2
Victoria Sta M3 . . . . .159 A3
Victoria Station App M3 . . . .159 A2
Victoria Terr
Bickershaw WN2 . . . . .74 F8
Heywood OL10 . . . . .29 C4
Manchester M12 . . . . .98 F4
Milnrow OL16 . . . . .32 A5
Victoria Way
Bramhall SK7 . . . . .132 D6
Leigh WN7 . . . . .75 E7
Royton OL2 . . . . .48 C6
Victoria Wlk 10 M9 . . . . .64 C5
Victory Cl M11 . . . . .160 F1
Victory Gr M34 . . . . .100 C7
Victory Rd Irlam M44 . . . . . .105 C4
Little Lever BL3 . . . . .43 B4
Victory St Bolton BL1 . . . . . .144 C8
Manchester M14 . . . . .98 C3
Victory Trad Est BL3 . . . . . . .148 A5
Vienna Rd SK3 . . . . .170 D6
Vienna Rd E SK3 . . . . .170 E6
View St BL3 . . . . .145 D5
Viewfield Wlk 10 M9 . . . . . .157 E7
Viewlands Dr SK9 . . . . .131 D2
Vigo Ave BL3 . . . . .146 B3
Vigo St Heywood OL10 . . . . . .29 E1
Oldham OL4 . . . . .67 D5
1 Wigan WN2 . . . . .37 F2
Viking Cl M11 . . . . .160 F1
Viking St Bolton BL3 . . . . . . .42 A4
Rochdale OL16 . . . . .31 A6
Villa Ave WN6 . . . . .37 A4
Villa Rd OL8 . . . . .66 F4
Village Circ M17 . . . . .96 D6
Village Ct Stretford M17 . . . . .96 C6
Wilmslow SK9 . . . . .137 C5
Village Dr 2 OL3 . . . . .69 B8
Village St M7 . . . . .81 C5
Village The M1 . . . . .106 F8
Village View 2 WN7 . . . . .76 B4
Village Way WN6 . . . . .131 D1
Village Way
(Ashburton Rd E) M17 . . . .96 C6
Village Wlk 3 M11 . . . . .83 C1
Villdale Ave SK2 . . . . .124 C7
Villiers Ct M45 . . . . .63 A6
Villiers Dr OL8 . . . . .66 D3
Villiers St Ashton-u-L OL6 . . . .85 D2
Bury BL9 . . . . .141 A3
Hyde SK14 . . . . .167 F2
Salford M6 . . . . .154 F4
Vinca Gr M7 . . . . .158 D3
Vincent Ave Eccles M30 . . . . .79 D4
Manchester M21 . . . . .97 A1
Oldham OL4 . . . . .67 C8
Vincent Ct BL3 . . . . .147 E3
Vincent St Bolton BL1 . . . . . .143 F4
Hyde SK14 . . . . .113 F8
Littleborough OL15 . . . . .16 A6
Manchester M11 . . . . .165 C8
Manchester M7 . . . . .155 E7
Middleton M24 . . . . .47 A2
1 Rochdale OL16 . . . . .15 B2
Vincent Way WN5 . . . . .54 D8
Vine Ave M27 . . . . .80 B8
Vine Cl Sale M33 . . . . .107 C5
Shaw OL2 . . . . .149 B7
Vine Ct Rochdale OL16 . . . . . .31 B6
Stretford M32 . . . . .96 D3
Vine Fold M40 . . . . .65 F1
Vine Gr Stockport SK2 . . . . .124 C6
Wigan WN3 . . . . .150 C7
Vine Pl OL11 . . . . .139 F5

Vine St Eccles M30 . . . . .79 C1
Hazel Grove SK7 . . . . .124 E3
Hindley WN2 . . . . .56 D6
Manchester M11,M18 . . . . . .99 E6
Manchester M7 . . . . .81 C8
Oldham OL9 . . . . .66 B3
Prestwich M25 . . . . .63 C5
Ramsbottom BL0 . . . . .11 A4
Wigan WN1 . . . . .37 D1
Vinery Gr M34 . . . . .100 E3
Vineyard Cl OL12 . . . . .15 C7
Vineyard St OL4 . . . . .67 B7
Viola Cl WN6 . . . . .19 D2
Viola St Bolton BL1 . . . . .143 E3
Droylsden M11 . . . . .83 D2
Violet Ave BL4 . . . . .42 A1
Violet Ct M22 . . . . .121 D3
Violet Hill Ct OL4 . . . . .67 E8
Violet St Ashton-in-M WN4 . . .73 B2
Droylsden M18 . . . . .99 F6
Ince-in-M WN3 . . . . .151 E6
Stockport SK2 . . . . .170 F6
Violet Way M24 . . . . .65 D7
Vip Centre Ind Est OL1 . . . . . .49 C1
Virgil St M15 . . . . .162 D6
Virginia Chase SK8 . . . . .131 F8
Virginia Cl M23 . . . . .120 D7
Virginia St Bolton BL3 . . . . . .146 B4
Rochdale OL11 . . . . .30 B4
Virginia Way WN5 . . . . .54 C8
Viscount Dr Gatley SK8 . . . . .131 D7
Wythenshawe M90 . . . . .129 F7
Viscount Rd WN5 . . . . .54 D8
Viscount St M14 . . . . .98 B2
Vista Ave WA12 . . . . .89 A4
Vista Rd WA11,WA12 . . . . . . .89 A6
Vista The M44 . . . . .105 C4
Vista Way WA12 . . . . .89 A4
Vivian Pl 9 M14 . . . . .98 C4
Vivian St OL11 . . . . .139 E5
Vixen Cl M21 . . . . .109 E7
Voewood Ho SK1 . . . . .124 B8
Voltaire Ave M6 . . . . .80 B3
Vorlich Dr OL9 . . . . .65 F8
Vulcan Cl WA12 . . . . .89 C4
Vulcan Dr WN1 . . . . .151 D7
Vulcan Ind Est WA12 . . . . . . .89 D1
Vulcan Rd WN5 . . . . .54 D8
Vulcan St OL1 . . . . .49 B1
Vyner Ave M33 . . . . .107 F6

W

Wadcroft Wlk 11 M9 . . . . . . .157 E8
Waddicor Ave OL6 . . . . .85 E6
Waddington Cl Bury BL8 . . . .26 E2
Golborne WA3 . . . . .90 F8
Waddington Fold OL16 . . . . . .31 C2
Waddington Rd BL1 . . . . .142 A2
Waddington St OL9 . . . . .152 C8
Wade Bank BL5 . . . . .57 F8
Wade Hill La OL3 . . . . .68 E8
Wade Ho 8 M30 . . . . .79 D1
Wade Row OL3 . . . . .69 A6
Wade St 4 Bolton BL3 . . . . . .147 F3
Middleton M24 . . . . .65 D6
Wade Wlk M11 . . . . .165 A8
Wadebridge Ave M23 . . . . . .120 D7
Wadebridge Cl 3 BL3 . . . . . .25 B1
Wadebrook Gr 4 SK9 . . . . . .131 E1
Wadeford Cl M4 . . . . .159 C3
Wadesmill Wlk M13 . . . . . . .163 B7
Wadeson Rd M13 . . . . .163 C7
Wadham Gdns SK6 . . . . .113 C5
Wadham Way WA15 . . . . . . .119 F1
Wadhurst Wlk 3 M13 . . . . . .163 C5
Wadlow Cl M3 . . . . .158 E3
Wadsworth Cl SK9 . . . . .131 E3
Wadsworth Dr WN6 . . . . .36 F2
Wadsworth Ind Pk BL3 . . . . .147 E4
Wadsworth Mews M43 . . . . . .83 F1
Waggon Rd Bolton BL2 . . . . . .42 D8
Mossley OL5 . . . . .86 C8
Waggoners Ct 2 M27 . . . . . . .79 F7
Wagner St BL1 . . . . .143 D3
Wagstaffe Dr M35 . . . . .83 F7
Wagstaffe St M24 . . . . .47 A2
Wagtail Cl M28 . . . . .78 D8
Wain Cl M30 . . . . .79 B2
Wain Stones Gn SK2 . . . . . .124 E6
Wainclife Ave M20,M21 . . . .110 D4
Wainfleet Cl WN2 . . . . .54 E2
Waingap Cres OL12 . . . . .14 D8
Waingap Rise
Rochdale OL12 . . . . .14 F4
Whitworth OL12 . . . . .4 F5
Wainman St M6,M7 . . . . .81 B5
Wainscot Cl M29 . . . . .77 B7
Wainwright Ave M34 . . . . . . .99 F3
Wainwright Cl Oldham OL4 . . .68 A7
Stockport SK2 . . . . .124 A7
Wainwright Rd WA14 . . . . . .119 C5
Wainwright St
Oldham OL8 . . . . .153 E5
Stalybridge SK16 . . . . .85 E1
Waithlands Rd OL16 . . . . .31 B6
Wakefield Cres
Romiley SK6 . . . . .113 A1
Standish WN6 . . . . .19 D1
Wakefield Dr Kearsley M27 . . .61 D4
Oldham OL1 . . . . .49 D4
Wakefield Mews SK15 . . . . . .86 B3
Wakefield St Golborne WA3 . . .90 A7
2 Manchester M1 . . . . .163 A7
Wakefield Wlk M34 . . . . .101 A1
Wakeling Rd M34 . . . . .112 E8
Walcot Pl WN3 . . . . .54 F7

Vau–Wal 257

Walcott Cl M13 . . . . .164 E5
Wald Ave M14 . . . . .110 E7
Waldeck St 1 BL1 . . . . .145 D8
Waldeck Wlk 24 M9 . . . . .64 E3
Walden 8 OL10 . . . . .46 C8
Walden Ave OL4 . . . . .49 D2
Walden Cl Hindley WN2 . . . . . .56 F4
Manchester M14 . . . . .110 A8
Walden Cres SK7 . . . . .124 C3
Walden Ave SK8 . . . . .122 D5
Waldon Cl BL3 . . . . .146 C4
Waldorf Cl WN3 . . . . .54 D2
Wales St OL1 . . . . .49 C1
Walford Rd WN4 . . . . .73 C3
Walford St M16 . . . . .97 E4
Walk Mill Cl OL12 . . . . .15 D4
Walk The Atherton M46 . . . . .58 D3
Rochdale OL16 . . . . .139 F7
Walkdale Brow SK13 . . . . . . .116 B7
Walkden Ave WN1 . . . . .37 B2
Walkden Ave E WN1 . . . . .37 C2
Walkden High Sch M28 . . . . . .60 E1
Walkden Market Pl M28 . . . . .60 D1
Walkden Rd Walkden M28 . . . .60 D1
Worsley M28 . . . . .78 E7
Walkden Sta M28 . . . . .60 D2
Walkdene Dr M28 . . . . .60 B3
Walkdens Ave M46 . . . . .58 A2
Walker Ave Bolton BL3 . . . . .147 F3
Failsworth M35 . . . . .84 B6
Stalybridge SK15 . . . . .86 C2
Walker Cl Hyde SK14 . . . . . . .167 F2
Kearsley BL4 . . . . .61 A6
Walker Fold BL2 . . . . .167 F2
Walker Fold Rd BL2 . . . . .23 D4
Walker Gn M28 . . . . .79 B5
Walker Ho 8 M30 . . . . .79 D1
Walker La SK14 . . . . .167 F2
Walker Rd Eccles M30 . . . . . .79 A4
Failsworth M9 . . . . .64 F4
Irlam M44 . . . . .93 F1
Manchester M9 . . . . .64 E4
Walker St Bolton BL1 . . . . . .145 D6
3 Bury BL9 . . . . .44 E8
Denton M34 . . . . .100 E4
Hadfield SK13 . . . . .104 A1
Heywood OL10 . . . . .29 C1
Middleton M24 . . . . .64 C7
Oldham OL8 . . . . .153 D6
4 Radcliffe M26 . . . . .44 C1
Rochdale OL16 . . . . .31 A7
Stockport SK1 . . . . .169 E1
Westhoughton BL5 . . . . .57 E8
Walker's Croft M3 . . . . .158 F2
Walker's La OL4 . . . . .68 A6
Walker's Rd OL8 . . . . .66 A6
Walkers Cl OL3 . . . . .69 B8
Walkers Ct Farnworth BL4 . . . .60 D8
Oldham OL4 . . . . .68 A6
Walkers Dr WN7 . . . . .76 A5
Walkerwood Dr SK15 . . . . . . .86 D2
Walkmill OL3 . . . . .50 F1
Walkway The BL3 . . . . .40 F5
Wall Hill Rd OL3 . . . . .50 E2
Wall St Oldham OL8 . . . . . . .153 F5
Salford M6 . . . . .154 F2
Shevington WN6 . . . . .36 A7
Wall Way M18 . . . . .99 E4
Wallace Ave M14 . . . . .98 D3
Wallace La M14 . . . . .37 E1
Wallace St 2 OL8 . . . . .66 F4
Wallasey Ave M14 . . . . .98 A1
Wallbank Dr OL12 . . . . .14 C8
Wallbrook Ave WN5 . . . . .53 D1
Wallbrook Cres M38 . . . . .60 B6
Wallbrook Gr BL4 . . . . .42 B2
Waller Ave M14 . . . . .110 C8
Walley St BL1 . . . . .143 E3
Wallgarth Cl WN3 . . . . .54 E2
Wallgate WN3 . . . . .150 B7
Wallgate Dr M35 . . . . .83 F7
Wallgate Sta WN1 . . . . .150 C8
Wallhead Rd OL16 . . . . .31 D7
Wallingford Rd
Handforth SK9 . . . . .131 C5
Urmston M41 . . . . .95 F3
Wallis St Failsworth M40 . . . .83 D5
Oldham OL9 . . . . .66 A4
Wallness La M6 . . . . .81 C3
Walls St WN2 . . . . .57 C2
Wallshaw Pl OL1 . . . . .67 A7
Wallshaw St OL1 . . . . .67 A7
Wallsuches BL6 . . . . .22 F4
Wallwork Cl OL11 . . . . .13 E1
Wallwork Rd Droylsden M11 . .99 E8
Wallwork St M11 . . . . .99 D5
Wallworth Ave M18 . . . . .99 D5
Wallworth Terr SK9 . . . . .136 E8
Wally Sq M7 . . . . .155 E6
Walmer Rd WN5 . . . . .57 A5
Walmer St 2 M14 . . . . .98 C3
Walmer St Manchester M14 . .98 C3
Manchester M18 . . . . .99 E6
Walmer St E M14 . . . . .98 C3
Walmersley Cl SK6 . . . . .125 F6
Walmersley Old Rd BL9 . . . . .27 F6
Walmersley Rd Bury BL9 . . . .27 F6
Failsworth M40 . . . . .65 E1
Walmersley Rd WN7 . . . . .75 E5

Walmesley St WN1 ....151 D7
Walmley Gr BL3 ....146 C3
Walmley Ave OL15 ....5 E3
Walmsley CE Prim Sch BL7 ..8 E1
Walmsley Gr M41 ....95 D2
Walmsley St ■ Bury BL8 ....27 B4
Newton-le-W WA12 ....89 D4
Reddish SK5 ....169 F3
Stalybridge SK15 ....102 A8
Walney Rd Wigan WN3 ....54 D2
Wythenshawe M22 ....121 D4
Walnut Ave WN7 ....121 D4
Walnut Ave Bury BL9 ....141 C3
Oldham OL4 ....67 D8
Wigan WN1 ....37 D2
Walnut Cl Hyde SK14 ....102 A2
Kearsley M27 ....61 D4
Wilmslow SK9 ....137 E8
Walnut Gr Leigh WN7 ....75 F8
Sale M33 ....108 A4
Walnut Rd Eccles M30 ....79 A4
Partington M31 ....105 D3
Walnut St Bolton BL1 ....143 F2
■ Manchester M18 ....99 D5
Walnut Tree Rd SK3 ....123 A8
Walnut Wlk ■ M32 ....96 C1
Walpole Ave WN3 ....54 F3
Walpole St OL16 ....31 A7
Walsall St M6 ....81 A5
Walsden Est OL14 ....6 B7
Walsden St M11 ....83 C2
Walsh Ave M9 ....64 D2
Walsh Cl WA12 ....89 C5
Walsh Fold BL7 ....9 D2
Walsh Ho M46 ....58 D4
Walshaw St Horwich BL6 .....22 B4
Oldham OL9 ....152 B6
Walshaw Brook Cl BL8 ....26 F4
Walshaw Dr M27 ....79 F7
Walshaw La BL8 ....26 F4
Walshaw Rd BL8 ....27 B4
Walshaw Wlk BL8 ....26 F5
Walshe St BL9 ....140 D2
Walsingham Ave
  Manchester M20 ....109 F4
  Middleton M24 ....65 A5
Walter Scott Ave WN1 ....37 B5
Walter Scott St ■ OL1 ....67 B8
Walter St Ashton-in-M WN4 ...73 D4
Droylsden M43 ....99 E6
Leigh WN7 ....75 B5
Manchester M16 ....97 C4
Manchester M9 ....157 D8
■ Oldham OL1 ....153 F6
Prestwich M25 ....62 F4
Radcliffe M26 ....43 F6
Walkden M28 ....60 D2
Wigan WN5 ....54 D6
Walters Dr OL8 ....67 A3
Walters Green Cres WA3 ......74 A2
Waltham Ave
  Glazebury WA3 ....92 C7
  Shevington WN6 ....36 F2
Waltham Dr SK8 ....132 B6
Waltham Gdns M26 ....43 E5
Waltham Rd M16 ....97 E1
Waltham St OL4 ....67 C4
Walthew House La WN5 ....36 B1
Walthew La
  Platt Bridge WN2 ....56 A2
  Wigan WN5 ....56 B2
Walton Cl Heywood OL10 .....46 D8
  Middleton M24 ....46 C1
Walton Ct BL3 ....147 F4
Walton Dr Bury BL9 ....27 E8
  Marple SK6 ....125 D7
Walton Hall Dr M19 ....99 D1
Walton Ho M35 ....83 F8
Walton Pl BL4 ....60 E7
Walton Rd
  Altrincham WA14 ....119 B5
  Culcheth WA3 ....91 F3
  Manchester M9 ....64 D6
  Sale M33 ....107 F2
Walton St Adlington PR7 ......21 A6
  Ashton-u-L OL7 ....84 F5
  Atherton M46 ....58 E4
  Heywood OL10 ....29 D1
  ■ Middleton M24 ....47 A2
  Stockport SK1 ....170 F7
Walton Way M34 ....101 B1
Walworth Dr M26 ....61 C7
Walwyn Cl M12 ....96 E1
Wanborough Cl WN7 ....75 F7
Wandsworth Ave M11 ....83 D2
Wanley Wlk ■ M9 ....64 E3
Wansbeck Cl M32 ....96 E1
Wansbeck Lock M32 ....96 E1
Wansfell Wlk M40 ....160 D2
Wansford St M14 ....98 A3
Wanstead Ave M9 ....65 B3
Wapping St BL1 ....143 D2
War Office Rd OL11 ....29 E6
Warbeck Cl Hindley WN2 ......56 E3
  Reddish SK5 ....100 A2
Warbeck Rd M40 ....65 D2
Warbreck Gr M33 ....108 D3
Warburton Bridge Rd
  WA13,WA3 ....105 A1
Warburton Cl
  Altrincham WA15 ....129 D6
  Lymm WA13 ....117 A4
  Romiley SK6 ....113 A1
Warburton La
  Partington M31 ....105 F4

Warburton La continued
  Partington M31,WA13 ....105 E2
Warburton Pl ■ M46 ....58 D3
Warburton Rd SK9 ....131 D4
Warburton St Bolton BL1 ....143 F2
  Eccles M30 ....79 E1
  ■ Manchester M20 ....110 B3
  Salford M5 ....161 B6
Warburton View WA3 ....105 A2
Warcock Rd OL4 ....67 C7
Ward La Diggle OL3 ....51 D3
Ward Rd M43 ....84 B1
Ward St Bredbury SK6 ....112 F3
  Hindley WN2 ....56 E7
  Hyde SK14 ....167 E2
  ■ Manchester M40 ....157 F8
  Manchester M40 ....64 C2
  Oldham OL1 ....153 D8
  Oldham OL9 ....152 C7
  Stockport SK1 ....124 A7
Warde St M15 ....162 E6
Warden La M40 ....83 B6
Warden St M40 ....83 B6
Wardend Cl M38 ....60 A6
Wardens Bank BL5 ....57 E5
Wardle Brook Ave SK14 ....102 D3
Wardle Brook Wlk SK14 ......102 D3
Wardle Cl Radcliffe M26 ......43 E5
  Stretford M32 ....96 E2
Wardle Ct M33 ....108 C4
Wardle Edge OL12 ....14 B4
Wardle Fold OL12 ....15 C7
Wardle Gdns OL12 ....15 C3
Wardle High Sch OL12 ....15 C4
Wardle Rd Rochdale OL12 ......15 C4
  Sale M33 ....108 C4
Wardle St Bacup OL13 ....3 D8
  Bolton BL2 ....148 C5
  Littleborough OL15 ....16 A6
  Manchester M40 ....160 E3
Wardley Ave
  Manchester M16 ....109 E8
  Manchester M16 ....97 E1
  Walkden M28 ....60 B3
Wardley CE Prim Sch
  M27 ....61 E2
Wardley Gr BL1 ....144 A7
Wardley Hall La M28 ....79 A8
Wardley Hall Rd M27,M28 .....61 B1
Wardley Ho M46 ....80 C4
Wardley Ind Est
  Swinton M28 ....61 C1
  Swinton M29 ....79 C8
Wardley Rd M29 ....77 D8
Wardley Sq M29 ....77 D8
Wardley St Swinton M27 ......79 F8
  Wigan WN5 ....54 B6
Wardlow Ave
  ■ Gamesley SK13 ....171 D1
  Wigan WN3 ....36 A1
Wardlow Fold ■ SK13 ....171 D1
Wardlow Gdns ■ SK13 ....171 D1
Wardlow Mews SK13 ....171 D1
Wardlow St BL3 ....146 B4
Wardlow Wlk ■ SK13 ....171 D1
Wardour St Atherton M46 .....58 C2
  Atherton M46 ....58 C3
Wards Pl ■ WN7 ....76 B4
Wardsend Wlk ■ M15 ....162 D6
Ware Cl WN4 ....73 D4
Wareham Gr M30 ....79 C3
Wareham St M8 ....64 B1
Warecing St M29 ....76 F8
Wareing Way BL3 ....145 E6
Wareings Yd ■ OL11 ....31 A4
Warfield Wlk ■ M9 ....64 E3
Warford Ave SK12 ....134 A2
Warford La WA16 ....136 B1
Warford St M4 ....159 B4
Warford Terr WA16 ....136 B2
Wargrave CE Prim Sch
  WA12 ....89 C1
Wargrave House Sch
  WA12 ....89 D1
Wargrave Mews WA12 ....89 C1
Wargrave Rd WA12 ....89 C2
Warham St SK9 ....137 B7
Warke The M25 ....78 F6
Warlands End Gate OL14 ....6 D5
Warley Cl SK8 ....122 E6
Warley Gr SK16 ....101 C8
Warley Rd M16 ....97 A3
Warley St OL15 ....16 B5
Warlingham Cl BL8 ....27 B1
Warlow Crest OL3 ....69 A4
Warlow Dr Leigh WN7 ....57 D1
  Oldham OL3 ....69 A4
Warmby Gdns OL8 ....66 F4
Warmington Dr M12 ....164 E6
Warminster Gr WN3 ....54 D2
Warmley Rd M23 ....120 D8
Warncliffe St ■ WN5 ....54 D5
Warne Ave M43 ....84 D2
Warnford Wlk ■ M11 ....160 F1
Warnford Cl M40 ....83 D4
Warnford St ■ WN1 ....37 C2
Warp Wlk ■ M4 ....159 C1
Warre St OL6 ....166 B3
Warren Ave SK8 ....122 D5
Warren Bank M9 ....64 D3
Warren Bruce Rd M17 ....96 D6
Warren Cl Atherton M46 ....58 E5
  Denton M34 ....100 D2
  Poynton SK12 ....133 B4
  Stockport SK2 ....123 D2

Warren Dr
  Altrincham WA15 ....129 D7
  Bacup OL13 ....4 C8
  Newton-le-W WA12 ....89 F4
  Swinton M27 ....79 D5
Warren Hey SK9 ....137 E8
Warren La OL8 ....67 B7
Warren Lea Poynton SK12 ....133 E5
  Romiley SK6 ....114 B2
Warren Rd Cheadle SK8 ....123 B2
  Stockport SK3 ....170 E6
Stretford M17 ....96 B6
Walkden M28 ....60 E3
Warren St ■ Bury BL8 ....27 B1
  Manchester M7 ....155 F8
  Manchester M9 ....64 C2
  Stockport SK1 ....169 F2
Warren Wood Prim Sch
  SK2 ....125 A6
Warrener St M33 ....108 D4
Waste St ■ OL1 ....67 A7
Wastwater St ■ OL1 ....49 A1
Watburn Rd SK2 ....127 D1
Watchgate Cl M24 ....46 D3
Water Dr WN6 ....37 B7
Water Gate OL3 ....69 B8
Water Grove Rd SK16 ....101 F7
Water La Droylsden M43 ......83 E1
  Edenfield BL0 ....1 D6
  Farnworth BL4 ....60 E7
  Hollingworth SK14 ....103 D5
  Milnrow OL16 ....32 A5
  Radcliffe M26 ....43 F3
  Wilmslow SK9 ....137 A7
Water Lane St
  Radcliffe M26 ....43 F3
  ■ Radcliffe M26 ....44 A4
Water Rd SK15 ....85 F2
Water Ski Ctr OL12 ....4 B2
Water St Adlington PR7 ....21 A6
  Ashton-u-L OL6 ....166 B3
  Atherton M46 ....58 D3
  Bolton BL1 ....145 F7
  Bolton BL7 ....8 D2
  Denton M34 ....100 F7
  Glossop SK13 ....104 E2
  Hyde SK14 ....167 D2
  Manchester M12 ....163 C8
  Manchester M3 ....162 D8
  Manchester M9 ....157 D8
  ■ Middleton M24 ....46 F1
  Newton-le-W WA12 ....89 C4
  Radcliffe M26 ....44 A3
  Ramsbottom BL0 ....138 B5
  Rochdale OL16 ....31 A7
  Royton OL2 ....49 A4
  Stalybridge SK15 ....86 A2
  Stockport SK1 ....169 F3
  ■ Wigan WN3 ....14 C8
  Wigan WN1 ....150 C8
Water''s Reach SK6 ....134 E7
Water's Edge BL4 ....42 A2
Water's Nook Rd BL5 ....58 A8
Waterbarn La OL13 ....11 B8
Waterbeck Cl WN3 ....37 F1
Waterbridge M28 ....79 A5
Watercroft OL11 ....13 D1
Waterdale Cl M28 ....78 B6
Waterdale Dr M45 ....62 F8
Waterfield Cl BL9 ....27 F7
Waterfield Way M35 ....84 A6
Waterfold La BL9 ....141 C1
Waterfoot Cotts SK14 ....103 A4
Waterfoot Cty Prim Sch
  BB4 ....2 F8

Waterford Ave
  Manchester M20 ....109 D3
  Romiley SK6 ....113 F2
Waterford Pl SK8 ....131 B8
Waterfront Quay M5 ....161 A7
Watergate M41 ....100 C8
Watergate Dr BL5 ....57 C7
Watergate La BL4,BL5 ....59 C7
Watergate Milne Ct ■
  OL4 ....67 D8
Waterhouse Cl OL12 ....15 C6
Waterhouse Nook M18 ....99 E4
Waterhouse St OL12 ....139 F8
Waterloo Ct Bury BL9 ....140 E8
  ■ Manchester M20 ....110 A5
  ■ Stalybridge SK15 ....86 A2
Waterloo Gdns OL6 ....85 E5
Waterloo Ind Pk BL1 ....143 F4
Waterloo Pk ■ SK1 ....112 A1
Waterloo Prim Sch OL7 ....85 A5
Waterloo Rd
  Ashton-u-L OL6 ....85 B5
  Bramhall SK7 ....132 F8
  Manchester M8 ....155 F6
  Manchester M8,M9 ....156 A6
  Poynton SK12 ....134 A2
  Romiley SK6 ....113 E2
  Stalybridge SK15 ....86 A2
  Stockport SK1 ....169 F1
Waterloo St Ashton-u-L OL6 ..85 B5
  Bolton BL1 ....143 F1
  Bury BL8 ....140 D2
  Manchester M1 ....163 A8
  Manchester M8 ....156 C8
  Manchester M9 ....47 A1
  ■ Wigan WN6 ....37 A1
Waterman View OL16 ....31 C8
Watermans Cl Horwich BL6 ...22 C4
  Manchester M9 ....157 F8
Watermead Cl SK3 ....123 E4
Watermede WN5 ....53 E3

Watermeetings La SK6 ....113 F1
Watermill Cl OL16 ....31 D6
Watermill Ct OL7 ....85 A5
Watermillock Gdns BL1 ....143 F4
Waterpark Rd M7 ....155 E8
Waters Edge SK6 ....126 B8
Waters Meeting Rd
  Bolton BL1 ....143 F1
  Bolton BL1 ....143 F3
  Bolton BL1 ....25 A2
Waters Reach
  Poynton SK12 ....133 F5
  Wigan WN1 ....151 F8
Watersedge Cl SK8 ....123 B3
Watersfield Cl SK8 ....131 F8
Watersheddings Com
  Prim Sch OL1 ....49 C1
Watersheddings St ■
  OL4 ....49 D1
Watersheddings Way ■
  OL4 ....49 D1
Waterside Hadfield SK13 .....104 A6
  Hattersley SK14 ....102 D2
  Marple SK6 ....125 F5
  Stretford M17 ....96 F6
Waterside Ave ■ SK6 ....125 F5
Waterside Cl
  Hattersley SK14 ....102 D2
  Manchester M21 ....109 D4
  Radcliffe M26 ....44 D4
Waterside Cotts OL3 ....69 C4
Waterside Ct SK14 ....102 D2
Waterside Dr WN3 ....150 B7
Waterside La OL16 ....31 B8
Waterside Rd Disley SK12 ....135 F7
  Ramsbottom BL9 ....11 C3
Waterside Trad Est ■
  WN7 ....76 B4
Waterside Wlk ■ SK14 ......102 D2
Waterslea M30 ....79 C2
Waterslea Dr BL1 ....40 F8
Watersmead Cl BL1 ....143 F2
Watersmead St BL1 ....143 F2
Watersmeet ■ M32 ....96 D4
Waterson Ave M40 ....83 A7
Waterton Ave OL5 ....68 B2
Waterton La OL5 ....68 B2
Waterview Cl OL16 ....32 B3
Waterview Pk WN7 ....75 E4
Waterworks Rd OL4 ....49 E1
Watfield Wlk ■ M9 ....157 D7
Watford Ave M14 ....98 B2
Watford Bridge Ind Est
  SK22 ....127 D1
Watford Bridge Rd SK22 ....127 D1
Watford Cl ■ BL1 ....143 E2
Watford La SK22 ....127 C2
Watford Rd
  Manchester M19 ....111 A6
  New Mills SK22 ....127 C2
Watkin Ave SK13 ....171 E4
Watkin Cl M13 ....163 C6
Watkin St Hyde SK14 ....102 A5
  Manchester M3 ....158 D3
  Rochdale OL16 ....31 B4
  Wigan WN1 ....150 C8
Watkins Dr M25,M8 ....63 F3
Watling St Bolton BL8 ....26 B7
  Bury BL8 ....26 F1
Watlington Cl OL1 ....49 D3
Watson Ave
  Ashton-in-M WN4 ....73 C3
  Golborne WA3 ....73 F1
Watson Gdns OL12 ....14 D2
Watson Rd BL4 ....59 F8
Watson St Denton M34 ....101 B3
  Eccles M30 ....79 C2
  Manchester M2,M3 ....162 F8
  Oldham OL4 ....67 C8
  Radcliffe M26 ....44 A4
  Swinton M27 ....79 F8
Watts St Horwich BL6 ....22 C2
  Manchester M19 ....111 B8
  Oldham OL8 ....66 D2
  Rochdale OL12 ....139 F8
  ■ Rochdale OL12 ....31 A8
Waugh Ave M35 ....83 F7
Wavell Dr M45 ....45 A1
Wavell Rd M22 ....121 D2
Waveney Dr
  Altrincham WA14 ....119 C6
  Handforth SK9 ....131 D2
Waveney Rd Oldham OL2 .....149 A8
  Wythenshawe M22 ....121 E4
Waverley Cl OL10 ....29 C2
  ■ Rochdale OL12 ....139 E8
Waverley Ave Kearsley BL4 ...60 F6
  Stretford M43 ....96 F3
Waverley Cres M43 ....84 A3
Waverley Ct WN3 ....54 D3
Waverley Dr SK8 ....132 B7
Waverley Gr WN7 ....76 D6
Waverley Rd Bolton BL1 ......143 E3
  Golborne WA3 ....74 D1
  Hindley WN2 ....56 C4
  Hyde SK14 ....113 D8
  Manchester M9 ....157 F7
  Middleton M24 ....47 A3
  Pendlebury M27 ....80 C7
  Sale M33 ....108 A2
  Stockport SK3 ....123 C7
  Walkden M28 ....60 B1
Waverley Rd W M9 ....157 F7
Waverley Sq M41 ....60 C6
Waverley St Oldham OL1 ......49 C1
  Rochdale OL11 ....30 C1

Waverton Ave SK4 ....111 D7
Waverton Rd M14 ....98 A1
Wavertree Ave M46 ....58 C4
Wavertree Ct 6 BL1 ......145 E8
Wavertree Rd M9 ....64 C4
Waybridge Ind Pk
  Stretford M17 ....96 C7
  Stretford M5 ....96 D8
Wayfarers Dr WA12 ....89 E2
Wayfarers Way M27 ......79 F7
Wayfaring BL5 ....39 F2
Wayford Wlk M9 ....156 C7
Wayland Rd M8 ....99 E4
Wayland Rd S M18 ....99 D3
Wayne Cl M43 ....84 C4
Wayne St M11 ....99 E8
Wayoh Croft BL7 ....9 D6
Wayside Dr SK12 ....133 C4
Wayside Gdns SK7 ....125 A2
Wayside Gr M28 ....60 E4
Weald Cl M13 ....163 C6
Wealdstone Gr BL2 ....25 B2
Weardale Rd M9 ....64 E5
Wearhead Cl Golborne WA3 .89 F7
  Golborne WA3 ....90 A7
Wearhead Row M5 ......154 F1
Wearish La BL5 ....57 C6
Weaste Ave M38 ....60 B4
Weaste Dr M5 ....154 D3
Weaste La M5,M6 ....154 D2
Weaste Rd M5 ....154 D2
Weaste Trad Est M6 .....154 D2
Weatherall St N M7 ......155 F7
Weatherley Cl OL8 ......67 A1
Weatherley Dr SK6 ......125 D6
Weaver Ave M26 ....60 A2
Weaver Cl WA14 ....119 C1
Weaver Ct M15 ....162 D6
Weaver Dr BL9 ....27 F8
Weaver Gr WN7 ....75 C4
Weaver Ho M47 ....81 C5
Weaver Rd WA3 ....92 A2
Weaver Wlk 5 M11 ......99 D7
Weaverham Cl 2 M13 ....98 F3
Weaverham Way SK9 .....131 E4
Weaverham Wlk M33 .....108 E3
Weavers Ct Bolton BL3 ...145 E5
  11 Middleton M24 ......46 F1
  Mottram-in-L SK14 ......103 A4
Weavers Gn BL4 ....60 D8
Weavers La SK7 ....132 D6
Weavers Rd M24 ....46 F1
Webb Gr SK14 ....102 F1
Webb La SK1 ....124 A8
Webb St Bury BL8 ....140 D3
  Horwich BL6 ....22 C3
Webb Wlk SK14 ....102 F1
Webdale Dr M40 ....83 A7
Weber Dr BL3 ....145 D5
Webster Gr M25 ....62 F2
Webster Jun Sch M15 ....98 A4
Webster St Bolton BL3 ...148 B5
  8 Mossley OL5 ....68 C2
  Oldham OL8 ....153 F5
Webster's St WN2 ....56 A3
Wedgewood Dr WN6 .....36 D3
Wedgewood St M40 .....160 F4
Wedgwood Rd M27 ......62 C2
Wedhurst St OL4 ....67 C7
Wedlock St OL1 ....67 A7
Wedneshough SK14 ......103 C5
Weedall Ave M5 ....161 A6
Weeder Sq OL2 ....49 E8
Weedon Ave WA12 ....89 B5
Weedon St OL16 ....31 B8
Weeton Ave BL2 ....42 F7
Weft Wlk 5 M4 ....159 C2
Weighbridge Ct M44 ....94 C3
Weint The WA3 ....105 B3
Weir Rd OL16 ....31 E7
Weir St Failsworth M35 ..83 E7
  Manchester M15 ....162 E5
Welbeck Ave
  Failsworth OL9 ....65 D3
  Littleborough OL15 .....16 A6
  Newton-le-W WA12 ......89 D2
  Urmston M41 ....95 F3
Welbeck Cl Milnrow OL16 .31 D6
  Whitefield M45 ....44 F2
Welbeck Gr M7 ....155 E7
Welbeck Ho 4 OL6 .....166 A2
Welbeck Rd
  Ashton-in-M WN4 ....73 C4
  Bolton BL1 ....144 A8
  Eccles M30 ....79 E4
  Hyde SK14 ....167 F2
  1 Radcliffe SK5 ....111 F8
  Rochdale OL16 ....31 B4
  Sale M30 ....79 B6
  Wigan WN3 ....54 E3
Welbeck St N OL6 ....99 E6
Welbeck St N OL6 ....166 A2
Welbeck St S OL6,OL7 ..166 A2
Welbeck Terr OL6 ....166 A2
Welburn Ave M22 ....121 E3
Welburn St OL11 ....139 F5
Welbury Rd M23 ....108 F1
Welby St M13 ....98 D4
Welch Rd SK14 ....167 F4
Welcomb Cl SK6 ....112 F4
Welcomb St M11 ....165 B7
Welcomb Wlk M11 ......62 F7
Welcome Par OL8 ....67 D3
Welcroft St SK1 ....170 F8
Weld Rd M20 ....110 D7
Weldon Ave BL3 ....146 A2
Weldon Cres SK3 ....123 E4

Weldon Dr M9 ....64 D5
Weldon Gr WN1 ....37 E2
Weldon Rd WA14 ....119 D6
Welfold Ho 8 OL4 ....67 B5
Welford Ave WA3 ....90 C7
Welford Cl SK9 ....137 E8
Welford Gn SK5 ....111 F5
Welford Rd M9 ....63 F3
Welford St M6 ....81 A4
Welkin Rd SK6 ....112 C3
Welkin Rd Ind Est SK6 ..112 C3
Well Ct WN6 ....19 E1
Well Gate SK13 ....104 E2
Well La M45 ....44 E2
Well Green Prim Sch
  WA15 ....120 C2
Well i' th' La OL11 ......31 A4
Well La M45 ....44 E2
Well Mdw SK14 ....167 D4
Well Mead Sk6 ....112 E3
Well Meadow La OL3 ....69 C8
Well Row SK14 ....115 A8
Well St Ainsworth BL2 ...26 C1
  Bolton BL1 ....148 A7
  Heywood OL10 ....29 E1
  Manchester M4 ....159 A2
  6 Rochdale OL1 ....31 A5
  Tyldesley M29 ....77 A8
Well St N BL0 ....1 C2
Newton le-W WA12 ......89 D3
Well-i-Hole Rd OL3 ......68 F4
Wellacre Ave M41 ....94 D2
Wellacre High Sch M41 ..94 D2
Wellacre Jun Sch M41 ...94 D2
Welland Ave OL10 ....29 A3
Welland Cl M15 ....162 D6
Welland Ct 4 M15 .....162 D6
Welland Rd
  Ashton-in-M WN4 ....73 E5
  Handforth SK9 ....131 E2
  Shaw OL2 ....149 A8
Welland St Droylsden M11 .99 D8
  Reddish SK5 ....99 F1
Welland The BL5 ....57 E8
Wellbank SK15 ....102 B8
Wellbank Ave OL6 ....85 E6
Wellbank Cl OL8 ....67 A4
Wellbank St BL8 ....26 F6
Wellbank View OL12 .....13 F2
Wellbeck Rd WN4 ....73 C3
Wellbridge Cl WN4 ......73 C3
Wellbrow Terr OL12 .....14 D2
Wellbrow Wlk 10 M9 ....64 E3
Wellburn Cl BL5 ....40 F2
Wellcross Rd WN8 ....53 B6
Wellens Way M24 ....46 F1
Weller Ave
  Manchester M21 ......109 D7
  Poynton SK12 ....133 D2
Weller Ct SK12 ....133 D2
Weller Gdns M21 ....109 D7
Wellesbourne Dr M23 ..120 F7
Wellesley Ave M18 ......99 D6
Wellesley Cl
  Newton-le-W WA12 ......89 B5
  Wigan WN5 ....54 E8
Wellfield SK6 ....113 C4
Wellfield Cl BL9 ....44 E6
Wellfield Gdns WA15 ...120 C3
Wellfield Inf Sch WA13 ..107 F6
Wellfield Jun Sch WA13 ..107 F6
Wellfield La WA15 ......120 C3
Wellfield Pl 6 OL11 .....31 A5
Wellfield Rd Bolton BL3 ..144 C5
  Culcheth WA3 ....91 F4
  Hindley WN2 ....57 A4
  Manchester M8 ....156 A8
  Stockport SK2 ....124 C6
  Wigan WN6 ....37 A3
  Wythenshawe M23 .....121 A7
Wellgate Ave M19 ......111 B8
Wellgreen Cl WA15 .....120 C3
Wellgreen Lo WA15 ....120 C3
Wellham Rd WN3 ....55 B3
Wellhead Cl M15 ....162 F5
Wellhouse Dr M40 ......65 C3
Welling Rd M40 ....83 E8
Welling St 2 BL2 ......25 B1
Wellington Ave M16 ....97 D2
Wellington Cl
  Newton-le-W WA12 .....89 A3
  Sale M33 ....108 C6
Wellington Clough OL7 ..85 A6
Wellington Cres M16 ....97 C3
Wellington Ct Bury BL8 ..26 F6
  8 Oldham OL8 ....67 B1
  Oldham OL8 ....64 D4
Wellington Ctr OL6 .....166 C2
Wellington Gdns Bury BL8 .27 B1
  Newton-le-W WA12 .....89 A3
Wellington Gr
  Ince-in-M WN3 ....151 D5
  Manchester M15 ......162 D6
  Stockport SK2 ....170 F7
Wellington Lo OL15 .....16 B6
Wellington Mill SK4 ....169 E1
Wellington Par SK16 ...166 B1
Wellington Pl
  Altrincham WA14 ......119 D4
  16 Rochdale OL16 .....31 A8
Wellington Rd
  Altrincham WA14 ......119 F6
  Ashton-u-L OL6 ......166 B3
  Atherton M46 ....58 F5
  Bury BL9 ....140 F1
  Eccles M30 ....79 F2

Wellington Rd continued
  Edgworth BL7 ....9 D4
  High Lane SK7 ....134 B8
  Manchester M14,M20 ..110 C8
  Manchester M16 ....97 E2
  Manchester M8 ....156 B8
  Oldham OL3 ....69 B6
  Oldham OL8 ....153 E5
  Swinton M27 ....79 F8
Wellington Rd N
  M19,SK3,SK4 ....169 D3
Wellington Rd S SK1,SK2 .170 F8
Wellington Sch The
  WA15 ....119 F6
Wellington Sq 6 BL8 ....27 B1
Wellington St
  Ashton-u-L OL6 ......166 B2
  Bolton BL3 ....145 E6
  Bury BL8 ....146 A4
  Chadderton OL9 ......152 B8
  Denton M34 ....100 F6
  Dukinfield SK14 ......101 C3
  2 Failsworth M35 ....66 A1
  Farnworth BL4 ....60 D8
  Hazel Grove SK7 ......124 F3
  1 Littleborough OL15 ..16 B5
  Manchester M18 ....99 D5
  Manchester M3 ....158 D2
  Milnrow OL16 ....32 A6
  Newton-le-W WA12 ....89 A3
  Oldham OL3 ....153 F6
  5 Radcliffe M26 ....44 C4
  10 Rochdale OL12 ....14 F1
  Stockport SK1 ....169 F1
  Stretford M32 ....96 E2
  Westhoughton BL5 .....39 E2
  Wigan WN1 ....151 D8
Wellington St E M7 ....155 E7
Wellington St W M7 ....155 D6
Wellington Terr
  13 Dukinfield SK16 ...166 B1
  Salford M5 ....154 D2
Wellington Wlk BL3 ....145 E6
Wellock St M10,M40 ....157 F5
Wellpark Wlk 13 M40 ...83 C5
Wells Ave Billinge WN5 ..71 D6
  Chadderton OL9 ....48 A1
  Manchester M25 ....63 C2
Wells Cl Droylsden M43 ..99 F8
  Gatley SK8 ....123 C1
  Middleton M24 ....64 C7
  Tyldesley M29 ....77 C8
Wells Ct SK16 ....101 C6
Wells Dr Dukinfield SK16 ..101 C6
  Wigan WN2 ....37 F2
Wells Pl WN1 ....151 E8
Wells Rd OL8 ....49 E5
Wells St Bury BL9 ......140 E1
Wellside Wlk 8 M8 ....156 A6
Wellstock La M38 ....59 F6
Wellwood Dr 11 M40 ...83 A7
Wellyhole St OL4 ....67 D6
Welney Rd M16 ....97 B3
Welshpool Cl M11 ......99 E7
Welshpool Way 2 M34 .101 A1
Welton Ave M20 ....110 C2
Welton Cl Leigh WN7 ...76 C5
  Wilmslow SK9 ....136 F4
Welton Dr SK9 ....136 E4
Welton Gr SK9 ....136 E4
Welwyn Cl M41 ....95 B5
Welwyn Dr M6 ....80 A5
Welwyn Wlk M40 ....160 D2
Wem St OL9 ....66 A4
Wembley Gr M14 ......110 C8
Wembley Rd M18 ....99 C3
Wembury St M9 ....157 E8
Wembury St N M9 .....157 E8
Wembury Wlk SK14 ....102 E3
Wemyslow Gr 2 BL4 ...60 C8
Wemyss Ave SK5 ....99 F1
Wendlebury Cl WN7 ....75 E1
Wendlebury Gr OL2 ...149 A5
Wendon Rd M23 ....121 B5
Wendover Dr BL3 ....147 D3
Wendover Rd Sale M23 .120 D8
  Urmston M41 ....95 C1
Wenfield Dr M9 ....65 B3
Wenlock Ave SK2 ....124 A6
Wenlock Cl
  Hazel Grove SK2 ......125 A6
  Horwich BL6 ....22 C6
Wenlock Ct M12 ....164 F6
Wenlock Gr 4 WN2 ....56 D4
Wenlock Rd Hindley WN2 ..56 D5
  Sale M33 ....108 A2
Wenlock St
  8 Hindley WN2 ......56 D5
  Swinton M27 ....79 D8
Wenlock Way M12 ....164 F6
Wenning Cl M45 ....45 C1
Wenning Wlk 3 WN2 ..56 A1
Wensley Ct M7 ....63 A1
Wensley Dr
  Hazel Grove SK7 ......133 D7
  Manchester M20 ....110 B5
Wensley Rd Cheadle SK8 .122 C6
  Salford M7 ....63 A1
Wensleydale Ave OL2 ..48 E5
  Whitefield BL9 ....45 A3
  Wythenshawe M23 ....120 F3

Wensleydale Rd WN7 ....76 C5
Wentbridge Rd BL1 ....145 D8
Wentworth Ave
  Altrincham WA15 ......120 A6
  Bury BL8 ....27 B4
  Farnworth BL4 ....60 C7
  Heywood OL10 ....46 D8
  Irlam M44 ....94 A3
  8 Manchester M18 ....99 D6
  Salford M6 ....80 C3
  Whitefield M45 ....62 D7
Wentworth Cl Marple SK6 .125 F8
  Middleton M24 ....64 E8
  Radcliffe M26 ....43 D4
  Westhoughton BL5 .....39 F7
Wentworth Ct M35 .....83 F6
Wentworth Dr
  Bramhall SK7 ....133 A7
  Sale M33 ....107 F5
Wentworth High Sch M27 .79 A6
Wentworth Rd Reddish SK5 .99 F1
  Salford M30 ....80 A4
  Swinton M27 ....79 D6
Wentworth Wlk 2 SK14 .101 F5
  1 Mossley OL5 ....68 C1
  Sale M33 ....108 B3
  Westhoughton BL5 .....57 D6
Wenworth Ave M41 ....95 B1
Werneth Ave Hyde SK14 ..113 F8
  Manchester M14 ....98 B2
  Hazel Grove SK7 ......124 F4
Werneth Cres OL8 ....66 D4
  Werneth Cl OL8 ....167 E1
Werneth Hall Rd OL8 ...153 D5
Werneth Hollow SK6 ...113 B6
Werneth Inf Sch OL8 ...153 E5
Werneth Jun Sch OL8 ..153 E5
Werneth Low Ctry Pk
  SK14 ....114 A7
Werneth Low Rd
  SK14,SK6 ....113 E5
Werneth Prep Sch OL8 .153 D5
Werneth Rd Glossop SK13 .116 A7
  Hyde SK14 ....167 F2
  Romiley SK6 ....113 C5
Werneth Rise 1 SK14 ..113 F7
Werneth Sch SK6 ......113 A2
Werneth St Denton M34 .100 F5
  Stockport SK1 ....112 B3
Werneth Sta OL9 ....153 D6
Werneth Wlk M34 ......100 F2
Wescoe Cl WN5 ....53 E5
Wesley Cl Rochdale OL12 ..15 C3
  Westhoughton BL5 .....26 E7
Wesley Ct Bury BL8 ....26 C7
  Manchester SK4 ....110 F2
  Walkden M28 ....60 D4
  Westhoughton BL5 .....39 E2
Wesley Dr Ashton-u-L OL6 .85 D6
  Worsley M28 ....78 F8
Wesley Gn M5 ....161 B8
Wesley Methodist
  Prim Sch M26 ....43 F5
Wesley News 6 BL2 ...148 B7
Wesley Sq M1 ....95 A2
Wesley St Atherton M46 ..58 E3
  Bolton BL3 ....145 E5
  Bolton BL7 ....25 A8
  Bury BL8 ....26 C8
  Eccles M30 ....79 C2
  Failsworth M35 ....66 A1
  Farnworth BL4 ....60 E7
  Glossop SK13 ....104 E2
  Hadfield SK13 ....104 A8
  Hazel Grove SK7 ......124 E3
  Heywood OL10 ....29 C2
  Manchester M11 ......165 A8
  Milnrow OL16 ....31 E6
  1 Rochdale OL12 .....15 B3
  Royton OL2 ....48 D8
  Stockport SK1 ....169 F1
  Stretford M32 ....96 E3
  Swinton M27 ....79 F8
  Westhoughton BL5 .....39 E2
  Wigan WN3 ....150 C7
Wessenden Bank E SK2 .124 D5
Wessenden Bank W SK2 .124 D5
Wessex Cl WN1 ....20 B1
Wessex Rd Chad OL9 ....149 B8
Wessex Rd WN5 ....36 D1
Wessington Bank 12
  SK13 ....171 E2
Wessington Fold 14 SK13 ..171 E2
Wessington Gn 18 SK13 ..171 E2
Wessington Mews SK13 .171 E2
West Ashton St M5 ....154 F1
West Ave Altrincham WA14 .119 A5
  Droylsden M43 ....99 E5
  Failsworth M40 ....66 B8
  Farnworth BL4 ....60 B8
  Gatley SK8 ....122 C1
  Golborne WN7 ....74 B1
  Leigh WN7 ....76 C3
  Littleborough OL12 .....15 C3
  Manchester M19 ....111 C8
  Stalybridge SK15 ......86 A3
  Walkden M28 ....60 C3
  Whitefield M45 ....44 E2
  Wigan WN6 ....37 A2

West Croft Ind Est M24 ..64 C7
West Crown Ave M5 ...161 B8
West Dean St M5 ....81 C1
West Downs Rd SK8 ...122 F3
West Dr Bury BL9 ....27 E5
  Droylsden M43 ....83 F1
  Gatley SK8 ....122 A4
  Pendlebury M27 ....80 B7
  Pendlebury M6 ....80 E6
  Tintwistle SK13 ....103 F7
West Duke St M5 ......158 D1
West Egerton St M5 ....81 B1
West End Ave
  1 Gatley SK8 ....122 A6
  West End Prim Sch OL7 .84 F2
  West End St OL9 ......153 D7
  West Gdns 8 SK13 .....3 B8
  West Gn M24 ....64 B7
  West Gr Manchester M13 .164 D5
  Sale M33 ....108 B3
  Westhoughton BL5 .....57 C6
  West High St M5 ....81 A2
  West Hill OL11 ....139 E6
  West Hill Cl SK15 .....85 F2
  West Hill Sch SK15 ...85 F2
  West Hollow BL5 ....57 C6
  Werneth Rd OL8 ......153 E1
  West King St M3 ......158 E2
  West Lea M34 ....101 A2
  West Liverpool Street
    Prim Sch M6 ....154 F2
  West Marwood St M7 ..155 E6
  West Mdw SK5 ....100 A1
  West Meade Bolton BL3 .147 D2
  Manchester M21 ......109 A7
  Swinton M27 ....79 A6
  West Mosley St M2 ...159 A1
  West Mount Orrell WN5 ..53 F6
  Wigan WN1 ....37 D2
  West Oak Pl SK8 ......122 F1
  West Over SK6 ....113 A1
  West Par M33 ....107 C3
  West Park Ave
    Denton M34 ....101 B2
    Poynton SK12 ....133 A4
  West Park Rd
    Stockport SK1 ....112 B2
    Stockport SK2 ....123 D2
    Manchester M25 ....161 B7
    West Pk SK14 ....113 E6
    West Pl M19 ....110 F7
  West Point Lo 1 M19 ..110 F8
  West Rd Altrincham WA14 ..119 C2
    Eccles M41 ....95 E6
    Prestwich M25 ....62 F5
    Stretford M32 ....96 A4
  West Row M25 ....62 D5
    West St Alderley Edge SK9 ..137 A1
    Ashton-u-L OL6 ......166 B3
    Bolton BL1 ....144 C7
    Droylsden M11 ....83 B2
    Dukinfield SK16 ......166 B1
    Failsworth M35 ....83 F7
    Farnworth BL4 ....42 E1
    Heywood OL10 ....29 D2
    Hindley WN2 ....56 A8
    Littleborough OL15 ....16 C5
    Middleton M24 ....47 A2
    Milnrow OL16 ....31 D7
    Oldham OL1 ....153 E7
    Oldham OL4 ....67 D3
    Oldham OL9 ....153 D6
    Ramsbottom BL0 ......138 B5
    Rawtenstall BB4 ....2 E8
    Rochdale OL16 ....31 A8
    Stalybridge SK15 ......85 F2
    Stockport SK3 ....169 D1
    Tintwistle SK13 ....103 F7
    Tyldesley M46 ....58 E1
    Wigan WN3 ....150 C7
  West Towers St M6 ....154 F1
  West Vale M26 ....44 A5
  West Vale Rd WA15 ...119 F6
  West View Bacup OL13 ....3 B8
    Denton M34 ....100 F7
    Hollinfare BB4 ....1 A7
    Littleborough OL15 ....16 C5
    Ramsbottom BL0 ....1 C2
  West View Gr M45 ....44 D1
  West View Rd M22 ...121 E8
  West Way Bolton BL1 ..25 B3
    Walkden M38 ....60 A5
  West Wlk BL7 ....9 E7
  West Works Rd M17,M32 ..96 C5
  Westage Gdns M23 ...121 A7
  Westbank Rd Bolton BL6 ..40 D6
    Manchester M20 ......110 D5
  Westbourne Ave
    Bolton BL3 ....42 B3
    Kearsley M27 ....61 D5
    Leigh WN7 ....75 E7
    Leigh WN7 ....75 F7
    Whitefield M45 ....44 D1
  Westbourne Dr OL7 ....84 F1
  Westbourne Gr
    Manchester M20 ......110 A6
    Manchester M9 ....157 D8
    Reddish SK5 ....111 F8

Westbourne Gr continued
Sale M33 ....108 A4
Westbourne Pk M41 ......95 D2
Westbourne Range
M18,M34 ....99 F4
Westbourne Rd
Denton M34 ....100 E2
Eccles M30 ....79 B4
Manchester M14 ....110 D8
Urmston M41 ....95 D2
Westbourne St OL9 ......153 D7
Westbridge Mews WN1 ..150 C7
Westbrook Ct BL2 ....148 A6
Westbrook Rd
Stretford M17 ....96 D7
Swinton M27 ....79 E7
Westbrook Sq M12 ......165 A6
Westbrook St BL2 ....148 A6
Westbrook Wlk ⊟ M20 ...110 A8
Westbury Ave Sale M33 ..107 C1
Wigan WN3 ....54 D2
Westbury Cl Bury BL8 ....27 A1
Westhoughton BL5 ....40 A1
Westbury Dr SK6 ....125 E6
Westbury Rd M8 ....64 B1
Westbury St
Ashton-u-L OL6 ....166 C3
Dukinfield SK14 ....69 E7
Westbury Street Ind Est
SK14 ....101 C5
Westbury Way OL1,OL2 ...48 D2
Westby Cl SK7 ....133 A7
Westby Gr BL2 ....148 C8
Westcliffe Ho ⊟ BL2 .....15 D4
Westcliffe Rd BL1 ....24 F6
Westcombe De BL8 ....27 C5
Westcott Ave M20 ......110 A6
Westcott Cl BL2 ....25 E5
Westcott Ct M15 ....162 D7
Westcott Dr WN3 ....54 C4
Westcourt Gr OL2 ....149 A5
Westcourt Rd Bolton BL3 .147 D3
Sale M33 ....108 A6
Westcraig Ave M40 ......65 C3
Westcroft Rd M19,M20 ...110 D4
Westdale Gdns M19 .....111 A5
Westdean Cres M19 .....110 C5
Westend Ave M27 ....19 D8
Westend St BL4 ....60 B8
Wester Hill Rd OL8 ......67 A1
Westerdale ⊟ OL4 ......67 C6
Westerdale Dr M9 ....77 B8
Westerdale Dr Bolton BL3 .144 A5
Royton OL2 ....48 C5
Westerham Ave M5 ......81 A1
Westerham Cl BL8 ....27 C7
Westerham Rd M26 ......97 E3
Westerling Way M27 .....62 D2
Western Circ M19 ....110 F6
Western Ct OL13 ....3 B8
Western Rd Bacup OL13 ...3 C8
Urmston M41 ....94 E1
Western St Manchester M18 .99 E6
Salford M6 ....154 E3
Westerton Ct BL3 ....145 D5
Westfield
Altrincham WA14 ......119 C3
Sale M33 ....154 E4
Westfield Ave
Ashton-in-M WN4 ......73 A4
Middleton M24 ....65 A7
Westfield Cl OL11 ....13 F1
Westfield Dr Romiley SK6 .113 D5
Uppermill OL4 ....68 E5
Westfield Gr Denton M34 ..100 E5
Wigan WN1 ....37 B3
Westfield Rd Bolton BL3 ..146 B2
Cheadle SK8 ....131 F8
Droylsden M43 ....83 E2
Manchester M21 ....97 B1
Tyldesley M46 ....58 E1
Westfield St
Manchester M7 ....63 D1
Oldham OL1,OL9 ....48 C1
Oldham OL9 ....152 C8
Westfields WA15 ....128 F8
Westgate Altrincham WA15 .119 E2
Sale M33 ....108 A4
Urmston M41 ....95 B1
Whitworth OL12 ....14 B7
Wilmslow SK9 ....137 A5
Westgate Ave Bolton BL1 ..144 C7
Bury BL9 ....140 E1
Westgate Dr M27 ....79 E6
Ramsbottom BL0 ....11 A2
Westgate Cl OL12 ....14 B7
Westgate Dr Orrell WN5 ..53 D5
Swinton M27 ....79 F6
Westgate Rd M6 ....80 C4
Westgate St OL7 ....166 A1
Westgrove Ave BL1 ......24 E6
Westhead Ave WA3 ......74 E1
Westhide Wlk ⊟ M9 .....64 F1
Westholm Ave SK4 ......111 B7
Westholme Ct SK9 ......137 A2
Westholme Rd
Manchester M20 ....110 B5
Prestwich M25 ....63 C7
Westhorne Fold ⊟ M8 ...63 E2
Westhoughton
Com Prim Sch BL5 ......39 F1
Westhoughton High Sch
BL5 ....57 F8

Westhoughton Parochial
CE Prim Sch BL5 ....57 E8
Westhoughton Rd PR6,PR7 .20 F8
Westhoughton Sta BL5 ...39 E2
Westhulme Ave OL1 .....48 D1
Westhulme St OL1 ....48 D1
Westhulme Way OL1 .....48 C1
Westinghouse Cl M16 ...150 A8
Westinghouse Rd M17 ...96 B5
Westlake Gr WN2 ....57 B4
Westlake St M11 ....165 C7
Westland Ave Bolton BL1 .142 A1
Farnworth BL4 ....60 D2
Stockport SK1 ....112 B1
Westland Dr M9 ....64 D4
Westlands M45 ....62 F6
Westlands The M27 ......80 C6
Westlea Dr M18 ....99 D3
Westleigh Dr M25 ....63 D3
Westleigh High Sch WN7 .57 D1
Westleigh La WN7 ....57 D1
Westleigh Meth Prim Sch
WN7 ....75 D8
Westleigh St M9 ....64 F1
Westleigh St Paul's
CE Prim Sch WN7 ......75 E8
Westleigh View WN7 .....75 E8
Westlock WN3 ....150 C6
Westman Wlk ⊟ M11 ....97 F4
Westmarsh Cl ⊟ BL1 ....143 E1
Westmead WN6 ....36 E8
Westmead Dr
Manchester M8 ....155 E5
Sale WA15 ....120 B7
Westmeade Rd M28 .....60 C5
Westmere Dr M9 ....156 C6
Westminster Ave
Ashton-u-L OL6 ....85 D7
Farnworth BL4 ....60 C8
Manchester M16 ....97 C2
Radcliffe M26 ....43 D4
Reddish SK5 ....111 E7
Royton OL2 ....48 C6
Whitefield M45 ....62 F8
Westminster Cl
Marple SK6 ....125 D7
Sale M33 ....107 D3
Shaw OL2 ....149 B8
Westminster Dr
Bramhall SK8 ....132 B6
Leigh WN7 ....76 E7
Wilmslow SK9 ....137 A4
Westminster Ho M3 .....158 E3
Westminster Rd
Altrincham WA15 ......120 A2
Bolton BL1 ....24 E5
Eccles M30 ....79 F3
Failsworth M35 ....84 B8
Urmston M41 ....95 E4
Walkden M28 ....60 C8
Westminster St Bury BL9 .140 E1
Farnworth BL4 ....60 C8
⊟ Manchester M19 .....99 B1
Oldham OL1 ....67 B8
Rochdale OL11 ....139 D5
Salford M15 ....161 C7
Swinton M27 ....61 E1
Wigan WN5 ....54 F6
Westminster Way SK16 .101 D6
Westminster Wlk ⊟ BL4 ..60 C8
Westmoor Gables SK4 ...168 A4
Westmoorland St ⊟ WN1 .37 E1
Westmoreland Ave
Altrincham WA14 ......128 B8
Bury BL9 ....44 E6
Westmorland Ave
Ashton-u-L OL7 ....166 B4
Dukinfield SK16 ....101 E8
Westmorland Cl SK5 ....112 C6
Westmorland Dr
Brinnington SK5 ....112 C6
Littleborough OL12 .....15 D6
Westmorland Rd
Manchester M20 ....110 A2
Partington M31 ....105 E2
Sale M33 ....108 C8
Salford M30 ....80 A4
Tyldesley M29 ....59 A2
Urmston M41 ....95 C1
Westmorland Wlk ⊟ OL2 .48 E4
Westmount Cl M40 ......156 C6
Weston Ave Failsworth M40 .65 C1
Kearsley M27 ....61 F4
Rochdale OL16 ....31 B4
Urmston M41 ....95 B1
Weston Ct M14 ....98 D2
Weston Dr Denton M34 ..101 A3
Stockport SK8 ....123 D4
Weston Gr Reddish SK4 ..111 C6
Wythenshawe M22 ....121 E8
Weston Pk WN6 ....36 D3
Weston Rd ⊟ Irlam M44 ..94 A2
Wilmslow SK9 ....137 E6
Weston St Atherton M46 ..58 E4
Bolton BL3 ....42 A4
Manchester M44 ......160 D2
Milnrow OL16 ....31 E6
Reddish SK5 ....169 E4
Westonby Ct WN4 ....73 D3
Westover Rd M41 ....95 C3
Westover St M27 ....61 F1
Westpark M20 ....110 B5
Westpoint Ent Pk M17 ...95 F7
Westray Cres M5 ....154 E1
Westray Rd M13 ....98 E2
Westrees WN7 ....76 A7
Westville Gdns M19 ....110 E5
Westward Ho OL16 .....31 F6

Westward Rd SK9 ....136 F6
Westway Droylsden M43 ..100 A8
Manchester M9 ....64 A6
Oldham OL4 ....67 E5
Shaw OL2 ....149 B6
Westwell Gdns ⊟ BL1 ...143 F1
Westwell Gr ⊟ WN7 .....75 E8
Westwell St WN7 ....75 E8
Westwick Terr ⊟ BL1 ....143 E2
Westwood WA14 ....119 B4
Westwood Ave
Altrincham WA15 ......119 F7
Failsworth M35 ....67 A1
Manchester M7 ....155 E8
Urmston M41 ....95 F1
Walkden M28 ....60 A3
Westwood Bsns Ctr OL9 .153 D6
Westwood Com Prim Sch
OL9 ....153 D7
Westwood Cotts ⊟ M16 .97 F4
Westwood Cres M30 ....79 B4
Westwood Dr Oldham OL9 .153 D7
Pendlebury M27 ....80 C6
Sale M33 ....108 B2
Westwood Ind Est OL9 ..152 C7
Westwood La WN1 ......151 D5
Westwood Pk
Com Prim Sch M30 .....79 B3
Westwood Rd Bolton BL1 .144 C8
Gatley SK8 ....131 B8
Stockport SK2 ....124 B4
Wigan WN3 ....150 C6
Westwood Terr WN1 .....151 E5
Westwood Trad Est SK6 .125 E5
Westworth Cl ⊟ BL1 ....145 D8
Wet Gate La WA13 ......117 E4
Wetheral Cl WN2 ....57 C3
Wetheral Dr BL3 ....147 E3
Wetherall St M19 ....99 B1
Wetherby Cl WA12 ......89 C5
Wetherby Dr
Hazel Grove SK7 ....125 A2
Royton OL2 ....48 D5
Wetherby St M11 ....99 E7
Wexford Wlk M22 ......121 E2
Wexham Gdns WN2 .....56 A3
Weybourne Cl WN2 .....56 C5
Weybourne Ave M9 .....65 A2
Weybourne Dr
Hazel Grove SK7 ......112 F4
Wigan WN3 ....54 E3
Weybourne Gr BL2 ......25 B4
Weybridge Cl ⊟ BL1 ....145 E8
Weybridge Rd M4 ......159 C2
Weybrook Rd M19,SK4 ..111 C7
Weycroft Cl BL2 ....43 A6
Weyhill Rd M23 ....121 A5
Weylands Gr M6 ....80 B5
Weymouth Dr WN2 .....57 A4
Weymouth Rd
Ashton-u-L OL6 ....85 F6
Eccles M30 ....79 B4
Weymouth St BL1 ......143 E2
Weythorne Dr Bolton BL1 .143 F4
Bury BL9 ....28 F4
Whalley Ave Bolton BL1 ..23 F3
Glazebury WA3 ....92 C7
Littleborough OL15 ....16 A6
Manchester M16 ......97 D3
Manchester M19 ......99 B2
Manchester M21 ......109 C7
Sale M33 ....108 C5
Urmston M41 ....95 E3
Whalley Cl
Altrincham WA15 ......119 F8
Milnrow OL16 ....31 D6
Whitefield M45 ....44 F1
Wigan WN3 ....55 B2
Whalley Dr BL8 ....26 F2
Whalley Gdns OL12 .....14 C4
Whalley Gr Ashton-u-L OL6 .85 C7
Leigh WN7 ....57 D1
Manchester M16 ......97 D2
Whalley Range High Sch
M14 ....109 F8
Whalley Rd
Altrincham WA15 ......119 D7
Heywood OL10 ....29 A2
Manchester M16 ......97 D3
Middleton M24 ....46 F3
Ramsbottom BL0 ......11 E7
Rochdale OL12 ....14 C2
Stockport SK2 ....124 C7
Whitefield M45 ....44 F1
Whalley St M40 ....160 D2
Wham Bar Dr OL10 .....29 B3
Wham Bottom La OL12 ..14 D4
Wham La OL3 ....33 D1
Wham St OL10 ....29 B2
Wharf Cots OL5 ....68 D1
Wharf End M17 ....161 A6
Wharf Rd
Altrincham WA14 ......119 D7
Sale M33 ....108 C5
Wharf St Dukinfield SK16 .166 C1
Oldham OL9 ....66 B3
Stockport SK3 ....169 E3
Wharf The OL3 ....51 A7
Wharfdale ⊟ WN7 ......76 A4
Wharfedale BL5 ....39 F2
Wharfedale Ave M40 ...65 A1
Wharfedale Rd SK5 .....111 E8
Wharfside Ave M30 ....155 D8

Wharfside Bsns Ctr M17 ..96 F6
Wharfside Way
(Trafford Park Rd) M17 ..96 E6
Wharmton Rise OL4 .....68 E6
Wharmton School Cotts
OL3 ....50 F1
Wharmton View
Oldham OL3 ....69 A6
Uppermill OL5 ....68 E3
Wharncliffe Cl SK13 .....171 E4
Wharncliffe St ⊟ WN2 ..56 D5
Wharton Ave M21 ......109 D7
Wharton La M38 ....59 E5
Wharton St M11 ....161 C8
Wharton La M30 ....79 E3
Wharton Prim Sch M38 ..59 E5
Wheat Cl M13 ....163 C5
Wheat Croft SK3 ....170 F5
Wheatcroft M33 ....171 E4
Wheater's Cres M7 .....158 D4
Wheater's Cl M7 ....158 D4
Wheater's Terr M7 ......158 D4
Wheatfield SK15 ....102 E7
Wheatfield Cl Bury BL9 ..27 F7
Romiley SK6 ....113 A4
Wheatfield Cres OL2 ....48 C3
Wheatfield Ho OL2 .....48 D3
Wheatfield St BL2 ......148 C5
Wheathill St ⊟ OL16 ...31 A4
Wheathill La Ind Est M19 .54 F1
Wheatlea Rd WN3 ......54 F2
Wheatley Ave WA12 ....89 C5
Wheatley Rd M27 ......61 D2
Wheatley Wlk M12 .....165 A6
Wheatsheaf Ctr The
OL16 ....139 F8
Wheatsheaf Ind Est M27 .62 B1
Wheatsheaf Wlk WN6 ...19 D1
Wheeldale OL4 ....67 D6
Wheeldale Cl BL1 ....143 E2
Wheeldon St M14 ......98 A3
Wheelock Cl SK9 ....131 D1
Wheelton Cl BL8 ....27 A1
Wheelwright Cl
Marple SK6 ....125 F8
Rochdale OL16 ....30 B4
Wheelwright Dr OL16 ...15 C3
Whelan Ave BL9 ....44 E7
Whelan Cl BL9 ....44 E7
Wheler St M11,M43 ....99 E8
Whelley Hospl (General)
WN1 ....37 E2
Whernside Ave
Ashton-u-L OL6 ....85 C7
Failsworth M40 ....83 A1
Whernside Cl SK4 ......169 E3
Whetmorhurst Rd SK6 ..126 E4
Whetstone Hill Cl OL1 ...49 B2
Whetstone Hill Rd OL1 ..49 B1
Whewell Ave BL9 ....44 E5
Whewell St ⊟ M29 .....59 A1
Whickham Cl M14 ......98 B3
Whiley St M13 ....98 F4
Whimberry Cl M5 ......161 C7
Whimbrel Ave WA12 ....89 C3
Whimbrel Rd
Hazel Grove SK2 ......125 A5
Tyldesley M29 ....77 C2
Whinberry Rd OL4 ......49 F4
Whinchat Ave WA12 ....89 C4
Whinchat Cl Golborne WA3 .90 E7
Hazel Grove SK2 ......125 A5
Whinfell Dr M24 ....46 C1
Whinfield Cl WN6 ......150 A8
Whingrove Wlk ⊟ M40 ..83 A6
Whinmoor Wlk M40 ....83 B7
Whins Ave BL4 ....59 E8
Whins Crest BL6 ....22 E6
Whinslee Cl BL6 ....40 C7
Whinslee Dr BL6 ....40 C7
Whinstone Way OL1,OL9 .47 F1
Whipp St OL10 ....29 B3
Whirley Cl SK4 ....111 D5
Whistlecroft Ct WN3 ...151 F6
Whistley St WN2 ....56 B3
Whiston Dr BL2 ....148 C6
Whiston Rd
Manchester M8 ....156 B8
Manchester M8 ....64 B1
Whit La Manchester M6 ..80 F6
Salford M6 ....81 A5
Whitaker St M24 ....64 F8
Whitbeam Gr WN2 ......56 A3
Whitbrook Way M24 ....47 C5
Whitburn Ave M13 ......98 E2
Whitburn Cl Bolton BL3 ..40 E4
Garswood WN4 ....72 D4
Whitburn Dr BL8 ....27 C5
Whitburn Rd M23 ......121 A4
Whitby Ave Heywood OL10 .29 C3
Manchester M14 ......110 E8
Manchester M16 ......97 D3
Salford M6 ....80 C3
Urmston M41 ....95 D2
Whitby Cl Bury BL8 .....26 F2
Cheadle SK8 ....122 C6
Poynton SK12 ....133 D4
Whitby Rd
Manchester M14 ......110 E8
Oldham OL8 ....67 C4
Whitby St Middleton M24 .47 C1
Rochdale OL11 ....31 A5
Whitchurch Dr M16 ....162 D5
Whitchurch Gdns ⊟ BL1 .143 E2

Whitchurch Rd M20 ....110 A7
Whitchurch St M3 ......158 E3
Whitchurch Sch SK5 ...112 C4
White Bank Ave SK5 ....112 C4
White Bank Rd OL8 .....66 E1
White Birk Cl BL8 ....10 F2
White Brook La
Oldham OL3 ....69 C8
Oldham OL3 ....69 D6
White Broom WA13 ....117 B4
White Carr La BL9 ......12 A1
White City Ret Pk M16 ..161 A5
White City Way M16 ....161 A5
White Croft ⊟ WN7 .....73 D4
White Hart SK14 ....167 D4
White Hill Cl OL12 ......14 D4
White Horse Cl BL6 .....22 C5
White Horse Gr BL5 ....40 A2
White Horse Mdws OL16 .31 C2
White House Ave M8 ...63 F3
White House Cl OL10 ...29 A2
White Lady Cl ⊟ M28 ...59 F3
White Lion Brow BL1 ...145 E7
White Lodge Dr WN4 ...73 D4
White Moss Ave M21 ...109 D8
White Moss Gdns M9 ...65 A2
White Moss Rd M9 .....64 E3
White Moss Rd E M9 ...65 A4
White Oak SK2 ....127 C2
White Slack Gate OL14 ..6 A6
White St Bury BL8 ......27 C1
Leigh WN7 ....76 C4
Manchester M15 ......162 D6
Salford M6 ....154 E1
⊟ Wigan WN5 ....54 B6
White Swallows Rd M27 .80 B6
White Swan Ind Est ⊟
OL1 ....67 C8
Whiteacre WN6 ....19 A2
Whiteacre Rd OL6 ......85 D4
Whiteacre Wlk M15 ....162 E5
Whiteacres M27 ....79 D7
Whitebeam Cl
Altrincham WA15 ......120 E5
Newhey OL16 ....32 A3
Salford M6 ....81 A3
Whitebeam Ct M6 ......81 A3
Whitebeam Wlk Sale M33 .107 D5
Westhoughton BL5 .....39 F2
Whitebeck Ct M9 ......65 A4
Whitebrook Rd M14 ....98 B1
Whitecar Ave M40 ......65 E1
Whitecarr La M23,WA15 .120 E3
Whitechapel Cl BL2 ....42 E7
Whitechapel St M20 ...110 B3
Whitecliff Cl M14 ....98 C3
Whitecroft Ave
Golborne WA3 ....74 E1
Shaw OL2 ....49 D7
Whitecroft Dr BL8 ......26 F2
Whitecroft Gdns ⊟ M19 .110 E4
Whitecroft Rd Bolton BL1 .142 A1
Marple SK6 ....126 C1
Wigan WN3 ....55 B2
Whitecroft St SK15 ⊟ OL1 ..49 C1
Whitefield Lymm WA13 ..117 A4
Manchester M45 ......169 D3
Pendlebury M6 ....80 D6
Whitefield Ave
Newton-le-W WA12 ....89 E2
Rochdale OL11 ....29 F8
Whitefield Cl
Golborne WA3 ....90 A8
Lymm WA13 ....117 A5
Whitefield Com Prim Sch
WA13 ....117 A4
Whitefield Cl WA13 .....91 F2
Whitefield Gr WA13 .....117 A4
Whitefield Prep Sch Ltd
M45 ....44 E1
Whitefield Rd
Bredbury SK6 ....112 E4
Bury BL9 ....44 D7
Sale M33 ....108 A5
Whitefield Sta M45 .....44 F1
Whitefriars Wlk ⊟ M22 .130 D8
Whitegate Bolton BL3 ...40 C2
Littleborough OL15 ....15 E4
Whitegate Ave
Culcheth WA3 ....91 F2
Oldham OL1 ....65 E1
Whitegate Ct M40 ......65 E1
Whitegate Dr Bolton BL1 .143 F4
Salford M5 ....154 D2
Swinton M27 ....62 B2
Whitegate End
Com Prim Sch OL9 .....65 E3
Whitegate La OL9 ......66 A4
Whitegate Pk M41 ......94 E2
Whitegate Rd OL9 ......65 E3
Whitegates La OL8 .....123 B5
Whitegates Rd
Cheadle SK8 ....122 D5
Middleton M24 ....47 C4
Whitehall Cl SK9 ....137 A5
Whitehall La Blackrod BL6 ..21 D3
Bolton BL1 ....24 D6
Oldham OL4 ....49 F4
Whitehall Rd
Manchester M20 ......110 C3
Sale M33 ....108 B3
Whitehall St
Ince-in-M WN3 ....151 E6
Oldham OL1 ....153 F8

Whitehall St *continued*
Rochdale OL12 139 F8
Rochdale OL12 14 F1
Whitehaven Gdns M20 110 A2
Whitehaven Pl SK14 101 C5
Whitehaven Rd SK7 132 C5
Whitehead Cres Bury BL8 27 C5
Kearsley M26 61 C7
Whitehead Rd
Stretford M21 108 F8
Swinton M27 62 B2
Whitehead St
Dukinfield M34 100 F7
Middleton M24 47 C1
Middleton OL16 31 E6
Newhey OL16 32 D4
Shaw OL2 48 F8
Walkden M28 60 D4
Whitehill Cotts BL7 24 D6
Whitehill Dr M40 83 A7
Whitehill Ind Est SK4,SK5 111 E5
Whitehill Prim Sch SK4 169 E4
Whitehill St SK4,SK5 111 E5
Whitehill St W SK4 169 E4
Whiteholme Ave M21 109 D4
Whitehouse Ave 4 OL4 67 C6
Whitehouse Dr
Altrincham WA15 129 B8
Wythenshawe M23 121 A5
Whitehouse La WA14 118 D8
Whitehurst Rd SK4 110 F4
Whitekirk Cl M13 163 B6
Whitelake Ave M41 94 F2
Whitelake View M41 94 F3
Whiteland Ave BL3 144 C5
Whitelands Rd
Ashton-u-L OL6,SK15 85 D2
Stalybridge OL6,SK16 166 C2
Whitelands Terr OL6 166 C2
Whitelea Dr SK3 170 D5
Whitelees Rd OL15 16 A5
Whitelegge St BL8 27 B4
Whiteley Dr M24 65 C7
Whiteley Pl WA14 119 D6
Whiteley St Droylsden M11 83 C2
Oldham OL9 66 B4
Whiteley's Pl 6 OL12 139 E8
Whitelow Rd
Manchester M21 109 A8
Manchester SK4 168 A3
Ramsbottom BL0 11 E5
Whitemoss OL12 14 B2
Whiteoak Cl SK6 125 E7
Whiteoak Ct M14 110 C8
Whiteoak Rd M14 110 C8
Whiteoak View BL3 42 D5
Whiteside Ave Hindley WN2 56 E7
2 Wigan WN6 37 A1
Whiteside Cl M5 154 D2
Whiteside Fold OL12 14 A1
Whitesmead Cl SK12 135 D5
Whitestone Cl BL6 40 D6
Whitestone Ho 10 OL1 153 E8
Whitestone Wlk M13 164 D5
Whitethorn Ave
1 Manchester M16 97 D3
3 Manchester M19 110 F7
Whitethorn Cl SK6 125 E7
Whitewater Dr M7 80 F8
Whiteway St M9 157 E7
Whitewell Cl Bury BL9 44 D7
Rochdale OL16 31 C8
Whitewillow Cl M35 84 A6
Whitewood Cl WN4 73 A6
Whitfield Ave SK13 116 C7
Whitfield Brows OL15 16 C7
Whitfield CE Prim Sch
SK13 116 B8
Whitfield Cres OL16 32 B3
Whitfield Cross SK13 116 D7
Whitfield Dr OL16 31 E5
Whitfield Pk SK13 116 C7
Whitfield Rise OL2 32 A1
Whitfield St Leigh WN7 76 C4
Manchester M3 159 A4
Whitford Wlk M40 160 D3
Whiting Gr BL3 40 E6
Whitland Ave BL1 40 F8
Whitland Dr OL8 66 B2
Whitle Rd SK22 127 C1
Whitledge Gn WN4 73 A5
Whitledge Rd WN4 73 A5
Whitley Cres
Abram Brow WN2 74 B7
Wigan WN1 37 C4
Whitley Gdns WA15 120 C7
Whitley Pl WA15 120 C7
Whitley Rd
Manchester M40 159 C4
Manchester SK4 168 B3
Orrell WN8 35 D3
Whitley St BL4 42 D2
Whitlow Ave
Altrincham WA14 119 B8
Golborne WA3 73 F1
Whitman St M40,M9 157 F8
Whitmore Rd M14 98 B1
Whitnall Cl M16 97 E4
Whitnall St SK14 101 D5
Whitsand Rd M22 121 E5
Whitsbury Ave
Hindley WN2 56 D4
Manchester M18 99 D3
Whitstable Cl OL9 152 B6
Whitstable Rd M40 65 C1
Whitsters Hollow BL1 142 B3
Whitsundale BL5 39 F2
Whitswood Cl 2 M16 97 E3
Whittaker Dr OL15 15 F2
Whittaker La
Littleborough OL15 16 E4
Prestwich M25 63 C4
Rochdale OL11 13 D1
Whittaker Moss Prim Sch
OL11 13 E1
Whittaker St
Ashton-u-L OL6 85 D5
Manchester M40 83 A8
Radcliffe M26 44 B4
Rochdale OL11 13 E1
Whittingham Dr BL0 11 C3
Whittingham Gr OL1 153 D8
Whittington St OL7 166 A1
Whittle Bank Rd SK22 127 B2
Whittle Ct WN3 54 E2
Whittle Dr Shaw OL2 49 D8
Walkden M28 60 D5
Whittle Gr Bolton BL1 142 B1
Walkden M28 60 E3
Whittle Hill BL7 8 E3
Whittle La OL10 46 B4
Whittle St Bury BL8 27 C3
Littleborough OL15 15 F5
Manchester M4 159 B2
Swinton M27 79 E7
Walkden M28 60 E3
Whittle's Croft M1 159 B1
Whittle's Terr 1 BL5 39 E1
Whittlebrook Gr OL10 46 E7
Whittles Ave M34 101 A2
Whittles St OL13 4 B8
Whittles Terr OL16 32 C4
Whittles Wlk M34 101 A2
Whitton Mews 5 BL6 22 B4
Whitwell Bank 4 SK13 171 D2
Whitwell Cl
3 Gamesley SK13 171 D2
Standish WN6 19 D2
Whitwell Fold 1 SK13 171 D2
Whitwell Gdns BL6 22 B5
Whitwell Gn 4 SK13 171 E2
Whitwell Lea 2 SK13 171 D2
Whitwell Way M18 165 C5
Whitwell Wlk 6 M13 98 E4
Whitworth Art Gall M15 98 B4
Whitworth Cl OL6 166 C4
Whitworth High Sch OL12 14 C8
Whitworth La M14 98 D1
Whitworth Park Mans
M14 98 A4
Whitworth Park Sch M14 98 A4
Whitworth Rake OL12 14 D8
Whitworth Rd OL12 14 F2
Whitworth Sq OL12 14 D8
Whitworth St Horwich BL6 22 C2
Manchester M1 163 A8
Manchester M11 165 B7
Milnrow OL16 31 F6
Rochdale OL16 15 C2
Whitworth St E M11 165 C7
Whitworth St W
M1,M3,M15 162 F8
Whixhall Ave M12 164 E6
Whoolden St BL4 42 C1
Whowell Fold BL1 142 C3
Whowell St BL3 145 E6
Wibbersley Pk M41 94 F2
Wibsey Cotts OL3 33 D2
Wichbrook Rd 13 M28 59 F3
Wicheaves Cres
11 Walkden M28 59 F3
Walkden M28 60 A3
Wicheries The M28 59 F3
Wicken Bank OL10 46 E7
Wicken St SK2 124 C7
Wickenby Dr M33 108 A4
Wickentree Holt OL12 14 A1
Wickentree La M35 66 A1
Wicker La WA15 129 C8
Wicket Gr M27 61 E4
Wickham Terr 11 M24 47 A2
Wickliffe St 17 BL1 145 E8
Wicklow Ave SK3 123 B7
Wicklow Dr M22 121 E2
Widcombe Dr BL2,BL3 42 F5
Widdop St OL9 153 D7
Widdow's St WN7 76 B4
Widdrington Rd WN1 37 D2
Widecombe Cl M41 95 B4
Widford Wlk BL6 21 E1
Widgeon Cl
Manchester M14 110 B8
Poynton SK12 133 B4
Widgeon Rd WA14 119 B8
Widnes St M11 165 C7
Wiend WN1 150 C8
Wigan & Leigh Coll
(Annexe) WN1 150 B8
Wigan & Leigh Coll
(Leigh Campus)
Leigh WN7 75 E3
Leigh WN7 75 E5
Wigan & Leigh Coll
(Linacre Bldg) WN1 37 B1
Wigan & Leigh Coll
(Mesnes Bldg) WN1 37 C1
Wigan & Leigh Coll
(Pagefield Bldg) WN1 37 B2
Wigan & Leigh Coll
(Parsons Wlk) WN1 150 B8
Wigan (North Western)
Sta WN3 150 C7
Wigan Athletic FC &
Wigan Warriors RLFC
(JJB Stad) WN5 54 F8
Wigan Gallery 2 WN1 150 C8
Wigan Hope Sch WN3 54 F2
Wigan Infmy WN1 37 C2
Wigan La
Adlington PR7,WN1 20 D7
Wigan WN1 37 C4
Wigan Lower Rd WN6 36 C3
Wigan Pier WN3 150 B7
Wigan Rd Ashton-in-M WN4 73 A5
Aspull WN2 38 B4
Atherton M46 58 B3
Billinge WN5 71 F7
Bolton BL3 144 B5
Bolton BL3 40 E3
Golborne WA3 74 B3
Leigh WN7 75 D7
Shevington WN6 36 B5
Standish WN6 37 A6
Westhoughton BL5 57 C7
Wigan Sq WN1 150 C8
Wigan St WN2 56 A1
Wiggins Wlk 13 M14 98 C3
Wightman Ave WA12 89 C5
Wighurst Wlk 6 M22 121 D1
Wigley St M12 164 E7
Wigmore Rd M8 156 B7
Wigmore St 15 OL6 85 D4
Wigsby Ave M40 65 C2
Wigsey La WA13 117 A7
Wigshaw Cl WN7 75 F1
Wigshaw La WA3 91 D2
Wigwam Cl SK12 133 C4
Wike St BL8 140 D3
Wilberforce Cl M15 162 F5
Wilbraham Prim Sch M14 98 A1
Wilbraham Rd
Manchester M14 98 B1
Manchester M14,M16,M21 97 C1
Manchester M21 109 B8
Walkden M28 60 E3
Wilbraham Regency Ct
M21 97 A1
Wilbraham St Leigh WN7 75 C5
Westhoughton BL5 57 E8
Wilby Ave BL3 43 B5
Wilby Cl BL8 27 D5
Wilby St M8 156 B6
Wilcock Rd WA11 89 B8
Wilcock St Manchester M16 97 E4
Wigan WN3 150 A7
Wilcockson Ho 4 BL4 60 D8
Wilcott Dr Sale M33 107 E5
Wilmslow SK9 136 F4
Wilcott Rd SK8 122 A5
Wild Arum Cl 8 WA3 90 E8
Wild Clough SK14 167 F1
Wild Ho OL8 153 F5
Wild St Bredbury SK6 112 F3
Dukinfield SK16 101 D8
Hazel Grove SK7 124 D2
Heywood OL10 29 E2
Oldham OL1 67 A7
Oldham OL4 67 E6
Radcliffe M26 44 D4
Shaw OL2 149 C6
Stockport SK2 124 A6
Wild's Pas WN7 75 F4
Wild's Sq 5 OL5 68 C2
Wildbank Chase SK15 102 E7
Wildbank Prim Sch SK15 86 D2
Wildbrook Cl M38 59 E3
Wildbrook Cres OL8 67 A2
Wildbrook Gr M38 59 E3
Wildbrook Rd M38 59 E3
Wildcroft Ave M40 65 A1
Wilde St M34 100 F3
Wilders Moor Rd 3 M28 78 C8
Wilderswood Ave BL6 22 C4
Wilderswood Cl M20 110 C5
Wilderswood Ct BL6 22 D4
Wildhouse La OL16 31 F8
Wilding St WN3 151 E6
Wildman La BL4 59 F8
Wildmoor Ave OL4 67 E4
Wilds Pl BL0 138 B5
Wildwood Cl BL0 11 A4
Wilford Ave M33 108 A2
Wilfred Dr BL9 141 B4
Wilfred Rd Eccles M30 95 A8
Walkden M28 60 D2
Wilfred St Bolton BL7 25 A7
Manchester M3,M7 158 E4
Manchester M40 83 A8
Oldham OL4 67 B6
Wigan WN5 54 F7
Wilfrid St M27 61 F1
Wilfrid's Pl WN6 19 F1
Wilham Ave 7 M30 79 D1
Wilkes St OL1 49 D3
Wilkesley Ave WN6 36 D8
Wilkin Croft SK8 122 E1
Wilkins La SK9 130 E5
Wilkinson Ave BL3 43 A5
Wilkinson Rd Bolton BL1 24 D5
Stockport SK4 169 E2
Wilkinson St
Ashton-u-L OL6 166 A2
Leigh WN7 75 E5
3 Sale M33 108 D4
Wilks Ave M22 121 F3
Will Griffith Wlk M11 164 E8
Willan Ent Ctr M17 96 C6
Willan Ind Est M5 154 F1
Willan Rd Eccles M30 79 E2
Manchester M9 64 C4
Willand Cl BL2 43 A6
Willand Dr BL2 43 A6
Willard Ave WN5 53 D3
Willard St SK7 124 D3
Willaston Cl M21 109 A7
Willaston Way 8 SK9 131 D5
Willbutts La OL11 30 C8
Willdale Cl M11 83 A2
Willdor Gr SK3 123 B6
Willenhall Rd M23 109 C2
Willerby Rd M7,M8 155 E5
Willesden Ave M13 98 E3
William Chadwick Cl 1
M40 159 C3
William Cl M41 95 C2
William Coates Ct 6 M16 97 D3
William Ford Ho SK14 103 A4
William Greenwood Cl
OL10 29 C2
William Henry St 2 OL11 31 A4
William Hulme's Gram Sch
M16 97 F1
William Hulme's Gram Sch
Prep Dept M21 97 C1
William Jessop Ct 18 M1 159 C1
William Kay Cl M16 97 E4
William Lister Cl M40 83 D4
William Murray Ct 4 M4 159 C2
William St Ashton-u-L OL7 166 A1
Ashton-u-L OL7 84 F2
Bacup OL13 4 C8
Failsworth M35 66 A1
Hindley WN2 56 E5
Horwich BL6 22 A3
Ince-in-M WN3 151 D6
8 Leigh WN7 76 A5
Leigh WN7 76 A5
Littleborough OL15 16 A5
Littleborough OL16 15 D4
5 Manchester M1 163 A7
Manchester M12 164 D8
Manchester M20 110 B3
Manchester M3 158 E2
Middleton M24 65 B8
Radcliffe M26 44 B4
Ramsbottom BL0 1 C1
Rochdale OL11 139 F6
Whitworth OL12 4 C1
William Wlk 2 WA14 119 D3
Williams Ave WA12 89 C5
Williams Cres OL9 65 F3
Williams Rd Failsworth M40 83 C7
Manchester M18 165 C5
Williams St Little Lever BL3 43 B3
Manchester M18 165 C5
Williamson Ave
Radcliffe M26 43 F6
Romiley SK6 113 A4
Williamson La M43 100 B8
Williamson St
Ashton-u-L OL6 166 B3
Manchester M4 159 B3
Reddish SK5 111 F7
Williamson's Yd 6 OL1 67 B7
Willingdon Cl BL8 27 C7
Willingdon Dr M25 63 B5
Willis Rd SK3 170 E6
Willis St BL3 146 C4
Williton Wlk 6 M22 121 F3
Willock St M7 155 F6
Willoughby Ave M20 110 C4
Willoughby Cl M33 108 A5
Willow Ave Cheadle SK8 122 F2
Middleton M24 65 C8
Newton-le-W WA12 89 E4
Reddish SK5 169 F4
Tyldesley M29 77 A6
Urmston M41 95 E2
Willow Bank
Altrincham WA15 120 A6
Bramhall SK8 132 A6
Manchester M14 110 C8
1 Manchester M9 157 E7
Oldham OL4 67 E8
Willow Bank Ct M20 122 B8
Willow Bank Est WA12 89 F4
Willow Cl Adlington PR6 21 B8
Bolton BL3 146 B4
Dukinfield SK16 101 F7
Poynton SK12 133 E3
Willow Cres WN7 75 E8
Willow Ct Gatley SK8 122 A6
Manchester M14 110 C8
Manchester M14 98 D1
Marple SK6 125 F5
Sale M33 108 E5
Willow Dr Handforth SK9 131 D3
Hindley WN2 56 F3
Sale M33 107 E2
Willow Fold M43 100 B8
Willow Gr Ashton-in-M WN4 73 E5
Chadderton OL9 152 B8
Denton M34 100 E3
Golborne WA3 74 A1
Manchester M18 99 E4
Marple SK6 125 F5
Willow Hill Rd M8 64 A1
Willow Lo 1 WN2 56 B1
Willow Pk M14 110 C8
Willow Rd Eccles M30 79 A4
High Lane SK6 134 F7
Newton-le-W WA12 89 E4
Oldham OL3 69 C7
Partington M31 105 E2
Prestwich M25,M45 63 A6
Wigan WN6 37 A3
Willow Rise OL15 15 F3
Willow St 2 Abram WN2 56 B1
Atherton M46 58 C4
Bury BL9 141 B3
Droylsden M11 83 A1
Heywood OL10 29 D2
Willow St *continued*
Manchester M8 158 E4
Oldham OL1 67 A7
Rawtenstall BB4 2 E8
Swinton M27 79 D5
Swinton M28 79 C7
Willow Tree Cl WN1 37 B4
Willow Tree Ct
1 Eccles M30 79 C1
Sale M33 108 B3
Willow Tree Mews SK8 122 B1
Willow Tree Rd WA14 119 D3
Willow Way Bramhall SK7 132 D7
Manchester M20 110 C3
Willow Wlk M43 84 C2
Willow Wood Cl OL6 85 E3
Willowbank M26 61 F8
Willowbank Ave BL2 148 B6
Willowbrook Ave M40 83 A7
Willowbrook Dr WN6 36 B7
Willowcroft Ave WN2 38 F3
Willowdale WA12 89 E3
Willowdale Ave SK8 122 B2
Willowdene Cl Bolton BL7 24 F8
3 Manchester M40 156 C5
Willowfield Gr WN4 73 A2
Willowfield Rd OL4 49 D2
Willowmead Way OL12 14 A2
Willowmoss Cl M28 60 E1
Willows Cotts OL16 31 E6
Willows Dr M35 83 F5
Willows End SK15 86 D3
Willows La Bolton BL3 146 C4
Milnrow OL16 31 E6
Willows Prim Sch WA15 120 A6
Willows Rd M5 154 D2
Willows The
5 Atherton M46 58 D3
Coppull PR7 19 E8
Little Lever BL3 43 A5
Manchester M21 109 A7
Manchester SK4 168 A3
Mossley OL5 68 E1
Partington M31 105 F3
Sale M33 107 D2
Whitworth OL12 14 C5
Wilma Ave M9 64 C4
Wilmans Wlk SK13 104 A6
Wilmcote Cl BL6 40 D6
Wilmcote Gdns 2 SK6 112 F3
Wilmcote Rd M40 159 C4
Wilmers OL15 6 D2
Wilmington Rd M32 96 B2
Wilmot Dr WA3 89 F7
Wilmot St BL1 142 C3
Wilmott St
Manchester M15 162 F7
Manchester M15 163 A6
Wilmslow Ave BL1 24 E5
Wilmslow Grange
Cty Prim Sch SK9 131 C4
Wilmslow High Sch SK9 137 B6
Wilmslow Old Rd M90 130 A6
Wilmslow Park Rd SK9 137 D7
Wilmslow Prep Sch SK9 137 B7
Wilmslow Rd
Alderley Edge SK9 137 A2
Cheadle SK8 122 D3
Cheadle SK8 122 D5
Gatley SK8,SK9 131 C6
Handforth SK9 131 D4
Manchester M14 98 C2
Manchester M14,M20 110 B5
Manchester M20 110 C1
Woodford SK7 132 C1
Wythenshaw M90,WA15,SK9
M90,WA15,SK9 129 F5
Wilmslow Sta SK9 137 C7
Wilmur Ave
Manchester M7 155 E6
Whitefield M45 63 A7
Wilpshire Ave 8 M12 99 B3
Wilsford Cl WA3 74 B1
Wilshaw Gr OL7 85 B6
Wilshaw La OL7 85 A5
Wilson Ave Heywood OL10 29 A2
Swinton M27 62 B2
Wigan WN6 37 B2
Wilson Cres OL6 85 E4
Wilson Fold Ave BL6 39 F8
Wilson Rd Manchester M9 64 D1
Manchester SK4 168 B4
Wilson St 7 Bolton BL3 145 F6
Bury BL9 141 A1
Farnworth BL4 60 E8
Horwich BL6 22 A4
Hyde SK14 167 E2
Manchester M11 165 A8
Manchester M12,M13 163 C6
Oldham OL3 69 A6
Oldham OL8 66 E4
Radcliffe M26 43 F4
Rochdale OL12 139 F8
1 Sale M33 108 B5
Stretford M32 96 E4
Wilson Way OL1 153 F8
Wilson's Terr SK13 116 B8
Wilsons Pk M40 157 E5
Wilsthorpe Cl M19 111 C7
Wilton Ave Gatley SK8 131 C7
Manchester M16 97 A3
Manchester M25 63 D2
Pendlebury M27 80 C7
Wigan WN2 37 F2
Wilton Cotts WA3 75 A2

Wilton Cres SK9 ....136 F2
Wilton Ct Middleton M25 ...63 E8
Reddish M34 ....100 A4
Wilton Dr
Ashton-in-M WA15 .....129 C8
Whitefield BL9 ....45 A5
Wilton Gdns M26 ......44 C5
Wilton Gr Heywood OL10 ...29 D1
Reddish M34 ....100 A4
Wilton La WA3 ....91 B5
Wilton Paddock M34 ...180 A4
Wilton Pl M3 ....158 D2
Wilton Rd Bolton BL1 .....24 E5
Manchester M21 ......109 B8
Manchester M8 ....64 A2
Salford M6 ....80 B4
Shevington WN6 ......36 A6
Wilton St Ashton-in-M WN4 ...73 A4
Bolton BL1 ....143 F3
Denton M34 ....100 E4
Heywood OL10 ....29 C2
Manchester M13 ......163 B6
Middleton M24 ....64 B2
Oldham OL9 ....66 B3
Prestwich M25 ....63 C4
Reddish SK5 ....99 F2
Whitefield M45 ....62 F7
Wigan WN1 ....151 D7
Wilton Terr OL12 .....139 E8
Wiltshire Ave SK5 ....112 C4
Wiltshire Cl BL9 ......45 A8
Wiltshire Dr Glossop SK13 ...116 F8
Haslingden BB4 ......1 B8
Wiltshire Pl WN5 .....54 C6
Wiltshire Rd
Failsworth M35 ......84 A6
Oldham OL9 ....152 B5
Partington M31 ......105 E2
Wiltshire St M7 ......155 E6
Wimberry Hill Rd BL5 ...39 D3
Wimbledon Dr
Rochdale OL11 ......139 D5
Stockport SK3 ....123 C7
Wimbledon Rd M35 ...84 B8
Wimborne Ave
Chadderton OL9 .....48 A1
Urmston M41 ....95 D3
Wimborne Cl Cheadle SK8 ...123 C4
Horwich BL6 ....22 F1
Wimborne Rd WN5 ...54 A8
Wimpenny Ho OL8 ...153 E5
Wimpole St
Ashton-u-L OL6 ......166 C3
Oldham OL1 ....49 A1
Wimpory St M11 .....99 D7
Winbolt St SK2 ......124 C4
Winby St M11 ....**1**..31 A4
Wincanton Ave M23 ...120 D8
Wincanton Dr BL1 ....24 D7
Wincanton Pk OL4 ....67 D6
Wince Cl M24 ....65 C6
Wincham Cl SK11 **51**...162 D6
Wincham Rd M33 ....107 E2
Winchcombe Cl WN7 ...75 F1
Winchester Ave
Ashton-in-M WN4 ....73 A3
Ashton-u-L OL6 ......85 D8
Chadderton OL9 .....47 F1
Denton M34 ....100 F1
Heywood OL10 ......46 C8
Manchester M25 ....63 C2
Tyldesley M29 ......77 C7
Winchester Cl Bury BL8 ...27 C8
Orrell WN5 ....53 F7
Rochdale OL11 ......30 A7
Wilmslow SK9 ....136 E5
Winchester Dr Sale M33 ...107 D4
Stockport SK4 ....168 B2
Winchester Ho M9 ....151 D6
Winchester Pk M20 ...109 F3
Winchester Rd
Altrincham WA11 ....120 C1
Ashton-in-M WA11 ...72 E1
Dukinfield SK16 ......102 A7
Longshaw WN5 .....53 D2
Radcliffe M26 ....43 D5
Salford M30 ....80 A4
Salford M6 ....80 C4
Urmston M41 ....95 E3
Winchester Way BL2 ...25 D1
Wincle Ave SK12 .....134 A2
Wincombe St M14 ....98 B2
Windale M28 ....60 B3
Windcroft Cl M11 ....165 A8
Winder Dr M44 ......159 C2
Winder St BL1 ....145 F8
Windermere Ave
Atherton M46 ....58 D5
Billinge WN5 ....43 A4
Pendlebury M27 .....80 A7
Reddish M34 ....100 B2
Sale M33 ....108 D2
Windermere Cl
Manchester M11 ....165 A8
Prestwich M25 .....62 F5
Stretford M32 .....96 C3
Windermere Cres OL7 ...84 F4
Windermere Dr
Adlington PR6 ....21 B8
Alderley Edge SK9 ...137 B5
Bury BL9 ....44 E7
Ramsbottom BL0 ....138 C7
Windermere Gr WN7 ...75 E6
Windermere Ho **3** M28 ...60 E2
Windermere Mews M46 ...46 E3

Windermere Rd
Abram WN2 ....74 B8
Dukinfield SK14 ......101 C5
Farnworth BL4 ......59 E7
Handforth SK9 ......131 C4
High Lane SK6 ......134 E8
Hindley WN2 ....56 E5
Ince-in-M WN2 .....56 B7
Leigh WN7 ....75 E5
Middleton M24 .....46 D3
Orrell WN5 ....53 F8
Royton OL2 ....48 D6
Stalybridge SK15 ...86 A4
Finchurst SK1,SK2 ..124 B7
Urmston M41 ......95 C1
Windermere St
Bolton BL1 ....143 F2
Wigan WN1 ....37 E1
Windermere Wlk **4** OL4 ...67 C7
Winders Way M6 .....81 B4
Windfields Cl SK8 ....123 B3
Windham St OL16 ....15 C1
Windle Ave M9 ......63 F3
Windle Ct SK2 ......124 E5
Windlehurst Dr M28 ...78 B7
Windlehurst Old Rd SK6 ...125 F2
Windlehurst Rd SK6 ...125 E2
Windleshaw St WN3 ...151 E6
Windley St BL7 ......148 A8
Windmill Ave M5 .....161 B7
Windmill Cl Reddish M34 ...100 B2
Walkden M28 ....60 C5
Wigan WN1 ....151 D8
Windmill Ct OL16 ....31 B6
Windmill Hts WN8 ....53 A8
Windmill La Denton M34 ...100 C2
Reddish SK5 ....100 A1
Tyldesley M29 ......76 F4
Windmill Lane Ind Est
M34 ....100 C2
Windmill Rd Sale M33 ...108 F3
Walkden M28 ......60 C5
Windmill St
Manchester M2 .....162 F8
2 Rochdale OL14 ...14 B6
Windover Cl BL5 ....59 A7
Windover St **1** BL3 ...146 A4
Windrush Ave M40 ...11 A2
Windrush Dr
Manchester M9 .....157 D7
Westhoughton BL5 ...39 F1
Windrush The OL12 ...14 C4
Windsor Ave Adlington PR7 ...20 F6
Failsworth M35 .....84 B8
Gatley SK8 ....122 A5
Heywood OL10 .....29 B2
Irlam M44 ....94 B3
Little Lever BL3 ....43 A3
Manchester SK4 ....168 A3
Newton-le-W WA12 ...89 D2
Oldham OL9 ....66 A4
Sale M33 ....108 B6
Swinton M27 ......62 A2
Tyldesley M29 .....77 A6
Urmston M41 .....94 F2
Walkden M38 .....60 A8
Whitefield M45 ....63 A7
Wilmslow SK9 .....136 F7
Windsor Cl Poynton SK12 ...133 D4
Ramsbottom BL8 ...11 A1
Windsor Comm High Sch
The M5 ....81 A2
Windsor Cres Appley Bridge WN7 ...38 D5
Manchester M25,M8 ...63 C2
Windsor Ct Bolton BL3 ...147 D2
Sale M33 ....107 F5
Windsor Dr
Ashton-in-M WA11 ...89 A7
Ashton-u-L OL7 ....84 F4
Bury BL8 ....44 B8
Droylsden M34 ....84 D1
Dukinfield SK16 ...101 F7
Horwich BL6 ......22 E2
Marple SK6 ....125 E5
Sale WA14 ....119 F8
Stalybridge SK15 ...86 A3
Windsor Gr Ashton-u-L OL6 ...85 C7
Bolton BL1 ....142 C1
Cheadle SK8 ......131 F8
Hindley WN2 ......57 B3
Kearsley M26 .....61 B7
Romiley SK6 ......113 E2
Windsor Rd
Ashton-in-M WN4 ...73 C1
Billinge WN5 ......71 F5
Bolton BL7 ....25 A7
Bredbury SK6 .....112 C3
Droylsden M43 ....83 E1
Failsworth M40 ....83 E4
Golborne WA3 ....90 C8
Hazel Grove SK7 ...124 F2
Hyde SK14 ....113 E7
Leigh WN7 ....76 E6
Manchester M19 ...99 A1
Manchester M9 ....157 E7
Oldham OL8 ......66 D4
Orrell WN8 ....53 A8
Reddish M34 .....100 A3
Windsor St Failsworth M35 ...84 A8
Failsworth M40 ....83 E4
Manchester M18 ...99 C4
Rochdale OL11 ....31 A5
Salford M5 ....81 B1
Stockport SK2 ....124 A6
Tyldesley M46 ....58 E2
Wigan WN1 ....37 D1
Windsor Terr Milnrow OL16 ...31 E6

Windsor Terr continued
Rochdale OL16 ......31 C7
Windy Bank Ave M40 ...170 F6
Windy Bank Ave WA3 ...90 E8
Windy Harbour La BL7 ...25 B8
Windybank M9 ......64 C5
Windyhill Dr BL3 ....146 A3
Winfell Dr M40 .....160 D3
Winfield Ave M20 ...110 D5
Winfield Dr M18 ....99 D6
Winfield Gr SK6 ....114 B1
Winfield St SK14 ....167 F2
Winford St M9 .....157 E8
Wingate Ave BL8 ...27 B2
Wingate Dr
Altrincham WA15 ...120 B5
Manchester M20 ...110 C2
Wingate Rd
Manchester SK4 ....168 C4
Walkden M38 .....60 B4
Wingate Rd OL11 ...13 E1
Wingates La BL5 ....39 D3
Wingates Ind Est BL5 ...39 D2
Wingates La BL5 ....39 E5
Wingates Rd WN1 ...37 C4
Wingates Sq BL5 ....39 E3
Wingfield Ave SK9 ...136 E6
Wingfield Gr WN6 ...37 A4
Wingfield Dr
Pendlebury M27 ....80 A6
Wilmslow SK9 .....136 E6
Wingfield St SK13 ...116 F7
Wingfield St M32 ...96 D4
Wingfield Villas OL15 ...16 C7
Wingrove Ho M6 ...154 F2
Wings Gr OL10 ....46 D7
Winhill Rd SK22 ...127 C1
Winifred Ave BL9 ...28 F4
Winifred Rd Failsworth M40 ...83 B7
Farnworth BL4 .....42 A1
Manchester M20 ...110 B3
Stockport SK2 ....124 A6
Urmston M41 .....95 D2
Winifred St **2** Eccles M30 ...79 B1
Hyde SK14 ....167 E4
Ince-in-M WN3 ....151 E6
Ramsbottom BL0 ...138 B5
Rochdale OL16 ....14 B1
Winmarith Dr WA15 ...120 B7
Winmarleigh Cl BL8 ...27 B3
Winmarleigh Gdns WN7 ...75 E3
Winnall Wlk **3** M40 ...83 C6
Winnard St WA3 ...74 B2
Winnats Cl SK13 ...116 F8
Winnington St M40 ...83 A8
Winning Hill Cl M18 ...99 D4
Winnington Gn SK2 ...124 D6
Winnington Rd SK6 ...125 F7
Winnipeg Quay M5 ...96 F7
Winnows The M34 ...100 D3
Winscar Rd WN2 ...56 D6
Winscombe Dr M40 ...159 C4
Winser St M1 ......163 A8
Winsfield Rd SK7 ....133 E8
Winsford Dr OL11 ...29 F5
Winsford Gr BL3 ....40 F5
Winsford Rd M14 ...98 A1
Winsford Wlk M33 ...108 E3
Winskill Rd M44 ....106 A8
Winslade Cl Oldham OL4 ...49 D1
Stockport SK7 ....124 A2
Winsley Rd M23 ...108 F2
Winslow Ave SK14 ...103 A2
Winslow Pl M19 ....110 F6
Winslow Rd BL3 ....40 D3
Winstanley Cl M5 ...165 A8
Winsmoor Dr WN2 ...56 E4
Winson Cl BL3 .....147 E4
Winstanley Cl **6** M6 ...80 D5
Winstanley Coll WN5 ...53 F3
Winstanley La SK9 ...136 C1
Winstanley Prim Sch WN3 ...54 C2
Winstanley Rd
Ashton-in-M WN2 ...73 F8
Garswood AVen &WNS ...72 B6
Garswood WN5 ....72 A8
Manchester M40 ...160 D3
Orrell WN5 ....53 F3
Sale M33 ....108 C5
Winstanley St WN5 ...54 F6
Winster Ave
Manchester M20 ...109 E4
Manchester M7 ....81 B6
Stretford M32 .....96 A3
Winster Cl Bolton BL2 ...25 F1
Whitefield M45 ....63 B8
Winster Dr Bolton BL2 ...25 F1
3 Middleton M24 ...46 E2
Winster Gn M30 ...95 B8
Winster Gr SK2 ....124 A6
Winster Mews **12** SK13 ...171 E2
Winster Rd M30 ...95 B8
Winston Ave
Little Lever BL3 ....43 C3
Newton-le-W WA12 ...89 C3
Rochdale OL11 ....29 C6
Winston Cl Marple SK6 ...125 D7
Radcliffe M26 .....43 E5
Winston Rd
Manchester M40,M9 ...157 F8
Manchester M9 ....64 F1
Sale M33 ....107 F5
Winswell Cl M11 ...83 B2
Winter Hey La BL6 ...22 B3
Winterbottom Gr SK14 ...102 F2

Winterbottom St OL9 ...153 D7
Winterbottom Wlk **4**
Manchester M4 .....159 B1
Winterbottom St M1 ...54 C2
Winterburn Ave Bolton BL2 ...25 E6
Manchester M21 ...109 D4
Winterburn Gn SK2 ...124 E5
Winterbutlee Gr OL14 ...6 A8
Winterdyne St M9 ...157 E7
Winterfield Dr BL3 ...146 A3
Winterford Ave M13 ...164 D5
Winterford Rd
Manchester M7,M8 ...155 F7
Mossley OL5 ......68 E1
Wintergreen Wlk **3** M31 ...105 F3
Wintermans Rd M21 ...109 C2
Winter St BL1 .....145 D8
Winterton Cl BL5 ...40 A1
Winterton Rd SK5 ...100 A1
Winthrop Ave M40 ...157 D5
Winton Ave Denton M34 ...100 D7
Failsworth M40 ....65 D1
Wigan WN5 ....54 D5
Winton Cl SK7 .....123 D1
Winton Ct WA14 ...119 C2
Winton Gn BL6 ....22 F1
Winton Gr BL3 ....40 E4
Winton Rd
Altrincham WA14 ...119 C2
Golborne WA3 ....90 B6
Pendlebury M6 ....80 D5
Winton St Ashton-u-L OL6 ...166 B3
Littleborough OL15 ...16 B5
2 Stalybridge SK15 ...86 B1
Winward St Bolton BL3 ...146 A4
Leigh WN7 ....75 B5
5 Westhoughton BL5 ...39 E1
Winwick La WA3 ...90 E3
Winwick Rd WA12 ...89 F1
Winwood Dr M24 ...47 B1
Winwood Fold M24 ...46 F4
Winwood Rd M20 ...122 C8
Wirral Cl Culcheth WA3 ...91 E4
Swinton M27 .....62 A2
Wirral Cres SK3 ...123 A8
Wirral Dr WN3 ....54 C2
Wisbech Dr M23 ...108 F1
Wisbeck Rd BL2 ...148 C8
Wiseley St M11 ....164 E8
Wiseman Terr M25 ...63 C4
Wishaw Sq M21 ...109 E7
Wisley Cl SK5 .....112 C4
Wistaria Rd M18 ...99 D5
Withall St M40 .....159 D8
Witham Ave M22 ...121 E5
Witham Cl Heywood OL10 ...29 A3
Withams The M45 ...19 D1
Witham St M6 .....85 E4
Withenfield Rd M23 ...120 F8
Withens Gr M23 ...124 E6
Withern **10** OL10 ...29 C2
Withington Ave M23 ...92 A4
Withington Dr M29 ...77 C7
Withington Girls Sch
M14 ....110 C8
Withington Gn M24 ...47 A4
Withington Hospl M20 ...109 F6
Withington La WN2 ...38 C2
Withington Rd
Manchester M16,M21 ...109 D8
Manchester M16,M21 ...97 D2
Withington St
Heywood OL10 ....46 E8
Salford M6 ....81 B2
Withins Ave M26 ...44 C5
Withins Dr BL2 ....42 E8
Withins Gr BL2 ....42 E8
Withins Gr BL2 ....42 E8
Withins La Bolton BL2 ...42 E8
Radcliffe M26 .....44 C5
Withins Rd Culcheth WA3 ...91 F3
Oldham OL8 ......66 B2
Withins St M26 ....44 C5
Withnell Cl WN6 ...37 A2
Withnell Dr BL8 ...27 A1
Withnell Rd M19 ...110 E6
Withy Gr M4 ......159 A2
Withy Tree Gr **1** M34 ...101 A2
Withycombe Pl M6 ...81 A5
Withypool Dr SK2 ...124 C5
Witley Dr M33 ....107 D6
Witley Rd OL16 ...31 B6
Witney Cl **11** BL1 ...143 E2
Wittenbury Rd SK4 ...168 B2
Wittenham Ho SK9 ...131 D2
Witterage Cl M12 ...164 F6
Witton Wlk M8 ....155 F6
Woburn Ave Bolton BL2 ...25 C3
Leigh WN7 ....57 D1
Newton-le-W WA12 ...89 D2
Woburn Cl Manchester M16 ...97 F3
Milnrow OL16 ....31 E6
Woburn Ct SK12 ...133 F4
Woburn Dr
Altrincham WA15 ...120 B2
Bury BL9 ....44 E8
Woburn Rd M16 ...161 C7
Woden St M5 .....161 C7
Woden's Ave M5 ...161 C7
Woking Rd SK8 ...132 A7
Woking Terr BL1 ...143 E1
Wolfenden Cty Prim Sch
BL1 ....143 E2
Wolfenden Gn BB4 ...2 F8
Wolfenden St BL1 ...143 E2
Wolfenden Terr **22** BL1 ...143 E2
Wolford Dr M29 ...59 C1

Wolfreton Cres M27 ...62 A3
Wolfson Sq WN4 ...72 F4
Wollaton Wlk M34 ...100 E1
Wolmer St WN4 ...73 A4
Wolseley Ho M33 ...108 C6
Wolseley Pl M20 ...110 B5
Wolseley Rd M33 ...108 C6
Wolseley St **1** Bury BL8 ...27 B1
Newhey OL16 .....32 A4
Wolsey Cl Ashton-in-M WN4 ...73 A5
Radcliffe M26 .....44 A3
Wolsey Dr WA14 ...119 A1
Wolsey St Heywood OL10 ...29 C2
Radcliffe M26 .....44 A3
Wolstenholme Ave BL9 ...27 F6
Wolstenholme Coalpit La
OL11,OL12 ....12 B2
Wolstenholme La
OL11,OL12 ....13 C2
Wolstencroft Cl M24 ...47 B1
Wolstenvale Cl M24 ...47 B1
Wolver Cl M38 ....60 A6
Wolverton Ave OL8 ...66 D3
Wolverton Dr SK9 ...131 D1
Wolvesey OL11 ...139 E6
Wolveton St M11 ...164 F7
Wood Bank Rd OL15 ...16 B6
Wood Bank Terr OL5 ...68 D2
Wood Brook La OL4 ...68 B7
Wood Brook Rd OL4 ...68 B7
Wood Cottage Cl **4** M28 ...59 F3
Wood Cotts SK6 ...113 A6
Wood Cres OL4 ...67 E3
Wood Edge Cl BL4 ...42 C2
Wood End SK7 ....123 D2
Wood Fold BL7 ....25 C6
Wood Gdns SK9 ...137 B2
Wood Gr Denton M34 ...100 F4
Romiley SK6 ......113 A5
Whitefield M45 ....44 F3
Wood Hey Gr M26 ...43 D3
Wood Hey Gr
2 Denton M34 ....101 A2
Rochdale OL12 ....14 B5
Wood La Altrincham WA15 ...120 B5
Altrincham WA16 ...129 B1
Altrincham WA16 ...129 D1
Ashton-u-L OL6,OL7 ...85 B5
Marple SK6 ....65 B7
Middleton M24 ....65 E7
Partington M31 ...105 D3
Wrightington Bar WN6 ...18 E8
Wood La N M33 ...134 B1
Wood Lea Bank **2** BB4 ...2 F8
Wood Lea Rd BB4 ...2 F8
Wood Mount WA15 ...120 B5
Wood Rd Manchester M16 ...97 D3
Manchester M16 ...161 B8
Wood Rd N M16 ...97 C3
Wood Road La Bury BL8 ...27 B8
Ramsbottom BL9 ...11 C1
Wood Sorrel Way WA3 ...90 C8
Wood Sq Droylsden M43 ...100 A8
Oldham OL3 ......69 B6
Wood St Altrincham WA14 ...119 D4
Ashton-u-L OL6 ...166 B2
Atherton M46 .....58 B4
Bolton BL1 ....145 F7
Bury BL8 ....27 C3
Cheadle SK8 .....122 D6
Denton M34 ......100 C4
Dukinfield SK16 ...101 C6
Eccles M30 ....79 F1
Glossop SK13 ....116 C8
Golborne WA3 ....90 B8
Hindley WN2 .....57 B3
Hollingworth SK14 ...103 D5
Horwich BL6 .....22 C3
Hyde SK14 ....167 E2
Littleborough OL15 ...16 B5
Manchester M11 ...165 B8
Manchester M3 ...158 F1
Middleton M24 ...64 F8
Newhey OL16 ....32 C4
Oldham OL1 ......67 B8
Radcliffe M26 .....61 E8
Ramsbottom BL0 ...138 B5
Rochdale OL16 ...31 A6
Shaw OL2 ....48 F8
3 Stalybridge SK15 ...85 F2
Stockport SK3 ....169 D1
Tyldesley M29 ....77 B8
Westhoughton BL5 ...57 F8
Wigan WN3 ......150 C7
Wood Terr BL1 ...26 D1
Wood Top Ave OL11 ...29 F5
Wood Top Cl SK2 ...124 E7
Wood View Heywood OL10 ...29 A4
Shevington WN6 ...36 B5
Wythenshawe M22 ...109 D1
Wood's Hospl SK13 ...104 C3
Wood's La WN4 ...73 C5
Wood's St WN1 ...150 C7
Woodacres Ct SK9 ...136 F6
Woodall Cl M33 ...108 D4
Woodark Cl OL4 ...67 F5
Woodbank Bolton BL2 ...25 D2
Woodbank Cl SK1 ...112 B1
Woodbank Ave
Bredbury SK6 .....112 E3
Stockport SK1 ....124 C8
Woodbank Dr BL8 ...27 C4
Woodbank Works Ind Est
SK1 ....112 B1
Woodbine Ave M44 ...105 D4
Woodbine Cres SK2 ...170 F7
Woodbine Rd Bolton BL3 ...146 C3

Woodbine Rd *continued*
Lymm WA13 117 B4
Woodbine St OL16 31 A5
Woodbine St E OL16 31 B5
Woodbine Terr 1 M44 94 A2
Woodbourne Ct M33 108 B2
Woodbourne Rd
Manchester SK4 111 C6
Sale M33 108 A2
Woodbray Ave M19 110 E5
Woodbridge Ave M34 100 E7
Woodbridge Gdns OL12 14 C2
Woodbridge Gr M23 109 A1
Woodbridge Rd M41 94 D3
Woodbrook Ave
Hyde SK14 167 F2
Oldham OL4 68 B7
Woodbrook Dr WN3 54 D4
Woodbrook Rd SK9 137 C1
Woodburn Dr BL1 142 B3
Woodburn Rd M22 121 D8
Woodburn Row M29 77 C3
Woodbury Cres SK16 101 B7
Woodbury Rd SK3 123 B7
Woodchurch WN1 37 F1
Woodchurch Cl 3 BL1 143 E1
Woodchurch Wlk
Oldham OL9 152 B6
5 Sale M33 108 F3
Woodcock Cl
Droylsden M43 84 C3
Rochdale OL11 29 F7
Woodcock Dr WN2 56 B2
Woodcock Gr SK13 104 E1
Woodcock Ho WN1 151 D8
Woodcock Sq 10 WN1 150 C8
Woodcote Ave SK7 123 C2
Woodcote Rd
Sale M14,M31 107 A2
Sale WA14 107 D1
Woodcote View SK9 131 F1
Woodcote Wlk M8 156 C8
Woodcott Bank BL1 143 E4
Woodcott Gr 3 SK9 131 E1
Woodcourt WN3 150 B6
Woodcroft
Appley Bridge WN6 35 E6
Stockport SK2 124 D6
Woodcroft Ave M19 110 E4
Wooddagger Cl WN2 56 F5
Woodeaton Cl OL2 49 A4
Wooded Cl BL9 27 F5
Woodedge WN4 73 A3
Woodend OL2 149 C8
Woodend Ct SK14 167 D1
Woodend Ctr Ind Pk OL5 68 D2
Woodend Dr SK15 102 D6
Woodend La
Altrincham WA16 129 E1
Hyde SK14 167 D1
Littleborough OL12 15 D6
Stalybridge SK15 102 D6
Woodend Mills OL4 67 F5
Woodend Rd
Stockport SK3 123 F4
Wythenshawe M22 121 D4
Woodend St Oldham OL1 48 E1
Oldham OL4 67 F5
Woodend View OL5 68 D2
Woodfield M22 121 D3
Woodfield Ave Hyde SK14 113 D8
Rochdale OL12 14 E2
Romiley SK6 113 A4
Woodfield Cl
Hadfield SK13 103 F5
Oldham OL8 66 C4
Woodfield Cres
Ashton-in-M WN4 73 A2
Bredbury SK6 112 F2
Woodfield Ct SK2 124 A4
Woodfield Dr M28 78 B6
Woodfield Gr Eccles M30 79 C1
Farnworth BL4 60 C6
Sale M33 108 A6
Woodfield Mews SK14 113 D8
Woodfield Prim Sch WN1 37 C4
Woodfield Rd
Altrincham WA14 119 C6
Bramhall SK8 132 B7
Manchester M24 64 E6
Manchester M8 64 A1
Salford M6 154 D4
Woodfield St Aspull WN2 38 A3
Bolton BL3 42 A3
Woodfield Terr OL10 29 E3
Woodfields Ret Pk BL9 140 F3
Woodfold Ave M19 99 A2
Woodfold Prim Sch WN6 36 D8
Woodfold Rd M35 84 A7
Woodford Ave
Dukinfield M34 101 A4
Eccles M30 79 B2
Golborne WA3 90 D7
Shaw OL2 49 D7
Woodford Ct
Droylsden M43 100 B8
3 Hindley WN2 56 E6
Woodford Dr M27 61 E2
Woodford Gdns M20 110 A2
Woodford Gr BL3 146 C4
Woodford Rd
Bramhall SK12 133 B6
Bramhall SK7 132 E4
Woodford St
4 Hindley WN2 56 E6
8 Wigan WN5 54 B6
Woodgarth WN7 75 C5
Woodgarth Ave M40 83 D5
Woodgarth Dr M27 79 E6
Woodgarth La M28 78 F5
Woodgate Ave Bury BL9 28 D4
Rochdale OL11 30 A6
Woodgate Cl SK6 112 F3
Woodgate Dr M25 63 C6
Woodgate Hill Rd
Bury BL9 141 C4
Bury BL9 28 D4
Woodgate Rd M16 97 E1
Woodgate St BL3 42 A3
Woodgrange Cl 2 M6 154 E2
Woodgreen Cl 1 WN2 56 D4
Woodgreen Dr M26 62 A8
Woodhall Ave
Manchester M20 110 A7
Whitefield M45 62 D6
Woodhall Cl Bolton BL2 25 C3
Bury BL8 27 D5
Woodford SK7 132 E3
Woodhall Cres SK5 112 A4
Woodhall Rd SK5 169 F4
Woodhall St M35 83 F8
Woodhalt Rd M8 156 A8
Woodham Rd M23 108 F1
Woodham Wlk BL3 145 D5
Woodhead Cl Oldham OL4 67 E7
Ramsbottom BL0 11 C4
Woodhead Dr WA15 119 F1
Woodhead Gr WN3 55 B2
Woodhead Rd
Altrincham WA15 119 F1
Glossop SK13 104 D4
Tintwistle SK13 104 B8
Woodhead St 6 M16 97 E4
Woodhey Ct M33 107 E1
Woodhey High Sch BL0 11 A3
Woodhey Rd BL0 11 A3
Woodheys SK4 110 F3
Woodheys Dr M33 107 D1
Woodheys Prim Sch M33 107 E2
Woodheys Rd OL15 16 A2
Woodheys St 1 M5 154 F1
Woodhill M24 46 F2
Woodhill Cl
Manchester M12 99 B4
Middleton M24 46 F2
Woodhill Dr M25 63 B3
Woodhill Fold BL8 140 D3
Woodhill Gr M25 63 B3
Woodhill Ho 3 M6 154 F3
Woodhill Rd Bury BL8 140 D3
Bury BL8 140 D4
Woodhill St BL8 140 D4
Woodhouse Ct M41 95 A4
Woodhouse Dr WN6 36 E2
Woodhouse Farm Cotts
OL12 13 D2
Woodhouse Knowl OL3 50 F4
Woodhouse La
Partington WA14 118 C4
Rochdale OL12 13 E3
Sale M33 107 C2
Sale M33 107 D2
Wigan WN6 36 E3
Wigan WN6 36 F2
Wigan WN6 37 A1
Wythenshawe M22 121 D4
Wythenshawe M22 130 D8
Wythenshawe M90 130 D7
Woodhouse La E WA15 108 A1
Woodhouse Park
Prim Sch M22 130 D8
Woodhouse Prim Sch
M41 95 A4
Woodhouse Rd Shaw OL2 32 C1
Urmston M41 94 F4
Urmston M41 95 A4
Wythenshawe M22 130 D8
Woodhouse St
Atherton M46 58 D2
Manchester M10,M40 157 F5
Manchester M18 99 E5
Woodhouses Prim Sch
M35 84 C6
Woodhurst Dr WN6 19 D1
Wooding Cl M31 106 A4
Woodlake Ave M21 109 C4
Woodland Ave Bolton BL3 42 B2
Hazel Grove SK7 124 E1
Hindley WN2 57 A3
Lymm WA13 117 A2
Newton-le-W WA12 89 F3
Reddish M18 99 E4
Woodland Cres M25 63 B2
Woodland Dr
Ashton-in-M WN4 73 B5
Lymm WA13 117 A2
Standish WN6 19 E2
Woodland Gr Bolton BL7 8 D2
Wigan WN1 37 D2
Woodland Pk OL2 48 B6
Woodland Rd
Heywood OL10 29 E3
Manchester M19 111 A7
Reddish M18 99 E4
Rochdale OL12 14 C2
Tyldesley M29 77 B7
Woodland St
Heywood OL10 29 D2
Manchester M12 165 B5
Rochdale OL12 15 A2
Woodland View BL7 25 B8
Woodland Way M24 64 F6
Woodlands Failsworth M35 83 E4
5 Urmston M41 95 C3
Woodlands Ave
Cheadle SK8 123 A2
Woodlands Ave *continued*
Eccles M30 95 A8
Ince-in-M WN3 151 F6
Irlam M44 94 A3
Leigh WN7 75 F3
Rochdale OL11 30 A6
Romiley SK6 113 A5
Stretford M32 96 D2
Swinton M27 79 D6
Urmston M41 94 C2
Whitefield M45 44 E1
Woodlands Cl
Cheadle SK8 132 A8
Mottram-in-L SK14 102 F1
Stalybridge SK15 102 D7
Tintwistle SK13 103 F6
Worsley M28 78 E7
Woodlands Ct
Altrincham WA15 119 E5
Stockport SK2 124 D8
Woodlands Dr
Atherton M46 58 F5
Romiley SK6 113 A5
Sale M23, M33 108 C1
Shevington WN6 35 F4
Stockport SK2 124 D8
Woodlands Gr Bury BL8 27 B3
Mottram-in-L SK14 102 F1
Woodlands Hospl M38 59 F4
Woodlands Ind Est WA12 89 C6
Woodlands La WA15 119 E5
Woodlands Park Rd SK2 124 D8
Woodlands Parkway
WA15 119 E6
Woodlands Rd
Altrincham WA14,WA15 119 E5
Ashton-u-L OL6 85 E6
Edenfield BL0 1 D2
Handforth SK9 131 E3
High Lane SK12 135 A6
Manchester M21 97 E1
Manchester M8 156 B7
Manchester SK4 110 E2
Milnrow OL16 31 F5
Sale M33 108 C4
Stalybridge SK15 102 D7
Wilmslow SK9 130 F1
Worsley M28 78 F7
Woodlands Road Sta M8 156 B7
Woodlands St M8 156 A8
Woodlands The Bolton BL6 40 C8
Bury BL8 140 D4
Heywood OL10 46 E8
Pendlebury M27 80 B7
Wigan WN1 37 D3
Woodlands View
Ramsbottom BL0 138 C6
Rochdale OL16 31 C8
Woodlark Cl M3 158 D1
Woodlawn Ct M16 97 C3
Woodlea Oldham OL9 65 D7
Worsley M28 78 E8
Woodlea Ave M19 110 E6
Woodlea Rd SK13 116 B7
Woodleigh WA14 119 A5
Woodleigh Ct SK9 137 A2
Woodleigh Dr M43 84 C4
Woodleigh Rd OL4 68 A7
Woodleigh St M9 64 F1
Woodles M30 79 C4
Woodley Ave M26 44 B1
Woodley Cl SK2 124 D7
Woodley Gr WN7 75 D5
Woodley Inf Sch SK6 113 C5
Woodley Jun Sch SK6 113 C5
Woodley Prec SK6 113 A5
Woodley St BL9 44 F8
Woodley Sta SK6 113 B6
Woodliffe St M16 161 C5
Woodlinn Wlk M9 157 D7
Woodman Dr BL9 27 E6
Woodman St SK1 169 E2
Woodmeadow Ct 9 OL5 68 C2
Woodmere Dr M9 64 E3
Woodmount Cl SK6 113 F2
Woodnook Rd WN6 35 E8
Woodpark Cl OL8 67 A3
Woodpecker Pl M28 78 D8
Woodridge Dr BL2 25 B1
Woodridings WA14 119 B3
Woodrow Way M44 105 F8
Woodrow Wlk M12 164 F6
Woodroyd Cl SK7 123 D1
Woodroyd Dr BL9 141 C3
Woodruff Wlk 7 M31 105 F3
Woodruffe Gdns SK6 125 A8
Woodrush Rd WN6 36 D3
Woods Ct Middleton M24 64 C7
Newton-le-W WA12 89 A3
Woods Gr SK8 132 B7
Woods La Bramhall SK8 132 B7
Uppermill OL3 51 A2
Woods Lea BL1 40 F7
Woods Rd Aspull WN2 38 C4
Irlam M44 105 F8
Woods The
4 Altrincham WA14 119 E6
Oldham OL4 68 B6
Rochdale OL11 30 C3
Woodseats La SK13 115 B6
Woodsend Circ M41 94 D3
Woodsend Crescent Rd
M41 94 D2
Woodsend Gn M41 94 D3
Woodsend Prim Sch M41 94 D3
Woodsend Rd M41 94 E3
Woodsend Rd S M41 94 E1
Woodshaw Gr 2 M28 78 C8
Woodside Manchester SK4 110 F1
Newhey OL16 32 C5
Shaw OL2 49 D8
Woodside Ave
Ashton-in-M WN4 73 A8
Manchester M19 110 F5
Walkden M28 60 F2
Woodside Cl WN8 53 C8
Woodside Com Specl Schs
BL1 40 E7
Woodside Ct M16 97 E2
Woodside Dr
High Lane SK6 134 F7
Hyde SK14 167 E1
Ramsbottom BL0 138 A5
Salford M6 80 C3
Woodside La SK12 133 E4
Woodside Mews SK7 123 C2
Woodside Pl BL2 148 C5
Woodside Rd Lymm WA13 117 B1
Manchester M16 97 B2
Woodside Sq BL2 148 C5
Woodside St SK15 86 E6
Woodsley Rd BL1 23 F2
Woodsmoor La SK2,SK3 124 A4
Woodsmoor Rd M27 79 D7
Woodsmoor Sta SK2 124 B4
Woodstock Ave
Bramhall SK8 132 A7
Newton-le-W WA12 89 D2
Reddish SK5 111 F5
Woodstock Cl
Heywood OL10 29 E2
Leigh WN7 75 E1
Woodstock Cres SK6 113 A5
Woodstock Dr Bolton BL1 142 A1
Bury BL8 26 D7
Eccles M28 79 A6
Pendlebury M27 80 B6
Woodstock Gn SK5 112 A5
Woodstock Rd
Altrincham WA14 119 C8
Failsworth M40 65 C1
Manchester M16 97 B3
Romiley SK6 113 A5
Woodstock St Oldham OL4 153 F6
12 Rochdale OL12 14 C1
Woodthorpe Cl M25 63 D2
Woodthorpe Dr SK8 123 A2
Woodthorpe Grange M25 63 D2
Woodvale
Altrincham WA14 119 C2
Middleton M24 47 A4
Woodvale Ave Aspull WN2 38 F3
Atherton M46 58 B5
Bolton BL3 147 D2
Woodvale Dr Bolton BL3 147 D2
Golborne WA3 74 E1
Woodvale Gdns BL3 147 D2
Woodvale Gr BL3 147 D2
Woodvale Wlk 18 M11 160 F1
Woodview Ave M19 110 F5
Woodville Dr Marple SK6 125 E4
Sale M33 108 A5
Stalybridge SK15 86 D3
Woodville Gr SK5 111 F6
Woodville Rd
Altrincham WA14 119 C3
Ince-in-M WN3 55 F4
Sale M33 108 A5
Woodville Terr 10 M40 64 F1
Woodward Cl BL9 27 F5
Woodward Ct M4 160 D2
Woodward Pl M4 159 C2
Woodward Rd M25 62 F2
Woodward St M4 159 C2
Woodwards Rd BL5 57 F6
Woodwise La M23 108 E1
Woodyates St WN5 54 F6
Wool Rd OL3 51 B2
Woolden Rd M44,WA3 105 B8
Woolden St Eccles M30 79 B3
8 Wigan WN5 54 F6
Woolfall Cl M12 164 F6
Woolfold Trad Est BL8 27 C3
Woollacot St 2 OL1 153 F6
Woollam Pl M3 162 D8
Woolley Ave SK12 133 D2
Woolley Bridge Rd SK13 103 E5
Woolley Cl SK14 171 D4
Woolley La
Hollingworth SK14 103 D6
Hollingworth SK14 171 D4
Woolley Mill La SK13 103 E7
Woolley St M8 159 A4
Woolley Terr 3 SK16 166 B1
Woolpack Gn 2 M6 154 F3
Woolston Dr M29 77 C8
Woolston Ho M6 80 C4
Woolton Cl
Ashton-in-M WN4 72 F5
3 Failsworth M40 65 C2
Wootton St SK14 167 D4
Worcester Ave
Brinnington SK5 112 C5
Denton M34 101 A1
Golborne WA3 90 B8
Hindley WN2 56 F6
Worcester Cl
Ashton-u-L OL6 85 D8
Romiley SK6 113 A1
Salford M6 80 C4
Whitefield BL9 45 A8
Worcester Gr SK13 116 F8
Worcester Rd
Cheadle SK8 123 A4
Little Lever BL3 42 F3
Middleton M24 64 F5
Worcester Rd *continued*
Sale M33 107 D3
Salford M6 80 C4
Swinton M27 61 D2
Worcester St
19 Bolton BL1 143 E1
Bury BL8 140 D4
Manchester M7 155 E6
Oldham OL9 152 B5
Rochdale OL11 30 E4
Wordsworth Ave
Atherton M46 58 E5
Bury BL9 44 F6
Droylsden M43 84 A2
Farnworth BL4 60 B7
Leigh WN7 75 D7
Longshaw WN5 53 D1
Manchester M8 156 A6
Orrell WN5 53 F6
Radcliffe M26 43 E4
Wigan WN1 37 C3
Wordsworth Cl SK16 102 A7
Wordsworth Cres
Ashton-u-L OL7 84 E5
Littleborough OL15 15 F2
Wordsworth Gdns M25 62 F3
Wordsworth Rd
Denton M34 113 A7
Manchester M16 97 B3
Middleton M24 47 B2
6 Oldham OL1 49 B1
Reddish SK5 99 D1
Swinton M27 61 E1
Walkden M38 60 B5
Wordsworth St
Bolton BL1 143 D2
Salford M6 81 C4
Wordsworth Trad Est
BL1 143 D2
Wordsworth Way OL11 29 E6
Workesleigh St 9 M40 83 C5
World Freight Terminal
M17 96 E5
World Way M90 130 B8
Worrall St Failsworth M40 83 A6
1 Rochdale OL12 14 D2
Salford M5 161 C7
Stockport SK3 170 E7
Worrell Cl M26 43 F4
Worsbrough Ave M28 60 C2
Worsefold St M40 83 A8
Worsel St BL3 146 C4
Worsley Ave
Manchester M40 65 A1
Walkden M28 60 A2
Worsley Brow M28 78 F6
Worsley Bsns Pk M28 77 E8
Worsley Cl WN5 54 C5
Worsley Cres SK2 124 B7
Worsley Ct 4 M14 98 C2
Worsley Gn WN5 54 B5
Worsley Gr
Manchester M19 99 A1
Walkden M28 60 A2
Worsley Mesnes
Com Prim Sch WN3 55 A4
Worsley Mesnes Dr WN3 150 A5
Worsley Pl Rochdale OL16 31 B7
Shaw OL2 149 A6
Worsley Rd Bolton BL3 146 A4
Eccles M30 79 B3
Farnworth BL4 60 D7
Swinton M27,M28 79 C6
Worsley Rd N M28 60 D5
Worsley St Bolton BL3 145 E5
Bury BL8 26 E7
Golborne WA3 90 A8
Manchester M15 162 D7
Manchester M3 158 E2
Manchester M3 162 E8
Oldham OL8 67 B5
Pendlebury M27 80 A7
Rochdale OL16 31 B7
Swinton M27 61 F2
Wigan WN5 54 B5
Worsley Terr WN1 37 C1
Worston Ave BL1 23 F3
Worth's La M34 113 A7
Worthing Cl SK2 124 D6
Worthing Gr M46 58 B3
Worthing St M14 98 B2
Worthington Ave
Heywood OL10 46 E7
9 Partington M31 105 F3
Worthington Cl
Ashton-u-L OL7 85 A5
7 Hattersley SK14 102 E2
Worthington Ct M33 108 E4
Worthington Dr M7 63 D1
Worthington Fold M46 58 B3
Worthington Prim Sch
M33 108 F4
Worthington Rd
Denton M34 101 B1
Sale M33 108 F4
Worthington St
Ashton-u-L OL7 85 A5
4 Bolton BL3 146 C3
Failsworth M40 83 C8
Hindley WN2 56 D6
Manchester M16 97 C4
Stalybridge SK15 85 F1
Worthington Way WN3 54 F2
Wortley Ave M6 80 C3
Wortley Gr M40 65 B2

Wotton Dr WN4 . . . . .73 D4
Wragby Cl BL8 . . . . .27 D5
Wrath Cl BL2 . . . . .25 B5
Wraxhall Cres WN7 . . . . . .75 D7
Wray Pl OL16 . . . . .31 C6
Wray St WN1 . . . . .151 E8
Wraysbury Wlk 15 M40 . . . .83 A7
Wrayton Lo M33 . . . . .108 B3
Wrekin Ave M23 . . . . .121 A3
Wren Ave M27 . . . . .62 B2
Wren Cl Droylsden M34 . . . .84 C1
   Farnworth BL4 . . . . .59 F8
   Hazel Grove SK2 . . . . .124 F5
   Wigan WN5 . . . . .36 B1
Wren Dr Bury BL9 . . . . .141 B4
   Irlam M44 . . . . .94 A4
Wren Gdns M24 . . . . .46 F1
Wren Gn OL16 . . . . .31 B6
Wren Nest Rd SK13 . . . . . .104 B1
Wren Nest Terr SK13 . . . . .104 C1
Wren St OL4 . . . . .67 C6
Wren's Nest Ave OL2 . . . .149 C8
Wrenbury Ave M20 . . . . . .109 F7
Wrenbury Cl 6 WN5 . . . . . .54 B5
Wrenbury Cres SK3 . . . . . .123 C6
Wrenbury Dr 2 Bolton BL7 .24 F6
   Cheadle SK8 . . . . .122 E6
   Rochdale OL16 . . . . .31 C3
Wrenbury Wlk M33 . . . . . .108 E3
Wrenswood Dr M28 . . . . . . .78 C8
Wrexham Cl OL8 . . . . .66 B2
Wrigglesworth Cl BL8 . . . .26 F3
Wright Robinson Cl M11 .164 E8
Wright Robinson High Sch
   M18 .99 F6
Wright St Abram Brow WN2 .74 B7
   Ashton-in-M WN4 . . . . .73 A6
   Ashton-u-L M34 . . . . .100 E8
   11 Ashton-u-L OL6 . . . . . . .85 D4
   Failsworth M35 . . . . .83 F8
   Horwich BL6 . . . . .22 B4
   Manchester M16 . . . . .161 C6
   15 Oldham OL1 . . . . .67 A7
   Oldham OL9 . . . . .152 B5
   Platt Bridge WN2 . . . . .56 A3
   Radcliffe M26 . . . . .43 F3
   6 Wigan WN1 . . . . .37 E1
Wright St 8 BL6 . . . . .22 B4
Wright Tree Villas M44 . . .105 E5
Wrightington Hospl WN6 .18 D2
Wrightington Mossy Lea
   Prim Sch WN6 . . . . .18 F6
Wrightington St WN1 . . . . .37 C1
Wrights Bank N SK2 . . . . .124 E5
Wrights Bank S SK2 . . . . .124 E5
Wrigley Cres M35 . . . . .83 F7
Wrigley Fold M24 . . . . .46 D3
Wrigley Head M35 . . . . .83 F8
Wrigley Head Cres M35 . . .83 F8
Wrigley Pl OL15 . . . . .15 F3
Wrigley Sq 1 OL4 . . . . .67 F6
Wrigley St Ashton-u-L OL6 .166 B4
   Oldham OL4 . . . . .67 B7
   Oldham OL4 . . . . .67 F6
   Oldham OL4 . . . . .68 B8
Wrington Cl WN7 . . . . .75 D8
Wroe St Manchester M3 . . .158 D2
   11 Oldham OL4 . . . . .67 C6
   Swinton M27 . . . . .61 F3
Wroe Terr M27 . . . . .61 F3
Wrotham Cl 2 M5 . . . . .81 A1
Wroxeter Wlk M12 . . . . . . .164 F6
Wroxham Ave
   Reddish M34 . . . . .100 A3
   Urmston M41 . . . . .95 B3
Wroxham Cl BL8 . . . . .27 D5

Wroxham Rd M9 . . . . .64 B3
Wuerdle Cl OL16 . . . . .15 E4
Wuerdle Farm Way 3
   OL16 . . . . .15 E4
Wuerdle Pl OL16 . . . . .15 E4
Wuerdle St 1 OL16 . . . . . .15 E4
Wyatt Ave M5 . . . . .161 C7
Wyatt Gr WN4 . . . . .73 D3
Wyatt St Dukinfield SK16 . .101 C8
   Stockport SK4 . . . . .169 E2
Wybersley Rd SK6 . . . . . . .135 A8
Wych Fold SK14 . . . . .113 E7
Wych St OL6 . . . . .166 B2
Wychbury St M5,M6 . . . . . .154 E2
Wychelm Rd M31 . . . . .105 F3
Wycherley Rd OL12 . . . . . . .14 B2
Wychwood WA14 . . . . .119 B1
Wychwood Cl M24 . . . . .65 B7
Wycliffe Ave SK9 . . . . .137 A7
Wycliffe Ct M41 . . . . .95 C2
Wycliffe Rd M41 . . . . .95 C2
Wycliffe St Eccles M30 . . . .79 C2
   Stockport SK4 . . . . .169 D2
Wycombe Ave M18 . . . . . . .99 E6
Wycombe Cl M41 . . . . .95 C5
Wycombe Dr M29 . . . . .77 B7
Wye Ave M35 . . . . .83 F7
Wye St OL6 . . . . .153 D5
Wyecroft Cl SK6 . . . . .113 B5
Wyke Pk OL4 . . . . .67 D6
Wykeham Cl WN3 . . . . .151 F6
Wykeham Gr OL12 . . . . .14 B1
Wykeham Mews BL1 . . . . .144 A7
Wykeham St M14 . . . . .98 A3
Wylam Wlk 4 M12 . . . . .99 B3
Wylde The BL9 . . . . .140 E2
Wynard Ave WN1 . . . . .37 D1
Wynchgate Rd SK7 . . . . . .125 A3
Wyndale Dr M35 . . . . .83 F5
Wyndale Rd OL8 . . . . .66 F3
Wyndcliff Dr M41 . . . . .94 E1
Wyndham Ave Bolton BL3 .146 A3
   Swinton M27 . . . . .61 F3
Wyndham Cl SK7 . . . . .132 E7
Wyne Cl SK7 . . . . .125 A3
Wynfield Ave M22 . . . . .130 F7
Wynford Sq M5 . . . . .154 F1
Wyngate Rd
   Altrincham WA15 . . . . .128 F8
   Cheadle SK8 . . . . .122 F1
Wynne Ave M27 . . . . .62 A3
Wynne Cl Denton M34 . . . .100 F1
   Manchester M11 . . . . .164 F8
Wynne Gr M34 . . . . .100 F1
Wynne St Bolton BL1 . . . . .143 E2
   Salford M6 . . . . .81 B3
   Tyldesley M29 . . . . .58 F1
   Walkden M38 . . . . .60 A4
Wynnstay Gr M14 . . . . .110 C8
Wynnstay Rd M33 . . . . . . .108 B5
Wynton Cl WN7 . . . . .75 E2
Wynyard Cl M33 . . . . .108 D2
Wynyard Rd M22 . . . . .121 C3
Wyre Ave WN2 . . . . .56 A2
Wyre Cl M45 . . . . .45 B1
Wyre Dr M28 . . . . .78 B7
Wyre St Manchester M1 . . .163 B8
   Mossley OL5 . . . . .68 C1
Wyresdale Rd BL1 . . . . . . .144 C8
Wyrevale Gr WN4 . . . . .73 C3
Wythall Ave M38 . . . . .60 A6
Wythburn Ave Bolton BL1 .142 A1
   Manchester M8 . . . . .156 C6
   Urmston M41 . . . . .95 B3
Wythburn Rd
   Middleton M24 . . . . .46 E3
   Stockport SK1 . . . . .124 B7
Wythburn St M5,M6 . . . . . .154 E2
Wythens Rd SK8 . . . . .131 B8

Wythenshawe Ctr M22 . . .121 D2
Wythenshawe Hall
   (Art Gal & Mus) M23 . . . .121 B8
Wythenshawe Hospl M23 .120 F5
Wythenshawe Rd
   Sale M33 . . . . .108 F4
   Wythenshawe M23 . . . . . . .109 B1
Wythop Gdns Salford M5 . .161 A8
   Salford M5 . . . . .81 A1
Wyvern Ave SK5 . . . . .111 E5
Wyverne Rd M21 . . . . .109 D8
Wyville Cl SK7 . . . . .125 A3
Wyville Dr Manchester M9 . .64 B6
   Salford M6 . . . . .154 F3
   Swinton M27 . . . . .79 E6

X

Xaverian Coll M14 . . . . .98 C3

Y

Yale St BL7 . . . . .9 D4
Yarburgh St M16 . . . . .97 E3
Yardley Ave M32 . . . . .96 A2
Yardley Cl M32 . . . . .96 A2
Yare St 1 BB4 . . . . .2 F8
Yarmouth Dr M23 . . . . .109 B1
Yarn Croft M29 . . . . .77 B8
Yarn Wlk 9 M4 . . . . .159 C1
Yarnton Cl OL2 . . . . .149 A5
Yarrow Cl OL11 . . . . .139 F5
Yarrow Gr BL6 . . . . .22 B4
Yarrow Pl BL1 . . . . .143 E1
Yarrow St WN2 . . . . .56 C4
Yarrow Wlk M45 . . . . .45 C1
Yarwell 22 OL12 . . . . .139 E8
Yarwood Ave M23 . . . . . . .120 F7
Yarwood Cl OL10 . . . . .29 E3
Yarwood St
   Altrincham WA14 . . . . .119 D3
   Bury BL9 . . . . .141 A2
Yasmin Gdns OL1 . . . . .48 D1
Yates Dr M28 . . . . .60 A3
Yates Gr WN6 . . . . .36 F4
Yates St Bolton BL2 . . . . . . .25 A1
   Leigh WN7 . . . . .75 E7
   Middleton M24 . . . . .64 C7
   Oldham OL1 . . . . .49 B1
   Stockport SK1 . . . . .112 B3
   Wigan WN3 . . . . .150 A2
Yattendon Ave M23 . . . . . .120 D8
Yea Fold OL15 . . . . .15 E3
Yeadon Rd M18 . . . . .99 D3
Yealand Ave SK4 . . . . .169 D3
Yealand Cl OL11 . . . . .30 B6
Yealand Gr WN2 . . . . .57 A5
Yeardsley Cl SK7 . . . . .123 E3
Yeargate Ind Est BB9 . . . . .28 D2
Yellow Brook Cl WN2 . . . . .38 C6
Yellow Lodge Dr BL5 . . . . . .40 B1
Yeoford Dr WA14 . . . . .119 B6
Yeoman Cl SK7 . . . . .124 D3
Yeoman Wlk M11 . . . . .160 F1
Yeoman's Cl OL16 . . . . .31 F7
Yeomanry Ct 3 M16 . . . . . .97 D3
Yeovil Wlk 10 M16 . . . . . . .97 F3
Yesoday HaTorah Sch
   M25 .63 B2
Yew Cl BL3 . . . . .146 B4
Yew Cres OL4 . . . . .67 B8
Yew Ct OL12 . . . . .15 B2
Yew Dale Gdns OL11 . . . . .30 B4
Yew St Bury BL9 . . . . .141 C3
   Denton M34 . . . . .100 F5
   Heywood OL10 . . . . .29 B2

Yew St continued
   Manchester M15 . . . . .162 E5
   Manchester M7 . . . . .81 C6
   Stockport SK4 . . . . .168 C1
Yew Tree Ave
   Cheadle SK7 . . . . .125 A1
   Hazel Grove SK7 . . . . .124 F1
   Manchester M14 . . . . .98 A2
   7 Manchester M19 . . . . . . .99 A1
   Newton-le-W WA12 . . . . . . .89 A4
   Wythenshawe M22 . . . . . . .109 D1
Yew Tree Cl Ashton-u-L OL7 .85 A6
   Marple SK6 . . . . .125 E5
   Wilmslow SK9 . . . . .137 D7
Yew Tree Com Prim Sch
   SK16 . . . . .101 E6
Yew Tree Cres M14 . . . . . . .98 B1
Yew Tree Ct OL14 . . . . .6 A8
Yew Tree Dr Bolton BL6 . . . .40 B6
   Bredbury SK6 . . . . .112 D3
   Chadderton OL9 . . . . .65 D7
   Prestwich M25 . . . . .63 B4
   Sale M33 . . . . .108 E4
   Urmston M41 . . . . .94 F4
   Wythenshawe M22 . . . . . . .109 D1
Yew Tree Farm Trad Est
   WA11 . . . . .89 A8
Yew Tree Gr Gatley SK8 . . .122 A3
   Rawtenstall BB4 . . . . .1 F8
Yew Tree Inf Sch OL9 . . . . .66 A4
Yew Tree Jun Sch OL9 . . . .66 A4
Yew Tree La Bolton BL1 . . . .25 A4
   Dukinfield SK16 . . . . .101 F7
Yew Tree Park Rd SK8 . . . .132 B6
Yew Tree Rd Denton M34 . .100 E1
   Manchester M14 . . . . .98 B2
   Poynton SK10 . . . . .134 B1
   Stockport SK10 . . . . .134 B1
Yew Tree Way WA3 . . . . . . .90 B7
Yew Tree Wlk 11 M31 . . . .105 E2
Yewbarrow Cl M29 . . . . .77 B7
Yewbarrow Rd M31 . . . . . .105 E2
Yewdale Shevington WN6 . . .36 B6
   Swinton M27 . . . . .62 B1
Yewdale Ave Billinge WA11 . .71 B1
   Bolton BL2 . . . . .25 F2
Yewdale Cres 3 WN1 . . . . .37 B3
Yewdale Dr M24 . . . . .46 E1
Yewdale Gdns BL2 . . . . .25 F2
Yewdale Rd
   Ashton-in-M WN4 . . . . .73 A7
   Stockport SK1 . . . . .124 B7
Yewlands Ave M9 . . . . .64 D5
Yewtree Ave M46 . . . . .58 C4
Yewtree La Poynton SK12 .133 F3
   Wythenshawe M23 . . . . . . .109 B2
York Ave Culcheth WA3 . . . .91 F2
   Haslingden BB4 . . . . .1 B8
   Little Lever BL3 . . . . .43 A3
   Manchester M16 . . . . .97 C2
   Manchester M25 . . . . .63 D2
   Oldham OL8 . . . . .66 D4
   Rochdale OL11 . . . . .30 A6
   Sale M33 . . . . .108 B5
   Swinton M27 . . . . .61 D2
   Tyldesley M29 . . . . .59 A2
   Urmston M41 . . . . .95 E3
York Cl Cheadle SK8 . . . . .123 A5
   Denton M34 . . . . .100 F4
York Cres SK9 . . . . .137 D8
York Dr Altrincham WA14 . .119 C1
   Hazel Grove SK7 . . . . .125 A2
   Ramsbottom BL0 . . . . .11 A4
   Wythenshawe M90 . . . . . . .129 F7
York Pl Adlington PR6 . . . . .21 A8
   Ashton-u-L OL6 . . . . .166 A2
   Manchester M13 . . . . .98 C4
   Ashton-in-M WN4 . . . . .73 B3

York Rd continued
   Chadderton OL9 . . . . .65 F8
   Denton M34 . . . . .100 F4
   Droylsden M43 . . . . .83 F3
   Hindley WN2 . . . . .56 F6
   Sale SK14 . . . . .113 E8
   Irlam M44 . . . . .105 D5
   Manchester M21 . . . . .109 B8
   Manchester M44 . . . . .111 B5
   Sale M33 . . . . .108 A5
York Rd E M24 . . . . .65 C5
York Rd S WN4 . . . . .73 C2
York Rd W M24 . . . . .65 C5
York Sq 1 OL2 . . . . .48 D4
York St Altrincham WA15 . .119 E3
   Ashton-u-L M34 . . . . .100 E8
   Atherton M46 . . . . .58 D3
   Bury BL9 . . . . .141 A2
   Farnworth BL4 . . . . .60 E8
   Glossop SK13 . . . . .104 E1
   Golborne WA3 . . . . .74 A1
   Heywood OL10 . . . . .29 D2
   Leigh WN7 . . . . .76 D4
   Manchester M1 . . . . .163 A8
   Manchester M1,M13 . . . . .163 A7
   Manchester M1,M2 . . . . . .159 A1
   Manchester M12 . . . . .162 E7
   Manchester M19 . . . . .111 A8
   Manchester M20 . . . . .110 B3
   Manchester M9 . . . . .157 E8
   Oldham OL9 . . . . .153 E6
   Radcliffe BL9 . . . . .44 D5
   Rochdale OL16 . . . . .31 B6
   Stockport SK3 . . . . .170 E8
   Whitefield M45 . . . . .62 F8
   Wigan WN1 . . . . .150 B8
York Terr 19 Bolton BL1 . . .143 E2
   Glossop SK13 . . . . .116 C8
   Sale M33 . . . . .108 A4
Yorkdale Rd OL4 . . . . .67 D6
Yorkshire Rd M31 . . . . .105 E2
Yorkshire St
   Ashton-u-L OL6 . . . . .166 B3
   Manchester M3 . . . . .158 E2
   Oldham OL1 . . . . .153 F7
   Rochdale OL16 . . . . .31 A8
   Rochdale OL16 . . . . .139 F8
Yorkshire Terr OL5 . . . . .68 C1
Yorkshire Way SK13 . . . . .116 F8
Youd St WN7 . . . . .75 F5
Youlgreave Cres SK13 . . . .171 D1
Young St Farnworth BL4 . . .60 E7
   Leigh WN7 . . . . .76 E4
   Manchester M3 . . . . .158 E1
   Radcliffe M26 . . . . .43 F5
   Ramsbottom BL0 . . . . .138 B6
Yulan Dr M33 . . . . .107 C4
Yule St SK3 . . . . .170 D8
Yvonne Cl WN4 . . . . .73 D5

Z

Zama St BL0 . . . . .11 A4
Zealand St OL4 . . . . .67 C8
Zebra St M7 . . . . .155 F7
Zedburgh 22 OL12 . . . . . . .139 E8
Zeta St M9 . . . . .157 F7
Zetland Ave BL3 . . . . .146 B2
Zetland Ave N BL3 . . . . . . .146 B2
Zetland Rd M21 . . . . .109 B8
Zetland St SK16 . . . . .101 C8
Zinnia Dr M44 . . . . .105 E8
Zion Cres M15 . . . . .162 E6
Zion Terr OL12 . . . . .13 E2
Zulu St BL2 . . . . .148 B7
Zurich Gdns SK7 . . . . .123 E3
Zyburn Ct M6 . . . . .80 A3